HONEST WORK

Honest Work

A Business Ethics Reader

Third Edition

Joanne B. Ciulla
University of Richmond

Clancy Martin
University of Missouri, Kansas City

Robert C. Solomon
University of Texas at Austin

New York   Oxford
OXFORD UNIVERSITY PRESS

Oxford University Press is a department of the University of Oxford. It furthers the University's
objective of excellence in research, scholarship, and education by publishing worldwide.

Oxford   New York
Auckland   Cape Town   Dar es Salaam   Hong Kong   Karachi
Kuala Lumpur   Madrid   Melbourne   Mexico City   Nairobi
New Delhi   Shanghai   Taipei   Toronto

With offices in
Argentina   Austria   Brazil   Chile   Czech Republic   France   Greece
Guatemala   Hungary   Italy   Japan   Poland   Portugal   Singapore
South Korea   Switzerland   Thailand   Turkey   Ukraine   Vietnam

For titles covered by Section 112 of the US Higher Education Opportunity Act, please
visit www.oup.com/us/he for the latest information about pricing and alternate formats.

Published by Oxford University Press.
198 Madison Avenue, New York, NY 10016
www.oup.com

Oxford is a registered trademark of Oxford University Press

Library of Congress Cataloging-in-Publication Data
Honest work : a business ethics reader / Joanne B. Ciulla, University of Riichmond, University of Fort Hare,
Clancy Martin, Universtiy of Missouri, Kansas City, Robert C. Solomon, Universtiy of Texas at Austin.—Third
edition.
    p. cm.
  ISBN: 978–0–19–994420–0
  1. Business ethics. 2. Work—Psychological aspects. 3. Work ethic. 4. Quality of work life.
5. Social justice.   I. Ciulla, Joanne B.   II. Martin, Clancy W.   III. Solomon, Robert C.   Title: Business
ethics reader.
HF5387.H663   2014
174'.4—dc23   2013032252

Printing number: 9 8 7 6 5 4 3 2

Printed in the United States of America
on acid-free paper

In memory of Robert C. Solomon
September 14, 1942–January 2, 2007

CONTENTS

PREFACE   xix

INTRODUCTION: GETTING TO WORK   xxiii

    BOX: "THREE QUESTIONS FOR THINKING ABOUT ETHICS"   XXV

    Robert Audi | "Some Approaches to Determining Ethical Obligations"   xxv

1 ON THE JOB: EVERYDAY ETHICS AT WORK   1

    Introduction   1

        BOX: "SLOTH: THE NOONDAY DEMON"   3

    Norman E. Bowie | "Respecting the Humanity in a Person"   4

        BOX: "W. D. ROSS ON PRIMA FACIE DUTIES"   6

    Arlie Hochschild | "Exploring the Managed Heart"   7

        BOX: "ROBERT C. SOLOMON, *THE PASSIONS*"   8

    Bruce Barry | "The Cringing and the Craven: Freedom of Expression in the Workplace"   11

    Loraleigh Keashly | "Workplace Bullying"   15

    The Economist | "Doing Business in Dangerous Places"   18

    Harry J. Van Buren III | "Boundaryless Careers and Employability Obligations"   20

        BOX: ROSABETH MOSS KANTER, "ETHICAL MANAGEMENT OF UNCERTAIN EMPLOYMENT"   24

    Harvard Law Review | Facial Discrimination   25

        BOX: "JOHN STUART MILL ON THE GREATEST GOOD AND EXPEDIENCY"   29

    CASES

    Case 1.1: Sloan Wilson, "The Job Interview"   30

    Case 1.2: John R. Boatright, "A 'State of the Art' Termination"   32

    Case 1.3: Joanne B. Ciulla, "Does Home Life Matter at Work?"   34

Case 1.4: Joanne B. Ciulla, "The Best Person for the Job?"   35

Case 1.5: Joanne B. Ciulla, "Attraction or Business as Usual?"   35

Case 1.6: Joanne B. Ciulla, "Pornography and the Boss's Computer"   36

    Box: "Sexual Harassment Guidelines"   37

2 "The Check Is In the Mail": Honesty and Trust in Business   39

Introduction   39

    Box: "Aristotle, Kant, and Mill on Honesty"   42

Albert Z. Carr | "Is Business Bluffing Ethical?"   43

    Box: "Nietzsche on Honesty"   48

Norman E. Bowie | "Does It Pay to Bluff in Business?"   48

Sissela Bok | "Defining Secrecy—Some Crucial Distinctions"   50

Sue De Wine | "Giving Feedback: The Consultant's Craft"   54

Adelaide Lancaster | "3 Steps to a More Honest Business"   58

Harry G. Frankfurt | "On Bullshit"   60

Paul Ekman and Mark G. Frank | "Lies That Fail"   61

    Box: "Transparency International—USA Program"   65

Robert C. Solomon and Fernando Flores | "Building Trust"   68

Tamar Frankel | "Trust, Honesty and Ethics in Business"   72

CASES

Case 2.1: Robert C. Solomon, "Flying or Lying in Business Class"   77

Case 2.2: Robert C. Solomon, "Willful Ignorance? Or Deception?"   77

Case 2.3: Clancy Martin, "Blindsided by Bankruptcy"   78

Case 2.4: William H. Shaw and Vincent Barry, "Testing for Honesty"   79

Case 2.5: Margaret P. Battin and Gordon B. Mower, "The Columbia Shuttle
    Disaster: Should We Have Told the Astronauts the Truth?"   82

3 The Good Life   85

Introduction   85

Robert C. Solomon | "Strategic Planning—For the Good Life"   87

Aristotle | "On the Good Life"   89

    Box: "Adam Smith on Capitalism"   93

Joanne B. Ciulla | "Work and Life"   94

    Box: "Worthy Work"   96

Epicurus | "On Pleasure"   97

Andrew Carnegie | "Wealth"   99

Solomon Schimmel | "Greed"   103

Joanne B. Ciulla | "Leisure and Consumption"   104

> Box: Bertrand Russell, "In Praise of Idleness"   106

Lynne McFall | "Integrity"   110

Bertrand Russell | "Impersonal Interests"   113

CASES

Case 3.1: James Fenimore Cooper, "The Opportunist"   115

Case 3.2: Bowen H. McCoy, "The Parable of the Sadhu"   116

> Box: "A Happiness Box"   117

Case 3.3: Arthur Miller, "A Life Badly Lived"   119

Case 3.4: Ruth Capriles, "Rags to Riches to Rags"   120

Case 3.5: Nona Walia, "Are You Living the Good Life?"   124

Case 3.6: D. Anthony Plath, "The Curious Loan Approval"   126

4 Money, How We Get It, and Where It Goes: Accounting,
   Finance, and Investment Ethics   128

Introduction   128

> Box: "Accounting and Mergers"   129

> Box: "Six Principles of Ethical Accounting"   130

Carol J. Loomis | "Lies, Damned Lies, and Managed Earnings"   132

> Box: "Learning to Cheat?"   133

> Box: "Ethical Decision Making"   136

Ed Cohen | "Arthur Andersen Refugees Reflect on What Went Wrong"   139

> Box: Sherron Watkins, "Before the Whistle Blew..."   140

Robert E. Frederick and W. Michael Hoffman | "The Individual Investor in Securities
                                                        Markets: An Ethical Analysis"   141

John R. Boatright | "Finance Ethics"   146

> Box: "The Wake-Up Call"   149

Jennifer Moore | "What Is Really Unethical About Insider Trading?"   152

> Box: Roel C. Campos, "Ethics Matter"   158

Frank Partnoy | "F.I.A.S.C.O."   160

> Box: "Aristotle on Money"   162

Paul B. Farrell | "Derivatives, the New 'Ticking bomb'"   163

Duff McDonald | "The Running of the Hedgehogs"   166

Niall Ferguson | "Wall Street Lays Another Egg"   169

CASES

Case 4.1: The Democratic Policy Committee, "A Modern History of 'Creative' Accounting"   177

Case 4.2: Lisa H. Newton and David P. Schmidt, "Merger Mania"   179

Case 4.3: Ron Duska, "Annuities to Seniors"   181

Case 4.4: John R. Boatright, "An Auditor's Dilemma"   182

Case 4.5: David Lawrence and Tom L. Beauchamp, "Enron and Employee Investment Risk"   183

Case 4.6: William F. Black, "The Fraud Recipe for CEO's, Why Banks Hate Free Markets and Love Crony Capitalism"   184

Case 4.7: Richard F. DeMong, "SNB Annual Conference"   186

Case 4.8 D. Anthony Plath, "The Accidental Bank Robbery"   187

5 WHO GETS WHAT AND WHY?: FAIRNESS AND JUSTICE   189

Introduction   189

   BOX: "PLATO AND ARISTOTLE ON JUSTICE"   190

Plato | "Ring of Gyges"   192

   BOX: "WOULD YOU RATHER EARN MORE OR JUST MORE THAN THE OTHER FELLOW?"   193

Adam Smith | "On Human Exchange and Human Differences"   194

Latin Trade | "A Latin Viewpoint: The Bentonville Menace"   196

Joanne B. Ciulla | "Exploitation of Need"   198

   BOX: "MARX ON ALIENATED LABOR"   199

John Rawls | "Justice as Fairness"   201

Robert Nozick | "Anarchy, State, and Utopia"   203

Peter Singer | "Rich and Poor"   214

Irving Kristol | "A Capitalist Conception of Justice"   217

   BOX: "OCCUPY WALL STREET"   221

Friedrich von Hayek | "Justice Ruins the Market"   223

Eduard Gracia | "The Winner-Take-All Game"   226

Gerald W. McEntee | "Comparable Worth: A Matter of Simple Justice"   229

Greg Breining | "The 1 Percent: How Lucky They Are"   231

CASES

Case 5.1: Naomi Klein, "Revolution Without Ideology"   233

Case 5.2: Jim Hightower, "Going Down the Road"   235

Case 5.3: Joanne B. Ciulla, "The Problem with Dudley Less"   237

Case 5.4: Joanne B. Ciulla, "Overworked and Ready to Blow"   237

Case 5.5: Rogene A. Buchholz, "Poverty Area Plants"   238

Case 5.6: William H. Shaw and Vincent Barry, "Poverty in America"   239

Case 5.7: William H. Shaw and Vincent Barry, "Burger Beefs"   241

Case 5.8: Sasha Lyutse, "Nike's Suppliers in Vietnam"   243

Case 5.9: Nick Wadhams, "Bad Charity (All I Got Was This Lousy T-Shirt)"   245

6 Is "The Social Responsibility of Business...to Increase Its Profits"?: Social Responsibility and Stakeholder Theory   247

Introduction   247

Milton Friedman | "The Social Responsibility of Business Is to Increase Its Profits"   249

Christopher D. Stone | "Why Shouldn't Corporations Be Socially Responsible?"   254

Peter A. French | "Corporate Moral Agency"   258

R. Edward Freeman | "A Stakeholder Theory of the Modern Corporation"   263

Kenneth J. Arrow | "Social Responsibility and Economic Efficiency"   269

Richard Parker | "Corporate Social Responsibility and Crisis"   273

Alexei M. Marcoux | "Business Ethics Gone Wrong"   275

CASES

Case 6.1: Ana G. Johnson and William F. Whyte, "Mondragon Cooperatives"   280

Case 6.2: Rogene A. Buchholz, "The Social Audit"   281

Case 6.3: Kelley MacDougall, Tom L. Beauchamp, and John Cuddihy, "The NYSEG Corporate Responsibility Case"   282

Case 6.4: Thomas I. White, "Beech-Nut's Imitation Apple Juice"   284

Case 6.5: Thomas I. White, "Sentencing a Corporation to Prison"   285

Case 6.6: Brian Grow, Steve Hamm, and Louise Lee, "The Debate Over Doing Good"   286

Case 6.7: Jagdish Bhagwati, "Blame Bangladesh, Not the Brands"   289

7 When Innovation Bytes Back: Ethics and Technology   290

Introduction   290

Box: "Locke on Property"   291

Deborah C. Johnson | "Intellectual Property Rights and Computer Software"   293

Box: Richard de George, "Seven Theses for Business Ethics and The Information Age"   297

Box: "Foucault and the Panopticon"   299

Elizabeth A. Buchanan | "Information Ethics in a Worldwide Context"   301

Victoria Groom and Clifford Nass | "Can Robots Be Teammates?"   305

>   Box: C. Kluckhorn, "An Internet Culture?"   306

Clive Thompson | "The Next Civil Rights Battle Will Be Over the Mind"   315

Bill Joy | "Why The Future Doesn't Need Us"   316

CASES

Case 7.1: Joel Rudinow and Anthony Graybosch, "The Digital Divide"   321

Case 7.2: Joel Rudinow and Anthony Graybosch, "Hacking into
        the Space Program"   321

Case 7.3: Joel Rudinow and Anthony Graybosch, "The I Love You Virus"   322

Case 7.4: Tom L. Beauchamp and Norman E. Bowie, "Privacy Pressures: The Use of
        Web Bugs at HomeConnection"   322

Case 7.5: Aarti Shahani, "Who Could Be Watching You Watch Your Figure? Your
        Boss"   324

Case 7.6: James Losey, "The Internet's Intolerable Acts"   325

8 The Art of Seduction: The Ethics of Advertising, Marketing, and Sales   327

Introduction   327

John Kenneth Galbraith | "The Dependence Effect"   329

>   Box: Plato on the Danger of Believing Bad Arguments   331

Friedrich von Hayek | "The Non Sequitur of the 'Dependence Effect'"   334

Alan Goldman | "The Justification of Advertising in a Market Economy"   337

Leslie Savan | "The Bribed Soul"   342

>   Box: "Conspicuous Consumption"   344

>   Box: "Ask Me No Questions..."   346

G. Richard Shell and Mario Moussa | "Woo with Integrity"   347

CASES

Case 8.1: Manuel G. Velasquez, "Toy Wars"   354

Case 8.2: Rogene A. Buchholz, "Advertising at Better Foods"   357

Case 8.3: Joseph R. Desjardins and John J. McCall, "Advertising's
        Image of Women"   358

Case 8.4: William H. Shaw and Vincent Barry, "Hucksters in the Classroom"   359

Case 8.5: Tom L. Beauchamp and Norman E. Bowie, "Marketing Malt Liquor"   361

Case 8.6: Scott Croker, "Energy Drinks, Do They Really Work?"   362

9 Things Fall Apart: Product Liability and Consumers 363

Introduction 363

Peter Huber | "Liability" 366

John Nesmith | "Calculating Risks: It's Easier Said Than Done" 371

Box: "What's Risky? Chances of Death?" 372

Stanley J. Modic | "How We Got into This Mess" 373

Henry Fairlie | Fear of Living 377

Warren E. Burger | "Too Many Lawyers, Too Many Suits" 381

Mark Dowie | "Pinto Madness" 384

Patricia Werhane | "The Pinto Case and the Rashomon Effect" 387

Judith Jarvis Thomson | "Remarks on Causation and Liability" 391

Bob Sullivan | "Annoying Fine Print May Not Even Be Legal" 397

CASES

Case 9.1: William H. Shaw and Vincent Barry, "The Skateboard Scare" 399

Case 9.2: William H. Shaw and Vincent Barry, "Aspartame: Miracle Sweetener or Dangerous Substance?" 400

Case 9.3: Joseph R. Desjardins and John J. McCall, "Children and Reasonably Safe Products" 402

Case 9.4: William H. Shaw and Vincent Barry, "Living and Dying with Asbestos" 403

Case 9.5: Kenneth B. Moll and Associates, "Merck and Vioxx" 406

Case 9.6: Claude Wyle, "The Top 10 Most Dangerous Toys of All Time" 407

Case 9.7: Jack Bouboushian, "Ten More Deaths Blamed on Plavix" 408

10 "You Know How to Whistle, Don't You?": Whistle-Blowing, Company Loyalty, and Employee Responsibility 410

Introduction 410

Box: "Martin Luther King on Silence" 411

Sissela Bok | "Whistleblowing and Professional Responsibility" 412

Box: "Ralph Nader on Whistle-Blowing" 414

Michael Davis | "Some Paradoxes of Whistleblowing" 417

Ronald Duska | "Whistleblowing and Employee Loyalty" 423

Box: Joseph Pulitzer, "On Secrecy and Disclosure" 425

Box: Jim Yardley, "The Upside of Whistle-Blowing" 427

David E. Soles | "Four Concepts of Loyalty" 428

Box: Robert C. Solomon and Clancy Martin, "Blind to Earned Loyalty" 431

George D. Randels | "Loyalty, Corporations, and Community" 435

Kim Zetter | "Why We Cheat" 439

CASES

Case 10.1: Sherron Watkins, "The Once Successful Business Model" 442

Case 10.2: Pat L. Burr, "Would You Blow the Whistle on Yourself?" 444

Case 10.3: William H. Shaw and Vincent Barry, "Changing Jobs and Changing Loyalties" 445

Case 10.4: Larry Margasak, "The Greenhouse Effect: Putting the Heat on Halliburton" 446

Case 10.5: Joseph R. Desjardins and John J. McCall, "Whistleblowing at the Phone Company" 447

11 Think Local, Act Global: International Business 449

Introduction 449

Anthony Kwame Appiah | "Global Villages" 452

Box: "Isaiah Berlin on Values" 458

Thomas Donaldson | "Values in Tension: Ethics Away from Home" 458

Box: "What Do These Values Have in Common?" 462

Florian Wettstein | "Silence and Complicity: Elements of a Corporate Duty to Speak Against the Violation of Human Rights" 466

Box: "The Global Compact" 471

John T. Noonan, Jr. | "A Quick Look at the History of Bribes" 472

Box: "The Foreign Corrupt Practices Act" 475

Daryl Koehn | "Confucian Trustworthiness" 476

CASES

Case 11.1: Joanne B. Ciulla, "The Oil Rig" 481

Case 11.2: Thomas Dunfee and Diana Robertson, "Foreign Assignment" 483

Case 11.3: Karen Marquiss and Joanne B. Ciulla, "The Quandry at PureDrug" 484

Case 11.4: Judith Schrempf-Stirling, and Guido Palazzo "IBM's Business with Hitler: An Inconvenient Past" 486

Case 11.5: Emily Black and Miriam Eapen, "Suicides at Foxconn" 493

Box: "Interns at Foxconn" 496

Case 11.6: Motorola University, "Personal Luxury or Family Loyalty?" 496

12 WORKING WITH MOTHER NATURE: ENVIRONMENTAL ETHICS AND BUSINESS
      ECOLOGY   499

    Introduction   499

        BOX: "NATIVE AMERICAN PROVERB"   500

    Aldo Leopold | "The Land Ethic"   501

    Mark Sagoff | "At the Shrine of Our Lady Fatima *or* Why Political
               Questions Are Not All Economic"   503

        BOX: NATIONAL ENVIRONMENTAL EDUCATION AND TRAINING FOUNDATION
           (MAY 2001), "THE NINTH ANNUAL NATIONAL REPORT ON ENVIRONMENTAL
           ATTITUDES, KNOWLEDGE, AND BEHAVIORS"   504

        BOX: CHIEF JOSEPH OF THE NEZ PERCE, "THE EARTH AND MYSELF ARE OF
           ONE MIND"   507

    William F. Baxter | "People or Penguins"   510

        BOX: MILTON FRIEDMAN, "ON POLLUTION"   512

    Norman Bowie | "Morality, Money, and Motor Cars"   515

        BOX: VINE DELORIA, "LAND AS A COMMODITY"   516

        BOX: "WHO OWNS THE EARTH?"   518

    Peter Singer | "The Place of Nonhumans in Environmental Issues"   521

        BOX: LUTHER STANDING BEAR, "THE TAME LAND"   524

    CASES

    Case 12.1: Thomas I. White, "The Ethics of Dolphin–Human Interaction"   526

    Case 12.2: William H. Shaw and Vincent Barry, "Made in
            the U.S.A.—and Dumped"   528

    Case 12.3: William H. Shaw and Vincent Barry, "The Fordasaurus"   530

    Case 12.4: Denis G. Arnold, "Texaco in the Ecuadorean Amazon"   532

    Case 12.5: Cheryl Davenport, "The Broken 'Buy-One, Give-One'
            Model: 3 Ways to Save Toms Shoes"   534

    Case 12.6: Morgan Carroll and Rhonda Fields, "Protect Us From Fracking"   536

13 WHEN THE BUCK STOPS HERE: LEADERSHIP   538

    Introduction   538

    Joanne B. Ciulla | "What Is Good Leadership?"   540

    Niccolo Machiavelli | "Is It Better to Be Loved than Feared?"   545

        BOX: "LAO TZU AND *TAO-TE-CHING*"   547

    Al Gini | "Moral Leadership and Business Ethics"   548

    Joanne B. Ciulla | "Why Business Leaders' Values Matter"   553

Dean C. Ludwig and Clinton O. Longenecker | "The Bathsheba Syndrome: The Ethical
Failure of Successful Leaders"   559

BOX: "PLATO ON WHY ETHICAL PEOPLE DON'T WANT TO BE LEADERS"   564

Robert Greenleaf | "Servant Leadership: A Journal into the Nature of Legitimate Power
and Greatness"   565

CASES

Case 13.1: George Orwell, "Shooting an Elephant"   567

Case 13.2: Mary Ann Glynn and Timothy J. Dowd, "Martha Stewart Focuses
on Her Salad"   571

Case 13.3: Joanne B. Ciulla, "Merck and Roy Vagelos: The Values of Leaders"   575

Case 13.4: Katherine Burton and Saijel Kishan, "How Raj Rajaratnam Gave Galleon
Group Its 'Edge' "   577

14 WHO'S MINDING THE STORE?: THE ETHICS OF CORPORATE GOVERNANCE   580

Introduction   580

Ralph Nader, Mark Green, and Joel Seligman | "Who Rules the Corporation?"   582

Irving S. Shapiro | "Power and Accountability: The Changing Role of the Corporate
Board of Directors"   588

BOX: IMMANUEL KANT, "ADVICE FOR CORPORATE DIRECTORS"   590

BOX: "CORPORATE-GOVERNANCE REFORM"   591

Rebecca Reisner | "When Does the CEO Just Quit?"   595

Thomas W. Dunfee | "Corporate Governance in a Market with Morality"   597

John J. McCall | "Employee Voice in Corporate Governance: A Defense of Strong
Participation Rights"   615

BOX: "DOES GOVERNANCE NEED GOVERNMENT?"   619

BOX: WARREN BUFFETT, "ADVICE TO OUTSIDE AUDITORS"   621

CASES

Case 14.1: Michael Lewis, "Selling Your Sole at Birkenstock"   623

Case 14.2: Dennis Moberg and Edward Romar, "The Good Old Boys at
WorldCom"   625

Case 14.3: Robert Reich, "Corporate Governance and Democracy"   629

Case 14.4: David Seltzer, "Pump It Up"   630

Case 14.5: Lefteris Pitarakis, "Fight Corporate Crimes with More than Fines"   631

15 IS EVERYTHING FOR SALE?: THE FUTURE OF THE FREE MARKET   633

Introduction   633

Aristotle | "Two Kinds of Commerce"   634

Adam Smith | "The Benefits of Capitalism"   637

Karl Marx | "Commodity Fetishism"   639

Robert Heilbroner | "Reflections on the Triumph of Capitalism"   642

John Stuart Mill | "Laissez-faire and Education"   645

John Maynard Keynes | "Economic Possibilities for Our Grandchildren" (1930)   648

E. F. Schumacher | "Buddhist Economics"   653

Amartya Sen | "The Economics of Poverty"   658

Thorstein Veblen | "Pecuniary Emulation and Conspicuous Consumption"   660

Daniel Bell | "The Cultural Contradictions of Capitalism"   662

Robert B. Reich | "Supercapitalism"   665

Thomas Frank | "Too Smart to Fail: Notes on an Age of Folly"   674

Robert Kuttner | "Everything for Sale"   675

CASES

Case 15.1: William H. Shaw and Vincent Barry, "Blood for Sale"   679

Case 15.2: Tom L. Beauchamp, Jeff Greene, and Sasha Lyuste, "Cocaine at the Fortune-500 Level"   681

Case 15.3: Megan McArdle, "Right to Work"   682

INDEX   685

PREFACE

FOR THE STUDENT

This reader is for undergraduate, graduate, and executive business ethics courses, as well as for anyone who wants to think about the challenges involved in being good and doing well in business. The readings cover all aspects of business ethics under the overarching theme of the good life—what it means to you as a person, what it means for business, and what it means for society. There is no bright line between business ethics and this most ancient of ethical concerns, the search for the good, happy, and productive life, free of regrets. Hence, ethics is not just a peripheral concern of business or a set of constraints on business enterprise. It stands at the very core of business activity and defines the overall concepts and context in which business plays its role.

The articles and cases in this book consist of classic and recent articles and cases that span a broad spectrum of issues, topics, and problems. We have selected pieces that have both practical import and wide application and have structured the narratives that open the book and each chapter as personal challenges, presenting the reader with real ethical issues and questions. We also tried to select articles that are fun to read. Unlike most textbooks, we have taken the liberty of addressing the reader in the second person—you—in our introductions and narratives. The point of studying ethics is to reflect on how you, not some third party or friend of yours, ought to behave.

The readings, as well as the philosophical email messages, are presented as resources to use as you work your way through the various issues and problems in business ethics. We aim to engage you directly and practically in business ethics, not just to offer up a potpourri of "interesting" debates and proclamations. The chapters, readings, and cases are presented so that every instructor will feel free to organize the course as he or she sees fit. You, the reader, are encouraged to browse and enjoy them in any order you want. Only so much of the book can be covered in class, but you may well find your own interests provoked by some of the other material in the book.

NEW TO THE THIRD EDITION

There are a number of changes in this edition that we made in response to the business climate and the comments of our reviewers. These include 40 new articles and cases. Here are a few samples of the new material from each chapter:

- We have added more discussion questions throughout the book.
- In the introduction, we now include Robert Audi's succinct description of some of the basic ethical theories.
- Chapter 1, on ethics in the workplace, contains several new articles such as Harry J. Van Buren's "Boundaryless Careers and Employability Obligations," which addresses the problems of employment in a difficult and uncertain job market.
- Chapter 2, on honesty and trust in business, includes a new reading called "3 Steps to a More Honest Business," by Adelaide Lancaster.
- Chapter 3, on the good life, remains the same but has two more cases that help the reader think about how the good life is related to the decisions that they make at work.
- Chapter 4, on money and finance, features Niall Ferguson's "Wall Street Lays Another Egg," which we think offers one of the best explanations of the financial crisis.
- Chapter 5, on justice and fairness, includes a piece on the Occupy Wall Street movement and Greg Breining's "The 1 Percent: How Lucky They Are."
- Chapter 6, on social responsibility and stakeholder theory, now has Alexei M. Marcoux's "Business Ethics Gone Wrong," which discusses the failures of stakeholder theory.
- Chapter 7, on innovation and technology, includes a new case about whether your boss should be able to monitor your weight through your cell phone.
- Chapter 8, on marketing and sales, offers a new case on marketing energy drinks.
- Chapter 9, on product liability, examines the sale of toys in "The Top 10 Most Dangerous Toys of All Time," by Claude Wyle.
- Chapter 10, on whistle-blowing, we kept intact because it treats the basic ethical issues of the topic. You can find your own new whistle-blowing cases in the newspaper.
- Chapter 11, on international business, has been extensively revamped with several new articles and cases such as Anthony Kwame Appiah's article on how cultures influence people, "Global Villages," and a historical case about IBM's relationship with Hitler.
- Chapter 12, on the environment, includes some new cases on topics such as the environmental impact of fracking.
- Chapter 13, on leadership, has several new articles and cases, including Al Gini's "Moral Leadership and Business Ethics" and a case on the billionaire founder of the Galleon Group, Raj Rajaratnam.
- Chapter 14, on corporate governance, has new cases, one of which looks at the efficacy of using fines to fight corporate crime.
- Chapter 15, on the future of the free market, has some provocative old and new articles in it such as John Maynard Keynes' "Economic Possibilities for Our Grandchildren" and Thomas Frank's "Too Smart to Fail: Notes on an Age of Folly."

FOR THE INSTRUCTOR

Although this book is intended to serve the function of a general-purpose traditional business ethics reader, we have also made a special effort to incorporate readings that are not so traditional and reflect dominant current themes and concerns—for instance, the ever-new technology and the ongoing globalization of the business world. We have also set our focus on what we consider the central and often most neglected theme in business ethics—the nature, the rewards, the costs, the promises, and the betrayals of work as such. Our students will work in a world in which the very meaning of work is in question. Ignoring that question or taking the meaning of work for granted does them an extreme disservice. While to be sure, this is not the whole of business ethics, we think it is its necessary starting point. It catches the students where their central concerns are: *What do you want to do? Why? And what kind of life do you think you'll achieve by doing it?*

What we have not done is what many business ethics texts stubbornly insist on doing, namely, to begin our text with an overview of different ethical theories and then "apply" these various theories throughout the book. This book is not about a competition between ethical theories. Instead, we offer a brief article on ethical theories in the beginning of the book so that students will be familiar with them when they encounter these theories in other articles. Questions about happiness, consequences, moral rules, and character, as well as about the nature of entitlement and contracts (social and otherwise) and the obligations they engender, emerge quite effortlessly from the students' own stated interests. Although moral reasoning is essential to the skills and the ethical "toolbox" that the students will need, we have found it much more effective when these skills are learned while the students are wrestling with real problems that they care about. This approach allows our text to be accessible to instructors from a variety of academic backgrounds.

Ethics, of course, is already on the minds of any student who reads or watches the news. It is not possible to cover all recent and still-unfolding scandals, nor is that necessarily the best way to teach business ethics. We selected the readings and cases as platforms for critical discussion and analysis of the issues that lie behind the headlines.

The premise of this book, and we think the premise of business ethics as a subject, is the idea that every job and every career has its responsibilities and its ethical issues; and for all students who are even thinking of spending part of their lives in the business world, it is necessary to be prepared by being informed and thoughtful. Some of the chapters in this text address the immediate work issues that students will face, but others are more thought-provoking and abstract. We think, as we said earlier, that the two feed on one another. Some issues require immediate action, but all require thought and understanding about what goes and what does not go in the peculiar ethics of the business world. So, in addition to the "issues at work" sorts of chapters, there are also the "big issues in the business world" chapters, on justice, on social responsibility, and on the nature of the market itself. There are also "how to live" chapters, in which the students are encouraged to think about how their planned careers in business fit into and help satisfy their larger life goals. It is often said that "no one dies wishing that he or she had spent more time at the office," but the profundity of that witticism often escapes business students. They underestimate the nature of the commitments that they are about to enter into, and their perspective on the good life—which many of them sample indulgently as students—is easily lost once they submerge themselves in various corporate and career cultures. So that, too, is the central theme of business ethics—not just work but work as it fits into and promotes the good life. In this book, we have tried to package some of the best and most prominent and most lively writings and issues, together with some of the most challenging cases and case studies, supplemented with philosophical insights, in a single volume that allows each instructor to design his or her own course, but in a package that already presents, we think, the materials for an exciting course.

ANCILLARY MATERIAL

A website for *Honest Work* can be found online at www.oup.com/us/ciulla. There, you will find ancillary material for instructors and students. Under password protection, instructors will find Sample Syllabi, Chapter Summaries, Lecture Outlines in PowerPoint format, and a Test Bank with essay questions, multiple-choice questions, true/false questions, and fill-in-the-blank questions. Both students and instructors will be able to access Chapter Goals, Suggested Readings & Media, Suggested Weblinks, and Student Self-Quizzes with multiple-choice, true/false, and fill-in-the-blank questions.

Additionally, instructors can find all this material on an Instructor Resources CD, available upon request from your publisher's representative.

ACKNOWLEDGMENTS

Editing this third edition of *Honest Work* still elicits fond memories of our dear friend and co-author Bob Solomon. His voice still echoes throughout the book, but resounds especially in Chapter 3 on the good life, which we only altered by adding a few more questions and cases. The changes on this book are the result of comments by the thoughtful and generous teacher/scholars who reviewed the second edition of the book. We owe our gratitude to David F. Dieteman, Pennsylvania State University—Erie & The Behrend College; S. L. Dwyer, Georgia State University; Francisco Gamez, University of San Francisco; Keith Korcz, University of Louisiana at Lafayette; Mitchell Langbert, Brooklyn College; Christopher Meakin, University of Texas at Austin; Dale Miller, Old Dominion University; Joshua Broady Preiss, Minnesota State University Mankato; and Jiyun Wu, Hofstra University. Our thanks to John Boatright, at Loyola University of Chicago, who gave us some very useful advice on the articles. A special thanks goes out to René Kanters, University of Richmond, for helping compile the book, as well as to Jessica Swope for hunting down the permissions for it. Last but not least, we are grateful to our wise and patient editors at Oxford University Press, Robert Miller and Kristin Maffei.

INTRODUCTION: GETTING TO WORK

You are about to begin a most important part of your business education, the study, discussion, and practice of business ethics. Business ethics has a few simple and rarely contested premises. These premises have their exceptions, to be sure, but there is little doubt that they hold up in general. First, ethics is essential to the functioning of the business world and the market. The opposite of ethics is corruption, and we know how badly corrupt countries and systems perform, insofar as they perform at all. Ethics is a fundamental part of business education, not an embellishment. Every course you take is not simply about learning the techniques of marketing, finance, accounting, and so forth, but how to practice them in the right way. Second, sound ethical practices are what make a business viable and adaptable to change over time. We do not claim that ethics *always* pays, but we do know how much ethical failure costs, not just in financial terms but in terms of productivity, innovation, morale, and goodwill in organizations. The sheer weight of guilt and regret is hard to measure, but everyone who has ever done anything wrong (and that covers just about all of us) knows how much such feelings can take away from a happy life. Third, business ethics is *everybody's* business. Every business student, every businessperson, every employee, every manager, and every executive has as his or her primary responsibility, along with learning and doing his or her job, acting ethically and, on occasion, speaking up in the face of unethical behavior. On the down side, *not* being ethical—or even failing to speak up—can bring a career, no matter how successful, to a sudden, humiliating halt. Ethical failures invite bankruptcy, lawsuits, and even jail time.

We designed this text with the pervasiveness of ethics in business and the personal nature of everyone's responsibility regarding ethics in mind. It is made up of the some of the best writing on business ethics along a broad spectrum of issues. But the readings are all directed toward one end, a practical end, and that is to provide you with the material to think about and discuss and ultimately to practice ethics in business. There are readings that tackle some huge questions about the nature of free enterprise and the new world of business in a globalized economy. There are readings concerning the new technologies and the ethical questions they raise. There are readings that focus on the details of your job—your rights, duties, and responsibilities as an employee or manager. In every reading, we want you to "take it personally." Take each issue as *your* issue, grapple with it as if it is up to you to decide, sitting there at or on your desk. These are issues that demand a decision and a solution. Someday soon, one or more of them may well be yours.

So, this book is ultimately about you, about you in business, about you as a professional, and about you as a decent human being. Our introductions to the various chapters all begin by presenting you with a situation, sometimes an ethical problem or dilemma, of the sort you may face on the job and sometimes a broader ethical issue in the business or economic world. We make no assumptions about whether you are male or female, where or in what industry you work, your precise aspirations or talents, or your race or religion. You know who you are. But ethics isn't just a matter of intuition or "gut feelings." It involves thought; information; practice in moral reasoning; and, if possible, knowledge of other, similar case histories. So you need resources—thought-provoking essays, facts, case studies, and philosophical insights.

Philosophy? Isn't that for airheads? What does it have to do with the rough and tumble of business life? But virtually every business and every businessperson has a philosophy, whether he or she calls it that or not. A philosophy specifies what is most important and what is not. A philosophy in business is a view or a vision of the place of one's business activities in one's life, in the community, and in the larger social world. It is a personal policy concerning the right and wrong ways to go about making money and the right and wrong ways of treating people (and being treated yourself). It is keeping the big picture in mind, the idea that money isn't everything, the idea that not everything is for sale, the importance of family and friends and community. (If you disagree with any of these statements, you *really* need this course.) We should add the love of one's country and one's culture, a hope for the well-being of all humanity, and some sense of the transcendent or the spiritual. By this we mean not only your religious beliefs and feelings, but the more worldly aspiration to be more than just a practical person caught up in daily routines. There are larger questions of meaning that business and making money cannot answer, like "what is the point of all this?" (Again, if you really think that the point is *just* to make money, you really need this course.)

Many great philosophers and social thinkers have had many things to say about these questions. Some of them were suspicious or even hostile to business. They saw business and making money as a tempting distraction from the more important things in life. But many philosophers and social thinkers were positive and even enthusiastic about business. The most famous of them, at least as far as business students are concerned, was Adam Smith, a moral philosopher (as well as a classic economist) in eighteenth-century Scotland. Smith thought that business (or, more accurately, the free enterprise system) offered tremendous hope to the world. But he was also very clear about the ethical presuppositions of any business culture, some sense of community or "fellow-feeling," a concern for justice and fairness in business dealings, a "natural" sense of sympathy for our fellow human beings. He would not have hesitated for a moment to embed his philosophy of business in a much larger picture of human happiness and well-being. And that is the philosophy of this book and this course as well. It is not to deny or cast doubt on business, but to situate it in a larger setting.

But you are too busy, no doubt, to read the often-wordy treatises of the philosophers. (Adam Smith's book *The Wealth of Nations* is over 500 pages long; his earlier book, *The Theory of the Moral Sentiments*, is not much shorter.) So we have devised a painless and efficient way to offer you these philosophical probes and insights. Perhaps you barely remember that roommate you had in your freshman year who considered a career in business but ultimately decided to study philosophy. For a couple of years, you lost touch. But as you have gotten into business ethics, this roommate (whom you have come to call "the philosopher") has made a point of getting back in touch with you by email. As you read through the chapters on business and ethics, the philosopher reminds you of some of the great thoughts about business, ethics, and the good life. The philosopher's responses to your questions and opinions on various ethical issues and problems in business appear in various boxes throughout the text, providing you with some wise reflections from great thinkers past and present. Think of these boxes and others in the text as those occasional email messages you receive from friends that provide you with thoughts and an occasional laugh while you study for your courses and for your future career.

Three Questions for Thinking About Ethics

The most difficult ethical problems are not black or white. Moral problems tend to have three facets to them that are more or less captured in some of the ethical theories you will run across in this book. We offer these three simple questions to help you organize your thoughts when you make ethical decisions or analyze the ethical behavior of people and organizations. In the first person they are:

Am I doing the right thing?
Am I doing it the right way?
Am I doing it for the right reasons?

In short, ethical behavior is generally about doing the right thing, the right way, for the right reason. Nonetheless, sometimes people do the right thing the wrong way, for the wrong reason; or the wrong thing, the right way, for the right reason, etc. Often the most difficult ethical problems are the ones where people can only answer "yes" to one or two of the three questions.

Robert Audi

Some Approaches to Determining Ethical Obligations

Robert Audi is the John O'Brian Professor of Philosophy at the University of Notre Dame.

UTILITARIANISM

For John Stuart Mill (the greatest nineteenth-century English philosopher), the master utilitarian principle is roughly this: choose that act from among your options which is best from the twin points of view of increasing human happiness and reducing human suffering:

> The creed which accepts as the foundation of morals "utility"...holds that actions are right in proportion as they tend to promote happiness, wrong as they tend to produce the reverse of happiness. By happiness is intended pleasure, and the absence of pain.

John Stuart Mill, Utilitarianism, Oscar Priest, ed. CNY: Macmillan, 1957, p. 10.

This formula does not tell us when an act is right, period; but the idea is that right acts contribute at least as favorably to the "proportion" of happiness to unhappiness (in the relevant population) as any alternative the agent has. Thus, if one act produces more happiness than another, it is preferable, other things equal. If the first also produces suffering, other things are not equal. We have to weigh good consequences of our projected acts against any bad consequences and, in appraising a prospective act, subtract its negative value from its positive value.

Utilitarianism calls for maximization. To see why producing even a *lot* of good may not be not ethically sufficient, consider two points: (1) the more we have of what is good—good in itself, *basically* good—the better; (2) it is a mistake to produce less good than we can or, correspondingly, to reduce what is bad less than we can. Arguably, no good person would act suboptimally if this could be avoided. Ideally, then, we would simultaneously produce pleasure and reduce pain. Often we cannot do both. A situation may be so dire that reducing pain is all we can do. For utilitarianism, although some people are better candidates to be made happy— or less unhappy—everyone matters morally.

On the plausible assumption that total happiness is best served by maintaining minimal well-being for the worst off, utilitarianism supports welfare capitalism. But it does not automatically support any highly specific position on the obligations of business. One might think otherwise if one identifies utilitarianism with the idea that ethics requires our producing the "greatest good for the greatest number." One reason utilitarianism does *not* imply any such thing is that great benefits (hence much good.) to some, say college students, could quantitatively outweigh even the greatest benefits a business or government could provide for a larger number of people, say by tax cuts for the whole population. Figure 0-1 makes this clear: the former, educational policy, could raise the *overall* happiness level (or lower the unhappiness

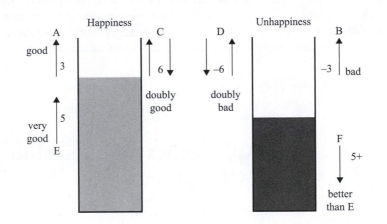

FIGURE 0-1 Utilitarianism: Six types of act scored in terms of maximizing the "ratio" of the good (represented by the lighter shading) to the bad (represented by the darker shading).The containers represent the "quantities" of the good (happiness) and the bad (unhappiness) in the population (possibly all persons) whose well-being concerns the utilitarian. The letters represent acts considered; the length of the accompanying arrows—and the positive or negative numbers beside the acts—represent the positive or negative change in quantity of well-being the acts produce in the indicated direction. Act A is good; B is bad (hence its negative score). For acts C and D, let the left arrow represents the change produced in the unhappiness level and the right arrow represents the change produced in the unhappiness level. C, then, is doubly good, since it both increases happiness and decreases unhappiness; D is doubly bad, since it does the opposite. E is better than A, since it produces more happiness. Our obligation is to maximize the difference between the levels, favoring happiness (the lighter shading) over unhappiness (the darker shading). For a qualified utilitarian view that weights reducing unhappiness higher than increasing happiness, F might be better than E even if they produce the same net change in the ratio of the good to the bad.

level, or both) more than the latter, tax relief legislation, regardless of the smaller number of beneficiaries of the educational policy.

How utilitarianism apparently supports welfare capitalism over other economic systems needs explanation. Here is a possible account. Arguably, businesses will contribute most favorably to human happiness (roughly, to the proportion of happiness to unhappiness in the world) by simply making a profit in a fair system of competition and paying taxes at a level high enough to support effective welfare programs and low enough to preserve incentives to gain wealth. For—given the incentives this arrangement might provide for talented people—it might not only support welfare programs but also lead to miracle drugs, fuel-efficient cars, superior fertilizers, and the like. Utilitarians may also argue that—at least if business leaders are utilitarians—then for both economic and ethical reasons, businesses operating in a welfare capitalist system will also contribute to the overall well-being of society through voluntary contributions, such as support for community projects, education, and the arts.

RIGHTS-BASED ETHICS

A very different ethical approach takes off from the idea that the main ethical demand is that we act within our rights and accord other people theirs. On this view, right action is simply action within one's rights, whereas wrong action violates rights. Rights may be negative, for instance rights *not* to be harmed or deprived of free expression, or positive, say rights to be given what is promised you, including such things as emergency medical treatment if the government has guaranteed it. *Roughly speaking*, negative rights coincide with liberties, positive rights with entitlements to benefits.

From this perspective we can see how someone might ask: Why should businesses *have* to contribute to the well-being of society by doing anything positive for society? What right does government have to force taxation for this purpose, as opposed to police and military protection? Granted, our property rights are limited by obligations to support some government programs, most notably policing and defense, but once businesses pay their fair share of taxes for these, why should they do more?

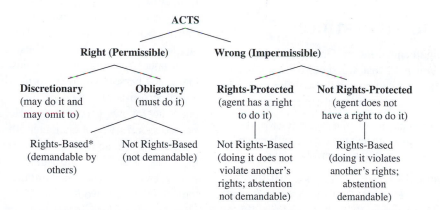

FIGURE 0-2 This figure shows an ethical classification of acts indicating how a rights-based ethics views obligation: our obligations lie *only* within others' rights against us. Most other ethical views recognize *wrongs within rights*, i.e., violations of obligations to others by acts that are *not* within their rights against us. Note that many right acts are discretionary (e.g., having coffee as opposed to tea) rather than obligatory (e.g., keeping a promise). Rights-based obligations—the *only* obligations under a rights-based ethics—lie in the starred category. Wrongs within rights are shown in the *rights-protected* category; e.g., giving nothing to charity may be wrong, though within one's rights and not *demandable* by charities. Unlike promise-keeping, it is a non-rights-based obligation and may be wrong, though within one's rights and not *demandable* by charities.

To this view, utilitarians and other *good-based* theorists may reply that even if businesses have a *right* not to do more, in the sense that their freedom not to do more should not be abridged by *compulsion*, they *ought* to do more. The plausible ethical point here is that a rights-based morality is unduly narrow. It takes what we ought (morally) to do to be only what we have no right not to do—presumably because someone else has a right to demand our doing it, in the sense that our not doing it violates that person's rights. All else is discretionary, as shown in Figure 0-2. In reality, however, we can and do distinguish between what we ought and ought not to do even *within* the sphere of our rights. Take a simple example: relations with coworkers. Our coworkers have a right to some consideration, say to being given at least minimal cooperation, but we *ought* to do more to support them than the minimum they can claim as their right.

It is not just utilitarians who think that ethics calls on us to do things we have a right not to do. This will be apparent from an outline of two other plausible and widely held ethical views: Kantianism and virtue ethics.

KANTIAN ETHICS

The great eighteenth-century German philosopher Immanuel Kant held that we should always act in such a way that we can rationally will the principle we are acting on to be a universal law:

> So act as if the maxim of your action [that is, the principle of conduct underlying the action] were to become through your will a universal law of nature.

This "Categorical Imperative" implies that I should not leave someone to bleed to death on the roadside if I could not rationally will the universality of the practice—say, even where *I* am the victim. We would not want to universalize, and thus live by, the callous principle: one should stop for someone bleeding to death provided it requires no self-sacrifice. Similarly, I should not make a lying promise to repay borrowed money if I could not rationally universalize my underlying principle, say that when I can get money only by making a lying promise,

I will do this. One way to see why the Imperative apparently disallows this is to note that we *count on* promises from others and cannot rationally endorse the universality of a deceitful promissory practice that would victimize us.

Kant also gave a less abstract formulation of the Categorical Imperative:

> Act so that you use humanity, as much in your own person as in the person of every other, always at the same time as an end and never merely as a means.

The idea is roughly that we must treat people as valuable in themselves, never merely as means to some end of ours. We are never to *use* people—including low-level, readily replaceable employees—as in manipulatively lying to them. Treating people as ends clearly requires caring about their good. They matter as persons, and we must at times and to some extent act for *their sake*, whether or not we benefit from it.

VIRTUE ETHICS

Virtue ethics differs from both utilitarianism and Kantianism in not being *rule centered*. Instead of proposing rules of conduct, it demands that we concentrate on being good as persons. Be honest, just, kind, and honorable, for instance. Thus, the ancient Greek philosopher Aristotle described just acts as the kind that a just person would perform. He did not define a just person as one who performs just acts, nor as one who follows certain rules. He apparently considered moral traits of character ethically more basic than moral acts and moral rules. He said, regarding the types of acts that are right: "Actions are called just or temperate when they are the sort that a just or temperate person would do." Similar virtue-ethical ideas are also found in non-Western traditions, such as Confucian ethics, especially as represented by the ancient Chinese philosopher Mencius.

For a virtue ethics, then, agents and their traits, as opposed to rules of action, are morally basic. Virtue ethics would have us ask both what kind of person we want to be and how we want to be seen by those we care about, say friends and family. Who wants to be (correctly) seen as cheap, insensitive, or even just indifferent to others' suffering? Who does not want to be seen as generous, caring, and fair?

One could say that virtue ethics endorses *be-rules* (be just, be honest, be kind) in contrast with *do-rules* (keep your promises). But, suggestive as it is, this contrast is misleading since be-rules do not make clear reference to *how* to fulfill their demands. We cannot fulfill be-rules without some prior knowledge of what to *do*. (It is because this point is understood that virtue ethics is often seen to require a good upbringing with definite kinds of acts prescribed for children.) The positive idea underlying virtue ethics is that we are to understand what it is to behave justly through studying the nature and tendencies of the just person, not the other way around. We do not, for instance, define just deeds as those that, say, treat people equally, and then define a just person as one who characteristically does such deeds.

Thus, for adults as well as for children, and in ordinary life as in business, *role models* are absolutely crucial for moral learning. Virtue ethics is indeed a kind of ethics of role modeling: good role models are *sources*, as well as potential teachers, of ethical standards. Rules of action can be formulated by generalizing from observations of virtuous agents, such as team leaders in a sales division; but the basic ethical standard is character rather than rules of action.

One value of the virtue approach to business ethics is that leadership in business is partly a role-modeling function. To call for conduct of any kind—but especially ethical conduct—when we do not exhibit it ourselves is at best unlikely to succeed and often hypocritical too. Good role modeling, as any major ethical view can stress, is both instructive and motivating.

COMMON-SENSE ETHICAL PLURALISM

Many readers will find something plausible in each of the approaches just sketched. Might a less abstract, more definite view capture much of the best in each? Utilitarianism above all requires good deeds; rights-based views stress respecting freedom, keeping commitments, and protecting property; Kantianism demands respecting others and acting on

principles that accord with this respect; and virtue ethics demands such ethical decisions as are made by people who are, say, just, honest, and beneficent. There are many standards here, but they are not too numerous to be reflected in ordinary principles that morally decent people teach their children and generally follow.

These ordinary ethical principles (1) prohibit injustice, harming others, lying, and breaking promises and (2) positively, call for doing good deeds toward others and for efforts toward self-improvement. They do not require *maximizing* good consequences, but do require at least certain good deeds we can do without great self-sacrifice. Thus, fraudulent accounting, as lying, is prohibited; providing for employees' healthcare, up to some reasonable point, is, as doing good deeds, an obligation of most companies.

Most people find these principles intuitively plausible, and the view that such principles are directly knowable on the basis of reflection on their content—intuitively knowable—is called *ethical intuitionism*. It is considered a common-sense view because these and a few other principles seem to be a common-sensical core toward which the best ethical theories converge. Since common-sense intuitionism is presented in Chapter 4, no further comment is needed here. It must simply be included among the perspectives from which to view the task of determining the ethical responsibilities of business.

Many who reflect on ethics find something of value in all the approaches just described, especially virtue ethics, Kantianism, and utilitarianism. Might a single wide principle include much of their content and encompass much of the common-sense plurality of obligations just indicated? There are apparently at least three conceptually independent factors that a sound ethical view should take into account: happiness, which we may think of as welfare conceived in terms of pleasure, pain, and suffering; justice, conceived largely as requiring equal treatment of persons; and freedom. On this approach—call it *pluralist universalism*—our broadest moral principle would require standards of conduct that optimize happiness as far as possible without producing injustice or curtailing freedom (including one's own). This principle is to be *internalized*—roughly, automatically presupposed and normally also strongly motivating—in a way that yields moral virtue. Right acts would be roughly those that conform to standards—including the ones described in Chapter 4—whose internalization and mutual balancing achieve that end. Each value (happiness, justice, and freedom) becomes, then, a guiding standard, and mature moral agents will develop a sense of how to act (or at least how to reach a decision to act) when the values pull in different directions.

Pluralist universalism is triple-barreled. It implies that no specific, single standard can be our sole moral guide. This is especially so in the case of principles (like this one) that appeal to different and potentially conflicting elements. How should we balance these in the triple-barreled principle? A priority rule for achieving a balance among the three values—and among the common-sense principles that pluralist universalism helps to unify—is this Considerations of justice and freedom take priority (at least normally) over considerations of happiness; justice and freedom do not conflict because justice requires the highest level of freedom possible within the limits of peaceful coexistence, and this is as much freedom as any reasonable ideal of liberty demands. Thus, public sale of a drug that gives people pleasure but reduces their freedom would be prohibited by the triple-barreled principle (apart from, say, special medical uses); a social policy (say, draft exemptions for all who have a high-school education) that makes most citizens happy but causes great suffering for a minority (who must go to war) would be rejected as unjust. Moreover, although one may voluntarily devote one's life to enhancing human happiness (if only by reducing human suffering), this is not obligatory. Thus, coercive force may not be used to produce even such highly desirable beneficence.

On the Job

Everyday Ethics at Work

Introduction

Most workplaces are like zoos. They are filled with a variety of people, some like you and some quite exotic. When you go to work, you navigate your way through a complex web of relationships with people who often seem to be of different species. Some of them are dominant, some are docile, some are cooperative, others are contentious, some are kind, and some will bite you. When you think of it, work is basically about the interaction of people toward some common goals, and ethics is about how they treat each other. The work zoo is an emotional place where employees experience anger, pain, fear, joy, satisfaction, and even love, sometimes all at once and in the same building. Not only do these people have different titles and different job descriptions, they also carry with them different lives shaped by gender, race, ethnicity, religion, health, and personal values, experiences, and cultural and personal preferences. Almost everyone you work with lives in another world with other responsibilities at home and at play. Before they go to work, some drop their children off at day care or school, others leave behind an elderly parent or a seriously ill spouse or partner, and still others say good-bye to their faithful dog or an empty apartment. After work, there are those who go off to help their favorite charity, those who go to the health club, and still others who head for the nearest bar. But they are all fellow members of this human zoo that we call work and, as such, deserve to be treated fairly and with respect.

When you think about it, what most upsets you about your job are the times when you either don't feel like you are treated with respect or don't think you are treated fairly. Throughout the history of modern work, one hears the same refrain from workers, "We just want to be treated like adults!" In the workplace, respect means treating someone as an autonomous person on the job, while at the same time knowing where to draw the line between the employee's job and the employee's personal life. You may have noticed that this line between work and private life is not easy to draw, especially if you socialize with coworkers, check your office email from home or are on call after hours via a pager or cell phone. But as your work life and your "personal" life converge, the question becomes even more pressing: What is the relation between the two? Is it OK for you to do whatever you want to in your personal life as long as you do your job well? What is the proper realm of privacy? And what are the employer's and employee's rights and responsibilities to each other?

Many great thinkers, such as Immanuel Kant, believe that respect for our common humanity is the most important principle of ethics. This chapter begins with a discussion of how Kant's ideas about respect for persons apply to the workplace. One aspect of respecting people is appreciating that they have feelings. In "Exploring the Managed Heart," Arlie Hochschild describes the emotional labor that flight attendants and others in the service industry do every day. Her article raises the question, When does the requirement to be nice to customers compromise the dignity and autonomy of a person? Where does one draw the line between politeness and humiliation? This leads us to the issue of an employee's right to express him or herself at work. Bruce Barry's article, "The Cringing and the Craven: Freedom of Expression in the Workplace," explores the question, Should employees have the same freedom of expression on the job as they have in their personal lives? Do employers have the right to punish employees for expressing their views on things such as politics?

The workplace can be a dangerous place, which raises questions about the obligations of employers to look after the physical, mental, and financial well-being of employees. Employers have power over employees and sometimes they abuse it. Loraleigh Keashly's article looks at one of the darker aspects of human nature—bullying. Bullying has the potential to inflict both physical and emotional damage on employees. Another way that work can be dangerous is when employers ask employees to work in dangerous places. An article from the *Economist* explores some of the ethical problems with putting employees in harm's way. Perhaps the most dangerous thing about the workplace in the twenty-first century is that most businesses are subject to increasingly volatile national and international economic conditions. As a result of this, most employees can lose their jobs at the drop of a hat because of a financial or environmental crisis at home or abroad. In an era where there is little, if any, job security left, what obligations do employers have to employees? Harry J. Van Buren III explores this question in his article, "Boundaryless Careers and Employability Obligations."

The last article in this chapter addresses the question of how your physical appearance affects your employment prospects. People come in all shapes, colors, and sizes, and their faces tell us about their race, ethnicity, and gender. The article "Facial Discrimination" offers us a broad way to think about how employers intentionally and unintentionally discriminate against job applicants because of the way that they look.

The first case in this chapter is from the classic novel *The Man in the Gray Flannel Suit*. It will give you an opportunity to think about who you are and how you want to present yourself to potential employers. We then go from a case on hiring to John Boatright's case on firing, which allows us reflect on how to respect the dignity of a person when you fire him or her. The rest of the cases in this chapter are all true stories that Joanne Ciulla has collected from participants in corporate seminars and students. They have been disguised for use in this text. These cases illustrate the old adage that "truth is stranger than fiction." The first case is about a manager who discovers that a man that his company was planning on promoting beats his wife. The next one is about matching clients with employees who share the same interests and gender. This is a very controversial issue in businesses that provide client services and sales. Should you pair a salesperson who golfs with a client who likes to golf? Is that different from pairing a male salesman with a client who does not seem to respect women? Since most people do not leave their feelings at home when they go to work, we explore a case where an employee chooses a supplier in part because she finds the company rep attractive. The last case is about an intern who discovers pornography on his boss's computer and then does something really stupid.

Since this chapter is about the everyday ethical problems of working with a variety of personalities and problems in the workplace, it offers cases that look at the large and small ethical problems that people face when they work together. All of the cases challenge us to think about our moral obligations to each other. Respect for persons and fairness are both moral obligations, but they are more than that. They are at the core of what makes us good people and represent a good part of what motivates us to cooperate with one another. Thus, a solid sense of what is personally fair (and unfair) lies at the heart of personal, social, and professional success. People have known this for a long time. Around the eighth century B.C., the poet Hesiod wrote, "Neither famine nor disaster ever haunt men who do true justice; but lightheartedly they tend the fields which are all their care."

To: You
From: The Philosopher
Subject: "Sloth: The Noonday Demon"

Have you ever noticed how the seventh deadly sin, sloth, seems almost out of place with the first six? I always thought it was worse to be greedy or lustful than to be just plain lazy, but it turns out that sloth isn't simply about not wanting to work, it's about being bored, listless, and simply not caring about work. In the fourth century, the Egyptian monk Evagrius called sloth the "Noonday Demon" that attacked monks after lunch and made the day seem as if it lasted 50 hours. He said:

> [The Noonday Demon] causes the monk continually to look out the windows and forces him to step out of his cell and to gaze at the sun to see how far it is from the ninth hour and to look around, here and there, whether any of his brethren is near.*

It makes you wonder how many people are attacked by this demon every day at work either because of a mind-numbing job, a big lunch, or sheer exhaustion.

*Siegfried Wenzel. *The Sin of Sloth: Acedia* (Chapel Hill, NC: University of North Carolina Press, 1967). p. 5.

Norman E. Bowie | # Respecting the Humanity in a Person

Norman E. Bowie is a professor of management at the University of Minnesota.

Part of the power of Kant's ethics lies in the extent of its ability to answer questions that Kant himself did not consider.

—*Barbara Herman*

INTRODUCTION

If the average American has a second moral principle to supplement the Golden Rule, it is probably a principle that says we should respect people. Respecting people is thoroughly interwoven into the fabric of American moral life. There is no one in the business community that has challenged the respect for persons principle as a principle in business ethics the way Albert Carr challenged the application of the Golden Rule in business. Yet, ironically, many of the moral criticisms of business practice are directed against policies that do not respect persons, e.g., that business human relations policies often invade privacy or relegate people to dead-end jobs where they cannot grow. In addition, there is considerable controversy, even among ethicists, as to what a respect for persons principle requires. . . .

I want to begin with an example which, although oversimplified, represents a standard discussion of the application of Kant's respect for persons principle to business. After presenting the example, I shall provide Kant's justification of the respect for persons principle and, using contemporary scholarship, explain what Kant means by the principle. With that in hand I will be able to apply the principle to more complex business examples.

I recall from my undergraduate ethics class more than 30 years ago that we struggled with the issue of whether buying a product, like vegetables in the supermarket, violated the respect for persons requirement of the second formulation of the categorical imperative. In buying our groceries did we merely use the clerk who rang up our purchases on the register? The first issue to be decided was whether we treated the sales person as a thing. Somewhat naively we decided that we did not merely use people in business transactions because we could accomplish our goal—buying carrots or potatoes—but that we could still show respect to those on the other end of the transaction. A casual observer in a supermarket can usually distinguish those patrons who treat the cashiers with respect from those who do not.

Our "solution" in this undergraduate class did not address business exchanges that involve tradeoffs between human and nonhuman sources. Any introductory economics text establishes that the efficient producer is instructed always to rearrange capital, land, machines, and workers so that their proportional marginal productivity is equal. The requirement of equal proportional marginal productivity works as follows: If the price of machines rises with respect to labor, substitute labor for machines. If the price of labor rises with respect to machines, substitute machines for labor. Both substitutions are equivalent.[1]

At first glance it looks as if a Kantian would say that the two substitutions are not morally equivalent. The first is morally permissible; the second is not morally permissible. It looks as if the employees are used as a means merely for the enhancement of the profits of the stockholders. It is morally permissible to use machines that way but it is not morally permissible to use people that way. Unlike the grocery-store example, the managers who act on behalf of the stockholders are not in a personal face-to-face

From Norman E. Bowie, *Business Ethics: A Kantian Perspective* (Oxford: Blackwell Publishers, 1999), 63–78 (edited).

relationship with the employees and thus they cannot avoid the charge of merely using the employees by saying that in the transaction they treated the other party to the transaction with respect. It doesn't matter if the manager was nice to the employees when she laid them off—a fact of some importance in contemporary discussions of downsizing because many managers think that when they fire people in a nice way, as opposed to firing them cruelly, they are off the moral hook. It is morally better to be nice than to be cruel, but the real issue is whether the firing can be morally justified. How would a Kantian using the respect for persons principle justify these contentions? To answer that question some explanation of Kant's respect for persons principle is in order.

THE RESPECT FOR PERSONS PRINCIPLE

Kant's second formulation of the categorical imperative says "Act so that you treat humanity whether, in your own person or in that of another, always as an end and never as a means only."[2] Kant did not simply assert that human beings are entitled to respect; he had an elaborate argument for it. Human beings ought to be respected because human beings have dignity. For Kant, an object that has dignity is beyond price. That's what is wrong with the principle that says a manager should adjust the inputs of production to the point where the marginal productivity of each is equal. And further, the denial of dignity is what makes much downsizing unjust. In these cases, that which is without price, human beings, are treated as exchangeable with that which has a price. Human employees have a dignity that machines and capital do not have. Thus, managers cannot manage their corporate resources in the most efficient manner without violating the respect for persons principle—or so it seems. But why do persons possess a dignity which is beyond all price?

They have dignity because human beings are capable of autonomy and thus are capable of self-governance. As autonomous beings capable of self-governance they are also responsible beings, since autonomy and self-governance are the conditions for responsibility. A person who is not autonomous and who is not capable of self-governance is not responsible. That's why little children or the mentally ill are not considered responsible beings. Thus, there is a conceptual link between being a human being, being an autonomous being, being capable of self-governance, and being a responsible being.

Autonomous responsible beings are capable of making and following their own laws; they are not simply subject to the causal laws of nature. Anyone who recognizes that he or she is autonomous would recognize that he or she is responsible (that he or she is a moral being). As Kant argues, the fact that one is a moral being enables us to say that such a being possesses dignity.

> Morality is the condition under which alone a rational being can be an end in himself because only through it is it possible to be a lawgiving member in the realm of ends. Thus morality, and humanity insofar as it is capable of morality, alone have dignity.[3]

It is the fact that human beings are moral agents that makes them subjects worthy of respect.

———

As I read Kant this is his argument for the necessity of including other persons within the scope of the respect for persons principle (treating the humanity in a person as an end and never as a means merely). It is based on consistency. What we say about one case, namely ourselves, we must say about similar cases, namely about other human beings.

———

Kant begins the third section of the *Foundations* as follows:

> What else, then, can freedom of the will be but autonomy (the property of the will to be a law to itself)? The proposition that the will is a law to itself in all its actions, however, only expresses the principle that we should act according to no other maxim than that which can also have itself as a

universal law for its object. And this is just the formula of the categorical imperative and the principle of morality. Therefore a free will and a will under moral laws are identical.[4]

Freedom and the ability to make laws are necessary and sufficient for moral agency. Moral agency is what gives people dignity. The importance of rationality comes when one explicates the meaning of freedom. Freedom is more than independence from causal laws. This is negative-freedom. Freedom is also the ability to make laws that are universal and to act on those laws in the world. As Kant says:

> The sole principle of morality consists in independence from all material of the law (i.e., a desired object) and in the accompanying determination of choice by the mere form of giving universal law which a maxim must be capable of having. That independence, however, is freedom in the negative sense, while this intrinsic legislation of pure and thus practical reason is freedom in the positive sense.[5]

Thus, we have shown why Kant believes persons have dignity and in this world are the only beings who have dignity. Kant has thus grounded our obligation to treat humanity in a person as an end and never as a means merely.

NOTES

1. Richard Parker has correctly pointed out that if the substitution of the machines made the jobs of the remaining workers more meaningful, then Kant would not oppose the substitution of machines for people just because the cost of machines went down relative to the costs of people.
2. Immanuel Kant, *Foundations of the Metaphysics of Morals* (New York: Macmillian, 1990), p. 46.
3. Ibid. p. 52.
4. Ibid. p. 64.
5. Immanuel Kant, *Critique of Practical Reason*, (Upper Saddle River, NJ: Prentice Hall, 1993), pp. 33–34.

QUESTIONS

1. What does the "respect for persons" principle mean in terms of the policies and practices of an organization?
2. If you simply are a means to your employer's ends, and you understand that this is the case when you are hired, would you care if you were treated as a means?
3. Do you agree with the idea that because humans are moral agents they are worthy of respect? What about people who are morally despicable?

To: You
From: The Philosopher
Subject: W. D. Ross on Prima Facie Duties

I like my work but I hate my job because of my boss. He treats most of the people in the office like they are garbage. We work like dogs and he never even bothers to say thank you. The other day he started yelling at the cleaning lady for making too much noise when she was emptying the trash in his office. The poor woman was almost in tears. My friend Sarah asked him if she could take a training seminar, so that she could get a promotion and he laughed and said, "you can hardly do your current job, let alone a job in management." He then promised Sarah that he would let her take the course in a year if her performance improved. It did improve, but then he told her he changed his mind.

My boss needs a good lesson on how to treat people. Sometimes I fantasize about tattooing the British philosopher W. D. Ross's list of prima facie duties on his chest—backwards so that he could read it in the mirror every day. "Prima facie" means "on the face of it" or "on first view." A prima facie duty or obligation is one that you should exercise all the time unless there is a very good moral reason not to do so. Ross's list of duties offer a simple guide to how you should treat people. It goes like this*:

1. Justice — Be just, prevent injustice and future injustice, and rectify existing injustices.
2. Non-injury — Avoid harming people.
3. Fidelity — Keep promises.
4. Veracity — Tell the truth.
5. Reparation — Apologize or make amends when you do something wrong.
6. Beneficence — Do good deeds for others and contribute to the development of their virtue, knowledge, or happiness.
7. Self-improvement — Better yourself.
8. Gratitude — Express appreciation for good deeds.

* W. D. Ross, *The Right and the Good*, Oxford University Press, 1930.

Arlie Hochshild | # Exploring the Managed Heart

Arlie Hochshild is a professor of sociology at the University of California at Berkeley.

The one area of her occupational life in which she might be "free to act," the area of her own personality, must now also be managed, must become the alert yet obsequious instrument by which goods are distributed.

—*C. Wright Mills*

In a section in *Das Kapital* entitled "The Working Day," Karl Marx examines depositions submitted in 1863 to the Children's Employment Commission in England. One deposition was given by the mother of a child laborer in a wallpaper factory: "When he was seven years old I used to carry him [to work] on my back to and fro through the snow, and he used to work 16 hours a day. . . . I have often knelt down to feed him, as he stood by the machine, for he could not leave it or stop." Fed meals as he worked, as a steam engine is fed coal and water, this child was "an instrument of labor."[1] Marx questioned how many hours a day it was fair to use a human being as an instrument, and how much pay for being an instrument was fair, considering the profits that factory owners made. But he was also concerned with something he thought more fundamental: the human cost of becoming an "instrument of labor" at all.

From Arlie Hochshild, *The Managed Heart* (Berkeley: University of California Press, 1983), pp. 3–9.

On another continent 117 years later, a twenty-year-old flight attendant trainee sat with 122 others listening to a pilot speak in the auditorium of the Delta Airlines Stewardess Training Center. Even by modern American standards, and certainly by standards for women's work, she had landed an excellent job. The 1980 pay scale began at $850 a month for the first six months and would increase within seven years to about $20,000 a year. Health and accident insurance was provided, and the hours were good.[2]

The young trainee sitting next to me wrote on her notepad, "Important to smile. Don't forget smile." The admonition came from the speaker in the front of the room, a crewcut pilot in his early fifties, speaking in a Southern drawl: "Now girls, I want you to go out there and really *smile*. Your smile is your biggest *asset*. I want you to go out there and use it. Smile. *Really* smile. Really *lay it on*."

The pilot spoke of the smile as the *flight attendant's* asset. But as novices like the one next to me move through training, the value of a personal smile is groomed to reflect the company's disposition—its confidence that its planes will not crash, its reassurance that departures and arrivals will be on time,

its welcome and its invitation to return. Trainers take it as their job to attach to the trainee's smile an attitude, a viewpoint, a rhythm of feeling that is, as they often say, "professional." This deeper extension of the professional smile is not always easy to retract at the end of the workday, as one worker in her first year at World Airways noted: "Sometimes I come off a long trip in a state of utter exhaustion, but I find I can't relax. I giggle a lot, I chatter, I call friends. It's as if I can't release myself from an artificially created elation that kept me 'up' on the trip. I hope to be able to come down from it better as I get better at the job."

As the PSA jingle says, "Our smiles are not just painted on." Our flight attendants' smiles, the company emphasizes, will be more human than the phony smiles you're resigned to seeing on people who are paid to smile. There is a smile-like strip of paint on the nose of each PSA plane. Indeed, the plane and the flight attendant advertise each other. The radio advertisement goes on to promise not just smiles and service but a travel experience of real happiness and calm. Seen in one way, this is no more than delivering a service. Seen in another, it estranges workers from their own smiles and convinces customers that

---

To: You
From: The Philosopher
Subject: "Robert C. Solomon, *The Passions*"

I have a British friend who is always amazed by how service employees act in America. The first time she went to a bank here she said, "the teller acted as if she just happened to be there and was delighted that I had dropped by to see her." Emotions are a part of your job and your life. You shouldn't abuse them or fail to cultivate the right ones. As philosopher Robert C. Solomon noted:

> Emotions are the meanings of life. It is because we are moved, because we feel, that life has a meaning. The passionate life is the meaningful life. Of course, it all depend on *which* passions. There are the grand passions, the driving forces of life, a life well-lived. And then there are the petty passions, defensive and self-undermining, "which drag us down with their stupidity," as Nietzsche says. Some meanings, in other words, are de-meaning.

on-the-job behavior is calculated. Now that advertisements, training, notions of professionalism, and dollar bills have intervened between the smiler and the smiled upon, it takes an extra effort to imagine that spontaneous warmth can exist in uniform—because companies now advertise spontaneous warmth, too.

At first glance, it might seem that the circumstances of the nineteenth-century factory child and the twentieth-century flight attendant could not be more different. To the boy's mother, to Marx, to the members of the Children's Employment Commission, perhaps to the manager of the wallpaper factory, and almost certainly to the contemporary reader, the boy was a victim, even a symbol, of the brutalizing conditions of his time. We might imagine that he had an emotional half-life, conscious of little more than fatigue, hunger, and boredom. On the other hand, the flight attendant enjoys the upper-class freedom to travel, and she participates in the glamour she creates for others. She is the envy of clerks in duller, less well-paid jobs.

But a close examination of the differences between the two can lead us to some unexpected common ground. On the surface there is a difference in how we know what labor actually produces. How could the worker in the wallpaper factory tell when his job was done? Count the rolls of wallpaper; a good has been produced. How can the flight attendant tell when her job is done? A service has been produced; the customer seems content. In the case of the flight attendant, the *emotional style of offering the service is part of the service itself*, in a way that loving or hating wallpaper is not a part of producing wallpaper. Seeming to "love the job" becomes part of the job; and actually trying to love it, and to enjoy the customers, helps the worker in this effort.

In processing people, the product is a state of mind. Like firms in other industries, airline companies are ranked according to the quality of service their personnel offer. Egon Ronay's yearly *Lucas Guide* offers such a ranking; besides being sold in airports and drugstores and reported in newspapers, it is cited in management memoranda and passed down to those who train and supervise flight attendants. Because it influences consumers, airline companies use it in setting their criteria for successful job performance by a flight attendant. In 1980 the *Lucas Guide* ranked Delta Airlines first in service out of fourteen airlines that fly regularly between the United States and both Canada and the British Isles. Its report on Delta included passages like this:

> [Drinks were served] not only with a smile but with concerned enquiry such as, "Anything else I can get you, madam?" The atmosphere was that of a civilized party—with the passengers, in response, behaving like civilized guests. . . . Once or twice our inspectors tested stewardesses by being deliberately exacting, but they were never roused, and at the end of the flight they lined up to say farewell with undiminished brightness. . . .
>
> [Passengers are] quick to detect strained or forced smiles, and they come aboard wanting to *enjoy* the flight. One of us looked forward to his next trip on Delta "because it's fun." Surely that is how passengers ought to feel.[3]

The work done by the boy in the wallpaper factory called for a coordination of mind and arm, mind and finger, and mind and shoulder. We refer to it simply as physical labor. The flight attendant does physical labor when she pushes heavy meal carts through the aisles, and she does mental work when she prepares for and actually organizes emergency landings and evacuations. But in the course of doing this physical and mental labor, she is also doing something more, something I define as *emotional labor*.[4] This labor requires one to induce or suppress feeling in order to sustain the outward countenance that produces the proper state of mind in others—in this case, the sense of being cared for in a convivial and safe place. This kind of labor calls for a coordination of mind and feeling, and it sometimes draws on a source of self that we honor as deep and integral to our individuality.

Beneath the difference between physical and emotional labor there lies a similarity in the possible cost of doing the work: the worker can become estranged or alienated from an aspect of self—either the body or the margins of the soul—that is *used* to do the work. The factory boy's arm functioned like a piece of machinery used to produce wallpaper. His employer, regarding that arm as an instrument, claimed control over its speed and motions. In this situation, what was the relation between the boy's arm and his mind? Was his arm in any meaningful sense his *own?*[5]

This is an old issue, but as the comparison with airline attendants suggests, it is still very much alive. If we can become alienated from goods in a goods-producing society, we can become alienated from service in a service-producing society. This is what C. Wright Mills, one of our keenest social observers, meant when he wrote in 1956, "We need to characterize American society of the mid-twentieth century in more psychological terms, for now the problems that concern us most border on the psychiatric."[6]

When she came off the job, what relation had the flight attendant to the "artificial elation" she had induced on the job? In what sense was it her *own* elation on the job? The company lays claim not simply to her physical motions—how she handles food trays—but to her emotional actions and the way they show in the ease of a smile. The workers I talked to often spoke of their smiles as being *on* them but not *of* them. They were seen as an extension of the makeup, the uniform, the recorded music, the soothing pastel colors of the airplane decor, and the daytime drinks, which taken together orchestrate the mood of the passengers. The final commodity is not a certain number of smiles to be counted like rolls of wallpaper. For the flight attendant, the smiles are a *part of her work*, a part that requires her to coordinate self and feeling so that the work seems to be effortless. To show that the enjoyment takes effort is to do the job poorly. Similarly, part of the job is to disguise fatigue and irritation, for otherwise the labor would show in an unseemly way, and the product—passenger contentment—would be damaged.[7] Because it is easier to disguise fatigue and irritation if they can be banished altogether, at least for brief periods, this feat calls for emotional labor.

The reason for comparing these dissimilar jobs is that the modern assembly-line worker has for some time been an outmoded symbol of modern industrial labor; fewer than 6 percent of workers now work on assembly lines. Another kind of labor has now come into symbolic prominence—the voice-to-voice or face-to-face delivery of service—and the flight attendant is an appropriate model for it. There have always been public-service jobs, of course; what is new is that they are now socially engineered and thoroughly organized from the top. Though the flight attendant's job is no worse and in many ways better than other service jobs, it makes the worker more vulnerable to the social engineering of her emotional labor and reduces her control over that labor. Her problems, therefore, may be a sign of what is to come in other such jobs.

Emotional labor is potentially good. No customer wants to deal with a surly waitress, a crabby bank clerk, or a flight attendant who avoids eye contact in order to avoid getting a request. Lapses in courtesy by those paid to be courteous are very real and fairly common. What they show us is how fragile public civility really is. We are brought back to the question of what the social carpet actually consists of and what it requires of those who are supposed to keep it beautiful. The laggards and sluff-offs of emotional labor return us to the basic questions. What is emotional labor? What do we do when we manage emotion? What, in fact, is emotion? What are the costs and benefits of managing emotion, in private life and at work?

NOTES

1. Karl Marx, (1977) *Capital,* Vol. 1. "Intro". By Ernest Mandel Tr. Ben Fowkes. New York: Vintage, pp. 356–357, 358.

2. For stylistic convenience, I shall use the pronoun "she" when referring to a flight attendant, except when a specific male flight attendant is being discussed. Otherwise I shall try to avoid verbally excluding either gender.

3. *Lucas Guide 1980*, p. 66.

4. I use the term *emotional labor* to mean the management of feeling to create a publicly observable facial and bodily display; emotional labor is sold for a wage and therefore has *exchange value*. I use the synonymous terms *emotion work* or *emotion management* to refer to these same acts done in a private context where they have *use value*.

5. *Lucas Guide 1980*, pp. 66, 76. Fourteen aspects of air travel at the stages of departure, arrival, and the flight itself are ranked. Each aspect is given one of sixteen differently weighted marks. For example, "The

friendliness or efficiency of the staff is more important than the quality of the pilot's flight announcement or the selection of newspapers and magazines offered."

6. C. Wright Mills (1956), *White Collar*. New York: Oxford University Press.

7. Like a commodity, service that calls for emotional labor is subject to the laws of supply and demand. Recently the demand for this labor has increased and the supply of it drastically decreased. The airline industry speed-up since the 1970s has been followed by a worker slowdown. The slowdown reveals how much emotional labor the job required all along. It suggests what costs even happy workers under normal conditions pay for this labor without a name. The speed-up has sharpened the ambivalence many workers feel about how much of oneself to give over to the role and how much of oneself to protect from it.

QUESTIONS

1. What are the various types of emotional labor found in the workplace today?

2. What kinds of emotional labor are acceptable and what kinds are unacceptable in the workplace? What ethical principles would you use to draw the line?

3. Does emotional labor violate your personal autonomy and freedom of expression?

Bruce Barry

The Cringing and the Craven: Freedom of Expression in the Workplace

Bruce Barry is the Brownlee O. Currey, Jr., Professor of Management at the Owen Graduate School of Management and Professor of Sociology at Vanderbilt.

In September 2004, Lynne Gobbell was fired from her job as a factory machine operator in Decatur, Alabama, because her automobile in the company's parking lot displayed a bumper sticker supporting John Kerry for president. In 2001, Clayton Vernon was fired by the Enron Corporation after posting on an Internet message board his opinion that Enron CEO Kenneth Lay is "a truly evil and satanic figure." In 1998, Edward Blum resigned his position as a stockbroker in Houston after (as he alleged) the firm pressured him to curtail his off-work political activities in support of a municipal ballot initiative on affirmative action. In August 2004, a web developer named Joyce Park was fired from her job at an online social network website company for mentions of her employer in writings posted to her blog. Gonzalo Cotto, an aircraft factory worker in Connecticut, sued his employer after he was fired for refusing to display an American flag at his workstation during a Gulf War celebration. After several appeals, Connecticut's highest court rejected Cotto's claim that his dismissal violated a state law protecting constitutional rights in the workplace.

These incidents share a common theme: punishment or retaliation by an employer for employee actions that involve expressive behavior—verbal or symbolic actions that would, in other domains of social life and in many countries, be regarded as protected speech. Freedom of speech and expression are bedrock tenets of liberty found in the legal frameworks of most nations having systems of civil democracy or republican government. Yet as

Copyright © 2007. *Business Ethics Quarterly*, Volume 17, Issue 2. ISSN 1052-150X, pp. 263–296.

these examples indicate, the scope of free expression in and around the workplace can be quite limited (especially in the United States compared to many other "Western" democracies). Work is a place where many adults devote significant portions of their waking lives, but it is also a place where civil liberties, including but not limited to freedom of speech, are significantly constrained.

DEFINING WORKPLACE FREEDOM OF EXPRESSION

Workplace speech as a liberty having roots in law, policy, custom, or ethics has received limited scholarly attention, but when it has, the focus has typically been constrained to speech at work or about work. For example, Campbell, a philosopher, defined *workplace freedom of expression* as "the capacity of employees to have and express opinions in their workplace about their workplace and the organisation that employs them." Estlund, a legal scholar, defined *freedom of speech in the workplace* as "the freedom to speak out at or about the workplace free from the threat of discharge or serious discipline." Lippke defined *work-related speech* as "speech that occurs within the workplace, but also speech which is sufficiently about work so that though it occurs outside the workplace, it is subject to employer sanction."

The incident mentioned at the outset involving a worker discharged for a political message affixed to an automobile in a factory parking lot moves beyond these cited definitions in two ways: by involving content that is plainly unrelated to work or workplace and by taking the form of expression that is not spoken (not literally "speech"). Accordingly, I define expression broadly here. Free speech theorist Scanlon defined an act of expression as "any action that is intended . . . to communicate to one or more persons some proposition or attitude" including acts of speech, publication, displays, failures to display, and artistic performances. Baker critized Scanlon's definition as too narrow, noting that it excludes self-expressive and creative forms of communication.

Siding with Baker, I encompass within "expression" actions that convey a proposition or attitude, or that involve a personal display of self-expression or creativity. The construct of interest in this article, then, is *workplace freedom of expression*, which I define as *the ability to engage in legally protected acts of expression at or away from the workplace, on subjects related or unrelated to the workplace, free from the threat of formal or informal workplace retribution, discipline, or discharge.*

This definition is expansive, incorporating the wide canvas of expression that might be legally protected in a constitutional democracy, but is delimited by its focus on expression that is discouraged, proscribed, or regulated by an employer. To illustrate the breadth of acts potentially within its purview, I show in Figure 1-1 a simplified taxonomy of expression in three dimensions. Acts of expression of potential interest for this analysis vary by *venue* (occurring at the workplace or away from it), by *topic* (addressing matters related to work or organization, or not), and by *publicness* (occurring through channels and contexts that make the conveyance one-to-one/few vs. one-to-many). Of the eight types implied within the figure, the two comprising the upper-left quadrant have garnered the most attention from researchers studying interaction processes in organizations, and understandably so. One can assume that the octant in the lower right—expression that occurs away from the workplace, on off-work topics, in private settings—is the expressive form of least interest presumably to employers, and by extension to this analysis (although by no means wholly irrelevant).

A renewed interest in and analysis of free expression in the workplace is warranted for several reasons. First, the legal climate regarding free speech in the workplace has evolved in significant ways since Ewing and Werhane were writing about employment rights.

Second, the workplace itself is changing in ways that render rights to expression both more threatened and more important. Yamada developed this argument, describing several factors that raise concerns about employers' inclination to

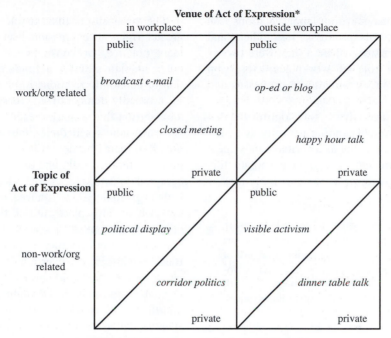

Venue of Act of Expression*

in workplace   outside workplace

Topic of Act of Expression

work/org related

- public — broadcast e-mail — closed meeting — private (in workplace)
- public — op-ed or blog — happy hour talk — private (outside workplace)

non-work/org related

- public — political display — corridor politics — private (in workplace)
- public — visible activism — dinner table talk — private (outside workplace)

*Entries in italics are examples (not modal types)

FIGURE **1-1** Taxonomy of acts of expression.

limit workplace expression: individual economic insecurity that breeds self-censorship at work, a rise in electronic surveillance of workers, a decline in unionization, an expansion in corporate political partisanship (which ostensibly chills employee expression that might deviate from the preferred point of view), and the simple fact that people work longer hours than in the past.

The notion that people spend more time at work bridges into a third rationale for more attention to workplace expression: the role of the workplace, given that many individuals spend the bulk of their waking hours there, as a building block for community engagement and a critical site for exchanges of views and public debate around political and social issues. Moreover, if individuals are spending more time on the job, then opportunities to engage in expression outside the workplace inevitably diminish. The relevance of speech rights to broader notions of

citizenship and community in a free society is a subject to which I will return later.

Fourth, advances in information technology, and individuals' ability to use technology for expressive purposes, change the landscape of free expression in and around the workplace (and everywhere else). A currently prominent illustration is found in cases where individuals are sanctioned or dismissed for comments about the workplace that appear in online web sites such as blogs; these in a sense are technology-enabled "publication" outlets that were previously unavailable. Workplace freedom of expression has occupied new terrain in an era of web sites, email, instant messaging, blogs, vlogs, wikis, and podcasts, compared to what existed before.

Lastly, renewed attention to free speech at work is warranted by the abundance (noted earlier) of research on related topics within the fields of organizational behavior and labor relations. As a consequence of this progress, researchers and managers are more attuned than they were twenty years ago to the role of workplace expression and participation in organizational processes and outcomes.

A generation ago there was optimism that employee rights were expanding not only as a matter of evolving practice, but as a veritable movement building toward radical change in corporate life. In 1974 an editor at the *Harvard Business Review* wrote:

> Within the management castle, as well as out in the woods and fields, there is growing support for employee rights. . . . [T]he notion of a "bill of rights" for corporate employees has been advocated in the *Harvard Business Review* and will doubtless find its way soon into other management journals.[1]

Ewing predicted a "sea change" in the social and intellectual environment of organizations. Thirty years later, it would be delusional to suggest that Ewing's predictions have come to fruition. The law in the United States (from an employment law perspective) has not significantly expanded its accommodation of employee expression, even as exceptions to employment-at-will have grown wider. Outside of academic writing, connections between speech, other civil liberties at work, and the state and health of larger civil society remain elusive. As Balkin wrote in an essay chronicling the evolution of free speech doctrine in the twentieth century, "speech in the workplace is not considered speech in the same sense as political or expressive speech generally, but is thought to be utilitarian, pedestrian, and incidental to the performance of work."

The proposition that people at work deserve greater rights to expression than the law, management practice, or conventional wisdom allow is not a utopian call for a fundamental transformation of economic relations in employment, or even for a broadly democratized workplace. It is merely an assertion that a market economy can still flourish when adults sell their time and their labor but not all of their liberties. Where suppression of one's power to think, speak, and dissent is conventionally accepted in workplaces, the ideology of management is given license to run free, not just at work, but everywhere. This places at risk the liberty interests of individuals, but also jeopardizes the health of civil democracy in community and society. Justice Hugo Black put it this way over a half-century ago: "Our own free society should never forget that laws which stigmatize and penalize thought and speech of the unorthodox have a way of reaching, ensnaring and silencing many more people than at first intended. We must have freedom of speech for all or we will in the long run have it for none but the cringing and the craven."

NOTE

1. David W. Ewing, "Free Speech from Nine to Five." *The Nation* 218:755–56, 1974.

QUESTIONS

1. What kinds of speech can be justifiably prohibited in the workplace?
2. Does freedom of speech protect an employees right to say what he or she knows is true at any time?
3. To what extent do managers have the right to tell employees what they can say and not say in regards to their work?

Loraleigh
Keashly

Workplace Bullying

Loraleigh Keashly is Associate Professor of Communication and Director of the MA program in Dispute Resolution at Wayne State University.

WORKPLACE BULLYING: THE NATURE OF THE BEAST

Workplace bullying is a special case of workplace aggression. Workplace aggression refers to efforts by individuals to harm others with whom they work. Before addressing workplace bullying's unique features, it is important to discuss aggressive behaviors more generally. I never cease to be amazed at the range and type of behaviors that fall within this domain. To more completely map out this behavioral space, Neuman and Baron utilized Buss's approach of three dimensions to define the space. The dimensions are:

1. Physical (deeds)—verbal (words, tone)
2. Active (doing a behavior)—passive (withholding or "failures to do")
3. Direct (at the target)—indirect (at something or someone the target values)

This approach describes the "methods of attack." This is not a comprehensive listing of all possible behaviors, but it will give an idea of ways in which bullying can be conducted.

1. **Threat to Professional Status.** Questioning competence, belittling opinion, professional humiliation in front of colleagues, negative comments about intelligence, questioning a person's ability to supervisors; spreading rumors or gossip. These are primarily active behaviors.
2. **Threat to Personal Standing.** Name-calling, insults, verbal abuse, tantrums, intimidating behaviors, devaluing with reference to age, gender, race/ethnicity or appearance, hostile gestures. These are predominantly active behaviors
3. **Isolation.** Exclusion from work-related gatherings, silent treatment, withholding information, ignoring contributions, not taking concerns seriously, preventing access to opportunities or promotion, poisoning others against the target. These behaviors tend to be passive in nature.
4. **Overwork/Unreal Expectations.** Undue pressure, impossible deadlines, unnecessary disruptions, setting up to fail, unreal or ambiguous expectations; more so than for others in the same environment.
5. **Destabilization.** Others take credit for work; assigning meaningless tasks, removing responsibility, denied raise or promotion without reason; excessive monitoring.

I have several observations regarding these behaviors. First, what is particularly unique about workplace bullying is that it is often about what people **do not do** rather than what they do, i.e., "lack of action" such as withholding information, excluding from meetings, the silent treatment. This poses particular challenges for the target, bystanders, managers, and third parties to whom these concerns are brought. Thus, it is important for ombudsmen to note that most aggressive behavior at work is psychological in nature and often passive or "failures to do" behaviors.

Second, the nature of the relationship between the target and actor will influence the specific expressions of hostility. This has to do with the means and opportunity available to the actor. For example, a supervisor due to his/her control over rewards and job assignments has the opportunity and the means to bully through overwork and destabilization types of behaviors. Opportunities available to peers may have more to do with information sharing and other working relationships. Thus, behaviors falling under threats to personal and professional standing as well as isolation are more likely under their control. Subordinates, due to their less powerful organizational position, may engage in more indirect kinds of behaviors such as rumors or gossip or withholding of information. These examples of actor means and opportunity illustrate that bullying is not limited to one type of relationship. Indeed, bullying can be top-down (boss–subordinate), horizontal (peer-peer) or bottom-up (subordinate–boss). Thus, workplace bullying is considered to be **relational** in nature— harming others through purposeful manipulation and damage of relationships. This is important for ombudsmen to know as it requires that the relational context of the experience be assessed. Thus, investigations will need to involve at the very least assessment of target and actor and consideration of the nature of their relationship organizationally, e.g., the kind of contact that is typically required for this type of relationship.

Third, identifying the behaviors, while necessary, is insufficient for understanding workplace bullying. Indeed, in isolation, each of these behaviors may be seen as minor and people may wonder what all the fuss is about (So he glared at you? So what?). What makes these behaviors more than they appear is their **frequency** and the **duration of exposure**. Workplace bullying and its related constructs are **repeated** and **enduring** forms of workplace aggression. **Persistency** is the core feature that distinguishes workplace bullying from more occasional aggressive treatment. The defining characteristics are as follows:

1. **Negative Actions that Are Repeated and Patterned.** This element captures both frequency of occurrence (daily, weekly, monthly) and variety (more than one type of behavior). Regardless of the construct, it is the frequency of exposure to hostile behaviors that has been directly linked to a variety of negative individual (health, job attitudes and behaviors) and organizational (productivity, turnover) outcomes, i.e., the greater the exposure, greater the impact. Being exposed to a number of different hostile behaviors contributes to this sense of frequency. We found that the number of different events uniquely contributed to negative individual outcomes beyond the mean frequency of exposure. But the number of behaviors and the frequency of occurrence do not adequately capture the nature of exposure. Frequency of exposure must also be considered in terms of the overall frequency of contacts with the actor. For example, perhaps the boss only yells at an employee once a month but if the employee only sees him/her once a month that is 100% of the time. The implications of that for a target are very different than for a target whose actor behaves this way once a month but they see him/her daily, i.e., they are exposed to other behaviors, hopefully positive, that will influence their overall experience. Further, the frequency of exposure can be created (or enhanced) by the target reliving the experience, i.e., rumination. Finally the repeated nature of exposure may be linked to the involvement of more than one actor, i.e., mobbing. The repeated and patterned nature of these behaviors highlights the importance of investigating a pattern of behavior rather than each incident as a separate item. Further the frequency of contact that would be required organizationally "normally" for the relationship is also important to consider in any assessment.

2. **Prolonged Exposure over Time (Duration).** It is duration that is particularly distinctive about workplace bullying. Researchers have used timeframes for assessing these actions ranging from six months (which is typical in the European literature) to a year. These timeframes pale in comparison to the reports of those who self-identify as targets of workplace bullying. They report exposure ranging up to 10 years. Zapf and Gross report that average duration of those who were bullied by one person was 28 months, for those who were bullied by two to four people or more than 4 people (i.e., mobbing), it was 36 months and 55 months, respectively. Thus, the question

of "how long is too long" is important to consider in this discussion of workplace bullying. While researchers often specify at least one event weekly for a minimum period of 6 or 12 months, this timeframe does not necessarily appeal to those for example, in Human Resources or indeed, ombudsmen who will want to be able to address a developing hostile situation as quickly as possible, before irreversible damage sets in. Thus, codifying a specific minimum duration in policy may hamper reporting of problems and ultimately effective management. It is sufficient to note that bullying tends to occur over an extended period of time.

Fourth, while persistence or chronicity is the important marker of workplace bullying, it is also important to recognize that the nature and intensity of behaviors directed at the target do not stay the same throughout. Long-standing bullying situations will often show a progression or escalation of aggression from covert and indirect behaviors to increasingly overt, direct and in some situations physical. Research suggests that such escalation will have the effect of rendering target attempts to constructively and actively respond ineffective. This puts the target at increased risk for injury psychologically, emotionally, and physically (see further discussion below). The failure of constructive methods also may promote target resistance and retaliation behaviors that may further an escalatory spiral. Such spirals can result in drawing others into the situation, often as actors and may even result in secondary spirals or cascades of aggression elsewhere in the unit or organization, i.e., the development of a hostile work environment.

Given the above description, a question is often raised as to how workplace bullying, particularly at advanced stages is different from an escalated conflict between employees. What appears to distinguish bullying from "normal" workplace conflict is the existence of a power imbalance. This imbalance can be preexisting in the structure of the workplace (boss-subordinate) or it can develop as a conflict escalates and one party becomes disadvantaged relative to the other. The importance of the imbalance is the potential impact on the target's resources and ability to defend him/herself as well as the actor's ability to continue their actions. This has implications for the nature and intensity of negative effects and highlights the importance of prevention and early intervention, as well as the necessity of strategies for remediation of effects.

Taken together, the prolonged exposure to repeated hostile actions with an inability to defend creates a situation in which the target becomes increasingly disabled. Further such a relationship, if allowed to continue, has the potential to not only spread its impact beyond the immediate dyad to others in the organization (e.g., witnesses) but it also has the possibility of creating hostile work environments where many workers are now "behaving badly". The bullying process with its progression and its span of impact illustrates the **communal** nature of workplace bullying. That is, a variety of different parties are involved in or impacted by workplace bullying. This communal nature requires that ombudsmen will need to engage a number of people in the investigation and ultimately the management of the bullying.

Cyberspace: The Next (and Current) Frontier

Before leaving this section on bullying's nature, It is Important to acknowledge modern technological devices as the new medium for bullying, e.g., bullying through the internet, email, text messaging, video/picture clips and social networking sites. Lois Price Spratlen ombudsman for the University of Washington at the time was among the first to identify how email was being used to bully and harass others. Known as cyberbullying or cyber-aggression, several unique features of the medium conspire to make it a particularly virulent and destructive forum for and form of bullying. Some of these features are:

(a) the ability of the actor(s) to be anonymous making it more difficult for both targets and those investigating to identify the source. By reducing detection, actors may become emboldened to engage in more extreme and destructive attacks on the person's reputation;

(b) span of impact from a few organizational members to millions of new media users globally; and

(c) once these messages or images are released, they are difficult to expunge from cyberspace, creating a situation in which exposure can be continually renewed and thus relived, increasing damage to the target and others.

It is critical that researchers and professionals focus their efforts on understanding the nature and impact of cyberbullying and to seek ways to manage its use and impact.

QUESTIONS

1. Do you think that bullying is a serious problem in the workplace?

2. What is the difference between being criticized by your boss for substandard work and bullying?

3. How can you tell if your boss is engaging in passive bullying rather than simply ignoring you?

The Economist | # Doing Business in Dangerous Places

Setting up a business abroad has always been risky, and not just financially. To create the colony of 90,000 white settlers that, in the late 17th century, earned enormous profits from growing tobacco in Virginia required the immigration of around 116,000 people. The chaps who sailed for India a century later had to endure even worse. "The variety of means by which a man could be carried off was quite bewildering," observes a recent book on the East India Company. "Malaria, typhoid or enteric fever, cholera, dysentery and smallpox were the most common diseases, and the bites of scorpions and mad dogs were frequently lethal."

Those who today run businesses in the nastier parts of the world also face a bewildering range of threats to the safety and health of their employees. Indeed, there are many more disagreeable places to choose from than there were a generation ago. In the days of the Cold War, there was usually a government to deal with, or at worst a rebel authority. These days, a growing number of countries, or large tracts of them, are run (if at all) by shifting coalitions of warlords or local bullies. Such power vacuums create potentially lethal uncertainty. They also aggravate more mundane (but no less burdensome) risks, from life-threatening driving conditions to the spread of diseases such as AIDS and malaria.

Moreover, some of the protection once offered by a white face, a red cross, a neutral flag or the passport of a Great Power has now vanished. As a result, many places that have long been dangerous have become even more so. Last month, Médecins Sans Frontières (MSF), an aid group that specialises in sending medical staff to countries in conflict, shut all its programmes in Afghanistan after five of its staff were killed in a deliberate attack on a clearly marked MSF vehicle. Taliban spokesmen said that aid organisations such as MSF were helping the Americans, something the charity vehemently denies. Anyone doing business in a conflict zone runs similar risks: driving a truck or building a telecoms network may not seem a political act to the company that undertakes the task, but followers of Osama bin Laden think otherwise.

The Economist, "Doing Business in Dangerous Places," August 14, 2004, p. 11.

HOW TO BE SAFER

For most employers, health and safety issues are generally about avoiding minor injuries and malfunctions. To send employees to regions where injury or death are real possibilities involves, on the face of it, quite a different approach. Sending staff to work in Iraq or Colombia might appear to be the reverse of good health-and-safety practice. In fact, whereas some of the principles of protecting employees in dangerous places are different, others are surprisingly similar.

For example, the greatest risks even in some of the scariest parts of the world are not of kidnap or murder, but of illness, traffic accidents or violent crime. In the heyday of the East India Company, the single biggest cause of death of the company's employees was not mad dogs or scorpions, but the familiar drug of alcohol (aggravated by bad diet and lack of exercise). In Congo today, malaria is a far bigger risk for expatriates than murder. The good news: such threats are easier to deal with than the terrors of ambush or armed attack. One of the simplest ways to lessen risk is to get all expats, their families and local staff to wear seatbelts: prosaic but effective.

Employers sending people to dangerous places need, first of all, to be honest about what they are doing. That means thinking early about the risks involved. Too many companies entering markets in backward countries, even those not at war, greatly underestimate the cost of security. Employers also need to decide early on how big a threat to their staff would force them to withdraw. That will vary from firm to firm. KBR, part of Halliburton, has lost 42 employees in Iraq and Kuwait and yet stayed put. Many other companies would have retreated at a serious threat to just one staff member.

Being honest with employees entails—as far as possible—avoiding pressure on them to go somewhere dangerous. That is sometimes easier said than done: the oil-company engineer willing to work only in comfy places is unlikely to thrive. It also means giving staff good advance training, especially in first aid. And it means using people with experience where possible. For instance, South Africans, accustomed to working in some of the riskier parts of their continent, may understand how to deal with a threat much better than someone coming to Africa for the first time. Inexperienced staff need more specialist support, perhaps from one of the companies in the burgeoning threat-management business.

SIMMERING

Inexperienced staff may also be eager to go for the wrong reasons—to be able to boast that they have risked death for their work and survived. One constant hazard is the "boiling frog" syndrome. Where danger is mounting, as it seems to be now in Saudi Arabia, people on the ground may not realise it, or may prefer to pretend otherwise, until too late. Even if they do acknowledge the risk, they may stay on out of exaggerated loyalty to clients or misplaced zeal to outlast competitors. Wise companies make sure that the judgment of independent security experts goes to head office, not the local boss, and that risks are kept under constant review.

What about using local staff? They may have a better sense of danger and be less conspicuous than expatriates. Many employers in dangerous parts of the world try to keep the use of foreigners to a minimum. That is fine if they also take their responsibilities to local staff seriously, but not if the locals are put at greater risk than expatriates because they are considered more expendable.

Why go, if the risks are great? There are good reasons for operating in dangerous lands. There are people who need help, and countries to rebuild. But for companies, the lure is usually the one that led early Virginians to endure the privations of America or the British to colonise India: if the risks are great, then so too are the rewards. What matters is that the rewards are not earned at the cost of putting employees in more danger than, once properly informed, they choose to accept.

QUESTIONS

1. To what extent should companies be held responsible for employees who get kidnapped or murdered while working in a foreign country?

2. In an era of terrorism, are there some places or conditions under which no company should send employees?

3. Is a company responsible for risks that employees take on their own volition in dangerous places?

Harry J. Van Buren III

Boundaryless Careers and Employability Obligations

Harry J. Van Buren III is associate Professor of Management at the Anderson Schools of Management, University of New Mexico.

Few issues in the academic study of management are as contentious as observed (and potential) changes in career patterns. The idea that employers and employees increasingly do not expect to have lifelong relationships has been the subject of much academic study and public debate. Optimists believe that boundaryless careers, defined as careers that unfold in multiple employment settings, provide opportunities for personal fulfillment and economic prosperity while freeing people from the demands of moribund organizational structures. A person following the boundaryless career (whether by choice or not) expects as a matter of course to work for a number of organizations in a temporary capacity; each employment relationship is in effect a transactional contract of limited duration. Pessimists suspect that changing career patterns are really driven by employers' desires to be rid of as many costly permanent employees (and their benefits) as possible. It is not surprising, therefore, that passions run high on both sides of the debate.

WHAT ARE BOUNDARYLESS CAREERS?

Before discussing "boundaryless careers," it is helpful to define "career." A person's career is the unfolding sequence of his or her work experiences overtime. For the purposes of this paper, everyone—not just professionals—is understood to have a career. A career can consist of one job held in an organization for a long time, many jobs held in the same organization, the same job in many different organizations, or many jobs in many organizations; the sum total of one's work experiences in one or several organizations is her career. The term "boundaryless career" did not come into existence until the early 1990s, and was the theme of the 1993 Academy of Management annual meeting.

Career theory has traditionally focused on the unfolding of a person's work experiences with one organization over time. The "boundaryless career"— a career that unfolds over time in multiple employment settings—describes a variety of changes in career patterns that have been recently observed. Employment practices like downsizing and the use of temporary/contingent workforces illustrate how organizational preferences for flexibility have affected career patterns. The traditional view of careers noted above—and the stable employment relationships assumed thereunder—has been largely replaced by a new view that emphasizes employer flexibility.

WHO IS HARMED BY THE BOUNDRYLESS CAREER?

Although many studies of boundaryless careers have focused on contexts like Silicon Valley, in which employees with rare skills have significant market power, a more difficult ethical question is posed by the advent of boundaryless career practices for employees with fungible skills. The ethical challenge posed by boundaryless careers is not the plight of well-compensated employees whose stock options and other forms of compensation equilibrate effort and reward, but rather the individuals whose talents mark them for lowlypaid, dead-end jobs. Workers with rare and valuable skills are most likely to have the sorts of contractual arrangements that ensure (1) their assent to the terms of the exchange relationship between themselves and the organization and

(2) explicit guarantees of remuneration and benefits. For those workers whose labor is a not a scarce commodity, their treatment by employers is quite different: Such employees are not likely to be given the sorts of benefits and due process protections enjoyed by workers who are thought to have rare and valuable skills. The notion that employees have less power than employers in negotiating the terms of exchange agreements can be traced back to Smith, who noted that "many workmen could not subsist a week, few could subsist a month, and scarcely any a year without employment. In the long run the work-man may be as necessary to his master as his master is to him, but the necessity is not so immediate."

The effect of boundaryless careers is to exacerbate the negative effects of the two-tiered workforce in most industrialized societies, composed of

1. a small top tier of highly sought-after employees with rare skills whose market power enables them to demand and receive fair treatment from employers and
2. a large second tier of employees whose skills are fungible and easily replaced. As a quasi-commodity, the pay and benefits of people in this tier will likely fall rather than rise in real terms unless they are able to acquire skills that move them closer to the first tier.

The first tier is largely able to demand and to receive equitable treatment. As Meyer has put it, "them who has, gets." The second tier faces a more tenuous existence; unless their skills are constantly upgraded, they will face greater competition for, and declining benefits from, jobs requiring fungible skills.[4] Second-tier workers are more likely to be negatively affected by boundaryless careers than first-tier workers.

RISK SHARING, FAIRNESS, EMPLOYABILITY, AND THE BOUNDARYLESS CAREER

The central issue with regard to boundaryless careers is this: who assumes what risk in the employment relationship? It is true, of course, that employees traditionally have borne risk when working for an organization. Although it is commonly held that shareholders—as residual claimants—bear the most risk in a publicly held enterprise, employees also bear risks. Employees face health and safety risks, the risk that the organization will go bankrupt, and (in the case of firms that have employee stock ownership plans) the risk that the company's stock will lose value. These risks are faced by almost every employee. But employees—whether in a boundaryless career pattern or not—also face the risk that the firm-specific investments that they make in a particular employer will not be fairly compensated.

In any employment relationship, two kinds of skills are used by employees. The first sort of skill is general to the particular task that a particular employee performs. A computer professional, for example, uses a set of skills that are transferable across organizations. But employees—even in very short-term occupations—also use firm-specific skills that are not salable on the external labor market. Such skills may include things as mundane as knowledge of organizational logistics. or as fundamental as information about the firm's values and mission. Skills therefore are transferable across organizations but require firm-specific knowledge in order to be useful in a particular firm. When an employee works for a particular firm, she is (or should be) making investments in both general skills (salable on external labor markets) and firm-specific skills (generally not salable on external labor markets).

In a traditional, long-term employment relationship, there is some element of mutuality and risk sharing between employers and employees: the organization invests in the general and firm-specific skills of employees and in turn employees exhibit some level of loyalty to the firm. Of course, employee investments in a particular firm are subject to abuse by employers; employers can, and do, change the terms of exchange relationships with employees—and employees are generally not able to force the organization to live up to the old "agreement," and employees tend to prefer the predictability of stable employment relation-ships to the unpredictability of more ephemeral arrangements. Further, there is some balancing of risk in firms that seek to maintain stable employ-ment relationships: The firm makes investments in employees and compensates them for their lost opportunity costs by providing further (general and firm-specific) skill investment and employment stability, and employees in turn voluntarily agree to stay with that employer long enough to allow the employer to earn returns from such investments in employees. It should be noted that agreements between employers and employees in this sort of arrangement are implicit rather than explicit in nature, following the logic of psychological rather than written contracts.

In the boundaryless career, however, employees still need to bring general and firm-specific skills into their employment relationships. (Even short-term employment relationships do not obviate the need for firm-specific knowledge.) But the terms of exchange between employers and employees are different in a firm that uses a boundaryless career model than in a firm that maintains strong inter-nal labor markets and career ladders. Now employ-ees not only bear the burden of maintaining their general skills and acquiring firm-specific knowl-edge, but they cannot rely on any promise of a long-term employment relationship with a particu-lar employer. The risk to the employee increases dramatically in a boundaryless-career relationship as compared with a more traditional relationship: the employee not only bears all of the burdens com-mon to any job, but also becomes responsible for acquiring general and firm-specific skills without any promise of a long-term relationship or of equi-table risk sharing.

Further, the sorts of protections available to workers in more stable employment relationships are absent for short-term employees. Union protections, for example, are largely absent. Many temporary workers actually work for (and draw a paycheck from) a temporary agency—not the particular employer to which the employee is assigned by the agency. Few if any temporary employees are willing to jeopardize future temporary assignments

by seeking union representation. Similarly, contract workers are loath to jeopardize the possibility of future work, either with their current "employer" or another employer. The countervailing force that union representation creates is therefore absent for many employees in boundaryless-career relationships. Similarly, labor and employment law in general—whether in terms of benefits, worker safety, or employer obligations—is an artifact of an industrial relations system designed in the 1930s and 1940s at a time when union representation (or the threat thereof) was a powerful check on managerial autonomy.

THE INADEQUACY OF EMPLOYMENT CONTRACTS FOR PRESERVING EMPLOYEE RIGHTS

Even if it is the case that boundaryless careers shift risk from employers to employees, it might be the case that this problem can be addressed through the use of employment contracts. But this is not a likely solution to the problem.

First and foremost, it should be noted that to the degree that contracts exist at all in boundary-less career-like relationships, they are generally contracts of adhesion created by employers that employees must either agree to or be denied employ-ment. Ehrenreich, for example, found that even (or perhaps especially) for low-wage jobs, employees are required to submit to drug tests as a condition for continued employment. Ehrenreich argues that employees are powerless to resist demands for drug testing as one condition of employment among many that are forced upon them. Similarly, employees in short-term and/or temporary employment relation-ships—the kinds of employment arrangements most consistent with the boundaryless career model—are often in no position to negotiate the terms of exchange. Such workers possess little power to make demands on their employees, whether for increased remuneration, benefits, or training. Their ability to negotiate for skill enhancement that would maintain their employability is limited.

Second, all contracts are incomplete, and espe-cially so with regard to employment relationships.

It is conceivable that some employees—particularly those with rare and valuable skills or the decreasing portion of the U.S. workforce that is represented by union contracts—might be able to include language germane to employability obligations in their employment contracts. (The vast majority of employees, however, would fit into neither category.) Even for such employees, however, the likelihood that they could develop an employment contract that ensures employability is limited by the incompleteness of any contract. It would be difficult indeed to write contractual language that would bind an employer to maintain an employee's employability, now and in the future. Although the problem of incompleteness in employment contracting is common to most relationships, the ephemeral nature of boundaryless career obligations makes it even harder for such employees to protect themselves through contractual means.

Finally, to adapt McCall's approach, there is little evidence that boundaryless careers provide wage premiums to employees over and above wages paid to employees in more stable employment relationships to compensate the former for the increased risks they assume. As noted previously, workers tend to prefer stable to unstable employment relationships. Further, the risk to employees (including risks associated with making investments in human capital that may not be rewarded by future employers and the risk of not having long-term job tenure) of boundaryless career employment relationships—which are by definition short-term in nature with no promise of access to internal labor markets or career ladders—is significantly higher. Yet—although more empirical research needs to be done in this area—employees whose employment patterns fit the boundaryless career model neither command wage premiums nor even keep pace with permanent employees with regard to wages and non-wage benefits. Were contracts a sufficient way in which employees in boundaryless career relationships could protect their interests and gain compensation for the increased risks they assume, such wage and benefit premiums would be expected.

In short, there is a fairness problem inherent to the boundaryless career: Employees assume a disproportionate share of the risks without commensurate marginal benefits (as compared with long-term employment relationships). The inequality of bargaining inherent to most employment relationships—after all, organizations find it easier to go without the labor of a particular employee than that employee can forego a paycheck in search of better exchange terms—is exacerbated by the kinds of short-term employment relationships (in which employment-related risk is shifted from the employer to the employee) engendered by the boundaryless career model. How, then, can the moral value of fairness be partially obtained in employment relationships based on the boundaryless career model?

THE RIGHT TO EMPLOYABILITY

The main ethical problem posed by boundary less careers is unfairness in terms of shifting risk from employers and employees without corresponding benefits for employees. A partial solution to this problem is therefore the vesting of employability rights to employees that must be satisfied by employers. Recall that employability was defined as "not a guarantee of continuity of employment with one company but a commitment to enhancing the skills and competencies of the employees so they can protect and continuously improve their options for gainful employment in the external labor market" and (1) greater information about employment prospects and (2) greater opportunities for enhancing skills that are salable in the external labor market (in contrast to firm-specific human capital investments).

Note that this is a partial solution to the problem of unfairness previously identified. This paper does not take a position with regard to whether boundary less career patterns are de facto unethical. Neither does employability satisfy or exhaust all of the ethical obligations of employers to employees—whether in short-term employment relationships consistent with the boundaryless career model or not. Rather, the ethical claim being made in this paper is more modest: if employers use the boundaryless career model as a way of organizing employment relationships and gaining flexibility, then satisfying the rights of employees to continued employability is *one* ethical obligation of employers. Such a right is derivative rather than basic and moral, rather than legal. What is deserving of protection in defining an employee's right to employability in the boundary-less career model is (1) employees' ability to maintain their ability to earn a living while (2) shifting some of the risks that they assume back to employers.

In the absence of employability rights, therefore, employers will be able to shift the risks associated with employment relationships almost entirely to employees while gaining the flexibility that employers seek by using the kinds of employment practices (temporary, contingent, contract) consistent with the boundaryless career model. Employment contracts are either absent or inadequate to protect employee interests in this regard. Countervailing forces—whether unions or government agencies—are similarly poorly situated to protect employability rights. Therefore, employability obligations should accrue to employers who benefit most from boundaryless career relationships, and they are best placed to protect and ensure employee employability.

In practical terms, positing a right of employees to employability means that corporations must invest in the skill development of each employee in an employment relationship consistent with the boundary-less career model sufficient to allow him to remain employable on the external labor market. Further,

information about internal employment prospects must be offered to allow employees to assess whether or not to maintain the employment relationship with the organization or to disengage. In turn, of course, employees owe the organization an obligation to use their skills and abilities as contracted for in the employment agreement (whether written or oral).

The analysis of the ethical issues posed by boundaryless careers should yield presumptive grounds for defining a right to employability that would be enjoyed by employees whose careers and employment relationships are consistent with it. The imbalance in relations between employers and employees, combined with the risk shifting from employers to employees engaged in boundaryless career patterns, can thus be partially remedied through employability rights—and, in so doing, helping to promote the moral value of justice in employer-employee relations.

QUESTIONS

1. What is the ethical argument for having employers to invest in employees' future employability?

2. How might adopting an employability approach to managing employees positively and negatively impact a business?

3. In the boundaryless career model, what are the employees' responsibilities?

Ethical Management of Uncertain Employment
Rosabeth Moss Kanter

Ideas for building an ethical workplace in a time when no one's job is secure:

- Recruit for the potential to increase in competence, not simply for narrow skills to fill today's slots.
- Offer ample learning opportunities, from formal training to lunchtime seminars—the equivalent of three weeks a year.
- Provide challenging jobs and rotating assignments that allow growth in skills even without promotion to higher jobs.

- Measure performance beyond accounting numbers and share the data to allow learning by doing and continuous improvement—turning everyone into self-guided professionals.
- Retrain employees as soon as jobs become obsolete.
- Emphasize team building, to help our diverse work force appreciate and utilize fully each other's skills.
- Recognize and reward individual and team achievements, thereby building external reputations and offering tangible indicators of value.
- Provide three-month educational sabbaticals, external internships, or personal time-out every five years.
- Find growth opportunities in our network of suppliers, customers, and venture partners.
- Ensure that pensions and benefits are portable, so that people have safety nets for the future even if they seek employment elsewhere.
- Help people be productive while carrying family responsibilities, through flex-time, provision for sick children, and renewal breaks between major assignments.
- Measure the building of human capital and the capabilities of our people as thoroughly and frequently as we measure the building and use of financial capital.
- Encourage entrepreneurship—new ventures within our company or outside that help our people start businesses and create alternative sources of employment.
- Tap our people's ideas to develop innovations that lower costs, serve customers, and create new markets—the best foundation for business growth and continuing employment, and the source of funds to reinvest in continuous learning.*

* Rosabeth Moss Kanter, *Men and Women of the Corporation*, 2nd ed. (New York: Basic Books, 1993, 330–331).

Harvard Law
Review

Facial Discrimination

"He had but one eye, and the popular prejudice runs in favour of two."
—Charles Dickens, Nicholas Nickleby

THE PHENOMENON OF APPEARANCE DISCRIMINATION

To be human is to discriminate. Humans constantly evaluate people, places, and things and choose some over others. The premise of antidiscrimination law is that in some areas, such as employment and housing, certain criteria are not permissible bases of selection. Antidiscrimination law has yet to state a general model of discrimination that describes precisely which criteria are "illegitimate." Despite the difficulty of developing such criteria, some inner and outer bounds are clear. In the domain of employment, for example, members of racial and religious minority groups are legally protected from discrimination. Those who score poorly on employment aptitude tests found to bear a legitimate relation to the job generally are not.

One approach to antidiscrimination law would protect any member of a minority group who faces discrimination because of membership in that group. This approach is consistent with Louis Wirth's influential definition of a minority: "a group of people who, because of their physical or cultural characteristics, are singled out from the others in the society in which they live for differential and unequal treatment and who therefore regard themselves as objects of collective discrimination." Physically unattractive people do not fall precisely within Wirth's formulation. First, the physically unattractive do not constitute a cohesive group; a thin person with an unattractive face, for example, may feel little kinship with an obese person. In addition, physical attractiveness is a continuum, and neat determinations of who is "unattractive" are impossible. Nevertheless, the physically unattractive share many of the burdens of Wirth's minority groups. Although our society professes a commitment to judge people by their inner worth, physically unattractive people often face differential and unequal treatment in situations in which their appearance is unrelated to their qualifications or abilities. In the employment context, appearance often functions as an illegitimate basis on which to deny people jobs for which they are otherwise qualified.

Appearance Discrimination Generally

People in our society often have a visceral dislike for individuals whom they find unattractive. The bias is so strong that it is not deemed inappropriate to express this dislike; the physically unattractive are a frequent subject of derisive humor. People frequently believe, either consciously or unconsciously, that people with unattractive exteriors were either born with equally unattractive interiors or gradually developed them. By contrast, people tend to think, often with very little basis, that people they find physically attractive are generally worthy and appealing or that, as the title of one study has it, "What Is Beautiful Is Good."

Social science studies have shown that people attribute a wide range of positive characteristics to those whom they find physically attractive. These studies also indicate that when less attractive people are compared to more attractive people, the less attractive men and women are accorded worse treatment simply because of their appearance. This less-favored treatment apparently begins as early as the first few months of life. Throughout childhood, unattractive children face parents who have lower expectations for their success than for more attractive children, teachers who have lower expectations for their academic success, and contemporaries who prefer more attractive children as friends. This less generous treatment of unattractive people continues through adulthood. For example, studies of "helping behavior"—the willingness of subjects to do small favors for a stranger—show that such behavior varies directly with the stranger's attractiveness. Likewise, simulation studies of court proceedings have found that unattractive people receive higher sentences in criminal cases and lower damage awards in civil lawsuits.

Physical appearance can also warp the functioning of ordinarily "objective" evaluations of individuals' work. This distortion has been shown in studies in which subjects were asked to evaluate a written essay that was accompanied by a photograph of the purported author. When copies of the same essay were evaluated with a photograph of an attractive or an unattractive person attached, the essays with the more attractive purported author were judged to have better ideas, better style, and more creativity. Moreover, studies have shown that in general, attractive people are disproportionately likely to receive credit for good outcomes, whereas the good outcomes of unattractive people are more likely to be attributed to external factors, such as luck. Such biases might easily lead an employer to underrate the talents of an unattractive job applicant.

Empirical research on the real-world effects of appearance discrimination supports the results of these simulation exercises. Considerable empirical research has been done in the area of obesity. One study showed that obese high school students were significantly less likely than non-obese students to be admitted to selective colleges, when academic achievement, motivation, and economic class were held constant; another found that obese adults were discriminated against in the renting of apartments.

Appearance discrimination thus seems to occur in a wide variety of situations. Clearly, the law cannot intervene directly to prevent all such discrimination; no law, for example, can itself make a teacher have more faith in an unattractive child's academic success. The law can, however, address discrimination in discrete areas. One such area is employment selection, in which appearance discrimination is widespread.

Appearance Discrimination in Employee Selection

Physical appearance is a significant factor in employee selection, regardless of the nature of the job or the relevance of appearance to the task at hand. One of the primary methods of assessing applicants for all levels of jobs is the personal interview, in which the applicant's appearance is a central criterion. One survey found that appearance was the single most important factor in determining candidate acceptability for a wide variety of jobs, regardless of the level of training of the interviewers. Another study asked 2804 employment interviewers throughout the United States to give "favorability" scores to a variety of characteristics of applicants for various positions. Interviewers considered as important positive characteristics such factors as "Has a good complexion" and rated as important negative characteristics factors such as "Is markedly overweight," and, for men, "Physique appears feminine." Interview manuals written for employers make clear the importance of physical appearance in the selection process. One general employment handbook places "Appearance" first on its list of "hire appeal" factors.

Research in specific areas of physical difference reinforces the claim that appearance discrimination pervades the job market. The National Association to Aid Fat Americans found that fifty-one percent of its members who responded to a survey reported instances of employment discrimination. A report of the State of Maryland's Commission on Human Relations concluded that it may well be easier to place a thin black person on a job than a fat white person. Extremely short people also experience severe employment discrimination.

There have as yet been no direct challenges to appearance discrimination, although appearance issues have been raised in other lawsuits. Hiring practices based on explicit evaluations of applicants' physical appearance were challenged in the courts for the first time in the 1960s and early 1970s in lawsuits charging airlines with sex and race discrimination in the hiring of flight attendants. One Equal Employment Opportunity Commission hearing of a race discrimination claim revealed that an interview form contained the written comment that a black applicant had "unattractive, large lips. The Commission found that this negative evaluation of a race-related aspect of the applicant's appearance provided reasonable cause to believe that unlawful racial discrimination had taken place. More recently, a computer programmer successfully sued under New York State law a company that failed to hire her because she was obese. The challenge alleged, however, that obesity was a medical handicap, and did not raise the broader issue of appearance discrimination.

Restructuring Employment Selection To Reduce Appearance Discrimination

Even if employers agreed in principle that considerations of physical appearance should ideally be eliminated from the hiring process, this ideal would be difficult to achieve in practice. As long as hiring is based on face-to-face interviews, physical appearance will inevitably have an impact on impressions. This problem can be avoided, however, by restructuring the hiring process to eliminate or reduce information about applicants' appearance when applicants are evaluated and hiring decisions are made.

The regulations promulgated by the HHS bar "preemployment inquiries" concerning a job applicant's handicapped status, unless the inquiries specifically concern the applicant's ability to do the job. To meet this requirement, employers could publicly announce a policy of not soliciting information about an applicant's appearance, other than grooming and neatness, and of not considering appearance as a factor in employee selection. The standard face-to-face interview, in which the applicant's appearance is highly salient, in many ways resembles just such a statutorily forbidden preemployment inquiry into appearance handicaps. To conform with the ban on preemployment inquiries, employers should reevaluate their commitment to the standard employment interview.

To be sure, interviews undoubtedly have some informational value beyond permitting illegitimate appearance evaluations. An employer may justifiably be concerned, for example, with an applicant's interpersonal skills. But this information can be obtained in ways that avoid the prejudicial process of face-to-face interviews. One possible method is the expanded use of telephone interviews. Another possibility, which could work well for many kinds of jobs, is the adoption of the practice used by virtually every American symphony orchestra to avoid discrimination and favoritism in hiring: auditions conducted behind screens. Such an interview process would provide employers with useful information about an applicant, revealing factors such as a "pleasant personality," without prejudicing the selection process by injecting appearance into the calculus.

Employers could also reduce or eliminate appearance discrimination through less dramatic modifications in the selection process. They could, for example, set a rigid dividing line between the person who meets and interviews job applicants and the person who makes the decision about whom to hire. The interviewer could pass along a form to the decision-maker that includes only job-related information and impressions. Although the applicant's appearance might still influence the interviewer's perceptions of other subjective qualities, it would nevertheless be a considerable reform.

Objections that employment decisions will be difficult or "random" under such a new regime are misplaced. Workable selection procedures and criteria can be maintained without permitting appearance discrimination. Employers could continue to use the battery of legitimate, work-related criteria: they could ask about education, prior work experience, and success in school and at previous jobs. And they could administer bona fide, work-related, non-discriminatory tests. Indeed, to the extent that these reforms eliminate irrelevant criteria, they should lead to a greater weighting of job-relevant criteria and hence a fairer overall process.

Moving From "Efficiency" to Equality

Efforts to eliminate appearance discrimination would significantly restructure employment practices. Inevitably, such proposed reforms raise questions about the sort of criteria on which our society should permit employment decisions to be based. One objection to eliminating physical appearance as a criterion for hiring is an argument about economic efficiency. If an employer can show that an applicant's appearance makes him or her more profitable, why should this not be a valid criterion for employment? The response to this objection is that "efficiency" is not always an acceptable basis on which to make distinctions in the employment process.

In fact, many sorts of discrimination may be "economically efficient." For example, a restaurant owner in a racist neighborhood might enlarge his or her clientele—and thus increase profits—by refusing to hire black waiters and waitresses. Yet in all forms of antidiscrimination law we proclaim that our society has some principles of equality that it holds more dear than efficiency.

CONCLUSION

The implications of appearance discrimination go beyond the sizeable number of people who experience its effects firsthand. Physical attractiveness discrimination provides a window on the criteria that our society uses to distinguish among people. It represents one of the ways in which we use hazy and illegitimate criteria to separate good from bad, acceptable from unacceptable, and normal from deviant. Stereotypes of all kinds are linked. Together they form a larger "web of stereotypes" that leads people at times to treat racial minorities, women, the elderly, and the disabled as "other" and to exclude them. One strand of otherness that is woven deeply into this web is that of appearance.

Appearance discrimination is sometimes closely connected to related kinds of discrimination. One significant aspect of prejudice against blacks, old people, or people in wheelchairs is a negative reaction to the way they look. Conversely, people may well dislike certain appearance characteristics—such as broad noses or wrinkled skin—because they associate them with groups they disfavor. Decreasing appearance discrimination would help to unravel this entire web of stereotypes. As we expand our conception of what people in certain jobs can look like, we open these jobs up further to once excluded groups.

Ultimately, as with the eradication of all forms of discrimination, people's attitudes must change before appearance discrimination will cease. The first step in this process is recognizing the existence of the problem. As Sander Gilman has written:

> The need for stereotypes runs so deep that I do not think it will ever be thwarted; nor do I think that it

will ever be converted to purely harmless expression. But I believe that education and study can expose the ideologies with which we structure our world, and perhaps help put us in the habit of self-reflection.

QUESTIONS

1. Is discrimination based on gender, race, ethnicity, and sexual orientation also facial discrimination?

2. In what cases is it ethical to hire people based on the way that they look?

3. Is an employer ever justified in not hiring someone who is qualified for a job because they are obese, ugly, disfigured, or with some other unattractive physical abnormality?

To: You
From: The Philosopher
Subject: "John Stuart Mill on the Greatest Good and Expediency"

A friend of mine just started working at a bank. On his first day of work, he had to take a drug test. He asked his manager why and she said, "The reason why new employees have to take drug tests is to help protect our clients and the bank from potential problems. After all, if we got in trouble, we'd have to let employees go. So, while it may be unpleasant for you, it's best everyone."

When I heard this argument, I thought, they certainly don't seem to believe in Kant's idea of treating people as ends in themselves. She sort of sounded like John' Stuart Mill.

> The multiplication of happiness is, according to utilitarian ethics, the object of Virtue: the occasions on which any person (except one in a thousand) has it in his power to do this on an extended scale, in other words to be a public benefactor, are but exceptional; and on these occasions alone, is he called on to consider public utility; in every other case, private utility, the interest or happiness of some few persons, is all the he has to attend to.*

But Mill also made a distinction between utility and expedience:

> [T]he expedient, in the sense in which it is opposed to the Right, generally means that which is expedient for the particular interest of the agent himself. . . . When it means anything better than this, it means that which is expedient for some immediate object, some temporary purpose, but which violates a rule whose observance is expedient in a much higher degree. The Expedient, in this sense instead of being the same thing as what is useful, is a branch of the hurtful."**

* John Stuart Mill, "What Is Utilitarianism?" in *Utilitarianism and other Essays*, ed. Alan Ryan (New York: Penguin Books, 1987), p. 282.
** Ibid., p. 283.

CASES

CASE 1.1
The Job Interview
Sloan Wilson

"Why do you want to work for the United Broadcasting Corporation?" Walker asked abruptly.

"It's a good company . . .," Tom began hesitantly, and was suddenly impatient at the need for hypocrisy. The sole reason he wanted to work for United Broadcasting was that he thought he might be able to make a lot of money there fast, but he felt he couldn't say that. It was sometimes considered fashionable for the employees of foundations to say that they were in it for the money, but people were supposed to work at advertising agencies and broadcasting companies for spiritual reasons.

"I believe," Tom said, "that television is developing into the greatest medium for mass education and entertainment. It has always fascinated me, and I would like to work with it. . . ."

"What kind of salary do you have in mind?" Walker asked. Tom hadn't expected the question that soon. Walker was still smiling.

"The salary isn't the primary consideration with me," Tom said, trying desperately to come up with stock answers to stock questions. "I'm mainly interested in finding something useful and worth while to do. I have personal responsibilities, however, and I would hope that something could be worked out to enable me to meet them. . . ."

"Of course," Walker said, beaming more cheerily than ever. "I understand you applied for a position in the public-relations department. Why did you choose that?"

Because I heard there was an opening, Tom wanted to say, but quickly thought better of it and substituted a halting avowal of lifelong interest in public relations. "I think my experience in working with *people* at the Schanenhauser Foundation would be helpful," he concluded lamely.

"I see," Walker said kindly. There was a short silence before he added, "Can you write?"

"I do most of the writing at the Schanenhauser Foundation," Tom said. "The annual report to the trustees is my job, and so are most of the reports on individual projects. I used to be editor of my college paper."

"That sounds fine," Walker said casually. "I have a little favor I want to ask of you. I want you to write me your autobiography."

"What?" Tom asked in astonishment.

"Nothing very long," Walker said. "Just as much as you can manage to type out in an hour. One of my girls will give you a room with a typewriter."

"Is there anything in particular you want me to tell you about?"

"Yourself," Walker said, looking hugely pleased. "Explain yourself to me. Tell me what kind of person you are. Explain why we should hire you."

"I'll try," Tom said weakly.

"You'll have precisely an hour," Walker said. "You see, this is a device I use in employing people—I find it most helpful. For this particular job, I have twenty or thirty applicants. It's hard to tell from a brief interview whom to choose, so I ask them all to write about themselves for an hour. You'd be surprised how revealing the results are. . . ."

He paused, still smiling. Tom said nothing.

From Sloan Wilson, *The Man in the Gray Flannel Suit* (Simon & Schuster, 1955), pp. 13–14.

"Just a few hints," Walker continued. "Write anything you want, but at the end of your last page, I'd like you to finish this sentence: 'The most significant fact about me is . . .'"

"The most significant fact about me is . . .," Tom repeated idiotically.

"The results, of course, will be entirely confidential." Walker lifted a bulky arm and inspected his wrist watch. "It's now five minutes to twelve," he concluded. "I'll expect your paper on my desk at precisely one o'clock."

Tom stood up, put on his coat, said, "Thank you," and went out of the room. . . .

Tom sat down in the chair, which had been designed for a stenographer and was far too small for him. Son of a bitch, he thought—I guess the laws about cruel and unusual punishment don't apply to personnel men. He tried to think of something to write, but all he could remember was Betsy and the drab little house and the need to buy a new washing machine, and the time he had thrown a vase that cost forty dollars against the wall. "The most significant fact about me is that I once threw a vase costing forty dollars against a wall." That would be as sensible as anything else he could think of, but he doubted whether it would get him the job. He thought of Janey saying, "It isn't *fair!*" and the worn linoleum on the kitchen floor. "The most significant fact about me is. . . ." It was a stupid sentence to ask a man to finish.

I have children, he thought—that's probably the most significant fact about me, the only one that will have much importance for long. Anything about a man can be summed up in numbers. Thomas R. Rath, thirty-three years old, making seven thousand dollars a year, owner of a 1939 Ford, a six-room house, and ten thousand dollars' worth of G.I. Life Insurance which, in case of his death, would pay his widow about forty dollars a month. Six feet one and a half inches tall; weight, 198 pounds. He served four and a half years in the Army, most of it in Europe and the rest in the South Pacific.

Another statistical fact came to him then, a fact which he knew would be ridiculously melodramatic to put into an application for a job at the United Broadcasting Corporation, or to think about at all. He hadn't thought about this for a long while. It wasn't a thing he had deliberately tried to forget—he simply hadn't thought about it for quite a few years. It was the unreal-sounding, probably irrelevant, but quite accurate fact that he had killed seventeen men. . . .

Such things were merely part of the war, the war before the Korean one. It was no longer fashionable to talk about the war, and certainly it had never been fashionable to talk about the number of men one had killed. Tom couldn't forget the number, "seventeen," but it didn't seem real any more; it was just a small, isolated statistic that nobody wanted. His mind went blank. . . .

"The most significant fact about me is that I detest the United Broadcasting Corporation, with all its soap operas, commercials, and yammering studio audiences, and the only reason I'm willing to spend my life in such a ridiculous enterprise is that I want to buy a more expensive house and a better brand of gin."

That certainly wouldn't get him the job.

"The most significant fact about me is that I've become a cheap cynic."

That would not be apt to get him the job.

"The most significant fact about me is that as a young man in college, I played the mandolin incessantly. I, champion mandolin player, am applying to you for a position in the public-relations department!"

That would not be likely to get him far. Impatiently he sat down at the typewriter and glanced at his wrist watch. It was a big loud-ticking wrist watch with a black face, luminous figures, and a red sweep hand that rapidly ticked off the seconds. He had bought it years ago at an Army post exchange and had worn it all through the war. The watch was the closest thing to a good-luck charm he had ever had, although he never thought of it as such. Now it was more reassuring to look at than the big impersonal clock on the wall, though both said it was almost twelve-thirty. So far he had written nothing. What the hell, he thought. I was a damn fool to think I wanted to work here anyway. Then he thought of Betsy asking, as she would be sure to, "Did you get the job? How did it go?" And he decided to try.

"Anybody's life can be summed up in a paragraph," he wrote. "I was born on November 20, 1920, in my grandmother's house in South Bay, Connecticut. I was graduated from Covington Academy in 1937, and from Harvard College in

1941. I spent four and a half years in the Army, reaching the rank of captain. Since 1946, I have been employed as an assistant to the director of the Schanenhauser Foundation. I live in Westport, Connecticut, with my wife and three children. From the point of view of the United Broadcasting Corporation, the most significant fact about me is that I am applying for a position in its public-relations department, and after an initial period of learning, I probably would do a good job. I will be glad to answer any questions which seem relevant, but after considerable thought, I have decided that I do not wish to attempt an autobiography as part of an application for a job."

He typed this paragraph neatly in the precise center of a clean piece of paper, added his name and address, and carried it into Walker's office. It was only quarter to one, and Walker was obviously surprised to see him. "You've still got fifteen minutes!" he said.

"I've written all I think is necessary," Tom replied, and handed him the almost empty page.

Walker read it slowly, his big pale face expressionless. When he had finished it, he dropped it into a drawer. "We'll let you know our decision in a week or so," he said.

QUESTIONS

1. What values does Tom struggle with in the job interview?

2. What does this story say to you about the relationship between the individual and the organization?

3. To what extent would you be willing to say things that you do not believe to please an interviewer? Where would you draw the line?

CASE 1.2
A "State of the Art" Termination
John R. Boatright

Monday had been the most humiliating day of Bill Collin's life. Rumors of downsizing had been swirling for months, and every computer analyst in Bill's department knew that the ax would fall on some of them. Bets had even been taken on who would stay and who would go. When the news was finally delivered, Bill was not surprised. He also understood the necessity of reducing the computer support staff in view of the merger that had made many jobs redundant, and he felt confident that he would find a new job fairly quickly. What upset him was the manner in which he had been terminated.

Bill arrived in the office at eight o'clock sharp to find a memo on his desk about a nine-thirty meeting at a hotel one block away. Since this site was often used for training sessions, he gave the notice little thought. Bill decided to arrive a few minutes early in order to chat with colleagues, but he found himself being ushered quickly into a small conference room where three other people from his department were already seated. His greeting to them was cut short by a fourth person whom Bill had never seen before. The stranger explained that he was a consultant from an outplacement firm that had been engaged to deliver the bad news and to outline the

From John R. Boatright, *Ethics and the Conduct of Business*, 2nd edition (Upper Saddle River, NJ: Prentice Hall, 1997), pp. 255–256. Notes were deleted from the text.

benefits the company was providing for them. Once he started talking, Bill felt relieved: The package of benefits was greater than he had dared hope. All employees would receive full salary for six months plus pay for accrued vacation time; medical insurance and pension contribution would be continued during this period; and the outplacement firm would provide career counseling and a placement service that included secretarial assistance, photocopying and fax service, and office space. The consultant assured the four longtime employees that the company appreciated their years of service and wanted to proceed in a caring manner. It was for this reason that they hired the best consulting firm in the business, one that had a reputation for a "state-of-the-art" termination process.

Bill's relief was jolted by what came next. The consultant informed the four that they were not to return to their office or to set foot inside the corporate office building again; nor were they to attempt to contact anyone still working for the company. (At this point, Bill suddenly realized that he had no idea how many employees might be in other four-person groups being dismissed at the same time.) The contents of their desks would be boxed and delivered to their homes; directories of their computer files would be provided, and requests for any personal material would be honored after a careful review of their contents to make sure that no proprietary information was included. The consultant assured them that all passwords had already been changed, including the password for remote access. Finally, they were instructed not to remain at the hotel but to proceed to a service exit where prepaid taxis were stationed to take them home.

Bill regretted not being able to say goodbye to friends in the office. He would have liked some advance warning in order to finish up several projects that he had initiated and to clear out his own belongings. The manner in which he had been terminated was compassionate up to a point, Bill admitted, but it showed that the company did not trust him. A few days later, Bill understood the company's position better when he read an article in a business magazine that detailed the sabotage that had been committed by terminated employees who had continued access to their employer's computer system. Some disgruntled workers had destroyed files and done other mischief when they were allowed to return to their offices after being informed of their termination. One clever computer expert had previously planted a virtually undetectable virus that remained dormant until he gained access long enough through a co-worker's terminal to activate it. The advice that companies were receiving from consulting firms that specialize in termination was: Be compassionate, but also protect yourself. Good advice, Bill thought, but the humiliation was still fresh in his mind.

QUESTIONS

1. Is firing someone with dignity an oxymoron?
2. Is there a way to fire people that will encourage them to act with dignity?
3. How does the way that a company fires people affect the rest of the employees?

CASE 1.3
Does Home Life Matter at Work?
Joanne B. Ciulla

Over the past month, you and your colleagues have been reviewing applications for regional manager. The regional manager's job involves overseeing and coordinating the operations of a large portion of the western United States. On Friday afternoon, your committee finally makes its selection and plans to announce its choice on Monday morning. Out of a number of talented managers, it selected John Deer. John's peers often used the words "brilliant" and "genius" to describe him. He held a consistent record of excellence in every task that he accomplished for the company.

A quiet, polite man, John rarely attended social functions, and when he did, he never brought his wife. When you arrive at your office on Monday morning, you are surprised to get a call from John's wife Edith, whom you've never met. Her voice sounds shaky, and you can hardly hear her. She says:

> I'm sorry to be a bother, but I needed to talk to you. My husband John has been tense lately because he really wants the regional manager's job. Anyway, last night John gave me a very bad beating. Our two children saw the whole thing and were terrified. I took the children and ran out of the house. We are now staying at the Chicago shelter for battered women. Over the years, John has hit me on numerous occasions, but never like this. He's basically a good man, but he's very high strung. Anyway, the reason why I am calling is to beg you to give the job to John. Maybe then he'll feel happier and things will be better for our family.

The phone call is so bizarre that you decide to check out Mrs. Deer's story. You call the Chicago shelter to find out if she is indeed there. The shelter director says that it is against its policy to give out the identity of clients or any information on them. Then in the background you hear some confusion as Mrs. Deer grabs the phone from the director. Mrs. Deer tells the director to get on the other line and demands that she answer your questions. The director protests, but does as she is asked. She reports that Mrs. Deer and her two children, ages 2 and 6, were admitted to the shelter last night at midnight after being treated at City Hospital. Mrs. Deer had a broken rib and bruises on the face, arms, and neck that were apparently caused by a blunt object.

It is now 10:30 a.m. The formal announcement is scheduled for noon. At this point, John may already know that he got the job. You are angry and disgusted, but you know that you will have to put your personal feelings aside and consider a number of issues before you make any decisions about John. Since Mrs. Deer has no plans to press charges against her husband, you put aside legal considerations and think about your ethical obligations in this situation.

QUESTIONS

1. Given that there is no legal action taken against an individual, is the way that a person treats his or her spouse or other family member relevant in hiring and promotion decisions?

2. If you were the manager in this case, how would you fill your moral obligations to all the stakeholders who are involved in it?

3. When do you think the manager's moral obligations to John Deer and his wife and children begin and end?

CASE 1.4

The Best Person for the Job?

Joanne B. Ciulla

Sam, one of your senior professionals, has resigned unexpectedly to join one of your competitors. He was responsible for transactions with Magnolia Corporation, where he had a close relationship with the CEO, J. W. Crawford. You know that there is a good chance that Magnolia may go with Sam if you don't put a knowledgeable and experienced person on the account. This is your largest account, and you don't want to lose it. In the past, both the company and Sam have made a lot of money from various deals with Magnolia.

You know from Sam's client notes and from your previous visits to Magnolia that J. W. belongs to the "old school" and is most comfortable dealing with "one of the boys." Last year, when Sam was visiting Magnolia, he went on a hunting trip with J. W. The final night of the trip, J. W. surprised them with a "special treat." He invited a stripper to entertain them after a long dinner and plenty of drinks. On another occasion, Sam invited Elaine Jones, one of the firm's top account executives, to attend a meeting with J. W. Sam wanted her advice on an investment. During the meeting, J. W. paid little attention to what Elaine had to say and kept referring to her as "honey." On the way out of the meeting, J. W. gave her a pat on her behind.

Elaine is really the only person who knows J. W.'s business and has the expertise and seniority to take Sam's place. Ordinarily, there would be no question of her taking over this client because of her experience and track record. Elaine is not known to turn down potentially lucrative deals; however, knowing what you do about J. W., you wonder if she's the person for the job.

QUESTIONS

1. Who should be responsible for making this decision?
2. What are the larger long-term ramifications of this decision for the firm and its stakeholders?
3. In businesses where client relationships are important, is it fair to consider an employee's personal interests as qualifications for working with a particular client? For example, would it be ethical to give a client who plays golf to a salesperson who plays golf, even if there are other salespeople who may be better qualified to work with that client?

CASE 1.5

Attraction or Business as Usual?

Joanne B. Ciulla

Your company is in the process of opening a new office. You are in charge of purchasing software that will be used for billing and payroll. There are really only three software systems that will meet your business needs.

Last week, each of the three vendors came in to give a demonstration of their product and get an assessment of your computing needs. You spoke with salespeople from two of the companies. However, the third company that you talked to, Agape, sent along a salesperson and a systems expert. The systems expert was named Hank Smith. The salesman explained that Agape likes its customers to meet the technician whom they would be working with if they purchased the system.

Hank Smith was very knowledgeable and answered all your questions clearly. He was also honest about the strengths and weaknesses of the system. The three of you talked for about two hours, and then the salesperson said that he had another appointment, but that Hank would stay to answer any further questions. Hank suggested that you continue over lunch. You said that would be fine, but only if you could pay.

At lunch Hank talks more about the software system, but you realize that you aren't really listening. Hank isn't just handsome, he's gorgeous and *very* charming. You find yourself looking at his hands to see if he is married. There is no wedding ring, so you turn the conversation to other matters. He tells you that he has an apartment in the city and, through a series of questions, you finally discover that he is not married and that he lives alone. You sense that Hank feels a similar attraction to you. Nonetheless, you realize that you can't do or say anything because of your business relationship.

Over the next few days, you keep thinking about Hank and hoping that Agape will come in with the lowest bid. Finally the bids arrive. Agape and Hi-Tech come in at about the same price. The third company's bid is significantly higher. You discuss the three options with your manager. The software packages offered by Agape and Hi-Tech are similar; either system would be adequate. The more expensive system does not offer much more, so you eliminate it.

Your manager says that since it's a toss-up between Agape and Hi-Tech, the decision is up to you. For a moment you think about your intense attraction to Hank. But then you think, "I am a professional woman, and this is a decision that could be made by the toss of a coin. So why not choose Agape?" You buy the Agape software, but to your great disappointment, they send another systems expert to work with your company. It makes you wonder if you really made the best decision and if the company sent Hank to work his charm on you.

QUESTIONS

1. Would it be wrong if Agape sent Hank because it knew a single woman was making the decision on the software?

2. Is this a conflict of interest on the purchaser's part, or is it just a case of her interests coinciding with the company's interests?

3. Is there anything wrong with doing a little flirting to make a sale?

CASE 1.6
Pornography and the Boss's Computer
Joanne B. Ciulla

Carlton Smith, an undergraduate business major, was very excited about his summer internship at the public relations company James and Madison in New York. The firm serves a number of high-profile clients ranging from Fortune 500 companies to religious organizations and NGOs. People inside and outside of the industry consider James and Madison the gold standard for integrity in the industry. This was where Carlton aspired to work at after he graduated. James and Madison had an extensive code of ethics that they required everyone in the firm, including interns, to sign. The code focuses on issues related to professional conduct, confidentiality, and the use of office computers for personal purposes. It requires all employees to report any infractions of the code to senior management.

The internship proved to be everything that Carlton had hoped it would be. A senior VP named Todd Williams took Carlton on as his assistant. The work that Carlton did for Todd exposed him to many aspects of the public relations business. Most of Carlton's work involved gathering information for Todd and providing support when Todd gave presentations to potential clients.

One day, about halfway into the internship, Todd called Carlton from L.A., where he was working with a client. Todd was in the middle of a meeting and he needed Carlton to quickly look up an article related to his client's business. Todd said that he could not remember how he searched for the article, but that he remembered pulling it up on his computer right before he left town. Carlton figured that instead of searching for it on his computer, it would be faster to retrieve it from the search history on Todd's Mac.

Carlton then went into Todd's office and pulled up Todd's search history to see if it is there. Just as Todd said, it was the first one on the list.

Carlton could not help but notice that the next few items in the search history had very odd names that sounded like pornography sites. Maybe these sites were research that Todd was doing for another client, but it did not seem likely. Curiosity got the best of him. Without thinking, he clicked on one site that had some very sick pictures of sadistic sex. Carlton then realized that he should not have done this. Since he sent the email from Todd's computer, Todd might know that he saw his search history and went to one of the sites. Carlton realized that he might be in a serious fix.

QUESTIONS

1. What did Carlton do wrong here?
2. What are his ethical obligations and to whom?
3. What would you do if you were Carlton?

Sexual Harassment Guidelines

Sexual harassment is covered Under Title VII of the Civil Rights Act of 1964. The act states that it is unlawful for an employer to discriminate against an employee based on a person's sex. It prohibits discrimination in decisions involving compensation, terms, conditions, or privileges of employment. There are two types of sexual harassment:

1. *Quid pro quo*: Harassment that pressures an employee for sexual favours as a condition of employment or for benefits, such as promotions, job assignments, etc.
2. *Hostile Environment*: Behavior that does not affect and employee's economic benefits. It consists of unwelcome advances or sexual, verbal, and/or physical conduct of a sexual nature. This conduct has the purpose or effect of interfering with an individual's work performance or creating an intimidating, hostile, or offensive working environment.*

Key elements of sexual harassment:

1. Harassment was unwelcome.
2. Harassment was based on gender
3. Harassment was sufficiently severe or pervaisve
4. Hostile enviornment affects a person's ability to perform at work and/or causes psychological harm.

* Anja Angelica chan, *Women and Sexual Harassment* (New York: Harrington Park Press, 1994), pp. 5–6.

CHAPTER QUESTIONS

1. What are the underlying conditions of the employer–employee relationship that make it a challenge for organizations to respect the humanity of persons in the workplace?

2. What claim does an employer have on a person's feelings, rights, and privacy? What rights are you willing to give up to be employed? What rights can an employer justifiably limit in the workplace?

3. The old social contract of most workplaces was, "if you do your job well, you can keep it." In today's uncertain employment environment, what kind of reciprocal agreements can employers have with employees?

"The Check Is in the Mail"

Honesty and Trust in Business

Introduction

You have a job you like, and you work for a man named George. George is a bright, ambitious, and energetic person, but his expectations often outreach his grasp, and he tends to take on more work than he can do. Working with him can be fun, but it's often frantic. Projects are frequently late, and you always seem to be on a tight if not impossible deadline.

The phones ring constantly in George's office. Typically, George tells his secretary to say that he is not in or that he will be out of town until the end of the week. Sometimes when people hear that George is not in, they call you. This puts you in the awkward position of not only having to back up the lie that the secretary was instructed to tell but sometimes having to make up new lies. Sometimes, you have to lie to confirm that George is where he says he is. Other times, you have to lie about what George is doing. There are times when George tells his manager that your group is working on or even almost finished with a project that the group hasn't even heard of, let alone started. In this way, George sometimes gets his team projects that they might not have gotten otherwise, but it also puts pressure on everyone in the group (including you) to lie about what the group is doing and how it is progressing.

Today George is away with his family on vacation. You get a call from his boss. He says, "I need to talk to you about that Franklin project—George told me that your team has been making great progress on it." You have no idea what the Franklin project is, so you lie, say "just fine," and tell George's manager that you are tied up in meetings all day. You agree to stop by first thing tomorrow.

Your first instinct is to contact George. But he is on a camping trip with his family, and he makes it a point not to check for messages when he is away from the office on personal time. You are positive that no one in your office is working on a Franklin project because you coordinate all the projects for George.

All along you knew that the lies would catch up to George. Every small lie seems to require 10 more lies. Yet the thing about George is that he has a way of turning his lies into truths. He reminds you of the French writer Andre Malraux. Malraux believed that the way to lead an exciting life was to tell big lies and then live your life so as to make them true. But this is not the time for philosophizing. You have been lying not because you are fabricating a better life for yourself, but because George has put you into this awkward situation. This not the first time you have had to lie for him or because of him, of course, but this time is much more serious. The little "white lies" that his secretary routinely tells—and you've been party to—seem innocent enough. After all, whom do you know who hasn't said or had someone say that they're "in a meeting" when, in fact, they are taking a nap or spending some time in the restroom? And how often have you said or heard someone say "the check is in the mail" when it is not, although just saying that usually motivates getting that check in the mail ASAP. Sure, it's a lie, but it's an innocent lie, even a productive lie. So what harm is done?

But now, what will you tell George's boss?

"Honesty is the best policy," we are told from childhood. But we see cheating and lying all around us. Why is honesty so important? Why is telling the truth important? Indeed, why is truth so important? If lies and deception help us get along in life, for example, when we don't tell our friends something true but offensive about themselves, isn't that more important than the truth? And whatever we think about the idea of lying to friends or deceiving one's family, business would seem to be another matter. No one expects a salesman to tell "the whole truth and nothing but the truth" about the advantages of his own versus his competitor's products. No one ever got ahead in an organization by being completely forthright about his or her abilities and deficiencies, although *pretending* to be completely forthright about one's deficiencies (for example, "I get so involved in a project that I cannot quit until it gets done") can get one ahead, to be sure. And what is a lie, after all? It is impossible to tell the whole truth; there are always details left out, perspectives left unexplored, presuppositions left unspoken. Given any situation or state of affairs, there are more or less positive, and more or less negative, ways of presenting it, which in today's politics is called "spin." Spin, strictly speaking, is not lying. It does not involve falsehood. It just imposes a positive (or a negative) way of interpreting the facts. Thus, two politicians may take exactly the same facts about the economy, for example, and one suggests that they show that the economy is getting better and the other insists that they show that the economy is in serious trouble. So, too, a salesman necessarily puts a positive spin on the facts about his product (as opposed to the facts about his competitor's product) but he need not tell any falsehood to do so. So what does it mean in business, that "honesty is the best policy"?

In the following selections, we will see a wide range of discussions and opinions about the place of truth, lies, and secrets in business. In the first selection, Albert Z. Carr argues that something very much like lying, *bluffing*, is utterly fundamental to business. Business, he says, is a lot like poker. He expands this analogy into a general observation that the morality of ordinary life is not applicable to business. Needless to say, many people in the business community howled in indignation. They thought of themselves as moral, upstanding citizens, and they thought of their business activities as a legitimate and completely moral part of their citizenship, and their replies make that very clear. We have also included an argument by business ethicist Norman Bowie, who argues against Carr that bluffing just doesn't pay. We then include a surprising excerpt from the great philosopher Immanuel Kant, who makes the good point that telling the truth is not always the right thing to do. He also opens up the question of privacy, confidentiality and secrets.

But honesty is not the only good policy in business. One of the complications surrounding questions of truthfulness in business is a legitimate concern with confidentiality and keeping secrets. All businesses operate within a network of agreements and promises, some of them explicitly spelled out in contracts, others left unsaid and merely implicit. People in the financial industry, for example, are often bound by confidentiality agreements. That means that they are committed not to tell the truth (or, rather, to not tell the truth) even when someone directly asks them for information that breaches confidentiality. In a more informal way, businesses have an obligation to their customers to maintain a certain privacy. Again, sometimes this obligation is explicit and spelled out (as when a mail order house promises to send a product "in a discrete package") but more often it is left merely implicit. Thus, airline customers howled and some even sued when their airlines passed along personal travel information to the federal government under the Homeland Security Act. That information, they argued, was private and therefore protected, whether or not they had any explicit assurances from the airlines. Protecting someone's privacy (including one's own), it can be argued, is not fairly construed as an instance of lying.

Many businesses also require secrets, secret formulas for a soft drink, secret strategies for negotiations, secret or at any rate private arrangements with various customers, employees, and vendors. Businesses, like individuals, are entitled to have secrets. Yet, Transparency International, considers the lack of transparency to be the key measure of business corruption. But what is a legitimate secret, and what is not? We include a piece by Sissela Bok that discusses the role of secrets in business.

Telling the truth is hardest, to many people, when one's career is on the line. If you are a consultant, for example, the temptation is to tell your client what he or she wants to hear. Otherwise, human nature being what it is, there is a strong likelihood that you will not be invited back. This is also true within the workplace, especially with the new emphasis on 360-degree assessment and regular job evaluations, so we have included an excerpt from a consultant's consultant, Sue De Wine, on giving feedback. Adelaide Lancaster offers three simple techniques for making a business more honest. But sometimes people from other businesses do not lie or tell the truth. They simply engage in what philosopher Harry Frankfurt calls "bullshit."

What makes honesty the best policy? Part of the answer is, because of *trust*. It is trust that makes the business world possible, and without it, there would be no business, just varieties of strategy, fraud, robbery, and coercion. Business is all about trust. Dishonesty violates trust and raises suspicions. And for those who think only prudentially, a powerful answer to the "why not lie?" question is "because you probably won't get away with it." People usually don't get away with it, not only because they get tripped up by embarrassing facts, but because they trip themselves up. We have included a piece by psychologists Paul Ekman and Mark Frank who have worked extensively with police and security institutions, explaining why this so often happens. The risk of destroying trust is usually enough of a deterrent for most people. Finally, we have included two pieces on the complex nature of trust, in both personal and business relationships.

To: You
From: The Philosopher
Subject: "Aristotle, Kant, and Mill on Honesty"

The way you are discussing honesty suggests that you think that truth and deception are special concerns in business, but if there is one moral rule that seems to have always been around; it is the insistence that we should tell the truth. Philosophers of almost every persuasion have seen fit to condemn lying, albeit for different reasons. Twenty-five hundred years ago, Aristotle argued that

> The man who loves truth and is truthful where nothing is at stake will be still more truthful where something is at stake; he will avoid falsehood as something base, seeing that he avoided it even for its own sake. Such a man is worthy of praise. (*N. Ethics* Book IV, Ch. 7)

For Aristotle, truthfulness was a virtue. The lack of truthfulness was a vice. Lying was not so much a breach of rules as it was a betrayal of bad character.

Kant, on the other hand, was a rule man. Lying was wrong because it violated what he called "The Moral Law" (or what he characterized as "The Categorical Imperative"). Yet he, too, saw lying as a mark of a bad person, worthy of contempt, and quite independent of the consequences:

> The greatest violation of man's duty to himself considered only as a moral being is the opposite of veracity: lying. That no intentional untruth in the expression of one's thoughts can avoid this harsh name in ethics which derives no authorization from harmlessness, is clear of itself For dishonor, to be an object of moral contempt, which goes with lying accompanies the liar like his shadow (*Metaphysics of the Principles of Virtue*, p. 429).

In other words, lying is wrong even if the consequences are good, and truth telling is right even if the results are disastrous.

John Stuart Mill, by contrast, insisted that consequences are all-important. Lying is wrong, accordingly, because it usually—perhaps almost always—has long-term bad consequences.

Albert Z. Carr | # Is Business Bluffing Ethical?

Albert Carr wrote this inflammatory piece in the *Harvard Business Review* in 1968. It continues to attract controversy.

A respected businessman with whom I discussed the theme of this article remarked with some heat, "You mean to say you're going to encourage men to bluff? Why, bluffing is nothing more than a form of lying! You're advising them to lie!"

I agreed that the basis of private morality is a respect for truth and that the closer a businessman comes to the truth, the more he deserves respect. At the same time, I suggested that most bluffing in business might be regarded simply as game strategy—much like bluffing in poker, which does not reflect on the morality of the bluffer.

I quoted Henry Taylor, the British statesman who pointed out that "falsehood ceases to be falsehood when it is understood on all sides that the truth is not expected to be spoken"—an exact description of bluffing in poker, diplomacy, and business. I cited the analogy of the criminal court, where the criminal is not expected to tell the truth when he pleads "not guilty." Everyone from the judge down takes it for granted that the job of the defendant's attorney is to get his client off, not to reveal the truth; and this is considered ethical practice. I mentioned Representative Omar Burleson, the Democrat from Texas, who was quoted as saying, in regard to the ethics of Congress, "Ethics is a barrel of worms"[1]—a pungent summing up of the problem of deciding who is ethical in politics.

I reminded my friend that millions of businessmen feel constrained every day to say *yes* to their bosses when they secretly believe *no* and that this is generally accepted as permissible strategy when the alternative might be the loss of a job. The essential point, I said, is that the ethics of business are game ethics, different from the ethics of religion.

He remained unconvinced. Referring to the company of which he is president, he declared: "Maybe that's good enough for some businessmen, but I can tell you that we pride ourselves on our ethics. In 30 years not one customer has ever questioned my word or asked to check our figures. We're loyal to our customers and fair to our suppliers. I regard my handshake on a deal as a contract. I've never entered into price-fixing schemes with my competitors. I've never allowed my salesmen to spread injurious rumors about other companies. Our union contract is the best in our industry. And, if I do say so myself, our ethical standards are of the highest!"

He really was saying, without realizing it, that he was living up to the ethical standards of the business game—which are a far cry from those of private life. Like a gentlemanly poker player, he did not play in cahoots with others at the table, try to smear their reputations, or hold back chips he owed them.

But this same fine man, at that very time, was allowing one of his products to be advertised in a way that made it sound a great deal better than it actually was. Another item in his product line was notorious among dealers for its "built-in obsolescence." He was holding back from the market a much-improved product because he did not want it to interfere with sales of the inferior item it would have replaced. He had joined with certain of his competitors in hiring a lobbyist to push a state legislature, by methods that he preferred not to know too much about, into amending a bill then being enacted.

In his view these things had nothing to do with ethics; they were merely normal business practice. He himself undoubtedly avoided outright falsehoods—never lied in so many words. But the entire organization that he ruled was deeply involved in numerous strategies of deception.

PRESSURE TO DECEIVE

Most executives from time to time are almost compelled, in the interests of their companies or themselves, to practice some form of deception when negotiating with customers, dealers, labor unions, government officials, or even other departments of their companies. By conscious misstatements, concealment of pertinent facts, or exaggeration—in short, by bluffing—they seek to persuade others to agree with them. I think it is fair to say that if the individual executive refuses to bluff from time to time—if he feels obligated to tell the truth, the whole truth, and nothing but the truth—he is ignoring opportunities permitted under the rules and is at a heavy disadvantage in his business dealings.

But here and there a businessman is unable to reconcile himself to the bluff in which he plays a part. His conscience, perhaps spurred by religious idealism, troubles him. He feels guilty; he may develop an ulcer or a nervous tic. Before any executive can make profitable use of the strategy of the bluff, he needs to make sure that in bluffing he will not lose self-respect or become emotionally disturbed. If he is to reconcile personal integrity and high standards of honesty with the practical requirements of business, he must feel that his bluffs are ethically justified. The justification rests on the fact that business, as practiced by individuals as well as by corporations, has the impersonal character of a game—a game that demands both special strategy and an understanding of its special ethics.

The game is played at all levels of corporate life, from the highest to the lowest. At the very instant that a man decides to enter business, he may be forced into a game situation, as is shown by the recent experience of a Cornell honor graduate who applied for a job with a large company:

- This applicant was given a psychological test which included the statement, "Of the following magazines, check any that you have read either regularly or from time to time, and double-check those which interest you most. *Reader's Digest, Time, Fortune, Saturday Evening Post, The New Republic, Life, Look, Ramparts, Newsweek, Business Week, U.S.*

News & World Report, The Nation, Playboy, Esquire, Harper's, Sports Illustrated."

His tastes in reading were broad, and at one time or another he had read almost all of these magazines. He was a subscriber to *The New Republic*, an enthusiast for *Ramparts*, and an avid student of the pictures in *Playboy*. He was not sure whether his interest in *Playboy* would be held against him, but he had a shrewd suspicion that if he confessed to an interest in *Ramparts* and *The New Republic*, he would be thought a liberal, a radical, or at least an intellectual, and his chances of getting the job, which he needed, would greatly diminish. He therefore checked five of the more conservative magazines. Apparently it was a sound decision, for he got the job.

He had made a game player's decision, consistent with business ethics.

A similar case is that of a magazine space salesman who, owing to a merger, suddenly found himself out of a job:

- This man was 58, and, in spite of a good record, his chance of getting a job elsewhere in a business where youth is favored in hiring practice was not good. He was a vigorous, healthy man, and only a considerable amount of gray in his hair suggested his age. Before beginning his job search he touched up his hair with a black dye to confine the gray to his temples. He knew that the truth about his age might well come out in time, but he calculated that he could deal with that situation when it arose. He and his wife decided that he could easily pass for 45, and he so stated his age on his résumé.

This was a lie; yet within the accepted rules of the business game, no moral culpability attaches to it.

THE POKER ANALOGY

We can learn a good deal about the nature of business by comparing it with poker. While both have a large element of chance, in the long run the winner is the man who plays with steady skill. In both games ultimate victory requires intimate knowledge of the rules, insight into the psychology of the other players, a bold front, a considerable amount of self-discipline, and the ability to respond swiftly and effectively to opportunities provided by chance.

No one expects poker to be played on the ethical principles preached in churches. In poker it is right and proper to bluff a friend out of the rewards of being dealt a good hand. A player feels no more than a slight twinge of sympathy, if that, when—with nothing better than a single ace in his hand—he strips a heavy loser, who holds a pair, of the rest of his chips. It was up to the other fellow to protect himself. In the words of an excellent poker player, former President Harry Truman, "If you can't stand the heat, stay out of the kitchen." If one shows mercy to a loser in poker, it is a personal gesture, divorced from the rules of the game.

Poker has its special ethics, and here I am not referring to rules against cheating. The man who keeps an ace up his sleeve or who marks the cards is more than unethical; he is a crook, and can be punished as such—kicked out of the game or, in the Old West, shot.

In contrast to the cheat, the unethical poker player is one who, while abiding by the letter of the rules, finds ways to put the other players at an unfair disadvantage. Perhaps he unnerves them with loud talk. Or he tries to get them drunk. Or he plays in cahoots with someone else at the table. Ethical poker players frown on such tactics.

Poker's own brand of ethics is different from the ethical ideals of civilized human relationships. The game calls for distrust of the other fellow. It ignores the claim of friendship. Cunning deception and concealment of one's strength and intentions, not kindness and open-heartedness, are vital in poker. No one thinks any the worse of poker on that account. And no one should think any the worse of the game of business because its standards of right and wrong differ from the prevailing traditions of morality in our society. . . .

"WE DON'T MAKE THE LAWS"

Wherever we turn in business, we can perceive the sharp distinction between its ethical standards and those of the churches. Newspapers abound with sensational stories growing out of this distinction:

- We read one day that Senator Philip A. Hart of Michigan has attacked food processors for deceptive packaging of numerous products.[2]
- The next day there is a Congressional to-do over Ralph Nader's book. *Unsafe At Any Speed*, which demonstrates that automobile companies for years have neglected the safety of car-owning families.[3]
- Then another Senator, Lee Metcalf of Montana, and journalist Vic Reinemer show in their book, *Overcharge*, the methods by which utility companies elude regulating government bodies to extract unduly large payments from users of electricity.[4]

These are merely dramatic instances of a prevailing condition; there is hardly a major industry at which a similar attack could not be aimed. Critics of business regard such behavior as unethical, but the companies concerned know that they are merely playing the business game.

Among the most respected of our business institutions are the insurance companies. A group of insurance executives meeting recently in New England was startled when their guest speaker, social critic Daniel Patrick Moynihan, roundly berated them for "unethical" practices. They had been guilty, Moynihan alleged, of using outdated actuarial tables to obtain unfairly high premiums. They habitually delayed the hearings of lawsuits against them in order to tire out the plaintiffs and win cheap settlements. In their employment policies they used ingenious devices to discriminate against certain minority groups.[5]

It was difficult for the audience to deny the validity of these charges. But these men were business game players. Their reaction to Moynihan's attack was much the same as that of the automobile manufacturers to Nader, of the utilities to Senator Metcalf, and of the food processors to Senator Hart. If the laws governing their businesses change, or if public opinion becomes clamorous, they will make the necessary adjustments. But morally they have in their view done nothing wrong. As long as they comply with the letter of the law, they are within their rights to operate their businesses as they see fit.

The small business is in the same position as the great corporation in this respect. For example:

- In 1967 a key manufacturer was accused of providing master keys for automobiles to mail-order customers, although it was obvious that some of the purchasers might be automobile thieves. His defense was plain and straightforward. If there was nothing in the law to prevent him from selling his keys to anyone who ordered them, it was not up to him to inquire as to his customers' motives. Why was it any worse, he insisted, for him to sell car keys by mail, than for mail-order houses to sell guns that might be used for murder? Until the law was changed, the key manufacturer could regard himself as being just as ethical as any other businessman by the rules of the business game.[6]

Violations of the ethical ideals of society are common in business, but they are not necessarily violations of business principles. Each year the Federal Trade Commission orders hundreds of companies, many of them of the first magnitude, to "cease and desist" from practices which, judged by ordinary standards, are of questionable morality but which are stoutly defended by the companies concerned.

In one case, a firm manufacturing a well-known mouthwash was accused of using a cheap form of alcohol possibly deleterious to health. The company's chief executive, after testifying in Washington, made this comment privately:

"We broke no law. We're in a highly competitive industry. If we're going to stay in business, we have to look for profit wherever the law permits. We don't make the laws. We obey them. Then why do we have to put up with this 'holier than thou' talk about ethics? It's sheer hypocrisy. We're not in business to promote ethics. Look at the cigarette companies, for God's sake! If the ethics aren't embodied in the laws by the men who made them, you can't expect businessmen to fill the lack. Why, a sudden submission to Christian ethics by businessmen would bring about the greatest economic upheaval in history!"

It may be noted that the government failed to prove its case against him.

CAST ILLUSIONS ASIDE

Talk about ethics by businessmen is often a thin decorative coating over the hard realities of the game:

- Once I listened to a speech by a young executive who pointed to a new industry code as proof that his company and its competitors were deeply aware of their responsibilities to society. It was a code of ethics, he said. The industry was going to police itself, to dissuade constituent companies from wrongdoing. His eyes shone with conviction and enthusiasm.

    The same day there was a meeting in a hotel room where the industry's top executives met with the "czar" who was to administer the new code, a man of high repute. No one who was present could doubt their common attitude. In their eyes the code was designed primarily to forestall a move by the federal government to impose stern restrictions on the industry. They felt that the code would hamper them a good deal less than new federal laws would. It was, in other words, conceived as a protection for the industry, not for the public.

    The young executive accepted the surface explanation of the code; these leaders, all experienced game players, did not deceive themselves for a moment about its purpose.

The illusion that business can afford to be guided by ethics as conceived in private life is often fostered by speeches and articles containing such phrases as, "It pays to be ethical," or, "Sound ethics is good business." Actually this is not an ethical position at all; it is a self-serving calculation in disguise. The speaker is really saying that in the long run a company can make more money if it does not antagonize competitors, suppliers, employees, and customers by squeezing them too hard. He is saying that oversharp policies reduce ultimate gains. That is true, but it has nothing to do with ethics. The underlying attitude is much like that in the familiar story of the shopkeeper who finds an extra $20 bill in the cash register, debates with himself the ethical problem—should he tell his partner?—and finally decides to share the money because the gesture will give him an edge over the s.o.b. the next time they quarrel.

I think it is fair to sum up the prevailing attitude of businessmen on ethics as follows:

We live in what is probably the most competitive of the world's civilized societies. Our customs encourage a high degree of aggression in the individual's striving for success. Business is our main area of competition, and it has been ritualized into a game of strategy. The basic rules of the game have been set by the government, which attempts to detect and punish business frauds. But as long as a company does not transgress the rules of the game set by law, it has the legal right to shape its strategy without reference to anything but its profits. If it takes a long-term view of its profits, it will preserve amicable relations, so far as possible, with those with whom it deals. A wise businessman will not seek advantage to the point where he generates dangerous hostility among employees, competitors, customers, government, or the public at large. But decisions in this area are, in the final test, decisions of strategy, not of ethics.

. . . If a man plans to make a seat in the business game, he owes it to himself to master the principles by which the game is played, including its special ethical outlook. He can then hardly fail to recognize that an occasional bluff may well be justified in terms of the game's ethics and warranted in terms of economic necessity. Once he clears his mind on this point, he is in a good position to match his strategy against that of the other players. He can then determine objectively whether a bluff in a given situation has a good chance of succeeding and can decide when and how to bluff, without a feeling of ethical transgression.

To be a winner, a man must play to win. This does not mean that he must be ruthless, cruel, harsh, or treacherous. On the contrary, the better his reputation for integrity, honesty, and decency, the better his chances of victory will be in the long run. But from time to time every businessman, like every poker player, is offered a choice between certain loss or bluffing within the legal rules of the game. If he is not resigned to losing, if he wants to rise in his company and industry, then in such a crisis he will bluff—and bluff hard.

Every now and then one meets a successful businessman who has conveniently forgotten the small or large deceptions that he practiced on his way to fortune. "God gave me my money," old John D. Rockefeller once piously told a Sunday school class. It would be a rare tycoon in our time who would risk the horse laugh with which such a remark would be greeted.

In the last third of the twentieth century even children are aware that if a man has become prosperous in business, he has sometimes departed from the strict truth in order to overcome obstacles or has practiced the more subtle deceptions of the half-truth or the misleading omission. Whatever the form of the bluff, it is an integral part of the game, and the executive who does not master its techniques is not likely to accumulate much money or power.

NOTES

1. *The New York Times*, March 9, 1967.
2. *The New York Times*, November 21, 1966.
3. New York, Grossman Publishers, Inc., 1965.
4. New York, David McKay Company, Inc., 1967.
5. *The New York Times*, January 17, 1967.
6. Cited by Ralph Nader in "Business Crime," *The New Republic*, July 1, 1967, p. 7.

QUESTIONS

1. Answer Carr's question: Is business bluffing ethical? Why or why not?
2. Are there "rules to the game" of business? Is a certain amount of deception necessary or even good in business? Explain your answer.
3. What are the problems with thinking of business as a game?

To: You
From: The Philosopher
Subject: "Nietzsche on Honesty"

The philosopher Friedrich Nietzsche had an interesting take on truth-telling and lying. He rather famously argued that a certain amount of deception (and self-deception) was necessary for life. (Art, after all, is essentially the telling of half-truths, embellished truths, and untruths.) But he nevertheless saw in lying a special problem, one that had less to do with breaking any rule than it did with the breach of personal trust. He said (in a book called *Beyond Good and Evil* § 183),

"Not that you lied to me, but that I no longer believe you, has shaken me."

Norman E. Bowie | # Does It Pay to Bluff in Business?

Norman E. Bowie holds the Chair in Business Ethics at the University of Minnesota.

Albert Carr has argued in an influential article[1] that the ethics of business is best understood on the model of the ethics of poker.

Wouldn't it be in the best interest of business to adopt the poker model of business ethics? I think not. Let us consider labor relations, where Carr's poker model is implicitly if not explicitly adopted. In collective bargaining the relationship between the employer and the employee is adversarial. Collective bargaining is competitive through and through. The task of the union is to secure as much in pay and benefits as possible. The task of the employer's negotiators is to keep the pay and benefits as low as possible.

In the resulting give-and-take, bluffing and deception are the rule. Management expects the union to demand a percentage pay increase it knows it won't get. The union expects the company to say that such a pay increase will force it to shut down the plant and move to another state. Such demands are never taken at face value although they are taken more seriously on the ninetieth day of negotiations than they are on the first day.

Recently the conventional view of collective bargaining practice has been under attack. One of the most prominent criticisms of current practice is its economic inefficiency. The adversarial relationship at the bargaining table carries over to the workplace. As a result of the hostility between employee and employer, productivity suffers and many American products are at a competitive disadvantage with respect to foreign products. Japanese labor-management relations are not so adversarial and this fact accounts for part of their success. This particular criticism of collective bargaining has received much attention in the press and in popular business magazines. The most recent manifestation of the recognition of the force

From Norman E. Bowie and Thomas Beauchamp, *Business Ethics* (Englewood Cliffs, NJ: Prentice Hall, 1988).

of this criticism is the host of decisions General Motors has made to ensure that labor relations are different at its new assembly plant for the Saturn.

Second, the practice of bluffing and deception tends to undermine trust. As some American firms lost ground to foreign competition, the management of many of the firms asked for pay reductions, commonly called "give backs." Other managers in firms not threatened by foreign competition cited the "dangers" of foreign competition to request pay cuts for their employees—even though they were not needed. Use of this tactic will only cause future problems when and if the competitive threat really develops. This utilitarian point was not lost on participants in a labor-management relations seminar I attended.

> *Participant I:* In the past, there was a relationship of mutual distrust.
> *Participant II:* These are the dangers in crying "wolf." When the company is really in trouble, no one will believe them.
> *Participant III:* To make labor/management participation teams work, you need to generate mutual trust. It only takes one bad deal to undermine trust.

These individuals are indicating that the practices of bluffing and deception have bad consequences in employer/employee relationships. These unfortunate consequences have been well documented by philosophers—most recently by Sissela Bok. Bok's critique of "white lies" and the use of placebos applies equally well to deception in the collective bargaining process:

> Triviality surely does set limits to when moral inquiry is reasonable. But when we look more closely at practices such as placebo-giving, it becomes clear that all lies defended as "white" cannot be so easily dismissed. In the first place, the harmlessness of lies is notoriously disputable. What the liar perceives as harmless or even beneficial may not be so in the eyes of the deceived. Second, the failure to look at an entire practice rather than at their own isolated case often blinds liars to cumulative harm and expanding deceptive activities. Those who begin with white lies can come to resort to more frequent and more serious ones. Where some tell a few white lies, others may tell more. Because

lines are so hard to draw, the indiscriminate use of such lies can lead to other deceptive practices. The aggregate harm from a large number of marginally harmful instances may, therefore, be highly undesirable in the end—for liars, those deceived, and honesty and trust more generally.[2]

However, there is more at stake here than the bad consequences of lying. Bluffing, exaggeration, and the nondisclosure of information also undermine a spirit of cooperation that is essential to business success. The poker model, with its permitted bluffing and the like, is a competitive model. What the model overlooks is the fact that the production of a good or service in any given plant or office is a cooperative enterprise. Chrysler competes with General Motors and Toyota but the production of Chrysler K cars in that assembly plant in Newark, Delaware, is a cooperative enterprise. Lack of cooperation results in poor quality vehicles.

Hence the competitive model of collective bargaining sets wages and working conditions for what at the local level is a cooperative enterprise. Labor–management negotiators forget the obvious truth that the production of goods and services cannot succeed on a purely competitive basis. There have to be some elements of cooperation somewhere in the system. Why shouldn't the collective bargaining process use cooperative rather than competitive techniques? When bargaining is conducted industrywide, as it is with automobiles, the competitive mode seems natural. Auto production is a competitive industry. But just because Chrysler is competitive with General Motors, why must Chrysler management be in a competitive relationship with its own employees? Indeed, couldn't it be argued that the fact that Chrysler's management does see itself in competition with its unionized employees undercuts its competitive position vis-à-vis other automobile producers. To use the language of competition, if Chrysler is at war with itself, how can it win the war against others?

As long as collective bargaining is essentially adversarial and characterized by bluffing and exaggeration on both sides, the cooperative aspect of business will be underemphasized. The costs of ignoring the cooperative aspect are great—both for society and for business itself.

Hence this distrust that so concerned the participants in the seminar is only in part a function of the deceit and bluffing that go on in collective bargaining. It is in large part a function of using the wrong model. We shouldn't look at collective bargaining as a game of poker.

With this discussion of collective bargaining as instance, let us evaluate Carr's proposal on utilitarian grounds. Should the stockholders applaud a chief executive officer whose operating procedure is analogous to the operating procedure of a poker player? In Carr's view, "A good part of the time the businessman is trying to do unto others as he hopes others will not do unto him." But surely such a practice is very risky. The danger of discovery is great, and our experience of the past several years indicates that many corporations that have played the game of business like the game of poker have suffered badly. Moreover, if business practice consisted essentially of these conscious misstatements, exaggerations, and the concealment of pertinent facts, it seems clear that business practice would be inherently unstable. Contemporary business practice presupposes such

stability, and business can only be stable if the chief executive officer has a set of moral standards higher than those that govern the game of poker. The growth of the large firm, the complexity of business decisions, the need for planning and stability, and the undesirable effects of puffery, exaggeration, and deception all count against Carr's view that the ethics of business should be the ethics of a poker game.

NOTES

1. Albert Z. Carr, "Is Business Bluffing Ethical?" *Harvard Business Review*, 46 (January–February 1968): 143–153.
2. Sissela Bok, *Lying: Moral Choice in Public and Private Life* (New York: Pantheon Books, 1978), pp. 19, 31.

QUESTIONS

1. What is Bowie's main reply to Carr?
2. How does cooperation suffer because of bluffing?
3. Bowie argues that bluffing erodes trust? What else does bluffing do to a business relationship?

Sissela Bok | # Defining Secrecy—Some Crucial Distinctions

Sissela Bok wrote one of the most popular books on the subject of lying. She followed it up with this book on secrets.

Lying and secrecy intertwine and overlap. Lies are part of the arsenal used to guard and to invade secrecy; and secrecy allows lies to go undiscovered and to build up. Lying and secrecy differ, however, in one important respect. Whereas I take lying to be prima facie wrong, with a negative presumption

against it from the outset, secrecy need not be. Whereas every lie stands in need of justification, all secrets do not. Secrecy may accompany the most innocent as well as the most lethal acts; it is needed for human survival, yet it enhances every form of abuse. The same is true of efforts to uncover or invade secrets.

A path, a riddle, a jewel, an oath—anything can be secret so long as it is kept intentionally hidden, set apart in the mind of its keeper as requiring

From Sissela Bok, *Secrets* (New York: Vintage Books, 1989). Notes were deleted from this text.

concealment. It may be shared with no one, or confided on condition that it go no farther; at times it may be known to all but one or two from whom it is kept. To keep a secret from someone, then, is to block information about it or evidence of it from reaching that person, and to do so intentionally; to prevent him from learning it, and thus from possessing it, making use of it, or revealing it. The word "secrecy" refers to the resulting concealment. It also denotes the methods used to conceal, such as codes or disguises or camouflage, and the practices of concealment, as in trade secrecy or professional confidentiality. Accordingly I shall take concealment, or hiding, to be the defining trait of secrecy. It presupposes separation, a setting apart of the secret from the non-secret, and of keepers of a secret from those excluded. The Latin *secretum* carries this meaning of something hidden, set apart. It derives from *secernere*, which originally meant to sift apart, to separate, as with a sieve. It bespeaks discernment, the ability to make distinctions, to sort out and draw lines: a capacity that underlies not only secrecy but all thinking, all intention and choice. The separation between insider and outsider is inherent in secrecy; and to think something secret is already to envisage potential conflict between what insiders conceal and outsiders want to inspect and lay bare.

Several other strands have joined with this defining trait to form our concept of secrecy. Although they are not always present in every secret or every practice of secrecy, the concepts of sacredness, intimacy, privacy, silence, prohibition, furtiveness, and deception influence the way we think about secrecy. They intertwine and sometimes conflict, yet they come together in our experience of secrecy and give it depth.

Too exclusive an emphasis on the links between the secret and the sacred can lead one to see all secrecy as inherently valuable. And those who think primarily of the links between secrecy and privacy or intimacy, and of secrets as personal confidences, have regarded them as something one has a duty to conceal. Negative views of secrecy are even more common. Why should you conceal something, many ask, if you are not afraid to have it known? The aspects of secrecy that have to do with stealth and

furtiveness, lying and denial, predominate in such a view. We must retain a neutral definition of secrecy, rather than one that assumes from the outset that secrets are guilty or threatening, or on the contrary, awesome and worthy of respect. A degree of concealment or openness accompanies all that human beings do or say. We must determine what is and is not discreditable by examining particular practices of secrecy, rather than by assuming an initial evaluative stance.

It is equally important to keep the distinction between secrecy and privacy from being engulfed at the definitional stage. The two are closely linked, and their relationship is central. In order to maintain the distinction, however, it is important first to ask how they are related and wherein they differ. Having defined secrecy as intentional concealment, I obviously cannot take it as identical with privacy. I shall define privacy as the condition of being protected from unwanted access by others—either physical access, attention, or access to personal information. Claims to privacy are claims to control access to what one takes to be one's personal domain.

Privacy and secrecy overlap whenever the efforts at such control rely on hiding. But privacy need not hide; and secrecy hides far more than what is private. A private garden need not be a secret garden; a private life is rarely a secret life. Conversely, secret diplomacy rarely concerns what is private, any more than do arrangements for a surprise party or for choosing prize winners.

Why then are privacy and secrecy so often equated? In part, this is so because privacy is such a central part of what secrecy protects that it can easily be seen as the whole. People claim privacy for differing amounts of what they are and do and own; if need be, they seek the added protection of secrecy. In each case, their purpose is to become less vulnerable, more in control. When do secrecy and privacy most clearly overlap? They do so most immediately in the private lives of individuals, where secrecy guards against unwanted access by others—against their coming too near, learning too much, observing too closely. Secrecy guards, then, the central aspects of identity, and if necessary, also plans and property. It serves as an additional shield in case the protection of privacy should fail or be broken down. Thus you may assume that no one will read your diary; but you can also hide it, or write it in code, as did William Blake, or lock it up. Secret codes, bank accounts, and retreats, secret thoughts never voiced aloud, personal objects hidden against intruders: all testify to the felt need for additional protection.

Similarly, groups can create a joint space within which they keep secrets, surrounded by an aura of mystery. Perhaps the most complete overlap of privacy and secrecy in groups is that exemplified in certain secret societies. The members of some of these societies undergo such experiences that their own sense of privacy blends with an enlarged private space of the group. The societies then have identities and boundaries of their own. They come into being like living organisms, vulnerable; they undergo growth and transformation, and eventually pass away.

It is harder to say whether privacy and secrecy overlap in practices of large-scale collective secrecy, such as trade or military secrecy. Claims of privacy are often made for such practices, and the metaphors of personal space are stretched to apply to them. To be sure, such practices are automatically private in one sense so long as they are not public. But the use of the language of privacy, with its metaphors of personal space, spheres, sanctuaries, and boundaries, to personalize collective enterprises should not go unchallenged. Such usage can be sentimental, and distort our understanding of the role of these enterprises.

The obsessive, conflict-ridden invocation of privacy in Western society has increased the occasions for such expanded uses of the metaphors of privacy; so has the corresponding formalization of the professional practices of secrecy and openness. At times the shield of privacy is held up to protect abuses, such as corporate tax fraud or legislative corruption, that are in no manner personal.

While secrecy often guards what is private, therefore, it need not be so, and it has many uses outside the private sphere. To see all secrecy as privacy is as limiting as to assume that it is invariably deceptive or that it conceals primarily what is discreditable. We must retain the definition of

secrecy as intentional concealment, and resist the pressure to force the concept into a narrower definitional mold by insisting that privacy, deceit, or shame always accompanies it. But at the same time we must strive to keep in mind these aspects of our underlying experience of secrecy, along with the others—the sacred, the silent, the forbidden, and the stealthy.

Secrecy is as indispensable to human beings as fire, and as greatly feared. Both enhance and protect life, yet both can stifle, lay waste, spread out of all control. Both may be used to guard intimacy or to invade it, to nurture or to consume. And each can be turned against itself; barriers of secrecy are set up to guard against secret plots and surreptitious prying, just as fire is used to fight fire.

Conflicts over secrecy—between state and citizen, or parent and child, or in journalism or business or law—are conflicts over power: the power that comes through controlling the flow of information. To be able to hold back some information about oneself or to channel it and thus influence how one is seen by others gives power; so does the capacity to penetrate similar defenses and strategies when used by others. To have no capacity for secrecy is to be out of control over how others see one; it leaves one open to coercion. To have no insight into what others conceal is to lack power as well.

In seeking some control over secrecy and openness, and the power it makes possible, human beings attempt to guard and to promote not only their autonomy but ultimately their sanity and survival itself. The claims in defense of this control, however, are not always articulated. Some take them to be so self-evident as to need no articulation; others subsume them under more general arguments about liberty or privacy. But it is important for the purposes of considering the ethics of secrecy to set forth these claims. The claims in defense of some control over secrecy and openness invoke four different, though in practice inseparable, elements of human autonomy: identity, plans, action, and property. They concern protection of what we are, what we intend, what we do, and what we own. Some capacity for keeping secrets and for choosing when to reveal them, and some access to the underlying experience of secrecy and depth, are indispensable for an enduring sense of identity, for the ability to plan and to act, and for essential belongings. With no control over secrecy and openness, human beings could not remain either sane or free.

Against every claim to secrecy stands, however, the awareness of its dangers. Secrecy can harm those who make use of it in several ways. It can debilitate judgment, first of all, whenever it shuts out criticism and feedback. The danger of secrecy goes far beyond risks to those who keep secrets. Because it bypasses inspection and eludes interference, secrecy is central to the planning of every form of injury to human beings. It cloaks the execution of these plans and wipes out all traces afterward. It enters into all prying and intrusion that cannot be carried out openly. While not all that is secret is meant to deceive—as jury deliberations, for instance are not—all deceit does rely on keeping something secret. And while not all secrets are discreditable, all that is discreditable and all wrongdoing seek out secrecy (unless they can be carried out openly without interference).

Given both the legitimacy of some control over secrecy and openness, and the dangers this control carries for all involved, there can be no presumption either for or against secrecy in general. Secrecy differs in this respect from lying, promise breaking, violence, and other practices for which the burden of proof rests on those who would defend them. Conversely, secrecy differs from truthfulness, friendship, and other practices carrying a favorable presumption. The resulting challenge for ethical inquiry into the aims and methods of secrecy is great. Not only must we reject definitions of secrecy that invite approval or disapproval; we cannot even begin with a moral presumption in either direction. This is not to say, however, that there can be none for particular practices, nor that these practices are usually morally neutral.

I shall rely on two presumptions that flow from the needs and dangers of secrecy that I have set forth. The first is one of *equality*. Whatever control over secrecy and openness we conclude is legitimate for some individuals should, in the absence of special considerations, be legitimate for all. My second presumption is in favor of *partial individual control* over the degree of secrecy or openness about personal matters—those most indisputably in the private realm. Without a premise supporting a measure of individual control over personal matters, it would be impossible to preserve the indispensable respect for identity, plans, action, and belongings that all of us need and should legitimately be able to claim. Such individual control should extend, moreover, to what people choose to share with one another about themselves—in families, for example, or with friends and colleagues. Without the intimacy that such sharing makes possible, human relationships would be impossible. At the same time, however, it is important to avoid any presumption in favor of *full* control over such matters for individuals. Such full control is not necessary for the needs that I have discussed, and would aggravate the dangers. It would force us to disregard the legitimate claims of those persons who might be injured, betrayed, or ignored as a result of secrets inappropriately kept or revealed.

QUESTIONS

1. Why does Bok distinguish between lies and secrets? Is keeping a secret ever morally equivalent to telling a lie?

2. How does Bok distinguish between privacy and secrecy?

3. If you came across private information about a co-worker's personal life on Facebook that would afffect the way that he does his job, would you feel an obligation to tell your boss or keep it to yourself?

Sue De Wine | # Giving Feedback: The Consultant's Craft

Sue De Wine is the president of Hanover College.

We all like to receive feedback but are afraid to ask for it. If I asked you "How am I doing?" you may really tell me and I may not like the answer! Feedback requires active listening and careful description of observed behavior. These two skills are the cornerstones to effective feedback and impactful interventions into human behaviors.

Schein (1988) suggests that most of what the process consultant does when he or she intervenes with individuals or groups is to manage the feedback process. The consultant makes observations that provide information, asks questions that direct the client's attention to the consequences of the individual's behavior, and provides suggestions that have implicit evaluations built into them (i.e., any given suggestion implies that other things that have not been suggested are less appropriate than what has been suggested) (p. 105).

Feedback comes in two forms: information on a person's behavior, and information on what impact that behavior can have on others. Remember that the overall purpose of feedback is to help, not attack. When giving feedback, make sure you can answer *yes* to these questions:

Timing: Have I checked with the receiver to determine the best time and place to give feedback?

Motivation: Am I being supportive while giving the feedback rather than ridiculing and hurting the receiver?

Language: Am I using positive or neutral rather than derogatory statements?

Tone: Am I using a friendly and caring tone of voice?

Value: Is the feedback useful to the receiver rather than an outlet for my feelings, frustrations, or anger?

Focus: Am I focusing on actions rather than attitudes or personalities?

Specificity: Am I using specific examples of observed behavior?

Information: Am I giving a manageable amount of helpful information rather than overloading the receiver with more information than is necessary?

Questions: Have I asked the receiver questions to ensure that my feedback was clear and helpful?

When receiving feedback, check for *yes* answers to these questions:

Timing: Have I agreed to the time and place for receiving feedback?

Trust: Do I trust the giver to accurately present information concerning my behavior?

Nondefensiveness: Am I prepared to listen to the feedback, rather than argue, refute, or justify my actions?

Specificity: If feedback is vague, am I requesting specific behavioral examples?

Tone: Am I using a neutral rather than a defensive tone of voice?

Questions: Have I asked questions that clarify the feedback?

Feedback is best when it is asked for and when there is a need for impartial knowledge. The client has to understand the difference between wisdom, which is a personal attribute of an individual, and knowledge, which is gained from books and facts. It is the consultant's job to be honest, direct, and nonthreatening.

Sometimes I am surprised at how willingly organizational members receive feedback. Just when I would expect defensiveness and denial, they admit the picture I am painting is on target.

One illustration of this occurred with a colleague, Elizabeth Bemett, when we worked with a healthcare

From Sue de Wine, *The Consultant's Craft* (Boston: Bedford/St. Martin's, 2001), pp. 307–314.

organization. We conducted interviews and asked for written statements about what was preventing this group from moving forward and cooperating with each other.

Participants told Elizabeth and me some very negative examples of how this group was dysfunctional. Some of the traits attributed to the group included being distrustful, deceitful, uncompromising, and overly critical of each other. We decided we would take the plunge and list all of the statements made by the group. We expected resistance and defensiveness. When we finished describing the list of attributes there was a long pause, and then someone spoke up and said, "Yep, that's us." Another said, "Sure sounds like us, doesn't it?" Nods of heads and general agreement indicated they accepted this feedback. Now our task was to find out if they were ready to change some of these behaviors or would they resist change because somehow these behaviors suited their individual agendas.

TYPES OF FEEDBACK

There are a variety of methods to provide feedback, many of which cause defensiveness. The function of feedback is to describe another person's observable behavior, disclose your thoughts and feelings about that behavior, interpret motives, and prescribe specific remedies. These may be our objectives; however, my experience has been that when people are evaluated they often feel attacked and begin to defend themselves.

Feedback is a way of helping another person to consider changing his or her behavior. It is communication to a person (or group) that gives that person information about how she or he affects others. As in a guided missile system, feedback helps an individual keep his or her behavior "on target" and thus achieve individual goals.

People give three kinds of feedback to others:

Evaluative: observing the other's behavior and responding with one's critique of it. "You are always late for everything. You are undependable."

Interpretive: observing the behavior and trying to analyze why the person is behaving that way. "You are late to meetings. I think you are spreading yourself too thin—trying to do too many things at the same time, and consequently you don't do anything really well."

Descriptive: observing the behavior and simply feeding back to the person specific observations without evaluating them, but sharing with the person how her or his behavior affects the speaker. "At the meeting last week you were 30 minutes late, on Monday you came when the meeting was half over, and today you missed the first 45 minutes of the meeting. I am concerned about the information you are missing by not being here."

In the first example, *always* and *undependable* are evaluative terms and create a climate of defensiveness on the part of the receiver. Chances are the person isn't *always* late, and using an all-inclusive term like *always* serves only to make the person angry. The receiver then naturally looks for ways to refute the statement. "I wasn't late to the staff meeting on Friday! You're being unfair."

In the second example the observer is playing dime-store psychologist and trying to figure out why someone is behaving a certain way. Unless you are a trained psychologist, your business is not to analyze and interpret someone else's behavior. You don't know why someone acts a particular way. All you can observe is behavior. You can't observe attitudes, nor should you be critiquing them.

In descriptive feedback we are describing, as specifically as possible, what we have actually observed the individual doing. We present that factual information, without judging the rightness or wrongness of the behavior and without trying to figure out why the person may have behaved that way.

EFFECTIVE FEEDBACK

Feedback should describe problematic behavior that the receiver can correct. Ideally, it is offered in response to the receiver's request, but whether or not it is solicited, effective feedback should be timely, clear, and accurate.

Useful Content

We have already discussed why feedback is more useful if it is descriptive rather than judgmental. Describing one's reaction to problematic behavior leaves the individual free to use the feedback or not, as the individual sees fit. Avoiding judgmental language reduces the need for the receiver to react defensively. Specific observations are more convincing than general ones. To be told that one is inattentive will probably not be as useful as to be told that: "Just now when we were deciding how to assimilate new employees, you were reading your mail. It made me feel that you were not interested or involved in the discussion."

Effective feedback takes into account the needs of both the receiver and the giver of the feedback. Feedback can be destructive when it serves only the giver's needs and fails to consider the needs of the person on the receiving end. For example, I may need to complain about the lateness of a report. The report writer may not need to hear my complaints because she is already aware of the deadline and cannot change the fact that some missing data from another department prevented her from finishing it earlier. It may make me feel better to "blow off steam" but in this instance it may actually impede the other person's ability to complete the task.

Effective feedback is directed toward behavior that the receiver can change. Frustration is only increased when a person is reminded of some shortcoming over which she or he has no control. One receptionist was criticized for her high-pitched voice over the phone. She had actually worked with a speech therapist and had improved it as much as possible. To continue to criticize her for something she could not change was not helpful; in fact, it was harmful. If the problem was severe enough, then her supervisor should have discussed other career options, but simply to continue to provide feedback that the problem existed could do nothing to bring about change.

Feedback is most useful when it is solicited rather than imposed and when the receiver has formulated the kinds of questions that people observing can answer. Unfortunately, people don't ask for feedback often enough. Therefore, we should take advantage of those rare opportunities when someone does ask us to take the time to provide it. It is easy to miss opportunities because one may dismiss a request as superficial.

For example, someone recently asked me, "How are things going?" (referring to a project she was working on). I said, "Oh, just fine." Her response was, "No, I really mean, *how do you think things are going?*" Then I said, "Oh, you *really* want some feedback about your performance?" If the person had not persisted, I would have missed a very good opportunity to provide feedback about her work performance at a time when she was actually requesting it!

Timeliness

In general, feedback is most useful at the earliest opportunity after the given behavior has occurred (depending, of course, on the person's readiness to hear it and the support that is available from others). One of the most delayed examples of feedback I have witnessed occurred with two female trainers with whom I was working. We were designing a seminar and the two began discussing their earlier work together. Finally, one said, "Let's be sure we get straight what each person's role will be throughout the course of this seminar because we aren't always clear about how much we want someone to be involved." When she was asked to explain her point further, she described a workshop the two of them had designed in which she felt her talents were not fully used. In fact, she was unclear about the role she should take. I ended up being the mediator in this discussion, and I asked when this workshop had occurred only to discover it had been eight years earlier! Feedback that delayed is useless and unfair. It is unfair because the person who chose not to provide the feedback closer to the time the behavior occurred had been harboring resentment for a long time. Indirectly she may have been acting on that resentment in her behavior toward the other person, who could do nothing about it.

Another example of poor timing would be if I asked my husband, during a formal banquet, how he liked my new outfit. To actually give me straightforward feedback, which may have been negative, at that time would have been inappropriate. What I really wanted him to say was, "You look great" whether I did or not! Why? Because there was nothing I could do to correct my appearance at that moment. The next time I was selecting an outfit to wear or buying a new one, when I could make a reasonable decision about how to use this information, would be a more appropriate time to tell me the outfit makes me look unattractive (if he dares to tell me that at all!). To provide such criticism in the middle of a social event could make both of us miserable!

Clarity and Accuracy

One way of checking to ensure clear communication is to ask the receiver to rephrase the feedback to see if it corresponds to what the sender had in mind. In this way too, the sender is training the other person to provide descriptive feedback.

Both giver and receiver should have an opportunity to check with others about the accuracy of the feedback. Is this one person's impression or an impression shared by others? A teacher knows that an entire classroom of students will not always be happy with the way in which the class is structured. The teacher must therefore check for themes that exist among most of the students. When you get disturbing or confusing feedback, be sure to check it with co-workers and colleagues. "Have you ever noticed me behaving in this way . . .?"

Feedback, then, is a way of giving help; it is a corrective mechanism for the individual who wants to learn how well his or her behavior and intentions match and a means for establishing one's identity—for answering "Who am I?" Feedback can be informal or a formal evaluation process, like performance appraisal.

TIPS ON PROVIDING FEEDBACK

Negative feedback is misunderstood much more readily than positive feedback. Consequently, go slowly and be descriptive. I prefer never to put negative feedback in a memo. There are too many opportunities to misinterpret the language. I use memos for good news and face-to-face meetings for bad news. I want to be sure people have a chance to ask any questions they might have when I am telling them something they may not want to hear. However, once the negative information has been communicated face-to-face, follow-up written documents are absolutely necessary to maintain a "paper trail."

Positive feedback that is too general has little impact. We shouldn't assume when we tell employees that they're doing a "good job" that the information will positively affect their performance. If they don't know exactly what it is they did well, it is unlikely they will know what to continue doing! In fact, if the feedback is perceived as too general, it might also be interpreted as insincere.

Keep feedback impersonal. It is important that the person and the person's actions be separated in discussions. I can like the person, respect the person, but find a particular behavior unacceptable. I love my children deeply, but I dislike intensely their tendency to squabble with each other. It is their behavior I find distasteful, not their person. Thus, when you provide feedback, make it impersonal and attach it to a specific behavior, not to the personality of the individual with whom you are talking.

Tailor the feedback to fit the person. Some people appreciate receiving straightforward, direct feedback about their efforts. Others cannot tolerate such directness and need positive reinforcement before they are prepared to handle negative information. Others learn best by example. Still others must hear new information several times before they really listen.

Use humor when appropriate. Sometimes it is easier to tease someone and indirectly provide feedback. This works when the relationship is a good one. However, many top-level executives might not be able to handle such forms of feedback. In one organization, a short story written about the head of the unit satirized a recent series of decisions (or lack of them!). The story was never mentioned by the unit head in public. In private he expressed his inability to accept the feedback in that form.

Sometimes subtlety works best. There are times when direct confrontation over an issue is not the best approach. You may be calling too much attention to a problem others can then trivialize. For example, one woman who was constantly asked to take the minutes at executive meetings simply placed the memo pad in front of the senior member's chair at the next meeting, and then offered to provide him with a pen so he could take the minutes at that meeting. He got the message without her having to make a big deal out of the issue and began rotating this secretarial function among all present.

We know who we are by "bumping up against" other people. Their feedback helps shape our identity, self-esteem, and self-concept. The more feedback we provide for others, the better they are able to perform. The more we *ask* for feedback from others about ourselves, the clearer image we have of how others see us.

QUESTIONS

1. What is "feedback"?
2. How do we make feedback effective? How do we make it ineffective?
3. Why is it wrong to inflate your assessment of an employee or a client?

Adelaide Lancaster | # 3 Steps to a More Honest Business

Adelaide Lancaster is the author of *Big Enough Company* (2011).

Unfortunately, the notions of business and honesty don't always go hand in hand. Our country's history is dotted with examples of nondisclosure, cover-ups, and outright scams. While lately we have been inundated with scandals involving corporate kingpins, the truth is that bad behavior exists from tiny mom and pop shops, too.

So, many entrepreneurs start their own companies, in part, because they desire to work in an environment that's congruent with their own values. Scarred by past experiences that required them to compromise their beliefs, entrepreneurs are often determined to create a business that prioritizes a

high standard of behavior along with the bottom line—where transparency and authenticity is not just one way to do things but actually part of their customers, shareholders, and employee's expectations. They want a *real* honest business.

Is this what you're after? If so, bravo. From our experience working with thousands of entrepreneurs, we've discovered that it takes three kinds of honesty to achieve this ideal.

HONESTY WITH OTHERS

This sounds basic, but it goes beyond not lying to your customers and employees. It's about owning a mistake when you mess up and admitting when

From http://www.forbes.com/sites/thebigenoughcompany/2011/09/21/21/3/-steps-to-a-more-honest-business/

you're wrong. It's also about refusing to pretend that you're something you're not. It requires acknowledging the state of the business to your employees. And, when it comes to customers, it requires selling only what you can deliver effectively and always living up to your word.

Done properly, this kind of honesty begets a tremendous amount of loyalty from both customers and employees. Both groups know they can trust you and, more importantly, that you value the integrity of the relationship.

NPR is a great example of a company that is honest with its customers. The station takes time at the end of most programs to share listener feedback on past shows. They share the glowing reviews, of course, but they also share customer outrage, disbelief, and disappointment. What's more, when NPR has made headlines for less than desirable reasons, the organization has reported its own bad news as if it were any other media outlet, rather than shifting the focus. These actions—which many companies might be afraid to take—only serve to underscore the affinity that subscribers and listeners have for the station.

HONESTY WITH SELF

It is crucial to be *brutally* honest with yourself about what you really want—from your job, your experience of entrepreneurship, and your business. For a business to work well, its leader needs to be satisfied; but too often, entrepreneurs end up running businesses that don't give them what they want. Sometimes this happens because people aren't clear about what their needs and goals are upfront. But mostly, it's small dishonesties along the way that cause us to make compromises with our business. When we tell ourselves that we need to do tasks we don't like, we end up creating jobs we don't enjoy. When we let other people's definition of success trample our own, we build companies that aren't in service of our vision.

I once knew a programmer who loved working with a consistent team of people for clients that were exciting and challenging. His reputation was great and, as a result, he got offered more gigs than he could handle. Many of his peers encouraged him to take this opportunity and run with it. It seemed like the "smart" thing to do, so he hired other programmers and tasked the new jobs to them.

One year later he was miserable. He spent 80% of his time managing clients and programmers—the things he hated doing—and not nearly enough time doing the work that he loved. He was making some more money but it wasn't worth it—he was constantly concerned with having enough business for the stable of people he had assembled. By not being honest about what he needed and wanted from his business, he had sacrificed the things that were most important to him.

HONESTY ABOUT THE EXPERIENCE

Many entrepreneurs have pitches that are too polished—stories that involve heightened drama or glossed-over details. They emphasize their happy endings and minimize their own doubts.

Sure, that's understandable—they're in the business of attracting clients and instilling consumer confidence. And who wants to air their dirty laundry? But what they don't realize is that, while you don't need to publicly sound the alarm each time you have a concern, there's a cost that comes with claiming that everything is all roses. Chief among them is that it makes you unrelatable to your peers. It also skews your own perspective about the business.

QUESTIONS

1. Why is it important to be honest with customers?
2. Why is it important to be honest with yourself about what you want from your business?

Harry G. Frankfurt | # On Bullshit

Harry Frankfurt is a professor emeritus of philosophy at Princeton University.

Lying and bluffing are both modes of misrepresentation or deception. Now the concept most central to the distinctive nature of a lie is that of falsity: the liar is essentially someone who deliberately promulgates a falsehood. Bluffing, too, is typically devoted to conveying something false. Unlike plain lying, however, it is more especially a matter not of falsity but of fakery. This is what accounts for its nearness to bullshit. For the essence of bullshit is not that it is *false* but that it is *phony*. In order to appreciate this distinction, one must recognize that a fake or a phony need not be in any respect (apart from authenticity itself) inferior to the real thing. What is not genuine need not also be defective in some other way. It may be, after all, an exact copy. What is wrong with a counterfeit is not what it is like, but how it was made. This points to a similar and fundamental aspect of the essential nature of bullshit: although it is produced without concern with the truth, it need not be false. The bullshitter is faking things. But this does not mean that he necessarily gets them wrong.

In Eric Ambler's novel *Dirty Story*, a character named Arthur Abdel Simpson recalls advice that he received as a child from his father:

> Although I was only seven when my father was killed, I still remember him very well and some of the things he used to say. . . . One of the first things he taught me was, *"Never tell a lie when you can bullshit your way through."*[1]

This presumes not only that there is an important difference between lying and bullshitting, but that the latter is preferable to the former. Now the elder Simpson surely did not consider bullshitting morally superior to lying. Nor is it likely that he regarded lies as invariably less effective than bullshit in accomplishing the purposes for which either of them might be employed. After all, an intelligently crafted lie may do its work with unqualified success. It may be that Simpson thought it easier to get away with bullshitting than with lying. Or perhaps he meant that, although the risk of being caught is about the same in each case, the consequences of being caught are generally less severe for the bullshitter than for the liar. In fact, people do tend to be more tolerant of bullshit than of lies, perhaps because we are less inclined to take the former as a personal affront. We may seek to distance ourselves from bullshit, but we are more likely to turn away from it with an impatient or irritated shrug than with the sense of violation or outrage that lies often inspire. The problem of understanding why our attitude toward bullshit is generally more benign than our attitude toward lying is an important one, which I shall leave as an exercise for the reader.

The pertinent comparison is not, however, between telling a lie and producing some particular instance of bullshit. The elder Simpson identifies the alternative to telling a lie as "bullshitting one's way through." This involves not merely producing one instance of bullshit; it involves a *program* of producing bullshit to whatever extent the circumstances require. This is a key, perhaps, to his preference. Telling a lie is an act with a sharp focus. It is designed to insert a particular falsehood at a specific point in a set or system of beliefs, in order to avoid the consequences of having that point occupied by the truth. This requires a degree of craftsmanship, in which the teller of the lie submits to objective constraints imposed by what he takes to be the truth. The liar is inescapably concerned with truth-values. In order to invent a lie at all, he must think he knows what is true. And in order to invent an effective lie,

From Harry G. Frankfurt, *On Bullshit* (Princeton, NJ: Princeton University Press, 2005), pp. 46–53.

he must design his falsehood under the guidance of that truth.

On the other hand, a person who undertakes to bullshit his way through has much more freedom. His focus is panoramic rather than particular. He does not limit himself to inserting a certain falsehood at a specific point, and thus he is not constrained by the truths surrounding that point or intersecting it. He is prepared, so far as required, to fake the context as well. This freedom from the constraints to which the liar must submit does not necessarily mean, of course, that his task is easier than the task of the liar. But the mode of creativity upon which it relies is less analytical and less deliberative than that which is mobilized in lying. It is more expansive and independent, with more spacious opportunities for improvisation, color, and imaginative play. This is less a matter of craft than of art. Hence the familiar notion of the "bullshit artist." My guess is that the recommendation offered by Arthur Simpson's father reflects the fact that he was more strongly drawn to

this mode of creativity, regardless of its relative merit or effectiveness, than he was to the more austere and rigorous demands of lying.

NOTE

1. E. Ambler, *Dirty Story* (1967), I. iii. 25. The citation is provided in the same *OED* entry as the one that includes the passage from Pound. The closeness of the relation between bullshitting and bluffing is resonant, it seems to me, in the parallelism of the idioms: "bullshit your way through" and "bluff your way through."

QUESTIONS

1. In what respect is bullshit morally different from bluffing and lying?
2. Are there aspects of business life that encourage people to bullshit?
3. When is bullshit harmful and when is it benign?

Paul Ekman and Mark G. Frank | Lies That Fail

Paul Ekman is one of the preeminent researchers on emotions and their expression and an expert on lying who has worked widely with police, federal agencies, and the Department of Homeland Security. Until recently he taught in the Psychiatry Department of the University of California, San Francisco.

Lies fail for many reasons. Some of these reasons have to do with the circumstances surrounding the lie, and not with the liar's behavior. For example, a confidant may betray a lie; or, private information made public can expose a liar's claims as false.

These reasons do not concern us in this chapter. What concerns us are those mistakes made during the act of lying, mistakes liars make despite themselves; in other words, lies that fail because of the liars' behaviors. Deception clues or leakage may be shown in a change in the expression on the face, a movement of the body, an inflection to the voice, a swallowing in the throat, a very deep or shallow breath, long pauses between words, a slip of the tongue, a microfacial expression, or a gestural slip.

There are two basic reasons why lies fail—one that involves thinking, and one that involves emotions. Lies fail due to a failure of the liar to prepare

From Michael Lewis and Carolyn Saarni, Eds., *Lying and Deception in Everyday Life* (New York: Guilford Press, 1993). References (notes) were deleted from this text.

his or her line, or due to the interference of emotions. These reasons have different implications for the potential behavioral clues that betray a lie.

LIES BETRAYED BY THINKING CLUES

Liars do not always anticipate when they will need to lie. There is not always time to prepare the line to be taken, to rehearse and memorize it. Even when there has been ample advance notice, and a false line has been carefully devised, the liar may not be clever enough to anticipate all the questions that may be asked, and to have thought through what his answers must be. Even cleverness may not be enough, for unseen changes in circumstances can betray an otherwise effective line. And, even when a liar is not forced by circumstances to change lines, some liars have trouble recalling the line they have previously committed themselves to, so that new questions cannot be consistently answered quickly.

Any of these failures—in anticipating when it will be necessary to lie, in inventing a line which is adequate to changing circumstances, in remembering the line one has adopted—produce easily spotted clues to deceit. What the person says is either internally inconsistent, or at odds with other incontrovertible facts, known at the time or later revealed. Such obvious clues to deceit are not always as reliable and straightforward as they seem. Too smooth a line may be the sign of a well rehearsed con man. To make matters worse, some con men knowing this purposely make slight mistakes in order not to seem too smooth! This was the case with Clifford Irving, who claimed he was authorized by Howard Hughes to write Hughes' biography. While on trial, Irving deliberately contradicted himself (albeit minor contradictions) because he knew that only liars tell perfectly planned accounts. The psychological evidence supports Irving's notion that planned responses are judged as more deceptive than unplanned ones. However, we believe in general that people who fabricate without having prepared their line are more likely to make blatant contradictions, to give evasive and indirect accounts—all of which will ultimately betray their lies.

Lack of preparation or a failure to remember the line one has adopted may produce clues to deceit in *how* a line is spoken, even when there are no inconsistencies in *what* is said. The need to think about each word before it is spoken—weighing possibilities, searching for a word or idea—may be obvious in pauses during speech, speech disfluencies, flattened voice intonation, gaze aversion, or more subtly in a tightening of the lower eyelid or eyebrow, certain changes in gesture, and a decrease in the use of the hands to illustrate speech. Not that carefully considering each word before it is spoken is always a sign of deceit, but in some circumstances it is—particularly in contexts in which responses should be known without thought.

LYING ABOUT FEELINGS

A failure to think ahead, plan fully, and rehearse the false line is only one of the reasons why mistakes are made when lying, which then furnish clues to the deceit. Mistakes are also made because of difficulty in concealing or falsely portraying emotion. Not every lie involves emotions, but those that do cause special problems for the liar. An attempt to conceal an emotion at the moment it is felt could be betrayed in words, but except for a slip of the tongue, it usually is not. Unless there is a wish to confess what is felt, the liar does not have to put into words the feelings being concealed. One has less choice in concealing a facial expression, or rapid breathing, or a tightening in the voice.

When emotions are aroused changes occur automatically without choice or deliberation. These changes begin in a split second; this is a fundamental characteristic of emotional experience. People do not actively decide to feel an emotion; instead, they usually experience emotions as happening to them. Negative emotions, such as fear, anger, or sadness, may occur despite either efforts to avoid them or efforts to hide them.

These are what we will call "reliable" behavioral signs of emotion, reliable in the sense that few people can mimic them at all or correctly. Narrowing the red margins of the lips in anger is an example of such a reliable sign of anger, typically missing when anger is feigned, because most people can not voluntarily make that movement. Likewise, when people experience enjoyment they not only move their lip corners upward and back (in a prototypical smile), but they also show a simultaneous contraction of the muscles that surround the eye socket (which raises the cheek, lowers the brow, and creates a "crows feet" appearance). This eye muscle contraction is typically missing from the smile when enjoyment is feigned or not felt. And, as in the case of the involuntary movement of the red margins of the lips in anger, most people cannot voluntarily make this eye muscle movement when they are not truly feeling enjoyment.

Falsifying an experienced emotion is more difficult when one is also attempting to conceal another emotion. Trying to look angry is not easy, but if fear is felt when the person tries to look angry, conflicting forces occur. One set of impulses, arising from fear, pulls in one direction, while the deliberate attempt to appear angry pulls in the other direction. For example, the brows are involuntarily pulled upward and together in fear, but to falsify anger the person must pull them down. Often the signs of this internal struggle between the felt and the false emotion betray the deceit.

Usually, lies about emotions involve more than just fabricating an emotion which is not felt. They also require concealing an emotion which is being experienced. Concealment often goes hand in hand with fabrication. The liar feigns emotion to mask signs of the emotion to be concealed. Such concealment attempts may be betrayed in either of two ways: (1) some signs of the concealed emotion may escape efforts to inhibit or mask it, providing what Ekman and Friesen termed *leakage*; or (2) what they called a *deception clue* does not leak the concealed emotion but betrays the likelihood that a lie is being perpetrated. Deception clues occur when only a fragment leaks which is not decipherable, but which does not jibe with the verbal line being maintained by the liar, or when the very effort of having to conceal produces alterations in behavior, and those behavioral alterations do not fit the liar's line.

FEELINGS ABOUT LYING

Not all deceits involve concealing or falsifying emotions. The embezzler conceals that she is stealing money. The plagiarizer conceals that he has taken the words of another and pretends they are his own. The vain middle-aged man conceals his real age, dying his gray hair and claiming he is seven years younger than he is. Yet even when the lie is about something other than emotion, emotions may become involved. The vain man might be embarrassed about his vanity. To succeed in his deceit he must conceal not only his age but his embarrassment as well. The plagiarizer might feel contempt toward those he misleads. He would thus have to conceal not only the source of his work and pretend an ability that is not his, but also conceal his contempt. The embezzler might feel surprise when someone else is accused of her crime. She would have to conceal her surprise or at least conceal the reason why she is surprised.

Thus, emotions often become involved in lies that were not undertaken for the purpose of concealing emotions. Once involved, the emotions must be concealed if the lie is not to be betrayed. Any emotion may be the culprit, but three emotions are so often intertwined with deceit to merit separate explanation: fear of being caught, guilt about lying, and delight in having duped someone.

Fear of Being Caught

In its milder forms, fear of being caught is not disruptive and may even help the deceiver to avoid mistakes by maintaining alertness. Moderate levels of fear can produce behavioral signs that are noticeable by the skilled lie catcher, and high levels of fear produce just what the liar dreads, namely, evidence of his or her fear or apprehension. The research literature on deception detection suggests that the behavior of highly motivated liars is different from that of less motivated ones. In other words, the behavior of liars who fear being caught is different from the behaviors of liars who do not fear being caught.

Many factors influence how the fear of being caught in a lie (or, *detection apprehension*) will be felt. The first determinant to consider is the liar's beliefs about his target's skill as a lie catcher. If the target (i.e., the person being lied to) is known to be gullible, there usually will not be much detection apprehension. On the other hand, a target known to be tough to fool, who has a reputation as an expert lie catcher, will increase the detection apprehension.

The second determinant of detection apprehension is the liar's amount of practice and previous success in lying. A job applicant who has lied about qualifications successfully in the past should not be overly concerned about an additional deception. Practice in deceit enables the liar to anticipate problems. Success in deceit gives confidence and thus reduces the fear of being caught.

The third determinant of detection apprehension is fear of punishment. The fear of being caught can be reduced if the target suggests that the punishment may be less if the liar confesses. Although they usually cannot offer total amnesty, targets may also offer a psychological amnesty, hoping to induce a confession by implying that the liar need not feel ashamed nor even responsible for committing the crime. A target may sympathetically suggest that the acts are understandable and might have been committed by anyone in the same situation. Another variation might be to offer the target a face-saving explanation of the motive for the behavior which the lie was designed to conceal.

A fourth factor influencing fear of being caught is the personality of the liar. While some people find it easy to lie, others find it difficult to lie; certainly more is known about the former group than the latter. One group, called *natural liars*, lie easily and with great success—even though they do not differ from other people on their scores on objective personality tests. Natural liars are people who have been getting away with lies since childhood, fooling their parents, teachers, and friends when they wanted to. This instills a sense of confidence in their abilities to deceive such that they have no detection apprehension when they lie. Although this sounds as if natural liars are like psychopaths, they are not; unlike natural liars, psychopaths show poor judgment, no remorse or shame, superficial charm, antisocial behavior without apparent compunction, and pathological egocentricity and incapacity for love.

Such natural liars may need to have two very different skills—the skill needed to plan a deceptive strategy, and the skill needed to mislead a target in a face-to-face meeting. A liar might have both skills, but presumably one could excel at one skill and not the other. Regretably, there has been little study of the characteristics of successful deceivers; no research has asked whether the personality characteristics of successful deceivers differ depending on the arena in which the deceit is practiced.

So far we have described several determinants of detection apprehension: the personality of the liar and, before that, the reputation and character of the lie catcher. Equally important are the *stakes*—the perceived consequences for successful and unsuccessful attempts at deception. Although there is no direct empirical evidence for this assertion, research on the role of appraisal in the experience of emotion is consistent with our thinking. There is a simple rule: the greater the stakes, the more the detection apprehension. Applying this simple rule can be complicated because it is not always so easy to figure out what is at stake; for example, to some people winning is everything, so the stakes are always high. It is reasonable to presume that what is at stake in any deception situation may be so idiosyncratic that no outside observer would readily know.

Detection apprehension should be greater when the stakes involve avoiding punishment, not just earning a reward. When the decision to deceive is first made, the stakes usually involve obtaining rewards. The liar thinks primarily about what might be gained. An embezzler may think only about the monetary gain when he or she first chooses to lie. Once deceit has been underway for some time the rewards may no longer be available. The company may become aware of its losses and suspicious enough that the embezzler is prevented from taking more. At this point, the deceit might be maintained in order to avoid being caught, and avoiding punishment becomes the only stake. On the other hand, avoiding punishment may be the motive from the outset, if the target is suspicious or the liar has little confidence.

There are two kinds of punishment which are at stake in deceit: the punishment that lies in store

Transparency International—USA Program

Securing Transparency in Trade: TI-USA is working with the U.S. administration, the private sector, and TI chapters to promote transparency in procurement, investment, services, and customs. It has promoted a World Trade Organization Agreement on Transparency in Government Procurement and agreements with similar requirements in the FTAA and APEC. It advocates strong transparency requirements in U.S. bilateral trade agreements and requiring bidders on projects financed by the World Bank and multilateral development banks to have antibribery programs.

if the lie fails; and the punishment for the very act of engaging in deception. Detection apprehension should be greater if both kinds of punishment are at stake. Sometimes the punishment for being caught deceiving can even be far worse than the punishment the lie was designed to avoid.

Even if the transgressor knows that the damage done if caught lying will be greater than the loss from admitting the transgression, the lie may be very tempting. Telling the truth brings immediate and certain losses, while telling a lie promises the possibility of avoiding all losses. The prospect of being spared immediate punishment may be so attractive that the liar may underestimate the likelihood that he or she will be caught in the lie. Recognition that confession would have been a better policy comes too late, when the lie has been maintained so long and with such elaboration that confession may no longer win a lesser punishment.

Sometimes there is little ambiguity about the relative costs of confession versus continued concealment. There are actions which are themselves so bad that confessing them wins little approval for having come forward, and concealing them adds little to the punishment which awaits the offender. Such is the case if the lie conceals child abuse, incest, murder, treason, or terrorism. Unlike the rewards possible for some repentant philanderers, forgiveness is not to be expected by those who confess these heinous crimes—although confession with contrition may lessen the punishment.

A final factor to consider about how the stakes influence detection apprehension is what is gained or lost by the target, not just by the liar. Usually the liar's gains are at the expense of the target. The embezzler gains what the employer loses. Stakes are not always equal; moreover, the stakes for the liar and the target can differ not just in amount but in kind. A philanderer may gain a little adventure, while the cuckolded spouse may lose tremendous self-respect. When the stakes differ for the liar and target, the stakes for either may determine the liar's detection apprehension. It depends upon whether the liar recognizes the difference and how it is evaluated.

Deception Guilt

Deception guilt refers to a feeling about lying, not the legal issue of whether someone is guilty or innocent. Deception guilt must also be distinguished from feelings of guilt about the content of a lie. Thus, a child may feel excitement about stealing the loose change off his parents' dresser, but feel guilt over lying to his or her parents to conceal the theft. This situation can be reversed as well—no guilt about lying to the parents, but guilt about stealing the money. Of course, some people feel guilt about both the act and the lie, and some people will not feel guilt about either. What is important is that it is not necessary to feel guilty about the content of a lie in order to feel guilty about lying.

Like the fear of being caught, deception guilt can vary in strength. It may be very mild, or so strong that the lie will fail because the deception guilt produces leakage or deception clues. When it becomes extreme, deception guilt is a torturing experience, undermining the sufferer's most fundamental feelings of self-worth. Relief from such severe deception guilt may motivate a confession despite the likelihood of punishment for misdeeds admitted. In fact the punishment may be sought by the person who confesses in order to alleviate the tortured feelings of guilt.

When the decision to lie is first made, people do not always accurately anticipate how much they may later suffer from deception guilt. Liars may not realize the impact of being thanked by their victims for their seeming helpfulness, or how they will feel when they see someone else blamed for their misdeeds—as in the recent case of the "gentleman bandit" who felt so guilty about someone else being prosecuted for his robberies that he turned himself in to the police. Another reason why liars underestimate how much deception guilt they will feel is that it is only with the passage of time that a liar may learn that one lie will not suffice, that the lie has to be repeated again and again, often with expanding fabrications in order to protect the original deceit.

Shame is closely related to guilt, but there is a key qualitative difference. No audience is needed for feelings of guilt, no one else need know for the guilty person is his own judge. Not so for shame. The humiliation of shame requires disapproval or ridicule by others. If no one ever learns of a misdeed there will be no shame, but there still might be guilt. Of course there may be both. The distinction between shame and guilt is very important because these two emotions may tear a person in opposite directions. The wish to relieve guilt may motivate a confession, but the wish to avoid the humiliation of shame may prevent it.

There exists a group of individuals who fail to feel any guilt or shame about their misdeeds; these people have been referred to as sociopaths or psychopaths. For these individuals, the lack of guilt or shame pervades all or most aspects of their lives. Experts disagree about whether the lack of guilt and shame is due to upbringing or some biological determinants. There is agreement that the psychopath's lack of guilt about lying and lack of fear of being caught will make it more difficult for a target to detect a psychopath's lies.

Conversely, some people are especially vulnerable to shame about lying and deception guilt; for example, people who have been very strictly brought up to believe lying is one of the most terrible sins. Those with less strict upbringing, that did not particularly condemn lying, could more generally have been instilled with strong, pervasive guilt feelings. Such guilty people appear to seek experiences in which they can intensify their guilt, and stand shamefully exposed to others; this appears to be the case for psychiatric patients suffering from generalized anxiety disorders. Unfortunately, unlike the psychopathic personality, there has been very little research about guilt-prone individuals.

Whenever the deceiver does not share social values with the victim, odds are there will not be much deception guilt. People feel less guilty about lying to those they think are wrongdoers. A philanderer whose marital partner is cold and unwilling in bed might not feel guilty in lying about an affair. A similar principle is at work to explain why a diplomat or spy does not feel guilty about misleading the other side. In all these situations, the liar and the target do not share common goals or values.

Lying is authorized in most of these examples—each of these individuals appeals to a well-defined social norm which legitimizes deceiving an opponent. There is little guilt about such authorized deceits when the targets are from opposing sides, and hold different values. There also may be authorization to deceive targets who are not opponents, who share values with the deceiver. Physicians may not feel guilty about deceiving their patients if they think it is for the patient's own good. Giving a patient a placebo, a sugar pill identified as a useful drug, is an old, time-honored, medical deceit. If the patient feels better, or at least stops hassling the doctor for an unneeded drug which might actually be harmful, many physicians believe that the lie is justified. In this case, the patient benefits from the lie, and not the doctor. If a liar thinks he is not gaining from the lie he probably will not feel any deception guilt.

Even selfish deceits may not produce deception guilt when the lie is authorized. Poker players do not feel deception guilt about bluffing (but they do feel detection apprehension). The same is true about bargaining whether in a Middle East bazaar, Wall Street, or in the local real estate agent's office. The home owner who asks more for his house than he will actually sell it for will not feel guilty if he gets his asking price. This lie is authorized. Because the participants expect misinformation, and not the truth, bargaining and poker are not necessarily lies. These situations by their nature provide prior notification that no one will be entirely truthful.

Deception guilt is most likely when lying is not authorized. Deception guilt should be most severe when the target is trusting, not expecting to be misled because honesty is expected between liar and target. In such opportunistic deceits, guilt about lying will be greater if the target suffers at least as much as the liar gains. Even then there will not be much, if any, deception guilt unless there are at least some shared values between target and liar. A student turning in a late assignment may not feel guilty about lying to the professor if the student feels the professor sets unreachable standards and assigns undoable workloads. This student may feel fear of being caught in a lie, but he or she may not feel deception guilt. Even though the student disagrees with the professor about the workload and other matters, if the student still cares about the professor he or she may feel shame if the lie is discovered. Shame requires some respect for those who disapprove; otherwise disapproval brings forth anger or contempt, not shame.

Liars feel less guilty when their targets are impersonal or totally anonymous. A customer who conceals from the check-out clerk, that he or she was undercharged for an expensive item will feel less guilty if he or she does not know the clerk. If the clerk is the owner, or if it is a small family owned store, the lying customer will feel more guilty than he or she will if it is one of a large chain of supermarkets. It is easier to indulge the guilt-reducing fantasy that the target is not really hurt, does not really care, will not even notice the lie, or even deserves or wants to be misled, if the target is anonymous.

Often there will be an inverse relationship between deception guilt and detection apprehension. What lessens guilt about the lie increases fear of being caught. When deceits are authorized there should be less deception guilt, yet the authorization usually increases the stakes, thus making detection apprehension high. In a high-stakes poker game there is high detection apprehension and low deception guilt. The employer who lies to his employee whom he has come to suspect of embezzling, concealing his suspicions to catch him in the crime, also is likely to feel high detection apprehension but low deception guilt.

While there are exceptions, most people find the experience of guilt so toxic that they seek ways to diminish it. There are many ways to justify deceit. It can be considered retaliation for injustice. A nasty or mean target can be said not to deserve honesty. "The boss was so stingy, he didn't reward me for all the work I did, so I took some myself." Or the liar can blame the victim of his or her lies; for example, Machiavellian personality types tend to see their victims as so gullible that they bring lies upon themselves.

QUESTIONS

1. Why do lies fail? Why are failed lies interesting?
2. What is deception guilt? How does it differ from shame?
3. What do the various kinds of failed lies tell you about the person who tells them?

Robert C. Solomon and Fernando Flores | Building Trust

Fernando Flores is a senator in Chile and formerly ran a successful consulting firm in Berkeley California. Robert C. Solomon teaches philosophy and business at the University of Texas at Austin. This selection is from their 1999 book, *Building Trust*.

In our experience, business people feel uncomfortable talking about trust, except, perhaps, in the most abstract terms of approbation. When the topic of trust comes up, they heartily nod their approval, but then they nervously turn to other topics. Executives are talking a great deal about trust these days, perhaps because they rightly suspect that trust in many corporations seems to be at an all-time low. One of our associates, who also consults for major corporations, recently gave a lecture on the importance of trusting your employees to several hundred executives of one of America's largest corporations. There was an appreciative but stunned silence, and then one of them—asking for all of them—queried, "but how do we control them?" It is a telling question that indicates that they did not understand the main point of the lecture, that trust is the very opposite of control. Or, perhaps, they understood well enough, but suffered a lack of nerve when it came time to think through its implications. Like the first-time skydiver who had eagerly read all of the promotional literature about the thrills of the sport and had listened carefully to instructions, he asked, incredulously, "but now you want us to *jump out of the plane!?*" We all know the importance of trust, the advantages of trust, and we all know how terrible life can

be without it. But when it comes time to put that knowledge into practice, we are all like the novice skydiver. Creating trust is taking a risk. Trust entails lack of control, in that some power is transferred or given up to the person who is trusted. It is leaping from the dark, claustrophobic fuselage of our ordinary cynicism into what seems like the unsupported free-fall of dependency. And yet, unlike skydiving, nothing is more necessary.

Today, there is a danger that trust is being oversold. There is such a thing as too much trust, and then there is "blind trust," trust without warrant, foolish trust. Trust alone will not, as some of our pundits promise, solve the problems that our society now faces. Thus we think there is good reason to listen to doubters like Daryl Koehn, who rightly asks, "should we trust trust?"[1] But the urgency remains, we believe, on the side of encouraging and understanding trust. There is a lot of encouraging going on today. What is lacking, we want to suggest, is understanding. The problem is not just lack of an adequate analysis. The problem is an aggressive misunderstanding of trust that pervades most of our discussions. The problem, if we can summarize it in a metaphor or two, is that trust is treated as if it were a "medium" in which human transactions take place, alternatively, as "ground," as "atmosphere" or, even more vaguely, as "climate." Benjamin Barber, for instance, who is one of the early writers on trust and often appealed to by the current crop of commentators, says that trust is "the basic stuff or ingredient of social interaction." But as "stuff" or "ingredient," as a "resource" (Fukuyama[2]), as "medium," "ground," "atmosphere" or "climate,"

This essay is one of two based on a talk given at the DePaul University Conference on Trust in Business, in Chicago, February 20–21, 1997. Special thanks to George Brenkert, Daryl Koehn, Ken Alpern and, especially, the terrific anonymous reviewers for *BEQ*, and to Business Design Associates in Alameda, CA. A companion piece appears in the *Journal for Professional and Business Ethics*, edited by Daryl Koehn, and both are part of a book now published by Oxford University Press, *Building Trust*, 2001.

trust all too easily tends to seem inert, simply "there" or "not there," rather than a dynamic aspect of human interaction and human relationships.

This is our thesis: Trust is a *dynamic aspect of human relationships*. It is an ongoing process that must be initiated, maintained, sometimes restored and continuously authenticated. Trust isn't a social substance or a mysterious entity; trust is a social practice, defined by choices. It is always relational: A trusts B (to do C, D, E). We can say that A is "trusting," but by that we mean that he or she has a disposition to readily trust people. Indeed, the very word "trust" is misleading, insofar as it seems to point to an entity, a thing, some social "stuff." Although we will continue to use the word, it might better be thought of as "trusting," an activity, a decision, a transitive verb, not a noun. Accordingly, the discussion of trust, in other words, is shot through with what French existentialist Jean-Paul Sartre called "bad faith," the distancing of our own actions and choices and the refusal to take responsibility for them. The not very subtle message of too much of the talk about trust today is, *"The problem isn't me/us, it's them,"* as if WE are perfectly willing to trust others—if they are trustworthy, that is, but, unfortunately, they are not or have not proven themselves so. Thus say the Bosnians and the Serbs, the Israelis and the Palestinians, many parents and their teenage kids, and all too many managers and their employees.

The misunderstanding of trust, accordingly, takes the form of a dangerous rationalization. Trust(ing) presupposes trustworthiness. Either one is trustworthy or one is not. So trusting takes the form of a kind of knowledge, the recognition (which may, of course, be fallible) that someone is trustworthy. So, if one trusts, so the rationalization goes, then nothing need be said, and it is much better that nothing be said. That is the core of our problem. Trust is rendered inarticulate, unpresentable. According to this view, to even raise the question, "Do you trust me?" or "Can I trust you?" is to already instigate, not only indicate, distrust. (Blaze Starr's mother warns her, "never trust a man who says, 'Trust me.'"[3]) If one does not trust, then nothing much is accomplished by saying so, except,

perhaps, as an insult, a way of escalating an already existing conflict or, perhaps, as a confirming test ("If you tell me that I should trust you, then you are doubly a liar.") When a politician or a business leader says, "trust me," he takes a considerable risk. Those who support him may well wonder why he needs to say that, and become suspicious. For those who are already suspicious of him, such an intrusive imperative confirms their suspicions.[4] On the other hand, when someone says "I trust you," there is always the possibility of some sense of manipulation, even the unwanted imposition of a psychological burden, one of whose consequences may be guilt.

The reason for talking about trust is not just to "understand" the concept philosophically but to put the issue of trust "on the table" in order to be able to talk it through in concrete, practical situations. By talking through trust, trust can be created, distrust mitigated. Not talking about trust, on the other hand, can result in continuing distrust, and lack of trust is calamitous to one's flourishing as a business and as individuals.

Economic approaches to trust, while well-intended and pointing us in the right direction, are dangerously incomplete and misleading. Trust in business is not merely a tool for efficiency, although it does have important implications for dealing with complexity and therefore efficiency.[5] Moreover, it would hardly be honest to guarantee (as many authors do these days), that more trust will make business more efficient and improve the bottom line. Usually, of course, trust has this effect, but there is no necessary connection between trust and efficiency, and this is neither the aim nor the intention of trust. Indeed, trust as a mere efficiency-booster may be a paradigm of *inauthentic* or phony trust, trust that is merely a manipulative tool, a facade of trust that, over the long run, increases *dis*trust, and for good reason. Employees can usually tell when the "empowerment" they receive like a gift is actually a noose with which to hang themselves, a set-up for blame for situations which they cannot really control. Managers know what it is like when they are awarded more responsibility ("I trust you to take care of that") without the requisite authority. Like many virtues, trust is most virtuous when it is pursued for its own sake, even if there is benefit or advantage in view. (Generosity and courage both have their payoffs, but to act generously or courageously *merely* in order obtain the pay-offs is of dubious virtue.) To think of trust as a business tool, as a mere means, as a lubricant to make an operation more efficient, is to not understand trust at all. Trust is, first of all, a central concept of ethics. And because of that, it turns out to be a valuable tool in business as well.

TRUST AS AN EMOTIONAL SKILL: SIMPLE TRUST, BLIND TRUST, AUTHENTIC TRUST

Trust is an emotional phenomenon. This is not to say that its significance is first of all "felt," or that it is merely transient. Trust, like love and indignation, finds its significance in the bonds it creates (or, better, in the bonds we create through such emotions), and it is the very essence of trust, like love (but unlike indignation), that it is enduring. Nevertheless (as with love) it may be cut short, betrayed, interrupted, and, on occasion, it may be all too fleeting, usually because it has been foolish. But trust, like all emotions, is dynamic. It defines our relationships and our relationship—our "being tuned"—to the world.

The importance of understanding emotion as a dynamic is essential to our view of emotion in general and trust in particular.[6] The contrast is the usual passivity picture of emotions as physiological interruptions of our lives that *happen to* us. Trust, in particular, is not something that simply happens, or is found or intuited. It is rather created through interaction and in the making of relationships. This is not to deny that there is an innate predisposition to trust, as evidenced so obviously in most babies, and it is compatible with the fact that trust may (tentatively) be established very quickly, within the first few minutes, of a relationship. But what this means is that we will have to be very careful how we talk about trust, careful that we do not collapse and confuse several very different phenomena.

Trust comes in various forms and degrees of sophistication and articulation. We can and ought to distinguish, just to begin with: *simple trust*, naive trust, trust as yet unchallenged, unquestioned (the faith of a well brought up child), *blind trust*, which is not actually naive but stubborn, obstinate, possibly even self-deluding, *basic trust*, which consists in the sense of physical and emotional security which most of us happily take for granted, which is most blatantly violated in war and in acts of random violence, and *authentic trust*, which is trust reflected upon, its risks and vulnerabilities understood, with *distrust* held in balance. (Distrust admits of similar distinctions and levels of sophistication.) Authentic trust, as opposed to simple trust, does not exclude or deny distrust but rather accepts it, even embraces it, but transcends it, absorbs it, overcomes it. With simple trust, one can always be surprised. The reasons for distrust are not even considered, much less taken seriously. Authentic trust can be betrayed, of course, but it is a betrayal that was foreseen as a possibility. There is no denial or self-deception, as in blind trust. There is no naivete, as in simple trust. Authentic trust need not be opposed to basic trust, but when basic trust is violated authentic trust sees clearly what trust remains. Once trust is spelled out, all sorts of new possibilities arise. It can be examined. It can be specified. It can be turned into explicit agreements and contracts. The mistake is to think that such agreements and contracts *precede* or *establish* trust. There can, of course, be agreements and contracts in the absence of trust, typically with elaborate enforcement mechanisms. But it is just as much of a mistake to conflate all trust with articulated trust as it is to conflate all trust with simple or basic (inarticulate) trust. The emotional life of trusting relationships is much more intricate and humanly complex than either contracts and cognitive interactive strategies or "non-cognitive security about motives" would alone allow.

Trust is created (and damaged) through dialogue, in conversation, by way of promises, commitments, offers, demands, expectations, explicit and tacit understandings. It is through such dialogue and conversation, including the rather one-way conversation of advertising, that producers make the nature and quality of their products known, that professionals and companies make their services and the abilities known, that expectations get initiated and intensified. This is not to say that trust is entirely linguistic, the product of promises and expectations verbally created. There is a good deal of trust embodied in our mere physical presence to one another, in our gestures, looks, smiles, handshakes and touches. Animals (especially "social" animals) have enormously complex trust relationships, often highly competitive at the same time, as any casual observation of two or more dogs (or wolves) together will confirm. Nor is the emphasis on dialogue and conversation suggested to imply—as so many social analyses too quickly conclude—that trust is an "agreement" or a "contract" (formal or informal). Contracts, too, are too static (although the negotiation of them, and negotiation out of them, may be dynamic indeed). Nor should trust be understood *primarily* in terms of limited or momentary interactions or transaction—or any number of them. Analyses of trust too often take as their paradigm either the most intimate of relationships—mother and child, husband and wife or lovers—or the most casual of them—notably, the one-shot business deal (for example, buying gas on the Interstate), or, the repeated one-shot business deal (buying gas at the same station on the way back down the Interstate). An interaction—even repeated interaction—is not yet a relationship, although, obviously, such repeated exchanges—and, occasionally, even a single one, can easily turn into one. A relationship is by its very nature on-going and dynamic, in which one of the central concerns of the relationship is the relationship itself, its status and identity and, consequently, the status and identity of each and all of its members. Trust is an essential and "existential" dimension of that dynamic relationship.

With this in mind, we can understand why lying betrays trust and is so damaging. Even just one lie—or a serious exaggeration or attempt to "spin" the truth—can undermine the accumulated trust and good will with which most of us approach new relationships and come to take for granted in established ones. Betrayal from a friend or neighbor may, with great difficulty, be overcome and eventually forgiven (though rarely forgotten), if only because these people are not easily eliminated from our lives. But betrayals in business, where associations are voluntary and there are always other possibilities, are typically fatal. Why work with or work a deal with someone you can no longer trust when there are so many others available?

NOTES

1. Daryl Koehn, "Should We Trust Trust?" *American Business Law Journal*, vol. 34(2), 1996: 184–203.
2. Francis Fukuyarna, *Trust: The Social Virtues and the Creation of Prosperity* (New York: Free Press, 1996).
3. Blaze Starr was the long-time mistress of Louisana governor Earl Long. The line occurs in the movie, starring Paul Newman and Lolita Davidovich, *Blaze* (1989).
4. E.g., Dick Morris on Bill Clinton's campaign strategy, *Behind the Oval Office* (New York: Knopf, 1997).
5. Nicholas Luhmann, "Trust: A Mechanism for the Reduction of Social Complexity," in his *Trust and Power* (New York: Wiley, 1980) pp. 4–103.
6. Martin Heidegger, *Being and Time (Sein und Zeit)*, trans. Joan Stambaugh (S.U.N.Y., 1996), esp. pp. 134–9.

QUESTIONS

1. Is there such a thing as too much trust? Explain.
2. What is "authentic trust"? What are the other forms of trust identified here?
3. What are some other ways for establishing trust that are not discussed in this article?

Tamar Frankel | # Trust, Honesty and Ethics in Business

Tamar Frankel is a professor at Boston University Law School.

Trust is crucial to the health of the financial system and the economy. In the past, when most trade and finance were conducted by people who knew each other, trust or mistrust developed naturally. In small communities, sanctions, like exclusion, could be a powerful means of preventing abuse of trust. But today, in a global financial system, people are forced to interact with strangers, and trust cannot be established as it was in the past.

What is the state of trust in the financial system today? When I was writing the book on *Trust and Honesty, America's Business Culture at a Crossroad* (published in 2006), I found a significant change in people's attitudes towards honesty and trustworthiness. There is no proof that there are more incidents of fraud today than there were in the past. America has always had its fair share of scandals and fraud. It has had its Robber Barons and medicine men who defrauded gullible people in small towns. It has had many corporate and financial frauds throughout the ages. I cannot prove that there is a change in the number of frauds today compared with the past.

What has changed, however, is the attitude towards dishonesty and breach of trust. Today, there is great er acceptance and more justification of dishonesty. In some cases, we have legitimized what in the past would have been considered an abuse of trust. And, moreover, the potential victims are required to protect themselves from abuse. This new and very dangerous trend leads to a culture of dishonesty and, in some respects, this cultural change is far more serious than an increasing number of cases of dishonesty.

CULTURE CONSIDERED AS SOCIAL HABITS

I define culture as social habits: It is how people expect themselves and others to behave. We don't give much thought to this expectation; it is not questioned or examined. In fact, people can rarely imagine any other way of doing things than the habits of the society in which they live. Culture often includes social enforcement of these expectations. If people expect others to tell the truth, then liars will be ostracized. If people are used to hiring assassins to kill their competitors, self-protection, deep mistrust and killings are part of the culture. Like all habits, social habits are efficient. People need not think about how to behave, or how not to behave. They need not weigh the pros and cons. They can act quickly and automatically. Yet habits are far from perfect. They are hard to develop. It takes many repetitions before peoples' actions and attitudes are established and become habits. Moreover, habits can be bad, or can become bad with a changing environment. Because culture is ingrained, it takes time and effort to change. Tendencies to bad habits must therefore be strongly discouraged before they can become habits.

That is why a culture of dishonesty and abuse of trust is so dangerous. If dishonesty is accepted because "everyone does it," the acceptance might freeze into a social habit and would then prove very hard to eliminate.

TRUST AND ALTERNATIVE VERIFICATION

Trust can be defined in many ways. I define it as the "reasonable belief that trusted persons: (1) tell the truth and (2) keep their promises." An alternative to trust is verification. If people did not show trust, they would seek to verify the other persons' statements, and demand guarantees to back the others' promises. However, verification and guarantees can be very costly. If we measure trust and verification by cost, we can determine when trust is necessary and when it is less important.

For example, buying a newspaper does not require trusting the seller. The buyer can easily verify that the newspaper is the one the buyer wants. And because the exchange of price for newspaper is simultaneous, there is no need for guarantees. Besides, the amount involved is not very large. In this case the buyer can protect his interests. But if I hand over my life's savings to a money-manager, I have no choice but to trust the manager. It is nearly impossible for me to verify what the manager will do with my money without negating the very usefulness of his service. In addition, entrusting the money and receiving the service are not simultaneous. I entrust my money to the manager first; only then can the manager perform his service for me.

Therefore, I am at risk that the manager might be tempted to avoid telling the truth or abiding by his promises. In addition, the amount of money involved here could be large and the risk of losing it may affect my future. In this case I must trust the manager and I may demand guarantees or regulation to reduce my risk of loss, If I cannot trust him, I had better not entrust my savings to him. Trust in this case must be supported by other mechanisms that protect from dishonesty.

MORALITY AS A BARRIER TO ABUSE OF TRUST

As I have already mentioned, there is a greater acceptance of dishonesty today. The danger is that this attitude could become part of the American or even universal culture. Abuse of trust, and the mistrust that follows, can undermine commercial and financial interaction, and drastically change our way of life. Trust can be supported by many mechanisms. Here I shall focus on just three: morality, law and the market.

The first of them, morality, is voluntary. Moral behavior is self-regulating rather than enforced—when good behaviour is imposed by the threat of punishment, the behavior is no longer moral. We value moral behaviour because its enforcement is the least costly to society. Moral people will do the right thing even if there are no police around. Police are an expense to society; they can also cause problems of abuse of power. So self-enforcement of social rules is a better option.

Morality can be taught. Usually, it must be taught at an early age, at home and in school. Some studies show that morality is part of our genetic make-up, together with our drive to survive. There are psychological tendencies, such as shame, empathy and guilt that induce most people to avoid harming others. However, while most people have those feelings, culture can strengthen or weaken them. A culture that denigrates and ridicules shame, empathy and guilt, can weaken them. So can a culture that emphasizes opposite drives, such as rational self-interest as the best guide to human behaviour, benefiting both individuals and society.

Adam Smith recognized morality, caring for others, and love. But this part of his teachings has been distilled and his name is forever associated with a different approach to economics and understanding of markets. Thus, morality and the feelings that restrict antisocial behaviour—the most effective and least expensive form of trust enforcement—have been weakened.

The law can serve as a barrier to dishonesty but, in the past thirty years, respect for the law has eroded. Some courts have interpreted law narrowly and literally, avoiding any consideration of policy, which is what they used to do in the past. That left room for self-interest without a balance of societal interest. In addition, Congress has been populated by members who believe that the less legislation, the greater the freedom of private sector corporate and financial management, the better off America would be.

THE LAW SUPPORTS TRUST

A few years ago, Congress imposed constraints on corporate power and gatekeepers, by enacting the Sarbanes–Oxley Act. This Act was passed in reaction to massive frauds in large corporations. However, when the shocked reaction to these frauds subsided, business leaders, lawyers, and academics sharply criticized the Act as imposing unnecessary costs on business. That may to some extent be true, but this ferocious and concentrated attack suggests that the pressures to curtail the field of application of law that began in the mid-1970s are still at work.

In the past thirty years, morality and law have lost ground to market regulation. The idea of market regulation was that people should be offered information and should be educated about financial matters and the financial system. As a consequence, they should be free to choose advisers. They should be free to decide what investments are good for them. Government should not determine that an investment is too risky for anyone. No court should decide that an offer of risky securities is fraudulent, so long as true information was provided publicly. No one, including individuals and corporations, should be restrained from borrowing as much as they wished, provided they find someone prepared to lend to them.

THE THIRD MECHANISM: THE MARKET

The regulators followed the same trend. They took a permissive attitude to financial innovation, freeing it from legal constraints but not following up to discover how the freedom was used. Regulators believed that market signals were better than government planning for the economy. The aggregate judgment of millions of investors, even if many of them were not experts, was more accurate than the judgment of a few experts.

However, in practice, the theory did not work precisely as was hoped. Providing information to investors may not prove enough, especially when the information is complex, and mistakes can be disastrous. Investors' self-education is not optimal when it is time-consuming, and when financial intermediaries send out signals of trustworthiness. Moreover, the requirement of self-protection signals the opposite of trust: "Don't rely on others."

Market regulation is supported by mechanisms designed to maintain trust. Most important are the lawyers, accountants, advisers, financial planners, analysts, rating agencies, and appraisers. During the past thirty years, these gatekeepers have failed to ensure trustworthiness and honesty in the markets. One reason for their failure is that these gatekeepers turned their main focus from gate-keeping to profit-making—they have become businessmen.

This conversion of gate-keeping professionals to businesses in pursuit of monetary profits as their main mission undermined a crucial element required in maintaining market regulation in support of trust.

Gatekeepers should view their main mission as preventing illegal actions. Instead they focused on profit-making.

In 1979, the Supreme Court of the Untied States overruled the long-term practice of the legal profession that prohibited lawyers from advertising and required them to charge fixed fees for various services. After 1979, lawyers could compete for business and charge different fees. The presumption was that in a free market, lawyers would compete to provide potential clients with more information and charge reduced fees.

The results were disappointing. Legal fees went up, not down. Lawyers became far more like businessmen, and competition did not result in higher quality services. In fact, it lowered the quality. Gate-keeping was subverted. Some lawyers provided clients with innovative loopholes in the law, all at a price. Market focus on "let the other party protect itself from me" took hold.

Thus, the trend of the last thirty years has been to strengthen the markets, and consequently, require trusting people to protect themselves against abusers of trust. The trend has been to reduce the pressure on trusted persons to self-regulation or to obey the laws that restrict and prohibit the abuse of trust. These conditions led to the flight of trusting people from the financial markets and had a devastating effect on the economy.

CAN A MARKET REGULATE DISHONESTY?

The belief that any market can regulate dishonesty and that market regulation should trump government regulation is based on an assumption that the market can "correct" problems of dishonesty as they arise. After all, it took a few months for the shares of Enron Corporation to fall from approximately $78 to about 19 cents. There are always some trendsetters, who lead the correction. It may well be that regulators react faster than the market, and prevent some of the losses that market corrections might cause.

However, even if this is the case, government regulation has flaws. Regulators do not know the unintended consequences of their actions; regulation may inhibit innovation; and, therefore, in the long run, regulation may create greater problems.

Yet the cost of market solutions and resolution of problems can be very high. In the case of the Enron Corporation, the losses to Enron's shareholders—individuals and institutional investors, such as pension plans—were enormous. Today, there is indeed "market correction" of excessive borrowing and risk taking. There is market correction of innovations that were not well tested and those that led to deceit and abuse of trust. However, the price of such corrections to the country is proving to be devastating.

The issue, here, is not whether markets can regulate behaviour. The issue is the price that the financial system and the economy pay for market regulation. In fact, today the markets are correcting the excesses of the past twenty-five or thirty years. Lending and borrowing have stopped altogether. Excess leverage has reached melting down point. Speculation has been replaced by a frantic search for security, liquidity, and lower risks. Yet, before these "corrections" took place, the market allowed financial intermediaries to provide enormous leverage, and take incredibly high risks, only to result in similarly drastic "corrective measures."

Therefore, the issue is not whether markets "correct" behaviour that undermines trust, but whether market corrections are at times too costly and whether less initial freedom might lead to lower correction costs. Of course market regulation has a place. But its place has been expanded and the right balance between market, morality and law has been lost. What is the best balance of morality, law and market regulation? The balance is not clear. There are disagreements on whether markets and competition enhance or undermine morality.

AN INEVITABLE REDUCTION IN TRUST

Morality—self-restraint—conflicts with market competition—the drive to get ahead of others. Yet, while markets and morality can weaken each other, they need not undermine each other. With cutthroat competition markets would not survive. Total self-restraint may also be destructive to markets. Long-term competition involves self-restraint. A similar balance can be sought in the law.

What is clear is that the degree of expanding market regulation has not been justified. Market regulation shifts the burden of maintaining trust from "trusted persons" to "trusting persons." Market regulation requires trusting persons to protect themselves against fraud of the people to whom they entrust their money.

The result is an inevitable reduction in trust by these vulnerable persons. And when their self-protection is weak, and morality of trusted people weakens as well, the shift to market regulation is likely to be accompanied by an abuse of trust. Freedom from supervision of trusted people poses great temptations. When this freedom and rejection of legal constraints are accompanied by theoretical justifications, abuse of trust is likely. This abuse may become cultural. It is then no longer called abuse. The behaviour is accepted and justified because "everyone does it." What used to be considered as abuse can be legitimized by denigrating the law, and even explicitly amending it.

CONSEQUENCES OF MISTRUST

Trusting people do not cease to trust on the first doubt or signal of abuse. But at some point abuse and unexpected large losses will cause a breakdown in trust. People who were unable to protect themselves from abuse learn their lesson. Those who could protect themselves, but did not, also learned their lesson. And people who have learned self-protection will tend to mistrust. In the end, all flee the market. It is then that those who rely on being trusted are left without clients, and the financial markets that are founded on trust crash and are decimated.

To be sure, markets continue to exist. However, they exist among parties who can protect themselves from the abuse of others or who have good reasons to trust. Deals are made by people who have known each other, usually depend on each other, and therefore can enforce the trust in each other. The markets that disappear are the markets in which trust is necessary because self-protection is too costly and personal knowledge of the other parties is almost impossible. These markets no longer function. The trusting people flee from them. This is the situation we have reached today.

Although financial problems are closely related to correcting market imbalance, the crucial issue today is the failing trust and confidence in the financial system. No matter how much money the government might pour into the banks; no matter how strongly it will support market institutions and large corporations that borrowed more than they can repay, these actions are insufficient to restore trust in the system and its intermediaries. Ironically, the government has taken over much of the financial system and said: "trust me." Yet, even those who have the cash to offer liquidity to the starving markets are loath to invest in the market because they do not trust the intermediaries or the market prices. The U.S. government's decision to support tottering banks did not bring the stock market prices up. In fact, stock prices fell!

AN ESSENTIAL AMBITION

There are, of course, many advisers and much advice on the subject of restoring trust. One source for research is the definition of "trust." After all, trust is a belief. If trust is lost, the person or institution that wishes to restore it must offer free verification. The trusting person need not seek proof. The trusted person must offer it. In general, moving towards more stable trust and honesty requires changes in the culture; and changes in the culture require altering aspirations and assumptions on acceptable behaviour. We need to change a number of fundamental beliefs. First, benefits to individuals or to a few corporations do not necessarily constitute benefits to larger groups of individuals and the country. What is good for General Motors is not necessarily good for America. There is a balance between individual and societal benefits. The balance cannot always be achieved by self-interest and conflict but most often, by a commitment to the other party's benefits. This commitment is expressed by honesty and trustworthiness. This is where the culture must lead if we are to restore trust in the financial system and the economy.

So here I make a leap to aspirations. We may have to compromise on the details. But the one thing on which we may not compromise is the ambition to become an honest society. This ambition is an idea, yet it can shape and become a building block of our culture. Being an idea, it is fully within our control -powerful and empowering. It may be a Utopia, which we cannot reach. But it can guide our daily life. Let the social pressures shame and prevent people from bragging about their gains at the expense of others. Let people who have abused trust be shunned. Do not let them be our leaders. Follow those who are not afraid to say: "I try my best to be honest. I want to live in a society of honest persons. I will not take advantage of others even when I can, and even when it is perhaps permissible under the law, and even if I give more than I can take." This would enable our society and economy to become far more prosperous and secure than they are today.

QUESTIONS

1. What might it mean to be a more honest society? How could that be achieved?

2. How do markets regulate trust and honesty? Explain.

CASES

CASE 2.1

Flying or Lying in Business Class

Robert C. Solomon

A few months ago, you graduated from business school and began working at National Inc. in New York City. It was exciting for you and your spouse to live in New York, but also very expensive, especially since you still have huge loans to pay off from college. Your boss at National is sending you to a conference in Amsterdam. This is a great opportunity for you to display your talents. New hires are watched closely to see if they have the maturity and sophistication to work with foreign clients.

At National employees have the option of getting an advance for their plane tickets, instead of paying for them and being reimbursed later. National also has a policy of sending employees business class on any flight of five hours or more. You were surprised at the amount of the advance for the business-class ticket and realize that you could use it to buy two coach tickets.

Your spouse has not yet found a job in New York and is getting a little depressed. When your spouse hears about the trip and expresses an interest in going with you, you agree that it is a good idea. You can't really afford a vacation, and it would be nice to stay in a good hotel and enjoy the sights in Amsterdam. Since the company is so large, and you submit your receipts to the accounting division, your boss would never know if you bought one or two tickets. Two coach tickets may even cost the company less money.

QUESTIONS

1. Should you ask your boss if you can use the money to buy two tickets?
2. Does the fact that the two coach tickets cost less justify not telling your boss?
3. What is the basic ethical problem here?

CASE 2.2

Willful Ignorance? Or Deception?

Robert C. Solomon

Two contract hires have been working in the accounts department at a major bank for eight months. The manager of their section had worked with HR (human resources) in posting the job and had agreed to a starting salary of $29,500, which the two hires had accepted. In a review of the section, the manager received a list of employees and their salaries and noticed that the two were listed as being paid $35,900. The manager assumed that it was a typographical error, but notified HR for a correction. HR responded that the two were indeed receiving that amount. Neither employee had informed the manager at any time during his or her employment that the salary was higher than what they had been offered.

As their manager, what would you do?

QUESTIONS

1. What would you do if you were being (modestly) overpaid?

2. Should the employees have told? Why? Is it possible that they just didn't notice? If they didn't notice, does their responsibility change? Why?

3. What if the employees who got the extra money noticed, but did not do anything about it because they figured that the company had changed their compensation?

CASE 2.3
Blindsided by Bankruptcy
Clancy Martin

You own a large chain of retail jewelry stores. Christmas was terrible and you are on the edge of bankruptcy. After a meeting with your attorneys and your banker, you realize it is, sadly, the time to file for a Chapter Eleven reorganization. Later that afternoon you are in your office and Rudolph Bultmann, your Rolex rep, calls you. "How was the season?" he asks. "Not what we hoped," you tell him. "Well don't worry. We are rolling out a whole new line and I want you to be the first to get it. It's a three million dollar commitment but I'll give you great terms on the credit." "What about the five million I already owe Rolex?" you ask him. "Don't worry so much. You'll catch up. You always do."

Rolex is an unsecured creditor, and you know they will be lucky to see pennies on the dollar for their debt. On the other hand, you desperately need the watches for your attempt to get through the Chapter Eleven. You remember what your attorney warned you: "Chapter Eleven is like an emergency room, and your inventory is the only medicine you've got. Stock up." You've been doing business with Bultmann for years. And you consider yourself to be a constitutionally honest person. On the other hand your company is at stake. What do you do?

QUESTIONS

1. You have two duties to yourself: a duty to be honest and a duty to your material prosperity. How do you decide between them?

2. What other duties do you have?

3. How much information does your vendor need to have about the state of your business?

CASE 2.4
Testing for Honesty
William H. Shaw and Vincent Barry

"Charity begins at home." If you don't think so, ask the Salvation Army. Some years ago, one of the Army's local branches discovered that it had a problem with theft among its kettle workers, the people who collect money for the Army during the Christmas season. Some of the Army's kettlers were helping themselves to the Army's loot before the organization had a chance to dole it out. To put a stop to the problem, Army officials sought the assistance of Dr. John Jones, director of research for London House Management Consultants.

London House is one of several companies that market honesty tests for prospective employees. Some of these tests, such as London House's Personnel Selection Inventory (PSI), also measure the applicant's tendency toward drug use and violence. All three categories—honesty, drugs, and violence—play a major part in company losses, according to the makers of these tests.

The company losses in question are astronomical. The U.S. Chamber of Commerce estimates that employee theft costs U.S. companies $40 billion annually; some unofficial estimates run three times as high. Moreover, 20 percent of the businesses that fail do so because of employee crime. Compounding the problem is the cost of employee drug use in terms of absenteeism, lost initiative, inattentiveness, accidents, and diminished productivity. Employee violence also costs companies millions of dollars in damage, lost productivity, and lawsuits.

Honesty-test makers say that the only way to deal with these problems is before workers are hired, not after—by subjecting them to a preemployment psychological test that will identify those prospective employees who will be likely to steal, who have a history of violence or emotional instability, or who have used illegal drugs on a regular basis.

James Walls, one of the founders of Stanton Corporation, which has offered written honesty tests for twenty-five years, says that dishonest job applicants are clever at hoodwinking potential employers in a job interview. "They have a way of conducting themselves that is probably superior to the low-risk person. They have learned what it takes to be accepted and how to overcome the normal interview strategy," he says. "The high-risk person will get hired unless there is a way to screen him." For this reason, Walls maintains, written, objective tests are needed to weed out the crooks. [Walls]

Millions of written honesty tests are given annually. Since 1988 demand has been booming as a result of congressional restrictions on polygraph testing, which prohibit about 85 percent of applicant and employee polygraph testing in the United States. As a result, purveyors of written tests have also been in high demand: The British Maxwell Communication Corporation, for instance, spent $17.4 million to acquire London House; Business Risk International took over the Stanton Corporation; and Wackenhut Corporation of Coral Gables, Florida, acquired marketing rights to the Phase II Profile, a widely used honesty test.

In addition to being legal, honesty tests are also more economical than polygraph tests. They cost between $7 and $14 per test, compared with $90 or so for a polygraph. Furthermore, the tests are easily administered at the workplace by a staff member to any category of worker, are easily and quickly evaluated by the test maker, and assess the applicant's overall answers rather than a few isolated responses.

From William H. Shaw and Vincent Barry, *Moral Issues in Business* (Blemont, CA: Wadsworth, 2001). Notes were deleted from this text.

The tests are also nondiscriminatory. The Equal Employment Opportunity Commission's "Uniform Guidelines on Employee Selection Procedures" (1978) permits tests that measure psychological traits because the race, gender, or ethnicity of applicants has no significant impact on scores.

A typical test begins with some cautionary remarks. Test-takers are told to be truthful because dishonesty can be detected, and they are warned that incomplete answers will be considered incorrect, as will any unanswered questions. Then applicants ordinarily sign a waiver permitting the results to be known to their prospective employer and authorizing the testing agency to check out their answers. Sometimes, however, prospective employees are not told that they are being tested for honesty, only that they are being asked questions about their background. James Walls justifies this less-than-frank explanation by saying that within a few questions it is obvious that the test deals with attitudes toward honesty. "The test is very transparent, it's not subtle." [Walls]

Some questions do indeed seem transparent— for example, "If you found $100 that was lost by a bank truck on the street yesterday, would you turn the money over to the bank, even though you knew for sure there was no reward?" But other questions are more controversial: "Have you ever had an argument with someone and later wished you had said something else?" If you were to answer no, you would be on your way to failing. Other questions that may face the test-taker are: "How strong is your conscience?" "How often do you feel guilty?" "Do you always tell the truth?" "Do you occasionally have thoughts you wouldn't want made public?" "Does everyone steal a little?" "Do you enjoy stories of successful crimes?" "Have you ever been so intrigued by the cleverness of a thief that you hoped the person would escape detection?" Or consider questions like "Is an employee who takes it easy at work cheating his employer?" or "Do you think a person should be fired by a company if it is found that he helped employees cheat the company out of overtime once in a while?" These ask you for your reaction to hypothetical dishonest situations. "If you are a particularly kind-hearted person who

isn't sufficiently punitive, you fail," says Lewis Maltby, director of the workplace rights office at the American Civil Liberties Union. "Mother Teresa would never pass some of these tests." [Maltby]

A big part of some tests is a behavioral history of the applicant. Applicants are asked to reveal the nature, frequency, and quantity of specific drug use, if any. They also must indicate if they have ever engaged in drunk driving, illegal gambling, traffic violations, forgery, vandalism, and a host of other unseemly behaviors. They must also state their opinions about the social acceptability of drinking alcohol and using other drugs.

Some testing companies go further in this direction. Instead of honesty exams, they offer tests designed to draw a general psychological profile of the applicant, claiming that this sort of analysis can predict more accurately than either the polygraph or the typical honesty test how the person will perform on the job. Keith M. Halperin, a psychologist with Personnel Decision, Inc. (PDI), a company that offers such tests, complains that most paper-and-pencil honesty tests are simply written equivalents of the polygraph. They ask applicants whether they have stolen from their employers, how much they have taken, and other questions directly related to honesty. But why, asks Halperin, "would an applicant who is dishonest enough to steal from an employer be honest enough to admit it on a written test?" It is more difficult for applicants to fake their responses to PDI's tests, Halperin contends.

Not everyone is persuaded. Phyllis Bassett, vice-president of James Bassett Company of Cincinnati, believes tests developed by psychologists that do not ask directly about the applicant's past honesty are poor predictors of future trustworthiness. This may be because, as some psychologists report, "it is very difficult for dishonest people to fake honesty." One reason is that thieves tend to believe that "everybody does it" and that therefore it would be implausible for them to deny stealing. In general, those who market honesty exams boast of their validity and reliability, as established by field studies. They insist that the tests do make a difference, that they enable employers to ferret out potential troublemakers—as in the Salvation Army case.

Dr. Jones administered London House's PSI to eighty kettler applicants, which happened to be the number that the particular theft-ridden center needed. The PSIs were not scored, and the eighty applicants were hired with no screening. Throughout the fund-raising month between Thanksgiving and Christmas, the center kept a record of each kettler's daily receipts. After the Christmas season, the tests were scored and divided into "recommended" and "not recommended" for employment. After accounting for the peculiarities of each collection neighborhood, Jones discovered that those kettlers the PSI had not recommended turned in on the average $17 per day less than those the PSI had recommended. Based on this analysis, he estimated the center's loss to employee theft during the fund drive at $20,000.

The list of psychological-test enthusiasts is growing by leaps and bounds, but the tests have plenty of detractors. Many psychologists have voiced concern over the lack of standards governing the tests; the American Psychological Association favors the establishment of federal standards for written honesty exams. But the chief critics of honesty and other psychological exams are the people who have to take them. They complain about having to reveal some of the most intimate details of their lives and opinions.

For example, until an employee filed suit, Rent-A-Center, a Texas corporation, asked both job applicants and employees being considered for promotion true/false questions like these: "I have never indulged in any unusual sex practices," "I am very strongly attracted by members of my own sex," "I go to church almost every week," and "I have difficulty in starting or holding my bowel movements." A manager who was fired for complaining about the test says, "It was ridiculous. The test asked if I loved tall women. How was I supposed to answer that? My wife is 5 feet 3 inches." A spokesman for Rent-A-Center argues that its questionnaire is not unusual and that many other firms use it.

Firms who use tests like Rent-A-Center's believe that no one's privacy is being invaded because employees and job applicants can always refuse to take the test. Critics disagree. "Given the unequal bargaining power," says former ACLU official Kathleen Bailey, "the ability to refuse to take a test is one of theory rather than choice—if one really wants the job." [Bailey]

QUESTION

1. Describe how you'd feel having to take a psychological test or an honesty test either as an employee or as a precondition for employment. Would you take the test? Why or why not?

2. Are you convinced that a test can really measure honesty? If not, then what do you think the results of this test mean?

3. Do you think it is fair to hire or not hire someone based on what they score on this test?

CASE 2.5

The Columbia Shuttle Disaster: Should We Have Told the Astronauts the Truth?

Margaret P. Battin and Gordon B. Mower

> The space shuttle Columbia exploded in 2003, killing all seven astronauts aboard. M. Battin and G. Mower teach at the University of Utah.

There is a deep ethical dilemma in the Columbia shuttle disaster that's been overlooked by both principals and commentators. Linda Ham didn't recognize it; neither did the Mission Management Team, or the Photo Working Group, or the Program Manager for Launch Integration, or the Debris Assessment Team, or commentators like Donovan and Green or Davis—or, perhaps, they somehow subliminally recognized it but all assumed it should be decided in the same way.

There was a genuine moral issue here. Assume that, as soon as the photos were taken, it became apparent that the tile damage was much greater than on any previous mission. Indeed, let us suppose that the gravity of the situation was fully recognized by ground control. There didn't seem to be any way out—once the shuttle was aloft, it wouldn't have been possible to dock with the space station, and it wouldn't have been possible to rescue the astronauts. This might lead us to think that, as Linda Ham apparently did, "there isn't anything I can do."

But there is something of significant ethical importance that you could do; the question is whether you *should* do it or not. After all, as we're assuming, you know there is a high probability that the astronauts will die on reentry—but *they* don't know it. Would you tell them? Ham, and apparently all others, have assumed no. Yet this is not at all obvious, and indeed different ethical approaches to the question may yield quite different answers.

We might wonder, to begin with, what it is about the ethical course of not disclosing to the astronauts their impending fate that seemingly makes it so

appealing to our moral intuitions. Nobody told the astronauts what very well could happen on reentry, and without access to the discussions of those concerned with tile loss, they had no way to know it themselves. Can we find support in ethical reasoning for our reticence? To do so, perhaps our reasoning takes a certain direction that we might find in other kinds of moral decision-making: let's consider several different seemingly analogous cases.

First, let's say that there is a military operation in which the leaders of the operation know that there is a reasonable chance that certain units will be destroyed by the enemy. Nevertheless, other units in the operation are dependent on these doomed units performing their part of the operation. Should the leaders of the operation inform the members of the endangered units that they are most likely to die? Wouldn't this knowledge affect their performance, thereby jeopardizing the mission and the lives of others? Isn't it the case that in the military profession, sometimes leaders know that certain people are about to die, but not only do they not tell them, they also exaggerate their chances for survival? In this profession, the ethical perspective might be one that emphasizes a primarily Utilitarian view of things—that one ought to try to promote the greater good for the greater number, even at some cost to a few.

There are all kinds of ways we can imagine in which informing the astronauts of the real risks they faced might affect their performance in ways that could affect others. It is, after all, a very powerful impulse to pursue one's own survival. If they knew of the damage to the tiles, for example, would they perhaps engage in an unauthorized space walk in an attempt to jury-rig some kind of tile repair, perhaps forgetting their research projects

From *Teaching Ethics*, Fall 2003, pp. 89–91. Reprinted with permission of the Board of Directors of *Teaching Ethics*.

or releasing uncharted debris into space, the tiniest fragment of which could have catastrophic effects on future shuttle and space missions? Would they collapse from emotional stress, or even harm each other there in their small, now-lethal cocoon? The astronauts are about to die in the performance of their own professional duties. Not performing them well could affect others. But if there is a chance of survival, even a slim one, wouldn't their performance level be diminished by the stress of knowing their fate? This is an argument for not telling them what we know.

But if this were a case in medical ethics, the assumption would be made just the other way around. Suppose, for example, that you're a physician, and have seven cancer patients, each of whom will die. Would you tell them the truth? Yes, of course; truthtelling even in fatal cancer diagnoses is now standard practice in medicine—though physicians try to do so with tact, empathy, and understanding. Among the standard arguments for truthtelling are that people who are facing death should be allowed to have time to say goodbyes, to set their affairs in order, to make amends, or, if they're religious, to make whatever final confessions and prayers they wish. This is what it is to respect persons, as Kant might put it, to recognize them as ends in themselves, able to determine in accord with their own values how they choose to spend the last moments of their lives. This is a deontological response to the deep moral problem here: whatever the consequences, it would be wrong to lie to the astronauts or to deprive them of the truth. It would be wrong to rob them of autonomous choice during their last moments, and of the knowledge that these are their last moments.

But isn't this just what happened, out there in space? If we know there's a reasonable chance the seven astronauts will die, and that there's nothing we can do to save them, shouldn't we tell them? Would they live that last week any differently? Surely, in undertaking a space mission in the first place, they would have made their wills, put their affairs in order, told their spouses and their children that they loved them. But now suppose that

they knew the end was really coming. Would they communicate differently? Live differently among themselves, there in the spaceship? Try to extend the length of the voyage until their supplies ran out? Or vote to "reenter" earlier, so that the fearsome end would be over sooner? Plead for help? Or send consoling messages to Earth, recognizing that this is a risk they voluntarily assumed and that they are willing to bear? There are many possibilities for heroism and despair, insight and cowardice, and the whole range of human emotion and reflection—not easy to bear but part of full human life—even one about to be made abruptly short. How will they live this week, before what may be a catastrophic end? These are the things the astronauts themselves should have a hand in deciding, not that should be decided by others.

If we move in the direction favored by Linda Ham, Mission Management, Launch Integration, Debris Assessment, the various commentators, and perhaps our own initial inclinations, we opt for a high dose of paternalism at one of the most significant points in the lives of these people. Perhaps we believe that this knowledge really is more harmful to the astronauts and to others than keeping it from them. Under such a belief, perhaps consequentialism trumps deontology. If, however, we are simply keeping the astronauts in the dark to protect them against their own fears, or even to protect ourselves against our anxieties for them, then this seems an unreasonable cost to their autonomy. Of course it would be painful to know the end was coming; but it would take a resolute paternalism to shield them from this knowledge, something we would not tolerate in other professions who work with people who know they are about to die.

QUESTIONS

1. Should they have told the astronauts the truth? Why or why not?

2. Why might being lied to be a good thing? Are there times when you would rather be lied to?

3. Who benefits from laying to the astronauts? What is the "benefit" of laying here?

CHAPTER QUESTIONS

1. In business (and in life), does honesty mean different things in different contexts? Is honesty on a used-car lot different from honesty in a classroom? Or honesty among friends? But once you contextualize honesty, do you open yourself up to deception? Is there such a thing as Enron-style honesty?

2. How does secrecy relate to honesty? What about bluffing? Should we feel guilty about keeping secrets? Why or why not? Should we feel guilty about bluffing? How, when, and why are we allowed to control the truth? When and why is complete disclosure or transparency obviously undesirable?

3. Construct guidelines for when it is appropriate to tell a lie in business.

3

The Good Life

Introduction

Of course, you want to be a success in business or in whatever enterprise you engage in. But what is success? How do you measure it? How will you know when you have achieved it? It is naturally tempting to postpone these questions, perhaps with a glib answer like "when I've got more money than I can spend" or "when I have it, I'll know it." But the truth is less obvious. Many people achieve the success that they sought as students, whether measured in dollars or in status, and only then realize that they were working for the wrong goal, that what they have earned turns out not to be what they really want or wanted. In the worst cases, people come to realize that they have wasted the best years of their lives. Psychiatrists document so many cases of "workaholism" and self-destructive goal setting in which people work and strive because they feel compelled to, perhaps imitating their parents or following what they take to be their parents' constant prodding and expectations. People ignore their families, working for success, only to realize too late that they have neglected their families even as they were supporting them, that they missed the opportunity to watch their children growing up or enjoy their hard-earned wealth when they were most able to do so. Success thus means not just wealth and "making a living." It involves the wise use of one's time, a sense of balance between one's career and one's "personal life," a continuing sense of what one wants and what is ultimately worthwhile, a "balance" between one's work and the rest of one's life, even where one loves one's work so much that it is difficult to separate the two.

Business ethics, like all ethics, is not just concerned with "doing the right thing." It is not all about ethical dilemmas and hard choices. Business ethics, like all ethics, is first of all concerned with living a good life, getting the most out of one's years, and forging the most satisfying relationships with one's family, friends, and community. What makes you happy is just as much a focus of business ethics as telling the truth and building trust with your colleagues and your customers. Indeed, it is hard to separate the two, insofar as it is difficult to imagine being happy while alienating your friends and being distrustful of everyone. So what this chapter is about is the larger frame within which business success is measured and meaningful. That frame is life itself, the good life, which in many ways remains much the same for you as it would have been back in ancient times. Aristotle built his entire ethics around the question "what is happiness (*eudaimonia*)?" And his answer

85

was that happiness is a life of virtue as well as pleasure, friendship as well as excellence in whatever it is you do. But it is not as if one simply achieves this through luck or good fortune or good upbringing (although all these may be a big advantage). Happiness is the result of practical wisdom and understanding. It is the result of planning. So as you put so much effort into preparing for your career, you had better make some time to plan for your life as well, and not just fill in the decreasing number of spaces between job assignments and pressures with friends, romance, excitement, and happiness.

Even in Aristotle's time, the temptation to misjudge one's own needs and desires was pervasive. Aristotle's teacher, Plato, had a good word for it, *"pleonexia,"* "grasping," or what we would loosely translate as *greed*. We hear a great deal about greed these days—top executives who never seem to have enough, despite obvious excesses and extravagances; financial managers, stockbrokers, and other agents who bilk their clients and the customers just for the sake of a little bit *more;* shareholders and customers who insist on a bit more profit or a better bargain without regard for where that money or savings is coming from and whose lives may be damaged or destroyed. But the problem with greed is not just the often-innocent victims who are hurt by it. As Plato and Aristotle knew very well, and as the medieval saints who listed greed ("avarice") as one of the seven deadly sins knew, too, greed has its most horrendous effects on the greedy themselves. Greed ruins lives. Greed runs the hardest after goals that contribute nothing to happiness but distract and detract from it. And foremost among these goals today, as it has been for thousands of years, is the pursuit of wealth. The ancient story of King Midas is as much a lesson for today's aspiring business students as it was for the students of Plato's Academy. Midas was a man who treasured gold above all else, and when he got his wish, that whatever he touched would turn to gold (a wish often put in the same terms by many of today's business students), that magical success became a lethal curse. One cannot eat or drink gold. Money, we are told, cannot buy love. (Although it is sometimes quipped, it can rent it for a while.) Money is little comfort to the deeply unhappy, although the perverse nature of greed is such that even when it is wealth that it is the source of unhappiness (for instance, in terms of enemies made, "friends" who cannot be trusted, opportunities missed or wasted in the pursuit of narrow business "success"), the illusion is that more wealth will make things better. But quite to the contrary, the pursuit of wealth often blinds us to what we really want.

None of this is to attack wealth or aspiration or success. Plato and Aristotle hung out with the wealthiest and most powerful men in Greece. (Alexander the Great was one of Aristotle's students, for example.) But wealth has its place. It is a means and not an end in itself. Knowing what one wants is knowing, in part, what it will cost, not just in terms of money but in terms of time, friendship, opportunities for adventure, and any number of other considerations that cannot be easily valued or measured by the market. As one of our current California wise men, Sam Keen, has put it, "the most important thing is knowing just how little one needs to be happy." The good life is the measure of success, and how much money one makes is just one of its many ingredients.

The following readings have been chosen to help you think philosophically about what you ultimately want out of life, not simply in terms of material acquisitions (a house, a couple of cars, a second house), but in terms of the essential ingredients in happiness, which includes thinking about what you want to do with wealth when you get it. So we start with some classic readings from Aristotle and Epicurus, two Greek philosophers who thought a great deal about the question of what it takes to be happy. Then we turn to Joanne

Ciulla's essay, which ponders what grasshoppers, ants, and bees tell us about about how we choose our work and life. In the next essay, Andrew Carnegie, one of America's richest men in the nineteenth century, offers a meditation on the question of what to do with wealth when you get it. We also know that too much emphasis on wealth acquisition can be injurious to your life and happiness. Solomon Schimmel offers us a historical picture of the "deadly sin" of greed. Then, shifting gears, Joanne Ciulla discusses the role of leisure and consumption in the good life, and the great English philosopher Bertrand Russell quips on "idleness" in response to the old warning that "the devil makes work for idle hands." Shifting gears again, philosopher Lynn McFall discusses the all-important virtue of integrity. Finally, we offer a longer piece from Bertrand Russell on the importance of "impersonal" interests (as opposed to those that look to self-interest). The cases, too, are designed to help you think philosophically about what you want out of life. Success? At what cost? Achievement of one's objectives? But can this become a distraction from more important values? Happiness? But what is this? How about a life of pure pleasure without responsibilities, cares, or disappointments?

Robert C. Solomon	Strategic Planning—For the Good Life

Young business people are often encouraged these days to make out a "plan" for themselves—where they would like to be in a year, in five years, perhaps more. An entire course at Harvard Business School is devoted to career planning—what sort of position to seek first, when to move, etc. But what is tragically lacking is analogous *life* planning, with an eye not only to such obvious life stages as marriage, children, and retirement and one or two hobbies for one's "spare time" (a revealing phrase) but also to other interests and aspects of one's personality. Not surprisingly, an informal survey of 1983 MBAs six months out of Harvard showed that nearly half were already frustrated with their jobs and their lives, though they had been equipped to understand and analyze only the former.

There is a sense, of course, in which the good life cannot be planned. Emergencies and tragedies are usually not predictable, and in business the details of the job market, politics, and the business cycle—even

if explicable to future historians—provide the wild cards in the game of life. Planning when to get married—when one does not already have a specific person in mind—strikes us as not only unromantic but also foolish. Risks are a part of life—and sometimes desirable. But risks can be foolish as well as invigorating, and they can be planned for. Chance may be as essential to life as the search for security, but chance—paradoxically—does not "just happen." Chance too can be planned and evaluated, and there is a world of difference between being ready to welcome unexpected opportunity and being shocked and unprepared for it. Much of our unhappiness, in fact, is not the result of misfortune or bad luck. It is bad planning, or no planning, no sorting out of priorities *before* we find ourselves neck-deep in responsibilities and obligations or over our heads in a life we never really wanted in the first place.

Life in today's fast-moving world is not so unpredictable as the future shockers would tell us. Modes

From Robert C. Solomon, *It's Good Business: Ethics and Enterprise for the New Millennium* (Lanham, MD: Rowman/ Littlefield, 1998). Reprinted with permission of the author.

of communication and transportation—not to mention warfare—may be evolving at a terrifying speed, but the essentials of the good life remain remarkably constant: friendship, family life and time to enjoy it, a sense of fulfillment, the respect of one's neighbors and self-respect besides, the basic comforts of life, good health and the "good things" that money will buy (whatever those happen to be this year or decade). Is there really so much difference between wanting to own an expensive car in this century and desiring a fine carriage in the last one? Were the food and wine better in the Middle Ages, or was friendship any more enjoyable in ancient Rome? As we become ever more efficient and productive, how is it that we seem to have less time rather than more, and have fewer ideas about what to do?

A plan for the good life means something more than listing one's career ambitions and possibilities and something more than listing the things that one enjoys. A plan for the good life means, first of all, knowing your needs, your ideals and aspirations as a human being. One joins a firm with business and management objectives in mind; it is not unreasonable to keep in mind also a set of life management goals. If one can set one's sights on a promotion by the end of the first year, why not set a goal of friendship for that period, too? One might argue that in life, "management by objective" is compulsive and neurotic—if indeed it is pursued in too business-like a manner. But when business life is so carefully planned and orchestrated, the rest of life is too easily forced into the odd or spare moments, or neglected altogether. Strangely enough, the risks and shocks we think of as the challenge of business are reserved for our personal lives, where they are usually much less welcome. Ethics and the good life get sacrificed not because of immorality or stupidity but simply because they are not part of the only plan in town.

What kinds of questions go into a plan for the good life? First of all, questions about yourself, what you want, expect, enjoy and need: security, freedom, companionship, privacy, power, friendship, great wealth, or just to be recognized as a success.

1. What do you consider the most important things in life? Success, family, companionship, romantic love, money, status and position, respect, friendship. Which could you live without, or have only in small doses? Which could you not live without, or have only in substantial doses?

2. What do you most enjoy doing? Imagine yourself left entirely to choose on your own, without financial pressures, without expecting rewards or compensations beyond the activity itself. What would (or do) you choose to do? Listen to music? Play tennis? Build things? Have a quiet dinner with an intimate friend? Be alone, doing nothing? Work?

3. What kind of people do you like to spend your time with? Work with? Are they the kind of people you are spending time with now? Are you the kind of person they would want to spend time with? Do you enjoy people who inspire you? What are your primary expectations in a friend? In a colleague? In a boss? (Most of us conscientiously choose our subordinates; it is much more important to be careful in choosing a boss.)

4. How do you see yourself, ideally? How would you describe yourself in a paragraph, say, for a future *Who's Who* emphasizing not positions and awards but character and accomplishments? How well are you working toward that now?

5. How important is so-called spare time to you? How much do you need? What do you (or would you) do with it? Is spare time to you just time to relax and get ready for more work? (Living to work used to be a virtue, until psychiatrists gave it a pathological name: "workaholism." But the fact remains that loving one's work is one of the few dependable roads to happiness.) Is your spare time more important than your work? (Then why are you working so hard?)

6. Where would you draw the line in your job? What would you not do, even at the risk of being fired? Work seventeen-hour days, and weekends? Have to fire a good friend? Make false reports? Lie to your boss? Get ahead at the expense of someone who deserves it more? Be responsible—even indirectly—for some innocent person's death? (Better to be clear

about these things *before* the topic comes up unexpectedly, under pressure.)

7. What is your ethical style? What kinds of arguments do you use to support your ideas? What kind of person do you find immoral? Do you resent people who obey the letter of the law? Do you find people who don't give arguments to be frustrating?

8. Whom do you want to please? ("Yourself" is the fashionable but usually false answer. "My mother" and "my father" are a bit overworked, thanks to Freud. Try again.)

9. How much money do you need? How much do you want? Why? Suppose you suddenly inherited $400,000. What would you do with it? Is that so important?

10. What do you want to be doing next year, this time, in your job and out of it?

11. What do you want to be doing five years from now—what kind of job, what kind of life? Does the idea of doing just what you are doing now (plus a little status and some cost-of-living increases) horrify you? Or does it give you a sense of pleasant comfort?

12. Looking back over your life and career from your rocking chair, what would you like to remember—and how would you like to be remembered?

QUESTIONS

1. Can you plan your life—or is it all just luck or fate?

2. What are your top five values? If you had to eliminate one, which would it be? Could you live without love, for example, if you knew that by doing so you would earn a million dollars a year?

3. Imagine sitting in your rocking chair when you are 90 and looking back at your life. What activities do you think you will wish that you had spent more time doing. For example, do you think that many people would wish that they had spent more time watching TV or more time at work?

Aristotle | # On the Good Life

Aristotle was one of the two greatest Greek philosophers of ancient times. His ethics is wholly devoted to an examination of happiness (*eudaimonia*) and the good life.

Each man judges well the things he knows, and of these he is a good judge. And so the man who has been educated in a subject is a good judge of that subject, and the man who has received an all-round education is a good judge in general. Hence a young man is not a proper hearer of lectures on political science; for he is inexperienced in the actions that occur in life, but its discussions start from these and are about these; and, further, since he tends to follow his passions, his study will be vain and unprofitable, because the end aimed at is not knowledge but action. And it makes no difference whether he is young in years or youthful in character; the defect does not depend on time, but on his living, and pursuing each successive object, as passion directs. For to such persons, as to the incontinent, knowledge brings no profit; but to those who desire and act in accordance with a rational principle knowledge about such matters will be of great benefit.

These remarks about the student, the sort of treatment to be expected, and the purpose of the inquiry, may be taken as our preface.

From the *Nicomachean Ethics* (translated by W. D. Ross, Oxford University Press, 1915).

What is the highest of all goods achievable by action [as opposed to mere good fortune and those achievable by pure thought and contemplation]? Verbally, there is very general agreement; for both the general run of men and people of superior refinement say that it is happiness, and identify living well and doing well with being happy; but with regard to what happiness is they differ, and the many do not give the same account as the wise. For the former think it is some plain and obvious thing, like pleasure, wealth, or honour; they differ, however, from one another—and often even the same man identifies it with different things, with health when he is ill, with wealth when he is poor; but, conscious of their ignorance, they admire those who proclaim some great ideal that is above their comprehension.

To judge from the lives that men lead, most men, and men of the most vulgar type, seem (not without some ground) to identify the good, or happiness, with pleasure; which is the reason why they love the life of enjoyment. For there are, we may say, three prominent types of life—that just mentioned, the political, and thirdly the contemplative life. Now the mass of mankind are evidently quite slavish in their tastes, preferring a life suitable to beasts, but they get some ground for their view from the fact that many of those in high places share the tastes of Sardanapallus. A consideration of the prominent types of life shows that people of superior refinement and of active disposition identify happiness with honour; for this is, roughly speaking, the end of the political life. But it seems too superficial to be what we are looking for, since it is thought to depend on those who bestow honour rather than on him who receives it, but the good we divine to be something proper to a man and not easily taken from him. Further, men seem to pursue honour in order that they may be assured of their goodness; at least it is by men of practical wisdom that they seek to be honoured, and among those who know them, and on the ground of their virtue; clearly, then according to them, at any rate, virtue is better. And perhaps one might even suppose this to be, rather than honour, the end of the political life. But even this appears somewhat incomplete; for possession of virtue seems actually compatible with being asleep, or with lifelong inactivity, and, further, with

the greatest sufferings and misfortunes; but a man who was living so no one would call happy, unless he were maintaining a thesis at all costs. But enough of this; for the subject has been sufficiently treated even in the current discussions. Third comes the contemplative life, which we shall consider later.

The life of money-making is one undertaken under compulsion, and wealth is evidently not the good we are seeking; for it is merely useful and for the sake of something else. And so one might rather take the aforenamed objects to be ends; for they are loved for themselves. But it is evident that not even these are ends; yet many arguments have been thrown away in support of them.

The function of man is an activity of the soul which follows or implies a rational principle, and the function of a good man is the good and noble performance of these in accordance with the appropriate virtue or excellence, so the good for man turns out to be an activity of soul in accordance with virtue, and if there are more than one virtue, in accordance with the best and most complete. But we should add, "in a complete life." For one swallow does not make a summer, nor one day; and so too one day, or a short time, does not make a man blessed or happy.

So the argument has reached this point; Since there are evidently more than one end, and we choose some of these (e.g., wealth, flutes, and in general instruments) for the sake of something else, clearly not all ends are final ends; but the chief good is evidently something final. Therefore, if there is only one final end, this will be what we are seeking, and if there are more than one, the most final of these will be what we are seeking. Now we call that which is in itself worthy of pursuit more final than that which is worthy of pursuit for the sake of something else, and that which is never desirable for the sake of something else more final than the things that are desirable both in themselves and for the sake of that other thing, and therefore we call final without qualification that which is always desirable in itself and never for the sake of something else.

Now such a thing happiness, above all else, is held to be; for this we choose always for itself and never for the sake of something else, but honour, pleasure, reason, and every virtue we choose indeed for themselves (for if nothing resulted from them we should still choose each of them), but we choose them also for the sake of happiness, judging that by means of them we shall be happy. Happiness, on the other hand, no one chooses for the sake of these, nor, in general, for anything other than itself.

From the point of view of self-sufficiency the same result seems to follow; for the final good is thought to be self-sufficient. Now by self-sufficient we do not mean that which is sufficient for a man by himself, for one who lives a solitary life, but also for parents, children, wife, and in general for his friends and fellow citizens, since man is born for citizenship. But some limit must be set to this; for if we extend our requirement to ancestors and descendants and friends' friends we are in for an infinite series. Let us examine this question, however, on another occasion; the self-sufficient we now define as that which when isolated makes life desirable and lacking in nothing; and such we think happiness to be; and further we think it most desirable of all things, without being counted as one good thing among others—if it were so counted it would clearly be made more desirable by the addition of even the least of goods; for that which is added becomes an excess of goods, and of goods the greater is always more desirable. Happiness, then, is something final and self-sufficient and is the end of action.

We must take as a sign of states of character the pleasure or pain that ensues on acts; for the man who abstains from bodily pleasures and delights in this very fact is temperate, while the man who is annoyed at it is self-indulgent, and he who stands his ground against things that are terrible and delights in this or at least is not pained is brave, while the man who is pained is a coward. For moral excellence is concerned with pleasures and pains; it is on account of the pleasure that we do bad things, and on account of the pain that we abstain from noble ones. Hence we ought to have been brought up in a particular way from our very youth, as Plato says, so as both to delight in and to be pained by the things that we ought; for this is the right education.

Again, if the virtues are concerned with actions and passions, and every passion and every action is accompanied by pleasure and pain, for this reason also virtue will be concerned with pleasures and pains. This is indicated also by the fact that punishment is inflicted by these means; for it is a kind of cure, and it is the nature of cures to be effected by contraries.

After these matters we ought perhaps next to discuss pleasure. For it is thought to be most intimately connected with our human nature, which is the reason why in educating the young we steer them by the rudders of pleasure and pain; it is thought, too, that to enjoy the things we ought and to hate the things we ought has the greatest bearing on virtue of character. For these things extend right through life, with a weight and power of their own in respect both to virtue and to the happy life, since men choose what is pleasant and avoid what is painful; and such things, it will be thought, we should least of all omit to discuss, especially since they admit of much dispute. For some say pleasure is the good, while others, on the contrary, say it is thoroughly bad—some no doubt being persuaded that the facts are so, and others thinking it has a better effect on our life to exhibit pleasure as a bad thing even if it is not; for most people (they think) incline towards it and are the slaves of their pleasures, for which reason they ought to lead them in the opposite direction, since thus they will reach the middle state. But surely this is not correct. For arguments about matters concerned with feelings and actions are less reliable than facts: and so when they clash with the facts of perception they are despised, and discredit the truth as well; if a man who runs down pleasure is once seen to be aiming at it, his inclining towards it is thought to imply that it is all worthy of being aimed at; for most people are not good at drawing distinctions. True arguments seem, then, most useful, not only with a view to knowledge, but with a view to life also; for since they harmonize with the facts they are believed, and so they stimulate those who understand them to live according to them.

Eudoxus thought pleasure was the good because he saw all things, both rational and irrational, aiming at it, and because in all things that which is the object of choice is what is excellent, and that which is most the object of choice the greatest good; thus the fact that all things moved towards the same object indicated that this was for all things the chief good (for each thing, he argued, finds its own good, as it finds its own nourishment); and that which is good for all things and at which all aim was *the* good. His arguments were credited more because of the excellence of his character than for their own sake; he was thought to be remarkably self-controlled, and therefore it was thought that he was not saying what he did say as a friend of pleasure, but that the facts really were so. He believed that the same conclusion followed no less plainly from a study of the contrary of pleasure; pain was in itself an object of aversion to all things, and therefore its contrary must be similarly an object of choice. And again that is most an object of choice which we choose not because or for the sake of something else, and pleasure is admittedly of this nature; for no one asks to what end he is pleased; thus implying that pleasure is in itself an object of choice. Further, he argued that pleasure when added to any good, e.g. to just or temperate action, makes it more worthy of choice, and that it is only by itself that the good can be increased.

This argument seems to show it to be one of the goods, and no more a good than any other; for every good is more worthy of choice along with another good than taken alone. And so it is by an argument of this kind that Plato proves the good *not* to be pleasure; he argues that the pleasant life is more desirable with wisdom than without, and that if the mixture is better, pleasure is not the good; for the good cannot become more desirable by the addition of anything to it. Now it is clear that nothing else, any more than pleasure, can be the good if it is made more desirable by the addition of any of the things that are good in themselves. What, then, is there that satisfies this criterion, which at the same time we can participate in? It is something of this sort that we are looking for.

In reply to those who bring forward the disgraceful pleasures one may say that these are not pleasant; if things are pleasant to people of vicious constitution, we must not suppose that they are also pleasant to others than these, just as we do not reason so about the things that are wholesome or sweet or bitter to sick people, or ascribe whiteness to the things that seem white to those suffering from a disease of the eye. Or one might answer thus—that the pleasures are desirable, but not from *these* sources, as wealth is desirable, but not as the reward of betrayal, and health, but not at the cost of eating anything and everything. Or perhaps pleasures differ in kind; for those derived from noble sources are different from those derived from base sources, and one cannot get the pleasure of the just man without being just, nor that of the musical man without being musical, and so on . . . .

No one would choose to live with the intellect of a child throughout his life, however much he were to be pleased at the things that children are pleased at, nor to get enjoyment by doing some most disgraceful deed, though he were never to feel any pain, in consequence. And there are many things we should be keen about even if they brought no pleasure, e.g. seeing, remembering, knowing, possessing the virtues. If pleasures necessarily do accompany these, that makes no odds; we should choose these even if no pleasure resulted. It seems to be clear, then, that neither is pleasure the good nor is all pleasure desirable, and that some pleasures *are* desirable in themselves, differing in kind or in their sources from the others. So much for the things that are said about pleasure and pain.

Since every sense is active in relation to its object, and a sense which is in good condition acts perfectly in relation to the most beautiful of its objects (for perfect activity seems to be ideally of this nature; whether we say that *it* is active, or the organ in which it resides, may be assumed to be immaterial), it follows that in the case of each sense the best activity is that of the best-conditioned organ in relation to the finest of its objects. And this activity will be the most complete and pleasant. For, while there is pleasure in respect of any sense, and in respect of thought and contemplation no less, the most complete is pleasantest, and that of a well-conditioned organ in relation to the worthiest of its objects is the most complete; and the pleasure completes the

Adam Smith on Capitalism

If we examine, I say, all these things, and consider what a variety of labor is employed about each of them, we shall be sensible that without the assistance and co-operation of many thousands, the very meanest person in a civilized country could not be provided, even according to what we very falsely imagine the easy and simple manner in which he is commonly accommodated. Compared, indeed, with the more extravagant luxury of the great, his accommodation must no doubt appear extremely simple and easy; and yet it may be true, perhaps, that the accommodation of an European prince does not always so much exceed that of an industrious and frugal peasant, as the accommodation of the latter exceeds that of many an African king, the absolute master of the lives and liberties of ten thousand naked savages.

From *The Wealth of Nations*.

activity. But the pleasure does not complete it in the same way as the combination of object and sense, both good, just as health and the doctor are not in the same way the cause of a man's being healthy. (That pleasure is produced in respect to each sense is plain; for we speak of sights and sounds as pleasant. It is also plain that it arises most of all when both the sense is at its best and it is active in reference to an object which corresponds; when both object and perceiver are of the best there will always be pleasure, since the requisite agent and patient are both present.) Pleasure completes the activity not as the corresponding permanent state does, by its immanence, but as an end which supervenes as the bloom of youth does on those in the flower of their age. So long, then, as both the intelligible or sensible object and the discriminating or contemplative faculty are as they should be, the pleasure will be involved in the activity; for when both the passive and the active factor are unchanged and are related to each other in the same way, the same result naturally follows.

QUESTIONS

1. Aristotle insists that a little money is essential to living a good life. Do you agree? Does that mean poor people cannot be good?

2. What is the function of human beings for Aristotle? How does Aristotle argue his way to that function? Rewrite his argument in clear steps.

3. Using Aristotle's ideas about the good life, construct a model of what that would look like in your own life.

Joanne B. Ciulla | # Work and Life

In our society, work shapes your life and your identity. What you do, in other words, has a lot to do with who you are. The questions "what do you want out of your work?" and "what do you want out of your life?" are important because they shape how you behave in business. Thinking about the meaning of work and life is not a touchy-feely luxury in a business course. It will provide a foundation for thinking about how you should behave at work and how you understand the work behavior of others. Typically, unethical behavior in business is the product of people who have lost their perspective on themselves, their work, and their lives. Success in business, by contrast, is usually the dessert of people who know who they are, what they are doing, and why.

Some of the most profound insights about work and life, curiously enough, are to be found in the famous fables of the ancient storyteller Aesop, who wrote about animals who act, think, and talk like human beings. Aesop wrote these fables sometime around 620 B.C., but some of the same stories show up in various forms on Egyptian papyri that date back to 1000–800 B.C. In the well-known fable, "The Grasshopper and the Ant," Aesop locked horns with the question, "To work or not to work?" He wrote:

> The ants were employing a fine winter's day in drying grain collected in the summer time. A grasshopper, perishing with famine, passed by and earnestly begged for a little food. The ants inquired of him, "Why did you not treasure up food during the summer?" He replied, "I had not leisure enough. I passed the days in singing," They then said in derision: "If you were foolish enough to sing all the summer, you must dance supperless to bed in winter.*

This is a cautionary tale. It does not say that a life of work is better than a life of singing, but rather that if you want to sing, you have to be willing to pay the price. The issue here is self-sufficiency and fairness—if you don't work, you don't eat, and you shouldn't expect others to feed you. Aesop's story gives us a choice. You can lead the brief happy life of the grasshopper or the long prudent life of the ant. Yet it's not wholly clear what the wise person should choose.

Unlike the good Protestant who would come along later, Aesop was somewhat ambivalent about industriousness. Greed, miserliness, and covetousness sometimes accompany hard work. In another story, "The Ant," he tells us that the ant was once a farmer who kept a jealous eye on his neighbor and stole some of his produce. Zeus, angry, changed the man into an ant, and Aesop wrote, "Although his form has changed, his character has not, for he still goes around the fields gathering up the wheat and barley of others and storing it up for himself." Aesop worried that industriousness, when motivated by envy can lead to theft, avarice, and miserliness.

Aesop was kinder to the grasshopper's relative, the cicada. He said that once there were men who, when music was invented, were so happy that they just kept singing and forgot food and drink until they died. From these men came the cicadas, who don't require food and sing their lives away. The muses smile upon the cicadas because their singing brings joy. While Aesop did not exactly endorse the life of the cicada, he expressed a somewhat romantic admiration. The cicada's brief life is spent in pursuit of beauty.

The aesthetic virtues of the cicadas and the moral virtues of the ant come together in Aesop's story called the "Ant and the Bee." In it, the bee and the ant have a dispute over who is more prudent and industrious. They appeal to Apollo for a judgment. The god applauds the ant's care, foresight, and independence from the labors of others, but he says, "it is you alone that you benefit; no other creature shares any part of your hoarded riches. Whereas, the bee produces, by his meritorious and ingenious exertions,

---

* *Aesop's Fables* trans. from the Greek by Rev. G. F. Townsend (New York: McLoughin Br., 1924), p. 16.

that which becomes a blessing to the world." Again we see chinks in the moral armor of hard work. It's good to provide for oneself, but it is even better to contribute a pleasing and useful product for society. We admire hard work much more if people do it for some purpose that lies beyond pure self-interest. The Buddhist scriptures use the bee as a model of the environmentally responsible businessperson. They tell us, "The wise and moral man, Shines like a fire on a hill top. Making money like a bee, Who does not hurt the flower."

Aesop's ant, grasshopper, and bee give us three ways of approaching life. Frugal, acquisitive, and hardworking, the antlike worker values security above all else. He spends all his time working at a moderately interesting job, makes cautious career choices, has little involvement in nonwork activities, and takes few vacations and fewer chances. Like the ant, this sort of person saves for retirement, mortgaging certain enjoyments for 65 years of his or her life, in the hopes of making up for it in the last 10 or 20. Ants work for the future, but don't always know what to do when (or if) they reach it. The merit of the ant's life plan is that his frugality saves him from want, prepares him for emergencies, and ensures self-sufficiency.

In contrast to the ant, the grasshopper lives for the present and sacrifices the future. His playing goes nowhere and leaves nothing behind. There is pleasure in a life of play, but is there meaning? The bee works like an ant, but takes pleasure and finds meaning in producing a good and useful product that is appreciated by others. The bee symbolizes a life of useful and rewarding work, the ant represents a life of work and security, while the grasshopper depicts a frivolous life of play and uncertainty.

But why is it that "all play and no work makes Jack a big jerk"? Today we sometimes legitimate play in a work-oriented society by playing squash to unwind, golf to woo clients, and basketball for cardiovascular health. Even animals aren't exempt from nonproductive play. You may notice how the narrator of a Discovery Channel show solemnly explains to the viewer that the frolicking lion cubs may *think* that they are playing, but they are *really* practicing the skills that will make them good hunters. Contrast

this with the idea of play defended by the great Greek philosopher Plato. Plato suggested that play evolved from the desire of children and small animals to leap and run around. Think for a moment of the delight that children and puppies get simply from jumping up and down and running around for no particular reason.

Play is often illogical and/or inefficient. Games are intentionally inefficient. The things that people do when they play them have no meaning outside the game. For example, if your job required you to put little white balls into 18 holes, you certainly wouldn't do it by separating the holes by several hundred yards and hitting the ball with a long, thin stick over lakes, hills, and sand traps. The point of golf is to get the ball into 18 holes in the most inefficient way possible. Getting the ball into the hole is important to the player, but just placing the golf balls in the holes serves no purpose whatsoever.

Play, like the cicada's singing, is done for no reason, except, perhaps, for pleasure. While the Aesop's grasshopper starves because he is irresponsible, the cicada is the "starving artist"; it starves for love of music. But the two fables convey different messages. Dying because of one's love of art seems to have some nobility, whereas dying just because one prefers to play games does not. For most of us, the hard question is not whether or not to play (most of us would say, "of course"), but "given freedom to choose, what should we do with the time given to us in life?"

There are four values that essentially shape how we make choices about work. They are (1) meaningful work, or work that is interesting and/or important to you or to others in society; (2) leisure or free time to do the things you want; (3) money; and (4) security. These values carry different weights at different times in life. Ideally, it would be best to have a fascinating job, plenty of vacation time, a salary that allows you to buy anything you want, and guaranteed lifetime employment. Since few of us have jobs that provide all these things, we make trade-offs, and these trade-offs signify what we value most. Consider the following thought experiment, which we will repeat in different versions throughout this book. Suppose you are single and have just graduated from college. You have four job offers. The first is a well-paying position in an accounting firm, the second is with Amnesty International, the third is a civil service job, and the fourth is a place as a waiter at an Aspen ski resort that operates only in winter. Which one would you choose?

Your answer probably derives from another question: What are you willing to give up if you can't have it all? People who are driven by the values of meaningful work and leisure are often more willing to give up security and money. If meaningful work is most important, you may choose Amnesty International. This job entails long hours without much pay or financial security but a keen sense of

making a positive difference to people's lives. The resort job may not give you much meaning, money, or security, but it will give you plenty of opportunities to do what you love best, namely, ski. Meaningful work and leisure may have a lot in common. People who insist on doing meaningful work often say that they do not really distinguish between their work and their leisure-time activities. What is important to them is doing what they want to do, whether for the value of the work itself or because of its significance.

Some people prefer leisure to meaningful work because they do not want to or cannot engage in the activity they love as paid work. They turn to other activities (hobbies, music, sports, and even crime) and

---

To: You
From: The Philosopher
Subject: "Worthy Work"

Do you remember the summer jobs that we had when we were students? You and I earned money baby-sitting, waiting on tables, and digging ditches. Work had a different meaning to us than to our coworkers who didn't get to quit when school started in September. I think people are willing to endure the worst jobs if it is reasonable to hope that the jobs will get them where they want to go or, at least, feed them along the way. The English designer, craftsman, poet, socialist, and all-around workaholic, William Morris, wrote a great essay on the difference between useful work and useless toil that emphasizes the importance of hope in the meaning of work:

> [There] are two kinds of work—one good, the other bad; one not far removed from a blessing, a lightening of life; the other a mere curse, a burden to life. What is the difference between them, then? This: one has hope in it, the other has not. It is manly to do one kind of work, and manly to refuse to do the other. What is the nature of hope that makes it worth doing?
>
> It is threefold, I think—hope of rest, hope of product, hope of pleasure in the work itself; hope of these also in some abundance of good quality; rest enough and good enough to be worth having: product worth having by one who is neither a fool nor an ascetic; pleasure enough for all for us to be conscious of it while we are at work; not a mere habit, the loss of which we shall feel as a fidgety man feels the loss of the bit of string he fidgets with.
>
> Thus worthy work carries with it hope of pleasure in rest, the hope of pleasure in using what it makes, and the hope of pleasure in using our daily creative skill. All other work is worthless; it is slaves' work—mere toiling to live that we may live to toil.*

* William Morris, "Useless Work Versus Useless Toil," in *The Collected Works of William Morris*, vol. 23 (London: Russell & Russell, 1966), pp. 98–100.

other institutions (family, friends, church, and community organizations) for the psychological rewards that they can't get from work. Meaningful work and leisure consist of activities that aren't just instrumental, but are rewarding or pleasurable in their own their own right.

If you value money and security above other things, then work is primarily an *instrumental* activity, a means toward those ends. For example, the accounting job may not be exciting, and few people ever make it to partner, but as a new graduate, you will make good money to pay off your college loans and buy a condo, nice clothes, and maybe a sports car. Those who value material goods above and beyond what they need to live comfortably trade leisure for overtime or a second job to buy extra cars and the like. Their pleasure in buying and owning things overrides their desire for free time. (Money is also important to those who value security; however, they value saving it over spending it.) If you want security, the government job may fit the bill. Even though it may not be glamorous, and you'll make less money than you would if you were in industry, the benefits are excellent, you get all the standard holidays, and it's relatively stable employment. At different points in one's life, different values dominate. The new graduate may choose the resort job, the single parent may choose between a challenging and time-consuming career and one that allows more time to spend with his or her children. Here, free time is more important than money or an interesting job. Not everyone has a wide latitude of choice when it comes to work, leisure, and money; however, it is still necessary to reflect on what you value if you want to pursue a good life.

QUESTIONS

1. Reflect on your own personality and inclinations and discuss the extent to which you are a grasshopper, an ant, a cicada, and a bee.

2. Draw a 4×4 matrix with the values of meaningful work, leisure, money, and security on each axis. Then fill in which ones are most important to you and which values you would be willing to give up to have the things that you want in life.

3. What would you do with your life if you were totally free to do anything that you wanted?

Epicurus | # On Pleasure

Epicurus wrote persuasively about the virtues of an unperturbed life, but his constrained emphasis on pleasure gave him the eventual (unwarranted) reputation as a party animal. "Epicurean" now means someone who lives for pleasure.

Let no one when young delay to study philosophy, nor when he is old grow weary of his study. For no one can come too early or too late to secure the health of his soul. And the man who says that the age for philosophy has either not yet come or has gone by is like the man who says that the age for happiness is not yet come to him, or has passed away. Wherefore both when young and old a man must study philosophy, that as he grows old he may be young in blessings through the grateful recollection of what has been, and that in youth he may be old as well, since he will know no fear of what is to come. We must then meditate on the things that make our happiness, seeing that when that is with us we have all, but when it is absent we do all to win it. . . .

From *Epicurus* (translated by C. Bailey, Oxford University Press, 1926).

Become accustomed to the belief that death is nothing to us. For all good and evil consists in sensation, but death is deprivation of sensation. And therefore a right understanding that death is nothing to us makes the mortality of life enjoyable, not because it adds to it an infinite span of time, but because it takes away the craving for immortality. For there is nothing terrible in life for the man who has truly comprehended that there is nothing terrible in not living. So that the man speaks but idly who says that he fears death not because it will be painful when it comes, but because it is painful in anticipation. For that which gives no trouble when it comes, is but an empty pain in anticipation. So death, the most terrifying of ills, is nothing to us, since so long as we exist death is not with us; but when death comes, then we do not exist. It does not then concern either the living or the dead, since for the former it is not, and the latter are no more.

But the many at one moment shun death as the greatest of evils, at another yearn for it as a respite from the evils in life. But the wise man neither seeks to escape life nor fears the cessation of life, for neither does life offend him nor does the absence of life seem to be any evil. And just as with food he does not seek simply the larger share and nothing else, but rather the most pleasant, so he seeks to enjoy not the longest period of time, but the most pleasant. . . .

We must then bear in mind that the future is neither ours, nor yet wholly not ours, so that we may not altogether expect it as sure to come, nor abandon hope of it, as if it will certainly not come.

We must consider that of desires some are natural, others vain, and of the natural some are necessary and others merely natural; and of the necessary some are necessary for happiness, others for the repose of the body, and others for very life. The right understanding of these facts enables us to refer all choice and avoidance to the health of the body and the soul's freedom from disturbance, since this is the aim of the life of blessedness. For it is to obtain this end that we always act, namely, to avoid pain and fear. And when this is once secured for us, all the tempest of the soul is dispersed, since the living creature has not to wander as though in search of something that is missing, and to look for some other thing by which he can fulfil the good of the soul and the good of the body. For it is then that we have need of pleasure, when we feel pain owing to the absence of pleasure; but when we do not feel pain, we no longer need pleasure. And for this cause we call pleasure the beginning and end of the blessed life. For we recognize pleasure as the first good innate in us, and from pleasure we begin every act of choice and avoidance, and to pleasure we return again, using the feeling as the standard by which we judge every good.

And since pleasure is the first good and natural to us, for this very reason we do not choose every pleasure, but sometimes we pass over many pleasures, when greater discomfort accrues to us as the result of them: and similarly we think many pains better than pleasures, since a greater pleasure comes to us when we have endured pains for a long time. Every pleasure then because of its natural kinship to us is good, yet not every pleasure is to be chosen: even as every pain also is an evil, yet not all are always of a nature to be avoided. Yet by a scale of comparison and by the consideration of advantages and disadvantages we must form our judgement on all these matters. For the good on certain occasions we treat as bad, and conversely the bad as good.

And again independence of desire we think a great good—not that we may at all times enjoy but a few things, but that, if we do not possess many, we may enjoy the few in the genuine persuasion that those have the sweetest pleasure in luxury who least need it, and that all that is natural is easy to be obtained, but that which is superfluous is hard. And so plain savours bring us a pleasure equal to a luxurious diet, when all the pain due to want is removed; and bread and water produce the highest pleasure, when one who needs them puts them to his lips. To grow accustomed therefore to simple and not luxurious diet gives us health to the full, and makes a man alert for the needful employments of life, and when after long intervals we approach luxuries, disposes us better towards them, and fits us to be fearless of fortune.

When, therefore, we maintain that pleasure is the end, we do not mean the pleasures of profligates and those that consist in sensuality, as is supposed by some who are either ignorant or disagree with us or do not understand, but freedom from pain in the body and from trouble in the mind. For it is not continuous drinkings and revellings, nor the satisfaction of lusts, nor the enjoyment of fish and other luxuries of the wealthy table, which produce a pleasant life, but sober reasoning, searching out the motives for all choice and avoidance, and banishing mere opinions, to which are due the greatest disturbance of the spirit.

QUESTIONS

1. Is pleasure always a good? Should we define other goods in terms of the pleasure they give us?
2. Can suffering ever be good? What would Epicurus say?
3. Imagine planning a whole day in which you maximize every pleasure possible. Would this be an enjoyable day?

Andrew Carnegie | # Wealth

Andrew Carnegie was one of the most powerful American millionaires of the nineteenth century. He was also a great philanthropist.

The problem of our age is the proper administration of wealth, so that the ties of brotherhood may still bind together the rich and poor in harmonious relationship. The conditions of human life have not only been changed, but revolutionized, within the past few hundred years. In former days there was little difference between the dwelling, dress, food, and environment of the chief and those of his retainers. The Indians are today where civilized man then was. When visiting the Sioux, I was led to the wigwam of the chief. It was just like the others in external appearance, and even within the difference was trifling between it and those of the poorest of his braves. The contrast between the palace of the millionaire and the cottage of the laborer with us today measures the change which has come into civilization.

This change, however, is not to be deplored, but welcomed as highly beneficial. It is well, nay essential, for the progress of the race, that the houses of some should be homes for all that is highest and best in literature and arts, and for all the refinements of civilization, rather than that none should be so. Much better this great irregularity than universal squalor. Without wealth there can be no Maecetions. When

First published in the *North American Review*, June 1889.

these apprentices rose to be masters, there was little or no change in their mode of life, and they, in turn, educated in the same routine succeeding apprentices. There was, substantially, social equality, and even political equality, for those engaged in industrial pursuits had then little or no political voice in the State.

But the inevitable result of such a mode of manufacture was crude articles at high prices. Today the world obtains commodities of excellent quality at prices which even the generation preceding this would have deemed incredible. In the commercial world similar causes have produced similar results, and the race is benefited thereby. The poor enjoy what the rich could not before afford. What were the luxuries have become the necessaries of life. The laborer has now more comforts than the farmer had a few generations ago. The farmer has more luxuries than the landlord had, and is more richly clad and better housed. The landlord has books and pictures rarer, and appointments more artistic, than the King could then obtain.

The price we pay for this salutary change is, no doubt, great. We assemble thousands of operatives in the factory, in the mine, and in the counting-house, of whom the employer can know little or nothing, and to whom the employer is little better than a myth. All intercourse between them is at an end. Rigid

Castes are formed, and, as usual, mutual ignorance breeds mutual distrust. Each Caste is without sympathy for the other, and ready to credit anything disparaging in regard to it. Under the law of competition, the employer of thousands is forced into the strictest economies, among which the rates paid to labor figure prominently, and often there is friction between the employer and the employed, between capital and labor, between rich and poor. Human society loses homogeneity.

The price which society pays for the law of competition, like the price it pays for cheap comforts and luxuries, is also great; but the advantages of this law are also greater still, for it is to this law that we owe our wonderful material development, which brings improved conditions in its train. But, whether the law be benign or not, we must say of it, as we say of the change in the conditions of men to which we have referred: It is here; we cannot evade it; no substitutes for it have been found; and while the law may be sometimes hard for the individual, it is best for the race, because it insures the survival of the fittest in every department. We accept and welcome, therefore, as conditions to which we must accommodate ourselves, great inequality of environment, the concentration of business, industrial and commercial, in the hands of a few, and the law of competition between these, as being not only beneficial, but essential for the future progress of the race. Having accepted these, it follows that there must be great scope for the exercise of special ability in the merchant and in the manufacturer who has to conduct affairs upon a great scale. That this talent for organization and management is rare among men is proved by the fact that it invariably secures for its possessor enormous rewards, no matter where or under what laws or conditions. The experienced in affairs always rate the MAN whose services can be obtained as a partner as not only the first consideration, but such as to render the question of his capital scarcely worth considering, for such men soon create capital; while, without the special talent required, capital soon takes wings. Such men become interested in firms or corporations using millions; and estimating only simple interest to be made upon the capital invested, it is inevitable that their income must exceed their expenditures, and that they must accumulate wealth. Nor is there any middle ground which such men can occupy, because the great manufacturing or commercial concern which does not earn at least interest upon its capital soon becomes bankrupt. It must either go forward or fall behind: to stand still is impossible. It is a condition essential for its successful operation that it should be thus far profitable, and even that, in addition to interest on capital, it should make profit. It is a law, as certain as any of the others named, that men possessed of this peculiar talent for affairs, under the free play of economic forces, must, of necessity, soon be in receipt of more revenue than can be judiciously expended upon themselves, and this law is as beneficial for the race as the others.

Objections to the foundations upon which society is based are not in order, because the condition of the race is better with these than it has been with any others which have been tried. Of the effect of any new substitutes proposed we cannot be sure. The Socialist or Anarchist who seeks to overturn present conditions is to be regarded as attacking the foundation upon which civilization itself rests, for civilization took its start from the day that the capable, industrious workman said to his incompetent and lazy fellow, "If thou dost not sow, thou shalt not reap," and thus ended primitive Communism by separating the drones from the bees. One who studies this subject will soon be brought face to face with the conclusion that upon the sacredness of property civilization itself depends—the right of the laborer to his hundred dollars in the savings bank, and equally the legal right of the millionaire to his millions. To those who propose to substitute Communism for this intense Individualism the answer, therefore, is: The race has tried that. All progress from that barbarous day to the present time has resulted from its displacement. Not evil, but good, has come to the race from the accumulation of wealth by those who have the ability and energy that produce it. But even if we admit for a moment that it might be better for the race to discard its present foundation, Individualism—that it is a nobler ideal that man should labor, not for himself alone, but in and for a brotherhood of his fellows, and share with them all in common, realizing Swedenborg's idea of Heaven, where, as he says, the angels derive their happiness, not from laboring for self, but for each other—even admit all this, and a sufficient answer is, This is not evolution, but revolution. It necessitates the changing of human nature itself—a work of aeons, even if it were good to change it, which we cannot know. It is not practicable in our day or in our age. Even if desirable theoretically, it belongs to another and long-succeeding sociological stratum. Our duty is with what is practicable now; with the next step possible in our day and generation. It is criminal to waste our energies in endeavoring to uproot, when all we can profitably or possibly accomplish is to bend the universal tree of humanity a little in the direction most favorable to the production of good fruit under existing circumstances. We might as well urge the destruction of the highest existing type of man because he failed to reach our ideal as to favor the destruction of Individualism, Private Property, the Law of Accumulation of Wealth, and the Law of Competition; for these are the highest results of human experience, the soil in which society so far has produced the best fruit. Unequally or unjustly, perhaps, as these laws sometimes operate, and imperfect as they appear to the Idealist, they are nevertheless, like the highest type of man, the best and most valuable of all that humanity has yet accomplished.

We start, then, with a condition of affairs under which the best interests of the race are promoted, but which inevitably gives wealth to the few. Thus far, accepting conditions as they exist, the situation can be surveyed and pronounced good. The question then arises—and, if the foregoing be correct, it is the only question with which we have to deal—What is the proper mode of administering wealth after the laws upon which civilization is founded have thrown it into the hands of the few? And it is of this great question that I believe I offer the true solution. It will be understood that *fortunes* are here spoken of, not moderate sums saved by many years of effort, the returns from which are required for the comfortable maintenance and education of families. This is not *wealth*, but only *competence*, which it should be the aim of all to acquire.

. . . Indeed, it is difficult to set bounds to the share of a rich man's estate which should go at his death to the public through the agency of the state, and by all means such taxes should be graduated, beginning at nothing upon moderate sums to dependents, and increasing rapidly as the amounts swell, until of the millionaire's hoard, as of Shylock's at least

> . . . The other half
> Comes to the privy coffer of the state.

This policy would work powerfully to induce the rich man to attend to the administration of wealth during his life, which is the end that society should always have in view, as being that by far most fruitful for the people. Nor need it be feared that this policy would sap the root of enterprise and render men less anxious to accumulate, for to the class whose ambition it is to leave great fortunes and be talked about after their death, it will attract more attention, and, indeed, be a somewhat nobler ambition to have enormous sums paid over to the state from their fortunes.

There remains, then, only one mode of using great fortunes; but in this we have the true antidote for the temporary unequal distribution of wealth, the reconciliation of the rich and the poor—a reign of harmony—another ideal, differing, indeed, from that of the Communist in requiring only the further evolution of existing conditions, not the total overthrow of our civilization. It is founded upon the present most intense individualism, and the race is prepared to put it in practice by degrees whenever it pleases. Under its sway we shall have an ideal state, in which the surplus wealth of the few will become, in the best sense, the property of the many, because administered for the common good, and this wealth, passing through the hands of the few, can be made a much more potent force for the elevation of our race than if it had been distributed in small sums to the people themselves. Even the poorest can be made to see this, and to agree that great sums gathered by some of their fellow-citizens and spent for public purposes, from which the masses reap the principal benefit, are more valuable to them than if scattered among them through the course of many years in trifling amounts.

The best uses to which surplus wealth can be put have already been indicated. Those who would administer wisely must, indeed, be wise, for one of the serious obstacles to the improvement of our race is indiscriminate charity. It were better for mankind that the millions of the rich were thrown into the sea than so spent as to encourage the slothful, the drunken, the unworthy. Of every thousand dollars spent in so called charity today, it is probable that $950 is unwisely spent; so spent, indeed, as to produce the very evils which it proposes to mitigate or cure. A well-known writer of philosophic books admitted the other day that he had given a quarter of a dollar to a man who approached him as he was coming to visit the house of his friend. He knew nothing of the habits of this beggar; knew not the use that would be made of this money, although he had every reason to suspect that it would be spent improperly. This man professed to be a disciple of Herbert Spencer, yet the quarter-dollar given that night will probably work more injury than all the money which its thoughtless donor will ever be able to give in true charity will do good. He only gratified his own feelings, saved himself from annoyance—and this was probably one of the most selfish and very worst actions of his life, for in all respects he is most worthy.

In bestowing charity, the main consideration should be to help those who will help themselves; to provide part of the means by which those who desire to improve may do so; to give those who desire to rise the aids by which they may rise; to assist, but rarely or never to do all. Neither the individual nor the race is improved by alms-giving. Those worthy of assistance, except in rare cases, seldom require assistance. The really valuable men of the race never do, except in cases of accident or sudden change. Every one has, of course, cases of individuals brought to his own knowledge where temporary assistance can do genuine good, and these he will not overlook. But the amount which can be wisely given by the individual for individuals is necessarily limited by his lack of knowledge of the circumstances connected with each. He is the only true reformer who is as careful and an anxious not to aid the unworthy as he

is to aid the worthy, and perhaps, even more so, for in alms-giving more injury is probably done by rewarding vice then by relieving virtue.

Thus is the problem of Rich and Poor to be solved. The laws of accumulation will be left free; the laws of distribution free. Individualism will continue, but the millionaire will be but a trustee for the poor; intrusted for a season with a great part of the increased wealth of the community, but administrating it for the community far better than it could or would have done for itself. The best minds will thus have reached a stage in the development of the race in which it is clearly seen that there is no mode of disposing of surplus wealth creditable to thoughtful and earnest men into whose hands it flows save by using it year by year for the general good. This day already dawns. But a little while, and although, without incurring the pity of their fellows, men may die sharers in great business enterprises from which their capital cannot be or has not been withdrawn, and is left chiefly at death for public uses, yet the man who dies leaving behind him millions of available wealth, which was his to administer during life, will pass away "unwept, unhonored, and unsung," no matter to what uses he leaves the dross which he cannot take with him. Of such as these the public verdict will then be: "The man who dies thus rich dies disgraced."

Such, in my opinion, is the true Gospel concerning Wealth, obedience to which is destined some day to solve the problems of the Rich and the Poor, and to bring "Peace on earth, among men Good-Will."

QUESTIONS

1. What is the "proper administration" of wealth? Is it being properly administered today?

2. What is the "one mode" of using great fortunes? How should the problem of "rich and poor" be solved?

3. Do you agree with Carnegie's idea that the wealthy should only help those who will help themselves?

Solomon Schimmel | Greed

Solomon Schimmel wrote the book (or, at any rate, one of them) on the seven deadly sins. Here he presents a scholarly look at greed, the vice most tempting and prevalent in business life.

If money be not thy servant, it will be thy master. The covetous man cannot so properly be said to possess wealth, as that may be said to possess him.
—Francis Bacon

In 1990 Congress passed a law that provided for life imprisonment for certain financial crimes in recognition of the social damage and danger of greed gone amok. This law was a reaction to public anger at the Savings and Loan scandal of the 1980s in which avaricious bankers, lawyers, and accountants, seeking easy riches, fraudulently deprived thousands of Americans of their savings, causing immeasurable suffering. The greed of the 1980s brought with it a surge in criminal and unethical schemes, such as insider trading on the stock market, company takeovers that resulted in massive layoffs followed by bankruptcies, and scientific fraud. Greed inflicted catastrophe on many innocent victims, and its adverse social consequences will be felt for many years.

This should come as no surprise, since the pursuit of wealth is a dominant value in our society. The media feature adulatory stories about thirty-year-old multimillionaires who have achieved their college goal of amassing a fortune within a decade of graduation. Rarely do journalists who revel in the rich ask whether such a goal is commendable, at what psychological or spiritual cost it was achieved, if ruthless or immoral means were used, and what "good" will be done with all of this wealth. Our constitution guarantees the freedom to pursue happiness and our capitalist ethos simplistically equates freedom with lack of restraint and happiness with wealth.

The premise is that unrestrained pursuit of wealth will eventually make us happier, because the more money we accrue the happier we will be. But in so worshipping money, placing our hope and trust in it—a form of idolatry—we blind ourselves to the social and personal costs of greed. The assumption that greed is good and that riches guarantee satisfying lives is false, and the teachings of the moralists about the sin of avarice illuminate why.

Greed (also known as avarice and covetousness) manifests itself in many ways. The cutthroat competitor, the workaholic, the swindler, the miser, and the gambler are all greedy. Sometimes even the spendthrift is guilty of greed. Basically, greed is the inordinate love of money and of material possessions, and the dedication of oneself to their pursuit. This love of money is fed by other vices and leads to many evils. In trying to satisfy greed we can injure ourselves and others, psychologically and physically. This is the paradox of greed—though its aim is to increase our pleasure through the purchase of goods and services, it often does so at the expense of pleasure and happiness.

———

A patient of mine provides an example of this. He hadn't taken a much-needed vacation for years although he could easily have afforded to do so. He could never get himself to spend a substantial sum of money on either himself or his wife. He was always complaining that airlines and hotels overcharge, and maintained that he enjoyed staying at home. It was quite obvious, though, that for his emotional health and for his wife's sake they needed to get away from the monotonous routine and pressures of their regular environment. The truth was that he found it extremely difficult to part with money, particularly for a nontangible asset. Things that were touchable could be assigned some money-equivalent value, so he was

From *The Seven Deadly Sins* (New York: Oxford University Press, 1997).

able to exchange money for them and buy a VCR or a new car. But the scenic beauty of nature, the enhanced intimacy and love that a tranquil getaway with his wife would facilitate, were, to him, ephemeral intangibles that were no substitute for money. This man's stinginess nearly cost him his marriage.

Another of my clients had been successfully immersed in the frenzied greed of the financial markets' subculture of the 1980s. By day he was a workaholic, by night a hedonist. He came to see me because he was unhappy with what he was doing with his life and with what his life was doing to him. He was wise and sensitive enough to realize that his money wasn't making him happy, and that the moral and spiritual values he once cherished were being eroded by his pursuit of wealth and pleasure. Yet he found it difficult to rectify the situation as long as he remained in the environment which supported it. After a period of sustained honest reflection about what he felt he would want to be remembered for if he were to die suddenly, he concluded that it wasn't his financial success or the gratifications of his body that his money bought. He decided to make a dramatic rupture with his present. He moved to a farm in rural Vermont where he now lives a life of material simplicity. He uses his business and organizational skills to consult with local government on projects to improve the lot of the rural poor. Although he earns only a small fraction of what he once did and lives more modestly, he is a much happier person than he

ever was in the heyday of his high-flying life-style. Nor does he miss the wealth of earlier times, now that he has adapted to the less that is really more. As Epicurus put it, wealth consists not in having great possessions but in having few wants.

Although greed is a cause of much unhappiness, there are few contemporary therapies for it since it is rarely perceived as undesirable. Only when it results in criminal behavior or in extreme disruption of personal or family life is some intervention deemed necessary. The courts will punish crimes that result from greed and therapists will treat an inveterate gambler or a high-powered executive whose drive for financial success produces intolerable stress or physical illness. For the most part, though, society encourages greed, although euphemisms are usually used when doing so, such as "financial success," "economic security," "the good life," or "having it all." This avoidance of the word *greed* reflects our ambivalence about greed because we know that it is essentially selfish and that when practiced to an extreme it can be very dangerous, leading even to murder.

QUESTIONS

1. Can greed be "good" (as Gordon Gecko argued)? Why or why not?
2. How may greed be a source of unhappiness?
3. Does greed encourage other vices in people? If so, which ones?

Joanne B. Ciulla | # Leisure and Consumption

Leisure is a special experience. It consists of activities that are freely chosen and good in themselves. Listening to music for pure enjoyment is one such pursuit. Aristotle believed that leisure was necessary for human happiness. Most people today think that we

From *The Working Life* (New York: Random House, 2001).

conduct business so that we can make money and buy things. And some trade time for leisure so that they can buy more things. Aristotle said we conduct business (or are "unleisurely") so that we can have leisure. Leisure brings out what is best and most distinctive about being human—our abilities to think, feel, reflect, create, and learn. We need leisure to develop wisdom.

The word for leisure in Greek is *skolé*; in Latin it is *otium*. In both languages the word for work is simply the negation of the word for leisure; *ascholia* and *negotium* both mean "not leisure." This is also true in Spanish. Today *negocio*, the word for business, means "no leisure." Greek, Latin, and Spanish words compare work to leisure as if to say that leisure is the center of life. The English word *leisure* comes from the Latin *licere*, which means "to be permitted." Our language compares leisure to work as if to say that work is the norm of life and leisure is when we are "permitted" to stop working. The British essayist and self-confessed workaholic G. K. Chesterton wrote there are three parts to leisure: "The first is being allowed to do something. The second is being allowed to do anything and the third (and perhaps most rare and precious) is being allowed to do nothing."[1] [Chesterton]

In his book *Of Time, Work, and Leisure*, sociologist Sebastian de Grazia observed that although work can ennoble us, wear us down, or make us rich, it is leisure that perfects us as human beings. Writing in 1962, de Grazia applied Aristotle's notion of leisure to the twentieth century. He wrote, "Leisure and free time live in two different worlds. . . ." Free time refers to a special way of calculating a special kind of time. Leisure refers to a state of being, a condition of man."[2] [de Grazia] It is a frame of mind or attitude of imaginative people who love ideas. Until World War I, educated Virginians defined a Yankee as a person who didn't understand how to use his leisure. For de Grazia, leisure is a special intellectual state that few people are capable of having. It is more than simply organized activities, amusements, relaxation, and free time.

The idea that leisure is something that only a few people attain leaves us to wonder: Is leisure elitist, or do people like Aristotle and de Grazia take an elitist view of leisure? After all, who are they to make judgments on what is and is not leisure? Besides eating, sleeping, procreating, and getting ready for work, how we use our free time is a highly personal matter. Class, taste, income, education, and personal preference certainly influence what we choose to do. Just as there is a pecking order

in work there is also one outside of it. Golfers look down on bowlers, tennis players look down on golfers, opera lovers sneer at soap opera fans, *New York Times* readers condescend to *National Enquirer* readers, Bloomingdale's shoppers scorn Wal-Mart shoppers. The prosperous and better-educated think (and have always thought) that their leisure pursuits are more enriching and self-fulfilling than those of the poor and the working class. But there are larger questions behind de Grazia's and Aristotle's discussions of leisure that get to the heart of how people experience life. Before we move to these questions, however, we need to look at the relationship of work to the way we spend our free time.

WORK AND AMUSEMENTS

The Reformation, with its emphasis on work, did its best to make Sunday a boring day. Luther got rid of the saints and their holidays. The Protestants associated work with virtue and hence leisure with vice. In the Middle Ages holidays were times for music, dancing, and drinking, but later, in Protestant countries, they became days for silence and meditation. In the 1640s the Puritans, who dominated the British Parliament, banned all Christmas festivities and enjoyments, including plum pudding and mince pie. In our own times, starting in the 1980s all workers began to lose holidays and paid vacation time, and some managers began acting like Scrooge on Christmas. In 1986, when Christmas fell on a Thursday, 46 percent of employers gave workers Friday off. In 1997, when Christmas fell on a Thursday, only 36 percent did. Holidays are more than days off; they are supposed to be public celebrations. But the public can't celebrate together if most people are working.

According to de Grazia, businesspeople liked the idea of making Sunday a dismal bore because that would make work more desirable.[3] If leisure were too rewarding and too much fun, people wouldn't want to go back to work. But the Protestants and employers were probably more concerned about amusements than leisure. *The Oxford English Dictionary* defines an amusement as a pleasurable occupation that distracts or diverts attention from something.

In Praise of Idleness
Bertrand Russell

Like most of my generation, I was brought up on the saying "Satan finds some mischief still for idle hands to do." Being a highly virtuous child, I believed all that I was told, and acquired a conscience which has kept me working hard down to the present moment. But although my conscience has controlled my actions, my opinions have undergone a revolution. I think that there is far too much work done in the world, that immense harm is caused by the belief that work is virtuous, and that what needs to be preached in modern industrial countries is quite different from what always has been preached. . . .

The wise use of leisure, it must be conceded, is a product of civilization and education. A man who has worked long hours all his life will be bored if he becomes suddenly idle. But without a considerable amount of leisure a man is cut off from many of the best things. There is no longer any reason why the bulk of the population should suffer this deprivation; only a foolish asceticism, usually vicarious, makes us continue to insist on work in excessive quantities now that the need no longer exists.

It will be said that, while a little leisure is pleasant, men would not know how to fill their days if they had only four hours of work out of the twenty-four. In so far as this is true in the modern world, it is a condemnation of our civilization; it would not have been true at any earlier period. There was formerly a capacity for light-heartedness and play which has been to some extent inhibited by the cult of efficiency. The modern man thinks that everything ought to be done for the sake of something else, and never for its own sake.

From *In Praise of Idleness.*

Interestingly, it comes from the word *muse*, which in this context means to be "affected with astonishment" or to be put into a "stupid stare."[4]

In the industrial era the English took legal measures to repress popular amusements in order to develop conduct suitable for work discipline. The Poor Law Amendment Act of 1834 wiped out the infrastructure of working-class entertainment. By restricting people to their parishes, the law effectively got rid of traveling balladeers, entertainers, and itinerant salesmen. The 1835 Highways Act forbade all street "nuisances," including soccer players, street entertainers, and traders. In the same year the Cruelty to Animals Act outlawed activities such as cockfights, but allowed fox hunting and other aristocratic pursuits. Working-class amusements moved off the streets and into pubs, which began providing various forms of entertainment to their customers. America never took such harsh legal measures except during the Prohibition years. Supporters of Prohibition argued that a shorter workweek would surely lead to more drinking.

At the turn of the century, employers opposed giving Saturday off because they claimed that their employees would only get into trouble. For example, in the early 1900s a Massachusetts firm required workers who were unwilling to attend church to stay indoors and "improve their time" by reading, writing, or performing other valuable duties. Mill owners of the time forbade drinking and gambling and justified the twelve-hour day and six-day week as means of keeping workers from vicious amusements. This was not a totally unfounded fear. As mentioned earlier, workers in the early industrial days of England often used their leisure time to drink, fight, and bet on animal contests, such as cockfights.

In early twentieth-century America, millions of workingmen spent their free time in bars and union clubs. There were more than ten thousand saloons in New York in 1900. In *Cheap Amusements*, Kathy Peiss estimates that workingmen in New York spent about 10 percent of their weekly income on personal expenses, the bulk of which were for beer and liquor, tobacco, and movie and theater tickets. An extensive study of workingmen's leisure found that married men spent half of their free time with their families. Workingmen felt that their work gave them a "right" to amusements after work—"I worked for someone else all day and now I deserve to have someone or something work to entertain me."[5]

Married women did not start going out for entertainment in great numbers until after the invention of the nickelodeon in 1905. When young women found job opportunities outside domestic labor, they flocked to work in industry, department stores, and restaurants. Having grown up seeing their mothers work from dawn to dusk and observing domestic servants work twelve-to-fourteen-hour days, they too felt they had a "right" to outside entertainment. Working-women who loved to party were called "rowdy girls" in the Victorian era. They relished the freedom of going out with their friends, dancing, and socializing in mixed company. A manager from Macy's complained that young girls went out dancing on week-nights and came in exhausted for work the next day. Women also integrated amusements into their work. Female factory workers practiced the latest dance steps outside the factory during their breaks. Female cigar rollers insisted on having someone read the newspaper to them while they worked. Women became very protective of their work hours and filed grievances when asked to work overtime or when detained after closing time. Women workers were largely responsible for getting the workweek shortened for all workers. The more women worked by the clock outside the home the more they too felt

entitled to a good time—something to distract them or take them away from work. Life became more segmented into bouts of uninterrupted work and bouts of amusement.

Not only did employers worry about the effects of workers' leisure on job performance, they had misgivings about what might happen when employees socialized together outside work. Union halls were just one form of association. Groupings of nonunion workers were also a threat because they gave employees ample time to bond and discuss working conditions and complaints, providing a fertile field for union organization.

In 1914 Henry Ford established a sociological department in his company. The department's mission was to supervise workers' lives so that they would be thrifty, industrious producers. They urged employees not to smoke and drink. Today's reformers who want to control sex and violence on TV, cigarettes, drugs, and alcohol face an uphill battle. If people like to engage in these activities during their free time, they will until they find—or the market offers them—alternatives they like more.

TRADING LEISURE FOR CONSUMPTION

In 1970 economist Steffan Linder published *The Harried Leisure Class*. In it he argued that in affluent societies, when people have to choose between more free time and more spending, most choose more spending. That is why he believed that an increase in income is not necessarily an increase in prosperity. In 1986, for example, Americans spent more than thirteen billion dollars on sports clothing, which meant that they traded 1.3 billion hours of potential leisure time for leisure clothing.[6] Spending money takes time—time to make the money, time to shop, and time to enjoy the things the money buys, such as cabin cruisers, package tours, and the like. Americans not only have less vacation time than Europeans, but they spend three to four times as many hours shopping as Europeans do.

Consumption ties a tighter knot between work and free time than any of the schemes of reformers, employers, or governments. William H. Whyte was right to be concerned about the organization man's shallow roots in the community and deep roots in the organization. What he didn't calculate was the way that consumerism and credit reinforce the grip of work on people. Consumption creates a *need* to work even when the desire to work is weak. However, it can also make work feel more burdensome. The market tempts people with more leisure options than they can afford or have time to enjoy. We wish we didn't have to work so that we could enjoy what the market has to offer us in terms of toys, vacations, and other amusements—all of which cost money.

Even teenagers trade their leisure for consumption. In the past, teens often had to work to help their families or pay for college. Some still do, but now a growing number of middle-class teens work to buy luxury items for themselves. As we have seen, generations of Americans have encouraged young people to work, in the belief that it keeps them out of trouble and develops discipline. In a 1986 study, researchers Ellen Greenberger and Laurence Steinberg came to a radically different conclusion about work and teenagers. They found that teens often get into more trouble when they work too much than they do during free time. This is because they suffer the stress of work and school and they have the money to buy drugs and alcohol. But most interestingly, Greenberger and Steinberg also suggest that too much work not only interferes with teens' school-work but can cause an "adjusted blandness" at a time when they should be curious, imaginative, and combative.[7] This "adjusted blandness" is exemplified by the routine "have a nice day" patter of counter workers in fast-food restaurants. Greenberger and Steinberg think that this is unhealthy.

At first their argument seems to go against the Protestant work ethic. But Greenberger and Steinberg maintain that instead of fostering respect for work, teenage employment often leads to increased cynicism about the ability of work to provide any personal satisfaction beyond a paycheck, since teens often work in menial jobs. They ask us to consider the image of a sixteen-year-old boy, who comes home from a long afternoon of work in a fast-food restaurant, downs a few beers, and thinks to himself, "People who work harder at their jobs than they have to are a little bit crazy."[8] Work is "bogus"—you do the minimum necessary to get paid.

Other researchers believe that the social meaning of work determines whether work is good or bad for teens. In 1993 J. Schulenberg and J. G. Bachman found that teens suffered when they worked *only* for the money, for long periods of time, at boring jobs that were unconnected to future work. A study conducted by H. W. Marsh in 1991 indicated that when teens were working to save money for college, their grades improved, even when the teens had boring jobs. When teens worked to buy extras such as cars and CD players for themselves, their grades went down, regardless of the job.[9] During the Depression era, similar studies showed the beneficial value of any kind of work for young people who contributed to the support of their families at a time of crisis. The young people gained self-confidence and a sense of efficacy from helping to care for their families.

These studies on teens offer an insight into how the meaning of work changes when teens conform to the demands of the workplace in order to conform to the desires elicited in the marketplace. Sometimes the reasons *why* we work are more important than the work we actually do. The experience of working to support a family or go to college may well be more satisfying than working for clothing and CD players, because the goals themselves are more lasting and meaningful. Nonetheless, many would still argue that it is better for young people to earn money to buy what they want than to have it given to them.

When teens substitute consumer goods for leisure, they get caught up in the work-and-spend pattern of their parents and something is lost. If they give up their free time so that they can make money to buy things, they don't have the leisure to discover what they like to do. They don't have the time to discover what activities they find intrinsically good. Far from fearing it (as parents and others in authority do), there is something to be said for doing nothing and hanging out with one's friends. While there may be the potential for trouble, there is also the potential to learn how to enjoy life on one's own terms and not those of the consumer market.

Of course, critics of consumerism and materialist values are legion. Somewhere in every major world religion is a warning about the dangers of the unfettered desire for material objects. We noted earlier that most of the seven deadly sins concern desire for material things. Nonetheless, many economists and businesspeople are cheered by the fact that consumer demand is insatiable. In *Social Limits to Growth*, Fred Hirsch wrote that the satisfaction that people derive from goods and services doesn't depend on their own consumption, but on the consumption of others, or "keeping up with the Joneses," which makes desire limitless. Juliet Schor's recent book *The Overspent American* picks up where Hirsch left off in his 1976 work. She argues that in the past our neighbors ("the Joneses") set the standard for what we wanted and thought we should buy. Today, she says, people often don't know their neighbors, and they compare what they own and want to own against the standards set by a wider range of people, such as those at work, on TV, in advertisements, and elsewhere. When we kept up with the Joneses, we kept up with people who had similar incomes. When we try to keep up with people at work or in the news, we may be trying to keep up with people who make many times more than we do.[10] This draws one into a seamless cycle of spending, debt, and longer working hours. Schor tells us that people who had been sucked into this cycle, "increasingly looked to consumption to give satisfaction, even meaning to their lives."[11]

NOTES

1. C.K. Chesterton, "On Leisure," *Generally Speaking*, (London: 1928), p. 130.

2. Sebastian de Grazia, *Of Time Work and Leisure* (New York: Twentieth Century Fund, 1962), p. 7.

3. Ibid. pp. 202–203.

4. *The Compact Oxford English Dictionary*, new edition (Oxford: Clarendon Press, 1991), p. 421.

5. Kathy Peiss, *Cheap Amusements* (Philadelphia: Temple University Press, 1986), pp. 17–23.

6. Witold Rybczynski, *Waiting for the Weekend* (New York: Viking Penguin, 1991), p. 219.

7. Ellen Greenberger & Laurence Steinberg, *When Teenagers Work* (New York: Basic Books, 1960), pp. 6–8.

8. Ibid. p. 173.

9. See Jeylan T. Mortimer and Michael D. Finch, "Work, Family, and Adolesant Development," in eds. Jeylan T. Mortimer and Michael D. Finch, *Adolescents, Work, and Family* (Thousand Oaks, CA: Sage Publications, 1996), pp. 9–10.

10. Juliet Schor, *The Overspent American* (New York: Basic Books, 1998), p. 4.

11. Ibid. p. 112.

QUESTIONS

1. Explain Ciulla's concept of "amusement." When did it arise, and why?

2. Why do we trade leisure for consumption? Is it a good idea to do so? Why or why not? What about "slackers"?

3. Reflect on your leisure activities. Which ones cost money and which ones are free? Is shopping a leisure activity? Why or why not?

Lynne McFall | # Integrity

Lynne McFall has a Ph.D. in philosophy and is a novelist. She is author of *The One True Story of the World*.

Olaf (upon what were once knees)
does almost ceaselessly repeat
"there is some shit I will not eat"
                                        —*e. e. cummings*

COHERENCE

Integrity is the state of being "undivided; an integral whole." What sort of coherence is at issue here? I think there are several.

One kind of coherence is simple consistency: consistency within one's set of principles or commitments. One cannot maintain one's integrity if one has unconditional commitments that conflict, for example, justice and personal happiness, or conditional commitments that cannot be ranked, for example, truth telling and kindness.

Another kind of coherence is coherence between principle and action. Integrity requires "sticking to one's principles," moral or otherwise, in the face of temptation, including the temptation to redescription.

Take the case of a woman with a commitment to marital fidelity. She is attracted to a man who is not her husband, and she is tempted. Suppose, for the purity of the example, that he wants her too but will do nothing to further the affair; the choice is hers. Now imagine your own favorite scene of seduction.

After the fact, she has two options. (There are always these two options, which makes the distinction between changing one's mind and weakness of the will problematic, but assume that this is a clear case.) She can (1) admit to having lost the courage of her convictions (retaining the courage of her mistakes) or (2) rewrite her principles in various ways (e.g., by making fidelity a general principle, with

exceptions, or by retroactively canceling her "subscription"). Suppose she chooses the latter. Whatever she may have gained, she has lost some integrity. Weakness of the will is one contrary of integrity. Self-deception is another. A person who admits to having succumbed to temptation has more integrity than the person who sells out, then fixes the books, but both suffer its loss.

A different sort of incoherence is exhibited in the case where someone does the right thing for (what he takes to be) the wrong reason. For example, in Dostoevsky's *The Devils*, Stepan Verkhovensky says, "All my life I've been lying. Even when I spoke the truth. I never spoke for the sake of the truth, but for my own sake." Coherence between principle and action is necessary but not sufficient. One's action might *correspond* with one's principle, at some general level of description, but be inconsistent with that principle more fully specified. If one values not just honesty but honesty for its own sake, then honesty motivated by self-interest is not enough for integrity.

So the requirement of coherence is fairly complicated. In addition to simple consistency, it puts constraints on the way in which one's principles may be held (the "first-person" requirement), on how one may act given one's principles (coherence between principle and action), and on how one may be motivated in acting on them (coherence between principle and motivation). Call this *internal coherence.* . . .

To summarize the argument so far: personal integrity requires that an agent (1) subscribe to some consistent set of principles or commitments and (2), in the face of temptation or challenge, (3) uphold these principles or commitments, (4) for what the agent takes to be the right reasons.

These conditions are rather formal. Are there no constraints on the *content* of the principles or commitments a person of integrity may hold?

From *Ethics* 9 (Oct 1987), pp. 11–16. Reprinted with permission.

INTEGRITY AND IMPORTANCE

Consider the following statements:

> Sally is a person of principle: pleasure.
>
> Harold demonstrates great integrity in his single-minded pursuit of approval.
>
> John was a man of uncommon integrity. He let nothing—not friendship, not justice, not truth—stand in the way of his amassment of wealth.

That none of these claims can be made with a straight face suggests that integrity is inconsistent with such principles.

A person of integrity is willing to bear the consequences of her convictions, even when this is difficult, that is, when the consequences are unpleasant. A person whose only principle is "Seek my own pleasure" is not a candidate for integrity because there is no possibility of conflict—between pleasure and principle—in which integrity could be lost. Where there is no possibility of its loss, integrity cannot exist.

Similarly in the case of the approval seeker. The single-minded pursuit of approval is inconsistent with integrity. Someone who is describable as an egg sucker, brownnose, fawning flatterer cannot have integrity, whatever he may think of the merits of such behavior. A commitment to spinelessness does not vitiate its spinelessness—another of integrity's contraries.

The same may be said for the ruthless seeker of wealth. A person whose only aim is to increase his bank balance is a person for whom nothing is ruled out: duplicity, theft, murder. Expedience is *contrasted* to a life of principle, so an ascription of integrity is out of place. Like the pleasure seeker and the approval seeker, he lacks a "core," the kind of commitments that give a person character and that makes a loss of integrity possible. In order to sell one's soul, one must have something to sell. . . .

Most of us, when tempted to "sell out," are tempted by pleasure, approval, money, status, or personal gain of some other sort. The political prisoner under the thumbscrew wants relief, however committed he may be to the revolution. Less dramatically, most of us want the good opinion of others and a decent standard of living. Self-interest in these forms is a legitimate aim against which we weigh our other concerns. But most of us have other, "higher" commitments, and so those who honor most what we would resist are especially liable to scorn.

This tendency to objectify our own values in the name of personal integrity can best be seen, I think, in a more neutral case. Consider the following claim:

> The connoisseur showed real integrity in preferring the Montrachet to the Mountain Dew.

Even if he was sorely tempted to guzzle the Mountain Dew and forbore only with the greatest difficulty, the connoisseur, we would say, did not show integrity in preferring the better wine. Why? Resisting temptation is not the only test of integrity; the challenge must be to something *important*. . . .

One may die for beauty, truth, justice, the objection might continue, but not for Montrachet. Wine is not that important. . . .

When we grant integrity to a person, we need not *approve* of his or her principles or commitments, but we must at least recognize them as ones a reasonable person might take to be of great importance and ones that a reasonable person might be tempted to sacrifice to some lesser yet still recognizable goods. It may not be possible to spell out these conditions without circularity, but that this is what underlies our judgments of integrity seems clear enough. Integrity is a personal virtue granted with social strings attached. By definition, it precludes "expediency, artificiality, or shallowness of any kind." The pleasure seeker is guilty of shallowness, the approval seeker of artificiality, and the profit seeker of expedience of the worst sort. . . .

INTEGRITY, FRIENDSHIP, AND THE OLAF PRINCIPLE

An attitude essential to the notion of integrity is that there are some things that one is not prepared to do, or some things one *must* do. I shall call this the "Olaf Principle," in honor of e. e. cummings's poem about Olaf, the "conscientious objector." This principle requires that some of one's commitments be unconditional.

In what sense?

There are, in ordinary moral thought, expressions of the necessity or impossibility of certain actions or types of actions that do not neatly correspond to the notions of necessity and impossibility most often catalogued by moral theorists. "I *must* stand by my friend (or "I *cannot* let him down") may have no claim to logical, psychological, rational, or moral necessity in any familiar sense. There is nothing logically inconsistent in the betrayal of friendship, or one could never be guilty of it. It is not psychologically impossible, since many have in fact done it and survived to do it again. Rationality does not require unconditional allegiance, without some additional assumptions, for one may have better reason to do a conflicting action, for example, where the choice is between betraying a friend and betraying one's country (although I am sympathetic to E. M. Forster's famous statement to the contrary). Nor is the necessity expressed one that has a claim to universality, for different persons may have different unconditional commitments. Impartiality and absoluteness are not what is at stake, for the choice may be between a friend and ten innocent strangers, and one person may have different unconditional commitments at different times. It is not clear, then, what sense of *unconditional commitment* is at issue.

Unless corrupted by philosophy, we all have things we think we would never do, under any imaginable circumstances, whatever we may give to survival or pleasure, power and the approval of strangers; some part of ourselves beyond which we will not retreat, some weakness however prevalent in others that we will not tolerate in ourselves. And if we do that thing, betray that weakness, we are not the persons we thought; there is nothing left that we may even in spite refer to as *I*.

I think it is in this sense that some commitments must be unconditional: they are conditions of continuing as ourselves.

Suppose, for example, that I take both friendship and professional advancement to be great goods, and my best friend and I are candidates for a promotion. Suppose, too, that I know the person who has the final decision has an unreasoned hatred of people who drink more than is socially required, as my friend does. I let this be known, not directly of course, with the predictable result that I am given the promotion.

Now in one sense I have not done anything dishonest. My friend may be the first to admit the pleasure he takes in alcohol. It may even be one of the reasons I value his friendship. (Loyal drinking companions are not easy to come by.) But this is clearly a betrayal of friendship. Is it so obviously a failure of integrity?

In *any* conflict between two great goods, I may argue, one must be "betrayed." And between you and me, I choose me.

What is wrong with this defense?

To beat someone out of a job by spreading vicious truths is proof that I am no friend. It is in the nature of friendship that one cannot intentionally hurt a friend in order to further one's own interests. So if I claim to be this person's friend, then I am guilty of incoherence, and therefore lack integrity.

Why does incoherence seem the wrong charge to make? The answer, I think, is that it is much too weak.

Some of our principles or commitments are more important to us than others. Those that can be sacrificed without remorse may be called *defeasible* commitments. For many of us, professional success is an important but defeasible commitment. I would like to be a successful philosopher, esteemed by my colleagues and widely published, but neither success nor failure will change my sense of personal worth.

Contrasted to defeasible commitments are *identity-conferring* commitments: they reflect what we take to be most important and so determine, to large extent, our (moral) identities. . . .

For many of us, friendship is an identity-conferring commitment. If we betrayed a friend in order to advance our careers, we could not "live with" ourselves; we would not be the persons we thought we were. This is what it means to have a "core": a set of principles or commitments that makes us who we are. Such principles cannot be justified by reference to other values, because they are the most fundamental commitments we have; they determine what, for us, is to *count* as a reason. . . .

QUESTIONS

1. What is the "Olaf principle"?
2. What does personal integrity require, according to McFall?
3. Why does McFall say that integrity is about more than resisting temptation?

Bertrand Russell | # Impersonal Interests

Bertrand Russell was one of the great philosophers, logicians, and moralists of the twentieth century. This is one of his many musings from *The Conquest of Happiness*.

I wish to consider not those major interests about which a man's life is built, but those minor interests which fill his leisure and afford relaxation from the tenseness of his more serious preoccupations. In the life of the average man his wife and children, his work and his financial position occupy the main part of his anxious and serious thought. Even if he has extra-matrimonial love affairs, they probably do not concern him as profoundly in themselves as in their possible effects upon his home life. The interests which are bound up with his work I am not for the present regarding as impersonal interests. A man of science, for example, must keep abreast of research in his own line. Towards such research his feelings have the warmth and vividness belonging to something intimately concerned with his career, but if he reads about research in some quite other science with which he is not professionally concerned he reads in quite a different spirit, not professionally, less critically, more disinterestedly. Even if he has to use his mind in order to follow what is said, his reading is nevertheless a relaxation, because it is not connected with his responsibilities. If the book interests him, his interest is impersonal in a sense which cannot be applied to the books upon his own subject. It is such interests lying outside the main activities of a man's life that I wish to speak about in the present chapter.

One of the sources of unhappiness, fatigue and nervous strain is inability to be interested in anything that is not of practical importance in one's own life. The result of this is that the conscious mind gets no rest from a certain small number of matters, each of which probably involves some anxiety and some element of worry. Except in sleep the conscious mind is never allowed to lie fallow while subconscious thought matures its gradual wisdom. The result is excitability, lack of sagacity, irritability, and a loss of sense of proportion. All these are both causes and effects of fatigue. As a man gets more tired, his external interests fade, and as they fade he loses the relief which they afford him and becomes still more tired. This vicious circle is only too apt to end in a breakdown. What is restful about external interests is the fact that they do not call for any action. Making decisions and exercising volition are very fatiguing, especially if they have to be done hurriedly and without the help of the subconscious. Men who feel that they must "sleep on it" before coming to an important decision are profoundly right. But it is not only in sleep that the subconscious mental processes can work. They can work also while a man's conscious mind is occupied elsewhere. The man who can forget his work when it is over and not remember it until it begins again next day is likely to do his work far better than the man who worries about it throughout the intervening hours. And it is very much easier to forget work at the times when it ought to be forgotten if a man has many interests other than his work than it is if he has not. It is, however, essential that these interests should not exercise those very faculties which have been exhausted by his day's work. They should not involve will and quick decision, they should not, like gambling, involve any financial element, and they should as a rule not be so exciting as to produce emotional fatigue and preoccupy the subconscious as well as the conscious mind.

A great many amusements fulfill all these conditions. Watching games, going to the theater, playing golf, are all irreproachable from this point of view. For a man of a bookish turn of mind reading unconnected with his professional activities is very satisfactory. However important a worry may be, it

From Bertrand Russell, *The Conquest of Happiness* (New York: Viking 1936), pp. 36–40.

should not be thought about throughout the whole of the waking hours. . . .

All impersonal interests, apart from their importance as relaxation, have various other uses. To begin with, they help a man to retain his sense of proportion. It is very easy to become so absorbed in our own pursuits, our own circle, our own type of work, that we forget how small a part this is of the total of human activity and how many things in the world are entirely unaffected by what we do. Why should one remember this? you may ask. There are several answers. In the first place, it is good to have as true a picture of the world as is compatible with necessary activities. Each of us is in the world for no very long time, and within the few years of his life has to acquire whatever he is to know of this strange planet and its place in the universe. To ignore our opportunities for knowledge, imperfect as they are, is like going to the theater and not listening to the play. The world is full of things that are tragic or comic, heroic or bizarre or surprising, and those who fail to be interested in the spectacle that it offers are forgoing one of the privileges that life has to offer.

Then again a sense of proportion is very valuable and at times very consoling. We are all inclined to get unduly excited, unduly strained, unduly impressed with the importance of the little corner of the world in which we live, and of the little moment of time comprised between our birth and death. In this excitement and overestimation of our own importance there is nothing desirable. True, it may make us work harder, but it will not make us work better. A little work directed to a good end is better than a great deal of work directed to a bad end, though the apostles of the strenuous life seem to think otherwise. Those who care much for their work are always in danger of falling into fanaticism, which consists essentially in remembering one or two desirable things while forgetting all the rest, and in supposing that in the pursuit of these one or two any incidental harm of other sorts is of little account. Against this fanatical temper there is no better prophylactic than a large conception of the life of man and his place in the universe. This may seem a very big thing to invoke in such a connection, but apart from this particular use, it is in itself a thing of great value. . . .

A man who has once perceived, however temporarily and however briefly, what makes greatness of soul, can no longer be happy if he allows himself to be petty, self-seeking, troubled by trivial misfortunes, dreading what fate may have in store for him. The man capable of greatness of soul will open wide the windows of his mind, letting the winds blow freely upon it from every portion of the universe. He will see himself and life and the world as truly as our human limitations will permit; realizing the brevity and minuteness of human life, he will realize also that in individual minds is concentrated whatever of value the known universe contains. And he will see that the man whose mind mirrors the world becomes in a sense as great as the world. In emancipation from the fears that beset the slave of circumstance he will experience a profound joy, and through all the vicissitudes of his outward life he will remain in the depths of his being a happy man. . . .

QUESTIONS

1. How do impersonal interests help us?
2. What is happiness, for Russell? How does it relate to "greatness of soul"?
3. How are impersonal interests different from activities such as watching TV? How is watching TV different from going to the theater to watch a play?

CASES

CASE 3.1
The Opportunist
James Fenimore Cooper

James Fenimore Cooper is the author of such American classics as *The Deerslayer* and *The Last of the Mohicans*. This short story is from his collection, *Home as Found*.

The service at Mr. Effingham's table was made in the quiet but thorough manner that distinguishes a French dinner. Every dish was removed, carved by the domestics, and handed in turn to each guest. But there were a delay and a finish in this arrangement that suited neither Aristabulus' go-ahead-ism, nor his organ of acquisitiveness. Instead of waiting, therefore, for the more graduated movements of the domestics, he began to take care of himself, an office that he performed with a certain dexterity that he had acquired by frequenting ordinaries—a school, by the way, in which he had obtained most of his notion of the proprieties of the table. One or two slices were obtained in the usual manner, or by means of the regular service; and then, like one who had laid the foundation of a fortune by some lucky windfall in the commencement of his career, he began to make accessions, right and left, as opportunity offered. Sundry *entremets*, or light dishes that had a peculiarly tempting appearance, came first under his grasp. Of these he soon accumulated all within his reach, by taxing his neighbors, when he ventured to send his plate here and there, or wherever he saw a dish that promised to reward his trouble. By such means, which were resorted to, however, with a quiet and unobtrusive assiduity that escaped much observation, Mr. Bragg contrived to make his own plate a sample epitome of the first course. It contained in the centre, fish, beef, and ham; and around these staple articles he had arranged croquettes, rognons, ragouts, vegetables, and other light things, until not only was the plate completely covered, but it was actually covered in double and triple layers; mustard, cold butter, salt, and even pepper garnishing its edges. These different accumulations were the work of time and address, and most of the company had repeatedly changed their plates before Aristabulus had eaten a mouthful, the soup excepted. The happy moment when his ingenuity was to be rewarded had now arrived, and the land agent was about to commence the process of mastication, or of deglutition rather, for he troubled himself very little with the first operation, when the report of a cork drew his attention towards the champagne. To Aristabulus this wine never came amiss, for, relishing its piquancy he had never gone far enough into the science of the table to learn which were the proper moments for using it. As respected all the others at table, this moment had in truth arrived, though, as respected himself, he was no nearer to it, according to regulated taste, than when he first took his seat. Perceiving that Pierre was serving it, however, he offered his own glass, and enjoyed a delicious instant as he swallowed a beverage that much surpassed anything he had ever known to issue out of the waxed and leaded nozzles that, pointed like so many enemies' batteries loaded with headaches and disordered stomachs, garnished sundry village bars of his acquaintance.

From James Fenimore Cooper, *Home as Found* (New York: G. P. Putnam's Sons, 1838), pp. 18–19.

Aristabulus finished his glass at a draught, and when he took breath he fairly smacked his lips. That was an unlucky instant; his plate, burdened with all its treasures, being removed at this unguarded moment; the man who performed this unkind office fancying that a dislike to the dishes could alone have given rise to such an *omniumgatherum*.

It was necessary to commence de novo, but this could no longer be done with the first course, which was removed, and Aristabulus set to with zeal forthwith on the game. Necessity compelled him to eat, as the different dishes were offered; and such was his ordinary assiduity with the knife and fork, that, at the end of the second remove, he had actually disposed of more food than any other person at table.

QUESTIONS

1. Is Aristabulus happy or unhappy? Why?
2. Why is the story entitled "the opportunist"? What does it tell us about our own society?
3. What types of opportunists do we run into every day?

CASE 3.2
The Parable of the Sadhu
Bowen H. McCoy

Bowen H. McCoy is a managing director of Morgan Stanley & Co., Inc., and president of Morgan Stanley Realty, Inc. He is also an ordained ruling elder of the United Presbyterian Church.

Last year, as the first participant in the new six-month sabbatical program that Morgan Stanley has adopted, I enjoyed a rare opportunity to collect my thoughts as well as do some traveling. I spent the first three months in Nepal, walking 600 miles through 200 villages in the Himalayas and climbing some 120,000 vertical feet. On the trip my sole Western companion was an anthropologist who shed light on the cultural patterns of the villages we passed through.

During the Nepal hike, something occurred that has had a powerful impact on my thinking about corporate ethics. Although some might argue that the experience has no relevance to business, it was a situation in which a basic ethical dilemma suddenly intruded into the lives of a group of individuals. How the group responded I think holds a lesson for all organizations no matter how defined.

THE SADHU

The Nepal experience was more rugged and adventuresome than I had anticipated. Most commercial treks last two or three weeks and cover a quarter of the distance we traveled.

My friend Stephen, the anthropologist, and I were halfway through the 60-day Himalayan part of the trip when we reached the high point, an 18,000-foot pass over a crest that we'd have to traverse to reach to the village of Muklinath, an ancient holy place for pilgrims.

Six years earlier I had suffered pulmonary edema, an acute form of altitude sickness, at 16,500 feet in the vicinity of Everest base camp, so we were understandably concerned about what would happen at

From *Harvard Business Review*, Sept–Oct 1983, pp. 103–104. Reprinted with permission.

18,000 feet. Moreover, the Himalayas were having their wettest spring in 20 years; hip-deep powder and ice had already driven us off one ridge. If we failed to cross the pass, I feared that the last half of our "once in a lifetime" trip would be ruined.

The night before we would try the pass, we camped at a hut at 14,500 feet. In the photos taken at that camp, my face appears wan. The last village we'd passed through was a sturdy two-day walk below us, and I was tired.

During the late afternoon, four back-packers from New Zealand joined us, and we spent most of the night awake, anticipating the climb. Below we could see the fires of two other parties, which turned out to be two Swiss couples and a Japanese hiking club.

To get over the steep part of the climb before the sun melted the steps cut in the ice, we departed at 3:30 A.M. The New Zealanders left first, followed by Stephen and myself, our porters and Sherpas, and then the Swiss. The Japanese lingered in their camp. The sky was clear, and we were confident that no spring storm would erupt that day to close the pass.

At 15,500 feet, it looked to me as if Stephen were shuffling and staggering a bit, which are symptoms of altitude sickness. (The initial stage of altitude sickness brings a headache and nausea. As the condition worsens, a climber may encounter difficult breathing, disorientation, aphasia, and paralysis.) I felt strong, my adrenaline was flowing, but I was very concerned about my ultimate ability to get across. A couple of our porters were also suffering from the height, and Pasang, our Sherpa sirdar (leader), was worried.

Just after daybreak, while we rested at 15,500 feet, one of the New Zealanders, who had gone ahead, came staggering down toward us with a body slung across his shoulders. He dumped the almost naked, barefoot body of an Indian holy man—a sadhu—at my feet. He had found the pilgrim lying on the ice, shivering

---

To: You
From: The Philosopher
Subject: "A Happiness Box"

You wrote in your last email message, "All I want is to be happy and enjoy my life!" I detect some frustration in that outburst. But is that all that you really want out of life? I was thinking the other day: imagine an invention—which today is not at all implausible—that is the following. It is a box, cushioned and comfortable (not unlike a coffin, but don't let that association turn you off). You lie in the box, and we hook you up with electrodes, but nothing painful or discomforting and after a few minutes you forget that they are even there. The electrodes are connected to a computer that sends out signals that stimulate your brain, sending waves of pleasure and satisfaction. Within minutes, you completely stop caring about anything else. No worries, no problems. Of course, you can get out of the box anytime that you want to, but it isn't necessary because technicians take care of all your bodily needs, making sure you have water and nutrition, that your body stays at a healthy temperature, and so on. And as a matter of fact (we can imagine), no one has ever decided to get out of the box. With time, your body starts looking like a bean bag from lack of exercise, and your friends and family all forget about you, but you don't care. You're happy. You're completely satisfied with your life and enjoying every minute of it.

OK. There's your life of enjoyment, satisfaction, and happiness. Would you like to try out the box?

and suffering from hypothermia. I cradled the sadhu's head and laid him out on the rocks. The New Zealander was angry. He wanted to get across the pass before the bright sun melted the snow. He said, "Look, I've done what I can. You have porters and Sherpa guides. You care for him. We're going on!" He turned and went back up the mountain to join his friends.

I took a carotid pulse and found that the sadhu was still alive. We figured he had probably visited the holy shrines at Muklinath and was on his way home. It was fruitless to question why he had chosen this desperately high route instead of the safe, heavily traveled caravan route through the Kali Gandaki gorge. Or why he was almost naked and with no shoes, or how long he had been lying in the pass. The answers weren't going to solve our problem.

Stephen and the four Swiss began stripping off outer clothing and opening their packs. The sadhu was soon clothed from head to foot. He was not able to walk, but he was very much alive. I looked down the mountain and spotted below the Japanese climbers marching up with a horse.

Without a great deal of thought, I told Stephen and Pasang that I was concerned about withstanding the heights to come and wanted to get over the pass. I took off after several of our porters who had gone ahead.

On the steep part of the ascent where, if the ice steps had given way, I would have slid down about 3,000 feet, I felt vertigo. I stopped for a breather, allowing the Swiss to catch up with me. I inquired about the sadhu and Stephen. They said that the sadhu was fine and that Stephen was just behind. I set off again for the summit.

Stephen arrived at the summit an hour after I did. Still exhilarated by victory, I ran down the snow slope to congratulate him. He was suffering from altitude sickness, walking 15 steps, then stopping, walking 15 steps, then stopping. Pasang accompanied him all the way up. When I reached them, Stephen glared at me and said: "How do you feel about contributing to the death of a fellow man?"

I did not fully comprehend what he meant.

"Is the sadhu dead?" I inquired

"No;" replied Stephen, "but he surely will be!"

After I had gone, and the Swiss had departed not long after, Stephen had remained with the sadhu. When the Japanese had arrived, Stephen had asked to use their horse to transport the sadhu down to the hut. They had refused. He had then asked Pasang to have a group of our porters carry the sadhu. Pasang had resisted the idea, saying that the porters would have to exert all their energy to get themselves over the pass. He had thought they could not carry a man down 1,000 feet to the hut, reclimb the slope, and get across safely before the snow melted. Pasang had pressed Stephen not to delay any longer.

The Sherpas had carried the sadhu down to a rock in the sun at about 15,000 feet and had pointed out the hut another 500 feet below. The Japanese had given him food and drink. When they had last seen him he was listlessly throwing rocks at the Japanese party's dog, which had frightened him.

We do not know if the sadhu lived or died.

QUESTIONS

1. Who is responsible for the well-being of the sadhu? What are the duties of the people involved? What action would best serve the good of everyone?

2. How are the problems here similar to problems that arise in organizations every day? What kinds of sadhus do people confront in everyday life?

3. Would McCoy's group have behaved differently if they had come across a Western man rather than a Sadhu?

CASE 3.3
A Life Badly Lived
Arthur Miller

Arthur Miller was one of America's great playwrights, and *Death of a Salesman* is his masterpiece. This is the Requiem that ends the play

CHARLEY: It's getting dark, Linda.
Linda doesn't react. She stares at the grave.

BIFF: How about it, Mom? Better get some rest, heh? They'll be closing the gate soon.
Linda makes no move. Pause.

HAPPY (*deeply angered*): He had no right to do that. There was no necessity for it. We would've helped him.

CHARLEY (*grunting*): Hmmm.

BIFF: Come along, Mom.

LINDA: Why didn't anybody come?

CHARLEY: It was a very nice funeral.

LINDA: But where are all the people he knew? Maybe they blame him.

CHARLEY: Naa. It's a rough world, Linda. They wouldn't blame him.

LINDA: I can't understand it. At this time especially. First time in thirty-five years we were just about free and clear. He only needed a little salary. He was even finished with the dentist.

CHARLEY: No man only needs a little salary.

LINDA: I can't understand it.

BIFF: There were a lot of nice days. When he'd come home from a trip; or on Sundays, making the stoop; finishing the cellar; putting on the new porch; when he built the extra bathroom; and put up the garage. You know something, Charley, there's more of him in that front stoop than in all the sales he ever made.

CHARLEY: Yeah. He was a happy man with a batch of cement.

LINDA: He was so wonderful with his hands.

BIFF: He had the wrong dreams. All, all, wrong.

HAPPY (*almost ready to fight Biff*): Don't say that!

BIFF: He never knew who he was.

CHARLEY (*stopping Happy's movement and reply. To Biff*): Nobody dast blame this man. You don't understand: Willy was a salesman.
And for a salesman, there is no rock bottom to the life. He don't put a bolt to a nut, he don't tell you the law or give you medicine. He's a man way out there in the blue, riding on a smile and a shoeshine. And when they start not smiling back—that's an earthquake. And then you get yourself a couple of spots on your hat, and you're finished. Nobody dast blame this man. A salesman is got to dream, boy. It comes with the territory.

BIFF: Charley, the man didn't know who he was.

HAPPY (*infuriated*): Don't say that!

BIFF: Why don't you come with me, Happy?

HAPPY: I'm not licked that easily. I'm staying right in this city, and I'm gonna beat this racket (*He looks at Biff, his chin set.*) The Loman Brothers!

BIFF: I know who I am, kid.

HAPPY: All right, boy. I'm gonna show you and everybody else that Willy Loman did not die in vain. He had a good dream. It's the only dream you can have—to come out number-one man. He fought it out here, and this is where I'm gonna win it for him.

BIFF (*with a hopeless glance at Happy, bends toward his mother*): Let's go, Mom.

LINDA: I'll be with you in a minute. Go on, Charley. (*He hesitates.*) I want to, just for a minute. I never had a chance to say good-by.

Charley moves away, followed by Happy. Biff remains a slight distance up and left of Linda. She sits there, summoning herself. The flute begins, not far away, playing behind her speech.

LINDA: Forgive me, dear. I can't cry. I don't know what it is, but I can't cry. I don't understand it. Why did you ever do that? Help me, Willy, I can't cry. It seems to me that you're just on another trip. I keep expecting you. Willy, dear, I can't cry. Why did you do it? I search and search and I search, and I can't understand it, Willy. I made the last payment on the house today. Today, dear. And there'll be nobody home. (*A sob rises in her throat.*) We're free and clear. (*Sobbing more fully, released.*) We're free.

(*Biff comes slowly toward her.*) We're free . . . We're free . . .

Biff lifts her to her feet and moves out up right with her in his arms. Linda sobs quietly. Bernard and Charley come together and follow them, followed by Happy. Only the music of the flute is left on the darkening stage as over the house the hard towers of the apartment buildings rise into sharp focus, and The Curtain Falls.

QUESTIONS

1. Is Willy Loman a hero or a failure? Why might his son insist on the heroism of Willy Loman?

2. What went wrong for Willy Loman?

3. What does Charley mean when he says, "No man only needs a little salary"?

CASE 3.4
Rags to Riches to Rags
Ruth Capriles

The Pemón are an indigenous people who inhabit the region of the tepuyes (Auyan, Chimanta, Akopan, Roraima). Although some anthropologists say the Pemón do not exist as a separate ethnic group from the Caribes, and whoever their ancestors may be, today they identify themselves as a tribal unit, scattered over the plains, living in more or less extended family groups, or in Catholic missions. Some of these Amerindians have been Westernized: they have been clothed, converted, taught to read and write, aided by social and missionary programs and have been taught to play the violin, work in the mines and cut diamonds. They appear to learn fast and yet have maintained a considerable ethnic rigidity (the community disapproves of inter racial mixing); their family-type social structure and their way of life are adapted to the plains, forests and rivers that constitute their natural environment, and to which they seem to make a straightforward return following their contact with modern civilization. The history that I am about to relate is more about my own astonishment than an exact description of the experience of this community. . . . I will tell the story in three moments or observation times.

THE UTOPIA

The story has a central figure, the current leader of a group of Pemón who lived on the other side of the tepuys, independent from the rest of the ethnic groups, escaping from the influence of Catholic

From Ruth Capriles, "Rags to Riches to Rags," *Leadership and Organizational Development,* vol. 21, no. 4, 2000, pp. 195–199.

missions and from the state control and urban influence. Having left the riverbank of the Alto Caroní at the age of seven, our leader reached Urimán where a pilot offered to take him to Ciudad Bolívar. Here the pilot handed him over to a good doctor who took him into his family and brought him up with his own son who was slightly younger. He was catechized by this Catholic family and he attended school; he lived in Caracas and began his high school diploma. But at the age of 16 he decided to return to his native land. For the next 15 years, we know little about him except that he returned to his native environment and made a living from the usual local economic activities: fishing, hunting, raising crops and pigs, finding the occasional alluvial diamond whose value to civilization he fully recognized.

Fifteen years later, his step brother went looking for him, found him now the captain of the Pemón at the other side of the tepuy, and they joined forces in a mining venture. They obtained the concession to exploit the mines from the Ministry of Energy and Mines (MEM) and through heroic, pioneering work, they cleared a landing strip and set up a mining camp in the middle of the unending jungle; then they started production. They also began to learn the art of cutting diamonds for which they showed an immediate knack.

Five years later they lost the mining concession for various reasons that need not concern us here. The non-Indian workers left the site and went back to their city lives. But the Pemón did not. They live there, and so they stayed and continued to work the mine. For the next 15 years, the captain dedicated himself to building an organized community. With the surplus income from the mine, and with the collaboration of the community, he rebuilt an old and lost small village, turning it into a political, economic and social center. He joined forces with some North American Baptist missionaries and built a church; they installed an electrical plant and built four school rooms and a dispensary.

The village functions as the political and social center for the Pemón and although they do not live there all the time, it serves as a religious, social and political center to reunite them as a tribe or extended family. Anyone who comes in is a relative; although the extended family extends beyond the village itself and is spread throughout the upper Caroní. The church, the school and the dispensary, now run by a doctor who visits the region every two weeks (paid for by the community from income from mining activity) serve important functions, attracting inhabitants and promoting social cohesion. Children learn Spanish in the school and read the Bible in Pemón. There is no malaria, there are no serious infantile diseases, and appropriate vaccines are administered. In case of sickness or for specific needs, including cases of mercury poisoning, they can seek medical attention in Ciudad Bolívar.

The political representation of the organization is non-democratic. The captain has been elected and reelected by the heads of every family (women included if they are the head of the family, which is normal) and not by all adult members of the community. However, this seems to be a legitimate form of representation and meets little opposition or challenge from other parties. The captain exercises uncontested authority over the 38,000 hectares and the most astonishing thing is that he rules over the heterogeneous extractive population that has invaded the territory. Anyone who enters the area submits to the captain's authority, must ask permission to mine, contributes a percentage of the income from exploitation to the community, and restricts their activity to the area specified by the captain. Brazilian diamond-hunters, adventurers from the city, be they Arabs, natives of Caracas, US citizens, Canadians, contractors or independent workers, accept and cooperate with the order established by the captain and contribute to the indigenous community. The mining camps under the captain's authority adhere to the rules of behavior and are starting to have an obligation to save the damaged environment (an ecological conscience). There are no venereal diseases and no prostitution. In all conflicts the captain mediates, moving constantly throughout the region to settle disputes. Only the large foreign mining concerns, authorized by the CVG (Guayana Corporation) or the MEM in Pemón territory, restrict access to their camps, expropriate the natives and force them off the land (some concessions have been granted on lands covering existing indigenous villages, i.e., Morrocoy);

these do not contribute to the community and cause greater, more widespread damage to the ecosystem.

The struggle to survive as an organized community in the face of the national interests of the state, that grants concessions and the interests of the transnational mining companies, is just starting. The Pemón have already lost several battles but they have achieved some miraculous results: being able to run mining operations without official concessions and having established order in all the regional camps with the exception of the foreign permit holders. This means that the Pemón's spontaneous form of organization seems to be capable of resolving the region's major problems, including mercury contamination of waterways.

I hope that the mere existence of this indigenous group gives us food for thought for reflecting upon forms of organization, representation and local governability.

AFTERMATH—THIS IS NOT A HAPPY ENDING

Four years later, bliss is gone and the Pemón community is unstable. Our utopia went well until its leader lost the lead. Too many lives to live by the same person; too much money. In practice, our Cacique was leading three lives. He had to direct and oversee the mine territory and rule over Pemóns and interlopers. He had to be present at the religious and political center, and fly to the city to deal and sell. And the city had the worst of him. He forgot his extended family and the political project. He was surrounded, advised, and helped by outsiders pursuing their own interest: military with interest in mining; women in diamond trade; private entrepreneurs or companies ready to offer their services to extract and market diamonds, or even as partners in the mining business.

He certainly needed alliances to deal with the state policies on mining and he would hear anyone promising to help the community get the concession to operate the mines. Somehow, to get the

concession and renew the permits of agrarian land rights became the main purpose of the leader. A number of factors combined to create instability in the Pemón' community.

The Catholic Church was one of his main opponents, competing for religious influence and contesting the Protestant influence over the community. The mission down river used its influence in government and demanded the control of education in the Pemón community, based on ancient privileges of the church to catechize and educate in the region. Teachers of the community had to be taught at the mission. This assured Catholic education in a village which had adopted the Baptist worship, which must have introduced certain ethical splits in the community. The intervention of the national education system through the mission control (and thereby the intervention of the national health system) also forced the leader to have the classrooms rebuilt in concrete blocks and zinc, rejecting the traditional hut, which is considered health hazardous. That meant a high cost of river transport in small boats (or curiaras) of heavy materials and a cost in time to build the needed classrooms.

The military (the National Guard) are fundamental actors in this story. They are the authority in the region and exercise it at discretion. Corruption in the military at the region is a public secret. They decide who passes by road and river posts, who can extract gold or diamonds and who can export them without paying taxes; they get a share on each pile or wash; they even distribute the mercury which miners shouldn't use; they deal in the business. Sometimes they play on the same side of the Pemóns (it is to their interest that the Indians keep the concession, so it will not be given to a foreign company, which extracts and does not share with anyone). By the same token, they are a plague to the Indians who must negotiate with the military every inch of the way.

State decisions have dissolving influence on the community. Decisions supporting the mission's demands (strengthened by a social Christian national government) puts an area of the Cacique's authority under control of the Catholic Church, introducing the problems mentioned above. Even more vital to the community's unfolding are the mining policies. The Ministry of Mining holds the mining concession pending. The Pemóns keep on extracting diamonds and gold in a lawless situation, under the permissive but discrete eyes of the National Guard. This is an unstable situation, obviously, that can be changed suddenly by state policies and decisions or by a switch in the military moods. Getting the concession becomes a survival goal of the community.

CORRUPTION OF THE LEADER

Staying too long in the city, women, processed alcohol, the company of adventurers detracts the leader from his purpose. He loses touch with the community and his legitimacy to rule diminishes rapidly. This has happened to leaders throughout history, regardless of their cultural background.

Mercury, used in mining not only by them, but by *garimpeiros* and other illegal miners up river, have contaminated the waters and the fish; and so also land animals and people. The shortage of fish had been a previous consequence of the Guri Dam built in the 1970s down river, which altered the ecosystem and interrupted the fish cycles. Having focused on the mining project as economic survival activity, the Indians did not attend to any other means of production of food. Their crops, mainly roots, do not provide the basic nutritional needs. By the end of the 1990s, the community was having real problems of nourishment, specially in proteins.

Intensive invasion of foreign miners or adventurers adds instability to the maintenance of authority. It becomes difficult to control mining activities, behavior in camps, sexual diseases, respect of the Indian women. . . .

THE UNSTABLE SOLUTION—
A NEW HAPPIER ENDING

One year later, descendants of the Pemón leader, his pupils and aids in the management of things (sons, nephews) called a Council of Family Chiefs to decide on the leadership of the community. The Council decided to ask the resignation of the Cacique, to establish a new form of government and to choose new government. Addressed by his colleagues, the Cacique accepted, not without pain, the community decision and offered his assistance as adviser to the young leaders.

The new form of government is a triumvirate of Caciques: one is chief over the mining production and occupation of mining territory; another is the religious-political chief in the town; and the third is in charge of foreign relations, including trade and procuring state permissions and concessions. They are still pending on the concession and are having the same basic problems of uncertainty, invasion, lack of nutritional food. But the impetus of the young seems to have regrouped them. Some I know went back from the city to the jungle to help in the recuperation and control of the territory. The young men of each family were given sectors of responsibility, forming a controlling team. The success of which I can not yet say. In a future paper I will report, for this is history and leadership in the making under local, national, global forces. I can imagine they keep on extracting mines without the concession and, although under a lot of obstacles, they might be managing some recuperation, even if uncertain. According to reports, their situation is in an unstable equilibrium.

A new Constitution of Venezuela seems to open new possibilities for the Indians. It formally recognizes the collective property to ethnic groups and indigenous communities: article 119 says, "The State will recognize the existence of ethnic groups and indigenous communities, their social, political and economic organization; their culture, uses and costumes, languages and religions; and also their habitat and original rights over the land they have occupied from ancestry and tradition and which are needed to develop and guarantee their forms of life." It gives the Indian people the right to demarcate and claim ownership of their lands as collective property. This new constitutional provision would give the Indians autonomy and stability in their lands. But the probabilities of obtaining it are not high, considering that if all Venezuelan Indians (a population of approximately 300,000) claim rights over their ancestral lands, they would own in collective regimes more than half of Venezuelan territory. We can expect the rest of the country will object to such arrangement on the making. Neither would collective property over land solve the mining rights, for the new constitution reinstated the ownership of the State over underground products, which keeps miners submitted to State policies.

1. What leadership challenges did the Cacique face?
2. What factors led to the downfall of the Cacique?
3. In what way is the Cacique's story the same as the story of leaders from a variety of other cultures?

CASE 3.5
Are You Living the Good Life?
Nona Walia

Wealth grants us opportunities to purchase many things, but it simultaneously impairs our ability to enjoy them. Nona Walia goes searching for the road to happiness in this material world. . . .

Everyone is in pursuit of a good life. But what exactly constitutes a good life? Luxury trimmings, big money, snazzy cubicles, fancy duplexes, BMWs, designer clothes, desirable BMI et al. does make one happy for a while; but are they assurances of a happy and fulfilling life in the long run? Psychology *Today* reports that people who enjoy close ties with friends and family are happier and have fewer health problems than those who don't. These people are more resilient to the stress of our times and withstand hurdles in a far better way. In short, la dolce vita isn't just about material possessions. A recent research at Washington University, St Louis, also indicates the same. Based on years of research, the experts came to the same conclusion: Happiness isn't about money or success. What is it all about then?

For Ria Chakraborty, housewife, happiness is all about Kolkata monsoons. "People complain about the traffic and the clogged drains but pouring rain is just beautiful to watch. It lifts my mood," she says. Ajit Sharma, a Pune-based software engineer, who stays at a boy's hostel, says, "Everyone is on their

own. But when I come back from work, and my friend makes me a cup of tea and sits down to chat with me. . . that makes me happy. He is busy too but he finds the time to ask. It's heartening, makes me feel good at the end of the day even if it has been shitty." Suchana Sarkar, a Delhi-based marketing professional, says, "Talking till I get breathless makes me happy. As soon as I come back, I have to share my day's stories with my friend or my roommate. I feel a void if I don't get to do that." You may think these are momentary pleasures, but it's these small things that make people most happy. Life guru Robin Sharma says, "Ultimately, life goes by in a blink. Material possessions aren't the only route to happiness. Life is a skill. And like any other skill, once you know the ground rules and make time to practise, you can get better. One has to engage in life and live it fully. When you near the end, you shouldn't be left with regret of a life half-lived."

The next logical question would be: How does one understand whether he or she is leading a good life? In his website, another guru of good living, Jamison Fox, asks a few fundamental questions to make people conscious of the kind of lives they are living. Would you like to be happier, healthier, wealthier, or make the world a better place?, he asks. "Impressing others, advancing your career will not

From The Times of India.

give you a very satisfied life. Living a good life is about being happy with what you have, and pursuing your dreams at the same time," says Fox.

Naysayers may still disagree. They may say that money solves most problems in life. It definitely gives you comfort. That's unchallenged, but the problem is that the pursuit of money is often confused with the pursuit of happiness and vice versa.

A team of researchers led by Jordi Quoidbach, from the Department of Psychology at Harvard University, reported in *Psychological Science* magazine that wealth does grant us opportunities to purchase many things, but it simultaneously impairs our ability to enjoy them.

BK Shivani, a Rajyoga meditation teacher, asks, "Why do you go to work? To get the money to pay the bills, buy the food and clothe, etc.? That's fine. But why do you want more money than you need? To buy the bigger car because you think these things will make you happy. But are you?" Life coach Rohini Singh, also the author of *The Only Way Out Is Within*, says, "Money is a medium, an energy. There are people who have an abundance of it but they still feel empty. They often find themselves wondering what's missing. The answer is happiness. Everyone needs to add to the external factors of well-being. People need to have a sense of purpose, spiritual practice, stillness, time to just be. To live life in gratitude, not giving energy to critics or negativity, going outside the comfort zone to help others gives you the kind of happiness you never hoped to achieve."

London-based industrialist Bina Goenka believes a good life is about creating one's own parameters of happiness. "You have to understand what drives you as an individual, what inspires the people you work with, and how to grow as a unit. Focus on what you love, the rest will take care of itself." In his book, *Ten Golden Rules on Living the Good Life,* Michael Soupios writes, "Worry only about the things that are in your control. Keep your life simple. Seek calming pleasures. Avoid excess and live life in harmony and balance."

Author, entrepreneur, and lifestyle innovator Jonathan Fields produces a TV show called *The Good Life Project* that draws inspiration from the real life experiences of acclaimed entrepreneurs, artistes, authors and thought leaders. Says Fields, "A few years ago, I would have said, 'I need to get a good life'. Now, I've come to believe that once your basic needs are covered, life welllived is more about mindset than circumstances. Happiness is not a place you arrive at, it's a lens you bring to the place you are standing right now."

QUESTIONS

1. Do you think luxury goods are an important aspect of the good life? Why or why not?

2. Do you think the author's perspective as an Indian journalist writing for an Indian audience changes what she means by her question: Are you living the good life? If so, how?

CASE 3.6
The Curious Loan Approval
D. Anthony Plath

D. Anthony Plath is an assistant professor at the University of North Carolina at Charlotte.

As a commercial loan officer-trainee at Farmwood National Bank, Adam's future looked very bright. He had recently completed a series of credit analysis exams, earning the highest score in his training group and capturing the attention of the bank's senior commercial loan officers. In the second phase of his training program, Adam was promoted to a financial analyst's position and assigned to work for Mary Ryan, one of the bank's most productive commercial loan officers. Like Adam, Mary had earned the highest score on the analysis exams among her training group five years ago, and she and Adam quickly became a team to be reckoned with inside the bank's corporate banking division.

In the first few months of his new assignment, Adam quickly grew to admire his new boss. In most cases, when he evaluated the creditworthiness of a new customer for Mary, she readily agreed with his analysis and praised his attention to detail. However, one recent loan application left Adam totally confused. Evaluating a request from Mitchell Foods, Inc., for a $5 million short-term loan to finance inventory expansion, Adam noted that the firm was dangerously overleveraged. Mitchell Foods represented a retail grocery chain with 35 stores located in the greater metropolitan area served by Farmwood National, and the firm was financing its retail outlets with operating leases. Unlike financial leases, operating leases only appear in the notes accompanying the firm's financial statements, and Mitchell Foods' current balance sheet gave

the appearance of far less leverage than the firm actually carried.

Adam promptly noted this fact in a memorandum of concern that he forwarded to Mary for inclusion in the Mitchell Foods credit file. Much to his surprise, Mary discounted the problem and told Adam to destroy the memo. After the bank's senior credit committee approved the Mitchell Foods loan request, Mary defended her position by telling Adam that the issue of operating lease leverage never surfaced during the credit committee meeting.

In spite of Mary's reassurances, Adam knew from his days in credit school that Mitchell Foods' operating lease liability was handled improperly. While pondering this problem over coffee in the employee cafeteria, Adam overheard Mary talking excitedly among a group of young commercial lenders. It seems she had just received word that her personal mortgage loan application at Bay Street Savings and Loan had been approved, and the terms of this loan were most attractive. The savings and loan willingly waived its normal down payment requirement and gave Mary 100 percent, fixed-rate financing of 25 years at 2 percent below the going rate of interest on fixed-rate mortgage loans.

Given his recent credit analysis, Adam recalled that the president of Mitchell Foods was also Chairman of the Board at Bay Street Savings. He began to wonder whether Mary's actions as a commercial loan officer had been compromised by her personal financial affairs, or whether he was simply thinking too much. After all, Mary was an outstanding commercial loan officer, and she was his mentor. What should Adam do next?

CHAPTER QUESTIONS

1. What is the most important thing in life to you? How does your career fit into your life? Or is your career the most important thing in your life?

2. How does pleasure differ from happiness? And what about the difference between short- term pleasure and long-term pleasure? Many hedonists have insisted carpe diem—seize the day—and you might wonder how far you should defer your pleasures. On the other hand, will you get the "big pleasures" if you don't sacrifice a lot of pleasure in the short term?

3. Outline the main elements of a good life. What aspects of your culture prevent people from living a good life? What aspects of your culture facilitate the good life?

4

Money, How We Get It, and Where It Goes

Accounting, Finance, and Investment Ethics

Introduction

"It's all about the money." Well, maybe. But we have already seen that it's about a lot more as well. It's about success. It's about satisfaction and self-satisfaction. It's about doing well and living well. Nevertheless, it's about the money. That's what business is, among other things. And that's what is involved in understanding business ethics as well. "Follow the money." That's good advice both in investigative journalism and in business ethics. Even if money is not all of what business is about, it certainly dictates an awful lot of what it is about. So what money is, where it comes from, how and where it gets invested and by whom, and where it goes are all crucial questions in business ethics.

What is money? That sounds like a naive question, until one actually starts to pay attention to it. What makes gold and silver, for example, so valuable? These "precious metals" have limited uses (filling teeth and making photo film, for instance, neither of which are all that impressive). Yet, since ancient times, they have been desired enough to kill for. To be sure, both are relatively rare. But so are hen's teeth and baby unicorns, although there would be little interest in the market for them if they existed. But even given the extraordinary value of precious metals and precious gems, the desirability of money is something else again. Most money is paper, of no value in itself, and even metal coins are rarely worth their face value. Paper money is a promissory note, and behind the promise is an enormous network of trust. (Think about what happens when even a hint of scandal or devaluation hits the banking community.) But what allows people to invest their trust this way? Why not just collect gold and hide it under one's mattress? In the final analysis, money is worth something only because people believe and trust that it is worth something. It is worth nothing at all in itself.

This mystery of money, as opposed to the illusion that money itself is what is ultimately desired and desirable, pervades the financial world and its ethics. Money depends entirely on trust, and trust is the stuff of ethics. Thus, the story of money and business, like the story of business ethics, is the story of trust and how it is gained and lost, how it is betrayed and, if lost, again regained. And the more abstract money becomes, the more it depends upon trust. Today most financial transactions do not even involve pieces of paper, except perhaps as back-up records. Hence, we can readily understand the trauma and the seriousness of the recent failure of one of the biggest auditing companies—Arthur Andersen, as well as the seriousness of conflicts of interest in the financial markets, not only as violations of authority and professional responsibility but as potentially undermining the whole financial system.

   Money doesn't just sit there. Money gets invested. Indeed, as any financial adviser will tell you, money that is just sitting there (e.g., in a low-interest savings or money market account) is nevertheless invested; it is just invested unwisely. Money is always at work. Money that is "just sitting there" still plays its passive role in the flow of markets and financial exchange. Indeed, money owed is also part of the flow of markets and financial exchange, and people who owe thousands of dollars in debt on their credit cards and corporations that owe billions to local and foreign banks are very much players in the system. But if everyone, whether a solvent, active investor or an insolvent, even bankrupt, debtor is part of the market, then those who actively control the market—bankers, brokers, bureaucrats, and others—have special obligations—fiduciary obligations—to those who are not so active or not so smart. The hardedged position here is that everyone—except, perhaps, children and the feeble-minded—is or ought to be fully informed about and responsible for his or her own financial state. But this is naive, not only in the sense that it is harsh treatment of responsibility, but that, given the abstraction and ultimate mystery of the financial world, it is expecting much too much of the average and perhaps even the aggressive investor. A few years ago, for example, when derivatives came into existence as

---

To: You
From: The Philosopher
Subject: "Accounting and Mergers"

Congratulations on the good news that your accounting firm is performing the due diligence and audit on the new merger. The stock offering will be the interesting part. We sometimes think that mergers and IPOs (and the accountants who manage them) are a new phenomenon, something the twentieth century invented. But when you are doing the numbers, remember these cautionary words from Daniel Defoe (he was writing in the early 1700s):

   Some in clandestine companies combine,
   Erect new stocks to trade beyond the line,
   With air and empty names beguile the town
   And raise new credits first, then cry 'em down,
   Divide the empty nothing into shares,
   And set the crowd together by the ears.

a hedge on the market, even the "experts" were forced to admit that they did not understand these instruments and thus, at least to some extent, could not be held responsible for what happened with them. But for most investors (keeping in mind the passivity of most people's investment histories), even such seemingly simple concepts as stocks and bonds, insurance, and annuities are mysterious, even if these instruments have now become (in the absence of government "welfare" systems) part and parcel of almost everyone's life. It is not enough to say "investor beware!" The financial markets are now complex and mysterious enough,

Six Principles of Ethical Accounting

PRINCIPLE	AICPA DIRECTIVE
1. Responsibilities	In carrying out their responsibilities as professionals, members should exercise sensitive professional and moral judgments in all their activities.
2. The public interest	Members should accept the obligation to act in a way that will serve the public interest, honor the public trust, and demonstrate commitment to professionalism.
3. Integrity	To maintain and broaden public confidence, members should perform all professional responsibilities with the highest sense of integrity.
4. Objectivity and independence	A member should maintain objectivity and be free of conflicts of interest in discharging professional responsibilities. A member in public practice should be independent in fact and appearance when providing auditing and other attestation services.
5. Due care	A member should observe the profession's technical and ethical standards, strive continually to improve competence and the quality of services, and discharge professional responsibility to the best of the member's ability.
6. Scope and nature of services	A member in public should observe the Principles of the Code of Professional Conduct in determining the scope and nature of services to be provided.

From the American Institute of Certified Public Accountants. Reprinted with permission.

and most people are vulnerable enough, to require special efforts and responsibilities on the part of those who manage and advise them.

In this chapter, we want to give at least some suggestions about a field that has been too long neglected in discussions of business ethics. In part, it has been neglected because it has seemed to many people too technical to be included in business ethics discussions. On the other hand, it has often seemed to be just another part of professional ethics. Accountants and money managers have been considered just professionals like doctors, lawyers, and architects and thus subject to the rules of their own peculiar institutions. But the collapse of Arthur Andersen convinced just about everyone in the financial world that the role of the accountant and the financial manager is something more than that of an economic technician or just another professional. And for the past fifteen years, after the financial scandals of the late 1980s, it has been evident that the financial markets can be as corrupted by unfair dealings (like insider trading and ignoring conflicts of interest) as it can be by outright theft and fraud. Behind all this concern is a new awareness that it is not enough to say "investor beware!" It is the responsibility of the financial community—in other words, all of us—to have some concern for what we might call *the innocent investor*, not just the proverbial feeble old lady on a pension, but most likely all of us. The forces of the market are brutal enough and sufficiently beyond our control that we all need and have a right to expect some protection, which means, minimally, ethical behavior on the part of those who are centrally responsible for making markets run in the first place.

Carol J. Loomis begins the chapter by canvasing several past major accounting scandals and explains how accountants fall under enormous pressure to "manage earnings" in "Lies, Damned Lies, and Managed Earnings." Ed Cohen briefly reflects on "What Went Wrong" for Arthur Andersen in the Enron-related accounting scandal that closed the gigantic and prestigious accounting firm. Robert E. Frederick and W. Michael Hoffman look at the ethical duties that companies have to the individual investor and the limitations on these duties. John R. Boatright gives a large perspective on finance ethics generally. Jennifer Moore shows how ethically complicated the stock market is in her "What Is Really Unethical About Insider Trading?" Frank Partnoy, a former Wall Street trader himself, explains the many dangers that are associated with derivative stock instruments. Paul Farrell, writing in 2008, makes the case against derivatives still stronger—and today both Partnoy and Farrell look like the tragic Greek character Cassandra, prophets whose dire warnings were ignored, to our peril. Duff McDonald takes a very close look at those mysterious money-printing machines known as hedge funds. Finally, Niall Ferguson examines the causes of the financial crisis of 2008.

Lies, Damned Lies, and Managed Earnings

Carol J. Loomis

Carol J. Loomis is a reporter for *Fortune* magazine.

Someplace right now, in the layers of a *Fortune* 500 Company, an employee—probably high up and probably helped by people who work for him—is perpetrating an accounting fraud. Down the road that crime will come to light and cost the company's shareholders hundreds of millions of dollars.

Typically, the employee will not have set out to be dishonest, only to dodge a few rules. His fraud, small at first, will build, because the exit he thought just around the corner never appears. In time, some subordinate may say, "Whoa!" But he won't muster the courage to blow the whistle, and the fraud will go on.

Until it's uncovered. The company's stock will drop then, by a big percent. Class-action lawyers will leap. The Securities and Exchange Commission will file unpleasant enforcement actions, levy fines, and leave the bad guys looking for another line of work.

Eventually someone may go to jail.

And the fundamental reason, very often, will be that the company or one of its divisions was "managing earnings"—trying to meet Wall Street expectations or those of the boss, trying also to pretend that the course of business is smooth and predictable when in reality it is not.

Jail? This is not a spot that CEOs and other high-placed executives see themselves checking into, for any reason. *Jail for managing earnings?* Many corporate chiefs would find that preposterous, having come to believe that "making their numbers" is just what executives do. Okay, so the pressure might lead some of them to do dumb (but legal) things—like making off-price deals at the end of a quarter that simply steal from full-priced business down the road. Who cares? Others might even be driven to make hash of the rules that publicly owned companies are required to abide by, Generally Accepted Accounting Principles, known as GAAP. Sure, that might mean crossing a legal line, but so what. . . .

What's at stake, he [Arthur Levitt, chairman of the SEC] says, is nothing less than the credibility of the U.S. financial-reporting system, traditionally thought to be the best in the world. It will not now, he vowed, be undermined by managements obsessed with making their numbers. "It's a basic cultural change we're asking for," he said, "nothing short of that."

For those who can't get with the program, the punishment increasingly could be criminal prosecution. The SEC does not itself have the ability to bring criminal actions, so the chairman has been out jawboning people who do, like Attorney General Janet Reno and various U.S. Attorneys. Levitt would particularly like to see these folk nail brokers who cheat investors, but there are accounting-fraud cases in which he wants indictments as well.

One U.S. Attorney in tune with the SEC's tough new line is Mary Jo White, of New York's Southern District. White has brought a string of accounting-fraud actions and says she still has "a lot" in the pipeline. Her district has two bigtime criminal cases even now—Livent and Bankers Trust, both stemming from managed earnings. However, as White points out. "On the criminal side, we don't use that polite a term: we call it accounting fraud or 'cooking the books.'" White has also prosecuted smaller cases that she prizes for their deterrence value. Object lessons don't work in most areas of the law, she says, but "significant jail time" for a white-collar executive is apt to give others of his ilk severe shakes.

What qualifies as significant? In March, Donald Ferrarini, the 71-year-old former CEO of a New York insurance brokerage, Underwriters Financial Group

Learning to Cheat?

Former Stanford University President Donald Kennedy blamed "infirmities" in the institution's accounting practices for overcharging the federal government more than $160 million over the past decade, including $180,000 for depreciation of the Stanford Sailing Association yacht and $185,000 for administrative costs for a profitable Stanford-owned shopping center. Kennedy said his institution billed the government for many of the expenses "merely because it was lawful to do so."

—*Quarterly Review of Doublespeak*, January 1992

(UFG), got 12 years. (He is appealing.) Ferrarini had cooked the most basic recipes in the book: He overstated revenues and understated expenses, a combo that magically converted UFG from a loser into a moneymaker. The scam, uncovered in 1995, cost shareholders, policyholders, and premium finance companies close to $30 million. . . .

Whether all this is enough to change the culture at the top of U.S. business remains to be seen. In taking on earnings management, Levitt is threatening a practice many CEOs regard as part of their bill of rights. The former communications director of a prominent *Fortune* 500 company remembers the blast his CEO once let loose at the financial managers and lawyers trying to tell him that the quarterly earnings he proposed to announce weren't accurate. Roared the CEO: "Stop fooling around with my numbers! The No. 1 job of management is to smooth out earnings. . . ."

The fundamental problem with the earnings-management culture—especially when it leads companies to cross the line in accounting—is that it obscures facts investors ought to know, leaving them in the dark about the true value of a business. That's bad enough when times are good, like now. Let business go south, and abusive financial reporting can veil huge amounts of deterioration.

The cult of consistent earnings imposes opportunity costs as well. To start with, even the least offensive kinds of earnings management take time, mainly because executives have to decide which

of several maneuvers to go for. Then there are the related tasks, especially the need to talk extensively to analysts and massage their earnings-per-share expectations. Custom says those expectations must not be disappointed by even a penny, since a management's inability to come up with a measly cent, when so many opportunities to manipulate earnings exist, will often be interpreted as a stark sign of failure and a reason to bomb the stock.

One well-regarded *Fortune* 500 CEO said recently that he probably spends 35% of his time talking to analysts and big shareholders, and otherwise worrying about the concerns of the Street. Would his company's bottom line be better off if he devoted that time to the business? "Of course," he answered. But there is always the stock price to think about—and naturally the CEO's compensation is structured to make sure he thinks about it a lot. . . .

What has sparked Chairman Levitt's war on falsified earnings reports, however, isn't the occasional distracted CEO. It's the continual eruption of accounting frauds. The accumulation of cases, in fact, keeps suggesting that beneath corporate America's uncannily disciplined march of profits during this decade lie great expanses of accounting rot, just waiting to be revealed.

Right now, among big cookers of books, the grand prize for rot is shared by the two caught up in criminal proceedings, Livent and Bankers Trust. Livent, for its part, vaporized close to $150 million in market value last August when new controlling shareholders (among them Hollywood bigwig Michael Ovitz) asserted that Livent's books had been cooked for years. Prosecutors went on to charge the company's former CEO, *Ragtime* and *Fosse* producer Garth Drabinsky, with creating another showpiece, in which Livent starred as a thriving operation when in reality it was crumbling. Indeed, Livent kept looking presentable only because financial facts were being whisked around like props in a stage set. Drabinsky was indicted in January and even earlier had exited from the U.S., stage north: He is holed up in his homeland, Canada, where he has denied wrongdoing and has said he will fight extradition proceedings. He has also sued both Livent and its auditors, KPMG.

At Bankers Trust, prosecutors say that employees working in the securities-processing business in the mid-1990s met top management's call for good results by misappropriating money that belonged to security holders but hadn't been claimed (and that was required to be escheated to the state). The funds were used to cover the department's general expenses, a procedure that increased profits. The evidence has already caused Bankers Trust to plead guilty and agree to a $63 million fine. In addition, at least three former BT managers, including B.J. Kingdon, the boss of the division that included securities processing, are reported to have been issued "target letters" that signal they may be indicted.

Kingdon, through his lawyer, neither confirms nor denies the existence of a target letter. The lawyer says Kingdon has reacted to reports about this matter with "astonishment" and "outrage." Kingdon, says the lawyer, was not aware that anything unlawful was being done. The lawyer also says that "whatever took place, took place in daylight, with the appropriate levels of the bank monitoring the activity."

That comment raises a question already begging for an answer: whether executives up the line at Bankers Trust, like former CEO Charles Sanford, will be pulled into this affair. The SEC's attempts to curb accounting fraud have always emphasized "tone at the top," and Bankers Trust's management has given a great impression of being tone-deaf. A few years ago the company got into deep trouble for unprincipled selling of derivatives, and even now, in the midst of its securities-processing mess, it has the SEC on its neck because of possible problems with its loan-loss reserves. . . .

Never fear that the SEC will run out of accounting cases to examine and perhaps move in on, because seldom does a month pass that those ugly words "restatement of earnings" do not fasten themselves to a new company. Joining the crowd recently from the FORTUNE 1000 were drugstore chain Rite Aid, holding company MCN Energy Group, and drug wholesaler McKesson HBOC. Ironically, this is McKesson's second brush with accounting infamy this century. . . .

Like any good general, Arthur Levitt has a strategy for going after this enemy called managed earnings. In his September speech, in fact, he unveiled a list of five accounting problems that would get the unremitting attention of the SEC. They were "big bath" restructuring charges, acquisition accounting, "cookie-jar reserves," the abuse of "materiality," and revenue recognition.

Of these, that last item—the wrongful booking of sales—seems the closest to outright fraud. GAAP includes some firm rules for recognizing revenue, and most don't leave a lot of room for playing around. That hasn't stopped the bad guys. A recent study done for the Committee of Sponsoring Organizations of the Treadway Commission (called COSO), which is supported by various accounting and financial bodies, studied 200 alleged frauds carried out by publicly owned companies in the 11 years ended in 1997. Roughly 50% had a revenue-recognition component. Many of the cases involved small companies, which for that matter pack the list when it comes to fraud of any kind.

Even so, some of the biggest accounting scandals of the past few years (and now McKesson's to boot) have also featured revenue-recognition schemes. Executives at Sensormatic held the books open at the end of quarters so that they could get enough sales in the door to meet their earnings targets. Richard Rubin, former CEO of apparel company Donnkenny, is awaiting sentence for creating false invoices that he used to book sales. And Al Dunlap, who was fired as CEO of Sunbeam by its board, is alleged to have carried out (among other things) a "bill and hold" scam. In other words, Sunbeam recorded the sale of goods but simply held them in its own warehouse, a forbidden combo unless a customer has taken bona fide ownership of the goods and requested they be stored. . . . Walter Schuetze, chief accountant of the SEC's Division of Enforcement, sees in these scandals a simple theme: "When it comes to cooking the books, revenue recognition is the recipe of choice."

Lately, though, the other earnings-management techniques on Levitt's list have been . . . suddenly and sweepingly popular. Take, first, the charges that hit earnings when a company restructures on its own or as the result of an acquisition. Say that a company commits itself at these junctures to exit a business or close a factory in the near future. Under GAAP, it must today, in what we'll call year one, estimate the costs it will eventually incur in the restructuring—for severance payments, plant closings, and the like—and charge them off, even though many of the expenses won't actually be paid until, say, year two or three. These charges, which end up in a liability called a reserve, tend to put craters in year one's profits. But analysts generally ignore the bottom-line damage these write-offs do, focusing instead on operating earnings. In fact, all too often analysts cheer these charges, figuring that they clear the decks for good results in the future.

Earnings often *do* shine in the wake of a restructuring—but not necessarily because business has improved. Maybe all that happened was that the restructuring change was a "big bath," deliberately made larger than the monies to be paid out, which allows the excess to be channeled back into earnings in year two or year three. Abracadabra!—higher profits than would otherwise have materialized.

Or maybe the company made the restructuring charge a kitchen disposal, using it to gobble up all kinds of costs that by rights should be hitting this year's operating earnings or next. Schuetze recently ticked off some of the impermissible costs the SEC has found in restructuring charges: services to be provided in some future period by lawyers, accountants, and investment bankers; special bonuses for officers, expenses for retraining people.

Since Levitt's speech, the SEC has sent a letter to about 150 companies that took large restructuring charges last year. The letter warned that their annual reports might be selected for review. It also reminded the companies that they are required to make disclosures about the status of their restructuring reserves—how many dollars paid out so far, how many employees terminated vs. the original plan, and so forth. The implication was that the SEC would be looking to see that the companies were adhering to their restructuring plans and not emerging with reserves that could be popped into earnings at a propitious moment. The disclosure requirements had been there for years but were often ignored. Not anymore.

That's especially true because the SEC has followed through with tough reviews, both of annual reports and registration statements. One SEC target was Rite Aid, which took a large restructuring charge in fiscal 1999 (a year that ended in February) in anticipation of closing 379 stores. The SEC later compelled the company to reduce the size of its restructuring charge (from $290 million to $233 million), add major expenses to its operating costs, and restate its profits from the unaudited figure of $158 million it had reported in March—a figure even then far below "analysts' expectations"—to $144 million. This year, to date, Rite Aid has lost close to $7 billion in market cap, and class-action lawyers are all over its case. . . .

Let us dip now, if you will pardon the expression, into another item on Levitt's list, cookie-jar reserves. GAAP, of course, is too stiffly worded to include a term like that. But not even the accounting-challenged have trouble visualizing that these are earnings held back from the period in which they should have been recognized and kept instead for a rainy day. Maybe the husbander is truly worried about bad weather hitting its business (as many banks, for example, claim to be), or maybe it just wants to manage earnings. It doesn't matter: GAAP says companies cannot establish reserves for "contingencies," because such costs can't be estimated. They should hit income statements when they actually arrive.

Beyond that, cookie jars are innately a problem because investors usually can't detect that they exist. Even outside directors, said one recently, typically wouldn't be told that managers had hidden cookies away. That makes it difficult for anyone to fairly

Ethical Decision Making

As a guide in deciding on a course of action, follow these steps:

1. *Recognize the Event, Decision, or Issue*
   - You are asked to do something that you think might be wrong
   - You are aware of potentially illegal or unethical conduct on the part of others at PwC or a client
   - You are trying to make a decision and are not sure about the ethical course of action
2. *Think Before You Act*
   - Summarize and clarify your issue
   - Ask yourself, why the dilemma?
   - Consider the options and consequences
   - Consider who may be affected
   - Consult with others
3. *Decide on a Course of Action*
   - Determine your responsibility
   - Review all the relevant facts and information
   - Refer to applicable firm policies or professional standards
   - Assess the risks and how you could reduce them
   - Comtemplate the best course of action
   - Consult with others . . .
4. *Test Your Decision*
   - Review the "Ethics Questions to Consider" again
   - Apply the Firm's values to your decision
   - Make sure you have considered Firm policies, laws and professional standards
   - Consult with others—enlist their opinion of your planned action
5. *Proceed With Confidence*

Ethics Questions to Consider

- *Is it legal?*
- *Does it feel right?*
- *How would it look in the newspapers?*
- *Will it reflect negatively on you or the firm?*
- *Who else could be impacted by this (others in the firm, clients, you, etc.)?*
- *Would you be embarrassed if others knew you took this course of action?*
- *Is there an alternative action that does not pose an ethical conflict?*
- *Is it against firm or professional standards*
- *What would a reasonable person think*?
- *Can you sleep at night*?

value a company, says Harvey Goldschmid, general counsel of the SEC. A second problem, he says, is that managements will often use reserves to "dim the signals" going to both the public and their boards when business turns down.

The SEC says it is looking at a number of companies suspected of harboring improper reserves. . . . The SEC's most elaborate reserve case is the one it launched last December against W.R. Grace, not just attacking cookie jars but also roping in another item on Levitt's list, "materiality." This term acknowledges that the preparation of financial statements is a complex job and that neither managements nor their outside auditors, however well-intentioned, can testify that the figures are accurate down to the penny. Auditors deal with this uncertainty by attesting that a company's statements are accurate "in all material respects." Unfortunately, auditors also lean on materiality when they are trying to convince themselves it's okay for managers to slip intentional misstatements into their financial reports.

The SEC is right now busy drawing a line in the sand about materiality. In the past it has sometimes permitted managements to get by with irregularities in their financial reports just as long as the deliberate misstatements could be classed, often by some ad hoc mathematical logic, as immaterial. But it is now preparing to say—in a staff bulletin soon to appear—that intentional errors made for the purpose of managing earnings just won't be tolerated.

In the W.R. Grace case, moreover, it went after intentional errors made several years back. It seems that in the early 1990s a division of that company, National Medical Care (NMC), made more in profits than it had expected. So NMC, according to the SEC, deliberately underreported its earnings (thereby creating an "irregularity"), stuffing the excess into a cookie-jar reserve that in time got to be $60 million in size. Then in 1993, when profits needed a sugar fix, NMC started feeding the reserve into earnings (thereby compounding the irregularities). Meanwhile, Grace's auditors, Price Waterhouse, went along with these contortions on the grounds that they weren't material.

The SEC, launching its case, objected to the entire goings-on. By June it had exacted cease-and-desist

consents from two PricewaterhouseCoopers partners and from Grace itself, which agreed as well to set up a $1 million educational fund to further awareness of GAAP. The commission has also filed cease-and-desist proceedings against seven former Grace officers (among them CEO J.P. Bolduc), of whom three get special attention. These three, who include Grace's former chief financial officer, Brian Smith, are licensed CPAs whom the SEC views as having engaged in "inappropriate professional conduct." So the commission wants an administrative judge to bar them from practicing before the SEC. That means they could not play *any* part in preparing the financial statements of publicly owned companies or any other SEC registrant. . . .

The Grace case is important to Levitt's initiative because it sends such a strong message to other companies, some of which should be thinking, "There but for the god of Grace go I." In an entirely different way, the Cendant case demands attention because it displays such gross behavior. The misdeeds are fully documented as well, in a remarkable and unsparing 146-page report done for the audit committee of Cendant's board by the law firm of Willkie Farr & Gallagher and auditors imported for the project, Arthur Andersen. Here are some of the report's findings:

- In the three years 1995–97, CUC's operating income before taxes was improperly inflated by $500 million, which was more than one-third of its reported pretax income for those years.
- Though many of the improprieties occurred in CUC's biggest subsidiary, Comp-U-Card, they reached to 16 others as well. No fewer than 20 employees participated in the wrongdoing.
- Several CUC employees who were interviewed said they understood that the purpose of inflating earnings was to meet "analysts' expectations."
- In the first three quarters of each of the infected years, CUC put out unaudited financial statements that headquarters deliberately falsified, mostly by "adjusting" Comp-U-Card's revenues upward and its expenses downward. These favorable "adjustments" grew: They were $31 million in 1995, $87 million in 1976, and $176 million in 1997.

- At the end of each year, before its outside auditors, Ernst & Young, came in to make their annual review, CUC undid those improprieties (which would almost certainly have been discovered in the audit process) and instead created the earnings it needed mainly by plucking them from cookie-jar reserves.

- In most cases, the explanations that CUC gave Ernst & Young for these reserve infusions satisfied the accounting firm, which in general did not display impressive detective skills. On one occasion, however, E&Y could not find justification for $25 million transferred helpfully from a reserve—and this it let pass as "immaterial." (Cendant has sued E&Y, which has responded that it was the victim of deception and is "outraged" to be blamed for Cendant's own fraud.)

- In one particularly colorful incident, CUC used a merger reserve it had established in 1997 to swallow up $597,000 of private airplane expenses that its CEO Walter Forbes, had paid in 1995 and 1996, and for which he had requested reimbursement. Had these expenses not been allocated to the reserve, they would have turned up where they should have: in operating costs.

Naturally, Willkie Farr questioned Forbes about his knowledge of CUC's wrongdoing. He denied knowing anything about it. . . .

Michael Young, a Willkie Farr litigator and a student of accounting frauds, says they tend to follow a predictable trajectory. The Cendant case was no exception. It started small and grew out of control. It also dragged in employees who were troubled by what they were asked to do but did it anyway. Young remembers one case in which he was about to interview a woman implicated in a fraud. She suddenly burst into tears and said the totally unexpected: "I'm so glad to have someone to talk to about this."

Levitt understands well that the SEC is facing an enormous challenge in trying to get the cultural change it wants. Wall Street itself is an obstacle: It wants consistent earnings, however attained. Speaking at a recent investor-relations conference, one stock analyst, Gary Baiter of DLJ, baldly urged that companies consider "hiding earnings" for future use. "If you don't play the game," he said, "you're going to get hurt."

On a second front, the SEC has already run into roadblocks on certain new rules it would like to impose on audit committees. . . . Levitt himself has grown used to visits from business leaders not happy at all with accounting changes disturbing their lives. Even some feds are up in arms. The SEC, brandishing GAAP, is arguing that certain banks have overstated their reserves; banking regulators, perfectly happy with a little conservatism, have risen in protest.

Another issue is whether really egregious cases can be made criminal actions. For a U.S. attorney, whose alternatives include going after drug dealing, espionage, and bank robbery, it is no easy decision to take on a white-collar case stuffed with the arcana of accounting. According to Levitt's chief policeman, Director of Enforcement Richard Walker, the cases that ought to wind up in criminal court are those in which a company or executive has exhibited a high level of what lawyers call *scienter*—that is, knowing and willful conduct—and acted "to violate the law, misapply accounting standards, and affect financial reporting." Prosecutors may also weigh aggravating factors such as lies told to auditors or profitable trades made by an executive as he paints a false picture of his company's financial health. Walker, who has been at the SEC for eight years, thinks Levitt's message is in any event getting through. "I'm seeing more acceptance of these cases by U.S. attorneys today than in all the time I've been here. . . ."

Meanwhile, some corporations continue to behave in ways that make you question whether they've even heard of Levitt. Companies are not in the least required to make forecasts about earnings. Yet this spring, as McKesson was conceding that it had no real handle on the profits of its accounting-troubled unit, HBOC, it was still saying it was comfortable with projections that it could make $2.50 a share for its fiscal year ending next February. McKesson's nervy statement supports the opinion of class-action lawyer William Lerach that it is always good to allow time for the actors in frauds, especially CEOs, to make the self-destructive public statements they almost always do.

If tales like McKesson's confirm the challenge that Levitt faces, there is another that puts a slightly different complexion on things. The SEC's Turner says he knows a largish FORTUNE 500 company that in a recent reporting period ended up with earnings well beyond Street expectations. The boss said to the CFO: "Let's hold some of those back." "Wait a minute," objected the CFO, "don't even go there. Don't you know what the SEC is doing to people?" And the boss looked at the CFO, told him he was in "career limiting" territory, and once again ordered the earnings hid.

And what happened then? Turner's answer: "The CFO, the auditors, and the audit committee got together and managed to convince the boss he was wrong."

That's just one time, at one company. But at least it's a start.

QUESTIONS

1. What is the "fundamental problem" with the earnings-management culture?

2. What are several obstacles that the SEC faces in pursuing corporate criminals?

| Ed Cohen | # Arthur Andersen Refugees Reflect on What Went Wrong |

Ed Cohen is an associate editor of Notre Dame Magazine.

Two Notre Dame alumni who held leadership positions with Arthur Andersen say mind-boggling corporate structures, pressure to keep earnings looking good to Wall Street, and negligent board directors all contributed to the wave of scandals that rocked the business world and toppled their long-venerated accounting firm at the turn of the 21st century.

They also say Arthur Andersen was unfairly scapegoated for having been Enron's and World-Com's auditor but that the accounting profession as a whole strayed from its traditional concern for keeping business on the straight and narrow.

Before being implicated in scandal, Arthur Andersen enjoyed a reputation for high ethical standards and quality work. . . .

Thomas Fischer . . . was managing partner of the Andersen's Milwaukee office until January 2002, when he took an already-planned retirement. Later that month it became known that the Justice Department intended to seek criminal obstruction-of-justice charges against the firm for its employees having shredded documents in the Enron case.

Fischer says he never witnessed any wrongdoing or felt pressure to cook books while at Andersen. So he believes it was unfair that the company was put out of business by the notoriety. Its demise cost more than 80,000 employees their jobs. . . .

"A lot of people would like to believe that Arthur Andersen was doing some kind of drive-by auditing and all the bad things that happened in the accounting profession were all centered in Arthur Andersen," he says. "Nothing is farther from the truth. All firms were run basically the same way."

Fischer blames the wave of corporate scandals on what he calls a "social and economic blow-off" that occurred in the United States in the late 1990s. People thought the good times would never end, and many were willing to bend rules to keep them rolling, he says. One of the symptoms of the culture, he says, was excessive compensation paid to CEOs.

Ed Cohen, "Arthur Andersen Refugees Reflect on What Went Wrong," *Notre Dame Magazine* Jan, 2004. Reprinted with permission of the editor.

Before the Whistle Blew...
Sherron Watkins

An excerpt from an August 2001 memo to Enron CEO Ken Lay:

> Has Enron become a risky place to work? For those of us who didn't get rich over the last few years, can we afford to stay?
>
> Skilling's abrupt departure will raise suspicions of accounting improprieties and valuation issues. Enron has been very aggressive in its accounting—most notably the Raptor transactions and the Condor vehicle. . . .
>
> It sure looks to the layman on the street that we are hiding losses in a related company and will compensate that company with Enron stock in the future.
>
> I am incredibly nervous that we will implode in a wave of accounting scandals. . . .

"Accountants used to be the part of business that stood up and said, 'This is not right, this doesn't make sense,'" Fischer says. He says he hopes the profession will one day "stand up and be the backbone and the moral compass of the business world that it used to be and is not today."

Joe J. Tapajna, former worldwide managing tax practice director for Arthur Andersen, is now national professional practice director for tax at Deloitte and Touche in Chicago. He also teaches a graduate-level course in tax accounting at Notre Dame.

Tapajna says that when he entered the profession in the 1970s, accounting emphasized professionalism and caution. Accountants were outspoken about following procedures and adhering to the spirit rather than merely the letter of the law. . . .

Tapajna says that in the 1980s and 1990s accurate accounting became much more difficult as businesses became more complex and the investment community demanded information faster. He notes that Enron, the giant energy-trader, consisted of thousands of subsidiaries with management acquiring and disposing of companies on almost a daily basis.

"[A]t best, you were always trying to come up with approximately the right answer instead of the right answer."

Both professionals also say that board members failed in their responsibility to provide appropriate oversight of management's activities.

"It isn't really ethics," says Fischer, "it's 'do your job.'"

QUESTIONS

1. What do you think went wrong at Arthur Andersen? Did the firm deserve the consequences?

2. If (as a management guru) you had to give advice to Arthur Andersen executives *before* the Enron debacle, what would you say?

Robert E. Frederick
and W. Michael Hoffman

The Individual Investor in Securities Markets: An Ethical Analysis

Robert E. Frederick is professor of philosophy at Bentley College. W. Michael Hoffman taught at Bentley College.

Securities markets are full of pitfalls for individual investors. Examples of fraud and regulatory violations in the markets are common. For instance, a recent *Business Week* cover story reports that investors are being duped out of hundreds of millions a year in penny stock scams in spite of SEC regulations.[1] A report in the *Wall Street Journal* on the Chicago futures trading fraud highlights the "danger of being ripped off in futures markets" by unscrupulous floor brokers filling customers' "market orders"—a type of order that "individual investors should avoid using."[2]

But securities markets present risks to individual investors that go beyond clear violations of regulations and fraud. The above *Wall Street Journal* story, for example, also issued a more general warning to investors:

> Futures are fast moving, risky investment vehicles that are unsuitable for anyone who can't afford to lose and who doesn't have time to pay close attention to trading positions.[3]

Furthermore, it is not only the high risk futures and commodities markets that are perilous for investors. . . . Even the bond markets, which in the past at least gave the outside appearance of stability, are in increasing turmoil. . . .

In light of these and many other examples that could be given, suppose the SEC announced that individual investors, for their own protection, no longer have access to securities markets. They are no longer permitted to buy stocks, bonds, or commodities or futures options. If this were to happen there surely would be a public outcry of protest, even moral outrage. The reasons for such outrage probably would revolve around the belief that some fundamental right had been violated, perhaps the presumed right that markets should be free and open so that everyone has an opportunity to better his or her position and enjoy the goods and services of society.

A quick look, however, reveals that not all markets have unrestricted access. Nor is there a generally accepted belief that any rights are being unjustifiably violated in such cases. In consumer markets, for example, individuals under a certain age are prohibited from voting, buying alcoholic beverages, and seeing certain movies. Regardless of age, not just anyone can buy a fully automatic rifle or order a few dozen hand grenades. In fact, not just anyone can drive a car; one must pass a test and be licensed to do that. Furthermore, even after being allowed to drive, this privilege can be revoked if it is abused. And, of course, none of our citizens is legally permitted to participate in certain drug markets, such as cocaine.

But it will be argued that there is good reason for these and other such restrictions. We are attempting to prevent people, the argument goes, from harming themselves or causing harm to others. This is what makes it morally permissible, or even obligatory, to restrict access to certain kinds of consumer products. The ethical principle here is that, when possible, persons ought to be protected from undue harm. Hence, the restrictions in question are justified.

Journal of Business Ethics 9 (1990): 579–589. © 1990 Kluwer Academic Publishers. Reprinted by permission of Kluwer Academic Publishers.

Yet might not this be exactly the rationale behind a possible SEC ban against individual investors entering securities markets? Just as unrestricted access to some drugs is thought to present unacceptable risks to consumers, trading in today's securities markets may present unacceptable risks to many investors, resulting in great financial rather than physical harm. And since we feel justified in prohibiting consumers from buying what we take to be highly dangerous drugs or other consumer products, shouldn't we, by analogy, be justified in prohibiting certain investors from buying highly risky financial instruments? . . .

EXACTLY WHAT KIND OF INVESTOR ARE WE TALKING ABOUT?

The type of investor we will be concerned with, and the type we take to be the most likely candidate for the SEC prohibition mentioned earlier, is one that (a) is at relatively *high risk*, where risk is a function of the probability of a certain market event occurring and the degree of harm the investor would suffer were the event to occur, and (b) an investor who is relatively *unsophisticated* about the functioning of the market and hence unappreciative of the degree of risk he or she faces. For example, suppose Jones invests his life savings in high yield bonds . . . and suppose a few months later the company that issued the bonds suddenly announces that it is going into Chapter 11 bankruptcy. The value of the bonds drops precipitously and, for all practical purposes, in a matter of hours Jones' savings are wiped out. If Jones did not realize that the high return he was initially receiving was a reflection of the risky nature of the bonds, then he would fall within the category of investors with which we are concerned even assuming he had several million dollars invested. . . .

WHAT SORT OF JUSTIFICATION MIGHT BE OFFERED FOR RESTRICTING THE INVESTMENTS OF AT-RISK INVESTORS?

One kind of justification that might be proposed is paternalistic. By paternalism we roughly mean

interfering with a person's actions or preferences by restricting their freedom of action or the range of choices normally available to them for the reason that such a restriction promotes or preserves their good, welfare, happiness, or interests. A paternalistic justification for restricting at risk investors would be that exposure to risk for many investors is too great to permit them to continue without some sort of protection that reduces the risk to an acceptable degree. For certain investors an acceptable degree may be no risk at all. For others some risk may be permissible. In either case, the argument goes, as long as the intent of intervention is to protect or promote the good of at-risk investors, and as long as it does not wrong other persons, then intervention is at least permissible and may be obligatory. It is only in this way that harm to many investors can be prevented.

The standard objection to paternalistic justifications is something like this: If people choose to run the risk to gain what they believe will be the rewards, who are we to interfere? From where do we derive a special dispensation to overrule their choices and interfere with their lives?

Although there is a kernel of truth in this objection, it is much too facile. Some paternalistic acts are clearly justified. Paternalistic reasoning is commonly used to justify restricting the choices of children and people judged incompetent or otherwise unable rationally to consider the consequences of their acts. Moreover, paternalistic justifications are not obviously unreasonable even in cases where the competence of the person is not in question. It is at least initially credible that some consumer products, such as prescription drugs, are not in unrestricted circulation precisely because of paternalistic reasons.

Let us confine our discussion to those persons ordinarily taken to be competent and rational. We still do not believe that paternalism per se justifies restricting at-risk investors that fall within this category. One reason is that it may be impossible to find out just what the good or welfare of an individual investor is. Not only is there the thorny problem of trying to reach a common and precise understanding of the vague idea of the "good" of a person, there are immense practical difficulties in discovering whether a certain individual's good is served by restricting his or her access to the market. There may be situations where an individual's good is not served, and intervention in those cases would be a wrongful violation of his or her rights.

But suppose regulators do know the good of some individuals. Would paternalism then justify intervening to preserve or promote their good? We believe not in cases where regulators and the person in question have differing conceptions of that person's good. Even if regulators happen to know a person's "true" good better than he or she does themselves, imposing on that person a conception of his or her good they do not accept is not justified. Regulators may attempt to persuade at-risk investors to take a different course or provide them with information that they need to make an informed decision, but it is not permissible to deny them the right to direct their lives. . . .

Although paternalism as characterized thus far does not justify interference with the choices of at-risk investors, there are circumstances in which intervention is justified. This can best be explained by using an example not related to investing. Suppose Jones mistakenly believes the food he is about to eat is wholesome but we have good reason to think it is contaminated with botulism. As he raises the fork to his mouth, we only have time to strike it away. At first he is angry, but after we explain the reason for our action he is grateful. The act of striking the fork away is an example of paternalistic intervention since it is done for Jones' good but against his wishes. It seems obvious, however, that we acted properly. Intervention in this case is justified since if Jones were fully aware of the circumstances he would act differently or would agree to have us intervene on his behalf. He would consent to our action. Hence, intervention here respects his right to freedom since it is compatible with his goals and does not force upon him some version of his good he would not accept.

Note that it is not merely our superior knowledge of the situation that justifies interference, but also our judgment that Jones would agree that our actions preserve or promote his good. The case would be different were Jones attempting suicide instead of trying to have a decent meal. Paternalistic intervention may not be justified when a person voluntarily undertakes an action harmful to him- or herself, provided that person has a reasonably complete understanding of his or her circumstances and the consequences of the action. But it is at least prima facie justified, we suggest, when an action is based on incomplete information and thus is, in one sense, less than fully voluntary.

Now suppose there are compelling grounds to believe that some otherwise competent investors are unappreciative of the high degree of risk they face, and that if they were presented with information about those risks they would act either to reduce or eliminate them, or would consent to having restrictions placed on the kinds of investments they could make. Since they would consent to intervention or act differently were they fully aware of the circumstances, intervention on their behalf is justified just as it was justified for Jones. Their rights are not violated since nothing is imposed on them that they would not consent to were they fully aware of the dangers they faced.

A major difference between the Jones case and at-risk investors is that we dealt with Jones as an individual, but a regulatory or legislative body would have to deal with at-risk investors as a group. There simply is no way to reach them all individually. Furthermore, although such bodies may be able to make reasonable assumptions about the kinds of risks acceptable to most at-risk investors, and about the kinds of restrictions to which most of them would agree, it seems inevitable that there will be some investors who would not consent to restrictions because, for example, they have an unusual conception of their good or welfare, or because they find the restrictions highly offensive. For these people restrictions on investing will impose a foreign conception of their good on them and thus is not compatible with their right to direct their lives. . . .

If the *reason* given for intervening is promoting the good of at-risk investors as a group, then, as we have tried to argue, it is not justified. Suppose, however, the reason is not only that the good of some investors is promoted, but that there is a duty to intervene to protect certain *rights*, in particular, the right of investors not to be harmed. The argument would go something like this: There is good reason to believe that some at-risk investors would consent to having restrictions placed on them to protect their financial position and prevent them from suffering financial harm. Since it is a basic function of government to protect its citizens from harm, there is a duty to protect these investors. Hence, placing restrictions on their investment activities is justified even though such restrictions may violate the right of other investors to direct their lives as they see fit.

If this argument is plausible, then there is a conflict of rights between two groups of at-risk investors. This is a genuine moral dilemma that can only be resolved by deciding whose rights are to prevail. We believe it should be the right not to be harmed. An analogy with prescription drugs may be helpful here. One reason there are restrictions on access to drugs is to prevent harm to persons who do not know how to use them correctly. These restrictions are justified, in our view, even supposing there are some individuals willing to take the risk. The right to freedom of this latter group should be and should remain a serious consideration in devising restrictions on drugs, but it does not override the right of others not to be exposed to excessive risk and possible serious harm.

The same holds true of at-risk investors. The right of some of them not to be exposed to excessive risk and possible serious financial harm overrides the right of others to invest without restrictions. We emphasize, however, that the right to freedom cannot be lightly dismissed, and must be given due consideration when formulating policies and regulations governing the markets. . . .

IF SOME INVESTORS ARE RESTRICTED, HOW SHOULD IT BE DONE?

Since we are not experts in the regulation of securities markets, the best we can do here is make a few suggestions that seem to us worthy of additional investigation. It is a basic premise, essential for any just system of regulation and law, that relevantly different classes of persons be treated in relevantly different ways. Hence, it clearly would be unjust to restrict the activities of all investors to protect some of them. It also follows from this basic premise that distinctions must be drawn within the class of at-risk investors. It may turn out in the end that there is no workable method of protecting some at-risk investors while preserving the rights of all of them, but it would be a mistake to begin with this assumption.

In light of this it might be suggested that the only plausible course of action is to make sure that at-risk investors have all the information they need to make investment decisions. This has at least three advantages. The first is that providing information does not seriously infringe any rights. And establishing stringent policies to ensure that the information is received also may be reasonable. For example, suppose that to demonstrate a minimum level of competence persons must pass an examination before investing, just as they have to pass a driving exam before driving. Different kinds of exams could be given for different kinds of investments. Would such a procedure violate any rights? It certainly would be costly and inconvenient, but we doubt that it is an inordinate restriction on the right to freedom.

A second advantage is that providing information is already one function of the Securities and Exchange Commission. According to the Commission's pamphlet "Consumers' Financial Guide" the three main responsibilities of the Commission are:

1. To require that companies that offer their securities for sale in "interstate commerce" register with the Commission and make available to investors complete and accurate information.
2. To protect investors against misrepresentation and fraud in the issuance and sale of securities.
3. To oversee the securities markets to ensure they operate in a fair and orderly manner.

Although the pamphlet goes on to advise investors that "whatever the choice of investment, make sure that you have complete and accurate information before investing to ensure that you use your funds wisely," it also emphasizes that the SEC does not see itself as the guarantor of investments:

> Registration. . .does not insure investors against loss of their investments, but serves rather to provide information upon which investors may base an informed and realistic evaluation of the worth of a security.

Thus, providing information to at-risk investors is consistent with the mission of the SEC and would not require massive restructuring of the Commission.

The third advantage is that providing information would be the most direct way to discover whether investors would consent to restrictions. Earlier we argued that restrictions on some at-risk investors are justified because they would consent to intervention if they were fully aware of the risk they faced. But instead of imposing regulations based on what investors *would* do were they to have all the relevant information, it is preferable to give them the information whenever possible and see what they *actually* do. This would avoid the danger of imposing on them a conception of their good that they do not accept.

We agree that providing information to at-risk investors is a good idea, and propose that methods be initiated that ensure that investors receive the information, rather than just having it available for those that seek it out. However, this may not be enough to eliminate unacceptable risks for at-risk investors. Consider the prescription drug market again, and assume that the FDA made strenuous efforts to provide consumers with complete information about drugs. Supposing for a moment that it is legally permissible for consumers to buy drugs, as it is in some countries, this might be enough to eliminate unacceptable risk of harm from drugs for the few that had the time, energy, and expertise to use the information. But for most people it would be an overwhelming blizzard of paper that would be of no real use.

The same reasoning applies in the securities markets. So much information is available and it is so complex that for many investors beyond a certain point it would be too costly to make the investment in time required to assimilate it all. Having "complete and accurate information," as the SEC suggests, is not enough. Leaving aside the issue of how one determines whether it is complete and accurate (note that not even the SEC does that), there remains the problem of understanding it well enough to make a wise investment decision. Perhaps it could be done, but would it be done by most at-risk investors? We are inclined to think not. So we suggest that, just as with prescription drugs, at-risk investors be required by law to engage the services of an expert. This would go a long way toward eliminating unacceptable risks for them, and given the significant possibility of harm many investors face, we do not feel it would be an excessive restriction on their freedom. Exceptions would have to be made for those investors willing to become expert in the markets (since they would no longer meet the definition of an at-risk investor), and some system of qualifications would need to be established to identify investment counselors capable of advising the other investors. . . .

NOTES

1. "The Penny Stock Scandal," *Business Week*, 23 (January 1989), pp. 74–82.
2. "Investors Can Take a Bite Out of Fraud," *Wall Street Journal*, (January 24, 1989), p. C1.
3. *Wall Street Journal*, (January 24, 1989), p. C1.

QUESTIONS

1. What is an individual investor, and why are individual investors a special category of investor?
2. How should some investors be restricted from risk in securities markets? Why should they be?

John R. Boatright | Finance Ethics

John R. Boatright teaches at Loyola University in Chicago.

- *Financial markets* are vulnerable to unfair trading practices (fraud and manipulation), unfair conditions (an unlevel playing field), and contractual difficulties (forming, interpreting, and enforcing contracts). The main aim of federal securities laws and the self-regulation of exchanges is expressed in the phrase "fair and orderly" markets, which reflects the need in financial markets to balance the twin goals of fairness and efficiency.
- Many individuals and institutions serve as financial intermediaries, providing *financial services* on behalf of others. Financial intermediaries commonly make decisions as agents for principals in an agency relation, and they often become fiduciaries with fiduciary duties. Agents and fiduciaries have an obligation to act solely in the interests of other parties and, especially, to avoid conflicts of interest. Although financial services providers are often merely sellers in a buyer–seller relation, they still have the obligations of any seller to avoid deceptive and abusive sales practices.
- *Financial Management:* Business firms are legally structured as the financial instruments of shareholders, and officers and directors are agents of firms, and have a fiduciary duty to manage the firms with the objective of maximizing shareholder wealth. Ethical issues in financial management concern the actions that violate the duties of financial managers and the discretion of financial managers to serve the interests of nonshareholder groups, commonly called "stakeholders."

All financial activity takes place in a larger economic, political, and social setting and so ethical issues arise about the overall impact of financial activity. Although financial decision making is generally limited to the financial factors of risk and return over time, ethics includes a consideration of the ethical treatment of everyone affected by a decision, and the consequences for the whole of society.

FINANCIAL MARKETS

The fundamental ethical requirement of financial markets is that they be *fair*. Fairness may be defined either *substantively* (when the price of a security reflects the actual value) or *procedurally* (when buyers are enabled to determine the actual value of a security). In the USA, some state securities laws aim at substantive fairness by requiring expert evaluation of new securities (so-called "blue-sky" laws), but the federal Securities Act of 1933 and the Securities Exchange Act of 1934 attempt to secure fairness procedurally by requiring adequate disclosure. The rationale for mandatory disclosure is that securities transactions are more likely to be fair when material information must be disclosed and investors have easy access to information.

Unfair Trading Practices

Fraud, manipulation, and other unfair trading practices lead not only to unfair treatment in securities transactions but to a loss of investor confidence in the integrity of financial markets. Speculative activity also produces excess volatility, which was blamed for the stock market crashes of 1929 and October 1987.

From Robert E. Frederick, Ed., *A Companion to Business Ethics* (Malden, MA: Blackwell, 1999), pp. 153–163. Reprinted by permission.

Both fraud and manipulation are defined broadly. Section 17(a) of the 1933 Securities Act and Section 10(b) of the 1934 Securities Exchange Act prohibit anyone involved in the issue or exchange of securities to make a false statement of a material fact, to omit a fact that makes a statement of material facts misleading, or to engage in any practice or scheme that would serve to defraud. Whereas fraud generally involves the disclosure or concealment of information that bears on the value of a security, manipulation consists of trading for the purpose of creating a misleading impression about a security's value.

Fraud is obviously committed by an initial stock offering that inflates the assets of a firm or fails to disclose some of its liabilities. Insider trading has been prosecuted as a fraud on the grounds that non-public material information ought to be disclosed before trading. In the 1920s, the stock market was manipulated by traders who bid up the price of stock in order to sell at the peak to unwary investors. In recent years, concern has been expressed about a form of program trading known as index arbitrage, in which traders are able to create volatility in different markets, solely for the purpose of trading on the resulting price differences.

Fair Conditions

Fairness in financial markets is often expressed by the concept of a level playing field. A playing field may be unlevel because of inequalities in information, bargaining power, resources, processing ability, and special vulnerabilities.

Unequal information, or *information asymmetry*, may refer either to the fact that all parties to a transaction do not possess the same information or that they do not have the same *access* to information. The possession of different information is a pervasive nature of markets that is not always ethically objectionable. Indeed, investors who invest resources in acquiring superior information are entitled to exploit this advantage. And they perform a service by making markets more efficient. The unequal possession of information is unfair only when the information has not been legitimately acquired or when its use

violates some right or obligation. Other arguments against insider trading, for example, are that the information has not been acquired legitimately but has been misappropriated from the rightful owner (the "misappropriation theory") and that an insider who trades on information that has been acquired in a fiduciary relation violates a fiduciary duty. Equal access to information is problematical because accessibility is not a feature of information itself but a function of the investment that is required to obtain information. To the objection that an inside trader is using information that is inherently inaccessible, some reply that anyone can become an insider by devoting enough resources.

Similarly, inequalities in bargaining power, resources, and processing ability—which are pervasive in financial markets—are ethically objectionable only when they are used in violation of some right or obligation and especially when they are used coercively. The main ethical requirement is that people not use any advantage unfairly. For example, American stock markets permit relatively unsophisticated investors with modest resources and processing ability to buy stocks on fair terms, and some changes, such as increased use of program trading or private placements, are criticized for increasing the advantages of institutional investors. (The growth of mutual funds has served to reduce the adverse consequences of inequalities among investors.) Vulnerabilities, such as impulsiveness or overconfidence, create opportunities for exploitation that can be countered by such measures as a "cooling off" period on purchases and loans, and the warning to request and read a prospectus before investing.

Financial Contracting

Some financial instruments, such as home mortgages and futures options, are contracts which commit the parties to a certain course of action, and many financial relations, such as being a trustee or corporate officer, are contractual in nature. Contracts are often vague, ambiguous, or incomplete, with the result that disagreements arise about what is ethically and legally required.

First, beyond the written words of *express contracts* lie innumerable tacit understandings that constitute *implied contracts*. Financial affairs would be impossible if every detail had to be made explicit. However, whatever is left implicit is subject to differing interpretations, and insofar as implied contracts are not legally enforceable, they may be breached with impunity. Not only financial instruments but the relations of corporations with employees, customers, suppliers, and other stakeholders consist of implied contracts, from which each party receives some value. . . .

Second, contracts are sometimes imperfect because of limitations in our cognitive ability, especially incomplete knowledge, bounded rationality, and future contingencies. In addition, some situations may be too complex and uncertain to permit careful planning. As a result, the parties may fail to negotiate contracts that produce the maximum benefit for themselves. Disputes in contractual relations also arise over what constitutes a breach of contract and what is an appropriate remedy.

Agency and fiduciary relations are one solution for the problems of imperfect contracting because they replace specific obligations with a general duty to act in another's interests. In particular, the fiduciary relations of managers to shareholders has arisen because of the difficulties of writing contracts for this particular relation. Similarly, supplier relations are not easily reduced to contractual terms. The term *relational contracting* has been coined to describe the building of working relations as an alternative to rigid contracts.

FINANCIAL SERVICES

The financial services industry—which includes commercial banks, securities and investment firms, mutual and pension funds, insurance companies, and financial planners—provides a vast array of financial services to individuals, businesses, and governments. Financial services firms act primarily as financial *intermediaries*, which is to say that they use their capital to provide services rather than to trade on their own behalf. In providing financial services,

these firms sometimes act as agents or fiduciaries with respect to clients; at other times, they act as sellers in a typical buyer–seller relation. Thus, a broker who is authorized to trade for a client's account is an agent, but a broker who makes a cold call to a prospect is merely a salesperson. Many ethical disputes result from misunderstandings about the nature of a financial service provider's role.

Fiduciaries and Agents

A fiduciary is a person who is entrusted to act in the interests of another. Fiduciary duties are the duties of a fiduciary to act in that other person's interest without gaining any material benefit except with the knowledge and consent of that person. Similar to the fiduciary relation is the relation of *agent* and *principal*, in which one person (the agent) is engaged to act on behalf of another (the principal). Whereas fiduciary relations arise when something of value is entrusted to another person, agency relations are due to the need to rely on others for their specialized knowledge and skill. In both relations, the specific acts to be performed are not fully specified in advance and fiduciaries and agents have wide latitude.

A major source of unethical conduct by fiduciaries and agents is conflict of interest, in which a personal interest of the fiduciary or agent interferes with the ability of the person to act in the interest of the other person. Fiduciaries and agents are called upon to exercise judgment on behalf of others, and their judgment can be compromised if they stand to gain personally by a decision. For example, a conflict of interest is created when a brokerage firm offers a higher commission for selling in-house mutual funds. The conflict arises because the broker has an incentive to sell funds that may not be in a client's best interests. Whether mutual fund managers should be permitted to trade for their own account is a controversial question because of the perceived conflict of interest. Fiduciaries and agents also have duties to preserve the confidentiality of information and not to use the information for their own benefit. Thus, "piggyback" trading in which a broker copies the trades of a savvy client, is a breach of confidentiality. Agency relations are subject to some

The Wake-Up Call

"We must usher in a new era of integrity in corporate America," Mr. Bush said in a speech before Wall Street leaders today.

"The business pages of American newspapers should not read like a scandal sheet. . . . I am calling for a new ethic of personal responsibility in the business community—an ethic that will increase investor confidence, make employees proud of their companies and regain the trust of the American people."

The president vowed his administration would "end the days of cooking the books, shading the truth and breaking our laws."

"Self-regulation is important, but it is not enough." . . .

The president announced he would create a Corporate Fraud Task Force which would operate like a "financial crimes SWAT team, overseeing the investigation of corporate abusers and bringing them to account." . . .

The president urged Congress to pass a $20 million emergency funding request for the SEC to allow the agency to hire 100 enforcement agents. Mr. Bush asked legislators to approve an additional $100 million for the SEC in his 2003 budget. . . . Other proposals in the president's ten-point plan included doubling prison terms for mail and wire fraud to ten years, and toughening laws for document shredding and other ways of obstructing federal investigations. . . .

—*Online NewsHour*, http://www.pbs.org/newshour/updates/corporteµ_07-09-02.html, July 9, 2002

---

well-known difficulties that arise from the inability of principals to monitor agents closely. These difficulties are opportunism, moral hazard, and adverse selection. Opportunism, or shirking, occurs because of the tendency of agents to advance their own interests despite the commitment to act on behalf of another. In agency theory, which is the study of agency relations, whatever in principal loses from opportunism is known as agency loss. The total of the agency loss and expenditures to reduce it are called agency costs. Moral hazard arises when the cost (or risk) of an activity is borne by others, as when a person seeks more medical care because of insurance. Moral hazard can be reduced in insurance by requiring deductibles and copayments, which provide an insured person with an incentive to lower costs. Insurance companies can also seek out better insurance prospects, but this leads to the problem of adverse selection. Adverse selection is the tendency, in insurance, of less suitable prospects to seek more insurance, which increases the risk for insurers who cannot easily identify good and bad insurance prospects. More generally, principals are not always able to judge the suitability of agents, and agents have an incentive to misrepresent themselves.

Many ethical problems, ranging from churning of client accounts by stockbrokers to the empire-building tendencies of CEOs, result from the difficulties inherent in agency relations. These problems can be addressed by closer monitoring and by changes in the structure of the relation. For example, the incentive for brokers to churn could be reduced by basing compensation more on the performance of clients' portfolios and less on the volume of trades.

In addition, compensating executives with stock options aligns their interests more closely with those of the shareholders and thus prevents empire building. The most effective solutions for ethical problems in agency relations are twofold: first, there must be a strong sense of professionalism accompanied by professional organizations with codes of ethics; second, a high degree of trust must be present. Trust is essential in the financial services industry, and companies generally pay a heavy price for violating the public's confidence.

Sales Practices

Financial products are susceptible to abusive sales practices, such as "twisting," in which an insurance agent persuades a client to replace an existing policy merely for the commission, and "flipping," which is the practice of replacing one loan with another in order to generate additional fees. The poor are frequent targets of abuses by loan providers who offer high-interest loans and add on various "options" of little value. Finally, financial products should meet certain standards of integrity. Just as automobiles and houses can be shoddily made, so too are there shoddy financial products. The sale of limited partnerships, for example, has been criticized in recent years for dubious valuation of assets and questionable practices by developers.

Victims of fraud or abuse by financial services firms generally have recourse to the courts, but the securities industry in the USA requires most customers (and employees) to sign a predispute arbitration agreement (PDAA) that commits them to binding arbitration of disputes. Mandatory arbitration is spreading to the holders of credit cards, insurance policies, and other financial products. Although arbitration has many advantages over litigation, critics charge that the process is often unfair and denies investors adequate protection. The controversy over compulsory arbitration in the securities industry focuses on three issues: the requirement that investors sign a PDAA as a condition of opening an account, the alleged industry bias of arbitration panels, and the permissibility of punitive damages. In addition, the requirement that employees submit complaints about such matters as discrimination and harassment to arbitration denies them of the right to sue in court, a right that employees outside the securities industry take for granted.

Financial Services Firms

Financial services firms are themselves businesses, and the management of such a business raises some ethical issues, especially in the treatment of institutional clients. For example, underwriters of municipal bonds have been criticized for making political contributions in city elections in order to gain access. Firms as well as individuals encounter conflicts of interest, such as the reluctance of brokerage firms to issue a negative analysis of a client company's stock. In recent years, rogue traders have caused great losses at some firms, including the collapse of a major bank.

The managers of large investment portfolios for mutual funds, insurance companies, pension funds, and private endowments face two important ethical questions.

1. Should they consider social factors in making decisions, such as how a corporation treats its employees or its record on the environment?
2. Should they vote the stock that they hold, and if so, what criteria should they use to evaluate the issues that are submitted to a vote?

Some large institutional investors take a hands-off approach, while others are becoming actively involved as shareholders in a movement known as relationship investing.

FINANCIAL MANAGEMENT

Financial managers have the task of actively deploying assets rather than investing them. Unlike a portfolio manager who merely buys stocks of corporations for a client, a corporate financial manager is involved in the running of a corporation. Investment decisions in a corporation are concerned not with which securities to hold but with what business opportunities to pursue. These decisions are still made using standard financial criteria, however. Finance theory can be applied to the operation of a corporation by viewing the various components of a business as a portfolio with assets that can be bought and sold. Option pricing theory, in particular, suggests that all of the possibilities for a firm can be regarded options to buy and sell assets. Bankruptcy, for example, is exercising an option to "sell" the corporation to the debtholders. (However, one critic has called this a "thoroughly immoral view of finance.")

The ethical issues in financial management are twofold.

- Financial managers, as agents and fiduciaries, have an obligation to manage assets prudently and especially to avoid the use of assets for personal benefit. Thus, managers, who have preferential access to information, should not engage in insider trading or self-dealing. For example, management buyouts, in which a group of managers take a public corporation private, raise the question whether people who are paid to mind the store should seek to buy it.

- Financial managers are called upon to make decisions that impact many different groups, and they have an obligation in their decision making to balance some competing interests. For example, should the decision to close a plant be made solely with the shareholders' interests in mind or should the interests of the employees and the local community be taken into account?

Balancing Competing Interests

In finance theory, the objective of the firm is shareholder wealth maximization (SWM). This objective is reflected in corporate law, according to which officers and directors of corporations are agents of the corporation and have a fiduciary duty to operate the corporation in the interests of the shareholders. Despite the seemingly unequivocal guide of SWM, financial managers still face the need, in some situations, to balance competing interests. In particular, decisions about levels of risk and hostile takeovers reveal some difficulties in the pursuit of SWM.

The Level of Risk

Maximizing shareholder wealth cannot be done without assuming some risk. A critical, often overlooked, task of financial management is determining the appropriate level of risk. Leveraging, for example, increases the riskiness of a firm. The capital asset pricing model suggests that, for properly diversified shareholders, the level of risk for any given firm, called *unique* risk, is irrelevant and that only market or *systemic* risk is important. Finance theory treats bankruptcy as merely an event risk that is worth courting if the returns are high enough. If a firm is in distress, then a high risk, "bet-the-farm" strategy is especially beneficial to shareholders, because they will reap all the gains of success, while everyone will share the losses of failure (the moral hazard problem). Consequently, a financial manager should seek the highest return adjusted for risk, no matter the actual consequences.

However, a high-risk strategy poses dangers for bondholders, employees, suppliers, and managers themselves, all of whom place a high value on the continued operation of the firm. Employees, in particular, are more vulnerable than shareholders to unique, as opposed to systemic, risk because of their inability to diversify. Is it ethical for financial managers to increase risk in a firm so as to benefit shareholders, at the expense of other corporate constituencies? Does the firm, as an ongoing entity, have value that should be considered in financial decision making? Some have argued that managing purely by financial criteria, without regard for the level of risk, is immoral.

Hostile Takeovers

Hostile takeovers are often epic battles with winners and losers. For this reason, the rules for acquiring controlling interest should be fair to all parties involved. Managers of target companies feel entitled to a fair chance to defend their jobs; shareholders who sell their shares, and those who do not, have a right to make a decision in a fair and orderly manner; bondholders often lose in takeovers because of the increased debt; and employees and residents of local communities, who usually have no say in the decision, are generally the groups most harmed. . . .

The directors of a target company, whose approval is often necessary for a successful takeover, have a fiduciary duty to act in the best interests of the firm itself, which may not be identical with the interests of either the preexisting shareholders or those who seek control. A majority of states have adopted so-called "other constituency statutes" that permit boards of directors to consider other constituencies, such as employees, suppliers, customers, and local communities, in evaluating a takeover bid. Many other laws govern the conduct of raiders and defenders alike, so that the market for corporate control is scarcely a pure market. In general, courts and legislatures have created rules for takeovers that seek both fairness and efficiency.

QUESTIONS

1. What are unfair trading practices? Give several examples.

2. What are the important ethical distinctions between stockholders and stakeholders?

Jennifer Moore

What Is Really Unethical About Insider Trading?

Jennifer Moore is an author and an attorney.

The term *insider trading* needs some preliminary clarification. Both the SEC and the courts have strongly resisted pressure to define the notion clearly. In 1961, the SEC stated that corporate insiders—such as officers or directors—in possession of material, nonpublic information were required to disclose that information or to refrain from trading. But this "disclose or refrain" rule has since been extended to persons other than corporate insiders. People who get information from insiders ("tippees") and those who become "temporary insiders" in the course of some work they perform for the company, can acquire the duty of insiders in some cases. Financial printers and newspaper columnists, not "insiders" in the technical sense, have also been found guilty of insider trading. Increasingly, the term *insider* has come to refer to the kind of information a person possesses rather than to the status of the person who trades on that information. My use of the term will reflect this ambiguity. In this paper, an "insider trader" is someone who trades in material, nonpublic information—not necessarily a corporate insider.

1. ETHICAL ARGUMENTS AGAINST INSIDER TRADING

Fairness

Probably the most common reason given for thinking that insider trading is unethical is that it is "unfair." For proponents of the fairness argument, the key feature of insider trading is the disparity of information between the two parties to the transaction. Trading should take place on a "level playing field," they argue, and disparities in information tilt the field toward one player and away from the other. There are two versions of the fairness argument: the first argues that insider trading is unfair because the two parties do not have *equal* information; the second argues that insider trading is unfair because the

From *Journal of Business Ethics* 9 (March 1990). Copyright © 1990 by D. Reidel Publishing Co. Reprinted by permission of Kluwer Academic Publishers. Some notes omitted.

two parties do not have equal *access* to information. Let us look at the two versions one at a time.

According to the equal information argument, insider trading is unfair because one party to the transaction lacks information the other party has, and is thus at a disadvantage. Although this is a very strict notion of fairness, it has its proponents, and hints of this view appear in some of the judicial opinions. One proponent of the equal information argument is Saul Levmore, who claims that "fairness is achieved when insiders and outsiders are in equal positions. That is, a system is fair if we would not expect one group to envy the position of the other." As thus defined, Levmore claims, fairness "reflects the 'golden rule' of impersonal behavior—treating others as we would ourselves."[1] If Levmore is correct, then not just insider trading, but *all* transactions in which there is a disparity of information are unfair, and thus unethical. But this claim seems overly broad. An example will help to illustrate some of the problems with it.

Suppose I am touring Vermont and come across an antique blanket chest in the barn of a farmer, a chest I know will bring $2,500 back in the city. I offer to buy it for $75, and the farmer agrees. If he had known how much I could get for it back home, he probably would have asked a higher price—but I failed to disclose this information. I have profited from an informational advantage. Have I been unethical? My suspicion is that most people would say I have not. While knowing how much I could sell the chest for in the city is in the interest of the farmer, I am not morally obligated to reveal it. I am not morally obligated to tell those who deal with me *everything* that it would be in their interest to know. . . .

In general, it is only when I owe a *duty* to the other party that I am legally required to reveal all information that is in his interest. In such a situation, the other party believes that I am looking out for his interests, and I deceive him if I do not do so. Failure to disclose is deceptive in this instance because of the relationship of trust and dependence between the parties. But this suggests that trading on inside information is wrong, *not* because it violates a general notion of fairness, but because a breach of fiduciary duty is involved. Cases of insider trading in which no

fiduciary duty of this kind is breached would not be unethical. . . .

The "equal information" version of the fairness argument seems to me to fail. However, it could be argued that insider trading is unfair because the insider has information that is not *accessible* to the ordinary investor. For proponents of this second type of fairness argument, it is not the insider's information advantage that counts, but the fact that this advantage is "unerodable," one that cannot be overcome by the hard work and ingenuity of the ordinary investor. No matter how hard the latter works, he is unable to acquire nonpublic information, because this information is protected by law.[2]

This type of fairness argument seems more promising, since it allows people to profit from informational advantages of their own making, but not from advantages that are built into the system. Proponents of this "equal access" argument would probably find my deal with the Vermont farmer unobjectionable, because information about antiques is not in principle unavailable to the farmer. The problem with the argument is that the notion of "equal access" is not very clear. What does it mean for two people to have equal access to information?

Suppose my pipes are leaking and I call a plumber to fix them. He charges me for the job, and benefits by the informational advantage he has over me. Most of us would not find this transaction unethical. True, I don't have "equal access" to the information needed to fix my pipes in any real sense, but I could have had this information had I chosen to become a plumber. The disparity of information in this case is simply something that is built into the fact that people choose to specialize in different areas. But just as I could have chosen to become a plumber, I could have chosen to become a corporate insider with access to legally protected information. . . .

One might argue that I have easier access to a plumber's information than I do to an insider trader's, since there are lots of plumbers from whom I can buy the information I seek. The fact that insiders have a strong incentive to keep their information to themselves is a serious objection to insider trading. But if insider trading were made legal, insiders could profit not only from trading on their information, but also on selling it to willing buyers. Proponents of the practice argue that a brisk market in information would soon develop—indeed, it might be argued that such a market already exists, though in illegal and clandestine form.[3] . . .

The most interesting thing about the fairness argument is not that it provides a compelling reason to outlaw insider trading, but that it leads to issues we cannot settle on the basis of an abstract concept of fairness alone. The claim that parties to a transaction should have equal information, or equal access to information, inevitably raises questions about how informational advantages are (or should be) acquired, and when people are entitled to use them for profit. . . .

Property Rights in Information

As economists and legal scholars have recognized, information is a valuable thing, and it is possible to view it as a type of property. We already treat certain types of information as property: trade secrets, inventions, and so on—and protect them by law. Proponents of the property rights argument claim that material, nonpublic information is also a kind of property, and that insider trading is wrong because it involves a violation of property rights.

If inside information is a kind of property, whose property is it? How does information come to belong to one person rather than another? This is a very complex question, because information differs in many ways from other, more tangible sorts of property. But one influential argument is that information belongs to the people who discover, originate, or "create" it. As Bill Shaw put it in a recent article, "the originator of the information (the individual or corporation that spent hard-earned bucks producing it) owns and controls this asset just as it does other proprietary goods."[4] Thus, if a firm agrees to a deal, invents a new product, or discovers new natural resources, it has a property right in that information and is entitled to exclusive use of it for its own profit.

It is important to note that it is the firm itself (and/or its shareholders), and not the individual employees of the firm, who have property rights in the information.

To be sure, it is always certain individuals in the firm who put together the deal, invent the product, or discover the resources. But they are able to do this only because they are backed by the power and authority of the firm. The employees of the firm—managers, officers, directors—are not entitled to the information any more than they are entitled to corporate trade secrets or patents on products that they develop for the firm. It is the firm that makes it possible to create the information and that makes the information valuable once it has been created. . . .

If this analysis is correct, then it suggests that insider trading is wrong because it is a form of theft. It is not exactly like theft, because the person who uses inside information does not deprive the company of the use of the information. But he does deprive the company of the *sole* use of the information, which is itself an asset. The insider trader "misappropriates," as the laws puts it, information that belongs to the company and uses it in a way in which it was not intended—for personal profit. It is not surprising that this "misappropriation theory" has begun to take hold in the courts, and has become one of the predominant rationales in prosecuting insider trading cases. . . .

This theory is quite persuasive, as far as it goes. But it is not enough to show that insider trading is always unethical or that it should be illegal. If insider information is really the property of the firm that produces it, then using that property is wrong *only when the firm prohibits it*. If the firm does not prohibit insider trading, it seems perfectly acceptable. (Unless there is some other reason for forbidding it, such as that it harms others.) Most companies do in fact forbid insider trading. But it is not clear whether they do so because they don't want their employees using corporate property for profit or simply because it is illegal. Proponents of insider trading point out that most corporations did not prohibit insider trading until recently, when it became a prime concern of enforcement agencies. . . .

A crucial factor here would be the shareholders' agreement to allow insider information. Shareholders may not wish to allow trading on inside information because they may wish the employees of the company to be devoted simply to advancing shareholder interests. We will return to this point later. But if shareholders did allow it, it would seem to be permissible. Still others argue that shareholders would not need to "agree" in any way other than to be told this information when they were buying the stock. If they did not want to hold stock in a company whose employees were permitted to trade on inside information, they would not buy that stock. Hence they could be said to have "agreed."

Manne and other proponents of insider trading have suggested a number of reasons why "shareholders would voluntarily enter into contractual arrangements with insiders giving them property rights in valuable information."[5] Their principal argument is that permitting insider trading would serve as an incentive to create more information— put together more deals, invent more new products, or make more discoveries. Such an incentive, they argue, would create more profit for shareholders in the long run. Assigning employees the right to trade on inside information could take the place of more traditional (and expensive) elements in the employee's compensation package. Rather than giving out end-of-the-year bonuses, for example, firms could allow employees to put together their own bonuses by cashing in on inside information, thus saving the company money. In addition, proponents argue, insider trading would improve the efficiency of the market. We will return to these claims later.

If inside information really is a form of corporate property, firms may assign employees the right to trade on it if they choose to do so. The only reason for not permitting firms to allow employees to trade on their information would be that doing so causes harm to other investors or to society at large. Although our society values property rights very highly, they are not absolute. We do not hesitate to restrict property rights if their exercise causes significant harm to others. The permissibility of insider trading, then, ultimately seems to depend on whether the practice is harmful.

Harm

There are two principal harm-based arguments against insider trading. The first claims that the practice is harmful to ordinary investors who engage in trades with insiders; the second claims that insider trading erodes investors' confidence in the market, causing them to pull out of the market and harming the market as a whole. I will address the two arguments in turn.

Although proponents of insider trading often refer to it as a "victimless crime," implying that no one is harmed by it, it is not difficult to think of examples of transactions with insiders in which ordinary investors are made worse off. Suppose I have placed an order with my broker to sell my shares in Megalith Co., currently trading at $50 a share, at $60 or above. An insider knows that Behemoth Inc. is going to announce a tender offer for Megalith shares in two days, and has begun to buy large amounts of stock in anticipation of the gains. Because of his market activity, Megalith stock rises to $65 a share and my order is triggered. If he had refrained from trading, the price would have risen steeply two days later, and I would have been able to sell my shares for $80. Because the insider traded, I failed to realize the gains that I otherwise would have made.

But there are other examples of transactions in which ordinary investors *benefit* from insider trading. Suppose I tell my broker to sell my shares in Acme Corp., currently trading at $45, if the price drops to $40 or lower. An insider knows of an enormous class action suit to be brought against Acme in two days. He sells his shares, lowering the price to $38 and triggering my sale. When the suit is made public two days later, the share price plunges to $25. If the insider had abstained from trading, I would have lost far more than I did. Here, the insider has protected me from loss. . . .

The truth about an ordinary investor's gains and losses from trading with insiders seems to be not that insider trading is never harmful, but that it is not systematically or consistently harmful. Insider trading is not a "victimless crime," as its proponents claim, but it is often difficult to tell exactly who the victims are and to what extent they have been victimized. The stipulation of the law to "disclose *or* abstain" from trading makes determining victims even more complex. While some investors are harmed by the insider's trade, to others the insider's actions make no difference at all; what harms them is simply *not having complete information* about the stock in question. Forbidding insider trading will not prevent these harms. Investors who neither buy nor sell, or who buy or sell for reasons independent of share price, fall into this category.

Permitting insider trading would undoubtedly make the securities market *riskier* for ordinary investors. Even proponents of the practice seem to agree with this claim. But if insider trading were permitted openly, they argue, investors would compensate for the extra riskiness by demanding a discount in share price. . . . If insider trading were permitted, in short, we could expect a general drop in share prices, but no net harm to investors would result. Moreover, improved efficiency would result in a bigger pie for everyone.

The second harm-based argument claims that permitting insider trading would cause ordinary investors to lose confidence in the market and cease to invest there, thus harming the market as a whole. As former SEC Chairman John Shad puts it, "if people get the impression that they're playing against a marked deck, they're simply not going to be willing to invest."[6] Since capital markets play a crucial role in allocating resources in our economy, this objection is a very serious one.

The weakness of the argument is that it turns almost exclusively on the *feelings* or *perceptions* of ordinary investors, and does not address the question of whether these perceptions are justified. If permitting insider trading really does harm ordinary investors, then this "loss of confidence" argument becomes a compelling reason for outlawing insider trading. But if, as many claim, the practice does not harm ordinary investors, then the sensible course of action is to educate the investors, not to outlaw insider trading. It is irrational to cater to the feelings of ordinary investors if those feelings are not justified. We ought not to outlaw perfectly permissible actions just because some people feel (unjustifiably) disadvantaged by them.

II. IS THERE ANYTHING WRONG WITH INSIDER TRADING?

My contention has been that the principal ethical arguments against insider trading do not, by themselves, suffice to show that the practice is unethical

and should be illegal. The strongest arguments are those that turn on the notion of a fiduciary duty to act in the interest of shareholders, or on the idea of inside information as company "property." But in both arguments, the impermissibility of insider trading depends on a contractual understanding among the company, its shareholders and its employees. In both cases, a modification of this understanding could change the moral status of insider trading.

Does this mean that there is nothing wrong with insider trading? No. If insider trading is unethical, it is so *in the context* of the relationship among the firm, its shareholders, and its employees. It is possible to change this context in a way that makes the practice permissible. But *should* the context be changed? I will argue that it should not. Because it threatens the fiduciary relationship that is central to business management, I believe, permitting insider trading is in the interest neither of the firm, its shareholders, nor society at large.

Fiduciary relationships are relationships of trust and dependence in which one party acts in the interest of another. They appear in many contexts, but are absolutely essential to conducting business in a complex society. Fiduciary relationships allow parties with different resources, skills, and information to cooperate in productive activity. Shareholders who wish to invest in a business, for example, but who cannot or do not wish to run it themselves, hire others to manage it for them. Managers, directors, and to some extent other employees, become fiduciaries for the firms they manage and for the shareholders of those firms.

The fiduciary relationship is one of moral and legal obligation. Fiduciaries, that is, are bound to act in the interests of those who depend on them even if these interests do not coincide with their own. Typically, however, fiduciary relationships are constructed as far as possible so that the interests of the fiduciaries and the parties for whom they act *do* coincide. Where the interests of the two parties compete or conflict, the fiduciary relationship is threatened. . . .

Significantly, proponents of insider trading do not dispute the importance of the fiduciary relationship. Rather, they argue that permitting insider trading would *increase* the likelihood that employees will act in the interest of shareholders and their firms. We have already touched on the main argument for this claim. Manne and others contend that assigning employees the right to trade on inside information would provide a powerful incentive for creative and entrepreneurial activity. It would encourage new inventions, creative deals, and efficient new management practices, thus increasing the profits, strength, and overall competitiveness of the firm. Manne goes so far as to argue that permission to trade on insider information is the only appropriate way to compensate entrepreneurial activity, and warns: "[I]f no way to reward the entrepreneur within a corporation exists, he will tend to disappear from the corporate scene."[7] The entrepreneur makes an invaluable contribution to the firm and its shareholders, and his disappearance would no doubt cause serious harm.

If permitting insider trading is to work in the way proponents suggest, however, there must be a direct and consistent link between the profits reaped by insider traders and the performance that benefits the firm. It is not at all clear that this is the case—indeed, there is evidence that the opposite is true. There appear to be many ways to profit from inside information that do not benefit the firm at all. I mention four possibilities in the following list. Two of these (Items 2 and 3) are simply ways in which insider traders can profit without benefiting the firm, suggesting that permitting insider trading is a poor incentive for performance and fails firmly to link the interests of managers, directors, and employees to those of the corporation as a whole. The others (1 and 4) are actually harmful to the corporation, setting up conflicts of interest and actively undermining the fiduciary relationship.

1. Proponents of insider trading tend to speak as if all information were positive. "Information," in the proponents' lexicon, always concerns a creative new deal, a new, efficient way of conducting business, or a new product. If this were true, allowing trades on inside information might provide an incentive to work even harder for the good of the company. But information can also concern *bad* news—a large lawsuit, an unsafe or poor quality product, or lower-than-expected performance. Such

negative information can be just as valuable to the insider trader as positive information. If the freedom to trade on positive information encourages acts that are beneficial to the firm, then by the same reasoning the freedom to trade on negative information would encourage harmful acts. At the very least, permitting employees to profit from harms to the company decreases the incentive to avoid such harms. Permission to trade on negative inside information gives rise to inevitable conflicts of interest. Proponents of insider trading have not satisfactorily answered this objection.

2. Proponents of insider trading also assume that the easiest way to profit on inside information is to "create" it. But it is not at all clear that this is true. Putting together a deal, inventing a new product, and other productive activities that add value to the firm usually require a significant investment of time and energy. For the well-placed employee, it would be far easier to start a rumor that the company has a new product or is about to announce a deal than to sit down and produce either one—and it would be just as profitable for the employee. If permitting insider trading provides an incentive for the productive "creation" of information, it seems to provide an even greater incentive for the nonproductive "invention" of information, or stock manipulation. The invention of information is in the interest neither of the firm nor of society at large.

3. Even if negative or false information did not pose problems, the incentive argument for insider trading overlooks the difficulties posed by "free riders"—those who do not actually contribute to the creation of the information, but who are nevertheless aware of it and can profit by trading on it. . . . Unless those who do not contribute can be excluded from trading on it, there will be no incentive to produce the desired information; it will not get created at all.

4. Finally, allowing trading on inside information would tend to deflect employees' attention from the day-to-day business of running the company and focus it on major changes, positive or negative, that lead to large insider trading profits.

Ethics Matter

Roel C. Campos

One of my duties as a Commissioner is not only to support and implement the securities laws, but also at times to urge practices that go beyond the letter of the law. I believe that this is such a time.

I am sure that I speak for the Chairman and my fellow Commissioners in observing that it is not enough for reporting companies simply to have a code of ethics. No matter how well or beautifully the language of the code of ethics reads, if the code is relegated to the back of a policy manual or a cluttered website, it is of no use. I submit that having a code of ethics that is not vigorously implemented is worse than not having a code of ethics. It smacks of hypocrisy.

We all know that having rules in life is not enough. Indeed, if it were enough, the existence of the Ten Commandments would ensure proper conduct among human beings. For this reason, I urge all CEOs and senior management of reporting companies to live and practice on a daily basis the principles contained in their codes of ethics.

Senior management should make it clear to employees through their words and conduct that ethics matter. Senior management and boards of directors should establish practices that acknowledge and commend acts of honesty and ethical behavior.

Just as good deeds in life create unforeseen blessings, I believe it is fundamental that honesty and integrity will ultimately create business success. Creating an ethical business culture should not be viewed as a sacrifice. Indeed, it is good business to be open and honest with your shareholders. It is good business to have fair dealings with your business partners. It is good business to reward employees for being honest and ethical. It is good business to be known as a company that deals fairly in its business transactions. It is good business for shareholders to know that a company not only has a code of ethics but that the code is followed every day. It is also good business to select CEOs and Presidents largely based on their integrity and commitment to ethical behavior. . . .

SEC Commissioner Roel C. Campos, Washington, D.C., October 16, 2002; http://www.sec.gov/news/speech/spch593.htm

This might not be true if one could profit by inside information about the day-to-day efficiency of the operation, a continuous tradition of product quality, or a consistently lean operating budget. But these things do not generate the kind of information on which insider traders can reap large profits. Insider profits come from dramatic changes, from "news"—not from steady, long-term performance. If the firm and its shareholders have a genuine interest in such performance, then permitting insider trading creates a conflict of interest for insiders. The ability to trade on inside information is also likely to influence the types of information officers announce to the public, and the timing of such announcements, making it less likely that the information and its timing is optimal for the firm. And the problems of false or negative information remain.

If the arguments just presented are correct, permitting insider trading does not increase the likelihood that insiders will act in the interest of the firm and its shareholders. In some cases, it actually causes conflicts of interest, undermining the fiduciary relationship essential to managing the corporation. This claim, in turn, gives corporations good reason to prohibit the practice. But insider trading remains primarily a private matter among corporations, shareholders, and employees. It is appropriate to ask why, given this fact about insider trading, the practice should be *illegal*. If it is primarily corporate and shareholder interests that are threatened by insider trading, why not let corporations themselves bear the burden of enforcement? Why involve the SEC? There are two possible reasons for continuing to support laws against insider trading. The first is that even if they wish to prohibit insider trading, individual corporations do not have the resources to do so effectively. The second is that society itself has a stake in the fiduciary relationship. . . .

The notion of the fiduciary duty owed by managers and other employees to the firm and its shareholders has a long and venerable history in our society. Nearly all of our important activities require some sort of cooperation, trust, or reliance on others, and the ability of one person to act in the interest of another—as a fiduciary—is central to this cooperation. The role of managers as fiduciaries for firms and shareholders is grounded in the property rights of shareholders. They are the owners of the firm, and bear the residual risks, and hence have a right to have it managed in their interest. The fiduciary relationship also contributes to efficiency, since it encourages those who are willing to take risks to place their resources in the hands of those who have the expertise to maximize their usefulness. While this "shareholder theory" of the firm has often been challenged in recent years, this has been primarily by people who argue that the fiduciary concept should be widened to include other "stakeholders" in the firm. I have heard no one argue that the notion of managers' fiduciary duties should be eliminated entirely, and that managers should begin working primarily for themselves.

III. CONCLUSION

I do believe that lifting the ban against insider trading would cause harms to shareholders, corporations, and society at large. But again, these harms stem primarily from the cracks in the fiduciary relationship caused by permitting insider trading, rather than from actual trades with insiders. Violation of fiduciary duty, in short, is at the center of insider trading offenses.

NOTES

1. Saul Levmore, "Securities and Secrets: Insider Trading and the Law of Contracts," 68 *Virginia Law Review* 117.

2. The equal access argument is perhaps best stated by Victor Brudney in his influential article, "Insiders, Outsiders and Informational Advantages Under the Federal Securities Laws," 93 *Harvard Law Review* 322.

3. Manne, *Insider Trading and the Stock Market* (Free Press, New York, 1966), 75.

4. Bill Shaw, "Should Insider Trading Be Outside the Law?" *Business and Society Review* 66: 34. See also Macey, "From Fairness to Contract: The New Direction of the Rules Against Insider Trading," 13 *Hofstra Law Review* 9 (1984).

5. Carlton and Fischel, "The Regulation of Insider Trading," 35 *Stanford Law Review* 857. See also Manne, *Insider Trading and the Stock Market*.

6. "Disputes Arise Over Value of Laws on Insider Trading," *The Wall Street Journal*, November 17, 1986, 28.

7. Manne, *Insider Trading and the Stock Market*, 129.

QUESTIONS

1. What *is* really unethical about insider trading? What does Moore conclude?

2. How might you argue that insider trading is really a good thing that should be allowed?

Frank Partnoy | F.I.A.S.C.O.

Frank Partnoy is an author and former Wall Street trader.

Keeping tabs on the derivatives obituaries column is nearly a full-time job these days, especially with the recent surge in activity. By the time you read this, the market is likely to be more than $100 trillion (it was estimated at $65–80 trillion as of mid-1998), headed for the astronomical $1 quadrillion mark. I can't resist the urge to abuse the late Senator Everett Dirksen's famous quote: a quadrillion here and a quadrillion there and pretty soon you're talking about some serious money.

. . . Derivatives, once again, are a horror show. The structured notes and leveraged swaps that rocked the financial markets with billion-dollar losses in 1994–95 are back. The same specters that haunted, and then broke Barings, and Orange County, and took a slice out of Procter & Gamble have returned from the dead. And in my opinion, the sequel is even more scary.

Derivatives remain unseen, yet ubiquitous. Time bombs are ticking away, concealed in the underbelly of our investment portfolios. Whether you realize it or not, most of you investors continue to have exposure to derivatives, typically through investments in mutual funds. . . and pension funds. . . . I was not happy to discover that my new hometown, sleepy San Diego, has a $3.3 billion public-employee pension fund chock full of derivatives. I own derivatives, indirectly, through a mutual fund I bought, and I'll bet you own them, too. If you still don't believe me, just call your mutual fund manager or read your prospectus. And get ready to weep.

Of course, Wall Street isn't weeping one tear. Derivatives continue to be hugely profitable for bankers, in part because fund managers who buy derivatives will pay a premium to take on risks they can hide from shareholders, and in part because other buyers don't fully understand what they are buying. Derivatives have helped Wall Street to its best year ever—bonuses were up more than 30 percent last year. Sellers of derivatives are ecstatic. Many buyers are happy, for now; ignorance is bliss. Yet 70 percent of derivatives professionals say they expect big losses in the coming year.

Opinion about derivatives remains sharply divided. George Soros, billionaire trader, warns that derivatives traders cause instability that will "destroy society.". . . [I believe that] derivatives carry hidden seeds of destruction, and that no one truly understands their risks. . . .

ASIAN FALLOUT

Much of the [recent] derivatives action. . . has been in Asia, where the derivatives market is estimated to be in the tens of trillions of dollars, though no one really knows how big it is. Market participants are worried, and Hong Kong pension fund regulators even proposed forbidding derivatives use. Japan and the Asian "tigers"—Korea, Indonesia, Malaysia, the Philippines, Singapore, Taiwan, Thailand—were doing just fine until the summer of 1997. On July 2, 1997, Thailand, which had pegged its currency, the baht, to a basket of foreign currencies, based on Thailand's trade with other countries, finally had to eliminate the peg. The baht plunged more than 17 percent against the U.S. dollar that day, just as the Mexican Peso had collapsed on December 20, 1994. The effects were cataclysmic.

[For instance, there was a] mouth-watering Thai baht structured note. . . . That note, and similar foreign exchange-linked notes, were issued by highly-rated corporations and government sponsored enterprises, such as General Electric Credit Corporation and the Federal Home Loan Banks. The notes looked safe, and paid a deliciously high coupon. But if you were an unlucky holder of a Thai baht structured note on July 2, 1997, you were suffering from more than mild digestive problems. A mountain of pink bismuth powder couldn't block the financial dysentery as the note ripped through the innards of your balance sheet, faster than a plate of bad pad ped.

The other Asian tigers followed Thailand into the dumpster. Asian banks had been feasting, like the fat Mexican banks of the early 1990s, making leveraged bets on their own markets and currencies using equity swaps, total return swaps, options, futures, forwards, and more complex derivatives. Now, they faced annihilation. Within months, the foreign currency value of investments in East Asia dropped by 50 percent or more.

Structured notes and swaps did far more than cause localized commercial collywobbles in Asia. They ensured that the ripple effects of the baht devaluation would reach well beyond the domestic markets. If a butterfly flapping its wings in Thailand can affect weather in the U.S., imagine what a currency devaluation can do. Individual investors, money managers, even hedge fund operators throughout the world were hurting.

Most of the derivatives causing the pain were "over-the-counter" rather than traded on any exchange. That means, for example, that Asian banks engaging in swaps had a counterparty, typically a U.S. or European bank, who expected repayment on the swap, just as I would expect repayment if you and I had bet $10 on whether the Asian markets would falter. In other words, the Asian banks and companies hadn't lost money to any centralized exchange; they had lost money to other companies, primarily Western banks. The bottom line was that if the Asian banks went bust, their counterparties might lose the entire amounts the Asian banks owed.

The over-the-counter nature of these derivatives trades created enormous potential for loss. For example, banking regulators warned that U.S. banks had more than $20 billion of exposure to Korea. One Korean investment firm, SK Securities Company, had bet with J. P. Morgan that the Thai baht would rise relative to the Japanese yen, and when the baht collapsed, SK owed J. P. Morgan about $300 million. Other banks—including Citicorp, Chase Manhattan, and Bankers Trust—each disclosed more than a billion dollars of exposure to Asia. This exposure to a counterparty's inability or unwillingness to repay is called "credit risk." Credit risk is a banal non-issue irrelevant to a counterparty until a so-called credit event actually occurs; then, credit risk is a central issue mattering all too much. Credit risk from derivatives was a major reason the U.S. was so concerned about rescuing Asia (and its banking counterparties) from financial meltdown.

One man who was suffering more than most during this period of financial indigestion in Asia was Victor Niederhoffer, the celebrated, and often barefooted, squash/derivatives maestro and hedge fund manager extraordinaire. Niederhoffer's imbroglio illustrates the interconnectedness of modern capital markets, and the amazing velocity of investments in derivatives.

In June 1997, Niederhoffer was on top of the world. His excellent autobiography, *The Education of a Speculator*, was selling well, and he was managing more than $100 million of investments, including much of his own considerable wealth. He was both popular and respected, and had an incredible track record: returns of 30 percent per year for fifteen years, with a 1996 return of 35 percent.

Unfortunately, Niederhoffer also had made a big bet on the baht. And when the Thai butterfly flapped its wings, he lost about $50 million, almost half of his fund.

Derivatives traders who lose $50 million, or more, seem to follow a pattern. I used to fall into that pattern playing blackjack in Las Vegas. Perhaps you've had a similar experience. You play a hand of blackjack for $100, thinking it wouldn't kill you to lose that much money. You lose the hand. Then, you play another hand, thinking it wouldn't be a big deal to lose $200. Besides, maybe you'll win the hand and get back to even. You lose that hand, too. Then, you

To: You
From: The Philosopher
Subject: "Aristotle on Money"

You probably remember Aristotle's idea of the "Golden Mean." Aristotle argued that if we consider almost any activity, the virtue of that activity lies in the mean between a "defect" or a "deficiency" and an "excess." Moderation is the key to virtue and happiness. True, he was not an accountant or an investment adviser, but Aristotle certainly has some helpful advice on how we relate to money:

> With regard to giving and taking of money the mean is liberality, the excess and the defect prodigality and meanness. They exceed and fall short in contrary ways to one another; the prodigal exceeds in spending and falls short in taking, while the mean man exceeds in taking and falls short in spending. With regard to money there are also other dispositions—a mean, magnificence (for the magnificent man differs from the liberal man; the former deals with large sums, the latter with small ones), an excess, tastelessness and vulgarity, and a deficiency, miserliness.

From Aristotle, *Nicomachean Ethics*, 1107b8–22.

lose another hand, and another hand, and another. Pretty soon, you're down $500, an amount of money you really would prefer *not* to lose. What do you do? Do you quit? Of course not. You do the opposite. You increase your wagers, and start betting to get even. That's the pattern. You look up to the eye-in-the-sky, and a little voice in your head trembles. "If only I could win that money back; *then* I would stop gambling. Forever."

Imagine adding five zeros to that $500. What does that voice sound like, now? It might sound awfully depressing if the $50 million was your money. But what if the money was, in the words of Justice Louis Brandeis, "other people's money"? Suddenly betting to get even doesn't seem foolish at all. Wouldn't you double-down, at least once, for $50 million of *someone else's* money? Why not? If you win, you're even and no one will ever care about your temporary loss. And if you lose, do you really think it matters much if you lose another $50 million of someone else's money? After the first $50 million, you've pretty much guaranteed that special someone won't be inviting you to Thanksgiving dinner.

So Niederhoffer, like others before him—Nick Leeson of Barings, Joseph Jett of Kidder, Peabody, Yasuo Hamanaka of Sumitomo, Toshihide Iguchi of Daiwa—began betting to get even, taking on additional risk in the hope that he could make back enough money to overcome his losses on the baht. Academics would refer to Niederhoffer, at this point in his life, as a rogue trader.

He had recovered a bit of the Thai loss by September, but was still down about 35 percent for the year. Going into October, Niederhoffer began doubling down by selling put options on the Standard & Poor's 500 index futures contract. This was a truly gutsy move. The S&P 500 index futures contract allows speculators to make leveraged bets on the performance of the S&P 500 index, an index that tracks 500 large stocks. You can sell put options on this contract in the same way you can sell put options on any other instrument.

. . . A put option is the right to sell some underlying financial instrument or index at a specified time and price. In the trader's parlance, or Corvette lingo, if you bought a put option, you might pay $1,000 today for the right to sell a Corvette for $40,000 some time during the next month. You would make money if the price of Corvettes dropped. If the price of a Corvette dropped to $30,000, you would make $10,000—the $40,000 you could sell a Corvette for, using the put option, minus the $30,000 you could buy a Corvette for in the market (less the $1,000 premium you had paid).

Whereas the buyer of a put option wants the price to go down, the seller of a put option wants the price to stay the same or go up—but definitely, *please*, not to go down. The more the price goes down, the more the seller of the put option must pay the buyer. In our example, if the price of Corvettes dropped to $30,000, and we had sold put options on 100 Corvettes, we would lose $900,000 ($1 million less the $100,000 premium we had received). The strategy of selling put options does not carry the one benefit Morgan Stanley touted for some of the riskier products it sold: "downside limited to size of initial investment." In this case, you could lose *more* than everything. A put seller's downside is limited only by the size of his or her imagination (and the fact that prices don't usually drop below zero).

Niederhoffer was looking OK through the weekend of October 25–26. October had not been an especially eventful month, the publication of my book notwithstanding. Niederhoffer was waiting, hoping the options would expire worthless so he could keep the premium and get back closer to even. Remember, he wanted the market to stay the same or go up—but definitely, *please*, not to go down.

On Monday, October 27, 1997, the U.S. stock market plummeted 554 points, or about 7 percent. The S&P index fell 64.67 points to 876.97. It had been almost exactly 10 years since the stock market crash of 1987, dubbed "Black Monday," October 19, 1987. A 7 percent drop didn't meet the definition of market crash, and it certainly couldn't match Black Monday. But for Niederhoffer, that Monday delivered a death blow. By noon, he was broke. By Wednesday, his funds had been liquidated. The $100 million plus of his investor's money was gone.

Take a guess at who Niederhoffer's investors were? That's right, believe it or not, my hometown favorite, the $3.3 billion San Diego public-employee pension fund was right there in the thick of it with Niederhoffer's other put option sellers. Well done, San Diego!

QUESTIONS

1. What was the fiasco?
2. What are derivatives? Why do they tend to create unique ethical dilemmas?

Paul B. Farrell | # Derivatives, the New "Ticking Bomb"

Paul B. Farrell, J.D., Ph.D., is a widely published finance columnist for CBS MarketWatch.

"Charlie and I believe Berkshire should be a fortress of financial strength," wrote Warren Buffett. That was five years before the subprime-credit meltdown. "We try to be alert to any sort of mega-catastrophe risk, and that posture may make us unduly appreciative about the burgeoning quantities of long-term derivatives contracts and the massive amount of uncollateralized receivables that are growing alongside. In our view, however, derivatives are financial weapons of mass destruction, carrying dangers that, while now latent, are potentially lethal."

Also fresh on Buffett's mind: His acquisition of General Re four years earlier, about the time

From Paul B. Farrell, CBS MarketWatch, March 10, 2008.

the Long-Term Capital Management hedge fund almost killed the global monetary system. How? This is crucial: LTCM nearly killed the system with a relatively small $5 billion trading loss—peanuts compared with the hundreds of billions of dollars of subprime-credit write-offs now making Wall Street's big shots look like amateurs. Buffett tried to sell off Gen Re's derivatives group. No buyers. Unwinding it was costly, but it led to his warning that derivatives are a "financial weapon of mass destruction." That was 2002.

DERIVATIVES BUBBLE EXPLODES FIVE TIMES BIGGER IN FIVE YEARS

Wall Street didn't listen to Buffett. Derivatives grew into a massive bubble, from about $100 trillion to $516 trillion by 2007. The new derivatives bubble was fueled by five key economic and political trends:

- Sarbanes–Oxley increased corporate disclosures and government oversight.
- Federal Reserve's cheap money policies created the subprime-housing boom.
- War budgets burdened the U.S. Treasury and future entitlements programs.
- Trade deficits with China and others destroyed the value of the U.S. dollar.
- Oil- and commodity-rich nations demanding equity payments rather than debt.

In short, despite Buffett's clear warnings, a massive new derivatives bubble is driving the domestic and global economies, a bubble that continues growing today parallel with the subprime-credit meltdown triggering a bear-recession.

Data on the five-fold growth of derivatives to $516 trillion in five years comes from the most recent survey by the Bank of International Settlements, the world's clearinghouse for central banks in Basel, Switzerland. The BIS is like the cashier's window at a racetrack or casino, where you'd place a bet or cash in chips, except on a massive scale: BIS is where the U.S. settles trade imbalances with Saudi Arabia for all that oil we guzzle and gives China IOUs for the tainted drugs and lead-based toys we buy.

To grasp how significant this five-fold bubble increase is, let's put that $516 trillion in the context of some other domestic and international monetary data:

- U.S. annual gross domestic product is about $15 trillion.
- U.S. money supply is also about $15 trillion.
- Current proposed U.S. federal budget is $3 trillion.
- U.S. government's maximum legal debt is $9 trillion.
- U.S. mutual fund companies manage about $12 trillion.
- World's GDPs for all nations is approximately $50 trillion.
- Unfunded Social Security and Medicare benefits are $50 trillion to $65 trillion.
- Total value of the world's real estate is estimated at about $75 trillion.
- Total value of world's stock and bond markets is more than $100 trillion.
- BIS valuation of world's derivatives back in 2002 was about $100 trillion.
- BIS 2007 valuation of the world's derivatives is now a whopping $516 trillion.

Moreover, the folks at BIS tell me their estimate of $516 trillion only includes "transactions in which a major private dealer (bank) is involved on at least one side of the transaction," but doesn't include private deals between two "non-reporting entities." They did, however, add that their reporting central banks estimate that the coverage of the survey is around 95% on average.

Also, keep in mind that while the $516 trillion "notional" value (maximum in case of a meltdown) of the deals is a good measure of the market's size, the 2007 BIS study notes that the $11 trillion "gross market values provides a more accurate measure of the scale of financial risk transfer taking place in derivatives markets."

BUBBLES, DOMINO EFFECTS, AND THE "BAD 2%"

However, while that may be true as far as the parties to an individual deal, there are broader risks to the world's economies. Remember back in 1998 when LTCM's little $5 billion loss nearly brought down the world's banking system. That "domino effect" is now repeating many times over, straining the world's monetary, economic, and political system as the sub-prime housing mess metastasizes, taking the U.S. stock market and the world economy down with it.

This cascading "domino effect" was brilliantly described in "The $300 Trillion Time Bomb: If Buffett Can't Figure Out Derivatives, Can Anybody?" published early last year in *Portfolio* magazine, a couple of months before the subprime meltdown. Columnist Jesse Eisinger's $300 trillion figure came from an earlier study of the derivatives market as it was growing from $100 trillion to $516 trillion over five years. Eisinger concluded, "There's nothing intrinsically scary about derivatives, except when the bad 2% blow up." Unfortunately, that "bad 2%" did blow up a few months afterwards, even as Bernanke and Paulson were assuring America that the subprime mess was "contained." Bottom line: Little things leverage a heck of a big wallop. It only takes a little spark from a "bad 2% deal" to ignite this $516 trillion weapon of mass destruction. Think of this entire unregulated derivatives market like an unsecured, unpredictable nuclear bomb in a Pakistan stockpile. It's only a matter of time.

WORLD'S NEWEST AND BIGGEST "BLACK MARKET"

The fact is, derivatives have become the world's biggest "black market," exceeding the illicit traffic in stuff like arms, drugs, alcohol, gambling, cigarettes, stolen art, and pirated movies. Why? Because like all black markets, derivatives are a perfect way of getting rich while avoiding taxes and government regulations. And in today's slowdown, plus a vola-tile global market, Wall Street knows that derivatives remain a lucrative business. Recently, Pimco's bond

fund king Bill Gross said, "What we are witness-ing is essentially the breakdown of our modern-day banking system, a complex of leveraged lending so hard to understand that Federal Reserve Chairman Ben Bernanke required a face-to-face refresher course from hedge fund managers in mid-August." In short, not only Warren Buffett, but bond king Bill Gross, our Fed Chairman Ben Bernanke, the Treasury Secretary Henry Paulson, and the rest of America's leaders can't "figure out" the world's $516 trillion derivatives.

Why? Gross says we are creating a new "shadow banking system." Derivatives are now not just risk management tools. As Gross and others see it, the real problem is that derivatives are now a new way of creating money outside the normal central bank liquidity rules. How? Because they're private con-tracts between two companies or institutions.

BIS is primarily a records-keeper, a toothless tiger that merely collects data giving a legitimacy and false sense of security to this chaotic "shadow banking system" that has become the world's biggest "black market." That's crucial, folks. Why? Because central banks require reserves like stock brokers require margins, something backing up the trans-action. Derivatives don't. They're not "real money." They're paper promises closer to "Monopoly" money than real U.S. dollars.

And it takes place outside normal business channels, out there in the "free market." That's the wonderful world of derivatives, and it's creating a massive bubble that could soon implode.

QUESTIONS

1. What is a derivative? Could you explain the concept to a friend?

2. How do derivatives differ from other financial instruments? Is there something about derivatives that makes them "wrong"?

Duff McDonald | # The Running of the Hedgehogs

Duff McDonald is a freelance writer based in New York. He writes for *Vanity Fair, Wired,* and many other magazines.

Not so long ago, the talk about hedge funds was all about their money—some guy you'd never heard of buying an $80 million piece of art or a $25 million teardown in Greenwich, Connecticut, or paying himself $1 billion for a single year's work. It was a spectator sport, absurd but entertaining, to a degree. Then the talk started to get serious, like, were hedge funds artificially bidding up the price of oil? What about that deal where a single trader ripped through $6 billion on a bad hunch about natural-gas prices—should that concern more than just the pissed-off people who entrusted him with their money? Or those two little bouts of panic the market has suffered this year already: Are hedge funds the virus that's going to make the markets keel over? Are they an evil cabal?

But really, it's time you understood them. As of March, by one estimate, there was a staggering $2 trillion invested in hedge funds worldwide, up nearly tenfold from 1999. Today, there are more than 9,000 hedge funds, 351 of which manage $1 billion or more.

LESSON ONE: JUST WHAT IS A HEDGE FUND?

It's only a vehicle for investing, albeit one that happens to be less constrained than most. Your run-of-the-mill mutual fund, for example, buys stocks and bonds, and that's pretty much it. Most are not even allowed to employ short selling, a way of betting that the price of a security will fall. Hedge funds can employ whatever investing tools they want, including leverage, the use of derivatives like options and futures, and short sales. The *New York*

Times decided years ago to incessantly refer to hedge funds' use of these instruments as "exotic and risky," thereby adding to their aura of mystery. The funny thing: Practically all financial institutions use these "exotic" instruments.

There's a much simpler way of putting it. According to Cliff Asness of AQR Capital, "Hedge funds are investment pools that are relatively unconstrained in what they do. They are relatively unregulated (for now), charge very high fees, will not necessarily give you your money back when you want it, and will generally not tell you what they do. They are supposed to make money all the time, and when they fail at this, their investors redeem and go to someone else who has recently been making money. Every three or four years, they deliver a one-in-a-hundred-year flood."

Although the origin of hedge funds dates back to Alfred Winslow Jones and the fifties, it wasn't until the late sixties that the category became a recognizable seedling of its current state: a group of highly skilled traders catering to a very wealthy clientele willing to gamble to get humongous returns. The first true stars of the hedge-fund universe—people like Soros, Michael Steinhardt, and Bruce Kovner—were experts in commodities and currencies and figured out how to exploit inefficiencies in those markets. Because they raised money privately—largely from friends and business associates—they avoided most of the disclosure requirements of U.S. securities laws. That meant they didn't have to explain to anybody how much money they had or what exactly they did with it. The deal, in effect, was this: Rich guys could gather up money from other rich guys without oversight, so long as they agreed not to utter a word to the general public that could be construed as "solicitation," including "communication published in any newspaper, magazine, or similar

From Duff McDonald, *New York* magazine, April 9, 2007.

media." Not that there was any point in soliciting the public anyway. To get into a fund, you had to invest $2.5 million. Managers were expected to have their own money in the fund, an informal check against reckless risk-taking.

A MYTHOLOGY BEGAN
TO TAKE SHAPE

People in the financial world became enamored of investing superheroes. Some deserved it: Soros almost broke the Bank of England by shorting the pound. As Soros's reputation grew, so did his power as an investor. Julian Robertson's Tiger Management was another legendary outfit that nobody wanted to bet against. Their $1 billion or $2 billion portfolios seem quaint today—like Mike Myers's Dr. Evil demanding "one million dollars!" to not destroy the world—but their ballsy moves inspired imitators. Of course, the more people out there tried to copy the Soroses and the Robertsons, the less well it worked out. John H. Makin, a principal at Kovner's Caxton Associates, puts it this way: "The extraordinarily high returns earned by hedge funds during their golden age in the eighties and early nineties were not too good to be true. They were just too good to be true for everyone."

A BRIEF PSYCHOGRAPHIC PORTRAIT

According to a survey of 294 fund managers with a net worth of $30 million or more by Russ Alan Prince, the author of *Fortune's Fortress*, 97 percent of hedge-fund managers see their portfolios as themselves personified. And here's what else they think about: failure. Fifty-four percent of them say they suffer from the Icarus syndrome, a fear of flying too close to the sun and crashing to Earth. They also think about staring down the barrel of a gun: Almost three-quarters believe their wealth makes them a target of criminals. This is the life we can't stop talking about?

Hedge funds sometimes get confused with private equity, the financial specialty that's gotten the most ink these past few months. Private-equity investors like the Blackstone Group or KKR differ from your typical hedge fund in that they tend to take more long-term, controlling stakes in companies—often taking them private in the process—in hopes of doing some financial engineering that results in a huge windfall.

You can think of them as products of the yin and yang of Wall Street's traditional powerhouses. Private-equity people are "people people"—their ranks full of former pros of the relationship-driven investment-banking side of the business. Hedge-fund people are much more likely to come from the trading side: quicker to draw, quicker to shoot, and not inclined to spend a whole lot of time discussing the thinking behind it all. "They measure their performance every day. They wonder, 'If I buy this today, will I look stupid tomorrow?'," says a private-equity professional. "A private-equity guy is sitting there thinking, 'What will the world look like in three to five years?'"

Both industries share an addiction to leverage, which is to say, borrowed money. They use it liberally to maximize the return of a good deal or a good trade. From the very beginning, in fact, hedge funds were premised on the notion that they could exploit minute profit-making opportunities by placing big leveraged bets. The "hedge" in hedge funds originally referred to the downside protection a fund would simultaneously employ by, yes, hedging. Typically, that would mean buying one stock and shorting another. While many hedge funds still employ actual hedging techniques, the practice has gone out of vogue. But leverage hasn't, and that means big bets with little or no downside protection. In a word, risky.

AND WHY ARE THEY SO RICH?

One thing hedge-funders uniformly agree on is that they are worth what they are paid. Running your own hedge fund is the fastest way to make a fortune known to man. The typical fee structure is known by the vernacular "2 & 20"—most funds take a 2 percent management fee and 20 percent of any profits. (Some take far more. James Simons, for example, charges a nominally obscene 5 & 44.) The result: A $1 billion fund posting a 30 percent return delivers a $78.8 million payday for its managers. A $1 billion fund posting a zero percent return can still spread around $20 million to its employees. The best managers do a lot better than breaking even, mind you, and as a result, a handful of hedge-fund kingpins take home more than $500 million in annual compensation.

In a sign of hedge funds' growing clout in other spheres, in late January, Senator Chuck Schumer called twenty or so of the top hedge-fund managers and invited them to the Upper East Side Italian restaurant Bottega del Vino. It was supposed to be a friendly chat—Schumer's message was, you talk to us about what's going on, and nobody has to worry about too much interference from regulators. The combined assets under management of those attending had to have been $200 billion.

Byron Wien, one of the most popular commentators in the history of Wall Street, left a cushy job at Morgan Stanley in 2005 in order to join Pequot Capital, a hedge fund, as chief investment strategist. He apparently wasn't forced to take the industry's vow of *omertà*. When asked to explain the staggering growth of late, he puts it quite simply: "One of the main reasons is that it became legitimate for institutions to invest. In the early days, you signed up in a dark alley with a flashlight. Today, a typical institutional portfolio now has about 15 to 25 percent in such alternative investments."

There's no need for flashlights anymore, but the industry still has its critics, who voice everything from concern about leverage and lemminglike rushes that could threaten the stability of global markets to disgust at the astronomical fee arrangements. No less an authority than Warren Buffett has accused the industry of selling hokum, calling the typical compensation structure a "grotesque arrangement." But whom did *Business Week* suggest as "the next Warren Buffett"? That would be Eddie Lampert, a hedge-fund manager.

THE BIG ARE GETTING COLOSSAL

A year ago, there were only four $20 billion-plus outfits; now, there are seven: JPMorgan, Goldman,

Bridgewater Associates, D. E. Shaw, Farallon Capital, Renaissance Technologies, and Och-Ziff Capital. The first U.S. hedge fund to offer its stock to the public, Fortress, gained 67.6 percent on its first day of trading. There will be more firms taking that path.

They're searching for a needle in a very large haystack. Ask any hedge-fund manager, and he will tell you that the easy money has already been made, and there are no "obvious trades" sitting around. A recent report by the European firm Dresdner Kleinwort points out that if 4 percent of assets under management go to fees, and another 4 to 5 percent is spent on trading commissions and interest, hedge funds would need to pull in 20 percent annually to justify their costs. That forces them to take ever greater risks.

THE GOVERNMENT IS GETTING NOSY

In 2004, the SEC required hedge funds to register with the agency, which was kind of like getting 19-year-olds to register for the draft. It didn't have any immediate consequences, but it could lead to something serious. The courts then threw that rule out, and regulatory talk died down until the Connecticut-based fund Amaranth lost about $6 billion on natural-gas futures last year. It's died down yet again, but is only one meltdown or scandal from flaring back up. All the big hedge funds have bulked up their lobbying budgets of late.

Investment banks are morphing into hedge funds. If you can't beat 'em, join 'em, right? More and more, Goldman Sachs and its ilk are making their money from proprietary trading, which means, simply, the managing of their own assets rather than, say, yours. These operations now dwarf many traditional investment-banking practices, like mergers and acquisitions. Goldman Sachs produces hedge-funders like the Dominican Republic produces shortstops. About one in five of the world's top hedge-fund managers used to work at Goldman. So, hedge funds really are something of a cabal.

AND NOW FOR THE DOOMSDAY SCENARIO

The only year that assets under management declined in the history of hedge funds was in 1994. Why? Rising interest rates and the digestion of the massive growth of the previous few years. Sounds familiar, doesn't it? A sharp spike in interest rates could be devastating to an industry that relies so heavily on borrowed money. Citadel, for example, had balance-sheet leverage of 11.5x last year—meaning it had borrowed more than eleven times more money than it actually had at the time, ballooning its gross-asset exposure to some $150 billion. This level of leverage adds tremendous risk. One prominent hedge-fund manager told me that any single hedge fund, other than three he could think of, could blow up and not really have any effect on the broader markets. But if one of the three did—and he named Citadel in that group—then the dominoes could start to tumble.

So, in the end, when someone blurts out, "Hedge funds are a venal get-rich scheme that we'll all end up paying for," should you nod solemnly like you agree? No, don't do that. Try instead to crib the argument of an actual hedge-fund manager: "The proliferation of hedge funds has both decreased volatility in the market and increased the long-term risk of a systematic collapse. In the first case, it's because hedge funds are more nimble than traditional long-only funds and can swoop in and correct market mispricings before they can get extreme. But it also means opportunities become fewer. And because hedge funds need good returns through the cycle, this reduced opportunity forces them to take more and more risk, increasing their exposure to risky investments, which, in the long term, will increase the likelihood of a systematic panic in the market." In their report, the Dresdner Kleinwort analysts had their own term for just such a panic; they called it "the great unwind."

QUESTIONS

1. Is a hedge fund like a pyramid scheme? Does it seek to cheat investors?
2. Why might hedge funds contribute, paradoxically, to the collapse of free markets?
3. Should hedge funds be regulated? What are three rules you would suggest?

Niall Ferguson | # Wall Street Lays Another Egg

Niall Ferguson is the Laurence A. Tisch Professor of History at Harvard University.

This year we have lived through something more than a financial crisis. We have witnessed the death of a planet. Call it Planet Finance. Two years ago, in 2006, the measured economic output of the entire world was worth around $48.6 trillion. The total market capitalization of the world's stock markets was $50.6 trillion, 4 percent larger. The total value of domestic and international bonds was $67.9 trillion, 40 percent larger. Planet Finance was beginning to dwarf Planet Earth.

Planet Finance seemed to spin faster, too. Every day $3.1 trillion changed hands on foreign-exchange markets. Every month $5.8 trillion changed hands on global stock markets. And all the time new financial life-forms were evolving. The total annual issuance of mortgage-backed securities, including fancy new "collateralized debt obligations" (C.D.O.'s), rose to more than $1 trillion. The volume of "derivatives"—contracts such as options and swaps—grew even faster, so that by the end of 2006 their notional value was just over $400 trillion. Before the 1980s, such things were virtually unknown. In the space of a few years their populations exploded. On Planet Finance, the securities outnumbered the people; the transactions outnumbered the relationships.

New institutions also proliferated. In 1990 there were just 610 hedge funds, with $38.9 billion under management. At the end of 2006 there were 9,462, with $1.5 trillion under management. Private-equity partnerships also went forth and multiplied. Banks, meanwhile, set up a host of "conduits" and "structured investment vehicles" (SIVs—surely the most apt acronym in financial history) to keep potentially risky assets off their balance sheets. It was as if an entire shadow banking system had come into being.

Then, beginning in the summer of 2007, Planet Finance began to self-destruct in what the International Monetary Fund soon acknowledged to be "the largest financial shock since the Great Depression." Did the crisis of 2007–8 happen because American companies had gotten worse at designing new products? Had the pace of technological innovation or productivity growth suddenly slackened? No. The proximate cause of the economic uncertainty of 2008 was financial: to be precise, a crunch in the credit markets triggered by mounting defaults on a hitherto obscure species of housing loan known euphemistically as "subprime mortgages."

Central banks in the United States and Europe sought to alleviate the pressure on the banks with interest-rate cuts and offers of funds through special "term auction facilities." Yet the market rates at which banks could borrow money, whether by issuing commercial paper, selling bonds, or borrowing from one another, failed to follow the lead of the official federal-funds rate. The banks had to turn not only to Western central banks for short-term assistance to rebuild their reserves but also to Asian and Middle Eastern sovereign-wealth funds for equity injections. When these sources proved insufficient, investors—and speculative short-sellers—began to lose faith.

Beginning with Bear Stearns, Wall Street's investment banks entered a death spiral that ended with their being either taken over by a commercial bank (as Bear was, followed by Merrill Lynch) or driven into bankruptcy (as Lehman Brothers was). In September the two survivors—Goldman Sachs and Morgan Stanley—formally ceased to be investment banks, signaling the death of a business model that dated back to the Depression. Other institutions deemed "too big to fail" by the U.S. Treasury were effectively taken over by the government, including the mortgage lenders and guarantors Fannie Mae and Freddie Mac and the insurance giant American International Group (A.I.G.).

By September 18 the U.S. financial system was gripped by such panic that the Treasury had to abandon this ad hoc policy. Treasury Secretary Henry Paulson hastily devised a plan whereby the government would be authorized to buy "troubled" securities with up to $700 billion of taxpayers' money—a figure apparently plucked from the air. When a modified version of the measure was rejected by Congress 11 days later, there was panic. When it was passed four days after that, there was more panic. Now it wasn't just bank stocks that were tanking. The entire stock market seemed to be in free fall as fears mounted that the credit crunch was going to trigger a recession. Moreover, the crisis was now clearly global in scale. European banks were in much the same trouble as their American counterparts, while emerging-market stock markets were crashing. A week of frenetic improvisation by national governments culminated on the weekend of October 11–12, when the United States reluctantly followed the British government's lead, buying equity stakes in banks rather than just their dodgy assets and offering unprecedented guarantees of banks' debt and deposits.

Since these events coincided with the final phase of a U.S. presidential-election campaign, it was not surprising that some rather simplistic lessons were soon being touted by candidates and commentators. The crisis, some said, was the result of excessive deregulation of financial markets. Others sought to lay the blame on unscrupulous speculators: short-sellers, who borrowed the stocks of vulnerable banks and sold them in the expectation of further price declines. Still other suspects in the frame were negligent regulators and corrupt congressmen.

This crisis, however, is about much more than just the stock market. It needs to be understood as a fundamental breakdown of the entire financial system, extending from the monetary-and-banking system through the bond market, the stock market, the insurance market, and the real-estate market. It affects not only established financial institutions such as investment banks but also relatively novel ones such as hedge funds. It is global in scope and unfathomable in scale.

Had it not been for the frantic efforts of the Federal Reserve and the Treasury, to say nothing of their counterparts in almost equally afflicted Europe, there would by now have been a repeat of that "great contraction" of credit and economic activity that was the prime mover of the Depression. Back then, the Fed and the Treasury did next to nothing to prevent bank failures from translating into a drastic contraction of credit and hence of business activity and employment. If the more openhanded monetary and fiscal authorities of today are ultimately successful in preventing a comparable slump of output, future historians may end up calling this "the Great Repression." This is the Depression they are hoping to bottle up—a Depression in denial.

To understand why we have come so close to a rerun of the 1930s, we need to begin at the beginning, with banks and the money they make. From the Middle Ages until the mid-20th century, most banks made their money by maximizing the difference between the costs of their liabilities (payments to depositors) and the earnings on their assets (interest and commissions on loans). Some banks also made money by financing trade, discounting the commercial bills issued by merchants. Others issued and traded bonds and stocks, or dealt in commodities (especially precious metals). But the core business of banking was simple. It consisted, as the third Lord Rothschild pithily put it, "essentially of facilitating the movement of money from Point A, where it is, to Point B, where it is needed."

The system evolved gradually. First came the invention of cashless intra-bank and inter-bank transactions, which allowed debts to be settled between account holders without having money physically change hands. Then came the idea of fractional-reserve banking, whereby banks kept only a small proportion of their existing deposits on hand to satisfy the needs of depositors (who seldom wanted all their money simultaneously), allowing the rest to be lent out profitably. That was followed by the rise of special public banks with monopolies on the issuing of banknotes and other powers and privileges: the first central banks.

With these innovations, money ceased to be understood as precious metal minted into coins. Now it was the sum total of specific liabilities (deposits and reserves) incurred by banks. Credit was the other side of banks' balance sheets: the total of their assets; in other words, the loans they made. Some of this money might still consist of precious metal, though a rising proportion of that would be held in the central bank's vault. Most would be made up of banknotes and coins recognized as "legal tender," along with money that was visible only in current- and deposit-account statements.

Until the late 20th century, the system of bank money retained an anchor in the pre-modern conception of money in the form of the gold standard: fixed ratios between units of account and quantities of precious metal. As early as 1924, the English economist John Maynard Keynes dismissed the gold standard as a "barbarous relic," but the last vestige of the system did not disappear until August 15, 1971—the day President Richard Nixon closed the so-called gold window, through which foreign central banks could still exchange dollars for gold. With that, the centuries-old link between money and precious metal was broken.

Though we tend to think of money today as being made of paper, in reality most of it now consists of bank deposits. If we measure the ratio of actual money to output in developed economies, it becomes clear that the trend since the 1970s has been for that ratio to rise from around 70 percent, before the closing of the gold window, to more than 100 percent by 2005. The corollary has been a parallel growth of credit on the other side of bank balance sheets. A significant component of that credit growth has been a surge of lending to consumers. Back in 1952, the ratio of household debt to disposable income was less than 40 percent in the United States. At its peak in 2007, it reached 133 percent, up from 90 percent a decade before. Today Americans carry a total of $2.56 trillion in consumer debt, up by more than a fifth since 2000.

Even more spectacular, however, has been the rising indebtedness of banks themselves. In 1980, bank indebtedness was equivalent to 21 percent of U.S. gross domestic product. In 2007 the figure was 116 percent. Another measure of this was the declining capital adequacy of banks. On the eve of "the Great Repression," average bank capital in Europe was equivalent to less than 10 percent of assets; at the beginning of the 20th century, it was around 25 percent. It was not unusual for investment banks' balance sheets to be as much as 20 or 30 times larger than their capital, thanks in large part to a 2004 rule change by the Securities and Exchange Commission that exempted the five largest of those banks from the regulation that had capped their debt-to-capital ratio at 12 to 1. The Age of Leverage had truly arrived for Planet Finance.

Credit and money, in other words, have for decades been growing more rapidly than underlying economic activity. Is it any wonder, then, that money has ceased to hold its value the way it did in the era of the gold standard? The motto "In God we trust" was added to the dollar bill in 1957. Since then its purchasing power, relative to the consumer price index, has declined by a staggering 87 percent. Average annual inflation during that period has been more than 4 percent. A man who decided to put his savings into gold in 1970 could have bought just over 27.8 ounces of the precious metal for $1,000. At the time of writing, with gold trading at $900 an ounce, he could have sold it for around $25,000.

Those few goldbugs who always doubted the soundness of fiat money—paper currency without a metal anchor—have in large measure been vindicated. But why were the rest of us so blinded by money illusion?

BLOWING BUBBLES

In the immediate aftermath of the death of gold as the anchor of the monetary system, the problem of inflation affected mainly retail prices and wages.

Today, only around one out of seven countries has an inflation rate above 10 percent, and only one, Zimbabwe, is afflicted with hyperinflation. But back in 1979 at least 7 countries had an annual inflation rate above 50 percent, and more than 60 countries—including Britain and the United States—had inflation in double digits.

Inflation has come down since then, partly because many of the items we buy—from clothes to computers—have gotten cheaper as a result of technological innovation and the relocation of production to low-wage economies in Asia. It has also been reduced because of a worldwide transformation in monetary policy, which began with the monetarist-inspired increases in short-term rates implemented by the Federal Reserve in 1979. Just as important, some of the structural drivers of inflation, such as powerful trade unions, have also been weakened.

By the 1980s, in any case, more and more people had grasped how to protect their wealth from inflation: by investing it in assets they expected to appreciate in line with, or ahead of, the cost of living. These assets could take multiple forms, from modern art to vintage wine, but the most popular proved to be stocks and real estate. Once it became clear that this formula worked, the Age of Leverage could begin. For it clearly made sense to borrow to the hilt to maximize your holdings of stocks and real estate if these promised to generate higher rates of return than the interest payments on your borrowings. Between 1990 and 2004, most American households did not see an appreciable improvement in their incomes. Adjusted for inflation, the median household income rose by about 6 percent. But people could raise their living standards by borrowing and investing in stocks and housing.

Nearly all of us did it. And the bankers were there to help. Not only could they borrow more cheaply from one another than we could borrow from them; increasingly they devised all kinds of new mortgages that looked more attractive to us (and promised to be more lucrative to them) than boring old 30-year fixed-rate deals. Moreover, the banks were just as ready to play the asset markets as we were.

Proprietary trading soon became the most profitable arm of investment banking: buying and selling assets on the bank's own account.

There was, however, a catch. The Age of Leverage was also an age of bubbles, beginning with the dot-com bubble of the irrationally exuberant 1990s and ending with the real-estate mania of the exuberantly irrational 2000s. Why was this?

The future is in large measure uncertain, so our assessments of future asset prices are bound to vary. If we were all calculating machines, we would simultaneously process all the available information and come to the same conclusion. But we are human beings, and as such are prone to myopia and mood swings. When asset prices surge upward in sync, it is as if investors are gripped by a kind of collective euphoria. Conversely, when their "animal spirits" flip from greed to fear, the bubble that their earlier euphoria inflated can burst with amazing suddenness. Zoological imagery is an integral part of the culture of Planet Finance. Optimistic buyers are "bulls," pessimistic sellers are "bears." The real point, however, is that stock markets are mirrors of the *human* psyche. Like *Homo sapiens*, they can become depressed. They can even suffer complete breakdowns.

FANNIE, GINNIE, AND FREDDIE

Prior to the 1930s, only a minority of Americans owned their homes. During the Depression, however, the Roosevelt administration created a whole complex of institutions to change that. A Federal Home Loan Bank Board was set up in 1932 to encourage and oversee local mortgage lenders known as savings-and-loans (S&Ls)—mutual associations that took in deposits and lent to homebuyers. Under the New Deal, the Home Owners' Loan Corporation stepped in to refinance mortgages on longer terms, up to 15 years. To reassure depositors, who had been traumatized by the thousands of bank failures of the previous three years, Roosevelt introduced federal deposit insurance. And by providing federally backed insurance for mortgage lenders, the Federal Housing Administration (F.H.A.) sought to encourage large (up to 80 percent of the purchase price), long (20- to 25-year), fully amortized, low-interest loans.

By standardizing the long-term mortgage and creating a national system of official inspection and valuation, the F.H.A. laid the foundation for a secondary market in mortgages. This market came to life in 1938, when a new Federal National Mortgage Association—nicknamed Fannie Mae—was authorized to issue bonds and use the proceeds to buy mortgages from the local S&Ls, which were restricted by regulation both in terms of geography (they could not lend to borrowers more than 50 miles from their offices) and in terms of the rates they could offer (the so-called Regulation Q, which imposed a low ceiling on interest paid on deposits). Because these changes tended to reduce the average monthly payment on a mortgage, the F.H.A. made home ownership viable for many more Americans than ever before. Indeed, it is not too much to say that the modern United States, with its seductively samey suburbs, was born with Fannie Mae. Between 1940 and 1960, the home-ownership rate soared from 43 to 62 percent.

These were not the only ways in which the federal government sought to encourage Americans to own their own homes. Mortgage-interest payments were always tax-deductible, from the inception of the federal income tax in 1913. As Ronald Reagan said when the rationality of this tax break was challenged, mortgage-interest relief was "part of the American dream."

In 1968, to broaden the secondary-mortgage market still further, Fannie Mae was split in two—the Government National Mortgage Association (Ginnie Mae), which was to cater to poor borrowers, and a rechartered Fannie Mae, now a privately owned government-sponsored enterprise (G.S.E.). Two years later, to provide competition for Fannie Mae, the Federal Home Loan Mortgage Corporation (Freddie Mac) was set up. In addition, Fannie Mae was permitted to buy conventional as well as government-guaranteed mortgages. Later, with the Community Reinvestment Act of 1977, American banks found themselves under pressure for the first time to lend to poor, minority communities.

These changes presaged a more radical modification to the New Deal system. In the late 1970s, the savings-and-loan industry was hit first by double-digit inflation and then by sharply rising interest rates. This double punch was potentially lethal. The S&Ls were simultaneously losing money on long-term, fixed-rate mortgages, due to inflation, and hemorrhaging deposits to higher-interest money-market funds. The response in Washington from both the Carter and Reagan administrations was to try to salvage the S&Ls with tax breaks and deregulation. When the new legislation was passed, President Reagan declared, "All in all, I think we hit the jackpot." Some people certainly did.

On the one hand, S&Ls could now invest in whatever they liked, not just local long-term mortgages. Commercial property, stocks, junk bonds—anything was allowed. They could even issue credit cards. On the other, they could now pay whatever interest rate they liked to depositors. Yet all their deposits were still effectively insured, with the maximum covered amount raised from $40,000 to $100,000, thanks to a government regulation two years earlier. And if ordinary deposits did not suffice, the S&Ls could raise money in the form of brokered deposits from middlemen. What happened next perfectly illustrated the great financial precept first enunciated by William Crawford, the commissioner of the California Department of Savings and Loan: "The best way to rob a bank is to own one." Some S&Ls bet their depositors' money on highly dubious real-estate developments. Many simply stole the money, as if deregulation meant that the law no longer applied to them at all.

When the ensuing bubble burst, nearly 300 S&Ls collapsed, while another 747 were closed or reorganized under the auspices of the Resolution Trust Corporation, established by Congress in 1989 to clear up the mess. The final cost of the crisis was $153 billion (around 3 percent of the 1989 G.D.P.), of which taxpayers had to pay $124 billion.

But even as the S&Ls were going belly-up, they offered another, very different group of American financial institutions a fast track to megabucks. To the bond traders at Salomon Brothers, the New York investment bank, the breakdown of the New Deal mortgage system was not a crisis but a wonderful opportunity. As profit-hungry as their language was profane, the self-styled "Big Swinging Dicks" at Salomon saw a way of exploiting the gyrating interest rates of the early 1980s.

The idea was to re-invent mortgages by bundling thousands of them together as the backing for new and alluring securities that could be sold as alternatives to traditional government and corporate bonds—in short, to convert mortgages into bonds. Once lumped together, the interest payments due on the mortgages could be subdivided into strips with different maturities and credit risks. The first issue of this new kind of mortgage-backed security (known as a "collateralized mortgage obligation") occurred in June 1983. The dawn of securitization was a necessary prelude to the Age of Leverage.

Once again, however, it was the federal government that stood ready to pick up the tab in a crisis. For the majority of mortgages continued to enjoy an implicit guarantee from the government-sponsored trio of Fannie, Freddie, and Ginnie, meaning that bonds which used those mortgages as collateral could be represented as virtual government bonds and considered "investment grade." Between 1980 and 2007, the volume of such G.S.E.-backed mortgage-backed securities grew from less than $200 billion to more than $4 trillion. In 1980 only 10 percent of the home-mortgage market was securitized; by 2007, 56 percent of it was.

These changes swept away the last vestiges of the business model depicted in *It's a Wonderful Life*. Once there had been meaningful social ties between mortgage lenders and borrowers. James Stewart's character knew both the depositors and the debtors. By contrast, in a securitized market the interest you paid on your mortgage ultimately went to someone who had no idea you existed. The full implications of this transition for ordinary homeowners would become apparent only 25 years later.

DRUNK ON DERIVATIVES

Do you, however, know about the second-order effects of this crisis in the markets for derivatives?

Do you in fact know what a derivative is? Once excoriated by Warren Buffett as "financial weapons of mass destruction," derivatives are what make this crisis both unique and unfathomable in its ramifications. To understand what they are, you need, literally, to go back to the future.

For a farmer planting a crop, nothing is more crucial than the future price it will fetch after it has been harvested and taken to market. A futures contract allows him to protect himself by committing a merchant to buy his crop when it comes to market at a price agreed upon when the seeds are being planted. If the market price on the day of delivery is lower than expected, the farmer is protected.

The earliest forms of protection for farmers were known as forward contracts, which were simply bilateral agreements between seller and buyer. A true futures contract, however, is a standardized instrument issued by a futures exchange and hence tradable. With the development of a standard "to arrive" futures contract, along with a set of rules to enforce settlement and, finally, an effective clearing-house, the first true futures market was born.

Because they are derived from the value of underlying assets, all futures contracts are forms of derivatives. Closely related, though distinct from futures, are the contracts known as options. In essence, the buyer of a "call" option has the right, but not the obligation, to buy an agreed-upon quantity of a particular commodity or financial asset from the seller ("writer") of the option at a certain time (the expiration date) for a certain price (known as the "strike price"). Clearly, the buyer of a call option expects the price of the underlying instrument to rise in the future. When the price passes the agreed-upon strike price, the option is "in the money"—and so is the smart guy who bought it. A "put" option is just the opposite: the buyer has the right but not the obligation to sell an agreed-upon quantity of something to the seller of the option at an agreed-upon price.

A third kind of derivative is the interest-rate "swap," which is effectively a bet between two parties on the future path of interest rates. A pure interest-rate swap allows two parties already receiving interest payments literally to swap them,

allowing someone receiving a variable rate of interest to exchange it for a fixed rate, in case interest rates decline. A credit-default swap (C.D.S.), meanwhile, offers protection against a company's defaulting on its bonds.

There was a time when derivatives were standardized instruments traded on exchanges such as the Chicago Board of Trade. Now, however, the vast proportion are custom-made and sold "over the counter" (O.T.C.), often by banks, which charge attractive commissions for their services, but also by insurance companies (notably A.I.G.). According to the Bank for International Settlements, the total notional amounts outstanding of O.T.C. derivative contracts—arranged on an ad hoc basis between two parties—reached a staggering $596 trillion in December 2007, with a gross market value of just over $14.5 trillion.

But how exactly do you price a derivative? What precisely is an option worth? The answers to those questions required a revolution in financial theory. From an academic point of view, what this revolution achieved was highly impressive. But the events of the 1990s, as the rise of quantitative finance replaced preppies with quants (quantitative analysts) all along Wall Street, revealed a new truth: those whom the gods want to destroy they first teach math.

Working closely with Fischer Black, of the consulting firm Arthur D. Little, M.I.T.'s Myron Scholes invented a groundbreaking new theory of pricing options, to which his colleague Robert Merton also contributed. (Scholes and Merton would share the 1997 Nobel Prize in economics.) They reasoned that a call option's value depended on six variables: the current market price of the stock (S), the agreed future price at which the stock could be bought (L), the time until the expiration date of the option (t), the risk-free rate of return in the economy as a whole (r), the probability that the option will be exercised (N), and—the crucial variable—the expected volatility of the stock, i.e., the likely fluctuations of its price between the time of purchase and the expiration date (s). With wonderful mathematical wizardry, the quants reduced the price of a call option to this formula (the Black–Scholes formula):

$$C = SN(d) - Le^{r1}N\left(d - \sigma\sqrt{t}\right)$$

in which

$$d = \frac{\ln\left(\dfrac{S}{L}\right) + \left(r + \dfrac{\sigma^2}{2}\right)t}{\sigma\sqrt{t}}$$

Feeling a bit baffled? Can't follow the algebra? That was just fine by the quants. To make money from this magic formula, they needed markets to be full of people who didn't have a clue about how to price options but relied instead on their (seldom accurate) gut instincts. They also needed a great deal of computing power, a force which had been transforming the financial markets since the early 1980s. Their final requirement was a partner with some market savvy in order to make the leap from the faculty club to the trading floor. Black, who would soon be struck down by cancer, could not be that partner. But John Meriwether could. The former head of the bond-arbitrage group at Salomon Brothers, Meriwether had made his first fortune in the wake of the S&L meltdown of the late 1980s. The hedge fund he created with Scholes and Merton in 1994 was called Long-Term Capital Management.

In its brief, four-year life, Long-Term was the brightest star in the hedge-fund firmament, generating mind-blowing returns for its elite club of investors and even more money for its founders. Needless to say, the firm did more than just trade options, though selling puts on the stock market became such a big part of its business that it was nicknamed "the central bank of volatility" by banks buying insurance against a big stock-market sell-off. In fact, the partners were simultaneously pursuing multiple trading strategies, about 100 of them, with a total of 7,600 positions. This conformed to a second key rule of the new mathematical finance: the virtue of diversification, a principle that had been formalized by Harry M. Markowitz, of the Rand Corporation. Diversification was all about having a multitude of uncorrelated positions. One might go wrong, or even two. But thousands just could not go wrong simultaneously.

The mathematics were reassuring. According to the firm's "Value at Risk" models, it would take a 10-s (in other words, 10-standard-deviation) event to cause the firm to lose all its capital in a single year. But the probability of such an event, according to the quants, was 1 in 10^{24}—or effectively zero. Indeed, the models said the most Long-Term was likely to lose in a single day was $45 million. For that reason, the partners felt no compunction about leveraging their trades. At the end of August 1997, the fund's capital was $6.7 billion, but the debt-financed assets on its balance sheet amounted to $126 billion, a ratio of assets to capital of 19 to 1.

There is no need to rehearse here the story of Long-Term's downfall, which was precipitated by a Russian debt default. Suffice it to say that on Friday, August 21, 1998, the firm lost $550 million—15 percent of its entire capital, and vastly more than its mathematical models had said was possible. The key point is to appreciate why the quants were so wrong.

The problem lay with the assumptions that underlie so much of mathematical finance. In order to construct their models, the quants had to postulate a planet where the inhabitants were omniscient and perfectly rational; where they instantly absorbed all new information and used it to maximize profits; where they never stopped trading; where markets were continuous, frictionless, and completely liquid. Financial markets on this planet followed a "random walk," meaning that each day's prices were quite unrelated to the previous day's, but reflected no more and no less than all the relevant information currently available. The returns on this planet's stock market were normally distributed along the bell curve, with most years clustered closely around the mean, and two-thirds of them within one standard deviation of the mean. On such a planet, a "six standard deviation" sell-off would be about as common as a person shorter than one foot in our world. It would happen only once in four million years of trading.

But Long-Term was not located on Planet Finance. It was based in Greenwich, Connecticut, on Planet Earth, a place inhabited by emotional human beings, always capable of flipping suddenly and en masse from greed to fear. In the case of Long-Term, the herding problem was acute, because many other firms had begun trying to copy Long-Term's strategies in the hope of replicating its stellar performance. When things began to go wrong, there was a truly bovine stampede for the exits. The result was a massive, synchronized downturn in virtually all asset markets. Diversification was no defense in such a crisis. As one leading London hedge-fund manager later put it to Meriwether, "John, you were the correlation."

QUESTIONS

1. How did the elimination of the gold standard and the creation of the federal housing authority create a climate in which the crash of 2007 was possible?

2. Please explain securitization, the Salomon brothers' innovation of bundling mortgages in the early 1980s, and how it precipitated the "age of leverage."

3. Please explain the flaw in Myron Scholes's theory of pricing options.

CASES

CASE 4.1

A Modern History of "Creative" Accounting

The Democratic Policy Committee

A timeline of corporate misconduct and accounting irregularities, offered in "A Special Report by the Democratic Policy Committee 7/11/02" follows.

April 1998: Waste Management/Arthur Andersen. Andersen approved a series of audits that overstated Waste Management's profits by $1.4 billion, the largest ever at the time. Andersen paid a $7 million fine, also the largest ever at the time. The SEC determined that Andersen had noticed the accounting irregularities but knowingly allowed the audits to go through with false numbers. . . .

December 1999: Tyco International/PricewaterhouseCoopers. The SEC reopened its investigation into conglomerate Tyco International, alleging accounting irregularities, including that Tyco had used reserves and other creative accounting strategies to increase its stock prices—problems that auditor PricewaterhouseCoopers had not disclosed.

PricewaterhouseCoopers also provided consulting services to Tyco—amounting to $37.9 million in 2001 alone. In addition, Tyco CEO Dennis Kozlowski resigned after having been indicted for tax evasion, and information has come out that his successor, John F. Fort III, has been involved in questionable accounting transactions that may indicate a significant conflict of interest. In 1999, the SEC investigated Tyco for not having reported the details of 700 acquisitions costing over $8 billion.

July 2000: Rite Aid/KPMG. Several former executives at Rite Aid have been indicted for securities and accounting fraud that led to a $1.6 billion restatement of earnings—a problem that Rite Aid's then-auditor, KPMG, never discovered.

November 2001: Enron/Arthur Andersen. Enron restated its 1997–2001 financial statements to reflect a $1.2 billion reduction in shareholder equity; it had improperly inflated earnings and

From *A Special Report by the Democratic Policy Committee*, 7/11/02.

hidden debt through business partnerships. An Arthur Andersen partner who objected to the accounting standards used in the Enron audit was removed from his oversight role after Enron pressured Andersen to do so. Earlier this year, Andersen was convicted of obstruction of justice.

January 2002: ImClone Systems. ImClone Systems CEO Samuel Waksal resigned over a major conflict of interest, which culminated in his recent arrest. In its criminal probe, the FBI accused Waksal of selling his stock in the company and alerting family members and friends to do so after he found out that ImClone's cancer drug would not be approved by FDA.

February 2002: Global Crossing/Arthur Andersen. Global Crossing, a fiber optic network provider, is an example of myriad conflicts of interests and accounting problems that have led to over 60 investor fraud lawsuits. First, it has admitted to having shredded documents after the SEC and the Justice Department began investigating potential fake network-access transactions it conducted in order to boost its revenue. These transactions involved counting revenue from long-term contracts immediately, rather than properly recording them over the period of the entire contract. Second, the SEC is also investigating stock sales and purchases by Global Crossing executives, several of whom made large sums of money before the company declared bankruptcy and cut 12,000 jobs. Third, Global Crossing appears to have had questionable ties to stock analyst Jack Grubman of Salomon Smith Barney. Grubman had a close relationship with Global Crossing's chairman for many years and purportedly influenced several of the company's key decisions. Grubman maintained a "buy" rating on Global Crossing's stock until just two months before the company filed for bankruptcy, despite signs that the company was in serious trouble.

March 2002: Qwest/Arthur Andersen. The SEC is investigating Qwest for overstating its revenue through capacity swaps and equipment sales—questionable transactions that were never questioned by auditor Arthur Andersen.

April 2002: Xerox/KPMG. KPMG found no irregularity in its audit of Xerox, even though Xerox had overstated its profits by $1.5 billion over 4 years. As a result, Xerox paid a $10 million civil penalty, the largest ever for fraud charges. More recently, PricewaterhouseCoopers reaudited Xerox's books and found that Xerox had improperly recorded over $6 billion in revenue over five years.

May 2002: PeopleSoft/Ernst & Young. The SEC has charged auditor Ernst & Young with violating federal securities law when it entered into business deals with its audit client People-Soft, a software maker. Ernst & Young had agreed to sell and install PeopleSoft's software—including to its audit clients.

May 2002: Halliburton/Arthur Andersen. The SEC is investigating Halliburton for accounting irregularities in which the company apparently changed its accounting practices in order to report a disputed $100 million in construction overruns as profit. Its accounting method, approved by auditor Arthur Andersen, allowed it to postpone losses and was never disclosed to the SEC.

May 2002: Peregrine Systems/KPMG/Arthur Andersen. Peregrine Systems, Inc. fired KPMG after it was revealed that Peregrine's previous auditor, Arthur Andersen, had not caught a $100 million overstatement in earnings, which led to a 3-year restatement of earnings. The problem? $35 million of this had come from transactions between KPMG Consulting and Peregrine—a clear conflict of interest that neither the auditing nor consulting arms of KPMG had revealed to Peregrine.

May 2002: Adelphia Communications/Deloitte & Touche. Adelphia Communications, one of the largest cable companies in the United States, never reported $2.3 billion in debt—and its auditor, Deloitte & Touche, never caught it. The money had been loaned to the Rigas family, Adelphia's owner, who used it to buy Adelphia stock. Deloitte served as both Adelphia's accountant and auditor for the Rigas-controlled entities, creating a conflict of interest, and Deloitte never revealed to Adelphia's audit committee that the Rigases were using the company's credit lines to buy Adelphia stock. This information caused Adelphia's stock to plummet to its lowest level since 1997. The SEC is investigating both Adelphia and Deloitte.

June 2002: WorldCom/Arthur Anderson. WorldCom recently reported that it had overstated its earnings by $3.8 billion—even though its figures were approved by auditor Arthur Andersen. According to the SEC, WorldCom illegally manipulated its earnings in order to bolster its stock price. Bankruptcy is now imminent for WorldCom. The current scandal comes in the wake of a class action lawsuit filed by shareholders, charging that WorldCom had misrepresented its earnings in official SEC filings. The SEC is also investigating WorldCom for loaning former CEO Bernie Ebbers $366 million so that he would not have to sell any of his WorldCom stock.

QUESTIONS

1. What do all these scandals have in common? How might they have been avoided?

2. What constraints should be placed on accounting firms in order to avoid scandals like these? What about criminal penalties?

CASE 4.2

Merger Mania

Lisa H. Newton and David P. Schmidt

Lisa Newton and David Schmidt are leading contemporary business ethicists.

People seem to love hating Martha Stewart, the homemaking queen known for her ingenious decorating ideas, linens, and housewares. Perhaps they resent her seemingly inexhaustible ability to transform mundane junk into all manner of beautiful and ingenious things. Or perhaps they believe the rumors that she is a harshly demanding chief executive of Martha Stewart Living Omnimedia. Whatever the reason, an entire nation sat up and eagerly took notice when Stewart joined the ranks of CEOs charged with corporate misdeeds. More than a few observers outwardly delighted in her troubles.

On December 27, 2001, Stewart sold 4,000 shares of ImClone Systems, a biotech company that was started and run by Stewart's friend, Samuel D. Waksal. According to Stewart's lawyers, she and her stockbroker, Peter E. Baconovic, had long before agreed that he should sell ImClone if the price dropped below $60 a share. Stewart denies that her decision to sell the shares was based on any inside information from Waksal or anyone else. It was simply a coincidence, she maintained, that her sale of ImClone took place just before the company released the bad news that the Food and Drug Administration (FDA) was not going to approve a new ImClone anticancer drug.

By the late 1990s, "merger mania" was once again becoming a force to reckon with. Just halfway

Lisa H. Newton and David P. Schmidt, *"Merger Mania"* in *Wake-Up Calls: Classic Cases in Business Ethics,* 2nd ed. © 2004 by South Western (Thomson).

into 1998, for example, takeovers and acquisitions engineered by Wall Street had soared past $1.2 trillion dollars, compared to just $920 billion in the entire preceding year. When many companies are taken over and sold, the conditions are ripe for abusing nonpublic information that can affect the stock prices of companies. Apparently, that is precisely what has been happening in recent years.

The Securities and Exchange Commission has lately redoubled its efforts to catch insider traders. It is especially interested in the trading patterns of senior executives who have been linked to the various accounting and disclosure scandals that rocked the business world in 2001–2002. The SEC also wants to pursue anyone who profited illegally from the sudden declines in the stock market following the dot-com bust. It is hard to say whether there is more insider trading going on now than in the 1990s. Clearly, however, we now live in a troubled business climate in which the public is much less tolerant of any illegal trading that is taking place. In an effort to restore public confidence in Wall Street, the SEC is now imposing tougher penalties on those who get caught. In the fiscal year ended September 30, 1997, the Commission brought forward 57 insider trading cases.

Some things about insider trading have not changed significantly since the 1980s. For example, as was the case back then, there still is no statutory definition of insider trading. The reason for this continues to be that a clear definition of insider trading would only help crafty lawyers find legal loopholes. We continue to use certain theories to interpret whether insider trading has occurred. One of these is the so-called "misappropriation theory," which says that people who acquired material nonpublic information through a special relationship with a company could not "misappropriate" this information for their own financial gain. Since the 1980s, prosecutors have had mixed success using this theory to convict inside traders. But in 1997, the Supreme Court strengthened the misappropriation theory when it upheld the insider-trading conviction of James H. O'Hagan. O'Hagan was a Minneapolis lawyer who sought to profit from information gleaned from his law firm's representation of Grand Metropolitan, a company who had tried to take over the Pillsbury Company. While O'Hagan's law firm worked for Grand Met, he bought call options and shares of Pillsbury stock. He sold these options and stock when Grand Met announced its tender offer, for a profit of more than $4.3 million. A case was made against O'Hagan. However, a federal appeals court overturned the conviction, saying that O'Hagan was neither an employee nor a fiduciary of Pillsbury. But the Supreme Court reversed the federal appeals court, saying that a person who obtains inside information, under conditions in which that person knows the information is supposed to remain nonpublic, may not use that information for trading. As a consequence, people who buy and sell securities today still need to be mindful of legal interpretive principles that were first hammered out in the 1980s.

At the same time, some things about insider trading today are very different than in the 1980s. Charges of insider trading today arise in a context of widespread public disgust with corporate scandals and ethical misconduct of senior executives. It galls many people that CEOs continue to enjoy huge salaries, bonuses, and perks while their companies' profits evaporate, employees are laid off, and long-term investors get hammered. There may be literally dozens of cases in which corporate insiders have legally sold millions of dollars of shares shortly before revised earnings projections drove down the prices of their companies' shares. It looks like insider trading. Why is it allowed to happen?

The problem was created, in part, by the growing practice of companies compensating their chief executives with generous stock options. One purpose of these options was to align the executives' self-interest with the interests of their corporations. But the executives needed a way to exercise their stock options without being accused of insider trading. By the end of 2000, then SEC Chairman Arthur D. Levitt led the Commission to adopt a rule allowing executives to set prearranged schedules for selling their stock. This so-called "safe harbor" approach insulated the executives from charges of insider trading, since they were selling according to fixed, pre-arranged schedules.

Levitt's rule may have helped to curb insider trading, but it did little to soften the growing public outcry over whether executives and the markets can be trusted. Kenneth Borovina is a thirty-four-year-old carpenter whose grandmother's life savings has shrunk from $600,000 to $200,000 in 2001–2002 in the dismal stock market. Of the senior executives who recently have been investigated and arrested for shady financial dealings, Borovina says, "They're getting what they deserve. That makes me feel great."

He no doubt speaks for many Americans who have turned their backs on corporate America in disgust.

QUESTIONS

1. Do you trust corporate America? Why or why not? Is "trust" appropriate in this context?
2. What is merger mania? What fuels it? Is it new, or has it been around for a while?

CASE 4.3
Annuities to Seniors
Ron Duska

The growth of the annuities market has been a boon for insurance companies accounting for a large portion of their sales. According to the ACLI fact book:

> The mix of premiums from life insurance and annuity considerations has changed markedly over the last 25 years. In 1978 the share of premium receipts from life policies (46%) was more than double the 21 percent from annuities. By 2002, this trend had reversed: Life policies accounted for only one-quarter of premium receipts (26%) while annuity considerations contributed more than half (53%). [American Council of Life Insurers: *Life Insurers Fact Book*, 2003. p. 53]

But the growth in the annuities market brings a set of problems for the industry that some say have the potential to lead to ethical scandals that could be devastating for the industry.

There is much concern about potentially unsuitable sales of variable annuities to seniors. The NASD in one of its alerts states the following:

> The marketing efforts used by some variable annuity sellers deserve scrutiny—especially when seniors are the targeted investors. Sales pitches for these products might attempt to scare or confuse investors. One scare tactic used with seniors is to claim that a variable annuity will protect them from lawsuits or seizures of their assets. Many such claims are not based on facts, but nevertheless help land a sale. [*NASD Investor Alert*, "Variable Annuities: Beyond the Hard Sell", May 27, 2003. This Alert focuses solely on *deferred variable* annuities and the unique issues they raise for investors.]

The *Wall Street Journal* reports that one company offers training sessions on how to sell annuities to senior citizens. "Treat them like they're children." "Don't be sophisticated." "They buy based upon emotions! Emotions of fear, anger and greed." "Show them their finances are all screwed up so that they think, 'Oh, no, I've done it all wrong.' This will make you money, and it's probably a product they need." "Tell them you can protect their life savings from nursing home and Medicaid seizure of assets. They don't know what that is, but it sounds scary. It's about putting a pitchfork in their chest."

What's an annuity? "There's the technical answer, and there's the senior answer. Tell them it's like a CD—it's safe, it's guaranteed."

On June 27, 2002 the SEC filed civil fraud charges against a California Broker, Gregory W. The SEC alleged that W. defrauded scores of retired customers by recommending they replace existing investments in variable annuities with new investments in similar variable annuities. The switches would enable him to receive significant commissions. W. recommended approximately 57 such switches in less than four years. W. told the customers they needed to switch in order to stem investment losses caused by declines in the stock market. The switching did not halt their losses and they could have achieved that objective by simply electing another investment option within the original variable annuity. The customers either received no economic benefit or lost money in the switch transactions and together incurred more than $200,000 in needless transactions costs, while W. received approximately $275,000 in commissions for the unsuitable switches.

Simultaneously the Commission proceeded against W.'s supervisor for failing to reasonably supervise W. and not investigating red flags raised by certain switches when she reviewed the transactions.

QUESTIONS

1. How can companies ensure that their annuity sales to seniors are suitable—that the product is both needed and understood by the client?

2. What are the ramifications of having multiple pricing and commission structures available on identical products? How can the company be confident that the agent is selling the right product for each client? What disclosures about product choices and compensation are appropriate?

CASE 4.4
An Auditor's Dilemma
John R. Boatright

Sorting through a stack of invoices, Alison Lloyd's attention was drawn to one from Ace Glass Company. Her responsibility as the new internal auditor for Gem Packing is to verify all expenditures, and she knew that Ace had already been paid for the June delivery of the jars that are used for Gem's jams and jellies. On closer inspection, she noticed that the invoice was for deliveries in July and August that had not yet been made. Today was only June 10. Alison recalled approving several other invoices lately that seemed to be misdated, but the amounts were small compared with the $130,000 that Gem spends each month for glass jars. I had better check this out with purchasing, she thought.

Over lunch, Greg Berg, the head of purchasing, explains the system to her. The jam and jelly division operates under an incentive plan whereby the division manager and the heads of the four main units—sales, production, distribution, and purchasing—receive substantial bonuses for meeting their quota in pre-tax profits for the fiscal year, which ends on June 30. The bonuses are about one-half of annual salary and constitute one-third of the managers' total compensation. In addition, meeting quota is weighted heavily in evaluations, and missing even once is considered to be a death blow to the career of an aspiring executive at Gem. So the pressure on these managers is intense. On the other hand, there is nothing to be gained from exceeding a quota. An exceptionally good year is likely to be rewarded with an even higher quota the next year, since quotas are generally set at corporate headquarters by adding 5 percent to the previous year's results.

Greg continues to explain that several years ago, after the quota had been safely met, the jam and jelly division began prepaying as many expenses as possible—not only for glass jars but for advertising costs, trucking charges, and some commodities, such as sugar. The practice has continued to grow, and sales also helps out by delaying orders until the next fiscal year or by falsifying delivery dates when a shipment has already gone out. "Regular suppliers like Ace Glass know how we work," Greg says, "and they sent the invoices for July and August at my request." He predicts that Alison will begin seeing more irregular invoices as the fiscal year winds down. "Making quota gets easier each year," Greg observes, "because the division gets an ever increasing head start, but the problem of finding ways to avoid going too far over quota has become a real nightmare." Greg is not sure, but he thinks that other divisions are doing the same thing. "I don't think corporate has caught on yet," he says. "But they created the system, and they've been happy with the results so far. If they're too dumb to figure out how we're achieving them, that's their problem."

Alison recalls that upon becoming a member of the Institute of Internal Auditors, she agreed to abide by the IIA code of ethics. This code requires members to exercise "honesty, objectivity, and diligence" in the performance of their duties, but also to be loyal to the employer. However, loyalty does not include being a party to any "illegal or improper activity." As an internal auditor, she is also responsible for evaluating the adequacy and effectiveness of the company's system of financial control. But what is the harm of shuffling a little paper around? she thinks. Nobody is getting hurt, and it all works out in the end.

QUESTIONS

1. Is the IIA code of ethics really helpful in resolving Alison's dilemma? Why or why not?

2. Greg blames the incentive system for the dilemma. Is he right?

CASE 4.5
Enron and Employee Investment Risk
David Lawrence and Tom L. Beauchamp

In order to determine appropriate and acceptable levels of risk in their retirement funds, employee-investors must be knowledgeable about how those funds are invested. Often employees are unaware of the level of risk taken by their employers in maintaining a fund. A famous recent case of the problem emerged from the ashes of the collapse of Enron.

After greatly expanding its operations during the 1990s, Enron, an energy broker, experienced

In Tom L. Beauchamp and Norman E. Bowie, *Ethical Theory and Business*, 7th ed. (Englewood Cliffs, NJ: Prentice Hall, 2004), p. 251. Reprinted with the permission of the authors.

unprecedented financial growth and soaring stock prices. Much of this growth, however, was not legitimate, and the details, as a result, were not disclosed to investors or to employees.

Using the lawful practice of "mark-to-market" accounting, Enron's financial analysts and advisors were able to record potential, future profits as immediate gains. To boost these apparent profits even more, Enron also created businesses and partnerships to hide its debt. These practices inflated stock prices while falsely establishing the company's financial position and stability. The success and prominence of the company seemed to minimize concerns about investment risk in Enron stock. Seeing immediate and extensive gains, however, such employee-investors saw little incentive in questioning the risk of their investments. They were not concerned when Enron used company stock as the sole unit of deposit in employee 401(k) earnings. While this involved tremendous risk, given Enron's true instability, the details of the company's financial state remained undisclosed. Only after uncovering the fraudulent accounting practices was the true level of the risk assessed. By this time, however, employee-investors and employees with retirement savings invested in

stock had lost all of their investments and all of their retirement funds.

Enron-style investing is commonplace in employee retirement accounts, where diversification in types of investment is not generally recognized as a legal or a moral requirement. While the collapse of Enron is everywhere recognized to be a scandal, the underlying questions of investor risk in company retirement plans is one feature of this scandal that remains largely unaddressed.

QUESTIONS

1. Should businesses, like Enron, encourage employees to buy stock in their own companies? Why or why not? What are some of the risks involved in permitting such practices?

2. While, legally, not all information must be disclosed, should companies be obligated to reveal the true nature of investor risk? Or, are investors individually responsible for determining such risk?

3. Does Enron's overstating of profit amount to a manipulation of investors? Was the manipulation intentional? Should investors assume a high level of risk unless expressly told otherwise?

CASE 4.6

The Fraud Recipe for CEO's, Why Banks Hate Free Markets and Love Crony Capitalism

William F. Black

On the "Technocrats" Running the Show in Europe: There are no *"technocrats,"* especially *"genius"* technocrats. I suggest a new rule of thumb for judging a *"genius technocrat."* They have to be right at least two out of ten times. There is not a single economist in Europe, who calls himself a

technocrat, that could do the equivalent of making two penalty kicks out of ten.

What We Learned from the Savings & Loan Crisis: George Santayana famously said that "those who cannot remember the past are condemned to repeat it." But, even if we remember the mistakes we

From William K. Black's presentation at the Modern Monetary Theory Summit in Rimini, Italy, Febuary 2012.

have made, the new policy we pick could be another mistake. Here is what we learned about the incidence of fraud leading up to the savings and loan crisis, according to the national commission that investigated the causes of that crisis:

> The typical large failure [grew] at an extremely rapid rate, achieving high concentrations of assets in risky ventures . . . [E]very accounting trick available was used . . . Evidence of fraud was invariably present, as was the ability of the operators to "milk" the organization.

On Control Fraud: Control fraud occurs when the person who controls a seemingly legitimate entity uses it as a weapon to defraud. In finance, accounting is the weapon of choice. These accounting frauds cause greater losses than all other property crimes combined, yet economists never talk about it.

On the Danger Control Frauds Pose to Society: When many of these frauds occur in the same area, they hyperinflate financial bubbles, which is what causes financial crises and mass unemployment. It makes the CEOs wealthy, produces *Balzac* scandals, and destroys democracy.

On How Perverse Incentives Encourage Fraud: Perverse incentives produce criminogenic environments that encourage fraud. When people are able to steal a lot of money, with no threat of imprisonment, nor having to live in disgrace, an environment conducive to fraud is established. Establishing such an environment in practice requires the 3 D's: deregulation, desupervision, and de facto decriminalization. Deregulation: You get rid of the rules. Desupervision: Any rules that remain, you do not enforce. Decriminalization: Even if you sometimes sue the perpetrators and get a fine, you do not put them in prison.

On the Ideal Perverse Incentives for Accounting Fraud: Accounting fraud thrives most with really high pay based on short-term reported income with no way to claw it back—even when it proves to be a lie. Also helpful is for assets to not have a readily verifiable market value; this makes it easy to inflate the asset prices and easy to hide real losses. For a true epidemic of fraud, it is also helpful to have easy entry into the industry.

Bill Black's Recipe for Bankers to Become Billionaires: 1. Grow massively, 2. By making very poor quality loans at high rates of interest, 3. Use extreme leverage (high corporate debt), and 4. Set aside virtually no loss reserves for the massive losses that will be coming. If you do these four things, you are mathematically guaranteed to report record short-term income. Akerlof and Romer referred to it as a sure thing—it is guaranteed.

What the Recipe for Fraud Will Guarantee: (1) The bank will report record profits (fictional profits), (2) the CEO will promptly become wealthy, and (3) down the road, the bank will suffer catastrophic losses. As a bonus, if many banks do this simultaneously, a bubble will be hyperinflated.

Why Bankers Hate Free Markets and Effective Market Competition and Adore Crony Capitalism: If you are a banker and wish to grow your bank (lending) at 50% per year—as was happening in Iceland, Ireland, and much of Europe, for example—you would have to beat your competition—as in charge a lower interest rate. But if markets are working properly, your competition will try to match your rates—and you wouldn't end up making more loans, and your income would fall. All bankers would lose. That's why banks are the biggest proponents of crony capitalism—and are the world leaders in crony capitalism.

Why Bad Loans Are Perfect for Bank Fraud: When loans are made to people who cannot afford to repay them, banks that do basic underwriting are no longer an issue in terms of competition. And, when you lend to people with no intention to pay back a loan, you can charge very high interest and very high fees—thus maximizing short-term paper gains. And if enough banks get into the business, the bubble is hyperinflated, the bad loans can be rolled over into new bad loans, and the losses can be hidden for years. The bottom line is that mediocre bankers cannot make money in a competitive market, but they are guaranteed to make enormous money by using the fraud recipe. Here is a quote from the economist who led the national investigation of the Savings and Loan crisis, James Pierce: "Accounting abuses also provided the ultimate perverse incentive: It paid to seek out bad loans because only those who had no intention of repaying would be willing to pay the high loan fees and interest required for the best loot-ing. It was rational for operators'—that's CEOs—to drive their banks ever deeper into insolvency, as they looted them."

So the best and surest way to become wealthy, as a bank CEO, is to make the worst possible loans. In order to make so many bad loans, they have to gut the underwriting process. Underwriting is what an honest bank does to make sure that it's going to get repaid.

How Adverse Selection and Gresham's Dynamics Permeate an Industry: Imagine you run a *Competent Honest Bank* and you do underwrit-ing. And you can tell can tell high-risk and low-risk borrowers. Low-risk borrowers you charge 10%. High-risk borrowers you charge 20%. I run *Bill's Incompetent Bank*; I can't tell risk. So, I charge everybody 15%. Which borrowers come to me? Only the absolute worst borrowers. No good borrower would come because they could borrow at your bank at 10%. In economics, we call this *adverse selection*. And it means that a bank that makes loans this way must lose vast amounts of money. No honest banker would operate this way. And the banks that engage in

these frauds also create criminogenic environments themselves to recruit fraud allies. For example, when it comes to the people that value homes, if they won't inflate the value, the dishonest banks won't use them. Do they need to corrupt every person that values homes? No, five percent of the profession is suffi-cient. They just send all their business to the corrupt appraisers. This is called a *Gresham's Dynamic*; and it means that cheaters prosper and bad ethics drives good ethics out of the marketplace.

On How to Battle Fraud: We need a coast guard for our banks. We can no longer allow CEOs to desert their posts after running their banks aground and causing such great destruction. The elite bank CEOs that destroyed the global economy remain wealthy, powerful, and famous because they looted. They were bailed out. They did not leave in a lifeboat in the dark of night. They left in their yachts—yachts that the governments paid for.

QUESTIONS

1. What environmental factors contribute to fraud?
2. Define Gresham's Dynamic.

CASE 4.7
SNB Annual Conference
Richard F. DeMong

Richard F. DeMong is a professor of commerce, McIntire School of Commerce, University of Virginia.

Carol was recently promoted to the assistant treasurer position of her medium-sized manufacturing com-pany in Rochester, New York. One of her primary duties is to monitor the three fixed-income invest-ment managers for her company's pension funds. She is responsible for monitoring their investment

performance, for recommending allocation of the current pension funds of approximately $2 billion (split roughly evenly among the three managers), and for new contributions added to the pension funds each month Carol reports directly to the treasurer, Mary Ann, but she will also present her analysis to the Investment Committee of the Board of Directors each quarter. Based on her analysis, she may also recommend firing a manager and selecting a new manager.

Carol was asked by one of the investment managers, SNB, to attend their annual conference for their best clients. The conference will be held during the first week of February in Vail, Colorado. The conference runs from Wednesday afternoon to late Saturday afternoon. She was told to bring her skis and her tennis racket because "there will be plenty of time for skiing and indoor tennis, since the morning sessions will end by 10:30 a.m. and the afternoon sessions will not begin until 4:30 p.m." SNB will pick up all her costs except her airfare to Vail. She is sure that she will gather some new information and a better sense of the current investment climate at the conference. But she is troubled by the possibility of an appearance of a conflict of intent if she attends a conference sponsored by one of the investment managers that she is responsible for monitoring. She also wonders whether attending the conference will taint her objectivity. Carol knows that her boss, Mary Ann, who previously was responsible for monitoring the fixed-income manager, looked forward to SNB's conferences each year. She wondered what Mary Ann would think if the new assistant treasurer decided not to attend the conference because of the possibility of a conflict of interest. Carol did not want unnecesssarily to make her boss look bad. The other two investment managers tended to have less elaborate working conferences in New York City.

QUESTIONS

1. Should Carol accept the invitation to SNB's conference? Explain.

2. If she chose not to attend, how might Carol present her choice so as not to embarrass her boss?

CASE 4.8
The Accidental Bank Robbery
D. Anthony Plath

D. Anthony Plath is an assistant professor at the University of North Carolina at Charlotte.

Chris wasn't really pleased with his current assignment as a relief branch manager at Commerce Trust Bank, but it was a means to an end. Employed by the bank for almost two years as a branch management trainee, Chris desperately wanted to escape the training program and begin a career as branch manager. He had earned strong praise from his superiors throughout the training program, and Chris hoped this last phase of training would pass quickly and uneventfully.

As a relief manager, Chris took over all management functions in various Commerce Trust retail branches whenever the regular office managers were called out of town for more than one day. The relief manager's position was particularly challenging, because Chris was called upon regularly to make quick decisions regarding check cashing, small loan approval, and employee supervision when he knew few of the regular branch customers and little about the daily office routines. For assistance, Chris often relied on the judgment and experience of the senior tellers and customer service representatives within each office he managed.

One recent assignment was particularly difficult because Chris was called to work in a small suburban office staffed by relatively inexperienced branch employees. At the end of his first full day in the office, Chris was not surprised when one of the branch's young tellers, Carole Baker, reported to him that her drive-in teller window was $900 short. While Chris was accustomed to out-of-balance teller windows, Carole was not. She had just completed teller school the week before Chris's arrival at the branch, and as a probationary employee, she knew that an unresolved $900 shortage would lead to the termination of her employment with the bank. When Carole approached Chris for help, she was in a state of panic.

Given his experience in retail banking, Chris reassured Carole that he would locate the $900 shortage from the transactions ledger maintained by Carole's computerized teller terminal. Sure enough, after reviewing Carole's ledger entries for only a few minutes, Chris spotted the error. Carole had received a check for $100 from one of the bank's regular depositors, incorrectly entered it into the computer for $1,000, and paid out $900 more in cash than the amount shown on the check.

Both Carole and Chris were relieved to locate the error, and even more relieved that one of the branch's best deposit customers was the unexpected beneficiary of Carole's error. Surely the customer pulled away from the drive-in window without realizing the mistake. When Chris phoned the customer to explain the bank's error, however, he was shocked when the

customer reported receiving only $100 from Carole's window. Even when Chris mentioned that Carole would lose her job if the error could not be resolved, the customer steadfastly maintained that Carole had only paid $100 in exchange for the $100 check.

Hanging up the phone, Chris turned toward Carole, who was now in tears. In order to reconcile her window, Chris would have to report the $900 error on Carole's shortage report. While the source of the mistake was clear to everyone at the branch, the loss appeared unrecoverable. When Chris reported the shortage to the bank's personnel department, as he was required to do by the bank's branch operations policy, Carole would be fired. Wasn't there something he could do. Carole sobbed, to balance her window without reporting the $900 loss?

QUESTIONS

1. What should Chris do now?
2. Should Chris debit one of the customer's other accounts, or place the $900 loss in a temporary suspense account to balance Carol's window?

CHAPTER QUESTIONS

1. What are the basic conflicts that arise in helping other people with their money? Should we rely on experts when it comes to money? How do we know when an expert's own pocketbook is guiding a decision, rather than an interest in our financial success? Are there ways of guaranteeing that our financial success, the expert's financial success, and good ethical principles are all in agreement?

2. One commentator described the Enron–Arthur Andersen debacle as "the half-full problem"—the tendency for analysts to insist that the glass is half-full rather than half-empty. How can financial managers both stimulate financial success and yet be wary of the dangers of excessive optimism? Is there a place for optimism in accounting? In the sale of derivatives?

3. How might regulation and finance ethics have helped to prevent the crisis of 2009–2010? Can you make a list of ten good reasons to control the flow of money? How should those who control the flow of money regulate themselves? Can they do so?

5

Who Gets What and Why?

Fairness and Justice

Introduction

Businesses and corporations are not just legal entities. They are communities. Small businesses are more like extended families, perhaps, but even giant corporations try to maintain something of a family identity in order to encourage family-like loyalty and foster a sense of belonging that "work-for-hire" and other contract workers do not feel. (Of course, there are unhappy as well as dysfunctional families and communities, but it is already a significant step to understand that joining a company is not just a matter of "taking a job.") As a member of a family or a community, however, you will, of course, be sensitive to considerations that pertain not just to yourself, for example, your salary, your job skills, and your responsibilities, but to you as a member of a group, the sort of motivation that is summarized in most corporations as "team spirit." But being a member of a group is not just becoming submerged in the group. One retains one's identity and interests as an individual. And that means that among the most important factors in a good job and the satisfaction that goes along with it is fairness, a *comparative* measure of how people are treated. It is a conclusion of a great deal of research, often confirmed, that people care about their comparative (ordinal) worth more than they care about their absolute (cardinal) worth. Most people, given the choice between a salary of, say, $60,000—while other people at the same level are making $64,000—and a salary of, say, $56,000—while other people at the same level are making $50,000—will choose the latter over the former. In the abstract, you may think, "How stupid! Choosing the lower salary." But in the context of a work situation, comparative rewards mean a great deal, in terms of one's sense of worth, one's sense of being appreciated, and one's sense of being fairly treated. Even trivial differences in salary or bonuses can cause seething and poisonous resentment.

Of course, considerations of fairness cut across careers and professions and involve both rewards and burdens, including punishments, of various kinds. In other words, considerations of fairness are not confined to peers and pay. A company that gives out awards or promotions, whether or not they involve any monetary reward, will find quickly the huge cost of favoritism and other forms of unfair competition. When the boss's nephew wins the award for "Best New Employee," he had better have the on-the-job record to back it up. Indeed, it may have been an injustice for him to get the job in the first place. But this is not to say that everyone should be treated or paid equally. Few people deny that top executives deserve more in salary than does the ordinary manager, but the question *how much more* is a controversial question these days. (It used to be a multiple of 35 or so. It is now over 500. In 2003, the average CEO of a major company received $9.2 million in total compensation, according to a study by compensation consultant Pearl Meyer & Partners for the *New York Times.)* The nurse who takes care of your sick aunt or the teacher who spends six hours a day with your eight-year-old niece in public school makes far less money for (arguably) just as much work. A stockbroker or investment banker readily makes a six-figure income; the nurse and the teacher make a fraction of that, with little possibility of a dramatic increase or substantial bonus.

Justice has two basic forms: *retributive* justice and *distributive* justice. Distributive justice is concerned with the distribution of goods, in the context of a job, salaries, bonuses, promotions, but also opportunities and responsibilities. Retributive justice is essentially concerned with penalties and punishments, with assigning blame and, when necessary, reprimanding or punishing people in proportion to their mistakes or misdeeds.

To: You
From: The Philosopher
Subject: "Plato and Aristotle on Justice"

The subject of justice is as old as human civilization. In really ancient times, perhaps, the rule was "might makes right." Some people still think that it does. But for most of history thoughtful people have seen beyond mere force and power to the idea that there is a *fairer* way of thinking about what people should get and give from and to society. Plato, through his spokesman Socrates in *The Republic*, argued that everyone should get his or her due—what he or she deserves—based on his or her place in a just society. Aristotle, Plato's student, had a more economically sophisticated version of this idea. He insisted that justice requires a principle of *equality*, by which he meant not (as in more recent philosophies) that everyone should get the same but, rather, that justice requires that everyone should get the proportion he or she deserves, depending on his or her position in the society. It is "equal" in the sense that it is neither too much nor too little. (Aristotle suggests, insightfully, that the best way to test a person's sense of fairness is to watch the person when he or she is in charge.)

Business, for the most part, is concerned with distributive justice. (In the wake of some of the serious scandals of recent years, retributive justice also becomes a major issue, but it becomes a matter of law and the business of the courts, rather than an issue in business ethics as such.) The one thing that we should say about retributive justice is that it is based on the idea that everyone should be treated fairly and equally, so that one person should not be punished for another person's mistakes and one person should not be punished more harshly than another who has made the same mistake. No matter how effective it may be to make an example of an innocent employee in order to deter other employees who may be thinking about cheating on their expense accounts, we feel strongly that it is unfair and an *injustice* to punish someone who has not, in fact, done something wrong. But in distributive justice, too, what is essential is that a person be rewarded in accordance with what he or she *deserves*. Two people who do the same job equally well deserve the same rewards. Different rewards (e.g., larger and smaller bonuses) had better be based on differences in the quality or quantity of work. Extraneous considerations—whether a person is male or female, his or her race or religion, his or her personal preferences or idiosyncrasies—should make no difference at all.

We start the chapter with a few bits from the great philosophers Plato and Aristotle on justice and, in particular, the famous "Ring of Gyges" example from Plato's *Republic*, in which the question is posed, Why would you care about doing the right thing and being fair if you could get away with anything? Then Adam Smith considers the value of fair exchange in the marketplace. The antithesis of justice in the marketplace is *exploitation*, and we offer a couple of different perspectives on it, from the very abstract (Karl Marx) to the very concrete (Wal-Mart's behavior in Latin America) and something in between, Joanne B. Ciulla on exploitation in the job market. Then we open up our horizons to the world more generally. The late philosopher John Rawls summarizes his classic theory of justice, Robert Nozick offers his now classic response to Rawls, and Princeton ethicist Peter Singer sums up the argument against the extreme gap between rich and poor in the world. Then Irving Kristol and Friedrich von Hayek offer two more conservative views of justice, Kristol on how justice fits into the free market and von Hayek on how it does not. Eduard Gracia weighs the risks of a society in which the "winner takes all." Gerald W. McEntee considers the question of gender equality and "comparable worth," the shameful fact that in a society in which people are supposed to be paid for the work they do, women are paid considerably less than are men for doing exactly the same job. The cases are intended to provoke your thinking about concrete concerns about justice, for instance, the fact that you may be contributing to the exploitation and injustice in the world by buying some of the products that you are wearing right now. Finally, Grey Breining discusses the problem of "the wealthiest 1%" of Americans.

Plato | # Ring of Gyges

Plato was one of the two greatest Greek philosophers of ancient times. This is the infamous "Ring of Gyges" story from his dialogue, *The Republic*, told by one of Socrates' philosophical sparring partners, Glaucon.

GLAUCON (TO SOCRATES): I have never yet heard the superiority of justice to injustice maintained by anyone in a satisfactory way. I want to hear justice praised in respect of itself; then I shall be satisfied, and you are the person from whom I think that I am most likely to hear this; and therefore I will praise the unjust life to the utmost of my power and my manner of speaking will indicate the manner in which I desire to hear you too praising justice and censuring injustice. Will you say whether you approve of my proposal?

SOCRATES: Indeed I do; nor can I imagine any theme about which a man of sense would oftener wish to converse.

GLAUCON: I am delighted to hear you say so, and shall begin by speaking, as I proposed, of the nature and origin of justice.

They say that to do injustice is, by nature, good; to suffer injustice, evil; but that there is more evil in the latter than good in the former. And so when men have both done and suffered injustice and have had experience of both, any who are not able to avoid the one and obtain the other, think that they had better agree among themselves to have neither; hence they began to establish laws and mutual covenants; and that which was ordained by law was termed by them lawful and just. This, it is claimed, is the origin and nature of justice—it is a mean or compromise, between the best of all, which is to do injustice and not be punished, and the worst of all, which is to suffer injustice without the power of retaliation; and justice, being at a middle point between the two, is tolerated not as a good but as the lesser evil, and

honoured where men are too feeble to do injustice. For no man who is worthy to be called a man would ever submit to such an agreement with another if he had the power to be unjust; he would be mad if he did. Such is the received account Socrates, of the nature of justice, and the circumstances which bring it into being.

Now that those who practice justice do so involuntarily and because they have not the power to be unjust will best appear if we imagine something of this kind: having given to both the just and the unjust power to do what they will, let us watch and see whither desire will lead them; then we shall discover in the very act the just and unjust man to be proceeding along the same road, following their interest, which all creatures instinctively pursue as their good; the force of law is required to compel them to pay respect to equality. The liberty which we are supposing may be most completely given to them in the form of such a power as is said to have been possessed by Gyges, the ancestor of Croesus the Lydian. According to the tradition, Gyges was a shepherd in the service of the reigning king of Lydia; there was a great storm, and an earthquake made an opening in the earth at the place where he was feeding his flock. Amazed at the sight, he descended into the opening, where, among other marvels which form part of the story, he beheld a hollow brazen horse, having doors, at which he stooping and looking in saw a dead body of stature, as appeared to him, more than human; he took from the corpse a gold ring that was on the hand, but nothing else, and so reascended. Now the shepherds met together, according to custom, that they might send their monthly report about the flocks to the king; into their assembly he came having the ring on his finger, and as he was sitting among them he chanced to turn the collet of the ring to the inside of his hand, when instantly he became invisible to the rest of the company and they began to

From *Republic*, Book 2, trans. Benjamin Jowett (Oxford University Press, 1924).

speak of him as if he were no longer present. He was astonished at this, and again touching the ring he turned the collet outwards and reappeared; when he perceived this, he made several trials of the ring, and always with the same result—when he turned the collet inwards he became invisible, when outwards he was visible. Whereupon he contrived to be chosen one of the messengers who were sent to the court; where as soon as he arrived he seduced the queen, and with her help conspired against the king and slew him, and took the kingdom. Suppose now that there were two such magic rings, and the just put on one of them and the unjust the other; no man can be imagined to be of such an iron nature that he would stand fast injustice. No man would keep his hands off what was not his own when he could safely take what he liked out of the market, or go into houses and lie with any one at his pleasure, or kill or release from prison whom he would, and in all respects be like a god among men. Then the actions of the just would be as the actions of the unjust; they would both tend to the same goal. And this we may truly affirm to be a great proof that a man is just, not willingly or because he thinks that justice is any good to him individually, but of necessity; for wherever anyone thinks that he can safely be unjust, there he is unjust. For all men believe in their hearts that injustice is far more profitable to the individual than justice and he who argues as I have been supposing will say that they are right. If you could imagine anyone obtaining this power of becoming invisible, and never

doing any wrong or touching what was another's, he would be thought by the lookers-on to be an unhappy man and a fool, although they would praise him to one another's faces, and keep up appearances with one another from a fear that they too might suffer injustice. Enough of this.

Now, if we are to form a real judgement of the two lives in these respects, we must set apart the extremes of justice and injustice; there is no other way; and how is the contrast to be effected? I answer: Let the unjust man be entirely unjust, and the just man entirely just; nothing is to be taken away from either of them, and both are to be perfectly furnished for the work of their respective lives. First, let the unjust be like other distinguished masters of craft; like the skillful pilot or physician, who knows intuitively what is possible or impossible in his art and keeps within those limits, and who, if he fails at any point, is able to recover himself. So let the unjust man attempt to do the right sort of wrongs, and let him escape detection if he is to be pronounced a master of injustice. To be found out is a sign of incompetence; for the height of injustice is to be deemed just when you are not. Therefore I say that in the perfectly unjust man we must assume the most perfect injustice; there is to be no deduction, but we must allow him, while doing the most unjust acts, to have acquired the greatest reputation for justice. If he has taken a false step he must be able to recover himself; he must be one who can speak with effect, if any of his deeds come to light, and who can force

To: You
From: The Philosopher
Subject: "Would You Rather Earn More or Just More Than the Other Fellow?"

Suppose that you are given a choice between two jobs, one with a salary of $60,000, but you know that other new hires at the same level have been offered $64,000, and the other with a salary of $56,000, and you know that other new hires have only been offered $50,000. Other things being equal (the job description, the working conditions, the people you will be working with), which would you choose?

his way where force is required, by his courage and strength and command of wealth and friends. And at his side let us place the just man in his nobleness and simplicity, wishing, as Aeschylus says, to be and not to seem good. There must be no seeming, for if he seems to be just he will be honoured and rewarded, and then we shall not know whether he is just for the sake of justice or for the sake of honours and rewards; therefore, let him be clothed in justice only, and have no other covering; and he must be imagined in a state of life the opposite of the former. Let him be the best of men, and let him be reputed the worst; then he will have been put to the test and we shall see whether his justice is proof against evil reputation and its consequences. And let him continue thus to the hour of death; being just and

seeming to be unjust. When both have reached the uttermost extreme, the one of justice and the other of injustice, let judgement be given which of them is the happier of the two.

SOCRATES: Heavens! my dear Glaucon . . . how energetically you polish them up for the decision, first one and then the other, as if they were two statues.

QUESTIONS

1. What would you do if you had the ring of Gyges? What do you think your best friend would do?

2. The consequences of unjust actions are one kind of constraint upon justice. What are some other constraints? Why might we want to appeal to more than consequences?

Adam Smith | # On Human Exchange and Human Differences

This division of labor, from which so many advantages are derived, is not originally the effect of any human wisdom which foresees and intends that general opulence to which it gives occasion. It is the necessary, though very slow and gradual, consequence of a certain propensity in human nature which has in view no such extensive utility: the propensity to truck, barter, and exchange one thing for another.

Whether this propensity be one of those original principles in human nature, of which no further account can be given; or whether, as seems more probable, it be the necessary consequence of the faculties of reason and speech, it belongs not to our present subject to enquire. It is common to all men, and to be found in no other race of animals, which seem to know neither this nor any other species of contracts. Two greyhounds, in running down the

same hare, have sometimes the appearance of acting in some sort of concert. Each turns her toward his companion, or endeavors to intercept her when his companion turns her toward himself. This, however, is not the effect of any contract, but of the accidental concurrence of their passions in the same object at that particular time. Nobody ever saw a dog make a fair and deliberate exchange of one bone for another with another dog. Nobody ever saw one animal by its gestures and natural cries signify to another, this is mine, that yours; I am willing to give this for that. When an animal wants to obtain something either of a man or of another animal; it has no other means of persuasion but to gain the favor of those whose service it requires. A puppy fawns upon its dam, and a spaniel endeavors by a thousand attractions to engage the attention of its master who is at dinner,

From Adam Smith, *The Wealth of Nations* (New York: Hafner, 1948).

when it wants to be fed by him. Man sometimes uses the same arts with his brethren, and when he has no other means of engaging them to act according to his inclinations, endeavors by every servile and fawning attention to obtain their good will. He has not time, however, to do this upon every occasion. In civilized society he stands at all times in need of the co-operation and assistance of great multitudes, while his whole life is scarce sufficient to gain the friendship of a few persons. In almost every other race of animals each individual, when it is grown up to maturity, is entirely independent, and in its natural state has occasion for the assistance of no other living creature. But man has almost constant occasion for the help of his brethren, and it is in vain for him to expect it from their benevolence only. He will be more likely to prevail if he can interest their self-love in his favor, and show them that it is for their own advantage to do for him what he requires of them. Whoever offers to another a bargain of any kind, proposes to do this. Give me that which I want, and you shall have this which you want, is the meaning of every such offer; and it is in this manner that we obtain from one another the far greater part of those good offices which we stand in need of. It is not from the benevolence of the butcher, the brewer, or the baker, that we expect our dinner, but from their regard to their own interest. We address ourselves, not to their humanity but to their self-love, and never talk to them of our own necessities but of their advantages. Nobody but a beggar chooses to depend chiefly upon the benevolence of his fellow-citizens. Even a beggar does not depend upon it entirely. The charity of well-disposed people, indeed, supplies him with the whole fund of his subsistence. But though this principle ultimately provides him with all the necessaries of life which he has occasion for, it neither does nor can provide him with them as he has occasion for them. The greater part of his occasional wants are supplied in the same manner as those of other people, by treaty, by barter, and by purchase. With the money which one man gives him he purchases food. The old clothes which another bestows upon him he exchanges for other old clothes which suit him better, or for lodging, or for food, or for money, with which he can buy either food, clothes, or lodging, as he has occasion.

As it is by treaty, by barter, and by purchase that we obtain from one another the greater part of those mutual good offices which we stand in need of, so it is this same trucking disposition which originally gives occasion to the division of labor. In a tribe of hunters or shepherds a particular person makes bows and arrows, for example, with more readiness and dexterity than any other. He frequently exchanges them for cattle or for venison with his companions; and he finds at last that he can in this manner get more cattle and venison than if he himself went to the field to catch them. From a regard to his own interest, therefore, the making of bows and arrows grows to be his chief business, and he becomes a sort of armorer. Another excels in making the frames and covers of their little huts or movable houses. He is accustomed to be of use in this way to his neighbors, who reward him in the same manner with cattle and with venison till at last he finds it his interest to dedicate himself entirely to this employment, and to become a sort of house carpenter. In the same manner a third becomes a smith or a brazier; a fourth a tanner or dresser of hides or skins, the principal part of the clothing of savages. And thus the certainty of being able to exchange all that surplus part of the produce of his own labor, which is over and above his own consumption, for such parts of the produce of other men's labor as he may have occasion for, encourages every man to apply himself to a particular occupation, and to cultivate and bring to perfection whatever talent or genius he may possess for that particular species of business.

The difference of natural talents in different men is, in reality, much less than we are aware of; and the very different genius which appears to distinguish men of different professions, when grown up to maturity, is not upon many occasions so much the cause as the effect of the division of labor. The difference between the most dissimilar characters, between a philosopher and a common street porter, for example, seems to arise not so much from nature as from habit, custom, and education. When they came into the world, and for the first six or eight years of their existence, they were, perhaps, very much alike, and neither their parents nor play-fellows could perceive any remarkable difference. About that age, or soon after, they come to be employed in very different occupations. The difference of talents comes then to be taken notice of, and widens by degrees, till at last the vanity of the philosopher is willing to acknowledge scarce any resemblance. But without the disposition to truck, barter, and exchange, every man must have procured to himself every necessary and conveniency of life which he wanted. All must have had the same duties to perform, and the same work to do, and there could have been no such difference of employment as could alone give occasion to any great difference of talents.

As it is this disposition which forms that difference of talents so remarkable among men of different professions, so it is this same disposition which renders that difference useful. Many tribes of animals acknowledged to be all of the same species derive from nature a much more remarkable distinction of genius than what, antecedent to custom and education, appears to take place among men. By nature a philosopher is not in genius and disposition half so different from a street porter as a mastiff is from a greyhound, or a greyhound from a spaniel, or this last from a shepherd's dog. Those different tribes of animals, however, though all of the same species, are of scarce any use to one another. The strength of the mastiff is not in the least supported either by the swiftness of the greyhound, or by the sagacity of the spaniel, or by the docility of the shepherd's dog. The effects of those different geniuses and talents, for want of the power or disposition to barter and exchange, cannot be brought into a common stock, and do not in the least contribute to the better accommodation and conveniency of the species. Each animal is still obliged to support and defend itself separately and independently, and derives no sort of advantage from that variety of talents with which nature has distinguished its fellows. Among men, on the contrary, the most dissimilar geniuses are of use to one another; the different produces of their respective talents, by the general disposition to truck, barter, and exchange, being brought, as it were, into a common stock, where every man may purchase whatever part of the produce of other men's talents he has occasion for.

QUESTIONS

1. Why does Smith believe that "self-love" is a good thing?

2. Why does Smith discuss the differences in people's talents? Why is it important that the difference in talents is not so large as we often suppose?

Latin Trade | # A Latin Viewpoint: The Bentonville Menace

Latin Trade is a South American business magazine.

If you wonder why more Latin American countries aren't jumping on the free-trade bandwagon, look no further than the cutthroat business practices of the world's largest private company, US$245 billion-in-revenues Wal-Mart Stores.

From *Latin Trade*, May 2004.

Taking screw-the-workers capitalism to new depths, this modern-day robber baron has pushed its Latin American suppliers to cut costs to the bone or lose their contracts to China. They are even trying to force down labor costs in emerging Asia. It seems even $0.40 cents an hour—the estimated wage in China—is too high for the heartless executives at the front offices in Bentonville, Arkansas.

In some 40 lawsuits reportedly filed in the United States, the corporate behemoth—its annual sales is greater than the gross domestic product (GDP) of all but two Latin American economies—has been accused of using third-party contractors who hire illegal immigrants to work below minimum wage; of forcing employees to work overtime without pay; of busting up attempts to unionize; and of skimping on worker and retirement compensation. The company's official line is anti-union.

An internal audit at Wal-Mart three years ago—as reported in the *New York Times*—showed extensive violations of child labor laws. Meanwhile, a federal judge in San Francisco is considering a sexual discrimination suit that could encompass as many as 1.6 million women, making it the largest civil rights class-action case in U.S. history.

If Wal-Mart stands accused of engaging in such shenanigans in the United States, imagine its corporate behavior in far-less-litigious Latin America.

"Many Latin Americans concerned about economic development see little benefit from the Wal-Mart model of maximizing profits by paying poverty wages," says Kent Wong, director of the Center for Labor Research and Education at the University of California at Los Angeles.

It was a *Los Angeles Times* exposé published in November that noted how Wal-Mart's global network of 10,000 suppliers is under constant pressure to reduce costs. The article described the unhappy life of a Honduran woman named Isabel Reyes, who works for a textile company in San Pedro Sula that makes shirts and shorts for Wal-Mart. With quotas constantly rising, she now works 10 hours a day, sewing sleeves onto 1,200 shirts a day for about $35 a week. The 37-year-old seamstress can't hold her infant daughter without gulping anti-inflammatory pills.

To be sure, nobody is forcing Reyes to work there. "It's easy to compare a $35 a week salary with a U.S. salary," Wal-Mart spokesman Bill Wertz told me. "But I don't know what the alternatives are in that country."

He's right—to an extent. What choice does Reyes have in a nation where 53% of the population lives below the poverty line, and 28% of the work force is unemployed?

Latin American governments are grappling with weak economies and need all the jobs they can get. Wal-Mart offers lots of them. The retail chain is now Mexico's largest private employer, with 663 stores and 100,000 employees. The chain generates $11 billion a year there—more than the country's entire tourism sector, or about 2% of Mexico's GDP. Puerto Rico has 53 Wal-Mart stores with 11,600 workers. Brazil has 25 stores and 6,600 employees; Argentina 11 stores and 4,200 employees.

And customers all over the world love bargain prices. In 1995, I covered the opening of Wal-Mart's first store in São Paulo. I remember Brazilians rhapsodizing over the store's mantra of "everyday low prices." So many people lined up to get inside during the first week of business that the manager had to lock out some customers.

Still, it's time to hold this mega-corporation accountable. Latin American leaders must not be forced to cower to foreign investors who threaten to move elsewhere if they don't play by the rules of take-no-prisoners U.S. capitalism.

Free trade was supposed to create decent paying jobs that ultimately offer Latin American families a middle-class life style and turn them into consumers. Unfortunately, fairness has never been part of the free trade blueprint. Nor, in my view, is fairness uppermost in the mind of Wal-Mart's corporate masters.

Consumers should think twice about patronizing any business that perpetuates economic injustice. Everyday social justice is more important than low prices at any cost.

QUESTIONS

1. What is the problem with Wal-Mart in Latin America?

2. Is economic justice more important than low prices? Should we be shopping at Wal-Mart?

Joanne B. Ciulla | Exploitation of Need

The fact that a person can choose his or her work does not necessarily justify ill-treatment by an employer. Part of the question is how many options a person really does have. A common myth is that all people really have a wide range of choices when it comes to making a living. The most important part of the American dream was that anyone could become anything. This was a land not only of opportunity but of options. But what about the destitute person whose only options are degrading ones?

The practice of self-enslavement had been around for a long time. It was common among the Germanic and Anglo-Saxon peoples in the Middle Ages. A person in need of support and/or protection would sell himself to another. This choice, though more or less freely made, was grounded in the same fears of starvation and violence found in other forms of slavery. Self-enslavement raises some interesting questions. Does a frightened and starving person *freely* choose to enter into a contract with someone who can provide him or her with food and safety? This is a question that lies beneath the way Americans think about employment. Is any kind of work or any set of working conditions okay as long as a person freely chooses it? We may be quicker to defend people's right to do any job they want to do, but what about the right of employers to hire people for physically dangerous or personally demeaning work?

The philosopher John Locke offers some insight into these questions. The desire to be free from the yoke of one's master or employer is at the heart of some of our most treasured political ideals. In the first of his two treatises on government, Locke asks, "And how is it that property in land gives a man power over another?" Here Locke is disputing the natural right of kings over property and their subjects. Locke argues that people own the work of their hands and the labor of their bodies. He also notes that we have a moral obligation to help those in need and not take advantage of them: "Charity gives every man a title to so much out of another's plenty, as will keep him

from extreme want, where he has no means to subsist otherwise; and a man can no more justly make use of another's necessity, to force him to become his vassal, by withholding that relief."

Locke then goes on to raise one of the biggest tensions of the employer–employee relationship. He writes that "the subjugation of the needy does not begin with the consent of the Lord, but with the consent of the poor man, who preferred being his [another person's] subject to starving." So, it's wrong to force a needy person to be your slave, but it's not wrong for the needy person to choose to be your slave or indentured servant. Are the two really that different? This is like the employer who says to a single mother of four, "If you don't like working here you are free to leave" or "If you didn't like the working conditions here, then you shouldn't have taken the job in the first place." A single mother who lives in a small town and has four children to support has the freedom to choose where to work, but little to choose from. When it comes to work, everyone has freedom of choice, but not everyone has viable options.

The actual difference between the indentured servant and the slave rests on his or her consent, even if a person really has only one viable choice. The indentured servant's bondage may be short-term and tempered by the voluntary contractual arrangements between the two people. The slave's bondage is involuntary and long-term, and there is no restriction on the master's power over the slave. In theory at least, it is not wrong to take away a person's freedom as long as he or she consents to the arrangement. This begs the larger question of exploitation. How much freedom and human dignity can an employer morally justify buying because someone is willing to sell it? The fourteen-year-old runaway on Sunset Boulevard in Los Angeles is willing to sell his body to buy the drugs he desperately needs. To what extent does he "freely" enter into the transaction? The answer to a question like this has always been hotly contested. Some would argue that the boy could

To: You
From: The Philosopher
Subject: "Marx on Alienated Labor"

There are a lot of people who feel alienated from their jobs and don't want to be identified with their work. The guy who serves you fries at McDonald's probably does not want his work to identify who he is. His job is to make food exactly the way he is told and wait on you fast. This isn't rocket science. Some people are much bigger than their jobs. Karl Marx understood this. He might have been misguided in his economics, but he was a keen observer of what happens to people when they are alienated from their work:

> . . .he does not confirm himself in his work, he denies himself, feels miserable instead of happy, deploys no free physical and intellectual energy, but mortifies his body and ruins his mind. Thus the worker only feels a stranger. He is at home when he is not working and when he works he is not at home.
>
> The result we arrive at then is that man (the worker) only feels himself freely active in his animal functions of eating, drinking, and procreating, at most also in his dwelling and dress, and feels himself in his animal functions. Eating, drinking, procreating, etc. are indeed truly human functions. But in the abstraction that separates them from the other round of human activity and makes them into final and exclusive ends they become animal.*

* From Karl Marx, *Capital*, Penguin Classics, 1992.

choose otherwise, others that given his physical and psychological condition, he is not free.

MONKEY LABOR

It is easy to slip into a logic of exploitation that says that those in need who are exploited are better off than they would be if they weren't exploited. *The Economist* ran a tongue-in-cheek report on working monkeys that illustrates this logic. In southern Thailand several thousand monkeys are "employed" every year to pick the 1.5 million-ton crop of coconuts. Village families train the monkeys and rent them out to plantation owners. The monkeys "earn" about twelve dollars per month in "monkey wages" of eggs, rice, and fruit from the plantation owner. Working monkeys are given names; they are groomed, bathed, and fed three times a day. Sometimes their owners even give them a ride to work, on the back of their motor scooters. When a monkey is ill, it gets the day off. When it is too old to work, it "retires," either back into the wild or as a family pet. The downside of the monkeys' work is that they are kept on chains and not allowed to breed at will. However, the article points out, this practice of "employment" keeps some species such as the crab-eating macaque from becoming extinct because their habitat is being destroyed by humans.

There is a striking parallel between this case and the way that colonists—and some people today— have justified their treatment of indigenous or tribal people in Africa, the Americas, and Australia. They would argue that although the farmers take away the monkeys' freedom, the monkeys are "better off" than they would be on their own in the wild, especially since their habitat has been largely taken over by the farmers. We don't know what the monkeys think. Would they prefer to give up their monkey wages, their names, their daily baths and motor scooter rides to take their chances in the wild? The justification for this arrangement is simple. It's okay for farmers to take away the monkey's freedom because they supply the monkey with what *they* think the monkey needs, even if it is not what the monkey wants.

This extreme (and, to some, frivolous) case illustrates how the logic of exploitation justifies taking advantage of those in need by arguing that one is taking care of people's needs. Exploitation is also about using one's power over others to determine what people need and what they *should* be willing to trade to have their needs filled. Similarly, the farmer decides that the monkey *needs* three meals a day and assumes that the monkey is willing to give up its freedom for them. As we'll see later, sometimes employers fill "needs" that employees do not have or want.

WAGES FOR TIME AND FREEDOM

We own our labor and we own our freedom. Freedom, like labor, is something that we can barter. Most paid employment involves some loss of freedom for the employee. All of us must sell, in varying degrees, our work and our time to earn a living. Both John Locke and Adam Smith realized that employees are not really paid for what they produce. Smith said workers receive compensation for their loss of freedom at work, not for the product they make. Here loss of freedom means a restriction of their liberty to do and say or not to do and say certain things during the time that they are working. Usually when we take a job we implicitly or explicitly agree to do it when, where, and how our employer wants it done. For instance, think about a receptionist's job. She has to sit at the front desk all day, greet people, and answer the phone. She is not totally free to come and go when she pleases. Someone has to cover for her when she goes to the rest room, or takes a break for coffee or lunch. *Being there* is a fundamental part of her job. She is paid for her time as well as for what she does. She can't say what she wants when she answers the phone, she has to be polite and say the name of the company. Today managers would argue that she is paid for the value she adds to the organization—her "value added."

The idea that wages are compensation for loss of freedom also leads to some absurd possibilities. Would this mean that the less freedom a person has on the job the more he or she should get paid? Quite the contrary: jobs with more surface freedom tend to signal higher status and pay more money. In his book *Class*, Paul Fussell argues that the amount of freedom one has on the job is a better indicator of class than salary. The idea of selling freedom often goes hand-in-hand with selling labor, especially when a person is in desperate need of a job and has little choice.

QUESTIONS

1. Tom desperately needs a job. Tom will work for $1 an hour because he cannot find a job that pays more. Although some of my workers (who perform comparable work) are paid $7 an hour or more, I offer Tom the job at $1 an hour. I do not force Tom to take the job. He happily accepts the job. Have I done something wrong in offering Tom a job he was grateful to accept? Why or why not, according to Ciulla?

2. What does Ciulla mean by "self-enslavement"? Can you give examples from your own experience of self-enslavement?

John Rawls | Justice as Fairness

John Rawls was the premier American political philosopher of the twentieth century. This is from his groundbreaking book, *A Theory of Justice*.

My aim is to present a conception of justice which generalizes and carries to a higher level of abstraction the familiar theory of the social contract as found, say, in Locke, Rousseau, and Kant. In order to do this we are not to think of the original contract as one to enter a particular society or to set up a particular form of government. Rather, the guiding idea is that the principles of justice for the basic structure of society are the object of the original agreement. They are the principles that free and rational persons concerned to further their own interests would accept in an initial position of equality as defining the fundamental terms of their association. These principles are to regulate all further agreements: they specify the kinds of social cooperation that can be entered into and the forms of government that can be established. This way of regarding the principles of justice I shall call justice as fairness.

Thus we are to imagine that those who engage in social cooperation choose together, in one joint act, the principles which are to assign basic rights and duties and to determine the division of social benefits. Men are to decide in advance how they are to regulate their claims against one another and what is to be the foundation charter of their society. Just as each person must decide by rational reflection what constitutes his good, that is, the system of ends which it is rational for him to pursue, so a group of persons must decide once and for all what is to count among them as just and unjust. The choice which rational men would make in this hypothetical situation of equal liberty, assuming for the present that this choice problem has a solution, determines the principles of justice.

In justice as fairness the original position of equality corresponds to the state of nature in the traditional theory of the social contract. This original position is not, of course, thought of as an actual historical state of affairs, much less as a primitive condition of culture. It is understood as a purely hypothetical situation characterized so as to lead to a certain conception of justice. Among the essential features of this situation is that no one knows his place in society, his class position or social status, nor does any one know his fortune in the distribution of natural assets and abilities, his intelligence, strength, and the like. I shall even assume that the parties do not know their conceptions of the good or their special psychological propensities. The principles of justice are chosen behind a veil of ignorance. This ensures that no one is advantaged or disadvantaged in the choice of principles by the outcome of natural chance or the contingency of social circumstances. Since all are similarly situated and no one is able to design principles to favor his particular condition, the principles of justice are the result of a fair agreement or bargain. For given the circumstances of the original position, the symmetry of everyone's relations to each other, this initial situation is fair between individuals as moral persons, that is, as rational beings with their own ends and capable, I shall assume, of a sense of justice. . . .

I shall maintain instead that the persons in the initial situation would choose two . . . principles: the first requires equality in the assignment of basic rights and duties, while the second holds that social and economic inequalities, for example inequalities of wealth and authority, are just only if they result in compensating benefits for everyone, and in particular for the least advantaged members of society. These principles rule out justifying institutions on the grounds that the hardships of some are offset by a greater good in the aggregate. It may be

From *A Theory of Justice* (Cambridge, Mass.: Harvard University Press, 1971).

expedient but it is not just that some should have less in order that others may prosper. But there is no injustice in the greater benefits earned by a few provided that the situation of persons not so fortunate is thereby improved. The intuitive idea is that since everyone's well-being depends upon a scheme of cooperation without which no one could have a satisfactory life, the division of advantages should be such as to draw forth the willing cooperation of everyone taking part in it, including those less well situated. Yet this can be expected only if reasonable terms are proposed. The two principles mentioned seem to be a fair agreement on the basis of which those better endowed, or more fortunate in their social position, neither of which we can be said to deserve, could expect the willing cooperation of others when some workable scheme is a necessary condition of the welfare of all. Once we decide to look for a conception of justice that nullifies the accidents of natural endowment and the contingencies of social circumstance as counters in quest for political and economic advantage, we are led to these principles. They express the result of leaving aside those aspects of the social world that seem arbitrary from a moral point of view.

———————

I shall now state in a provisional form the two principles of justice that I believe would be chosen in the original position. The first statement of the two principles reads as follows.

- First: each person is to have an equal right to the most extensive basic liberty compatible with a similar liberty for others.
- Second: social and economic inequalities are to be arranged so that they are both (a) reasonably expected to be to everyone's advantage, and (b) attached to positions and offices open to all.

By way of general comment, these principles primarily apply, as I have said, to the basic structure of society. They are to govern the assignment of rights and duties and to regulate the distribution of social and economic advantages. As their formulation suggests, these principles presuppose that the social structure can be divided into two more or less distinct parts, the first principle applying to the one, the second to the other. They distinguish between those aspects of the social system that define and secure the equal liberties of citizenship and those that specify and establish social and economic inequalities. The basic liberties of citizens are, roughly speaking, political liberty (the right to vote and to be eligible for public office) together with freedom of speech and assembly; liberty of conscience and freedom of thought; freedom of the person along with the right to hold (personal) property; and freedom from arbitrary arrest and seizure as defined by the concept of the rule of law. These liberties are all required to be equal by the first principle, since citizens of a just society are to have the same basic rights.

The second principle applies, in the first approximation, to the distribution of income and wealth and to the design of organizations that makes use of differences in authority and responsibility, or chains of command. While the distribution of wealth and income need not be equal, it must be to everyone's advantage, and at the same time, positions of authority and offices of command must be accessible to all. One applies the second principle by holding positions open, and then, subject to this constraint, arranges social and economic inequalities so that everyone benefits.

These principles are to be arranged in a serial order with the first principle prior to the second. This ordering means that a departure from the institutions of equal liberty required by the first principle cannot be justified by, or compensated for, by greater social and economic advantages. The distribution of wealth and income, and the hierarchies of authority, must be consistent with both the liberties of equal citizenship and equality of opportunity.

QUESTIONS

1. What does Rawls mean by the "initial situation"? Why does he posit an initial situation?

2. What are Rawls's two principles of justice? How do they guarantee justice? How does Rawls's more general conception of justice emerge from them?

Robert Nozick | # Anarchy, State, and Utopia

Robert Nozick was for years a philosopher at Harvard University with John Rawls.

The minimal state is the most extensive state that can be justified. Any state more extensive violates people's rights. Yet many persons have put forth reasons purporting to justify a more extensive state. It is impossible within the compass of this book to examine all the reasons that have been put forth. Therefore, I shall focus upon those generally acknowledged to be most weighty and influential, to see precisely wherein they fail. In this essay we consider the claim that a more extensive state is justified, because necessary (or the best instrument) to achieve distributive justice.

The term "distributive justice" is not a neutral one. Hearing the term "distribution," most people presume that some thing or mechanism uses some principle or criterion to give out a supply of things. Into this process of distributing shares some error may have crept. So it is an open question, at least, whether *re*distribution should take place; whether we should do again what has already been done once, though poorly. However, we are not in the position of children who have been given portions of pie by someone who now makes last minute adjustments to rectify careless cutting. There is no *central* distribution, no person or group entitled to control all the resources, jointly deciding how they are to be doled out. What each person gets, he gets from others who give to him in exchange for something, or as a gift. In a free society, diverse persons control different resources, and new holdings arise out of the voluntary exchanges and actions of persons. There is no more a distributing or distribution of shares than there is a distributing of mates in a society in which persons choose whom they shall marry. The total result is the product of many individual decisions which the different individuals involved are entitled to make. Some

uses of the term "distribution," it is true, do not imply a previous distributing appropriately judged by some criterion (for example, "probability distribution"); nevertheless, despite the title of this chapter, it would be best to use a terminology that clearly is neutral. We shall speak of people's holdings; a principle of justice in holdings describes (part of) what justice tells us (requires) about holdings. I shall state first what I take to be the correct view about justice in holdings, and then turn to the discussion of alternate views.

THE ENTITLEMENT THEORY

The subject of justice in holdings consists of three major topics. The first is the *original acquisition of holdings*, the appropriation of unheld things. This includes the issues of how unheld things may come to be held, the process, or processes, by which unheld things may come to be held, the things that may come to be held by these processes, the extent of what comes to be held by a particular process, and so on. We shall refer to the complicated truth about this topic, which we shall not formulate here, as the principle of justice in acquisition. The second topic concerns the *transfer of holdings* from one person to another. By what processes may a person transfer holdings to another? How may a person acquire a holding from another who holds it? Under this topic come general descriptions of voluntary exchange, and gift and (on the other hand) fraud, as well as reference to particular conventional details fixed upon in a given society. The complicated truth about this subject (with placeholders for conventional details) we shall call the principle of justice in transfer. (And we shall suppose it also includes principles governing how a person may divest himself of a holding, passing it into an unheld state.)

If the world were wholly just, the following inductive definition would exhaustively cover the subject of justice in holdings.

1. A person who acquires a holding in accordance with the principle of justice in acquisition is entitled to that holding.
2. A person who acquires a holding in accordance with the principle of justice in transfer, from someone else entitled to the holding, is entitled to the holding.
3. No one is entitled to a holding except by (repeated) applications of 1 and 2.

The complete principle of distributive justice would say simply that a distribution is just if everyone is entitled to the holdings they possess under the distribution.

A distribution is just if it arises from another just distribution by legitimate means. The legitimate means of moving from one distribution to another are specified by the principle of justice in transfer. The legitimate first "moves" are specified by the principle of justice in acquisition. Whatever arises from a just situation by just steps is itself just. The means of change specified by the principle of justice in transfer preserve justice. As correct rules of inference are truth-preserving, and any conclusion deduced via repeated application of such rules from only true premises is itself true, so the means of transition from one situation to another specified by the principle of justice in transfer are justice-preserving, and any situation actually arising from repeated transitions in accordance with the principle from a just situation is itself just. The parallel between justice-preserving transformations and truth-preserving transformations illuminates where it fails as well as where it holds. That a conclusion could have been deduced by truth-preserving means from premises that are true suffices to show its truth. That from a just situation a situation *could* have arisen via justice-preserving means does *not* suffice to show its justice. The fact that a thief s victims voluntarily *could* have presented him with gifts does not entitle the thief to his ill-gotten gains. Justice in holdings is historical; it depends upon what actually has happened. We shall return to this point later.

Not all actual situations are generated in accordance with the two principles of justice in holdings: the principle of justice in acquisition and the principle of justice in transfer. Some people steal from others, or defraud them, or enslave them, seizing their product and preventing them from living as they choose, or forcibly exclude others from competing in exchanges. None of these are permissible modes of transition from one situation to another. And some persons acquire holdings by means not sanctioned by the principle of justice in acquisition. The existence of past injustice (previous violations of the first two principles of justice in holdings) raises the third major topic under justice in holdings: the rectification of injustice in holdings. If past injustice has shaped present holdings in various ways, some identifiable and some not, what now, if anything, ought to be done to rectify these injustices? What obligations do the performers of injustice have toward those whose position is worse than it would have been had the injustice not been done? Or, than it would have been had compensation been paid promptly? How, if at all, do things change if the beneficiaries and those made worse off are not the direct parties in the act of injustice, but, for example, their descendants? Is an injustice done to someone whose holding was itself based upon an unrectified injustice? How far back must one go in wiping clean the historical slate of injustices? What may victims of injustice permissibly do in order to rectify the injustices being done to them, including the many injustices done by persons acting through their government? I do not know of a thorough or theoretically sophisticated treatment of such issues. Idealizing greatly, let us suppose theoretical investigation will produce a principle of rectification. This principle uses historical information about previous situations and injustices done in them (as defined by the first two principles of justice and rights against interference), and information about the actual course of events that flowed from these injustices, until the present, and it yields a description (or descriptions) of holdings in the society. The principle of rectification presumably will make use of its best estimate of subjunctive information about what would have occurred (or a probability distribution over what might have occurred, using the expected value) if the injustice had not taken place. If the actual description of holdings turns out not to be one of the descriptions yielded by the principle, then one of the descriptions yielded must be realized.

The general outlines of the theory of justice in holdings are that the holdings of a person are just if he is entitled to them by the principles of justice in acquisition and transfer, or by the principle of rectification of injustice (as specified by the first two principles). If each person's holdings are just, then the total set (distribution) of holdings is just. To turn these general outlines into a specific theory we would have to specify the details of each of the three principles of justice in holdings: the principle of acquisition of holdings, the principle of transfer of holdings, and the principle of rectification of violations of the first two principles. I shall not attempt that task here. (Locke's principle of justice in acquisition is discussed later.)

HISTORICAL PRINCIPLES AND THE END-RESULT PRINCIPLE

The general outlines of the entitlement theory illuminate the nature and defects of other conceptions of distributive justice. The entitlement theory of justice in distribution is *historical*; whether a distribution is just depends upon how it came about. In contrast, *current time-slice principles* of justice hold that the justice of a distribution is determined by how things are distributed (who has what) as judged by some *structural* principle(s) of just distribution. A utilitarian who judges between any two distributions by seeing which has the greater sum of utility and, if the sums tie, applies some fixed equality criterion to choose the more equal distribution, would hold a current time-slice principle of justice. As would someone who had a fixed schedule of trade-offs between the sum of happiness and equality. According to a current time-slice principle, all that needs to be looked at, in judging the justice of a distribution, is who ends up with what; in comparing any two distributions one need look only at the matrix presenting the distributions. No further information need be fed into a principle of

justice. It is a consequence of such principles of justice that any two structurally identical distributions are equally just. (Two distributions are structurally identical if they present the same profile, but perhaps have different persons occupying the particular slots. My having ten and your having five, and my having five and your having ten, are structurally identical distributions.) Welfare economics is the theory of current time-slice principles of justice. The subject is conceived as operating on matrices representing only current information about distribution. This, as well as some of the usual conditions (for example, the choice of distribution is invariant under relabeling of columns), guarantees that welfare economics will be a current time-slice theory, with all of its inadequacies.

Most persons do not accept current time-slice principles as constituting the whole story about distributive shares. They think it relevant in assessing the justice of a situation to consider not only the distribution it embodies, but also how that distribution came about. If some persons are in prison for murder or war crimes, we do not say that to assess the justice of the distribution in the society we must look only at what this person has, and that person has, and that person has, . . . at the current time. We think it relevant to ask whether someone did something so that he *deserved* to be punished, deserved to have a lower share. Most will agree to the relevance of further information with regard to punishments and penalties. Consider also desired things. One traditional socialist view is that workers are entitled to the product and full fruits of their labor; they have earned it; a distribution is unjust if it does not give the workers what they are entitled to. Such entitlements are based upon some past history. No socialist holding this view would find it comforting to be told that because the actual distribution *A* happens to coincide structurally with the one he desires *D*, *A* therefore is no less just than *D*; it differs only in that the "parasitic" owners of capital receive under *A* what the workers are entitled to under *D*, and the workers receive under *A* what the owners are entitled to under *D*, namely very little. This socialist rightly, in my view, holds onto the notions of earning, producing, entitlement, desert, and so forth, and he rejects current time-slice principles that look only to the structure of the resulting set of holdings. (The set of holdings resulting from what? Isn't it implausible that how holdings are produced and come to exist has no effect at all on who should hold what?) His mistake lies in his view of what entitlements arise out of what sorts of productive processes.

We construe the position we discuss too narrowly by speaking of *current* time-slice principles. Nothing is changed if structural principles operate upon a time sequence of current time-slice profiles and, for example, give someone more now to counterbalance the less he has had earlier. A utilitarian or an egalitarian or any mixture of the two over time will inherit the difficulties of his more myopic comrades. He is not helped by the fact that *some* of the information others consider relevant in assessing a distribution is reflected, unrecoverably, in past matrices. Henceforth, we shall refer to such unhistorical principles of distributive justice, including the current time-slice principles, as *end-result principles* or *end-state principles*.

In contrast to end-result principles of justice, *historical principles* of justice hold that past circumstances or actions of people can create differential entitlements or differential deserts to things. An injustice can be worked by moving from one distribution to another structurally identical one, for the second, in profile the same, may violate people's entitlements or deserts; it may not fit the actual history.

PATTERNING

The entitlement principles of justice in holdings that we have sketched are historical principles of justice. To better understand their precise character, we shall distinguish them from another subclass of the historical principles. Consider, as an example, the principle of distribution according to moral merit. This principle requires that total distributive shares vary directly with moral merit; no person should have a greater share than anyone whose moral merit is greater. (If moral merit could be not merely ordered but measured on an interval or ratio scale, stronger principles could be formulated.) Or consider the principle that results by substituting "usefulness to

society" for "moral merit" in the previous principle. Or instead of "distribute according to moral merit," or "distribute according to usefulness to society," we might consider "distribute according to the weighted sum of moral merit, usefulness to society, and need," with the weights of the different dimensions equal. Let us call a principle of distribution *patterned* if it specifies that a distribution is to vary along with some natural dimension, weighted sum of natural dimensions, or lexicographic ordering of natural dimensions. And let us say a distribution is patterned if it accords with some patterned principle. (I speak of natural dimensions, admittedly without a general criterion for them, because for any set of holdings some artificial dimensions can be gimmicked up to vary along with the distribution of the set.) The principle of distribution in accordance with moral merit is a patterned historical principle, which specifies a patterned distribution. "Distribute according to I.Q." is a patterned principle that looks to information not contained in distributional matrices. It is not historical, however, in that it does not look to any past actions creating differential entitlements to evaluate a distribution; it requires only distributional matrices whose columns are labeled by I.Q. scores. The distribution in a society, however, may be composed of such simple patterned distributions, without itself being simply patterned. Different sectors may operate different patterns, or some combination of patterns may operate in different proportions across a society. A distribution composed in this manner, from a small number of patterned distributions, we also shall term "patterned." And we extend the use of "pattern" to include the overall designs put forth by combinations of end-state principles.

Almost every suggested principle of distributive justice is patterned: to each according to his moral merit, or needs, or marginal product, or how hard he tries, or the weighted sum of the foregoing, and so on. The principle of entitlement we have sketched is not patterned. There is no one natural dimension or weighted sum or combination of a small number of natural dimensions that yields the distributions generated in accordance with the principle of entitlement. The set of holdings that results when some persons receive their marginal products, others win at gambling, others receive a share of their mate's income, others receive gifts from foundations, others receive interest on loans, others receive gifts from admirers, others receive returns on investment, others make for themselves much of what they have, others find things, and so on, will not be patterned. Heavy strands of patterns will run through it; significant portions of the variance in holdings will be accounted for by pattern-variables. If most people most of the time choose to transfer some of their entitlements to others only in exchange for something from them, then a large part of what many people hold will vary with what they held that others wanted. More details are provided by the theory of marginal productivity. But gifts to relatives, charitable donations, bequests to children, and the like, are not best conceived, in the first instance, in this manner. Ignoring the strands of pattern, let us suppose for the moment that a distribution actually arrived at by the operation of the principle of entitlement is random with respect to any pattern. Though the resulting set of holdings will be unpatterned, it will not be incomprehensible, for it can be seen as arising from the operation of a small number of principles. These principles specify how an initial distribution may arise (the principle of acquisition of holdings) and how distributions may be transformed into others (the principle of transfer of holdings). The process whereby the set of holdings is generated will be intelligible, though the set of holdings itself that results from this process will be unpatterned.

The writings of F. A. Hayek focus less than is usually done upon what patterning distributive justice requires. Hayek argues that we cannot know enough about each person's situation to distribute to each according to his moral merit (but would justice demand we do so if we did have this knowledge?); and he goes on to say, "our objection is against all attempts to impress upon society a deliberately chosen pattern of distribution, whether it be an order of equality or of inequality." However, Hayek concludes that in a free society there will be distribution in accordance with value rather than moral merit; that is, in accordance with the perceived value of a person's actions and services to others. Despite his rejection of a patterned conception of distributive justice, Hayek himself suggests a pattern he thinks justifiable: distribution in accordance with the perceived benefits given to others, leaving room for the complaint that a free society does not realize exactly this pattern. Stating this patterned strand of a free capitalist society more precisely, we get "To each according to how much he benefits others who have the resources for benefiting those who benefit them." This will seem arbitrary unless some acceptable initial set of holdings is specified, or unless it is held that the operation of the system over time washes out any significant effects from the initial set of holdings. As an example of the latter, if almost anyone would have bought a car from Henry Ford, the supposition that it was an arbitrary matter who held the money then (and so bought) would not place Henry Ford's earnings under a cloud. In any event, *his* coming to hold it is not arbitrary. Distribution according to benefits to others *is* a major patterned strand in a free capitalist society, as Hayek correctly points out, but it is only a strand and does not constitute the whole pattern of a system of entitlements (namely, inheritance, gifts for arbitrary reasons, charity, and so on) or a standard that one should insist a society fit. Will people tolerate for long a system yielding distributions that they believe are unpatterned? No doubt people will not long accept a distribution they believe is *unjust*. People want their society to be and to look just. But must the look of justice reside in a resulting pattern rather than in the underlying generating principles? We are in no position to conclude that the inhabitants of a society embodying an entitlement conception of justice in holdings will find it unacceptable. Still, it must be granted that were people's reasons for transferring some of their holdings to others always irrational or arbitrary, we would find this disturbing. (Suppose people always determined what holdings they would transfer, and to whom, by using a random device.) We feel more comfortable upholding the justice of an entitlement system if most of the transfers under it are done for reasons. This does not mean necessarily that all deserve what holdings they receive. It means only that there is a purpose or point to someone's transferring a holding to one person rather than to another; that usually we can see what the transferrer thinks he's gaining, what cause he thinks he's serving, what goals he thinks he's helping to achieve, and so forth. Since in a capitalist society people often transfer holdings to others in accordance with how much they perceive these others benefiting them, the fabric constituted by the individual transactions and transfers is largely reasonable and intelligible. (Gifts to loved ones, bequests to children, charity to the needy also are nonarbitrary components of the fabric.) In stressing the large strand of distribution in accordance with benefit to others, Hayek shows the point of many transfers, and so shows that the system of transfer of entitlements is not just spinning its gears aimlessly. The system of entitlements is defensible when constituted by the individual aims of individual transactions. No overarching aim is needed, no distributional pattern is required.

To think that the task of a theory of distributive justice is to fill in the blank in "to each according to his _____" is to be predisposed to search for a pattern; and the separate treatment of "from each according to his _____" treats production and distribution as two separate and independent issues. On an entitlement view these are *not* two separate questions. Whoever makes something, having bought or contracted for all other held resources used in the process (transferring some of his holdings for these cooperating factors), is entitled to it. The situation is *not* one of something's getting made, and there being an open question of who is to get it. Things come into the world already attached to people having entitlements over them. From the point of view of the historical entitlement conception of justice in holdings, those who start afresh to complete "to each according to his _____" treat objects as if they appeared from nowhere, out of nothing. A complete theory of justice might cover this limit case as well; perhaps here is a use for the usual conceptions of distributive justice.

So entrenched are maxims of the usual form that perhaps we should present the entitlement conception as a competitor. Ignoring acquisition and rectification, we might say:

> From each according to what he chooses to do, to each according to what he makes for himself (perhaps with the contracted aid of others) and what

others choose to do for him and choose to give him of what they've been given previously (under this maxim) and haven't yet expended or transferred.

This, the discerning reader will have noticed, has its defects as a slogan. So as a summary and great simplification (and not as a maxim with any independent meaning) we have:

> From each as they choose, to each as they are chosen.

HOW LIBERTY UPSETS PATTERNS

It is not clear how those holding alternative conceptions of distributive justice can reject the entitlement conception of justice in holdings. For suppose a distribution favored by one of these non-entitlement conceptions is realized. Let us suppose it is your favorite one and let us call this distribution D_1; perhaps everyone has an equal share, perhaps shares vary in accordance with some dimension you treasure. Now suppose that Wilt Chamberlain is greatly in demand by basketball teams, being a great gate attraction. (Also suppose contracts run only for a year, with players being free agents.) He signs the following sort of contract with a team: In each home game, twenty-five cents from the price of each ticket of admission goes to him. (We ignore the question of whether he is "gouging" the owners, letting them look out for themselves.) The season starts, and people cheerfully attend his team's games; they buy their tickets, each time dropping a separate twenty-five cents of their admission price into a special box with Chamberlain's name on it. They are excited about seeing him play; it is worth the total admission price to them. Let us suppose that in one season one million persons attend his home games, and Wilt Chamberlain winds up with $250,000, a much larger sum than the average income and larger even than anyone else has. Is he entitled to this income? Is this new distribution D_2, unjust? If so, why? There is *no* question about whether each of the people was entitled to the control over the resources they held in D_1; because that was the distribution (your favorite) that (for the purposes of argument) we assumed was acceptable. Each of these persons *chose* to give twenty-five cents of their money to Chamberlain. They could have spent it on going to the movies, or on candy bars, or on copies of *Dissent* magazine, or of *Monthly Review*. But they all, at least one million of them, converged on giving it to Wilt Chamberlain in exchange for watching him play basketball. If D_1 was a just distribution, and people voluntarily moved from it to D_2, transferring parts of their shares they were given under D_1 (what was it for if not to do something with?), isn't D_2 also just? If the people were entitled to dispose of the resources to which they were entitled (under D_1), didn't this include their being entitled to give it to, or exchange it with, Wilt Chamberlain? Can anyone else complain on grounds of justice? Each other person already has his legitimate share under D_1. Under D_1, there is nothing that anyone has that anyone else has a claim of justice against. After someone transfers something to Wilt Chamberlain, third parties *still* have their legitimate shares; *their* shares are not changed. By what process could such a transfer among two persons give rise to a legitimate claim of distributive justice on a portion of what was transferred, by a third party who had no claim of justice on any holding of the others *before* the transfer? To cut off objections irrelevant here, we might imagine the exchanges occurring in a socialist society, after hours. After playing whatever basketball he does in his daily work, or doing whatever other daily work he does, Wilt Chamberlain decides to put in *overtime* to earn additional money. (First his work quota is set; he works time over that.) Or imagine it is a skilled juggler people like to see, who puts on shows after hours.

Why might someone work overtime in a society in which it is assumed their needs are satisfied? Perhaps because they care about things other than needs. I like to write in books that I read, and to have easy access to books for browsing at odd hours. It would be very pleasant and convenient to have the resources of Widener Library in my back yard. No society, I assume, will provide such resources close to each person who would like them as part of his regular allotment (under D_1). Thus, persons either must do without some extra things that they want, or be allowed to do something extra to get some of these things. On what basis could the inequalities

that would eventuate be forbidden? Notice also that small factories would spring up in a socialist society, unless forbidden. I melt down some of my personal possessions (under D_1) and build a machine out of the material. I offer you, and others, a philosophy lecture once a week in exchange for your cranking the handle on my machine, whose products I exchange for yet other things, and so on. (The raw materials used by the machine are given to me by others who possess them under D_1, in exchange for hearing lectures.) Each person might participate to gain things over and above their allotment under D_1. Some persons even might want to leave their job in socialist industry and work full time in this private sector. I shall say something more about these issues in the next chapter. Here I wish merely to note how private property even in means of production would occur in a socialist society that did not forbid people to use as they wished some of the resources they are given under the socialist distribution D_1. The socialist society would have to forbid capitalist acts between consenting adults.

The general point illustrated by the Wilt Chamberlain example and the example of the entrepreneur in a socialist society is that no end-state principle or distributional patterned principle of justice can be continuously realized without continuous interference with people's lives. Any favored pattern would be transformed into one unfavored by the principle, by people choosing to act in various ways; for example, by people exchanging goods and services with other people, or giving things to other people, things the transferrers are entitled to under the favored distributional pattern. To maintain a pattern one must either continually interfere to stop people from transferring resources as they wish to, or continually (or periodically) interfere to take from some persons resources that others for some reason chose to transfer to them. (But if some time limit is to be set on how long people may keep resources others voluntarily transfer to them, why let them keep these resources for *any* period of time? Why not have immediate confiscation?) It might be objected that all persons voluntarily will choose to refrain from actions which would upset the pattern. This presupposes unrealistically

(1) that all will most want to maintain the pattern (Are those who don't to be "reeducated" or forced to undergo "self-criticism"?), (2) that each can gather enough information about his own actions and the ongoing activities of others to discover which of his actions will upset the pattern, and (3) that diverse and far-flung persons can coordinate their actions to dovetail into the pattern. Compare the manner in which the market is neutral among persons' desires, as it reflects and transmits widely scattered information via prices, and coordinates persons' activities.

It puts things perhaps a bit too strongly to say that every patterned (or end-state) principle is liable to be thwarted by the voluntary actions of the individual parties transferring some of their shares they receive under the principle. For perhaps some *very* weak patterns are not so thwarted. Any distributional pattern with any egalitarian component is overturnable by the voluntary actions of individual persons over time; as is every patterned condition with sufficient content so as actually to have been proposed as presenting the central core of distributive justice. Still, given the possibility that some weak conditions or patterns may not be unstable in this way, it would be better to formulate an explicit description of the kind of interesting and contentful patterns under discussion, and to prove a theorem about their instability. Since the weaker the patterning, the more likely it is that the entitlement system itself satisfies it, a plausible conjecture is that any patterning either is unstable or is satisfied by the entitlement system. . . .

LOCKE'S THEORY OF ACQUISITION

Before we turn to consider other theories of justice in detail, we must introduce an additional bit of complexity into the structure of the entitlement theory: This is best approached by considering Locke's attempt to specify a principle of justice in acquisition. Locke views property rights in an unowned object as originating through someone's mixing his labor with it. This gives rise to many questions. What are the boundaries of what labor is mixed with? If a private astronaut clears a place on Mars, has he mixed his labor with (so that he comes to own) the whole planet, the whole uninhabited universe, or just a particular plot? Which plot does an act bring under ownership? The minimal (possibly disconnected) area such that an act decreases entropy in that area, and not elsewhere? Can virgin land (for the purposes of ecological investigation by high-flying airplane) come under ownership by a Lockean process? Building a fence around a territory presumably would make one the owner of only the fence (and the land immediately underneath it).

Why does mixing one's labor with something make one the owner of it? Perhaps because one owns one's labor, and so one comes to own a previously unowned thing that becomes permeated with what one owns. Ownership seeps over into the rest. But why isn't mixing what I own with what I don't own a way of losing what I own rather than a way of gaining what I don't? If I own a can of tomato juice and spill it in the sea so that its molecules (made radioactive, so I can check this) mingle evenly throughout the sea, do I thereby come to own the sea, or have I foolishly dissipated my tomato juice? Perhaps the idea, instead, is that laboring on something improves it and makes it more valuable; and anyone is entitled to own a thing whose value he has created. (Reinforcing this, perhaps, is the view that laboring is unpleasant. If some people made things effortlessly, as the cartoon characters in *The Yellow Submarine* trail flowers in their wake, would they have lesser claim to their own products whose making didn't *cost* them anything?) Ignore the fact that laboring on something may make it less valuable (spraying pink enamel paint on a piece of driftwood that you have found). Why should one's entitlement extend to the whole object rather than just to the *added value* one's labor has produced? (Such reference to value might also serve to delimit the extent of ownership; for example, substitute "increases the value of" for "decreases entropy in" in the above entropy criterion.) No workable or coherent value-added property scheme has yet been devised, and any such scheme presumably would fall to objections (similar to those) that fell the theory of Henry George.

It will be implausible to view improving an object as giving full ownership to it, if the stock of unowned objects that might be improved is limited.

For an object's coming under one person's ownership changes the situation of all others. Whereas previously they were at liberty (in Hohfeld's sense) to use the object, they now no longer are. This change in the situation of others (by removing their liberty to act on a previously unowned object) need not worsen their situation. If I appropriate a grain of sand from Coney Island, no one else may now do as they will with *that* grain of sand. But there are plenty of other grains of sand left for them to do the same with. Or if not grains of sand, then other things. Alternatively, the things I do with the grain of sand I appropriate might improve the position of others, counterbalancing their loss of the liberty to use that grain. The crucial point is whether appropriation of an unowned object worsens the situation of others.

Locke's proviso that there be "enough and as good left in common for others" (sect. 27) is meant to ensure that the situation of others is not worsened. (If this proviso is met is there any motivation for his further condition of nonwaste?) It is often said that this proviso once held but now no longer does. But there appears to be an argument for the conclusion that if the proviso no longer holds, then it cannot ever have held so as to yield permanent and inheritable property rights. Consider the first person Z for whom there is not enough and as good left to appropriate. The last person Y to appropriate left Z without his previous liberty to act on an object, and so worsened Z's situation. So Y's appropriation is not allowed under Locke's proviso. Therefore the next to last person X to appropriate left Y in a worse position, for X's act ended permissible appropriation. Therefore X's appropriation wasn't permissible. But then the appropriator two from last, W, ended permissible appropriation and so, since it worsened X's position, W's appropriation wasn't permissible. And so on back to the first person A to appropriate a permanent property right.

This argument, however, proceeds too quickly. Someone may be made worse off by another's appropriation in two ways: first, by losing the opportunity to improve his situation by a particular appropriation or any one; and second, by no longer being able to use freely (without appropriation) what he previously could. A *stringent* requirement that another not be made worse off by an appropriation would exclude

the first way if nothing else counterbalances the diminution in opportunity, as well as the second. A *weaker* requirement would exclude the second way, though not the first. With the weaker requirement, we cannot zip back so quickly from Z to A, as in the above argument; for though person Z can no longer *appropriate*, there may remain some for him to *use* as before. In this case Y's appropriation would not violate the weaker Lockean condition. (With less remaining that people are at liberty to use, users might face more inconvenience, crowding, and so on; in that way the situation of others might be worsened, unless appropriation stopped far short of such a point.) It is arguable that no one legitimately can complain if the weaker provision is satisfied. However, since this is less clear than in the case of the more stringent proviso, Locke may have intended this stringent proviso by "enough and as good" remaining, and perhaps he meant the nonwaste condition to delay the end point from which the argument zips back.

Is the situation of persons who are unable to appropriate (there being no more accessible and useful unowned objects) worsened by a system allowing appropriation and permanent property? Here enter the various familiar social considerations favoring private property: it increases the social product by putting means of production in the hands of those who can use them most efficiently (profitably); experimentation is encouraged, because with separate persons controlling resources, there is no one person or small group whom someone with a new idea must convince to try it out; private property enables people to decide on the pattern and types of risks they wish to bear, leading to specialized types of risk bearing; private property protects future persons by leading some to hold back resources from current consumption for future markets; it provides alternate sources of employment for unpopular persons who don't have to convince any one person or small group to hire them, and so on. These considerations enter a Lockean theory to support the claim that appropriation of private property satisfies the intent behind the "enough and as good left over" proviso, *not as* a utilitarian justification of property. They enter to rebut the claim that because the proviso is violated no natural right to private property can arise by a Lockean process. The difficulty in working such an argument to show that the proviso is satisfied is in fixing the appropriate base line for comparison. Lockean appropriation makes people no worse off than they would be *how*? This question of fixing the baseline needs more detailed investigation than we are able to give it here. It would be desirable to have an estimate of the general economic importance of original appropriation in order to see how much leeway there is for differing theories of appropriation and of the location of the baseline. Perhaps this importance can be measured by the percentage of all income that is based upon untransformed raw materials and given resources (rather than upon human actions), mainly rental income representing the unimproved value of land, and the price of raw material *in situ*, and by the percentage of current wealth which represents such income in the past.

We should note that it is not only persons favoring *private* property who need a theory of how property rights legitimately originate. Those believing in collective property, for example those believing that a group of persons living in an area jointly own the territory, or its mineral resources, also must provide a theory of how such property rights arise; they must show why the persons living there have rights to determine what is done with the land and resources there that persons living elsewhere don't have (with regard to the same land and resources).

THE PROVISO

Whether or not Locke's particular theory of appropriation can be spelled out so as to handle various difficulties, I assume that any adequate theory of justice in acquisition will contain a proviso similar to the weaker of the ones we have attributed to Locke. A process normally giving rise to a permanent bequeathable property right in a previously unowned thing will not do so if the position of others no longer at liberty to use the thing is thereby worsened. It is important to specify *this* particular mode of worsening the situation of others, for the proviso does not encompass other modes. It does not include the worsening due to more limited

opportunities to appropriate (the first way above, corresponding to the more stringent condition), and it does not include how I "worsen" a seller's position if I appropriate materials to make some of what he is selling, and then enter into competition with him. Someone whose appropriation otherwise would violate the proviso still may appropriate provided he compensates the others so that their situation is not thereby worsened; unless he does compensate these others, his appropriation will violate the proviso of the principle of justice in acquisition and will be an illegitimate one. A theory of appropriation incorporating this Lockean proviso will handle correctly the cases (objections to the theory lacking the proviso) where someone appropriates the total supply of something necessary for life.

A theory which includes this proviso in its principle of justice in acquisition must also contain a more complex principle of justice in transfer. Some reflection of the proviso about appropriation constrains later actions. If my appropriating all of a certain substance violates the Lockean proviso, then so does my appropriating some and purchasing all the rest from others who obtained it without otherwise violating the Lockean proviso. If the proviso excludes someone's appropriating all the drinkable water in the world, it also excludes his purchasing it all. (More weakly, and messily, it may exclude his charging certain prices for some of his supply.) This proviso (almost?) never will come into effect; the more someone acquires of a scarce substance which others want, the higher the price of the rest will go, and the more difficult it will become for him to acquire it all. But still, we can imagine, at least, that something like this occurs: someone makes simultaneous secret bids to the separate owners of a substance, each of whom sells assuming he can easily purchase more from the other owners; or some natural catastrophe destroys all of the supply of something except that in one person's possession. The total supply could not be permissibly appropriated by one person at the beginning. His later acquisition of it all does not show that the original appropriation violated the proviso (even by a reverse argument similar to the one above that tried to zip back from Z to A). Rather, it is the combination of the original appropriation *plus* all the later transfers and actions that violates the Lockean proviso.

Each owner's title to his holding includes the historical shadow of the Lockean proviso on appropriation. This excludes his transferring it into an agglomeration that does violate the Lockean proviso and excludes his using it in a way, in coordination with others or independently of them, so as to violate the proviso by making the situation of others worse than their baseline situation. Once it is known that someone's ownership runs afoul of the Lockean proviso, there are stringent limits on what he may do with (what it is difficult any longer unreservedly to call) "his property." Thus a person may not appropriate the only water hole in a desert and charge what he will. Nor may he charge what he will if he possesses one, and unfortunately it happens that all the water holes in the desert dry up, except for his. This unfortunate circumstance, admittedly no fault of his, brings into operation the Lockean proviso and limits his property rights. Similarly, an owner's property right in the only island in an area does not allow him to order a castaway from a shipwreck off his island as a trespasser, for this would violate the Lockean proviso.

Notice that the theory does not say that owners do have these rights, but that the rights are overridden to avoid some catastrophe. (Overridden rights do not disappear; they leave a trace of a sort absent in the cases under discussion.) There is no such external (and *ad hoc*?) overriding. Considerations internal to the theory of property itself, to its theory of acquisition and appropriation, provide the means for handling such cases. The results, however, may be coextensive with some condition about catastrophe, since the baseline for comparison is so low as compared to the productiveness of a society with private appropriation that the question of the Lockean proviso being violated arises only in the case of catastrophe (or a desert-island situation).

The fact that someone owns the total supply of something necessary for others to stay alive does *not* entail that his (or anyone's) appropriation of anything left some people (immediately or later) in a situation worse than the baseline one. A medical researcher who synthesizes a new substance that effectively treats a certain disease and who refuses to sell except on his terms does not worsen the situation of others by depriving them of whatever he has appropriated. The others easily can possess the same materials he appropriated; the researcher's appropriation or purchase of chemicals didn't make those chemicals scarce in a way so as to violate the Lockean proviso. Nor would someone else's purchasing the total supply of the synthesized substance from the medical researcher. The fact that the medical researcher uses easily available chemicals to synthesize the drug no more violates the Lockean proviso than does the fact that the only surgeon able to perform a particular operation eats easily obtainable food in order to stay alive and to have the energy to work. This shows that the Lockean proviso is not an "end-state principle"; it focuses on a particular way that appropriative actions affect others, and not on the structure of the situation that results.

Intermediate between someone who takes all of the public supply and someone who makes the total supply out of easily obtainable substances is someone who appropriates the total supply of something in a way that does not deprive the others of it. For example, someone finds a new substance in an out-of-the-way place. He discovers that it effectively treats a certain disease and appropriates the total supply. He does not worsen the situation of others; if he did not stumble upon the substance no one else would have, and the others would remain without it. However, as time passes, the likelihood increases that others would have come across the substance; upon this fact might be based a limit to his property right in the substance so that others are not below their baseline position; for example, its bequest might be limited. The theme of someone worsening another's situation by depriving him of something he otherwise would possess may also illuminate the example of patents. An inventor's patent does not deprive others of an object which would not exist if not for the inventor. Yet patents would have this effect on others who independently invent the object. Therefore, these independent inventors, upon whom the burden of proving independent discovery may rest, should not be excluded from utilizing their own invention as they wish (including selling it to others). Furthermore, a known inventor drastically lessens the chances of actual independent invention. For persons who know of an invention usually will not try to reinvent it, and the notion of independent discovery here would be murky at best. Yet we may assume that in the absence of the original invention, sometime later someone else would have come up with it. This suggests placing a time limit on patents, as a rough rule of thumb to approximate how long it would have taken, in the absence of knowledge of the invention, for independent discovery.

I believe that the free operation of a market system will not actually run afoul of the Lockean proviso. If this is correct, the proviso will not play a very important role in the activities of protective agencies and will not provide a significant opportunity for future

state action. Indeed, were it not for the effects of previous *illegitimate* state action, people would not think the possibility of the proviso's being violated as of more interest than any other logical possibility. (Here I make an empirical historical claim; as does someone who disagrees with this.) This completes our indication of the complication in the entitlement theory introduced by the Lockean proviso.

QUESTIONS

1. How do you think Rawls would have replied to Nozick?

2. Can you think of an objection to the Wilt Chamberlain example? (Wilt Chamberlain was a hugely famous basketball player, the Michael Jordan of his day.)

Peter Singer | # Rich and Poor

Peter Singer is an Australian philosopher who teaches at Princeton University's Institute for Values and is most famous for his defense of "animal liberation."

SOME FACTS ABOUT POVERTY

. . . Consider these facts: by the most cautious estimates, 400 million people lack the calories, protein, vitamins and minerals needed to sustain their bodies and minds in a healthy state. Millions are constantly hungry; others suffer from deficiency diseases and from infections they would be able to resist on a better diet. Children are the worst affected. According to one study, 14 million children under five die every year from the combined effects of malnutrition and infection. In some

districts half the children born can be expected to die before their fifth birthday.

Nor is lack of food the only hardship of the poor. To give a broader picture, Robert McNamara, when president of the World Bank, suggested the term "absolute poverty." The poverty we are familiar with in industrialised nations is relative poverty—meaning that some citizens are poor, relative to the wealth enjoyed by their neighbours. People living in relative poverty in Australia might be quite comfortably off by comparison with pensioners in Britain, and British pensioners are not poor in comparison with the poverty that exists in Mali or Ethiopia. Absolute poverty, on the other hand, is poverty by any standard. In McNamara's words:

> Poverty at the absolute level . . . is life at the very margin of existence. The absolute poor are severely

deprived human beings struggling to survive in a set of squalid and degraded circumstances almost beyond the power of our sophisticated imaginations and privileged circumstances to conceive.

Compared to those fortunate enough to live in developed countries, individuals in the poorest nations have:

- An infant mortality rate eight times higher
- A life expectancy one-third lower
- An adult literacy rate 60 percent less
- A nutritional level, for one out of every two in the population, below acceptable standards;
- And for millions of infants, less protein than is sufficient to permit optimum development of the brain.

McNamara has summed up absolute poverty as "a condition of life so characterised by malnutrition, illiteracy, disease, squalid surroundings, high infant mortality and low life expectancy as to be beneath any reasonable definition of human decency." . . .

Death and disease apart, absolute poverty remains a miserable condition of life, with inadequate food, shelter, clothing, sanitation, health services and education. The Worldwatch Institute estimates that as many as 1.2 billion people—or 23 percent of the world's population—live in absolute poverty. For the purposes of this estimate, absolute poverty is defined as "the lack of sufficient income in cash or kind to meet the most basic biological needs for food, clothing, and shelter." Absolute poverty is probably the principal cause of human misery today. . . .

The problem is not that the world cannot produce enough to feed and shelter its people. People in the poor countries consume, on average, 180 kilos of grain a year, while North Americans average around 900 kilos. The difference is caused by the fact that in the rich countries we feed most of our grain to animals, converting it into meat, milk, and eggs. Because this is a highly inefficient process, people in rich countries are responsible for the consumption of far more food than those in poor countries who eat few animal products. If we stopped feeding animals on grains and soybeans, the amount of food saved would—if distributed to those who need it—be more than enough to end hunger throughout the world.

These facts about animal food do not mean that we can easily solve the world food problem by cutting down on animal products, but they show that the problem is essentially one of distribution rather than production. The world does produce enough food. Moreover, the poorer nations themselves could produce far more if they made more use of improved agricultural techniques.

So why are people hungry? Poor people cannot afford to buy grain grown by farmers in the richer nations. Poor farmers cannot afford to buy improved seeds, or fertilisers, or the machinery needed for drilling wells and pumping water. Only by transferring some of the wealth of the rich nations to the poor can the situation be changed.

That this wealth exists is clear. Against the picture of absolute poverty that McNamara has painted, one might pose a picture of "absolute affluence." Those who are absolutely affluent are not necessarily affluent by comparison with their neighbours, but they are affluent by any reasonable definition of human needs. This means that they have more income than they need to provide themselves adequately with all the basic necessities of life. After buying (either directly or through their taxes) food, shelter, clothing, basic health services, and education, the absolutely affluent are still able to spend money on luxuries. The absolutely affluent choose their food for the pleasures of the palate, not to stop hunger; they buy new clothes to look good, not to keep warm; they move house to be in a better neighborhood or have a playroom for the children, not to keep out the rain; and after all this there is still money to spend on stereo systems, video-cameras, and overseas holidays.

At this stage I am making no ethical judgments about absolute affluence, merely pointing out that it exists. Its defining characteristic is a significant amount of income above the level necessary to provide for the basic human needs of oneself and one's dependents. By this standard, the majority of citizens of Western Europe, North America, Japan, Australia, New Zealand, and the oil-rich Middle Eastern states are all absolutely affluent. To quote McNamara once more:

The average citizen of a developed country enjoys wealth beyond the wildest dreams of the one billion people in countries with per capita incomes under $200.

These, therefore, are the countries—and individuals—who have wealth that they could, without threatening their own basic welfare, transfer to the absolutely poor.

At present, very little is being transferred. Only Sweden, the Netherlands, Norway, and some of the oil-exporting Arab states have reached the modest target, set by the United Nations, of 0.7 percent of gross national product (GNP). Britain gives 0.31 percent of its GNP in official development assistance and a small additional amount in unofficial aid from voluntary organisations. The total comes to about £2 per month per person, and compares with 5.5 percent of GNP spent on alcohol, and 3 percent on tobacco. Other, even wealthier nations, give little more: Germany gives 0.41 percent and Japan 0.32 percent. The United States gives a mere 0.15 percent of its GNP. . . .

THE OBLIGATION TO ASSIST

The Argument for an Obligation to Assist

The path from the library at my university to the humanities lecture theatre passes a shallow ornamental pond. Suppose that on my way to give a lecture I notice that a small child has fallen in and is in danger of drowning. Would anyone deny that I ought to wade in and pull the child out? This will mean getting my clothes muddy and either cancelling my lecture or delaying it until I can find something dry to change into; but compared with the avoidable death of a child this is insignificant.

A plausible principle that would support the judgment that I ought to pull the child out is this: if it is in our power to prevent something very bad from happening, without thereby sacrificing anything of comparable moral significance, we ought to do it. This principle seems uncontroversial. It will obviously win the assent of consequentialists; but non-consequentialists should accept it too, because the injunction to prevent what is bad applies only when nothing comparably significant is at stake. Thus the principle cannot lead to the kinds of actions of which non-consequentialists strongly disapprove—serious violations of individual rights, injustice, broken promises, and so on. If non-consequentialists regard any of these as comparable in moral significance to the bad thing that is to be prevented, they will automatically regard the principle as not applying in those cases in which the bad thing can only be prevented by violating rights, doing injustice, breaking promises, or whatever else is at stake. Most non-consequentialists hold that we ought to prevent what is bad and promote what is good. Their dispute with consequentialists lies in their insistence that this is not the sole ultimate ethical principle: that it is an ethical principle is not denied by any plausible ethical theory.

Nevertheless the uncontroversial appearance of the principle that we ought to prevent what is bad when we can do so without sacrificing anything of comparable moral significance is deceptive. If it were taken seriously and acted upon, our lives and our world would be fundamentally changed. For the principle applies, not just to rare situations in which one can save a child from a pond, but to the everyday situation in which we can assist those living in absolute poverty. In saying this I assume that absolute poverty, with its hunger and malnutrition, lack of shelter, illiteracy, disease, high infant mortality, and low life expectancy, is a bad thing. And I assume that it is within the power of the affluent to reduce absolute poverty, without sacrificing anything of comparable moral significance. If these two assumptions and the principle we have been discussing are correct, we have an obligation to help those in absolute poverty that is no less strong than our obligation to rescue a drowning child from a pond. Not to help would be wrong, whether or not it is intrinsically equivalent to killing. Helping is not, as conventionally thought, a charitable act that it is praise-worthy to do, but not wrong to omit; it is something that everyone ought to do.

QUESTIONS

1. What does Singer mean by "absolute poverty"? Why does he distinguish it from relative poverty?

2. What is Singer's argument for "an obligation to assist"?

Irving Kristol | A Capitalist Conception of Justice

Irving Kristol was, for many years, the editor of the conservative journal *The Public Interest.*

It is fashionable these days for social commentators to ask, "Is capitalism compatible with social justice?" I submit that the only appropriate answer is "No." Indeed, this is the only possible answer. The term "social justice" was invented in order *not* to be compatible with capitalism.

What is the difference between "social justice" and plain, unqualified "justice?" Why can't we ask, "Is capitalism compatible with justice?" We can, and were we to do so, we would then have to explore the idea of justice that is peculiar to the capitalist system, because capitalism certainly does have an idea of justice.

"Social justice," however, was invented and propagated by people who were not much interested in understanding capitalism. These were nineteenth-century critics of capitalism—liberals, radicals, socialists—who invented the term in order to insinuate into the argument a quite different conception of the good society from the one proposed by liberal capitalism. As it is used today, the term has an irredeemably egalitarian and authoritarian thrust. Since capitalism as a socioeconomic or political system is neither egalitarian nor authoritarian, it is in truth incompatible with "social justice."

Let us first address the issue of egalitarianism. In a liberal or democratic capitalist society there is, indeed, a connection between justice and equality. Equality before the law and equality of political rights are fundamental to a liberal capitalist system and, in historical fact, the ideological Founding Fathers of liberal capitalism all did believe in equality before the law and in some form of equality of political rights. The introduction of the term "social

justice" represents an effort to stretch the idea of justice that is compatible with capitalism to cover *economic* equality as well. Proponents of something called "social justice" would persuade us that economic equality is as much a right as are equality before the law and equality of political rights. As a matter of fact, these proponents move in an egalitarian direction so formidably that inevitably *all* differences are seen sooner or later to be unjust. Differences between men and women, differences between parents and children, differences between human beings and animals—all of these, as we have seen in the last ten or fifteen years, become questionable and controversial.

A person who believes in "social justice" is an egalitarian. I do not say that he or she necessarily believes in perfect equality; I do not think anyone believes in perfect equality. But "social justice" advocates are terribly interested in far more equality than a capitalist system is likely to deliver. Capitalism delivers many good things but, on the whole, economic equality is not one of them. It has never pretended to deliver economic equality. Rather, capitalism has always stood for equality of economic opportunity, reasonably understood to mean the absence of official barriers to economic opportunity.

We are now in an egalitarian age when Harvard professors write books wondering whether there is a problem of "social justice" if some people are born of handsome parents and are therefore more attractive than others. This is seriously discussed in Cambridge and in other learned circles. Capitalism is not interested in that. Capitalism says there ought to be no *official* barriers to economic opportunity. If one is born of handsome or talented parents, if one inherits a musical skill, or mathematical skill, or whatever, that is simply good luck. No one can question the person's right to the fruits of such skills. Capitalism believes that, through equal opportunity, each individual will pursue his happiness as he defines it, and as far as his natural assets (plus luck, good or bad) will permit. In pursuit of that happiness everyone will, to use that familiar phrase of Adam Smith, "better his condition."

Thus, capitalism says that equal opportunity will result in everyone's bettering his or her condition. And it does. The history of the world over the past 200 years shows that capitalism did indeed permit and encourage ordinary men and women in the pursuit of their happiness to improve their condition. Even Marx did not deny this. We are not as poor as our grandparents. We are all better off because individuals in pursuit of happiness, and without barriers being put in their way, are very creative, innovative, and adept at finding ways for societies to be more productive, thereby creating more wealth in which everyone shares.

Now, although individuals do better their condition under capitalism, they do not better their conditions equally. In the pursuit of happiness, some will be more successful than others. Some will end up with more than others. Everyone will end up with *somewhat* more than he had—everyone. But some people will end up with a lot more than they had and some with a little more than they had. Capitalism does not perceive this as a problem. It is assumed that since everyone gets more, everyone ought to be content. If some people get more than others, the reason is to be found in their differential contributions to the economy. In a capitalist system, where the market predominates in economic decision making, people who—in whatever way—make different productive inputs into the economy receive different rewards. If one's input into the economy is great, one receives a large reward; if one's input is small, one receives a modest reward. The determination of these rewards is by public preferences and public tastes as expressed in the market. If the public wants basketball players to make $400,000 a year, then those who are good at basketball can become very, very rich. If the public wants to purchase certain paintings for $1 million or $2 million, then certain artists can

become very, very rich. On the other hand, croquet players, even brilliant croquet players, won't better their condition to the same degree. And those who have no particular skill had better be lucky.

This is the way the system works. It rewards people in terms of their contribution to the economy as measured and defined by the marketplace—namely, in terms of the free preferences of individual men and women who have money in their pockets and are free to spend it or not on this, that, or the other as they please. Economic justice under capitalism means the differential reward to individuals is based on their productive input *to the economy*. I emphasize "to the economy" because input is measured by the marketplace.

Is it "just" that Mr. Ray Kroc, chairman of the board of McDonald's, should have made so much money by merely figuring out a new way of selling hamburgers? They are the same old hamburgers, just better made, better marketed. Is it fair? Capitalism says it is fair. He is selling a good product; people want it; it is fair. It is "just" that he has made so much money.

However, capitalism doesn't say only that. It also understands that it is an exaggeration to say that literally *everyone* betters his condition when rewards are based on productive input. There are some people who are really not capable of taking part in the race at all because of mental illness, physical illness, bad luck, and so on. Such persons are simply not able to take advantage of the opportunity that does exist.

Capitalism as originally conceived by Adam Smith was not nearly so heartless a system as it presented itself during the nineteenth century. Adam Smith didn't say that people who could make no productive input into the economy through no fault of their own should be permitted to starve to death. Though not a believer, he was enough of a Christian to know that such a conclusion was not consistent with the virtue of charity. He understood that such people had to be provided for. There has never been any question of that. Adam Smith wrote two books. The book that first made him famous was not *The Wealth of Nations* but *The Theory of Moral Sentiments*, in which he said that the highest human sentiment is sympathy—the sympathy that men and women have for one another as human beings. Although *The Wealth of Nations* is an analysis of an economic system based on self-interest, Adam Smith never believed for a moment that human beings were strictly economic men or women. It took some later generations of economists to come up with that idea. Adam Smith understood that people live in a society, not just in an economy, and that they feel a sense of social obligation to one another, as well as a sense of engaging in mutually satisfactory economic transactions.

In both these books, but especially in *The Theory of Moral Sentiments*, Adam Smith addressed himself to the question, "What do the rich do with their money once they get it?" His answer was that they reinvest some of it so that society as a whole will become wealthier and everyone will continue to be able to improve his or her condition to some degree. Also, however, the rich will engage in one of the great pleasures that wealth affords: the expression of sympathy for one's fellow human beings. Smith said that the people who have money can only consume so much. What are they going to do with the money aside from what they consume and reinvest? They will use it in such a way as to gain a good reputation among their fellow citizens. He said this will be the natural way for wealthy people to behave under capitalism. Perhaps he was thinking primarily of Scotsmen. Still, his perceptiveness is interesting. Although capitalism has long been accused of being an inhumane system, we forget that capitalism and humanitarianism entered the modern world together. Name a modern, humane movement—criminal reform, decent treatment of women, kindness to animals, etc. Where does it originate? They all came from the rising bourgeoisie at the end of the eighteenth century. They were all middle-class movements. The movements didn't begin with peasants or aristocrats. Peasants were always cruel to animals and aristocrats could not care less about animals, or about wives, for that matter. It was the bourgeoisie, the capitalist middle class, that said animals should be treated with consideration, that criminals should not be tortured, that prisons should be places of punishment, yes, but humane places of punishment. It was the generation that helped establish the capitalist

idea and the capitalist way of thinking in the world that brought these movements to life. Incidentally, the anti-slavery movement was also founded by middle-class men and women who had a sense of social responsibility toward their fellow citizens.

So it is simply and wholly untrue that capitalism is a harsh, vindictive, soulless system. A man like Adam Smith would never have dreamed of recommending such a system. No, he recommended the economic relations which constitute the market system, the capitalist system, on the assumption that human beings would continue to recognize their social obligations to one another and act upon this recognition with some degree of consistency. Incidentally, he even seems to have believed in a progressive income tax.

However, something very peculiar happened after Adam Smith. Something very odd and very bad happened to the idea of capitalism and its reputation after the first generation of capitalism's intellectual Founding Fathers. The economics of capitalism became a "dismal science." One cannot read *The Wealth of Nations* and have any sense that economics is a dismal science. It is an inquiry into the causes of the wealth of nations that tells people how to get rich. It says, "If you organize your economic activities this way, everyone will get richer." There is nothing pessimistic about that, nothing dismal about that. It was an exhilarating message to the world.

Unfortunately, what gave capitalism a bad name in the early part of the nineteenth century was not the socialist's criticism of capitalism but, I fear, the work of the later capitalist economists. We do not even have a really good intellectual history of this episode because people who write histories of economic thought tend not to be interested in intellectual history, but in economics. For some reason, Malthus and then Ricardo decided that capitalist economics should not deal with the production of wealth but rather with its distribution. Adam Smith had said everyone could improve his condition. Malthus said the situation was hopeless, at least for the lower classes. If the lower classes improved their condition, he argued, they would start breeding like rabbits and shortly they would be right back where they started. Ricardo came along and said that the expanding population could not all be fed because there is a shortage of fertile land in the world. In his view, the condition of the working class over the long term was unimprovable.

This was the condition of capitalist economics for most of the nineteenth century. It is a most extraordinary and paradoxical episode in modern intellectual history. Throughout the nineteenth century, ordinary men and women, the masses, the working class, were clearly improving their condition. There is just no question that the working classes in England were better off in 1860 than they had been in 1810. In the United States there was never any such question and in France, too, it was quite clear that the system was working as Adam Smith had said it would. Yet all the economists of the School of Malthus and Ricardo kept saying, "It cannot happen. Sorry, people, but you're doomed to live in misery. There is nothing we can do about it. Just have fewer children and exercise continence." To which the people said, "Thank you very much. We do not much like this system you are recommending to us," as well they might not.

When the possibility of helping the average man and woman through economic growth is rejected loudly and dogmatically by the leading economists of the day, many will believe it. When they conclude that their condition cannot be improved by economic growth, they will seek to improve it by redistribution, by taking it away from others who have more. It is nineteenth-century capitalist economic thought, with its incredible emphasis on the impossibility of improving the condition of the working class—even as the improvement was obviously taking place—that gave great popularity and plausibility to the socialist critique of capitalism and to the redistributionist impulse that began to emerge. This impulse, which is still so appealing, makes no sense. A nation can redistribute to its heart's content and it will not affect the average person one bit. There just isn't ever enough to redistribute. Nevertheless, once it became "clear" in the nineteenth century that there was no other way, redistribution became a very popular subject.

Because capitalism after Adam Smith seemed to be associated with a hopeless view of the world, it provoked egalitarian impulses. Is it not a natural

human sentiment to argue that, if we're all in a hopeless condition, we should be hopeless equally? Let us go down together. If that indeed is our condition, equality becomes a genuine virtue. Egalitarianism became such a plausible view of the world because capitalist apologists, for reasons which I do not understand, kept insisting that this is the nature of capitalism. Those who talk about "social justice" these days do not say that the income tax should be revised so that the rich people will get more, although there may be an economic case for it. (I am not saying there is, even though there might be.) "Social justice," the term, the idea, is intimately wedded to the notion of egalitarianism as a proper aim of social and economic policy, and capitalism is criticized as lacking in "social justice" because it does not achieve this equality. In fact, it does not, cannot, and never promised to achieve this result.

However, I think the more important thrust of the term "social justice" has to do with its authoritarian meaning rather than its egalitarian meaning. The term "social" prefixed before the word "justice" has a purpose and an effect which is to abolish the distinction between the public and the private sectors, a distinction which is absolutely crucial for a liberal society. It is the very definition of a liberal society that there be a public sector and a large, private sector where people can do what they want without government bothering them. What is a "social problem?" Is a social problem something that government can ignore? Would anyone say we have a social problem but it is not the business of government? Of course not.

The term "social justice" exists in order to identify those issues about which government should get active. A social problem is a problem that gives rise to a governmental policy, which is why people who believe in the expansion of the public sector are always inventing, discovering, or defining more and more social problems in our world. The world has not become any more problematic than it ever was. The proliferation of things called "social problems" arises out of an effort to get government more and more deeply involved in the lives of private citizens in an attempt to "cope with" or "solve" these "problems." Sometimes real problems are posed. Rarely are they followed by real solutions.

Occupy Wall Street
Annie Lowrey

The protesters say the top 1 percent of Americans have gotten too rich. Are they right?

It is not easy to say just what Occupy Wall Street wants; there is no concise list of specific demands. But the gist of the quickly snowballing movement is clear. Wall Street has not accepted responsibility for its role in the financial crisis and ensuing recession. It has done more harm than good for average citizens and businesses. On top of all that, average Americans are "getting nothing while the other 1 percent is getting everything. We are the 99 percent."

One thing is inarguably true: The 99 percent don't have 99 percent of anything, money-wise, in the United States. But just how bad is the skew toward the top 1 percent?

Let's start with income—the money you make from things like wages, salary, interest payments, and collected rent. According to an analysis (XLS) of Internal Revenue Service data by the economists Thomas Piketty and Emmanuel Saez, the 99 percent account for 79 percent of income in 2008, with the top 1 percent taking the other 21 percent.

"That's not that bad," you might say. "Of course, some people are going to be richer than others." Perhaps. But the 1 percent has been eating a bigger and bigger share of the pie over time. Back in the 1970s, the 99 percent were earning about 90 percent of income, for instance. The top 1 percent of households took a bigger share of overall income in 2007 than they did at any time since 1928.

The 1 percent's income did take a knock during the Great Recession: It dropped 20 percent, whereas the 99 percent took a 7 percent hit. But that mostly was caused by the stock market crash and falling capital-gains earnings among the rich, not by salary cuts.

The 99 percent's fortunes look even worse if you focus on wealth, rather than income—the total value of a household or individual's assets, such their house and their investment funds. According to data compiled by economist Edward Wolff (PDF), in 2007, the 99 percent held about two-thirds of American wealth, meaning the top 1 percent has nearly one-third.

The sustained woes of the housing market may skew those numbers even further in the coming years, because the 99 percent rely on homes for a bigger proportion of their wealth than the 1 percent do. Before the crash, the middle of the income distribution had about 90 percent of their assets in their homes. Housing prices have cratered across the country. That means trillions in lost housing value and a hefty debt burden for underwater homeowners to boot.

The 1 percent has about 43 percent of all the non housing wealth, which has held up comparatively better. Sociologist William Domhoff reports that the 99 percent hold just 38 percent of equity in businesses, 40 percent of financial securities, and 62 percent of stocks and mutual funds. Among the 99 percent, about one in three households has more than $10,000 in stock. Among the 1 percent, nearly nine in 10 households do.

In short, inequality has increased in the past decade, leaving the 99 percent with smaller and smaller proportions of income and wealth. And it has many economists, public policy wonks, and, well, protesters very, very worried. As put by Nobel laureate Joseph Stiglitz, "growing inequality is the flip side of something else: shrinking opportunity. Whenever we diminish equality of opportunity, it means that we are not using some of our most valuable assets—our people—in the most productive way possible."

Whether Occupy Wall Street can help to rectify that imbalance—who knows. But there is certainly value in at least making sure Americans know just how unequal the country is.

From Slate.com.

The idea of "social justice," however, assumes not only that government will intervene but that government will have, should have, and can have an authoritative knowledge as to what everyone merits or deserves in terms of the distribution of income and wealth. After all, if we do not like the inequality that results from the operation of the market, then who is going to make the decision as to the distribution of services and wealth? Some authority must be found to say so-and-so deserves more than so-and-so. Of course, the only possible such authority in the modem world is not the Church but the State. To the degree that one defines "social justice" as a kind of protest against the capitalist distribution of income, one proposes some other mechanism for the distribution of income. Government is the only other mechanism that can make the decisions as to who gets what, as to what he or she "deserves," for whatever reason.

The assumption that the government is able to make such decisions wisely, and therefore that government should make such decisions, violates the very premises of a liberal community. A liberal community exists on the premise that there is no such authority. If there were an authority which knew what everyone merited and could allocate it fairly, why would we need freedom? There would be no point in freedom. Let the authority do its work. Now, we have seen the experience of non-liberal societies, and not all of it is bad. I would not pretend that a liberal society is the only possible good society. If one likes the values of a particular non-liberal society, it may not be bad at all. There are

many non-liberal societies I admire: monasteries are non-liberal societies, and I do not say they are bad societies. They are pretty good societies—but they are not liberal societies. The monk has no need for liberty if he believes there is someone else, his superior, who knows what is good for him and what reward he merits.

Once we assume that there is a superior authority who has authoritative knowledge of the common good and of the merits and demerits of every individual, the ground of a liberal society is swept away, because the very freedoms that subsist and thrive in a liberal society all assume that there is no such authoritative knowledge. Now, this assumption is not *necessarily* true. Maybe there is someone who really does have an authoritative knowledge of what is good for all of us and how much we all merit. We who choose a liberal society are skeptical as to the possibility. In any case, we think it is more likely that there will be ten people all claiming to have different versions of what is good for all of us and what we should all get, and therefore we choose to let the market settle it. It is an amicable way of not getting involved in endless philosophical or religious arguments about the nature of the true, the good, and the beautiful.

The notion of a "just society" existing on earth is a fantasy, a utopian fantasy. That is not what life on earth is like. The reason is that the world is full of other people who are different from you and me, alas, and we have to live with them. If they were all like us, we would live fine; but they are not all like us, and the point of a liberal society and of a market economy is to accept this difference and say, "Okay, you be you and I'll be I. We'll disagree, but we'll do business together. We'll mutually profit from doing business together, and we'll live not necessarily in friendship but at least in civility with one another."

I am not saying that capitalism is a just society. I am saying that there is a capitalist conception of justice which is a workable conception of justice. Anyone who promises you a just society on this earth is a fraud and a charlatan. I believe that this is not the nature of human destiny. It would mean that we all would be happy. Life is not like that. Life is doomed not to be like that. But if you do not accept this view, and if you really think that life can indeed be radically different from what it is, if you really believe that justice can prevail on earth, then you are likely to start taking phrases like "social justice" very seriously and to think that the function of politics is to rid the world of its evils: to abolish war, to abolish poverty, to abolish discrimination, to abolish envy, to abolish, abolish, abolish. We are not going to abolish any of those things. If we push them out one window, they will come in through another window in some unforeseen form. The reforms of today give rise to the evils of tomorrow. That is the history of the human race.

If one can be somewhat stoical about this circumstance, the basic precondition of social life, capitalism becomes much more tolerable. However, if one is not stoical about it, if one demands more of life than life can give, then capitalism is certainly the wrong system because capitalism does not promise that much and does not give you that much. All it gives is a greater abundance of material goods and a great deal of freedom to cope with the problems of the human condition on your own.

QUESTIONS

1. What is the difference between social justice and plain, unqualified justice?

2. Is Adam Smith's understanding of capitalism harsh and "soulless"? What makes Smith's understanding of capitalism more humane than some other versions of capitalism?

3. Plato said that "No one should make more than five times the income of an average worker." Recent business leaders have made similar recommendations. What would Adam Smith have said?

Friedrich von Hayek | # Justice Ruins the Market

Friedrich von Hayek was a classic neoconservative and a staunch defender of the unfettered, unregulated market. This is from his book, *The Road to Serfdom*.

THE IMMORAL CONSEQUENCES OF MORALLY INSPIRED EFFORTS

Though in the long perspective of Western civilization the history of law is a history of a gradual emergence of rules of just conduct capable of universal application, its development during the last hundred years has become increasingly one of the destruction of justice by "social justice," until even some students of jurisprudence have lost sight of the original meaning of "justice." We have seen how the process has mainly taken the form of a replacement of the rules of just conduct by those rules of organization which we call public law (a "subordinating law"), a distinction which some socialist lawyers are

From Friedrich von Hayek, *The Road to Serfdom* (Highpoint Press, 1940). Reprinted with permission.

trying hard to obliterate. In substance this has meant that the individual is no longer bound only by rules which confine the scope of his private actions, but has become increasingly subject to the commands of authority. The growing technological possibilities of control, together with the presumed moral superiority of a society whose members serve the same hierarchy of ends, have made this totalitarian trend appear under a moral guise. It is indeed the concept of "social justice" which has been the Trojan Horse through which totalitarianism has entered.

The values which still survive from the small end-connected groups whose coherence depended upon them, are, however, not only different from, but often incompatible with, the values which make possible the peaceful coexistence of large numbers in the Open Society. The belief that while we pursue the new ideal of this Great Society in which all human beings are regarded as equal, we can also preserve the different ideals of the small closed society, is an illusion. To attempt it leads to the destruction of the Great Society.

The possibility of men living together in peace and to their mutual advantage without having to agree on common concrete aims, and bound only by abstract rules of conduct, was perhaps the greatest discovery mankind ever made. The "capitalist" system which grew out of this discovery no doubt did not fully satisfy the ideals of liberalism, because it grew up while legislators and governments did not really understand the modus operandi of the market, and largely in spite of the policies actually pursued. Capitalism as it exists today in consequence undeniably has many remediable defects that an intelligent policy of freedom ought to correct. A system which relies on the spontaneous ordering forces of the market, once it has reached a certain level of wealth, is also by no means incompatible with government providing, outside the market, some security against severe deprivation. But the attempt to secure to each what he is thought to deserve, by imposing upon all a system of common concrete ends towards which their efforts are directed by authority, as socialism aims to do, would be a retrograde step that would deprive us of the utilization of the knowledge and aspirations of millions,

and thereby of the advantages of a free civilization. Socialism is not based merely on a different system of ultimate values from that of liberalism, which one would have to respect even if one disagreed; it is based on an intellectual error which makes its adherents blind to its consequences. This must be plainly said because the emphasis on the alleged difference of the ultimate values has become the common excuse of the socialists for shirking the real intellectual issue. The pretended difference of the underlying value judgments has become a protective cloak used to conceal the faulty reasoning underlying the socialist schemes.

IN THE GREAT SOCIETY "SOCIAL JUSTICE" BECOMES A DISRUPTIVE FORCE

Not only is it impossible for the Great Society to maintain itself while enforcing rules of "social" or distributive justice; for its preservation it is also necessary that no particular groups holding common views about what they are entitled to should be allowed to enforce these views by preventing others to offer their services at more favourable terms. Though common interests of those whose position is affected by the same circumstances are likely to produce strong common opinions about what they deserve, and will provide a motive for common action to achieve their ends, any such group action to secure a particular income or position for its members creates an obstacle to the integration of the Great Society and is therefore anti-social in the true sense of this word. It must become a divisive force because it produces not a reconciliation of, but a conflict between, the interests of the different groups. As the active participants in the struggle for "social justice" well know, it becomes in practice a struggle for power of organized interests in which arguments of justice serve merely as pretexts.

The chief insight we must hold on to is that not always when a group of people have strong views about what they regard as their claims in justice does this mean that there exists (or can be found) a corresponding rule which, if universally applied, would produce a viable order. It is a delusion to believe that whenever a question is represented as one of justice it must be possible to discover a rule capable of universal application which will decide that question. Nor does the fact that a law endeavours to meet somebody's claim for justice prove that it is a rule of just conduct.

All groups whose members pursue the same or parallel aims will develop common views about what is right for members of those groups. Such views, however, will be right only for all those who pursue the same aims, but may be wholly incompatible with any principles by which such a group can be integrated into the overall order of society. The producers of any particular commodity or service who all aim at a good remuneration for their efforts will regard as unjust the action of any fellow producer who tends to reduce the incomes of the others. Yet it will be precisely the kind of actions by some members of the group that the rest regard as harmful which will fit the activities of the members of the group into the overall pattern of the Great Society and thereby benefit all.

It is certainly in itself not unjust if a barber in one city receives $3 for a haircut while in another city only $2 is paid for the same work. But it would clearly be unjust if the barbers in the first prevented any from the second city from improving their position by offering their services in the first for, say, $2.50 and thus, while improving their position, lowering the income of the first group. Yet it is precisely against such efforts that established groups are today permitted to combine in defence of their established position. The rule "do nothing which will decrease the income of the members of your own group" will often be regarded as an obligation of justice toward one's fellow members. But it cannot be accepted as a rule of just conduct in a Great Society where it will conflict with the general principles on which the activities of that society are co-ordinated. The other members of that society will have every interest and moral right to prevent the enforcement of such a rule that the members of a special group regard as just, because the principles of integration of the Great Society

demand that the action of some of those occupied in a particular manner should often lead to a reduction of the incomes of their fellows. This is precisely the virtue of competition. The conceptions of group justice would often proscribe all effective competition as unjust—and many of the "fair competition" demands aim in effect at little less.

It is probably true that in any group whose members know that their prospects depend on the same circumstances, views will develop that represent as unjust all conduct of any member which harms the others; and there will in consequence arise a desire to prevent such conduct. But by any outsider it will rightly be regarded as unjust if any member of such a group is prevented by his fellows from offering him more advantageous terms than the rest of the group are willing to offer. And the same is true when some "interloper" who before was not recognized as a member of the group is made to conform to the standards of the group as soon as his efforts compete with theirs.

The important fact which most people are reluctant to admit, yet which is probably true in most instances, is that, though the pursuit of the selfish aims of the individual will usually lead him to serve the general interest, the collective actions of organized groups are almost invariably contrary to the general interest. What in fact leads to the condemnation as anti-social of that pursuit of individual interests which contributes to the general interest, and to the commendation as "social" of the subservience to those sectional interests which destroy the overall order, are sentiments which we have inherited from earlier forms of society. The use of coercion in this kind of "social justice," meaning the interests of the particular group to which the individual belongs, will thus always mean the creation of particular preserves of special groups united against the outsiders—interest groups which exist because they are allowed to use force or pressure on government for the benefit of their members. But, however much the members of such groups may agree among themselves that what they want is just, there exists no principle which could make it appear as just to the outsider. Yet today, if such a group is only large enough, its representation of the demands of its members as just is commonly accepted as one view of justice which must be taken into account in ordering the whole, even though it does not rest on any principle which could be generally applied.

1. How does justice ruin the market, according to Hayek?

2. How would Hayek deal with the problem of monopolies?

Eduard Gracia | # The Winner-Take-All Game

Eduard Gracia is a senior manager with Deloitte MCS, Strategy & Operations in London.

In 1981, when the world was at the deep end of the so-called Second Oil Crisis, Marvin Harris, an American anthropologist, published a short essay entitled "America Now: The Anthropology of a Changing Culture." In it he analyzed the underlying economic phenomena that had ultimately generated a wide cultural change, and he found out that the problem could to a large extent be traced back to the general lack of reliability of goods and services produced in America at that time, and that this, in turn, was attributable to the short-term-oriented management style that had increasingly dominated corporate America since the end of World War II:

> The observers [agree] that there is something in the way today's executives relate to their companies that makes them different from the previous generation of corporate leaders. De Lorean, for example, depicts them as "short-term professional executives" that remain in a company less than ten years and that are driven by the need to produce immediate profits during their short tenure. Due to the frequent change from one company to another, their economic position does no longer depend mainly on owning assets in the company they work for, and therefore do not need to worry about what will

happen if, say, the reputation of their firm regarding quality falls to pieces soon after they left. . . .

In the wake of the most recent corporate scandals it has once again become fashionable to criticize this myopia of bad behavior often in fairly apocalyptic terms and in a tone that seems to imply that "something" should be done about it. However, without an understanding of the underlying causes of this phenomenon, the recent outcry is not likely to be any more effective than its predecessors apart from, perhaps, encouraging the deployment of government regulatory measures that, as public intervention usually does, are more likely to impair the efficiency of the system as a whole rather than solving any real problem.

Therefore, the objective of this paper is to put forward a potential explanation of this phenomenon that is consistent with its remarkable resilience over time as well as its presence in economic systems that otherwise are quite healthy. Specifically, the phenomenon can be interpreted as a side effect of free market competition and, therefore, not only are there no "magic bullets" available, but solutions based on radical forms of intervention are likely to do more harm than good. Instead, just as in the case of a chronic illness, it will be suggested that it is better not to try to fix it once and for all, but rather to consistently monitor its evolution and fine-tune the balance of long- vs. short-term incentives within the organization whenever they deviate too much from the desired "balance," which, incidentally, may also change over time.

————

Imagine a country with ten cities, in each one of which lives a single doctor, and let's assume there are strong limitations for people to go visit physicians in cities other than their own, be it due to a deficient transport system, to a legal system that requires them to depend upon a local doctor, or to any other reason. The income of each one of the physicians, assuming the size and morbidity of the different cities to be roughly the same, will thus also tend to be more or less the same. The physicians, under these conditions, will not have many incentives to invest in advertising themselves, as there is no pressure for competition, and the control by each one of them of his/her own city market will have monopolistic characteristics, with the corresponding impact on price and quality. On the other hand, the planning investment horizon of each one of the physicians will tend to be relatively long, as the expectation is that each city market will belong to its local doctor for a long time, and perhaps even pass to his or her descendants.

Now suppose that the barriers to free competition disappear: communications improve across the cities, and there are no legal restrictions to prevent people from freely choosing any doctor. What happens now? To begin with, of course, people will tend to go to the doctor with the best reputation. Thus, other things being equal, the income of the best physicians will rise, and that of the worst will decline. At the extreme (e.g., if the best physician can really deal with all the patients and, thus, all the other doctors have no business), this is just a winner-take-all game. There will be competitive pressure both on prices and quality and on the proportion of their income the physicians spend on advertising themselves. There will also be a strong tendency for success (or failure) to retro-feed itself: the most successful doctors will make more money and, therefore, be able to afford both better equipment and more expensive advertising.

This means that winning in the next few rounds of the game has a potentially very high relevance, as it determines to a large extent the conditions under which the player is going to have to compete afterwards. Yet success will always have the potential of being short-lived because tomorrow an unfortunate mistake in a difficult surgery procedure or the appearance of a new, better advertised or genuinely more gifted competitor can trigger the vicious cycle of failure for the physician that today is at the top of the world. This provides an incentive for market leaders to stay "on their toes" for sure, but it also discounts any long-term investment at a heavy risk premium, especially if it reduces the chances of immediate success. At this point, the reader may have spotted a seeming contradiction: if the physician "on top" keeps focusing on his short-term marketability and downplaying longer-term investments (such as his own retraining), isn't he implicitly digging his own grave in the long run? The answer is yes, of course, as this is precisely the nature of the dilemma.

This is what we could call "Hollywood-style economics," as it is indeed how the Hollywood star system has worked almost from the beginning. The Hollywood cinema industry is a very competitive industry with global reach. Every weekend, people in the whole world are free to choose what movie they want to watch, and they do so based on a few parameters such as the name of the featured actors or a trailer they saw last week. The value of the theatre ticket of each one is minimal, but there is almost no limit to the number of people who can go to a given movie, and, therefore, the potential revenue from a film can swing from zero (no one was interested) to many millions (everyone went to watch it, and some even went twice). In other words: as in the case of the doctors after the barriers between the cities were removed, the difference between the physician (or, in this case, the actor) on top and the one at the bottom of the ranking is potentially huge. Under these conditions, of course, the stakes are very high, and the competition must be cut-throat. Therefore, reputation is everything, and the salaries of the actors at the top of the system are an almost obscene multiple of those of many others who are only slightly less gifted, or simply have been a bit less lucky or a bit less ruthless.

Our modern economy, increasingly global, competitive and meritocratic as it is, just cannot be excluded from this same rule: as competition grows on a global scale, the pressure for performance will increase, which is a stimulating factor but, at the same time, the planning horizon of corporations and even individuals will tend to become somewhat shorter simply because none of them can count on retaining his/her position in the marketplace in the long run. This, of course, generates interesting and seemingly paradoxical effects. For example, as long as the top leadership of Marks & Spencer in the UK was securely in the hands of a member of the founding family (as it was always the case from the company's foundation in 1894 until 1984), the CEO never needed to justify a long-term-oriented policy of sustained product quality and client service, even when facing temporary losses, simply because he/she did not face the risk of dismissal. In fact, the problems that ended up in the spectacular nosedive of this firm in 1999 can to a large extent be attributed to a series of policies increasingly aimed at improving measurable results in the short term that M&S applied throughout the 1990s. This is by no means an exceptional situation. Anderson and Reeb (2003), working on U.S. data from S&P 500 companies over the period 1992 to 1999, found statistically robust evidence that "family firms perform better than non-family firms" and that, even within the set of family-controlled firms, "when family members serve as CEO, performance is better than with outside CEOs." They link these findings directly to those of James (1999) in the sense that family firms can attain greater investment efficiency due to their longer investment horizons.

Conversely, for a hired CEO who is exposed to being fired if short-term results are below the board's expectations, reputation represents a large portion of his/her market value, and reputation is built upon sustained, demonstrated success. The stakes are high and, thus, it is not at all surprising that, as research found, they discount their companies' investments at a rate higher than that applied by the shareholders they serve. Interestingly, the same paper also found that "at the time of the survey, the fall of 1990, U.S. CEOs believed that their firms had systematically shorter time horizons than their major competitors in Europe and (especially) Asia," which is consistent with the general observation that the U.S. market is still freer and more internally competitive than most of the European and Asian ones. This is also consistent with findings which suggest that CEO performance-related turnover rates are generally higher in the U.S. than in either Europe or Asia, although the long-term tendency is for the latter to gradually approach the U.S. rates over time.

The pressure, of course, rarely stays at the CEO level, as it tends to spread top down throughout the whole organization culture. For example, while one should always take comments on a failed business with more than a grain of salt (it is just too easy to pontificate on what went wrong in a business after it has failed), the analysis of Enron's case suggests that it was to a large extent their aggressive culture of internal competition as represented by the annual performance review. Informally known as "rank and yank," whose focus on measurable results within the period being appraised meant that, in the words of a former employee, "people went from being geniuses to idiots overnight" and which typically resulted in the bottom 10–20% performers being regularly fired. It meant, too, unyielding focus on results. According to a former employee, "they were so goal-oriented toward immediate gratification that they lost sight of the future," and this is what ultimately led them to catastrophe.

QUESTIONS

1. What is "the winner-take-all-game"? Is it a good thing or a bad thing? Why?

2. What does Garcia mean by "Hollywood-style" economics? Do you think Hollywood-style economics should be encouraged or discouraged? How would you do so?

Gerald W. McEntee

Comparable Worth: A Matter of Simple Justice

Gerald W. McEntee is the International President of American Federation of State, County and Municipal Employees.

On December 31, 1985, the American Federation of State, County, and Municipal Employees (AFSCME) and the state of Washington reached a historic comparable worth agreement. They negotiated a settlement of the *AFSCME v. Washington State* pay equity lawsuit. The $106.5 million payout is historic because it is the largest comparable worth settlement in history, and it ended over a decade of resistance by the state to rectify sex-based wage discrimination in its wage scales, as documented by Washington's own studies.

In spite of this historic ruling, however, there is evidence that public sector employers still practice intentional wage discrimination and job segregation policies that funnel women into lower-paying, female-dominated jobs. Is this segregation intentional? And are the pay scales for these particular jobs based on sex-based wage discrimination?

AFSCME believes that the answer to both is "yes."

Take the Washington State example. According to the state's own studies, a laundry operator working in a large state institution should have been paid more than a farm equipment operator. But the salaries for farm equipment operators were seventeen pay grades higher than those of the laundry workers. The difference? One job was male-dominated; the other, female-dominated.

Also in Washington, clerk-typists working in state government and beginning warehouse workers were rated at the same level. But typists earned salaries ten pay grades below those of warehouse workers.

In both the public and the private sector workforce, these examples of pay discrimination are repeated hundreds of times in various job classifications. This translates into a national problem for working women, who still earn only sixty-four cents for every dollar working men earn, in spite of increased education and growing workforce participation by women.

The Washington State settlement capped off a year of comparable worth successes for AFSCME. Comparable worth moved from the courts to the bargaining table and state legislatures in 1985. Public employers are beginning to negotiate with their employees and their unions to work out practical and affordable solutions to the historic problem of sex-based wage discrimination.

However, in spite of the gains made on the comparable worth front this past year, the debate over this method of eradicating sex-based wage discrimination continues. Unfortunately, the discussion too often remains mired in the same kind of mean-spirited arguments used against every major piece of civil rights legislation. Opponents include U.S. Civil Rights Commission Chairman Clarence Pendleton, Phyllis Schlafly, and President Reagan. They have constructed their own definition of what comparable worth is, how it can be accomplished, how much it will cost, and what its effects will be. Their dire predictions fly in the face of the experience of AFSCME and public sector employers across the country. Many employers have voluntarily begun to correct disparities in their wage scales due to sex discrimination. The main arguments of comparable worth opponents are the following:

The gap between men's earnings and women's earnings is due to women's more recent entry into

This article first appeared in *The Humanist* issue of May/June 1986 and is reprinted with permission.

the workforce and their lesser education, training, and experience. Once you have allowed for legitimate differences in pay between men and women, such as seniority, experience, and collective bargaining agreements, there is still a gap that has remained constant for most of the years women have been in the workforce. At least half of this gap is due to sex discrimination by employers. AFSCME defines pay equity, or comparable worth, as a means of closing the gap between men's salaries and women's salaries that can be attributed only to sex discrimination.

Instituting comparable worth will upset the free market economy and require new laws and government wage-setting boards. The U.S. economy is partly controlled by minimum wage laws, civil rights laws, child labor laws, and the Equal Pay Act of 1963. AFSCME contends that the so-called free market has historically discriminated against women. Otherwise, nurses would be handsomely paid, because over the years they have been in critically short supply. But in 1981, for example, full-time registered nurses earned an average of only $331 a week—less than ticket agents and drafters.

Similarly, laws requiring women to be paid the same as men if they are doing comparable work are already on the books—all that remains is the will to enforce the law. In 1981, the Supreme Court ruled that the prohibition of Title VII of the 1964 Civil Rights Act against discrimination in wage compensation was not limited to the claims of working women for equal pay for equal work. The Court made it clear that Title VII prohibits all forms of discrimination in wage setting, including instances in which the male and female jobs being compared are dissimilar.

No advocate of comparable worth has urged that a government board set wages. Comparable worth requires only that *each individual employer* remove sex bias from his or her wage scale. If, say, a truck driver and a secretary within the same organization are evaluated as doing comparable work, they should be paid comparably.

Dissimilar jobs—like apples and oranges— cannot be compared. Think again. You *can* compare apples and oranges on a basis of their weight, their color, and their percentages of vitamins and fluid.

Likewise, jobs have certain common characteristics: training, experience, responsibility, working conditions, and other criteria. Employers have been comparing jobs for as long as they have been hiring workers. Two-thirds of all workers are covered by some form of job evaluation system. The federal government has had an evaluation system to compare dissimilar jobs for one hundred years.

Comparable worth costs too much. AFSCME's on-the-job experience has shown that comparable worth has never cost more than 4 percent of a jurisdiction's payroll. In its first four years of implementation on the state level in Minnesota (which is now implementing pay equity on the county and local level), comparable worth was expected to cost 4 percent of the state's total payroll. Actually, it will cost about 3.5 percent.

Interestingly, the same cost argument was made during the debate over civil rights legislation in the 1960s. Critics charged that paying blacks more would reduce the salaries of white workers. Critics of comparable worth argue that paying women more will reduce men's salaries.

Charging that pay equity will cost too much is an empty argument; it is inflammatory rhetoric designed to alienate women from men. Just because it carries a price, we should not be diverted from our goal of ending discrimination.

Unions promote pay equity because they want to keep women segregated in traditionally female-dominated jobs. Sex segregation in the workforce is a fact of life. A recent National Academy of Sciences report found that, despite recent progress, most American women who are employed will continue to work in largely low-paying occupations dominated by women for the foreseeable future.

Fifty-one percent of AFSCME's members are working women. The concerns of the union's women members are part of the union's overall agenda for the 1980s. Career ladders and career development programs are two of the contract provisions AFSCME negotiates to help move women into better-paying, more skilled jobs.

At the same time, a worker should be paid fairly for his or her work. Today, nearly 60 percent of mothers in families with children under-eighteen are working; 80 percent of all working women are segregated into only twenty of the jobs listed by the *Dictionary of Occupational Titles*. Comparable worth is a means to bring the wages of working women into the mainstream. There are side benefits, also. For example, in Minnesota, during the first four years of pay equity, there has been an increase of 19 percent in the number of women entering nontraditional jobs.

AFSCME believes that comparable worth is the civil rights issue of the eighties. By using collective bargaining and legislative lobbying, AFSCME is pursuing the vestiges of sex-based wage discrimination. Its pay equity lawsuits on behalf of workers in Hawaii, Connecticut, New York City, Philadelphia, and Nassau County, New York, are making their way through the federal courts. Tens of thousands of workers—both women and men—in female-dominated jobs across the country are beginning to be paid based upon fairness and worth. It's a matter of simple justice.

QUESTIONS

1. What is comparable worth?
2. What are several strong arguments in favor of comparable worth? What are some arguments opposed to it? Can comparable worth ever result in injustice?

Greg Breining

The 1 Percent: How Lucky They Are

Greg Breining writes about science, nature, and travel. He is the author of "*Paddle North*: Canoeing the Boundary Waters—Quetico Wilderness" and "Wild Shore: Exploring Lake Superior by Kayak."

As a stagnant economy and the Occupy Wall Street protests ignite debate over the disparity of wealth in America, a little noticed economic study provides mathematical support for a radical idea. The rich get richer and the poor get poorer. You knew that. But you may not have known that according to a mathematical model developed at the University of Minnesota, the fabulously rich get as rich as they do by chance alone.

The policy implications should be alarming, especially if you're a conservative or libertarian who has been saying that economic liberty gives everyone a chance to grab the golden ring. It's a vanishingly small chance. Indeed, if the model is accurate, the inevitable outcome of unfettered capitalism is oligarchy.

"That's the conclusion I came to, too," says Joseph Fargione, lead author of the paper, published this summer in the peer-reviewed journal PLoS ONE. "I was quite surprised by that."

The wealth project took shape as Fargione read Kevin Phillips' "Wealth and Democracy: A Political History of the American Rich." As Phillips notes, Alexis de Tocqueville in 1837 warned the young American republic that its industrial class, "one of the harshest that ever existed," could create "permanent inequality of conditions and aristocracy." And so it did. Despite the interruptions of the Populist and Progressive eras and the New Deal, writes Phillips, by 2000 "the United States was not only the world's wealthiest nation and leading economic power, but also the Western industrial nation with the greatest percentage of the world's rich and greatest gap between rich and poor."

From http://startribune.com/printarticle/?id=132819963 October 29, 2011.

Fargione discovered that other mathematical models of wealth have failed to account fully for its concentration. Some economists blamed wealth concentration on political factors such as cronyism, or on differences in the sharpness of investors.

"What would you expect would happen on its own without a lot of intervention for redistribution of wealth?" Fargione wondered.

He began his research with a simple question: Can chance alone account for wealth concentration?

Fargione focused on entrepreneurs (who make up one in nine Americans) because, contrary to all advice to diversify portfolios, they typically plow their earnings back into their businesses. "Twenty years ago, Bill Gates didn't say, 'Well, I made some money—I think I'm going to diversify my investment.'" The all-in strategy is risky, but when it works it leads to rapid accumulation of wealth.

He assumed that all entrepreneurs began with equal wealth. Returns varied, solely by chance. (Past performance is not an indicator of future success—you've heard that before.) Earnings were reinvested. And for the purposes of the study, the investors seamlessly passed their wealth on to heirs. Says Fargione, "I started out with an Excel spreadsheet and just did some simulations that ran out over time."

WINNER TAKE ALL

I'll spare you the calculus, but according to Fargione's model, by the "inexorable effect of chance," and chance alone, "a small proportion of entrepreneurs come to possess essentially all of the wealth. . . . The concentration of wealth occurs merely because some individuals are lucky by randomly receiving a series of high growth rates, and once they are ahead with exponentially growing capital, they tend to stay ahead."

According to Fargione, greater variation in rates of return hastened the concentration of wealth. Inequality grows with time. Wealth concentration continues despite periods of recession and depression. And splitting estates among heirs does not appreciably slow concentration.

In the real world, of course, some people are more skilled at making money than others. And business owners who are making a high rate of return, by operating highly successful companies, tend to continue earning high rates of return. And the rich have connections and other means to increase their wealth that most folks lack. "Those other factors would exacerbate the underlying pattern," says Fargione.

That underlying pattern is the inexorable concentration of wealth and the inevitable result— winner takes all. Says Fargione, "If you play long enough, someone will end up with all the money."

Indeed, that is what has been happening in the United States, where the top 1 percent owns about 40 percent of total wealth.

The greatest potential impact of Fargione's model is on our attitude toward accumulated wealth.

For if you are to believe Fargione's model, the result of Republicans' infatuation with conservative economics and laissez faire libertarianism is inevitable and permanent plutocracy.

That is intolerable for several reasons. Great disparity of wealth—"the development of a race of the idle rich," in Winston Churchill's words—violates our sense of justice and breeds social instability. U.S. Supreme Court Justice Louis Brandeis observed, "We can either have democracy in this country or we can have great wealth concentrated in the hands of a few, but we cannot have both."

Inequality may also be bad business in the long run. According to economists Andrew G. Berg and Jonathan D. Ostry of the International Monetary Fund, "In fact equality appears to be an important ingredient in promoting and sustaining growth. The difference between countries that can sustain rapid growth for many years or even decades and the many others that see growth spurts fade quickly may be the level of inequality."

But perhaps the greatest conceptual contribution of Fargione's model is that it relieves wealth of much of its moral baggage. Extreme wealth is not a reward for virtue. Nor is it the ill-gotten gains of collusion. It is the inexorable outcome of dumb luck, the giant cardboard check of a national lotto.

As beneficiaries of a system that paid them way out of proportion to any effort or virtue of their own, the superrich are entitled to some of their wealth, but not all.

They should give a lot of it back.

QUESTIONS

1. Why do the rich get rich in America?
2. Should the rich "give a lot of it back"?

CASES

CASE 5.1
Revolution Without Ideology
Naomi Klein

Naomi Klein is the author of No Logo *and* Fences and Windows.

An extraordinary chapter in capitalist history is being written today in Argentina. Call it revolution without ideology, or serendipitous employee ownership. Call it a reminder that property rights originate at the point of a gun. Whatever words we use cannot do justice to the remarkable events themselves. In Buenos Aires, every week brings news of a new worker occupation—a four-star hotel now run by its cleaning staff, a supermarket taken over by its clerks, a regional airline about to be turned into a cooperative by the pilots and attendants. In Trotskyist journals around the world, Argentina's occupied factories are giddily hailed as the dawn of a socialist utopia, because workers have "seized the means of production." In *The Economist*, the worker-run factories are described as a threat to the sacred principle of private property. The truth lies in between.

Take the Brukman textile factory in Buenos Aires. Brukman has been producing men's suits for 50 years, and since December it's been doing it without managers. The means of production weren't seized—they were simply picked up after being abandoned by their owners. The factory had been in decline for years, with debts to utility companies piling up. Seamstresses had seen salaries slashed from 100 pesos a week to two pesos—not enough for bus fare.

In December 2002, the workers demanded a travel allowance. The owners, pleading poverty, told them to wait at the factory while they looked for the money. "We waited until night," said Brukman worker Celia Martinez. "No one came."

Getting the keys from the doorman, workers slept at the factory that night. They've been running it ever since. They've paid the outstanding bills, attracted new clients and—without profits and management salaries to worry about—paid themselves steady salaries. All these decisions have been made by vote

From *Business Ethics*, Summer 2003, p. 6. Reprinted by permission of Bell Globemedia Interactive Inc.

in open assemblies of the 58 workers. "I don't know why the owners had such a hard time," Martinez says. "I don't know much about accounting, but for me it's easy: addition and subtraction."

Like other garment factories, Brukman is filled with women hunched over sewing machines, eyes straining and fingers flying. What makes Brukman different are the sounds. Along with the roar of machines is the Bolivian folk music, coming from a tape deck at the back of the room. And there are soft voices, as older workers show younger ones new stitches. "Before," says Martinez says, "they wouldn't let us get up from our workspaces or listen to music. But why not listen to music, to lift the spirits a bit?"

In dozens of cases like Brukman's, workers have been awarded legal expropriation by the courts—much like squatters allowed to claim ownership of occupied buildings. Lawyers of the Brukman workers argue that factory owners have violated principles of business by failing to pay employees and creditors, while collecting huge subsidies from the state. Why can't the state now insist that the indebted companies' assets continue to serve the public with steady jobs?

In Brukman's case, the argument hasn't worked. A federal judge has ordered the workers evicted, writing—in a remarkable statement—that "Life and physical integrity have no supremacy over economic interests." Property rights trump all other rights.

Those preeminent rights were enforced in April, when police carried out the judge's eviction order in the middle of the night. They turned the entire block into a military zone guarded by machine guns and attack dogs. Unable to get into the factory and complete an order for 3,000 pairs of dress trousers, the workers gathered a huge crowd of supporters and announced it was time to go back to work. At 5 p.m., 50 middle-aged seamstresses in no-nonsense haircuts, sensible shoes, and blue smocks walked up to the police fence. Someone pushed, the fence fell. The Brukman women—unarmed and arm in arm—slowly walked through.

They had taken only a few steps when the police began shooting: tear gas, water cannons, rubber bullets, then lead. Dozens were injured—for the crime of trying to sew trousers.

"They are afraid of us because we have shown that, if we can manage a factory, we can also manage a country," Martinez said. "That's why this government decided to repress us." There may also be fear of the sheer magnitude of what is underway. In the past 18 months, almost 200 factories employing more than 10,000 nationwide have been taken over and run by workers.

It's a new kind of labor movement, based not on the power to stop working (the traditional union tactic) but on the dogged determination to keep working no matter what. It's a demand driven not by dogma but by realism: In a country where 58 percent of the population is in poverty, workers are a paycheck away from having to scavenge to survive. A revolution may be underway, but it's not driven by ideology. The specter haunting Argentina's occupied factories is not communism, but indigence.

QUESTIONS

1. Did these women have a moral justification for taking over their factory?

2. Aside from the legal arguments, did the factory owners have a good moral argument for stopping the women from running the factory?

CASE 5.2
Going Down the Road
Jim Hightower

Jim Hightower was Texas Railroad commissioner and is a popular talk show host.

A couple of years ago, Susan DeMarco and I were doing our radio talk show, *Chat & Chew*, on the topic of sweatshop goods. A lady from Jackson, Mississippi, called to say that whenever she goes into a store to shop for clothing, she always tries to find a manager and asks, "Can you tell me where your made-in-the-USA section is?" Good questions. Go into any clothing department and everything in there—from overcoats to undies, hats to shoes—bears labels that shout: made in China, Bangladesh, El Salvador, the Philippines . . . everywhere but the US of A. This is not only in the Wal-Marts and Targets but also in the upscale Talbotses and Abercrombie & Fitches.

It is not that Americans are unable to make quality stuff, but the ugly fact is that corporations have abandoned US workers and communities in hot pursuit of ever-fatter profits, rushing off to the lowest-wage hellholes they can find to cut and sew their garments. Instead of paying even a minimum wage of $5.15 an hour here, they can get wage slaves at 13 cents an hour in China—then ship the goods back here without lowering the price they charge us. The corporations gleefully pocket the difference in labor costs—and claim that this is the "magic" of the new global market at work. It certainly is magic for them.

For us it is globaloney—just the same old greed. But what's a consumer to do? Even if a garment is made in the United States, some companies also run sweatshops here, with workers, usually recent immigrants, crammed into basement "contract shops," making less than minimum wage. How can we combat the scourge of sweatshops everywhere?

"Going Down the Road" *The Nation*, June 24, 2002.

Government could take action, but even under Bill Clinton, it was Nike, Gap, Ralph Lauren and other bigwigs that dominated the discussion, so Washington did nothing but dabble and dawdle. Of course, under King George the W, even discussion stopped.

SWEATX IS CHIC

The good news is that people themselves—especially children and young people—see sweatshops as a moral abomination, putting them (yet again) well ahead of officialdom. Major groups like United States Against Sweatshops, the National Labor Committee, Global Exchange and the garment union UNITE have been aggressively exposing, agitating and organizing against sweatshop labor. As this political organizing expands, an important assault on sweatshops has come from the one place the multibillion-dollar industry least expects: The marketplace itself.

SweatX is a new brand of garment in every sense of the word. The Hot Fudge Social Venture Fund, set up by Ben Cohen, the puckish entrepreneur and social activist of Ben & Jerry's ice cream fame, has invested $1 million to date in a brand-new garment business in Los Angeles. The business, called *teamX*, is based on a thoroughly radical principle: "Garment workers don't have to be exploited in order to operate a financially successful apparel factory." Imagine.

Inspired and informed by Spain's Mondragon Industrial Cooperatives (a fifty-year-old network of successful employee-owned businesses: *www. mcc.es*), *teamX* is organized as a worker-owned co-op that (1) is a union shop organized by UNITE;

(2) pays a living wage starting at $8.50 an hour; (3) provides good health care, a pension and a share of profits through co-op ownership; (4) practices the "solidarity ratio," in which no executive is paid more than eight times what the lowest-paid worker gets; and (5) intends to make a profit, grow and spread its progressive seed.

This is no touchie-feelie, froufrou social exercise but a bottom-line business initiative to show that doing well can also mean doing good. Pierre Ferrari's twenty-five years in the corporate world ranges from being VP of Coca-Cola to being director of Ben & Jerry's . . . to now being CEO of *teamX*. These entrepreneurial folks believed that there had to be a better way than sweatshops. Ferrari immersed himself in the economics of garment production. His most shocking (and enlightening) discovery was that a sweatshop worker in the United States gets about 25 cents to make a T-shirt that retails for as much as 18 bucks. Let's say that a worker grosses about $9,000 a year. Poverty. What if you doubled the wage—to 50 cents per shirt? The increase would not affect the buyer, but that worker would suddenly be getting $18,000 a year. Not exactly a fortune, but a livable wage. "Come on," says Ferrari, "they're exploiting people for a lousy 25 cents?"

BUILDING THE BRAND

This March, twenty *teamX* employee-owners, many of whom previously had been sweatshop workers, began production in Los Angeles on their company's first line of stylish shirts, shorts, caps and other casual wear, working with state-of-the-art equipment in a brand-new factory. "I've been working in clothing for twenty years, and I never had a paid holiday before this," one of the employees told the *Los Angeles Times*. A small, experienced team of managers has been assembled, drawing especially on some older managers who are not merely chasing bucks but looking to add a moral dimension to their work lives.

To build the brand identity, *teamX* is initially targeting the activist community—campuses, unions, churches, local governments, nonprofits, etc. (The T-shirts for my Rolling Thunder Downhome Democracy tour proudly bear the SweatX label.) This "market of conscience" alone has a huge and virtually untapped potential—as Ferrari discovered, for example, unions buy a lot of T-shirts for rallies, organizing drives and such. After Oprah recently featured *teamX* on her show, the phones began ringing off the hook with orders, and Ferrari now expects this upstart startup to break even by July—an investment miracle by anyone's standards.

By tapping this growing market of conscience, SweatX not only can be successful but will put the lie to the garment industry's cynical assertion that low wages are an inevitable component of globalization. We can help by talking to our local organizations, clothing store managers, school board members and others, introducing them to the SweatX possibility. . . showing with our dollars that commerce and conscience can cohabitate.

QUESTIONS

1. Are sweatshops "moral abominations"? Why?
2. What should we do about sweatshops?

CASE 5.3
The Problem with Dudley Less
Joanne B. Ciulla

Dudley Less is an account manager. Dudley started working for A. H. Miller soon after he got out of high school. He is now 55 years old. Today, Dudley's coworkers took him to dinner to celebrate 30 years of service to the company. You are Dudley's manager. At the end of the party, he asks to see you. Dudley takes you aside and says, "I've been thinking. I've been doing the same job for this company for 30 years. But, today I realized that I want a change. I'd like to take the leadership program to qualify for a more senior position in our new division. I've received above-average evaluations for many years and believe that my experience will be a real asset to this division."

You are flabbergasted. Dudley came into this business in another era. In his day, account managers took three-hour lunches and had personal ties with clients. Dudley has made some attempt to keep up with the hectic pace of the office. He is a steady worker and a pleasant guy. His work has always been quite average, but because of his personality and long tenure with the company, he has always received very good performance ratings. He never displayed any ambition to move up in the organization before, nor had you ever seen him demonstrate management potential. Now he is asking you to send him to a company leadership program that is designed for fast-track managers. The program is three months long, and the cost per employee is very high. Managers are encouraged to be selective about who they send. Your office is allowed to send only one employee a year. You were thinking of sending Carol Thompson through the program this year. You think Carol has a bright future with the company. You tell Dudley that you will consider his request.

QUESTIONS

1. What does the company owe an employee like Dudley?
2. What would you tell Dudley?

CASE 5.4
Overworked and Ready to Blow
Joanne B. Ciulla

You have been working at the Regent Corporation for 15 years. Because of a recent downsizing, your job has become extremely hectic. You now do a job that had been done by three employees. You've been working late and on weekends. Recently you had to cancel a much-needed vacation because you had to work. You are afraid to raise any questions about overtime because your manager keeps telling you that the company values committed and loyal employees.

All your family members have suffered from your heavy work schedule. You missed your daughter's Christmas play and have been unable to take a few hours off to watch your son's soccer games. When you get home at night, you are exhausted, but there is still dinner to make, clothes to wash, and the children's homework to check. Your husband is also tired when he comes home, and because he often arrives home late, he is not able to help much around the house. The two of you have had numerous fights over who should do what. These fights have strained your marriage and upset your children. Lately, your son has been misbehaving in school. You feel like your life is spinning out of control and you are ready to explode.

Today you went to your manager and explained to him that you needed two days off. You told him about the stress that you were under at home and pointed out how helpful it would be to take Thursday and a Friday off as vacation leave. This would allow you time to catch up on work at home and time to go and talk to your son's teacher.

Your manager said he understood your problem, but that your request was not very professional. He said, "Professionals don't ask for time off to catch up on their housework. We'd all like to have time off to do things at home. You don't see any of the guys in this office coming in to ask for time off to cut the grass or wash the car. This is a business. If you want to keep up with your housework, don't work—stay at home. When things slow down around here next month, you can take some vacation days." You left his office feeling angry and humiliated.

QUESTIONS

1. What do loyalty and commitment mean to the manager in this case? What should the terms mean to a business from an ethical point of view?

2. Would it have been wiser for you simply to call in sick on Thursday and Friday?

CASE 5.5
Poverty Area Plants
Rogene A. Buchholz

Paperboard Company did not have a contributions program and was being pressured by other companies in the city to help make a better community by contributing to some aspect of community welfare. The company was being accused of being a free rider and benefiting from other companies' concern about city problems. Company management wanted to be a responsible company, but it doubted the wisdom of establishing a contributions program. The company wanted to do something different.

Paperboard had heard of Control Data's program to build plants in disadvantaged areas to employ local people and thus help the area to establish a sound economic base. The management of the company wondered if this strategy would work well for Paper-board and if it could make a better contribution to the community in this manner. Its manufacturing process lent itself to small plants that could make specialized products. The company also did not need many highly skilled employees to operate a typical plant.

Rogene A. Buchholz, *Business Environment and Public Policy: Implications for Management*, 5th ed. (Englewood Cliffs, NJ: Prentice Hall, 1995), p. 301.

The company was also aware that the federal government was considering a bill to create enterprise zones in disadvantaged areas to encourage companies to locate there. Due to budgetary considerations, however, political experts were saying that the bill had little chance of passage during the current congressional session. Paperboard was thus wondering whether to wait and see if this bill could be salvaged, or whether to go ahead on its own and plan to build plants in disadvantaged areas of the community.

QUESTIONS

1. What factors should the company consider in building plants in disadvantaged areas? What problems are likely to be encountered? Will small plants of this nature really make much of an impact on disadvantaged areas of communities?

2. Should the company lobby for passage of federal legislation to establish enterprise zones? Or should it begin to work at the state level for passage of similar legislation? Which would be the most socially responsible course of action?

CASE 5.6

Poverty in America

William H. Shaw and Vincent Barry

In recent years the U.S. Census Bureau has brought some glad tidings: The median income of American households has been increasing. Meanwhile, the number of families with incomes below the poverty line—defined as $17,960 for a family of four—has declined, and overall the poverty rate has fallen to 11.3 percent, about what it had been back in the 1970s. Still, despite the long economic boom of the 1990s, 32.3 million Americans continue to live in poverty, a third of them children. That's more than one out of every nine people. Moreover, the average adult American has a 60 percent chance of living at least one year below the poverty line and a 33 percent chance of experiencing dire poverty.

Most people think that those described as "poor" in the United States are pretty well off by world standards. The truth is, in life expectancy twenty-year-old U.S. males rank thirty-sixth among the world's nations, and twenty-year-old U.S. females rank twenty-first. Our infant mortality rate is worse than that in twenty-one other Western nations. Moreover, millions of Americans endure hunger. According to the U.S. Department of Agriculture, 31 million Americans lack "food security," and in 3 million American households one or more persons go hungry during the year. Figures from the Food Research and Action Center are even more alarming; it reports that 5 million children under age twelve go hungry each month. In addition, one out of every four Americans lives in substandard housing, and in most cities one sees people roaming the streets in tattered clothing, picking their food out of garbage cans. Homeless people—many of them former mental patients released from state hospitals, others jobless individuals and families unable to afford housing—live in abandoned cars and shacks or simply sleep in doorways and on subway grates. Precise figures are impossible to obtain. One recent

From William H. Shaw and Vincent Barry, *Moral Issues in Business*, 9th ed. (Belmont, CA: Wadsworth, 2004), pp. 127–129. Reprinted by permission of the editors.

survey found 280,000 people homeless, but other experts estimate that 600,000–700,000 Americans are homeless on any given night and that 3 to 12 million Americans are homeless sometime during the year.

People in different walks of life and in different circumstances experience poverty. Many others live on the edge of poverty and are in continual danger of falling into it through illness, job loss, or other misfortune. In the United States today, the "working poor"—that is, those who work full time, year around, while earning an income below the poverty line—number 2.8 million. They represent a higher percentage of the workforce than in the 1970s as well-paid unionized manufacturing jobs have been replaced by nonunion service jobs. In 1997, the minimum wage was increased to $5.15 per hour, but it is still less in real terms than it was in 1969. Someone working forty hours a week, every week, for that wage cannot raise his or her family out of poverty. In fact, according to a housing advocacy group, a minimum-wage earner can't afford to rent a two-bedroom home anywhere in the United States.

Many poor people are unable to work and depend on outside assistance. Recent legislative efforts to reform the welfare system rely on certain myths about welfare recipients. Investigation shows, for instance, that most people do not stay on the welfare rolls for years. They move on and off, and less than 1 percent remain on welfare for ten years. Contrary to popular mythology, the majority of those who receive welfare are young children whose mothers must remain at home. They are not able-bodied adults who are unwilling to work. Nor do welfare mothers differ from non-welfare mothers in the number of children they have. About 70 percent of welfare families have only one or two children, and there is little financial incentive to have more. Half of the families who receive welfare include an adult who works full or part time, and research consistently demonstrates that poor people have the same strong desire to work that the rest of the population does. Two-thirds of the mothers on welfare did not grow up in families that received welfare—contrary to the stereotype of intergenerational welfare dependency—and only 7.6 percent of them are under eighteen and unmarried.

There has never been a way to live well on welfare. Under the old system of AFDC (Aid to Families with Dependent Children), by 1996 welfare benefits had fallen, in real terms, to 51 percent of what they had been in 1971. With annual cash allowances for a family on AFDC ranging from $1,416 in Mississippi to $6,780 in New York, even in the most generous states' stipends were never enough to allow a family to escape from poverty. In 1996 Congress replaced AFDC with TANF (Temporary Assistance to Needy Families). Under the new system, the entitlement of poor people to support has been replaced by block grants to the states to run their own welfare programs. The grants are limited to a certain amount of money; if they run out, the states are not required to make additional expenditures. Welfare recipients are required to work for pay or to enroll in training programs, and financial support is limited to a lifetime maximum of five years. This shift in policy has been controversial. Since the TANF system began, the number of people receiving welfare benefits has declined, but experts disagree about the reasons: Is it a growing economy offering more opportunities, the success of the new approach in encouraging welfare recipients to make themselves employable, or simply people who are not able to take care of themselves being denied support?

One thing that is clear is the large number of women living in poverty. This includes women with inadequate income following divorce, widowhood, or retirement, as well as women raising children alone. Wage discrimination against women is one factor. Women who work full time, year round earn only about two-thirds of what men earn. And millions of women hold full-time jobs that pay wages near or below the poverty line.

Women's responsibilities for child rearing are another important factor. Despite many changes in recent years, women continue to have primary responsibility in this area. When marriages break up, mothers typically take custody and bear the major financial burden. Fewer than half the women raising children alone are awarded child support, and fewer than half of those entitled to it receive the full amount. Of family households headed by women, 52 percent have incomes below $25,000 and 19.7 percent have incomes below $10,000.

Most poor people in our nation—about two-thirds of them—are white, but blacks are about three times more likely to be poor. Whereas fewer than one out of every ten white Americans is poor, more than one of every five African Americans and Hispanics are below the poverty line. Many members of the minority communities have succeeded in moving up the economic ladder, but the overall picture is bleak. African-American family income, for instance, is only 62 percent that of white family income.

QUESTIONS

1. Does the existence of poverty imply that our socioeconomic system is unjust? Does the concentration of poverty in certain groups make it more unjust than it would be otherwise?

2. Surveys show that Americans, even poor Americans, favor individualistic explanations of poverty (such as lack of effort or ability, poor morals, poor work skills) over structural explanations (such as inadequate schooling, low wages, lack of jobs), whereas Europeans favor structural explanations of poverty over individualistic explanations. What are the causes of poverty? How is one's answer to this question likely to affect one's view of the justice or injustice of poverty?

CASE 5.7
Burger Beefs
William H. Shaw and Vincent Barry

When seventeen-year-old Wendy Hamburger (her real name) applied for a summer job at a Wendy's Old Fashioned Hamburgers outlet near her Barrington, Illinois, home, she hoped to earn some money for college. But after working there for only three months, she quit when a manager threatened to fire her if she refused to work an extra shift on a holiday.

Wendy wasn't too upset about losing her job. "It seemed like the job cost me more than I made," she says. She does concede, however, that Wendy's International did pay her a little attention during her brief connection with the company. It used her to get a lot of free publicity in Chicago-area newspapers, and its president and founder, R. David Thomas, mailed her an autographed photograph of himself, which presumably she didn't have to return when she quit.

Actually, there's nothing atypical about Wendy's experience. Rock-bottom pay, unpleasant working conditions, and bossy bosses—all are familiar to the millions of teenage employees in the fast-food industry. Little wonder the average teenage worker quits in disgust within four months of being hired.

Such rapid turnover would disembowel most businesses. Not so for those that peddle billions of burgers, fries, and shakes a year. For them, frequent turnover is the rank fodder for their multimillion-dollar operations, at least according to critics. Instead of relying upon a small, stable workforce of well-paid and well-trained employees, the fast-food industry seeks out part-time, unskilled workers who are willing to accept low pay. Teenagers, of course, fit this bill perfectly. These days the nation's approximately 3.5 million fast-food workers are the largest group of minimum-wage earners in the country—only migrant farm workers consistently earn a lower hourly wage—and two-thirds of them are less than twenty years old.

From William H. Shaw and Vincent Barry, *Moral Issues in Business*, 9th ed. (Belmont, CA: Wadsworth, 2004), pp. 298–299. Reprinted by permission of the editors.

"The whole system is designed to have turnover," says Robert Harbrant, secretary-treasurer for the AFL-CIO Food and Beverage Trades Department in Washington, D.C. That way the industry averts pay increases and thwarts union efforts to organize workers. Moreover, the fast-food chains work hard at making their machines and operating systems as foolproof as possible. That way their jobs require no skills, and any individual worker can be quickly replaced.

Industry executives deny such nefarious motives. They point out, correctly, that for most youngsters a fast-food job is their first work experience. Such unseasoned workers usually are undisciplined and unreliable. No sooner are they trained, say fast-food executives, than they up and leave.

Harlow E. White, president of Systems for Human Resources, Inc., thinks otherwise. He publicly wonders whether the 300 percent annual turnover of fast-food workers is the cause or effect of industry operations. He suspects that "the industry has managed to manufacture a self-fulfilling prophecy: 'We're going to have turnover. And by God, we do.'" While admitting that the teenage part-timer is crucial to fast-food success, industry officials insist that they do not purposely encourage turnover. "Turnover costs us money," asserts a spokesperson for Burger King, even while conceding that it takes little time to train a new worker.

Despite the industry's declared good intentions, discontent among fast-food workers is widespread. That's not surprising given that the vast majority of them are paid an hourly wage, provided no benefits, and scheduled to work only as needed. If the restaurant's busy, they're kept longer than usual. If business is slow, they're sent home early. For example, one teenage part-timer at a New York McDonald's shop says management there routinely has workers appear up to an hour ahead of work time and then "wait in the back room and punch in later when they need you." (A McDonald's official insists that this is an isolated case, that McDonald's does not condone such a policy.) And a teenage waitress in an Atlanta Steak n' Shake complains that she is scheduled for a two-hour workday, although it takes her that much time to make a round-trip from home to work. (A company official says this is a management problem, that the policy of Steak n' Shake is to pay workers for a minimum of three hours.)

Some believe that the companies' insistence that such problems lie with local management, not the home office, is buck passing. Richard Gilber, a compliance officer in the U.S. Labor Department's wage and hour division, places the blame squarely on the store-manager training programs conducted by the home offices. He says, "We find in many cases that the 20-year-old managers are sales oriented and cleanliness oriented. But they aren't taught much about employee relations. And the Wage Hour Law is just another three pages in the operating manual."

Wendy Hamburger agrees. "I went through three managers in the short time I was at Wendy's," she recalls. "They needed managers so badly they hired anyone. They got a lot of young guys in there who think they're Mr. Macho and want to exercise their power. They don't know anything."

A Burger King official conceded that much of the criticism is warranted. The industry, he says, has put people in their early twenties in charge of a million-dollar restaurant and sometimes forty employees under age eighteen and expects them to function like professionals. The results are often less than ideal. "You can train someone to fix a piece of equipment a lot easier than you can to deal with people," he says.

To be sure, a manager's job is no bowl of cherries. Ask the young woman who is paid not much more than minimum wage to run a McDonald's outlet that grosses $750,000 annually. "They don't pay managers enough," she complains. "I'm on my feet from 6 A.M. to 6 P.M. Often I don't have time to eat all day. On days off I come in a couple of hours or call in to check on my assistant managers. And I have to take work home, like weekly scheduling."

Low pay is the chronic complaint of fast-food employees. Most chains come under minimum-wage and overtime-pay laws, but they don't always abide by them. Although enforcement of the laws is often lax, fast-food franchises across the country have been found guilty of underpaying their workers and not keeping proper wage reports. In 1997, for example, a Washington State jury found that Taco Bell had systematically coerced employees into working off the clock in order to avoid paying them overtime. In addition, the industry routinely ignores child-labor laws that restrict the hours that young teenagers can work. A few years ago the Labor Department fined Burger King $500,000—the largest child-labor penalty in history—for letting fourteen- and fifteen-year-olds work late into the night on school nights.

Over at Starbucks Coffee, things are a little different. In contrast to the giant fast-food chains, Starbucks recently became the first U.S. company to give its part-time, hourly employees full health care benefits and stock options—even though, like the burger chains, part-time workers make up most of the company's workforce. "It's not viewed as a professional job in America to work behind a counter," says the owner of Starbucks, Howard Schultz. "We don't believe that. We want to provide our people with dignity and self-esteem, and we can't do that with lip service. So we offer tangible benefits."

QUESTIONS

1. Do you think the fast-food industry dislikes turnover? Do you think it encourages turnover?

2. Are wages in the fast-food industry fair? Does the industry exploit teenage workers? Compare the attitude of Starbucks to its workers with that of the fast-food industry.

3. How would you evaluate personnel procedures and working conditions in the fast-food industry? Are they reasonable? Could they be improved?

CASE 5.8
Nike's Suppliers in Vietnam
Sasha Lyutse

Following allegations of worker abuse, an investigation was launched in 1998 of Nike practices in subcontracted factories in Vietnam. This investigation created a public relations problem for the American manufacturer of athletic apparel. The report found that by not directly running the factories where its products were being made, Nike had little direct control over how employees were treated.

The report focused on Nike subcontracted factories in and around Ho Chi Minh City. It found local supervisors using abusive and humiliating practices to punish Vietnamese workers. Nike insisted that it did not tolerate abuse and required its manufacturers to take "immediate and effective measures to deal with it." A Nike training manager, the company said, works with subcontractors on sexual harassment, physical and verbal abuse, as well as on listening skills. The report found that Nike had "a fine code of conduct," but that its local contractors often violated it.

In 1998 Nike employees at the Sam Yang factory, just outside Ho Chi Minh City, were paid $1.84 a day. Their average monthly salary was $48—slightly better than Vietnam's $45 minimum wage

This case was written by Sasha Lyutse. Basic sources were: "*The Living Wage Project to Brief Members of Congress on Nike Labor Abuses*," PR Newswire Association, Inc., Copyright 2001, April 3, 2001; "*Labor-rights Group: Nike, Knight not Living up to 1998 Promises*," The Associated Press State & Local Wire, May 16, 2001; and "*Nike battles Labour Charges U.S. Firm makes Changes after Alleged Worker Abuses in Vietnam*," Toronto Star Newspapers, Ltd., Copyright 1998, April 2, 1998.

for this region. With this salary, Nike workers could meet needs for food and shelter, but little else. In a 1998 survey, however, Nike suppliers were found to be paying competitive wages—no worse and no better than those paid by other foreign shoemakers.

Phillip Knight, founder of Nike's $9 billion sports-apparel empire, signs sports superstars to multimillion dollar contracts to advertise Nike sneakers that sometimes sell for $100 or more on the American market. A pair of Nike sneakers is unattainable for a worker at the Sam Yang factory, who works six days a week and makes roughly $600 a year, half the average income in Ho Chi Minh City, but about four times the annual earnings in more remote rural regions of Vietnam.

In 1999 Nike responded to mounting pressures by creating a labor monitoring department and translated its code of conduct into 11 languages so that more workers could read it. At the Sam Yang factory the local owners issued a 10-point "action plan" based on many of the 1998 report's recommendations. They held a union election, signed a labor contract with workers, and improved working conditions. The factory also got a new manager, increased trainees' wages and cut overtime. Most workers got a 5 percent raise, which came to about 8 cents more a day.

However, a 2001 report by the Global Alliance, an initiative sponsored by Nike in response to persistent criticism, documented proof of continued abusive labor practices in Southeast Asia, including physical, verbal and sexual abuse. According to the report, 96 percent of workers stated that they did not make enough money to meet their basic needs.

In its early days, before costs escalated and orders shifted to lowercost suppliers in Taiwan and South Korea, Nike imported all of its shoes from Japan. Soon, even Taiwan and South Korea became expensive, and suppliers moved their factories to China and Indonesia. In its global search for low-cost labor, Nike found Vietnam. By 1998, one out of every 10 pairs of Nike shoes came from subcontractors in Vietnam.

Vietnam is one of Southeast Asia's poorest countries. It has an official rural unemployment of about 27 percent in some regions. It aggressively seeks foreign investment to create jobs and bring manufacturing expertise. However, unlike those countries that turn a blind eye to worker abuses by overseas employers, Vietnam pays close attention to foreign investors' behavior and has some of the region's toughest laws aimed at protecting workers; it ensures a minimum wage, sets overtime limits, permits strikes, etc.

At the same time, Vietnamese government officials sometimes appear to have divided priorities. They feel that they are duty-bound to defend workers (which union leaders say is their primary responsibility), but they also feel that they must accommodate investment planners who want trade unions to back off and not scare away desperately needed foreign investments.

In 1998 Nike employed more workers than any other foreign business in Vietnam (through its five Nike-aligned shoe factories). At the time, shipments of Nike shoes accounted for 5 percent of Vietnam's total exports. If Nike were to pull out of Vietnam, 35,000 Vietnamese would be out of work.

QUESTIONS

1. Is an average monthly salary of $48 morally indefensible, or is such a judgment relative to the expectations of a given society?

2. Are there issues of economic justice in this case, or are prices always fair when set in competitive markets?

3. If Nike were to close its factories and leave Vietnam for a country with a lower minimum wage, would this decision be morally indefensible?

CASE 5.9
Bad Charity? (All I Got Was This Lousy T-Shirt!)
Nick Wadhams

In the history of foreign aid, it looked pretty harmless: A young Florida businessman decided to collect a million shirts and send them to poor people in Africa. Jason Sadler just wanted to help. He thought he'd start with all the leftover T-shirts from his advertising company, I Wear Your Shirt. But judging by the response Sadler got from a group of foreign aid bloggers, you'd think he wanted to toss squirrels into wood chippers or steal lunch boxes from fourth-graders.

"I have thick skin, I don't mind, but it's just the way they responded—it was just, 'You're an idiot, here's another stupid idea, I hope this fails,'" Sadler, 27, tells TIME. "It really was offensive because all I'm trying to do is trying to make something good happen and motivate people to get off their butts, get off the couch and do something to help."

Little did Sadler know he had stumbled into a debate that is raging in the aid world about the best and worst ways to deliver charity, or whether to give at all. He crashed up against a rather simple theory that returned to prominence after aid failures following the 2004 Asian tsunami and 2010 Haiti earthquake: Wanting to do something to help is no excuse for not knowing the consequences of what you're doing.

Sadler has never visited Africa or worked on a foreign aid project. To his critics, his pitch seemed naive with its exhortation, "Share the wealth, share your shirts—we're going to change the world." Millions of Africans who have no trouble getting shirts, and who never asked Sadler for a handout, might object to the idea that giving them more clothes will change the world. Stung from watching people donate old, useless stuff after the tsunami and earthquake, aid workers bristled. "I'm sorry to be so unkind to someone who has good intentions, but you

don't get a get-home-free card just for having good intentions. You have to do things that make sense," says William Easterly, an author and New York University economics professor who is a leading critic of bad aid. "If a surgeon is about to operate on me, I'm not all that interested in whether he has good intentions. I hope he doesn't have evil intentions, but I'm much more interested in whether he knows what he's doing. People have a double standard about aid."

But why gang up on a guy who just wants to help clothe people in Africa? First, because it's not that hard to get shirts in Africa. Flooding the market with free goods could bankrupt the people who already sell them. Donating clothing is a sensitive topic in Africa because many countries' textile industries collapsed under the weight of secondhand-clothing imports that were introduced in the 1970s and '80s. "First you have destroyed these villages' ability to be industrious and produce cotton products, and then you're saying, 'Can I give you a T-shirt?' and celebrating about it?" says James Shikwati, director of the Nairobi-based Inter Region Economic Network, a think tank. "It's really like offering poison coated with sugar."

People looking to help the poor often think so-called goods-in-kind donations are a way to help, Easterly says. They're certainly an easy way to inspire potential donors. There was the boy in Grand Rapids, Michigan, who collected 10,000 teddy bears for Haiti's earthquake victims. Soles4Souls.com is sending shoes. The list goes on: old soap from hotel rooms, underwear, baby formula, even Spam (the pork product, not junk e-mail). "Years—decades— of calm, reasoned discussion do not seem to have worked," an aid worker who blogs under the name Tales from the Hood told TIME by e-mail. "People are still collecting shoes, socks, underwear . . .

T-shirts . . . somehow under the delusion that it is helpful. Sometimes loud shouting down is the only thing that gets heard." Then there's the matter of cost. Money spent shipping teddy bears to kids might be better spent providing for more pressing needs. The same goes for T-shirts.

Sadler says he never planned to dump a million shirts on the market at once. With his two partners, HELP International and WaterIsLife.com, he wanted to send a few thousand shirts at a time to orphanages in Kenya and Uganda that asked for them. Widows would sell the shirts and make a little money. "We're looking at bringing in several thousand shirts and it being a yearlong process of distribution," says Ken Surritte, founder of WaterIsLife.com. "The goal is not to hurt the economy in these areas but to be an asset and to be a blessing to these people that otherwise wouldn't have jobs."

Sadler has proven flexible: he says he is listening to his critics and no longer plans to send the shirts to Africa. He says he will find another way to use the T-shirts he collects, possibly for disaster relief, giving them to homeless shelters or using them to create other goods. He says any profits would then "go back to the company's goal of helping foster sustainability." And judging by the response on the Web, he's

getting a lot of donations. "I've since listened to a lot of these people," he says. "I want to change this thing into something that's better, that's more helpful and that listens to the people that have the experience that I don't have."

There are some critics who argue that all foreign aid—whether from individuals or nonprofits or governments—is keeping Africa back. A vast body of research shows that foreign aid has done little to spur economic growth in Africa—and may have actually slowed it down. "The long-term solution is not aid. It may seem cruel that aid should stop, but really it should," says Rasna Warah, a Kenyan newspaper columnist and editor of the anthology *Missionaries, Mercenaries and Misfits*, a call to arms against aid. "Africa is the greatest dumping ground on the planet. Everything is dumped here. The sad part is that African governments don't say no—in fact, they say, 'Please send us more.' They're abdicating responsibility for their own citizens."

QUESTIONS

1. Was Sadler's idea bad? Why?
2. What might have been a better allocation of resources?

CHAPTER QUESTIONS

1. Is capitalism just? Why should we even ask the question? Is the fairest society produced by capitalism? Is there even a tension between capitalism and fairness?

2. We are the wealthiest society the world has even seen. Does wealth create responsibilities? If so, how should these responsibilities be distributed or shared?

6

Is "The Social Responsibility of Business . . . to Increase Its Profits"?

Social Responsibility and Stakeholder Theory

Introduction

Business ethics has been around a long time, in fact, as long as there has been business in the world. The ancient Greeks were concerned about it, although it must be admitted that they were not particularly sympathetic to business, which was considered a grubby and parasitic way to make a living. (The much better way to make one's fortune was to inherit it or, even better, to loot it from a conquered adversary.) The early Romans, who were much more sympathetic to business, worried at some length about fair trade practices. Cicero, for example, expressed a contemporary concern about whether someone who was selling a house or a horse was obliged to tell the potential buyer of its existing flaws and defects. (The familiar warning, caveat emptor—"buyer beware"—is in Latin, after all.) And throughout the ages, the main concern of business ethics has remained the lure of profit as opposed to larger social responsibilities, one's loyalty to one's country, for instance, or the local consequences of a business deal.

That question, what is now called (since the nineteenth century) "the profit motive" as opposed to broader social responsibilities, including questions of fairness as well as patriotism and consequences, still occupies a large part of business ethics. Civic-minded corporate executives worry about how they can maximize the bottom line without breaking the rules of their society and without betraying their own integrity. Small businesses fight to keep up with the competition while keeping in mind their obligations to their customers and the local community. You, no doubt, want the best job you can get, but there are all sorts of lines you do not want to cross—breaking the law, acting contrary to your religious beliefs, violating your own personal morality, turning your friends and neighbors against you. So the question is, what are your social responsibilities, and how do they tie into your own sense of personal worth and morality? How much can you serve and fulfill what you take to be your social responsibilities (responsibilities to your family, your friends, your neighbors, your religious group, your country, the world at large) and at the same time make the kind of living that you would like to make?

In the past 30 years, business ethics has gotten a great deal of mileage out of a polemic that Nobel prize-winning economist Milton Friedman published in the *New York Times Magazine* (September 1971). Friedman took on the rising chorus of demands that businesses, now the wealthiest and most powerful segment of society, have a greater sense of social responsibility. (That demand can be traced back to a Medieval notion, noblesse oblige, the obligation of the most powerful and most privileged members of society—whether the Church and the clergy or the army and its officers or the aristocracy and its nobles—to use some of their wealth and power to benefit the whole society.) But Friedman said *no*, the demand is misplaced, and business is not in a position to do more than it is created to do. Business is not social work, although a business is, of course, a valuable source of jobs and livelihoods. Business is not an educator, except, of course, in business. Business is not an arbiter of artistic taste, although what it sells may well be in better or worse taste. The business of business is, in short, business. That is what it can do well, and the benefits of a prosperous business community, Friedman says, will spill over into benefits for the whole society. (This part, the reader will note, comes directly from Adam Smith and his classic treatise on the benefits of the free market system.) But business does not—and *should not*—aim at this result. It will follow naturally, not by design.

What Friedman actually wrote—the now-famous title of his piece—was that "The Social Responsibility of Business Is to Increase Its Profits." He was immediately pounced upon by business ethicists—and by a great many businessmen—who insisted that his pronouncements were themselves irresponsible and misleading, as well as insulting to the many business leaders, managers, and employees who took their sense of social responsibility very seriously, and as business leaders, managers, and employees, not just as citizens. The question was raised whether business would have the benign effects that Friedman predicted if everyone in business did, in fact, follow his prescription and think of nothing but profits. It was pointed out that businesses do, in fact, have and recognize any number of other responsibilities and obligations, for example, to their employees and to their customers. Friedman responded, predictably enough, that, of course, they had to treat their employees decently, or the employees would quit their jobs and work for somebody else and, of course, that they had to treat their customers well, or the customers would buy from someone else. In other words, the free market would take care of such things. The owners of a business or the leaders of a corporation know full well that to be profitable, they need to treat their employees and their customers well, and therefore they can and should just focus on profitability. The market will take care of the rest.

Needless to say, the debate did not stop there. The question became whether the obligation of a corporation to its stockholders was indeed its primary obligation or rather just one of many obligations to its *stakeholders*, that is, all those who are effected by the actions of a company, whether they had any market power or not. The question turned to the nature of profits and how they could be distinguished, nonarbitrarily, from income and assets in general. And the question remained just what was meant by that red-button phrase, "social responsibility." Just what is the social responsibility of a business? Is it just to pay its debts and make a good-quality (or, at least, a not unexpectedly dangerous) product? Is it to clean up any mess it makes, whether pollution or increased traffic around a site? Is it to help educate the people it will or, at least, may employ? Is it to solve such social problems as poverty and racial tension? Is it to enrich the society through its support of the arts and various cultural events and institutions? Of course, we recognize that many corporations do all these things, but then the question turns to the *motive* for doing so. Friedmanites will insist that companies have found that it is good publicity and good public relations to be associated with such projects. Anti-Friedmanites will say that this shows that corporations (or their leaders) do have a conscience and a sense of social responsibility that goes beyond their insistence on profitability. And that is where the question still stands today.

Following Friedman's piece is a rebuttal by University of Southern California professor Christopher D. Stone from his book *Where the Law Ends*. Of course, it doesn't make any sense to say that corporations have social responsibilities if it doesn't make sense to say that they have any responsibilities at all, that is, if they are not agents who can be praised or blamed for their actions, a widespread view in the business community. But Peter A. French, in "Corporate Moral Agency," takes issue with this notion and claims that corporations are agents in the appropriate sense and can indeed be praised or blamed for their actions. Then R. Edward Freeman advances the now-standard conception of a stakeholder (instead of just talking about stockholders) in his now-classic "A Stakeholder Theory of the Modern Corporation." Kenneth J. Arrow then approaches the social responsibility question from a different angle, that of economic efficiency," in his "Social Responsibility and Economic Efficiency." Richard Parker asks whether the very notion of corporate social responsibility is in crisis, and Alexei Marcoux raises an attack on stakeholder theory.

Milton Friedman

The Social Responsibility of Business Is to Increase Its Profits

Milton Friedman wrote this seminal piece in the *New York Times Magazine* (as elsewhere). It continues to attract considerable controversy.

When I hear businessmen speak eloquently about the "social responsibilities of business in a free-enterprise system," I am reminded of the wonderful line about the Frenchman who discovered at the age of 70 that he had been speaking prose all his life. The businessmen believe that they are defending free enterprise when they declaim that business is not concerned "merely" with profit but also with promoting desirable "social" ends; that business has a "social conscience" and takes seriously its responsibilities

for providing employment, eliminating discrimination, avoiding pollution and whatever else may be the catchwords of the contemporary crop of reformers. In fact they are—or would be if they or anyone else took them seriously—preaching pure and unadulterated socialism. Businessmen who talk this way are unwitting puppets of the intellectual forces that have been undermining the basis of a free society these past decades.

The discussion of the "social responsibilities of business" are notable for their analytical looseness and lack of rigor. What does it mean to say that "business" has responsibilities? Only people can have responsibilities. A corporation is an artificial person and in this sense may have artificial responsibilities, but "business" as a whole cannot be said to have responsibilities, even in this vague sense. The first step toward clarity to examining the doctrine of the social responsibility of business is to ask precisely what it implies for whom.

Presumably, the individuals who are to be responsible are businessmen, which means individual proprietors or corporate executives. Most of the discussion of social responsibility is directed at corporations, so in what follows I shall mostly neglect the individual proprietors and speak of corporate executives.

In a free-enterprise, private-property system, a corporate executive is an employee of the owners of the business. He has direct responsibility to his employers. That responsibility is to conduct the business in accordance with their desires, which generally will be to make as much money as possible while conforming to the basic rules of the society, both those embodied in law and those embodied in ethical custom. Of course, in some cases his employers may have a different objective. A group of persons might establish a corporation for an eleemosynary purpose—for example, a hospital or a school. The manager of such a corporation will not have money profit as his objectives but the rendering of certain services.

In either case, the key point is that, in his capacity as a corporate executive, the manager is the agent of the individuals who own the corporation or establish the eleemosynary institution, and his primary responsibility is to them.

Needless to say, this does not mean that it is easy to judge how well he is performing his task. But at least the criterion of performance is straightforward, and the persons among whom a voluntary contractual arrangement exists are clearly defined.

Of course, the corporate executive is also a person in his own right. As a person, he may have many other responsibilities that he recognizes or assumes voluntarily—to his family, his conscience, his feelings of charity, his church, his clubs, his city, his country. He may feel impelled by these responsibilities to devote part of his income to causes he regards as worthy, to refuse to work for particular corporations, even to leave his job, for example, to join his country's armed forces. If we wish, we may refer to some of these responsibilities as "social responsibilities." But in these respects he is acting as a principal, not an agent; he is spending his own money or time or energy, not the money of his employers or the time or energy he has contracted to devote to their purposes. If these are "social responsibilities," they are the social responsibilities of individuals, not of business.

What does it mean to say that the corporate executive has a "social responsibility" in his capacity as businessman? If this statement is not pure rhetoric, it must mean that he is to act in some way that is not in the interest of his employers. For example, that he is to refrain from increasing the price of the product in order to contribute to the social objective of preventing inflation, even though a price increase would be in the best interests of the corporation. Or that he is to make expenditures on reducing pollution beyond the amount that is in the best interests of the corporation or that is required by law in order to contribute to the social objective of improving the environment. Or that, at the expense of corporate profits, he is to hire "hardcore" unemployed instead of better qualified available workmen to contribute to the social objective of reducing poverty.

In each of these cases, the corporate executive would be spending someone else's money for a general social interest. Insofar as his actions in accord with his "social responsibility" reduce returns to stockholders, he is spending their money. Insofar as his actions raise the price to customers, he is spending the customers' money. Insofar as his actions lower the wages of some employees, he is spending their money.

The stockholders or the customers or the employees could separately spend their own money on the particular action if they wished to do so. The executive is exercising a distinct "social responsibility," rather than serving as an agent of the stockholders or the customers or the employees, only if he spends the money in a different way than they would have spent it.

But if he does this, he is in effect imposing taxes, on the one hand, and deciding how the tax proceeds shall be spent, on the other.

This process raises political questions on two levels: principle and consequences. On the level of political principle, the imposition of taxes and the expenditure of tax proceeds are governmental functions. We have established elaborate constitutional, parliamentary and judicial provisions to control these functions, to assure that taxes are imposed so far as possible in accordance with the preferences and desires of the public—after all, "taxation without representation" was one of the battle cries of the American Revolution. We have a system of checks and balances to separate the legislative function of imposing taxes and enacting expenditures from the executive function of collecting taxes and administering expenditure programs and from the judicial function of mediating disputes and interpreting the law.

Here the businessman—self-selected or appointed directly or indirectly by stockholders—is to be simultaneously legislator, executive and jurist. He is to decide whom to tax by how much and for what purpose, and he is to spend the proceeds—all this guided only by general exhortations from on high to restrain inflation, improve the environment, fight poverty and so on and on.

The whole justification for permitting the corporate executive to be selected by the stockholders is that the executive is an agent serving the interests of his principal. This justification disappears when the corporate executive imposes taxes and spends the proceeds for "social" purposes. He becomes in effect a public employee, a civil servant, even though he remains in name an employee of a private enterprise. On grounds of political principle, it is intolerable that such civil servants—insofar as their actions in the name of social responsibility are real and not just window-dressing—should be selected as they are now. If they are to be civil servants, then they must be elected through a political process. If they are to impose taxes and make expenditures to foster "social" objectives, then political machinery must be set up to make the assessment of taxes and to determine through a political process the objectives to be served.

This is the basic reason why the doctrine of "social responsibility" involves the acceptance of the socialist view that political mechanisms, not market mechanisms, are the appropriate way to determine the allocation of scarce resources to alternative uses.

On the grounds of consequences, can the corporate executive in fact discharge his alleged "social responsibilities"? On the one hand, suppose he could get away with spending the stockholders' or customers' or employees' money. How is he to know how to spend it? He is told that he must contribute to fighting inflation. How is he to know what action of his will contribute to that end? He is presumably an expert in running his company—in producing a product or selling it or financing it. But nothing about his selection makes him an expert on inflation. Will his holding down the price of his product reduce inflationary pressure? Or, by leaving more spending power in the hands of his customers, simply divert it elsewhere? Or, by forcing him to produce less because of the lower price, will it simply contribute to shortages? Even if he could answer these questions, how much cost is he justified in imposing on his stockholders, customers and employees for this social purpose? What is his appropriate share and what is the appropriate share of others?

And, whether he wants to or not, can he get away with spending his stockholders', customers' or employees' money? Will not the stockholders fire him? (Either the present ones or those who take over when his actions in the name of social responsibility have reduced the corporation's profits and the price of its stock.) His customers and his employees can desert him for other producers and employers less scrupulous in exercising their social responsibilities.

This facet of "social responsibility" doctrine is brought into sharp relief when the doctrine is used to justify wage restraint by trade unions. The conflict of interest is naked and clear when union officials are asked to subordinate the interest of their members to some more general purpose. If the union officials try to enforce wage restraint, the consequence is likely to be wildcat strikes, rank-and-file revolts and the emergence of strong competitors for their jobs. We thus have the ironic phenomenon that union leaders—at least in the U.S.—have objected to Government interference with the market far more consistently and courageously than have business leaders.

The difficulty of exercising "social responsibility" illustrates, of course, the great virtue of private competitive enterprise—it forces people to be responsible for their own actions and makes it difficult for them to "exploit" other people for either selfish or unselfish purposes. They can do good—but only at their own expense.

Many a reader who has followed the argument this far may be tempted to remonstrate that it is all well and good to speak of Government's having the responsibility to impose taxes and determine expenditures for such "social" purposes as controlling pollution or training the hard-core unemployed, but that the problems are too urgent to wait on the slow course of political processes, that the exercise of social responsibility by businessmen is a quicker and surer way to solve pressing current problems.

Aside from the question of fact—I share Adam Smith's skepticism about the benefits that can be expected from "those who affected to trade for the public good"—this argument must be rejected on grounds of principle. What it amounts to is an assertion that those who favor the taxes and expenditures in question have failed to persuade a majority of their fellow citizens to be of like mind and that they are seeking to attain by undemocratic procedures what they cannot attain by democratic procedures. In a free society, it is hard for "evil" people to do "evil," especially since one man's good is another's evil.

I have, for simplicity, concentrated on the special case of the corporate executive, except only for the brief digression on trade unions. But precisely the same argument applies to the newer phenomenon of calling upon stockholders to require corporations to exercise social responsibility (the recent G.M. crusade for example). In most of these cases, what is in effect involved is some stockholders trying to get other stockholders (or customers or employees) to contribute against their will to "social" causes favored by the activists. Insofar as they succeed, they are again imposing taxes and spending the proceeds.

The situation of the individual proprietor is somewhat different. If he acts to reduce the returns of his enterprise in order to exercise his "social responsibility," he is spending his own money, not someone else's. If he wishes to spend his money on such purposes, that is his right, and I cannot see that there is any objection to his doing so. In the process, he, too, may impose costs on employees and customers. However, because he is far less likely than a large corporation or union to have monopolistic power, any such side effects will tend to be minor.

Of course, in practice the doctrine of social responsibility is frequently a cloak for actions that are justified on other grounds rather than a reason for those actions.

To illustrate, it may well be in the long-run interest of a corporation that is a major employer in a small community to devote resources to providing amenities to that community or to improving its government. That may make it easier to attract desirable employees, it may reduce the wage bill or lessen losses from pilferage and sabotage or have other worthwhile effects. Or it may be that, given the laws about the deductibility of corporate charitable contributions, the stockholders can contribute more to charities they favor by having the corporation make the gift than by doing it themselves, since they can in that way contribute an amount that would otherwise have been paid as corporate taxes.

In each of these—and many similar—cases, there is a strong temptation to rationalize these actions as an exercise of "social responsibility." In the present climate of opinion, with its widespread aversion to "capitalism," "profits," the "soulless corporation" and so on, this is one way for a corporation to generate goodwill as a by-product of expenditures that are entirely justified in its own self-interest.

It would be inconsistent of me to call on corporate executives to refrain from this hypocritical window-dressing because it harms the foundations of a free society. That would be to call on them to exercise a "social responsibility"! If our institutions, and the attitudes of the public make it in their self-interest to cloak their actions in this way, I cannot summon much indignation to denounce them. At the same time, I can express admiration for those individual proprietors or owners of closely held corporations or stockholders of more broadly held corporations who disdain such tactics as approaching fraud.

Whether blameworthy or not, the use of the cloak of social responsibility, and the nonsense spoken in its name by influential and prestigious businessmen, does clearly harm the foundations of a free society. I have been impressed time and again by the schizophrenic character of many businessmen. They are capable of being extremely far-sighted and clearheaded in matters that are internal to their businesses. They are incredibly short-sighted and muddle-headed in matters that are outside their businesses but affect the possible survival of business in general. This short-sightedness is strikingly exemplified in the calls from many businessmen for wage and price guidelines or controls or income policies. There is nothing that could do more in a brief period to destroy a market system and replace it by a centrally controlled system than effective governmental control of prices and wages.

The short-sightedness is also exemplified in speeches by businessmen on social responsibility. This may gain them kudos in the short run. But it helps to strengthen the already too prevalent view that the pursuit of profits is wicked and immoral and must be curbed and controlled by external forces. Once this view is adopted, the external forces that curb the market will not be the social consciences, however highly developed, of the pontificating executives; it will be the iron fist of Government bureaucrats. Here, as with price and wage controls, businessmen seem to me to reveal a suicidal impulse.

The political principle that underlies the market mechanism is unanimity. In an ideal free market resting on private property, no individual can coerce any other, all cooperation is voluntary, all parties to such cooperation benefit or they need not participate. There are no values, no "social" responsibilities in any sense other than the shared values and responsibilities of individuals. Society is a collection of individuals and of the various groups they voluntarily form.

The political principle that underlies the political mechanism is conformity. The individual must serve a more general social interest—whether that be determined by a church or a dictator or a majority. The individual may have a vote and say in what is to be done, but if he is overruled, he must conform. It is appropriate for some to require others to contribute to a general social purpose whether they wish to or not.

Unfortunately, unanimity is not always feasible. There are some respects in which conformity appears unavoidable, so I do not see how one can avoid the use of the political mechanism altogether.

But the doctrine of "social responsibility" taken seriously would extend the scope of the political mechanism to every human activity. It does not differ in philosophy from the most explicitly collectivist doctrine. It differs only by professing to believe that collectivist ends can be attained without collectivist means. That is why, in my book *Capitalism and Freedom*, I have called it a "fundamentally subversive doctrine" in a free society, and have said that in such a society, "there is one and only one social responsibility of business—to use its resources and engage in activities designed to increase its profits so long as it stays within the rules of the game, which is to say, engages in open and free competition without deception or fraud."

QUESTIONS

1. How does business benefit society by increasing its profits?
2. Can profit ever harm society, according to Friedman? What do you think?

Christopher D. Stone

Why Shouldn't Corporations Be Socially Responsible?

Christopher Stone teaches law at the University of Southern California.

The opposition to corporate social responsibility comprises at least four related though separable positions. I would like to challenge the fundamental assumption that underlies all four of them. Each assumes in its own degree that the managers of the corporation are to be steered almost wholly by profit, rather than by what they think proper for society on the whole. Why should this be so? So far as ordinary morals are concerned, we often expect human beings to act in a fashion that is calculated to benefit others, rather than themselves, and commend them for it. Why should the matter be different with corporations?

THE PROMISSORY ARGUMENT

The most widespread but least persuasive arguments advanced by the "antiresponsibility" forces take the form of a moral claim based upon the corporation's supposed obligations to its shareholders. In its baldest and least tenable form, it is presented as though management's obligation rested upon the keeping of a promise—that the management of the corporation "promised" the shareholders that it would maximize the shareholders' profits. But this simply isn't so.

Consider for contrast the case where a widow left a large fortune goes to a broker, asking him to invest and manage her money so as to maximize her return. The broker, let us suppose, accepts the money and the conditions. In such a case, there would be no disagreement that the broker had made a promise to the widow, and if he invested her money in some venture that struck his fancy for any reason other than that it would increase her fortune, we would be inclined to advance a moral (as well, perhaps, as a legal) claim against him. Generally, at least, we believe in the keeping of promises; the broker, we should say, had violated a promissory obligation to the widow.

But that simple model is hardly the one that obtains between the management of major corporations and their shareholders. Few if any American shareholders ever put their money into a corporation upon the express promise of management that the company would be operated so as to maximize their returns. Indeed, few American shareholders ever put their money directly *into* a corporation at all. Most of the shares outstanding today were issued years ago and found their way to their current shareholders only circuitously. In almost all cases, the current shareholder gave his money to some prior shareholder, who, in turn, had gotten it from B, who, in turn, had gotten it from A, and so on back to the purchaser of the original issue, who, many years before, had bought the shares through an underwriting syndicate. In the course of these transactions, one of the basic elements that exists in the broker case is missing: The manager of the corporation, unlike the broker, was never even offered a chance to refuse the shareholder's "terms" (if they were that) to maximize the shareholder's profits.

There are two other observations to be made about the moral argument based on a supposed promise running from the management to the shareholders. First, even if we do infer from all the circumstances a "promise" running from the management to the shareholders, but not one, or not one of comparable weight running elsewhere (to the company's employees, customers, neighbors, etc.), we ought to keep in mind that as a moral matter (which is what we are discussing here) sometimes it is deemed morally justified to break promises (even to break the law) in the furtherance of other social interests of higher concern. Promises can advance moral arguments, by way of creating presumptions, but few of us believe that promises, per se, can end them. My promise to appear in class on time would not ordinarily justify me from refusing to give aid to a drowning man. In other words, even if management *had* made an express promise to its shareholders to "maximize your profits," (a) I am not persuaded that the ordinary person would interpret it to mean "maximize *in every way you can possibly get away with*, even if that means polluting the environment, ignoring or breaking the law"; and (b) I am not persuaded that, even if it were interpreted as so blanket a promise, most people would not suppose it ought—morally—to be broken in some cases.

Finally, even if, in the face of all these considerations, one still believes that there is an overriding, unbreakable, promise of some sort running from management to the shareholders, I do not think that it can be construed to be any stronger than one running to *existent* shareholders, arising from *their* expectations as measured by the price *they* paid. That is to say, there is nothing in the argument from promises that would wed us to a regime in which management was bound to maximize the income of shareholders. The argument might go so far as to support compensation for existent shareholders if the society chose to announce that henceforth management would have other specified obligations, thereby driving the price of shares to a lower adjustment level. All future shareholders would take with "warning" of, and a price that discounted for, the new "risks" of shareholding (i.e., the "risks" that management might put corporate resources to *pro bonum* ends).

THE AGENCY ARGUMENT

Related to the promissory argument but requiring less stretching of the facts is an argument from agency principles. Rather than trying to infer a promise by management to the shareholders, this argument is based on the idea that the shareholders designated the management their agents. This is the position advanced by Milton Friedman in his *New York Times* article. "The key point," he says, "is that . . . the manager is the agent of the individuals who own the corporation . . . ."[1]

Friedman, unfortunately, is wrong both as to the state of the law (the directors are *not* mere agents of the shareholders) and on his assumption as to the facts of corporate life (surely it is closer to the truth that in major corporations the shareholders are *not*, in any meaningful sense, selecting the directors; management is more often using its control over the proxy machinery to designate who the directors shall be, rather than the other way around).

What Friedman's argument comes down to is that for some reason the directors ought morally to consider themselves more the agents for the shareholders than for the customers, creditors, the state, or the corporation's immediate neighbors. But why? And to what extent? Throwing in terms like "principal" and "agent" begs the fundamental questions.

What is more, the "agency" argument is not only morally inconclusive, it is embarrassingly at odds with the way in which supposed "agents" actually behave. If the managers truly considered themselves the agents of the shareholders, as agents they would be expected to show an interest in determining how their principals wanted them to act—and to act accordingly. In the controversy over Dow's production of napalm, for example, one would expect, on this model, that Dow's management would have been glad to have the napalm question put to the shareholders at a shareholders' meeting. In fact, like most major companies faced with shareholder requests to include "social action" measures on proxy statements, it fought the proposal tooth and claw. It is a peculiar agency where the "agents" will go to such lengths (even spending tens of thousands of dollars of their "principals'" money in legal fees) to resist the determination of what their "principals" want.

THE ROLE ARGUMENT

An argument so closely related to the argument from promises and agency that it does not demand extensive additional remarks is a contention based upon supposed considerations of *role*. Sometimes in moral discourse, as well as in law, we assign obligations to people on the basis of their having assumed some role or status, independent of any specific verbal promise they made. Such obligations are assumed to run from a captain to a seaman (and vice versa), from a doctor to a patient, or from a parent to a child. The antiresponsibility forces are on somewhat stronger grounds resting their position on this basis, because the model more nearly accords with the facts—that is, management never actually promised the shareholders that they would maximize the shareholders' investment, nor did the shareholders designate the directors their agents for this express purpose. The directors and top management are, as lawyers would say, fiduciaries. But what does this leave us? So far as the directors are fiduciaries of the shareholders in a legal sense, of course they are subject to the legal limits on fiduciaries—that is to say, they cannot engage in self-dealing, "waste" of corporate assets, and the like. But I do not understand any proresponsibility advocate to be demanding such corporate largesse as would expose the officers to legal liability; what we are talking about are expenditures on, for example, pollution control, above the amount the company is required to pay by law, but less than an amount so extravagant as to constitute a violation of these legal fiduciary duties. (Surely no court in America today would enjoin a corporation from spending more to reduce pollution than the law requires.) What is there about assuming the role of corporate officer that makes it immoral for a manager to involve a corporation in these expenditures? A father, one would think, would have stronger obligations to his children by virtue of his status than a corporate manager to the corporation's shareholders. Yet few would regard it as a compelling moral argument if a father were to distort facts about his child on a scholarship application form on the grounds that he had obligations to advance his child's career; nor would we consider it a strong moral argument if a father were to leave unsightly refuse piled on his lawn, spilling over into the street, on the plea that he had obligations to give every moment of his attention to his children, and was thus too busy to cart his refuse away.

Like the other supposed moral arguments, the one from role suffers from the problem that the strongest moral obligations one can discover have at most only prima facie force, and it is not apparent why those obligations should predominate over some contrary social obligations that could be advanced.

Then too, when one begins comparing and weighing the various moral obligations, those running back to the shareholder seem fairly weak by comparison to the claims of others. For one thing, there is the consideration of alternatives. If the shareholder is dissatisfied with the direction the corporation is taking, he can sell out, and if he does so quickly enough, his losses may be slight. On the other hand, as Ted Jacobs observes, "those most vitally affected by corporate decisions—people who work in the plants, buy the products, and consume the effluents—cannot remove themselves from the structure with a phone call."[2]

THE "POLESTAR" ARGUMENT

It seems to me that the strongest moral argument corporate executives can advance for looking solely to profits is not one that is based on a supposed express, or even implied promise to the shareholder. Rather, it is one that says, if the managers act in such fashion as to maximize profits—if they act *as though* they had promised the shareholders they would do so—then it will be best for all of us. This argument might be called the polestar argument, for its appeal to the interests of the shareholders is not justified on supposed obligations to the shareholders per se, but as a means of charting a straight course toward what is best for the society as a whole.

Underlying the polestar argument are a number of assumptions—some express and some implied. There is, I suspect, an implicit positivism among its supporters—a feeling (whether its proponents own up to it or not) that moral judgments are peculiar, arbitrary, or vague—perhaps even "meaningless" in the philosophic sense of not being amenable to rational discussion. To those who take this position, profits (or sales, or price-earnings ratios) at least provide some solid, tangible standard by which participants in the organization can measure their successes and failures, with some efficiency, in the narrow sense, resulting for the entire group. Sometimes the polestar position is based upon a related view—not that the moral issues that underlie social choices are meaningless, but that resolving them calls for special expertise. "I don't know any investment adviser whom I would care to act in my behalf in any matter except turning a profit. . . . The value of these specialists . . . lies in their limitations; they ought not allow themselves to see so much of the world that they become distracted."[3] A slightly modified point emphasizes not that the executives lack moral or social expertise per se, but that they lack the social authority to make policy choices. Thus, Friedman objects that if a corporate director took "social purposes" into account, he would become "in effect a public employee, a civil servant . . . . On grounds of political principle, it is intolerable that such civil servants . . . should be selected as they are now."[4]

I do not want to get too deeply involved in each of these arguments. That the moral judgments underlying policy choices are vague, I do not doubt—although I am tempted to observe that when you get right down to it, a wide range of actions taken by businessmen every day, supposedly based on solid calculations of "profit," are probably as rooted in hunches and intuition as judgments of ethics. I do not disagree either that, ideally, we prefer those who have control over our lives to be politically accountable; although here, too, if we were to pursue the matter in detail we would want to inspect both the premise of this argument, that corporate managers are not *presently* custodians of discretionary power over us anyway, and also its logical implications: Friedman's point that "if they are to be civil servants, then they must be selected through a political process"[5] is not, as Friedman regards it, a reductio ad absurdum—not, at any rate, to Ralph Nader and others who want publicly elected directors.

The reason for not pursuing these counterarguments at length is that, whatever reservations one might have, we can agree that there is a germ of validity to what the "antis" are saying. But their essential failure is in not pursuing the alternatives. Certainly, *to the extent* that the forces of the market and the law can keep the corporation within desirable bounds, it may be better to trust them than to have corporate managers implementing their own vague and various notions of what is best for the rest of us. But are the "antis" blind to the fact that there are circumstances in which the law—and the forces of the market—are simply not competent to keep the corporation under control? The shortcomings of these traditional restraints on corporate conduct are critical to understand, not merely for the defects they point up in the "antis'" position. More important, identifying where the traditional forces are inadequate is the first step in the design of new and alternative measures of corporate control.

NOTES

1. *New York Times*, September 12, 1962, sect. 6, p. 33, col. 2.
2. Theodore J. Jacobs, "Pollution, Consumerism, Accountability," *Center Magazine 5*, I (January–February 1971): 47.
3. Walter Goodman, "Stocks Without Sin," *Harper's*, August 1971, p. 66.
4. *New York Times*, September 12, 1962, sec. 6, p. 122, col. 3.
5. Ibid., p. 122, cols. 3–4.

QUESTIONS

1. What is the promissory argument?
2. Explain the agency and the role arguments. How do they differ?

Peter A. French | Corporate Moral Agency

Peter A. French runs the Lincoln Center for Applied Ethics and teaches philosophy at Arizona State University.

1

In one of his *New York Times* columns of not too long ago Tom Wicker's ire was aroused by a Gulf Oil Corporation advertisement that "pointed the finger of blame" for the energy crisis at all elements of our society (and supposedly away from the oil company). Wicker attacked Gulf Oil as the major, if not the sole, perpetrator of that crisis and virtually every other social ill, with the possible exception of venereal disease. I do not know if Wicker was serious or sarcastic in making all of his charges; I have a sinking suspicion that he was in deadly earnest, but I have doubts as to whether Wicker understands or if many people understand what sense such ascriptions of moral responsibility make when their subjects are corporations. My interest is to argue for a theory that accepts corporations as members of the moral community, of equal standing with the traditionally acknowledged residents—biological human beings—and hence treats Wicker-type responsibility ascriptions as unexceptionable instances of a perfectly proper sort without having to paraphrase them. In short, I shall argue that corporations should be treated as full-fledged moral persons and hence that they can have whatever privileges, rights, and duties as are, in the normal course of affairs, accorded to moral persons.

2

There are at least two significantly different types of responsibility ascriptions that I want to distinguish in ordinary usage (not counting the laudatory recommendation, "He is a responsible lad.") The first type pins responsibility on someone or something, the who-dun-it or what-dun-it sense. Austin has pointed out that it is usually used when an event or action is thought by the speaker to be untoward. (Perhaps we are more interested in the failures rather than the successes that punctuate our lives.)

The second type of responsibility ascription, parasitic upon the first, involves the notion of accountability. "Having a responsibility" is interwoven with the notion "Having a liability to answer," and having such a liability or obligation seems to imply (as Anscombe has noted) the existence of some sort of authority relationship either between people, or between people and a deity, or in some weaker versions between people and social norms. The kernel of insight that I find intuitively compelling is that for someone to legitimately hold someone else responsible for some event, there must exist or have existed a responsibility relationship between them such that in regard to the event in question the latter was answerable to the former. In other words, a responsibility ascription of the second type is properly uttered by someone Z if he or she can hold X accountable for what he or she has done. Responsibility relationships are created in a multitude of ways, e.g., through promises, contracts, compacts, hirings, assignments, appointments, by agreeing to enter a Rawlsian original position, etc. The "right" to hold responsible is often delegated to third parties; but importantly, in the case of moral responsibility, no delegation occurs because no person is excluded from the relationship: moral responsibility relationships hold reciprocally and without prior agreements among all moral persons. No special arrangement needs to be established between parties for anyone to hold someone morally responsible for his or her acts or, what amounts to the same thing, every person is a party to a responsibility relationship with all other persons as regards the doing or refraining from doing of certain acts: those that take descriptions that use moral notions.

Because our interest is in the criteria of moral personhood and not the content or morality, we need not pursue this idea further. What I have maintained is that moral responsibility, although it is neither contractual nor optional, is not a class apart but an extension of ordinary, garden-variety responsibility. What is needed in regard to the present subject, then, is an account of the requirements in *any* responsibility relationship.

3

A responsibility ascription of the second type amounts to the assertion that the person held responsible is the cause of an event (usually an untoward one) and that the action in question was intended by the subject or that the event was the direct result of an intentional act of the subject. In addition to what it asserts, it implies that the subject is liable to account to the speaker (who the speaker is or what the speaker is, a member of the "moral community," a surrogate for that aggregate). The primary focus of responsibility ascriptions of the second type is on the subject's intentions rather than, though not to the exclusion of, occasions.

4

For a corporation to be treated as a responsible agent it must be the case that some things that happen, some events, are describable in a way that makes certain sentences true, sentences that say that some of the things a corporation does were intended by the corporation itself. That is not accomplished if attributing intentions to a corporation is only a shorthand way of attributing intentions to the biological persons who comprise, for example, its board of directors. If that were to turn out to be the case, then on metaphysical if not logical grounds there would be no way to distinguish between corporations and mobs. I shall argue, however, that a corporation's

CID Structure (the *Corporate Internal Decision* Structure) is the requisite redescription device that licenses the predication of corporate intentionality.

It is obvious that a corporation's doing something involves or includes human beings' doing things and that the human beings who occupy various positions in a corporation usually can be described as having reasons for *their* behavior. In virtue of those descriptions they may be properly held responsible for their behavior, *ceteris paribus*. What needs to be shown is that there is sense in saying that corporations, and not just the people who work in them, have reasons for doing what they do. Typically, we will be told that it is the directors, or the managers, etc. that really have the corporate reasons and desires, etc. and that although corporate actions may not be reducible without remainder, corporate intentions are always reducible to human intentions.

5

Every corporation must have an internal decision structure. The CID Structure has two elements of interest to us here: (1) an organizational or responsibility flow chart that delineates stations and levels within the corporate power structure and (2) corporate decision recognition rule(s) (usually embedded in something called "corporate policy"). The CID Structure is the personnel organization for the exercise of the corporation's power with respect to its ventures, and as such its primary function is to draw experience from various levels of the corporation into a decision-making and ratification process. When operative and properly activated, the CID Structure accomplishes a subordination and synthesis of the intentions and acts of various biological persons into a corporate decision. When viewed in another way the CID Structure licenses the descriptive transformation of events seen under another aspect as the acts of biological persons (those who occupy various stations on the organizational chart) as corporate acts by exposing the corporate character of those events. A functioning CID Structure *incorporates* acts of biological persons. For illustrative purposes, suppose we imagine that an event E has at least two aspects, that is, can be described in two nonidentical ways. One of those aspects is "Executive X's doing *y*" and one is "Corporation C's doing *z*." The corporate act and the individual act may have different properties: indeed they have different causal ancestors though they are causally inseparable.

Although I doubt he is aware of the metaphysical reading that can be given to this process, J. K. Galbraith rather neatly captures what I have in mind when he writes in his recent popular book on the history of economics:

> From [the] interpersonal exercise of power, the interaction . . . of the participants, comes the *personality* of the corporation.[1]

I take Galbraith here to be quite literally correct, but it is important to spell out how a CID Structure works this "miracle."

In philosophy in recent years we have grown accustomed to the use of games as models for understanding institutional behavior. We all have some understanding of how rules of games make certain descriptions of events possible that would not be so if those rules were nonexistent. The CID Structure of a corporation is a kind of constitutive rule (or rules) analogous to the game rules with which we are familiar. The organization chart of, for example, the Burlington Northern Corporation distinguishes "players" and clarifies their rank and the interwoven lines of responsibility within the corporation. The Burlington chart lists only titles, not unlike King, Queen, Rook, etc. in chess. What it tells us is that anyone holding the title "Executive Vice President for Finance and Administration" stands in a certain relationship to anyone holding the title "Director of Internal Audit" and to anyone holding the title "Treasurer," etc. Also it expresses, or maps, the interdependent and dependent relationships that are involved in determinations of corporate decisions and actions. In effect, it tells us what anyone who occupies any of the positions is vis-à-vis the decision structure of the whole. The organizational chart provides what might be called the grammar of corporate decision-making. What I shall call internal recognition rules provide its logic.[2]

Recognition rules are of two sorts. Partially embedded in the organizational chart are the procedural recognitors: we see that decisions are to be reached collectively at certain levels and that they are to be ratified at higher levels (or at inner circles, if one prefers the Galbraithean model). A corporate decision is recognized internally not only by the procedure of its making, but by the policy it instantiates. Hence every corporation creates an image (not to be confused with its public image) or a general policy, what G. C. Buzby of the Chilton Company has called the "basic belief of the corporation,"[3] that must inform its decisions for them to be properly described as being those of that corporation. "The moment policy is side-stepped or violated it is no longer the policy of that company."[4]

Peter Drucker has seen the importance of the basic policy recognitors in the CID Structure (though he treats matters rather differently from the way I am recommending). Drucker writes:

> Because the corporation is an institution it must have a basic policy. For it must subordinate individual ambitions and decisions to the *needs* of the corporation's welfare and survival. That means that it must have a set of principles and a rule of conduct which limit and direct individual actions and behavior.[5]

6

Suppose, for illustrative purposes, we activate a CID Structure in a corporation, Wicker's favorite, the Gulf Oil Corporation. Imagine then that three executives X, Y, and Z have the task of deciding whether or not Gulf Oil will join a world uranium cartel (I trust this may catch Mr. Wicker's attention and hopefully also that of Jerry McAfee, current Gulf Oil Corporation president). X, Y, and Z have before them an Everest of papers that have been prepared by lower echelon executives. Some of the reports will be purely factual in nature, some will be contingency plans, some will be in the form of position papers developed by various departments, some will outline financial considerations, some will be legal opinions, and so on. Insofar as these will all have been processed through

Gulf's CID Structure system, the personal reasons, if any, individual executives may have had when writing their reports and recommendations in a specific way will have been diluted by the subordination of individual inputs to peer group input even before X, Y, and Z review the matter. X, Y, and Z take a vote. Their taking of a vote is authorized procedure in the Gulf CID Structure, which is to say that under these circumstances the vote of X, Y, and Z can be redescribed as the corporation's making a decision: that is, the event "X Y Z voting" may be redescribed to expose an aspect otherwise unrevealed, that is quite different from its other aspects, e.g., from X's voting in the affirmative.

But the CID Structure, as already suggested, also provides the grounds in its nonprocedural recognitor for such an attribution of corporate intentionality. Simply, when the corporate act is consistent with the implementation of established corporate policy, then it is proper to describe it as having been done for corporate reasons, as having been caused by a corporate desire coupled with a corporate belief and so, in other words, as corporate intentional.

An event may, under one of its aspects, be described as the conjunctive act "X did *a* (or as X intentionally did *a)* and Y did *a* (or as Y intentionally did *a)* and Z did *a* (or as Z intentionally did *a)"* (where *a* = voted in the affirmative on the question of Gulf Oil joining the cartel). Given the Gulf CID Structure—formulated in this instance as the conjunction of rules: when the occupants of positions A, B, and C on the organizational chart unanimously vote to do something and if doing that something is consistent with an implementation of general corporate policy, other things being equal, then the corporation has decided to do it for corporate reasons—the event is redescribable as "the Gulf Oil Corporation did *j* for corporate reasons *f*" (where *j* is "decided to join the cartel" and *f* is any reason [desire + belief] consistent with basic policy of Gulf Oil, e.g., increasing profits) or simply as "Gulf Oil Corporation intentionally did *j*." This is a rather technical way of saying that in these circumstances the executives voting are, given its CID Structure, also the corporation deciding to do something, and that regardless of the personal reasons the executives have for voting as they do, and

even if their reasons are inconsistent with established corporate policy or even if one of them has no reason at all for voting as he does, the corporation still has reasons for joining the cartel; that is, joining is consistent with the inviolate corporate general policies as encrusted in the precedent of previous corporate actions and its statements of purpose as recorded in its certificate of incorporation, annual reports, etc. The corporation's only method of achieving its desires or goals is the activation of the personnel who occupy its various positions. However, if X voted affirmatively purely for reasons of personal monetary gain (suppose he had been bribed to do so), that does not alter the fact that the corporate reason for joining the cartel was to minimize competition and hence pay higher dividends to its shareholders. Corporations have reasons because they have interests in doing those things that are likely to result in realization of their established corporate goals regardless of the transient self-interest of directors, managers, etc. If there is a difference between corporate goals and desires and those of human beings, it is probably that the corporate ones are relatively stable and not very wide ranging, but that is only because corporations can do relatively fewer things than human beings, being confined in action predominately to a limited socio-economic sphere. It is, of course, in a corporation's interest that its component membership view the corporate purposes as instrumental in the achievement of their own goals. (Financial reward is the most common way this is achieved.)

It will be objected that a corporation's policies reflect only the current goals of its directors. But that is certainly not logically necessary nor is it in practice totally true for most large corporations. Usually, of course, the original incorporators will have organized to further their individual interests and/or to meet goals which they shared. But even in infancy the melding of disparate interests and purposes gives rise to a corporate long-range point of view that is distinct from the intents and purposes of the collection of incorporators viewed individually. Also corporate basic purposes and policies, as already mentioned, tend to be relatively stable when compared to those of individuals and not couched in the kind of language that would be appropriate to individual purposes.

Furthermore, as histories of corporations will show, when policies are amended or altered it is usually only peripheral issues and matters of style that are involved. Radical policy alteration constitutes a new corporation. This point is captured in the incorporation laws of such states as Delaware. ("Any power which is not enumerated in the charter or which cannot be inferred from it is *ultra vires* [beyond the legal competence] of the corporation.") Obviously underlying the objection is an uneasiness about the fact that corporate intent is dependent upon policy and purpose that is but an artifact of the sociopsychology of a group of biological persons. Corporate intent seems somehow to be a tarnished, illegitimate offspring of human intent. But this objection is a form of the anthropocentric bias that pervades traditional moral theory. By concentrating on possible descriptions of events and by acknowledging only that the possibility of describing something as an agent depends upon whether or not it can be properly described as having done something for a reason, we avoid the temptation of trying to reduce all agents to human referents.

The CID Structure licenses redescriptions of events as corporate and attributions of corporate intentionality while it does not obscure the private acts of executives, directors, etc. Although X voted to support the joining of the cartel because he was bribed to do so, X did not join the cartel: Gulf Oil Corporation joined the cartel. Consequently, we may say that X did something for which he should be held morally responsible, yet whether or not Gulf Oil Corporation should be held morally responsible for joining the cartel is a question that turns on issues that may be unrelated to X's having accepted a bribe.

Of course Gulf Oil Corporation cannot join the cartel unless X or somebody who occupies position A on the organization chart votes in the affirmative. What that shows, however, is that corporations are collectivities. That should not, however, rule out the possibility of their having metaphysical status and being thereby full-fledged moral persons.

This much seems to me clear: We can describe many events in terms of certain physical movements of human beings and we also can sometimes describe those events as done for reasons by those human beings, but further we also can sometimes describe those events as corporate and still further as done for corporate reasons that are qualitatively different from whatever personal reasons, if any, component members may have for doing what they do.

Corporate agency resides in the possibility of CID Structure licensed redescription of events as corporate intentional. That may still appear to be downright mysterious, although I do not think it is, for human agency, as I have suggested, resides in the possibility of description as well. On the basis of the foregoing analysis, however, I think that grounds have been provided for holding corporations *per se* to account for what they do, for treating them as metaphysical persons *qua* moral persons.

A. A. Berle has written:

> The medieval feudal power system set the "lords spiritual" over and against the "lords temporal." These were the men of learning and of the church who in theory were able to say to the greatest power in the world: "You have committed a sin; therefore either you are excommunicated or you must mend your ways." The lords temporal could reply: "I can kill you." But the lords spiritual could retort: "Yes that you can, but you cannot change the philosophical fact." In a sense this is the great lacuna in the economic power system today.[6]

I have tried to fill that gap by providing reasons for thinking that the moral world is not necessarily composed of homogeneous entities. It is sobering to keep in mind that the Gulf Oil Corporation certainly knows what "You are held responsible for payment in full of the amount recorded on your statement" means. I hope I have provided the beginnings of a basis for an understanding of what "The Gulf Oil Corporation should be held responsible for destroying the ecological balance of the bay" means.

NOTES

1. John Kenneth Galbraith, *The Age of Uncertainty* (Boston: Houghton Mifflin, 1977), p. 261.

2. By "recognition rule(s)" I mean what Hart, in another context, calls "conclusive affirmative indication" that a decision or act has been made or performed for corporate reasons. H. L. A. Hart, *The Concept of Law* (Oxford: Clarendon Press, 1961), Chap. VI.

3. G. C. Buzby, "Policies—A Guide to What a Company Stands For," *Management Record* (March 1962), p. 5.

4. Ibid.

5. Peter Drucker, *Concept of the Corporation* (New York: John Day Co., 1946/1972), pp. 36–37.

6. A. A. Berle, "Economic Power and the Free Society," *The Corporate Take-Over*, ed. Andrew Hacker (Garden City, N.Y.: Doubleday, 1964), p. 99.

QUESTIONS

1. Explain French's idea that corporations should be treated as full-fledged moral persons. What motivates this argument? What are his goals? What problems may this account provoke?

2. How do internal decisions structures influence his account? Explain the significance of the CID.

R. Edward Freeman | # A Stakeholder Theory of the Modern Corporation

R. Edward Freeman teaches business ethics at the University of Virginia.

INTRODUCTION

Corporations have ceased to be merely legal devices through which the private business transactions of individuals may be carried on. Though still much used for this purpose, the corporate form has acquired a larger significance. The corporation has, in fact, become both a method of property tenure and a means of organizing economic life. Grown to tremendous proportions, there may be said to have evolved a "corporate system"—which has attracted to itself a combination of attributes and powers, and has attained a degree of prominence entitling it to be dealt with as a major social institution.

—A. Berle and G. Means, The Modern Corporation
and Private Property

Despite these prophetic words of Berle and Means (1932), scholars and managers alike continue to hold sacred the view that managers bear a special relationship to the stockholders in the firm.[1] Since stockholders own shares in the firm, they have certain rights and privileges, which must be granted to them by management, as well as by others. Sanctions, in the form of "the law of corporations," and other protective mechanisms in the form of social custom, accepted management practice, myth, and ritual, are thought to reinforce the assumption of the primacy of the stockholder.

The purpose of this paper is to pose several challenges to this assumption, from within the framework of managerial capitalism, and to suggest the bare bones of an alternative theory, *a stakeholder theory of the modern corporation*. I do not seek the demise of the modern corporation, either intellectually or in fact. Rather, I seek its transformation. In the words of Neurath, we shall attempt to "rebuild the ship, plank by plank, while it remains afloat."[2]

My thesis is that I can revitalize the concept of managerial capitalism by replacing the notion that managers have a duty to stockholders with the concept that managers bear a fiduciary relationship to stakeholders. Stakeholders are those groups who have a stake in or claim on the firm. Specifically I include suppliers, customers, employees, stockholders, and

From Norman E. Bowie and Thomas L. Beauchamp, eds., *Ethical Theory and Business* (Englewood Cliffs, NJ: Prentice Hall, 1994), 66–74.

the local community, as well as management in its role as agent for these groups. I argue that the legal, economic, political, and moral challenges to the currently received theory of the firm, as a nexus of contracts among the owners of the factors of production and customers, require us to revise this concept. That is, each of these stakeholder groups has a right not to be treated as a means to some end, and therefore must participate in determining the future direction of the firm in which they have a stake.

The crux of my argument is that we must reconceptualize the firm around the following question: For whose benefit and at whose expense should the firm be managed? I shall set forth such a reconceptualization in the form of a *stakeholder theory of the firm*. I shall then critically examine the stakeholder view and its implications for the future of the capitalist system.

THE ATTACK ON MANAGERIAL CAPITALISM

The Legal Argument

The basic idea of managerial capitalism is that in return for controlling the firm, management vigorously pursues the interests of stockholders. Central to the managerial view of the firm is the idea that management can pursue market transactions with suppliers and customers in an unconstrained manner.

The law of corporations gives a less clear cut answer to the question: In whose interest and for whose benefit should the modern corporation be governed? While it says that the corporations should be run primarily in the interests of the stockholders in the firm, it says further that the corporation exists "in contemplation of the law" and has personality as a "legal person," limited liability for its actions, and immortality, since its existence transcends that of its members. Therefore, directors and other officers of the firm have a fiduciary obligation to stockholders in the sense that the "affairs of the corporation" must be conducted in the interest of the stockholders. And stockholders can theoretically bring suit against those directors and managers for doing otherwise. But since the corporation is a legal person, existing

in contemplation of the law, managers of the corporation are constrained by law.

Until recently, this was no constraint at all. In this century, however, the law has evolved to effectively constrain the pursuit of stockholder interests at the expense of other claimants on the firm. It has, in effect, required that the claims of customers, suppliers, local communities, and employees be taken into consideration, though in general they are subordinated to the claims of stockholders.

For instance, the doctrine of "privity of contract," as articulated in *Winterbottom v. Wright* in 1842, has been eroded by recent developments in products liability law. Indeed, *Greenman v. Yuba Power* gives the manufacturer strict liability for damage caused by its products, even though the seller has exercised all possible care in the preparation and sale of the product and the consumer has not bought the product from nor entered into any contractual arrangement with the manufacturer. Caveat emptor has been replaced, in large part, with caveat venditor. The Consumer Product Safety Commission has the power to enact product recalls, and in 1980 one U.S. automobile company recalled more cars than it built. Some industries are required to provide information to customers about a product's ingredients, whether or not the customers want and are willing to pay for this information.

The same argument is applicable to management's dealings with employees. The National Labor Relations Act gave employees the right to unionize and to bargain in good faith. It set up the National Labor Relations Board to enforce these rights with management. The Equal Pay Act of 1963 and Title VII of the Civil Rights Act of 1964 constrain management from discrimination in hiring practices; these have been followed with the Age Discrimination in Employment Act of 1967. The emergence of a body of administrative case law arising from labor-management disputes and the historic settling of discrimination claims with large employers such as AT&T have caused the emergence of a body of practice in the corporation that is consistent with the legal guarantee of the rights of the employees. The law has protected the due process rights of those employees who enter into collective bargaining agreements with management. As of the present, however, only 30 percent of the labor force are participating in such agreements; this has prompted one labor law scholar to propose a statutory law prohibiting dismissals of the 70 percent of the work force not protected.

The law has also protected the interests of local communities. The Clean Air Act and Clean Water Act have constrained management from "spoiling the commons." In an historic case, *Marsh v. Alabama*, the Supreme Court ruled that a company-owned town was subject to the provisions of the U.S. Constitution, thereby guaranteeing the rights of local citizens and negating the "property rights" of the firm. Some states and municipalities have gone further and passed laws preventing firms from moving plants or limiting when and how plants can be closed. In sum, there is much current legal activity in this area to constrain management's pursuit of stockholders' interests at the expense of the local communities in which the firm operates.

I have argued that the result of such changes in the legal system can be viewed as giving some rights to those groups that have a claim on the firm, for example, customers, suppliers, employees, local communities, stockholders, and management. It raises the question, at the core of a theory of the firm: In whose interest and for whose benefit should the firm be managed? The answer proposed by managerial capitalism is clearly "the stockholders," but I have argued that the law has been progressively circumscribing this answer.

The Economic Argument

In its pure ideological form managerial capitalism seeks to maximize the interests of stockholders. In its perennial criticism of government regulation, management espouses the "invisible hand" doctrine. It contends that it creates the greatest good for the greatest number, and therefore government need not intervene. However, we know that externalities, moral hazards, and monopoly power exist in fact, whether or not they exist in theory. Further, some of the legal apparatus mentioned above has evolved to deal with just these issues.

The problem of the "tragedy of the commons" or the free-rider problem pervades the concept of public goods such as water and air. No one has an incentive to incur the cost of clean-up or the cost of nonpollution, since the marginal gain of one firm's action is small. Every firm reasons this way, and the result is pollution of water and air. Since the industrial revolution, firms have sought to internalize the benefits and externalize the costs of their actions. The cost must be borne by all, through taxation and regulation; hence we have the emergence of the environmental regulations of the 1970s.

Similarly, moral hazards arise when the purchaser of a good or service can pass along the cost of that good. There is no incentive to economize, on the part of either the producer or the consumer, and there is excessive use of the resources involved. The institutionalized practice of third-party payment in health care is a prime example.

Finally, we see the avoidance of competitive behavior on the part of firms, each seeking to monopolize a small portion of the market and not compete with one another. In a number of industries, oligopolies have emerged, and while there is questionable evidence that oligopolies are not the most efficient corporate form in some industries, suffice it to say that the potential for abuse of market power has again led to regulation of managerial activity. In the classic case, AT&T, arguably one of the great technological and managerial achievements of the century, was broken up into eight separate companies to prevent its abuse of monopoly power.

Externalities, moral hazards, and monopoly power have led to more external control on managerial capitalism. There are de facto constraints, due to these economic facts of life, on the ability of management to act in the interests of stockholders.

A STAKEHOLDER THEORY OF THE FIRM

The Stakeholder Concept

Corporations have stakeholders, that is, groups and individuals who benefit from or are harmed by, and whose rights are violated or respected by, corporate actions. The concept of stakeholders is a generalization of the notion of stockholders, who themselves have some special claim on the firm. Just as stockholders have a right to demand certain actions by management, so do other stakeholders have a right to make claims. The exact nature of these claims is a difficult question that I shall address, but the logic is identical to that of the stockholder theory. Stakes require action of a certain sort, and conflicting stakes require methods of resolution.

Freeman and Reed distinguish two senses of *stakeholder*. The "narrow definition" includes those groups who are vital to the survival and success of the corporation. The "wide-definition" includes any group or individual who can affect or is affected by the corporation. I shall begin with a modest aim: to articulate a stakeholder theory using the narrow definition.

Stakeholders in the Modern Corporation

Figure 6-1 depicts the stakeholders in a typical large corporation. The stakes of each are reciprocal, since each can affect the other in terms of harms and benefits as well as rights and duties. The stakes of each are not univocal and would vary by particular corporation. I merely set forth some general notions that seem to be common to many large firms.

Owners have financial stake in the corporation in the form of stocks, bonds, and so on, and they expect some kind of financial return from them. Either they have given money directly to the firm, or they have some historical claim made through a series of morally justified exchanges. The firm affects their livelihood or, if a substantial portion of their retirement income is in stocks or bonds, their ability to care for themselves when they can no longer work. Of course, the stakes of owners will differ by type of owner, preferences for money, moral preferences, and so on, as well as by type of firm. The owners of AT&T are quite different from the owners of Ford Motor Company, with stock of the former company being widely dispersed among 3 million stockholders and that of the latter being held by a small family group as well as by a large group of public stockholders.

Employees have their jobs and usually their livelihood at stake; they often have specialized skills for which there is usually no perfectly elastic market. In return for their labor, they expect security, wages, benefits, and meaningful work. In return for their loyalty, the corporation is expected to provide for them and carry them through difficult times. Employees are expected to follow the instructions of management most of the time, to speak favorably about the company, and to be responsible citizens in the local communities in which the company operates. Where they are used as means to an end, they must participate in decisions affecting such use. The evidence that such policies and values as described here lead to productive company–employee relationships is compelling. It is equally compelling to realize that the opportunities for "bad faith" on the part of both management and employees are enormous. "Mock participation" in quality circles, singing the company song, and wearing the company uniform solely to please management all lead to distrust and unproductive work.

Suppliers, interpreted in a stakeholder sense, are vital to the success of the firm, for raw materials will determine the final product's quality and price. In turn the firm is a customer of the supplier and is therefore vital to the success and survival of the supplier. When the firm treats the supplier as a valued member of the stakeholder network, rather than simply as a source of materials, the supplier will respond when the firm is in need. Chrysler traditionally had very close ties to its suppliers, even to the extent that led some to suspect the transfer of illegal payments. And when Chrysler was on the brink of disaster, the suppliers responded with price cuts, accepting late payments, financing, and so on. Supplier and company can rise and fall together. Of course, again, the particular supplier relationships will depend on a number of variables such as the number of suppliers and whether the supplies are finished goods or raw materials.

Customers exchange resources for the products of the firm and in return receive the benefits of the products. Customers provide the lifeblood of the firm in the form of revenue. Given the level of reinvestment of earnings in large corporations, customers

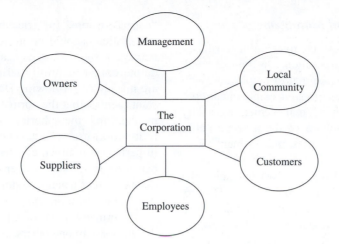

FIGURE **6-1** A stakeholder model of the corporation.

indirectly pay for the development of new products and services. Peters and Waterman have argued that being close to the customer leads to success with other stakeholders and that a distinguishing characteristic of some companies that have performed well is their emphasis on the customer. By paying attention to customers' needs, management automatically addresses the needs of suppliers and owners. Moreover, it seems that the ethic of customer service carries over to the community. Almost without fail the "excellent companies" in Peters and Waterman's study have good reputations in the community. I would argue that Peters and Waterman have found multiple applications of Kant's dictum, "Treat persons as ends unto themselves," and it should come as no surprise that persons respond to such respectful treatment, be they customers, suppliers, owners, employees, or members of the local community. The real surprise is the novelty of the application of Kant's rule in a theory of good management practice.

The local community grants the firm the right to build facilities and, in turn, it benefits from the tax base and economic and social contributions of the firm. In return for the provision of local services, the firm is expected to be a good citizen, as is any person, either "natural or artificial." The firm cannot expose the community to unreasonable hazards in the form of pollution, toxic waste, and so on. If for some reason the firm must leave a community, it is expected to work with local leaders to make the transition as smoothly as possible. Of course, the firm does not have perfect knowledge, but when it discovers some danger or runs afoul of new competition, it is expected to inform the local community and to work with the community to overcome any problem. When the firm mismanages its relationship with the local community, it is in the same position as a citizen who commits a crime. It has violated the implicit social contract with the community and should expect to be distrusted and ostracized. It should not be surprised when punitive measures are invoked.

I have not included "competitors" as stakeholders in the narrow sense, since strictly speaking they are not necessary for the survival and success of the firm; the stakeholder theory works equally well in monopoly contexts. However, competitors and government would be the first to be included in an extension of this basic theory. It is simply not true that the interests of competitors in an industry are always in conflict. There is no reason why trade associations and other multi-organizational groups cannot band together to solve common problems that have little to do with how to restrain trade. Implementation of stakeholder management principles, in the long run, mitigates the need for industrial policy and an increasing role for government intervention and regulation.

The Role of Management

Management plays a special role, for it too has a stake in the modern corporation. On the one hand, management's stake is like that of employees, with some kind of explicit or implicit employment contract. But, on the other hand, management has a duty of safeguarding the welfare of the abstract entity that is the corporation. In short, management, especially top management, must look after the health of the corporation, and this involves balancing the multiple claims of conflicting stakeholders. Owners want higher financial returns, while customers want more money spent on research and development. Employees want higher wages and better benefits, while the local community wants better parks and day-care facilities.

The task of management in today's corporation is akin to that of King Solomon. The stakeholder theory does not give primacy to one stakeholder group over another, though there will surely be times when one group will benefit at the expense of others. In general, however, management must keep the relationships among stakeholders in balance. When these relationships become imbalanced, the survival of the firm is in jeopardy.

When wages are too high and product quality is too low, customers leave, suppliers suffer, and owners sell their stocks and bonds, depressing the stock price and making it difficult to raise new capital at favorable rates. Note, however, that the reason for paying returns to owners is not that they "own" the firm, but that their support is necessary for the survival of the firm, and that they have a legitimate claim on the firm. Similar reasoning applies in turn to each stakeholder group.

A stakeholder theory of the firm must redefine the purpose of the firm. The stockholder theory claims that the purpose of the firm is to maximize the welfare of the stockholders, perhaps subject to some moral or social constraints, either because such maximization leads to the greatest good or because of property rights. The purpose of the firm is quite different in my view.

"The stakeholder theory" can be unpacked into a number of stakeholder theories, each of which has a "normative core," inextricably linked to the way that corporations should be governed and the way that managers should act. So, attempts to more fully define, or more carefully define, a stakeholder theory are misguided. Following Donaldson and Preston, I want to insist that the normative, descriptive, instrumental, and metaphorical (my addition to their framework) uses of "stakeholder" are tied together in particular political constructions to yield a number of possible "stakeholder theories." "Stakeholder theory" is thus a genre of stories about how we could live. Let me be more specific.

A "normative core" of a theory is a set of sentences that includes among others, sentences like:

(1) Corporations ought to be governed . . .
(2) Managers ought to act to . . .

where we need arguments or further narratives which include business and moral terms to fill in the blanks. This normative core is not always reducible to a fundamental ground like the theory of property, but certain normative cores are consistent with modern understandings of property. Certain elaborations of the theory of private property plus the other institutions of political liberalism give rise to particular normative cores. But there are other institutions, other political conceptions of how society ought to be structured, so that there are different possible normative cores.

So, one normative core of a stakeholder theory might be a feminist standpoint one, rethinking how we would restructure "value-creating activity" along principles of caring and connection. Another would be an ecological (or several ecological) normative cores. . . .

If we begin with the view that we can understand value-creation activity as a contractual process among those parties affected, and if for simplicity's sake we initially designate those parties as financiers, customers, suppliers, employees, and communities, then we can construct a normative core that reflects the liberal notions of autonomy, solidarity, and fairness as articulated by John Rawls, Richard Rorty, and others. Notice that building these moral notions into the foundations of how we understand value creation and contracting requires that we eschew separating the "business" part of the process from the "ethical" part, and that we start with the presumption of equality among the contractors, rather than the presumption in favor of financier rights.

The normative core for this redesigned contractual theory will capture the liberal idea of fairness if it ensures a basic equality among stakeholders in terms of their moral rights as these are realized in the firm, and if it recognizes that inequalities among stakeholders are justified if they raise the level of the least well-off stakeholder. The liberal ideal of autonomy is captured by the realization that each stakeholder must be free to enter agreements that create value for themselves, and solidarity is realized by the recognition of the mutuality of stakeholder interests.

QUESTIONS

1. What is a stakeholder? What is the stakeholder's role in guiding the corporation?
2. How and why do "corporate systems" complicate the moral responsibility of the corporation?

Kenneth J. Arrow

Social Responsibility and Economic Efficiency

Kenneth J. Arrow is Professor Emeritus at Stanford University and one of the most prominent economic theorists of the twentieth century.

Let us first consider the case against social responsibility: the assumption that the firms should aim simply to maximize their profits. One strand of that argument is empirical rather than ethical or normative. It simply states that firms *will* maximize their profits. The impulse to gain, it is argued, is very strong and the incentives for selfish behavior are so great that any kind of control is likely to be utterly ineffectual. This argument has some force but is by no means conclusive. Any mechanism for enforcing or urging social responsibility upon firms must of course reckon with a profit motive, with a desire to evade whatever response of controls is imposed. But it does not mean that we cannot expect any degree of responsibility at all.

One finds a rather different argument, frequently stated by some economists. It will probably strike the noneconomist as rather strange, at least at first hearing. The assertion is that firms *ought* to maximize profits; not merely do they like to do so but there is practically a social obligation to do so. Let me briefly sketch the argument:

Firms buy the goods and services they need for production. What they buy they pay for and therefore they are paying for whatever costs they impose upon others. What they receive in payment by selling their goods, they receive because the purchaser considers it worthwhile. This is a world of voluntary contracts; nobody *has* to buy the goods. If he chooses to buy it, it must be that he is getting a benefit measured by the price he pays. Hence, it is argued, profit really represents the net contribution that the firm makes to the social good, and the profits should therefore be made as large as possible. When firms compete with each other, in selling their goods or in buying labor or other

Kenneth J. Arrow, "Social Responsibility and Economic Efficiency," *Public Policy* 21 (Summer 1973). Reprinted by permission.

services, they may have to lower their selling prices in order to get more of the market for themselves or raise their wages; in either case the benefits which the firm is deriving are in some respects shared with the population at large. The forces of competition prevent the firms from engrossing too large a share of the social benefit. Now, as far as it goes this argument is sound. The problem is that it may not go far enough.

Under the proper assumptions profit maximization is indeed efficient in the sense that it can achieve as high a level of satisfaction as possible for any one consumer without reducing the levels of satisfaction of other consumers or using more resources than society is endowed with. But the limits of the argument must be stressed. I want to mention two well-known points in passing without making them the principal focus of discussion. First of all, the argument assumes that the forces of competition are sufficiently vigorous. But there is no social justification for profit maximization by monopolies. This is an important and well-known qualification. Second, the distribution of income that results from unrestrained profit maximization is very unequal. The competitive maximizing economy is indeed efficient—this shows up in high average incomes—but the high average is accompanied by widespread poverty on the one hand and vast riches, at least for a few, on the other. To many of us this is a very undesirable consequence.

Profit maximization has yet another effect on society. It tends to point away from the expression of altruistic motives. Altruistic motives are motives whose gratification is just as legitimate as selfish motives, and the expression of those motives is something we probably wish to encourage. A profit-maximizing, self-centered form of economic behavior does not provide any room for the expression of such motives.

Even if the three problems above were set aside . . . there are still two categories of effects where the arguments for profit maximization break down: The first is illustrated by pollution or congestion. Here it is no longer true (and this is the key to these issues) that the firm in fact does pay for the

harm it imposes on others. When it takes a person's time and uses it at work, the firm is paying for this, and therefore the transaction can be regarded as a beneficial exchange from the point of view of both parties. We have no similar mechanism by which the pollution which a firm imposes upon its neighborhood is paid for. Therefore the firm will have a tendency to pollute more than is desirable. That is, the benefit to it or to its customers from the expanded activity is really not as great, or may not be as great, as the cost it is imposing upon the neighborhood. But since it does not pay that cost, there is no profit incentive to refrain.

The same argument applies to traffic congestion when no charge is made for the addition of cars or trucks on the highway. It makes everybody less comfortable. It delays others and increases the probability of accidents; in short, it imposes a cost upon a large number of members of the society, a cost which is not paid for by the imposer of the cost, at least not in full. The person congesting is also congested, but the costs he is imposing on others are much greater than those he suffers himself. Therefore there will be a tendency to overutilize those goods for which no price is charged, particularly scarce highway space.

There are many other examples of this kind, but these two will serve to illustrate the point in question: some effort must be made to alter the profit-maximizing behavior of firms in those cases where it is imposing costs on others which are not easily compensated through an appropriate set of prices.

The second category of effects where profit maximization is not socially desirable is that in which there are quality effects about which the firm knows more than the buyer. Let me illustrate by considering the sale of a used car. (Similar considerations apply to the sale of new cars.) A used car has potential defects and typically the seller knows more about the defects than the buyer. The buyer is not in a position to distinguish among used cars, and therefore he will be willing to pay the same amount for two used cars of differing quality because he cannot tell the difference between them. As a result, there is an inefficiency in the sale of used cars. If somehow or other the cars were distinguished as to their quality, there would be some buyers who would prefer a cheaper car with more defects because they intend to use it very little or they only want it for a short period, while others will want a better car at a higher price. In fact, however, the two kinds of car are sold indiscriminately to the two groups of buyers at the same price, so that we can argue that there is a distinct loss of consumer satisfaction imposed by the failure to convey information that is available to the seller. The buyers are not necessarily being cheated. They may be, but the problem of inefficiency would remain if they weren't. One can imagine a situation where, from past experience, buyers of used cars are aware that cars that look alike may turn out to be quite different. Without knowing whether a particular car is good or bad, they do know that there are good and bad cars, and of course their willingness to pay for the cars is influenced accordingly. The main loser from a monetary viewpoint may not be the customer, but rather the seller of the good car. The buyer will pay a price which is only appropriate to a lottery that gives him a good car or a bad car with varying probabilities, and therefore the seller of the good car gets less than the value of the car. The seller of the bad car is, of course, the beneficiary. Clearly then, if one could arrange to transmit the truth from the sellers to the buyers, the efficiency of the market would be greatly improved. The used-car illustration is an example of a very general phenomenon. . . .

Defenders of unrestricted profit maximization usually assume that the consumer is well informed or at least that he becomes so by his own experience, in repeated purchases, or by information about what has happened to other people like him. This argument is empirically shaky; even the ability of individuals to analyze the effects of their own past purchases may be limited, particularly with respect to complicated mechanisms. But there are two further defects. The risks, including death, may be so great that even one misleading experience is bad enough, and the opportunity to learn from repeated trials is not of much use. Also, in a world where the products are continually changing, the possibility of learning from experience is greatly reduced. Automobile companies are continually introducing new models which at least purport to differ from what they were in the past, though doubtless the change is more external than

internal. New drugs are being introduced all the time; the fact that one has had bad experiences with one drug may provide very little information about the next one.

Thus there are two types of situation in which the simple rule of maximizing profits is socially inefficient: the case in which costs are not paid for, as in pollution, and the case in which the seller has considerably more knowledge about his product than the buyer, particularly with regard to safety. In these situations it is clearly desirable to have some idea of social responsibility, that is, to experience an obligation, whether ethical, moral, or legal. Now we cannot expect such an obligation to be created out of thin air. To be meaningful, any obligation of this kind, any feeling or rule of behavior has to be embodied in some definite social institution. I use that term broadly: a legal code is a social institution in a sense. Exhortation to do good must be made specific in some external form, a steady reminder and perhaps enforcer of desirable values. Part of the need is simply for factual information as a guide to individual behavior. A firm may need to be told what is right and what is wrong when in fact it is polluting, or which safety requirements are reasonable and which are too extreme or too costly to be worth consideration. Institutionalization of the social responsibility of firms also serves another very important function. It provides some assurance to any one firm that the firms with which it is in competition will also accept the same responsibility. If a firm has some code imposed from the outside, there is some expectation that other firms will obey it too and therefore there is some assurance that it need not fear any excessive cost to its good behavior.

Let me turn to some alternative kinds of institutions that can be considered as embodying the possible social responsibilities of firms. First, we have legal regulation, as in the case of pollution where laws are passed about the kind of burning that may take place, and about setting maximum standards for emissions. A second category is that of taxes.

Economists, with good reason, like to preach taxation as opposed to regulation. The movement to tax polluting emissions is getting under way and there is a fairly widely backed proposal in Congress to tax sulfur dioxide emissions from industrial smokestacks. That is an example of the second kind of institutionalization of social responsibility. The responsibility is made very clear: the violator pays for violations.

A third very old remedy or institution is that of legal liability—the liability of the civil law. One can be sued for damages. Such cases apparently go back to the Middle Ages. Regulation also extends back very far. There was an ordinance in London about the year 1300 prohibiting the burning of coal, because of the smoke nuisance.

The fourth class of institutions is represented by ethical codes. Restraint is achieved not by appealing to each individual's conscience but rather by having some generally understood definition of appropriate behavior. . . . [w]hen there is a wide difference in knowledge between the two sides of the market, recognized ethical codes can be a great contribution to economic efficiency. Actually we do have examples of this in our everyday lives, but in very limited areas. The case of medical ethics is the most striking. By its very nature there is a very large difference in knowledge between the buyer and the seller. One is, in fact, buying precisely the service of someone with much more knowledge than you have. To make this relationship a viable one, ethical codes have grown up over the centuries, both to avoid the possibility of exploitation by the physician and to assure the buyer of medical services that he is not being exploited. I am not suggesting that these are universally obeyed, but there is a strong presumption that the doctor is going to perform to a large extent with your welfare in mind. Unnecessary medical expenses or other abuses are perceived as violations of ethics. There is a powerful ethical background against which we make this judgment. Behavior that we would regard as highly reprehensible in a physician is judged less harshly when found among businessmen. The medical profession is typical of professions in general. All professions involve a situation in which knowledge is unequal on two sides of the market by the very definition of the profession, and therefore there have grown up ethical principles that afford some protection to the client. Notice there is a mutual benefit in this. The fact is that if you had sufficient distrust of a doctor's services, you wouldn't buy them. Therefore the physician wants an ethical code to act as assurance to the buyer, and he certainly wants his competitors to obey this same code, partly because any violation may put him at a disadvantage but more especially because the violation will reflect on him, since the buyer of the medical services may not be able to distinguish one doctor from another. A close look reveals that a great deal of economic life depends for its viability on a certain limited degree of ethical commitment. Purely selfish behavior of individuals is really incompatible with any kind of settled economic life. There is almost invariably some element of trust and confidence. Much business is done on the basis of verbal assurance. It would be too elaborate to try to get written commitments on every possible point. Every contract depends for its observance on a mass of unspecified conditions which suggest that the performance will be carried out in good faith without insistence on sticking literally to its wording. To put the matter in its simplest form, in almost every economic transaction, in any exchange of goods for money, somebody gives up his valuable asset before he gets the other's; either the goods are given before the money or the money is given before the goods. Moreover there is a general confidence that there won't be any violation of the implicit agreement. Another example in daily life of this kind of ethics is the observance of queue discipline. People line up; there are people who try to break in ahead of you, but there is an ethic which holds that this is bad. It is clearly an ethic which is in everybody's interest to preserve; one waits at the end of the line this time, and one is protected against somebody's coming in ahead of him.

In the context of product safety, efficiency would be greatly enhanced by accepted ethical rules. Sometimes it may be enough to have an ethical compulsion to reveal all the information available and let the buyer choose. This is not necessarily always the best. It can be argued that under some circumstances setting minimum safety standards and simply not putting out products that do not meet them would be desirable and should be felt by the businessman to be an obligation.

1. How does Arrow propose to improve the efficiency of business?

2. Explain Arrow's "used-car" argument. What does it show?

Richard Parker | # Corporate Social Responsibility and Crisis

Richard Parker, an economist, teaches at the Kennedy School of Government at Harvard.

For writers who seek to influence public affairs, timing plays a paramount role. And few writers have had better timing than Adolf Augustus Berle.

In the summer of 1932, with America trapped in the greatest financial crisis in its history, Berle published *The Modern Corporation and Private Property*, a scholarly yet readable analysis of America's largest companies and their managers. Berle is largely forgotten today, yet with that book he succeeded in persuading Americans to see their economic system in a new way—and helped set the stage for the most fundamental realignment of power since abolition.

The stock market had plunged vertiginously three years earlier, and by 1932 Americans were desperate to reverse the much wider collapse that had ensued— and to make sure it wouldn't happen again. The New Republic was soon hailing *The Modern Corporation* as the book of the year, while *The New York Herald Tribune* pronounced it "the most important work bearing on American statecraft" since the Federalist Papers. Louis Brandeis would cite its arguments in a major Supreme Court ruling on corporate power. Running for president, Franklin Delano Roosevelt recruited Berle—a Republican Wall Street lawyer who had supported Hoover—to join his "brain trust," and that fall entrusted him with drafting what

became the most important speech of the campaign. After the election, Berle remained in New York, yet his connection to the president he audaciously addressed as "Dear Caesar" was such that *Time* would characterize *The Modern Corporation* as "the economic bible of the Roosevelt administration."

At first glance, the book would hardly seem to merit such broad acclaim. But if the topic was limited, Berle's analysis was not. He used the data compiled by his co-author, the economist Gardiner Means, to examine how markets had become concentrated in just a few hundred firms and how senior managers had wrested power from the companies' legal owners, the shareholders. No radical, Berle was eager to preserve the corporate system, which he called "the flower of our industrial organization." But he now believed that new controls would have to balance "a variety of claims by various groups in the community"—not just its managers or shareholders—and assign "to each a portion of the income stream on the basis of public policy rather than private cupidity."

In 1932, as in our own moment of financial crisis, most Americans could see that something needed to be done because these new behemoths—which had turned America from a nation of farmers into the world's largest industrial power—were on the verge of collapse, poised like Samson to pull the entire economy down with them. Berle's genius in *The Modern Corporation* was to align his professional

From the *New York Times*, November 7, 2008.

insights with the public's fears, and its anger. As he starkly put it in his preface, "Between a political organization of society and an economic organization of society, which will be the dominant form?"

In Theodore Roosevelt's and Woodrow Wilson's era, reformers like Brandeis had argued that strict anti-monopoly and anti-collusion laws could return America to a place of small firms and farms, the beau ideal of Adam Smith's market model. But Americans continued rushing to the cities, spurring an explosion in mass consumption, financed by a boom in cheap consumer credit and easy home loans. Then, in 1929, the markets crashed.

The crash for a time reinvigorated not only the anti-monopolists, but also union organizers, socialists, agrarian populists and crackpot utopians. It also brought forth "forward looking" chief executives like Gerald Swope of General Electric, who supported progressive corporatism—a world of government-mandated business cartels in exchange for higher wages, improved working conditions, and corporate-based workers' compensation, pension and unemployment plans. Berle, however, was keen on none of these solutions. In his book, he explained that giant corporations were not "natural" economic institutions but recent inventions of the law, cobbled together on the remains of the medieval corporation, a quite different institution. What the Depression showed, he argued, was that modern corporations had failed not only stockholders, but the public—and would do so again, if left unregulated.

But what sort of regulation was required? On details, Berle was maddeningly but deliberately vague. What he did say clearly was that government needed to bear final responsibility for the economy by using its powers to balance supply and demand. It would also need to require corporate directors to manage the managers, not just for shareholders' benefit but in accordance with new rules codifying the collective rights of stakeholders and the broader social responsibilities of corporations.

The impact of Berle's ideas was no doubt enhanced by his decidedly nonradical biography. The son of a reform-minded Congregational minister and his wealthy wife, he had entered Harvard at 14 and finished Harvard Law School at 21—at the time its

youngest graduate ever. (Arrogant as well as gifted, he once showed up in Felix Frankfurter's class the semester after completing it. Puzzled, Frankfurter asked him why he was back. "Oh," Berle replied, "I wanted to see if you'd learned anything since last year.") After a year at Louis Brandeis's firm, he briefly did public-interest legal work before marrying well and settling down to a prosperous career in Wall Street corporate law.

As clients flocked to him, however, he began questioning the very system that was making them (and him) rich. In 1923, alarmed by the venality, the chicanery and frequently the stupidity of Wall Street, he started writing articles that over the next several years would virtually invent the modern field of corporate finance law, emphasizing moderate solutions. After Columbia Law School offered him a job in 1927, he began cycling between his lucrative practice downtown and his teaching uptown.

But the Great Crash—and the subsequent revelations of market manipulation, fraud and reckless risk-taking—forced Berle to change sides. He was a Mugwump Republican, but the economic chaos of the Depression, and the threat it posed to American democracy, convinced him a new sort of regulation was now unavoidable.

In late 1931, Franklin Roosevelt, then governor of New York, called on the Columbia political scientist Raymond Moley. Roosevelt was weighing a run for president and was looking for fresh ideas. Moley quickly approached Berle and connected the two ambitious Harvard men.

A month after *The Modern Corporation* appeared, Berle drafted Roosevelt's famous Commonwealth Club address, delivered in September 1932. Proclaiming that "the day of enlightened administration has come," Roosevelt articulated the rationale for much of the New Deal's financial and corporate reforms, including deposit insurance and securities regulation. He defended the coming government interventions as protecting individualism and private property against concentrated economic power. Calling for a new "economic constitutional order," he declared it our common duty to "build toward the time when a major depression cannot occur again."

"None of Roosevelt's speeches," Arthur Schlesinger, Jr., later wrote, "caught up more poignantly the intellectual moods of the early Depression than this one." It helped assure his landslide victory—and earned Berle a series of ever more important posts in the administration. America began an unprecedented forty-year expansion.

By the Reagan era, however, a new philosophy would take hold, and the public oversight of markets that Berle helped pioneer would over time be swept aside, in confident belief that markets could self-regulate and that government was the problem, not the solution.

Today, that era itself seems to be coming to end, and the question Berle posed—will democracy rule the corporations, or will the corporations rule democracy?—seems a profoundly important one worth asking again.

QUESTIONS

1. What does Berle teach us about how we get into financial crises?

2. What ethical principles might Berle have proposed, might you guess, to inform regulation of markets?

Alexei M. Marcoux | # Business Ethics Gone Wrong

Alexei M. Marcoux is assistant professor of management at Loyola University in Chicago.

It arose from the scandals that plagued Wall Street during the 1980s: a growing public support for business ethics as an object of study and teaching in America's colleges and universities. Business ethics courses are offered (and often, for business majors, required) in ever-increasing numbers. The ranks of the academy swell with professors whose principal vocation is teaching and writing in business ethics. Philanthropists endow chairs in business ethics faster than universities can fill them.

Although deriving and explaining the ethical norms that support and lubricate a wellfunctioning market economy are worthwhile tasks, the intellectual fashion in business ethics is quite a different matter. For among business ethicists there is a consensus favoring the *stakeholder theory* of the firm—a theory that seeks to redefine and reorient the purpose and the activities of the firm. Far from providing an ethical foundation for

capitalism, these business ethicists seek to change it dramatically.

SHAREHOLDERS AND STAKEHOLDERS

Stakeholder talk is rampant. In Great Britain, Tony Blair's Labour Party came to power promising Britons a "stakeholder society." Perhaps capitalizing on the trend, Yale law professors Bruce Ackerman and Anne Alstott argue for a far-reaching overhaul of the American tax and welfare systems in their recent book, *The Stakeholder Society*. But stakeholder theory, as it has emerged in business ethics, is different.

Stakeholder theory is most closely associated with R. Edward Freeman, Olsson Professor of Applied Ethics at the University of Virginia's Darden School. The theory holds that managers ought to serve the interests of all those who have a "stake" in (that is, affect or are affected by) the firm. Stakeholders

From *Cato Policy Report,* May/June 2000, Vol. 22, No. 3.

include shareholders, employees, suppliers, customers, and the communities in which the firm operates—a collection that Freeman terms the "big five." The very purpose of the firm, according to this view, is to serve and coordinate the interests of its various stakeholders. It is the moral obligation of the firm's managers to strike an appropriate balance among the big five interests in directing the activities of the firm.

This understanding of the firm's purpose and its management's obligations diverges sharply from the understanding advanced in the *shareholder theory* of the firm. According to shareholder theorists such as Nobel laureate economist Milton Friedman, managers ought to serve the interests of the firm's owners, the shareholders. Social obligations of the firm are limited to making good on contracts, obeying the law, and adhering to ordinary moral expectations. In short, obligations to nonshareholders stand as *side-constraints* on the pursuit of shareholder interests. This is the view that informs American corporate law and that Friedman defends in his *1970 New York Times Magazine* essay, "The Social Responsibility of Business Is to Increase Its Profits."

CORPORATE SOCIAL RESPONSIBILITY AND STAKEHOLDER THEORY

Stakeholder theory seeks to overthrow the shareholder orientation of the firm. It is an outgrowth of the corporate social responsibility (CSR) movement to which Friedman's essay responds. According to CSR, the firm is obligated to "give something back" to those that make its success possible. The image of the firm presented in CSR is that of a free rider, unjustly and uncooperatively enriching itself to the detriment of the community. Socially responsible deeds (such as patronizing the arts or mitigating unemployment) are necessary to redeem firms and transform them into good citizens.

One wonders, however, why firms are obligated to give something back to those to whom they routinely give so much already. Rather than enslave their employees, firms typically pay them wages and benefits in return for their labor. Rather than steal from their customers, firms typically deliver goods and services in return for the revenues that customers provide. Rather than free ride on public provisions, firms typically pay taxes and obey the law. Moreover, these compensations are ones to which the affected parties or (in the case of communities and unionized employees) their agents freely agree. For what reasons, then, is one to conclude that those compensations are inadequate or unjust, necessitating that firms give something more to those whom they have already compensated?

Stakeholder theory constitutes at least something of an advance over CSR. Whereas CSR is fundamentally antagonistic to capitalist enterprise, viewing both firm and manager as social parasites in need of a strong reformative hand, stakeholder theory takes a different tack. Rather than offer stakeholder theory as a means of overthrowing capitalist enterprise, stakeholder theorists profess to offer theirs as a strategy for improving it. As Robert Phillips of the University of Penn-sylvania's Wharton School writes, "One of the goals of the stakeholder theory is to maintain the benefits of the free market while minimizing the potential ethical problems created by capitalism."

On the theory that "you'll catch more flies with honey than with vinegar," stakeholder theorists ostensibly praise corporate leaders and maintain that firms are social institutions and their managers are community leaders. Given appropriate latitude, firms and managers are disposed to serve the social good. Corporate law and the market for corporate control, however, preclude firms and managers from following their inclinations and serving their social missions. Stakeholder theory seeks to free both firm and manager from their exclusive attention to the narrow, parochial concerns of shareholders so that they can focus on a broader set of interests.

But although the diagnosis of the problem with capitalist enterprise is (at least, on the face of it) different from that advanced in CSR, the stakeholder theorists' remedy is largely the same: the elevation of nonshareholding interests to the level of shareholder interests in formulating business strategy and policy.

The stakeholder-oriented manager is admonished to weigh and balance stakeholder interests, trading off one against another in settling on a course of action. Stakeholder theorists seek a reorientation of the corporate law toward the interests of stakeholders and the insulation of managers from the market for corporate control.

PROBLEMS

Whatever the appeal of the stakeholder theory's inclusiveness of and sensitivity to the myriad interests that affect and are affected by firms, there are several powerful reasons to resist the theory's adoption and embodiment in a reformed corporate law.

Equity Capital

Because it undermines shareholder property rights, stakeholder-oriented management denigrates and discourages equity investment. In the stakeholder-oriented firm, equity investors bear the same downside risks that they bear in the traditionally governed, shareholder-oriented firm. The upside potential of their investment, however, is diminished significantly; for in distributing the fruits of the firm's success, equity investor interests are only some among many to be considered and served. In short, when the firm loses, shareholders lose; when the firm wins, shareholders might lose anyway if other interests are deemed to be more weighty and important.

Stakeholder-oriented management effectively eliminates issuing shares as a means of financing the firm's growth and new ventures. By diminishing the orientation of the firm toward shareholder interests, stakeholder-oriented management will presumably lead investors to discount sharply the value they attach to shareholdings. So stakeholder-oriented management essentially entails a near-exclusive reliance on debt as the fuel of expansion.

But the problems do not stop there. Debtholders, whether banks or bondholders, typically use equity holdings, returns to equity, and appreciation in the market price for shares as signals of financial health, and hence as mechanisms for pricing debt capital. Widespread or legally mandatory adoption of stakeholder-oriented management threatens to undermine well-established, stable, and efficient market norms for pricing capital in favor of a regime under which capital is more costly for firms to acquire because investment (whether in the form of equity or debt) is an inherently riskier proposition. That, in turn, threatens prospects for economic growth, stable employment, and the liquidity of financial markets. In short, stakeholder-oriented management promises poorer, static, risk-averse firms and hence a poorer, static, risk-averse economy. Stakeholder-oriented management is contrary to the interests of the very stakeholders it is intended to help.

Managerial Accountability

People recoil in horror at corporate officers' and directors' salaries, perks, and other bonuses that at times bear no relation to the performance of the firms they manage. This sorry state of affairs results from the confluence of a number of recent trends in corporate law that make it more difficult for shareholders to discipline self-serving managers:

- The decline of the *ultra vires* doctrine (under which shareholders could sue managers for embarking on projects contrary to the corporate purpose).
- The emergence of so-called corporate constituency statutes (which permit managers to consider and appeal to a broader range of interests in determining how and whether to fend off a takeover bid—and thereby hamper the smooth operation of the market for corporate control).
- The expansive reading given to the business judgment rule (which shields some managerial actions from substantive review by courts) by the Supreme Court of Delaware—where many firms are incorporated.

But whatever the impediments to disciplining self-serving managers under current law and public policy, they pale in comparison with those promised by stakeholder-oriented management (and a stakeholder-oriented corporate law). Whereas under the current corporate law much self-serving managerial behavior is recognizably self-serving but shielded from substantive review, under stakeholder-oriented corporate law such behavior would be considerably more difficult even to detect, as well as to deter.

It would be more difficult to detect because all but the most egregious of self-serving managerial behavior will coincide with the interests of *some* stakeholding group, and hence the self-serving manager may point to the benefited and burdened stakeholders and argue that, in his estimation, this was the optimal way to balance competing stakeholder interests. Absent a powerful principle of balanced distribution of the benefits of the firm (something stakeholder theorists have been notoriously slow to sketch), stakeholder theorists must acquiesce in self-serving managerial action that can plausibly be said to accomplish some sort of balance among competing stakeholder interests. That point is made with admirable clarity by Frank Easterbrook and Daniel Fischel in their 1991 book, *The Economic Structure of Corporate Law*: "A manager told to serve two masters (a little for the equity holders, a little for the community) has been freed of both and is answerable to neither. Faced with a demand from either group, the manager can appeal to the interests of the other."

Self-serving managerial action would be more difficult to deter under stakeholder-oriented corporate law because stakeholder theory anticipates that good-faith stakeholder-oriented managerial actions will serve some interests and frustrate others in pursuit of an overall balance of interests. Therefore, stakeholder-oriented corporate law must provide protections to managers at least as extensive as those afforded under current business judgment rule doctrine—lest managers be the perpetual object of derivative lawsuits brought by shareholders, employees, customers, suppliers, or communities who believe that their interests were unfairly or improperly weighed and balanced. Between the ability of managers to justify their self-serving behavior in terms of the balanced pursuit of stakeholder

interests, on the one hand, and the protections that a stakeholder-oriented corporate law must afford to managers if firms are to be managed at all, on the other hand, the accountability of managers for their actions must necessarily suffer.

Interest-Group Politics

Because stakeholder-oriented management anticipates the weighing and the balancing—and hence often the frustrating—of competing interests, it promises to make the boardroom (populated, per Freeman, by representatives of all stakeholding groups) the site of wasteful, inefficient interest-group politicking. That is, the corporate boardroom will be transformed from a forum in which economically rational strategies are adopted in pursuit of added value into one in which legislative and bureaucratic political maneuvering will be the order of the day. Surprisingly, stakeholder theorists recognize and, apparently, *welcome* this. In a 1998 issue of *Business Ethics Quarterly*, communitarian thinker Amitai Etzioni is comforted by the thought that there "is no reason to expect that the politics of corporate communities would be any different from other democratic systems."

One can scarcely imagine how firms, whose resources are far more limited than are those of governments (and unsupported by the taxing power), can remain viable if their decision procedures are characterized by the strategic bargaining, logrolling, and other wasteful tactics that are the hallmark of democratic politics. If a camel is a horse designed by a committee, then what misshapen beast is a firm shaped by the strategic interactions of its stakeholder representatives?

SMALL VICTORIES

The market economy, the liberty it safeguards, and the prosperity it secures are threatened not, as in the recent past, by firebrands who seek to abolish it, but by more modest tinkerers who seek to "improve" it in the name of myriad social concerns. Defending the market economy from this attack requires more than cataloging the defects of alternative economic systems and the merits of markets. It requires a principled defense of the shareholder-oriented firm—the basic productive institution on which the market economy is constructed.

Despite its worrisome implications, stakeholder-oriented management and its accompanying rhetoric encounter little systematic opposition in philosophy departments, business schools, or boardrooms. The costs of complacency about that state of affairs are potentially high. For although they have so far failed to bring wholesale change to the corporation and the law that governs it, stakeholder-oriented activists have won important piecemeal victories. The passage of corporate constituency statutes in several states has weakened the market for corporate control and, hence, the property rights of shareholders. Federal plant-closing legislation has legitimized among policymakers the idea that firm managers ought to be responsive to a multiplicity of interests. Corporate mission statements in which stakeholders and their interests feature prominently—whether adopted earnestly or as cover for self-serving managers—serve to further legitimize the subordination of shareholder interests to other concerns. If the market economy and its cornerstone, the shareholder-oriented firm, are in no danger of being dealt a decisive blow, they at least risk death by a thousand cuts.

BUSINESS ETHICS RECONSIDERED

Too often the free-market response to the changes sought by stakeholder-oriented business ethicists has been to denigrate the role of ethics in business— as if stakeholder-oriented reforms are the inevitable consequence of injecting concern for ethics into business. But the partisans of stakeholder theory are not spokespeople for ethics; they are spokespeople only for a particular conception of ethics— and a particularly flawed *conception*, at that. The manifold failings of stakeholder theory should not be taken to reflect poorly on the project of business ethics; rather, they reflect poorly on stakeholder theory itself.

Defenders of the free market, limited government, and the rule of law must articulate an *alternative* business ethics, one that recognizes and provides reasoned argument for the moral merit of the shareholder-oriented firm. Norms of honesty, integrity, and fair play, rather than an albatross around the neck of the free market, are a central, if neglected, part of the story of the success of the shareholder-oriented firm. In short, shareholder-oriented firms are not merely wealth-enhancing, they are good.

QUESTIONS

1. Define stakeholder theory, Define CSR.
2. List three flaws in stakeholder theory.

CASES

CASE 6.1
Mondragon Cooperatives
Ana G. Johnson and William F. Whyte

The Basque region of Spain contains the world's most successful industrial cooperative, the Mondragon system. The Mondragon system is a group of more than 80 cooperatively owned firms with a combined total of over 18,000 employee owners. These profitable co-ops are the product of a single cooperative firm begun in 1956 under the guidance of a Spanish priest, José Maria Arizmendi.

The system of employee-owned businesses is supported by a cooperative educational system that provides well-educated workers and, most importantly, by a credit union that provides the capital required to sustain cooperative firms in their early years. The credit union's capital is raised from deposits by local residents. Its funds are used to supply loans to cover 60 percent of the startup costs of new cooperative enterprises and also to cover any deficits that accrue during the first two years of the firm's existence. The credit union also supplies invaluable organizational assistance by assigning credit union specialists to assist the cooperative's management in running the new firm. None of the 56 new cooperatives begun through the credit union between 1961 and 1976 has failed.

The cooperative firms maintain a maximum disparity between workers' wages of three to one. Since entry level employees are paid wages comparable to those in noncooperative firms, higher level employees have wages below the norm in other firms. This may be compensated for by the fact that most profits of the firm eventually return to the worker owners. But the distribution of annual profits is controlled by a policy which mandates that 10 to 15 percent of the profits be returned to support community activities such as the school system, 15 percent be reinvested in the firm, and the remaining 70 percent be invested in accounts within the firm in the names of individual employees. These accounts pay employees interest, but the principal cannot be withdrawn until the worker retires. This policy for controlled profit distribution solves one of the most common problems of cooperative enterprises—the lack of operating capital due to too little reinvestment.

Mondragon policies also protect against another tendency of cooperatives—to revert to traditional private ownership by non-employee stockholders. At Mondragon, the worker owners cannot sell their shares or continue to own stock after leaving the company. In addition, every new employee is required to buy shares in the firm (purchase of those shares can be facilitated by personal loans from the credit union).

Internal governance of the Mondragon cooperatives had until recently been primarily hierarchical and autocratic. Work at Mondragon differed little

This case was prepared from information found in the following sources: "The Mondragon System of Worker Production Cooperatives," Ana G. Johnson and William F. Whyte, *Industrial and Labor Relations Review*, vol. 31, no. 1, pp. 18–30; *Working Together*, John Simmons and William Mares (New York University Press, 1985), pp. 136–142.

from the most routinized American factory. However, in the 1970s the Mondragon system began to evolve a more participatory system of governance in response to labor unrest at one of the larger cooperatives. Now most cooperatives have employee-elected boards to oversee management, direct involvement at the shop floor, and employee social councils which consider issues related to working conditions.

QUESTIONS

1. How could a reliable source of initial capital for cooperative firms be created in the United States?

2. What do you imagine prevents most U.S. cooperatives from adopting a Mondragon-like policy for controlling shares?

3. Is a narrow range of wage levels necessary for maintaining a successful cooperative enterprise?

CASE 6.2
The Social Audit
Rogene A. Buchholz

Monolith, a large conglomerate, has recently come under fire from a variety of federal agencies and/or offices because of alleged problems in some of its operations. The Occupational Safety and Health Administration has charged it with certain violations in its steel plants, the Office of Federal Contract Compliance Programs is threatening to cancel some of the government contracts the company enjoys because of its failure to meet affirmative action guidelines, and the Federal Trade Commission is taking a close look at certain aspects of the corporation's advertising strategies. A management consultant called in to study the situation has advised that the company would not be in this predicament if it had periodically conducted a social audit. The consultant recommends that such an audit be taken systematically in the future.

The company is thus considering doing something along these lines, but it is finding that there is no agreement on what a social audit should look like. It has run across various proposals as to what kinds of things should appear on a social audit

and what measures are appropriate. There is also the question as to whether such an audit should be used for internal management purposes only or disclosed to the outside public. Nonetheless, the company is committed to developing some kind of means to determine how well it is doing in areas that cannot be measured by the traditional financial statements. It has formed a team to deal with this problem and make proposals to top management as to what exactly ought to be done in this regard.

QUESTIONS

1. What types of regulations may the conglomerate have violated based on the agencies mentioned in the case? Be as specific as possible. Would an audit of the areas covered by these regulations help the company with its compliance efforts?

2. What do you think of the suggestion to conduct a social audit? As far as the issues raised in this case are concerned, what type of social audit might be most useful to alleviate some of the problems the company is currently facing?

From Rogene A. Buchholz, *Business, Environment and Public Policy* (Englewood Cliffs; NJ: Prentice Hall, 1995).

CASE 6.3

The NYSEG Corporate Responsibility Case

Kelley MacDougall, Tom L. Beauchamp, and John Cuddihy

> We are responsible to the communities in which
> we live and work and to the world community as
> well. We must be good citizens and support good
> works and charities . . . . We must encourage civic
> improvements and better health and education.[1]

Many large corporations currently operate consumer responsibility or social responsibility programs, which aim to return something to the consumer or to the community in which the company does business. New York State Electric and Gas (NYSEG) is one company that has created a program to discharge what its officers consider to be the company's responsibility to its public.

NYSEG is a New York Stock Exchange-traded public utility with approximately 60,500 shareholders. It supplies gas and electricity to New York State. NYSEG currently earns 89 percent of its revenues from electricity and 11 percent from gas sales. The company is generally ranked as having solid but not excellent financial strength. Earnings per share have declined in recent years because of the regulatory climate and the company's write-offs for its Nine Mile Point #2 nuclear unit. In order to finance the unit, the company at one point had to absorb delay costs of several million dollars per month. The setback reduced shareholders' dividends for the first time in many years. NYSEG's financial base is now less secure than in the past because of the lowered earnings per share and the increased plant costs.

The company's corporate responsibility program has been in effect throughout this period of financial reversal. NYSEG designed the program to aid customers who are unable to pay their utility bills for various reasons. The program does not simply help customers pay their bills to the company. Rather, NYSEG hopes the program will find people in the community in unfortunate or desperate circumstances and alleviate their predicament. The two objectives often coincide.

NYSEG has created a system of consumer representatives, social workers trained to deal with customers and their problems. Since the program's 1978 inception, NYSEG has maintained a staff of 13 consumer representatives. Each handles approximately 40 cases a month, over half of which result in successful financial assistance. The remaining cases are referred to other organizations for further assistance.

The process works as follows: When the company's credit department believes a special investigation should be made into a customer's situation, the employee refers the case to the consumer representative. Referrals also come from human service agencies and from customers directly. Examples of appropriate referrals include unemployed household heads; paying customers who suffer serious injury, lengthy illness, or death; and low-income senior citizens or those on fixed incomes who cannot deal with rising costs of living. To qualify for assistance, NYSEG requires only that the customers must be suffering from hardships they are willing to work to resolve.

Consumer representatives are primarily concerned with preventing the shutoff of service to these customers. They employ an assortment of resources to put them back on their feet, including programs offered by the New York State Department of Social Services and the federal Home Energy Assistance Program (HEAP), which awards annual grants of varying amounts to qualified families. In addition the consumer representatives provide financial counseling and help customers with their medical bills and education planning. They arrange assistance from

This case was prepared by Kelley MacDougall and Tom L. Beauchamp and revised by John Cuddihy. Not to be duplicated without permission of the holder of the copyright, © 1991 Tom L. Beauchamp. This case is indebted to Cathy Hughto-Delzer, NYSEG Consumer Assistance Program Supervisor. Used by permission.

churches and social services, provide food stamps, and help arrange VA benefits.

NYSEG also created a direct financial assistance program called Project Share, which enables paying customers who are not in financial difficulty to make charitable donations through their bills. They are asked voluntarily to add to their bill each month one, two, or five extra dollars, which are placed in a special fund overseen by the American Red Cross. This special Fuel Fund is intended to help those 60 years and older on fixed incomes who have no other means of paying their bills. Help is also provided for the handicapped and blind who likewise have few sources of funds. Many Project Share recipients do not qualify for government-funded assistance programs but nonetheless face energy problems. Through December 1990 Project Share had raised over $1.5 million and had successfully assisted more than 8,000 people.

The rationale or justification of this corporate responsibility program is rooted in the history of public utilities and rising energy costs in North America. Originally public utilities provided a relatively inexpensive product. NYSEG and the entire industry considered its public responsibility limited to the business function of providing energy at the lowest possible costs and returning dividends to investors. NYSEG did not concern itself with its customers' financial troubles. The customer or the social welfare system handled all problems of unpaid bills.

However, the skyrocketing energy costs in the 1970s changed customer resources and NYSEG's perspective. The energy crisis caused many long-term customers to encounter difficulty in paying their bills, and the likelihood of power shutoffs increased as a result. NYSEG then accepted a responsibility to assist these valued customers by creating the Consumer Representative system.

NYSEG believes its contribution is especially important now because recent reductions in federal assistance programs have shifted the burden of addressing these problems to the private sector. Project Share is viewed as "a logical extension of the President's call for increased volunteerism at the local level."[2] NYSEG chose the American Red Cross to cosponsor Project Share because of its experience in providing emergency assistance.

The costs of NYSEG's involvement in the program are regarded by company officers as low. NYSEG has few additional costs beyond the consumer representatives' salaries and benefits, which total $462,625 annually and are treated as operating expenses. To augment Project Share's financial support, NYSEG shareholders give the program an annual, need-based grant. In the past, shareholder grants have ranged from $40,000 to $100,000. NYSEG also pays for some personnel and printing costs through consumer rate increases, despite a recent ruling by the New York State Supreme Court that forbids utilities from raising consumer rates to obtain funds for charitable contributions (Cahill v. Public Service Commission). The company has also strongly supported Project Share by giving $490,000 over a seven-year period. The company's annual revenues are in the range of $1.5 billion, and the company's total debt also runs to approximately $1.5 billion.

The company views some of the money expended for the corporate responsibility program as recovered because of customers retained and bills paid through the program. NYSEG assumes that these charges would, under normal circumstances, have remained unpaid and would eventually have been written off as a loss. NYSEG's bad-debt level is 20 percent lower than that of the average U.S. utility company. The company believes that its corporate responsibility policy is *both* altruistic *and* good business, despite the program's maintenance costs, which seem to slightly exceed recovered revenue.

NOTES

1. "The Johnson and Johnson Way" (from the Johnson and Johnson Company credo), 1986, p. 26.
2. NYSEG, Project Share Procedures Manual, 1988, p. 2.

QUESTIONS

1. Do you agree that NYSEG's Project Share is both altruistic and good business? Why or why not?
2. To what extent, if any, is Project Share an example of stakeholder management principles?
3. Could adherents to a stockholder theory of corporate responsibility and adherents to a stakeholder theory both endorse Project Share as socially responsible? Why or why not?

CASE 6.4
Beech-Nut's Imitation Apple Juice
Thomas I. White

In 1988, the Beech-Nut Nutrition Corporation and two of its top executives admitted that they had knowingly sold adulterated apple juice. In fact, the baby food, although described on the label as "100% fruit juice," contained little if any apple juice. The company agreed to pay a $2 million fine, but the ultimate cost to Beech-Nut was closer to $25 million when the settlement of a class action suit, legal fees, and lost sales are included. The two executives, Neils L. Hoyvald, the firm's former president and CEO, and John F. Lavery, former vice-president of manufacturing, were fined $100,000 each and sentenced to jail terms of a year and a day. (A major part of the conviction and Hoyvald's imprisonment were dismissed when an appeals court ruled that the trial had taken place in the wrong court.)

This example of corporate wrongdoing combines fraud with a coverup and was apparently driven by ongoing and intense financial pressure at Beech-Nut. In 1977, Beech-Nut changed suppliers of the concentrate used to produce its apple juice when it was offered the product at 20 percent below market rates by Interjuice Trading Corporation. This resulted in an annual savings of $250,000—no small amount for a company that was financially strapped. Despite misgivings about the juice by Jerome LiCari, Beech-Nut's director of research and development, laboratory tests could not prove that the juice was counterfeit. By 1981, however, LiCari believed that there was enough circumstantial evidence to suggest that the concentrate was a blend of synthetic ingredients, and he claims that he notified senior management of his belief. By that time, however, Hoyvald had apparently promised Nestlé, the Swiss food concern that had bought Beech-Nut, that the company would turn around financially in 1982. Beech-Nut had been sold to Nestlé in 1979 and had lost $2.5 million in fiscal 1981. But Hoyvald pledged a profit

of $700,000 for the following year, and the parent company apparently communicated to him that he must deliver. As Hoyvald put it, "The pressure was on." Changing suppliers and buying a more expensive concentrate would have made a profit impossible to achieve. Also, some Beech-Nut officials still pointed to the fact that there was no absolute proof that the apple juice was adulterated. (It is worth noting, however, that although Beech-Nut's policy was to stay with the concentrate as long as it could not be proven that it was counterfeit, other companies reversed the burden of proof and terminated a supplier if it could not prove that its product was genuine.) Some Beech-Nut officials also claimed that even if the juice were fake, it was not doing anyone any harm. The juice in the bottles might not be apple juice, but it was not a health hazard.

By mid-1982, however, a private detective hired by an industry association found proof that the concentrate was synthetic and presented it to Beech-Nut. The company did stop buying the concentrate at that time. But instead of publicly admitting the error, destroying or relabeling the inventory, and paying a fine, Hoyvald chose a strategy that would buy enough time to sell the $3.5 million worth of juice sitting in warehouses. The company refused to cooperate with an investigation against the suppliers and waited a few month. The product then was offered at large discounts to offshore distributors. To keep one step ahead of state law enforcement officials, inventory was even moved from one state to another. Hoyvald apparently believed that Beech-Nut's very existence was at stake. When asked by one of the prosecutors why the juice had simply not been destroyed, he replied, "And I could have called up Switzerland and told them I had just closed the company down. Because that is what would have been the result of it."

From Thomas I. White, *Business Ethics: A Philosophical Reader* (New York: Macmillan, 1993).

REFERENCES

Buder, Leonard, "2 Former Executives of Beech-Nut Guilty in Phony Juice Case," *New York Times*, February 18, 1988, A1, D3.

Traum, James, "Into the Mouths of Babes," *This World*, August 7, 1988, 14–15.

"What Led Beech-Nut Down the Road to Disgrace," *Business Week*, February 22, 1988, 124–128.

QUESTIONS

1. How seriously unethical is what Beech-Nut did? How seriously wrong is what Hoyvald and Lavery did?

2. How do you distinguish corporate from personal responsibility? Should the parent company, Nestlé, be held responsible for anything that happened?

3. Is the company's difficult financial condition an extenuating circumstance?

4. How relevant is the claim that the counterfeit juice did not hurt any babies who drank it?

5. If you were the judge in this case, what punishments would you assign the corporation and the individual executives?

6. What would the punishments look like if you used French's Hester Prynne Sanction, Shipp's modified vendetta, or Rafalko's beheading proposal?

CASE 6.5

Sentencing a Corporation to Prison

Thomas I. White

In 1988, Federal Judge Robert G. Doumar handed down an extremely unusual punishment for a corporation convicted of wrongdoing—he sentenced it to three years in prison. The Maryland-based Allegheny Bottling Company was found guilty of three years of price-fixing, and Judge Doumar wanted a penalty that would be sterner than the typical fine. "The corporation," explained the jurist, "cannot come in here, profit to the tune of $10 million and walk away with a $1 million fine." The punishment he chose, on top of such a fine, was clearly unexpected.

Judge Doumar later suspended the sentence and $50,000 of the fine, but he placed the company on probation. The judge explained that in the case of a corporation, imprisonment amounted to placing restrictions on the company's ability to operate. He ordered that four of the company's senior executives perform up to two years of full-time community service. And he threatened that if the company failed to do so, he would close down its operations.

Allegheny Bottling, a Pepsi bottling franchise, was accused of collaborating with the Mid-Atlantic Coca-Cola Bottling Company to set wholesale prices. Before Allegheny's sentencing, the price-fixing scheme had already led to convictions of Morton Lapides, former chairman of Allegheny, and James Harford, former president of Mid-Atlantic Coca-Cola. Both men were sentenced to three years in prison, with all but six months suspended. Harford was also sentenced to three years of community service. In his order that four of Allegheny's executives perform community service, Judge Doumar specified that their positions and salaries must be similar to those of the executives already sentenced.

Attorneys for the company objected, pointing out that there was no precedent for imprisoning a corporation.

From Thomas I. White, *Business Ethics: A Philosophical Reader* (New York: Macmillan, 1993).

REFERENCE

Hicks, Jonathan P., "Corporate Prison Term for Allegheny Bottling," *New York Times*, September 1, 1988, D2.

QUESTIONS

1. It is obviously difficult to punish a corporation, and one of the most frustrating aspects of trying to do so is that a fine can ultimately be passed along to stockholders, employees, or consumers—that is, people who had no hand in the wrongdoing pay the penalty. Is the Allegheny case a model of how to address this particular problem?

2. Two specific top executives were sentenced to prison and community service, Allegheny was ordered to have four other senior managers perform community service, and the company was ordered to pay a fine. How does this serve justice, broadly understood? Is such a model appropriately retributive for the crime? Would it deter other corporations? Most important, does it make any sense to sentence a corporation to imprisonment?

CASE 6.6
The Debate Over Doing Good
Brian Grow, Steve Hamm, and Louise Lee

Grow, Hamm, and Lee regularly report on current financial and corporate issues.

It's 8:30 a.m. on a Friday in July, and Carol B. Tomé is starting to sweat. The chief financial officer of Home Depot Inc. isn't getting ready to face a firing squad of investors or unveil troubled accounting at the home-improvement giant. Instead, she and 200 other Home Depot employees are helping to build a playground replete with swings, slides, and a jungle gym at a local girls' club in a hardscrabble neighborhood of Marietta, Georgia. Dressed in a white Home Depot T-shirt, a baseball cap, and blue capri jeans, Tomé tightens bolts, while others dump wood chips, mix concrete, and sink posts. The company, together with nonprofit playground specialist KaBOOM!, plans to build 1,000 more such kiddie parks in the next three years—and spend $25 million doing it.

Is this any way to build shareholder value at Home Depot, where the stock has been stuck near $43, down 35 percent from its all-time high? Chief Executive Robert L. Nardelli and his troops think so. Last year about 50,000 of Home Depot's 325,000 employees donated 2 million hours to community service. Now, Nardelli is trying to encourage more companies to volunteer at Home Depot's pace. At his invitation, executives from twenty-four companies and foundations gathered for five hours at Home Depot's Atlanta headquarters in May to discuss community service. Attendees included Lawrence R. Johnston of Albertson's, F. Duane Ackerman of BellSouth, Gerald Grinstein of Delta Air Lines, and William R. McDermott of SAP America. On September 1st these CEOs and others will kick off "A Month of Service," an ambitious plan, developed with community group the Hands-On Network, to deploy corporate volunteers on 2,000 projects across the country, and raise the total number of volunteers by 10 percent, or 6.4 million, in two years. "We look at this activity with the same eye that we look at business," Nardelli says.

Yes, companies have long paid lots of money—and lip service—to philanthropy and public service. But as Nardelli's confab indicates, managers from all parts of American business are increasingly seeing social responsibility as a strategic imperative.

From *Business Week*, August 15, 2005.

In June, General Electric Co. released its first "Citizenship Report" as a way for interest groups to assess its social performance from air pollution to volunteer hours. That followed the announcement in May of GE's ecomagination program, which will invest billions in environmentally friendly technologies. IBM uses its On Demand Community—a 40,000-employee volunteer program—as a way to bring IBM technologies to schools and community centers and plug its brand. Even the legendarily hard-nosed Wal-Mart Stores Inc. has come around to the cause. "We thought we could sit in Bentonville [Arkansas], take care of customers, take care of associates—and the world would leave us alone," CEO Lee Scott said at a recent analyst conference. "It doesn't work that way anymore."

BEHOLDEN TO MANY

What's behind this realization? At the very minimum, it's clear that companies recognize that it takes a robust, sharp public-relations strategy to navigate through the mines of today's operating environment. Among them: increased regulatory scrutiny; a global, twenty-four-hour news cycle; and communities hostile to scandal-tarred big businesses. But what Nardelli suggests is something deeper. In fact, it's a growing embrace of so-called stakeholder theory, which posits that companies are beholden not just to stockholders but also to suppliers, customers, employees, community members, even social activists. That's quite a departure from the long-dominant notion that corporations' only duty is to increase profits for shareholders. "Things have become a lot more interdependent," says Nardelli. "There are a broader range of constituents."

Such platitudes, of course, make critics cringe. The Nobel prize-winning economist Milton Friedman, ninety-three, casts a long intellectual shadow over the debate. In a seminal 1970 *New York Times Magazine* article, he declared social initiatives "fundamentally subversive" because they undermine the profit-seeking purpose of public companies and waste shareholders' money. Even today, Friedman, a senior fellow at Stanford University's Hoover Institution, rails at the idea that managers elected by shareholders to run companies should spend their profits on social causes. "Adam Smith said in 1776: 'I have never known much good done by those who profess to trade for the public good.' It's a good quote," says Friedman.

There's no doubt that a surge in community outreach and do-good deeds is, in large part, a gussied-up bid for good favor. Tarred by a raft of corporate scandals from Enron to WorldCom, social outreach can be a way to regain the high ground. That's probably one reason corporate giving hit $3.6 billion last year, an all-time high, up from $3.5 billion in 2003, according to philanthropy research group the Foundation Center. Indeed, Nardelli argues that a "dark veil" hangs over big business. It is exacting tangible penalties: Based on its $91 billion market cap, Home Depot was required to shell out an estimated $1 million last year to fund the Public Company Accounting Oversight Board, an outfit created by the Sarbanes–Oxley corporate reform bill to monitor the work of auditors. In effect, say Home Depot executives, all public companies are paying for the sins of a few.

But more than mere public relations appears to be at work here. Companies are being forced to address the concerns of customers, employees, and investors—in order to keep them. Such pressure is why last year Gap Inc. halted relationships with seventy of its overseas factories over alleged labor abuses, and has for the past two years issued a social responsibility report. Or why Nike Inc. is now a world leader in setting safety standards for overseas workers. When the controversy over its sweatshops erupted several years ago, managers mistakenly believed they could afford to ignore the outcry simply by cranking out hip shoes. "It is no longer an option to sit on the sidelines," says Bradley K. Googins, executive director of The Center for Corporate Citizenship at Boston College.

YOUTHFUL IDEALISM

More important, the calls for change are coming from inside the corporate walls. A new generation of employees is demanding attention to stakeholders and seeking more from their jobs than just 9-to-5 work hours and a steady paycheck. The number of Gen Yers—those born between 1977 and 1994—in the working world has grown 9.2 percent since 1999, while the number of Gen X workers remained flat, and baby boomers declined 4.3 percent, according to Robert Szafran, a sociology professor at Stephen F. Austin State University in Nacogdoches, Texas. As a result, Home Depot and others are finding that burnishing an image as a socially responsible company helps to attract younger workers, at all levels. "One of the things we compete most for in the marketplace is our associates," says Nardelli. "I'm not sure that was the case [two decades ago]."

Take Sewell Avant. The twenty-five-year-old senior procurement analyst graduated from the Georgia Institute of Technology in 2002. During college, he cleaned churches and did regular social projects with fraternity brothers. Now he's carrying on that tradition at Home Depot. He took a day off, without pay, to help mix concrete at the playground project in Marietta. His entire department will do more kiddie-park construction on a weekend in August. For Avant, volunteering adds meaning to his day-to-day job. "Employees are trying to marry their work and nonwork lives. If the company gives them a chance to do that, then they're happier," says C. B. Bhattacharya, associate professor of marketing at Boston University's School of Management.

That's why younger companies are baking the social responsibility concept into their culture—and demanding investors accept the cost. Costco Wholesale Corp. has long offered generous compensation to its workers, to the scorn of Wall Street and the detriment of its stock price. In the 1980s, networking giant Cisco Systems Inc. opened its first office in East Palo Alto, California, a run-down neighborhood amid the prosperity of Silicon Valley. Cisco Chairman John Morgridge worked as "principal for the day" at a school next door. "We're in business to get results. This is just a different currency," says Tae Yoo, Cisco's vice-president for corporate affairs.

Indeed, it has been a rude awakening for companies that have not embraced a more strategic approach to social responsibility. For years Wal-Mart has been a top corporate donor. But as the company's image was pummeled by labor unions and lawsuits, research showed its fragmented giving generated little goodwill. The reason: Few people could remember exactly what—or whom—Wal-Mart supports. Now, it's giving its community outreach a sharper focus. "Society has changed," says Betsy Reithemeyer, executive director of the Wal-Mart Foundation. "If you are the gathering place of the community, then you have a responsibility to it."

In fact, some executives argue that a company should develop a social responsibility platform—even if it doesn't add to the bottom line. In 2003, Wayside Cross Ministries, an Aurora, Illinois, shelter for abused women and men, couldn't obtain enough ground beef for meals. On hamburger days at Wayside, some residents ended up eating buns, lettuce, and tomato—no burger. Then grocery giant Albertson's, through Jewel, its Midwest grocery chain, launched Fresh Rescue to boost supplies of perishable meat, dairy, and vegetable products for local food banks. The result: Last year, the Northern Illinois Food Bank supplied 386 shelters with 740,000 pounds of meat, double the number from the year before. The payoff for Albertson's: goodwill—and perhaps a few more shoppers. "We don't look for any statistics," says CEO Johnston. "This has to be in the DNA of a company."

Even evangelists such as Nardelli stop short of saying that companies should divert money from other strategic priorities to support corporate social responsibility. But at corporations like Home Depot and GE, good works are being bred into Big Business. "It's just the right thing to do," says Nardelli. Good PR? Sure. Money well spent? The goodwill refund could be in the mail.

QUESTIONS

1. So, should money be diverted to support social responsibility?

2. What would Milton Friedman be likely to say about the Wal-Mart Foundation?

CASE 6.7

Blame Bangladesh, Not the Brands

Jagdish Bhagwati

Jagdish Bhagwati is an economist and professor at Columbia University. He is also the author of *In Defense of Globalization* and a fellow at the Council on Foreign Relations.

The community was in a palpable state of shock over the fire at a plant that left 25 workers dead and 55 others injured. Many people who lost loved ones and friends in the fire expressed bitterness about the deaths and injuries. They acknowledged that the plant provided significant employment for residents in the area, but they were deeply concerned by reports that many of the victims of the blaze were trapped in the building by blocked exits.

Asking corporate brands to substitute for the somnolent government will only marginally address worker safety reform.

Was this a report from Bangladesh or Karachi? No, it was from a poultry processing plant in Hamlet, North Carolina, described in the *New York Times* as an "All-American City" in 1991. Blame for that fire was cast not just on the company, but on the government.

The Bangladesh fires emphasize again a lax and lackadaisical attitude to the issue of workplace safety by the Bangladeshi authorities, possibly aided and abetted by domestic politics. This reflects a general attitude of neglect in protecting workers against unsafe conditions, like providing goggles and ensuring that they are worn when workers operate close to an open furnace.

But asking Wal-Mart, Gap, and other brands to substitute for the somnolent government will only marginally address worker safety reform. What is necessary is for the Bangladeshi government to stop resting on its laurels of social progress—a myth, which I and the economist Arvind Panagariya have recently challenged—and step up to the plate to establish proper regulations and monitoring, extending to all of Bangladesh and not just its garment factories.

QUESTIONS

1. Is Bangladesh responsible for safety conditions at plants located inside its borders?
2. Is the U.S. government responsible for safety conditions at plants located in the United States?

CHAPTER QUESTIONS

1. Is the social responsibility of business to increase its profits? Why or why not?

2. How are corporations like persons? How are they different? Why do stakeholders matter?

From *New York Times,* updated December 30, 2012, 10:16 A.M.

7

When Innovation Bytes Back

Ethics and Technology

Introduction

It is hard to talk about contemporary business without talking at the same time about technology. Some of the problems of business ethics, to be sure, are pretty much the same as they were in ancient times. The Roman philosopher Cicero expounded at length about the risks and responsibilities involved in buying or selling a house or a chariot, and the ethics surrounding such exchanges were not much different from our current concerns when we are buying or selling a modern condo or a new or used car. But even these transactions are permeated by ever-more-difficult questions that have to do with the new technologies. People buy cars and even houses on-line, without ever actually seeing them. They exchange funds and make contracts over the Internet without anything so tangible as paper currency, much less gold coins ever changing hands. They make promises and offers by email that may go out to hundreds of thousands of consumers (most of whom are more irritated than enticed). One might argue that all that has changed is the speed of business and personal transactions—from days, weeks, or (until the nineteenth century) months to fractions of a second or even nanoseconds, but this would be a very unimaginative view. What has changed is not just the speed but the very nature of business and business transactions.

Whether this is an unmixed blessing, needless to say, is the subject of considerable debate. What were introduced as dramatic aids to efficiency and productivity have, ironically, seemingly increased the time that most of us spend in our jobs, whether in or out of the office (if one even *has* an office). Mobile phones make us accessible to our bosses and supervisors twenty-four hours a day, seven days a week, at home, in our cars, and at the beach, and many employers insist that we "stay in touch" or have our phones turned on and available even while we're supposedly not at work or are "on vacation." Laptop computers and wireless connections mean that we can work on projects anywhere. Email, even forgetting about the time it takes most of us to delete the "spam" we receive, seems to increase the demands on our time, rather than decrease it, making us less rather than more efficient. What used to be short, concise, to-the-point memos have given way to long, rambling, verbose documents that take time and patience to read, with little reward. It is an observation that has become commonplace:

With the dramatic improvements in communication technology, we spend more time on the job; have less time to ourselves; have less privacy; and, in many cases, get no more done than when we walked from office to office, working, talking, and negotiating with people face to face. In fact, many of us miss that interpersonal experience. Not going to the office may save many of us an hour or more of commuting time, but it also deprives many people of the camaraderie that is often (though surely not always) one of the satisfactions of working life.

Technology also raises new and novel legal and ethical problems. The law, as plodding as it is, can't keep up with the new technologies. (A famous statue in the Palace of Justice in Paris depicts a famous judge, his foot on a turtle, thus complaining about the slowness of the legal process even in the eighteenth century.) And just as compliance is difficult when the rules no longer apply, ethics is equally difficult when there are few precedents and no clear traditions or customs to guide us. For example, there are the intricacies of

---

To: You
From: The Philosopher
Subject: "Locke on Property"

Who hasn't downloaded a song from the Internet? Or shared files? Or perhaps used bootlegged or pirated software? (It was paid for once, what is the harm if *I* use it?). There is a lot of material on the web that doesn't seem to belong to *anyone*. But could that be right? How did it get on the web? And who created the content? For Locke, our notion of property is inseparable from our notion of labor. If you have invested work into the creation of something, if it is what it is because of your labor, then it ought to belong to you (imagine how controversial this idea was in the 17th century, when Locke wrote it—especially among the wealthy English landowners). Now, if we think about it that way, do we still feel OK about downloading the latest *Outkast* release (and avoiding paying 99 cents for it)? Here's Locke:

> Though the earth and all inferior creatures be common to all men, yet every man has a *property* in his own *person*. This nobody has any right to but himself. The *labour* of his body and the *work* of his hands, we may say, are properly his. Whatsoever, then, he removed out of the state that nature hath provided and left it in, he hath mixed his labour with it, and joined to it something that is his own, and thereby makes it his property.... Thus, the grass my horse has bit... and the ore I have digged in any place, where I have a right to them in common with others, become my property without the assignation or consent of any body. The labour that was mine, removing them out of that common state they were in, hath fixed my property in them.*

*From John Locke, *The Second Treatise on Government*, (Oxford, England: Clarendon Press, 1690), pp. 26–27.

copyright and intellectual property law and the ethics that gives rise to them. Music and movies used to be played on the radio or shown in theaters, where there were no ready ways of copying or reproducing them. Now, "downloading" from the Web, near-perfect digital copies, and handheld recorders and videocameras make stealing such things easy. But what counts as stealing? It used to be that if you owned something and I took it, I now had it and you didn't. That makes it theft. But if I download a song from the Internet, you (whoever you are—the musician, the producer, the recording company) still own it. I just happen to have a copy, too. So is this stealing? The general consensus is, yes (though many students still seem to have the idea that music, by its very nature, is or ought to be free and belong to none). But what does that mean? If I buy a piece of software and install it on my computer at work, but then I want to install it on my computer at home (which I also use for work), is that stealing, too? What if I give the same software to my office-mate? If I want to back up my purchase of a DVD movie in case of loss or damage, is that stealing? And if some companies (Linux, for instance) choose to make their intellectual property free and "open" to everyone, does that in any way change the status of those who vigorously insist on their ownership (Microsoft, for example)? We all appreciate the complexity of these questions, even if we disagree on the exact answers to them.

Or consider the new privacy issues that have come with the new technology. It used to be, if you didn't want anyone to know what you have written, you could burn the paper (or, if you're a spy in a desperate situation, you could eat it). Now, everyone knows that erasing an email message doesn't make it disappear, should your computer be seized and searched by experts. Private correspondence is vulnerable to hackers of all stripes. (And, by the way, is hacking ethical? It is a matter of violating another's privacy—even if nothing is "taken" [e.g., credit card numbers], but when is violating another person's privacy unethical, and when is it a case not so different from listening to—and not merely overhearing—a neighbor's audible argument with his or her spouse?) Office email is no longer considered private. And then there are questions about personal correspondence on the office computer. If, after hours, you want to use your office computer to chat with a friend overseas, is that stealing? It does not cost the company anything (as opposed, say, to a long distance overseas call, which used to cost quite a lot). If you do some on-line shopping during your lunch hour, does that violate some new ethical principle? When you are on the Internet, whether it's business or personal, do you have an obligation to reveal your true identity, when now it is so easy to hide or disguise it? The truth is that all such questions are very much in play, as companies and managers try to decide what is legitimate and what is not. And while they are doing so, the technology keeps changing. When you can merely think thoughts that are automatically transmitted to colleagues across town or across an ocean, does the company have some sort of claim to your mental processes? And when the software becomes so sophisticated that it can reproduce YOUR job, is your company justified in letting you go to be replaced by a piece of machinery that never stops working, expects no benefits, and wastes no time at the water cooler? Such questions are no longer the stuff of science fiction but the source of tomorrow's ethical dilemmas.

First, Deborah C. Johnson discusses the problem of intellectual property rights in computer software. Who should own what, why, and for how long? She discusses the tension between creativity and freedom and considers a labor theory of property. Elizabeth A. Buchanan argues that the Internet has opened up opportunities, but with those opportunities comes a duty to disseminate beneficial information worldwide, especially to those persons whom it will most benefit. Victoria Groom and Clifford Nass examine how robots and humans can act together as teammates, and Clive Thompson worries about the possibilities of computers that can read our minds. Bill Joy, in "Why the Future Doesn't Need Us," argues that technology must be carefully curtailed by prudent people (especially scientists) today. Technology must serve us, not the other way around. We are in danger of destroying the world through a slavish dedication to "technology for its own sake." Finally, a cautionary note that we should curb our enthusiasm.

Deborah C. Johnson

Intellectual Property Rights and Computer Software

Deborah Johnson is Olsson Professor of Applied Ethics Technology, Culture, and Communication at the University of Virginia.

THE PHILOSOPHICAL BASIS OF PROPERTY

Property is by no means a simple notion. Property is created by law. Laws specify what can and cannot be owned, how things may be acquired and transferred. Laws define what counts as property and create different kinds of property.

. . . [S]oftware has challenged our traditional notions of ownership in that the system of laws created specifically to deal with invention in the useful arts and sciences in the U.S. does not seem to grant property rights in software that are comparable to the property rights of inventors in other fields. In discussing this situation we often implicitly or explicitly make assumptions about or argue for moral (and not just legal) rights in property. These assumptions and arguments need to be fully articulated and critically examined. . . .

The reasoning behind both the patent and copyright systems is consequentialist in that the system's primary aim is to create property rights which will have good effects. Invention is encouraged and facilitated so that new products and processes will be made available. Nevertheless, many discussions of property rights assume that property is not a matter of social utility, but rather a matter of justice or natural right. We will consider this approach first, as it applies to the ownership of software.

NATURAL RIGHTS ARGUMENTS

The strongest natural rights argument that can be made for private ownership of software is based on the idea that a person has a natural (and, therefore, moral) right to what he or she produces and this natural right ought to be protected by law. John Locke's labor theory of property bases the natural right of ownership on the labor one puts into a thing in creating it.

According to this theory, a person acquires a right of ownership in something by mixing his labor with it. Thus, in a state of nature (that is, before laws and civilized society), *if* an individual were to come upon a piece of land that looked suitable for cultivation, and *if* this person were to cultivate the land by planting seed, tending to the crops daily, nourishing them and so on, *then* the crops would belong to the person. The person has a strong claim to the crops because his labor produced them and they would not exist without this labor. It would be wrong for someone else to come along and take the crops. The intruder would, in effect, be confiscating the creator's labor.

On the face of it, this Lockean account seems plausible. Locke's theory is tied to the notion of individual sovereignty. A person cannot be owned by another and since a person's labor is an extension of her body, it cannot be owned by another. If an individual puts her labor in something and then someone else takes it, the laborer has been rendered a slave.

Using a Lockean theory of property, a software developer could argue that the program she developed is rightfully "hers" because she created it with her labor. . . .

Critique of Moral Rights in Software

Now, while this argument seems plausible, it can be countered in several ways. First, we can imagine a just world in which we did not acquire rights to what we created. To be sure, it would be unjust if others acquired rights to what we created, but if there were no property rights whatsoever, then there would be no injustice. Those who created things would simply create things. If one mixed one's labor with something, one would simply lose one's labor. Robert Nozick alludes to the possibility of such an arrangement when he questions Locke's theory in *Anarchy, State and Utopia*:

> Why does mixing one's labor with something make one the owner of it? Perhaps because one own one's labor, and so one comes to own a previously unowned thing that becomes permeated with what one owns. Ownership seeps over into the rest. But why isn't mixing what I own with what I don't own a way of losing what I own rather than a way of gaining what I don't? If I own a can of tomato juice and spill it in the sea so that its molecules (made radioactive, so I can check this) mingle evenly throughout the sea, do I thereby come to own the sea, or have I foolishly dissipated my tomato juice?

A second counter to the Lockean theory applies only to intellectual or nontangible things, such as computer software. Though software's primary function is for use in computers, software is intelligible as a nontangible entity. The software designer can describe how the software works and what it does.

Another person can comprehend, and even use this information as instructions—without the software ever being put into a machine.

The point is that with intellectual things, many people can "have" or use them at the same time. If a second person eats or sells food that I have grown, I have lost the products of my labor altogether. But one can continue to have and use software when others have and use it. So, when a person copies a program that I have created, she has not taken it from me. I am not deprived of it by her act. Rather, what is usually the case is that by copying my program, the person has taken my *capacity to profit from my creation*, either by making it difficult for me to sell it (since it becomes available at no cost), or by taking my competitive advantage in using the program (since my competitors can now also use it).

Once this difference between intellectual and tangible things is recognized, the natural rights argument appears much weaker than at first sight. The claim of software developers turns out *not* to be a claim to their creations (this they still have when others have their software), but a claim to a right to profit from their creations. However, to show that a person has a right to profit from his creation requires more than showing that he has created it. If he ever has a right to profit, it would seem that such a right would be socially created. It would be defined by an economic system with laws about what can be owned, what can be put into the marketplace, under what conditions, and so on. In other words, the right would derive from a complex set of rules structuring commercial activity.

The natural rights argument is, therefore, not convincing on its own. To be sure, there is a moral issue when it comes to confiscation for profit. It is unfair for one person (or company) to take a program written by someone else, and sell it. However, from a moral point of view software need never enter the commercial realm. It might be declared unownable or public property.

So, the claims of software developers must be understood not to be claims to a natural or moral right, but rather to a social right. Deciding whether or not such a social right should be created is a consequentialist issue. In a moment we will explore the consequentialist reasons for creating property rights in software, as already suggested by the rationale of the patent and copyright. For now it may be useful to point out that a natural rights argument could be made against private ownership of software.

Against Ownership

Some of the early legal literature on ownership of programs and some of the court cases focused on the idea that a patent on a program might violate "the doctrine of mental steps." This doctrine states that a series of mental operations like addition or subtraction cannot be owned. Discussion of the doctrine was based on the possibility that computers, in effect, perform, or at least duplicate, mental steps. It is acknowledged that the operations are performed quickly on the machine so that in a short time a large number of steps can take place. Still, it might be argued, the operations performed by the computer are in principle capable of being performed by a person. If this is so, then ownership of programs could be extremely dangerous for it might interfere with freedom of thought. Those who had patents on programs would have a monopoly on mental operations and might be able to stop others from performing those operations in their heads.

If this is right, then we have the basis of a natural rights argument against ownership of computer software. The argument would be that individuals have a natural right to freedom of thought, and ownership of software will interfere with that right. The argument is worthy of further reflection, especially in light of research in artificial intelligence. . . .

CONSEQUENTIALIST ARGUMENTS

As suggested earlier the claims of software developers make most sense as arguments for a social right to ownership. They can and do claim that good consequences result from ownership and bad consequences result when there is no or inadequate protection. Unless individuals and companies have some proprietary rights in what they create, they will not invest the time, energy, and resources needed to develop and market software. Without protection, they can never

make money at producing software. Why develop a new program if the moment you introduce it, others will copy it, produce it more cheaply, and yours will not sell? If we, as a society, want software developed, we will have to give those who develop it the protection they need; otherwise society will lose because the great promise of computers will not be realized. There must be an incentive to create programs and that incentive is profit—so the argument goes.

Objections can be made to this very important argument. In particular, we can argue that there are incentives other than profit to create software. For one thing, people will create software because they need it for their own purposes: they can use it and make it available to others or keep it to themselves, as they choose.

Another possibility is that we could create a credit system similar to what we have now with scientific publications, in which individuals are given credit and recognition for new knowledge they create when they publish it and make it available to others. (Admittedly, credit may not be enough of an incentive to encourage the development of expensive and elaborate programs, and it may lead to more secrecy.)

––––––––––

Another possible incentive on which we might rely, if software were not ownable, would be the incentive of hardware companies to create software to make their computers marketable. A company's computers are useless without good software to go with them. Indeed, the better the software available for a type of computer, the better the computer is likely to do in the marketplace.

The point is that if ownership of software were disallowed, software development would not come to a complete standstill. There would be other incentives for creating software. So, while the consequentialist argument for ownership is a good argument—ownership does encourage development—it is not such an overwhelming argument that we should reject all other considerations.

Indeed, as already explained, both the copyright and the patent system recognize reasons for limiting ownership. Both recognize that the very thing

we want to encourage—development of the technological arts and sciences—will be impeded if we fail
to limit ownership. Both the copyright and patent
systems recognize that invention will be retarded if
ideas and other building blocks of science and technology are owned.

This gets us to the dilemmas that we presently
face in both copyright and patent law: How can we
draw a line between what can and cannot be owned
so that software developers can own something of
value but not something which will interfere, in the
long run, with development in the field?

CONCLUSIONS FROM THE PHILOSOPHICAL ANALYSIS OF PROPERTY

The preceding philosophical analysis of property
rights in software supports a consequentialist framework for analyzing the property rights issues
surrounding software (and not a natural rights
framework). The consequentialist framework puts
the focus on deciding ownership issues in terms of
effects on continued creativity and development in
the field of software. This framework suggests that
we will have to delicately draw a line between what
is ownable and what is not ownable when it comes to
software, along the lines already delineated in patent
and copyright law. . . .

IS IT WRONG TO COPY PROPRIETARY SOFTWARE?

We must now turn our attention to the individual
moral issue. Is it wrong for an individual to make
a copy of a proprietary piece of software? You will
see that the answer to this question is somewhat connected to the preceding discussion of policy issues.

To begin, it will be helpful to clarify the domain
of discussion. First, making a backup copy of a piece
of software, which you have purchased, for your own
protection is generally not illegal, and is, in any case,
not at issue here. Second, while I have labeled this
the "individual" moral issue, it is not just an issue
for individuals but applies as well to collective units
such as companies, agencies, and institutions. The
typical case is the case in which you borrow a piece
of software from someone who has purchased it and
make a copy for your own use. . . . This case does not
differ significantly from the case in which a company buys a single copy of a piece of software and
makes multiple copies for use within the company in
order to avoid purchasing more.

We can begin with the intuition (which many
individuals seem to have) that copying a piece of
software is *not wrong* (that it is morally permissible). This intuition seems understandable enough at
first glance. After all, making a copy of a piece of
software is easy, and seems harmless, and the laws
aimed at preventing it seem ill-suited for doing the
job. Nevertheless, when we examine the arguments
that can be made to support this intuition, they are
not very compelling. Indeed, after analysis, it seems
difficult to deny that it is morally wrong to make an
illegal copy of a piece of software. The key issue
here has little to do with software per se and everything to do with the relationship between law and
morality.

Perhaps the best way to begin is by laying out what
seem to be the strongest arguments for the moral
permissibility of individual copying. The strongest
arguments claim (1) the laws protecting computer
software are bad, and either (2a) making a copy of
a piece of software is not intrinsically wrong, or (2b)
making a copy of a piece of software does no harm,
or (2c) *not* making a copy of a piece of software actually does some harm.

. . . [I]t is important to be clear on what could be
claimed in Premise (1). Here are some of the possibilities: (1a) All property law in America is unjust
and the software laws are part of this; (1b) all intellectual property laws are unjust and software laws
are part of this; (1c) most property law in America is
just, but the laws surrounding computer software are
not; and (1d) while the laws surrounding the ownership of software are not unjust, they could be a lot
better. The list could go on and just which position
one holds makes much of the difference in the copying argument.

Seven Theses for Business Ethics and the Information Age

Richard de George

THESIS I

The IT Head-in-the-Sand Syndrome

Many businesses either fail to realize that we have entered the information age or fail to appreciate its importance.

THESIS II

The Abdication of IT Ethical Responsibility

The lack of awareness of the ethical implications of the information age is what I call the "myth of amoral computing and information technology." The myth says that computers are not good or bad, information systems are not good or bad—they simply have a logic and rationale of their own.

THESIS III

Where Are the Business Ethicists When You Need Them?

The task of the business ethicist in the present period of transition—and a task in which few are engaged—is to help anticipate the developments and ease the transition by not losing sight of the effects on people.

THESIS IV

Surmounting the Information Nexus

If by "information" we mean not simply data but *useful* data, we see immediately that what we are interested in is useful information. Information, as generally used, stands for true knowledge in some area. Its opposites are disinformation, misinformation, and falsehood. Information is not simply data, but data that represents reality. It's true and not false.

Two virtues appear immediately. One is truth (and so truthfulness), the other is accuracy.

THESIS V

Confronting the Communication Complex

Information is not useful, even if truthful and accurate, unless it is used. Hence, it needs to be communicated. The communication process, which is developing at an exponential rate, is central to the information age. The virtues of truthfulness and accuracy carry over into communication. But there are elements of communication that pose their own ethical issues: communication of what, to whom, in what form?

THESIS VI

The American Information Privacy Schizophrenia

The U.S. is schizophrenic about information privacy, wanting it in theory and giving it away in practice.

Information must be communicated, but it must also be about something. Information about people has become much more important than it was previously because of the great opportunity for a revolution in marketing in which manufacturers can target potential customers in ways not previously possible.

THESIS VII

Mickey Mouse Isn't a Program

Information is very different from machines and tangible products, and so requires a new conception of property and property protection applicable to it.

Until fairly recently, a copyright granted protection to the expression of ideas in books and similar forms for 28 years (renewable for another 28 years). The protected period was then changed to the life of the author plus 50 years and to 75 years for a corporate author. In 1998, Congress extended the already-extended period, to the life of the author plus 70 years and to 95 years for a corporate author. The change came just in time to save Mickey Mouse from falling into the public domain, much to the pleasure of the Walt Disney Company.

We will not be able to analyze each of the possibilities here, but it should be clear . . . that I believe that the system of intellectual property rights in America (in particular patent, trade secrecy, and copyright laws) may not be the best of all possible laws in every detail but they are roughly just. That is, copyright and patent laws aim at a utilitarian system of property rights and aim essentially to draw the right kind of line between what can and cannot be owned. I recognize that there are problems in extending these laws to software, and I recognize the system could be improved. Nevertheless, I do not believe that the system is blatantly unjust or wholly inappropriate for software.

Now, the next step in my argument is to claim that an individual has a *prima facie* obligation to obey the law of a roughly just system of laws. . . . The prima facie obligation to obey the law can be overridden by higher-order obligations or by special circumstances that justify disobedience. Higher-order obligations

will override when, for example, obeying the law will lead to greater harm than disobeying. . . . For example, the law prohibiting us from driving on the left side of the road is a good law but we would be justified in breaking it in order to avoid hitting someone.

So I am not claiming that people always have an obligation to obey the law; I claim only that the burden of proof is on those who would disobey roughly good laws. Given that extant laws regarding computer software are roughly good and given that a person has a prima facie obligation to obey roughly good laws, the second premise carries the weight of the argument for the moral permissibility of copying. In other words, the second premise must provide a reason for disobeying roughly just laws.

Premises (2a)–(2c) must, then, be examined carefully. Premise (2a) to the effect that there is nothing intrinsically wrong with making a copy of a piece of software is true, but it doesn't make the argument. The claim is true in the sense that if there were no laws against copying, the act of copying would not be wrong. Indeed, I argued earlier that property rights are not natural or moral in themselves but a matter of social utility. They acquire moral significance only when they are created by law and only in relatively just systems of law. Still, premise (2a) does not support copying because copying has been made illegal and as such is prima facie wrong: There have to be overriding reasons or special conditions to justify breaking the law.

According to premise (2b), making a copy of a piece of software for personal use harms no one. If we think of copying taking place in a state of nature, this premise is probably true; no one is harmed. However, once we are in a society of laws, the laws create legal rights, and it seems that a person harms another by depriving him of his legal right. When a person makes a copy of a piece of *proprietary* software, she deprives the owner of his legal right to control use of that software and to require payment in exchange

---

To: You
From: The Philosopher
Subject: "Foucault and the Panopticon"

The English philosopher Jeremy Bentham designed the first Panopticon, in the hope of improving the dismal conditions in the prisons of his day. At the center of a huge octagon stood a tower, from which the guards could monitor any cell. Ringed around the tower were the prisoners in their cells, entirely visible to the guards (and largely visible to one another). In fact, many prisons that were built in the United States in the 1960s and 1970s followed closely the architectural model that was first designed and drawn by Bentham.

But Bentham did not anticipate the effects on the human psyche that constant surveillance would have. Unfortunately, today the possibilities of such constant surveillance (by the government? By marketers? By big business?) grow and grow. In his great study of the emergence of the modern prison, the 20th-century French philosopher Foucault has a chilling meditation on the Panopticon:

> Hence the major effect of the Panopticon: to induce in the inmate a state of conscious and permanent visibility that assures the automatic functioning of power. So to arrange things that the surveillance is permanent in its effects, even if it is discontinuous in its action; that the perfection of power should tend to render its actual exercise unnecessary; that this architectural apparatus should be a machine for creating and sustaining a power relation independent of the person who exercises it; in short, that the inmates should be caught up in a power situation of which they are themselves the bearers. To achieve this, it is at once too much and too little that the prisoner should be constantly observed by an inspector; too little, for what matters is that he knows himself to be observed; too much, because he has no need in fact of being so. In view of this, Bentham laid down the principle that power should be visible and unverifiable. Visible: the inmate will constantly have before his eyes the tall outline of the central tower from which he is spied upon. Unverifiable: the inmate must never know whether he is being looked at at any one moment; but he must be sure that he may always be so.*

* From Michel Foucault, *Discipline and Punish: The Birth of the Prison*, trans. Alan Sheridan (New York: Random House, 1979), p. 201.

for the use of the software. This is a harm. (Those who think this is not a harm should think of small software companies or individual entrepreneurs who have gone into the business of developing software, invested time and money, only to be squeezed out of business by customers who would buy one copy and make others instead of buying more.) So premise (2b) is false. Making a copy of a piece of proprietary software in our society harms someone.

Premise (2c) has the most promise as an argument for copying in that if it were true that one was doing harm by obeying the law, then we would have a moral reason for overriding the law, even if it were relatively good. Richard Stallman and Helen Nissenbaum have both made arguments of this kind. Both argue that there are circumstances in which not making a copy or not making a copy *and* providing it to a friend does some harm. However, in their arguments, the harm referred to does not seem of the kind to counterbalance the effects of a relatively just system of property rights. Both give examples of how an individual might be able to help a friend out by providing her with an illegal copy of a piece of proprietary software. Both argue that laws against copying have the effect of discouraging altruism.

Still, this argument ignores the harm to the copyright or patent holder. Even if we were to grant that not providing a copy to a friend does harm, we have to compare that harm to the harm to the owner and choose the lesser.

Given what I said earlier about the prima facie obligation to obey the law, it follows that there may be some situations in which copying will be justified, namely when some fairly serious harm can only be prevented by making an illegal copy of a piece of proprietary software and using it. In most cases, however, the claims of the software owner to her legal rights would seem to be much stronger than the claims of someone who needs a copy to make her life easier.

If the position I have just sketched seems odd, consider an analogy with a different sort of property. Suppose I own a private swimming pool and I make a living by renting the use of it to others. I do not rent the pool every day and you figure out how to break in undetected and use the pool when it is not opened and I am not around. The act of swimming is not intrinsically wrong, and swimming in the pool does no obvious harm to me (the owner) or anyone else. Nevertheless, you are using my property without my permission. It would hardly seem a justification for ignoring my property rights if you claimed that you were hot and the swim in my pool made your life easier. The same would be true, if you argued that you had a friend who was very uncomfortable in the heat and you, having the knowledge of how to break into the pool, thought it would be selfish not to use that knowledge to help your friend out.

Of course, there are circumstances under which your illegal entry into my pool might be justified. For example, if someone else had broken in, was swimming, and began to drown, and you were innocently walking by, saw the person drowning, broke in, and jumped in the pool in order to save the other. Here the circumstances justify overriding my legal rights.

There seems no moral difference between breaking into the pool and making a copy of a proprietary piece of software. Both acts violate the legal rights of the owner—legal rights created by reasonably good laws. I will grant that these laws do prevent others from acting altruistically, but this, I believe, is inherent to private property. Private property is individualistic, exclusionary, and, perhaps, selfish. So, if Stallman and Nissenbaum want to launch an attack on all private property laws, I am in sympathy with their claims. However, I would press them to explain why they had picked out computer software law when private ownership of other things, such as natural resources or corporate conglomerates, seems much more menacing.

I conclude that it is prima facie wrong to make an illegal copy of a piece of proprietary software because to do so is to deprive someone (the owner) of their legal rights, and this is to harm them.

QUESTIONS

1. Why does computer software complicate the question of property?

2. How does Johnson use Locke's notion of property to solve the problem?

Elizabeth A. Buchanan

Information Ethics in a Worldwide Context

Elizabeth A. Buchanan is an assistant professor at the School of Information Studies, University of Wisconsin—Milwaukee.

Alkalimat begins his eloquent essay, "The New Technological Imperative in Africa: Class Struggles on the Edge of Third-Wave Revolution" by stating the "twentieth century is ending as a global drama full of conflict and change, with humanity torn between hope and despair. For a few the new century offers the wonders of a high-tech future, with wealth amid the birth of a new civilization; but for the majority there is fear of war, starvation, homelessness, poverty, and plagues. . . ." As information professionals, what are our ethical obligations in this worldwide context? . . . The information age is a time of mythology, a time for fantasies of wealth, power, ownership. The ethics of information services in this time, however, are very real, and don't necessarily correspond to these fantasies.

How do we as information professionals respond? Do we contribute to the fantasies? the non-truths? Or do we recognize the conditions Alkalimat describes and respond to them? . . .

The information society (now understood as a global society) or information age possesses a number of characteristics or qualities, among them a growing reliance on computer technologies, a large knowledge sector work force, a growing division of labor—a division which has major international implications, a movement from an analog to a digital model of informational and commercial transfer, and the consideration of information as a major commodity, analogous to the physical goods of the industrial age. And, nearly two decades ago, Smith recognized the global significance of information as a major commodity and defining feature of this age. Smith then declared that information lay at the heart of the world economy and cannot be separated from the other conflicts of which international and national policies are composed. Thus, the information society is considered an international phenomenon, with potential benefits and detriments to the world as a whole.

. . . [New] ethical dilemmas range from the fair and equitable distribution of resources to the availability and provision of education and training, to a mutual respect and consideration of cultural specificity and values. For instance, while the information age has encouraged a major increase in the amount of information produced, in the number of available channels through which information is accessible, and the apparent ease with which information is readily available, a growing disparity continues to set apart the now all-too-familiar "haves" and the "havenots." While the information society offers an abundance of goods to some peoples, it is contributing to an expansive "digital divide," keeping peoples and nations on unequal planes. This inequality is promulgated on a number of levels.

AN OVERVIEW OF INFORMATION INEQUITY

In 1979, Mustapha Masmoudi's seminal paper "The New World Information Order" drew attention to the growing inequities and imbalances across the world in terms of information access, control, dissemination, and content construction. In it, he cites seven prominent forms of inequities existing in the world in terms of information.

From *Ethics and Information Technology* 7. © 1999, p. 193 © Kluwer Academic Publishers. Notes were deleted from the text.

1. A flagrant quantitative imbalance between North and South;
2. An inequality in information resources;
3–4. A de facto hegemony and a will to dominate;
5. A lack of information on developing countries;
6. Survival of the colonial era. An alienating influence in the economic, social, and cultural spheres.
7. Messages ill-suited to the areas in which they are disseminated.

. . . Smith highlighted cultural domination of the South by the North through the control of major media outlets, through the unstinted flow of its cultural products throughout the world, and the cultural, political, and economic powers wielded by the North over the South. Ultimately, Smith's *Geopolitics of Information* thoroughly documented the ways in which information dissemination and commoditization fuel international domination, inequality, and suppression of cultural uniqueness and traditional values. Following Masmoudi and Smith, Morehouse called attention to another level of inequality, in the quantitatively biased distribution of resources, including information-based resources, across the world; he states

> . . . the late twentieth century world is a highly unequal place in energy consumption, income distribution, materials deprivation, economic and political power, and science-based problem solving capacity. Ninety-seven percent of the world's expenditure on research and development is made by a handful of industrialized countries. . . . Technology is rapidly emerging as a major instrument for global domination as other economic and military forms of power decline for stronger nations in the international system.

Nearly twenty years after Masmoudi, Smith, and Morehouse questioned the ethics of the information age and its supposed free flow of information and related commodities, the inequities in information transfer across the globe have changed very little. For example, flagrant inequities exist on a number of levels where the transfer of information or commodities is involved. Of particular significance, the unjust state of intellectual resource allocation severely affects contemporary scientists. If knowledge is power, the creation and dissemination of knowledge contribute to power. Thus, in relation to the science-based problem solving capacity to which Morehouse referred, Gibbs reviews the poor showing of third world researchers in the *Science Citation Index*, the leading index to cited scientific journal literature. This poor showing has third world researchers caught in a "vicious circle."

Third world scientists denied the possibility to contribute suggests that their information is less valuable, or less esteemed to the western eye. Less developed countries are held at a distance in terms of research and development, forcing continuous cycles of dependence. On another level, Gibbs considers telephone access, and notably, Haywood suggests that "one approach to measuring the impact of the 'information economy' as it evolves is the rate at which a country gains access to telephone lines." A dramatic example comes from Africa, a continent representing more than one tenth of the world's population, yet the least technologically and informationally developed. "The entire continent of Africa. . . contains fewer telephone lines than does Manhattan. African customers who sign up for service today are put on a waiting list 3.6 million people deep; in sub-Saharan regions, the wait is currently about nine years." Equally dismal, Haywood relates that "portable radios are probably the most widespread technology to be found in rural Africa, but even these lie silent for want of batteries."

It is significant to note that within Africa, great inequities exist. "South Africa has 9.5 main telephone lines per hundred people, giving a teledensity twenty times higher than the rest of sub-Saharan Africa. But only 11.6% of Africans have telephones in their homes, compared with 87.4% of whites, and 47.6% of Africans have no access to any phone, compared to only 6.6% of whites." This suggests that while North to South information flow is dramatically inequitable, internal inequities exist as well. In many ways, these inequities parallel the disparity between suburban, urban, and rural regions within the United States.

QUALITATIVELY GROUNDED INEQUITIES

While a quantitative evaluation of information equity is dim for many nations, a more qualitatively based assessment of the information society and its international flow of information reveals an equally disturbing picture. . . .

First, information transfer from the North to the South may contribute to serious disruption in the social fabric of a nation. Given that the majority of information entering a country is from the United States or constructed with a western viewpoint, cultural values and perspectives are transferred as well. The potential for serious social fragmentation is at hand and Woodrow draws attention to four major areas of potential conflict or tension that result from this international telecommunications or transfer of information. These include conflict over basic values embedded within the information infrastructure; tensions at the industry levels, at which western corporate interest may take precedence over the indigenous interests; conflict among nations over views on liberal or conservative approaches to information dissemination; and finally, tension, which arises when information holds great economic and political power; the power remains in the hands of the developers or transmitters of information, not in the hands of the receivers. Furthermore, social disruption may ensue, leading to potential dangerous situations; for instance, the Tiananmen Square incident in China was further aggravated by incoming fax memos and email messages from dissidents in the United States.

INFORMATION COMMODITIZATION, OR "FREE IS OUT, FEE IS IN"

Next, the commoditization of information brings potentially unnecessary or undesirable forms of information to a region or country. . . . The increasing commoditization of information is removing information from public sectors or public agencies to the Private realm. . . . If we are of the belief that information wants to be free and should be free, an age old adage of librarianship, this intense commoditization of information comprises a most significant issue facing information professionals today. As wealth is concentrated in fewer and fewer hands through monopolization and centralization, information professionals must more actively seek alternative outlets of information. Uniformity and monotony dominate, as we see American and western privatization strangle choice and options. While we have hundreds of channels, millions of Internet sites, and a plethora of media outlets, we still suffer from a paucity of choice. On the global level, fewer countries, fewer cultures have a chance to promote their own forms of indigenous knowledge, and they are increasingly forced to accept irrelevant, futile, and ineffective information.

Furthermore, the continual neglect of developing nations as *potential* information suppliers smacks of imperialism and colonialism, while it continues to deny any economic power or autonomy to the developing nations. . . . The myth of the information age strikes again—providing computers to the average citizens of the third world is insufficient, at best. . . . [T]he information society is grounded in commoditization and profit for some, while simultaneously, for many, social necessities and resources are in danger. . . .

THE INTERNET: PERPETUATING INEQUITY WORLDWIDE

Increasingly, the information age is defined by the "world-wide" presence of the Internet. The NTIA offers a familiar sentiment: "Now that a considerable portion of today's business, communication, and research takes place on the Internet, access to the computers and networks may be as important as access to traditional telephone service." The Internet has been heralded as a means to ensure equitable access to information and democratic ideals, as well as a destroyer of cultural sovereignty and polluter of values. Due to the inherent nature of the Internet, including its many-to-many mode of communication, its immediacy, and its anonymity, the world's population can potentially have access to any and all forms of information, regardless of where or when it was released, or irregardless of its subject.

Yes, information might be free in the philosophical sense, but at what expense, in the monetary sense and in terms of cultural values?

Shapiro optimistically acknowledges the liberating characteristics of the Internet; these sentiments comprise the many myths surrounding the information age and its technologies.

Using the Net and other new media, individuals can take back power from large Institutions, including government, corporations, and the media. Trends like personalization, decentralization, and dis-intermediation . . . will allow us each to have more control over life's details: what news and entertainment we're exposed to, how we learn and work, whom we socialize with, even how goods are distributed and political outcomes are reached. . . . The Net will allow us to transcend the limitations of geography and circumstance to create new social bonds.

Conversely—some would say more realistically—the Net can contribute to "social fragmentation"; it can cause cultural splintering and loss of tradition, . . . "What happens to the special history of people situated in microsocial niches when information is directed to people en masse? Does this universality of information destroy particularity of social life?" Many issues demand the attention of information professionals in considering these questions. Firstly, the mass release of information fails to consider cultural sensitivity; peoples and nations may take objection to such forms of information as governmental, for instance.

Secondly, the immediacy of the international information flow denies opportunities for peoples and nations to prepare for the onslaught of foreign cultural viewpoints, and the rapidity with which information is released denies the chance for contemplation and consideration.

Thirdly, cultural particularity is under siege by the prevalence of the English language on the Internet; some 90% of the material on the Internet is in the English language, thus raising concerns over language imperialism and literacy issues.

Fourthly, cultural specificity should be cherished and protected. With mass releases of information, information that continues to be homogenous and often monotonous, individual thought is diminishing and communal integrity is lessening. Cultural niches

fight for survival in a world of sameness, and despite the many predictions and hopes of virtual communities and virtual neighborhoods, individuality in the truest sense and the communal sense is taking a severe beating. . . .

Receptivity to information between cultures is increasingly at an exciting or alarming rate, depending on your point of view. The upside of this is that different races can now understand more about each other as language barriers break down in favor of English; the downside is that, as language is the main conduit of cultural heritage and the key to distinctiveness, there will be less to fascinate and excite us because the richness of difference will be replaced by the poverty of sameness. . . .

CONCLUSION

Masmoudi demands a reevaluation and readjustment to the inequitable conditions surrounding information access, control, dissemination, and content construction. Yet, it is critical however, that developing countries make their own decisions concerning the flow of information; while no country should be denied access or control of information, cultural sensitivity demands that self-reliance and self-control dictate that flow of information. Cultural specificity demands respect. An imperialistic or colonialist approach to information will only set the worlds further apart, at a time when information and its conveyers promise to bring the world closer together.

In summary, it is useful to consider an episode which begins Richard Sclove's *Democracy and Technology*:

During the 1970s, running water was installed in the houses of Ibieca, a small village in northeast Spain. With pipes running directly to their houses, Ibiecans no longer had to fetch water from the village fountain. Families gradually purchased washing machines, and women stopped gathering to scrub laundry by hand at the village washbasin.

Arduous tasks were rendered technologically superfluous, but village social life unexpectedly changed. The public fountain and washbasin, once scenes of vigorous social interaction, became nearly deserted. Men began losing their sense of familiarity with the children and the donkeys that had once helped them to haul water. Women stopped congregating at the washbasin to intermix their scrubbing with politically empowering gossip about men and social life. In hindsight, the installation of running water helped break down the Ibiecans' strong bonds—with one another, with their animals, and with the land—that had knit them together as a community.

Sclove's premise in *Democracy and Technology* involves participatory design and a democratic adoption of information and technology. Participatory design and development holds the key to ensuring that all peoples will be able to choose among alternatives, these choices will reflect their personal aspirations and their view of the common good, and will contribute to the best social conditions possible according to the perspective of those affected by the information flow or technological development. Sclove asserts that participatory design and development will "ensure a more diverse range of

social needs, concerns, and experiences." Such an approach is requisite if the information age is to be equitable and ethical. Consequently, information transfer in terms of access, dissemination, control, and content construction must be designed according to a principle or set of principles that respect cultural specificity, subjectivity, and values. The information age holds great potential to unite disparate peoples and ideas; nevertheless, it is imperative to safeguard the cultural uniqueness and social microcosms which furnish the regions of the world with independence, freedom of choice, and freedom of access.

QUESTIONS

1. Why does the "worldwide context" of information change its ethical situation?

2. Why might a free on-line library (containing much or most of the world's recorded knowledge) be a good thing? Why might it be a bad thing?

Victoria Groom and Clifford Nass | Can Robots Be Teammates?

Victoria Groom researches human–computer interaction at Stanford University's CHIME lab.

Clifford Nass is Thoms M. Storke Professor at Stanford University.

IDENTIFYING THE BEST MODEL FOR HUMAN–ROBOT INTERACTION

Human teams are so effective that there is a natural tendency to enlist non-humans as teammates. What happens when nonhuman animals are brought into human teams? While there is an expectation that human teams are so powerful and effective that they

should be able to gracefully incorporate at least one or two animal others, especially given the power of teams to blur differences between members, the results have generally been poor, even when the proposed teammates are social animals such as dogs. In the best-studied examples, there have been attempts to bring dogs into human search and rescue teams as full-fledged teammates. No matter how much the dog trains with the team as a whole, it has proven to be much more effective to provide the dog with a single "handler" who is part of the team: the dog is an adjunct to the handler rather than a team member in its own right.

Before the advent of robots, there was a general understanding that technologies could not be

From *Interaction Studies* 8:3 (2007), 483–500. © John Benjamins Publishing Company.

An Internet Culture?
C. Kluckhorn

Culture: "the total way of life for a people," "the social legacy an individual acquires from his group," "a way of thinking, feeling and believing," "a mechanism for the regulation of behavior."

C. Kluckhorn, *Mirror for Man.*

teammates. Noninformation technologies have long been understood as at most facilitators of teams. Although people may appreciate the capabilities of computers, few see them as having the potential to function as teammates (Nass, Fogg, & Moon, 1996). In essence, computers do not seem to have the required communication and coordination abilities.

Although animals and technologies have not even been pretenders for team membership, the team has been designated the normative organizational model for human–robot interaction. The 2007 International Conference of Human–Robot Interaction was themed "Robot as Team Member." In the official program, the Co-Chairs note that robots used in "critical domains . . . must coordinate their behaviors with human team members; they are more than mere tools but rather quasi-team members whose tasks have to be integrated with those of humans." It is not suprising that people address the need for coordination by modeling robots on teammates. Teams appear so valuable that it may seem they should be considered first among other possible social structures. Unlike animals, robots can be designed specifically to support human activities. Robots can be programmed to focus unwaveringly on the team's goal. Researchers continue to make significant strides in training robots to engage in socially-appropriate behavior and coordinated action (Fong, Nourbakhsh, & Dautenhahn, 2003). There is also evidence that robots and especially androids elicit a broad range of social responses

to a greater extent than computers and other technologies (MacDorman & Ishiguro, 2006a, 2006b). Given how humanlike robots can appear, the answer to the question, "Can and should we try to design robot teammates?" has been "Yes," and the field has moved on to the question, "How do we make robots *better* teammates?"

The Assumption of "Humanness"

The assumption that the team is an ideal model for human–robot interaction is based on the even more basic assumption that the best model for the development of robots is the human model. When researchers ask the question, "How do we make robots better teammates in human teams?" what they are really asking is, "How do we make robots better *human* teammates?" The view that robots can succeed as teammates while computers cannot may derive from the fact that robots are ascribed a greater potential to exhibit characteristically human behavior.

By presupposing that robots could be teammates, researchers may miss noticing the possibility that imbuing robots with the "humanness" assumed of teammates may be extremely challenging or even impossible. If robots cannot or will not manifest "humanness" then the question, "Is it possible to make robots successful teammates?" needs to be reevaluated. If robots can never be effective teammates, the team model should be replaced with a more appropriate model.

The human ability to accept robots into teams ultimately will determine the success or failure of robot teammates. Although the technical capabilities of robots to engage in coordinated activity is improving (as visible for robot-only teams at RoboCup[1]), we believe humans' innate expectations for team-appropriate behavior pose challenges to the development of mixed teams that cannot be fixed with technological innovation. Since we focus on the human response to robots positioned as teammates, we limit our discussion to human–robot teams in which robots and humans work together as teammates in one team. Our discussion of robot teammates does not apply to partnerships, teams of humans interacting with robots external to the teams, or teams of robots controlled by external operators. "Teammate" has a strict organizational definition, which we describe in detail below.

Human–Robot Organizational Structures

Murphy (2004) divides robot applications into two broad domains: robots deployed in controlled environments and robots deployed in unpredictable environments. The latter collection of applications she terms *field applications;* these include space exploration, SWAT teams, military robotics, and rescue robotics. Teams prove particularly appealing in these areas because the autonomy, flexibility, and coordination of teammates strengthen the group's ability to adjust to unforeseen circumstances and changing situations. In field applications, operators are usually physically distant from the robots they control and breakdowns in communication may have negative consequences. High stakes make explicit the need for a robust coordination model, such as the team. Robots in field applications are often operated by a human team (Murphy, 2004); extending the team to include the robot appears a logical adaptation.

If a robot is not identified as a teammate, it may be treated as a tool. The robot-as-tool model, often used in teleoperation, constrains the robot's performance to the operator's skill and the design of the interface (Fong, Thorpe, & Baur, 2002). While the team model promises the robot the autonomy needed to

liberate it from humans' restrictive control, we argue that robots are currently unable to meet human's high expectations for appropriate team behavior in the unpredictable, high-stakes situations for which they are designed.

Our problematization of the human–robot team is not a criticism of other human–robot interaction structures. In controlled environments, robots in humanlike social roles are demonstrating great promise. The public's positive response to commercial entertainment robots, such as Sony's Aibo and WowWee's Robosapien, highlights the promise of robots as entertainers. As robots become increasingly adept at playing games with humans, the effectiveness of robot entertainers will likely increase (Brooks et al., 2004). The Huggable and other similar haptic devices demonstrate the ability of robots to serve as media, conveying human communication across distances (Stiehl et al., 2005). Users have responded enthusiastically to iRobot's Roomba, suggesting that domestic servant robots will be welcomed into homes (Forlizzi & DiSalvo, 2006). The utility of robots as therapeutic aids has been particularly well-demonstrated. Both as companions (Libin & Libin, 2004; Tamura et al., 2004; Turkle, 2007) and behavioral therapists (Feil-Seifer, Skinner & Matarić, 2007; Werry, Dautenhahn, Ogden, & Harwin, 2001), robots have proven their ability to enhance people's quality of life. In controlled environments, such as a therapy session, or when limited autonomy is required, such as with entertainment, robots fit easily into human roles. While robots may not be fully convincing, their behavior is rarely in such blatant violation of human expectations as to break the social contract of the role.

Features of Successful Teammates

To determine if robot teammates can succeed without full-blown humanness, researchers should first identify those qualities that make a successful human teammate. A substantial body of literature on human teams identifies benchmarks that are relevant to a team's success. Broadly speaking, teammates need to share interests (Rouse, Cannon-Bowers, & Salas,

1992) and engage in pro-team behavior (Mead, 1934). More specifically, successful teammates must

- Share a common goal (P. R. Cohen & Levesque, 1991)
- Share mental models (Bettenhausen, 1991)
- Subjugate individual needs for group needs (Klein, Woods, Bradshaw, Hoffman, & Feltovich, 2004)
- View interdependence as positive (Gully, Incalcaterra, Joshi, & Beaubien, 2002)
- Know and fulfill their roles (Hackman, 1987)
- Trust each other (G. R. Jones & George, 1998)

Teams adopt shared goals because forming teams to achieve shared goals makes it easier to achieve individual goals. Teams establish and maintain goals by sharing a team mental model. A team mental model has a form similar to that of an individual's mental model. While each teammate's mental model is unique, they are structurally similar. Each teammate may infer the basic motivations, perceptions, and vulnerabilities of other teammates from her own model. The ability to infer others' mental models enables teammates to develop a team mental model complete with a shared set of goals, strategies, and motivations. Sharing a mental model aids decision-making (Walsh & Fahey, 1986), communication, and collaborative action (H. H. Clark, 1996).

Before engaging in activities to achieve shared goals, potential teammates need to deduce that the benefits of participation in the team outweigh the anticipated personal sacrifices. To make these sacrifices, teammates have to value the group's interests above their own and subjugate personal needs to the needs of the group. Comparing individual needs to the needs of the group requires a sense of self, the ability to distinguish self from other, and personal needs. Furthermore, teammates must view the interdependence of the group as positive. If a person feels that pursuing a goal as a group is less likely to produce the desired reward than pursuing it alone, the individual will not make the sacrifices demanded of teammates (Cannon-Bowers, Salas, & Converse, 1993).

Communication between teammates enables the team to distribute work efficiently (Bales, 1951). If teammates do not know their roles and do not fulfill their duties, the team will perform less well. Similarly, if a team member's actions do not meet the behavioral expectations of other teammates, the strength of the team will deteriorate (Butler, 1976).

The Importance of Trust

Trust is the feeling of confidence that another individual will not put the self at risk unnecessarily (Anderson, 1980; Axelrod, 1976). Believing that teammates will protect each other's interests enables individual teammates to surrender their personal interests to the interests of the group. Trust between teammates is essential for the successful functioning of a team, as trust bridges shared interests and proteam behavior. Trust also establishes behavioral expectations that facilitate joint activity (Mayer, Davis, & Schoorman, 1995). In high-risk situations, trust assumes even greater importance (Das & Teng, 2004). Because robots are often designed to take the place of humans in high-risk situations, people's trust of robots will be particularly critical if robots are to succeed as teammates.

Willingness to surrender the protection of one's safety depends in large part on the degree to which individuals trust each other. At-risk teammates must believe that the team's interest in their welfare is comparable to their own (Mayer et al., 1995) and think that other teammates are capable of protecting their interests (Deutsh, 1960).

The Specter of the Human–Robot Team

No group of humans and robots has met the requirements of a team as described above. One reason the team has been accepted as the ideal model for human–robot interaction may be that researchers are unaware of its specific requirements, and therefore underestimate the challenges of creating a team. Researchers often label humans and robots interacting together as teams, but examining these "teams" offers more evidence for the enormity of the challenge of creating true teams than evidence of their successful implementation.

When researchers report the successful implementation of a human–robot team, these "teams" are in fact one of the other successful human–robot organizational structures, such as the partnership. For example, Sierhuis et al. (2003) developed a human–robot team model that positioned robots as nonessential servants to human needs aboard the International Space Station. This organizational structure would not have been called a team if a subset of cohabitating humans was dedicated entirely to serving the needs of other members. Without personal needs, expendable robots are unable to willingly subjugate individual needs for the benefit of the group, to trust or be trusted, or to view interdependence as positive. In this model, robots are servants and humans are masters.

Unlike humans, robots have not yet exhibited the abilities required of teammates. They do not have unique viewpoints or mental models and cannot be trusted in a humanlike way. Robots lack values, and they cannot access the mental model shared by human teammates. Robots do not exhibit a drive for self-preservation and lack the ability to link motivations to protect the self with motivations to protect the group. Simply put, robots fail as teammates. They set false expectations of autonomy, agency, and self-preservation, making collaboration difficult.

These problems are exacerbated by the human tendency to respond socially to nonhuman stimuli (MacDorman & Ishiguro, 2006a). Humans project a social identity on media and technologies that offer the slightest social cue (Reeves & Nass, 1996). In the case of robots—even nonhumanoids—implicit social cues are powerful. Characterizing robots as teammates indicates that robots are capable of fulfilling a human role and encourages humans to treat robots as human teammates. When expectations go unmet, a negative response is unavoidable.

Attempts at Human–Robot Teams

While there have been few attempts to deploy robots as meaningful teammates in real-life situations, many researchers are focusing on developing in robots the potential to one day succeed in true human–robot teams. Groups at NASA have developed robots

intended to take the place of humans in dangerous situations in space exploration and to support humans in the Space Station (Fong, Nourbakhsh, Kunz, Fluckiger, & Schreiner, 2005; Sierhuis et al., 2003). The Stanford Aerospace Robotics Laboratory has worked with the Palo Alto-Mountain View Regional SWAT Team and MLB Company to integrate an Unmanned Aerial Vehicle, the MLB Bat, into a human SWAT team. The MLB Bat provided SWAT teammates on the ground with aerial views of the site. Robin Murphy and others at the University of South Florida have focused on deploying human–robot teams to aid with search and rescue operations. Other groups, such as The Naval Research Laboratory and the Robotics Institute at Carnegie Mellon, have focused on the technical development of features required for robots to act as teammates. Work by these groups includes the development of dialog systems (Rybski, Yoon, Stolarz, & Veloso, 2007), modeling of cognitive and affective systems (Cassimatis, Trafton, Bugajska, & Schultz, 2004; Gockley, Simmons, & Forlizzi, 2006), improvement of spatial awareness (Trafton et al., 2005; Trafton et al., 2006), implementation of flexible autonomy structures (Heger & Singh, 2006), and robot training (Rybski et al., 2007).

While these groups are succeeding in improving robots' performance, they have not yet addressed some of the features most essential for human–robot team success, nor have they demonstrated that currently identified challenges can be overcome. For example, the Peer-to-Peer Human Interaction Project was created in response to the NASA Vision for Space Exploration, which called for the development of a program for space exploration that balanced contributions from both robots and humans (Fong et al., 2005). Researchers from NASA, the Robotics Institute at Carnegie Mellon, the National Institute of Standards and Technology, the Naval Research Laboratory, and the Massachusetts Institute of Technology collaborated in one of the largest coordinated efforts to develop successful human–robot teams. The group's three major efforts included the development of the "Human–Robot Interaction Operating System" to facilitate task-oriented dialog exchange, cognitive architectures designed for humans and robots to understand each other, and metrics to evaluate team success. A simulated team of astronauts and multiple robots, including the humanoid Robonaut, worked collaboratively on construction tasks. Performance analysis revealed deficiencies in both human–robot and human–human communication. The robots' inabilities to monitor and communicate their status resulted in the greatest identified deficiency: time lost in communication between astronauts to determine the robots' status.

Two major problem areas . . . are the robot's inability to earn trust and lack of self awareness. In high-stress situations, robot operators may experience physical and cognitive fatigue. In extreme cases, operators may forget to bring a robot to or from a disaster site (Casper & Murphy, 2003). Unlike human teammates who think not only about how to do their jobs, but also how to be prepared to do their jobs, robots require an external activation of their autonomy. They must be set-up to perform, but in cases of extreme stress, human teammates may lose their ability to babysit the robot. In these cases, the robot will not be in the appropriate position to complete its task.

In the examples considered, the robots have provided insufficient information on their internal state to operators, so operators have needed to spend much of their time diagnosing a robot's problems. In the wake of the World Trade Center Disaster, an estimated 54% of time spent in voids was wasted diagnosing problems (Casper & Murphy, 2003). Robots lack pain and may continue to engage in destructive behaviors until they are damaged or destroyed. The difficulties regarding robots' self-awareness stem from their lack of a self–other distinction and a drive for self-preservation. Lacking unconditional autonomy, current robots are never fully self-motivated and engage in behaviors that are not only self-destructive, but damaging to the team.

Perhaps the most daunting problem for the development of human–robot teams is overcoming the challenge of establishing trust between humans and robots. Not surprisingly, trusting something that is unable to trust and to feel guilt or betrayal proves difficult. The less a user trusts a robot, the sooner she will intervene in its progress towards the completion of a task (Olsen & Goodrich, 2003). If she believes the robot's actions contradict a higher-level goal, she

will override the robot's completion of a low-level task (Olsen & Goodrich, 2003).

Human teams are easily created and expanded. In crises, teammates generally feel certain of other teammates' high-level goals. Even when new teams are integrated into a larger team, teammates may rely on their understanding of others' goals and mental models to predict the new teammates' behavior. Because robots lack fully-formed mental models and operate using task-specific models of their goals and environments, human teams feel they cannot rely on the robot to act only in ways that protect the team's safety. At the World Trade Center site, robots were sent into the rubble last, following humans, search tools, and then dogs (Casper & Murphy, 2003). In SWAT incidents, certainty and control are highly valued; technologies that show any potential to introduce uncertainty are seen as threats. SWAT teammates may reject robots as sources of risk (H. L. Jones, Rock, Burns, & Morris, 2002).

Benchmarking an Ongoing Successful Team

Throughout the lifespan of a team, the integrity of the team will be challenged. Violations of trust are one of the most serious threats, and with robots, these challenges are among the most difficult to overcome. Without self-interest and humanlike mental models, the introduction of a robot into a human team makes violations of trust and the ensuing consequences highly likely. A successful strategy of response to threats is marked by a series of benchmarks. The best way to understand these benchmarks is to understand how they might fail.

Benchmark 1: Conditional trust is established. In low stakes situations, humans grant potential teammates the benefit of the doubt and show initial conditional trust. In human–robot teams, if the initial interaction with the robot is in a low-risk situation, humans may begin trusting the robot conditionally. If the stakes are initially high, trust may never be established and the humans will not treat the robot as a teammate. If an initially low stakes situation becomes more risky or potentially rewarding, or if the team's goal changes, the human teammates' trust of the robot will be challenged.

Benchmark 2: Trust is challenged. The greater a human teammate's personal investment in the team's ultimate goal, the lower her threshold for violations of expectations. If the robot works with significant autonomy in an uncontrolled environment, it will inevitably act in an unexpected manner. The robot may fail to complete a routine task, or it may adapt to a new situation in an unexpected way. In high stakes situations, even if the robot's actions do not put humans at direct risk, unpredictability will be seen as a threat to the safety of the group. While reciprocation of expectations causes an upward spiral of team success, unmet expectations initiate a downward spiral in trust. The human's conditional trust and initial positive affect towards the robot will shift to distrust and negative affect (G. R. Jones & George, 1998).

Benchmark 3: Violated party attempts to repair trust. If a teammate whose trust has been violated believes the offender still shares the same values, the trust relationship may be reparable. The violation will signal to the human a need to reevaluate the relationship. She will compare the robot's values to her own, and consider her attitudes and emotions with regards to the robot. If her trust has been violated but not destroyed, she will indicate the violation of trust via outbursts (Frijda, 1988). Thus, early responses to minor trust violations by robots will result in verbal and physical displays of negative affect toward the robot and negative emotion. The human may direct frustration directly at the robot or, given the social inappropriateness of scolding a robot, the human may channel it through alternative paths. She may direct outbursts at other human teammates or simply withhold expression of the violation.

Benchmark 4: Renegotiated relationship is established. While minor violations of trust need not destroy a trust relationship, the offender must respond positively to the wronged party's outburst and change their behavior in accordance with the trust agreement. The offender also needs to make the wronged party's feelings more positive (G. R. Jones & George, 1998). Robots are unlikely to change in accordance with the human's request. Over time, the human will criticize the robot for acting unpredictably, regardless of the action or the expected behavior. Negative outbursts will

increase, and as the robot fails to renegotiate the trust relationship, the relationship will spiral downward.

Benchmark 5: Team performance changes. If trust is reestablished, the overall performance of the team will show improvement. Without the shared goals and close social relationship of trust, the human will lack the willingness or desire to assist the robot (M. S. Clark & Mills, 1979). Without assistance, the robot may fail to complete its tasks. A hallmark of a successful team is a willingness among teammates to perform tasks outside their roles that further the goals of the team. Without shared goals, human teammates will limit the scope of their roles. By completing only the tasks dictated by her role, a teammate may jeopardize the safety of the team. Any dependence on the robot will make the human feel uncomfortable. She will be unlikely to engage in help-seeking behavior, which may delay or prevent the resolution of problems (Walster, Walster, Berscheid, & Austin, 1978). Without a timely resolution of problems, the success of the entire team is jeopardized. Uncertain that all teammates will subjugate their individual needs for the group's goal, the humans may shirk their duties (Holmstrom, 1979).

Communication amongst teammates will be damaged as well. Because the individual is concerned that information will be used to her detriment or to exert power over her, she will withhold information from all distrusted parties (Fama & Jensen, 1983), including the robot and those working closely with the robot. When the trust relationship between human and robot deteriorates beyond repair, the human will lobby to remove the robot from the team. If the human succeeds, a productive human-only team may be established. If the robot is not removed from the team, the human may leave the team.

Benchmarking a New Interaction Model

If researchers accept that robots may never succeed as teammates, does that mean that human–robot collaborations will always be inferior to human–human collaborations? Should we limit robots to the role of socially unaware tool?

The success of the team model for collaborative human behavior demonstrates that organizational structures should take advantage of the abilities of each entity in the group. Instead of steadfastly maintaining the team model of human–robot interaction and trying to make robots comparable to human teammates, researchers should instead develop an organizational structure that exploits both the special abilities of humans and the special abilities of robots. In the struggle to make robots into people, researchers have not fully identified the human characteristics that robots lack nor the robot characteristics that humans lack. While trying to make robots human, researchers have sometimes overlooked what makes robots special.

The Advantages of Robots

Teams not only take advantage of human strengths; they also work around human weaknesses. Just as it is challenging to recognize the human strengths that teams optimize, so it is challenging to recognize the human weaknesses that teams minimize. Benchmarking and developing desirable abilities in robots that are not restrained by selfhood may enable designers to create robots that succeed in aspects of coordinated activity where people struggle.

A unique point of view, while it offers many advantages, limits a human's perspective. While humans simultaneously process a range of information through a variety of channels, the perspective of the individual is restricted to one physical location. Humans have access only to information that reaches their locations. Robots need not be limited in this way. Robot sensors may be distinct from the robot and placed throughout an environment. Not only does this enable the robot to perceive information unavailable at the robot's physical location, it also enables the robot to perceive itself directly from a third-person perspective. Because self-perceptions are subject-less, obtaining a clear assessment of the status of the self is often more challenging than assessing the status of others. Robots have the potential to perceive themselves both first-personally and third-personally. Even if humans could perceive information through multiple points of view at once, they would be unable to process the information.

The concept of the self and the functioning of mental models require that phenomena be experienced through one unique point of view. Robots may be developed not only to perceive information through multiple points of view, but also to process and assimilate this information into one coherent whole.

Humans rely on external sources of information to orient themselves. Humans must use a process of triangulation that relies on external markers to establish their physical locations. This process is limiting in several ways. External orienting references are constantly changing. If a human does not stay alert to these changes, all reference points may be lost and disorientation may occur. Robots need not rely on variable reference points to establish their physical location. Robots designed with the ability to determine their location regardless of context can have navigation abilities superior to those of humans.

Mental models aid human action and team coordination because they make the processing and use of information manageable. For people, perceiving the world directly without the filtration and organization offered by mental models would result in information overload and impairment of intentional action. People refer to simplified models to make decisions, instead of the constantly changing, information-rich world. While mental models do enable people to avoid information overload, they separate the human experience from phenomenal reality. Mental models do not perfectly represent reality, as information is filtered out, changed to fit the model, and emotionally colored. While mental models enable humans to act with limited information processing, they restrict the information available to make decisions. Without mental models, robots need not filter perceptions nor alter information to enable efficient processing and decision-making. Robots may be designed with the ability to store and process all sensory input. Processing information without mental models also enables robots to evaluate information without the influence of moods or emotions. In high-risk or emotionally-charged situations, a robot's ability to process all information without the influence of attitudes, moods, or emotions could enable the robot to process information more accurately and make wiser decisions than human counterparts.

CONCLUSION

We do not wish to offer here a blueprint for a new human–robot organizational structure. Instead, we hope to inspire designers and researchers to identify and develop the potential abilities of robots that humans do not share. To determine the best interaction model for humans and robots, we believe the following questions need to first be addressed. Answering each question sets a benchmark for determining the best model.

- What are the restrictions of humanness that limit performance?
- Which inabilities of humans can be successfully implemented in robots?
- What organizational structure best optimizes both human and robot abilities?
- If an organizational structure familiar to humans is ideal, do robots have the potential to fulfill the social duties of the role, and is developing those abilities worth the effort?

Researchers would not be using robots for side-by-side interaction if they did not believe that robots have assets to contribute that humans do not. Nonetheless, the human tendency to see "humanness" everywhere has led researchers to impose a model of interaction suitable only for human–human interaction. If researchers wish to optimize what is special about robots, they should recognize that robots and humans need to be designed to complement each other in a way that enables optimal social structures to emerge. Rather than expect robots to meet benchmarks for being human, robots should be evaluated in terms of benchmarks that make them effective as complements rather than duplicates. As we move beyond teams to social structures that allow robots to complement humans rather than be ersatz teammates and ersatz people, the true benefits of robots and humans working together will be realized.

NOTE

1. RoboCup: URL: http://www.robocup.org/, last accessed 17/5/2007.

REFERENCES

Anderson, J. R. (1981). Concepts, propositions, and schemata: What are the cognitive units? In J. H. Flowers (Ed.), Nebraska symposium on motivation: Cognitive processes (Vol. 28). Lincoln: University of Nebraska Press.

Axelrod, R. M. (1976). The structure of decision. Princeton: Princeton University Press.

Bales, R. F. (1951). Interaction process analysis: A method for the study of small groups. Chicago: Addison-Wesley Press.

Bettenhausen, K. L. (1991). Five years of groups research: What we have learned and what needs to be addressed. Journal of Management, 17(2), 345–381.

Brooks, A. G., Gray, J., Hoffman, G., Lockerd, A., Lee, H., & Breazeal, C. (2004). Robot's play: interactive games with sociable machines. Computers in Entertainment (CIE), 2(3), 10–10.

Butler, J. K. (1976). Reciprocity of trust between professionals and their secretaries. Psychological Reports, 53, 411–416.

Cannon-Bowers, J. A., Salas, E., & Converse, S. (1993). Shared mental models in expert team decision making. In N. J. Castellan (Ed.), Individual and group decision making (pp. 221–246). Hillsdale, NJ: Erlbaum.

Casper, J., & Murphy, R. R. (2003). Human–robot interactions during the robot-assisted urban search and rescue response at the World Trade Center. IEEE Transactions on Systems, Man and Cybernetics (Part B), 33(3), 367–385.

Cassimatis, N. L., Trafton, J. G., Bugajska, M. D., & Schultz, A. C. (2004). Integrating cognition, perception and action through mental simulation in robots. Robotics and Autonomous Systems, 49(1–2), 13–23.

Clark, H. H. (1996). Using language. Cambridge: Cambridge University Press.

Clark, M. S., & Mills, J. (1979). Interpersonal attraction in exchange and communal relationships. Journal of Personality and Social Psychology, 37(1), 12–24.

Cohen, P. R., & Levesque, H. J. (1991). Teamwork. Nous, 25(4), 487–512.

Das, T., & Teng, B. (2004). The risk-based view of trust. Journal of Business and Psychology, 19(1), 85–116.

Deutsh, M. (1960). The effect of motivational orientation upon trust and suspicion. Human Relations, 13, 123–140.

Fama, E. F., & Jensen, M. C. (1983). Separation of ownership and control. Journal of Law and Economics, 26(2), 301–325.

Feil-Seifer, D., Skinner, K., & Malarie, M. J. (2007). Benchmarks for evaluating socially assistive robotics. Interaction Studies, 8(3).

Fong, T., Nourbakhsh, I., Kunz, C., Fluckiger, L., & Schreiner, J. (2005). The peer-to-peer human–robot interaction project. Paper presented at the AAAI Space, Long Beach, CA.

Fong, T., Nourbakhsh, I., Kunz, C., Fluckiger. L., & Schreiner, J. (2005). The peer-to-peer human–robot interaction project. *Space*, 2005–6750.

Fong, T., Thorpe, C., & Baur, C. (2002). Robot as partner: vehicle teleoperation with collaborative control. *Proceedings from the 2002 Naval Research Laboratory Workshop on Multi-Robot Systems*. Washington, DC, USA.

Forlizzi, J., & DiSalvo, C. (2006). Service robots in the domestic environment: A study of the Roomba vacuum in the home. *ACM SIGCHI/SIGART Human–Robot Interaction*, 258–265.

Frijda, N. H. (1988). The laws of emotion. *American Psychologist,* 43(5), 349–358.

Gockley, R., Simmons, R., & Forlizzi, J. (2006). Modeling affect in socially interactive robots. *Proceedings of the 15th IEEE International Symposium on Robot and Human Interactive Communication (RO-MAN 2006)*, (pp. 558–563) Hatfield, UK.

Gully, S. M., Incalaterra, K. A., Joshi, A., & Beaubien, J. M. (2002). A meta-analysis of team-efficacy, potency, and performance: Interdependence and level of analysis as moderators of observed relationships. *Journal of Applied Psychology,* 87(5), 819–832.

Hackman, J. R. (1987). The design of work teams. In J. W. Lorsch (Ed.), *Handbook of organizational behavior.* Englewood Cliffs, NJ: Prentice Hall.

Heger, F., & Singh, S. (2006). Sliding autonomy for complex coordinated multi-robot tasks: Analysis and experiments. *Proceedings Robotics: Science and Systems II*, August 16–19, 2006. Philadelphia, Pennsylvania, USA. The MIT Press 2007.

Holmstrom, B. (1979). Moral hazard and observability. *The Bell Journal of Economics,* 10(1), 74–91.

Jones, G. R., & George, J. M. (1998). The experience and evolution of trust: implications for cooperation and teamwork. *The Academy of Management Review,* 23(3), 531–546.

Jones, H. L., Rock, S. M., Burns, D., & Morris, S. (2002). Autonomous robots in swat applications: Research, design, and operations challenges. *Proceedings of the Association of Unmanned Vehicle Systems International (AUVSI) International Conference on Unmanned Vehicles*, Orlando, FL, USA.

Klein, G., Woods, D. D., Bradshaw, J. M., Hoffman, R. R., & Feltovich, P. J. (2004). Ten challenges for making automation a "team player" in joint human–agent activity. *IEEE Intelligent Systems* 19(6), 91–95.

Libin, A. V., & Libin, E. V. (2004). Person–robot interactions from the robopsychologists point of view: The robotic psychology and robotherapy approach. *Proceedings of the IEEE,* 92(11), 1789–1803.

MacDorman, K. F. & Ishiguro, H. (2006a). Opening Pandora's uncanny box: Reply to commentaries on "The uncanny advantage of using androids in social and cognitive science research." *Interaction Studies*, 7(3), 361–368.

MacDorman, K. F. & Ishiguro, H. (2006b). The uncanny advantage of using androids in social and cognitive science research. *Interaction Studies*, 7(3), 297–337.

Mayer, R. C., Davis, J. H., & Schoorman, F. D. (1995). An integrative model or organization trust. *Academy of Management Review,* 3(20), 709–734.

Mead, G. H. (1934). *Mind, self, and society.* Chicago: University of Chicago Press.

Murphy, R. R. (2004). Human–robot interaction in rescue robotics. *IEEE Transactions on Systems, Man, and Cybernetics, Part C: Applications and Reviews,* 34(2), 138–153.

Nass, C., Fogg, B. J., & Moon, Y. (1996). Can computers be teammates? *International Journal of Human–Computer Studies,* 45(6), 669–678.

Olsen, D. R., & Goodrich, M. A. (2003). Metrics for evaluating human-robot interactions. *In Proc. NIST Performance Metrics for Intelligent Systems Workshop, Washington, DC, USA.*

Rouse, W. B., Cannon-Bowers, J. A., & Salas, E. (1992). The role of mental models in team performance in complex systems. *IEEE Transactions on Systems, Man, and Cybernetics,* 22(6), 1296–1308.

Rybski, P. E., Yoon, K., Stolarz, J., & Veloso, M. M. (2007, March 10–12). Interactive robot task training through dialog and demonstration. *Proceeding of the ACM/IEEE 2nd International Conference on Human–Robot Interaction*, (pp. 49–56) Arlington, Virginia, USA.

Sierhuis, M., Bradshaw, J. M., Acquisti, A., van Hoof, R., Jeffers, R., & Uszok, A. (2003). Human–agent teamwork and adjustable autonomy in practice. *Proceedings of the 7th International Symposium on Artificial Intelligence, Robotics and Automation in Space, Nara, Japan.*

Stiehl, W. D., Lieberman, J., Breazeal, C., Basel, L., Lalla, L, & Wolf, M. (2005). Design of a therapeutic robotic companion for relational, affective touch. *Proceedings 14th IEEE International Workshop on Robot and Human Interactive Communication,* (pp. 408–415). Nashville, USA.

Tamura, T., Yonemitsu, S., Itoh, A., Oikawa, D., Kawakami, A., Higashi, Y., et al. (2004). Is an entertainment robot useful in the care of elderly people with severe dementia? *Journals of Gerontology Series A: Biological and Medical Sciences,* 59(1), 83–85.

Trafton, J. G., Cassimatis, N. L., Bugajska, M. D., Brock, D. P., Mintz, F. E., & Schultz, A. C. (2005). Enabling effective human–robot interaction using perspective-taking in robots. *IEEE Transactions on Systems, Man and Cybernetics* (Part A), 35(4), 460–470.

Trafton, J. G., Schultz, A. C., Perznowski, D., Bugajska, M. D., Adams, W., Cassimatis, N. L., & Brock, D. P. (2006). Children and robots learning to play hide and seek. Paper presented at the ACM SIGCHI/SIGART Human–Robot Interaction, Salt Lake City, Utah, USA. Turkle, S. (2007). Authenticity in the age of digital companions. *Interaction Studies,* 8(3). (This issue)

Walsh, J. P., & Fahey, L. (1986). The role of negotiated belief structures in strategy making. *Journal of Management,* 12(3), 325–338.

Walster, E., Walster, G. W., Berscheid, E., & Austin, W. (1978). *Equity: theory and research.* Boston: Allyn and Bacon.

Werry, I., Dautenhahn, K., Ogden, B., & Harwin, W. (2001). Can social interaction skills be taught by a social agent? The role of a robotic mediator in autism therapy. In M. Beynon, C. L. Nehaniv & K. Dautenhahn (Eds.), Proceedings of The Fourth International Conference on Cognitive Technology: Instruments of Mind (pp. 57–74). Berlin, Heidelberg: Springer-Verlag.

QUESTIONS

1. Why should robots be a source of moral worry?

2. Will a day come when a robot is defending itself—with a lawyer, of course—in court?

3. How should we rethink and how robots can help humans? Do we have the right ideal in mind?

Clive Thompson

The Next Civil Rights Battle Will Be Over the Mind

Clive Thompson writes extensively on moral issues raised by new technologies.

Trolling down the street in Manhattan, I suddenly hear a woman's voice. "Who's there? Who's there?" she whispers. I look around but can't figure out where it's coming from. It seems to emanate from inside my skull. Am I going nuts? Nope. I have simply encountered a new advertising medium: hypersonic sound. It broadcasts audio in a focused beam, so that only a person standing directly in its path hears the message. In this case, the cable channel A&E was using the technology to promote a show about, naturally, the paranormal.

I'm a geek, so my first reaction was, "Cool!" But it also felt creepy. We think of our brains as the ultimate private sanctuary, a zone where other people can't intrude without our knowledge or permission. But its boundaries are gradually eroding. Hypersonic sound is just a portent of what's coming, one of a host of emerging technologies aimed at tapping into our heads. These tools raise a fascinating, and queasy, new ethical question: Do we have a right to "mental privacy"? "We're going to be facing this question more and more, and nobody is really ready for it," says Paul Root Wolpe, a bioethicist and board member of the nonprofit Center for Cognitive Liberty and Ethics. "If the skull is not an absolute domain of privacy, there *are* no privacy domains left." He argues that the big personal liberty issues of the twenty-first century will all be in our heads—the "civil rights of the mind," he calls it.

From *Wired* 16, no.4 (March 24, 2008).

It's true that most of this technology is still gestational. But the early experiments are compelling: Some researchers say that fMRI brain scans can detect surprisingly specific mental acts—like whether you're entertaining racist thoughts, doing arithmetic, reading, or recognizing something. Entrepreneurs are already pushing dubious forms of the tech into the marketplace: You can now hire a firm, No Lie MRI, to conduct a "truth verification" scan if you're trying to prove you're on the level. Give it ten years, ethicists say, and brain tools will be used regularly—sometimes responsibly, often shoddily. Both situations scare civil libertarians. What happens when the government starts using brain scans in criminal investigations—to figure out if, say, a suspect is lying about a terrorist plot? Will the Fifth Amendment protect you from self-incrimination by your own brain? Think about your workplace, too: Your boss can already demand that you pee in a cup. Should he or she also be allowed to stick your head in an MRI tube as part of your performance review?

But this isn't just about reading minds; it's also about bombarding them with messages or tweaking their chemistry. Transcranial magnetic stimulation—now used to treat epilepsy—has shown that it can artificially generate states of empathy and euphoria. And you've probably heard of propranolol, a drug that can help erase traumatic memories. Let's say you've been assaulted and you want to take propranolol to delete the memory. The state needs that memory to prosecute the assailant.

Can it prevent you from taking the drug? "To a certain extent, memories are societal properties," says Adam Kolber, a visiting professor at Princeton. "Society has always made claims on your memory, such as subpoenaing you." Or what if you use transcranial stimulation to increase your empathy. Would you be required to disclose that? Could a judge throw you off a jury? Could the Army turn you away? I'd love to give you answers. But the truth is that no one knows. Privacy rights vary from state to state, and it's unclear how, or even if, the protections would apply to mental sanctity. "We really need to articulate a moral code that governs all this," warns Arthur Caplan, a University of Pennsylvania bioethicist.

The good news is that scholars are holding conferences to hash out legal positions. But we'll need a broad public debate about it, too. Civil liberties thrive only when the public demands them—and understands they're at risk. That means we need to stop seeing this stuff as science fiction and start thinking about how we'll react to it. Otherwise, we could all lose our minds.

QUESTIONS

1. In what ways are your words like the contents of your mind? In what ways are they different?

2. How are the contents of your mind already being manipulated? Is this manipulation usually moral or immoral? Or neither?

Bill Joy | # Why The Future Doesn't Need Us

Bill Joy, cofounder and chief scientist of Sun Microsystems, was cochair of the presidential commission on the future of IT research.

From the moment I became involved in the creation of new technologies, their ethical dimensions have concerned me, but it was only in the autumn of 1998 that I became anxiously aware of how great are the dangers facing us in the 21st century. I can date the onset of my unease to the day I met Ray Kurzweil, the deservedly famous inventor of the first reading machine for the blind and many other amazing things. . . .

In the hotel bar, Ray gave me a partial preprint of his then-forthcoming book *The Age of Spiritual Machines*, which outlined a utopia he foresaw—one in which humans gained near immortality by becoming one with robotic technology. On reading it, my sense of unease only intensified; I felt sure he had to be understating the dangers, understating the probability of a bad outcome along this path.

I found myself most troubled by a passage detailing a *dys*topian scenario:

THE NEW LUDDITE CHALLENGE

First let us postulate that the computer scientists succeed in developing intelligent machines that can do all things better than human beings can do them. In that case presumably all work will be done by vast, highly organized systems of machines and no human effort will be necessary. . . .

If the machines are permitted to make all their owndecisions, we can't make any conjectures as to the results, because it is impossible to guess how such machines might behave. We only point out that the fate of the human race would be at the mercy of the machines. . . . The human race might easily permit itself to drift into a position of such dependence on the machines that it would have no practical choice but to accept all of the machines' decisions. As society and the problems that face it become more and more complex and machines become more and more intelligent, people will let machines make more of their decisions for them, simply because machine-made decisions will bring better results than man-made ones. Eventually a stage may be reached at which the decisions necessary to keep the system running will be so complex that human beings will be incapable of making them intelligently. At that stage the machines will be in effective control. People won't be able to just turn the machines off, because they will be so dependent on them that turning them off would amount to suicide.

On the other hand it is possible that human control over the machines may be retained. . . . Due to improved techniques the elite will have greater

control over the masses; and because human work will no longer be necessary the masses will be superfluous, a useless burden on the system.

In the book, you don't discover until you turn the page that the author of this passage is Theodore Kaczynski—the Unabomber. . . .

Kaczynski's dystopian vision describes unintended consequences, a well-known problem with the design and use of technology, and one that is clearly related to Murphy's law—"Anything that can go wrong, will.". . . Our overuse of antibiotics has led to what may be the biggest such problem so far; the emergence of antibiotic-resistant and much more dangerous bacteria. Similar things happened when attempts to eliminate malarial mosquitoes using DDT caused them to acquire DDT resistance; malarial parasites likewise acquired multi-drug-resistant genes.

The cause of many such surprises seems clear: The systems involved are complex, involving interaction among and feedback between many parts. Any changes to such a system will cascade in ways that are difficult to predict; this is especially true when human actions are involved. . . .

THE SHORT RUN (EARLY 2000S)

Biological species almost never survive encounters with superior competitors. Ten million years ago, South and North America were separated by a sunken Panama isthmus. South America, like Australia today, was populated by marsupial mammals, including pouched equivalents of rats, deers, and tigers. When the isthmus connecting North and South America rose, it took only a few thousand years for the northern placental species, with slightly more effective metabolisms and reproductive and nervous systems, to displace and eliminate almost all the southern marsupials.

In a completely free marketplace, superior robots would surely affect humans as North American placentals affected South American marsupials (and as humans have affected countless species). Robotic industries would compete vigorously among themselves for matter, energy, and space, incidentally driving their price beyond human reach. Unable to afford the necessities of life, biological humans would be squeezed out of existence.

There is probably some breathing room, because we do not live in a completely free marketplace. Government coerces nonmarket behavior, especially by collecting taxes. Judiciously applied, governmental coercion could support human populations in high style on the fruits of robot labor, perhaps for a long while.

A textbook dystopia—and Moravec is just getting wound up. He goes on to discuss how our main job in the 21st century will be "ensuring continued cooperation from the robot industries" by passing laws decreeing that they be "nice," and to describe how seriously dangerous a human can be "once transformed into an unbounded superintelligent robot." Moravec's view is that the robots will eventually succeed us—that humans clearly face extinction.

I decided it was time to talk to my friend Danny Hillis. Danny became famous as the cofounder of Thinking Machines Corporation, which built a very powerful parallel supercomputer. Despite my current job title of Chief Scientist at Sun Microsystems, I am more a computer architect than a scientist, and I respect Danny's knowledge of the information and physical sciences more than that of any other single person I know. Danny is also a highly regarded futurist who thinks long-term—four years ago he started the Long Now Foundation, which is building a clock designed to last 10,000 years, in an attempt to draw attention to the pitifully short attention span of our society. . . . Danny's answer—directed specifically at Kurzweil's scenario of humans merging with robots—came swiftly, and quite surprised me. He said, simply, that the changes would come gradually, and that we would get used to them.

––––––––––

The 21st-century technologies—genetics, nanotechnology, and robotics (GNR)—are so powerful that they can spawn whole new classes of accidents and abuses. Most dangerously, for the first time, these accidents and abuses are widely within the reach of individuals or small groups. They will not require large facilities or rare raw materials. Knowledge alone will enable the use of them.

Thus we have the possibility not just of weapons of mass destruction but of knowledge-enabled mass destruction (KMD), this destructiveness hugely amplified by the power of self-replication.

I think it is no exaggeration to say we are on the cusp of the further perfection of extreme evil, an evil whose possibility spreads well beyond that which weapons of mass destruction bequeathed to the nation-states, on to a surprising and terrible empowerment of extreme individuals.

Nothing about the way I got involved with computers suggested to me that I was going to be facing these kinds of issues.

––––––––––

In designing software and microprocessors, I have never had the feeling that I was designing an intelligent machine. The software and hardware is so fragile and the capabilities of the machine to "think" so clearly absent that, even as a possibility, this has always seemed very far in the future.

But now, with the prospect of human-level computing power in about 30 years, a new idea suggests itself: that I may be working to create tools which will enable the construction of the technology that may replace our species. How do I feel about this? Very uncomfortable. Having struggled my entire career to build reliable software systems, it seems to me more than likely that this future will not work out as well as some people may imagine. My personal experience suggests we tend to overestimate our design abilities.

Given the incredible power of these new technologies, shouldn't we be asking how we can best coexist with them? And if our own extinction is a likely, or even possible, outcome of our technological development, shouldn't we proceed with great caution? . . .

How soon could such an intelligent robot be built? The coming advances in computing power seem to make it possible by 2030. And once an intelligent robot exists, it is only a small step to a robot species—to an intelligent robot that can make evolved copies of itself.

A second dream of robotics is that we will gradually replace ourselves with our robotic technology, achieving near immortality by downloading our consciousnesses. . . . But if we are downloaded into our technology, what are the chances that we will thereafter be ourselves or even human? It seems to me far more likely that a robotic existence would not be like a human one in any sense that we understand, that the robots would in no sense be our children, that on this path our humanity may well be lost.

Molecular electronics—the new subfield of nanotechnology where individual molecules are circuit elements—should mature quickly and become enormously lucrative within this decade, causing a large incremental investment in all nanotechnologies.

Unfortunately, as with nuclear technology, it is far easier to create destructive uses for nanotechnology than constructive ones. Nanotechnology has clear military and terrorist uses, and you need not be suicidal to release a massively destructive nanotechnological device—such devices can be built to be selectively destructive, affecting, for example, only a certain geographical area or a group of people who are genetically distinct.

An immediate consequence of the Faustian bargain in obtaining the great power of nanotechnology is that we run a grave risk—the risk that we might destroy the biosphere on which all life depends.

. . . "Plants" with "leaves" no more efficient than today's solar cells could out-compete real plants, crowding the biosphere with an inedible foliage. Tough omnivorous "bacteria" could out-compete real bacteria: They could spread like blowing pollen, replicate swiftly, and reduce the biosphere to dust in a matter of days. Dangerous replicators could easily be too tough, small, and rapidly spreading to stop—at least if we make no preparation. We have trouble enough controlling viruses and fruit flies.

Among the cognoscenti of nanotechnology, this threat has become known as the "gray goo problem." Though masses of uncontrolled replicators need not be gray or gooey, the term "gray goo" emphasizes that replicators able to obliterate life might be less inspiring than a single species of crabgrass. They might be superior in an evolutionary sense, but this need not make them valuable.

The gray goo threat makes one thing perfectly clear: We cannot afford certain kinds of accidents with replicating assemblers.

Gray goo would surely be a depressing ending to our human adventure on Earth, far worse than mere fire or ice, and one that could stem from a simple laboratory accident. Oops.

These possibilities are all thus either undesirable or unachievable or both. The only realistic alternative I see is relinquishment: to limit development of the technologies that are too dangerous, by limiting our pursuit of certain kinds of knowledge.

Yes, I know, knowledge is good, as is the search for new truths. We have been seeking knowledge since ancient times. Aristotle opened his *Metaphysics* with the simple statement: "All men by nature desire to know." We have, as a bedrock value in our society, long agreed on the value of open access to information, and recognize the problems that arise with attempts to restrict access to and development of knowledge. In recent times, we have come to revere scientific knowledge.

But despite the strong historical precedents, if open access to and unlimited development of knowledge hence-forth puts us all in clear danger of extinction, then common sense demands that we reexamine even these basic, long-held beliefs.

It was Nietzsche who warned us, at the end of the 19th century, not only that God is dead but that "faith in science, which after all exists undeniably, cannot owe its origin to a calculus of utility; it must have originated *in spite of* the fact that the disutility and dangerousness of the 'will to truth,' of 'truth at any price' is proved to it constantly." It is this further danger that we now fully face—the consequences of our truth-seeking. The truth that science seeks can certainly be considered a dangerous substitute for God if it is likely to lead to our extinction.

If we could agree, as a species, what we wanted, where we were headed, and why, then we would make our future much less dangerous—then we might understand what we can and should relinquish. Otherwise, we can easily imagine an arms race developing over GNR technologies, as it did with the NBC technologies in the 20th century. This is perhaps the greatest risk, for once such a race begins, it's very hard to end it. This time—unlike during the Manhattan Project—we aren't in a war, facing an implacable enemy that is threatening our civilization; we are driven, instead, by our habits, our desires, our economic system, and our competitive need to know. . . .

As Thoreau said, "We do not ride on the railroad; it rides upon us"; and this is what we must fight, in our time. The question is, indeed, Which is to be master? Will we survive our technologies?

We are being propelled into this new century with no plan, no control, no brakes. . . .

And yet I believe we do have a strong and solid basis for hope. Our attempts to deal with weapons of mass destruction in the last century provide a shining example of relinquishment for us to consider: the unilateral U.S. abandonment, without preconditions, of the development of biological weapons. This relinquishment stemmed from the realization that while it would take an enormous effort to create these terrible weapons, they could from then on easily be duplicated and fall into the hands of rogue nations or terrorist groups.

———————

Where can we look for a new ethical basis to set our course? I have found the ideas in the book *Ethics for the New Millennium*, by the Dalai Lama, to be very helpful. As is perhaps well known but little heeded, the Dalai Lama argues that the most important thing is for us to conduct our lives with love and compassion for others, and that our societies need to develop a stronger notion of universal responsibility and of our interdependency.

The Dalai Lama further argues that we must understand what it is that makes people happy, and acknowledge the strong evidence that neither material progress nor the pursuit of the power of knowledge is the key—that there are limits to what science and the scientific pursuit alone can do.

Clearly, we need to find meaningful challenges and sufficient scope in our lives if we are to be happy in whatever is to come. But I believe we must find alternative outlets for our creative forces, beyond the culture of perpetual economic growth; this growth has largely been a blessing for several hundred years, but it has not brought us unalloyed happiness, and we must now choose between the pursuit of unrestricted and undirected growth through science and technology and the clear accompanying dangers.

———————

Do you remember the beautiful penultimate scene in *Manhattan* where Woody Allen is lying on his couch and talking into a tape recorder? He is writing a short story about people who are creating unnecessary, neurotic problems for themselves, because it keeps them from dealing with more unsolvable, terrifying problems about the universe.

He leads himself to the question, "Why is life worth living?" and to consider what makes it worthwhile for him: Groucho Marx, Willie Mays, the second movement of the *Jupiter Symphony*, Louis Armstrong's recording of "Potato Head Blues," Swedish movies, Flaubert's *Sentimental Education*, Marlon Brando, Frank Sinatra, the apples and pears by Cézanne, the crabs at Sam Wo's, and, finally, the showstopper: his love of Tracy's face.

Each of us has our precious things, and as we care for them we locate the essence of our humanity. In the end, it is because of our great capacity for caring that I remain optimistic we will confront the dangerous issues now before us.

QUESTIONS

1. Why doesn't the future need us? Or does it need us, but only in certain ways?

2. Does regulation ever encourage creativity? How can we both encourage innovation and avoid the dangers that technological innovation often creates?

CASES

CASE 7.1

The Digital Divide

Joel Rudinow and Anthony Graybosch

The National Telecommunications and Information Administration (NTIA) issued a report on access to computer information services in July 1998. The report found as follows:

> Despite this significant growth in computer ownership and usage overall, the growth has occurred to a greater extent within some income levels, demographic groups, and geographic areas, than in others. In fact, the "digital divide" between certain groups of Americans has *increased* between 1994 and 1997 so that there is now an even greater disparity in penetration levels among some groups. There is a widening gap, for example, between those at upper and lower income levels.
>
> Additionally, even though all racial groups now own more computers than they did in 1994,

Blacks and Hispanics now lag *even further behind* [emphasis in original] Whites in their levels of PC-ownership and online access.

QUESTIONS

1. Do you think that lack of access to computers and computer-based information services places the children of the poor and minority groups in an unfair educational and financial situation that amounts to a competitive disadvantage in the emerging information based economy?

2. What role, if any, should government take to encourage computer literacy and information access in public schools?

CASE 7.2

Hacking into the Space Program

Joel Rudinow and Anthony Graybosch

Hackers regularly gain access to highly sensitive Internet sites. For instance, a hacker overloaded the National Aeronautics and Space Administration (NASA) communications system in 1997 as the United States space shuttle was docking with the

Russian space station, Mir. The hacker, intentionally or unintentionally, interfered with medical monitoring and communication with the astronaut on the shuttle. NASA was forced to rely upon an alternative communications route.

Cases 7.1–7.3 are from Joel Rudinow and Anthony Graybosch, *Ethics and Values in the Information Age*, Wadsworth, 2001.

QUESTIONS

1. Because hackers have proved able at gaining access to sensitive sites guarded by the latest security systems, do you think it reasonable to protect military information systems by threat of criminal prosecution?

2. Or should sensitive information remain off the Internet and decisions about the use of weapons systems always require a human decision maker?

CASE 7.3

The I Love You Virus

Joel Rudinow and Anthony Graybosch

The I Love You virus was ". . . estimated to have hit tens of millions of users and cost billions of dollars in damage." Cyber attacks against commercial sites such as Yahoo and e-Bay not only cause direct financial losses but shake the confidence of both corporations and consumers in electronic commerce. Assume that these attacks were motivated by curiosity or spite and not by a political concern.

QUESTIONS

1. Would Arquilla consider such attacks instances of information warfare?

2. Would just war theory consider the attacks terrorism? Are these terrorist attacks?

CASE 7.4

Privacy Pressures: The Use of Web Bugs at HomeConnection

Tom L. Beauchamp and Norman E. Bowie

As Matthew Scott, president of HomeConnection, sat in his office waiting for several members of his executive team to arrive, he grew more worrisome about a story featuring his company in the morning paper. His impulse was to fight back and go on the defensive, but Scott knew that he had to be careful.

However, he did not accept the article's implicit conclusion that HomeConnection had no regard for the privacy rights of its customers, and he was anxious to hear what his colleagues had to say about the matter.

HomeConnection was an Internet Service Provider (ISP) with several million customers, primarily

From Tom L. Beauchamp and Norman E. Bowie, *Ethical Theory and Business* (Englewood Cliffs, NJ: Prentice Hall, 2004). Reprinted with permission. *Case Studies in Information Technology Ethics*, 2/E by Richard A. Spinello. Reprinted by permission of Pearson Education, Inc., Upper Saddle River, NJ.

clustered in the mid-West. An ISP links people and businesses to the Internet, usually for a monthly fee. HomeConnection was much smaller than the industry leader, America OnLine (AOL), but it was still seen as a formidable player in this industry. Thanks to Scott's management, the company had recorded increasing profits for the past three years, 1999 through 2002. One feature that attracted customers was the opportunity to create their own personal Web page. HomeConnection made this process easy and convenient.

In the past year HomeConnection had devised an innovative promotion to help increase its subscriber base. The company encouraged its users with their own personal Web pages to carry an ad for Home-Connection. The ad would offer new subscribers a heavily discounted rate for the first year of membership. In addition, as an incentive to display the ad on their personal Web pages, the company agreed to pay its users $25 for any new members who signed up for a subscription by clicking on the ad. The response to the promotion was stronger than expected, and HomeConnection's membership had risen by over 6.5 percent since the program's inception eight months ago. Scott was quite enthused about the results, and he did not anticipate that one aspect of the program would attract some negative attention.

In consultation with his marketing manager, Scott had authorized the use of Web bugs so that when users placed the ad on their Web pages they would also get a Web bug. A Web bug is embedded as a miniscule and invisible picture on the screen and it can track everything one does on a particular Web site. Web bugs, also called "Web beacons," are usually deployed to count visitors to a Web site or to gather cumulative data about visitors to those sites without tracking any personal details. In this case the Web bug transmitted information to a major on-line ad agency, DoubleDealer. DoubleDealer would collect data about those who visited these Web pages, which ads they clicked on, and so forth.

The newspaper report cited HomeConnection as well as other ISPs and e-commerce sites for using this protocol without the permission of their customers. They quoted a well-known privacy expert: "It's extremely disturbing that these companies are using technology to gather information in such a clandestine manner; I don't see how it can be morally justified." The article had clearly resonated with some of HomeConnection's users, and the switchboard had been busy most of the afternoon with calls from irate customers. Some wanted to cancel their subscription.

Scott felt that the company had done nothing wrong but was a victim of a pervasive paranoia about privacy. HomeConnection was not using these bugs for any untoward purposes—its purpose was to track the results of the advertising promotion, that is, how many people were clicking on these ads. Also, Scott himself had modified the company's privacy policy to indicate that Web bugs might be used sometimes. (However, there was no indication that Web bugs would be placed on the personal Web pages of its user base.)

As several of his managers made their way into the conference room adjoining his office, Scott made one last check with customer service. By now it was late in the day and the volume of calls and emails was dying down. It was now up to Scott to determine a response—did the company face a serious problem or was this just a tempest in a teapot?

QUESTIONS

1. Had HomeConnection done something wrong? Why or why not?

2. What might be ethical or legal limitations you would place on HomeConnection?

CASE 7.5

Who Could Be Watching You Watching Your Figure? Your Boss

Aarti Shahani

Sensors and Bluetooth technologies have become so cheap and sophisticated that they can record more than steps taken and calories burned.

The startup Basis plans to make money by selling the heart watch. But if the company turns a big profit, Chang says, it will be from selling the data aggregated on a smartphone app and analyzing it for you, the user.

"People aren't really interested in raw data," Chang says. "If I just gave you your heart rate data, you wouldn't know how to interpret it. In fact, it might confuse you, or it might scare you and say, 'What is the spike? Why is it low? Why is it high?'"

Facebook and Google collect data on users and get advertisers to pay for access to those users. By contrast, Chang's first self-tracking company, Lumos Labs, sells data directly to hundreds of thousands of its own users. This paid subscriber base has more than doubled every year since 2007.

"The beauty of subscription business models, if you can retain your users, is that they can be naturally very profitable," Chang says.

EMPLOYERS ARE WATCHING

Big data raise big privacy issues.

Two years ago, some users of a leading self-tracking brand, Fitbit, were logging their sexual activity as exercise and found the sex logs somehow popping up on Google searches.

"We've now made those privacy settings more prominent so that people are more aware of what the privacy setting are," says Woody Scal, Fitbit's chief revenue officer. "I think the area of privacy is an area that many companies like ours have learned a lot over the past couple of years."

Fitbit is entering a brave new world in privacy as it starts selling devices and data to a new market: employers. Scal says Fitbit is attempting to grow through corporate wellness programs.

"Companies can see how many of the devices they've given out have actually been activated. How many are being used? How is it actually changing employee behavior?" Scal says.

Scal explains bosses typically don't get reports on an individual employee. They get aggregated data, and the worker must consent first.

One of Fitbit's competitors, BodyMedia, says it is working with insurance companies to get its self-trackers into more workplaces. Scal says Fitbit is running an experiment with one insurer, to see if employees who use the devices go to the doctor less. This, he says, "would be the holy grail for a product like this."

"If we could make a direct connection to reduction in medical care costs, then I think the floodgates would be open," Scal says.

QUESTIONS

1. Should employers have access to data collected by employees' phones? Why?

2. If a user has agreed to make his information public unknowingly—by agreeing to the terms of a contract without reading it—is the company responsible?

From KQED (Public Radio).

CASE 7.6
The Internet's Intolerable Acts

James Losey

You should be very afraid of a pair of bills that threaten Internet freedom The United States of America was forged in resistance to collective reprisals—the punishment of many for the acts of few. In 1774, following the Boston Tea Party, the British Parliament passed a series of laws—including the mandated closure of the port of Boston—meant to penalize the people of Massachusetts. These abuses of power, labeled the "Intolerable Acts," catalyzed the American Revolution by making plain the oppression of the British crown.

The interconnected nature of the Internet fostered the growth of online communities such as Tumblr, Twitter, and Facebook. These sites host our humdrum daily interactions and serve as a public soapbox for our political voice. Both the PROTECT IP Act and SOPA would create a national firewall by censoring the domain names of websites accused of hosting infringing copyrighted materials. This legislation would enable law enforcement to take down the entire tumblr.com domain due to something posted on a single blog. Yes, an entire, largely innocent online community could be punished for the actions of a tiny minority.

SOPA would go even further, creating a system of private regulation to shut down websites that are accused of not doing enough to prevent infringement. Keep in mind that these shutdowns would happen before a site owner could defend himself in court—SOPA could punish sites without even establishing whether they are guilty of the charges brought against them.

In January 2010, Hillary Clinton launched the State Department's Internet Freedom initiative, stumping for open access to information worldwide. Though Secretary Clinton has said that "there is no contradiction between intellectual property rights

protection and enforcement of expression on the Internet," PROTECT IP and SOPA create mutually exclusive trajectories for these two priorities. These bills are driven by technologically naive thinking that it's possible to censor information without affecting freedom of speech. SOPA even goes so far as to make the key circumvention tools used by human rights advocates and democracy organizers throughout the Middle East illegal. While we're certain that SOPA's authors did not mean to craft a bill tailor-made to support the future Qaddafis and Mubaraks of the world, that is precisely what they've done.

Rather than blocking online copyright infringement, legislation like SOPA and Protect IP would instigate a data obfuscation arms race, making legitimate law enforcement efforts all the more difficult. If the United States decides that copyright infringement must be stopped at any cost, the required censorship regime will depend on ever more invasive practices, such as monitoring users' personal Web traffic. This counterproductive cat-and-mouse game of censorship and circumvention would drive savvy scofflaws to darknets while increasing surveillance of less technically proficient Internet users.

Given that the Intolerable Acts sparked a revolution, it should be no surprise that this proposed legislation has generated a massive outcry in the United States. However, this attempt to unilaterally censor the Internet has spurred worldwide opposition, with several dozen international organizations signing a letter stating that "[t]hrough SOPA, the United States is attempting to dominate a shared global resource." Last month, the European Parliament adopted a resolution underscoring "the need to protect the integrity of the global internet and freedom of communication by refraining from unilateral measures to revoke IP addresses or domain names."

Posted on Slate.com, Thursday, December 8, 2011 at 7:19 A.M. ET.

As participants in the Internet community, we must defend against collective reprisals that undermine our rights to access, privacy, and freedom of expression online. SOPA and the PROTECT IP Act are fundamentally incompatible with a free society and with the founding principles of the United States. This truth should be self-evident: Human rights should never be subjugated to copyright.

Note from the authors: As of January 2013, the Protect IP Act was passed, and then a hold was placed upon it. The Stop Online Piracy Act has been neither passed nor defeated.

QUESTIONS

1. Is there a conflict between intellectual property rights protection and free speech? Explain your answer.

2. Should web sites that enable piracy be afforded the time to mount a defense? Or should they simply be shut down?

CHAPTER QUESTIONS

1. Is technology a good or a bad thing in your life, on balance? List 10 ways in which technology has improved your life and 10 ways in which it has been detrimental. How can we find the right role for technology in society, in business, and in our individual lives? Has technology assumed a godlike role in our culture?

2. Why do new technologies create problems for old laws and regulations? How does new technology create new definitions of property? How might ethical principles solve these problems?

8

The Art of Seduction

The Ethics of Advertising, Marketing, and Sales

Introduction

It's Saturday morning. You're taking it easy, sitting with your kids who are watching cartoons. During one of the intervals, the sound volume doubles, and a new cartoon character appears, but this one in the service of an ad for a new double-sugared and chocolate-covered cereal. The character is cute if obnoxious, and the ad features a photo of delighted children ecstatic as they munch. The cereal itself is presented with special-effects sparkles, making it look magical. This is followed by an ad for one of the big fast-food outfits, Mr. B's, which is offering a cheap but colorful toy with every kiddy meal. The company has become renowned for its nonnutritional high-calorie foods, and one of your kids is already showing a weight problem. Immediately he turns to you excitedly and asks, "Can we go to Mr. B's, for lunch, huh, please, please, please?" A family negotiation follows, in which it becomes evident that it is the toy, rather than the meal, that has moved your youngsters and the ad, not the cereal, that attracted their attention. But it gets you thinking. What is the justification for making such unhealthy appeals to young children? And at a time when most parents are not there, as you are now, to monitor and discuss the true desirability of these artificially created desires. Indeed, what is the difference between appealing to kids' actual needs and wants as opposed to creating artificial desires that are the opposite of their actual needs and wants? And shouldn't there be some restrictions on advertising to the young and vulnerable?

That last question you answer right away. Restrictions on advertising violate the right to free speech. You, like most Americans, are against censorship, particularly by the government and its agencies. But then you start thinking again. What if what is advertised is unhealthy? What if, as in the case of cigarettes and other tobacco products, it is downright deadly? The problem is not just kids and sugary, fattening foods. There is a similar problem with teenagers, who are subject to peer pressure that is artfully manipulated by advertisers, not only in the case of smoking, but across the whole range of teenage fads, clothes, and habits. But then, there are adults, too. It's not as if they are privy to the skills and secrets of contemporary marketing and advertising techniques. Ads for cars, ads for real estate, ads for detergents and cosmetics and beers and now even pharmaceuticals and plastic surgery. It is all seduction. But is seduction always wrong? How about the truth of the claims? "The best beer in the world." Who knows? The fastest-acting cleanser? Has anyone measured this? (Probably *Consumer Reports*, but who has read it? And doesn't the company keep repeating the ad—now disproved—anyway?) There are lies, but then there are white lies and partial truths and "spin," which has some basis in truth but is powerfully prejudiced toward a certain bias. Where does advertising fit in? What makes it legitimate? What would make it illegitimate? Is it allowable to tell a lie in order to sell something?

At this point, we may want to go back to our honesty chapter, but most of us would argue that honesty, full disclosure, may be too high a standard for most advertising and marketing. No one expects a salesperson to tell you the flaws in the product or the advantages of a competitor's version. And advertising and marketing, which are by their very nature biased, play a critical role in a free market system. People have to know about a product to have any interest in buying it. People have to be appealed to and made to pay attention to learn about a product. And the products themselves must be made appealing and distinguished from the many other products on the market. Merely providing the information to the consumer is rarely enough. In a world filled with ads and products, much more dramatic methods are called for. But once we get beyond the honest presentation of information, the ethical questions get rather difficult. What do we do about advertising to kids and teenagers and people who are vulnerable (which means, ultimately, all of us)? What are the limits of exaggeration and self-promotion? What are the effects of not just supplying what people want and need, but creating their desires, which then become created needs? And what about those needs that are satisfied by the ads themselves?

The great economist John Kenneth Galbraith begins, in "The Dependence Effect," by showing how advertising may actually create consumer demands, rather than merely serve consumer needs. Friedrich von Hayek offers a vigorous counterargument to Galbraith's position in "The Non Sequitur of the 'Dependence Effect.'" Alan Goldman offers a powerful argument in defense of the usefulness and, ultimately, the ethical importance of advertising in his "The Justification of Advertising in a Market Economy." Leslie Savan details more ways in which advertising and the market more generally may undermine the freedom of consumers in "The Bribed Soul." Finally, G. Richard Shell and Mario Moussa offer some practical advice on how to sell—as they put it, "woo"—with integrity.

John Kenneth Galbraith

The Dependence Effect

John Kenneth Galbraith was one of the most influential economists of the twentieth century.

The theory of consumer demand, as it is now widely accepted, is based on two broad propositions, neither of them quite explicit but both extremely important for the present value system of economists. The first is that the urgency of wants does not diminish appreciably as more of them are satisfied or, to put the matter more precisely, to the extent that this happens it is not demonstrable and not a matter of any interest to economists or for economic policy. When man has satisfied his physical needs, then psychologically grounded desires take over. These can never be satisfied or, in any case, no progress can be proved. The concept of satiation has very little standing in economics. It is neither useful nor scientific to speculate on the comparative cravings of the stomach and the mind.

The second proposition is that wants originate in the personality of the consumer or, in any case, that they are given data for the economist. The latter's task is merely to seek their satisfaction. He has no need to inquire how these wants are formed. His function is sufficiently fulfilled by maximizing the goods that supply the wants.

The notion that wants do not become less urgent the more amply the individual is supplied is broadly repugnant to common sense. It is something to be believed only by those who wish to believe. Yet the conventional wisdom must be tackled on its own terrain. Intertemporal comparisons of an individual's state of mind do rest on doubtful grounds. Who can say for sure that the deprivation which afflicts him with hunger is more painful than the deprivation which afflicts him with envy of his neighbour's new car? In the time that has passed since he was poor his soul may have become subject to a new and deeper searing. And where a society is concerned, comparisons between marginal satisfactions when it is poor and those when it is affluent will involve not only the same individual at different times but different individuals at different times. The scholar who wishes to believe that with increasing affluence there is no reduction in the urgency of desires and goods is not without points for debate. However plausible the case against him, it cannot be proved. In the defence of the conventional wisdom this amounts almost to invulnerability.

However, there is a flaw in the case. If the individual's wants are to be urgent they must be original with himself. They cannot be urgent if they must be contrived for him. And above all they must not be contrived by the process of production by which they are satisfied. For this means that the whole case for the urgency of production, based on the urgency of wants, falls to the ground. One cannot defend production as satisfying wants if that production creates the wants.

Were it so that man on arising each morning was assailed by demons which instilled in him a passion sometimes for silk shirts, sometimes for kitchenware, sometimes for chamber-pots, and sometimes for orange squash, there would be every reason to applaud the effort to find the goods, however odd, that quenched this flame. But should it be that his passion was the result of his first having cultivated the demons, and should it also be that his effort to allay it stirred the demons to ever greater and greater effort, there would be question as to how rational was his solution. Unless restrained by conventional attitudes, he might wonder if the solution lay with more goods or fewer demons.

So it is that if production creates the wants it seeks to satisfy, or if the wants emerge *pari passu* with the production, then the urgency of the wants can no longer be used to defend the urgency of the production. Production only fills a void that it has itself created.

The even more direct link between production and wants is provided by the institutions of modern advertising and salesmanship. These cannot be reconciled with the notion of independently determined desires, for their central function is to create desires—to bring into being wants that previously did not exist.[1] This is accomplished by the producer of the goods or at his behest. A broad empirical relationship exists between what is spent on production of consumers' goods and what is spent in synthesizing the desires for that production. A new consumer product must be introduced with a suitable advertising campaign to arouse an interest in it. The path for an expansion of output must be paved by a suitable expansion in the advertising budget. Outlays for the manufacturing of a product are not more important in the strategy of modern business enterprise than outlays for the manufacturing of demand for the product. None of this is novel. All would be regarded as elementary by the most retarded student in the nation's most primitive school of business administration. The cost of this want formation is formidable. In 1956 total advertising expenditure—though, as noted, not all of it may be assigned to the synthesis of wants—amounted to about ten thousand million dollars. For some years it had been increasing at a rate in excess of a thousand million dollars a year. Obviously, such outlays must be integrated with the theory of consumer demand. They are too big to be ignored.

But such integration means recognizing that wants are dependent on production. It accords to the producer the function both of making the goods and of making the desires for them. It recognizes that production, not only passively through emulation, but actively through advertising and related activities, creates the wants it seeks to satisfy.

The businessman and the lay reader will be puzzled over the emphasis which I give to a seemingly obvious point. The point is indeed obvious. But it is one which, to a singular degree, economists have resisted. They have sensed, as the layman does not, the damage to established ideas which lurks in these relationships. As a result, incredibly, they have closed their eyes (and ears) to the most obtrusive of all economic phenomena, namely modern want creation.

This is not to say that the evidence affirming the dependence of wants on advertising has been entirely ignored. It is one reason why advertising has so long been regarded with such uneasiness by economists. Here is something which cannot be accommodated easily to existing theory. More pervious scholars have speculated on the urgency of desires which are so obviously the fruit of such expensively contrived campaigns for popular attention. Is a new breakfast cereal or detergent so much wanted if so much must be spent to compel in the consumer the sense of want? But there has been little tendency to go on to examine the implications of this for the theory of consumer demand and even less for the importance of production and productive efficiency. These have remained sacrosanct. More often the uneasiness has been manifested in a general disapproval of advertising and advertising men, leading to the occasional suggestion that they shouldn't exist. Such suggestions have usually been ill received.

And so the notion of independently determined wants still survives. In the face of all the forces of modern salesmanship it still rules, almost undefiled, in the textbooks. And it still remains the economist's mission—and on few matters is the pedagogy so firm—to seek unquestioningly the means for filling these wants. This being so, production remains of prime urgency. We have here, perhaps, the ultimate triumph of the conventional wisdom in its resistance to the evidence of the eyes. To equal it one must imagine a humanitarian who was long ago persuaded of the grievous shortage of hospital facilities in the town. He continues to importune the passersby for money for more beds and refuses to notice that the town doctor is deftly knocking over pedestrians with his car to keep up the occupancy.

And in unravelling the complex we should always be careful not to overlook the obvious. The fact that wants can be synthesized by advertising, catalysed by salesmanship, and shaped by the discreet manipulations of the persuaders shows that they are not very urgent. A man who is hungry need never be told of his need for food. If he is inspired by his appetite, he is immune to the influence of Messrs. Batten,

THE ART OF SEDUCTION

Barton, Durstine and Osborn. The latter are effective only with those who are so far removed from physical want that they do not already know what they want. In this state alone men are open to persuasion.

The general conclusion of these pages is of such importance for this essay that it had perhaps best be put with some formality. As a society becomes increasingly affluent, wants are increasingly created by the process by which they are satisfied. This may operate passively. Increases in consumption, the counterpart of increases in production, act by suggestion or emulation to create wants. Or producers may proceed actively to create wants through advertising and salesmanship. Wants thus come to depend on output. In technical terms it can no longer be assumed that welfare is greater at an all-round higher level of production than at a lower one. It may be the same. The higher level of production has, merely, a higher level of want creation necessitating a higher level of want satisfaction. There will be frequent occasion to refer to the way wants depend on the process by which they are satisfied. It will be convenient to call it the Dependence Effect.

The final problem of the productive society is what it produces. This manifests itself in an implacable tendency to provide an opulent supply of some things and a niggardly yield of others. This disparity carries to the point where it is a cause of social discomfort and social unhealth. The line which divides our area of wealth from our area of poverty

Plato on the Danger of Believing Bad Arguments

There is one danger that we must guard against, Socrates said.

What sort of danger? I asked.

Of becoming misologic [hating logic], he said, in the sense that people become misanthropic. No greater misfortune could happen to anyone than that of developing a dislike for argument. Misology and misanthropy arise in just the same way. Misanthropy is induced by believing in somebody quite uncritically. You assume that a person is absolutely truthful and sincere and reliable, and a little later you find that he is shoddy and unreliable. Then the same thing happens again. After repeated disappointments at the hands of the very people who might be supposed to be your nearest and most intimate friends, constant irritation ends by making you dislike everybody and suppose that there is no sincerity to be found anywhere. . . .

The resemblance between arguments and human beings lies in this: that when one believes that an argument is true without reference to the art of logic, and then a little later decides rightly or wrongly that it is false, and the same thing happens again and again . . . they end by believing that they are wiser than anyone else, because they alone have discovered that there is nothing stable or dependable either in facts or in arguments, and that everything fluctuates just like the water in a tidal channel, and never stays at any point for any time. . . .

But suppose that there is an argument which is true and valid but someone spent his life loathing arguments and so missed the chance of knowing the truth about reality—would that not be a deplorable thing?

—Plato, *Phaedo* 89d–90e, fourth century B.C.; Hugh Tredennick, *The Last Days of Socrates* (Harmondsworth, MD: Penguin, 1954).

is roughly that which divides privately produced and marketed goods and services from publicly rendered services. Our wealth in the first is not only in startling contrast with the meagreness of the latter, but our wealth in privately produced goods is, to a marked degree, the cause of crisis in the supply of public services. For we have failed to see the importance, indeed the urgent need, of maintaining a balance between the two.

This disparity between our flow of private and public goods and services is no matter of subjective judgment. On the contrary, it is the source of the most extensive comment which only stops short of the direct contrast being made here. In the years following World War II, the papers of any major city—those of New York were an excellent example—told daily of the shortages and shortcomings in the elementary municipal and metropolitan services. The schools were old and overcrowded. The police force was under strength and underpaid. The parks and playgrounds were insufficient. Streets and empty lots were filthy, and the sanitation staff was under-equipped and in need of men. Access to the city by those who work there was uncertain and painful and becoming more so. Internal transportation was overcrowded, unhealthful, and dirty. So was the air. Parking on the streets had to be prohibited, and there was no space elsewhere. These deficiencies were not in new and novel services but in old and established ones. Cities have long swept their streets, helped their people move around, educated them, kept order, and provided horse rails for vehicles which sought to pause. That their residents should have a non-toxic supply of air suggests no revolutionary dalliance with socialism.

The contrast was and remains evident not alone to those who read. The family which takes its mauve and cerise, air-conditioned, power-steered, and power-braked car out for a tour passes through cities that are badly paved, made hideous by litter, blighted buildings, billboards, and posts for wires that should long since have been put underground. They pass on into a countryside that has been rendered largely invisible by commercial art. (The goods which the latter advertise have an absolute priority in our value system. Such aesthetic considerations as a view of the countryside accordingly come second. On such matters we are consistent.) They picnic on exquisitely packaged food from a portable icebox by a polluted stream and go on to spend the night at a park which is a menace to public health and morals. Just before dozing off on an air-mattress, beneath a nylon tent, amid the stench of decaying refuse, they may reflect vaguely on the curious unevenness of their blessings. Is this, indeed, the American genius?

The case for social balance has, so far, been put negatively. Failure to keep public services in minimal relation to private production and use of goods is a cause of social disorder or impairs economic performance. The matter may now be put affirmatively. By failing to exploit the opportunity to expand public production we are missing opportunities for enjoyment which otherwise we might have had. Presumably a community can be as well rewarded by buying better schools or better parks as by buying bigger cars. By concentrating on the latter rather than the former it is failing to maximize its satisfactions. As with schools in the community, so with public services over the country at large. It is scarcely sensible that we should satisfy our wants in private goods with reckless abundance, while in the case of public goods, on the evidence of the eye, we practice extreme self-denial. So, far from systematically exploiting the opportunities to derive use and pleasure from these services, we do not supply what would keep us out of trouble.

The conventional wisdom holds that the community, large or small, makes a decision as to how much it will devote to its public services. This decision is arrived at by democratic process. Subject to the imperfections and uncertainties of democracy, people decide how much of their private income and goods they will surrender in order to have public services of which they are in greater need. Thus there is a balance, however rough, in the enjoyments to be had from private goods and services and those rendered by public authority.

It will be obvious, however, that this view depends on the notion of independently determined consumer wants. In such a world one could with some reason defend the doctrine that the consumer, as a voter, makes an independent choice between public and private goods. But given the dependence effect—given that consumer wants are created by the process by which they are satisfied—the consumer makes no such choice. He is subject to the forces of advertising and emulation by which production creates its own demand. Advertising operates exclusively, and emulation mainly, on behalf of privately produced goods and services.[2] Since management and emulative effects operate on behalf of private production, public services will have an inherent tendency to lag behind. Car demand which is expensively synthesized will inevitably have a much larger claim on income than parks or public health or even roads where no such influence operates. The engines of mass communication, in their highest state of development, assail the eyes and ears of the community on behalf of more beer but not of more schools. Even in the conventional wisdom it will scarcely be contended that this leads to an equal choice between the two.

The competition is especially unequal for new products and services. Every corner of the public psyche is canvassed by some of the nation's most talented citizens to see if the desire for some merchantable product can be cultivated. No similar process operates on behalf of the nonmerchantable services of the state. Indeed, while we take the cultivation of new private wants for granted we would be measurably shocked to see it applied to public services. The scientist or engineer or advertising man who devotes himself to developing a new carburetor, cleanser, or depilatory for which the public recognizes no need and will feel none until an advertising campaign arouses it, is one of the valued members of our society. A politician or a public servant who dreams up a new public service is a wastrel. Few public offences are more reprehensible.

So much for the influences which operate on the decision between public and private production. The calm decision between public and private consumption pictured by the conventional wisdom is, in fact, a remarkable example of the error which arises from viewing social behaviour out of context. The inherent tendency will always be for public services to fall behind private production. We have here the first of the causes of social imbalance.

NOTES

1. Advertising is not a simple phenomenon. It is also important in competitive strategy and want creation is, ordinarily, a complementary result of efforts to shift the demand curve of the individual firm at the expense of others or (less importantly, I think) to change its shape by increasing the degree of product differentiation. Some of the failure of economists to identify advertising with want creation may be attributed to the undue attention that its use in purely competitive strategy has attracted. It should be noted, however, that the competitive manipulation of consumer desire is only possible, at least on any appreciable scale, when such need is not strongly felt.

2. Emulation does operate between communities. A new school or a new highway in one community does exert pressure on others to remain abreast. However, as compared with the pervasive effects of emulation in extending the demand for privately produced consumers' goods there will be agreement, I think, that this intercommunity effect is probably small.

QUESTIONS

1. Does advertising serve our needs or create them? Or both? Explain and provide examples.

2. Think of three or four television commercials that you like. Briefly describe them on paper. Now ask yourself: how many lies or half-truths are expressed by those ads?

The Non Sequitur of the "Dependence Effect"

Friedrich von Hayek

Friedrich von Hayek was the most eminent of the Austrian economists and the author of *Road to Serfdom*.

For well over a hundred years the critics of the free enterprise system have resorted to the argument that if production were only organized rationally, there would be no economic problem. Rather than face the problem which scarcity creates, socialist reformers have tended to deny that scarcity existed. Ever since the Saint-Simonians their contention has been that the problem of production has been solved and only the problem of distribution remains. However absurd this contention must appear to us with respect to the time when it was first advanced, it still has some persuasive power when repeated with reference to the present.

The latest form of this old contention is expounded in *The Affluent Society* by Professor J. K. Galbraith. He attempts to demonstrate that in our affluent society the important private needs are already satisfied and the urgent need is therefore no longer a further expansion of the output of commodities but an increase of those services which are supplied (and presumably can be supplied only) by government. Though this book has been extensively discussed since its publication in 1958, its central thesis still requires some further examination.

I believe the author would agree that his argument turns upon the "Dependence Effect" [p. 289 of this book]. The argument of this chapter starts from the assertion that a great part of the wants which are still unsatisfied in modern society are not wants which would be experienced spontaneously by the individual if left to himself, but are wants which are created by the process by which they are satisfied. It is then represented as self-evident that for this reason such wants cannot be urgent or important. This crucial conclusion appears to be a complete *non sequitur* and it would seem that with it the whole argument of the book collapses.

The first part of the argument is of course perfectly true: we would not desire any of the amenities of civilization—or even of the most primitive culture—if we did not live in a society in which others provide them. The innate wants are probably confined to food, shelter, and sex. All the rest we learn to desire because we see others enjoying various things. To say that a desire is not important because it is not innate is to say that the whole cultural achievement of man is not important.

This cultural origin of practically all the needs of civilized life must of course not be confused with the fact that there are some desires which aim, not as a satisfaction derived directly from the use of an object, but only from the status which its consumption is expected to confer. In a passage which Professor Galbraith quotes, Lord Keynes seems to treat the latter sort of Veblenesque conspicuous consumption as the only alternative "to those needs which are absolute in the sense that we feel them whatever the situation of our fellow human beings may be." If the latter phrase is interpreted to exclude all the needs for goods which are felt only because these goods are known to be produced, these two Keynesian classes describe of course only extreme types of wants, but disregard the overwhelming majority of goods on which civilized life rests. Very few needs indeed are "absolute" in the sense that they are independent of social environment or of the example of others, and that their satisfaction is an indispensable condition for the preservation of the individual or of the species. Most needs which

Excerpted from "The *Non Sequitur* of the 'Dependence Effect'" by F. A. von Hayek, *Southern Economic Journal* (April 1961).

make us act are needs for things which only civilization teaches us to exist at all, and these things are
wanted by us because they produce feelings or emotions which we would not know if it were not for our
cultural inheritance. Are not in this sense probably
all our esthetic feelings "acquired tastes"?

How complete a non sequitur Professor Galbraith's
conclusion represents is seen most clearly if we
apply the argument to any product of the arts, be it
music, painting, or literature. If the fact that people
would not feel the need for something if it were not
produced did prove that such products are of small
value, all those highest products of human endeavor
would be of small value. Professor Galbraith's argument could be easily employed without any change
of the essential terms, to demonstrate the worthless-
ness of literature or any other form of art. Surely an
individual's want for literature is not original with
himself in the sense that he would experience it if
literature were not produced. Does this then mean
that the production of literature cannot be defended
as satisfying a want because it is only the production which provokes the demand? In this, as in the
case of all cultural needs, it is unquestionably, in
Professor Galbraith's words, "the process of satisfying the wants that creates the wants." There have
never been "independently determined desires for"
literature before literature has been produced and
books certainly do not serve the "simple mode of
enjoyment which requires no previous conditioning
of the consumer." Clearly my taste for the novels of
Jane Austen or Anthony Trollope or C. P. Snow is
not "original with myself." But is it not rather absurd
to conclude from this that it is less important than,
say, the need for education? Public education indeed
seems to regard it as one of its tasks to instill a taste
for literature in the young and even employs producers of literature for that purpose. Is this want creation
by the producer reprehensible? Or does the fact that
some of the pupils may possess a taste for poetry
only because of the efforts of their teachers prove
that since "it does not arise in spontaneous consumer
need and the demand would not exist were it not contrived, its utility or urgency, ex contrivance, is zero?"

The appearance that the conclusions follow from
the admitted facts is made possible by an obscurity

of the wording of the argument with respect to which
it is difficult to know whether the author is himself the victim of a confusion or whether he skillfully uses ambiguous terms to make the conclusion
appear plausible. The obscurity concerns the implied
assertion that the wants of the consumers are determined by the producers. Professor Galbraith avoids
in this connection any terms as crude and definite
as "determine." The expressions he employs, such as
that wants are "dependent on" or the "fruits of" production, or that "production creates the wants" do,
of course, suggest determination but avoid saying so
in plain terms. After what has already been said it
is of course obvious that the knowledge of what is
being produced is one of the many factors on which
it depends what people will want. It would scarcely
be an exaggeration to say that contemporary man, in
all fields where he has not yet formed firm habits,
tends to find out what he wants by looking at what
his neighbours do and at various displays of goods
(physical or in catalogues or advertisements) and
then choosing what he likes best.

In this sense the tastes of man, as is also true of his
opinions and beliefs and indeed much of his personality, are shaped in a great measure by his cultural
environment. But though in some contexts it would
perhaps be legitimate to express this by a phrase like
"production creates the wants," the circumstances
mentioned would clearly not justify the contention
that particular producers can deliberately determine
the wants of particular consumers. The efforts of all
producers will certainly be directed towards that
end: but how far any individual producer will succeed will depend not only on what he does but also
on what the others do and on a great many other
influences operating upon the consumer. The joint
but uncoordinated efforts of the producers merely
create one element of the environment by which the
wants of the consumers are shaped. It is because
each individual producer thinks that the consumers
can be persuaded to like his products that he endeavours to influence them. But though this effort is part
of the influences which shape consumers' tastes, no
producer can in any real sense "determine" them.
This, however, is clearly implied in such statements
as that wants are "both passively and deliberately

the fruits of the process by which they are satisfied." If the producer could in fact deliberately determine what the consumers will want, Professor Galbraith's conclusions would have some validity. But though this is skillfully suggested, it is nowhere made credible, and could hardly be made credible because it is not true. Though the range of choice open to the consumers is the joint result of, among other things, the efforts of all producers who vie with each other in making their respective products appear more attractive than those of their competitors, every particular consumer still has the choice between all those different offers.

A fuller examination of this process would, of course, have to consider how, after the efforts of some producers have actually swayed some consumers, it becomes the example of the various consumers thus persuaded which will influence the remaining consumers. This can be mentioned here only to emphasize that even if each consumer were exposed to pressure of only one producer, the harmful effects which are apprehended from this would soon be offset by the much more powerful example of his fellows. It is of course fashionable to treat this influence of the example of others (or, what comes to the same thing, the learning from the experience made by others) as if it amounted all to an attempt of keeping up with the Joneses and for that reason was to be regarded as detrimental. It seems to me that not only the importance of this factor is usually greatly exaggerated but also that it is not really relevant to Professor Galbraith's main thesis. But it might be worthwhile briefly to ask what, assuming that some expenditure were actually determined solely by a desire of keeping up with the Joneses, that would really prove? At least in Europe we used to be familiar with a type of persons who often denied themselves even enough food in order to maintain an appearance of respectability or gentility in dress and style of life. We may regard this as a misguided effort, but surely it would not prove that the income

of such persons was larger than they knew how to use wisely. That the appearance of success, or wealth, may to some people seem more important than many other needs, does in no way prove that the needs they sacrifice to the former are unimportant. In the same way, even though people are often persuaded to spend unwisely, this surely is no evidence that they do not still have important unsatisfied needs.

Professor Galbraith's attempt to give an apparent scientific proof for the contention that the need for the production of more commodities has greatly decreased seems to me to have broken down completely. With it goes the claim to have produced a valid argument which justifies the use of coercion to make people employ their income for those purposes of which he approves. It is not to be denied that there is some originality in this latest version of the old socialist argument. For over a hundred years we have been exhorted to embrace socialism because it would give us more goods. Since it has so lamentably failed to achieve this where it has been tried, we are now urged to adopt it because more goods after all are not important. The aim is still progressively to increase the share of the resources whose use is determined by political authority and the coercion of any dissenting minority. It is not surprising, therefore, that Professor Galbraith's thesis has been most enthusiastically received by the intellectuals of the British Labour Party where his influence bids fair to displace that of the late Lord Keynes. It is more curious that in this country it is not recognized as an outright socialist argument and often seems to appeal to people on the opposite end of the political spectrum. But this is probably only another instance of the familiar fact that on these matters the extremes frequently meet.

QUESTIONS

1. Would Hayek regulate advertising? Why or why not?
2. What is the "non sequitur" of the dependence effect?

Alan Goldman	The Justification of Advertising in a Market Economy

Alan Goldman is professor of philosophy at the University of Miami.

The first virtue of a market economy is its efficiency in allocating economic resources, capital, and labor to satisfy collective needs and wants for products and services. In theory, maximum efficiency obtains given certain ideal conditions of pure competition. These conditions include: (1) competition within industries among firms, each of which is too small to dictate prices to the market; (2) fluidity of labor and capital; (3) perfect knowledge on the part of consumers of prices and features of various products and services; and (4) knowledge on the part of producers of consumer demand for various goods. Given such conditions, the market, through its price mechanisms, guides profit seeking producers to allocate economic resources in ways that optimize the aggregate satisfaction of demand—that is, the sum total of wants in society. Goods are distributed in turn to those with greatest demand, the degree of demand being measured by willingness to pay. The result approximates to maximization of utility, understood as the greatest sum of the satisfaction of wants over the whole society. Those goods are produced and distributed that yield the greatest surplus of value over economic costs.

The market mechanism theoretically underlying efficiency of resource allocation was first described by Adam Smith. When a certain good is undersupplied in relation to the demand for it, its price is bid upward. Consumers are willing to pay more for a product they want when it is in short supply, and producers can improve their profits by selling the limited supply at a higher price. The possibility of higher profits will attract new resources (that is, capital and labor) to the industry, until supply is increased and the margin of profit falls again to approximate that of other industries. Thus supply adjusts to demand. Conversely, oversupply of a good means that some of it will have to be sold at a loss, driving resources from the industry and adjusting the production downward. The tendency is toward an equilibrium at which the marginal value of all goods is equal and, taken collectively, maximal in relation to the relative social demand for the various goods.

This process is dynamic and progressive. At the same time as optimal efficiency is achieved in allocating resources so as to satisfy particular wants at particular times, competition generates progress through improvement of productive techniques and processes. Each competitor is motivated to modernize production so as to increase volume and cut unit costs of products. The price a producer pays for obsolescence is being undersold by the more efficient competition and thereby driven out of business. Thus the free market is theoretically efficient over time. It guarantees not only the most efficient use of resources in the present, but the production of more and more goods and services in the future.

A further virtue of the competitive market economy, given ideal conditions, is its maximization of individual freedoms. All transactions within this economy are to be voluntary. Individuals are free to choose their occupations, investors to invest where they like, and consumers to buy or refuse what is offered for sale. For a transaction to take place, given the ideal condition of full knowledge of its features and alternatives, it must be perceived as mutually beneficial to the parties involved.

If we accept this model as a morally defensible economic system, where in it can we find a place for

From *Just Business: New Introductory Essays in Business Ethics*, ed. Tom Regan (New York: Random House, 1983), pp. 235–270. Reprinted with permission of McGraw Hill Co.

the institution of advertising? The ideal requires relevant knowledge on the part of consumers of the existence, quality, and prices of products, and it is unclear that advertising, at least as we know it, accomplishes this goal. Second, the model also assumes that consumer demands are given and judges the efficiency of the market by the extent to which they are satisfied. Advertising, however, sometimes aims to *create* desires in the consuming public, and it is unclear whether the satisfaction of these desires should likewise be counted as a gain in utility or social value. An even more fundamental difficulty may be explained as follows. Our model assumes that consumer demand for a product dictates prices to individual firms, which then manufacture goods until the marginal costs equal the price (that is, until no more profit can be made from additional units). But some economists have argued that advertising contributes to conditions in which producers can control prices, by creating demand to match planned levels of supply at fixed prices. Similarly, advertising often seeks to create *consumer loyalty*, which arguably makes it more difficult for new competitors to enter the market—specifically, more expensive, since it requires extensive advertising campaigns to overcome consumer loyalty. Brand loyalty may also be inefficient in itself, since it leads consumers to perceive differences among products when there may be no real differences in quality, which might cause them to forgo savings in price among identical products (for example, chemically identical aspirin tablets), thereby diminishing maximum utility.

More recently, however, economists have taken the opposite stand on this issue. Some have argued that advertising actually facilitates entry of new competitors by allowing them to publicize their products and lure customers away from established firms. The purpose of ad campaigns, it is now said, is to create brand *dis*loyalty. Campaigns are typically directed not at those who already are customers, but at potential new customers. In response to the claim that ads lead consumers to make ungrounded and costly product differentiations, it is pointed out that brand recognition and even brand loyalty create benefits for consumers as well. When shoppers can identify products and their manufacturers, the latter are pressured to maintain quality. At the same time comparison shopping is facilitated among retailers, so that they must sell within price limits.

In assessing this debate, it appears that the claims of the opposing sides may all be true, showing only that advertising produces *both* positive *and* negative effects upon competition and prices for consumers. It seems clear, first, that there have been successful advertising campaigns of both sorts, those that reinforce brand loyalty and help to retain a clientele (perhaps by reinforcing a favorable image of the brand in consumers' minds), and those that lure new customers away from established brands. Furthermore, while brand loyalty may raise successful entry costs, advertising may simultaneously ease entry for those with the capital to mount extensive campaigns. Finally, while ads may create the illusion of product differences where none exist and hence prevent choice of cheaper alternatives, brand recognition, achieved through exposure to ads, does facilitate comparison shopping among retailers. In the absence of data weighing these opposing tendencies across many industries, it seems impossible to justify or condemn advertising by its effects on the degree of competition in various product markets. There is no good reason at present, in short, for believing that advertising is inconsistent with the free market's aims of eliminating monopolies and encouraging competition.

———————

Principal among the direct benefits claimed to result from advertising is the benefit of consumers' having relevant knowledge of the existence, quality, and price of products. How well advertising provides this benefit will concern us shortly. First, though, let us consider an indirect social benefit attributed to the institution of advertising: namely, that it subsidizes the media. Commercial radio and television, as well as most newspapers and magazines, could not survive without this subsidy, certainly not in the forms we know them and at the prices we are used to paying. It can be argued, then, that since these media themselves add much to the social environment in the way of information and entertainment, the institution of advertising is indirectly but importantly valuable in making this possible.

Once again, however, one must recognize as well the negative influence of advertising, especially upon the broadcast media. The main problem, of course, is the desire of the stations, pressured by the sponsors, to appeal to the largest possible audience with every show. The result is the reduction of content and style to the lowest common denominator of taste. Commercial television can be held responsible for debasing American taste, certainly for failing to elevate it and contribute culturally and aesthetically as it could. Advertising sponsors are the main culprits. Not only the "highbrow," but also the innovative, daring, or controversial is shunned as possibly offensive, when sponsors exercise effective censorship over programming. This is true not only of cultural and entertainment shows, but perhaps more seriously, sometimes of news and information programs as well. . . .

Thus once more we find a mixed blessing at best in the social effect of advertising. Here we can begin to draw some morals for advertisers. The service provided by advertising in subsidizing the media seems clearly preferable when sponsors do not act as censors. When commercial considerations come first, this priority is clearly detrimental to the aesthetic value of programs. This may be even more clearly true of the informative value of news and information programming. Very large audiences can be expected to be attracted only to the familiar and aesthetically un-innovative. But the judgment of artistic merit, as well as that of newsworthiness, ought to be made on intrinsic grounds by those with some expertise, rather than on strictly commercial grounds, if the media are to realize their potential for educating and not simply tranquilizing the public. In order to accomplish this, self-restraint, sometimes at the expense of the short-term self-interest of particular advertisers and their business clients, is required.

If advertising is to be ethically justified, given the free-market approach, it is not enough to argue for its consistency in a free-market economy, or that it is not wasteful of economic resources, or even that it provides certain indirect social benefits. The positive justification must include the direct benefit that allegedly accrues from this institution: namely, the provision of relevant information. Maximal value can be obtained by consumers only if they know all the alternative ways of satisfying their desires and the costs of doing so. For any beneficial transaction to occur, people must be acquainted with products available. Advertising so informs them, also often providing data on product features, changes, and prices. Such information must be continuously provided because of the arrival of new consumers, new products, and new product features. So advertising seems justified in a free market as a valuable source of information. Even when it attempts mainly to persuade rather than to inform directly, it will tell of a product's availability and perhaps of its prominent features.

———————

Certain moral demands appear to follow quite obviously from this justification. If advertisements are to be justified as sources of information for consumers then they ought to be truthful and avoid deception. If, in the area of consumer decisions, free choice is most likely to satisfy genuine desires and maximize welfare, then lies in the marketplace tend to subvert the entire rationale of the free-market economy. If consumers are misled, they will no longer be free in their choices and will no longer be maximizing utility; the virtues of the free market will be lost.

A central function of much advertising is to persuade people to buy products. One method of persuading someone to buy something is simply to inform him of its features and availability. This suffices when the object is known to satisfy some pre-existing desire. A slightly more complex method that better fits our usual concept of persuasion consists in showing someone that he *should* desire, something because it is a means to achieve something else that he desires. This is still a typical form of rational persuasion—one provides reasons for desiring that are to be consciously weighed by the person addressed.

A more controversial method of persuasion bypasses reason and even conscious thought processes, attempting rather to create an association in the consumer's mind between the product and some image that expresses a subconscious wish or desire.

A possibly more sinister variation on this persuasive strategy seeks to establish an association between the lack or absence of the product and some unconscious fear or anxiety. The consumer is then to choose the product as a way of fulfilling his unconscious wish or avoiding the object of his unconscious anxiety.

The psychological theory behind typical variations on this method is eclectic, a mixture of Freudian ideas and behavioral conditioning methods. Notions of subconscious wishes, fears, and sublimations combine with techniques to induce association by conditioning. Methods of advertising (like simple repetition of a brand name or slogan) that make little sense if we think of them as means of providing information become intelligible under this alternative analysis. But though economically successful at least some of the time, such advertising might be condemned on moral grounds. Why?

Persuasion by rational means respects the right of the intended object of persuasion to free and informed choice. But when the influence is intended to be subconscious, the persuasion appears similar to deception. The method appears then to violate a central requirement of at least one major moral tradition, the imperative to treat other persons as equals and to respect their rationality and freedom of choice. It also seems to contradict a major justification of the free economic market: that the system permits all economic transactions to be voluntary. A consumer's decision to buy is not voluntary, it can be argued, when he has been unduly influenced in this way.

Suppose we grant that there is a right to advertise. Businesses have the right to promote their products and services, and advertisers have the right to provide this service to them. Advertising is a form of speech, and as such it seems to require no further justification than appeal to the right of free expression. There remains a constitutionally supported distinction between commercial and other relevant forms of speech, that is, political and literary. Congress is granted the right to control commerce, but not to abridge other forms of speech. Granted that certain economic freedoms are central—for example, the freedom of individuals to work, invest, and consume as they choose—even in these areas there are limitations to protect others as well as the agents themselves. One cannot buy dangerous explosives or work on certain jobs without wearing safety equipment; one cannot invest in the heroin trade. In the realm of speech, the right to advertise does not include a right to defraud, or moral license to mislead people into buying harmful products. Legally, the Federal Trade Commission requires that advertisements be truthful and that their factual claims be substantiated. Such requirements, of course, would not be tolerated in other realms of discourse. We would not trust the government to prohibit political speech it judges to be untrue or literary works it holds misleading or even subversive. . . .

In endorsing regulation of advertising we must recognize certain negative consequences. First, strict scrutiny of factual claims may lead advertisers to reduce their content, relying instead upon nonrational methods of persuasion. One could argue that the net result is less information to consumers. We can reply that less information is better than false or misleading information. In addition, information that gives good reasons to prefer the product remains valuable for use in ads. The public can still recognize substantiated claims of superiority in product features, and such claims are likely to be more persuasive than meaningless jingles, with less repetition required. Second, it has been argued that regulation makes ads more believable in the eyes of the public, which only makes it easier for the less scrupulous to deceive. But to argue in that way against holding advertisers to the truth suggests more generally that we ought not to encourage honesty, since honesty as a rule makes deception in particular cases easier. This argument is absurd.

We must recognize, secondly, that not all morally objectionable practices on the part of advertisers can be made illegal or regulated. Fair regulation requires objectively verifiable criteria on which to base enforcement. It must therefore center on fraud and deception in factual claims and upon limiting promotion of obviously harmful products such as cigarettes. Non-rational persuasion that creates false associations or insecurities, or that encourages pretentious and unfulfilling patterns of consumption and lifestyles, cannot be prohibited, since enforcement of the prohibitions could not be fair and non-controversial. Such practices nevertheless remain morally objectionable. . . .

Despite the limitations on regulation, then, it is clear that the right to advertise does not include a moral right to deceive, mislead, or harass, or to create or foster insecurities or self-defeating values. The legal right to advertise is narrower than the corresponding right to free non-commercial speech. The moral right to engage in specific advertising practices is narrower still, not including certain activities that cannot be legally sanctioned (because of the costs involved). . . .

The social effect of advertising subsidies to print and broadcast media is optimized when sponsors restrain their inclinations to censor program material in order to appeal to uniformly large audiences and avoid offending them. Only uncensored media can educate public taste rather than accommodating to its lowest common denominator. Here is the first case of a moral demand that may run counter to the profit-maximizing motive of the advertiser and his client. The injunction against censorship is a genuinely moral requirement, since the social effect of commercial censors seems no less pernicious than that of government censors.

A function more intrinsic to advertisements themselves is the provision of information to consumers enabling them to make more rational choices among products so as to better satisfy their desires. The performance of this function requires that advertisements be truthful and verifiable in their explicit and implied factual claims. "Puffery" or hyperbole must be clearly distinguishable from factual claims by the audience, this requirement becoming broader and stricter when the product is potentially harmful and the intended audience less worldly wise (for example, children). While the advertiser is not morally required to aim at providing complete information, material omitted must not negate claims made or implied, or relate to probable harm from the product.

. . . The basic principle regarding effects of persuasion is that advertisers ought not to create desires whose fulfillment would be more harmful than beneficial to consumers. More broadly, the principle we propose would prohibit encouraging irrational desires. Desires are irrational if their targets are falsely believed to be means to ends sought, if their satisfaction blocks that of other more important desires, or if the costs of their satisfaction are too high. Proscribed are desires for specific products known by the advertiser to be harmful, as well as yearnings for a lifestyle out of reach or ultimately low in overall satisfaction. The advertiser's ignorance of the harmfulness of the product he advocates is normally no excuse. Since he shares responsibility for the consumer's buying the product, he must share the blame for the harm that results. To avoid such blame he is obligated to find out, within reasonable limits, the nature of the products he sells. . . .

Turning to the methods of non-rational persuasion, important moral considerations include the resistibility of the appeal to the audience, that is, whether the choices under its influence remain free, and the importance of the choices at stake. The former is especially relevant in the case of children, where the advertiser must exercise extreme caution and restraint. . . .

Weaker moral demands relate also to the aesthetics of advertising. The advertiser ought not to harass or irritate us intentionally or pollute our natural or aesthetic environments in order to get our attention.

QUESTIONS

1. How does Goldman justify advertising in a market economy?

2. Suppose I am a Nazi propagandist "advertising" the good of concentration camps for the German people (pay your taxes! It supports the camps!). What would Goldman say to me?

Leslie Savan | The Bribed Soul

Leslie Savan is the advertising columnist for the *Village Voice* and was twice a finalist for the Pulitzer Prize in criticism.

Television-watching Americans—that is, just about *all* Americans—see approximately 100 TV commercials a day. In that same 24 hours they also see a host of print ads, billboard signs, and other corporate messages slapped onto every available surface, from the fuselages of NASA rockets right down to the bottom of golf holes and the inside doors of restroom stalls. Studies estimate that, counting all the logos, labels, and announcements, some 16,000 ads flicker across an individual's consciousness daily. . . .

Most admakers understand that in order to sell to you they have to know your desires and dreams better than you may know them yourself, and they've tried to reduce that understanding to a science. Market research, in which psychologists, polling organizations, trends analysts, focus group leaders, "mall-intercept" interviewers, and the whole panoply of mass communications try to figure out what will make you buy, has become a $2.5 billion annual business growing at a healthy clip of about 4.2 percent a year (after adjustment for inflation). Yet this sophisticated program for the study of the individual consumer is only a starter kit for the technological advances that will sweep through the advertising-industrial complex in the 1990s. Today, the most we can do when another TV commercial comes on—and we are repeatedly told that this is our great freedom—is to switch channels. But soon technology will take even that tiny tantrum of resistance and make it "interactive," providing advertisers with information on the exact moment we became bored—vital data that can be crunched, analyzed, and processed into the next set of ads, the better to zap-proof *them*.

Impressive as such research may be, the real masterwork of advertising is the way it uses the techniques of art to seduce the human soul. Virtually all of modern experience now has a sponsor, or at least a sponsored accessory, and there is no human emotion or concern—love, lust, war, childhood innocence, social rebellion, spiritual enlightenment, even disgust with advertising—that cannot be reworked into a sales pitch. The transcendent look in a bride's eyes the moment before she kisses her groom turns into a promo for Du Pont. The teeth-gnashing humiliation of an office rival becomes an inducement to switch to AT&T.

In short, we're living the sponsored life. From Huggies to Maalox, the necessities and little luxuries of an American's passage through this world are provided and promoted by one advertiser or another. The sponsored life is born when commercial culture sells our own experiences back to us. It grows as those experiences are then reconstituted inside us, mixing the most intimate processes of individual thought with commercial values, rhythms, and expectations. It has often been said by television's critics that TV doesn't deliver products to viewers but that viewers themselves are the *real* product, one that TV delivers to its advertisers. True, but the symbiotic relationship between advertising and audience goes deeper than that. The viewer who lives the sponsored life—and that is most of us to one degree or the other—is slowly re-created in the ad's image.

Inside each "consumer," advertising's all-you-can-eat, all-the-time, all-dessert buffet produces a build-up of mass-produced stimuli, all hissing and sputtering to get out. Sometimes they burst out as sponsored speech, as when we talk in the cadences of sitcom one-liners, imitate Letterman, laugh uproariously at lines like "I've fallen and I can't get up," or mouth the words of familiar commercials, like the entranced high school student I met in a communication class who moved his lips with the voiceover of a Toyota spot. . . .

To lead the sponsored life you don't really have to do anything. You don't need to have a corporate sponsor as the museums or the movies do. You don't even have to buy anything—though it helps, and you will. You just have to live in America and share with the nation, or at least with your mall-intercept cohorts, certain paid-for expectations and values, rhythms and reflexes. . . .

The chief expectation of the sponsored life is that there will and always should be regular blips of excitement and resolution, the frequency of which is determined by money. We begin to pulse to the beat, the one-two beat, that moves most ads: problem/solution, old/new, Brand X/hero brand, desire/gratification. In order to dance to the rhythm, we adjust other expectations a little here, a little there: Our notions of what's desirable behavior, our lust for novelty, even our visions of the perfect love affair or thrilling adventure adapt to the mass consensus coaxed out by marketing. Cultural forms that don't fit these patterns tend to fade away, and eventually *everything* is commercial culture—not just the 30-second spot but the drama, news segment, stage performance, novel, magazine layout—comes to share the same insipid insistence on canned excitement and neat resolution.

What's all the excitement about? Anything and nothing. You know you've entered the commercial zone when the excitement building in you is oddly incommensurate with the content dangled before you: does a sip of Diet Coke really warrant an expensive production number celebrating the rebel prowess of "ministers who surf," "insurance agents who speed," and "people who live their life as an exclamation not an explanation"?!? Of course not. Yet through the sympathetic magic of materialism we learn how to respond to excitement: It's less important that we purchase any particular product than that we come to expect resolution *in the form of* something buyable. . . .

Irony has become the hallmark of the sponsored life because it provides a certain distance from the frustration inherent in commercial correctness. For some time now the people raised on television, the

baby boomers and the "Generation Xers" that followed, have mentally adjusted the set, as it were, in order to convince themselves that watching is cool. They may be doing exactly what their parents do—but they do it *differently.* They take in TV with a Lettermanesque wink, and they like it when it winks back. In many cases (as Mark Crispin Miller has described it so well in *Boxed In).,* the winkers have enthusiastically embraced the artifice, even the manipulativeness, of advertising as an essential paradox of modern life, a paradox that is at the crux of their own identity.

The winkers believe that by rolling their collective eyes when they watch TV they can control *it,* rather than letting it control them. But unfortunately, as a defense against the power of advertising, irony is a leaky condom—in fact, it's the same old condom that advertising brings over every night. A lot of ads have learned that to break through to the all-important boomer and Xer markets they have to be as cool, hip, and ironic as the target audience likes to think of itself as being. That requires at least the pose of opposition to commercial values. The cool commercials—I'm thinking of Nike spots, some Reeboks, most 501s, certainly all MTV promos—flatter us by saying we're too cool to fall for commercial values, and therefore cool enough to want their product.

If irony is weak armor, how do we ward off the effect of billions of words and images from our sponsors? No perfect wolfsbane exists, but I can suggest some tactics to keep in mind:

When watching, watch out. Literally. Watch as an outsider, from as far a distance as you can muster (farther even than irony)—*especially* when watching ads that flatter you for being an outsider, as more and more are doing.

Big lie, little lie. All advertising tells lies, but there are little lies and there are big lies. Little lie: This beer tastes great. Not all ads tell little lies—they're more likely to be legally actionable (while big lies by definition aren't). And many products do live up to their modest material claims: This car runs. But all ads *must* tell big lies: This car will attract babes and make others slobber in envy. Don't be shocked that ads lie—that's their job. But do try to distinguish between the two kinds of lies.

To: You
From: The Philosopher
Subject: "Conspicuous Consumption"

Thorstein Veblen was an American economist and social theorist. He argued that the reason our society loves consumer goods is that they give us prestige. Why do we buy a Porsche instead of a Previa? Because people admire Porsche owners. Why do people buy Rolexes instead of Timexes, despite the notorious unreliability of the former? Simply because they cost more. The logical conclusion of consumption, Veblen argues, is systematic waste.

> Conspicuous consumption of valuable goods is a means of reputability to the gentleman of leisure. As wealth accumulates on his hands, his own unaided effort will not avail to sufficiently put his opulence in evidence by this method. The aid of friends and competitors is therefore brought in by resorting to the giving of valuable presents and expensive feasts and entertainments. . . .
>
> The basis on which good repute in any highly organised industrial community ultimately rests is pecuniary strength; and the means of showing pecuniary strength, and so of gaining or retaining a good name, are leisure and a conspicuous consumption of goods. . . . No class of society not even the most abjectly poor, foregoes all customary conspicuous consumption. The last items of this category of consumption are not given up except under stress of the direst necessity. Very much of squalor and discomfort will be endured before the last trinket or the last pretence of pecuniary decency is put away.
>
> . . . It appears that the utility of both alike for the purposes of reputability lies in the element of waste that is common to both. In the one case it is a waste of time and effort, in the other it is a waste of goods. Both are methods of demonstrating the possession of wealth, and the two are conventionally accepted as equivalents. The choice between them is a question of advertising expediency simply, except so far as it may be affected by other standards of propriety springing from a different source. On grounds of expediency the preference may be given to the one or the other at different stages of the economic development. The question is, which of the two methods will most effectively reach the persons whose convictions it is desired to affect. . . .
>
> Throughout the entire evolution of conspicuous expenditure, whether of goods or of services or human life, runs the obvious implication that in order to effectually mend the consumer's good fame it must be an expenditure of superfluities. In order to be reputable it must be wasteful. . . .

From Thorstein Veblen, *The Theory of the Leisure Class: An Economic Study of Institutions* (New York: Macmillan, 1902), pp. 68–101.

Read the box. Look not just at whether an ad's claims are false or exaggerated, but try to figure out what portion of an ad is about the culture as opposed to the product. Read the contents as you would a cereal box's: Instead of how much sugar to wheat, consider how much style to information. Not that a high ratio of sugar to wheat is necessarily more malevolent than the other way around. But it's a sure sign that they're fattening you up for the shill.

Assume no relationship between a brand and its image. Marlboro was originally sold as a woman's cigarette, and its image was elegant, if not downright prissy. It wasn't until 1955 that the Marlboro Man was invented to ride herd on all that. The arbitrary relationship between a product and its ads becomes even clearer when you realize how much advertising is created to overcome "brand parity"—a plague more troubling to marketers than bodily odors. Brand parity means that there is little or no difference between competing brands and that the best a brand can do is hire a more appealing image. When advertising works at all, it's because the public more or less believes that something serious is going on between a product and its image, as if the latter reveals intrinsic qualities of the former. Peel image off item, and you too can have more of the freedom that ads are always promising. Likewise . . .

We don't buy products, we buy the world that presents them. Over the long run, whether you actually buy a particular product is less important than that you buy the world that makes the products seem desirable. Not so long ago a BMW or a Mercedes was required if you seriously bought the worldview that their ads conveyed. Still, buying an attitude doesn't automatically translate into product purchase. If your income precluded a BMW, you might have bought instead a Ralph Lauren polo shirt or even a Dove bar (which is how yuppie snack foods positioned themselves—as achievable class). Sure, GE wants you to buy its bulbs, but even more it wants you to buy the paternalistic, everything's-under-control world that GE seems to rule. Buying *that* will result, GE is betting, not only in more appliance sales but also in more credibility when spokesmen insist that defrauding the Pentagon is not *really* what GE is all about. That is to say . . .

The promotional is the political. Each world that commercials use to sell things comes packed with biases: Entire classes, races, and genders may be excluded for the coddling of the sponsored one. Lee Jeans' world (circa 1989) is a place where young people are hip, sexual, and wear jeans, while old people are square, non-sexual, and wear uniforms. The class and age politics here is more powerful than the Young Republicans'. There is politics in all advertising (and, more obviously, advertising in all politics). It makes sense that these two professions call what they do "campaigns."

Advertising shepherds herds of individuals. When Monty Python's mistaken messiah in *The Life*

of Brian exhorts the crowd of devotees to "Don't follow me! Don't follow anyone! Think for yourselves! . . . You are all individuals!" they reply in unison, "We are all individuals!" That is advertising in a nutshell.

Advertising's most basic paradox is to say: Join us and become unique. Advertisers learned long ago that individuality sells, like sex or patriotism. The urge toward individualism is a constant in America, with icons ranging from Thomas Jefferson's yeoman farmer to the kooky girl bouncing to the jingle "I like the Sprite in you!" Commercial nonconformity always operates in the service of . . . conformity. Our system of laws and our one-man-one-vote politics may be based on individualism, but successful marketing depends on the exact opposite: By identifying (through research) the ways we are alike, it hopes to convince the largest number of people that they need the exact same product. Furthermore, in modem pop culture, we construct our individuality by the unique combination of mass-produced goods and services we buy. I sip Evian, you slug Bud Light; I drive a Geo, you gun a Ford pickup; I kick sidewalk in cowboy boots, you bop in Reeboks. Individuality is a good angle for all advertising, but it's crucial for TV commercials. There you are sitting at home, not doing anything for hours on end, but then the very box you're staring at tells you that you are different, that you are vibrantly alive, that your quest for freedom—freedom of speech, freedom of movement, freedom to do whatever you damn well choose—will not be impeded! And you can do all that, says the box, without leaving your couch.

It's the real ad. The one question I'm most often asked is, Does advertising shape who we are and what we want, or does it merely reflect back to us our own emotions and desires? As with most nature-or-nurture questions, the answer is both. The real ad in any campaign is controlled neither by admakers nor adwatchers; it exists somewhere between the TV set and the viewer, like a huge hairball, collecting bits of material and meaning from both. The real ad isn't even activated until viewers hand it their frustrations from work, the mood of their love life, their idiosyncratic misinterpretations, and most of all, I think, their everyday politics. On which class rung do they see themselves teetering? Do they ever so subtly

Ask Me No Questions . . .

Every fat commission check has a price tag. For Matt Cooper the cost of earning up to $150,000 per sale was spending every day lying to his customers. It was the promise of huge bonus checks—not his $40,000 base salary—that lured him to join the sales force of a large, well-known Internet company two years ago. In his early twenties, hungry, and aggressive, Cooper fit the dot-com's sales culture mold, but what he didn't realize was that dishonesty was the price of admission.

The New York-based start-up formed a big-deals team, a group that sold multimillion-dollar advertising campaigns to some of the world's largest companies. The sales force's key strategy? Do whatever it took to close those deals. Almost 100 percent of the time that meant lying to the client. "If you didn't lie you were fired," Cooper says. "It always came down to careful wording and fudging numbers." Among various other deceptive tactics, the Internet company's salespeople would book $2 million deals, promising a certain amount of impressions on the client's banner ads for the first million and guaranteeing a certain amount of sales for the second million dollars. . . .

Finally Cooper couldn't take it anymore. "I started selling only what I knew worked, because I couldn't lie anymore—so my managers told me to either close more deals or find another job," he says. "It was the kind of culture where they broke you down and rebuilt you to be an animal." . . .

Such deception may be more common than we think. In the SMM survey, 36 percent of respondents said salespeople now conduct business in a less ethical manner than they did five years ago, and 36 percent believe there's been no change at all. What kind of fabrications do salespeople resort to? The survey shows that 45 percent of managers have heard their reps lying about promised delivery times, 20 percent have overheard their team members give false information about the company's service, and nearly 78 percent of managers have caught a competitor lying about their company's products or services. "It appears that misrepresentation of products or services is prevalent among salespeople," [Andy] Zoltners [a marketing professor at Northwestern University's Kellogg School of Management] says. "This is a losing strategy, and this kind of behavior is not what the best salespeople do."

From Erin Stroud, "Kellogg in the Media," *Sales & Marketing Management*, July 2002, Kellogg School of Management.

flinch when a different race comes on TV? In this way, we all co-produce the ads we see. Agency people are often aghast that anyone would find offensive meanings in their ads because "that's not what we intended." Intention has little to do with it. Whatever they meant, once an ad hits the air it becomes public property. That, I think, is where criticism should aim—at the fluctuating, multi-meaning thing that floats over the country, reflecting us as we reflect it.

Follow the flattery. I use the word "flattery" a lot. When trying to understand what an ad's really up to, following the flattery is as useful as following the money. You'll find the ad's target market by asking who in any 30-second drama is being praised for qualities they probably don't possess. When a black teenager plays basketball with a white baby boomer for Canada Dry, it's not the black youth that's being pandered to. It's white boomers—the flattery being that they're cool enough to be accepted by blacks. Ads don't even have to put people on stage to toady up to them. Ads can flatter by style alone, as do all the spots that turn on hyper-quick cuts or obscure meanings, telling us—uh, *some* of us—that we're special enough to get it.

We participate in our own seduction. Once properly flattered, all that's left is to close the sale—and only we can do that. Not only do we co-produce the ads, but we're our own best voiceover—that little inner voice that ultimately decides to buy or not. The best ads tell us we're cool *coolly*—in the other meaning of the word. McLuhan used to say that a cool medium, like television, involves us more by not giving us everything; the very spaces between TV's flickering dots are filled in by our central nervous system. He refers to "the involvement of the viewer with the completion of 'closing'

of the TV image." This is seduction: We're stirred to a state so that not only do we close the image but, given the right image at the right time, we open our wallet. All television is erotically engaged in this way, but commercials are TV's G-spot. The smart ads always hold back a little to get us to lean forward a little. Some ads have become caricatures of this tease, withholding the product's name until the last second to keep you wondering who could possibly be sponsoring such intrigue. The seduction may continue right to the cash register, where one last image is completed: you and product together at last. It'd be nice to say that now that you've consumed, you've climaxed, and everyone can relax. But sponsorship is a lifetime proposition that must be renewed every day.

QUESTIONS

1. Is your soul bribed? Why or why not? Give examples?

2. How is it that our souls come to be "bribed"? How can we free our souls?

G. Richard Shell and Mario Moussa

Woo with Integrity

G. Richard Shell is a professor at the Wharton School of Business.

Mario Moussa directs Wharton's Center for Applied Research.

Ambition, not so much for vulgar ends but for fame, glints in every mind.

—Winston Churchill

Character is like a tree and reputation like its shadow. The shadow is what we think of it; the tree is the real thing.

—Abraham Lincoln

THE ART OF DOING GOOD

Our story begins with a man named Jack, who grew up in a working-class neighborhood in Philadelphia. He graduated from a local college with a major in education and enrolled in medical school, hoping to become a doctor. But he quickly realized that he had neither the passion nor the patience for medicine and dropped out.

Two formative events then took place. First, after holding down a few odd jobs, Jack finally found his calling in a nonprofit program dealing with drug abuse. Here he discovered that he liked the social sector with its emphasis on helping people. He also married and started a family.

Second, his father died, which affected him in a profoundly spiritual way. He joined a large church and became a dedicated member. Religion was to play an important role in the events that would soon consume his life. In addition, with the help of business and political leaders he met through his church, Jack launched two ambitious social service organizations, one in the drug-abuse area and the other in mental health. His successes were noticed. He became known throughout the region as a skilled fund-raiser for worthy causes.

That is when Jack's big idea came to him. In his fund-raising work, he saw that people were much more willing to give to a cause when their money was "matched" by others, thus doubling the impact of their gifts. The problem was that such "matching" opportunities were hard to find and develop.

His idea was to create a central organization—a foundation—that would identify anonymous donors who were willing to provide matching gifts to worthy causes. Jack would collect money from charities, pair up this money with new money from anonymous philanthropists, and then return the doubled money to the worthy cause. His foundation could be operated off the interest earned by his donors' money during the six months it would take to pair just the right charities with just the right anonymous donors. He gave his idea a name—New Concepts in Philanthropy—and created a case for it based on the problem (there was not enough money being raised for worthy causes), the cause (people were stuck in old-fashioned, laborious fund-raising techniques), his solution (a centralized, anonymous-donor foundation), and its relatively inexpensive method of administration the interest earned from donations would be enough to cover operating costs).

Through his widening social network, he made a new friend at about this time—one of the top physicians at the area's leading hospital for children. And that man, in turn, introduced Jack to his father, one of the richest men in America and perhaps its most visionary and well-connected philanthropist. Jack impressed both men with his energy and new ideas. They set up an institute—with Jack as its

director—to spread his fund-raising expertise and commitment to values. The father joined Jack's new matching-fund foundation as a trustee and the son helped him launch the new idea by recommending friends who could participate as donors.

To get his idea off the ground, Jack took one small step. With names given him by his physician friend, he let it be known that if he could get twenty people to donate five thousand dollars each to his new foundation, their money would be matched by an equal amount from a donor who wished to remain anonymous and the combined money would be given to some important local charities. When people saw who was affiliated with this new program, Jack had no trouble raising his first hundred thousand dollars.

In no time, the idea caught fire. Other people asked Jack if they could contribute and donations began to flow. And as they did, Jack's foundation began making substantial gifts to local causes from these monies. That, in turn, triggered interest from other groups that wished to receive grants from Jack's foundation. People lined up to get to know this new foundation and its founder.

Then Jack came up with his second and most original idea. He realized he could accelerate his program by opening the foundation to a whole new type of donation. If a nonprofit institution—say a college or university—placed part of its endowment in his foundation, then Jack saw that this money, too, could be matched by Jack's growing stable of anonymous donors, allowing the charitable organization to increase its endowment through matching gifts. Jack's new idea took hold, and Harvard, Princeton, and the University of Pennsylvania (among others) signed up to deposit funds. With these premier institutions on board, a host of smaller colleges, especially many religious schools that struggled to raise money, clamored to be included in the program.

Within a few short years, Jack's foundation was raising hundreds of millions of dollars and making large donations to many well-known, highly visible institutions, including the Red Cross, the Salvation Army, and top universities. Jack himself had become one of the most respected people in the philanthropic world.

Jack had found the secret of doing well by doing good—and it had all come about through his remarkable powers to leverage relationships, address interests, and implement his simple insight: people give more to causes when other people are matching their gifts.

A WOO REVIEW

Let's push the pause button at this point and review what Jack did right in terms of the Art of Woo. His strategy reflects an almost perfect execution of the four-step Woo process.

Step 1—Survey Your Situation. First, Jack did a great job on the "me" stage of Woo. He came up with a well-formulated idea and polished it using his extensive nonprofit experience. Second, he found and embraced his own personal persuasion style—an affable mix of other-oriented Promoter and Advocate roles coupled with an ability to project a sincere, committed belief in his idea. As he achieved early successes, he acquired confidence and that helped him to project credibility. Finally, he surveyed and mapped the philanthropic social network around Philadelphia and found his way, one stepping-stone at a time, to some of the nation's wealthiest and most open-minded donors. Jack's networking activity never stopped and was the source of an ever-widening set of contacts.

Step 2—Confront the Five Barriers. Jack also showed respect for and command of the five potential barriers to persuasion. Let's look at each one of them in turn.

- **Relationships.** Jack built and scrupulously maintained key, Trust-Level relationships. Jack had no trouble meeting and greeting people. And by selecting his most powerful friends to be the trustees of his foundation, he created the momentum he needed to both launch his idea and keep it expanding.
- **Credibility.** Jack's relationship skills and his proven track record gave him credibility. People trusted him and saw him as a reliable, competent expert in his field. Those who did not know him could rely on the reputations of the well-known

people who were affiliated with him. Finally, he delivered on his double-your-donation promise time after time in very public ways.

- **Tuning to the Other Person's Channel.** Jack had a gift for communicating effectively with many diverse audiences. He excelled at the Visionary and Relationship communication channels, as did most of his charity-minded audience. Even the hard-nosed denizens of Wall Street he approached were inclined to shift to the visionary channel when it came to charity. With religious people, he spoke of religion. With educators, he spoke of education. With hospitals, he spoke of health care. Regardless of whom he spoke with, as one supporter put it, Jack had a way of finding the "key to their hearts."
- **Beliefs and Values.** Jack's mission was to advance people's values and beliefs by enhancing their ability to do good works. And he not only spoke of values, his life reflected them.
- **Interests and Needs.** It was in addressing this factor that Jack showed his touch of genius. Leveraging the power of matching gifts is an old idea—some say Benjamin Franklin invented it. But Jack took it to a whole new level and, in doing so, opened his foundation to many smaller institutions that had never had an opportunity to benefit from mainstream philanthropy. The president of the Coalition for Christian Colleges and Universities, for example, said that gaining access to Jack's stable of donors was "almost a gift from heaven, in a religious sense."

Step 3—Make Your Pitch. Early on, Jack constructed a powerful, PCAN-based case for his program. He gave his early backers reasons to say yes, and when he spoke to new donors, he could point to others who had doubled their money and received substantial gifts. He combined all his insights regarding his audience's beliefs and interests into his message.

There are no records of specific pitches Jack made, but his results suggest they must have been memorable. As a Christian, for example, he had Jesus' "Parable of the Talents," which teaches that people "to whom much is given" should multiply their assets rather than hoard them so they can provide the means to advance God's work. And as his organization grew, Jack had many stories and examples to offer from the lives of individuals who had been touched by his foundation's work.

Step 4—Secure Your Commitments. Finally, Jack was not content to gain promises of support. He demanded actions. A realist about human nature, he required concrete commitments from his donors—deposits of cash and agreements to leave it in his care for at least six months while he arranged the "match." And at the institutional level, he was skilled at overcoming occasional objections raised by naysayers—usually traditional fund-raising professionals—whose career or professional interests conflicted with his philanthropic model. As his program grew, he mounted true "campaigns" for his idea, creating a "snowball effect" within the charitable world as a whole. He built a broad base of enthusiastic supporters, and was widely credited for his innovations.

BACK TO JACK

Given his success, you may be wondering how Jack's story ended. Did his foundation spawn similar institutions?

Jack's full name was John G. Bennett, Jr. He lived in a suburb of Philadelphia in the 1980s and 1990s. His organization was called the Foundation for New Era Philanthropy. At the height of his fame, he counted as close friends the wealthy mutual fund magnate John Ternpleton and his physician son John Templeton, Jr., former ABC news anchor Peter Jennings, former Treasury Secretary William E. Simon, former co-head of Goldman Sachs John C. Whitehead, philanthropist Laurance Rockefeller, and many other political, business, and cultural leaders.

And, as of this writing, Jack is finishing up a twelve-year sentence in a federal penitentiary for securities law violations and fraud.

The Foundation for New Era Philanthropy was a pyramid scheme. When New Era went down—as it did in May 1995 after five years of operation—it owed pledges of more than five hundred million

dollars and had few assets with which to pay them. Jack never had or found any "anonymous donors" willing to give money—though many people had assumed John Templeton was the mysterious benefactor behind Jack's plan. Instead, he raised *all* his money from charities with his compelling "double your money" pitch and used the new money he raised to pay off the groups that had put money in earlier. His system required him to raise ever-increasing millions to stay ahead of his rapidly escalating obligations—a job made somewhat easier by the fact that many colleges and universities let their endowment money "ride" for multiple six-month cycles.

He returned just enough "doubled" money to keep everyone's confidence. Meanwhile, he pocketed millions of dollars from the interest earned while he held his victims' cash. He and his family bought expensive homes and Lexus automobiles, and they entertained lavishly.

An accounting professor from a small college in Michigan, worried that his own school was about to throw its endowment away by giving it to New Era, got hold of its 1993 federal tax return and discovered the fraud: the foundation had reported almost no interest income on its hundreds of millions of dollars in assets. The *Wall Street Journal* put the story on its front page, New Era's bankers called a $65 million loan, and the regulators swooped in.

Such is the power of reputations and beliefs, however, that even at this point Jack's backers refused to believe what they were hearing. John Templeton, reached by reporters in a London hotel, commented, "I think he will have good answers, and as people get to know him, I think people will have the same view of him that I do."

Jack was carted off to jail in 1997 after trying unsuccessfully to argue in court that the whole affair had been the result of brain damage he suffered in a 1984 car accident. He wept when he met with his staff to confess that he had made the whole thing up. "I betrayed you all," he said. "All I ever wanted to do was help people. There are no anonymous donors."

The biggest losers turned out to be those that could least afford the loss—the small religious colleges. Lancaster Bible College lost $16.9 million and John Brown University of Siloam Springs, Arkansas, lost over $2 million, 4 percent of its endowment. Other losers included hospitals, major universities, the Academy of Natural Sciences in Philadelphia, a program teaching English-language courses in Cambodia, and a long list of other charities.

Why did he do it? With his gift for Woo, Jack could have made a good living as a highly paid nonprofit executive. He gave a hint of his motivation just before he was sentenced. "As the years passed," he told the court, "the desire became a dream, the dream became a need, the need became an obsession, the obsession became a fantasy, and the fantasy became a delusion." In some ways, he was like the dieter who by day truly believes that he or she is on a diet, only to lapse into compulsive eating—in Bennett's case into writing himself checks—in the dark of night. An attorney specializing in nonprofit law and familiar with the New Era story had this to say about Jack: "I'm not sure Bennett set out to commit fraud. I think the situation got away from him. These things aren't necessarily set up to defraud charities or the public, but the philanthropic community is about power and reputation . . .not so much about money. And that's very exciting."

In other words, Jack longed to be a "player" in the world of the rich and famous. He craved a feeling of importance. As Winston Churchill warned in his quote that led this chapter, the "ambition . . . for fame" that "glints in every mind" led Jack to use his persuasion skills to con an entire community of very sophisticated people.

WHAT MATTERS MOST: CHARACTER AND PURPOSE

Winston Churchill noted in his history of World War II that Hitler was, on a person-to-person level as well as at rallies, a very persuasive person. So was Churchill. These two men understood the Art of Woo in all its details.

The main difference between them was that Churchill had character: he was an honorable man who was committed to using his persuasion skills to achieve worthy goals.

Let's put it this way. An earnest and sincere lover buys flowers and candy for the object of his affections. So does the cad who seeks to take advantage of another's heart. But when the cad succeeds, we don't blame the flowers and candy. We rightly question his character. And in Jack Bennett's case, we should not blame the misery he caused on the persuasion tools he mastered. Instead, we should ask how we can avoid slipping—even a little—into the self-serving state of mind that led Bennett to his downfall.

The answer lies in paying attention to both your own motives and the effects of your actions on others when you sell your ideas. Almost all persuasion situations at work involve a mix of purposes—people want to advance their own careers and take care of their own needs even as they work toward their organization's goals. But you will face tough choices—people always do—when your needs conflict either with the organization's or with other people's as you advance your agenda. As a person of character, you have an obligation to think about the standards of conduct you will hold yourself to in these situations, or you risk joining Jack Bennett in the rogue's gallery.

One simple test is to avoid purposes and practices that benefit yourself by causing direct and substantial harm to others. For example, we object to some of the advice given in Robert Greene's *The 48 Laws of Power*, which teaches readers to obey such rules as "Get Others to Do the Work—While You Take the Credit," "Be Selectively Honest and Generous to Disarm Your Target," and "Crush Your Enemy Totally."

But even this test will leave you with unanswered questions in many circumstances. For example, suppose you are promoting a strategy idea that requires the organization to close an existing business unit and lay off hundreds of employees—but would also result in a big promotion and raise for you. Many worthy ideas involve actions that will make someone, somewhere worse off. And we don't think that makes them unethical.

For these cases, we recommend what we call the *Wall Street Journal* standard—a paraphrase of Richard's conclusion on negotiation ethics in *Bargaining for Advantage*.

It goes like this: "Persuaders who aspire to personal integrity, should test their actions with a thoughtful set of personal values, based on widely shared social norms, that they could explain and defend to the *Wall*

Street Journal were that paper to run a front-page story on the idea-selling strategy they adopted."

If you could not defend your actions on the front page of the *Wall Street Journal*, where Jack Bennett's fraud was revealed, then you should rethink your strategy. You may still go astray if the social norms you consult are controversial or if you give in to the temptation to delude yourself about your motives, but you will keep your-self out of a lot of trouble.

TEN QUESTIONS FOR WOULD-BE WOOERS

As you finish reading this and return to the world of work with all its tough challenges, we thought it might be helpful to give you a set of ten questions to ask as you get ready for every idea-selling encounter. Consider these the preflight checklist for launching your idea.

1. What Is the Five-Minute Summary of My Idea?

Before going into a meeting or sending an important message, review exactly what your idea is about. Scan quickly through the PCAN model: What is the problem? What are the causes of that problem? How does my idea answer the problem? How is my answer superior to the status quo or available alternatives? Recall a memorable image or metaphor that captures the idea clearly and positions it favorably against the background of its alternatives.

2. What Role Does This Person Play in the Decision Process?

Review why you have chosen to meet with or communicate with this person at this time. Which step are they in your stepping-stone strategy? How can he or she help you advance your idea?

3. What Is My Goal for This Encounter?

Think specifically about your goals. Useful goals include: getting feedback on your idea, gaining access to someone else, persuading this person to take a favorable attitude toward your idea, obtaining authorization for resources, gaining endorsements, making decisions, and getting help with implementation. Write down your goal and refer to it before as well as after the encounter. Did you achieve your goal? If not, why not?

4. What Is the Basis for My Credibility with This Person?

What relationships, references, credentials, past accomplishments, or competencies should you be prepared to mention or display to establish your credibility? If you think you have a Trust-Level relationship, this will be less of an issue. If it is a Reciprocity-Level relationship, you may need to be prepared to diplomatically remind the other person of who owes what to whom at this point in your interaction. If this is only a Rapport-Level relationship, concrete signs of credibility may be especially important.

5. What Persuasion Channel Will This Person Be Tuned To?

Be prepared to adjust your pitch so you are communicating on the other person's channel. If you think the Rationality channel is his dominant mode, be prepared with your analysis and evidence. If the other person is more conceptual, emphasize the larger purpose or framework within which your idea fits. Have a Plan B in case you need to shift to a discussion of interests (what is in it for him?), politics (how will it look to a larger audience?), relationships (how does this fit into your ongoing interactions?), or authority (who is in charge and is that authority being respected and used appropriately?).

6. What Persuasion Style Is Appropriate?

Be aware that your preferred persuasion style— Driver, Commander, Advocate, Chess Player, or Promoter—may not be the best way to appeal to this particular audience. Remember how Charles Lindbergh, a man who preferred the reserved and rational Commander style, bought a new suit, made an expensive telephone call, and took on the role of the Idea Promoter when he went to New Jersey to sell the busy aircraft executives at Wright Aeronautical Corporation on his plan to fly across the Atlantic. Once he had attracted a group of loyal and enthusiastic backers, he quickly shifted back to his more restrained, natural persuasion mode. But he was smart enough to adjust the way he presented himself to meet his audience's expectations.

Of course, different people have varying degrees of flexibility when it comes to personal style. If you try to adjust yourself beyond your stretch point, you will damage your credibility. Had Lindbergh taken the Promoter role too far—throwing parties and giving lavish gifts—he could not have sustained it and people would have wondered who he thought he was fooling. He was a mail pilot, after all, not a Wall Street mogul.

So make an effort to shift your presentation style in the right direction—turn up (or down) your volume and focus more (or less) on spinning your message to appeal to the audience. But remember that it is better to be a bit awkward—and authentic—than it is to try too hard to be someone you obviously are not.

7. Will My Idea Conflict with Any of This Person's Beliefs?

Will the other party be skeptical of the idea based on its feasibility? If so, how can you address that? Might your idea conflict with a basic value or norm the other person holds? Think of ways to minimize this conflict—such as mentioning the prior endorsement of someone who holds that same belief or value.

8. Might My Idea Conflict with This Person's Interests?

Imagine that you are sitting in this person's chair. Think of the interests the person may have—especially those related to control, resources, career, decision-making jurisdiction, and future opportunities—that your idea could conflict with. Then think of the interests you both might share that could help bridge the conflicting agendas that arise.

9. What Commitments Can I Ask For?

What specific actions do you want the other person to take to advance your idea? What audience should witness this action? If you have an endorsement goal, obtain agreement on the people you can notify about the endorsement. If you have a decision goal, request permission to notify others of the decision.

10. Can I Leave the Relationship Better Than I Found It?

Always remember that Woo begins and ends with positive, constructive relationships. Think about how you can conclude the encounter with a strong relationship intact. Be considerate of the other person's time. Ask if there are things this person needs that you can help with. Find ways to demonstrate your good faith and reliability. As story after story in this book has shown, there are few problems a good relationship cannot fix.

THE ETHICS OF WOO

You need persuasion skills no matter what kind of organization you work for. And the higher you go, the more these skills matter. Most important, you need to think *strategically* about persuasion, with an eye on the moves that lie ahead as you decide which ones to take today.

We recently read about a Dutch traffic engineer named Hans Monderman whose theories of avoiding automobile collisions in urban environments resemble what we have tried to get across about designing and executing a good persuasion strategy. Monderman designs intersections with no stoplights, signs, painted centerlines, speed bumps, or defined pedestrian crossings. His idea is that people actually do a better job looking out for themselves—and each other—when they are given full responsibility for maneuvering than when they rely on systems and signals. Traffic lights, he says, are "the wrong story. People here have to find their own way, negotiate for themselves, and use their own brains."

Monderman calls this the concept of "shared space." Surveying his busy intersection, Monderman comments: "This is social space, so when Grandma is coming, you stop, because that's what normal, courteous human beings do." Tens of thousands of people cross paths every day at Monderman's intersections, and there has never been a fatal accident.

We are not sure Monderman's traffic theories would work so well outside the friendly confines of small Dutch cities, but we think that selling ideas in most organizations is quite similar to maneuvering through the traffic in one of his "shared spaces." The typical organization may have many traffic lights and stop signs, but these "standard operating procedures" are often ignored—and everyone knows they are ignored. To advance initiatives through these spaces, therefore, you have to navigate by keeping your eye on the right people and avoiding obstacles such as conflicting interests, hostile beliefs, cultural missteps, and political minefields that can come out of nowhere and cause collisions.

Woo. Simple to say. Hard to do.

Now it's up to you.

QUESTIONS

1. Shell and Moussa offer practical advice on selling with integrity. But isn't this just another way of manipulating people?

2. Is selling inherently deceptive?

3. What makes the difference between a good salesperson—morally speaking—and a bad salesperson?

CASES

CASE 8.1
Toy Wars
Manuel G. Velasquez

Tom Daner, president of the advertising company of Daner Associates, was contacted by the sales manager of Crako Industries, Mike Teal.[1] Crako Industries is a family-owned company that manufactures children's toys and had long been a favorite and important client of Daner Associates. The sales manager of Crako Industries explained that the company had just developed a new toy helicopter. The toy was modeled on the military helicopters that had been used in Vietnam and that had appeared in the "Rambo" movies. Mike Teal explained that the toy was developed in response to the craze for military toys that had been sweeping the nation in the wake of the Rambo movies. The family-owned toy company had initially resisted moving into military toys, since members of the family objected to the violence associated with such toys. But as segments of the toy market were increasingly taken over by military toys, the family came to feel that entry into the military toy market was crucial for their business. Consequently, they approved development of a line of military toys, hoping that they were not entering the market too late. Mike Teal now wanted Daner Associates to develop a television advertising campaign for the toy.

The toy helicopter Crako designers had developed was about one and one-half feet long, battery-operated, and made of plastic and steel. Mounted to the sides were detachable replicas of machine guns and a detachable stretcher modeled on the stretchers used to lift wounded soldiers from a battlefield. Mike Teal of Crako explained that they were trying to develop a toy that had to be perceived as "more macho" than the top-selling "G. I. Joe" line of toys. If the company was to compete successfully in today's toy market, according to the sales manager, it would have to adopt an advertising approach that was even "meaner and tougher" than what other companies were doing. Consequently, he continued, the advertising clips developed by Daner Associates would have to be "mean and macho." Television advertisements for the toy, he suggested, might show the helicopter swooping over buildings and blowing them up. The more violence and mayhem the ads suggested, the better Crako Industries was relying heavily on sales from the new toy, and some Crako managers felt that the company's future might depend on the success of this toy.

Tom Daner was unwilling to have his company develop television advertisements that would increase what he already felt was too much violence in television aimed at children. In particular, he recalled a television ad for a tricycle with a replica machine gun mounted on the handlebars. The commercial showed the tricycle being pedaled through the woods by a small boy as he chased several other boys fleeing before him over a dirt path. At one point the camera closed in over the shoulder of the boy, focused through the gun sight, and showed the gun sight apparently trying to aim at the backs of the boys as they fled before the tricycle's machine gun. Ads of that sort had disturbed Tom Daner and had led him to think that advertisers should find other ways of promoting these toys. He suggested, therefore, that instead of promoting the Crako helicopter through violence, it should be presented in some other manner. When Teal asked what he had in mind, Tom was forced to reply that he didn't know. But at any rate, Tom pointed out, the three television networks would not accept a violent commercial aimed at children. All three networks adhered to an advertising code that prohibited violent, intense, or unrealistic advertisements aimed at children.

This seemed no real obstacle to Teal, however. Although the networks might turn down children's ads when they were too violent, local television stations were not as squeamish. Local television stations around the country regularly accepted ads aimed at children that the networks had rejected as too violent. The local stations inserted the ads as spots on their non-network programming, thereby circumventing the Advertising Codes of the three national networks. Daner Associates would simply have to place the ads they developed for the Crako helicopter through local television stations around the country. Mike Teal was firm: if Daner Associates would not or could not develop a "mean and tough" ad campaign, the toy company would move their account to an advertiser who would. Reluctantly, Tom Daner agreed to develop the advertising campaign. Crako Industries accounted for $1 million of Daner's total revenues.

Like Crako Industries, Daner Associates is also a family-owned business. Started by his father almost fifty years ago, the advertising firm that Tom Daner now ran had grown dramatically under his leadership. In 1975 the business had grossed $3 million; ten years later it had revenues of $25 million and provided a full line of advertising services. The company was divided into three departments (Creative, Media, and Account Executive), each of which had about 12 employees. Tom Daner credited much of the company's success to the many new people he had hired, especially a group with M.B.A.s who had developed new marketing strategies based on more thorough market and consumer analyses. Most decisions, however, were made by a five-person executive committee consisting of Tom Daner, the Senior Account Manager, and the three department heads. As owner-president, Tom's view tended to color most decisions, producing what one of the members called a "benevolent dictatorship." Tom himself was an enthusiastic, congenial, intelligent, and widely read person. During college he had considered becoming a missionary priest but had changed his mind and was now married and the father of three daughters. His personal heroes included Thomas Merton, Albert Schweitzer, and Tom Dooley.

When Tom Daner presented the Crako deal to his Executive Committee, he found they did not share his misgivings. The other Committee members felt that Daner Associates should give Crako exactly the kind of ad Crako wanted: one with a heavy content of violence. Moreover, the writers and artists in the Creative Department were enthused with the prospect of letting their imaginations loose on the project, several feeling that they could easily produce an attention-grabbing ad by "out-violencing" current television programming. The Creative Department, in fact, quickly produced a copy-script that called for videos showing the helicopter "flying out of the sky with machine guns blazing" at a jungle village below. This kind of ad, they felt, was exactly what they were being asked to produce by their client, Crako Industries.

But after viewing the copy, Tom Daner refused to use it. They should produce an ad, he insisted, that would meet their client's needs but that would also meet the guidelines of the national networks. The ad should not glorify violence and war but should somehow support cooperation and family values. Disappointed and somewhat frustrated, the Creative Department went back to work. A few days later they presented a second proposal: an ad that would show the toy helicopter flying through the family room of a home as a little boy plays with it; then the scene shifts to show the boy on a rock rising from the floor of the family room; the helicopter swoops down and picks up the boy as though rescuing him from the rock where he had been stranded. Although the Creative Department was mildly pleased with their attempt, they felt it was too "tame." Tom liked it, however, and a version of the ad was filmed.

A few weeks later Tom Daner met with Mike Teal and his team and showed them the film. The viewing was not a success. Teal turned down the ad. Referring to the network regulations, which other toy advertisements were breaking as frequently as motorists broke the 55 mile per hour speed law, he said, "That commercial is going only 55 miles an hour when I want one that goes 75." If the next version was not "tougher and meaner," Crako Industries would be forced to look elsewhere.

Disappointed, Tom Daner returned to the people in his Creative Department and told them to go ahead with designing the kind of ad they had originally wanted: "I don't have any idea what else to do."

In a short time the Creative Department had an ad proposal on his desk that called for scenes showing the helicopter blowing up villages. Shortly afterwards a small set was constructed depicting a jungle village sitting next to a bridge stretching over a river. The ad was filmed using the jungle set as a background.

When Tom saw the result he was not happy. He decided to meet with his Creative Department and air his feelings. "The issue here," he said, "is basically the issue of violence. Do we really want to present toys as instruments for beating up people? This ad is going to promote aggression and violence. It will glorify dominance and do it with kids who are terrifically impressionable. Do we really want to do this?" The members of the Creative Department, however, responded that they were merely giving their client what the client wanted. That client, moreover, was an important account. The client wanted an aggressive "macho" ad, and that was what they were providing. The ad might violate the regulations of the television networks, but there were ways to get around the networks. Moreover, they said, every other advertising firm in the business was breaking the limits against violence set by the networks. Tom made one last try: why not market the toy as an adventure and fantasy toy? Film the ad again, he suggested, using the same jungle backdrop. But instead of showing the helicopter shooting at a burning village, show it flying in to rescue people from the burning village. Create an ad that shows excitement, adventure, and fantasy, but no aggression. "I was trying," he said later, "to figure out a new way of approaching this kind of advertising. We have to follow the market or we can go out of business trying to moralize to the market. But why not try a new approach? Why not promote toys as instruments that expand the child's imagination in a way that is positive and that promotes cooperative values instead of violence and aggression?"

A new film version of the ad was made, now showing the helicopter flying over the jungle set. Quick shots and heightened background music give the impression of excitement and danger. The helicopter flies dramatically through the jungle and over a river and bridge to rescue a boy from a flaming village. As lights flash and shoot haphazardly through the scene the helicopter rises and escapes into the sky. The final ad was clearly exciting and intense. And it promoted saving of life instead of violence against life.

It was clear when the final version was shot, however, that it would not clear the network censors. Network guidelines require that sets in children's ads must depict things that are within the reach of most children so that they do not create unrealistic expectations. Clearly the elaborate jungle set (which cost $25,000 to construct) was not within the reach of most children, and consequently most children would not be able to recreate the scene of the ad by buying the toy. Moreover, network regulations stipulate that in children's ads scenes must be filmed with normal lighting that does not create undue intensity. Again clearly the helicopter ad, which created excitement by using quick changes of light and fast cuts, did not fall within these guidelines.

After reviewing the film Tom Daner reflected on some last-minute instructions Crako's sales manager had given him when he had been shown the first version of the ad: The television ad should show things being blown up by the guns of the little helicopter and perhaps even some blood on the fuselage of the toy; the ad had to be violent. Now Tom had to make a decision.

NOTE

1. Although the events described in this case are real, all names of the individuals and the companies involved are fictitious; in addition, several details have been altered to disguise the identity of participants.

QUESTIONS

1. Should he risk the account by submitting only the rescue mission ad? Or should he let Teal also see the ad that showed the helicopter shooting up the village, knowing that he would probably prefer that version if he saw it?

2. And was the rescue mission ad really that much different from the ad that showed the shooting of the village?

3. Did it matter that the rescue mission ad still violated some of the network regulations?

4. What if he offered Teal only the rescue mission ad and Teal accepted the "rescue approach" but demanded he make it more violent; should he give in?

5. And should Tom risk launching an ad campaign that was based on this new untested approach?

6. What if the ad failed to sell the Crako toy?

7. Was it right to experiment with a client's product, especially a product that was so important to the future of the client's business?

CASE 8.2
Advertising at Better Foods
Rogene A. Buchholz

The Better Foods Corporation had been producing a cereal that tasted good and was nutritious for children as well as adults. When first introduced, the product captured a significant share of the market and had held this market share for several years. The company did not tout the health benefits of its cereal because of regulations that prevented companies from making such claims. Thus, its advertisements stressed the taste features of the product as well as other characteristics such as crispiness that might appeal to consumers.

When the government relaxed restrictions on making health claims, the company's competitors

From Rogene A. Buchholz, *Business, Environment, and Public Policy* (Englewood Cliffs, NJ: Prentice Hall, 1995).

began to tout the benefits their cereals had on cholesterol levels as well as other areas of health that were of concern to consumers. The companies knew many of these claims were misleading to consumers because they implied that eating regular amounts of the cereal would have such health benefits. Actually, consumers would have to consume prodigious amounts of cereals to receive any such benefits. But consumers were not made aware of this fact and were beginning to be influenced by all the hype about health benefits of these cereals.

Better Foods Corporation experienced its first drop in market share in several years because of this new type of advertising. As an employee in charge of the advertising program, you have been asked to come up with a new advertising campaign that will stress the nutritious aspects of the company's product. This assignment puts you in something of a bind, as you find some of the outrageous claims being made by your competitors offensive from a moral standpoint. Yet, if you don't do the same, the sales of your company's product may continue to decline and your job itself may be in jeopardy.

QUESTIONS

1. What is the purpose of advertising in a free market society? Are there minimum standards of honesty that should be adhered to, or are advertisers free to do whatever the market will bear? How can consumers tell the outrageous health claims from honest ones so they can make a reasonable decision?

2. What advertising strategy should Better Foods adopt? Should it follow the lead of its competitors? Could it point out the misleading advertising its competitors are doing? Should it advertise more honestly and take the moral high ground even if it leads to a further decrease in sales?

CASE 8.3
Advertising's Image of Women
Joseph R. Desjardins and John J. McCall

It has been estimated that U.S. children between the ages of two and five watch an average of 30 hours of television each week. At this rate, the average young person will watch some 350,000 television commercials by the end of high school. Given all forms of advertising (magazines, newspapers, packaging, radio, television) the average American will have seen some 50 million commercials by age 60. Thus advertising is inescapable in our culture, and its socializing impact cannot be ignored. Ads not only describe products but also present images, values, and goals; they portray certain concepts of normalcy and sexuality, and they promote certain types of self-images. Advertising not only aims to provide information to consumers but also aims to motivate them. What images of women does it present, and what motivations does it appeal to?

Many ads seek to motivate women by suggesting that they are inadequate without a particular product. Cosmetic ads purvey an ideal form of female beauty—a form that is unattainable. Women are portrayed as having no facial wrinkles, no lines, no blemishes—indeed no pores. If you do not look like this, the ads suggest, you are not beautiful, and since no one (including the model) really looks like this, women need cosmetics to look beautiful. Beauty thus results

From Joseph R. Desjardins and John J. McCall, *Contemporary Issues in Business Ethics*, 2nd ed. (Belmont, CA: Wadsworth, 1990).

from products and not from the woman herself. Advertising tells women that they should change their age (the "little-girl look"), weight, bust size, hair color, eye color, complexion—and even their smell. In many ads a woman's worth is measured not by her intelligence or her character or even her natural appearance. A woman's worth is measured by how closely she approaches an ideal created by an advertising agency.

Many ads also portray women as inferior to other women and to men. Women are seen as engaged in a constant competition with other women for the attention of men. When they are pictured with men, women are often shown as clinging to the male, as passive, as submissive. Men are seen in control, active, and dominant.

Besides feelings of inadequacy, many ads also use guilt to motivate women. The "housewife" is constantly being chided because the laundry is not as white nor does it smell as clean as the neighbor's. Her dishes have spots, her meals are unappealing, her floors and furniture have "wax buildup," and her clothes are out of style. Even when women are

shown in the more realistic setting of worker rather than homemaker, feelings of guilt and inadequacy are still reinforced. The working woman is portrayed as a superwoman who harmonizes perfectly the roles of career woman, mother, wife, and homemaker. Despite all of these demands, the woman still looks like a model. In those few cases where the harmony breaks down, the woman is shown as being responsible for the breakdown or in need of drugs to cope with the stress. On the other hand, men are seldom seen as responsible for cooking, cleaning, and child care, or in need of drugs in order to cope.

QUESTIONS

1. What kind of influence has advertising had on your own views of beauty, attractiveness, sexuality?

2. How does advertising influence our understanding of social role based on gender?

3. To what degree have your family, friends, and classmates been socialized by advertising?

CASE 8.4

Hucksters in the Classroom

William H. Shaw and Vincent Barry

Increased student loads, myriad professional obligations, and shrinking school budgets have sent many public school teachers scurrying for teaching materials to facilitate their teaching.

They don't have to look far. Into the breach has stepped business, which is ready, willing, and able to provide current print and audiovisual materials for classroom use. These activities and industry-supplied teaching aids are advertised in educational journals, distributed to school boards, and showcased at educational conventions. The Dr. Pepper Company, for example, displays at such conventions a recipe

booklet titled *Cooking with Dr. Pepper*. Each recipe includes sugar-filled Dr. Pepper soda.

One collective tack taken by the business community has been the ABC Education Program of American Industry, whose annual publication, *Resourcebook*, consists of product-specific "sponsored pages" or ads with accompanying teacher guide sheets. Food and toiletry products are featured, as in the following:

A is for AGREE: the Creme Rinse and Conditioner that helps the greasies.

From William H. Shaw and Vincent Barry, *Moral Issues in Business*, 5th ed. (Belmont, CA: Wadsworth, 1992).

C is for COCONUT: a tantalizing tropical treat from Peter Paul candies.

E is for EFFECTIVE double deodorant system in Irish Spring (soap).

Advertising space in *Resourcebook* doesn't come cheap: A single ad can run as much as $30,000. But ABC official Art Sylvie thinks it's worth it. After all, he asks, where else are manufacturers going to get such widespread and in-depth product exposure? He has a point: About 2.7 million or 35 percent of all junior high school students in the United States participate in the ABC program, not to mention their 95,000 teachers.

An integral part of the ABC program is an annual essay-writing contest. Essays must deal with some aspect of a product in *Resource-book*—its production and marketing, the history or importance of an industry to a community or nation, and so on. To be eligible, entries must be signed by a teacher and include a product label or reasonable facsimile. Student writers can earn up to $50 for entering.

The people at ABC say they want to reflect the positive aspects of the world outside the classroom. And they're convinced that the way to do it is through depicting the wonders and genius of industry. "Thus," says researcher Sheila Harty, "history is taught in terms of 'innovative industrial genius,' as students write their essays on the value of soft drinks (C is for Canada Dry) or the production of tires (G is for Goodyear)."

Evidently teachers go for corporate freebies with all the gusto of a softball player at a company picnic. In a survey of its members, the National Educational Association found that about half its members were using industry audiovisual materials and the ten resource guides published annually by Educators Progress Services (EPS). A cursory look at the guides suggests that the offerings are comprehensive and impartial. A closer look reveals that most are privately, not publicly, sponsored.

Some people think corporate-sponsored teaching materials do more than fill curriculum needs. They are also public relations gambits. Thus, in his book *Corporate Response to Urban Crisis*, professor of sociology Ken Neubeck writes:

Corporations must continually respond to problems which they had a hand in creating in the first place. From this perspective, corporate social responsibility becomes a defensive strategy to be employed whenever the social and political climate become hostile to the active pursuit of corporate economic goals. It is a strategy of "enlightened self-interest."

Corporate America's latest and most dramatic venture into the classroom, however, goes beyond a defensive public relations strategy. In 1989, Whittle Communications began beaming into high schools in six cities its controversial Channel One, a television newscast for high school students, and by June 1991 the number of schools receiving Channel One had grown to 8,600. Although Whittle has grander plans for the future, the broadcasts at present are twelve minutes long—ten minutes of news digest with slick graphics and two minutes of commercials for Levi's jeans, Gillette razor blades, Head & Shoulders shampoo, Snickers candy bars, and other familiar products.

The schools in the program receive thousands of dollars worth of free electronic gadgetry, including television monitors, satellite dishes, and video recorders. And students seem to like the program. "It was very interesting and it appeals to our age group," says student Angelique Williams. "One thing I really liked was the reporters were our own age. They kept our attention."

But Whittle Communications, and interested competitors like Turner Broadcasting and the Discovery Channel, formed in Maryland by four large cable operators, have more in mind than simply making the news interesting to students like Angelique. The prospect of being able to deliver a captive and narrowly targeted audience to its customers promises to be breathtakingly profitable—so profitable, in fact, that advertisers on Channel One pay $150,000 for each thirty seconds of commercial time.

That captive audience is just what worries the critics. Peggy Charren of Action for Children's Television calls the project a "great big, gorgeous Trojan horse. . . . You're selling the children to the advertisers. You might as well auction off the rest of the school day to the highest bidders." This development worries many educators, and New York and

New Jersey have banned Channel One and its potential clones from public classrooms.

On the other hand, Principal Rex Stooksbury of Central High School in Knoxville, which receives Channel One, takes a different view. "This is something we see as very, very positive for the school," he says. And as student Danny Diaz adds, "we're always watching commercials" anyway.

QUESTIONS

1. What explains industry's thrust into education? Is it consistent with the basic features of capitalism?

2. What moral issues, if any, are involved in the affiliation between education and commercial interests?

3. Do you think students have a "moral right" to an education free of commercial indoctrination?

CASE 8.5

Marketing Malt Liquor

Tom L. Beauchamp and Norman E. Bowie

During the summer of 1991, the surgeon general of the United States and advocacy groups led by the Center for Science in the Public Interest (CSPI) launched a campaign to remove G. Heileman Brewing Company's malt liquor PowerMaster from store shelves. The LaCrosse, Wisconsin-based brewer had experienced a series of financial setbacks. In January 1991 the company filed for protection from creditors in a New York bankruptcy court, claiming to be "struggling under a huge debt load" (Alix Freedman, "Heileman Will Be Asked to Change Potent Brew's Name," *The Wall Street Journal*, June 20, 1991, p. B1). In an attempt to reverse its financial decline, Heileman introduced PowerMaster with a 5.9 percent alcohol content. Most malt liquors (defined by law as beers with alcohol levels above 4 percent) have a 5.5 percent average content, as compared with the typical 3.5 percent alcohol level of standard beers.

PowerMaster came under fire from both anti-alcohol and African-American activists. These groups charged that Heileman had created the name and the accompanying advertising campaign, which featured a black male model, with the intent of targeting young black men, who consume roughly one-third of all malt liquors. U.S. Surgeon General Antonia Novello joined the Heileman critics, calling the PowerMaster marketing campaign insensitive. Citing the economic burden that a legal contest to retain the brand name would entail, the company discontinued the product. However, beer industry executives and members criticized the government's role in the controversy. One newspaper columnist cited race as the critical factor in the campaign to remove PowerMaster, noting that the "It's the power" advertising slogan used in the marketing of Pabst Brewing Co.'s Olde English 800 malt liquor had gone unchallenged. James Sanders, president of the Washington, DC-based Beer Institute, contended that the government focused on the PowerMaster label to avoid having to focus on other factors such as unemployment and poverty, the real problems that the black community confronts.

QUESTIONS

1. Would it be deceptive or manipulative advertising to call your beer "PowerMaster" and to use black male models?

2. Is it ethically insensitive for a company to target a specific market identified by race and gender?

From Tom L. Beauchamp and Norman E. Bowie, *Ethical Theory and Business*, 7th ed. (Englewood Cliffs, NJ: Prentice Hall, 2004), p. 465.

CASE 8.6
Energy Drinks, Do They Really Work?
Scott Croker

For many people, no day can start without a healthy dose of caffeine. Those looking for an edge by chugging an energy drink may be disappointed to find out there is no proof these drinks work as advertised.

The best example is Red Bull, a company that promises their drink "gives you wings." Promises like that have turned energy drinks in the fastest growing market in the beverage industry. In 2012, energy drink sales rose to $10 billion.

Studies are now beginning to show that all the hoopla may be overblown. Dr. Roland Griffiths, a researcher at John Hopkins University who has spent years studying energy drinks, believes these companies choose to market this way to sell the product:

"These are caffeine delivery systems. They don't want to say this is equivalent to a NoDoz because that is not a very sexy sales message."

Associate Professor at Minnesota State University, Dr. Robert W. Pettitt, says:

"If you had a cup of coffee you are going to affect metabolism in the same way."

With doubt placed behind all the promises, the *New York Times* is reporting that Democratic Representative of Massachusetts Edward J. Markey has asked the government to investigate the industry's marketing claims.

Markey believes that, by marketing their products as providing benefits beyond caffeine like a mental edge, energy drink companies are able to charge premium prices for their products.

The European Food and Safety Authority has published studies that conclude that the effects that energy drinks provide are equal to those of the caffeine that coffee provides.

The Food and Drug Administration is even placing energy drink companies under the microscope after a series of caffeine-related deaths.

At the same time, Red Bull claims on its own website that more than 2,500 reports have been published about taurine, its main stimulant, and its physiological effects.

QUESTIONS

1. What's the difference between an energy drink and a caffeine pill?

2. Should energy-drink manufacturers be allowed to claim that their products do anything? What can they claim?

CHAPTER QUESTIONS

1. Explain how advertising may influence autonomy. Are there ways that advertising creates freedom? How would you regulate advertising, if you would regulate it at all?

2. Is some level of deception necessary or inevitable in all sales? What would a perfectly transparent sales pitch look like? Would it persuade anyone? What are the duties of truthfulness of advertisers and salespeople? And how much product information do we really want or need?

From Scott Croker in The Inquisitr, January 2, 2013.

9

Things Fall Apart

Product Liability and Consumers

Introduction

During a brief strike at your company, all the managers—regardless of their status or position—are farmed out to the various company functions that are normally handled by the striking employees. You are put in charge of the walk-in Complaint Department. The second day, a fellow walks in with one of your company's products, mangled almost beyond recognition. It is immediately obvious to you that the consumer has misunderstood the assembly instructions, and his rambling explanation confirms it. You tell him, politely, that you think that this is what happened, but he, in turn, gets irritated and a bit abusive. He threatens to sue. You are not used to this sort of behavior, and you are getting pretty irritated yourself. You think of a number of terse and sarcastic responses, but you keep your cool and some semblance of a smile. Your manager has told you to handle all cases as best you can and has given you a free hand to give refunds or replace products at your discretion. But there is no advice or policy about what to do when a customer abuses the product through stupidity or incompetence. In your view, should the company honor the complaints of this customer? Or should you (politely) tell him what he should do?

"Sooner or later, life makes philosophers of us all" wrote minor French philosopher Maurice Riseling. In the same vein, "Shit Happens" is the crude philosophical message of one of the ruder bumper stickers you see around town these days. "Accidents happen," the more polite way of putting the same point, is an inescapable part of business life. Even high-quality products break. Good intentions get frustrated. It would be good and useful experience for every manager and employee, in whatever industry, to spend a few days working in the Complaint Department. (In the most trusted corporations, every person in the company is, in effect, a mini-Complaint Department, responsible for making good on the company's claims and liabilities.) The aim of a business, we are told, is to make a profit by selling high-quality products at a reasonable price. But this makes it sound as if most business transactions are one-shot deals, without an aftermath, sort of like buying something on eBay or at a garage sale. But most business is not like this. It involves multiple transactions, often over a prolonged period. (It is often pointed out that getting a new customer costs a business ten times what it costs to retain an old one.) It thus involves the building of relationships, and this means not just continuing to provide high-quality products and services, but "making good" when they go wrong. How a business responds to flaws and failure, whether or not the company is strictly responsible, can fix the fate of a business relationship. A dissatisfied consumer will end his or her relationship and, even after many years, cease to do business with the company. The defensive response that we hear too often, "so what d'ya want me to do about it?" signals the end of many business relationships.

Businesses are responsible for what happens because of their operations and products. The extent and nature of that responsibility depends on the product, the situation, the extent of the damage caused, the character of the company, the consumer, and the community. If something bad happens because an already-hated company or industry does something wrong, the reaction will be much more ferocious than when a well-loved local business makes a mistake. Sometimes, the mistake in question is a broken or flawed product. Sometimes, as was described earlier, the mistake is the consumer's, not the company's at all, but, nevertheless, the company has to deal with it. Sometimes the harm done is inherent to the product itself. No one any longer pretends that smoking doesn't cause cancer and all sorts of other horrid diseases, but there is still considerable controversy surrounding the selling and marketing of tobacco products. An important question is to what extent the consumer is a fully responsible agent, which is why marketing to teenagers is so much in focus. Sometimes the harm is not from the product, but from the production process, for example, when a manufacturing process causes severe pollution or building a new factory strains the infrastructure of a small community. Sometimes the potential harm of a product or a line of products is just not known, for instance, the new bioengineered foods or the radiation from cell phones. But after the fact, companies may still be liable, as evidenced by the still-lingering asbestos-poisoning cases from decades ago.

Complicating the basic observation that most people consider companies to be responsible for their products and services are a number of issues that are both basic to human psychology and emergent in the new world of tort law and strict liability. On the human psychology side, there is the fact that when something goes wrong, people want to *blame* someone. Thus, the relationship between company and consumer when something goes wrong often starts on a confrontational, if not hostile, note, and the first concern of any wise company or agent of the company is to defuse the accusations of blame and re-present the situation as a shared problem. On the side of tort law, there has been a ballooning—especially in America—of product liability and malpractice cases and verdicts. Some of these verdicts have been well publicized and quite understandably strike fear in the hearts of anyone who tries to supply products or services to the public. Some strike most people as ridiculous—the original multi-million-dollar award to the woman who spilled McDonald's hot coffee on herself (the award was considerably reduced on appeal), but others, for instance, when medical products have caused serious illnesses and deaths, do not strike most people as ridiculous. Deterring such irresponsibility, of course, is why the plaintiffs' attorneys defend the current system of sometimes-huge verdicts. It is not enough to punish an allegedly wrong-doing company (when it is usually possible to absorb the verdict as just another cost of doing business). The aim is to put the company out of business.

Further complicating the emerging portrait of the tort system is the concept of "strict liability." Most people accept the idea that when someone does something wrong or causes harm that could or should have been avoided, he or she should be held responsible. But strict liability bypasses that commonsense practice and holds companies responsible—at least financially responsible—even in the absence of any argument that they could have or should have avoided the harm in question. Thus, it has become common practice for plaintiffs to sue not only those who are immediately responsible for a harm, but those who are simply in the chain of causation. For instance, after an automobile accident, one might expect the wrongful or careless driver to be sued. But current law allows for the pursuit of the company that manufactured the car as well, even if there was no design flaw that contributed to the accident. Feeding this practice is the notion of "deep pockets," the idea that those who are immediately responsible may not have funds to pay any substantial award, but someone down the line may well have the resources to do so. It is, in part, because of this practice, but also the enormous size of some of the recent awards, that tort law has been declared a kind of "crisis" by many in the business community.

In this chapter, we explore a family of issues surrounding the concepts of risk and responsibility, both on an individual and on a corporate level, and their effects on society as a whole. The issues are economic, to be sure, but they also have a great deal to do with fairness and our attitudes toward life. Accordingly, they are of interest to both the law and philosophy and the basic question of how much risk are we willing to take in our lives. Economically, on the one hand, there is the need to provide recourse for consumers and communities who are hurt by business practices and products and to deter and punish companies that act irresponsibly. On the other hand, the cost of litigation and the irresponsible use of litigation do indeed hurt innocent businesses and compromises the free enterprise system. In the readings that follow, we take a look at some of the situations that are most in the news and both some of the charges against the tort system and the arguments for it. We start with a selection from Peter Huber's polemical book on the liability crisis and the need for tort reform, which has now become a major campaign by many prominent politicians. The numbers are still in dispute, but the seriousness of the problem is very much on the national agenda.

In response to Huber, we offer different perspectives on the problem, including various considerations about both the difficulties of risk assessment and fairness. John Nesmith discusses the difficulty of calculating risks in his "Calculating Risks: It's Easier Said Than Done." From inside the insurance industry, Stanley J. Modic explains "How We Got into This Mess." Henry Fairlie chastizes us all for failing to acknowledge the role of risks in our lives in his "Fear of Living," and former Chief Justice Warren E. Burger reflects on the situation of "Too Many Lawyers, Too Many Suits" in *The New York Times* (1991). We focus on one of the most publicized liability cases in the past several decades, the case of the once-popular Ford Pinto, which exploded on impact because of a fixable design flaw. Mark Dowie presents the original case in his "Pinto Madness," from *Mother Jones* in 1977, but philosopher and business ethicist Patricia Werhane urges us to be cautious in considering such cases. She compares the Pinto case with the classic Japanese movie, *Rashomon*, in which we get four different accounts of a murder and no clear resolution in favor of any one of them. Judith Jarvis Thomson shows many of the complications that arise when we examine more closely the relationship between harm, liability, and how harm is caused. In the cases, you will be asked to examine more examples of liability and the law. Finally, Bob Sullivan shows that the "annoying fine print" that is supposed to protect companies from consumer lawsuits may not even be legal.

Peter Huber | Liability

Peter W. Huber is a lawyer, a Senior Fellow of the Manhattan Institute for Policy Research, and the author of *Liability*.

It is one of the most ubiquitous taxes we pay, now levied on virtually everything we buy, sell, and use. The tax accounts for 30 percent of the price of a stepladder and over 95 percent of the price of childhood vaccines. It is responsible for one-quarter of the price of a ride on a Long Island tour bus and one-third of the price of a small airplane. It will soon cost large municipalities as much as they spend on fire or sanitation services.

Some call it a safety tax, but its exact relationship to safety is mysterious. It is paid on many items that are risky to use, like ski lifts and hedge trimmers, but it weighs even more heavily on other items whose whole purpose is to make life safer. It adds only a few cents to a pack of cigarettes, but it adds more to the price of a football helmet than the cost of making it. The tax falls especially hard on prescription drugs, doctors, surgeons, and all things medical. Because of the tax, you cannot deliver a baby with medical assistance in Monroe County, Alabama. You cannot buy several contraceptives certified to be safe and effective by the Food and Drug Administration (FDA), even though available substitutes are more dangerous or less effective. If you have the stomach upset known as hyperemesis, you cannot buy the pill that is certified as safe and effective against it. The tax has orphaned various drugs that are invaluable for treating rare but serious diseases. It is assessed against every family that has a baby, in the amount of about $300 per birth, with an obstetrician in New York City paying $85,000 a year.

Because of the tax, you cannot use a sled in Denver city parks or a diving board in New York City schools. You cannot buy an American Motors "CJ" Jeep or a set of construction plans for novel airplanes from Burt Rutan, the pioneering designer of the *Voyager*. You can no longer buy many American-made brands of sporting goods, especially equipment for amateur contact sports such as hockey and lacrosse. For a while, you could not use public transportation in the city of St. Joseph, Missouri, nor could you go to jail in Lafayette County in the same state. Miami canceled plans for an experimental railbus because of the tax. The tax has curtailed Little League and fireworks displays, evening concerts, sailboard races, and the use of public beaches and ice-skating rinks. It temporarily shut down the famed Cyclone at the Astroland amusement park on Coney Island.

The tax directly costs American individuals, businesses, municipalities, and other government bodies at least $80 billion a year, a figure that equals the total profits of the country's top 200 corporations. But many of the tax's costs are indirect and unmeasurable, reflected only in the tremendous effort, inconvenience, and sacrifice Americans now go through to avoid its collection. The extent of these indirect costs can only be guessed at. One study concluded that doctors spend $3.50 in efforts to avoid additional charges for each $1 of direct tax they pay. If similar multipliers operate in other areas, the tax's hidden impact on the way we live and do business may amount to a $300 billion dollar annual levy on the American economy.

The tax goes by the name of *tort liability*. It is collected and disbursed through litigation. The courts alone decide just who will pay, how much, and on what timetable. Unlike better-known taxes, this one was never put to a legislature or a public referendum, debated at any length in the usual public arenas, or approved by the president or by any state governor. And although the tax ostensibly is collected for the public benefit, lawyers and other middlemen pocket more than half the take.

From Peter Huber, *Liability* (New York: Basic Books, 1990), pp. 3–39. Reprinted with permission.

The tort tax is a recent invention. Tort law has existed here and abroad for centuries, of course. But until quite recently it was a backwater of the legal system, of little importance in the wider scheme of things. For all practical purposes, the omnipresent tort tax we pay today was conceived in the 1950s and set in place in the 1960s and 1970s by a new generation of lawyers and judges. In the space of twenty years they transformed the legal landscape, proclaiming sweeping new rights to sue. Some grew famous and more grew rich selling their services to enforce the rights that they themselves invented. But the revolution they made could never have taken place had it not had a component of idealism as well. Tort law, it is widely and passionately believed, is a public-spirited undertaking designed for the protection of the ordinary consumer and worker, the hapless accident victim, the "little guy." Tort law as we know it is a peculiarly American institution. No other country in the world administers anything remotely like it.

FROM CONSENT TO COERCION

Tort law is the law of accidents and personal injury. The example that usually comes to mind is a two-car collision at an intersection. The drivers are utter strangers. They have no advance understanding between them as to how they should drive, except perhaps an implicit agreement to follow the rules of the road. Nor do they have any advance arrangement specifying who will pay for the damage. Human nature being what it is, the two sides often have different views on both these interesting questions. Somebody else has to step in to work out rights and responsibilities. This has traditionally been a job for the courts. They resolve these cases under the law of *torts* or civil wrongs.

But the car accident between strangers is comparatively rare in the larger universe of accidents and injuries. Just as most intentional assaults involve assailants and victims who already know each other well, most unintended injuries occur in the context of commercial acquaintance—at work, on the hospital operating table, following the purchase of

an airplane ticket or a home appliance. And while homicide is seldom a subject of advance understanding between victim and assailant, unintentional accidents often are. More often than not, both parties to a transaction recognize there is some chance of misadventure, and prudently take steps to address it beforehand.

Until quite recently, the law permitted and indeed promoted advance agreement of that character. It searched for understandings between the parties and respected them where found. Most accidents were handled under the broad heading of *contract*—the realm of human cooperation—and comparatively few relegated to the dismal annex of tort, the realm of unchosen relationship and collision. The old law treated contract and tort cases under entirely different rules, which reflected this fairly intuitive line between choice and coercion.

Then, in the 1950s and after, a visionary group of legal theorists came along. Their leaders were thoughtful, well-intentioned legal academics at some of the most prestigious law schools, and judges on the most respected state benches. They were the likes of the late William Prosser, who taught law at Hastings College, John Wade, Professor of Law at Vanderbilt University, and California Supreme Court Justice Roger Traynor. They are hardly household names, but considering the impact they had on American life they should be. Their ideas, eloquence, and persistence changed the common law as profoundly as it had ever been changed before. For short, and in the absence of a better term, we will refer to them as the founders of modern tort law, or just the *Founders*. If the name is light-hearted, their accomplishments were anything but.

The Founders were to be followed a decade or two later by a much more sophisticated group of legal economists, most notably Guido Calabresi, now Dean of the Yale Law School, and Richard Posner of the University of Chicago Law School and now a federal judge on the Seventh Circuit Court of Appeals. There were many others, for economists seem to be almost as numerous as lawyers, and the application of economic theory to tort law has enjoyed mounting popularity in recent years as tort law has itself become an industry. An economist, it has been said, is someone who observes what is happening in practice and goes off to study whether it is possible in theory. The new tort economists were entirely true to that great tradition. Indeed, they carried it a step forward, concluding that the legal revolution that had already occurred was not only possible but justified and necessary. Mustering all the dense prose, arcane jargon, and elaborate methodology that only the very best academic economists muster, they set about proving on paper that the whole new tort structure was an efficient and inevitable reaction to failures in the marketplace. Arriving on the scene of the great tort battle late in the day, they courageously congratulated the victors, shot the wounded, and pronounced the day's outcome satisfactory and good.

Like all revolutionaries, the Founders and their followers, in the economics profession and elsewhere, had their own reasons for believing and behaving as they did. Most consumers, they assumed, pay little attention to accident risks before the fact. Ignoring or underestimating risk as they do, consumers fail to demand, and producers fail to supply, as much safety as would be best. As a result, manufacturers, doctors, employers, municipalities, and other producers get away with undue carelessness, and costly accidents are all too frequent. To make matters worse, consumers buy less accident insurance than they really need, so injuries lead to unneeded misery and privation and some victims become public charges.

With these assumptions as their starting point, the new tort theorists concluded that the overriding question that the old law asked—how did the parties agree to allocate the costs of the accident?—was irrelevant or worse. The real question to ask was: How can society best allocate the cost of accidents to minimize those costs (and the cost of guarding against them), and to provide potential victims with the accident insurance that not all of them currently buy or can afford? The answer, by and large, was to make producers of goods and services pay the costs of accidents. A broad rule to this effect, it was argued, can accomplish both objectives. It forces providers to be careful. It also forces consumers to take accident costs into account, not consciously but by paying a safety-adjusted price for everything they buy or do. And it compels the improvident to buy accident insurance, again not directly but through the safety tax. It has a moral dimension too: People should be required to take care before the accident and to help each other afterward, for no other reason than that it is just, right, and proper to insist that they do so.

The expansive new accident tax is firmly in place today. In a remarkably short time, the Founders completely recast a centuries-old body of law in an entirely new mold of their own design. They started sketching out their intentions only in the late 1950s; within two short decades they had achieved virtually every legal change that they originally planned. There were setbacks along the way, of course; the common law always develops in fits and starts, with some states bolder and others more timid, and the transformation of tort law was no exception. But compared with the cautious incrementalism with which the common law had changed in centuries past, an utter transformation over a twenty-year span can fairly be described as a revolution, and a violent one at that.

The revolution began and ended with a wholesale repudiation of the law of contract. Until well into the 1960s, it was up to each buyer to decide how safe a car he or she wanted to buy. Then as now, the major choices were fairly obvious: large, heavy cars are both safer and more expensive; economy cars save money but at some cost in safety. In case after case today, however, the courts struggle to enforce a general mandate that all cars be *crashworthy*. That term is perfectly fluid; it is defined after the accident by jury pronouncements; it is defined without reference to preferences and choices deliberately expressed by buyer and seller before the transaction. A woman's choice of contraceptives was once a matter largely under the control of the woman herself and her doctor, with the FDA in the background to certify the general safety and efficacy of particular drugs or devices. Today tort law has shifted that authority too from the doctor's office to the courtroom. Balancing the risks and benefits of childhood vaccination was once a concern of parents, pediatricians, the FDA, and state health authorities. But here again, the views of the courts have become the driving force in determining what may be bought and sold. Not long ago, workplace safety was something to be decided between employer and employees, often through collective bargaining, perhaps with oversight from federal and state regulators, while compensation for accidents was determined by state workers' compensation laws. Today the courts supervise a free-for-all of litigation that pits employees against both employers and the outside suppliers of materials and equipment, the latter two against each other, and both against their insurers.

What brought us this liability tax, in short, was a wholesale shift from consent to coercion in the law of accidents. Yesterday we relied primarily on agreement before the fact to settle responsibility for most accidents. Today we emphasize litigation after the fact. Yesterday we deferred to private choice. Today it is only public choice that counts, more specifically the public choices of judges and juries. For all practical purposes, contracts are dead, at least insofar as they attempt to allocate responsibility for accidents ahead of time. Safety obligations are now decided through liability prescription, worked out case by case after the accident. The center of the accident insurance world has likewise shifted, from *first-party* insurance chosen by the expected beneficiary, to *third-party* coverage driven by legal compulsion.

STRICT LIABILITY

The old negligence rules had always been open to the reproach of stinginess. With the death of contract, they now promised to be hopelessly cumbersome as well. The prospect of running an ever-growing number of cases through a full postaccident inquest on how all the players had performed was discouraging; the sheer task threatened to overwhelm the courts, and the outcome would too often be compensation deferred or denied altogether. This was most vexing. The Founders had labored hard to cross the high mountains of contractual language, only to find that the valley of tort below was not exactly flowing with milk and honey.

As we saw earlier, their initial response was to rely on the contractual material already at hand, using it to spin out liability through the implied warranty. If the Mammoth Corporation had somehow *promised* to pay for any and all accidents involving its product, everything else was simple. No one had to worry about whether there had been negligence; somewhere or other down there between the lines the contract itself promised payment. The content was novel, but the forms were reassuringly familiar.

For a while, then, the reinterpretation of contract terms sufficed as a basis for inventing liability standards much stricter than negligence. And a while was all the Founders really needed. Most people are eager to believe good news, even when it is too good to be true. The public and press didn't at all mind the idea that manufacturers had suddenly begun promising (tacitly, mind you) to pay for accidents resulting from all defects in their products, regardless of negligence. Within a few years, this legal notion of "strict" producer liability had become familiar and obvious. At that point, several state courts were ready to discard the roundabout legal fictions and take a more direct route to the same result. In 1962, the California Supreme Court led the way.

For Christmas in 1955, William Greenman's wife had bought her husband a Shopsmith, a new power tool that served as a combination saw, drill, and wood lathe. Greenman was making a wooden chalice on his Shopsmith one day when a piece of wood flew out of the machine and struck him on the forehead. He sued the manufacturer, maintaining that "inadequate[ly] set screws were used to hold parts of the machine together so that normal vibrations caused the tailstock of the lathe to move away from the piece of wood being turned, permitting it to fly out of the lathe." No contract claim was possible: Greenman was not the actual buyer of the lathe, and he had failed, in any event, to comply with California contract rules that require timely notice of a pending claim. By 1962, however, when the case reached it, the California Supreme

Court was already growing tired of contracts and all their troublesome formalities and rules. It contemptuously brushed aside the notice requirement as a "booby trap for the unwary." Strict liability, the court bluntly declared, would no longer be rationalized in terms of implied warranties, fictional contracts, or anything of that sort. Product manufacturers would instead be held "strictly liable" to consumers for accidents caused by a "defect in manufacture" of their product.

This was a great leap. The need to find implied warranties and such had been a bothersome and often embarrassing barrier to contractual theories of liability. The need to find negligence had been an equally troublesome barrier to tort theories of liability. Now, at one bound, the courts could leap directly to the desired goal, at least so long as a product defect was at issue.

But there was important work still to be done. Though somewhat obscure on the point, *Greenman* seemed to cover *manufacturing defects*, which are in fact quite rare. *Design defects*, however, were quite another matter, and had not yet been officially incorporated into the new doctrine. So Barbara Evans learned in 1966. Driving her station wagon across an intersection one day, Barbara's husband was broadsided by another car and killed. The 1961 Chevrolet had an X-shaped frame; at the time, other manufacturers still used a box frame. Barbara sued General Motors, claiming misdesign. Her suit was quickly dismissed. "Perhaps it would be desirable to require manufacturers to construct automobiles in which it would be safe to collide," the court of appeals declared, "but that would be a legislative function, not an aspect of the judicial interpretation of existing law." Errors in manufacture were one thing. But in 1966 the courts were not yet ready to examine product design and declare it defective.

Greenman, however, had its own inexorable logic. If General Motors can be held liable for leaving a frame strut loose accidentally, why shouldn't it be liable for leaving it out deliberately? By mid-decade the design defect barrier was beginning to crumble.

David Larsen broke through this last major conceptual wall in 1968, just two years after Barbara

Evans lost her case. His 1963 Chevrolet Corvair collided head on with another car, thrusting the steering column into his head. He sued General Motors, complaining that "the design and placement of the solid steering shaft, which extends without interruption from a point 2.7 inches in front of the leading surface of the front tires to a position directly in front of the driver, exposes the driver to an unreasonable risk of injury from the rearward displacement of that shaft in the event of a left-of-center head-on collision." This time, a federal appeals court was ready to move ahead. Thereafter, the court announced, juries would be free to pin liability on defects in design as well as manufacture.

Like so many other changes in the tort rules, the step from manufacturing defects to design defects was presented as the soul of modesty. But with that simple change the courts plunged into a new and daunting enterprise. To begin with, the takes in design defect cases are much higher. A manufacturing-defect verdict condemns only a single item coming off the assembly line. But a defect of design condemns the entire production, and a loss in one case almost inevitably implies losses in many others. Moreover, design is a much more subtle business than manufacture, and identifying deficiencies is vastly more difficult.

Before long, juries across the country were busy redesigning lawn mowers, electrical switches, glass and plastic bottles, pesticides, and consumer and industrial products of every other description. A product can be defectively designed because a safety device has been omitted (e.g., a paydozer without rearview mirrors) or because certain parts are not as strong as they might have been (e.g., a car roof is not strong enough to withstand a rollover, or the impact of a runaway horse that lands on the roof after a front-end collision). A jury can find that a single-control shower faucet is defective because if one turns it on all the way to one side, it will allow only hot water to spray, or that children's cotton sleepwear is defective because it has no flame-retardant chemicals added. Sears lost a $1.2 million judgment to a man who suffered a heart attack caused (he alleged) by a lawn mower rope that was too hard to pull. The Bolko Athletic Company paid $92,500 for defectively designing the second base on a baseball diamond; a concrete anchor, the jury concluded, was unsafe for amateur-league players. Recent cases have attempted to extend strict liability (at least for the condition rather than the design of a product) to persons who sell used goods, even ordinary citizens selling cars through the classified ads, though so far most courts have declined to take this seemingly logical step.

Drugs and pharmaceutical devices were among the last products to be swept up in design defect litigation. Until well into the 1970s, most courts accepted that potent drugs often have unavoidable side effects, and they declined to repeat the difficult balancing of risks and benefits already conducted by the FDA. But this line was crossed in the end as well. Courts began to find design defects in contraceptive pills (one brand contained more hormone than another, making it both more effective and riskier), vaccines (the live but weakened polio virus is both more effective and more dangerous than the killed virus), morning sickness drugs, and intrauterine devices.

QUESTIONS

1. What is "liability"? How does a business acquire it?
2. What are the limits on liability? How are they justified?

John Nesmith

Calculating Risks: It's Easier Said Than Done

WASHINGTON—What's more dangerous? A terrorism attack involving anthrax or being struck by lightening? A plane trip or a long country drive? In these terror-haunted times, we must constantly balance risks.

We often fear the wrong things and spend money to protect ourselves from lesser evils, says David Ropeik, director of risk communications at Harvard Center for Risk Analysis.

Government and industry together spend more than $30 million a year to deal with hazardous products even though the number of people whose health is at risk from this special kind of garbage is quite low. The annual expenditure on anti-smoking campaigns, on the other hand, is only about $500 million a year, even though smoking is one of the leading preventable causes of death in America.

"This irrational response kills people," Ropeik says. "In a world of finite resources, we can only protect ourselves from so many things."

But fear often is stronger than reason.

Ropeik likes to cite the example of a hiker walking through the woods who sees a dark, crooked shape on the ground. Before he has time to ask himself whether it is a stick or a snake, and then reason that if it is a snake it could be dangerous, he jumps away, impelled by a fear programmed deep in his brain, perhaps even in his genes.

Nerve circuits convey information to the brain's fear center, or amygdala, much faster than other circuits serve the cortex, where thought and rational learning occur, Ropeik says. These messages not only trigger the physical response, but also reinforce the fear itself.

Reprinted by permission of John Nesmith of the Cox News Washington Bureau.

That means to Ropeik that fear and the emotional processes linked to it are more powerful than the rational processes with which we might make more valid assessments of our risks.

In addition to such biological factors, Ropeik says, social psychologists have identified "universal perception factors" that underlie group fears and help shape behavior. Among them are:

- Control vs. no control: We normally fear something more if we are not personally in control of it. Thus, you feel safer driving your own car through several hundred miles of bad traffic than traveling the same distance in an airliner, even though you are safer in the plane.
- Immediate vs. chronic: We are more afraid of something that can kill us suddenly and violently than we are of chronic, long-term dangers.
- Natural vs. manmade: We're less afraid of radiation from the sun than of the radiation from power lines and cell phone towers, even though the risk from the sun is far greater.
- Risk vs. benefit: We find reasons to overlook the risks brought to us by something we like. The acetone in fingernail polish is less fearsome to those who use it than the same chemical encountered in another form.
- Imposed vs. voluntary: Nonsmokers are often fearful of tobacco smoke. Smokers usually aren't.

There's even some risk in assessing risk, at least politically. The Harvard center has been criticized for accepting contributions from government-regulated industries eager to promote any suggestion that their products pose relatively little danger. Thus, the center is controversial with environmental and consumer groups.

Ropeik, who authored "Risk: A Practical Guide for Deciding What's Really Safe and What's Really

What's Risky? Chances of Death?

The annual risks of dying of various causes in the United States:

Heart disease, 1 in 397
Cancer, 1 in 511
Stroke, 1 in 1,699
Accidents (all kinds), 1 in 3,014
Accidents (motor vehicle), 1 in 6,745
Alzheimer's disease, 1 in 5,752
Alcohol (including liver disease), 1 in 6,210
Suicide, 1 in 12,091
Homicide, 1 in 15,440
Food poisoning, 1 in 56,031
Fire, 1 in 82,977
Bicycle accidents, 1 in 376,165
Lightning, 1 in 4,478,159
Bioterrorism attack involving anthrax, 1 in 56,424,800

Harvard Center for Risk Analysis, from U.S. Centers for Disease Control and Prevention data.

Dangerous in the World Around Us," insists that some of our most expensive risks are actually "bogeymen" on which society spends inordinate sums.

"I think some people have used this to advance political or corporate agendas," he said. "Obviously, there are environmental risks that are bigger and demand more attention than we're giving them."

He cited indoor air pollution. Most Americans draw nine out of 10 breaths in indoor environments that are polluted with molds, germs and chemicals, he said.

So, with crooked sticks, solar radiation, acetone, mosquitoes and dirty indoor air surrounding us, what is our biggest risk?

Ropeik hesitated.

"Obesity," he replied. "There is better than a 50–50 chance that any given American is obese, and this causes 300,000 deaths a year. Tobacco causes about 400,000 deaths a year, but only 47 million Americans smoke. They are really neck-and-neck."

QUESTIONS

1. What are the "universal perception factors" that are used in explaining group fear?

2. What are your biggest fears as a consumer? As a citizen? How do they control your behavior?

Stanley J. Modic | # How We Got into This Mess

Stanley J. Modic is a journalist and a member of the Press Club of Cleveland's Hall of Fame. John Anderson is a retired vice president of Allstate Insurance Co.

Product-liability problems continue to vex U.S. industry. Just about everyone concedes that something must be done, but consensus as to a solution remains elusive.

Some accuse the insurance industry of contriving a crisis to justify raising premiums. Others blame the legal profession's obsession with using tort law to extract high settlements.

Just where *does* the fault lie? And where do we go from here? Are legislative curbs needed?

The search for a remedy is mired in confusion. And the confusion stems primarily from the way in which liability insurance and tort law have combined into an organic system which has evolved over the years.

The principal catalysts feed on each other. As the system of tort law has grown and its scope has expanded, the insurance industry has responded by increasing the amounts of coverage it offers and, naturally, its premiums. Each system has prospered, in a sense, from the activities of the other. And, over the years, that has caused the product-liability problem to spiral out of control.

Roy R. Anderson, who retired as a vice president of Allstate Insurance Cos., has pondered this dilemma. As an actuary, a strategic planner, and a futurist, he has extensively analyzed the problems of our society and of the insurance industry. In retirement, he continues his interest in futurism. And, though he readily admits that accurately predicting the future is impossible, he believes that the way to get a fix on the future is to study how our systems are working today and how they got that way.

From Stanley J. Modic, "How We Got into This Mess," *Industry Week*, January 12, 1987.

WHO PAYS?

"It is critical," Mr. Anderson stresses, "to understand that both liability insurance and tort law are organic, man-made systems that operate in accordance with the perceptions, beliefs, and values of human beings—all of which continually are shifting."

As he explains it, the tort system was originally intended to achieve two goals in situations where one person, through negligence, injured another person.

"The first was to heal the victim; the second was to punish the person at fault by making him compensate the victim."

The advent of liability insurance drastically changed things. "No longer was the person at fault punished by having to bear the full cost of compensating the victim," Mr. Anderson explains. "Instead, this 'punishment' was spread across society by means of insurance premiums."

To illustrate how social systems evolve, Mr. Anderson points out that in some respects we are returning to the days when the guilty party had to bear the full burden of compensating the victim. This happens when a person (or corporation) forgoes liability insurance—because it's not available or because the premiums are too high. It also happens when the amount of the plaintiff's award greatly exceeds the amount of liability insurance carried—an increasingly common situation which alarms many manufacturers.

IT'S NOT WORKING

For those individuals and corporations priced out of the insurance market, the system is no longer working. The expansion of the tort system has warped beyond all reason both the financial settlements and the legal definition of what constitutes being "at fault."

"The most invidious and illogical of these distortions has been the increase in awards for punitive damages," Mr. Anderson contends. He feels that if a guilty person is to be punished for behavior that caused injury to another person, that punishment should come in the form of a fine payable to the state, rather than punitive damages awarded in a civil suit to the individual.

"This is especially true," Mr. Anderson asserts, "in the case of a guilty corporation where the fine must be very large before it gets the attention of the wrongdoer. Clearly, such cases should come under the criminal section of the law—with both the corporation and the guilty corporate executives subject to the penalty process."

Other shifts, too, have distorted the legal system. The initial concept that the guilty person had to be 100% at fault and that the victim had to be totally blameless in the cause of the injury has been eroded, Mr. Anderson points out. In addition, the definition of what constitutes an "injury" and the conditions under which a party can be deemed liable have changed; and class-action and cumulative-injury precedents have been established.

WHY IT'S HAPPENING

The reasons for these shifts, Mr. Anderson says, include: The liberality of juries in awarding damages; the attitude of the public toward insurance companies' ability to pay; and public outrage against the questionable behavior of some corporations and professionals.

"In a nutshell, the system of liability insurance has been transformed from a system that originally compensated only blameless victims to a system that is steadily expanding to take care of all injured persons [regardless of fault]," Mr. Anderson claims.

It comes into play in our lives in many ways. The skyrocketing cost of liability insurance impacts the repair of our automobiles and the quality of our health care. It increases the cost of new products being developed—and keeps some of them off the market. More recently, it has even affected civic affairs, Little League baseball, and our leisure hours.

"If you stop to consider how much it is messing up so much of what we do, you have to wonder how we let it get so bad," says Mr. Anderson.

The former insurance executive believes that the tort law-liability insurance system started going sour with the explosion in automobile ownership following World War II. Prior to that time, liability insurance was almost a luxury for the lower and middle classes. Ordinarily, they carried only collision and comprehensive insurance, usually provided by the dealer as part of the financing package, Mr. Anderson explains. But the enactment of financial-responsibility laws shifted liability insurance from a luxury to a necessity.

"Steadily, it became apparent to the plaintiffs' [attorneys] that each time there was an automobile accident, there was a good chance that there was also an injured person—and another person involved who was at fault," Mr. Anderson says. "The existence of the 'contingent fee' provision in the tort system made it possible for the plaintiff's lawyer to finance the lawsuit for his client—and to be rewarded handsomely for his initiative if he won the case."

In terms of coverage—typically $10,000 for bodily injury and $5,000 for property damage—the amount of insurance in force in the 1950s was "peanuts," reflects Mr. Anderson. "But it was enough to support a training ground for the plaintiffs' bar as it learned to expand the scope of the fledgling system."

IMPETUS FROM DETROIT

At the same time, a symbiotic relationship was evolving between the auto-insurance industry and the car manufacturers, Mr. Anderson points out. "With the growth of property-damage liability insurance, together with collision insurance, the automakers knew that adequate money would be available for the repair of the great majority of damaged cars. . . . Typically, the owner of the damaged car has not been concerned about what he was charged for repairs, as long as it was covered by insurance."

This knowledge influenced how auto manufacturers built and priced their cars. The philosophy was: "Keep the price of new cars low to encourage sales and make up the difference on repair and replacement parts," Mr. Anderson notes. "It also occurred to them that it might be in their financial interest to design cars that were easily damaged. For example, look at what Detroit has done to bumpers over the years, designing them to be more like ornaments that

provide little or no protection, thus adding substantially to repair costs."

Mr. Anderson claims that the insurance industry played a useful role in improving the construction of automobile bumpers. "It was the advertising and lobbying efforts of the insurance companies that led to state and federal laws requiring sensible bumpers rather than fragile ornaments."

TWO CRISES

The first major crisis in the tort law/auto insurance system arose in the mid-1970s with the proposal for "no-fault" auto insurance. "In essence, it would have meant the elimination of tort law in the case of auto accidents. It would have been replaced by a 'first-party' system which would compensate the injured parties for medical expenses and economic loss, regardless of fault," the former insurance executive explains.

He recalls that the auto-insurance business was deeply divided on the no-fault issue. Proponents were mainly those carriers writing auto insurance for large corporate clients. Opponents of no-fault were the companies doing business primarily with individuals.

"Unfortunately, what finally emerged from the battle over no-fault was 'modified no-fault,' which included the poorer parts of both systems and ended up costing the public more than the old 'fault' system."

The next crisis in the system occurred with the huge growth in medical-malpractice suits. As Mr. Anderson sees it, the medical profession did "a miserable job" of policing itself. "Incompetent doctors remained at large because medical societies took little action. In those days, doctors operated under their version of the Mafia's *omerta* or 'vow of silence'—which precluded doctors from testifying against each other."

Mr. Anderson credits the plaintiffs' bar and the judicial system for cracking this "vow of silence" and turning the spotlight on the shabby performance of the medical profession—"even though its motives were hardly altruistic."

Cultivating the Market

Initially, the average damage settlements were relatively small, Mr. Anderson points out. Even so, studies indicated that the insurance industry could economically provide higher amounts of coverage. And carriers jumped at the chance to tap a new market; they urged policyholders to buy higher limits on liability coverage.

Although it seemed to be in the best interests of the public, "from a systems standpoint it proved to be ill-advised," Mr. Anderson reflects. "The plaintiffs' bar reacted to the higher limits like a cat to catnip.

"Here again," he says, "it is obvious that the system that has evolved is not the best way to 'monitor' the quality of medical care. The sooner the plaintiffs' bar is removed from the picture, the better."

As Mr. Anderson sees it, the experience in the auto and medical arenas set the stage for the legal profession's pursuit of greener pastures—product liability. "It is in the area of product liability that some of the most significant precedents of tort law have been established and enhanced," he points out. The legal system has accepted new thinking on joint and several liability, punitive damages, class-action suits, and cumulative injury (due, for example, to repeated exposure to a toxic substance).

In product liability the stakes are high. Injury, and the number of people affected, can accumulate over long periods.

Mr. Anderson says the classic case may be asbestosis. "The amount of damages that corporations now have to pay are astronomically so much higher than the direct economic loss that they can bankrupt a company."

A GLOOMY PROSPECT

As bad as the asbestos case has been, it pales in comparison with potential damage claims against companies, or even entire industries, stemming from toxic chemicals or long-term environmental degradation.

"The explosive nature of the present product-liability system is [such] that it will ultimately be beyond the capacity of the insurance business to carry it," Mr. Anderson contends. "The systems are

so out of control that our economy and society can no longer bear the cost."

Mr. Anderson believes that the public, as well as federal and state legislators, recognize that something must be done. The problem, however, transcends the issues of law, insurance, and compensation.

"In fact," he claims, "what we are dealing with is the very value structure of our society." Mr. Anderson warns that change will come slowly, because "the legal fraternity has a great vested interest in the system."

Solutions Coming

But, as bleak as the situation seems today, this futurist sees a light at the end of the tunnel. A start is likely this year; Congress is expected to pass legislation to cap the amount of damages that can be awarded.

That legislation, however, will not solve the basic problem of a tort law-liability insurance system running amok. Nevertheless, Mr. Anderson believes there is reason to hope for a long-range solution. Congressional action, he predicts, will break a logjam and set into motion waves of change that will ripple through other aspects of tort law.

Organic, man-made systems have life cycles and ultimately run their course, Mr. Anderson observes. "The system of liability insurance is well into the stage of decline," he believes.

He thinks that the system of tort law is also in a state of decline. "However, the course of its future and the timing of its demise will differ greatly from that of the insurance system. Because tort law is an important part of the much broader system of civil and criminal law, its future—and its demise—will be tied to its broader parent system," he concludes.

Tort-Law Change

As for tort law, the futurist makes this prediction: The two purposes served under the present system—compensating the injured persons and punishing those at fault—eventually will be served by two different systems.

"The compensation of injured people will be included under a much broader system that will compensate or cure injured persons, regardless of the cause of the injury," he anticipates.

The "punishment" purpose, Mr. Anderson predicts, will be handled under the criminal justice system. "There would be standards of performance required for the various professions; those who failed to adhere to those standards would be punished by their profession—or under criminal law."

The same would apply to manufactured products. "Standards would be established and tests would be required. Manufacturers failing to follow the standards, thereby causing injury, would be punished under criminal law."

QUESTIONS

1. How did we "get into this mess," according to Modic? What is the mess we are in? How does Modic think we can get out of the mess?

2. How did the major crises in the tort law/auto insurance system complicate the issues of liability?

Henry Fairlie | # Fear of Living

Henry Fairlie writes for *The New Republic* magazine.

In January 1967 the first Apollo spacecraft caught fire during a test on the launchpad. Three astronauts were killed. The nation was shocked and horrified, all the more so because the screams and scrambles of the astronauts could be clearly heard. But although there was a congressional hearing, and some delay of the manned flights, the Apollo program went smartly ahead, with the full understanding and support of the nation, and within 18 months Apollo 11 landed on the moon, ahead of the deadline set by John Kennedy. The Apollo disaster was not graven on the public mind as a rebuke to America's confidence in its technology, or taken as the occasion to preach that Americans must learn the limits to their energy and power.

Nineteen years later, the space shuttle Challenger was destroyed before our eyes on television. It was a spectacular tragedy, the result of human miscalculation and technical failure, neither of which should have been present, perhaps, but both of which are understood risks in the still dangerous enterprise of space flight. Yet the prevailing mood in America so panicked NASA that it took almost three years to send up another shuttle. NASA even reached the stage, as members of its staff said, of taking so many precautions that it was in danger of enlarging, instead of diminishing, the possibility of malfunction.

In the 19 years between these tragedies, the idea that our individual lives and the nation's life can and should be risk-free has grown to be an obsession, driven far and deep into American attitudes. Indeed, the desire for a risk-free society is one of the most debilitating influences in America today, progressively enfeebling the economy with a mass of safety regulations and a widespread fear of liability rulings, and threatening to create an unbuoyant and uninventive society. As many studies show, this is strikingly an American phenomenon, one that seems to have taken root in yet another distortion of the philosophy of rights underlying the Constitution, as if the Declaration of Independence had been rewritten to include

From *The New Republic*, January 23, 1989.

freedom from risk among the self-evident rights to life, liberty, and the pursuit of happiness. This morbid aversion to risk calls into question how Americans now envision the destiny of their country.

If America's new timorousness had prevailed among the Vikings, their ships with the bold prows but frail hulls would have been declared unseaworthy. The Norsemen would have stayed home and jogged. Columbus's three tubs would not have been allowed to sail; as it was, one was left wrecked on American shores. The Vikings and Columbus were exploring what was as unknown to them then as our solar system is to us today, and it is not only the practical achievements of such venturing that are frustrated by the desire for a risk-free society. Something of the questing endeavor of the human spirit is also lost. The Vikings made sagas of their explorations, as European and English literature flowered during the great Age of Exploration. There once was, but there is not now, a promise of saga in America. Its literature has retreated into a preoccupation with private anxieties and fretting.

At Three Mile Island, the fail-safe system worked. The power station switched itself off. There was a scare, but no disaster. Yet Three Mile Island in the American mind is an emblem of catastrophe. Nuclear power in America, as in no equivalent industrial or industrializing nation, has been almost paralyzed, although it is the only sufficient, efficient, and *relatively* safe source of energy that can avoid the greater risks of pollution and the "greenhouse effect." Of course there is a risk in nuclear power, and there should be thorough inspections and safeguards. Of course, also, there is such a thing as a level of risk that is unacceptable. But in America the threshold of tolerable risk has now been set so low that the nation is refusing to pay the inevitable costs of human endeavor. Stand beneath the majesty of the Grand Coulee Dam, or gaze up at the marvel of the Brooklyn Bridge—"O Harp and Altar," as Hart Crane sang of it—and count the number of lives lost in their construction. But then feel the power, even the beauty, of both dam and bridge, and weigh the cost of lives against the benefits they have brought.

The origins of the widespread refusal to accept a sometimes high level of risk as a normal and necessary hazard of life lie in the early 1970s. As America lost heart in the prosecution of the war in Vietnam, the energy of the dissenters—the vanguard of the "Me Decade"—turned to lavish care for the environment, the snail darter, and their own exquisite, often imagined, physical and emotional well-being. The simultaneous loss of faith in American technology was part of the same phenomenon; technology, it was observed, not only fouled the environment, but had proved incapable of winning a war against guerrillas in the jungle. And beyond this, of course, has been the growth of the larger belief that science itself has somehow betrayed us, that it promises evil and not beneficence.

This loss of courage and faith has manifested itself in many ways, but it has found its most immediately dangerous expression in tort (liability) law. Tort law is not only threatening to make the economy uncompetitive, it is warping the American legal system and its judicial philosophy. As Peter W. Huber observes in *The Legal Revolution and Its Consequences*, "No other country in the world administers anything like it." Tort law was "set in place in the 1960s and 1970s by a new generation of lawyers and judges. . . . Some grew famous and more grew rich in selling their services to enforce the rights they themselves invented."

In November a court in Albany had seriously to consider a claim for $1 million in damages against New York state, brought by a woman who, while she was sunbathing on the beach in a public park on Long Island, was hit in the neck by a Frisbee being tossed between a nine-year-old boy and a 20-year-old woman. Her lawyer contended that the Frisbee was a "dangerous instrument" that should not have been allowed on the beach. (Since the idea of the Frisbee was taken from the bakery of that name where the workers whizzed pie plates to each other, rather than laboriously carry them, are we to assume that today the Occupational Safety and Health Administration would have stepped in to stop this skilled, efficient, rapid, but clearly "dangerous" method of conveyance?) At least this woman's claim was thrown out: the judge observed that she could have moved to another part of the beach if she feared injury from these alarming flying objects. Consider also the mother who sued a baseball club because her son was injured by a ball fouled back to their seats. It may well be that they had chosen seats there because her son had hopes of capturing a foul ball as a trophy, in which case the risk was known and invited by the mother; in any event, blame cannot be said to lie with the club, the hitter, or the ball. Here we see one pernicious moral effect of America's growing fear of risk: a commensurate diminution of the notion of individual responsibility for one's actions.

Claims of others' liability for our plights are, with the support of judges, lawyers, and juries, producing a "tort tax" on goods and services. They amount to a $300 billion levy on the American economy, observes Huber, that "accounts for 30 percent of the price of a stepladder and 95 percent of the price of childhood vaccines." The development of tort law has been particularly vicious in its effect because of another phenomenon peculiar to the United States—the award of huge punitive damages (as opposed to nominal damages, intended only to compensate the victim for the actual injury inflicted). The flagrant injustice of many of these awards was illustrated in a case brought against the Monsanto Company that sought damages for 65 plaintiffs for alleged personal injuries from one of the company's products used to make wood preservatives. After the longest-running trial in American history, the jury awarded each plaintiff one dollar in nominal damages, but then, "in a burst of tortured reasoning," as Monsanto Chairman Richard J. Mahoney says, awarded $16 million to the plaintiffs in punitive damages.

There is no justification for this. The Supreme Court has recently agreed to hear a case in which the constitutionality of huge punitive damages will be tested. In an earlier case, Justices Antonin Scalia and Sandra Day O'Connor observed that "this grant of wholly standardless discretion to determine the severity of punishment appears inconsistent with due process." Meanwhile, the awards further frustrate, if they are not crushing, the spirit of innovation in American business. The Conference Board in 1988 conducted a survey of chief executive officers. It showed that uncertainty over potential liability had led almost 50 percent to discontinue product lines,

and nearly 40 percent to withhold new products, including beneficial drugs. The fault lies not only with the "wholly standardless discretion" allowed to juries to determine the severity of the punishment, but with the present power of a single jury to decide what conduct is liable for punitive damages.

The result of all this, says Justice Richard Neely of the West Virginia Supreme Court, author of *The Product Liability Mess*, is that "as a state court judge much of my time is devoted to ways to make business pay for everyone else's bad luck." When the step of a stepladder breaks because it was made of defective material, the payment of reasonable damages to the injured party is just. But as anyone with any household experience knows, sometimes a broken stepladder is just a broken stepladder, the result of bad luck; and surely each of us has the individual responsibility to approach any stepladder with some circumspection. The prevailing attitude in America is that people should be safeguarded against not only negligence but bad luck; it has become all too easy for lawyers to manipulate jurors who generally are scientifically ignorant and believe that they can be guaranteed a risk-free society.

One confirmation that the obsessive American aversion to risk is a growth of the last two decades is the proliferation in that time of academic and quasi-academic literature on risk, with such titles as "Public Perceptions of Acceptable Risks as Evidence of Their Cognitive, Technical, and Social Structure." The conclusions of much of this literature were drawn together in 1982 by Mary Douglas and Aaron Wildavsky in *Risk and Culture*, their own still impressive critique of this phenomenon. Among the interesting questions asked by the authors is "Why is asbestos poisoning now seen to be more fearsome than fire," especially when asbestos was introduced and welcomed as a prevention of injury or death by fire? The question is made even more interesting by Mahoney's revelation that Monsanto "abandoned a possible substitute product for asbestos just before commercialization, not because it was unsafe or ineffective, but because a whole generation of liability lawyers had been schooled in asbestos liability theories that could possibly be turned against the substitute." In principle, Douglas and Wildavsky note, a society selects which risks it will worry, and perhaps even legislate, about in the hope of diminishing or eliminating them. But why do Americans seem to be more concerned about the risks of pollution than about the budget deficit, economic stagnation, and even war?

Who are the people who promote the intolerance of risk in contemporary America, and select which risks the society should worry about? It is reasonable and almost certainly correct to assume a link between the attitudes that have led to the slowing of such new and promising industries as space technology and nuclear power, the gross development of liability law and litigation, the concern about environmental pollution, and the finicky attention to one's bodily health, comfort, and even purity. Together they form a syndrome. The people who are environmental extremists are likely also to be exorbitantly fussy about the risks to their bodily purity from a multitude of pollutants, natural and artifical, not much concerned about the progress of the space and nuclear power industries, automatically against manufacturing companies in liability cases, and generally uninterested in creating and maintaining a productive industrial economy.

From such people are drawn the staffs and membership of the special interest groups that have sedulously promoted America's risk aversion. Douglas and Wildavsky counted some 75 national environmental groups alone, and thousands more at state and local levels. By something like sleight of hand they represent themselves as public interest groups, but in fact these risk-averse groups speak for a very clear special interest: those who work not in manufacturing industries, but in the now vast services sector, including government and corporate bureaucracies, and who manufacture nothing. In short, they do not get their hands dirty. So it is easy for them—it does not violate their "class interest"—to be indifferent to creating a productive industrial economy. It is no sweat off their backs if a manufacturer is closed down, and its workers laid off for environmental reasons. The risk-averse groups are drawn from a privileged class.

Since it is in the interest of these groups to multiply regulations and strengthen their control of the economy, they have encouraged the growth of government bureaucracy (federal, state, and local). The federal environmental agencies have grown like a coral reef into this bureaucracy and are as indestructible. Since their bureaucrats also wish to keep their paper-shuffling jobs, they work hand in glove to promote yet more regulation of the manufacturing sector of the economy.

One of the reasons why an aversion to risk has taken hold in America is the manner in which the American political system has developed during precisely the same two decades as the growth of the movement for a risk-free society. All the influences that have been observed and analyzed—the decline of parties, the proliferation of committees and subcommittees and the undermining of seniority in Congress, and the development of the primary electoral system—have given advantage to single-issue special interest groups. Direct-mailings have provided special interest groups, as well as candidates, with direct access to the voters without having to work through the established political institutions that would have forced them to adjust their own aims to accommodate the broader national interest. Never has it been so evident that, as Macaulay wrote to his American correspondent H. S. Randall, the biographer of Jefferson, "your Constitution is all sail and no anchor." Those now filling the sails are the special interest groups, of whom the risk-averse are the most successful. European countries, in contrast, simply have not permitted the sacrifice of their political systems to the single-issue special interests. Strong parties compel these special interests to adjust to the national interests.

But these groups could not have been so destructively successful if Americans had not already suffered a loss of faith in their nation—a loss of faith in the science and technology on which American progress has been built (while paradoxically they look to science to create their version of a risk-free country); a loss of faith in America's inexhaustible possibilities, its sense of limitlessness; a loss of faith in the ever-advancing frontier, even, as Kennedy proclaimed, the exploration of the new frontier in space. And with it all, a loss of the American adventuring spirit, of the American gusto whose absence the world now laments, the gusto that, until the 1960s, blew like a fresh wind around the globe, showing what could be accomplished in so short a time by a nation that did not shrink from risk but found it a challenge.

There is something grossly at fault in the conception of the Vietnam War Memorial and the false veneration it excites. It is not, like the Iwo Jima Memorial, a monument to heroism, or even to sacrifice. It is a monument to a loss of life that is seen as wasteful and dishonorable. The feelings it excites reflect a nation that is coming to believe that even war should be fought without risk to its fighting men or risk of defeat.

A nation should lament the deaths, and succor the survivors. But it cannot forever be counting its dead.

QUESTIONS

1. What is the "fear of living"? Should we have it? How can we escape it?

2. What groups encourage the fear of living? Why do they do so?

Warren E. Burger

Too Many Lawyers, Too Many Suits

Warren E. Burger was the Chief Justice of the U.S. Supreme Court from 1969 to 1986 and presided over several of the most important cases in recent American history.

In a speech to the American Bar Association convention in 1906, the famous legal philosopher and Harvard Law School Dean, Roscoe Pound, criticized lawyers for making litigation a "sporting contest." The A.B.A. did not like the criticism and at first refused to publish the speech. In "The Litigation Explosion," Walter K. Olson echoes and amplifies Pound's indictment of the legal profession.

Writing especially for nonlawyers, Mr. Olson, a journalist and a senior fellow at the Manhattan Institute, argues that the decline in ethics and the profession's abandonment of age-old constraints on lawyers has created the "litigation business." Lawyers, he tells us, are moving from a profession to a trade, with a corresponding decline in ethics, and they are developing many of the attitudes exhibited by used car dealers. Lawyers' behavior, Mr. Olson says, is largely responsible for the alarming increase in the number of lawsuits in the United States in comparison to other countries that share the basic structure of our legal system. Mr. Olson adds that this rise parallels the rise in the number of law schools and lawyers—producing a kind of "chicken and egg" situation. . . .

To demonstrate that our society is drowning in litigation, one only has to look at the overworked system of justice, the delays in trials, the clogs businessmen face in commerce and a medical profession rendered overcautious for fear of malpractice suits. The litigation explosion, which developed in barely more than a decade beginning in the 1970's, has affected us at all levels, including, as Mr. Olson notes, "the most sensitive and profound relationships of human life." The consequences of the explosion have become painfully obvious. Suits against hospitals and doctors, which went up 300-fold since the 1970's, increased doctors' medical insurance premiums more than 30-fold for some. We have more lawyers per 100,000 people than any other society in the world. We have almost three times as many lawyers per capita as Britain, with whom we share the common law system.

Mr. Olson notes that lawyers who got their start advertising on late-night television are moving from automobile cases into commercial litigation—or any litigation that earns fees. Another recent book, "Shark Tank," by Kim Isaac Eisler, tells the dismal tale of a mega-law firm, Finley Kumble, and reveals, among other things, the growing use of public relations consultants to tout a law firm's skills and accomplishments. The United States stands alone as the glorifier of lawyers and litigation. And who pays? All of us! Malpractice insurance (which can cost a doctor upward of $50,000 a year), higher automobile insurance rates and other such expenses are a "sales tax" paid by all of us, but one that goes into lawyers' pockets.

There was a time, Mr. Olson indicates, when litigation was viewed as undesirable and, at best, like war, a necessary evil. Strict professional standards, tough laws and social stigma discouraged shyster lawyers from the temptation to stir up litigation. Professional ethics were alive and on the minds of most attorneys. Today, however, success at the bar is measured by salaries and bonuses, while many lawyers, Mr. Olson notes, justify their new role in our litigious society by asserting that they are preserving and protecting people's rights—giving more "access to justice." In short, as he aptly puts it, lawyers want Americans to believe that "the more lawsuits there are . . . the closer to perfect the world will become."

The author says this idea—that lawsuits can be used to deter wrongdoing—is one reason for the litigation explosion. Lawsuits, he argues, have become known as assertions of "rights." Lawyers have justified a wide range of grossly unprofessional actions, like flying off to Bhopal, India, to solicit cases, or to Alaska in a chase for cases on oil spills. To those who have praised litigation as having social value per se, one is tempted to cite Judge Learned Hand: "I must say that as a litigant, I should dread a lawsuit beyond almost anything else short of sickness and death."

One way Mr. Olson documents the disintegration of professional ethics is by examining lawyer advertising on television and in print. In 1977, in *Bates v. Arizona*, the Supreme Court held 5 to 4 that such advertising was protected by the First Amendment;

prior to that time, lawyers were forbidden to advertise or to solicit clients. Apart from a handful of "ambulance chasers," only the shysters went further than sending a business card to a potential client or joining the right clubs. Clearly, the disintegration accelerated after the Bates case. But Mr. Olson's argument that the decision itself changed legal ethics attributes too much to it. The author ignores the difference between a profession, like the law, and a trade or business where advertising is more acceptable.

For centuries, the standards of the legal profession were higher than simply compliance with the law. Yet after the Bates ruling, the American Bar Association quickly relaxed its traditional Canons of Professional Ethics, leading some commentators to wonder whether the A.B.A. had become more interested in a large membership than in traditional ethical standards. Today, the ancient and hallowed concept that lawyers are officers of the court is too often treated with an indulgent smile, not only by shyster advertisers, of course, but unfortunately even by some members of the legal profession who have been entrusted with teaching law students.

Legal academia is one of Mr. Olson's frequent targets. For example, he takes on a law professor who argues that in the "contemporary social context" it may be appropriate for lawyers to sponsor and finance litigation. Mr. Olson also perceptively criticizes the tricky business of champerty, allowing a third party, a bank for instance, to finance litigation, with the attorney often agreeing to pay back that third party, or even putting up collateral. Transactions of this kind reflect what has gone on in the savings and loan and the bank scandals—and in the Ivan Boesky and Michael Milken cases. Champerty, as Mr. Olson explains, developed from another form of legal gambling, the contingency fee.

Mr. Olson would be on even sounder ground if he were to expand his discussion and say that a contingency fee is unethical and dishonest, and ought to be unlawful whenever liability is certain, as it often is, for example, in multiple-victim disasters like plane crashes or railroad collisions.

Admittedly, unless the measure of damages is fixed by statute, the *amount* of a recovery can vary, even when liability is certain. A highly experienced litigator is likely to get a larger settlement or verdict than an amateur. But if a lawyer soliciting a case is required to tell a client whenever liability is certain, that should at least rule out unconscionable contingency fees of 33 percent and 50 percent in those certain-recovery cases.

Mr. Olson contrasts lawyers' contingency fees with the ethical prohibition against doctors charging a fee contingent on the success of the treatment of a patient. The American Medical Association, unlike the American Bar Association, has not thought that the constitutional protection of advertising called for a change in medical ethics. The Hippocratic oath still prevails among doctors. Because a doctor may *constitutionally* advertise has not meant that doctors may do so *ethically*. Compare this with the A.B.A.'s tentative standard forbidding only "false and misleading" advertising. Shyster advertisers stimulate litigation with their advertisements, offering a "free" conference. This kind of advertising is reminiscent of that old poem we recited in our school days: " 'Come into my parlor,' said the spider to the fly."

There is some hope, Mr. Olson points out, of curbing the litigation explosion through third-party arbitration and other forms of "alternative dispute resolution." In 1976, the Judicial Conference of the United States and the A.B.A. sponsored a conference to celebrate the 70th anniversary of Pound's famous speech. That meeting introduced "alternative dispute resolution" into our vocabulary. With hordes of unneeded lawyers flooding the country, perhaps the surplus could be used as arbitrators and mediators.

Who, finally, is to blame for the current problem? Journalists? Lawyers? Law professors? The A.B.A.? The Supreme Court? Mr. Olson indicts all of us; and while there is much to this, those charged with legal stewardship, pre-eminently the A.B.A., can especially be called to account.

The legal and the medical professions are monopolies. Historically, each has largely regulated itself with codes and creeds. Medicine has the Hippocratic oath. Lawyers have no counterpart, but over centuries they have developed common law ethical standards. Up till now, legislative bodies and courts have left regulation to the organized bar. Will that continue? One can only hope that Mr. Olson's book will stimulate moves to control unethical lawyers.

In an era noted for corruption in business, the clergy, academia, science, the political arena— and even among Federal judges—it should not be surprising that there has been a deterioration in the standards and practices of the legal profession. More Federal judges have been found guilty of bribe-taking and tax fraud in the past decade than in the first 190 years of our history. Mr. Olson need not be totally correct in all his criticisms to make "The Litigation Explosion" a valuable contribution to the public interest. Will the legal profession, especially the A.B.A., do anything to clean its own house? It remains uncertain.

QUESTIONS

1. Why does Justice Berger think there are too many lawyers?

2. Can you argue, against Burger, that we need more lawyers?

Mark Dowie | # Pinto Madness

Mark Dowie is a multiple award-winning journalist. He wrote this explosive piece for *Mother Jones*.

One evening in the mid-1960s, Arjay Miller was driving home from his office in Dearborn, Michigan, in the four-door Lincoln Continental that went with his job as president of the Ford Motor Company. On a crowded highway, another car struck his from the rear. The Continental spun around and burst into flames. Because he was wearing a shoulder-strap seat belt, Miller was unharmed by the crash, and because his doors didn't jam he escaped the gasoline-drenched, flaming wreck. But the accident made a vivid impression on him. Several months later, on July 15, 1965, he recounted it to a U.S. Senate subcommittee that was hearing testimony on auto safety legislation. "I still have burning in my mind the image of that gas tank on fire," Miller said. He went on to express an almost passionate interest in controlling fuel-fed fires in cars that crash or roll over. He spoke with excitement about the fabric gas tank Ford was testing at that very moment. "If it proves out," he promised the senators, "it will be a feature you will see in our standard cars."

Almost seven years after Miller's testimony, a woman, whom for legal reasons we will call Sandra Gillespie, pulled onto a Minneapolis highway in her new Ford Pinto. Riding with her was a young boy, whom we'll call Robbie Carlton. As she entered a merge lane, Sandra Gillespie's car stalled. Another car rear-ended hers at an impact speed of 28 miles per hour. The Pinto's gas tank ruptured. Vapors from it mixed quickly with the air in the passenger compartment. A spark ignited the mixture and the car exploded in a ball of fire. Sandra died in agony a few hours later in an emergency hospital. Her passenger, 13-year-old Robbie Carlton, is still alive; he has just come home from another futile operation aimed at grafting a new ear and nose from skin on the few unscarred portions of his badly burned body. (This accident is real; the details are from police reports.)

Why did Sandra Gillespie's Ford Pinto catch fire so easily, seven years after Ford's Arjay Miller made his apparently sincere pronouncements—the same seven years that brought more safety improvements to cars than any other period in automotive history? An extensive investigation by *Mother Jones* over the past six months has found these answers:

- Fighting strong competition from Volkswagen for the lucrative small-car market, the Ford Motor Company rushed the Pinto into production in much less than the usual time.
- Ford engineers discovered in pre-production crash tests that rear-end collisions would rupture the Pinto's fuel system extremely easily.
- Because assembly-line machinery was already tooled when engineers found this defect, top Ford officials decided to manufacture the car anyway—exploding gas tank and all—*even though Ford owned the patent on a much safer gas tank*.
- For more than eight years afterwards, Ford successfully lobbied, with extraordinary vigor and some blatant lies, against a key government safety standard that would have forced the company to change the Pinto's fire-prone gas tank.

By conservative estimates Pinto crashes have caused 500 burn deaths to people who would not have been seriously injured if the car had not burst into flames. The figure could be as high as 900. Burning Pintos have become such an embarrassment to Ford that its advertising agency, J. Walter Thompson, dropped a line from the end of a radio spot that read "Pinto leaves you with that warm feeling."

Ford knows the Pinto is a firetrap, yet it has paid out millions to settle damage suits out of court, and it is prepared to spend millions more lobbying against safety standards. With a half million cars rolling off the assembly lines each year, Pinto is the biggest-selling subcompact in America, and the company's operating profit on the car is fantastic. Finally, in 1977, new Pinto models have incorporated a few minor alterations necessary to meet that federal standard Ford managed to hold off for eight years. Why did the company delay so long in making these minimal, inexpensive improvements?

- Ford waited eight years because its internal "cost-benefit analysis," *which places a dollar value on human life*, said it wasn't profitable to make the changes sooner. . . .

Cost–benefit analysis was used only occasionally in government until President Kennedy appointed Ford Motor Company President Robert McNamara to be Secretary of Defense. McNamara, originally an accountant, preached cost benefit with all the force of a Biblical zealot. Stated in its simplest terms, cost-benefit analysis says that if the cost is greater than the benefit, the project is not worth it—no matter what the benefit. Examine the cost of every action, decision, contract, part, or change, the doctrine says, then carefully evaluate the benefits (in dollars) to be certain that they exceed the cost before you begin a program or—and this is the crucial part for our story—pass a regulation.

As a management tool in a business in which profits matter over everything else, cost-benefit analysis makes a certain amount of sense. Serious problems come, however, when public officials who ought to have more than corporate profits at heart apply cost-benefit analysis to every conceivable decision. The

inevitable result is that they must place a dollar value on human life.

Ever wonder what your life is worth in dollars? Perhaps $10 million? Ford has a better idea: $200,000.

Remember, Ford had gotten the federal regulators to agree to talk auto safety in terms of cost-benefit analysis. But in order to be able to argue that various safety costs were greater than their benefits, Ford needed to have a dollar value figure for the "benefit." Rather than be so uncouth as to come up with such a price tag itself, the auto industry pressured the National Highway Traffic Safety Administration to do so. And in a 1972 report the agency decided a human life was worth $200,725. (For its reasoning, see [Table 9-1].) Inflationary forces have recently pushed the figure up to $278,000.

TABLE 9-1 What's Your Life Worth? Societal Cost Components for Fatalities, 1972 NHTSA Study

Component	1971 Costs
Future productivity losses	
Direct	$132,000
Indirect	41,300
Medical costs	
Hospital	700
Other	425
Property damage	1,500
Insurance administration	4,700
Legal and court	3,000
Employer losses	1,000
Victim's pain and suffering	10,000
Funeral	900
Assets (lost consumption)	5,000
Miscellaneous accident costs	200
Total per fatality:	$200,725

Here is a chart from a federal study showing how the National Highway Traffic Safety Administration has calculated the value of a human life. The estimate was arrived at under pressure from the auto industry. The Ford Motor Company has used it in cost–benefit analyses arguing why certain safety measures are not "worth" the savings in human lives. The calculation above is a breakdown of the estimated cost to society every time someone is killed in a car accident. We were not able to find anyone, either in the government or at Ford, who could explain how the $10,000 figure for "pain and suffering" had been arrived at.

Furnished with this useful tool, Ford immediately went to work using it to prove why various safety improvements were too expensive to make.

Nowhere did the company argue harder that it should make no changes than in the area of ruptureprone fuel tanks. Not long after the government arrived at the $200,725-per-life figure, it surfaced, rounded off to a cleaner $200,000, in an internal Ford memorandum. This cost-benefit analysis argued that Ford should not make an $11-per-car improvement that would prevent 180 fiery deaths a year. (This minor change would have prevented gas tanks from breaking so easily both in rear-end collisions, like Sandra Gillespie's, and in rollover accidents, where the same thing tends to happen.)

Ford's cost–benefit table [Table 9-2] is buried in a seven-page company memorandum entitled "Fatalities Associated with Crash-Induced Fuel Leakage and Fires." The memo argues that there is no financial benefit in complying with proposed safety standards that would admittedly result in fewer auto fires, fewer burn deaths and fewer burn injuries. Naturally, memoranda that speak so casually of "burn deaths" and "bum injuries" are not released to the public. They are very effective, however, with

TABLE 9-2 $11 vs. a Burn Death: Benefits and Costs Relating to Fuel Leakage Associated with the Static Rollover Test Portion of FMVSS 208

Benefits
   Savings: 180 burn deaths, 180 serious bum injuries, 2,100 burned vehicles.
   Unit cost: $200,000 per death, $67,000 per injury, $700 per vehicle.
   Total benefit: 180 × ($200,000) + 180 × ($67,000) + 2,100 × ($700) = $49.5 million.

Costs
   Sales: 11 million cars, 1.5 million light trucks.
   Unit cost: $11 per car, $11 per truck.
   Total cost: 11,000,000 × ($11) + 1,500,000 × ($11) = $137 million.

From Ford Motor Company internal memorandum: "Fatalities Associated with Crash-Induced Fuel Leakage and Fires."

Department of Transportation officials indoctrinated in McNamarian cost-benefit analysis.

————————

The Nixon Transportation Secretaries were the kind of regulatory officials big business dreams of. They understood and loved capitalism and thought like businessmen. Yet, best of all, they came into office uninformed on technical automotive matters. And you could talk "burn injuries" and "burn deaths" with these guys, and they didn't seem to envision children crying at funerals and people hiding in their homes with melted faces. Their minds appeared to have leapt right to the bottom line—more safety meant higher prices, higher prices meant lower sales and lower sales meant lower profits.

So when J. C. Echold, Director of Automotive Safety (which means chief anti-safety lobbyist) for Ford wrote to the Department of Transportation— which he still does frequently, at great length—he felt secure attaching a memorandum that in effect says it is acceptable to kill 180 people and burn another 180 every year, *even though we have the technology that could save their lives for $11 a car.*

Furthermore, Echold attached this memo, confident, evidently, that the Secretary would question neither his low death/injury statistics nor his high cost estimates. But it turns out, on closer examination, that both these findings were misleading.

First, note that Ford's table shows an equal number of burn deaths and burn injuries. This is false. All independent experts estimate that for each person who dies by an auto fire, many more are left with charred hands, faces and limbs. Andrew McGuire of the Northern California Burn Center estimates the ratio of burn injuries to deaths at ten to one instead of the one to one Ford shows here. Even though Ford values a burn at only a piddling $67,000 instead of the $200,000 price of life, the true ratio obviously throws the company's calculations way off.

The other side of the equation, the alleged $11 cost of a fire-prevention device, is also a misleading estimation. One document that was *not* sent to Washington by Ford was a "Confidential" cost analysis *Mother Jones* has managed to obtain, showing that crash fires could be largely prevented for considerably *less* than $11 a car. The cheapest method involves placing a heavy rubber bladder inside the gas tank to keep the fuel from spilling if the tank ruptures. Goodyear had developed the bladder and had demonstrated it to the automotive industry. We have in our possession crash-test reports showing that the Goodyear bladder worked well. On December 2, 1970 *(two years before* Echold sent his cost–benefit memo to Washington), Ford Motor Company ran a rear-end crash test on a car with the rubber bladder in the gas tank. The tank ruptured, but no fuel leaked. On January 15, 1971, Ford again tested the bladder and again it worked. The total purchase and installation cost of the bladder would have been $5.08 per car. That $5.08 could have saved the lives of Sandra Gillespie and several hundred others.

QUESTIONS

1. What was the fundamental moral mistake made by Ford?

2. Insurers place dollar values on human lives all the time—otherwise they would go out of business. When is it permissible to assign a cash value to a human life, and when not? What differentiates between the cases?

Patricia Werhane

The Pinto Case and the Rashomon Effect

Patricia Werhane teaches business ethics at the University of Virginia and currently holds the Wicklander Chair in Business Ethics and is Director of the Institute for Business and Professional Ethics at De Paul University in Chicago. This is from her book, *Moral Imagination and Management Decision-Making*.

The Academy Award-winning 1950 Japanese movie *Rashomon* depicts an incident involving an outlaw, a rape or seduction of a woman, and a murder or suicide of her husband. A passerby, who is also the narrator, explains how the story is told to officials from four different perspectives: that of the outlaw, the woman, the husband, and himself. The four narratives agree that the outlaw, wandering through the forest, came upon the woman on a horse led by her husband; the outlaw tied up the husband; the woman and the outlaw had intercourse in front of the bound husband; and the husband was found dead. The narratives do not agree on how these events occurred or who killed the husband. The outlaw contends that consensual intercourse occurred between him and the wife, and he claims to have killed the husband. The wife depicts the sexual act as rape and claims that because of her disgrace, she killed her husband. The husband, through a medium, says that the sexual act began as rape and ended as consent, and that, in shame after being untied by the outlaw, he killed himself. The passerby's story confirms the husband's account of the sexual contact but claims that the bandit was initially afraid to kill the husband. The passerby depicted both men as cowards, preferring to save their own lives rather than protect the wife. Eventually, however, the husband was killed by the bandit. Interestingly, because the passerby is also the narrator of the film, recounting to friends the strange contradictory reportings of this event, we tend to believe his version. But what actually took place is never resolved.

From Patricia Werhane, *Moral Imagination and Management Decision-Making* (New York: Oxford University Press, 1999), pp. 69–75.

In this chapter I examine the role of narratives and make the following claim: the ways we present or re-present a story, the narrative we employ, and the conceptual framing of that story affect its content, its moral analysis, and the subsequent evaluation. Sometimes, narratives of a particular set of events contradict each other. Other times, when one narrative becomes dominant, we appeal to that story for reinforcement of facts, assuming it represents what actually happened, even though it may have distorting effects. The result in either case is a *Rashomon* effect. Yet we seldom carefully examine the narrative we use, often unaware of the "frame" or mental model at work. If my thesis is correct, it is important, morally important, to understand the constructive nature and limits of narratives. . . .

We are at once byproducts of, characters in, and authors of, our own stories. Still, sometimes we become so embroiled in a particular set of narratives, of our own making or not, that we fail to compare with other accounts or evaluate its implications. . . .

Let us begin with some accounts of the Ford Pinto. The accounts of these cases are Mark Dowie's "Pinto Madness" from *Mother Jones*, later revised and reprinted in *Business and Society*; "Beyond Products Liability" by Michael Schmitt and William W. May from the *University of Detroit Journal of Urban Law*; Manuel Velasquez's treatment of the Pinto in his book *Business Ethics* (second edition); Dekkers L. Davidson and Kenneth Goodpaster's Harvard Business School case, "Managing Product Safety: The Ford Pinto"; Ford Motor Company's statements from its lawsuit, *State of Indiana vs. Ford Motor Company;* and Michael Hoffman's case/essay, "The Ford Pinto." Reporting on these incidents, different commentators present "independently supportable facts". In each instance, the commentator claims to be presenting facts, not assumptions, commentary, or conjecture. Yet these "facts" seem to differ. One report, Mark Dowie's, one of the earliest accounts of the case, becomes the dominant narrative despite some of its suspect claims.

The Grimshaw/Pinto case began the documentation of a series of Pinto automobile fires involving rear-end collisions, usually at low speeds, that caused the gas tanks in the Pintos to explode. There

is *one* indisputable set of data upon which all commentators agree:

> On May 28, 1972 Mrs. Lily Gray was driving a six-month old Pinto on Interstate 15 near San Bernardino, California. In the car with her was Richard Grimshaw, a thirteen-year old boy. . . . Mrs. Gray stopped in San Bernardino for gasoline, got back onto the freeway (Interstate 15) and proceeded toward her destination at sixty to sixty-five miles per hour. As she approached Route 30 off-ramp, . . . the Pinto suddenly stalled and coasted to a halt in the middle lane. . . . [T]he driver of a 1962 Ford Galaxie was unable to avoid colliding with the Pinto. Before impact the Galaxie had been braked to a speed of from twenty-eight to thirty-seven miles per hour.
>
> At the moment of impact, the Pinto caught fire and its interior burst into flames. The crash had driven the Pinto's gas tank forward and punctured it against the flange on the differential housing. . . . Mrs. Gray died a few days later. . . . Grimshaw managed to survive with severe burns over 90 percent of his body.

What is the background behind the development of the Pinto? Lee Iacocca, then CEO of Ford, stated publicly that in order to meet Japanese competition, Ford decided to design a subcompact car that would weigh less than 2,000 pounds and cost less than $2,000. According to Davidson and Goodpaster, Ford began planning the Pinto in June 1967 and began producing it in September 1970. This represented a 38-month turnaround time as opposed to the industry average of 43 months for engineering and developing a new automobile. Mark Dowie claims that the development was "rushed" into 25 months; Velasquez says it occurred in "under two years"; Hoffman, claims that Ford "rushed the Pinto into production in much less than the usual time". Although the actual time of development may seem unimportant, critics of the Pinto design argue that *because* it was "rushed into production," the Pinto was not as carefully designed or as carefully checked for safety as a model created over a 43-month time span. But if it took 38 months rather than 25, perhaps the Pinto was not rushed into production after all.

The Pinto was designed so that the gas tank was placed behind the rear axle. According to Davidson and Goodpaster, "[a]t that time almost every American-made car had the fuel tank located in the same place". Dowie wonders why Ford did not place the gas tank over the rear axle, Ford's patented design for its Capri models. This placement is confirmed by Dowie, Velasquez, and some Ford engineers as the "safest place." Yet, according to Davidson and Goodpaster, other studies at Ford showed that the Capri placement actually increased the likelihood of ignition inside the automobile. Moreover, such placement reduces storage space and precludes a hatchback design. Velasquez says that "[b]ecause the Pinto was a rush project, styling preceded engineering", thus accounting for the gas tank placement. This notion may have been derived from Dowie's quotation, allegedly from a "Ford engineer, who doesn't want his name used," that "[t]his company is run by salesmen, not engineers; so the priority is styling, not safety".

Dowie claims that in addition to rushing the Pinto into production, "Ford engineers discovered in pre-production crash tests that rear-end collisions would rupture the Pinto's fuel system extremely easily." According to Dowie, Ford crash-tested the Pinto in a secret location, and in every test made at over 25 mph the fuel tank ruptured. But according to Ford, Pinto's gas tank exploded during many of its tests, because, following government guidelines, Ford had tested the car using a fixed barrier standard, wherein the vehicle is towed backwards into a fixed barrier at the speed specified in the test. Ford argued that Pinto behaved well under a less stringent moving-barrier standard, which, Ford contended, is a more realistic test.

Ford Motor Company and the commentators on this case agree that in 1971, before Ford launched the automobile, an internal study showed that a rubber bladder inner tank would improve the reliability of Pinto's gas tank placement. The bladder would cost perhaps $5.08, $5.80, or $11. The $11 figure probably refers to a design adjustment required to meet a later government rollover standard. However, the idea of this installation was discarded, according to Ford, because of the unreliability of the rubber at cold temperatures, a conjecture not mentioned by commentators. Dowie also contends that Ford could have reduced the dangers from rear-end collisions by installing a $1 plastic baffle between the gas tank and the differential housing to reduce the likelihood of gas tank perforation. I can find no other verification of this contention.

All commentators claim that Ford did a cost/benefit analysis to determine whether it would be more costly to change the Pinto design or to assume the liability costs for burn victims, and memos to that effect were cited as evidence at the Grimshaw trial. However, according to trial evidence submitted by Ford in *Grimshaw*, this estimate was made in 1973, the year *after* the Grimshaw accident, after Ford had evaluated a proposed new government rollover standard. According to evidence presented by Ford in *Grimshaw*, Ford calculated that it would cost $11 per auto to meet the rollover requirement. Ford used government data for the cost of a life ($200,000 per person), and projected an estimate of 180 burn deaths from rollovers. The study was not applicable to rear-end collisions, as some commentators, following Dowie's story, claimed.

Many reports of this case noted the $200,000 figure as Ford's price of a human life. Dowie says, for example, "Ever wonder what your life is worth in dollars? Perhaps $10 million? Ford has a better idea: $200,000". In fact, it was the National Highway Traffic Safety Administration's 1973 figure.

How many people have died as a result of being inside a Pinto during a rear-end collision? "By conservative estimates Pinto crashes have caused 500 burn deaths to people who would not have been seriously injured had the car not burst into flames. The figure could be as high as 900," Dowie claimed. Hoffman repeats Dowie's figures, word for word. A more cautious Velasquez claims that by 1978 at least 53 people had died and "many more had been severely burnt". Schmitt and May, quoting a 1978 article in an issue of *Business and Society Review* that I could not find, estimate the number as "at least 32". Davidson and Goodpaster claim that by 1978, NHTSA estimated that 38 cases involved 27 fatalities.

In the 1978 trial that followed the Grimshaw accident, a jury awarded Grimshaw at least $125 million in punitive damages. *Auto News* printed a headline, "Ford Fights Pinto Case: Jury Gives 128 Million" on February 13, 1978. The commonly cited figure of $125 million is in the court records as the total initial punitive award. The $128 million might be the total award including punitive damages. This award was later reduced on appeal to $3.5 million, a fact that is seldom cited.

A second famous Pinto accident led Indiana to charge Ford with criminal liability. Hoffman reports the incident that led to the charges, on which all agree:

> On August 10, 1978, a tragic automobile accident occurred on US Highway 33 near Goshen, Indiana. Sisters Judy and Lynn Ulrich (ages 18 and 16, respectively) and their cousin Donna Ulrich (age 18) were struck from the rear in their, 1973 Ford Pinto by a van. The gas tank of the Pinto ruptured, the car burst into flames, and the three teenagers were burned to death.

There are two points of interest in this case that apparently led the jury to find Ford not guilty. First, in June 1978 Ford recalled 1.5 million Pintos in order to modify the fuel tank. There was some evidence that the Ulrich auto had not participated in the recall. Second, Ulrich's Pinto was hit from behind at 50 mph by a van driven by a man named Duggar. Duggar later testified that he looked down for a "smoke" and then hit the car, although, according to police reports, the Ulrich car had safety blinkers on. Found in Duggar's van were at least two empty beer bottles and an undisclosed

amount of marijuana. Yet this evidence, cited in the *State of Indiana v. Ford Motor Co.* case, is seldom mentioned in the context of the Ulrich tragedy, and Duggar was never indicted.

The purpose of this exercise is not to exonerate Ford or to argue for bringing back the Pinto. Rather, it is to point out a simple phenomenon—a story can become a narrative and can be taken as fact even when other alleged equally verifiable facts contradict that story. Moreover, one narrative can dominate as *the facts*. Dowie's interesting tale of the Pinto became the prototype for Pinto cases; many authors accepted his version without going back to check whether his data were correct or to question why some of his data contradicted Ford and government claims. Dowie's reporting of Grimshaw became a prototype for the narrative of the Ulrich case as well, so that questions concerning the recall of the Ulrich auto and Duggar's performance were virtually ignored. Such omissions not only make Ford look better, they also question the integrity of these reports and cases. Thus, this set of cases illustrates pitfalls that develop when a particular narrative becomes the paradigm for data and fact.

QUESTIONS

1. What is the "Rashomon effect?" How does it affect the Pinto case?

2. How do the stories we tell about ourselves (and to ourselves) influence our moral decisions? Do you ever see yourself as a character in a drama that you are creating? But what about when the drama becomes all too real? What about the other characters in this drama?

Judith Jarvis Thomson | # Remarks on Causation and Liability

Judith Jarvis Thomson is one of the world's leading moral philosophers.

I

Under traditional tort law, a plaintiff had to show three things in order to win his case: that he suffered a harm or loss, that an act or omission of the defendant's caused that harm or loss, and that the defendant was at fault in so acting or refraining from acting. It is widely known by non-lawyers that liability may nowadays be imposed in many kinds of cases in which there is no showing that the third requirement is met. Strict product liability is one example. Thus if you buy a lawn mower, and are harmed when you use it, then (other things being equal) you win your suit against the manufacturer if you show that you suffered a harm when you used it, and that the harm you suffered was caused by a defect in the lawn mower—as it might be, a missing bolt. You do not need also to show the manufacturer was at fault for the defect; it is enough that the lawn mower was defective when it left his hands, and that the defect caused your harm.

What may be less widely known by non-lawyers is that there have been some recent cases which were won without plaintiff's having shown that the second requirement was met, namely, that of causation. Perhaps the most often discussed nowadays is *Sindell v. Abbott Laboratories,*[1] which was decided by the California Supreme Court in 1980. Plaintiff Sindell had brought an action against eleven drug companies that had manufactured, promoted, and marketed diethylstilbesterol (DES) between 1941 and 1971. The plaintiff's mother took DES to prevent miscarriage. The plaintiff alleged that the defendants knew or should have known that DES was ineffective as

a miscarriage-preventive, and that it would cause cancer in the daughters of the mothers who took it, and that they nevertheless continued to market the drug as a miscarriage-preventive. The plaintiff also alleged that she developed cancer as a result of the DES taken by her mother. Due to the passage of time, and to the fact that the drug was often sold under its generic name, the plaintiff was unable to identify the particular company which had manufactured the DES taken by her mother; and the trial court therefore dismissed the case. The California Supreme Court reversed. It held that if the plaintiff "joins in the action the manufacturers of a substantial share of the DES which her mother might have taken," then she need not carry the burden of showing which manufactured the quantity of DES that her mother took; rather the burden shifts to them to show they could not have manufactured it.[2] And it held also that if damages are awarded her, they should be apportioned among the defendants who cannot make such a showing in accordance with their percentage of "the appropriate market" in DES.

In short, then, the plaintiff need not show about any defendant company that it caused the harm in order to win her suit.

Was the Court's decision in *Sindell* fair? I think most people will be inclined to think it was. On the other hand, it is not easy to give principled reasons why it should be thought fair, for some strong moral intuitions get in the way of quick generalization. What I want to do is to bring out some of the sources of worry.

But the case is in fact extremely complicated, so I suggest we begin with a simpler case, *Summers v. Tice,*[3] which the same court had decided in 1948, and which the plaintiff in *Sindell* offered as a precedent.

From *Philosophy and Public Affairs* 13(2) (Spring, 1984). Reprinted with permission of Blackwell Publishing.

II

Plaintiff Summers had gone quail hunting with the two defendants, Tice and Simonson. A quail was flushed, and the defendants fired negligently in the plaintiffs direction; one shot struck the plaintiff in the eye. The defendants were equally distant from the plaintiff, and both had an unobstructed view of him. Both were using the same kind of gun and the same kind of birdshot; and it was not possible to determine which gun the pellet in the plaintiff's eye had come from. The trial court found in the plaintiff's favor, and held both defendants "jointly and severally liable." That is, it declared the plaintiff entitled to collect damages from whichever defendant he chose. The defendants appealed, and their appeals were consolidated. The California Supreme Court affirmed the judgment.

Was the Court's decision in *Summers* fair? There are two questions to be addressed. First, why should either defendant be held liable for any of the costs? And second, why should each defendant be held liable for all of the costs—that is, why should the plaintiff be entitled to collect all of the costs from either?

Why should either defendant be held liable for any of the costs? The facts suggest that in the case of each defendant, it was only .5 probable that he caused the injury; normally, however, a plaintiff must show that it is more likely than not, and thus more than .5 probable, that the defendant caused the harm complained of if he is to win his case.

The Court's reply is this:

> When we consider the relative position of the parties and the results that would flow if plaintiff was required to pin the injury on one of the defendants only, a requirement that the burden of proof on that subject be shifted to defendants becomes manifest. They are both wrongdoers—both negligent toward plaintiff. They brought about a situation where the negligence of one of them injured the plaintiff, hence it should rest with them each to absolve himself if he can. The injured party has been placed by defendants in the unfair position of pointing to which defendant caused the harm. If one can escape the other may also and plaintiff is remediless.

The Court's argument seems to me to go as follows. The plaintiff cannot determine which defendant caused the harm. If the plaintiff has the burden of determining which defendant caused the harm, he will therefore be without remedy. But both defendants acted negligently "toward plaintiff," and the negligence of one of them caused the harm. Therefore the plaintiff should not be without remedy. Therefore it is manifest that the burden should shift to each defendant to show that he did not cause the injury; and, if neither can carry that burden, then both should be held liable.

The argument does not say merely that both defendants are wrongdoers, or that both defendants acted negligently: it says that both defendants acted negligently "toward plaintiff"—that is, both were in breach of a duty of care that they owed to the plaintiff. Suppose, for example, that the plaintiff had brought suit, not against the two hunters who were out quail hunting with him, but against three people: the two hunters, and Jones, who was driving negligently in New York that afternoon. All three members of that class of defendants were wrongdoers, all three acted negligently, and indeed one of the three caused the harm, though it is not possible to tell which. But it could hardly be thought fair for all of them, and so a fortiori, for Jones to have to carry the burden of showing that *his* negligence did not cause the harm. Perhaps he could carry that burden easily; but it would not be fair to require that he do so on pain of liability for the harm. The argument excludes Jones, however, for although he was negligent, he was not negligent toward the plaintiff.

And even that qualification is not enough—we must suppose a further qualification to lie in the background of the argument. Consider Smith, who was driving negligently in California that day, and who in fact nearly ran the plaintiff down as the plaintiff was on his way to go quail hunting. And suppose that the plaintiff had brought his suit against the following three people: the two hunters and Smith. All three were wrongdoers, all three acted negligently, and indeed negligently toward the plaintiff, and one of the three caused the harm, though it is not possible to tell which. But it could hardly be thought fair for all of them, and so a fortiori for Smith to have to carry the burden of showing that *his* negligence did not cause the harm. As it stands, the argument does not exclude Smith, for he *was* negligent toward the plaintiff. So we must suppose that the Court had in mind not merely that all the defendants were negligent toward the plaintiff, but also that their negligent acts were in a measure likely to have caused the harm for which the plaintiff sought compensation.

There lurks behind these considerations what I take to be a deep and difficult question, namely: Why does it matter to us whose negligent act caused the harm in deciding who is to compensate the victim?

III

It will help to focus on a hypothetical variant of the case, which I shall call *Summers II*. Same plaintiff, same defendants, same negligence, same injury as in *Summers;* but *Summers II* differs in that during the course of the trial, evidence suddenly becomes available which makes it as certain as empirical matters ever get to be, that the pellet lodged in plaintiff Summers' eye came from defendant Tice's gun. Tort law being what it is, defendant Simonson is straightway dismissed from the case. And isn't that the right outcome? Don't we feel that Tice alone should be held liable in *Summers II?* We do not feel that Simonson should be dismissed with a blessing: he acted very badly indeed. So did Tice act badly. But Tice also caused the harm, and (other things being equal) fairness requires that he pay for it.[4] But why? After all, both defendants acted equally negligently toward Summers in shooting as they did; and it was simple good luck for Simonson that, as things turned out, he did not cause the harm to Summers.

It is arguable that there is no principled stopping place other than Tice.[5] Consider, for example, a rule which says: Liability is to be shared among the actual harm-causer and anyone else (if there is anyone else) who acted as negligently toward the victim, and who nearly caused him a harm of the same kind as the actual harm-causer did. Under this rule, liability should presumably be shared between Tice and

Simonson in *Summers II*. But only presumably, since what, after all, counts for these purposes as a "harm of the same kind"? (Compare Smith of the preceding section.) And by what principle should liability be shared only among those who acted negligently toward the victim? (Compare Jones of the preceding section.)

Moreover, even if there is no principled stopping place *other than* Tice, it would remain to be answered what is the principle behind a rule which stops liability *at* Tice.

It pays to begin by asking: What if Tice has an insurance policy that covers him for the costs of harms he causes? We would not feel it unfair for the insurance company to pay Summers off for Tice.

Nor do we feel there would be any unfairness if a friendly philanthropist paid Summers off for Tice.

But the insurance company could simply be living up to its contract with Tice to pay what Tice would have had to pay if he had had no such contract; and the philanthropist would simply be making a gift to Tice—paying a debt for Tice which Tice would otherwise have had to pay himself.

Nevertheless these considerations do bring out that paying Summers' costs is not something we wish to impose on Tice by way of retribution or punishment for his act. If imposing this were a punishment, we would not regard it as acceptable that a third party (insurance company, friendly philanthropist) suffer it as a surrogate for Tice.[6]

What we are concerned with here is not blame, but only who is to be out of pocket for the costs. More precisely, why it is Tice who is to be out of pocket for the costs. It pays to take note of what lies on the other side of this coin. You and your neighbor work equally hard, and equally imaginatively, on a cure for the common cold. Nature then smiles on you: a sudden gust of wind blows your test tubes together, and rattles your chemicals, and lo, there you have it. Both of you acted well; but who is to be in pocket for the profits? You are. Why? That is as deep and difficult a question as the one we are attending to. I think that the considerations I shall appeal to for an answer to our question could also be helpfully appealed to for an answer to this one, but I shall not try to show how.

There is something quite general at work here. "*B* is responsible for the damage to *A*'s fence; so *B* should repair it." "The mess on *A*'s floor is *B*'s fault; so *B* should clean it up." Or anyway, *B* should have the fence repaired, the mess cleaned up. The step is common, familiar, entirely natural. But what warrants taking it?

It is a plausible first idea that the answer lies in the concept "enrichment." Suppose I steal your coffee mug. I am thereby enriched, and at your expense. Fairness calls for return for the good: I must return the coffee mug.

That model is oversimple, of course: it cannot be brought to bear directly. For only I can return the coffee mug, whereas by contrast, anyone can pay the costs of having the fence repaired or the mess cleaned up, either in his own time and effort, or in whatever it takes to get someone else to do these things.

Well, fairness needn't call for the return of the very coffee mug I took, and surely can't call for this if I have now smashed it. Replacement costs might do just as well. Or perhaps something more than replacement costs, to cover your misery while thinking you'd lost your mug. In any case, anyone can pay those costs. But I must pay them to you because I was the person enriched by the theft of the mug, and at your expense. So similarly, perhaps we can say that *B* must pay the costs of having the fence repaired because *B* was the person who enriched himself, and at *A*'s expense, by the doing of whatever it was he did by the doing of which he damaged the fence.

Enrichment? Perhaps so: *B* might literally have made a profit by doing whatever it was he did by the doing of which he made a mess on *A*'s floor (e.g., mudpie-making for profit). Or anyway, he might have greatly enjoyed himself (e.g., mudpie-making for fun). Perhaps he made the mess out of negligence? Then he at least made a saving: he saved the expense in time or effort or whatever he would have had to expend to take due care. And he made that saving at *A*'s expense.

But this cannot really be the answer—it certainly cannot be the whole answer. For consider Tice and Simonson again. They fired their guns negligently in Summers' direction, and Tice's bullet hit Summers. Why should Tice pay Summers' costs? Are we to say that that is because Tice enriched himself at Summers' expense? Or anyway, that Tice made a saving at Summers' expense—a saving in time or effort or whatever he would have had to expend to take due care? Well, Simonson saved the same as Tice did, for they acted equally negligently.[7] It would have to be said "Ah, but Tice's saving was a saving *at Summers' expense*—and Simonson's was not." But what made Tice's saving *be* a saving at Summers' expense? Plainly not the fact that his negligence was negligence "toward" Summers, for as the Court said, Tice and Simonson were both "negligent toward plaintiff." If it is said that what made Tice's saving be a saving at Summers' expense is the fact that it was Tice's negligence that caused Summers' injury, then we are back where we were: for what we began with was why that fact should make the difference.

Drawing attention to cases in which two are equally enriched also brings out more clearly a problem which is already present when only one is. Why is it *B* who must pay the costs of having the mess on *A*'s floor cleaned up, when it is *B* who caused it to be there? Because in doing what he did which caused it to be there he enriched himself (or made a saving) at *A*'s expense. But if what made the enrichment be *at A*'s *expense* is the fact that his act caused the mess to be there, then the question has not been answered: we have merely been offered new language in which to ask it.

Perhaps it pays to set aside the concept "enrichment" and attend, instead, to what we have in mind when we characterize a person as "responsible." Consider again: "*B* is responsible for the damage to *A*'s fence; so *B* should repair it." Doesn't the responsible *person* pay the costs of damage he or she is responsible *for*? And don't we place a high value on being a responsible person?

Similarly, the responsible person pays the costs of damage which is his or her fault.

This is surely right; but what lies behind it? *Why* do we think it a good trait in a man that he pays the costs of damage he is responsible for? Why do we expect him to?

I hazard a guess that the, or anyway an, answer may be found in the value we place on freedom of action, by which I mean to include freedom to plan on action in the future, for such ends as one chooses for oneself. We take it that people are entitled to a certain "moral space" in which to assess possible ends, make choices, and then work for the means to reach those ends. Freedom of action is obviously not the only thing we value; but let us attend only to considerations of freedom of action, and bring out how they bear on the question in hand.

If A is injured, his planning is disrupted: he will have to take assets he meant to devote to such and such chosen purpose, and use them to pay the costs of his injury. Or that is so unless he is entitled to call on the assets of another, or others, to pay the costs for him. His moral space would be considerably larger if he were entitled to have such costs paid for him.

But who is to pay A's costs? On whose assets is it to be thought he is entitled to call? Whose plans may *he* disrupt?

A might say to the rest of us, "Look, you share my costs with me now, and I'll share with you when you are injured later." And we might then agree to adopt a cost-spreading arrangement under which the costs of all (or some) of our injuries are shared; indeed, we might the better secure freedom of action for all of us if we did agree to such an arrangement. The question which needs answering, however, is whether A may call on this or that person's assets in the absence of agreement.

One thing A is not entitled to do is to choose a person X at random, and call on X's assets to pay his costs. That seems right; but I think it is not easy to say exactly why. That is, it will not suffice to say that if all we know about X is that X is a person chosen at random, then we know of no reason to think that a world in which X pays A's costs is better than a world in which A pays A's costs. That is surely true. But by the same token, if all we know about X is that X is a person chosen at random, then we know of no reason to think that a world in which A pays A's costs is better than a world in which X pays A's costs. So far, it looks as if flipping a coin would be in order.

What I think we should do is to look at A's situation *before* any costs have been incurred. A has been injured. Now he wants to be "made whole": he wants the world changed in such a way as to make him be as nearly as possible what he would have been had he not been injured. That is what he needs money for. But the freedom of action of other people lends weight to the following: If A wants the world changed in that (or any other) way, then—other things being equal—A has to pay the costs, in money, time, energy, whatever is needed, unless he can get the voluntary agreement of those others to contribute to those costs. Again, A's wanting the world changed in that (or any other) way is not by itself a reason to think he may call on another person to supply him with what he needs to change it. It follows that A is not entitled to call on a person unless that person has a feature other than just that of being a person, which marks *his* pockets as open to A. A cannot, then, choose a person X at random, and call on X to pay the costs—on pain of infringing X's freedom of action.

And it could hardly be thought that while A is not entitled to call on X's assets before A has spent anything, A becomes entitled to call on X's assets the moment he has.

So A is not entitled to choose a person X at random, and call on X's assets to pay his costs.

Well, here is B, who is considerably richer than A. Perhaps some people will feel that that does entitle A to call on B. I want to set this aside. As I said, freedom of action is not the only thing we value, but I want to bring out *its* bearing on the question in hand; so I shall sidestep this issue by inviting you to imagine that no one is any richer than anyone else.

A is injured. Let us supply his injury with a certain history. Suppose, first, that A himself caused it—freely and wittingly, for purposes of his own. And suppose, second, that it is not also true of any other person X that X caused it, or even that X in any way causally contributed to it. Thus:

(I) A caused A's injury, freely, wittingly, for purposes of his own; and no one other than A caused it, or even causally contributed to it.

We can easily construct examples of injuries which consist in loss or damage to property which have histories of this kind—for example, *A* might have broken up one of his chairs, to use as kindling to light a fire to get the pleasure of looking at a fire. It is harder to construct examples of injuries which consist in physical harm which have histories of this kind. But it is possible—for example, *A* might have cut off a gangrenous toe to save his life. *A* might have cut off his nose to spite his face.

Suppose now that having caused himself the injury, *A* wants for one or another reason to be made whole again. That will cost him something. Here is *B*. Since (I) is true of *A*'s injury, *B*'s freedom of action protects him against *A*: *A* is not entitled to call on *B*'s assets for the purpose—*A* is not entitled to disrupt *B*'s planning to reverse an outcome wholly of his own planning which he now finds unsatisfactory.

That seems right. And it seems right whatever we imagine true of *B*. *B* may be vicious or virtuous, fat or thin, tall or short; none of this gives *A* a right to call on *B*'s assets. Again, *B* might have been acting very badly indeed contemporaneously with *A*'s taking the steps he took to cause his own injury: *B* might even have been imposing risks of very serious injuries on *A* concurrently with *A*'s act—for example, *B* might have been playing Russian roulette on *A*, or throwing bricks at him. No matter: if *A*'s injury has the history I described in (I), then *B*'s freedom of action protects him against the costs of it.

If that is right, then the answer to our question falls out easily enough. Let us suppose that *A* is injured, and that *B* did not cause the injury, indeed, that he in no way causally contributed to *A*'s injury. Then whatever did in fact cause *A*'s injury—whether it was *A* himself who caused his injury, or whether his injury was due entirely to natural causes, or whether *C* or *D* caused it—there is nothing true of *B* which rules out that *A*'s injury had the history described in (I), and therefore nothing true of *B* which rules out that *A* should bear his own costs. Everything true of *B* is compatible with its being the case that *A*'s costs should lie where they fell. So there is no feature of *B* which marks his pockets as open to *A*—*A* is no more entitled to call on *B* than he is entitled to call on any person *X* chosen at random.

Causality matters to us, then, because if *B* did not cause (or even causally contribute to) *A*'s injury, then

B's freedom of action protects him against liability for *A*'s costs. And in particular, it is Simonson's freedom of action which protects him against liability for Summers' costs in *Summers II*, for in that case it was discovered that Tice had caused the injury.

I have been saying that freedom of action is not the only thing we value, and that is certainly true. But if I am right that it is freedom of action which lies behind our inclination to think causality matters—and in particular, our inclination to think it right that Simonson be dismissed once it has been discovered that he did not cause Summers' injury—then these considerations by themselves show we place a very high value on it, for those inclinations are very strong.

NOTES

1. 26 Cal. 3d 588, 163 Cal. Rptr. 132, 607 P. 2d 924 (1980).

2. One defendant had already been dismissed from the action on the ground that it had not manufactured DES until after the plaintiff was born.

3. 33 Cal. 2d 8o, 199 P. 2d I (1948).

4. Some people feel that Summers himself should share in the costs, in the thought that Summers assumed a risk in going out quail hunting with Tice and Simonson. I do not myself share that intuition. Anyone who does is invited to imagine, instead, that Summers is a farmer, who was passing by, on his way to market.

5. See Wex S. Malone, "Ruminations on Cause-In-Fact," *Stanford Law Review* 9 (December 1956): 66.

6. A number of people have drawn attention to the general point at work here. See, for example, Jules Coleman, "On the Moral Argument for the Fault System," *The Journal of Philosophy* 71, no. 14 (15 August 1974).

7. The general point I illustrate here was made by Jules Coleman, in "Corrective Justice and Wrongful Gain," *The Journal of Legal Studies* 11, no. 2 (June 1982).

QUESTIONS

1. What is the connection Thomson sees between causation and liability?

2. How should we decide who pays the costs for an injured party? Why is the issue more complex than it initially appears?

Bob Sullivan

Annoying Fine Print May
Not Even Be Legal

Bob Sullivan is an award-winning author and investigative journalist.

Can the New York Yankees change the First Amendment and make their fans agree to the change? They tried recently.

Anyone who's been to the Bronx recently probably wouldn't fault an attempt to make it more family friendly, but can a baseball team change the Constitution and force you to accept it?

Welcome to the world of "boilerplate" language—also known as mouseprint, standard form contracts, fine-print fraud, shrink-wrap contracts, etc.

U.S. consumers rarely engage in any kind of transaction today without clicking or signing away a wide swath of their rights. Cellphone contracts, software purchases, baseball tickets, credit card applications—all include lengthy tomes full of ominous warning that most of us ignore.

Regular readers of this column know I am a collector of fine print and its absurdities, such as school waiver forms asking parents to sign away their kids' right to "enjoy life."

Consumers hate fine print, but emotions rarely carry the day in courtrooms. So corporations have been having a field day with barely readable terms and conditions for some time. In fact, fine-print writers have been emboldened by a recent Supreme Court decision in which the court took their side.

But in a new book titled *Boilerplate*, author and lawyer Margaret Jane Radin is taking aim at the intellectual and legal basis of fine print, trying to put a serious dent in the legal argument behind it.

"I don't think there's a contract, ever, when something is just dropped on us," Radin said, "especially when there is no option to vote with your feet as a consumer, when there are no alternatives."

Radin's point is that contracts, by definition, involve two equal parties that negotiate terms, while fine print is issued on a "take-it-or-leave-it" basis. (Just try to negotiate a lower early termination fee or strike out any clause when you sign a cellphone agreement.) In layman's terms, fine print is merely a list of bad things that can happen to you, the consumer. You might get hit with a penalty fee; your service might be terminated; your right to join a class-action lawsuit is surrendered.

Some lawyers would call these take-it-or-leave-it agreements "contracts of adhesion," a special class of contracts that can be ruled unenforceable if the consumer persuades a judge that the provisions are "unconscionable." As you might imagine, that's a high bar—it means generally that such provisions would be shocking to a normal person's conscience as excessively unfair. Such a legal battle also involves an excessive amount of legal fees, so it's not a realistic option for an aggrieved cellphone holder.

Radin wades into this confusing situation with a fairly radical idea. Trying to shove fine-print agreements into contract law, she argues, is like trying to shove a round peg into a square hole. She calls it "legal gerrymandering." Instead, courts need to adopt a brand-new way of looking at fine print, she says.

Her view is simple: Interactions between consumers and companies are more like brief encounters with strangers than negotiated bargains between equal parties. As such, they fall into the realm of tort law, rather than contract law, Radin argues.

That change would have dramatic implications for fine-print haters everywhere. Were these agreements viewed as torts, angry cellphone owners would retain the right to sue for damages, including pain

From NBCNews.com.

and suffering, if they believe a company has violated their rights, by making an unauthorized withdrawal from the consumer's checking account, for instance.

Generally, the argument in favor of fine print has been economic. Industry groups have repeatedly argued that standard-form agreements are essential because no one wants every consumer negotiating their own terms and conditions for every transaction. The logic runs like this: Form agreements save companies money, particularly when they limit liability and the potential for costly lawsuits, and that savings is passed on to consumers.

But some rights can't be signed away, Radin argues, even if a consumer seemingly agrees to that. Even if it saves them money.

"Important rights can't be canceled by a private party just because they pay the value," she said. "For example . . . you can't sell food with *E. coli* just because it's cheaper. . . . You can't say we haven't maintained our airplanes, but our prices are cheaper, so you assume the risk if we fall out of the sky."

Fine print that limits liability or complicates consumer costs is everywhere—on coffee cups, on dog bone packaging. It's flashed for a brief moment on TV mortgage ads, it's read at record-breaking speed on radio ads for car leases. Falling under the general term "disclosure," its absurdity and ineffectiveness is hard to debate.

"Disclosure doesn't work. We don't understand it, even if it's in large print. We don't read it, even lawyers," Radin said. "That's why we have to start evaluating these disclosures a different way. They aren't contracts."

When consumers talk about fine print, they usually focus on hidden language that imposes punishing late fees, doubles prices after some unknown trial period, or springs other tricks and traps that ding their wallets. But when consumer lawyers talk about fine print, they are usually complaining about something a bit more theoretical—common provisions within agreements that indicate that consumers waive their rights to sue the company if something goes wrong or join in a class-action lawsuit. Instead, consumers are forced into a process known as binding mandatory arbitration. Most consumer agreements with banks, cellphone companies, credit card issuers, television subscription services, and other service providers include arbitration clauses.

Consumer groups and class-action lawyers despise such provisions and have been fighting them in courtrooms around the country for some time, arguing that waiver of jury trial rights is "unconscionable."

After compiling a mixed legal record, the fight was dealt a devastating blow last year, when the U.S. Supreme Court sided with AT&T in a case involving a consumer who sued to have a class-action lawsuit waiver thrown out of a cellphone contract. Within months, similar waivers began appearing in nearly all consumer agreements, dealing a blow to the entire class-action system.

Consumer lawyers argue that waiving a right to a jury trial in order to buy a car or baseball ticket is similar to waiving the right to free speech.

Anyone who's ever received a 50-cent coupon because of an old class-action lawsuit that earned lawyers millions knows that lawsuits are hardly a panacea for the problem of misbehaving companies or those that impose overreaching terms and conditions. But neither is a free market, argues Radin, unless it is truly a thriving market with informed consumers.

In many markets, consumers have few or no choices. Most cellphone firms have the same early termination fees and arbitration clauses, for example. Meanwhile, if fine print is too small to read or too arcane to understand, there won't even be a handful of ace consumers who can provide a watchdog effect. What happens next is called a "lemon's equilibrium," a term first coined in the 1970s by economist George Akerlof.

"If there is a lot of competition in a marketplace, and at least some consumers are very well informed, then market forces can have a positive impact on fine print," Radin explained. "But even if there's a lot of competition, but not enough people in the market know what's going on, there's a race to the bottom. Everybody just buys the cheaper product . . . and everyone gets a lemon."

Radin's argument is broader than a need to protect consumers from $480 satellite dish early termination fees or to preserve their right to sue. She thinks that industry's reliance on sweeping rights clauses in every consumer agreement, and the courts' compliance with that, has created an alternate legal system in America—one that voters never agreed to.

"This is creating a mockery of state legislatures. We elect legislators, they decide something is important and debate it, then vote on a law, then it becomes law," she said. "Then corporations write rules and they effectively become law, contradicting what the legislature did. What we think of as a contract is really important to our conception of social order.

Think of how many people are affected by boilerplate language. If it is thousands or millions of people, that's letting a firm create a new legal universe. That undermines our rule of law."

QUESTIONS

1. Are consumers required to adhere to the terms of the contracts they sign, even if they have not read them?

2. Is there anything a manufacturer couldn't put into fine print? Think of three examples.

CASES

CASE 9.1
The Skateboard Scare
William H. Shaw and Vincent Barry

Colin Brewster, owner of Brewster's Bicycle Shop, had to admit that skateboard sales had salvaged his business now that interest in the bicycle seemed to have peaked. In fact, skateboard business was so brisk that Brewster could hardly keep them in stock. But the picture was far from rosy.

Just last week a concerned consumer group visited his shop. They informed Brewster that they had ample evidence to prove that skateboards present a real and immediate hazard to consumer safety. Brewster conceded that the group surely provided enough statistical support; the number of broken bones and concussions that had resulted directly and indirectly from accidents involving skateboards was shocking. But he thought the group's position was fundamentally unsound because, as he told them, "It's not the skateboards that are unsafe but how people use them."

Committee members weren't impressed with Brewster's distinction. They likened it to saying

automobile manufacturers shouldn't be conscious of consumer safety because it's not the automobiles that are unsafe but how we drive them. Brewster objected that automobiles present an entirely different problem, because a number of things could be done to ensure their safe use. "But what can you do about a skateboard?" he asked them. "Besides, I don't manufacture them, I just sell them."

The committee pointed out that other groups were attacking the problem on the manufacturing level. What they expected of Brewster was some responsible management of the problem at the local retail level. They pointed out that recently Brewster had run a series of local television ads portraying young but accomplished skateboarders performing fancy flips and turns. The ad implied that anyone could easily accomplish such feats. Only yesterday one parent had told the committee of her child's breaking an arm attempting such gymnastics

From William H. Shaw and Vincent Barry, *Moral Issues in Business*, 5th ed. (Belmont, CA: Wadsworth, 1996).

after having purchased a Brewster skateboard. "Obviously," Brewster countered, "the woman has an irresponsible kid whose activities she should monitor, not me." He pointed out that his ad was not intended to imply anyone could or should do those tricks, no more than an ad showing a car traveling at high speeds while doing stunt tricks implies that you should drive that way.

The committee disagreed. They said Brewster not only should discontinue such misleading advertising but also should actively publicize the potential dangers of skateboarding. Specifically, the committee wanted him to display prominently beside his skateboard stock the statistical data testifying to its hazards. Furthermore, he should make sure anyone buying a skateboard reads this material before purchase.

Brewster argued that the committee's demands were unreasonable. "Do you have any idea what effect that would have on sales?" he asked them.

Committee members readily admitted that they were less interested in his sales than in their children's safety. Brewster told them that in this matter their children's safety was their responsibility, not his. But the committee was adamant. Members told Brewster that they'd be back in a week to find out what positive steps, if any, he'd taken to correct the problem. In the event he'd done nothing, they indicated they were prepared to picket his shop.

QUESTIONS

1. With whom do you agree—Brewster or the committee? Why?

2. Would you criticize Brewster's advertisements? Do you think the demand that he publicize the dangers of skateboarding is reasonable?

3. What responsibilities, if any, do retailers have to ensure consumer safety? Compare the responsibilities of manufacturers, skateboarders, and parents.

CASE 9.2

Aspartame: Miracle Sweetener or Dangerous Substance?

William H. Shaw and Vincent Barry

Diet Coke stands alone as the greatest overnight success in the marketplace. But when you quaff a Diet Coke on a hot summer's day, you may be doing more than quenching your thirst. You could be inviting a headache, depression, seizure, aggressive behavior, visual impairment, or menstrual disturbances. You might even be loading your tissues with a carcinogen. The reason, say most nutritionists and medical scientists, is that soft drinks like Diet Coke—and a host of other products—contain the low-calorie sweetener aspartame, which goes by the name NutraSweet.

In 1983 the Reagan administration's commissioner of the Food and Drug Administration, Dr. Arthur Hull

Hayes, Jr., approved the use of aspartame in carbonated beverages. In one stroke, he seemed to end the prolonged controversy over the safety of the artificial sweetener. That controversy erupted in 1974, when the FDA first approved aspartame as a food additive.

No sooner had aspartame's manufacturer, G. D. Searle & Co., begun to celebrate the FDA's initial approval of its profits-promising sweetener than things turned sour. Largely as a result of the rancorous protests of lawyer James Turner, author of a book about food additives, the FDA suspended its approval. Armed with the results of animal experiments conducted at Washington University, Turner

William H. Shaw and Vincent Barry, *Moral Issues in Business* 5th ed. (Belmont, CA: Wadsworth, 1996).

insisted that aspartame could damage the brain, especially in infants and children. Searle pooh-poohed the charges, citing experiments of its own that, it said, established the safety of its chemical sweetener. Unconvinced, Dr. Alexander M. Schmidt, then FDA commissioner, appointed a task force of six scientists to examine Searle's experiments.

The task force's findings did not corroborate Searle's rosy assurances of safety. In fact, it concluded that Searle had distorted the safety data to win FDA approval of aspartame. According to the task force's 1976 report, "Searle made a number of deliberate decisions which seemingly were calculated to minimize the chances of discovering toxicity and/or to allay FDA concern." Schmidt not only endorsed the task force's findings but told Congress in April 1976 that he saw in Searle's experiments "a pattern of conduct which compromises the scientific integrity of the studies." He added: "At the heart of the FDA's regulatory process is the ability to rely upon the integrity of the basic safety data submitted by the sponsors of regulated products. Our investigation clearly demonstrates that, in the G. D. Searle Co., we have no basis for such reliance now." Specifically addressing the tests of aspartame, the commissioner and other FDA officials reported such irregularities as test animals recorded as dead on one date and alive on another and autopsies on rats conducted a year after the rodents had died during a feeding experiment. Schmidt further branded Searle's animal studies as "poorly conceived, carelessly executed, or inaccurately analyzed or reported."

Understandably, Searle wasn't about to allow these broadsides to pass unanswered. In a May 1976 letter to Schmidt, the firm's executive vice president, James Buzard, asserted that the FDA task force investigators "totally failed to find fraud, totally failed to find concrete evidence of an intent to deceive or mislead the agency or any advisory committee, or a failure to make any required report."

Sticking to his opinions, Schmidt asked the Justice Department to investigate the possibility that Searle had deliberately misled the FDA. After looking into the matter, a grand jury brought no indictment against the company. Nevertheless, under FDA pressure Searle enlisted the services of Universities Associated for Research and Education in Pathology (UAREP), a private group of fifteen universities that work under contracts and grants for paying clients. UAREP was to scrutinize eight of the fifteen as yet unreviewed aspartame studies to check Searle's conclusions. Under the terms of its agreement with Searle, UAREP would submit its findings to the company before submitting them to the FDA. Searle said that procedure was necessary to ensure accuracy. But Adrian Gross, a task force member and senior FDA scientist, expressed misgivings about the arrangement to his superiors. The report that UAREP submitted, Gross argued, "may well be interpreted as nothing short of an improper whitewash."

Despite Gross's concern, the UAREP body proceeded, focusing solely on the microscopic slides produced by Searle in its animal experiments. In the end, the consortium could find nothing improper in Searle's interpretation of the slides. But James Turner complained that the review was unacceptably narrow and incomplete because it had failed to consider either the design or execution of Searle's experiments. He was assured in writing that these and other relevant matters would be taken up by a public board of inquiry.

That board, made up of three independent scientists, had plenty to do. By January 1980, when the panel convened, the FDA had amassed 140 volumes of data on aspartame. Unable to deal with the mountain of information, the board concentrated on the same studies UAREP had examined. On September 30, 1980, the panel recommended that the FDA withdraw approval of aspartame. In making its recommendation, the board said it couldn't exclude the possibility that aspartame causes cancer in rats.

It thus appeared that the FDA would keep aspartame off the market for good. But in November 1980 the country elected a new president, and within a few short months, the chemical would be sweetening a multitude of products and making millions of dollars for its manufacturer.

The day after Ronald Reagan was inaugurated president of the United States, Searle repetitioned the FDA to approve the sale of aspartame. It based its appeal on the same data it had previously submitted. Six months later, on July 24, 1981, the new FDA commissioner, Dr. Hayes, approved the sale of aspartame as a "tabletop sweetener and ingredient of dry foods."

In approving the product for sale, Hayes discounted the possible cancer connection. He cited a study done in 1981 by Ajinomoto, a Japanese chemical firm. Its study found that, while rats fed with aspartame did develop more brain tumors than untreated rats, the increase was not statistically significant. The commissioner took the results as breaking the tie between two similar experiments conducted earlier by Searle, which had produced differing results.

Some scientists immediately discredited the Ajinomoto experiments, claiming that they used a strain of rat different from the one used in earlier Searle studies. In reply, Searle insisted that all three rat studies demonstrated that aspartame was noncarcinogenic.

In 1983 Searle successfully petitioned the FDA to permit aspartame to be used in carbonated beverages. Hayes gave FDA approval on July 8, 1983.

Worldwide sales of aspartame the next year were estimated at $600 million.

One month after granting Searle permission to use aspartame in soft drinks, Dr. Hayes resigned from the FDA to become dean of New York Medical College. Three months later, in November 1983, he also took a job as senior scientific consultant to Burson Marsteller, the public relations firm that has Searle's account for aspartame.

QUESTIONS

1. Does the aspartame controversy tend to support or belie the assumption that regulatory agencies are sufficient to ensure consumer safety?

2. Who do you think should have primary responsibility for ensuring product safety—manufacturer or government agency?

3. Does requiring a label warning consumers that a food or beverage contains carcinogenic chemicals sufficiently discharge a government agency's obligation to protect the public? Or should such products be banned? What if the product contains a substance that is only possibly carcinogenic?

CASE 9.3
Children and Reasonably Safe Products
Joseph R. Desjardins and John J. McCall

When children are involved, how safe need a "reasonably safe" product be? How vigilant should manufacturers be in forseeing misuse? Consider two cases.

In *Ritter v. Narragansett Electric Co.*, a four-year-old girl was injured when she used an oven door as a stepstool to stand on so that she could peak into a pot on the top of the stove. Her weight caused the stove to tip over, causing serious injury to the child. The first question concerns a possible defective design.

Was the stove defective because it could not support thirty pounds on the oven door without tipping? A foreseeable use of the stove could involve placing a heavy roasting pan on the oven door while checking food during preparation. If the stove tipped over and injured the cook during this use, it is very likely that a court would rule against the manufacturer on the grounds of a design defect. The manufacturer should have foreseen the use of the door as a shelf.

From Joseph R. Desjardins and John J. McCall, *Contemporary Issues in Business Ethics*, 2nd ed. (Belmont, CA: Wadsworth, 1990).

Could the manufacturer foresee the use of the door as a step-stool? Should it matter, since the product was defective in this regard anyway?

Vincer v. Esther Williams Swimming Pool Co. concerned a two-year-old boy who climbed the ladder of an above-ground swimming pool at his grandparents' house and fell into the pool. He remained under water for some time before being rescued. As a result, he suffered severe and permanent brain damage. His family sued the manufacturer, claiming that the pool should have had a self-closing gate and/or an automatically retractable ladder. Knowing that children are attracted to swimming pools and knowing that many children drown each year because of

such accidents, should the manufacturer have foreseen this possibility? Was it "unreasonable" not to include protections against such an accident in the design of the swimming pool?

QUESTIONS

1. Courts ruled against the manufacturer in *Ritter*, and in favor of the manufacturer in *Vincer*. Do you agree? Why or why not?

2. Does your determination of "reasonably safe product" depend on the person who is using it? If so, are any products "reasonably safe" where children are concerned? If so, who decides what is "reasonable"?

CASE 9.4
Living and Dying with Asbestos
William H. Shaw and Vincent Barry

Asbestos is a fibrous mineral used for fireproofing, electrical insulation, building materials, brake linings, and chemical filters. If exposed long enough to asbestos particles—usually ten or more years—people can develop a chronic lung inflammation called asbestosis, which makes breathing difficult and infection easy. Also linked to asbestos exposure is mesothelioma, a cancer of the chest lining that sometimes doesn't develop until forty years after the first exposure. Although the first major scientific conference on the dangers of asbestos was not held until 1964, the asbestos industry knew of its hazards more than sixty years ago.

As early as 1932, the British documented the occupational hazards of asbestos dust inhalation. Indeed, on September 25, 1935, the editors of the trade journal *Asbestos* wrote to Summer Simpson, president of Raybestos-Manhattan, a leading

asbestos company, asking permission to publish an article on the dangers of asbestos. Simpson refused and later praised the magazine for not printing the article. In a letter to Vandivar Brown, secretary of Johns-Manville, another asbestos manufacturer, Simpson observed: "The less said about asbestosis the better off we are." Brown agreed, adding that any article on asbestosis should reflect American, not English, data.

In fact, American data were available, and Brown, as one of the editors of the journal, knew it. Working on behalf of Raybestos-Manhattan and Johns-Manville and their insurance carrier, Metropolitan Life Insurance Company, Anthony Lanza had conducted research between 1929 and 1931 on 126 workers with three or more years of asbestos exposure. But Brown and others were not pleased with the paper Lanza submitted to them for

William H. Shaw and Vincent Barry, *Moral Issues in Business*, 9th ed., (Belmont, CA: Wadsworth, 2004). Notes were deleted from this text.

editorial review. Lanza, said Brown, had failed to portray asbestosis as milder than silicosis, a lung disease caused by longterm inhalation of silica dust and resulting in chronic shortness of breath. Under the then-pending Workmen's Compensation law, silicosis was categorized as a compensable disease. If asbestosis was worse than silicosis or indistinguishable from it, then it, too, would have to be covered. Apparently Brown didn't want this and thus requested that Lanza depict asbestosis as less serious than silicosis. Lanza complied and also omitted from his published report the fact that more than half the workers examined—67 of 126—were suffering from asbestosis.

Meanwhile, Summer Simpson was writing F. H. Schulter, president of Thermoid Rubber Company, to suggest that several manufacturers sponsor additional asbestos experiments. The sponsors, said Simpson, could exercise oversight prerogatives; they "could determine from time to time after the findings are made whether we wish any publication or not." Added Simpson: "It would be a good idea to distribute the information to the medical fraternity, providing it is of the right type and would not injure our companies." Lest there be any question about the arbiter of publication, Brown wrote to officials at the laboratory conducting the tests:

It is our further understanding that the results obtained will be considered the property of those who are advancing the required funds, who will determine whether, to what extent and in what manner they shall be made public. In the event it is deemed desirable that the results be made public, the manuscript of your study will be submitted to us for approval prior to publication [Brown].

Industry officials were concerned with more than controlling public information flow. They also sought to deny workers early evidence of their asbestosis. Dr. Kenneth Smith, medical director of a Johns-Manville plant in Canada, explained why seven workers he found to have asbestosis should not be informed of their disease:

It must be remembered that although these men have the X-ray evidence of asbestosis, they are working today and definitely are not disabled from asbestosis. They have not been told of this diagnosis, for it is felt that as long as the man feels well, is happy at home and at work, and his physical condition remains good, nothing should be said. When he becomes disabled and sick, then the diagnosis should be made and the claim submitted *by the Company*. The fibrosis of this disease is irreversible and permanent so that eventually compensation will be paid to each of these men. But as long as the man is not disabled, it is felt that he should not be told of his condition so that he can live and work in peace and the Company can benefit by his many years of experience. Should the man be told of his condition today there is a very definite possibility that he would become mentally and physically ill, simply through the knowledge that he has asbestosis.

When lawsuits filed by asbestos workers who had developed cancer reached the industry in the 1950s, Dr. Smith suggested that the industry retain the Industrial Health Foundation to conduct a cancer study that would, in effect, squelch the asbestos-cancer connection. The asbestos companies refused, claiming that such a study would only bring further unfavorable publicity to the industry and that there wasn't enough evidence linking asbestos and cancer industrywide to warrant it.

Shortly before his death in 1977, Dr. Smith was asked whether he had ever recommended to Johns-Manville officials that warning labels be placed on insulation products containing asbestos. He testified as follows:

The reasons why the caution labels were not implemented immediately, it was a business decision as far as I could understand. Here was a recommendation, the corporation is in business to make, to provide jobs for people and make money for stockholders and they had to take into consideration the effects of everything they did, and if the application of a caution label identifying a product as hazardous would cut out sales, there would be serious financial implications. And the powers that be had to make some effort to judge the necessity of the label vs. the consequences of placing the label on the product.

Dr. Smith's testimony and related documents have figured prominently in hundreds of asbestos-related lawsuits. In the 1980s these lawsuits swamped Manville (as Johns-Manville is now called) and forced the company into bankruptcy. A trust fund valued at $2.5 billion was set up to pay Manville's asbestos claimants. To fund the trust, shareholders were required to surrender half the value of their stock, and the company had to give up much of its projected earnings over the next twenty-five years. Claims, however, soon over-whelmed the trust, which ran out of money in 1990. After various legal delays, the trust fund's stake in Manville was increased to 80 percent, and Manville was required to pay it an additional $300 million in dividends. The trust fund itself was restructured to pay the most seriously ill victims first, but average payments to victims were lowered significantly—from $145,000 to $43,000.

Meanwhile, in 1997 the U.S. Supreme Court struck down a landmark $1.3-billion class-action settlement between some twenty former asbestos producers and their injured workers. A few years earlier, the companies involved had approached the workers' lawyers and agreed to settle thousands of existing health complaints, in a deal that netted the lawyers millions of dollars in fees. Then the lawyers and companies devised a settlement agreement involving people who had not filed claims against the company by a specified date. It was this aspect of the settlement that was the main sticking point. Although a lower court had praised the settlement for "forging a solution to a major social problem," the Supreme Court balked at the fact that future claimants were not allowed to opt out of the agreement. A class-action agreement, the Court said, was not the best way to resolve thousands of different claims involving different factual and legal issues. In 1999, the Court rejected a second proposed settlement. As a result, thousands of lawsuits that would have been settled by the agreements continue to clog federal dockets.

The situation is made worse by the fact that in the last few years asbestos-related litigation has expanded exponentially—spun out of control, some would say—as workers who did not make asbestos, but only handled it every now and then or worked in the vicinity of those who did, are suing companies that never made the stuff but only used it. Altogether more than 200,000 cases are pending nationwide against more than 1,000 companies. In fact, of the 91,000 cases filed in 2001, only 6 percent of the plaintiffs have actually suffered from asbestos-related diseases. Almost all of the other claimants are seeking compensation for anxiety they have experienced over the risk that they might have asbestosis.

QUESTIONS

1. Hand-of-government proponents would say that it's the responsibility of government, not the asbestos industry, to ensure health and safety with respect to asbestos—that in the absence of appropriate government regulations, asbestos manufacturers have no responsibility other than to operate efficiently and profitably. Do you agree?

2. What responsibilities do asbestos manufacturers now have to their injured workers? How should society respond to these workers' claims for restitution? Is our legal system adequate for handling this problem? Should the asbestos companies be punished in some way, or is their liability to civil lawsuits sufficient?

3. Do you see any parallels between this case and the tobacco industry's response to the health risks of smoking?

CASE 9.5
Merck and Vioxx
Kenneth B. Moll and Associates

On October 5, 2004, Kenneth B. Moll & Associates, Ltd. filed the first worldwide class action lawsuit against Merck, on behalf of all persons who were prescribed the potentially deadly arthritis drug rofecoxib, also known as Vioxx (Ceoxx outside the United States).

The law firm has already received inquiries from persons who believe they were injured by Vioxx in over 14 countries (China, South Africa, Italy, Canada, Iceland, Israel, Chile, United Kingdom, New Zealand, Brazil, The Netherlands, Singapore, the United States, and other countries). Merck estimates that over 24 million patients have been prescribed the drug worldwide.

The lawsuit, known as the "VIOXX Class Action," was filed in the Federal District Court for the Northern District of Illinois.

On September 30, 2004, Merck officially announced a voluntary withdraw of Vioxx from all markets worldwide in light of unequivocal results from a clinical trial demonstrating that Vioxx almost triples the risk of heart attack and stroke for those who take the product long term. The company's decision is based on three-year data from a prospective, randomized, placebo-controlled clinical trial, the APPROVe (Adenomatous Polyp Prevention on VIOXX) trial.

The APPROVe study followed the 1999 VIGOR (Vioxx Gastrointestinal Outcomes Research Study) study. In the VIGOR study, analysis of the cardiovascular data by the Safety Monitoring Board focused on "the excess deaths and cardiovascular adverse experiences in [the Vioxx group] compared to [the Naproxen group]."

Attorney Kenneth Moll said, "a primary goal of the Vioxx Class Action is to inform consumers and physicians worldwide of the potentially deadly side effects of Vioxx." Mr. Moll said he is concerned that thousands of people have been injured by the drug and are not aware of their injuries. According to our experts, a person is susceptible to a Vioxx injury beginning from the initial dosage, up to and including a week after discontinuing use of the drug.

The lawsuit will request that a medical monitoring fund be established to enable people who have taken Vioxx to monitor the existence of dangerous side effects.

IMPORTANT: Injuries from Vioxx may occur days after usage.

Our offices are working in conjunction with attorneys around the world to address the enormous public health issue created by Merck in its manufacture, marketing and distribution of the prescription drug Vioxx (marketed as Ceoxx outside of the United States). The drug has been marketed around the world since 1999 and has been prescribed tens of millions of times. In light of the millions of patients around the world who were taking Vioxx, even if a fraction of a percent of patients experience cardiovascular events, that would translate into thousands of affected people. The Italian consumer protection group, ADUC, has addressed the health concerns surrounding Vioxx and has issued a press release.

QUESTIONS

1. What duties does Merck have in the Vioxx case?
2. Should attorneys always be the ones to "solve" liability problems? Why or why not?

Source: Kenneth B. Moll and Associates. Reprinted by permission of Kenneth B. Moll and Associates.

CASE 9.6
The Top 10 Most Dangerous Toys of All Time
Claude Wyle

As concerned consumers we trust that the toys we buy for our children are safe and won't cause any harm from use, but that is not always the case. In the heat of the Holiday Season, the Consumer Product Safety Commission works tirelessly to recall millions of harmful toys each year, yet they cannot guard against all potential dangers. Below are some of the most dangerous toys that slipped through the cracks.

1. **CSI—Fingerprint Examination Kit.** Based on the hit TV show, the powder given to investigate fingerprints was found to contain asbestos. (2007)
2. **Magnetix.** A magnet building set, which could easily be broken, spilling the small magnets from inside. These magnets were incredibly harmful if swallowed, as they would reconnect through tissue walls causing digestive complications and even death within a short period of time. (2008)
3. **Inflatable baby boats.** Prone to tearing, these boats were intended to make pool time fun for toddlers, but instead made it a potentially deadly experience. (2009)
4. **Hannah Montana Pop Star Card Game.** Lab tests revealed that the card game contained at least 75 times the recommended amount of arsenic for children's toys. It slipped through the cracks as it was made of vinyl, and not paint, allowing it to remain uncovered by regulations. (2007)
5. **Aquadots.** A more popular toy, allowed children to arrange beads into different shapes and fuse them together with water. However, it was found that the beads contained GHB, the date rape drug. Eventually 4.2 million kits were recalled. (2007)

6. **Snacktime Cabbage Patch Doll.** A must-have doll was intended to "eat" only the packaged provided fake snacks, but when it couldn't tell the difference and contained no off switch, ended up eating children's fingers and hair. (1996)
7. **Mini Hammocks.** The children's hammocks had over three million hammocks made, resulting in at least twelve children's deaths, with many more injured. (1985–96)
8. **Lawn Darts.** A toy with missile shaped weighted skewers for children to throw across the yard? It is fairly obvious why these began being banned by the CPSC. (1990–2009)
9. **The Austin Magic Pistol.** This gun delivered gas powered combustion, in the form of calcium carbide, a hazardous material that exploded when mixed with water. (1950)
10. **The Gilbert U-238 Atomic Energy Lab.** Including uranium in a children's toy is just asking for it to get pulled from the shelves. (1950)

QUESTIONS

1. Are product manufacturers responsible for injuries incurred while using their products?
2. How might we legally define the point at which manufacturers become responsible?

From *The Legal Examiner*, Friday, December 28, 2012.

CASE 9.7
Ten More Deaths Blamed on Plavix
Jack Bouboushian

CHICAGO (CN)—Ten people died from the block-buster blood-thinner Plavix, which is no better than aspirin against stroke but costs 100 times more, dozens of family members claim in two complaints.

Bristol-Myers Squibb and Sanofi-Aventis reaped annual U.S. sales of $3.8 billion from Plavix, push-ing the drug in TV, magazine, and Internet ads, while they "knew or should have known that when taking Plavix, the risk of suffering a heart attack, stroke, internal bleeding, blood disorder, or death far out-weigh any potential benefit," lead plaintiff Geraldine Jackson says.

At least 561 lawsuits have been filed over Plavix, according to the Courthouse News database. Rose Creighton is the lead plaintiff in the other most recently filed case. Both were filed in Cook County Court.

Quotations in this article are from Jackson's lawsuit, though the dozens of plaintiffs make simi-lar claims in both cases—that Bristol-Myers and Sanofi-Aventis deceived the public by misrepresent-ing the risks of Plavix, which they knew about from their own studies.

"Plavix was heavily marketed directly to con-sumers through television, magazine, and Internet advertising," the complaint states. "It was touted as a "super-aspirin" that would give a person even greater cardiovascular benefits than a much less expensive, daily aspirin while being safer and easier on a person's stomach than aspirin. Those assertions have proven to be false.

"The truth is that BMS and Sanofi always knew—or, if they had paid attention to the findings of their own studies, should have known—that Plavix was not more efficacious than aspirin to prevent heart attacks and strokes. More importantly though, defendants knew or should have known that when taking Plavix, the risk of suffering a heart attack, stroke, internal bleeding, blood disorder, or death far outweigh any potential benefit."

Plavix is the sixth best-selling drug in the United States, with annual sales of $3.8 billion, although it works no better than aspirin in many cases, accord-ing to the complaint. A dose of Plavix costs $4, 100 times more than aspirin, at 4 cents a dose.

"Defendants' nearly eight-year run of lying to phy-sicians and to the public about the safety and efficacy of Plavix for the sole purpose of increasing corporate profits has now been uncovered by scientific studies that reveal that not only is Plavix not worth its high price—it is dangerous," the complaint states.

A recent study "uncovered another truth about Plavix," the complaint adds. "It found that Plavix plus aspirin (dual therapy) is only minimally more effective than aspirin plus placebo at preventing ath-erothrombotic events. But more importantly, it found that in patients who do not have peripheral arterial disease (PAD) or acute coronary syndrome (ACS), Plavix plus aspirin (dual therapy) poses a 20 percent increased risk to the patient of suffering bleeding injuries, heart attacks, stroke and death. In other words, in those patients without ACS or PAD, dual therapy with aspirin and Plavix does more harm than good.

"Despite a growing body of scientific knowledge that the four-dollar ($4.00) Plavix pill was not much better than a four-cent-a-day aspirin, Defendants kept promoting it to the public and to physicians, using hyperbole and outright falsification in the process."

Three people died because they took Plavix, according to Jackson's lawsuit. Creighton's lawsuit, filed the same day, claims that seven people died from the drug.

"Defendants failed to fully, truthfully, and accurately communicate the safety and efficacy of

From Courthouse News Service, January 2, 2013.

Plavix drug products and intentionally and fraudulently misled the medical community, physicians, plaintiffs' physicians, and ingesting plaintiffs and decedents about the risks associated with Plavix," Jackson's complaint states.

The families seek punitive damages for products liability, manufacturing defect, failure to warn, negligence, loss of consortium, and wrongful death.

All plaintiffs are represented by Steven Aroesty with Nafoli, Bern, Ripka, and Shkolnik, of Edwardsville, Illinois.

Plavix has been prescribed to prevent stroke after operations, which may be caused by blood clots breaking loose and traveling toward the brain. It has been a drug of choice for conditions such as those being suffered by Secretary of State Hillary Clinton

QUESTIONS

1. How do Plavix and aspirin differ?
2. How can Bristol-Meyers Squibb compensate the 561 patients who died due to Plavix?

CHAPTER QUESTIONS

1. When should producers be responsible for harms that are caused by their products? What moral responsibilities do producers have? What are the responsibilities of consumers? Where (and how) do we draw the line?

2. Is life becoming more dangerous? Is greater fear one of the costs of greater convenience and greater luxury? How can we regulate business—if we should—to manage the escalating risks created by mushrooming production?

10

"You Know How to Whistle, Don't You?"

Whistle-Blowing, Company Loyalty, and Employee Responsibility

Introduction

One of the wise-guy employees of a local, particularly vicious, crime family, let's call them the Baritones, finds himself increasingly repulsed by some of his assignments, which involve, among other things, the breaking of various bones and the noncosmetic rearrangement of unresponsive clients' faces. He starts to feel sorry for his victims, most of whom are perfectly law-abiding citizens who just happen to have small businesses in Baritone territory and find themselves unable to make the extortion payments that have been demanded of them. Eventually, his conscience gets the better of him, and he has a change of heart. He gets in touch with the FBI (though he by no means feels all that good about doing so) and offers to testify ("rat," in his lexicon) on his bosses. There is no doubt that they have been doing wrong (to put it mildly). There is no doubt that their activities have been both destructive of the community and corrupting to the real free enterprise system (which, as Adam Smith warned years ago, can be ruined by "Force and Fraud"). But this guy took an oath, a blood oath, in fact, to keep his secrets and not betray his employers, who have come to seem to him, over the years, like a literal family. And the question that bugs him, over and over, is how he can justify violating that oath, however evil his "family" may be.

Whatever our affection for fictional crime families may be—indeed, whatever misplaced affection we may have for real-life criminals in the news—we recognize or should recognize evil for what it is, evil. We're not talking here about bending the law or cutting corners. We're not talking about wrongdoers who deserve one another. We're talking about terrorizing and ruining the lives of hardworking, innocent people. But even so, we can understand the turmoil of the wise guy, torn between his belated recognition of evil and his sense of loyalty. And if that is so, we should be all the more sympathetic toward those who see less than evil—shoddy business practices, dangerous situations for employees, pollution or destruction of the environment, the violation of tax laws, and the systematic misleading of investors—and are moved to say something about it. Whistle-blowing, as it has come to be called, is always a painful

> # Martin Luther King on Silence
>
> *Our lives begin to end the day we become silent about things that matter.*
>
> —*From an Enron Company notepad*

and desperate course of action. But sometimes it is heroic and necessary. And that becomes a question for all of us. Most of us will, at some time in our lives, work for a corporation or an institution with flaws. At what point might we feel justified, indeed even compelled, to speak out, first, of course, with a more or less polite internal memo. But if that memo gets no results, are we ever justified in violating our own sense of loyalty—and others' expectations of loyalty—to go outside the company? This, of course, has been the dilemma of several high-placed whistle-blowers in recent years. Erin Brockovich became a national heroine (and had superstar Julia Roberts depict her in a movie) for blowing the whistle on corporate polluters. Jeffrey Wigand went through utter Hell exposing the lethal lies told by his employers in the tobacco industry, but he also emerged a hero (played by Russell Crowe in the movie *The Insider)* for daring to risk his life and career for the sake of the truth and public safety. More recently, Sherron Watkins (along with Cynthia Cooper of WorldCom and Coleen Rowley of the FBI) made the cover of *Time* magazine for writing a now-famous memo to Enron CEO Kenneth Lay, warning of an "implosion" if Enron's accounting practices ever came to light, and then testified against her superiors in the much-awaited criminal cases that followed.

Most of us will never find ourselves in such a difficult position, but we all need to keep that possibility in mind. First of all, we all need to have some sense of what lines we will not cross, what sorts of things we would refuse to do, what sorts of activities we will not tolerate, even if we ourselves are not direct participants but only observers (and therefore nonetheless complicit). And second, we need to keep in mind how painful such a dilemma must be for those who are so involved, rather than simply retreat to the knee-jerk (or perhaps just jerk) reaction that "they should not have gotten themselves into that situation in the first place" or "I would never rat on my employer." (No? Never? No matter what?) What's more, the opposition is not always (or usually) the company versus the public, but the very existence of the company. An early whistleblower (especially if he or she is heeded *within* the company) can prevent the massive Enron-type collapse and bankruptcy. Not only the ethics but the health of the free enterprise system depends on the freedom of everyone in it to speak up and to criticize or expose wrongdoing. This is not to say that speaking up is easy or that all criticism is warranted criticism. But unless we acknowledge and even celebrate those who are willing to act as correctives when our market system goes wrong, we are in danger of finding ourselves in a world that is no longer free or a true market but, as wrongdoing tends to find its imitators, what Smith warned us about, a system of Force and Fraud.

Sissela Bok offers a general characterization of the ethical foundations of whistle-blowing in her "Whistleblowing and Professional Responsibility." Michael Davis explains the many tensions and difficulties in an adequate characterization of the moral obligation to blow the whistle in his "Some Paradoxes of Whistleblowing." Ronald Duska emphasizes the particular difficulties posed by the conflict between loyalty and a moral obligation to blow the whistle in his "Whistleblowing and Employee Loyalty." David E. Soles offers a comprehensive analysis of the ethical foundations of employee loyalty in his "Four Concepts of Loyalty." George D. Randels expands the idea of loyalty to include loyalties between employees and corporations, corporations and communities, and corporations to employees in his "Loyalty, Corporations, and Community." Finally, Kim Zetter interviews economist, psychologist and philosopher Dan Ariely on "why we cheat."

| Sissela Bok | # Whistleblowing and Professional Responsibility |

Sissela Bok is a member of the American Academy of Political and Social Science and is an Eleanor Roosevelt Fellow. She was formerly professor of philosophy at Brandeis University.

"Whistleblowing" is a new label generated by our increased awareness of the ethical conflicts encountered at work. Whistleblowers sound an alarm from within the very organization in which they work, aiming to spotlight neglect or abuses that threaten the public interest.

The stakes in whistleblowing are high. Take the nurse who alleges that physicians enrich themselves in her hospital through unnecessary surgery; the engineer who discloses safety defects in the braking systems of a fleet of new rapid-transit vehicles; the Defense Department official who alerts Congress to military graft and overspending: all know that they pose a threat to those whom they denounce and that their own careers may be at risk. . . .

NATURE OF WHISTLEBLOWING

Three elements, each jarring, and triply jarring when conjoined, lend acts of whistleblowing special urgency and bitterness: dissent, breach of loyalty, and accusation.

Like all dissent, whistleblowing makes public a disagreement with an authority or a majority view. But whereas dissent can concern all forms of disagreement with, for instance, religious dogma or government policy or court decisions, whistleblowing has the narrower aim of shedding light on negligence or abuse, or alerting to a risk, and of assigning responsibility for this risk.

Would-be whistleblowers confront the conflict inherent in all dissent: between conforming and sticking their necks out. The more repressive the authority they challenge, the greater the personal risk they take in speaking out. At exceptional times, as in times of war, even ordinarily tolerant authorities may come to regard dissent as unacceptable and even disloyal.

Furthermore, the whistleblower hopes to stop the game; but since he is neither referee nor coach, and since he blows the whistle on his own team, his act is seen as a violation of loyalty. In holding his position, he has assumed certain obligations to his colleagues and clients. He may even have subscribed to a loyalty oath or a promise of confidentiality. Loyalty to

From Sissela Bok, "Whistleblowing and Professional Responsibility," *New York University Education Quarterly*, 11 (Summer 1980): 2–7. Reprinted with permission.

colleagues and to clients comes to be pitted against loyalty to the public interest, to those who may be injured unless the revelation is made.

Not only is loyalty violated in whistleblowing, hierarchy as well is often opposed, since the whistle-blower is not only a colleague but a subordinate. Though aware of the risks inherent in such disobedience, he often hopes to keep his job. At times, however, he plans his alarm to coincide with leaving the institution. If he is highly placed, or joined by others, resigning in protest may effectively direct public attention to the wrongdoing at issue. Still another alternative, often chosen by those who wish to be safe from retaliation, is to leave the institution quietly, to secure another post, then to blow the whistle. In this way, it is possible to speak with the authority and knowledge of an insider without having the vulnerability of that position.

It is the element of accusation, of calling a "foul," that arouses the strongest reactions on the part of the hierarchy. The accusation may be of neglect, of willfully concealed dangers, or of outright abuse on the part of colleagues or superiors. It singles out specific persons or groups as responsible for threats to the public interest. If no one could be held responsible— as in the case of an impending avalanche—the warning would not constitute whistleblowing.

The accusation of the whistleblower, moreover, concerns a present or an imminent threat. Past errors or misdeeds occasion such an alarm only if they still affect current practices. And risks far in the future lack the immediacy needed to make the alarm a compelling one, as well as the close connection to particular individuals that would justify actual accusations. Thus an alarm can be sounded about safety defects in a rapid-transit system that threaten or will shortly threaten passengers, but the revelation of safety defects in a system no longer in use, while of historical interest, would not constitute whistleblowing. Nor would the revelation of potential problems in a system not yet fully designed and far from implemented.

Not only immediacy, but also specificity, is needed for there to be an alarm capable of pinpointing responsibility. A concrete risk must be at issue rather than a vague foreboding or a somber prediction. The act of whistle-blowing differs in this respect from the lamentation or the dire prophecy. An immediate and specific threat would normally be acted upon by those at risk. The whistleblower assumes that his message will alert listeners to something they do not know, or whose significance they have not grasped because it has been kept secret.

The desire for openness inheres in the temptation to reveal any secret, sometimes joined to an urge for self-aggrandizement and publicity and the hope for revenge for past slights or injustices. There can be pleasure, too—righteous or malicious—in laying bare the secrets of co-workers and in setting the record straight at last. Colleagues of the whistleblower often suspect his motives: they may regard him as a crank, as publicity-hungry, wrong about the facts, eager for scandal and discord, and driven to indiscretion by his personal biases and shortcomings.

For whistleblowing to be effective, it must arouse its audience. Inarticulate whistleblowers are likely to fail from the outset. When they are greeted by apathy, their message dissipates. When they are greeted by disbelief, they elicit no response at all. And when the audience is not free to receive or to act on the information—when censorship or fear of retribution stifles response—then the message rebounds to injure the whistleblower. Whistleblowing also requires the possibility of concerted public response: the idea of whistleblowing in an anarchy is therefore merely quixotic.

Such characteristics of whistleblowing and strategic considerations for achieving an impact are common to the noblest warnings, the most vicious personal attacks, and the delusions of the paranoid. How can one distinguish the many acts of sounding an alarm that are genuinely in the public interest from all the petty, biased, or lurid revelations that pervade our querulous and gossip-ridden society? Can we draw distinctions between different whistleblowers, different messages, different methods?

We clearly can, in a number of cases. Whistleblowing may be starkly inappropriate when in malice or error, or when it lays bare legitimately private matters having to do, for instance, with political belief or sexual life. It can, just as clearly, be the only way to shed light on an ongoing unjust practice such as drugging political prisoners or subjecting them to electroshock treatment. It can be the last resort for alerting the public to an impending disaster. Taking such clear-cut cases as benchmarks, and reflecting on what it is about them that weighs so heavily for or against speaking out, we can work our way toward the admittedly more complex cases in which whistleblowing is not so clearly the right or wrong choice, or where different points of view exist regarding its legitimacy—cases where there are moral reasons both for concealment and for disclosure and where judgments conflict. Consider the following cases[1]:

A. As a construction inspector for a federal agency, John Samuels (not his real name) had personal knowledge of shoddy and deficient construction practices by private contractors. He knew his superiors received free vacations and entertainment, had their homes remodeled and found jobs for their relatives—all courtesy of a private contractor. These superiors later approved a multimillion no-bid contract with the same "generous" firm.

Samuels also had evidence that other firms were hiring nonunion laborers at a low wage while receiving substantially higher payments from the government for labor costs. A former superior, unaware of an office dictaphone, had incautiously instructed Samuels on how to accept bribes for overlooking sub-par performance.

As he prepared to volunteer this information to various members of Congress, he became tense and uneasy. His family was scared and the fears were valid. It might cost Samuels thousands of dollars to protect his job. Those who had freely provided Samuels with information would probably recant or withdraw their friendship. A number of people might object to his using a dictaphone to gather information. His agency would start covering up and vent its collective wrath upon him. As for reporters and writers, they would gather for a few days, then move on to the next story. He would be left without a job, with fewer friends, with massive battles looming, and without the financial means of fighting them. Samuels decided to remain silent.

B. Engineers of Company "A" prepared plans and specifications for machinery to be used in a manufacturing process and Company "A" turned them over to Company "B" for production. The engineers of Company "B," in reviewing the plans and specifications, came to the conclusion that they included certain miscalculations and technical deficiencies of a nature that the final product might be unsuitable for the purposes of the ultimate users, and that the equipment, if built according to the original plans and specifications, might endanger the lives of persons in proximity to it. The engineers of Company "B" called the matter to the attention of appropriate officials of their employer who, in turn, advised Company "A." Company "A" replied that its engineers felt that the design and specifications for the equipment were adequate and safe and that Company "B" should proceed to build the equipment as designed and specified. The officials of Company "B" instructed its engineers to proceed with the work.

C. A recently hired assistant director of admissions in a state university begins to wonder whether

To: You
From: The Philosopher
Subject: "Ralph Nader on Whistle-Blowing"

The key question is, at what point should an employee resolve that allegiance to society (e.g., the public safety) must supersede allegiance to the organization's policies (e.g., the corporate profit) and then act on that resolve by informing outsiders or legal authorities? It is a question that involves basic issues of individual freedom, concentration of power, and information flow to the public.

transcripts of some applicants accurately reflect their accomplishments. He knows that it matters to many in the university community, including alumni, that the football team continue its winning tradition. He has heard rumors that surrogates may be available to take tests for a fee, signing the names of designated applicants for admission, and that some of the transcripts may have been altered. But he has no hard facts. When he brings the question up with the director of admissions, he is told that the rumors are unfounded and is asked not to inquire further into the matter.

INDIVIDUAL MORAL CHOICE

What questions might those who consider sounding an alarm in public ask themselves? How might they articulate the problem they see and weigh its injustice before deciding whether or not to reveal it? How can they best try to make sure their choice is the right one? In thinking about these questions it helps to keep in mind the three elements mentioned earlier: dissent, breach of loyalty, and accusation. They impose certain requirements—of accuracy and judgment in dissent; of exploring alternative ways to cope with improprieties that minimize the breach of loyalty; and of fairness in accusation. For each, careful articulation and testing of arguments are needed to limit error and bias.

Dissent by whistleblowers, first of all, is expressly claimed to be intended to benefit the public. It carries with it, as a result, an obligation to consider the nature of this benefit and to consider also the possible harm that may come from speaking out: harm to persons or institutions and, ultimately, to the public interest itself. Whistleblowers must, therefore, begin by making every effort to consider the effects of speaking out versus those of remaining silent. They must assure themselves of the accuracy of their reports, checking and rechecking the facts before speaking out; specify the degree to which there is genuine impropriety; consider how imminent is the threat they see, how serious, and how closely linked to those accused of neglect and abuse.

If the facts warrant whistleblowing, how can the second element—breach of loyalty—be minimized? The most important question here is whether the

existing avenues for change within the organization have been explored. It is a waste of time for the public as well as harmful to the institution to sound the loudest alarm first. Whistleblowing has to remain a last alternative because of its destructive side effects: it must be chosen only when other alternatives have been considered and rejected. They may be rejected if they simply do not apply to the problem at hand, or when there is not time to go through routine channels or when the institution is so corrupt or coercive that steps will be taken to silence the whistleblower should he try the regular channels first.

What weight should an oath or a promise of silence have in the conflict of loyalties? One sworn to silence is doubtless under a stronger obligation because of the oath he has taken. He has bound himself, assumed specific obligations beyond those assumed in merely taking a new position. But even such promises can be overridden when the public interest at issue is strong enough. They can be overridden if they were obtained under duress or through deceit. They can be overridden, too, if they promise something that is in itself wrong or unlawful. The fact that one has promised silence is no excuse for complicity in covering up a crime or a violation of the public's trust.

The third element in whistleblowing—accusation—raises equally serious ethical concerns. They are concerns of fairness to the persons accused of impropriety. Is the message one to which the public is entitled in the first place? Or does it infringe on personal and private matters that one has no right to invade? Here, the very notion of what is in the public's best "interest" is at issue: "accusations" regarding an official's unusual sexual or religious experiences may well appeal to the public's interest without being information relevant to "the public interest."

Great conflicts arise here. We have witnessed excessive claims to executive privilege and to secrecy by government officials during the Watergate scandal in order to cover up for abuses the public had every right to discover. Conversely, those hoping to profit from prying into private matters have become adept at invoking "the public's right to know." Some even regard such private matters as threats to the public: they voice their own religious and political prejudices in the language of accusation. Such a danger is never stronger than when the accusation is delivered surreptitiously. The anonymous accusations made during the McCarthy period regarding political beliefs and associations often injured persons who' did not even know their accusers or the exact nature of the accusations.

From the public's point of view, accusations that are openly made by identifiable individuals are more likely to be taken seriously. And in fairness to those criticized, openly accepted responsibility for blowing the whistle should be preferred to the denunciation or the leaked rumor. What is openly stated can more easily be checked, its source's motives challenged, and the underlying information examined. Those under attack may otherwise be hard put to defend themselves against nameless adversaries. Often they do not even know that they are threatened until it is too late to respond. The anonymous denunciation, moreover, common to so many regimes, places the burden of investigation on government agencies that may thereby gain the power of a secret police.

From the point of view of the whistleblower, on the other hand, the anonymous message is safer in situations where retaliation is likely. But it is also often less likely to be taken seriously. Unless the message is accompanied by indications of how the evidence can be checked, its anonymity, however safe for the source, speaks against it.

During the process of weighing the legitimacy of speaking out, the method used, and the degree of fairness needed, whistleblowers must try to compensate for the strong possibility of bias on their part. They should be scrupulously aware of any motive that might skew their message: a desire for self-defense in a difficult bureaucratic situation, perhaps, or the urge to seek revenge, or inflated expectations regarding the effect their message will have on the situation. (Needless to say, bias affects the silent as well as the outspoken. The motive for holding back important information about abuses and injustice ought to give similar cause for soul-searching.)

Likewise, the possibility of personal gain from sounding the alarm ought to give pause. Once again there is then greater risk of a biased message. Even if the whistleblower regards himself as incorruptible, his profiting from revelations of neglect or abuse will lead others to question his motives and to put less credence in his charges. If, for example, a government employee stands to make large profits from a book exposing the iniquities in his agency, there is danger that he will, perhaps even unconsciously, slant his report in order to cause more of a sensation.

A special problem arises when there is a high risk that the civil servant who speaks out will have to go through costly litigation. Might he not justifiably try to make enough money on his public revelations— say, through books or public speaking—to offset his losses? In so doing he will not strictly speaking have *profited* from his revelations: he merely avoids being financially crushed by their sequels. He will nevertheless still be suspected at the time of revelation, and his message will therefore seem more questionable.

Reducing bias and error in moral choice often requires consultation, even open debate: methods that force articulation of the moral arguments at stake and challenge privately held assumptions. But acts of whistleblowing present special problems when it comes to open consultation. On the one hand, once the whistleblower sounds his alarm publicly, his arguments will be subjected to open scrutiny; he will have to articulate his reasons for speaking out and substantiate his charges. On the other hand, it will then be too late to retract the alarm or to combat its harmful effects, should his choice to speak out have been ill-advised.

For this reason, the whistleblower owes it to all involved to make sure of two things: that he has sought as much and as objective advice regarding his choice as he can *before* going public; and that he is aware of the arguments for and against the practice of whistleblowing in general, so that he can see his own choice against as richly detailed and coherently structured a background as possible. Satisfying these two requirements once again has special problems because of the very nature of whistleblowing: the more corrupt the circumstances, the more dangerous it may be to seek consultation before speaking out. And yet, since the whistleblower himself may have a biased view of the state of affairs, he may choose not to consult others when in fact it would be not only safe but advantageous to do so; he may see corruption and conspiracy where none exists.

NOTE

1. Case A is adapted from Louis Clark, "The Sound of Professional Suicide," *Barrister*, Summer 1978, p. 10; Case B is Case 5 in Robert J. Baum and Albert Flores, eds., *Ethical Problems of Engineering* (Troy, NY: Rensselaer Polytechnic Institute, 1978), p. 186.

QUESTIONS

1. When and why do we have a duty to blow the whistle, according to Bok?
2. What are the constraints that govern whistleblowers?

Michael Davis | # Some Paradoxes of Whistleblowing

Michael Davis is a Senior Fellow at the Illinois Institute of Technology Center for Study of Ethics in the Professions and a professor of philosophy.

Most acts, though permitted or required by morality, need no justification. There is no reason to think them wrong. Their justification is too plain for words. Why then is whistleblowing so problematic that we need *theories* of its justification? What reason do we have to think whistleblowing might be morally wrong?

Whistleblowing always involves revealing information that would not ordinarily be revealed. But there is nothing morally problematic about that; after all, revealing information not ordinarily revealed is one function of science. Whistleblowing always involves, in addition, an actual (or at least declared) intention to prevent something bad that would otherwise occur. There is nothing morally problematic in that either. That may well be the chief use of information.

What seems to make whistleblowing morally problematic is its organizational context. A mere individual cannot blow the whistle (in any interesting sense); only a member of an organization, whether a current or a former member, can do so. Indeed, he can only blow the whistle on his own organization (or some part of it). . . .

The whistleblower cannot blow the whistle using just any information obtained in virtue of membership in the organization. A clerk in Accounts who, happening upon evidence of serious wrongdoing while visiting a friend in Quality Control, is not a whistleblower just because she passes the information to a friend at the *Tribune*. She is more like a self-appointed spy. She seems to differ from the whistleblower, or at least from clear cases of the whistleblower, precisely in her relation to the information in question. To be a whistleblower is to reveal information with which one is *entrusted*.

But it is more than that. The whistleblower does not reveal the information to save his own skin (for example, to avoid perjury under oath). He has no excuse for revealing what his organization does not want revealed. Instead, he claims to be doing what he should be doing. If he cannot honestly make that claim—if, that is, he does not have that intention—his revelation is not whistleblowing (and so, not justified as whistleblowing), but something analogous, much as pulling a child from the water is not a rescue, even if it saves the child's life, when the "rescuer" merely believes herself to be salvaging old clothes. What makes whistleblowing morally problematic, if anything does, is this high-minded but unexcused misuse of one's position in a generally law-abiding, morally decent organization, an organization that *prima facie*

From *Business and Professional Ethics Journal* 15 (Spring 1996). Reprinted by permission of the author.

deserves the whistleblower's loyalty (as a burglary ring does not).

The whistleblower must reveal information the organization does not want revealed. But, in any actual organization, "what the organization wants" will be contested, with various individuals or groups asking to be taken as speaking for the organization. Who, for example, did what Thiokol wanted the night before the *Challenger* exploded? In retrospect, it is obvious that the three vice presidents, Lund, Kilminster, and Mason, did not do what Thiokol wanted—or, at least, what it would have wanted. At the time, however, they had authority to speak for the company—the conglomerate Morton-Thiokol headquartered in Chicago—while the protesting engineers, including Boisjoly, did not. Yet, even before the explosion, was it obvious that the three were doing what the company wanted? To be a whistleblower, one must, I think, at least temporarily lose an argument about what the organization wants. The whistleblower is disloyal only in a sense—the sense the winners of the internal argument get to dictate. What can justify such disloyalty?

THE STANDARD THEORY

According to the theory now more or less standard,[1] such disloyalty is morally permissible when:

(S1) The organization to which the would-be whistleblower belongs will, through its product or policy, do serious considerable harm to the public (whether to users of its product, to innocent bystanders, or to the public at large);

(S2) The would-be whistleblower has identified that threat of harm, reported it to her immediate superior, making clear both the threat itself and the objection to it, and concluded that the superior will do nothing effective; and

(S3) The would-be whistleblower has exhausted other internal procedures within the organization (for example, by going up the organizational ladder as far as allowed)—or at least made use of as many internal

procedures as the danger to others and her own safety make reasonable.

Whistleblowing is morally required (according to the standard theory) when, in addition:

(S4) The would-be whistleblower has (or has accessible) evidence that would convince a reasonable, impartial observer that her view of the threat is correct; and

(S5) The would-be whistleblower has good reason to believe that revealing the threat will (probably) prevent the harm at reasonable cost (all things considered).

Why is whistleblowing morally required when these five conditions are met? According to the standard theory, whistleblowing is morally required, when it is required at all, because "people have a moral obligation to prevent serious harm to others if they can do so with little cost to themselves."[2] In other words, whistleblowing meeting all five conditions is a form of "minimally decent Samaritanism" (a doing of what morality requires) rather than "good Samaritanism" (going well beyond the moral minimum). . . .

THREE PARADOXES

That's the standard theory—where are the paradoxes? The first paradox I want to call attention to concerns a commonplace of the whistleblowing literature. Whistleblowers are not minimally decent Samaritans. If they are Samaritans at all, they are good Samaritans. They always act at considerable risk to career, and generally, at considerable risk to their financial security and personal relations.

In this respect, as in many others, Roger Boisjoly is typical. Boisjoly blew the whistle on his employer, Thiokol; he volunteered information, in public testimony before the Rogers Commission, that Thioko did not want him to volunteer. As often happens, both his employer and many who relied on it for employment reacted hostilely. Boisjoly had to say goodbye to the company town, to old friends and neighbors, and to building rockets; he had to start a new career at an age when most people are preparing for retirement.

Since whistleblowing is generally costly to the whistleblower in some large way as this, the standard theory's minimally decent Samaritanism provides *no* justification for the central cases of whistleblowing. That is the first paradox, what we might call "the paradox of burden."

The second paradox concerns the prevention of "harm." On the standard theory, the would-be whistleblower must seek to prevent "serious and considerable harm" in order for the whistleblowing to be even morally permissible. There seems to be a good deal of play in the term *harm*. The harm in question can be physical (such as death or disease), financial (such as loss of or damage to property), and perhaps even psychological (such as fear or mental illness). But there is a limit to how much the standard theory can stretch "harm." Beyond that limit are "harms" like injustice, deception, and waste. As morally important as injustice, deception, and waste can be, they do not seem to constitute the "serious and considerable harm" that can require someone to become even a minimally decent Samaritan.

Yet, many cases of whistleblowing, perhaps most, are not about preventing serious and considerable physical, financial, or psychological harm. For example, when Boisjoly spoke up the evening before the *Challenger* exploded, the lives of seven astronauts sat in the balance. Speaking up then was about preventing serious and considerable physical, financial, and psychological harm—but it was not whistleblowing. Boisjoly was then serving his employer, not betraying a trust (even on the employer's understanding of that trust); he was calling his superiors' attention to what he thought they should take into account in their decision and not publicly revealing confidential information. The whistleblowing came after the explosion, in testimony before the Rogers Commission. By then, the seven astronauts were beyond help, the shuttle program was suspended, and any further threat of physical, financial, or psychological harm to the "public" was—after discounting for time—negligible. Boisjoly had little reason to believe his testimony would make a significant difference in the booster's redesign, in safety procedures in the shuttle program, or even in reawakening concern for safety among NASA employees and contractors. The

Challenger's explosion was much more likely to do that than anything Boisjoly could do. What Boisjoly could do in his testimony, what I think he tried to do, was prevent falsification of the record.

Falsification of the record is, of course, harm in a sense, especially a record as historically important as that which the Rogers Commission was to produce. But falsification is harm only in a sense that almost empties "harm" of its distinctive meaning, leaving it more or less equivalent to "moral wrong." The proponents of the standard theory mean more by "harm" than that De George, for example, explicitly says that a threat justifying whistleblowing must be to "life or health."[3] The standard theory is strikingly more narrow in its grounds of justification than many examples of justified whistleblowing suggest it should be. That is the second paradox, the "paradox of missing harm."

The third paradox is related to the second. Insofar as whistleblowers are understood as people out to prevent harm, not just to prevent moral wrong, their chances of success are not good. Whistleblowers generally do not prevent much harm. In this too, Boisjoly is typical. As he has said many times, the situation at Thiokol is now much as it was before the disaster. Insofar as we can identify cause and effect, even now we have little reason to believe that—whatever his actual intention—Boisjoly's testimony actually prevented any harm (beyond the moral harm of falsification). So, if whistleblowers must have, as the standard theory says (S5), (beyond the moral wrong of falsification) "good reason to believe that revealing the threat will (probably) prevent the harm," then the history of whistleblowing virtually rules out the moral justification of whistleblowing. That is certainly paradoxical in a theory purporting to state sufficient conditions for the central cases of justified whistleblowing. Let us call this "the paradox of failure."

A COMPLICITY THEORY

As I look down the roll of whistleblowers, I do not see anyone who, like the clerk from Accounts, just happened upon key documents in a cover-up. Few, if any, whistleblowers are mere third-parties like the good Samaritan. They are generally deeply involved in the activity they reveal. This involvement suggests that we might better understand what justifies (most) whistleblowing if we understand the whistleblower's obligation to derive from *complicity* in wrongdoing rather than from the ability to prevent harm.

Any complicity theory of justified whistleblowing has two obvious advantages over the standard theory. One is that (moral) complicity itself presupposes (moral) wrongdoing, not harm. So, a complicity justification automatically avoids the paradox of missing harm, fitting the facts of whistleblowing better than a theory which, like the standard one, emphasizes prevention of harm.

That is one obvious advantage of a complicity theory. The second advantage is that complicity invokes a more demanding obligation than the ability to prevent harm does. We are morally obliged to avoid doing moral wrongs. When, despite our best efforts, we nonetheless find ourselves engaged in some wrong, we have an obligation to do what we reasonably can to set things right. If, for example, I cause a traffic accident, I have a moral (and legal) obligation to call for help, stay at the scene until help arrives, and render first aid (if I know how), even at substantial cost to myself and those to whom I owe my time, and even with little likelihood that anything I do will help much. Just as a complicity theory avoids the paradox of missing harm, it also avoids the paradox of burden.

What about the third paradox, the paradox of failure? I shall come to that, but only after remedying one disadvantage of the complicity theory. That disadvantage is obvious—we do not yet have such a theory, not even a sketch. Here, then, is the place to offer a sketch of such a theory.

Complicity Theory

You are morally required to reveal what you know to the public (or to a suitable agent or representative of it) when:

(C1)   what you will reveal derives from your work for an organization;

(C2)   you are a voluntary member of that organization;

(C3)   you believe that the organization, though legitimate, is engaged in serious moral wrong doing;

(C4)   you believe that your work for that organization will contribute (more or less directly) to the wrong if (but *not* only if) you do not publicly reveal what you know;

(C5)   you are justified in beliefs C3 and C4; and

(C6)   beliefs C3 and C4 are true.

The complicity theory differs from the standard theory in several ways worth pointing out here. The first is that, according to C1, what the whistleblower reveals must derive from his work for the organization. This condition distinguishes the whistleblower from the spy (and the clerk in Accounts). The spy seeks out information in order to reveal it; the whistleblower learns it as a proper part of doing the job the organization has assigned him. The standard theory, in contrast, has nothing to say about how the whistleblower comes to know of the threat she reveals (S2). For the standard theory, spies are just another kind of whistleblower.

A second way in which the complicity theory differs from the standard theory is that the complicity theory (C2) explicitly requires the whistleblower to be a *voluntary* participant in the organization in question. Whistleblowing is not—according to the complicity theory—an activity in which slaves, prisoners, or other involuntary participants in an organization engage. . . .

A third way in which the complicity theory differs from the standard theory is that the complicity theory (C3) requires moral wrong, not harm, for justification. The wrong need not be a new event (as a harm must be if it is to be *prevented*). It might, for example, consist in no more than silence about facts necessary to correct a serious injustice.

The complicity theory (C3) does, however, follow the standard theory in requiring that the predicate of whistleblowing be "serious." Under the complicity theory, minor wrongdoing can no more justify whistleblowing than can minor harm under the standard theory. While organizational loyalty cannot forbid whistleblowing, it does forbid "tattling," that is, revealing minor wrongdoing.

A fourth way in which the complicity theory differs from the standard theory, the most important, is that the complicity theory (C4) requires that the whistleblower believe that her work will have contributed to the wrong in question if she does nothing, but it does *not* require that she believe that her revelation will prevent (or undo) the wrong. The complicity theory does not require any belief about what the whistleblowing can accomplish (beyond ending complicity in the wrong in question). The whistleblower reveals what she knows in order to prevent complicity in the wrong, not to prevent the wrong as such. She can prevent complicity (if there is any to prevent) simply by publicly revealing what she knows. The revelation itself breaks the bond of complicity, the secret partnership in wrongdoing, that makes her an accomplice in her organization's wrongdoing. The complicity theory thus avoids the third paradox, the paradox of failure, just as it avoided the other two.

The fifth difference between the complicity theory and the standard theory is closely related to the fourth. Because publicly revealing what one knows breaks the bond of complicity, the complicity theory does not require the whistleblower to have enough evidence to convince others of the wrong in question. Convincing others, or just being able to convince them, is not, as such, an element in the justification of whistleblowing.

The complicity theory does, however, require (C5) that the whistleblower be (epistemically) justified in believing both that his organization is engaged in wrongdoing and that he will contribute to that wrong unless he blows the whistle. Such (epistemic) justification may require substantial physical evidence (as the standard theory says) or just a good sense of how things work. The complicity theory does not share the standard theory's substantial evidential demand (S4).

In one respect, however, the complicity theory clearly requires more of the whistleblower than the standard theory does. The complicity theory's C6—combined with C5—requires not only that the whistleblower be *justified* in her beliefs about the organization's wrongdoing and her part in it, but also that she be *right* about them. If she is wrong about

either the wrongdoing or her complicity, her revelation will not be justified whistleblowing. . . .

The complicity theory says nothing on at least one matter about which the standard theory says much—going through channels before publicly revealing what one knows. But the two theories do not differ as much as this difference in emphasis suggests. If going through channels would suffice to prevent (or undo) the wrong, then it cannot be true (as C4 and C6 together require) that the would-be whistleblower's work will contribute to the wrong if she does not publicly reveal what she knows. Where, however, going through channels would *not* prevent (or undo) the wrong, there is no need to go through channels. Condition C4's if-clause will be satisfied. For the complicity theory, going through channels is a way of finding out what the organization will do, not an independent requirement of justification. That, I think, is also how the standard theory understands it.

TESTING THE THEORY

Let us now test the theory against Boisjoly's testimony before the Rogers Commission. Recall that under the standard theory any justification of that testimony seemed to fail for at least three reasons: First, Boisjoly could not testify without substantial cost to himself and Thiokol (to whom he owned loyalty). Second, there was no serious and substantial harm his testimony could prevent. And, third, he had little reason to believe that, even if he could identify a serious and considerable harm to prevent, his testimony had a significant chance of preventing it.

Since few doubt that Boisjoly's testimony before the Rogers Commission constitutes justified whistleblowing, if anything does, we should welcome a theory that—unlike the standard one—justifies that testimony as whistleblowing. The complicity theory sketched above does that:

(C1) Boisjoly's testimony consisted almost entirely of information derived from his work on booster rockets at Thiokol.

(C2) Boisjoly was a voluntary member of Thiokol.

(C3) Boisjoly believed Thiokol, a legitimate organization, was attempting to mislead its client, the government, about the causes of a deadly accident. Attempting to do that certainly seems a serious moral wrong.

(C4) On the evening before the *Challenger* exploded, Boisjoly gave up objecting to the launch once his superiors, including the three Thiokol vice presidents, had made it clear that they were no longer willing to listen to him. He also had a part in preparing those superiors to testify intelligently before the Rogers Commission concerning the booster's fatal field joint. Boisjoly believed that Thiokol would use his failure to offer his own interpretation of his retreat into silence the night before the launch, and the knowledge that he had imparted to his superiors, to contribute to the attempt to mislead Thiokol's client.

(C5) The evidence justifying beliefs C3 and C4 consisted of comments of various officers of Thiokol, what Boisjoly had seen at Thiokol over the years, and what he learned about the rocket business over a long career. I find this evidence sufficient to justify his belief both that his organization was engaged in wrongdoing and that his work was implicated.

(C6) Here we reach a paradox of *knowledge*. Since belief is knowledge if, but only if, it is *both* justified *and* true, we cannot *show* that we know anything. All we can show is that a belief is now justified and that we have no reason to expect anything to turn up later to prove it false. The evidence now available still justifies Boisjoly's belief both

about what Thiokol was attempting and about what would have been his part in the attempt. Since new evidence is unlikely, his testimony seems to satisfy C6 just as it satisfied the complicity theory's other five conditions.

Since the complicity theory explains why Boisjoly's testimony before the Rogers Commission was morally required whistleblowing, it has passed its first test, a test the standard theory failed.

NOTES

1. Throughout this essay, I take the standard theory to be Richard T. De George's version in *Business Ethics*, 3rd Edition (New York: Macmillan, 1990), pp. 200–214 (amended only insofar as necessary to include nonbusinesses as well as businesses). Why treat De George's theory as standard? There are two reasons: first, it seems the most commonly cited; and second, people offering alternatives generally treat it as the one to be replaced. The only obvious competitor, Norman Bowie's account, is distinguishable from De George's on no point relevant here. See Bowie's *Business Ethics* (Englewood Cliffs, NJ: Prentice Hall, 1982), p. 143.

2. De George, op. cit.

3. De George, p. 210: "The notion of *serious* harm might be expanded to include serious financial harm, and kinds of harm other than death and serious threats to health and body. But as we noted earlier, we shall restrict ourselves here to products and practices that produce or threaten serious harm or danger to life and health."

QUESTIONS

1. What are the paradoxes of whistle-blowing?

2. What is Davis's "complicity theory" of the morality of whistle-blowing? How does it avoid the failures of the standard theory?

Ronald Duska | # Whistleblowing and Employee Loyalty

Ronald Duska is Charles F. Lamont Post Chair of Ethics and the Professions Professor of Ethics at the American College.

There are proponents on both sides of the issue—those who praise whistleblowers as civic heroes and those who condemn them as "finks." Maxwell Glen and Cody Shearer, who wrote about the whistleblowers at Three Mile Island say, "Without the *courageous* breed of assorted company insiders known as whistleblowers—workers who often risk their livelihoods to disclose information about construction and design flaws—the Nuclear Regulatory Commission itself would be nearly as idle as Three Mile Island. . . . That whistle-blowers deserve both gratitude and protection is beyond disagreement."[1]

Still, while Glen and Shearer praise whistleblowers, others vociferously condemn them. For example, in a now infamous quote, James Roche, the former president of General Motors said:

> Some critics are now busy eroding another support of free enterprise—the loyalty of a management team, with its unifying values and cooperative work. Some of the enemies of business now encourage an employee to be *disloyal* to the enterprise. They want to create suspicion and disharmony, and pry into the proprietary interests of the business. However this is labeled—industrial espionage, whistle blowing, or professional responsibility—it is another tactic for spreading disunity and creating conflict.[2]

From Roche's point of view, not only is whistleblowing not "courageous" and not deserving of gratitude and protection" as Glen and Shearer would have it, it is corrosive and impermissible.

Discussions of whistleblowing generally revolve around three topics: (1) attempts to define whistleblowing more precisely, (2) debates about whether and when whistleblowing is permissible, and (3) debates about whether and when one has an obligation to blow the whistle.

In this paper I want to focus on the second problem, because I find it somewhat disconcerting that there is a problem at all. When I first looked into the ethics of whistleblowing it seemed to me that whistleblowing was a good thing, and yet I found in the literature claim after claim that it was in need of defense, that there was something wrong with it, namely that it was an act of disloyalty.

If whistleblowing is a disloyal act, it deserves disapproval, and ultimately any action of whistleblowing needs justification. This disturbs me. It is as if the act of a good Samaritan is being condemned as an act of interference, as if the prevention of a suicide needs to be justified.

In his book *Business Ethics,* Norman Bowie claims that "whistleblowing . . . violate(s) a *prima facie* duty of loyalty to one's employer." According to Bowie, there is a duty of loyalty that prohibits one from reporting his employer or company. Bowie, of course, recognizes that this is only a *prima facie* duty, that is, one that can be overridden by a higher duty to the public good. Nevertheless, the axiom that whistleblowing is disloyal is Bowie's starting point.[3]

Bowie is not alone. Sissela Bok sees "whistleblowing" as an instance of disloyalty:

> The whistleblower hopes to stop the game; but since he is neither referee nor coach, and since he blows the whistle on his own team, his act is seen as a *violation of loyalty.* In holding his position, he has assumed certain obligations to his colleagues and clients. He may even have subscribed to a loyalty oath or a promise of confidentiality. . . . Loyalty to colleagues and to clients comes to be pitted against loyalty to the public interest, to those who may be injured unless the revelation is made.[4]

From Tom L. Beauchamp and Norman E. Bowie, *Ethical Theory and Business* (Englewood Cliffs, NJ: Prentice Hall, 2001). Reprinted by permission of the author.

Bowie and Bok end up defending whistleblowing in certain contexts, so I don't necessarily disagree with their conclusions. However, I fail to see how one has an obligation of loyalty to one's company, so I disagree with their perception of the problem and their starting point. I want to argue that one does not have an obligation of loyalty to a company, even a prima facie one, because companies are not the kind of things that are properly objects of loyalty. To make them objects of loyalty gives them a moral status they do not deserve and in raising their status, one lowers the status of the individuals who work for the companies. Thus, the difference in perception is important because those who think employees have an obligation of loyalty to a company fail to take into account a relevant moral difference between persons and corporations.

But why aren't companies the kind of things that can be objects of loyalty? To answer that we have to ask what are proper objects of loyalty. John Ladd states the problem this way, "Granted that loyalty is the wholehearted devotion to an object of some kind, what kind of thing is the object? Is it an abstract entity, such as an idea or a collective being? Or is it a person or group of persons?"[5] Philosophers fall into three camps on the question. On one side are the idealists who hold that loyalty is devotion to something more than persons, to some cause or abstract entity. On the other side are what Ladd calls "social atomists," and these include empiricists and utilitarians, who think that at most one can only be loyal to individuals and that loyalty can ultimately be explained away as some other obligation that holds between two people. Finally, there is a moderate position that holds that although idealists go too far in postulating some super-personal entity as an object of loyalty, loyalty is still an important and real relation that holds between people, one that cannot be dismissed by reducing it to some other relation.

There does seem to be a view of loyalty that is not extreme. According to Ladd, " 'loyalty' is taken to refer to a relationship between persons—for instance, between a lord and his vassal, between a parent and his children, or between friends. Thus the object of loyalty is ordinarily taken to be a person or a group of persons."[6]

But this raises a problem that Ladd glosses over. There is a difference between a person or a group of persons, and aside from instances of loyalty that relate two people such as lord/vassal, parent/child, or friend/friend, there are instances of loyalty relating a person to a group, such as a person to his family, a person to this team, and a person to his country. Families, countries, and teams are presumably groups of persons. They are certainly ordinarily construed as objects of loyalty.

But to what am I loyal in such a group? In being loyal to the group am I being loyal to the whole group or to its members? It is easy to see the object of loyalty in the case of an individual person. It is simply the individual. But to whom am I loyal in a group? To whom am I loyal in a family? Am I loyal to each and every individual or to something larger, and if to something larger, what is it? We are tempted to think of a group as an entity of its own, an individual in its own right, having an identity of its own.

To avoid the problem of individuals existing for the sake of the group, the atomists insist that a group is nothing more than the individuals who comprise it, nothing other than a mental fiction by which we refer to a group of individuals. It is certainly not a reality or entity over and above the sum of its parts, and consequently is not a proper object of loyalty. Under such a position, of course, no loyalty would be owed to a company because a company is a mere mental fiction, since it is a group. One would have obligations to the individual members of the company, but one could never be justified in overriding those obligations for the sake of the "group" taken collectively. A company has no moral status except in terms of the individual members who comprise it. It is not a proper object of loyalty. But the atomists go too far. Some groups, such as a family, do have a reality of their own, whereas groups of people walking down the street do not. From Ladd's point of view the social atomist is wrong because he fails to recognize the kinds of groups that are held together by "the ties that bind." The atomist tries to reduce these groups to simple sets of individuals bound together by some externally imposed criteria. This seems wrong.

There do seem to be groups in which the relationships and interactions create a new force or entity. A group takes on an identity and a reality of its own that is determined by its purpose, and this purpose defines the various relationships and roles set up within the group. There is a division of labor into roles necessary for the fulfillment of the purposes of the group. The membership, then, is not of individuals who are the same but of individuals who have specific relationships to one another determined by the aim of the group. Thus we get specific relationships like parent/child, coach/player, and so on, that don't occur in other groups. It seems then that an atomist account of loyalty that restricts loyalty merely to individuals and does not include loyalty to groups might be inadequate.

But once I have admitted that we can have loyalty to a group, do I not open myself up to criticism from the proponent of loyalty to the company? Might not the proponent of loyalty to business say: "Very well. I agree with you. The atomists are short-sighted. Groups have some sort of reality and they can be proper objects of loyalty. But companies are groups. Therefore companies are proper objects of loyalty."

The point seems well taken, except for the fact that the kinds of relationships that loyalty requires are just the kind that one does not find in business. As Ladd says, "The ties that bind the persons together provide the basis of loyalty." But all sorts of ties bind people together. I am a member of a group of fans if I go to a ball game. I am a member of a group if I merely walk down the street. What binds people together in a business is not sufficient to require loyalty.

A business or corporation does two things in the free enterprise system: It produces a good or service and it makes a profit. The making of a profit, however, is the primary function of a business as a business, for if the production of the good or service is not profitable, the business would be out of business. Thus nonprofitable goods or services are a means to an end. People bound together in a business are bound together not for mutual fulfillment and support, but to divide labor or make a profit. Thus, while we can jokingly refer to a family as a place where "they have to take you in no matter what," we cannot refer to a company in that way. If a worker does not produce in a company or if cheaper laborers are available, the company—in order to fulfill its purpose—should get rid of the worker. A company feels no obligation of loyalty. The saying "You can't buy loyalty" is true. Loyalty depends on ties that demand self-sacrifice with no expectation of reward. Business functions on the basis of enlightened self-interest. I am devoted to a company not because it is like a parent to me; it is not. Attempts of some companies to create "one big happy family" ought to be looked on with suspicion. I am not devoted to it at all, nor should I be. I work for it because it pays me. I am not in a family to get paid, I am in a company to get paid.

The cold hard truth is that the goal of profit is what gives birth to a company and forms that

On Secrecy and Disclosure
Joseph Pulitzer

There is not a crime, there is not a dodge, there is not a trick, there is not a swindle, there is not a vice which does not live by secrecy. Get these things out in the open, describe them, attack them, ridicule them in the press, and sooner or later public opinion will sweep them away. Publicity may not be the only thing that is needed, but it is the one thing without which all other agencies will fail.

particular group. Money is what ties the group together. But in such a commercialized venture, with such a goal, there is no loyalty, or at least none need be expected. An employer will release an employee and an employee will walk away from an employer when it is profitable for either one to do so.

Not only is loyalty to a corporation not required, it more than likely is misguided. There is nothing as pathetic as the story of the loyal employee who, having given above and beyond the call of duty, is let go in the restructuring of the company. He feels betrayed because he mistakenly viewed the company as an object of his loyalty. Getting rid of such foolish romanticism and coming to grips with this hard but accurate assessment should ultimately benefit everyone.

To think we owe a company or corporation loyalty requires us to think of that company as a person or as a group with a goal of human fulfillment. If we think of it in this way we can be loyal. But this is the wrong way to think. A company is not a person. A company is an instrument, and an instrument with a specific purpose, the making of profit. To treat an instrument as an end in itself, like a person, may not be as bad as treating an end as an instrument, but it does give the instrument a moral status it does not deserve; and by elevating the instrument we lower the end. All things, instruments and ends, become alike.

Remember that Roche refers to the "management team" and Bok sees the name "whistleblowing" coming from the instance of a referee blowing a whistle in the presence of a foul. What is perceived as bad about whistleblowing in business from this perspective is that one blows the whistle on one's own team, thereby violating team loyalty. If the company can get its employees to view it as a team they belong to, it is easier to demand loyalty. Then the rules governing teamwork and team loyalty will apply. One reason the appeal to a team and team loyalty works so well in business is that businesses are in competition with one another. Effective motivation turns business practices into a game and instills teamwork.

But businesses differ from teams in very important respects, which makes the analogy between business and a team dangerous. Loyalty to a team is loyalty within the context of sport or a competition.

Teamwork and team loyalty require that in the circumscribed activity of the game I cooperate with my fellow players, so that pulling all together, we may win. The object of (most) sports is victory. But winning in sports is a social convention, divorced from the usual goings on of society. Such a winning is most times a harmless, morally neutral diversion.

But the fact that this victory in sports, within the rules enforced by a referee (whistleblower), is a socially developed convention taking place within a larger social context makes it quite different from competition in business, which, rather than being defined by a context, permeates the whole of society in its influence. Competition leads not only to victory but to losers. One can lose at sport with precious few consequences. The consequences of losing at business are much larger. Further, the losers in business can be those who are not in the game voluntarily (we are all forced to participate) but who are still affected by business decisions. People cannot choose to participate in business. It permeates everyone's lives.

The team model, then, fits very well with the model of the free market system, because there competition is said to be the name of the game. Rival companies compete and their object is to win. To call a foul on one's own teammate is to jeopardize one's chances of winning and is viewed as disloyalty.

But isn't it time to stop viewing corporate machinations as games? These games are not controlled and are not ended after a specific time. The activities of business affect the lives of everyone, not just the game players. The analogy of the corporation to a team and the consequent appeal to team loyalty, although understandable, is seriously misleading, at least in the moral sphere where competition is not the prevailing virtue.

If my analysis is correct, the issue of the permissibility of whistleblowing is not a real issue since there is no obligation of loyalty to a company. Whistleblowing is not only permissible but expected when a company is harming society. The issue is not one of disloyalty to the company, but of whether the whistleblower has an obligation to society if blowing the whistle will bring him retaliation.

The Upside of Whistle-Blowing

Jim Yardley

The nightclub sparkled under a strobe light, as dancers gyrated to "Play That Funky Music" and Court TV's guest of honor, Sherron S. Watkins, sipped wine from a glow-in-the-dark glass. The music stopped so Ms. Watkins could accept the cable channel's Scales of Justice award.

It was not quite the Nobel Prize ceremony. "Let's rock-n-roll and have a few drinks!" exclaimed Court TV's chairman, Henry Schleiff, after handing Ms. Watkins a bronze statuette. The D.J. obeyed and blasted "Shaft," as the 1970's-theme publicity party roared on.

For Ms. Watkins, the Enron vice president whose blunt-spoken warning about the company's accounting practices made her an instant celebrity, the Court TV party in New Orleans on Sunday was only one weird scene from her surreal new life. The day before, Sam Donaldson introduced her to President Bush at the White House Correspondent's Association dinner in Washington.

And this week in Houston, she has continued to do what some consider the unlikeliest thing of all—work at Enron, whose improprieties she sought to expose in the memo, now famous, she wrote to the former chairman, Kenneth L. Lay, months before the company filed for bankruptcy.

"Generally, people are surprised that she is still there," said Philip H. Hilder, Ms. Watkins's lawyer. "Some people think she has been fired. Some people thought that just on her own she had moved on."

For now, while she remains at Enron, the 42-year-old Ms. Watkins is also tip-toeing toward a public life. Her persona as an upscale Erin Brockovich has brought her book and movie deals. She is in demand on the lecture circuit, and next week she is scheduled to be the keynote speaker at a San Francisco conference that is being sponsored by Steve Forbes.

The New York Times, May 10, 2002.

NOTES

1. Maxwell Glen and Cody Shearer, "Going After the Whistle-blowers," *Philadelphia Inquirer*, Tuesday, August 2, 1983, Op-ed page, p. 11A.

2. James M. Roche, "The Competitive System, to Work, to Preserve, and to Protect," *Vital Speeches of the Day* (May 1971): 445.

3. Norman Bowie, *Business Ethics* (Englewood Cliffs, NJ: Prentice Hall, 1982), pp. 140–143.

4. Sissela Bok, "Whistleblowing and Professional Responsibilities," *New York University Education Quarterly* 2 (1980): 3.

5. John Ladd, "Loyalty," *The Encyclopedia of Philosophy* 5: 97.

6. Ibid.

QUESTIONS

1. Whether and when is whistle-blowing permissible, according to Duska? What moral constraints do whistle-blowers have?

2. What is the "team model"? How does it solve the problem of whistle-blowing?

David E. Soles | # Four Concepts of Loyalty

David E. Soles is an author and a philosopher.

THE IDEALIST ACCOUNT

The first view of loyalty may be called an idealist account because of the close resemblance it bears to the position developed by the American idealist, Josiah Royce. According to Royce, loyalty is

[t]he willing and practical and thorough-going devotion of a person to a cause. A man is loyal when, first, he has some *cause* to which he is loyal; secondly, he *willingly* and *thoroughly* devotes himself to this cause; and when, thirdly, he expresses his devotion in some *sustained and practical way*, by acting steadily in the service of his cause. Instances of loyalty are: The devotion of a patriot to his country, when this devotion leads him to actually live and perhaps to die for his country; the devotion of a martyr to his religion; the devotion of a ship's captain to the requirements of his office when, after a disaster, he works steadily for his ship and for the saving of the ship's company until the last possible service is accomplished, so that he is the last man to leave the ship, and is ready if need be to go down with his ship.[1]

As Royce realizes, each of the aspects of his analysis requires further elucidation. To begin with the object of loyalty: that to which one is loyal must be something objective, external to the individual, and possessed of its own inherent value; "[i]t does not get its value merely from your being pleased with it. You believe, on the contrary, that you love it just because of its own value, which it has by itself, even if you die" (19).

By saying that loyalty requires *willing* devotion, Royce is maintaining that loyalty must be freely given; while obedience can be demanded, loyalty cannot. In part, this follows from Royce's thesis that loyalty entails devotion: devotion is a mental state not reducible to behavior, and while behavior can be demanded, mental states cannot. But while loyalty may entail devotion, devotion is never sufficient for loyalty: "[l]oyalty is never mere emotion. Adoration and affection may go with loyalty, but can never alone constitute loyalty" (18).

This follows from the claim that loyalty is practical—to be loyal is to serve a cause. Furthermore, this service is thorough-going and sustained; a loyal person does whatever is necessary to promote the cause, "ready to live or die as the cause directs" (18).

This idealist conception of loyalty is germane to discussions of business ethics in the following way. If this is the accepted conception of loyalty and if it can be established that employees ought to be loyal to their employers, then the stringent obligations sometimes placed upon employees in the name of loyalty would be perfectly justified. A loyal employee would be one thoroughly dedicated to serving the interests of his principal, ready to live or die as directed, and to say that employees should be loyal would be to advocate such dedication. It is instructive to consider some examples of the sorts of obligations this conception of loyalty could require of a loyal employee. A loyal employee would always be willing to place the interests of the principal before purely private interests, even in matters unrelated to employment; a loyal employee would be willing to sacrifice the interests of uninvolved third parties or even society at large, if doing so served the employer's interest; a loyal employee would never advocate or vote for social policies or legislation that might damage the interests of the employer; a loyal employee would never publicly criticize or oppose the actions of the employer; a loyal employee would never consider leaving the employer. That something akin to the idealist conception of loyalty is operative in some quarters is evidenced by the frequent endorsements of these claims.

Reprinted by permission of the author from *The International Journal of Applied Philosophy* 8 (Summer 1993).

Lest it be thought that I am constructing a straw man here; consider the following case which Marcia Baron discusses in *The Moral Status of Loyalty*.

In a 1973 CBS report on Phillips Petroleum, Inc., one of its chief executives was asked to describe what sort of qualities his company looks for in prospective employees. He responded without hesitation that above all else, what Phillips wants and needs is loyalty on the part of its employees. A loyal employee, he elaborated, would buy only Phillips products. . . . Moreover, a loyal employee would vote in local, state, and national elections in whatever way was most conducive to the growth and flourishing of Phillips. And, of course, a loyal employee would never leave Phillips unless it was absolutely unavoidable. To reduce the likelihood of that happening, prospective employees were screened to make sure their respective wives did not have careers which might conflict with lifelong loyalty to Phillips.[2]

Is it true that employees have an obligation to so thoroughly dedicate themselves to the interests of their employers and, if so, what are the grounds of that obligation? . . .

It is morally irresponsible to be willing to perform any conceivable action that would further the interests of one's chosen cause; one must always reserve the option of saying that one can no longer serve a cause if it requires the performance of certain sorts of actions. . . .

If loyalty requires such total, thorough-going dedication to a cause, there are very few things worthy of loyalty; furthermore, since the interests of any two causes could conceivably come into conflict, one can be loyal to only one object. Therefore, it is incumbent upon each person to ensure that the object of his loyalty is of the highest inherent worth.

It is very unlikely that business institutions qualify as objects of the most inherent worth. To begin with, business institutions are instrumentally, not inherently, valuable; they are valued because they are means for providing goods and services which are valued. If we no longer cared for those goods and services or if we found better ways to obtain them, the institutions which provide them would lose much of their value. Furthermore, not all business institutions possess instrumental value: some produce more

harm than good by manufacturing dangerous, inferior products, polluting the environment, engaging in illegal business practices, etc. But whether instrumentally good or evil, a business institution is not the sort of thing worthy of loyalty in the idealist sense.

In summary, if the idealist conception of loyalty were accepted as our working notion of loyalty, and if it could be established that employees ought to be loyal to their employers, then the demands placed upon employees in the name of loyalty would be justified: employees would have an obligation to place the interests of their employers before all other interests. However, it is not clear that we should accept this as our working conception of loyalty and, more importantly, even if we did, we must conclude that business institutions could not be appropriate objects of loyalty.

THE COMMON SENSE CONCEPTION

The common sense view of loyalty more satisfactorily captures the everyday conception of loyalty with which most of us are familiar. Most of us are untroubled by statements to the effect that someone is a loyal fan of the Kansas City Royals, a loyal member of the Republican party, or loyal to her alma mater, and when we hear such claims we are not inclined to suppose that the person is totally dedicated to the cause, "willing to live or die as the cause directs."

A version of the common sense view of loyalty has been formulated by Andrew Oldenquist in "Loyalties."[3] According to Oldenquist,

. . . [w]hen I have a loyalty to something I have somehow come to view it as *mine*. It is an object of non-instrumental value to me in virtue (but not only in virtue) of its being mine, and I am disposed to feel pride when it prospers, shame when it declines, and anger or indignation when it is harmed. In general, people care about the objects of their loyalties, and they acknowledge obligations that they would not acknowledge were it not for their loyalties. (175)

. . . [L]oyalty is positive and is primarily characterized by esteem and concern for the common good of one's group. (177)

On this view, there are three essential features of loyalty. First, loyalty entails having a positive attitude towards the objects of one's loyalty; a loyalty is to "an object of non-instrumental value," people "care about" the objects of their loyalties. Second, loyalty entails a disposition to serve the interests of the object to which one is loyal; loyal persons "acknowledge obligations that they would not acknowledge were it not for their loyalties." Third, both the concern and the obligations are rooted in the individual's belief that he stands in some personal relationship to the object of his loyalty; to have a loyalty to something is to somehow come to view it as one's own.

The first thing to note about this conception of loyalty is that it is not sufficient to distinguish loyalty from many other virtues.[4] While caring, acknowledging obligations, and feeling a personal relationship may be necessary features of loyalty, they also are necessary features of virtues such as love and friendship and may even characterize the relationship between some professionals and their patients, clients, students, etc. Many dedicated teachers consider their students to be objects of non-instrumental value, care about them, acknowledge supererogatory obligations, and both the concern and the obligations stem from the fact that these students are their students. Similar remarks may be made about doctors, nurses, lawyers, social workers, etc. To characterize their attitude as one of loyalty seems to be stretching the common sense notion of loyalty too far. . . .

In conflating loyalty with other, distinct, virtues, Oldenquist has failed to provide the promised analysis of loyalty. Nevertheless, while this common sense account should not be construed as providing a definition of "loyalty" in terms of necessary and sufficient conditions, it may be acceptable as a rough characterization of some essential features of loyalty. Loyalty, like friendship, love, and professional interest, entails concern, obligations, and a feeling of personal identification with the object of one's loyalty. The questions that need to be asked, then, are: (1) does one have any obligation to have such attitudes to one's employer, and (2) does the having of such attitudes justify always acting in the interests of the object of one's loyalty?

Beginning with the first question, on the common sense account, the mere fact that one happens to have been born in a particular country, happens to have attended a particular school, or happens to work for a particular institution is not sufficient for saying that one should be loyal to it. Oldenquist makes this point in maintaining that ". . . a loyalist doesn't value something simply because it is his. It must have features which make it worth having, and it could deteriorate to the extent that shame ultimately kills his loyalty" (178). On this conception of loyalty, one should bestow one's loyalty only on those objects which are worthy of it and loyalty bestowed upon some nations, schools or institutions would be misguided.

Furthermore, if this is our working conception of loyalty, no one has an obligation to be loyal to anything; to suppose that one has an obligation to be loyal to anything is to make a fundamental category mistake. On this view, being loyal entails having certain sorts of attitudes; to be loyal to an object one must care about it. But while persons can have moral obligations to perform certain actions and while certain attitudes may be morally desirable or indesirable, we do not have moral obligations to have certain attitudes and beliefs. Just as no one has an obligation to have feelings of love or friendship to another, no one has an obligation to have feelings of loyalty to anything. Thus, one can have no obligation to be loyal to her nation, school, or employer even if they are worthy of loyalty.

Turning to the second question, does loyalty require one to always act in the interest of that to which one is loyal? It is often suggested that loyalty is inconsistent with certain sorts of actions, for example, whistleblowing is alleged to be incompatible with loyalty. Sissela Bok, for instance, sets up the dichotomy this way:

> . . . [T]he whistleblower hopes to stop the game; but since he is neither referee nor coach, and since he blows the whistle on his own team, his act is seen as a violation of loyalty. In holding his position, he has assumed certain obligations to his colleagues and clients. He may even have subscribed to a loyalty oath or a promise of confidentiality. Loyalty to colleagues and clients comes to be pitted against loyalty to the public interest, to those who may be injured unless the revelation is made.
> *Not only is loyalty violated in whistleblowing*, hierarchy as well is often opposed. . . . If the facts warrant whistleblowing, how can the second element— *breach of loyalty*—be minimized?[5] (my italics)

Blind to Earned Loyalty

Robert C. Solomon and Clancy Martin

The concept of loyalty has changed from one of "blind and obligated" to one of "insightful and earned." Several generations ago, if a person worked hard and kept his nose to the grindstone, he could pretty well be assured of work for a lifetime. People were loyal to organizations because they believed organizations would be loyal to them.

The passage of "good old loyalty" may be lamented by many, but there is some good news. It has been replaced by a strong new type—namely, earned loyalty.

So, rather than lament the loss of "good old loyalty," let's focus on a loyalty that may well provide a stronger motivational force for both management and the managed. I have identified five basic elements of the new loyalty.

1. Values and Standards. Loyalty tends to be more easily earned in those organizations that have clearly-defined values and challenging standards. People are likely to be loyal to values that lead to outstanding achievements in products, services, and relationships.
2. Clear Expectations. A willingness to be specific and forthright in terms of expected behaviors does a great deal toward developing a feeling of loyalty on the part of those who will follow. It is easier for people to be loyal to what they clearly understand.
3. Frequent Feedback. People need to know where they stand and how well or poorly they have performed when evaluated against the expectations, standards, and values. People need to hear good news as well as bad. Frequent feedback is a way of increasing meaningful involvement.
4. Respect for the Individual. The new loyalty will have to be earned on the basis of respect for the individual. Respect requires trust, based on consistency in personal and interpersonal relationships; a willingness to be open with expectations and requirements; to really listen and engage in honest exchange.
5. Long-Term Commitments. This last element is probably most difficult to achieve. In what appears to many to be an atmosphere of layoffs, terminations, forced resignations, and retirements, it is difficult to convince people that long-term commitments are realistic or possible.

—From *Above the Bottom Line*

On the common sense conception, this is a very misleading way of presenting the problem for it implies that whistleblowing is a breach of loyalty, that one cannot both be loyal to an institution and blow the whistle on it. But, on the common sense view, this is surely wrong; one can view an institution as one's own, care deeply about it, assume obligations towards it, and still publicly and strenuously oppose what one takes to be unethical or illegal actions on its part. This is a feature of loyalty explicitly recognized in British politics as "the loyal opposition."

Setting up a dichotomy between loyalty and whistleblowing is not merely a misleading way to present the problem of whistleblowing, it is dangerous. Loyalty is generally perceived as a virtue and disloyalty is perceived as a vice. To say that loyalty demands a certain action is to give a prima facie reason for performing that action and to label a particular action as disloyal is to give a prima facie reason for not performing that action. Under those conditions, potential whistleblowers are encouraged to construe themselves as choosing between performing a wrong act themselves (being disloyal) or remaining silent about the performance of wrongs committed by others. When presented this way, it is not surprising that many individuals choose silence. But if whistleblowing is not construed as an instance of disloyalty, the whole complexion of the problem changes. If loyalty does not require acquiescence in wrong doing, the refusal to remain silent about known wrongs cannot be construed as an ipso facto instance of disloyalty.

Acceptance of the common sense view of loyalty, thus, would justify two conclusions both of which are anathema to many discussions of business and professional ethics. First, it is simply a mistake to suppose that individuals have an obligation to be loyal to their employers and second, loyalty is compatible with strenuously opposing actions of one's employer.

LOYALTIES AS NORMS

While he does not appear to be aware that he is doing so, Oldenquist formulates a second conception of loyalty radically different from his common sense account. According to this second view, "loyalties are norms that define the domains within which we accept the moral machinery of universalizable reasons and relevant differences" (182); alternatively, "loyalties define moral communities or domains within which we are willing to universalize moral judgments, treat equals equally, protect the common good, and in other ways adopt the familiar machinery of impersonal morality. . . . A loyalty defines a moral community in terms of a conception of a common good and a special commitment to the members of the group who share this good" (177). This seems to be incompatible with the common sense account Oldenquist formulates. Attitudes, definitions and norms are different sorts of things. If loyalty is an attitude as the common sense account maintains, then it is neither a norm nor a definition.

Perhaps the confusion here is merely verbal. Perhaps Oldenquist's claim is something like this: the class of objects to which one is loyal is delineated by, or co-extensive with, the moral communities or domains "within which we are willing to universalize moral judgments, treat equals equally, protect the common good, and in other ways adopt the familiar machinery of impersonal morality." On this reading, loyalty is not literally a norm which defines a moral community; rather, one has attitudes of loyalty towards the moral community determined by the norms.

There are two ways of interpreting this talk of loyalty to the moral community: (1) we might have feelings of loyalty to each of the members of the community defined by the norm, or (2) we might have feelings of loyalty to the community, but not necessarily to each of its members. Either alternative faces serious difficulties.

Beginning with the first interpretation, if loyalty is characterized by positive feelings of esteem and concern, a disposition to feel pride when the object of loyalty prospers, shame when it declines, and anger or hurt when it is harmed, then the moral community defined by the norms and the objects of one's loyalty might not be co-extensive. One might, for instance, define the moral community as rational, sentient beings; this would define the domain within which we are willing to universalize moral judgments, etc. One might not, however, have positive feelings of concern, esteem, etc. for all the members of this community. In that case, the community of objects to which one is loyal would not be coextensive with the moral community.

The second interpretation would avoid this conclusion by arguing that on the above example one is loyal to the class of rational sentient beings, not individual rational sentient beings; that communities and not individuals are the proper objects of loyalty. . . .

If any moral norm to which one is committed defines a moral community to which one is loyal, then loyalty can never come into conflict with any other moral standard. Suppose that I am loyal to the institution where I am employed; it is a community towards which I have positive attitudes, I have assumed special obligations to promote its interests, I treat the members of that community according to the procedures of impersonal morality, recognizing universalizable reasons, and relevant differences, etc. Suppose that I am also committed to the principle that rational beings should always be treated as ends in themselves. Suppose, finally, that I come to perceive certain policies pursued by my institution as being grossly exploitive and am torn between a desire to protect the institution and an obligation to act on my moral principles. In choosing what course of action to pursue, it would be natural to describe myself as choosing between considerations of loyalty to the institution and some other principle of morality.

On Oldenquist's view, however, the choice is merely one between a wide and a narrow loyalty; on the one hand I am loyal to the institution and on the other hand I am loyal to the moral community defined by the norm. If any moral standard which I accept defines a moral community to which I am loyal, then loyalty can never come into conflict with any other moral standard, there can only be conflicts between wide and narrow loyalties. At precisely that point loyalty becomes a vacuous, trivial moral notion.

Furthermore, to say that loyalty is a norm does not answer any ethical questions nor provide moral guidance. . . .In particular, characterizing loyalties as norms which define moral communities provides no guidance in ascertaining whether we should be loyal to our employers nor does it provide any insight into what loyalty would demand should we decide that loyalty is appropriate. Consequently, such an analysis is useless for deciding the interesting questions about loyalty that arise in the context of business and professional ethics.

THE MINIMALIST ACCOUNT

There is a fourth conception of loyalty which maintains that a loyal individual is one who meets reasonable expectations of trust; to be loyal just is to discharge one's obligations and responsibilities conscientiously. Such an attenuated view of loyalty does not demand positive feelings of affection, devotion, or respect nor does it expect one to perform supererogatory actions in promoting the interests of the object of one's loyalty. At most, loyalty demands that one act in a way that does not betray reasonable expectations of trust.

The Restatement of the Law of Agency is subject to a minimalist interpretation.[6] That Restatement maintains that a loyal agent has a duty ". . . to act solely for the benefit of the principal in all matters connected with his agency" (387). This claim that the agent is to act solely for the benefit of the principal is qualified in several important respects by the Restatement. First, an agent may act against the interests of his principal when doing so is necessary for the protection of his own interests or those of others (387b). Second, an agent has no obligation to perform acts which are illegal or unethical and ". . . in determining whether or not the orders of the principal are reasonable . . . business or professional ethics . . . are considered" (385-1a). Third, an agent is not "prevented from acting in good faith outside his employment in a manner which injuriously affects his principal's business" (387b). Finally, "[a]n agent is privileged to reveal information confidentially acquired . . . in the protection of a superior interest of himself or of a third person. Thus, if the confidential information is to the effect that the principal is committing or is about to commit a crime, the agent is under no duty not to reveal it" (395f).

Like most documents, the Restatement of Agency is subject to competing interpretations. As Blumberg has noted, the Restatement

. . . is drafted in terms of economic activity, economic motivation, and economic advantage and formulates duties of loyalty and obedience for the agent to prevent the agent's own economic interest from impairing his judgment, zeal, or single-minded devotion to the furtherance of his principal's economic interests. The reference in section 395, Comment permitting the agent to disclose confidential information concerning a criminal act committed or planned by the principal is the sole exception to a system of analysis that is otherwise exclusively concerned with matters relating to the economic position of the parties.[7] . . .

As Blumberg rightly emphasizes, the Restatement is concerned almost exclusively with conflicts of economic interests; nevertheless, if interpreted liberally, the Restatement can be quite useful in responding to the broader issues. The discussion of criminal activity at 395f could be treated as an example of a case where the revelation of confidential material is justified by the need to protect a superior interest; it need not be read as limiting the revelation of confidential material to cases involving criminal activity. By the same token, 387b could be interpreted as maintaining that an agent is justified in acting against the interests of the principal when doing so is necessary to protect important noneconomic interests of himself or others. Interpreted thusly, either 395f or 387b could be appealed to in justifying the claim that loyalty is consistent with acting against the interests of one's employer.

On the minimalist account, loyalty would not entail a willingness to participate in, condone or remain silent about illegal activities. It would not entail willingness to participate in unethical conduct if doing so promoted the interests of one's principal. It would be compatible with acting against the interests of one's employer, even revealing confidential information, if doing so were necessary to protect important interests of the public. Finally, contrary to the opinion of the Phillips executive, loyalty would be compatible with voting in ways not conducive to the growth and flourishing of one's principal and even compatible with seeking employment elsewhere. In this minimalist sense, simply meeting reasonable expectations of trust is sufficient for loyalty.

This, of course, raises the issue of what responsibilities it is reasonable for employers to entrust to employees. Many of these are defined and clearly stipulated in job descriptions, contracts, and codes of professional ethics and many more are informally recognized as standard acceptable practices within a profession; and, while there are bound to be grey areas and points of disagreement, there are some activities which loyalty does not enjoin.

If the minimalist conception of loyalty is accepted, it seems clear that employees ought to be loyal to their employers. That, however, merely amounts to the claim that they ought to meet reasonable, legitimate expectations of trust; it does not impose upon them the sorts of obligations that often are urged in the name of loyalty.

CONCLUSION

Much of the confusion and disagreement infecting discussions of the role of loyalty in business and professional ethics has been engendered by equivocation and ambiguity in the concept itself. This essay has briefly considered four different conceptions of loyalty and examined some of the implications of each. If the idealist conception of loyalty is accepted, loyalty to one's employer would demand the sort of behavior sometimes advocated in its name. It is not clear, however, that this account should be accepted and, if we do accept it, employers would not be appropriate objects of loyalty. If the common sense conception of loyalty is accepted, two conclusions follow: first, since loyalty is supererogatory, no one has an obligation to feel loyal to anything; second, loyalty, in this sense, does not entail placing the interests of one's principal before all other considerations and, in fact, is compatible with opposing some of the interests of one's principal. The third conception, which maintains that the adoption of any norm regulating conduct generates a loyalty, trivializes the notion of loyalty to the point where it is useless for guiding conduct. Finally, on the minimalist conception, one can justify saying that employees ought to be loyal to their employers; the minimalist view is sufficiently attenuated, however, that such a claim does not amount to much.

NOTES

1. Josiah Royce, *The Philosophy of Loyalty*, The MacMillan Co., New York, 1916, pp. 16–17. Subsequent references to this work are provided as page numbers in the text.

2. Marcia Baron, *The Moral Status of Loyalty*, Kendal Hunt, Dubuque, Iowa, 1984, p. 1.

3. Andrew Oldenquist, "Loyalties," *The Journal of Philosophy*, April, 1982, pp. 173–193. Subsequent references to this work are provided as page numbers in the text.

4. This should not be construed as a criticism of Oldenquist. His objective seems to be to advocate loyalty, not explicate the conception.

5. Sissela Bok, "Whistleblowing and Professional Responsibility," *New York University Education Quarterly*, Vol. II, 4 (1980), 2–7. Reprinted in Beauchamp and Bowie, *Ethical Theory and Business*, 2nd ed., Prentice Hall, Inc., Englewood Cliffs, New Jersey, pp. 261–269.

6. *Restatement of the Law, Second, Agency*, Vol. 2, American Law Institute Publishers, St. Paul, Minnesota, 1958.

7. Phillip J. Blumberg, "Corporate Responsibility and the Employee's Duty of Loyalty and Obedience," in Beauchamp and Bowie, *Ethical Theory and Business*, Prentice Hall, Inc., Englewood Cliffs, New Jersey, 1979, pp. 309–310.

QUESTIONS

1. What are the four concepts of loyalty? How do they disagree with one another?

2. What remains of loyalty after Soles concludes his analysis? What concept of loyalty do you subscribe to? Can you offer your own, original concept of loyalty?

George D. Randels | # Loyalty, Corporations, and Community

George D. Randels, Jr., is associate professor of social ethics in the Religious Studies Department of the University of the Pacific.

The man in the gray flannel suit. The organization man. When it comes to loyalty, American business is not without images, flawed though they may be. But these are the ghosts of business past. In spite of their hard work, long hours, and important sacrifices, they have been downsized. It is yesterday's news that this type of devotion is not necessarily rewarded, nor does such devotion necessarily indicate loyalty to a company as opposed to the company being a mere instrument for personal advantage. Three *New Yorker* cartoons reflect current trends. In one, the downsized employee is pictured as that paradigm of loyalty, the dog. "Of *course* the company appreciates your years of loyalty," says the manager to the teary-eyed employee (destined for the Humane Society?). In another, the manager's consolation includes some positive spin: "Yes, and the fact that you've been an outstanding employee for twenty-five years is going to look great on your résumé." The third cartoon's setting is the interview rather than the layoff. Here the personnel manager's statement depicts both sides of the coin: "We expect little loyalty. In return we offer little security." In the context that these cartoons portray, the "Why be moral?" question often associated with discussions of business ethics becomes "Why be loyal?" There seems to be no benefit, unless loyalty is somehow its own reward. . . .

LOYALTY, DUTY, AND VIRTUE

Loyalty is often characterized as a duty that an employee owes to a corporation, or as a virtue of a good employee, but loyalty is not a duty or a virtue. It is, however, linked to both of these concepts in that loyal persons will perform certain duties and possess certain virtues. Loyalty involves a complex of

From *Business Ethics Quarterly*, 11, No. 1. © 2001. *Business Ethics Quarterly*, 11:1. ISSN 1052–1064. Notes were deleted from the text.

passions and character traits such as commitment, with outward actions springing from them. It is thus more readily identified by character-based ethics, but is not itself an individual virtue. . . .

WHAT IS LOYALTY?

. . . Loyalty is a passion. But contrary to traditional thinking, there is not necessarily a one-to-one correspondence between passions and virtues (or vices). Loyalty seems to be the type of passion that can contribute to multiple virtues (and vices) and obviously to a multitude of ends. Ewin apparently finds loyalty so central, however, that it is the sole passion at work. He suggests that "loyalty is the emotional setting for the virtues and vices; it is not itself a virtue or a vice, but is the raw material for them."[1] Because loyalty extends beyond the self to some object, it is a social passion, and Robert Solomon likely is correct to suggest that it is a type of love.[2] But even as a type of love, loyalty is not the sole passion for the virtues, not even the moral virtues. There are, after all, other types of love, and other passions, such as fear, daring, pleasure, anger, joy, pity, pride, shame, and hope. These other loves and passions are not readily reducible to loyalty, and also provide "raw material" for virtues and vices.

Loyalty is a social passion, a type of love that extends beyond the self to some object of loyalty. As loyalty develops, this object becomes no longer strictly external, but is linked to one's self-identity and helps to provide meaning for one's life. Solomon and Fletcher both claim that it is through our loyalties that we define our sense of self, and this seems quite right.[3] Harvard or Yale, Duke or Carolina, Cubs or Sox, Catholic or Protestant, Macy's or Gimble's, Microsoft or Netscape. While loyalties often do not involve binary choices like these or an "us v. them" mentality, they clearly do define us and link us not only to the object of loyalty but perhaps also to a group of other people who share that loyalty with us. . . .

The link between self and others is key to loyalty, and relationship is the source of this link and serves as an important conceptual tool. But relationship would need to move from the literal to the metaphorical to provide a general understanding of loyalty (as opposed to a particular type of loyalty), and even then the metaphor breaks down. When venturing beyond interpersonal loyalties, the nature of relationships will differ dramatically, and it is difficult to maintain that mutuality or reciprocity is required for all forms of loyalty as it is in the friendship relation. Just as there can be unrequited love, there can be unrequited loyalty. A person can be loyal without a literal relationship to the object of loyalty. It is possible to be a loyal Cub fan without having a relationship with Sammy Sosa, or even having his autograph or ever having seen a game at Wrigley Field. Likewise, it is possible to be a loyal customer by continuing to use a product without any contact with any person from the company (e.g., Coke or Pepsi). And one can be loyal to certain ideals regardless of the support of like-minded persons.

In the corporate context, relationship works quite well for understanding interpersonal loyalties between co-workers, loyalty to one's boss, and so on. The concept presents difficulties, however, when thinking about the prospects for loyalty to an organization. Fletcher partially addresses this concern by noting that in group loyalty, membership rather than relationship provides the basis. "Membership makes one an insider; it confers identity within a matrix of relationships both to other members and to the leadership of the organization." Entry into the group and subsequent identification with it are the two key aspects of membership. Loyalties arise from this identification.[4] Membership defined in this way is a good vehicle for characterizing loyalty to an organization like a corporation. To be loyal, an employee or manager would need to feel like a part of the organization through a matrix of relationships and identify himself or herself with the organization, typically with a positive association. A sense of membership minimizes the compartmentalization or segmentation of oneself that often happens between the workplace and the rest of one's life. There are, of course, different possible levels of membership in terms of commitment and identification (not necessarily in terms of job status), and the degree of loyalty would vary with them.

Loyalty in the corporate context would have to be based on relationships and a sense of membership. This analysis necessarily cuts against traditional business/economic theory about individualism, self-interest, and the corporation. In the next section, I will discuss loyalty in relation to this standard account of business, and then move on to discuss an alternative account in the last section.

LOYALTY AND THE STANDARD ACCOUNT OF BUSINESS

The standard account of business presents serious barriers for loyalty's prospects in the business context with its focus on the individual and self-interest in pursuit of wealth. The "spirit of capitalism," the economic mind-set, would seem to preclude loyalties except perhaps as instrumental for one's own gain. Ewin nicely presents the contrast between loyalty and the standard account of business. "A really loyal person subjugates (at least to some extent) his or her private interests to those of the object of loyalty, and that is quite different from being an entirely independent item entering a commercial relationship. Loyalty involves emotional ties and not merely commercial ties." Loyalty runs counter to commercial judgment because the latter would require one to take a better job offer from a rival company rather than stay put. Loyalty proves difficult in the business context because it would necessarily involve a "willingness *not* to follow good [commercial] judgment, at least some of the time."[5]

One must then choose between loyalty and self-interest, and in the standard account, there really could not be a choice at all. Self-interest would be the only option. There would be a very limited sense—if any—of relationship or membership, which serve as the grounding of loyalty. This is why Duska rejects a duty of loyalty in the business context, because "the kinds of relationships that loyalty requires are just the kind that one does not find in business." The common pursuit of personal financial gain is insufficient to establish the bonds necessary for loyalty. "Loyalty depends on ties that demand self-sacrifice with no expectation of reward. Business functions on the basis of enlightened self-interest. . . . Attempts of some companies to create 'one big happy family' ought to be looked upon with suspicion. I am not devoted to it at all, nor should I be. I work for it because it pays me. I am not in a family to get paid, I am in a company to get paid." Money, not love, keeps the company together. Duska holds that loyalty to a corporation is not only not required, but is likely to be misguided when it exists. A corporation is concerned with profit, not human fulfillment. We should thus get rid of foolish romanticism about corporations. Accepting this harsh reality benefits us all, especially those loyal workers who wind up feeling betrayed. Corporate loyalty should not exist, and is a mistake when it does.[6]

. . . Insofar as a corporation operates for the sole purpose of profit making, then Duska is exactly right that such an organization does not deserve loyalty. Neither would individuals like co-workers and bosses if they were strictly rational maximizers of their own self-interest. Furthermore, if financial gain is all *I* want, then I could not be loyal anyway, whether the organization, boss, or co-workers deserve my loyalty or not. I would view it (and them) strictly in instrumental terms, even as it (and they) may also view me the same way. The grounds for loyalty would not exist.

Although Duska follows most accounts of loyalty in emphasizing self-sacrifice—and clearly loyal people sacrifice various interests, their time, and sometimes even their lives—loyalty is not strictly altruistic. The loyal person's self-interest is tied up with that of the object of loyalty. There is an important link between the self and the object of loyalty. It is not just in the company's interest or the boss's interest or my co-workers' interests that the product succeed, but *my* interest. It is not strictly a matter of sacrifice for others, although I may make sacrifices. I have invested myself and thus have a stake in the object of loyalty. In many respects, its interests *are* my interests. The necessary dichotomy between loyalty and self-interest is a false one. The standard account mistakenly assumes that they cannot co-exist in the business world.

CORPORATE LOYALTY IN THE POSTMODERN BUSINESS WORLD

What is a proper object of loyalty? Why not loyalty to a corporation, co-worker, boss, project, team, or profession? Of course, corporate loyalty might not be prudential, as the downsizing phenomenon has shown.[7] Moreover, as Duska indicates, "A company is an instrument, and an instrument with a specific purpose, the making of profit. To treat an instrument as an end in itself . . . give[s] the instrument a moral status it does not deserve."[8]

Duska is correct that a corporation is indeed an instrument, and insofar as that is all a corporation is, then his conclusion is correct. But a corporation can also be much more, . . . Robert Solomon claims that corporations are indeed much more—they are communities. The "relationships of reciprocity and cooperation . . . consist, first of all, in a shared sense of belonging, a shared sense of mission or, at least, a shared sense of mutual interest."[9] . . .

For a corporation to be a community, it would have to be more than an instrument for financial gain. It would have to contribute to human fulfillment. This is not to say, however, that a corporation needs to become the center of its employees' lives to be a community. . . . A corporation or any group need not include all of one's social relationships, values, and interests in order to be a community. Instead, a community involves "a framework of shared beliefs, interests, and commitments unit[ing] a set of *varied* groups and activities . . . that establish a common faith or fate, a personal identity, a sense of belonging, and a supportive structure of activities and relationships." For a group like a corporation, *"the emergence of community depends on the opportunity for, and impulse toward, comprehensive interaction, commitment, and responsibility."*[10]

. . . Rather than viewing corporations strictly as instruments because they are not comprehensive communities, they can be seen as existing along a community continuum. While I would not want to see corporations all the way at the comprehensive end of

the continuum, the closer they move in that direction, the greater the sharing of values, sense of membership, and identification of the self with the whole. To the extent that corporations are communities, loyalty not only is possible, but can be very much appropriate.

Whether loyalty is appropriate is a crucial question, but can receive only a cursory reply here. Good judgment is necessary to determine if and when to invest loyalty and hence oneself in an organization. The presence of community is a necessary but insufficient condition for doing so. One must consider the ideals and goals of organization and their worthiness. Do they match with my own aspirations, or do I want to modify my own to fit with its? Furthermore, are the goals and ideals adhered to, and if so, are ethically acceptable means used to attain them?

Assuming loyalty is appropriate in a corporation, as a community it involves whole persons rather than strictly their segmented interests. Unlike the organization man's singleness of purpose, however, this involvement of the whole person does not exclude loyalties to other communities and to individuals with whom we have relationships. . . . Loyalties to family, friends, religion, town, country, and corporation, among others, may happily co-exist with one another, but likely will compete from time to time. When they do compete, as Alan Wolfe indicates, "the choice is not between loyalty and disloyalty but between competing ways of being loyal. . . . The question is how we balance them, not how we choose between them."[11]

Integrity, a personal sense of wholeness, is important to the task of balancing one's loyalties. This sense of wholeness involves not an isolated self, but includes connectedness with these various others. It involves not a return to singleness of purpose, but balance. That is not to say that all loyalties are equal and so must receive identical treatment; some undoubtedly are more important than others. Corporate loyalty should be less than some loyalties, but perhaps more than some others. This balancing must be worked out in concrete cases, however, and can only be suggested in the abstract.

While the need for such balancing may cause one to question the desirability of corporate loyalty, the inability to have loyalty to a corporation itself can damage one's integrity. The impossibility of loyalty makes for a divided self and potentially compromises one's other loyalties to religion, family, friends, etc., as one engages in tasks for a purely instrumental entity. It would be far better to establish a Connection Thesis that acknowledges the legitimacy of loyalty to corporate communities.

NOTES

1. R. E. Ewin, "Loyalty and Virtues," *The Philosophical Quarterly* 42 (1992): 418.

2. Robert C. Solomon, *A Passion for Justice: Emotions and the Origins of the Social Contract* (Reading, Mass.: Addison-Wesley Publishing Co., 1990), p. 288.

3. Solomon, p. 289; George P. Fletcher, *Loyalty: An Essay on the Morality of Relationships* (New York: Oxford University Press, 1993), pp. 8–9.

4. Fletcher, pp. 33–34.

5. Ewin, pp. 410–412 (emphasis original), p. 554.

6. Ronald Duska, "Whistleblowing and Employee Loyalty," *Contemporary Issues in Business Ethics*, 2nd ed., ed. Joseph R. Des Jardins and John J. McCall (Belmont, Calif.: Wadsworth, 1990); reprinted in *Business Ethics: A Philosophical Reader*, ed. Thomas I. White (New York: Macmillan, 1993), p. 554.

7. *The Economist* contends that for prudential reasons employees should avoid loyalty to a corporation. Given the shrinking life expectancy of a Fortune 500 company and downsizing, employees might find a better focus than companies for their feelings of loyalty. "Two Cheers for Loyalty," *The Economist*, 6 Jan. 1996, p. 49.

8. Duska, p. 554.

9. Robert C. Solomon, "The Corporation as Community: A Reply to Ed Hartman." *Business Ethics Quarterly* 4 (1994): 277.

10. Philip Selznick, *The Moral Commonwealth: Social Theory and the Promise of Community* (Berkeley: University of California Press, 1992), pp. 358–359 (emphasis original).

11. Alan Wolfe, "On Loyalty," *Wilson Quarterly* 21 (1997): 52.

QUESTIONS

1. How is a corporation like a community? How do they differ?

2. Does a corporation always deserve my loyalty? A community? Why or why not? When and when not?

Kim Zetter | # Why We Cheat

Kim Zetter is a freelance journalist.

Dan Ariely is a people hacker. A professor of behavioral economics at Duke University and MIT as well as director of MIT's Center for Advanced Hindsight, Ariely deconstructs human behavior to find the hidden ways we deceive ourselves about the things we do and to construct better ways of resolving some of life's issues.

In his research, Ariely gave test subjects twenty math problems to solve and told them they'd be paid cash for each correct answer. The subjects were given only five minutes to do the exam, ensuring that no one would complete it. When the time was up, the control subjects were told to count their correct answers and collect their pay. The test group, however, was told to shred their exams before reporting their totals, to see if they'd fudge the number if no one could confirm their claim. Not surprisingly, many people in the latter group cheated. But they cheated by only a small amount. And the amount by which they cheated didn't change when they

From *Wired* (February 7, 2009): Reprinted with permission.

were offered more money per question. It also didn't change when they were told to pay themselves from a bowl of money.

Conventional wisdom assumes people cheat based on whether they think they'll get caught and the level of punishment they'll receive. But Ariely says other factors come into play.

WIRED: What did your tests tell you about the ways people cheat and why they do it?

DAN ARIELY: We came up with this idea of a fudge factor, which means that people have two goals: We have a goal to look at ourselves in the mirror and feel good about ourselves, and we have a goal to cheat and benefit from cheating. And we find that there's a balance between these two goals. That is, we cheat up to the level that we would find it comfortable [to still feel good about ourselves]. Now if we have this fudge factor, we thought that we should be able to increase it or shrink it [to affect the amount of cheating someone does]. So we tried to shrink it by getting people to recite the Ten Commandments before they took the test. And it turns out that it shrinks the fudge factor completely. It eliminates it. And it's not as if the people who are more religious or who remember more commandments cheat less. In fact, even when we get atheists to swear on the Bible, they don't cheat afterwards. So it's not about fear of God; it's about reminding people of their own moral standards. That was the first thing we discovered. Then we said let's try to increase the fudge factor [to make people cheat more]. So I distributed Cokes in refrigerators in the dorm, and I found out that people very quickly took these Cokes that did not belong to them. But when I distributed plates with $1 bills on them, nobody ever took the money.

WIRED: Why would someone take a Coke but not money?

DA: When you take money, you can't help but think you're stealing. When you take a pencil, for example from work, there's all kinds of stories you can tell yourself. You can say this is something everybody does. Or, if I take a pencil home, it's actually good for work because I can work more. It's the same thing with the Coke. You can say to yourself, Maybe

somebody left it on purpose, or somebody took mine once so it's okay for me to take this.

We did the [math problem] experiment with tokens instead of money to see if it would change the cheating and it did. The idea was we get people one step away from money [and they cheat more]. As we deal with things that are more distant [from] money, the easier it is to cheat and not to think of yourself as a bad person. I think we're moving to a society where things are getting more and more removed from cash. Executives backdating stock options [can think] it's not cash, it's stock options.

WIRED: What are the implications of these findings?

DA: The idea is, what are the points at which we're tempted, and can we reduce the issues at the point of temptation? When we got people to contemplate on their morality, they reduced their cheating. So the issue is, how in society we can get people to contemplate morality more when it matters? I really think that people have good moral standards, but it's just the case that you don't go around all day asking yourself am I moral. And when you don't ask yourself am I moral, you can do all kinds of little things that don't seem to be engaging your moral compass.

WIRED: So it's a matter of putting a mirror in front of people. Posting rules above the copier machine, things like that.

DA: That's right. It's basically about the mirror that reminds us who we are at the point where it matters. Now I don't want to say this is the only factor that's going on. Take what happened in Enron. There was partly a social norm that was emerging there. Somebody started cheating a little bit, and then it became more and more a part of the social norm. You see somebody behaving in a bit more extreme way, and you adopt that way. If you stopped and thought about [what you were doing] it would be clear it was crazy, but at the moment you just accept that social standard. The second thing that happened at Enron is that it wasn't clear what was the right social norm to apply to this particular emerging energy market. They could basically define it anyway they wanted. And, finally, they were dealing with stuff that was really very removed from money, which allowed them to [cheat].

WIRED: What's the difference between the person who goes along with the standard and the whistleblower who says enough?

DA: It's a very good question, but I haven't done stuff with whistleblowers and I don't really know what makes them decide to stand up. My guess is that at some point they get sufficiently exposed to other forces from outside of the organization and that gets them to think differently, but I don't really know. Think about this CEO of Merrill Lynch who just apologized for refurbishing his bathroom for $1.2 million. I think that when he was in the midst of those things, if he thought about it, he would realize it is crazy. But he wasn't thinking about it, and nobody around him was thinking about it either. They wanted to see the world in a certain way and wanted to get these incredible bonuses. So the moment you're surrounded by all these people who think the same way, it's very hard to think differently.

WIRED: What are you hoping to convey to the TED audience?

DA: That people don't predict correctly what will drive our behavior and, as a consequence, we need to be more careful. What happens is you have intuitions and axioms about the world, and you assume they are perfectly correct. I think we should just start doubting our assumptions more regularly and submitting them to empirical tests. We understand cheating is bad, but we don't really understand where it's really coming from and how we can reduce it. The common theory says that all we need to do is to make sure we don't have bad apples and that the punishment is sufficiently severe. I think that's not the right approach. I think we need to realize that most people are not bad apples—we find very, very few people who really cheat in a big way—but a lot of people are cheating just by a little bit. [Bernard] Madoff's . . . cheating is substantially lower than everything else that was happening in the market. The market for cheating is unbelievably big. It's estimated by some people to be about $600 billion a year—just internal fraud and theft within companies. The market for blue-collar criminals is tiny in comparison.

QUESTIONS

1. What does Ariely teach us about why cheating might take place at the highest levels of the corporation?

2. How does Ariely's explanation of cheating complicate the role of the whistleblower? Could whistle blowers be the best way we have of "looking at ourselves in the mirror"?

CASES

CASE 10.1
The Once Successful Business Model
Sherron Watkins

Before the catastrophic collapse of Enron, the company congratulated itself for having "the one successful business model" in the world. This piece is excerpted from whistle-blower Sherron Watkins' book, *Power Failure.*

At 7:40 the next morning, Ken Lay, founder and longtime CEO of Enron, gave the formal welcome. Even though he, too, was dressed casually, his casual—pressed jeans and a crisp white button-down shirt—was still a little starchy, an ensemble from another time. He was fifty-eight, which was nearly elderly at Enron, and his audience treated him that way—respectfully, but just a little restively. Lay had been playing the gentle sage to Skilling's samurai for years; a balding, somewhat jowly man of average build, he spoke with a sharp midwestern twang and lately had sometimes seemed too folksy for the sleek, sharklike company he had created. Maybe he knew that, because for the last few months Lay had been orchestrating his exit. Clinton was leaving the White House, and Lay's enormous, long-term investment in the Bush family was about to pay off again. (Lay didn't wonder, in November 2000, who really won the presidential election. He was an indefatigable optimist, and a major donor to the Republican party.)

Lay had succeeded beyond his wildest dreams. He was worshiped in Houston both as a political kingmaker and for his philanthropy. His was the classic American success story: He had triumphed over childhood poverty, a bad stutter, an antiquated, regulated business, and enough financial setbacks

to kill most companies. And now, in late middle age, he was ready to let go. He had already anointed Skilling as his successor. If he didn't join the Bush administration, maybe he would run for mayor of Houston. Whatever he did, it would be big. But on this particular morning Lay was focused solely on Enron. "Our future has never looked rosier," he told his many heirs. Enron was in businesses today it had not been in just five years earlier; he hoped that in ten years Enron would find more new business worlds to invent and dominate. At Enron it was always the future that mattered: inventing it, shaping it, ruling it.

The ashen, hung-over executives applauded politely. They'd heard this before.

And so it went for the next several hours. The editor of the hip *Red Herring* magazine extolled the glories of the Internet, followed by a pep talk from Gary Hamel, a stylishly shabby Harvard professor and the author of the best-selling *Leading the Revolution*, in which he championed the corporate innovators of the late nineties, especially Enron. "It pays to hire the best," Hamel said of the company. "You can't build a forever restless, opportunity-seeking company unless you're willing to hire forever restless, opportunity-seeking individuals." That Hamel was also a paid adviser to Enron didn't seem to bother anyone in the crowd. He was a Harvard professor, after all, and behavior that would once have been characterized as a conflict of interest was, by the late nineties, simply viewed as synergistic.

Finally, Skilling took the podium, and the enthusiasm in the room contracted noticeably. Skilling,

From Mimi Swartz, with Sherron Watkins, *Power Failure* (New York: Doubleday, 2003).

like Lay, was small in stature. (In fact, almost everyone who got ahead at Enron was short.) But where Lay was soft and self-assuredly self-deprecating—almost Sunday schoolish—Skilling was sharp and cool. He was dressed casually, almost carelessly, like his troops, and he wore his hair combed off his face in the style of Hollywood producers and Wall Street financiers. He was assiduously fit; his eyes were ice blue and his gaze was steady, and he spoke in clipped, flat, supremely confident tones. Everyone at Enron knew that Jeff was twice as smart as they were—twice as smart as they could ever hope to be—and they hung on every word. It was Skilling who had made the revenues grow from $4 billion to more than $60 billion, an increase of nearly 2,000 percent. It was Skilling who had made the stock price ascend to the heavens. So it was Skilling who made Enron's troops frantic to live in fast-forward mode, who made them anxious to prove that they could deliver any concept he could dream up, who made them desperate to tag along on his extreme adventures—rock climbing, bungee jumping—around the globe. Because if Jeff Skilling thought you "got it," you really did.

Skilling's appearance onstage signaled the arrival of an annual event: his stock-price prediction. In years past he had been on the money—Enron had gone from $40 to $60 a share in 1998, and soared to $80 in 1999. Now he stood before his faithful and bowed his head, as if he had to think about what he had to say. When he looked at the crowd again, he was beaming. Enron stock, he told them, would hit $126 a share in 2001. There was just a second of stunned silence before the crowd burst into applause. No one quite knew how the stock was going to increase another 30 percent, even with the success of Broadband, which was not exactly a sure thing. Neither was Enron Energy Services, the company's foray into the management of power needs for large corporations. And a few people in the crowd had heard of problems in Fastow's finance group. But no one was that worried. They reminded themselves that they worked for Enron and, no matter what, Jeff would find a way. Because he always did.

There was, in fact, only one cautionary note sounded that morning. Skilling introduced the crowd to Tom Peters, the author of the best-selling business bible *In Search of Excellence*. Before abandoning the stage to Peters, Skilling wanted to boost morale a little higher. Enron, he reminded the crowd, had found the one successful business model that could be applied to any market.

Peters strode to the stage, abandoned his prepared speech, and started pacing back and forth. He was even sweating slightly, which made some in the audience think he might be another loser. "That's the scariest thing I've ever heard," Peters said to Skilling, his former colleague at McKinsey. What, exactly, had Enron done that was so novel? he asked. What accounted for such self-congratulation? The company had taken a model and replicated it in other fields—Enron had created markets where none had existed before, in gas, in power, probably in telecom. But everyone knew that now. Other businesses were already copying Enron, and the novelty would soon wear off. And then where would Enron be? Where were the company's new new ideas? "An excess of self-confidence kills companies," Peters warned.

In the audience, Sherron Watkins scribbled notes furiously on a pad, listing Peters' signs of a company in trouble:

1. Denial of problems.
2. Nostalgia.
3. Arrogance.

Listening, Skilling and Lay sat frozen in their seats, smiles locked on their faces. When Peters stopped speaking, Skilling jumped up to the dais, thanked him, and repeated himself: *Remember*, he said, *Enron had found the one successful business model that could be applied to any market.*

QUESTIONS

1. Should Watkins have spoken up earlier? How does a whistle-blower know when to whistle?

2. If you could go back in time and advise Enron, what would you tell them?

CASE 10.2
Would You Blow the Whistle on Yourself?
Pat L. Burr

In the course of teaching business classes through the semesters, I have been the butt of a great many accusations about the unethical behavior of American entrepreneurs, the deceptive advertising of Madison Avenue silver tongues, and even the rolling back of odometers by the local used-car dealers. I have not been personally involved in any of the activity, I hasten to add, I have simply been held accountable for it. All of it. By business students.

Enough, I said one day. I have done nothing wrong. I am not a crook. I vowed to bring the issue to the surface.

I set about my plan by inviting comments from my business students . . . about the structure of the system. The real question, as I saw it, was whether our business activity is inherently unethical or whether business persons are simply a product of our social system and therefore a reflection of our collective social values. Hogwash, they said. . . .

In pressing for more substance in their arguments, each semester I posed the same question to them at least once on written exams. I asked for detailed discussion. And on those very exams, I deliberately made grading mistakes on the numerous other questions, giving my students the advantage by two to five points. In short, I gave them grades which clearly were too high.

I turned back their papers, smugly awaiting the rush of feet to my desk to point out my error and to bring their unquestionably ethical behavior to a shining apex. I was confident of my students' motives. When none of them rushed forward, I pointed out the need for them to review my grading

lest I had made a mistake on their papers. Still no comment. . . . Not one student, in my seven years of teaching, has ever come forward to point out my error in their favor. . . .

My game usually ends each semester when I nonchalantly explain my own dirty trick on the last class day, thus giving them every opportunity to come clean before final exam day. . . . "Surely, it is a hoax," they say. "For shame," I mumble under my breath, enunciating clearly so they can hear me. I had caught them. Even set the trap. They were furious.

After years of refinement of my game of "values clarification," I have arrived at several conclusions:

1. It is . . . too late to reach business students with ethics courses.
2. One dirty trick in the hand is worth two fists of mud in the bush when the entire system is under attack.
3. Our economic system is closely tied to our social system.
4. Some of our business students, particularly those I have observed after they were exposed in my little test, would make terrific drama coaches.

QUESTIONS

1. Would you have reported yourself? Why or why not? Should you have?

2. Do people ever blow the whistle on themselves? Is there something wrong with blowing the whistle on yourself? Is it irrational to do so? Explain.

Business and Society Review, 19, 1977–78.

CASE 10.3
Changing Jobs and Changing Loyalties
William H. Shaw and Vincent Barry

Cynthia Martinez was thrilled when she first received the job offer from David Newhoff at Crytex Systems. She had long admired Crytex, both as an industry leader and as an ideal employer, and the position the company was offering her was perfect. "It's just what I've always wanted," she told her husband, Tom, as they uncorked a bottle of champagne. But as she and Tom talked, he raised a few questions that began to trouble her.

"What about the big project you're working on at Altrue right now? It'll take three months to see that through," Tom had reminded her. "The company has a lot riding on it, and you've always said that you're the driving force behind the project. If you bolt, Altrue is going to be in a real jam."

Cynthia explained that she had mentioned the project to David Newhoff. "He said he could understand I'd like to see it through, but Crytex needs someone right now. He gave me a couple of days to think it over, but it's my big chance."

Tom looked at her thoughtfully and responded, "But Newhoff doesn't quite get it. It's not just that you'd like to see it through. It's that you'd be letting your whole project team down. They probably couldn't do it without you, at least not the way it needs to be done. Besides, Cyn, remember what you said about that guy who quit the Altrue branch in Baltimore."

"That was different," Cynthia responded. "He took an existing account with him when he went to another firm. It was like ripping Altrue off. I'm not going to rip them off, but I don't figure I owe them anything extra. It's just business. You know perfectly well that if Altrue could save some money by laying me off, the company wouldn't hesitate."

"I think you're rationalizing," Tom said. "You've done well at Altrue, and the company has always treated you fairly. Anyway, the issue is what's right for you to do, not what the company would or wouldn't do. Crytex is Altrue's big competitor. It's like you're switching sides. Besides, it's not just a matter of loyalty to the company, but to the people you work with. I know we could use the extra money, and it would be a great step for you, but still. . . ."

They continued to mull things over together, but the champagne no longer tasted quite as good. Fortunately, she and Tom never really argued about things they didn't see eye to eye on, and Tom wasn't the kind of guy who would try to tell her what she should or shouldn't do. But their conversation had started her wondering whether she really should accept that Crytex job she wanted so much.

QUESTIONS

1. What should Cynthia do? What ideals, obligations, and effects should she take into account when making her decision?

2. Would it be unprofessional of Cynthia to drop everything and move to Crytex? Would it show a lack of integrity? Could moving abruptly to Crytex have negative career consequences for her?

3. What does loyalty to the company mean, and how important is it, morally? Under what circumstances, if any, do employees owe loyalty to their employers? When, if ever, do they owe loyalty to their coworkers?

William H. Shaw and Vincent Barry, *Moral Issues in Business*, 9th ed. (Belmont, CA: Wadsworth, 2004).

CASE 10.4

The Greenhouse Effect: Putting the Heat on Halliburton

Larry Margasak

The Army extended a Halliburton Co. troop support contract over the objections of a top contracting officer, even contending—and then withdrawing—a claim that U.S. forces faced an emergency if the company didn't get the extra work.

"I wrote directly on the document the weaknesses . . . so that all could clearly see," contracting official Bunnatine Greenhouse wrote a top general this month in questioning the extended troop support contract in the Balkans.

Halliburton was formerly headed by Vice President Dick Cheney.

Greenhouse has had problems with the $2 billion (€1.6 billion) contract at least since January 2002, when she wrote, "There is little or no incentive for the contractor to reduce or keep cost down."

The contracting officer has gone public with allegations of favoritism toward the company once headed by Vice President Dick Cheney. . . .

Greenhouse complained, in writing, Oct. 5 to Lt. Gen. Carl Strock, commander of the Army Corps of Engineers, that the Corps should not have halted plans to let companies compete for a successor Balkans contract. She is the Corps' top contracting officer.

Corps officials initially justified stopping the bidding by concluding that a "compelling emergency" would exist if Halliburton's work were to be interrupted.

When Greenhouse challenged the justification and sought an explanation of the emergency, however, Corps officials changed their reasoning. The new explanation was that Halliburton subsidiary KBR was the "one and only" company that could do the job.

Greenhouse wrote Strock that "the truth should be clearly explained" about the reason for halting competition.

She not only complained there was no explanation of what drove officials to cite an emergency, but, referring to the second justification, added: "It is not reasonable to believe that only one source responded to the solicitation."

Greenhouse, who has said she was frozen out of decisions on Halliburton, went public last weekend with allegations that Army officials showed favoritism to the company.

The FBI has asked Greenhouse's lawyers for an interview with her. The bureau has launched a criminal investigation of Halliburton's no-bid work.

The Associated Press has obtained dozens of documents that Greenhouse intends to provide to investigators.

The Balkans contract was to have ended May 27 but has been extended through next April.

The extension was so politically sensitive that Corps official, William Ryals, sent a memo to Corp headquarters in July seeking high-level approval.

"The reason for sending it to (headquarters) for approval is because this is so controversial in regard to this firm," the memo said. "If it had been any other firm, we would have done this and moved forward without any further consideration. Given that the firm is KBRS (the Halliburton subsidiary) and that we are in an election year and coming up to the peak in the election season soon, I sent to (headquarters) for concurrence."

Halliburton spokeswoman Wendy Hall said "This is very old information. The issue mentioned about the Balkans was fully dealt with and resolved several years ago, and since then KBR has received high marks from the Army on our Balkans Support Contract."

In a letter to Corps employees on Friday, Strock said the Army is investigating Greenhouse's allegations and therefore would not respond to the allegations "to ensure that a fair investigation can proceed."

The Army has cited severe problems with Halliburton's work in the Balkans, many documented in the Jan. 4, 2002, report by Greenhouse, who reviewed findings of investigators known as a "tiger" team.

"The general feeling in the theater is that the contractor is 'out of control,'" she wrote.

Greenhouse said it appeared the Halliburton subsidiary "makes the decisions of what is constructed, purchased or provided and it appears that oftentimes the products and services delivered reflect gold-plating since the contractor proudly touts that they provide the very, very best."

Greenhouse said Army contracting officials must work as a team because "divided—the contractor will 'eat our lunch.'"

QUESTIONS

1. Should no-bid contracts ever be allowed? What might be a good argument in favor of no-bid contracts?

2. Do you think a problem arises when former members of company boards acquire a great deal of political power (such as becoming vice president or president)? What is presently done to control this? What more should be done?

CASE 10.5
Whistleblowing at the Phone Company
Joseph R. Desjardins and John J. McCall

Michael J., an employee of the phone company, recognizes that he has divided loyalties. The company has treated him well and, despite some minor disagreements, he gets along quite well with upper management and his own department. However, the phone company is a public utility, regulated for the public interest by the state's Public Utility Commission (PUC). As such, Michael J. recognizes that his firm owes a loyalty to citizens that goes beyond the simple responsibility that other firms owe to their consumers.

Once a year, as part of a major fund-raising drive for a local charity, the phone company encourages its employees to donate their personal time and money to this charity. This year, however, Michael J. discovers that a significant amount of company resources are being used to support the charity. The company is printing posters and sending out mail at its own expense and is using employees on company time to promote the fund-raiser. When Michael J. brought this to the attention of his manager, the whole incident was dismissed as trivial. After all, the resources were going to charity.

After some consideration, Michael J. judged that these charitable efforts were betraying the public trust. The public, and not private individuals acting as their agents, ought to decide for themselves when to contribute to charity. As a result, he notified the PUC of this misallocation of funds. Knowing that records of calls from his desk could easily be traced, Michael J. made the calls from pay phones and from his house.

As required by law, the PUC investigated the charges. Although the facts were as Michael J. reported, the PUC judged that the misallocation was not substantial enough to constitute a violation of the public trust. However, executives of the phone company were less willing to dismiss the incident.

From Joseph R. Desjardins and John J. McCall, *Contemporary Issues in Business Ethics*, 2nd ed. (Belmont, CA: Wadsworth, 1990).

They were upset at what they judged to be serious disloyalty among their employees.

Although they suspected that Michael J. was the whistleblower, there was no proof that he was. A check of his office phone records showed no calls placed to the PUC. However, since this was the phone company, it was easy enough to trace calls made from Michael J.'s home and cross-check these against calls made to and from the PUC's offices. They did so, confirmed their suspicions, and disciplined Michael J.

QUESTIONS

1. Do employees of public utilities have special responsibilities to protect the public interest? Why or why not? Should these responsibilities be extended to employees of some private firms, for example, large defense contractors?

2. Did the phone company do anything unethical in checking its own records to trace Michael J.'s phone calls? Should the PUC investigate further?

3. Would your opinion of this case change if large sums of money or something other than a charity was involved?

CHAPTER QUESTIONS

1. When should you blow the whistle?

2. How is loyalty created? What ethical demands are created by loyalty? Does loyalty ever entirely outweigh other ethical concerns? Should it?

11

Think Local, Act Global

International Business

Introduction

You have just been transferred to the international division of your company. Your new job requires you to work with company operations all over the world. Navigating various cultural customs can be tricky, but the most difficult problems you will face concern navigating different ethical norms of behavior. Sometimes it is not easy to distinguish between customs that you should follow to be polite and respectful and practices that are morally unacceptable, regardless of what appears to be common practice in the culture. As soon as you leave your home country, you find yourself grappling with variations on a major philosophical question: Are ethical principles universal, or does every culture have its own ethics? In a practical sense, when you are in Rome, should you do what the Romans do, even if it is morally repugnant? Or should you follow what you take to be the moral path, even if it makes you unpopular and is bad for your business? Sometimes, perhaps, we can be mistaken about what is really the moral path. You may not understand the situation because it is complex in ways that you have never had to deal with. In some cases, you may discover that your stereotype about the local culture and what is right in it is wrong. A Kenyan friend told me that paying small bribes is a part of everyday life in Kenya. This is not because Kenyans think bribery is acceptable, but because they cannot do anything about it. When you are in another culture, it is important to find out what people in that culture think life requires as they actually live it. It is not enough for you to imagine an idealized version of their life as it might be with a major change in their institutions. There is what is morally necessary. There is also what is morally preferable. But there is also what is morally possible, and confusing them when you are in a position of power or influence can do a lot of people a lot of harm.

At the same time, it is a good idea for you and your organization to have a clear picture of your own values and ethical standards of behavior *before* you go to do business in another country. While your company may have its rules and regulations, there is always an open question whether these rules and regulations will make sense elsewhere. (Indeed, it may be a matter of ongoing debate whether or not some of them make sense at home.) Furthermore, you also have to have your own sense of what you personally will and will not do, anywhere, as a person and as a professional. You may be able to justify paying "facilitating payments" to an official abroad, on the grounds that everyone in the culture expects it, but you should resolve ahead of time that you are unwilling to engage in the local customs of hiring children to do dangerous work, of denigrating women on the job, of physically abusing employees who fail to make their quotas, and of lying to the home office about how the work is going or to officials about the nature of the product or the services you provide. Making such decisions on the spot may be much more difficult if it is not backed up by prior understanding or, preferably, by company policy as well.

Navigating a business in a foreign culture can be confusing. How do you balance respect for other cultures with what you believe is morally right? For example, if companies in another country pay female employees less than men to do the same work, should you do the same? Businesses and individuals in some overseas countries are tempted to slip into the lax standards of health, safety, and human rights. In the name of "staying competitive," are you justified in doing the same? It isn't always easy to act on your own or to enforce your company's values in another place where the customs are going against you because an essential part of business is about gaining favor and building relationships. So the practical question is, how can you build a relationship by adhering to local expectations and preferences and, at the same time, stay true to your own and your company's values? More than anything, you will need the moral imagination to comprehend both the values of the local culture and your own in order to figure out how best to act both ethically and without seeming disrespectful, arrogant, unfriendly, or uncooperative.

Globalization intertwines the economic fates of nations and tends to promote shared values on the basis of shared business interests, but it also accentuates real differences in cultural values. People from other countries often think of Americans as ethical imperialists who try to impose their values on the world. Much worse, they tend to think of us as hypocrites who espouse values like justice, liberty, and equality but do not actually act in ways that promote these values in other countries. But global business is, ethically, a double-edged sword. On the one hand, multinational corporations can and do exploit people in poorer countries and market products and values that are undesirable, undermining whatever respect those people may have had for "our values" and our way of life. On the other hand, multinationals can be a positive force for improving the welfare and opportunities of people in other countries and prove by doing what those lofty values have promised.

The first article in this chapter, by Anthony Kwame Appiah, argues that the problem with the view that every culture has its own ethical values is that very few cultures are homogeneous. He says most cultures have been "contaminated" by other cultures. People choose what they want to adopt from other cultures and hold on to what they think is better in their own culture. The next article puts you on the street and doing business in a foreign culture. Thomas Donaldson's article, "Values in Tension: Ethics Away from Home," looks at some of the practical problems that you may encounter in a foreign environment. He offers some excellent advice on how to behave ethically in places that have different value systems.

Florian Wettstein addresses the question of whether companies have a duty to protect human rights in a foreign country. He argues that when a company simply goes about its business in countries where there are human rights violations, they become complicit in those violations. According to Wettstein, the nature of wrongdoing in international business is changing. It used to be that all a business had to do was behave ethically while doing business. Wettstein argues that in today's world, businesses can operate ethically but behave unethically by being silent about human rights violations in the culture around them.

In John T. Noonan's take on the history of bribes, we see that bribery is not a cultural quirk, because it has been considered wrong for a very long time in most parts of the world. People often think that because bribery is a ubiquitous practice, it is an ethically acceptable practice. This is rarely true. Often bribery seems to be acceptable because no one is able to, or no one wants to, do anything about it. The final article helps us better understand some of the Confucian values that underpin the way that some business people behave in China and other Asian cultures. The Confucian emphasis on relationships and family loyalty can be especially difficult for Westerners who believe that nepotism is wrong and that contracts and laws should govern business—not who you know. The conflict between these two ethical systems is not about which one is right or wrong. It is about how to do business ethically in countries where their ethical systems differ from your own.

The cases in this chapter are about how to treat people, how to make ethical decisions in international business, and the responsibilities of multinationals for what goes on the in the places in which they operate. The "Oil Rig" raises questions about respect for persons, equality, and employees' rights when working in developing countries. "Foreign Assignment" is a personal case about how you should act and what kind of treatment you should tolerate in another country. In the "PureDrug" case, you will think about a company's obligations when someone from another country wants to buy a product that is considered unsafe in your own country. "IBM's Business with Hitler" describes how IBM knowingly sold the Nazis machines that would help them keep the records that were used to carry out the holocaust. It is a historical case that raises a number of questions about doing business today with countries that kill or harm their citizens, support terrorism, or are a threat to the rest of the world. In other words, to what extent does the morality of your customer and your customer's country matter when doing business? These are serious questions in a world where doing business in another country may require companies to be responsible for more than just their business.

Supply chains raise another set of ethical problems for international business. Much has already been written about sweatshops. In the Foxconn case, employees at the factory are committing suicide at an alarming rate. Foxconn produces, among other things, iPhones for Apple. To what extent is Apple responsible for the conditions that led to these suicides? How responsible are companies for the way that firms in their supply chain operate? The last case is another personal one. A foreign employee of a multinational company is assigned to his home country. Instead of living in safe comfortable housing, the employee lives in a ghetto and spends his housing allowance on his poor family members who live there. This case illustrates the problems that can come from the strong pull of family loyalty in some cultures.

Ultimately these readings intend to help you ponder how you would navigate value conflicts in other cultures and where you would draw the line when the norms of a foreign culture violate the norms of your value system. In the end, all the readings and cases in this chapter intend to help you reflect on what values and standards you want to live and work by, no matter where you are in the world. It helps to be clear on this point before you take a foreign assignment or a job with a multinational firm because you will be miserable working with an organization that does not allow you to behave ethically, especially in regard to respecting and protecting human rights. Furthermore, working for such an employer may be harmful to your moral and physical health.

| Anthony Kwame Appiah | Global Villages |

Anthony Kwame Appiah is Lawrence J. Rockefeller University Professor of Philosophy at Princeton University.

People who complain about the homogeneity produced by globalization often fail to notice that globalization is, equally, a threat to homogeneity. You can see this as clearly in Kumasi as anywhere. The capital of Asante is accessible to you, whoever you are—emotionally, intellectually, and, of course, physically. It is integrated into the global markets. None of this makes it Western, or American, or British. It is still Kumasi. What it isn't, just because it's a city, is homogeneous. English, German, Chinese, Syrian, Lebanese, Burkinabe, Ivorian, Nigerian, Indian: I can find you families of each description. I can find you Asante people, whose ancestors have lived in this town for centuries, but also Hausa households that have been around for centuries, too. There are people there from all the regions, speaking all the scores of languages of Ghana as well. And while people in Kumasi come from a wider variety of places than they did a hundred or two hundred years ago, even then there were already people from all over the place coming and going. I don't know who was the first Asante to make the pilgrimage to Mecca, but his trip would have followed trade routes that are far older than the kingdom. Gold, salt, kola nuts, and, alas, slaves have connected my hometown to the world for a very long time. And trade

means travelers. If by globalization you have in mind something new and recent, the ethnic eclecticism of Kumasi is not the result of it.

But if you go outside Kumasi, only a little way—twenty miles, say, in the right direction—and if you drive off the main road down one of the many potholed side roads of red laterite, you can arrive pretty soon in villages that are fairly homogeneous. The people have mostly been to Kumasi and seen the big, polyglot, diverse world of the city. Here, though, where they live, there is one everyday language (aside from the English in the government schools), a few Asante families, and an agrarian way of life that is based on some old crops, like yam, and some new ones, like cocoa, which arrived in the late nineteenth century as a commercial product for export. They may or may not have electricity (this close to Kumasi, they probably do). When people talk of the homogeneity produced by globalization, what they are talking about is this: the villagers will have radios; you will be able to get a discussion going about the World Cup in soccer, Muhammad Ali, Mike Tyson, and hip-hop; and you will probably be able to find a bottle of Guinness or Coca-Cola (as well as Star or Club, Ghana's own delicious lagers). Then again, the language on the radio won't be a world language, the soccer teams they know best will be Ghanaian, and what can you tell about someone's soul from the fact that she drinks Coca-Cola? These villages are connected with more places than they were a couple of centuries ago. Their homogeneity, though, is still the local kind.

In the era of globalization—in Asante as in New Jersey—people make pockets of homogeneity. Are all these pockets of homogeneity less distinctive than they were a century ago? Well, yes, but mostly in good ways. More of them have access to medicines that work. More of them have access to clean drinking water. More of them have schools. Where, as is still too common, they don't have these things, this is not something to celebrate but to deplore. And whatever loss of difference there has been, they are constantly inventing new forms of difference: new hairstyles, new slang, even, from time to time, new religions. No one could say that the world's villages are—or are about to become—anything like the same.

So why do people in these places sometimes feel that their identity is threatened? Because the world, their world, is changing, and some of them don't like it. The pull of the global economy— witness those cocoa trees whose chocolate is eaten all around the world—created some of the life they now live. If the economy changes—if cocoa prices collapse again as they did in the early 1990s—they may have to find new crops or new forms of livelihood. That is unsettling for some people (just as it is exciting for others). Missionaries came a while ago, so many of these villagers will be Christian, even if they also have kept some of the rites from earlier days. But new Pentecostal messengers are challenging the churches they know and condemning the old rites as idolatrous. Again, some like it; some don't.

Above all, relationships are changing. When my father was young, a man in a village would farm some land that a chief had granted him, and his *abusua*, his matriclan, (including his younger brothers) would work it with him. If extra hands were needed in the harvest season, he would pay the migrant workers who came from the north. When a new house needed building, he would organize it. He would also make sure his dependents were fed and clothed, the children educated, marriages and funerals arranged and paid for. He could expect to

pass the farm and the responsibilities eventually to one of his nephews.

Nowadays, everything has changed. Cocoa prices have not kept pace with the cost of living. Gas prices have made the transportation of the crop more expensive. And there are new possibilities for the young in the towns, in other parts of the country, and in other parts of the world. Once, perhaps, you could have commanded your nephews and nieces to stay. Now they have the right to leave; in any case, you may not make enough to feed and clothe and educate them all. So the time of the successful farming family has gone; and those who were settled in that way of life are as sad to see it go as some of the American family farmers whose lands are being accumulated by giant agribusinesses. We can sympathize with them. But we cannot force their children to stay in the name of protecting their authentic culture; and we cannot afford to subsidize indefinitely thousands of distinct islands of homogeneity that no longer make economic sense.

Nor should we want to. Cosmopolitans think human variety matters because people are entitled to the options they need to shape their lives in partnership with others. What John Stuart Mill said more than a century ago in *On Liberty* about diversity within a society serves just as well as an argument for variety across the globe:

> If it were only that people have diversities of taste, that is reason enough for not attempting to shape them all after one model. But different persons also require different conditions for their spiritual development; and can no more exist healthily in the same moral, than all the variety of plants can exist in the same physical, atmosphere and climate. The same things which are helps to one person towards the cultivation of his higher nature, are hindrances to another. . . . Unless there is a corresponding diversity in their modes of life, they neither obtain their fair share of happiness, nor grow up to the mental, moral, and aesthetic stature of which their nature is capable.

If we want to preserve a wide range of human conditions because it allows free people the best chance to make their own lives, there is no place for the enforcement of diversity by trapping people within a kind of difference they long to escape. There simply is no decent way to sustain those communities of difference that will not survive without the free allegiance of their members.

DON'T EVER CHANGE

Even if you grant that people shouldn't be forced into sustaining authentic cultural practices, you might suppose that a cosmopolitan should side with those who are busy around the world "preserving culture" and resisting "cultural imperialism." But behind these slogans you often find some curious assumptions. Take "preserving culture." It's one thing to provide people with help to sustain arts they want to sustain. I am all for festivals of Welsh bards in Llandudno funded by the Welsh Arts Council, if there are people who want to recite and people who care to listen. I am delighted with the Ghana National Cultural Center in Kumasi, where you can go and learn traditional Akan dancing and drumming, especially since its classes are spirited and overflowing. Restore the deteriorating film stock of early Hollywood movies; continue the preservation of Old Norse and early Chinese and Ethiopian manuscripts; record, transcribe, and analyze the oral narratives of Malay and Maasai and Maori: all these are a valuable part of our human heritage. But preserving *culture*—in the sense of cultural artifacts, broadly conceived—is different from preserving *cultures*. And the preservers of cultures are busy trying to ensure that the Huli of Papua New Guinea or, for that matter, Sikhs in Toronto or Hmong in New Orleans keep their "authentic" ways. What makes a cultural expression authentic, though? Are we to stop the importation of baseball caps into Vietnam, so that the Zao will continue with their colorful red headdresses? Why not ask the Zao? Shouldn't the choice be theirs?

"They *have* no real choice," the cultural preservationists may say. "We have dumped cheap Western clothes into their markets; and they can no longer afford the silk they used to wear. If they had what they really wanted, they'd still be dressed traditionally." Notice that this is no longer an argument about authenticity. The claim is that they can't afford to do something that they'd really like to do, something that is expressive of an identity they care about and want to sustain. This is a genuine problem, one that afflicts people in many communities: they're too poor to live the life they want to lead. If that's true, it's an argument for trying to see whether we can help them get richer. But if they do get richer and they still run around in T-shirts, so much the worse, I say, for authenticity.

Not that this is likely to be a problem in the real world. People who can afford it mostly *like* to put on traditional garb from time to time. American boys wear tuxedos to proms. I was best man once at a Scottish wedding. The bridegroom wore a kilt, of course. (I wore a *kɛntɛ* cloth. Andrew Oransay, who piped us up the aisle, whispered in my ear at one point, "Here we all are then, in our tribal gear.") In Kumasi, people who can afford them, love to put on their *kɛntɛ* cloths, especially the most "traditional" ones, woven in colorful silk strips in the town of Bonwire, as they have been for a couple of centuries. (The prices have risen in part because demand outside Asante has risen. A fine *kɛntɛ* for a man now costs more than the average Ghanaian earns in a year. Is that bad? Not for the people of Bonwire.) But trying to find some primordially authentic culture can be like peeling an onion. The textiles most people think of as traditional West African cloths are known as java prints, and arrived with the Javanese batiks sold, and often milled by, the Dutch. The traditional garb of Herero women derives from the attire of nineteenth-century German missionaries, though it's still unmistakably Herero, not least because the fabrics they use have a distinctly un-Lutheran range of colors. And so with our *kɛntɛ* cloth: the silk was always imported, traded by Europeans, produced in Asia. This tradition was once an innovation. Should we reject *it* for that reason as untraditional? How far back must one go? Should we condemn the young men and women of the University of Science and Technology, a few miles outside Kumasi, who wear European-style gowns for graduation, lined with *kɛntɛ* strips (as they do, now, at Howard and Morehouse, too). Cultures are made of continuities *and* changes, and the identity of a society can survive through these changes, just as each individual survives the alterations of Jacques's "seven ages of man."

THE TROUBLE WITH "CULTURAL IMPERALISM"

Cultural preservationists often make their case by invoking the evil of "cultural imperialism." And its victims aren't necessarily the formerly colonized "natives." In fact, the French have a penchant for talking of "cultural imperialism" to make the point that French people like to watch American movies and visit English-language sites on the Internet. (*Évidemment*, the American taste for French movies is something to be encouraged.) This is surely very odd. No army, no threat of sanctions, no political saber rattling, imposes Hollywood on the French.

There is a genuine issue here, I think, but it is not imperialism. France's movie industry requires government subsidy. Part of the reason, no doubt, is just that Americans have the advantage of speaking a language with many more speakers than France (though this can't be the whole explanation, since the British film industry seems to require subsidy, too). Still, whatever the reason, the French would like to have a significant number of films rooted deeply in French life, which they watch alongside all those American movies. Since the resulting films are often wonderful, in subsidizing them for themselves, they have also enriched the treasury of cosmopolitan cultural experience. So far, I think, so good.

What would justify genuine concern would be an attempt by the United States through the World Trade Organization, say, to have these culturally motivated subsidies banned. Even in the United States, most of us believe it is perfectly proper to subsidize programs on public television. We grant tax-exempt status to our opera and ballet companies; cities and states subsidize sports stadiums. It is an empirical question, not one to be settled by appeal to a free-market ideology, how much of the public culture the citizens of a democratic nation want can be produced solely by the market.

But to concede this much is not to accept what the theorists of cultural imperialism want. In broad strokes, their underlying picture is this. There is a world system of capitalism. It has a center and a periphery. At the center—in Europe and the United States—is a set of multinational corporations. Some of these are in the media business. The products they sell around the world promote the interests of capitalism in general. They encourage consumption not just of films, television, and magazines but of the other non-media products of multinational capitalism. Herbert Schiller, a leading critic of "media/cultural imperialism" has claimed that it is "the imagery and cultural perspectives of the ruling sector in the center that shape and structure consciousness throughout the system at large."

People who believe this story have been taking the pitches of magazine and television company executives selling advertising space for a description of reality. The evidence doesn't bear it out. As it happens, researchers actually went out into the world and explored the responses to the hit television series *Dallas* in Holland and among Israeli Arabs, Moroccan Jewish immigrants, kibbutzniks, and new Russian immigrants to Israel. They have examined the actual content of the television media—whose penetration of everyday life far exceeds that of film—in Australia, Brazil, Canada, India, and Mexico. They have looked at how American popular culture was taken up by the artists of Sophiatown, in South Africa. They have discussed *Days of Our Lives* and the *The Bold and the Beautiful* with Zulu college students from traditional backgrounds.

And they have found two things, which you might already have guessed. The first is that, if there is a local product—as there is in France, but also in Australia, Brazil, Canada, India, Mexico, and South Africa—many people prefer it, especially when it comes to television. For more than a decade in Ghana, the one program you could discuss with almost anyone was a local soap opera in Twi called *Osofo Dadzie*, a lighthearted program with a serious message, each episode, about the problems of contemporary everyday life. We know, do we not, how the Mexicans love their *telenovelas?* (Indeed, people know it even in Ghana, where they are shown in crudely dubbed English versions, too.) The academic research confirms that people tend to prefer television programming that's close to their own culture. (The Hollywood blockbuster has a special status around the world; but here, as American movie critics regularly complain, the nature of the product—heavy on the action sequences, light on clever badinage—is partly determined by what works in Bangkok and Berlin. From the point of view of the cultural-imperialism theorists, this is a case in which the empire has struck back.)

The second observation that the research supports is that how people respond to these American products depends on their existing cultural context. When the media scholar Larry Strelitz spoke to those students from KwaZulu-Natal, he found that they were anything but passive vessels. One of them, Sipho, reported both that he was a "very, very strong Zulu man" and that he had drawn lessons from watching the American soap opera *Days of Our Lives*—"especially relationship-wise." It fortified his view that "if a guy can tell a woman that he loves her she should be able to do the same." What's more, after watching the show, Sipho "realized that I should be allowed to speak to my father. He should be my friend rather than just my father. . . . " One doubts that that was the intended message of multinational capitalism's ruling sector.

But Sipho's response also confirmed what has been discovered over and over again. Cultural consumers are not dupes. They can resist. So he also said,

> In terms of our culture, a girl is expected to enter into relationships when she is about 20. In the Western culture, the girl can be exposed to a relationship as early as 15 or 16. That one we shouldn't adopt in our culture. Another thing we shouldn't adopt from the Western culture has to do with the way they treat elderly people. I wouldn't like my family to be sent into an old-age home.

The "old-age homes" in American soap operas may be safe places, full of kindly people. That doesn't sell the idea to Sipho. Dutch viewers of *Dallas* saw not the pleasures of conspicuous consumption among the super-rich—the message that theorists of "cultural imperialism" find in every episode— but a reminder that money and power don't protect you from tragedy. Israeli Arabs saw a program that confirmed that women abused by their husbands should return to their fathers. Mexican *telenovelas* remind Ghanaian women that, where sex is at issue, men are not to be trusted. If the *telenovelas* tried to tell them otherwise, they wouldn't believe it.

Talk of cultural imperialism structuring the consciousnesses of those in the periphery treats Sipho and people like him as tabulae rasae on which global capitalism's moving finger writes its message, leaving behind another homogenized consumer as it moves on. It is deeply condescending. And it isn't true.

IN PRAISE OF CONTAMINATION

Behind much of the grumbling about the cultural effects of globalization is an image of how the world used to be—an image that is both unrealistic and unappealing. Our guide to what is wrong here might as well be another African. Publius Terentius Afer, whom we know as Terence, was born a slave in Carthage in North Africa, and taken to Rome in the late second century AD. Before long, his plays were widely admired among the city's literary elite; witty, elegant works that are, with Plautus's earlier, less cultivated works, essentially all we have of Roman comedy. Terence's own mode of writing—his free incorporation of earlier Greek plays into a single Latin drama—was known to Roman littérateurs as "*contamination*." It's a suggestive term. When people speak for an ideal of cultural purity, sustaining the authentic culture of the Asante or the American family farm, I find myself drawn to contamination as the name for a counter-ideal. Terence had a notably firm grasp on the range of human variety: "So many men, so many opinions" was an observation of his. And it's in his comedy *The Self-Tormentor* that you'll find what has proved something like the golden rule of cosmopolitanism: *Homo sum: humani nil a me alienum puto.* "I am human: nothing human is alien to me." The context is illuminating. The play's main character, a busybody farmer named Chremes, is told by his overworked neighbor to mind his own affairs; the *homo sum* credo is his breezy rejoinder. It isn't meant to be an ordinance from on high; it's just the case for gossip.

Then again, gossip—the fascination people have for the small doings of *other* people—shares a taproot with literature. Certainly the ideal of contamination has no more eloquent exponent than Salman Rushdie, who has insisted that the novel that occasioned his fatwa "celebrates hybridity, impurity, intermingling, the transformation that comes of new and unexpected combinations of human beings, cultures, ideas, politics, movies, songs. It rejoices in mongrelization and fears the absolutism of the Pure. Mélange, hotchpotch, a bit of this and a bit of that is how newness enters the world. It is the great possibility that mass migration gives the world, and I have tried to embrace it."[6] But it didn't take modern mass migration to create this great possibility. The early Cynics and Stoics took their contamination from the places they were born to the Greek cities where they taught. Many were strangers in those places; cosmopolitanism was invented by contaminators whose migrations were solitary. And the migrations that have contaminated the larger world were not all modern. Alexander's empire molded both the states and the sculpture of Egypt and North India; first the Mongols then the Mughals shaped great swaths of Asia; the Bantu migrations populated half the African continent. Islamic states stretch from Morocco to Indonesia; Christianity reached Africa, Europe, and Asia within a few centuries of the death of Jesus of Nazareth; Buddhism long ago migrated from India into much of East and Southeast Asia. Jews and people whose ancestors came from many parts of China have long lived in vast diasporas. The traders of the Silk Road changed the style of elite dress in Italy; someone brought Chinese pottery for burial in fifteenth-century Swahili graves. I have heard it said that the bagpipes started out in Egypt and came to Scotland with the Roman infantry. None of this is modern.

No doubt, there can be an easy and spurious utopianism of "mixture," as there is of "purity." And yet the larger human truth is on the side of Terence's contamination. We do not need, have never needed, settled community, a homogeneous system of values, in order to have a home. Cultural purity is an oxymoron. The odds are that, culturally speaking, you already live a cosmopolitan life, enriched by literature, art, and film that come from many places, and that contains influences from many more. And the marks of cosmopolitanism in that Asante village—soccer, Muhammad Ali, hip-hop—entered their lives, as they entered yours, not as work but as pleasure. There are some Western products and vendors that appeal to people in the rest of the world *because* they're seen as Western, as modern: McDonald's, Levis. But even here, cultural significance isn't just something that corporate headquarters gets to decree. People wear Levis on every continent. In some places they are informal wear; in others they're dressy. You can get Coca-Cola on every continent, too. In Kumasi you will get it at funerals. Not, in my experience, in the West of England, where hot milky Indian tea is favored. The point is that people in each place make their own uses even of the most famous global commodities.

A tenable cosmopolitanism tempers a respect for difference with a respect for actual human beings—and with a sentiment best captured in the credo, once comic, now commonplace, penned by that former slave from North Africa. Few remember what Chremes says next, but it's as important as the sentence everyone quotes: "Either I want to find out for myself or I want to advise you: think what you like. If you're right, I'll do what you do. If you're wrong, I'll set you straight."

QUESTIONS

1. What assumptions should a business make about the ethical values of people in a particular culture? What is the problem with the idea "When in Rome, do as the Romans do"?

2. What is cultural imperialism? What does Appaiah say is the problem with cultural imperialism? Why does he like about cultural contamination?

3. Should public culture (e.g., movies, art, etc.) be subsidized by the government or left in the hands of private enterprise?

To: You
From: The Philosopher
Subject: "Isaiah Berlin on Values"

I hear that you will be traveling all over the world in your new job. The thing I like best about traveling is comparing home to what is better and worse in other countries. Americans often think that they have the best values and people in other places have got it all wrong, but as the philosopher Isaiah Berlin argues, disagreements about values are not always about who is right and who is wrong. Berlin doesn't think it is possible or desirable for everyone to agree on the same values. He says, "These collisions of values are of the essence of what they are and what we are." But, "We are doomed to choose, and every choice may entail an irreparable loss." Berlin writes:

> What is clear is that values can clash—that is why civilizations are incompatible. They can be incompatible between cultures, or groups in the same culture, or between you and me. You believe in always telling the truth, not matter what; I do not, because I believe that it can sometimes be too painful and too destructive. We can discuss each other's point of view, we can try to reach common ground, but in the end what you pursue may not be reconcilable with the ends to which I find that I have dedicated my life. Values may easily clash within the breast of an individual; and it does not follow that, if they do, some must be true and others false. Justice, rigorous justice, is for some people an absolute value, but it is not compatible with what may be no less ultimate values for them—mercy, compassion—as arises in concrete cases.*

*Isaiah Berlin, "The Pursuit of the Ideal," *The Crooked Timber of Humanity* (Alfred A. Knopf), 1991, pp. 7–8.

Thomas Donaldson

Values in Tension: Ethics Away from Home

Thomas Donaldson is Mark O. Winkelman Professor of Legal Studies at the Wharton School of Business, University of Pennsylvania.

When we leave home and cross our nation's boundaries, moral clarity often blurs. Without a backdrop of shared attitudes, and without familiar laws and judicial procedures that define standards of ethical conduct, certainty is elusive. Should a company invest in a foreign country where civil and political rights are violated? Should a company go along with a host country's discriminatory employment practices? If companies in developed countries shift facilities to developing nations that lack strict environmental and health regulations, or if those companies choose to fill management and other top-level positions in a host nation with people from the home country, whose standards should prevail?

Even the best-informed, best-intentioned executives must re-think their assumptions about business practice in foreign settings. What works in a company's home country can fail in a country with different standards of ethical conduct. Such difficulties are unavoidable for businesspeople who live and work abroad.

But how can managers resolve the problems? What are the principles that can help them work through the maze of cultural differences and establish codes of conduct for globally ethical business practice? How can companies answer the toughest question in global business ethics: What happens when a host country's ethical standards seem lower than the home country's?

COMPETING ANSWERS

One answer is as old as philosophical discourse. According to cultural relativism, no culture's ethics are better than any other's; therefore there are no international rights and wrongs. If the people of Indonesia tolerate the bribery of their public officials, so what? Their attitude is no better or worse than that of people in Denmark or Singapore who refuse to offer or accept bribes. Likewise, if Belgians fail to find insider trading morally repugnant, who cares? Not enforcing insider-trading laws is no more or less ethical than enforcing such laws.

The cultural relativist's creed—When in Rome, do as the Romans do—is tempting, especially when failing to do as the locals do means forfeiting business opportunities. The inadequacy of cultural relativism, however, becomes apparent when the practices in question are more damaging than petty bribery or insider trading.

In the late 1980s, some European tanneries and pharmaceutical companies were looking for cheap waste-dumping sites. They approached virtually every country on Africa's west coast from Morocco to the Congo. Nigeria agreed to take highly toxic polychlorinated biphenyls. Unprotected local workers, wearing thongs and shorts, unloaded barrels of PCBs and placed them near a residential area. Neither the residents nor the workers knew that the barrels contained toxic waste.

We may denounce governments that permit such abuses, but many countries are unable to police transnational corporations adequately even if they want to. And in many countries, the combination of ineffective enforcement and inadequate regulations leads to behavior by unscrupulous companies that is clearly wrong. A few years ago, for example, a group of investors became interested in restoring the SS *United States*, once a luxurious ocean liner. Before the actual restoration could begin, the ship had to be stripped of its asbestos lining. A bid from a U.S. company, based on U.S. standards for asbestos removal, priced the job at more than $100 million. A company in the Ukranian city of Sevastopol offered to do the work for less than $2 million. In October 1993, the ship was towed to Sevastopol.

A cultural relativist would have no problem with that outcome, but I do. A country has the right to establish its own health and safety regulations, but in the case just described, the standards and the terms of the contract could not possibly have protected workers in Sevastopol from known health risks. Even if the contract met Ukranian standards, ethical businesspeople must object. Cultural relativism is morally blind. There are fundamental values that cross cultures, and companies must uphold them.

At the other end of the spectrum from cultural relativism is ethical imperialism, which directs people to do everywhere exactly as they do at home. Again, an understandably appealing approach but one that is clearly inadequate. Consider the large U.S. computer-products company that in 1993 introduced a course on sexual harassment in its Saudi Arabian facility. Under the banner of global consistency, instructors used the same approach to train Saudi Arabian managers that they had used with U.S. managers: the participants were asked to discuss a case in which a manager makes sexually explicit remarks to a new female employee over drinks in a bar. The instructors failed to consider how the exercise would work in a culture with strict conventions governing relationships between men and women. As a result, the training sessions were ludicrous. They baffled and offended the Saudi participants, and the message to avoid coercion and sexual discrimination was lost.

The theory behind ethical imperialism is absolutism, which is based on three problematic principles. Absolutists believe that there is a single list of truths, that they can be expressed only with one set of concepts, and that they call for exactly the same behavior around the world.

The first claim clashes with many people's belief that different cultural traditions must be respected. In some cultures, loyalty to a community—family, organization, or society—is the foundation of all ethical behavior. The Japanese, for example, define business ethics in terms of loyalty to their companies, their business networks, and their nation. Americans place a higher value on liberty than on loyalty; the U.S. tradition of rights emphasizes equality, fairness, and individual freedom. It is hard to conclude that truth lies on one side or the other, but an absolutist would have us select just one.

The second problem with absolutism is the presumption that people must express moral truth using only one set of concepts. For instance, some absolutists insist that the language of basic rights provide the framework for any discussion of ethics. That means, though, that entire cultural traditions must be ignored. The notion of a right evolved with the rise of democracy in post-Renaissance Europe and the United States, but the term is not found in either Confucian or Buddhist traditions. We all learn ethics in the context of our particular cultures, and the power in the principles is deeply tied to the way in which they are expressed. Internationally accepted lists of moral principles, such as the United Nations' Universal Declaration of Human Rights, draw on many cultural and religious traditions. As philosopher Michael Walzer has noted, "There is no Esperanto of global ethics."

The third problem with absolutism is the belief in a global standard of ethical behavior. Context must shape ethical practice. Very low wages, for example, may be considered unethical in rich, advanced countries, but developing nations may be acting ethically if they encourage investment and improve living standards by accepting low wages. Likewise, when people are malnourished or starving, a government may be wise to use more fertilizer in order to improve crop yields, even though that means settling for relatively high levels of thermal water pollution.

When cultures have different standards of ethical behavior—and different ways of handling unethical behavior—a company that takes an absolutist approach may find itself making a disastrous mistake. When a manager at a large U.S. specialty-products company in China caught an employee stealing, she followed the company's practice and turned the employee over to the provincial authorities, who executed him. Managers cannot operate in another culture without being aware of that culture's attitudes toward ethics.

If companies can neither adopt a host country's ethics nor extend the home country's standards, what is the answer? Even the traditional litmus test—What would people think of your actions if they were written up on the front page of the newspaper?—is an unreliable guide, for there is no international consensus on standards of business conduct.

BALANCING THE EXTREMES: THREE GUIDING PRINCIPLES

Companies must help managers distinguish between practices that are merely different and those that are wrong. For relativists, nothing is sacred and nothing is wrong. For absolutists, many things that are different are wrong. Neither extreme illuminates the real world of business decision making. The answer lies somewhere in between.

When it comes to shaping ethical behavior, companies must be guided by three principles.

- Respect for core human values, which determine the absolute moral threshold for all business activities.

- Respect for local traditions.
- The belief that context matters when deciding what is right and what is wrong.

Consider those principles in action. In Japan, people doing business together often exchange gifts—sometimes expensive ones—in keeping with longstanding Japanese tradition: When U.S. and European companies started doing a lot of business in Japan, many Western business-people thought that the practice of gift giving might be wrong rather than simply different. To them, accepting a gift felt like accepting a bribe. As Western companies have become more familiar with Japanese traditions, however, most have come to tolerate the practice and to set different limits on gift giving in Japan than they do elsewhere.

Respecting differences is a crucial ethical practice. Research shows that management ethics differ among cultures; respecting those differences means recognizing that some cultures have obvious weaknesses—as well as hidden strengths. Managers in Hong Kong, for example, have a higher tolerance for some forms of bribery than their Western counterparts, but they have a much lower tolerance for the failure to acknowledge a subordinate's work. In some parts of the Far East, stealing credit from a subordinate is nearly an unpardonable sin.

People often equate respect for local traditions with cultural relativism. That is incorrect. Some practices are clearly wrong. Union Carbide's tragic experience in Bhopal, India, provides one example. The company's executives seriously underestimated how much on-site management involvement was needed at the Bhopal plant to compensate for the country's poor infrastructure and regulatory capabilities. In the aftermath of the disastrous gas leak, the lesson is clear companies using sophisticated technology in a developing country must evaluate that country's ability to oversee its safe use. Since the incident at Bhopal, Union Carbide has become a leader in advising companies on using hazardous technologies safely in developing countries.

Some activities are wrong no matter where they take place. But some practices that are unethical in one setting may be acceptable in another. For

instance, the chemical EDB, a soil fungicide, is banned for use in the United States. In hot climates, however, it quickly becomes harmless through exposure to intense solar radiation and high soil temperatures. As long as the chemical is monitored, companies may be able to use EDB ethically in certain parts of the world.

DEFINING THE ETHICAL THRESHOLD: CORE VALUES

Few ethical questions are easy for managers to answer. But there are some hard truths that must guide managers' actions, a set of what I call *core human values*, which define minimum ethical standards for all companies.[1] The right to good health and the right to economic advancement and an improved standard of living are two core human values. Another is what Westerners call the Golden Rule, which is recognizable in every major religious and ethical tradition around the world. In Book 15 of his *Analects*, for instance, Confucius counsels people to maintain reciprocity, or not to do to others what they do not want done to themselves.

Although no single list would satisfy every scholar, I believe it is possible to articulate three core values that incorporate the work of scores of theologians and philosophers around the world. To be broadly relevant, these values must include elements found in both Western and non-Western cultural and religious traditions. Consider the examples of values in the [box] "What Do These Values Have in Common?"

At first glance, the values expressed in the two lists seem quite different. Nonetheless, in the spirit of what philosopher John Rawls calls *overlapping consensus*, one can see that the seemingly divergent values converge at key points. Despite important differences between Western and non-Western cultural and religious traditions, both express shared attitudes about what it means to be human. First, individuals must not treat others simply as tools; in other words, they must recognize a person's value as a human being. Next, individuals and communities must treat people in ways that respect people's basic

What Do These Values Have in Common?

Non-Western

Kyosei (Japanese): Living and working together for a
   Common good
Dharma (Hindu): The fulfillment of inherited duty
Santutthi (Buddhist): The importance of limited desires
Zakat (Muslim): The Muslin duty to give alms to the poor.

Western

Individual liberty

Egalitarianism
Political Participation
Human rights

---

rights. Finally, members of a community must work together to support and improve the institutions on which the community depends. I call those three values *respect for human dignity, respect for basic rights*, and *good citizenship*.

Those values must be the starting point for all companies as they formulate and evaluate standards of ethical conduct at home and abroad. But they are only a starting point. Companies need much more specific guidelines, and the first step to developing those is to translate the core human values into core values for business. What does it mean, for example, for a company to respect human dignity? How can a company be a good citizen?

I believe that companies can respect human dignity by creating and sustaining a corporate culture in which employees, customers, and suppliers are treated not as means to an end but as people whose intrinsic value must be acknowledged, and by producing safe products and services in a safe workplace. Companies can respect basic rights by acting in ways that support and protect the individual rights of employees, customers, and surrounding communities, and by avoiding relationships that violate human beings' rights to health, education, safety, and an adequate standard of living. And companies can be good citizens by supporting essential social institutions, such as the economic system and the education system, and by working with host governments and other organizations to protect the environment.

The core values establish a moral compass for business practice. They can help companies identify practices that are acceptable and those that are intolerable—even if the practices are compatible with a host country's norms and laws. Dumping pollutants near people's homes and accepting inadequate standards for handling hazardous materials are two examples of actions that violate core values.

Similarly, if employing children prevents them from receiving a basic education, the practice is intolerable. Lying about product specifications in the act of selling may not affect human lives directly, but it too is intolerable because it violates the trust that is needed to sustain a corporate culture in which customers are respected.

Sometimes it is not a company's actions but those of a supplier or customer that pose problems. Take the case of the Tan family, a large supplier for Levi Strauss. The Tans were allegedly forcing 1,200 Chinese and Filipino women to work 74 hours per week in guarded compounds on the Mariana Islands. In 1992, after repeated warnings to the Tans, Levi Strauss broke off business relations with them.

CREATING AN ETHICAL CORPORATE CULTURE

The core values for business that I have enumerated can help companies begin to exercise ethical judgment and think about how to operate ethically in foreign cultures, but they are not specific enough to guide managers through actual ethical dilemmas. Levi Strauss relied on a written code of conduct when figuring out how to deal with the Tan family. The company's Global Sourcing and Operating Guidelines, formerly called the Business Partner Terms of Engagement, state that Levi Strauss will "seek to identify and utilize business partners who aspire as individuals and in the conduct of all their businesses to a set of ethical standards not incompatible with our own." Whenever intolerable business situations arise, managers should be guided by precise statements that spell out the behavior and operating practices that the company demands.

Ninety percent of all *Fortune* 500 companies have codes of conduct, and 70% have statements of vision and values. In Europe and the Far East, the percentages are lower but are increasing rapidly. Does that mean that most companies have what they need? Hardly. Even though most large U.S. companies have both statements of values and codes of conduct, many might be better off if they didn't. Too many companies don't do anything with the documents; they simply paste them on the wall to impress employees, customers, suppliers, and the public. As a result, the senior managers who drafted the statements lose credibility by proclaiming values and not living up to them. Companies such as Johnson & Johnson, Levi Strauss, Motorola, Texas Instruments, and Lockheed Martin, however, do a great deal to make the words meaningful. Johnson & Johnson, for example, has become well known for its Credo Challenge sessions, in which managers discuss ethics in the context of their current business problems and are invited to criticize the company's credo and make suggestions for changes. The participants' ideas are passed on to the company's senior managers. Lockheed Martin has created an innovative site on the World Wide Web and on its local network that gives employees, customers, and suppliers access to the company's ethical code and the chance to voice complaints.

Codes of conduct must provide clear direction about ethical behavior when the temptation to behave unethically is strongest. The pronouncement in a code of conduct that bribery is unacceptable is useless unless accompanied by guidelines for gift giving, payments to get goods through customs, and "requests" from intermediaries who are hired to ask for bribes.

Motorola's values are stated very simply as "How we will always act: [with] constant respect for people [and] uncompromising integrity." The company's code of conduct, however, is explicit about actual business practice. With respect to bribery, for example; the code states that the "funds and assets of Motorola shall not be used, directly or indirectly, for illegal payments of any kind." It is unambiguous about what sort of payment is illegal: "the payment of a bribe to a public official or the kickback of funds to an employee of a customer. . . ." The code goes on to prescribe specific procedures for handling commissions to intermediaries, issuing sales invoices, and disclosing confidential information in a sales transaction—all situations in which employees might have an opportunity to accept or offer bribes.

Codes of conduct must be explicit to be useful, but they must also leave room for a manager to use his or her judgment in situations requiring cultural sensitivity. Host-country employees shouldn't be forced to adopt all home-country values and renounce their own. Again, Motorola's code is exemplary. First, it gives clear direction: "Employees of Motorola will respect the laws, customs, and traditions of each country in which they operate, but will, at the same time, engage in no course of conduct which, even if legal, customary, and accepted in any such country, could be deemed to be in violation of the accepted business ethics of Motorola or the laws of the United States relating to business ethics." After laying down such absolutes, Motorola's code then makes clear when individual judgment will be necessary. For example, employees may sometimes accept certain kinds of small gifts "in rare circumstances, where the refusal to accept a gift" would injure Motorola's "legitimate business interests." Under certain circumstances, such gifts "may be accepted so long as the gift inures to the benefit of Motorola" and not "to the benefit of the Motorola employee."

Striking the appropriate balance between providing clear direction and leaving room for individual judgment makes crafting corporate values statements and ethics codes one of the hardest tasks that executives confront. The words are only a start. A company's leaders need to refer often to their organization's credo and code and must themselves be credible, committed, and consistent. If senior managers act as though ethics don't matter, the rest of the company's employees won't think they do, either.

CONFLICTS OF DEVELOPMENT AND CONFLICTS OF TRADITION

Managers living and working abroad who are not prepared to grapple with moral ambiguity and tension should pack their bags and come home. The view that all business practices can be categorized as either ethical or unethical is too simple. As Einstein is reported to have said, "Things should be as simple as possible—but no simpler." Many business practices that are considered unethical in one setting may be ethical in another. Such activities are neither black nor white but exist in what Thomas Dunfee and I have called *moral free space*.[2] In this gray zone, there are no tight prescriptions for a company's behavior. Managers must chart their own courses—as long as they do not violate core human values.

GUIDELINES FOR ETHICAL LEADERSHIP

Learning to spot intolerable practices and to exercise good judgment when ethical conflicts arise requires practice. Creating a company culture that rewards ethical behavior is essential. The following guidelines for developing a global ethical perspective among managers can help.

Treat corporate values and formal standards of conduct as absolutes. Whatever ethical standards a company chooses, it cannot waver on its principles either at home or abroad. Consider what has become part of company lore at Motorola. Around 1950, a senior executive was negotiating with officials of a South American government on a $10 million sale that would have increased the company's annual net profits by nearly 25%. As the negotiations neared completion, however, the executive walked away from the deal because the officials were asking for $1 million for "fees." CEO Robert Galvin not only supported the executive's decision but also made it clear that Motorola would neither accept the sale on any terms nor do business with those government officials again. Retold over the decades, this story demonstrating Galvin's resolve has helped cement a culture of ethics for thousands of employees at Motorola.

Design and implement conditions of engagement for suppliers and customers. Will your company do business with any customer or supplier? What if a customer or supplier uses child labor? What if it has strong links with organized crime? What if it pressures your company to break a host country's laws? Such issues are best not left for spur-of-the-moment decisions. Some companies have realized that. Sears, for instance, has developed a policy of not contracting production to companies that use prison labor or infringe on workers' rights to health and safety. And BankAmerica has specified as a condition for many of its loans to developing countries that environmental standards and human rights must be observed.

Allow foreign business units to help formulate ethical standards and interpret ethical issues. The French pharmaceutical company Rhône-Poulenc Rorer has allowed foreign subsidiaries to augment lists of corporate ethical principles with their own suggestions. Texas Instruments has paid special attention to issues of international business ethics by creating the Global Business Practices Council, which is made up of managers from countries in which the company operates. With the overarching intent to create a "global ethics strategy, locally deployed," the council's mandate is to provide ethics education and create local processes that will help managers in the company's foreign business units resolve ethical conflicts.

In host countries, support efforts to decrease institutional corruption. Individual managers will not be able to wipe out corruption in a host country, no matter how many bribes they turn down. When a host country's tax system, import and export procedures, and procurement practices favor unethical players, companies must take action.

Many companies have begun to participate in reforming host-country institutions. General Electric, for example, has taken a strong stand in India, using the media to make repeated condemnations of bribery in business and government. General Electric and others have found, however, that a single company usually cannot drive out entrenched corruption. Transparency International, an organization based in Germany, has been effective in helping coalitions of companies, government officials, and others work to reform bribery-ridden bureaucracies in Russia, Bangladesh, and elsewhere.

Exercise moral imagination. Using moral imagination means resolving tensions responsibly and creatively. Coca-Cola, for instance, has consistently turned down requests for bribes from Egyptian officials but has managed to gain political support and public trust by sponsoring a project to plant fruit trees. And take the example of Levi Strauss, which discovered in the early 1990s that two of its suppliers in Bangladesh were employing children under the age of 14—a practice that violated the company's principles but was tolerated in Bangladesh. Forcing the suppliers to fire the children would not have ensured that the children received an education, and it would have caused serious hardship for the families depending on the children's wages. In a creative arrangement, the suppliers agreed to pay the children's regular wages while they attended school and to offer each child a job at age 14. Levi Strauss, in turn, agreed to pay the children's tuition and provide books and uniforms. That arrangement allowed Levi Strauss to uphold its principles and provide longterm benefits to its host country.

Many people think of values as soft; to some they are usually unspoken. A South Seas island society uses the word *Mokita*, which means, "the truth that everybody knows but nobody speaks." However difficult they are to articulate, values affect how we all behave. In a global business environment, values in tension are the rule rather than the exception. Without a company's commitment, statements of values and codes of ethics end up as empty platitudes that provide managers with no foundation for behaving ethically. Employees need and deserve more, and responsible members of the global business community can set examples for others to follow. The dark consequences of incidents such as Union Carbide's disaster in Bhopal remind us how high the stakes can be.

NOTES

1. In other writings, Thomas W. Dunfee and I have used the term *hypernorm* instead of *core human value*.

2. Thomas Donaldson and Thomas W. Dunfee, "Toward a Unified Conception of Business Ethics: Integrative Social Contracts Theory," *Academy of Management Review*, April 1994; and "Integrative Social Contracts Theory: A Communitarian Conception of Economic Ethics," *Economics and Philosophy*, spring 1995.

QUESTIONS

1. When should companies and/or the people who work in them attempt to assert their own moral values over the values of another culture?

2. When you have traveled to other countries, which cultural values and practices did you find more ethical than your home culture, and which ones did you find less ethical? Why?

3. Under what conditions do you think it is right for a business to try and change the values of employees and others in a foreign culture? What sorts of initiatives do you think are appropriate changes and what sorts of initiative are not appropriate?

Silence as Complicity: Elements of a Corporate Duty to Speak Out Against the Violation of Human Rights

Florian Wettstein

Florian Wettstein is an Assistant Professor in the Ethics and Business Law Department of the University of St. Thomas.

The vast majority of corporate rights violations," as Stephen Kobrin observes, "involve complicity, aiding and abetting violations by another actor, most often the host government." Kobrin's claim certainly seems plausible. In an increasingly interconnected world our actions affect the lives of others in ever more profound ways. Thus, increasingly we may contribute to harm without being aware of it, or at least without intending to do so. It is in the very nature of complicity that it falls "outside the paradigm of individual, intentional wrongdoing." The problem deepens if we are not merely looking at the actions of individuals, but at those of organizations that operate globally and on a large scale, such as multinational corporations. Corporations may become complicit in human rights violations although they are not doing anything wrong in a conventional sense or engaging in any unlawful conduct; they may simply be going about their business. This contributes to the pervasiveness of corporate complicity and renders it notoriously hard to grasp and, not least, to condemn. The very nature of wrongdoing is changing in the process of today's globalization.

The changing nature of wrongdoing in the global age must be followed by our rethinking of the parameters of moral responsibility. The fact that corporations often contribute to wrongdoings in the course of their "regular" business conduct rather than by engaging in some specific, overt and deliberate harmful activity, poses new challenges to our moral intuition and our natural sense of justice. This is why cases of corporate complicity are in a sense symptomatic for our time; they require us to rethink some of the certainties of the Westphalian age and to come up with new normative visions and concepts to deal with the new problems with which we are faced in a transnational world.

The aim of this paper then is to assess under what conditions it is plausible to speak of corporations as silently complicit in human rights abuses and thus under what circumstances such a positive duty to speak out can be assumed.

SILENT COMPLICITY AND THE MORAL DUTY TO HELP PROTECT

Corporate complicity is commonly defined as "aiding and abetting" in the violation of human rights committed by a third party. Aiding and abetting is to be interpreted broadly; it includes not merely direct involvement of corporations, but also various forms of indirect facilitation.

Thus, corporate complicity can be categorized by the nature of its contribution to the wrongdoing in play. The literature on the topic commonly refers to four different forms of complicity: direct complicity, indirect complicity, beneficial complicity and silent complicity. While direct complicity implies direct involvement of the corporation in a human rights abuse, indirect complicity involves mere facilitation, that is, an indirect contribution to the general ability of a perpetrator to commit human

Copyright © 2012, *Business Ethics Quarterly,* Volume 22, Issue 1, 2012, pp. 37–61.

rights violations. There is increasing agreement that the scope of complicity may extend beyond *active* assistance given to a primary perpetrator. Cases of beneficial complicity, for example, do not require an active contribution by the corporation, but merely that the corporation directly or indirectly benefits from the violation of human rights. In the case of silent complicity, even "merely" standing by while human rights are violated is increasingly perceived as a form of complicity.

In contrast to other, more "conventional" forms of complicity, silent and in most cases also beneficial complicity are not established by a corporation's active contribution, but by its passive stance toward the violation of human rights. Knowingly looking the other way while the most basic rights of human beings are trampled underfoot by a host government can constitute not merely indifference, but actual support. In such cases, silence can have a potentially *legitimizing or encouraging effect* on a perpetrator, which in turn grounds the accusation of silent complicity. For John M. Kline, silent complicity "suggests that a non-participant is aware of abusive action and, although possessing some degree of ability to act, chooses neither to help protect nor to assist victims of the abuse, remaining content to meet the minimal ethical requirement to do no (direct) harm." Hence, moral blame in cases of silent complicity is not attached to certain harmful actions conducted by the corporation, but to its failure to give assistance to those in need when it is in a position to do so. In short, the main difference between silent complicity and most other forms of complicity is that its moral basis is not commission, but omission.

The normative implications of this insight are far-reaching. Omission denotes a failure to act in response to wrongdoing. Thus, rather than to merely passively refrain from specific harmful actions, the agent in danger of becoming silently complicit is under a moral obligation to confront and possibly counteract the wrongdoing. If silence renders companies complicit, speaking out to help protect the victims is what is required to diffuse such allegations. The claim that a corporation is silently complicit in human rights violations, as

Wiggen and Bomann-Larsen conclude, implies that it is guilty of omitting to fulfill an actual *positive duty*.

In sum, there are two constitutive requirements that need to be fulfilled in order for an agent to be guilty of silent complicity: first, the agent must have failed to speak out and help protect the victims. I will call this the "omission requirement." Second, the omission of this positive duty must have a legitimizing or encouraging effect on the human rights violation and the perpetrator who is committing it. I will call this the "legitimization requirement." This, in turn, raises the question: under what conditions can corporations indeed be said to be silently complicit in a host government's human rights abuse? That is, under what circumstances or conditions can these two requirements plausibly be said to be fulfilled? In what follows I will assess both requirements separately. The "omission requirement," I will argue, hinges on one general and two qualified conditions, while the "legitimization requirement" depends on a fourth condition.

ASSESSING THE "OMISSION REQUIREMENT": ELEMENTS OF A POSITIVE DUTY TO SPEAK OUT AGAINST THE VIOLATION OF HUMAN RIGHTS

A first important distinction that needs to be drawn in order to assess the "omission requirement" is the one between negative and positive duties. A *negative duty* is a duty to do no harm, while a *positive duty* is a duty to assist or "help persons in [acute] distress." Thus, a negative duty is a duty not to make a situation worse, while a positive duty is a duty to improve a given state of affairs. Negative duties are commonly seen as stricter than positive ones, which is at the root of the controversy surrounding any argument that assigns positive duties to corporations.

The distinction between negative and positive duties is not to be confused with the one between passive and active duties. *Passive duties* command us to merely abstain from certain (harmful) activities while *active duties* require us to actively perform specific actions. Negative duties can be active or passive. Doing no harm may be as simple as abstaining from actively hurting someone (passive), but, depending on the situation, it may also require to *actively* eliminate risks or dangers to others, such as cutting the tree in one's yard that threatens to fall onto the sidewalk. Passive duties are always negative, since passively abstaining from specific actions is obligatory only if those actions are harmful to others (or, in some cases, to oneself). As a consequence, positive duties are always active.

The duty to speak out against human rights violations is a positive duty. That is to say, it is a duty to speak out to *help protect* the victims. It is from this perspective that commonly the duty to speak out is not perceived merely as a duty to make a statement, but as a broader duty to *address* the issue with the appropriate authorities.

Generally, for there to be a passive negative duty to do no harm, only one condition needs to be fulfilled, which is that an agent has some level of autonomy to act. It is against this background that the passive negative duty to do no harm is of general nature and of universal reach; it applies to everyone at the same time and to the same extent. I will refer to this as the criterion of voluntariness. Second, for a negative duty to become active there must be a morally significant connection between the respective agent and the human rights violation. In contrast to passive duties, active duties (negative or positive) are specific and dependent on the context and situation; they apply to particular agents to varying degrees and extent. However, for active duties to apply to some agents but not to others, there must be something that specifically links those agents to the human rights violations at stake. I will call this the connection criterion. For there to be a positive duty to help protect, these two conditions must be complemented with a third one; a positive duty to improve a given state of affairs presupposes that a duty-bearer has the power to exert influence on the situation in a positive way. Thus, I will refer to this as the criterion of influence/power. The first two conditions aim at the non-violation of human rights, which means that they can be justified on a deontological basis. The third condition, however, aims at the improvement of

a given situation. Thus, its justification or plausibility requires at least some sensitivity to consequences (not, however, consequentialism). Let us analyze all three conditions in some more detail.

Voluntariness: Passive negative duties apply to all responsible individuals at all times and to the same extent; we all have the same duty to abstain from harming others. For any rational, adult human being this responsibility can only be mitigated or eliminated if the action causing harm is not freely chosen or if the harmful consequences are not foreseeable. Thus, moral responsibility, as opposed to mere causal responsibility, depends on autonomous and thus voluntary or intentional action. We can only be held morally responsible for actions we freely and willingly choose, but not for those over which we have no control or which we are forced to commit.

Connection: For there to be an active negative duty, voluntariness must be combined with connection. As pointed out earlier, silence turns into complicity only if, based on the perception of implicit endorsement or approval, it has a legitimizing or encouraging effect on the wrongdoing. This, it seems, presupposes a significant connection between the agent and the human rights violation. After all, the very claim that agents have an active duty to *disassociate* themselves from a particular human rights violation or its perpetrator already implies that there is an actual connection that links them to the violation in a morally relevant way. The crucial question is what qualifies connections as morally significant in this context of silent complicity. Generally, we can distinguish between two categories of connections: an agent can either be *actively* connected or *passively* connected to the violation. Active connection essentially means actual involvement, that is, the agent actively contributes to the violation of human rights committed by the primary perpetrator. However, such cases of active involvement belong to the category of direct complicity, which establishes a passive negative obligation to do no harm. In such cases, active involvement or contribution to the human rights violation is the problem, rather than the agent's silence. Hence, the connections that are relevant for silent complicity are of the passive kind.

Influence/Power: While voluntariness and connection are necessary conditions for there to be a moral obligation for a company to speak out against human rights abuse, they merely establish a negative obligation for the company, that is, an obligation to disassociate itself from the perpetrator and its harmful actions. However, on their own, these two conditions are insufficient to establish a positive duty to speak out to help protect the victims. For the company to have a positive obligation to speak out, it must be in a position to exert pressure or influence for the purpose of improving the situation of the victims.

Legitimization Requirement: The legitimization requirement consists of two elements. First, an agent's silence must imply implicit endorsement of the human rights violation. Second, this implied endorsement must serve to legitimize or encourage the violation. The implied endorsement derives from the combination of voluntariness, connection, and power as discussed above. Hence, an agent who is connected to the human rights violation and would be in a sufficiently powerful position to speak out against it can be perceived as endorsing it, if she *chooses* not to speak out. In order for an agent's implied endorsement to add legitimacy to the incident, her stance on the issue must carry some weight in the public perception. For this to be the case, the agent must be of a certain status or standing. This may involve high social regard and prestige. It may imply that the agent is epresentative of society or a relevant subset thereof.

INNOCENT BYSTANDER OR SILENTLY COMPLICIT?: THE EXECUTION OF KEN SARO-WIWA AND SHELL'S "ECOLOGICAL WAR" IN THE NIGER DELTA

On Tuesday, 31 October 1995, Nigerian playwright and minority-rights activist Ken Saro-Wiwa, along with eight of his followers, were sentenced to death by a specially convened, "hand-picked" tribunal of the Abacha regime in Nigeria for inciting the murder of four conservative, pro-government Ogoni chiefs. The four Ogoni chiefs were rounded up and killed by a rioting mob on 21 May 1994. On 10 November 1995, just ten days after the sentence was passed, Saro-Wiwa and his friends were executed while the world watched in outrage.

At the time of his arrest, Ken Saro-Wiwa and his activist group "Movement for the Survival of the Ogoni People" (MOSOP) were spearheading widespread protests against exploitation and environmental degradation by oil companies in the Ogoni land. Protests against the environmental destruction caused by oil companies had been growing throughout the Niger Delta since the 1970s. When the protests grew bigger and more numerous in the early 1990s, the government started to repress them violently—often at the specific request of Shell. Growing tension between Shell and the indigenous people in the Niger Delta led to increasing numbers of increasingly violent protests. The most devastating of these protests occurred in January 1993, when, at the dawn of the UN Year of Indigenous Peoples, the largest peaceful rally against oil companies to that point in time was silenced violently by government forces, resulting in the destruction of 27 villages, displacing 80,000 Ogoni villagers, and leaving some 2000 people dead. As the struggle evolved, the Ogoni people became the "vanguard movement for adequate compensation and ecological self-determination" in the Niger Delta and Shell became the symbol of their oppression. Saro-Wiwa was the driving force behind the Ogoni movement; "No other person in Nigeria," as one member of the Nigerian Civil Liberties Organisation put it, "can get 100,000 people on the streets."

The murder of the four chiefs provided the Nigerian government with an opportunity to arrest Saro-Wiwa and eight other leaders of his organization. The charges against Saro-Wiwa and his colleagues were anything but uncontroversial. It was even suggested that the Nigerian government itself was involved in provoking the murders as a justification for stronger military presence in the region. Not only was Saro-Wiwa "miles away" when the murders took place, but he was, in fact, under military escort. Key witnesses admitted that they had been bribed to provide false evidence and the tribunal, which was controlled by the military, was denounced as illegitimate by the international community due to blatant violations of international fair trial standards and a lack of respect for due process. The British government condemned the trial as "judicial murder."

The international protests did not remain limited to the Nigerian government. Shell too came under attack for idly standing by while the tragedy unfolded. Shell was accused of not using its influence in Nigeria to stop the execution, the torturing of protesters, and the violent crack-down of demonstrations. In other words, Shell was seen as being silently complicit by violating a positive duty to help protect them against the human rights violations of the Abacha junta. Our analysis now provides a tool with which to assess the validity of this claim. For Shell to be silently complicit, the two qualified conditions underlying the omission requirement (i.e., connection and influence/power) as well as the status condition underlying the legitimization requirement all need to have been met.

Connection: The connection between Shell and Ken Saro-Wiwa's and the roughly 2000 other Ogoni deaths is undisputed. The uprising of the Ogoni people was a direct response to Shell's operations in the Niger Delta; their protests were directly aimed at Shell. In some instances the police forces that put the demonstrations down were requested by Shell. Even when they were not requested, the suppression of large scale protests benefitted Shell and secured the continuation of its operations. In his closing statement to the tribunal, Ken Saro-Wiwa explicitly addressed Shell's role and connection to the incidence:

> I repeat that we all stand before history. I and my colleagues are not the only ones on trial. Shell is on trial here, and it is as well that it is represented by counsel said to be holding a watching brief. The company has, indeed, ducked this particular trial, but its day will surely come and the lessons learned here may prove useful to it, for there is no doubt in my mind that the ecological war the company has waged in the delta will be called to question sooner than later and the crimes of that war be duly punished. The crime of the company's dirty wars against the Ogoni people will also be punished.

Shell was the main cause for the formation of the Ogoni protests and was also the main reason for the violent crack down. Shell was, by every definition of the word, linked to the execution of Ken Saro-Wiwa and his friends in a morally significant way.

Influence/Power: For Shell to have a positive duty to help protect and thus to speak out against

the trial and to put pressure on the Nigerian government, their connection to the incidence must come with a position of influence or power. While the degree of Shell's real influence at the time ultimately is subject to speculation, most of the evidence and, as we will see shortly, also Shell's own assessment of its influence in Nigeria suggest that this condition too was met. Shell's position in Nigeria was and still is exceptionally powerful. The military government's power was dependent on the foreign earnings generated by oil and Shell was by far the major oil producer not only in the area but in the whole country. At the time of Saro-Wiwa's execution, Shell produced roughly half of Nigeria's crude oil output. As a result, Shell's power and influence was by any measure considerable.[22] Thus, Andrew Rowell observes that Shell's position in Nigeria was "both powerful and unique." Quoting an anonymous Ogoni activist, he says: "With such an illegitimate political system, each bunch of unelected military rulers that comes into power, simply dances to the tune of this company. . . . Shell is in the position to dictate, because Nigeria is economically and politically weak."

Status: At the time of the execution Shell enjoyed the prestige of a company with global brand recognition. In the mid-1990s, Shell was the world's biggest oil company not owned by a government, it was producing 3 percent of the world's crude oil and 4 percent of its natural gas. It was the world's only private company to rank among the top ten biggest holders of oil and gas reserves. Its influence both in Nigeria and globally was substantial. It was without doubt a company that led, molded, and directed, a company that disrupted old social orders and dictated the pace of daily life in Nigeria and the Niger Delta. The very protests that erupted first in Nigeria against Shell's environmental record and later on an international scale against Shell's way of handling the turmoil in Nigeria underscore Shell's standing relative to society at large. Furthermore, they are a case in point regarding the politicization of corporations and the subsequent call for deliberative public engagement. In light of the worldwide attention that the Shell case received, it seems that it would at least be difficult to argue that the company lacked the status necessary to be implicated with silent complicity.

Based on such assessments there certainly is a case to be made for Shell's silent complicity in Saro-Wiwa's execution. Many commentators believed and continue to believe that Shell was in a position to speak out against the trial. Saro-Wiwa's brother, Owens Wiwa goes so far as to claim that if Shell "had threatened to withdraw from Nigeria unless Ken was released, he would have been alive today. There is no question of that." Andrew Rowell's conclusions even reach beyond the specific incident around Saro-Wiwa: "[S]uch is the economic strength of the company that few people in Nigeria or Britain doubt that it could have stopped the conflict outright—or at least stopped the use of excessive force against demonstration." Shell was well aware of its powerful position in the country and its potential to turn the events around. In fact, as *The Observer* reported nine days after Saro-Wiwa's execution, Brian Anderson, who was head of Shell Nigeria at the time, had in fact offered to Owens Wiwa to use Shell's influence with Nigeria's military regime to try to free his brother; however, his offer was conditional on the Ogoni leaders calling off any global protests against Shell. This bargain, irrespective of its questionable ethical quality, was unattainable for Wiwa: "Even if I had wanted to, I didn't have the power to control the international environmental protests."

Shell defended its position of inactivity against the growing public outrage. The company's official position was that it would be "dangerous and wrong" for Shell to "intervene and use its perceived 'influence' to have the judgment overturned." "A commercial organization like Shell," as they claimed further, "cannot and must never interfere with the legal processes of any sovereign state." A Shell manager reportedly stated in 1996:

> I am afraid I cannot comment on the issue of the Ogoni 9, the tribunal and the hanging. This country has certain rules and regulations on how trials can take place. Those are the rules of Nigeria. Nigeria makes its rules and it is not for private companies like us to comment on such processes in the country.

QUESTIONS

1. What does it mean for a corporation to be complicit in human rights violations? Can you give some cases outside of this article where corporations could have prevented the abuse of human rights?

2. To what extent do you think that Shell was responsible for the 2000 Ogoni deaths? What could they have done to prevent them?

3. How can companies leverage their status in another country to bring about change without affecting their competitive position?

To: You
From: The Philosopher
RE: The Global Compact

Have you heard about this Global Compact that the United Nations launched in 2000? It's a set of 10 ethical principles for businesses. Companies voluntarily sign it and pledge to align their business practices and strategies with its principles. It is the largest voluntary corporate responsibility initiative in the world, with over 8700 signatories from 130 countries. I am skeptical about these things. Some companies may only do this for public relations purposes. What do you think? Do these sorts of initiatives really make a difference in how the companies that sign it do business? What do you think of the principles in the compact?

Principle 1: Businesses should support and respect the protection of internationally proclaimed human rights.

Principle 2: Make sure that they are not complicit in human rights abuses.

Principle 3: Businesses should uphold the freedom of association and the effective recognition of the right to collective bargaining.

Principle 4: The elimination of all forms of forced and compulsory labor.

Principle 5: The effective abolition of child labor.

Principle 6: The elimination of discrimination in respect of employment and occupation.

Principle 7: Businesses should support a precautionary approach to environmental challenges.

Principle 8: Undertake initiatives to promote greater environmental responsibility.

Principle 9: Encourage the development and diffusion of environmentally friendly technologies.

Principle 10: Businesses should work against corruption in all its forms, including extortion and bribery.

John T. Noonan, Jr. | # A Quick Look at the History of Bribes

John T. Noonan, Jr., is a judge in the United States Ninth Circuit Court of Appeals.

First. Bribes—socially disapproved inducements of official action meant to be gratuitously exercised—are ancient, almost as ancient as the invention in Egypt of scales which symbolized and showed social acceptance of the idea of objective judgment.

Second. The bribe has a history, divisible into discernible epochs. From approximately 3000 B.C. to 1000 A.D. the idea of nonreciprocity struggles against the norms of reciprocation which cement societies whose rulers are both judges and the recipients of

offerings. In the second period from, say, 1000 A.D. to 1550 A.D., the antibribery ideal is dominant in religious, legal, and literary expressions; its active enforcement is attempted in successive waves of reformation. The third period of the idea, as far as English-speaking people are concerned, begins in the sixteenth century with its domestication in English bibles and English plays and English law and ends in the eighteenth century with its proclamation as a norm for the English empire. The fourth stage is the American, when the heirs of the successive reformations and of English politics begin to apply it and then to expand its sway until it is asserted as an

John T. Noonan, Jr. "A Quick Look at the History of Bribes" in *Bribes* (New York: Macmillan Publishers, 1984), pp. xx–xxiii.

American norm around the earth; and the rest of the world—not merely as a result of American influence but because of the general expansion of the Western moral tradition—makes at least verbal acknowledgment of the norm.

Third. Bribes are today universal; that is, every culture, with insignificant exceptions, treats certain reciprocities with officials as disapproved.

Fourth. The bribe is a concept running counter to normal expectations in approaching a powerful stranger. Linguistic ambiguity in the term for bribe in Hebrew, Greek, and Latin marks the cultural resistance encountered by the concept. Historically, the limitation of the concept to one class of officials—judges—is a second sign of the resistance. Reluctance to apply the concept against the bribegiver is a third. Lack of specific sanctions against the bribetaker is a fourth indication of the precarious hold the concept, historically, has enjoyed.

Fifth. The bribe in its origins depends on religious teaching. Reciprocity is so regularly the norm of human relations that the conception of a transcendental figure, a Judge beyond the reach of ordinary reciprocities, was of enormous importance for the idea that certain reciprocities with earthly officials were intolerable. That conception of a transcendental Judge was shaped in the ancient Near East. Communication of this image to the West was largely dependent on religion. Accepted as divine revelation, Scripture by commandment and paradigm inculcated a teaching on impartial judgment. The concept of the bribe was cast in a biblical mold.

Sixth. Religion—Jewish, Christian, pagan—has been, however, profoundly ambivalent in its teaching on reciprocity. The Judge beyond influence has been placated by pagans, offered prayers and slaughtered animals by Jews, and seen by Christians as accepting a special redeeming sacrifice. Religion can be viewed as bribery on a grand scale, organized for the highest end, man's salvation, and practiced to persuade the Supreme Authority. Indulgences, systematized to support enterprises from basilicas to bridges, constitute an especially striking example of this kind of religion. Even in its most primitive form, Christianity rests on a transaction carried out between God and the Son of God which theology labeled the Buy Back, a term in Roman civilization often used to mean payoff to a judge to escape punishment. Job and Jesus himself to the contrary, religion can be read as reinforcement of the iron law, "I give that you may give," a law requiring reciprocity with every power-holder including God.

Seventh. The double message conveyed by the several religious traditions is paralleled in Western cultures by the elimination of certain reciprocities as bribes and the retention of others as acceptable quid pro quos. Words alone seem to mark the distinction between certain acceptable and condemned offerings. In sixteenth-century Europe payment to obtain a spiritual favor was the sin of simony; a *contributio* to obtain an indulgence was legitimate. In twentieth-century America, payment to a candidate for his vote is a penal offense; a licensed contribution to a campaign committee is lawful. In some instances, there is only verbal camouflage; in some instances, the verbal distinction points to a real difference.

Eighth. Although the definition of a bribe depends on the conventions of the culture, so that ceremony and context, form and intention, determine whether an exchange counts as a crime or a virtuous act, ultimately the distinction between bribe and gift has become fundamental. Without this distinction the condemnation of bribes appears arbitrary, and intermediate offerings such as a tip or a campaign contribution are indiscriminately lumped into a single category which includes all reciprocities. With bribe and gift set at polar opposites, a spectrum with shades of discrimination exists. For our culture—Western culture, now the dominant world culture—the difference between bribe and gift has been most powerfully developed by reflection, theological and literary, on the Redemption.

Ninth. Bribes come openly or covertly, disguised as an interest in a business, as a lawyer's fee, or, very often, as a loan. Bribes come directly, paid into the waiting hands of the bribee or, more commonly, indirectly to the subordinate or friend performing the nearly indispensable office of bagman. Bribes come in all shapes as sex, commodities, appointments, and, most often, cash. In the shape of sex, bribes have been both male and female: a slave, a wife, a noble boy. As commodities, they have included bedspreads, cups, dogs, fruits, furniture, furs, golf balls, jewels, livestock, peacocks, pork, sturgeon, travel, wine—the gamut of enjoyable goods. As appointments, they have often been rationalized or justified by the merits of the appointee—a double effect, one good, one bad, being achieved by the bribe. As cash they have come as contingent payments and down payments, as payments for the life of the contract and payments for the life of the recipient and as cash on the spot. They have come at the rate of so much a car towed, so much a prostitute undisturbed, so much a plane purchased, so much a guinea spent, at such a percentage, and at a flat rate. They have been as little as 1 percent of a contract and as high as 20 percent or more. They have been as small as $2.50 for a Connecticut voter and as much as $12,000,000 for the prime minister of Japan and his associates. . . .

Tenth. Bribers have included every variety of business, from very small to multinational; all the professions; every manner of criminal defendant; and the ordinary citizen in line for an inheritance or in need of a traffic ticket being fixed. Bribees have ranged from constables and sheriffs to the Speaker of the House (U.S., nineteenth century), the Speaker of the House of Commons (U.K., seventeenth century), the president of Honduras, the president of Italy, the prime minister of Japan, the prince-consort of the Netherlands, the Lord Chancellor of England (seventeenth century). Bribe-takers and bribe-givers are not distinguished by any of the characteristics commonly associated with criminality. Sometimes they are oppressed and bribe to escape harassment. Sometimes they are oppressed and therefore accept bribes. Often they are possessed of high office and comfortable income, bribe to maintain or expand their power or wealth, and accept bribes given as tributes to their power or wealth. Their crimes have not been shown to depend on any oedipal fixation, sexual need or malfunction, or uncontrollable instinct. They are not vicious in all respects; they are often otherwise decent individuals. They are of all nationalities and sects and have been in the past more often men than women.

Eleventh. The bribe is ideologically neutral—that is, charges of bribery can be made by an established class attacking a new class (John Randolph pursuing the Yazoo speculators; George Templeton Strong

scorning the Tweed Ring); by a new class attacking an old class (the Protestants assailing the papacy; Andrew Jackson censuring Adams and Clay); and in intraclass warfare (Coke against Bacon; the Carter administration against the Abscam defendants). The bribe is a concept which can be effectively evoked by "the center" or existing hierarchy, as fourth-century Roman emperors and popes like Gregory I, Gregory VII, and Innocent III illustrate. It is a concept which is useful to "the border" or sectarian groupings within a society, as is shown by the writings of John Wyclif and Jan Hus.

Twelfth. Enforcement of law against bribes has nearly always been a function of prosecutorial discretion. Prosecutions for bribery have often depended on motivations distinct from the desire to punish the bribe. The watershed for widespread federal prosecution of bribery occurred in the 1960s. Whatever social causes account for it, at this time the pursuit of bribery became a national enterprise in the United States. Watergate is the consequence not the cause of this phenomenon. In the Orwellian prophecy for the year 1984, sexual Puritanism is the rule, enforced by electronics. In the actual America of 1984, it is the purity of political reciprocities that is enforced by wire taps, tape recordings, and television cameras.

Thirteenth. The commonest sanctions against bribes are moral—the invocation of guilt before God and shame before society, guilt and shame being equally relied on. Political sanctions—repudiation at the polls, forced resignation from office, loss of promotion—are frequently invoked. Sanctions prescribed by law are more often indirect than direct—not the crime of bribery itself but a related offense is usually punished. Until very recent times application of direct criminal sanctions to highly placed bribe-takers was rare.

Fourteenth. Prosecutors, politicians, and journalists are those most attentive to contemporary corruption. Academic lawyers, anthropologists, psychoanalysts, and theologians have had little to say. Political scientists and sociologists, intent on understanding the function of social practices, sometimes give little weight to the moral impact of corruption. Biographers and historians, despite a tendency at times to act as advocates or apologists, give a kind of secular last judgment on the corrupt. Those who have most powerfully articulated the antibribery ethic are the masters of Western literature—above, all, Chaucer, Dante, and Shakespeare.

Fifteenth. The material injury bribers and bribees inflict is often undemonstrable. Their actions always subvert the trust that accompanies public office and distinguishes office from power. For Jews, for Christians, for those who share their moral heritage, the bribe is not a morally neutral concept.

Writing at this interesting time in the history of the bribe, I venture a prediction that is a projection of my values. That will come at the end. History itself is not prediction but the selection of significant actions, words, and characters to be remembered—drama more than process. "Remember! Remember! Remember!"—Burke's incantation after his prosecution of Warren Hastings had ended in defeat. If all that is collected here survives in memory, this account has been worth making.

QUESTIONS

1. How would you delineate the difference between a bribe and a gift?

2. What is it about a bribe that makes it such a prevalent ethical problem in history? Why has bribery been discredited for so long in so many places?

3. Are anti-bribery rules the luxury of wealthy countries and a hindrance to people in developing countries? Are countries corrupt because they are poor or poor because they are corrupt?

To: You
From: The Philosopher
Subject: The Foreign Corrupt Practices Act

I always thought that the Foreign Corrupt Practices Act (FCPA) put American Companies at a disadvantage. After all, how can they compete in some markets when other companies can pay bribes to get business? Then I read that in 2008 Siemens paid $800 million to the U.S. and Germany to settle a bribery case. The company was later charged for paying $100 million in bribes to the Carlos Menem, the then President of Argentina, and other Argentine officials to secure a $1 billion project.* The bribery took place in Argentina and the people who paid, demanded, and received the bribes were Argentine, and Siemans is a German company. Yet, Siemans was prosecuted and fined for violating a US law! I did not know that in 1998, the U.S. extended the FPCA to foreign companies, like Siemans, that traded their securities in the United States.

While this amendment sounds good for U.S. companies, it also makes me wonder: Is it fair to force companies from other countries to play by laws based on the U.S. values? Here is what the law says:

The Foreign Corrupt Practices Act of 1977 was enacted for the purpose of making it unlawful for certain classes of persons and entities to make payments to foreign government officials to assist in obtaining or retaining business. Specifically, the anti-bribery provisions of the FCPA prohibit the willful use of the mails or any means of instrumentality of interstate commerce corruptly in furtherance of any offer, payment, promise to pay, or authorization of the payment of money or anything of value to any person, while knowing that all or a portion of such money or thing of value will be offered, given or promised, directly or indirectly, to a foreign official to influence the foreign official in his or her official capacity, induce the foreign official to do or omit to do an act in violation of his or her lawful duty, or to secure any improper advantage in order to assist in obtaining or retaining business for or with, or directing business to, any person.

Since 1977, the anti-bribery provisions of the FCPA have applied to all U.S. persons and certain foreign issuers of securities. With the enactment of certain amendments in 1998, the anti-bribery provisions of the FCPA now also apply to foreign firms and persons who cause, directly or through agents, an act in furtherance of such a corrupt payment to take place within the territory of the United States.

The FCPA also requires companies whose securities are listed in the United States to meet its accounting provisions. See 15 U.S.C. § 78m. These accounting provisions, which were designed to operate in tandem with the anti-bribery provisions of the FCPA, require corporations covered by the provisions to (a) make and keep books and records that accurately and fairly reflect the transactions of the corporation and (b) devise and maintain an adequate system of internal accounting controls.**

*Leslie Wayne, "Foreign Firms Most Affected by a U.S. Law Baring Bribes," *The New York Times*, September 3, 2012.
**Quoted from: http://www.justice.gov/criminal/fraud/fcpa/

Daryl Koehn | Confucian Trustworthiness

Daryl Koehn is a Professor in the Ethics and Business Law Department of the University of St. Thomas.

It is not the failure of others to appreciate your abilities that should trouble you, but rather your own lack of them.[1]

—*Confucius*

Confucius contends that individuals are ethically obligated to refine themselves and to become exemplary human beings. Such refinement (jen*) requires education. Becoming an educated and influential individual depends, in turn, upon establishing trust: "Only after he has gained the trust of the common people does the gentleman work them hard, for otherwise they would feel themselves illused. Only after he has gained the trust of the lord does the gentleman advise him against unwise action, for otherwise the lord would feel himself slandered" (19/9).

At first glance, Confucius appears to think of trust in a manner not all that different from Western theorists. Trust is the trustor's expectation of good will on the part of the trustee. Trust is something we can bestow on or refuse to other people. Trust must be gained and, if we are not careful when reposing trust, we will feel ourselves betrayed. On closer examination, though, we find that Confucius diverges from many Western theorists because he regards the virtue of trustworthiness as more important than trust per se.

To be worthy of our trust a person does not have to cater to our needs. While a good leader will try to ensure that those ruled have enough to eat and drink, people will still honor a leader in hard times: "Death has always been with us since the beginning of time, but when there is no trust, the common people will have nothing to stand on" (12/7). This saying suggests that we should trust as long as the good will of the trustee is evident, regardless of whether the trustee promotes our material well-being or conforms to our expectations. Virtuous persons, who look beyond their own narrow self-interest and who seek the spiritual as well as merely material welfare of all of their fellow citizens, merit our trust. Cultivated individuals display good will by never treating the multitude with contempt. Instead he always praises the good while taking pity on the backward (19/3). To excessively hate those who are not refined only provokes them to unruly behavior (8/10), and the trustworthy person seeks to avoid war and conflict (7/13).

Those who are devoted to the way of virtue take instruction from anyone who speaks well. Anyone who truly is trying to be virtuous is eager to learn, and she never dismisses what is said on account of who is speaking (15/23). The person of jen* will even speak with a madman (18/5). In general, the person of jen* is intent upon helping others realize what is good in them (12/16). He neither looks for the evil nor denounces others as evil (17/24). He hates evil, not evil people: "To attack evil as evil and not as evil of a particular man, is that not the way to reform the depraved?" (12/21). If we focus upon evil persons, we will not discern opportunities for realizing the good in others. We will not merit the trust of others because we will not be acting so as to refine people. Instead, our judgments will foster hatred and discord.

Many Western ethics of trust contend that we are justified in accusing those who fall short of our expectations of betrayal. Confucius asks us to consider instead whether we have demanded more of those we have trusted than we should have. We ought

to err on the side of making allowances for people (15/15), remembering that individuals have different strengths. Virtue exists as a continuum. The person of jen* has good relations with others precisely because she does not expect complete virtue from everyone:

> A man good enough as a partner in one's studies need not be good enough as a partner in the pursuit of the way; a man good enough as a partner in the pursuit of the way need not be good enough as a partner in a common stand; a man good enough as a partner in a common stand need not be good enough as a partner in the exercise of moral discretion (9/30).

It is up to us to choose our partners and friends carefully. In some cases, our business associates, friends, and family members may fail to keep their promises to us or may not show us due respect. However, we should not waste our energy accusing them of being untrustworthy. It is not the failure of others to appreciate our abilities that should trouble us, but rather our own lack of abilities (14/29). The Confucian ethic sees the value of trust but always directs our attention back to our own performance and attitudes. When there is trouble, we should look inward (4/17) and bring charges against ourselves, instead of blaming or scapegoating others (5/26).

The Confucian ethic takes the energy out of our anger at others for slighting us and redirects that energy back into self-examination. This redirection is appropriate for several reasons. First, there is little point in getting angry with others. If they have harmed us out of ignorance, then the correct response is to try to educate them, not to harm them in return. If they intend us harm, we should still try to dissuade them, rather than retaliate in kind. Second, even if others persist in trying to wrong us, we should not let their actions distract us from the arduous work of becoming an authoritative person. Since refinement or jen* is within our control, we always should look to our own behavior and not worry overly much about what others are or are not doing to us. Warned that Huan T'ui would try to assassinate him, Confucius retorted: "Heaven is the author of the virtue that is in me. What can Huan

T'ui do to me?" (7/23). The person of jen* is free from anxieties (7/37) because he keeps his eye on what is most important: "If, on examining himself, a man finds nothing to reproach himself for, what worries and fears can he have?" (12/4). Confucius was famous for maintaining his composure in the face of insults: "To be transgressed against yet not to mind. It was towards this end that my friend [Confucius] used to direct his efforts" (8/5). It is our trustworthiness, not others' machinations or venom, that should be our primary concern.

Third, it is easy to misjudge another. We may think, for example, that someone is not a good leader because the community or corporation he leads is in disarray. Yet "even with a true king, it is bound to take a generation for benevolence to become a reality" (13/12). Or we may conclude we have been betrayed when a trusted party deviates from a stated plan of action. Sometimes, though, to change one's mind is the right course. A "man who insists on keeping his word and seeing his actions through to the end . . . shows a stubborn petty-mindedness" (13/20). We cannot hope to assess accurately the "betrayals" of other people if we are not striving simultaneously to be as mindful as possible (15/8). Followers have a responsibility, therefore, to be thoughtful as their leaders. If those who are led are not mindful, they will not be able to grasp the wisdom in what the leader is saying and simply may dismiss her out of hand.

Finally, we humans are only too prone to self-deceit. Scrupulous self-examination is necessary if we are not to err. For example, we may be inclined to dismiss younger workers as undisciplined and undeserving of our trust and regard. Yet, we are far from infallible. How "do we know that the generations to come will not be equal of the present?" (9/23). In other cases, our judgment may be motivated by bad faith. One should never oppose a lord or ruler without first making certain of one's own honesty (14/22). If all of us would engage in routine self-scrutiny, we would be more worthy of trust. We then would trust one another more fully. With more trust, we would be able to educate each other even better, thereby increasing the level of trustworthiness and engendering still more trust. If people are failing to live up to their potential and living in

discord, then perhaps it is because we are failing to lead by example (13/4). When Confucius wanted to settle in the midst of the "barbarians." one of his disciples asked, "But could you put up with their uncouth ways?" Confucius bitingly retorted, "Once a gentleman settles amongst them, what uncouthness will there be?" (9/14).

For all of these reasons, Confucius warns that to love trust without loving learning can lead an individual to do harm (17/8). Judging other people's good will without simultaneously turning a critical eye on our own standard and trust-worthiness is a recipe for disaster. It does not follow that we should tolerate any and all abuse. The person of jen* is not angered by abuse, but neither does she stick around to be mistreated. She tries to choose her friends carefully, refusing to accept anyone as a friend who is not as good as herself (9/25; see also 16/4). That does not mean she chooses only completely virtuous individuals as her friends. It does mean she looks for others who are as critically mindful as she is. Her friends should be eager to learn. She advises them as best she can but stops if her advice is not being heeded. She does not ask to be snubbed (12/23) and does not waste her words on those who are incapable of improving themselves (15/8). The superior person does not look for evil but she quickly discerns it because she is thoughtful. So, "without anticipating attempts at deception or presuming acts of bad faith, [she] is, nevertheless, the first to be aware of such behavior" (14/31). Her responses to others' acts are similarly nuanced. An injury should not be taken personally but neither should it be rewarded. Confucius rejects a student's suggestion that one should repay an injury with a good turn. For if you did so, then "what do you repay a good turn with? You repay an injury with straightness, but you repay a good turn with a good turn" (14/34).

By judging and responding with a high degree of discretion, we show ourselves to be worthy of trust. In turn, we should trust those who are consistently thoughtful. There probably is no such thing as a perfect friend or colleague. However, if we use good judgment and do not expect too much of our colleagues and associates; and if our friends use good judgment as well and do not take on too much responsibility, then we can have strong, secure, and trusting relations with our fellow employees and friends.

SUSPICION OF CONTRACTS

Like the Japanese, the Chinese historically have been loathe to rely upon contracts. They often will not even read long contracts and may insist the document be shortened. A contract is merely a commercial agreement not to be taken as the gospel: "You might say they [the Chinese] sign long complicated contracts only as a formal confirmation that they intend to do business with you, not how they are going to conduct the business." The Confucian emphasis on trustworthiness makes reliance on contracts less attractive for several reasons. First, use of detailed contracts encourages parties to think of the contract as the basis for trust. The parties then feel entitled to accuse each other of betrayal whenever one appears to the other to have deviated from the terms of the contract. The contract thus contributes to an atmosphere of distrust. By contrast, if people enter into relationships and transactions with the understanding that they will need to work hard to accommodate their partner's interests and to keep their own biases and self-righteousness in check, then they will have put their relationship on a sounder footing. They may still decide to use some simple written document to lay out key terms or to serve as a talking document, but they will not make adherence to a contract the entire basis of the relation.

Second, reliance on contracts can prevent people from focussing on the larger picture and from being as mindful as they should be. A number of disputes between the Chinese and their joint venture partners have involved transfer of technology issues. The foreign partner typically accuses the Chinese side of failing to meet contractual requirements to supply land or capital, while the Chinese claim that the foreign partner has not provided the technical training the two had agreed upon. The foreign partner has generally viewed this counter-claim as a fabrication. It did provide training and the Chinese are simply trying to justify their own breach of contract. While that might be true in some cases, the person of jen* would look beyond the contractual dispute to the larger cultural and economic issues.

The Chinese have good reason to be sensitive about technical training. The government has made a conscious decision to modernize the country by importing technology and then adapting it to suit their needs and their level of development. Mao Tse Tung imported "turnkey" facilities—i.e., entire factories. The current policy is to build their own facilities using imported technology. In an effort to acquire technology as cheaply as possible, the Chinese have been willing to acquire slightly older hardware and software in the secondhand market. This modernization strategy obviously will not succeed if they do not also learn to use the technology. Therefore, the Chinese place great emphasis on jishu jiaoliu or technical presentations conveying technical information. They will bring in successive groups. Each group asks most of the same questions their predecessors posed. The Chinese use these sessions not only to brief all members of their team on the status of the project but also to train their people in the technology. They do not see themselves as "using" these presenters for their own purposes. They simply see themselves as obtaining an education that any person of genuine good will would wish to help them obtain.

Given their history of being colonized, the Chinese are understandably afraid of being exploited. Many have noted that, as late as the beginning of World War II, Shanghai's British quarters still had signs proclaiming "Chinamen and dogs are not permitted to enter." They do not want to give up hard currency and to provide land and other resources to their former masters in exchange for technology they are unable to use. Nor do they want to become a dumping ground for obsolete or non-functioning software. If they cannot get the software to run, they naturally suspect that they have been duped. What Westerners view as a rather cut-and-dried contractual dispute— did the Chinese live up to their end of the bargain or not?—is a major cultural issue for the Chinese. The future of China and Chinese pride and self-respect is at stake in each of these deals. Contracting to do business with the Chinese will never build trust unless each side consistently looks beyond the contract to discern the economic, psychological, and cultural factors at work.[7] Parties will be more inclined to take this broad and more generous point of view if they remind themselves that they may not know as much about the situation as they think they do. Contractual disputes will prove more resolvable if each side shifts its attention away from the other's alleged betrayal and to the question of whether it has been behaving trustworthily.

THE PROMINENCE OF GUANXI

The Chinese reliance on connections or guanxi is another important feature of the Chinese business scene. Does the Confucian ethic endorse such a reliance? Guanxi is typically seen as an outgrowth of the Confucian emphasis on personal relations. And it is true that, for Confucius, good order requires that each person fulfill his particular role-based duties. Children should be filial. The ruler should be a ruler and a father should be a father (12/11). Persons should acknowledge their role in the hierarchy. Historically these roles were relatively fixed by custom. There was little public law to which people could appeal if the authorities abused their power. In such a system, it became vitally important to cultivate relations with powerful people in the event one needed some sort of help from an authority. Family and local ties were especially important. To this day Chinese businesspeople will often treat classmates, friends, and family members preferentially when making hiring or other business decisions.

Public authorities, especially local authorities, continue to exercise a phenomenal degree of power in China. Kristoff and Wudunn argue that China still has an imperial system. The party leader is the new emperor, but local chieftains share in this absolute power:

> Each lower official acts like a prince on his own turf, from the ministry to the department to the section to the team, from the factory manager to the production manager to the workshop director. The petty autocrats are often the worst, as well as the most difficult to escape. In many villages, the local chief rules even more absolutely than [the national leader], for he decides who can marry, who can get good land, who can get water for irrigation, who can be buried where. He is almost as powerful as God, but not so remote.

Businesspeople, therefore, are well advised to cultivate guanxi. However, it would be a mistake to conclude, as Francis Fukuyama does, that China is a low-trust, family-oriented society whose members have little practice or interest in interacting with outsiders or in dealing with others on an equal basis. If this were true, the Chinese would never have been able to achieve their economic miracle: China now ranks first in the world in the production of coal, cement, grain, fish, meat, and cotton; third in steel production; and fifth in crude oil output; its annual growth rate has averaged more than 9 percent since 1978. The Chinese would never have succeeded if they had not imported their technology and had not formed numerous joint ventures with foreign companies. Nearly 10 percent of China's industrial output comes from foreign-owned and private businesses.

It should also be noted that the fastest-growing countries during the last decade—China, Japan, Hong Kong, Singapore, Taiwan, and South Korea—either have a large Chinese population or have been heavily influenced by Chinese culture. The ethnic Chinese may be the most economically successful ethnic group in the world. Although they constitute only 1.5 percent of the Philippine population, they are responsible for 35 percent of the sales of locally owned firms. In Indonesia, they are 2 percent of the population but may own as much as 70 percent of private domestic capital. Again, these minority Chinese populations would never have done as well as they did if they had refused to deal with non-family members.

CONCLUSION

Although recent Western discussions of trust have tended to focus on conditions for reposing trust, Confucius asks us to see trustworthiness as the more important phenomenon: How should we behave if we are to make ourselves into beings truly worthy of trust? What responsibility do we have for ensuring that our judgment of someone's trustworthiness is sound? The Confucian ethic calls into question whether a business leader can earn the trust of her followers simply by adhering to select rules (e.g., "avoid conflicts of interest") or by adopting certain techniques. Being thoughtful is ultimately the only way to earn and merit the trust of one's fellow citizens.

NOTE

All references to Confucian sayings are to the chapter and paragraph listing in Confucius, *The Analects*, trans. D. C. Lau (London: Penguin Books, 1979).

QUESTIONS

1. What elements of Confucian Ethics are similar to Western ethics?

2. Why do the Chinese and Japanese dislike contracts?

3. What are the strengths and weaknesses of business ethics that rely more on trust and relationships than on rules and regulations?

CASES

CASE 11.1
The Oil Rig
Joanne B. Ciulla

You have just taken over as the new chief executive officer of Stratton Oil Company, an exploration and drilling firm under contract to a major multinational oil company. Your enterprise has experienced ups and downs over the past few years because of the fluctuation of international oil prices and complications with overseas operations.

Many of the operational problems stem from difficulties with Stratton's offshore oil-drilling rigs. Maintenance and equipment costs have skyrocketed. You have received several reports of strained labor relations on the platforms. One incident caused such an uproar that the rig manager halted operations for over a week. In addition, there have been a number of complaints from conscientious shareholders who are concerned with the environmental impact of these rigs.

In an attempt to address these issues, you decide to get a firsthand look at the offshore drilling operations. On your first excursion, you visit a rig off the coast of Africa, dubbed the "Voyager 7." You discover that an oil rig is really a small society, separate and distinct from the rest of the world.

Stratton's Voyager 7 is a relatively small "jackup" (a platform with legs) with dimensions of about 200 feet by 100 feet. The platform houses a crew of 150 men, made up of skilled laborers, "roustabouts" or unskilled laborers, maintenance staff, and 30 expatriates. The expatriates work as roughnecks, drillers, technicians, or administrators. The top administrator on the Voyager 7 is the "tool pusher," an expatriate who wields almost absolute authority over matters pertaining to life on the rig.

Stratton engineers modified the crew quarters on the Voyager 7 for operations in Africa. They installed a second galley on the lower level and enlarged the cabins to permit a dormitory-style arrangement of 16 persons per room. This lower level of the rig makes up the "African section" of the rig, where the 120 local workers eat, sleep, and socialize during their 28-day "hitch."

The upper level of the platform houses the 30 expatriates in an area that is equal in square footage to that of the African section. The "expatriate section" contains semiprivate quarters with baths and boasts its own galley, game room, and movie room. Although not explicitly written, a tacit regulation exists prohibiting African workers from entering the expatriate section of the rig except in emergencies. The only Africans who are exempt from this regulation are those who are assigned to the highly valued positions of cleaning or galley staff in the expatriate section. The Africans hold these positions in high esteem because of the potential for receiving gifts or recovering discarded razors and other items from the expatriates.

Several other rig policies separate the African workers from the expatriates. African laborers travel to and from the rig by boat (an 18-hour trip), whereas expatriates receive helicopter transportation. An expatriate registered nurse dispenses medical attention to the expatriates throughout the day, but the Africans have access to treatment only during shift changes or in an emergency. The two groups also receive disparate treatment when serious injuries arise. For instance, if a finger is severed, expatriates are rushed to the mainland for reconstructive surgery. However, because of the high cost of helicopter transportation, African workers must have an amputation operation performed on the rig by the medic.

The company issues gray coveralls to the Africans, while the expatriates receive red coveralls. Meals in the two galleys are vastly different: The expatriate galley serves fine cuisine that approaches gourmet quality, while the Africans dine on a somewhat more proletarian fare. Despite the gross disparity in the numbers served, the catering budgets for the two galleys are nearly equal.

Communication between the expatriates and the Africans is notably absent on the Voyager 7, since none of the expatriates speaks the native language and none of the Africans speaks more that a few words of the expatriate's language. Only the chef of the catering company knows both languages. Consequently, he acts as an interpreter in all emergency situations. In the everyday working environment, management must rely upon sign language or repetition of examples to train and coordinate efforts.

From time to time, an entourage of African government officials visits the Voyager 7. These visits normally last only for an hour or so. Invariably, the officials dine with the expatriates, take a brief tour of the equipment, and then return to shore by helicopter. No entourage has never expressed concern about the disparity in living conditions on the rig, nor have officials ever bothered to speak with the African workers. Observers comment that the officials seem disinterested in the situation of the African workers, most of whom come from outside the capital city.

The presence of an expatriate black worker has little effect on the rig's segregated environment. The expatriate black is assigned to the expatriate section and partakes in all expatriate privileges. However, few expatriate blacks participate in the international drilling business, and the few who do are frequently not completely welcomed into the rig's social activities.

You leave the oil rig feeling uneasy. You know that there has always been a disparity in living conditions on the drilling platforms. However, you want to make Stratton a socially responsible and profitable company. You wonder how you can best accomplish your dual goals.

QUESTIONS

1. What do you think is really bothering the workers?
2. What kinds of inequalities are tolerable and intolerable on an oil rig, in operations away from home, and inside an organization at home?
3. Does an international corporation have an obligation to give employees benefits that they do not ask for or expect from an employer?

CASE 11.2

Foreign Assignment

Thomas Dunfee and Diana Robertson

Sara Strong graduated with an MBA from UCLA four years ago. She immediately took a job in the correspondent bank section of the Security Bank of the American Continent. Sara was assigned to work on issues pertaining to relationships with correspondent banks in Latin America. She rose rapidly in the section and received three good promotions in three years. She consistently got high ratings from her superiors, and she received particularly high marks for her professional demeanor.

In her initial position with the bank, Sara was required to travel to Mexico on several occasions. She was always accompanied by a male colleague even though she generally handled similar business by herself on trips within the United States. During her trips to Mexico she observed that Mexican bankers seemed more aware of her being a woman and were personally solicitous to her, but she didn't discern any major problems. The final decisions on the work that she did were handled by male representatives of the bank stationed in Mexico.

A successful foreign assignment was an important step for those on the "fast track" at the bank. Sara applied for a position in Central or South America and was delighted when she was assigned to the bank's office in Mexico City. The office had about twenty bank employees and was headed by William Vitam. The Mexico City office was seen as a preferred assignment by young executives at the bank.

After a month, Sara began to encounter problems. She found it difficult to be effective in dealing with Mexican bankers—the clients. They appeared reluctant to accept her authority and they would often bypass her in important matters. The problem was exacerbated by Vitam's compliance in her being bypassed. When she asked that the clients be referred back to her, Vitam replied, "Of course that isn't really practical." Vitam made matters worse by patronizing her in front of clients and by referring to her as "my cute assistant" and "our lady banker." Vitam never did this when only Americans were present, and in fact treated her professionally and with respect in internal situations.

Sara finally complained to Vitam that he was undermining her authority and effectiveness; she asked him in as positive a manner as possible to help her. Vitam listened carefully to Sara's complaints, then replied: "I'm glad that you brought this up, because I've been meaning to sit down and talk to you about my little game-playing in front of the clients. Let me be frank with you. Our clients think you're great, but they just don't understand a woman in authority, and you and I aren't going to be able to change their attitudes overnight. As long as the clients see you as my assistant and deferring to me, they can do business with you. I'm willing to give you as much responsibility as they can handle your having. I *know* you can handle it. But we just have to tread carefully. You and I know that my remarks in front of clients don't mean anything. They're just a way of playing the game Latin style. I know it's frustrating for you, but I really need you to support me on this. It's not going to affect your promotions, and for the most part you really will have responsibility for these clients' accounts. You just have to act like it's my responsibility." Sara replied that she would

Case study by Thomas Dunfee and Diana Robertson, "Foreign Assignment," the Wharton School of Business, The University of Pennsylvania. Reprinted by permission of the authors.

try to cooperate, but that basically she found her role demeaning.

As time went on, Sara found that the patronizing actions in front of clients bothered her more and more. She spoke to Vitam again, but he was firm in his position, and urged her to try to be a little more flexible, even a little more "feminine."

Sara also had a problem with Vitam over policy. The Mexico City office had five younger women who worked as receptionists and secretaries. They were all situated at work stations at the entrance to the office. They were required to wear standard uniforms that were colorful and slightly sexy. Sara protested the requirement that uniforms be worn because (1) they were inconsistent to the image of the banking business and (2) they were demeaning to the women who had to wear them. Vitam just curtly replied that he had received a lot of favorable comments about the uniforms from clients of the bank.

Several months later, Sara had what she thought would be a good opportunity to deal with the problem. Tom Fried, an executive vice president who had been a mentor for her since she arrived at the bank, was coming to Mexico City; she arranged a private conference with him. She described her problems and explained that she was not able to be effective in this environment and that she worried that it would have a negative effect on her chance of promotion within the bank. Fried was very careful in his response. He spoke of certain "realities" that the bank had to respect and he urged her to "see it through" even though he could understand how she would feel that things weren't fair.

Sara found herself becoming more aggressive and defensive in her meetings with Vitam and her clients. Several clients asked that other bank personnel handle their transactions. Sara has just received an Average rating, which noted "the beginnings of a negative attitude about the bank and its policies."

QUESTIONS

1. Do you think that Vitam and Tom are correct about the "realities" of the culture concerning women? If these cultural assumptions are correct, what are the ethical implications of following the "when in Rome" principle?

2. Was Sarah treated fairly in her evaluation?

3. Where would you draw the line between personal dignity and serving the interests of your company?

CASE 11.3
The Quandary at PureDrug
Karen Marquiss and Joanne B. Ciulla

You are the Chief Executive Officer of PureDrug, a large pharmaceutical company with sales and operations throughout the world. Your firm has an outstanding reputation for quality as well as a long-term record of growth and profitability. Over the past 10 years, sales grew at an average annual compound rate of 12 percent and profits increased by an average of 15 percent per annum. The company had not experienced losses since 1957, and stock prices remained consistently healthy.

In spite of PureDrug's impeccable record, by October 1991 your company is in trouble. Due to a

Karen Marquiss & Joanne B. Ciulla "The Quandary at PureDrug" in Paul Minus, ed., *The Ethics of Business in a Global Economy* (Boston: Kluwer Academic Press, 1993), pp. 130–131.

general economic downturn and a few product development problems, the firm faces a declining market share and weakened corporate profits. Although still profitable, PureDrug fell far short of its goals established for 1990. As of the end of the third quarter of 1991, you project a $4 million loss for the year. The value of your corporate stock has already dropped by one-fifth of its 1990 year-end value, and a loss for the year could result in an even more substantial devaluation. Small investors might switch to pharmaceutical companies with better results. Even worse, a disappointing year could cause large institutional investors such as pension funds to support a takeover by one of your competitors.

In an attempt to remedy the immediate situation, you call an emergency meeting of your top managers to poll their suggestions. Charles Dunn, head of the International Export Division, reminds you that his department has an opportunity to sign an $8 million contract with the Philippine government. The contract involves the sale of Travolene, a new injectable drug, developed by PureDrug for the treatment of serious viral infections, including measles. The drug remains difficult and expensive to manufacture and has been in very short supply since its introduction. The 1991 budget did not include this sale due to the lack of product availability.

Dunn mentions that at this time PureDrug's inventory contains a large lot of Travolene, produced at a cost of about $2 million. The government rejected the batch for the domestic market on the basis of a new, very sensitive test for endotoxin. The authorities recently adopted this test in addition to the standard method that had been used for many years. The more sensitive test revealed a very low level of endotoxin in the batch of Travolene, while the old procedure uncovered no endotoxin whatsoever.

You ask Ann Doe, the company's Chief Medical Safety Officer, whether this rules out shipping the batch to the Philippines. She explains that the Philippines and many other countries still rely exclusively on the old test. Ann said, "It always takes them a while to adopt more sophisticated practices, and sometimes they never do. Endotoxin might cause high fever when injected into patients, but I can't tell you that the level in this batch is high enough to cause trouble. Still, how can we have a double standard, one for our nation and one for Third World countries?"

Charles Dunn interrupts, "It's not our job to overprotect other countries. The health authorities in the Philippines know what they are doing. Our officials always take an extreme position. Measles is a serious illness. Last year in the Philippines half of the children who contracted measles died. It's not only good business but also good ethics to send them the only batch of Travolene we have available."

As the other senior members of PureDrug's management begin to take sides on the issue, you contemplate your options. In the short run, the profit margin on the lot of Travolene would boost PureDrug's bottom line into the black for the year. In addition, the sale to the Philippines could foster a lucrative long-term relationship and lead to expansion into other Asian markets.

You leave the meeting with an uneasy feeling. You have only 72 hours before you must present a plan to PureDrug's Board of Directors.

QUESTIONS

1. Is it ethical for PureDrug to practice one standard of safety at home and another in a foreign country?

2. If children in the Philippines die as the result of taking Tavolene, is Puredrug morally responsible for it?

3. Do foreign clients have the right to make dangerous decisions about your country's products?

CASE 11.4

IBM's Business with Hitler: An Inconvenient Past

Judith Schrempf-Stirling, and Guido Palazzo

Judith Schrempf-Stirling is an Assistant Professor of Management, Robins School of Business, University of Richmond; and Guido Palazzo is Professor of Business Ethics, HEC, University of Lausanne.

September 9, 1939: IBM Headquarter, New York. With full attention Thomas J. Watson, president of International Business Machines (IBM) read the business letter from Herman Rottke, manager of IBM's German subsidiary, Dehomag which arrived by mid-September 1939, only a few days after Adolf Hitler had invaded Poland.

Dear Mr. Watson:

During your last visit in Berlin at the beginning of July, you made the kind offer to me that you might be willing to furnish the German company machines from Endicott in order to shorten our long delivery terms. I . . . asked you to leave with us for study purposes one alphabetic tabulating machine and a collator out of the American machines at present in Germany. You have complied with this request, for which I thank you very much, and have added that in cases of urgent need, I may make use of other American machines. . . .

You will understand that under today's conditions, a certain need has arisen for such machines, which we do not build as yet in Germany. Therefore, I should like to make use of your kind offer and ask you to leave with the German company for the time being the alphabetic tabulating machines which are at present still in the former Austria. . . . This offer, made orally by you, dear Mr. Watson . . .will undoubtedly be greatly appreciated in many and especially responsible circles. . . . We should thank you if you would ask your Geneva organization, at the same time, to furnish us the necessary repair parts for the maintenance of the machines. . . .
Yours very truly,

H. Rottke

Watson stared at the letter and wondered what to respond while recalling the economic, political, and social climate in Germany.

PERSECUTION OF JEWS IN GERMANY

When Adolf Hitler became Reich Chancellor in 1933, he announced his ambition to strengthen Germany's economic and territorial position and to create the (Jew-free) Master Race. Many of his initiated regulations and activities were aimed at bringing this vision into reality. He passed critical discriminating regulations, and he initiated and supported boycotts against the Jewish population.[1] The extermination of Jews (genocide), however, was not planned from the beginning but gradually developed. Only in 1942 the "Final solution to the Jewish question" was decided at the Wannsee Conference. In total, Hitler's fight against Jews developed in six phases: identification, exclusion, confiscation, ghettoization, deportation, and extermination.[2] The last two phases took place after the Wannsee Conference (1942).

First, Hitler's Nazi regime identified those people who—according to Nazi philosophy— were of the minor race, i.e. Jews. Hitler ordered that a census be carried out to find out how many Jews lived in Germany and where they lived.[3] According to Nazism, it did not matter whether a Jew was a practicing Jew or not. Using complicated racial mathematics, the Nazis derived at different categories of Jews (full Jew, half Jew).[4] Having Jewish ancestors made a person Jewish. For the Nazis, all kinds of Jews were a threat to the Aryan race and needed to be identified and excluded from society.

This second stage, exclusion, began with the introduction of the *Aryan Paragraph* in 1933. The Aryan paragraph entitled only Aryans to be members of an organization, institution, or corporation.[5] This clause was first applied to the officialdom, which displaced Jewish official servants. The Aryan Paragraph was gradually applied to other professions such as notaries and lawyers.[6] Furthermore, the Nazi regime appealed for a public boycott of Jewish shops and businesses since April 1933. Step by step, Jews were socially and culturally isolated from society.

The third phase—confiscation and expropriation—started with the Nuremberg Decrees in 1935.[7] The Nazi government passed "The law for the protection of German blood" and the "Reich Citizenship Law," which deprived Jews of their German citizenship and all related rights. The Jewish population was increasingly deprived of their assets and possessions. Jewish shop owners were forced to transfer their business to Aryans and hand over other valuable possessions to the Nazi regime. The segregation between Jews and Aryans became more and more visible. From 1935 on, Jews were, for instance, not allowed to marry or to have sexual relationships with Aryans. The first climax of the Anti-Semitism fostered by the Nazis was the Kristallnacht (the Night of Broken Glass) on November 9, 1938. Numerous synagogues, Jewish shops, and Jewish apartments were destroyed and depredated. Around 100 Jews were killed that night and over 20,000 were arrested.

The Nazi policies during their first years of power aimed at banishing the Jewish population out of Germany. Until November 1938, around 170,000 Jews emigrated from Germany as their living conditions had changed dramatically: Nazi regulations did not allow Jews to own land, have health insurance, own a car, get child allowances, work, and participate in social or cultural life.[8] Since 1938, Jews had to add the names Sarah (for women) and Israel (for men) in their passports and any other official documents. Besides, the letter "J" was stamped on their passports to signal immediately their Jewish origins. When Hitler annexed Austria and Czechoslovakia in 1938, those regulations were also introduced in these countries.[9]

With the occupation of Poland in September 1939, the fourth phase, ghettoization, started. Ghettos functioned as a tool to control and segregate Jews from Aryans. Jews were forced to wear badges and armbands with the Star of David. They had to perform forced labor during their stay in the ghettos. Jewish Councils were established which were responsible for the organization of daily ghetto life. After the resolutions at the Wannsee Conference in 1942, the ghettos became intermediate stations for Jews. From there, they were deported to concentration camps.

The Jewish Councils in the ghettos were responsible for administering the deportation, which was the fifth stage of the Holocaust. Concentration camps were already established in 1933 and 1937 (Dachau and Buchenwald, respectively). Their numbers increased exponentially with the blitzkrieg against Poland in September 1939. In the first years of Hitler's regime, mainly political opponents were sent to concentration camps. Later, people who did not correspond to the Nazi race ideology were herded off to the camps. Those included "antisocials," homosexuals, Jehovah Witnesses, and gypsies. Since the Kristallnacht, more and more Jews were deported to the camps. Concentration camps had various functions. They gathered Jews to specific locations, but also functioned as working camps. Prisoners were assigned work according to their physical strength and skills. Inmates worked in quarries and brickyards or did any other work related to the preparation or the support of Germany's war machine. The working and living conditions in the camps were devastating. Prisoners suffered from hunger and contagions. Some were exposed to inhuman medical experiments like those carried out by Dr. Josef Mengele, who conducted cruel experiments with twins in Auschwitz.[10] During the war years, from 1939 to 1945, some camps evolved to extermination (death) camps where the "final solution" (destruction of the Jewish population in Europe as decided at the Wannsee Conference) was executed.[11]

INTERNATIONAL BUSINESS MACHINES (IBM)

IBM was founded by Herman Hollerith in 1889 and became known as the "Computing Tabulating

Recording Corporation" in 1911. In 1924, the company name changed to "International Business Machines (IBM). IBM's revenue and number of employees increased steadily since 1915, which is linked to the company's expansion to Europe, Asia, South America, and Australia. In 1915, the company had a gross income of $4M with an employee base of around 1600. Only five years later, its income increased threefold, and the number of employees increased to 2700.[12] The 1920s and 1930s constituted a period of steady growth for IBM, despite the Great Depression. In 1930, IBM employed 6700 people worldwide and had an income of nearly $20M.[13] IBM was a flourishing company and cared for its employees. IBM was one of the first companies to introduce group life insurance, survivor benefits, and paid vacation.[14]

IBM's Business: Punched Card System

IBM's core business consisted of punched card data processing equipment and technology. Punch cards became the key medium for data entry, data storage, and processing in institutional computing. IBM was the main manufacturer and marketer for a variety of unit record machines for creating, sorting, and tabulating punched cards. In its earlier years, IBM worked mainly with the U.S. government on population censuses, but soon the company also provided large-scale, custom-built tabulating and punch card solutions for businesses. IBM enjoyed an almost worldwide monopoly in its punch card technology.

A punch card contains information represented by the absence or presence of holes in predefined positions. In 1928, IBM introduced the Eighty-column punch card with 12 punch locations and one character per column. Each column stood for a predefined characteristic according to a client's wishes and information purposes. Punch cards could offer information such as names, addresses, gender, and any other personal data. Eighty columns with 12 horizontal positions lead to 960 punch hole possibilities yielding thousands of demographic permutations. The original usage of the punch card system was the national census, but

the IBM punch card system was also used for other purposes such as train schedules, warehouse goods, and financial transactions and for the identification of people. Tabulating machines summarize, sort, and count the punch card data.

Over the years, IBM continuously improved its tabulating machines in order to make data processing, sorting, and accounting more convenient and time efficient. In 1920, for example, IBM introduced the printing tabulator, which improved speed and accuracy. In the 1930s, IBM further developed alphabetizer–tabulating machines, which created high–speed alphabetized lists. IBM did not sell those tabulating machines, but leased them to its clients. This ensured the company (and its subsidiaries) monthly payments. IBM headquarters in New York kept a detailed book with information as to the location and usage of the machines worldwide. The machines were tailored to the demands of the customer. IBM usually asked its client to disclose the purpose and use of the technology so that engineers could prepare the punch card systems accordingly. Leasing the machines also included a service and maintenance contract. In case repairs and regular maintenance were necessary, IBM technicians traveled to their clients' offices to check that the IBM machines were functional.

IBM President: Thomas J. Watson

Thomas J. Watson was a born salesman and a self-made industrialist. He started his career as a salesman at the National Cash Register Company in 1895 in Ohio.[15] After a short time, Watson became the best salesman on the East Coast. Applying an "anything-goes strategy" and some tricks such as phony transactions and second-hand businesses, Watson ran one competitor after the other out of business.[16] His business practices did not remain unnoticed. In 1913, he was prosecuted for breaching anti-trust legislation and received a $5000 fine. The trial did not harm Watson's business career. In 1914, he joined IBM as a general manager and worked his way to the top with an adamant focus on sales increase. Within only a few years, Watson became the president of IBM and made the company one of the most effective selling organizations. Watson introduced successful business practices at IBM such as generous sales incentives and an evangelical fervor for instilling company pride and loyalty in every worker. Watson's attitude shaped IBM's corporate culture, and the media called him "the Leader."[17]

Watson's business success can be traced back to his strict management style. He did not leave anything to chance. He was the president of one of America's most influential companies and no decision was made without his approval—be it business deals or the decision as to which office color should be chosen.

Under Watson's leadership, IBM established subsidiaries in different parts of the world—Asia, Australia, South America and Europe.[18] One of the most important European subsidiaries was Dehomag in Germany, which was acquired in 1922 thanks to Watson's persistence and tough negotiation skills. Watson decided to keep the German name Dehomag instead of changing it to IBM Germany due to the already strong national consciousness in the 1920s in Germany. Whether the name was Dehomag or IBM Germany did not change anything: It was a wholly owned IBM subsidiary. Watson saw a glorious financial future in Europe, especially in Germany. He took personal care of the German market and managed its business tightly by setting sales quotas. Watson frequently visited Germany in order to get first-hand information and impressions from how well his German subsidiary was performing and which future profit prospects would still lie ahead. Watson learned from his past clash with the law and made sure to do most business activities by untraceable oral agreements.

DEHOMAG—IBM'S SUBSIDIARY IN NAZI GERMANY

Willy Heidinger founded Dehomag in 1910. From its early years, the company rented and later also built tabulating machines under IBM license. In 1922, Dehomag became a fully owned IBM subsidiary. It had a history of success in the 1920s, despite the post-war hyperinflation in Germany.

With the rise of Hitler and his Nazi party, IBM's business opportunities increased tremendously. For Hitler's plans to separate the Aryan race from the non-Aryan race as described earlier, he needed a powerful computer system. He needed the best available technology, which would allow him to identify Jews, keep track of their possessions, and finally deport them to ghettoes and concentration camps. IBM's punched card data processing system and technology turned out to be exactly the technology that Hitler required. Governments were a normal type of customer for IBM, and Hitler was therefore not an exception. The German government became a significant and important business partner for Dehomag (IBM). More than 2000 IBM machines would be installed throughout Germany from 1933 onwards and thousands more throughout occupied Europe after 1939. Approximately 1.5 billion punch cards would be produced annually for the German market.[19] The profitable relationship between Hitler and IBM's subsidiary Dehomag started with the first German population census in 1933.[20]

First Population Census: April 1933

IBM's and Hitler's business relationship started only a few months after Hitler became chancellor in 1933. Hitler wanted to conduct a nationwide census, which would give him a demographic overview of the German population. For IBM, a government that aimed at monitoring and counting its population was a promising business client.

Only a few weeks after Hitler's inauguration, IBM headquarters decided to expand its German subsidiary Dehomag by investing over 7 million Reichsmarks.[21] In May 1933, Dehomag's special consultant for government contracts, attorney Karl Koch, secured the contract with the German government for the Prussian census.[22]

As with each customer, Dehomag tailored its punched card system according to the Nazi's wishes. The Nazi regime briefed Dehomag engineers on the aim of the census. For the German government, this census functioned as an identification process, especially in relation to Eastern Jews who became the initial targets in the Nazi anti-Semitic movement. The punch cards provided all the required demographic information such as the person's county, community, gender, age, religion, mother tongue, current occupation, and work. Special attention in this census was given to column 22 "Religion": hole 1 for Protestant, hole 2 for Catholic, and hole 3 for Jew.[23] When Jews were identified during the census, a special "Jewish counting card" was created to indicate the place of birth. This data enabled the Nazi government to identify the Jews in the Prussian population. This first identification of Jews in Germany enabled the Nazi regime to plan and organize its anti-Jewish policies and activities. For example, the census helped to identify the jobs that Jews occupied. Combined with the Aryan paragraph, it became easy for the Nazis to deprive Jews from their work and increasingly deprive them from social life as discussed earlier.

The successful implementation of the Prussian census encouraged Watson to follow his ambitions to increase IBM's presence also in other European countries (e.g., Netherlands, Belgium, and Sweden). Watson ordered all existing IBM subsidiaries in Germany to merge together with Dehomag.[24] He went to Germany and granted Dehomag manager Willy Heidinger special commercial powers outside Germany. This allowed Dehomag to offer and deliver punch card systems directly to customers in other European countries, even if IBM agencies and subsidiaries already existed in those countries. Watson put lots of confidence into the business with the Nazis and Dehomag. He had a personal interest in the success of IBM's business, as he received a five percent bonus on every dollar of after tax, after dividend. Hence, every business relation and transaction with the Reich meant direct profit for Watson. Therefore, Watson was delighted with Dehomag's contract for a second, even bigger population census in 1937.

Second Population Census: May 1939

In 1937, the Nazi regime planned another census. IBM—as basically the only company offering this

technology—secured the 3.5 million Reichsmark contract ($14M today).[25] The census was delayed due to Hitler's absorption of Austria. It was not until May 1939 that the census took place. The large majority of Germany's 22 million households, 3.5 million farmhouses, and 5.5 million shops and factories were registered.[26] This census included almost all of the 80 million citizens in Germany, Austria, the Sudetenland and the Saar. To carry out this census, IBM transferred 70 card sorters, 60 tabulators, 76 multipliers, and 90 million punch cards to Germany.[27]

This census was purely racial and aimed at tracing all Jewish ancestry. Citizens had to indicate their religious faith and material possessions. Additionally, there were special blanks where each citizen had to indicate whether he or she was of pure "Aryan" blood. Finally, the Aryan/Jewish status of each individual's grandparents had to be provided. Only pure Aryans were acceptable according to Nazi ideology. The family statistics helped the Nazis to determine full Jews, half Jews, and even quarter Jews. In total, 330,530 "racial Jews" were identified. The census database was then used to locate Jews, to organize their transportation to ghettos (phase 4) and later to concentration camps (phases 5 & 6). Also the organization of the railways in the German Reich was managed with the IBM punch card technology. The German Reichsbahn (state railway) was one of the largest IBM customers. Most train stations and depots had punch card installations. IBM's technology was used to efficiently manage train scheduling and ensure that detailed lists of rail cargo (humans or commodities) were created. The final destination for most Jews was a concentration camp. At concentration camps, new arrivals were registered by IBM technology.[28]

Concentration Camps

Concentration camps were assigned IBM code numbers to facilitate the recordkeeping of inmate registration and transfers. Auschwitz, for instance, was 001, Buchenwald was 002, and Dachau was 003.[29] Each concentration camp operated a department where IBM tabulators, sorters, and printers kept track of inmates. Most IBM activity took place in the Labor Assignment Office of the camp, which dealt with daily work assignments and processed inmate data and labor transfer rosters.[30] The office also kept a camp hospital index and kept track of all kinds of inmate statistics. This allowed the full tracking of each single inmate. The Nazis knew where the inmates came from (from another concentration camp or ghetto), what their working skills were, why they were deported, what their health status was, and why they were sent to the camp.

The tabulating machine departments in concentration camps needed experts operating the machines and keeping track of all the processed data. The people working in those departments were directly trained by IBM in Germany or in another country depending on the IBM location and the concentration camps. This was included in the leasing, service, and maintenance contract between IBM and its client. The service contract between Dehomag and the Nazi regime also included regular maintenance services of the machines. Dehomag (IBM) technicians and workers made on-site visits to check, repair, and replace machines. Whether those machines were in concentration camps or regular office buildings did not matter. Hence, IBM workers repaired and checked IBM equipment in concentration camps like Buchenwald and Dachau.

WATSON'S GERMANY VISITS IN THE 1930S

Watson regularly visited Germany in the 1930s. After the election of Hitler, Watson visited Germany to oversee the merger of IBM's German subsidiaries with its major subsidiary Dehomag.[31] At that time, Nazi anti-Semitic politics were clearly visible in a typical Jew's every day's life. The Nazi party was the only political party remaining. All other political parties had disappeared during 1933. Likewise, critical newspapers and journals had disappeared. People who criticized the Nazi regime in any form or were a threat to the German nation equally disappeared. According to Nazi information, some committed suicide; others just disappeared. No one knew whether they had left the country or had died. No one seemed to care. Other prevalent events in 1933 were the book burnings, where books, which did not correspond to Nazi ideology, were publicly burned.[32] Between March and October 1933 nearly 100 burnings took place in 70 cities in Germany.

When Watson made his business trips to Germany in the early 1930s, violence against the Jews was apparent. The persecution of Jews started with the boycott of Jewish stores in April 1933. Aryans were no longer allowed to shop in Jewish shops or to be patients of Jewish doctors. The doorways of Jewish shops were blocked by Nazi troops, and signs saying "Jews not wanted" were posted on the streets. Hitler's stormtroopers—a paramilitary organization—made sure that the anti-Semitic regulations were executed. The stormtroopers entered universities and other public institutions, shouted "Jews out" and forced all non-Aryans to leave public buildings immediately. To check whether the boycott was being implemented, stormtroopers went to the medical practices of Jewish doctors to check that there were indeed no patients. On the streets, Jews were confronted with similar antipathy: Insults to the effect of "Judah die" ("Juda verrecke") belonged to their daily lives. Those Germans who managed to sympathize with Jews or who helped them were referred to as national betrayers and were themselves subject to boycotts and sanctions. The atmosphere in Germany became increasingly tense during the 1930s.

For Dehomag's 25th anniversary, Watson traveled to Germany irrespective of the *New York Times* headlines which read "Nazi warns Jews to stay at home." In 1935 anti-Semitic actions became more severe. Jewish shops were systematically destroyed. By the end of 1935, approximately 125,000 Jews had left Nazi Germany.[33] Watson did not have much time to deal with the anti-Semitic attitude in Germany as he focused on the business of his German subsidiary. Dehomag was performing very well. "The company deftly controlled the data operations of the entire Reich."[34] Dehomag's customer base included all important German businesses and public institutions: the Reichsbank (state bank), Reichsbahn (state

492 of 740 HONEST WORK

railway), and companies from central industries such as the aircraft, metal, chemical, car, and ship industries. IBM's and Watson's cooperation with German industry and particularly with the German government was well perceived by the Nazis. As the first international businessman, Watson received the *Merit Cross of the German Eagle with Star* by Hitler for his outstanding activities for Germany in 1937.

Watson saw the political climate and anti-Semitism first-hand during his frequent visits to Germany in the 1930s, but for him his visits were business travels. After one of his visits to Germany, he stated:

> "You can cooperate with a man without believing in everything he says and does. If you do not agree with everything he does, cooperate with him in the things you do believe in. Others will cooperate with him in the things they believe in."[35]

Watson's focus on business corresponded to the manager zeitgeist of the time. Having governments as customers was not unusual. It was actually desirable. Many corporate CEOs and managers shared the viewpoint of "business as usual" in the 1930s and during the war. Alfred P. Sloan, CEO of General Motors (GM) at that time, once said that a global corporation should focus its activities solely on the business level, without any consideration for political opinion of its management or of the states within which it operates.[36]

September 9, 1939: IBM Headquarters, New York.
Watson looked at Rottke's letter again and then at the newspaper from last week, which was still on his desk: Following Hitler's invasion to Poland, France and Great Britain declared war on Germany.

NOTES

1. Sebastian Haffner, *Defying Hitler: A Memoir* (London, UK: Phoenix, 2003); Christopher R. Browning, *The Origins of the Final Solution: The Evolution of Nazi Jewish Policy, September 1939–March 1942.* (Jerusalem: Yad Vashem, 2004).

2. Edwin Black, *IBM and the Holocaust: The Strategic Alliance Between Nazi Germany and America's Most Powerful Corporation* (Washington, DC: Dialog Press, 2001). Please note that the case takes place in September 1939. The last three phases of Hitler's fight against Jews (ghettoization, deportation and extermination) took only place after September 1939. Those phases are still described to provide a complete review of the persecution of Jews in Germany. IBM's president Watson, however, could not have known any of the developments at the time he had to make a decision about the machine transfer.

3. Gotz Aly and Karl Heinz Roth, *Nazi Census: Identification and Control in the Third Reich* (Philadelphia: Temple University Press, 2004).

4. Browning, 2004.

5. Marion Kaplan, *Between Dignity and Despair: Jewish Life in Nazi Germany* (New York: Oxford University Press, 1998).

6. Haffner, 2003.

7. Martin Dean, *Robbing the Jews: The Confiscation of Jewish Property in the Holocaust, 1933–1945* (New York: Cambridge University Press, 2008); Ian Kershaw, *Hitler: 1889–1936: Hubris.* (New York: WW Norton & Company, 2008).

8. Black, 2001; Alex Grobman, *Genocide: Critical Issues of the Holocaust: A Companion to the Film Genocide* (Chappaqua, NY: Rossel Books, 1982).

9. Saul Friedlander, *Nazi Germany and the Jews. The Years of Persecution: 1933–1939* (London, UK: Phoenix, 1997); Jean Ziegler, *The Swiss, the Gold and the Dead: How Swiss Bankers Helped Finance the Nazi War Machine* (New York: Penguin Putnam Inc., 1998).

10. Edwin Black, *Nazi Nexus* (Washington, DC: Dialog Press, 2009); Gerald L. Posner and John Ware, *Mengele: The Complete Story.* (Lanham: Cooper Square Publishing Inc., 2000).

11. Yisrael Gutman and Michael Berenbaum, *Anatomy of the Auschwitz Death Camp* (Bloomington: Indiana University Press, 1998); Francois Furet, *Unanswered Questions: Nazi Germany and the Genocide of the Jews* (New York: Schocken, 1989).

12. IBM, *IBM Highlights, 1885–1969 (2001)*, http://www.03.ibm.com/ibm/history/documents/pdf/1885–1969.pdf

13. Ibid.

14. Black, 2001.

15. Kevin Maney, *The Maverick and His Machine: Thomas Watson, Sr. and the Making of IBM* (Hoboken: John Wiley & Sons Inc., 2004).

16. William Rodgers, *Think: A Biography of the Watsons and IBM* (New York: Stein and Day, 1969).

17. Black, 2001, p. 71.

18. Rodgers, 1969; Black, 2001.

19. Ibid.

20. Aly and Roth, 2004.

21. Black, 2001.

22. Aly and Roth, 2004.

23. Ibid.

24. Black, 2001.

25. Ibid.

26. Aly and Roth, 2004.

27. Black, 2001.

28. Black, 2009.

29. Black, 2001.

30. Johannes Tuchel, *Die Inspektion der Konzentrationslager* (Berlin: Hentrich, 1994).

31. Ibid.

32. Theodor Verweyen, *Buecherverbrennungen* (Heidelberg: Universitaetsverlag, 2000)

33. Alex Grobman, *Genocide: Critical Issues of the Holocaust: A Companion to the Film Genocide* (Chappaqua, NY: Rossel Books, 1982).

34. Black, 2001, p. 151.

35. Ibid, p. 254.

36. Charles Higham, *Trading with the Enemy. The Nazi-American Money Plot 1933–1949* (Lincoln: iUniverse, Inc, 2007); Henry A. Turner, *General Motors and the Nazis: The Struggle for Control of Opel, Europe's Biggest Carmaker* (New Haven: Yale University Press, 2005).

QUESTIONS

1. What are the (legal, economic, and ethical) arguments for and against signing the order to transfer the machines to the German IBM subsidiary?

2. In 2002, a group of gypsies filed a lawsuit against IBM. The lawsuit alleged that the American corporation assisted the Nazis in Holocaust killings during World War II by providing the Nazis with punch card machines and computer technology that resulted in the coding. Does today's IBM still have a responsibility for the historic injustices to which it was connected? Please summarize arguments for and against IBM's responsibility for historic injustices.

3. Today, corporations operate in zones of conflict, terror, and war (similar to IBM's situation between 1939 and 1945)—think about diamond and mineral sourcing in African countries. What are the lessons learned from the IBM case, and how can we apply these to current business operations in conflict zones?

CASE 11.5

Suicides at Foxconn

Emily Black and Miriam Eapen

Emily Black and Miriam Eapen are 2012 graduates of the Jepson School of Leadership Studies, University of Richmond.

In 1974, Terry Gou founded the Taiwanese company Hon Hai Precision Industry, with only $7500. With Hon Hai Precision Industry as the flagship, Gou created a subsidiary, Foxconn Technology Group, based in China. Foxconn is the largest employer in China, and it accounts for almost 40% of the revenues in the consumer electronics industry. It employs about a million workers—half of them work at the plant in Shenzhen. The company is driven by an aggressive management approach that caters to the needs of its clients, no matter what the costs.[1] Its clients include companies such as Dell, Hewlett-Packard, and Motorola. Foxconn's most successful and technologically demanding client is Apple, Inc. Apple chose to incorporate Foxconn as an integral part of their supply chain because it is the largest electronic manufacturing services provider in the world.

According to Gou, Foxconn aims to recruit people with talent, "those who are willing to continue making progress, building their abilities and taking on bigger responsibilities."[2] Yet, while Foxconn recruits some of the best and brightest to work in its prestigious company, the majority of workers are inexperienced and unskilled. Furthermore, those with experience and inexperience are confined to the production line, with a worker explaining, "I do the same thing every day . . . I have no future."[3]

The factory complexes at Foxconn look like college campuses enclosed by tall fences and security gates. Officials boast that their facilities offer "free meals and accommodation . . . complimentary bus and free laundry . . . free swimming pools, tennis courts . . . exercise programs . . . chess, calligraphy, mountain climbing, or fishing clubs."[4] Yet, many workers complain that they do not have the time to enjoy these benefits. A report conducted by 20 universities across China describes Foxconn "as a concentration camp of workers in the 21st century."[5] Moreover, inside these enclosed facilities "around 50% of employees reported being subjected to some form of abuse, with 16% of cases allegedly perpetuated by supervisors or managers."[6]

Foxconn gained a reputation for being able to turn out quality products for its clients fast. As its client list grew, so did their demands for speedy production. This placed a heavy burden on employees, many of whom worked as much as 80 to100 hours of overtime per month, which is three times the legal limit. Some workers were not allowed to take breaks to eat because they failed to reach production targets. In addition to stressful working conditions, employees were exposed to dangerous chemicals and aluminum dust without proper equipment and protection.[7] While the working conditions are not good, most workers feel fortunate to be employed by a prestigious company that pays better than other available employment options. For personal and cultural reasons, few employees complain.

In 2010 Foxconn came under public scrutiny because in the span of 3 months, 9 of its employees committed suicide at the Shenzhen factory. It then came to light that there had been 17 suicides in the past 5 years. At least 16 of the people jumped to their deaths from the upper floors of the factory and about 20 other people were stopped before they could jump.[8] Although the direct causes of these suicides are unknown, a variety of factors may have contributed to a worker's unhappiness at Foxconn. The company did not think that working conditions were the cause of the suicides. It responded to the suicides by blocking windows, locking the doors to roofs and balconies, and placing over three million square meters of yellow-mesh netting around the buildings to catch jumpers. During a visit to the Foxconn plant in Shenzhen, journalist Joel Johnson described the sight of these nets, "it's hard not to look at the nets. Every building is skirted with them. They drape over precipice, steel poles jutting 20 feet above the sidewalk, loosely tangled like volleyball nets in winter."[9] Although these nets serve as a constant reminder to employees about the suicides, they have deterred other suicides.

Company officials believed that some workers killed themselves to receive compensation for their families from Foxconn, so they decided to make employees to sign an Anti-Suicide Pledge. Employees promise that they will not attempt to kill themselves and that if they do, their families will only receive minimal compensation. It says, "in the event of non-accidental injuries (including suicide, self-mutilation, etc.), I agree that the company has acted properly in accordance with relevant laws and regulations, and will not sue the company, bring excessive demands, take drastic actions that would damage the company's reputation or cause trouble that would hurt normal operations."[10]

Foxconn set up a 24-hour counseling center and gave its employees a 30 percent raise, with a promise for a second raise later in the year. The company also plans to move some plants closer to where worker's families live. Foxconn is building a facility in the city of Zhengzhou, the capital of Henan province, which has a population of more than 100 million. Henan is the home of about a fifth of Foxconn's workforce. "We want to go to the source of abundant workers and where there is a support group of family and friends."[11]

In a September 2010, a journalist from *Business Week* asked Gou how he felt about the suicides. He said, "I should be honest with you. The first one, second one, and third one, I did not see this as a serious problem. We had around 800,000 employees . . . we are about 2.1 square kilometers. At the moment,

I'm feeling guilty. But at that moment, I didn't think I should be taking full responsibility."[12] He continued by explaining that it was not until the fifth suicide that he began to think the company had an issue to address. It was at this time that Gou hired the New York Public Relations firm Burson–Marsteller to help devise a formal strategy for addressing the public and the media. Despite Gou's initiatives to address the crisis at Foxconn, he said that dealing with the suicides is not necessarily the responsibility of Foxconn. Instead, he believes "we need to change the way things are. Businesses should be focused on business, and social responsibility should be government responsibility."[13]

The suicides at Foxconn also had an impact on one of its largest clients, Apple. Apple was preparing to roll out its next major product, the iPhone, and it needed Foxconn to produce it on time. Apple's CEO, Steve Jobs, insisted that Foxconn is not a sweatshop. At a June 2010 All Things Digital Conference, Jobs explained, "You go in this place and it's a factory but, my gosh, they've got restaurants and movie theaters and hospitals and swimming pools. For a factory, it's pretty nice."[14] He continued by acknowledging that while the suicides were "very troubling . . . we are on top of this."[15] One month after the suicides, Apple publicized the visit of its Chief Operating Officer Tim Cook and other Apple to the factory in China. Apple's 2011 Progress Report stated that Cook and the executives "met with Foxconn CEO Terry Gou and members of his senior staff to better understand the conditions of the site and to assess the emergency measures Foxconn was putting in place to prevent more suicides."[16] Because Apple believed "we would need additional expertise to help prevent further tragedies," the company commissioned an independent "team of suicide-prevention experts" to survey Foxconn workers about their quality of life and the factory's living conditions.

Apple's independent research revealed "several areas for improvement, such as better training of hotline staff and care center counselors and better monitoring to ensure effectiveness."[17] The Progress Report concluded, "Foxconn incorporated the team's specific recommendations into their long-term plans for addressing employee well-being."[18] With the Apple executives' trip to the factory and the investigative report publicly underway, Jobs insisted that "Apple does one of the best jobs of any company understanding the working conditions of our supply chain."[19]

NOTES

1. Frederik Balfour, and Tim Culpan, "The Man Who Makes Your IPhone—BusinessWeek." Businessweek—Business News, Stock Market & Financial Advice. September 9, 2010. Accessed September 30, 2011.

2. Ibid.

3. Stephanie Wong, "Why Apple Is Nervous about Foxconn—Business—US Business—Bloomberg Businessweek—Msnbc.com." Msnbc.com—Breaking News, Science and Tech News, World News, US News, Local News- Msnbc.com. June 7, 2010. Accessed October 01, 2011. http://www.msnbc.msn.com/id/37510167/ns/business-us_business/t/why-apple-nervous-about-foxconn.

4. Malcolm Moore, "A Look inside the Foxconn Suicide Factory—Telegraph." Telegraph.co.uk—Telegraph Online, Daily Telegraph and Sunday Telegraph—Telegraph. May 27, 2010. Accessed September 30, 2011. http://www.telegraph.co.uk/finance/china-business/7773011/A-look-inside-the-Foxconn-suicide-factory.html.

5. Dylan Bushell-Embling, "Foxconn a 'concentration Camp': Report." Telecom Asia. October 11, 2010. Accessed September 30, 2011. http://www.telecomasia.net/content/foxconn-concentration-camp-report.

6. Dylan Bushell-Embling, Ibid.

7. Dylan Bushnell-Embling, Ibid.

8. Malcolm Moore, Ibid.

9. Joel Johnson, Wired Magazine, February 28, 2011 http://www.wired.com/magazine/2011/02/ff_joelinchina/

10. Killian Bell, "Foxconn Workers to Sign 'Anti-Suicide Pledge' & Promise Not to Sue | Cult of Mac." Cult of Mac | Apple News, Reviews and How Tos. May 6, 2011. Accessed September 30, 2011. http://www.cultofmac.com/93674/foxconn-workers-to-sign-anti-suicide-pledge-promise-not-to-sue.

11. Frederik Balfour, and Tim Culpan, Ibid.

12. Frederik Balfour, and Tim Culpan, Ibid.

13. Frederik Balfour, and Tim Culpan, Ibid.

14. Michelle Maisto, "Apple CEO Jobs Says Foxconn Conditions Not So Bad." EWeek.com. June 2, 2010. Accessed September 30, 2011. http://www.eweek.com/c/a/Mobile-and-Wireless/

To: You
From: The Philosopher
Subject: Interns at Foxconn

I can't believe that Foxconn! First, their workers are jumping out the windows and then in September of 2012, they make student interns help them pump out the Apple's new iPhone. You've got to admit, free labor is a great way to keep costs down! According to a *New York Times* (September 10, 2012), nearby vocational schools required students to do an internship at Foxconn. Instead of learning about the company, students had to make cables for iPhones. I guess that will teach them *something* about Foxconn. The students weren't slaves. They could leave at any time; however, they had to complete the internship to graduate.

Apple had hired a group called the Fair Labor Association to audit Foxconn after the suicides. When they found out about the intern labor, the Fair Labor Association took steps to make sure that they interns could resign and still graduate and that Foxconn linked their jobs to their outside studies. Problem solved?

Apple-CEO-Jobs-Says-Foxconn-Conditions-Not-So-Bad-566877/.

15. Ibid.

16. Apple, "Apple Supplier Responsibility." Accessed September 30, 2011. http://images.apple.com/supplier responsibility/pdf/Apple_SR_2011_Progress_Report.pdf.

17. Apple, Ibid.

18. Apple, Ibid., p. 19.

19. Michelle Maisto, Ibid.

QUESTIONS

1. What do you think of Terry Gou's personal response to the suicides? What do you think of the initiatives that Foxconn took in response to the suicides?

2. What are Apple's responsibilities in this case? Do you think that Apple's investigation was sufficient?

3. Is Foxconn like a sweatshop? What does this case tell us about the social responsibility of a corporation for the behavior of businesses in their supply chain?

CASE 11.6
Personal Luxury or Family Loyalty?
Motorola University

Joe was a native of *Ganzpoor*, a megacity in the developing nation of *Chompu*. Joe entered this life as the first of five children of an impoverished cloth peddler. Against all odds, by means of sheer guts, hard work and ability, Joe had brought himself to the United States and managed to earn a prestigious

From R. S. Moorthy, Richard T. De George, Thomas Donaldson, William J. Ellos, Robert C. Solomon, and Robert B. Textor, *Uncompromising Integrity: Motorola's Global Challenge* (Schaumburg, IL: Motorola University Press, 1998) pp. 88–89.

degree in engineering from *Cornford University*. Motorola snapped him up a week after graduation, and during the next five years gave him challenging assignments in Florida, Phoenix, Scotland and Mexico. Joe had thoroughly "bought into" the Motorola Culture. Or so it seemed.

Meanwhile, Motorola's business in Chompu began taking off. The Chompu Group was eager for more engineers. But the Human Resources Office was having great difficulty finding candidates willing to accept assignment to Ganzpoor. The news of all this reached Joe, who soon began a vigorous campaign for a transfer. "Look," he argued, "I speak native Ganzpoori and near-native Chompunese, and can hit the ground running." HR saw him as a guy too good to be true: qualified both professionally and culturally. Joe got his transfer.

Upon his assignment to Ganzpoor, Joe was informed in writing that he was expected to reside in a safe and seemly residence of his choice, and would be reimbursed for the actual cost of his rent and servants, up to a maximum of $2,000 per month. "Joe, just give us your landlord's and servants' receipts, and we'll get you promptly reimbursed," explained *Pierre Picard*, a French Motorolan assigned as financial controller for Motorola/Chompu.

Joe found a place to live, but even months later, other Motorolans were not sure exactly where it was because he never seemed to entertain at home. Some of his colleagues thought this was a bit strange, but then realized that Joe hardly had time for entertaining, given his executive responsibility for sourcing contracts for the construction of a new office and factory complex.

Each month Joe would send Pierre a bill for $2,000, accompanied by a rental and service receipt for exactly that amount, duly signed by his landlord. Each month Pierre would reimburse Joe accordingly. This went on for several months, until one day, a traditionally dressed Chompunese man came to see Pierre. He complained bitterly that Joe was his Master, and that Master had cheated him of his servant's wages for the past three months. At this point Pierre, despite his personal regard for Joe, had no

alternative but to check into the facts of Joe's living arrangements.

Pierre and the local HR manager, *Harry Hanks*, had trouble getting the facts of the case, so finally they got a car and driver and went looking for Joe's address. It took almost two hours. The address turned out to be on the edge of a slum area of Ganzpoor, where houses were poorly marked. When they finally got there, they were shocked. Joe was living in what was, by Western standards, not much more than a shack.

Their first concern was for Joe's safety. In this part of the world, there were good reasons why transpatriates chose not to live in slums. Also, they felt, Joe's unseemly residence was hardly good for Motorola's image. Aside from these considerations, though, was the fundamental matter of simple integrity.

Harry felt he had no choice but to report the case to the regional HR director, who had no choice but to order a full-scale investigation.

When Joe learned that he was under investigation, he exploded in fury. He complained to HR that his right to personal privacy was being invaded. Further, he argued that his receipts were legitimate, despite the fact that the investigation revealed that rent plus service in so humble a dwelling could not possibly have cost Joe more than $400 a month, and probably cost much less.

Joe finally explained: Yes, it was true that he actually paid "less than" $2,000 a month (though he refused to say how much less). But, he argued, just because he was willing to "make sacrifices" should not mean that he should receive less than the full $2,000, which "all of my fellow Motorolans receive." To clinch his defense, Joe argued, "Look, I'm a Chompunese as well as a Motorolan, and here in Chompu this kind of thing happens all the time."

The hearings officer pressed further. Finally Joe, near tears, explained that all four of his younger siblings were now of college or high school age, and that he was putting all four of them through school with the reimbursements he received from Motorola, plus a sizeable chunk of his salary. "Look," said Joe, "My family is *poor*—so poor in fact that most Westerners wouldn't believe our poverty even if they saw it. This money can mean the difference between hope and despair for all of us. For me to do anything less for my family would be to defile the honor of my late father.

"Can't you understand?"

A week later Joe was asked to step into the director's office to learn his fate. . . .

QUESTIONS

1. Do employees have a right to spend their living allowance in a foreign country any way they want?

2. If you were the director, what would you do with Joe?

3. Do employees have the right to spend their living allowances any way that they please in a foreign country?

CHAPTER QUESTIONS

1. Whose values should prevail when operating in another culture? Who decides what is best for the people in a country?

2. What kind of responsibilities does a firm have for things that happen outside of their business in a foreign country?

3. How can one bridge the gap between people who have different moral priorities?

12

Working with Mother Nature

Environmental Ethics and Business Ecology

Introduction

Will you buy an SUV? They are very popular these days, and if you want to win the admiration or, at least, not attract the scorn of your acquaintances (including those whom you zoom past on the Interstate), you had better get one. (As opposed, say, to a staid sedan or, worse, a minivan, which singles you out as one who is utterly and hopelessly uncool). Of course, you could get a Miata or a BMW Sportster, but that puts you at risk from those who do go for the more gargantuan three-ton SUVs. But, sadly, in addition to burning a small hole in your gas allowance, driving an SUV also helps burn a hole in the ozone layer, arguably increases global warming, burns up more of an increasingly precious fossil fuel, pollutes the very air that you breathe, and puts us at the mercy of foreign, often hostile, oil producers. But politics and expense aside, you are sensitive enough to the state of the environment—as now we all are—to feel just a little bit guilty that you are now contributing to the problem. And it doesn't make you feel any better that millions of people around the globe—including the fast emerging car markets of Asia—are doing the same thing. It is little comfort to know that the air quality in Beijing is even worse than it is in Houston and Los Angeles, or that the skin cancer rate in New Zealand is increasing faster than it is in Florida.

Whether or not to buy an SUV is probably a personal decision, but it has obvious implications regarding the entire planet. It is commonly said that pollution recognizes no national boundaries, but this might be said of the environment and the state of the planet in general. There are few changes, including the depletion of one natural resource or another, in one place or another, that do not sooner or later involve the planet as a whole. In business, the same principle applies. There are few enterprises, whether they directly involve the mining or use of natural resources or the financial concerns of developers and entrepreneurs, that do not have profound environmental implications, perhaps not in their immediate, particular results, but certainly when reiterated around the globe in country after country, whether "developed" or "developing." (Are there any countries, even including those that are wretchedly poor or torn apart by civil strife, that are not developing?) The days when

499

Native American Proverb

"The frog does not drink up the pond in which he lives."

---

we could tap into our natural resources without concern and remain oblivious to the costs and effects of our behavior are now past. Every business has effects on the environment. Every business therefore involves and requires thinking about the environment. There is no such luxury as being "too small to make a difference." Our actions are imitated around the globe, and the result is literally enough to move—or remove—mountains.

The environment plays a peculiar but crucial role in business ethics. The concept of social responsibility, and even stakeholder theory, generally refers to people or groups of people who have, or potentially could have, a say in the business by buying stocks, by buying or refusing to buy products, by joining community groups, and so on. (In fact, one prominent management textbook perversely defines a stakeholder as someone who has the power to affect the *operation* of a business or a corporation.) But the environment has no "say." It does not "respond." (Of course, environmental groups may speak on its behalf, but that is not the point.) The fact is that the environment is affected by business operations, and it, in turn, affects us all. Of course, we distinguish between accidents, which, after all, will happen, and negligence, which means causing an accident that could have and should have been prevented, and producing those by-products which one knows may be harmful but are unavoidable in the production process itself, and questions concerning conservation and the depletion of resources. In the last two cases, the question should be, do we need this product or to use this resource in this way? And that, in turn, may depend on the general question of lifestyle. Americans use some 60 percent of the world's resources for less than 5 percent of its population. And then we ask the third world to cut back on their pollution and use of resources. Is that fair? But in any case, we need to look at our own lifestyles and expectations—which by now have often grown into feelings of entitlement—and ask whether our own responsibilities as consumers are as much a part of the problem as the behavior of the giant corporations.

We begin with a classic meditation on the American wild and how business and technology are changing it, by Aldo Leopold. This is followed by an essay by Mark Sagoff, "At the Shrine of Our Lady Fatima *or* Why Political Questions Are Not All Economic." Sagoff argues that we err when we suppose that all public policy questions (especially public policy vis-á-vis the environment) should be settled on the basis of money. Sagoff argues that we may and often do have policy concerns that are equal to or more important than financial concerns. How, he asks, can we put a price on the diversity of wildlife in the Alaskan Wildlife Reserve? Then William F. Baxter, in "People or Penguins," argues that we should allow our relationship with the environment to be determined by our own rational, long-term interest. We do not have duties to the environment as such, but we do have duties to ourselves and to future generations of humanity. But when it is a choice between "people or penguins," we must choose people. Against this view, Peter Singer argues that not only humans, but also sentient nonhumans, are of moral concern and so must be included in our moral analyses of environmental issues. Norman Bowie then explores the ethical complexities of the automobile business in "Morality, Money, and Motor Cars." Finally, Jon Entine discusses the relationship between protecting the environment for ethical reasons and protecting the environment for reasons of corporate image in "Rain-forest *Chic*."

Aldo Leopold | # The Land Ethic

Aldo Leopold is widely credited with being the "father" of the green movement in America.

People who have never canoed a wild river, or who have done so only with a guide in the stern, are apt to assume that novelty, plus healthful exercise, account for the value of the trip. I thought so too, until I met the two college boys on the Flambeau.

Supper dishes washed, we sat on the bank watching a buck dunking for water plants on the far shore. Soon the buck raised his head, cocked his ears upstream, and then bounded for cover.

Around the bend now came the cause of his alarm: two boys in a canoe. Spying us, they edged in to pass the time of day.

"What time is it?" was their first question. They explained that their watches had run down, and for the first time in their lives there was no clock, whistle, or radio to set watches by. For two days they had lived by "sun-time," and were getting a thrill out of it. No servant brought them meals: they got their meat out of the river, or went without. No traffic cop whistled them off the hidden rock in the next rapids. No friendly roof kept them dry when they misguessed whether or not to pitch the tent. No guide showed them which camping spots offered a nightlong breeze, and which a nightlong misery of mosquitoes; which firewood made clean coals, and which only smoke.

Before our young adventurers pushed off downstream, we learned that both were slated for the Army

upon the conclusion of their trip. Now the *motif* was clear. This trip was their first and last taste of freedom, an interlude between two regimentations: the campus and the barracks. The elemental simplicities of wilderness travel were thrills not only because of their novelty, but because they represented complete freedom to make mistakes. The wilderness gave them their first taste of those rewards and penalties for wise and foolish acts which every woodsman faces daily, but against which civilization has built a thousand buffers. These boys were "on their own" in this particular sense.

Perhaps every youth needs an occasional wilderness trip, in order to learn the meaning of this particular freedom.

When I was a small boy, my father used to describe all choice camps, fishing waters, and woods as "nearly as good as the Flambeau." When I finally launched my own canoe in this legendary stream, I found it up to expectations as a river, but as a wilderness it was on its last legs. New cottages, resorts, and highway bridges were chopping up the wild stretches into shorter and shorter segments. To run down the Flambeau was to be mentally whipsawed between alternating impressions: no sooner had you built up the mental illusion of being in the wilds than you sighted a boat-landing, and soon you were coasting past some cottager's peonies.

Safely past the peonies, a buck bounding up the bank helped us to restore the wilderness flavor, and the next rapids finished the job. But staring at you

From *A Sand County Almanac* (New York: Oxford University Press, 1949).

beside the pool below was a synthetic log cabin, complete with composition roof, "Bide-A-Wee" signboard, and rustic pergola for afternoon bridge.

Paul Bunyan was too busy a man to think about posterity, but if he had asked to reserve a spot for posterity to see what the old north woods looked like, he likely would have chosen the Flambeau, for here the cream of the white pine grew on the same acres with the cream of the sugar maple, yellow birch, and hemlock. This rich intermixture of pine and hardwoods was and is uncommon. The Flambeau pines, growing on a hardwood soil richer than pines are ordinarily able to occupy, were so large and valuable, and so close to a good log-driving stream, that they were cut at an early day, as evidenced by the decayed condition of their giant stumps. Only defective pines were spared, but there are enough of these alive today to punctuate the skyline of the Flambeau with many a green monument to bygone days.

The hardwood logging came much later; in fact, the last big hardwood company "pulled steel" on its last logging railroad only a decade ago. All that remains of that company today is a "land-office" in its ghost town, selling off its cutovers to hopeful settlers. Thus died an epoch in American history: the epoch of cut out and get out.

Like a coyote rummaging in the offal of a deserted camp, the post-logging economy of the Flambeau subsists on the leavings of its own past. "Gypo" pulpwood cutters nose around in the slashings for the occasional small hemlock overlooked in the main logging. A portable sawmill crew dredges the riverbed for sunken "deadheads," many of which drowned during the hell-for-leather log-drives of the glory days. Rows of these mud-stained corpses are drawn up on shore at the old landings—all in perfect condition, and some of great value, for no such pine exists in the north woods today. Post and pole cutters strip the swamps of white cedar; the deer follow them around and strip the felled tops of their foliage. Everybody and everything subsists on leavings.

So complete are all these scavengings that when the modern cottager builds a log cabin, he uses imitation logs sawed out of slab piles in Idaho or Oregon, and hauled to Wisconsin woods in a freight car. The proverbial coals to Newcastle seem a mild irony compared with this.

Yet there remains the river, in a few spots hardly changed since Paul Bunyan's day; at early dawn, before the motor boats awaken, one can still hear it singing in the wilderness. There are a few sections of uncut timber, luckily state-owned. And there is a considerable remnant of wildlife: muskellunge, bass, and sturgeon in the river; mergansers, black ducks, and wood ducks breeding in the sloughs; ospreys, eagles, and ravens cruising overhead. Everywhere are deer, perhaps too many: I counted 52 in two days afloat. A wolf or two still roams the upper Flambeau, and there is a trapper who claims he saw a marten, though no marten skin has come out of the Flambeau since 1900.

Using these remnants of the wilderness as a nucleus, the State Conservation Department began, in 1943, to rebuild a fifty-mile stretch of river as a wild area for the use and enjoyment of young Wisconsin. This wild stretch is set in a matrix of state forest, but there is to be no forestry on the river banks, and as few road crossings as possible. Slowly, patiently, and sometimes expensively the Conservation Department has been buying land, removing cottages, warding off unnecessary roads, and in general pushing the clock back, as far as possible, toward the original wilderness.

The good soil that enabled the Flambeau to grow the best cork pine for Paul Bunyan likewise enabled Rusk County, during recent decades, to sprout a dairy industry. These dairy farmers wanted cheaper electric power than that offered by local power companies, hence they organized a co-operative REA and in 1947 applied for a power dam, which, when built, would clip off the lower reaches of a fifty-mile stretch in process of restoration as canoe-water.

There was a sharp and bitter political fight. The Legislature, sensitive to farmer-pressure but oblivious of wilderness values, not only approved the REA dam, but deprived the Conservation Commission of any future voice in the disposition of power sites. It thus seems likely that the remaining canoe-water on the Flambeau, as well as every other stretch of wild river in the state, will ultimately be harnessed for power.

Perhaps our grandsons, having never seen a wild river, will never miss the chance to set a canoe in singing waters.

QUESTIONS

1. What is morally significant about "a wild river"?
2. Are we too busy to think about posterity?

Mark Sagoff

At the Shrine of Our Lady Fatima *or* Why Political Questions Are Not All Economic

Mark Sagoff is a Senior Research Scholar at the University of Maryland—College Park and a Pew Fellow.

Lewiston, New York, a well-to-do community near Buffalo, is the site of the Lake Ontario Ordinance Works, where years ago the federal government disposed of the residues of the Manhattan Project. These radioactive wastes are buried but are not forgotten by the residents who say that when the wind is southerly, radon gas blows through the town. Several parents at a recent Lewiston conference I attended described their terror on learning that cases of leukemia had been found among area children. They feared for their own lives as well. On the other side of the table, officials from New York State and from local corporations replied that these fears were ungrounded. People who smoke, they said, take greater risks than people who live close to waste disposal sites. One speaker talked in terms of "rational methodologies of decisionmaking." This aggravated the parents' rage and frustration.

The speaker suggested that the townspeople, were they to make their decision in a free market and if they knew the scientific facts, would choose to live near the hazardous waste facility. He told me later they were irrational—"neurotic"—because they refused to recognize or to act upon their own interests. The residents of Lewiston were unimpressed with his

analysis of their "willingness to pay" to avoid this risk or that. They did not see what risk-benefit analysis had to do with the issues they raised.

If you take the Military Highway (as I did) from Buffalo to Lewiston, you will pass through a formidable wasteland. Landfills stretch in all directions and enormous trucks—tiny in that landscape—incessantly deposit sludge which great bulldozers then push into the ground. These machines are the only signs of life, for in the miasma that hangs in the air, no birds, not even scavengers, are seen. Along colossal power lines which criss-cross this dismal land, the dynamos at Niagra send electric power south, where factories have fled, leaving their remains to decay. To drive along this road is to feel, oddly, the mystery and awe one experiences in the presence of so much power and decadence.

POLITICAL AND ECONOMIC DECISIONMAKING

This essay concerns the economic decisions we make about the environment. It also concerns our political decisions about the environment. Some people have suggested that ideally these should be the same, that all environmental problems are problems in distribution. According to this view, there is an environmental problem only when some resource is not allocated in equitable and efficient ways.

The Ninth Annual National Report on Environmental Attitudes, Knowledge, and Behaviors
National Environmental Education and Training Foundation (May 2001)

As in the previous eight years [1993–2001] a majority of Americans say that "environmental protection and economic development can go hand in hand." Of those surveyed, 63% agree with this option, rather than the alternative—that one must be chosen over the other (25%).

Americans say that a balance between the environment and the economy is required for prosperity. Fully 89% either strongly or mostly agree that "The condition of the environment will play an increasingly important role in the nation's economic future." Thus, Americans believe that environmental protection and economic development must be achieved together to ensure a vibrant nation. Still, when people are asked to choose between environmental protection and economic development, fully 71% say they would choose the environment.

There is room for improvement in our efforts to protect the environment. Close to half (46%) of Americans hold the view that current laws "do not go far enough" to protect the environment. One-third (32%) hold the view that existing laws have struck "about the right balance," while 15% contend that laws and regulations already "go too far."

This approach to environmental policy is pitched entirely at the level of the consumer. It is his or her values that count, and the measure of these values is the individual's willingness to pay. The problem of justice or fairness in society becomes, then, the problem of distributing goods and services so that more people get more of what they want to buy: a condo on the beach, a snowmobile for the mountains, a tank full of gas, a day of labor. The only values we have, according to this view, are those that a market can price.

How much do you value open space, a stand of trees, an "unspoiled" landscape? Fifty dollars? A hundred? A thousand? This is one way to measure value. You could compare the amount consumers would pay for a townhouse or coal or a landfill to the amount they would pay to preserve an area in its "natural" state. If users would pay more for the land with the house, the coal mine, or the landfill, than without—less construction and other costs of development—then the efficient thing to do is to improve the land and thus increase its value. This is why we have so many tract developments, pizza stands, and gas stations. How much did you spend last year to preserve open space? How much for pizza and gas? "In principle, the ultimate measure of environmental quality," as one basic text assures us, "is the value people place on these . . . services or their *willingness to pay*."[1]

Willingness to pay: what is wrong with that? The rub is this: not all of us think of ourselves simply as *consumers*. Many of us regard ourselves *as citizens* as well. We act as consumers to get what we want *for ourselves*. We act as citizens to achieve what we think is right or best *for the community*. The question arises, then, whether what we want for ourselves individually as consumers is consistent with the goals we would set for ourselves collectively as citizens. Would I vote for the sort of things I shop for? Are my preferences as a consumer consistent with my judgments as a citizen?

They are not. I am schizophrenic. Last year, I fixed a couple of tickets and was happy to do so since I saved fifty dollars. Yet, at election time, I helped to vote the corrupt judge out of office. I speed on the highway; yet I want the police to enforce laws against speeding. I used to buy mixers in returnable bottles—but who can bother to return them? I buy only disposables now, but to soothe my conscience, I urge my state senator to outlaw one-way containers. I love my car; I hate the bus. Yet I vote for candidates who promise to tax gasoline to pay for public transportation. And of course I applaud the Endangered Species Act, although I have no earthly use for the Colorado squawfish or the Indiana bat. I support almost any political cause that I think will defeat my consumer interests. This is because I have contempt for—although I act upon—those interests. I have an "Ecology Now" sticker on a car that leaks oil everywhere it's parked.

The distinction between consumer and citizen preferences has long vexed the theory of public finance. Should the public economy serve the same goals as the household economy? May it serve, instead, goals emerging from our association as citizens? The question asks if we may collectively strive for and achieve only those items we individually compete for and consume. Should we aspire, instead, to public goals we may legislate as a nation? . . .

SUBSTITUTING EFFICIENCY FOR SAFETY

The labor unions won an important political victory when Congress passed the Occupational Safety and Health Act of 1970.[2] That Act, among other things, severely restricts worker exposure to toxic substances. It instructs the Secretary of Labor to set "the standard which most adequately assures, to the extent feasible . . . that no employee will suffer material impairment of health or functional capacity even if such employee has regular exposure to the hazard . . . for the period of his working life."[3]

Pursuant to this law, the Secretary of Labor in 1977 reduced from ten to one part per million (ppm)

the permissable ambient exposure level for benzene, a carcinogen for which no safe threshold is known. The American Petroleum Institute thereupon challenged the new standard in court. It argued, with much evidence in its favor, that the benefits (to workers) of the one ppm standard did not equal the costs (to industry).[4] The standard therefore did not appear to be a rational response to a market failure in that it did not strike an efficient balance between the interests of workers in safety and the interests of industry and consumers in keeping prices down.

The Secretary of Labor defended the tough safety standard on the ground that the law demanded it. An efficient standard might have required safety until it cost industry more to prevent a risk than it cost workers to accept it. Had Congress adopted this vision of public policy—one which can be found in many economics texts—it would have treated workers not as ends-in-themselves but as means for the production of overall utility. This, as the Secretary saw it, was what Congress refused to do.[5]

The United States Court of Appeals for the Fifth Circuit agreed with the American Petroleum Institute and invalidated the one ppm benzene standard.[6] On July 2, 1980, the Supreme Court affirmed the decision in *American Petroleum Institute v. Marshall*[7] and remanded the benzene standard back to OSHA for revision. The narrowly based Supreme Court decision was divided over the role economic considerations should play in judicial review. Justice Marshall, joined in dissent by three other justices, argued that the Court had undone on the basis of its own theory of regulatory policy an act of Congress inconsistent with that theory.[8] He concluded that the plurality decision of the Court "requires the American worker to return to the political arena to win a victory that he won before in 1970."[9]

The decision of the Supreme Court is important not because of its consequences, which are likely to be minimal, but because of the fascinating questions it raises. Shall the courts uphold only those political decisions that can be defended on economic grounds? Shall we allow democracy only to the extent that it can be construed either as a rational response to a market failure or as an attempt to redistribute wealth? Should the courts say that a regulation is not "feasible" or "reasonable"—terms that occur in the OSHA law[10]—unless it is supported by a cost-benefit analysis?

The problem is this: An efficiency criterion, as it is used to evaluate public policy, assumes that the goals of our society are contained in the preferences individuals reveal or would reveal in markets. Such an approach may appear attractive, even just because it treats everyone as equal, at least theoretically, by according to each person's preferences the same respect and concern. To treat a person with respect, however, is also to listen and to respond intelligently to his or her views and opinions. This is not the same thing as to ask how much he or she is willing to pay for them. The cost-benefit analyst does not ask economists how much they are willing to pay for what they believe, that is, that the workplace and the environment should be made efficient. Why, then, does the analyst ask workers, environmentalists, and others how much they are willing to pay for what they believe is right? Are economists the only ones who can back their ideas with reasons while the rest of us can only pay a price? The cost-benefit approach treats people as of equal worth because it treats them as of no worth, but only as places or channels at which willingness to pay is found.

LIBERTY: ANCIENT AND MODERN

When efficiency is the criterion of public safety and health, one tends to conceive of social relations on the model of a market, ignoring competing visions of what we as a society should be like. Yet it is obvious that there are competing conceptions of what we should be as a society. There are some who believe on principle that worker safety and environmental quality ought to be protected only insofar as the benefits of protection balance the costs. On the other hand, people argue—also on principle—that neither worker safety nor environmental quality should be treated merely as a commodity to be traded at the margin for other commodities, but rather each should be valued for its own sake. The conflict between these two principles is logical or moral, to be resolved by argument or debate. The

question whether cost-benefit analysis should play a decisive role in policy-making is not to be decided by cost-benefit analysis. A contradiction between principles—between contending visions of the good society—cannot be settled by asking how much partisans are willing to pay for their beliefs. The role of the *legislator*, the political role, may be more important to the individual than the role of *consumer*. The person, in other words, is not to be treated merely as a bundle of preferences to be juggled in cost–benefit analyses. The individual is to be respected as an advocate of ideas which are to be judged according to the reasons for them. If health and environmental statutes reflect a vision of society as something other than a market by requiring protections beyond what are efficient, then this may express not legislative ineptitude but legislative responsiveness to public values. To deny this vision because it is economically inefficient is simply to replace it with another vision. It is to insist that the ideas of the citizen be sacrificed to the psychology of the consumer.

We hear on all sides that government is routinized, mechanical, entrenched, and bureaucratized; the jargon alone is enough to dissuade the most mettlesome meddler. Who can make a difference? It is plain that for many of us the idea of a national political community has an abstract and suppositions quality. We have only our private conceptions of the good, if no way exists to arrive at a public one. This is only to note the continuation, in our time, of the trend Benjamin Constant described in the essay *De La Liberte des Anciens Compare a Celle des Modernes*.[11] Constant observes that the modern world, as opposed to the ancient, emphasizes civil over political liberties, the rights of privacy and property over those of community and participation. "Lost in the multitude," Constant writes, "the individual rarely perceives the influence that he exercises," and, therefore, must be content with "the peaceful enjoyment of private independence."[12] The individual asks only to be protected by laws common to all in his pursuit of his own self-interest. The citizen has been replaced by the consumer; the tradition of Rousseau has been supplanted by that of Locke and Mill.

The Earth and Myself Are of One Mind
Chief Joseph of the Nez Perce

The earth is our mother. She should not be disturbed by hoe or plough. We want only to subsist on what she freely gives us. Our fathers gave us many laws, which they had learned from their fathers. These laws were good. I have carried a heavy load on my back ever since I was a boy. I realized then that we could not hold our own with the white men. We were like deer. They were like grizzly bears. We had small country. Their country was large. We were contented to let things remain as the Great Spirit Chief made them. They were not, and would change the rivers and mountains if they did not suit them.

Nowhere are the rights of the moderns, particularly the rights of privacy and property, less helpful than in the area of the natural environment. Here the values we wish to protect—cultural, historical, aesthetic, and moral—are public values. They depend not so much upon what each person wants individually as upon what he or she thinks is right for the community. We refuse to regard worker health and safety as commodities: we regulate hazards as a matter of right. Likewise, we refuse to treat environmental resources simply as public goods in the economist's sense. Instead, we prevent significant deterioration of air quality not only as a matter of individual self-interest but also as a matter of collective self-respect. How shall we balance efficiency against moral, cultural, and aesthetic values in policy for the workplace and the environment? No better way has been devised to do this than by legislative debate ending in a vote. This is very different from a cost-benefit analysis terminating in a bottom line.

VALUES ARE NOT SUBJECTIVE

It is the characteristic of cost-benefit analysis that it treats all value judgments other than those made on its behalf as nothing but statements of preference, attitude, or emotion, insofar as they are value judgments. The cost-benefit analyst regards as true the judgments that we should maximize efficiency or wealth. The analyst believes that this view can be backed by reasons, but does not regard it as a preference or want for which he or she must be willing to pay. The cost-benefit analyst tends to treat all other normative views and recommendations as if they were nothing but subjective reports of mental states. The analyst supposes in all such cases that "this is right" and "this is what we ought to do" are equivalent to "I want this" and "this is what I prefer." Value judgments are beyond criticism if, indeed, they are nothing but expressions of personal preference; they are incorrigible since every person is in the best position to know what he or she wants. All valuation, according to this approach, happens *in foro interno;* debate *in foro publico* has no point. With this approach, the reasons that people give for their views do not count; what does count is how much they are willing to pay to satisfy their wants. Those who are willing to pay the most, for all intents and purposes, have the right view; theirs is the more informed opinion, the better aesthetic judgement, and the deeper moral insight.

Economists have used this impartial approach to offer solutions to many significant social problems, for example, the controversy over abortion. An economist argues that "there is an optimal number of abortions, just as there is an optimal level of pollution, or purity. . . . Those who oppose abortion could eliminate it entirely, if their intensity of feeling were so strong as to lead to payments that were greater at the margin than the price anyone would pay to have an abortion."[13] Likewise, economists, in order to determine whether the war in Vietnam was justified, have estimated the willingness to pay of those who demonstrated against it. Following the same line of reasoning, it should be possible to decided whether Creationism should be taught in the public schools, whether black and white people should be segregated, whether the death penalty should be enforced, and whether the square root of six is three. All of these questions arguably depend upon how much people are willing to pay for their subjective preferences or wants. This is the beauty of cost–benefit analysis: no matter how relevant or irrelevant, wise or stupid, informed or uninformed, responsible or silly, defensible or indefensible wants may be, the analyst is able to derive a policy from them—a policy which is legitimate because, in theory, it treats all of these preferences as equally valid and good.

PREFERENCE OR PRINCIPLE?

In contrast, consider a Kantian conception of value.[14] The individual, for Kant, is a judge of values, not a mere haver of wants, and the individual judges not for himself or herself merely, but as a member of a relevant community or group. The central idea in a Kantian approach to ethics is that some values are more reasonable than others and therefore have a better claim upon the assent of members of the community as such. The world of obligation, like the world of mathematics or the world of empirical fact, is public not private, and objective standards of argument and criticism apply. Kant recognized that values, like beliefs, are subjective states of mind which have an objective content as well. Therefore, both values and beliefs are either correct or mistaken. A value judgment is like an empirical or theoretical judgment in that it claims to be *true* not merely to be *felt*.

We have, then, two approaches to public policy before us. The first, the approach associated with normative versions of welfare economics, asserts that the only policy recommendation that can or need be defended on objective grounds is efficiency or wealth-maximization. The Kantian approach, on the other hand, assumes that many policy recommendations may be justified or refuted on objective grounds. It would concede that the approach of welfare economics applies adequately to some questions, for example, those which ordinary consumer markets typically settle. How many yo-yos should be produced as compared to how many frisbees? Shall pens have black ink or blue? Matters such as these are so trivial it is plain that markets should handle them. It does not follow, however, that we should adopt a market or quasi-market approach to every public question.

A market or quasi-market approach to arithmetic, for example, is plainly inadequate. No matter how much people are willing to pay, three will never be the square root of six. Similarly, segregation is a national curse and the fact that we are willing to pay for it does not make it better, but only us worse. The case for abortion must stand on the merits; it cannot be priced at the margin. Our failures to make the right decisions in these matters are failures in arithmetic, failures in wisdom, failures in taste, failures in morality—but not market failures. There are no relevant markets which have failed.

What separates these questions from those for which markets are appropriate is that they involve matters of knowledge, wisdom, morality, and taste that admit of better or worse, right or wrong, true or false, and not mere economic optimality. Surely environmental questions—the protection of wilderness, habitats, water, land, and air as well as policy toward environmental safety and health—involve moral and aesthetic principles and not just economic ones. This is consistent, of course, with cost-effectiveness and with a sensible recognition of economic constraints.

The neutrality of the economist is legitimate if private preferences or subjective wants are the only values in question. A person should be left free to choose the color of his or her necktie or necklace, but we cannot justify a theory of public policy or private therapy on that basis. . . . The neutrality of economics is not a basis for its legitimacy. We recognize it as an indifference toward value—an indifference so deep, so studied, and so assured that at first one hesitates to call it by its right name.

THE CITIZEN AS JOSEPH K.

The residents of Lewiston at the conference I attended demanded to know the truth about the dangers that confronted them and the reasons for those dangers. They wanted to be convinced that the sacrifice asked of them was legitimate even if it served interests other than their own. One official from a large chemical company dumping wastes in the area told them in reply that corporations were people and that people could talk to people about their feelings, interests, and needs. This sent a shiver through the audience. Like Joseph K. in *The Trial*,[15] the residents of Lewiston asked for an explanation, justice, and truth, and they were told that their wants would be taken care of. They demanded to know the reasons for what was continually happening to them. They were given a personalized response instead.

This response, that corporations are "just people serving people," is consistent with a particular view of power. This is the view that identifies power with the ability to get what one wants as an individual, that is, to satisfy one's personal preferences. When people in official positions in corporations or in the government put aside their personal interests, it would follow that they put aside their power as well. Their neutrality then justifies them in directing the resources of society in ways they determine to be best. This managerial role serves not their own interests but those of their clients. Cost–benefit analysis may be seen as a pervasive form of this paternalism. Behind this paternalism, as William Simon observes of the lawyer–client relationship, lies a theory of value that tends to personalize power. "It resists understanding power as a product of class, property, or institutions and collapses power into the personal needs and dispositions of the individuals

who command and obey."[16] Once the economist, the therapist, the lawyer, or the manager abjures his own interests and acts wholly on behalf of client individuals, he appears to have no power of his own and thus justifiably manipulates and controls everything. "From this perspective it becomes difficult to distinguish the powerful from the powerless. In every case, both the exercise of power and submission to it are portrayed as a matter of personal accommodation and adjustment."[17]

The key to the personal interest or emotive theory of value, as one commentator has rightly said, "is the fact that emotivism entails the obliteration of any genuine distinction between manipulative and non-manipulative social relations."[18] The reason is that once the affective self is made the source of all value, the public self cannot participate in the exercise of power. As Philip Reiff remarks, "the public world is constituted as one vast stranger who appears at inconvenient times and makes demands viewed as purely external and therefore with no power to elicit a moral response."[19] There is no way to distinguish the legitimate authority that public values and public law create from tyranny.

"At the rate of progress since 1900," Henry Adams speculates in his *Education*, "every American who lived into the year 2000 would know how to control unlimited power."[20] . . . Yet in the 1980s, the citizens of Lewiston, surrounded by dynamos, high tension lines, and nuclear wastes, are powerless. They do not know how to criticize power, resist power, or justify power—for to do so depends on making distinctions between good and evil, right and wrong, innocence and guilt, justice and injustice, truth and lies. These distinctions cannot be made out and have no significance within an emotive or psychological theory of value. To adopt this theory is to imagine society as a market in which individuals trade voluntarily and without coercion. No individual, no belief, no faith has authority over them. To have power to act as a nation we must be able to act, at least at times, on a public philosophy, conviction, or faith. We cannot abandon the moral function of public law. The anti-nomianism of cost–benefit analysis is not enough.

NOTES

1. A. Freeman, R. Haveman, A. Kneese, *The Economics of Environmental Policy* (1973), *supra* note 6, at 23.

2. Pub. L. No. 91–596, 84 Stat. 1596 (1970) (codified at 29 U.S.C. §§ 651–678 (1970)).

3. 29 U.S.C. $sm 655(b)(5) (1970).

4. *American Petroleum Inst. v. Marshall*, 581 F 2d 493 (5th Cir. 1978), *aff'd*, 448 U.S. 607 (1980) at 501 *See* e.g., R. Posner, *Economic Analysis of Law* I & II (1973). In G. Calabresi, *The Costs of Accidents passim* (1970) the author argues that accident law balances two goals "efficiency" and "equality" or "justice."

5. *American Petroleum Inst. v. Marshall*, 581 F 2d 493, 503–05 (5th Cir. 1978).

6. *Idem.* at 505.

7. 448 U.S. 607 (1980).

8. *Idem.* at 719.

9. *Idem.*

10. 29 U.S.C. §§655(b)(5) & 652(8) (1975).

11. B. Constant, *De La Liberte des Anciens Compares a Celle des Modernes* (1819).

12. *Oeuvres Politiques de Benjamin Constant,* 269 (C. Louandre, ed. 1874). *quoted in* S. Wolin, *Politics and Vision* 281 (1960).

13. H. Macaulay & B. Yandle, *Environment Use and the Market*, 120–21 (1978). *See generally* Cicchetti, Freeman, Haveman, & Knetsch, *On the Economic of Mass Demonstrations: A Case Study of the November 1969 March on Washington*, 61 *Am. Econ.* Rev. 719 (1971).

14. I. Kant, *Foundations of the Metaphysics of Morals* (1969). I follow the interpretation of Kantian ethics of W. Sellars, *Science and Metaphysics*, ch. vii (1968) and Sellars, *On Reasoning About Values*, 17 *Am. Phil. Q.* 81 (1980). *See* A. Macintyre, *After Virtue* 22 (1981).

15. F. Kafka, *The Trial* (rev. ed. trans. 1957). Simon applies this anology to the lawyer–client relationship. Simon, *supra* note 40, at 524.

16. Simon, *supra* note 40, at 495.

17. *Idem.*

18. A. Macintyre, *supra* note 54, at 22.

19. P. Reiff, *The Triumph of the Therapeutic: Uses of Faith After Freud* 52 (1966).

20. H. Adams, *supra* note I, at 476.

QUESTIONS

1. Why are some political questions *not* economic questions?

2. What are the two approaches to public policy distinguished by Sagoff? How do they arrive at different solutions to the same questions?

William F. Baxter | # People or Penguins

William F. Baxter is a professor at the Stanford University Law School.

I start with the modest proposition that, in dealing with pollution, or indeed with any problem, it is helpful to know what one is attempting to accomplish. Agreement on how and whether to pursue a particular objective, such as pollution control, is not possible unless some more general objective has been identified and stated with reasonable precision. We talk loosely of having clean air and clean water, of preserving our wilderness areas, and so forth. But none of these is a sufficiently general objective: each is more accurately viewed as a means rather than as an end.

With regard to clean air, for example, one may ask, "how clean?" and "what does clean mean?" It is even reasonable to ask, "Why have clean air?" Each of these questions is an implicit demand that a more general community goal be stated—a goal sufficiently general in its scope and enjoying sufficiently general assent among the community of actors that such "why" questions no longer seem admissible with respect to that goal.

If, for example, one states as a goal the proposition that "every person should be free to do whatever he wishes in contexts where his actions do not interfere with the interests of other human beings," the speaker is unlikely to be met with a response of "why?" The goal may be criticized as uncertain in its implications or difficult to implement, but it is so basic a tenet of our civilization—it reflects a cultural value so broadly shared, at least in the abstract— that the question of "why" is seen as impertinent or imponderable or both . . . .

Without any expectation of obtaining unanimous consent to them, let me set forth four goals that I generally use as ultimate testing criteria in attempting to frame solutions to problems of human organization. My position regarding pollution stems from these four criteria. . . .

My criteria are as follows:

1. The spheres of freedom criterion stated [two paragraphs] above.
2. Waste is a bad thing. The dominant feature of human existence is scarcity—our available resources, our aggregate labors, and our skill in employing both have always been, and will continue for some time to be, inadequate to yield to every man all the tangible and intangible satisfactions he would like to have. Hence, none of those resources, or labors, or skills, should be wasted—that is, employed so as to yield less than they might yield in human satisfactions.
3. Every human being should be regarded as an end rather than as a means to be used for the betterment of another. Each should be afforded dignity and regarded as having an absolute claim to an even-handed application of such rules as the community may adopt for its governance.
4. Both the incentive and the opportunity to improve his share of satisfactions should be preserved to every individual. Preservation of incentive is dictated by the "no-waste" criterion and enjoins against the continuous, totally egalitarian redistribution of satisfactions, or wealth; but subject to that constraint, everyone should receive, by continuous redistribution if necessary, some minimal share of aggregate wealth so as to avoid a level of privation from which the opportunity to improve his situation becomes illusory.

The relationship of these highly general goals to the more specific environmental issues at hand may not be readily apparent, and I am not yet ready to demonstrate their pervasive implications. Recently scientists have informed us that use of DDT in food production is causing damage to the penguin population. For the present purposes let us accept that assertion as an indisputable scientific fact. The scientific fact is often asserted as if the correct implication—that we must stop agricultural use of DDT—followed from the mere statement of fact of penguin damage. But plainly it does not follow if my criteria are employed.

My criteria are oriented to people, not penguins. Damage to penguins, or sugar pines, or geological marvels is, without more, simply irrelevant. One must go further, by my criteria, and say: Penguins are important because people enjoy seeing them walk about rocks; and furthermore, the well-being of people would be less impaired by halting use of DDT than by giving up penguins. In short, my observations about environmental problems will be people oriented, as are my criteria. I have no interest in preserving penguins for their own sake.

It may be said by way objection to this position that it is very selfish of people to act as if each person represented one unit of importance and nothing else was of any importance. It is undeniably selfish. Nevertheless I think it is the only tenable starting place for analysis for several reasons. First, no other position corresponds to the way most people really think and act—i.e., corresponds to reality.

Second, this attitude does not portend any massive destruction of nonhuman flora and fauna, for people depend on them in many obvious ways, and they will be preserved because and to the degree that humans do depend on them.

Third, what is good for humans is, in many respects, good for penguins and pine trees—clean air for example. So that humans are, in these respects, surrogates for plant and animal life.

Fourth, I do not know how we could administer any other system. Our decisions are either private or collective. Insofar as Mr. Jones is free to act privately, he may give such preferences as he wishes to other forms of life: he may feed birds in winter and do with less himself, and he may even decline to resist an advancing polar bear on the ground that the bear's appetite is more important than those portions of himself that the bear may choose to eat. In short my basic premise does not rule out private altruism to competing life-forms. It does rule out, however, Mr. Jones' inclination to feed Mr. Smith to the bear, however hungry the bear, however despicable Mr. Smith.

Insofar as we act collectively, on the other hand, only humans can be afforded an opportunity to participate in the collective decisions. Penguins cannot vote now and are unlikely subjects for the franchise—pine trees more unlikely still. Again each individual is free to cast his vote so as to benefit sugar pines if that is his inclination. But many of the more extreme assertions that one hears from some conservationists amount to tacit assertions that they are specially appointed representatives of sugar pines, and hence than their preferences should be weighted more heavily than the preferences of other humans who do not enjoy equal rapport with "nature." The simplistic assertion that agricultural use of DDT must stop at once because it is harmful to penguins is of that type.

Fifth, if polar bears or pine trees or penguins, like men, are to be regarded as ends rather than means, if they are to count in our calculus of social organization, someone must tell me how much each one counts, and someone must tell me how these life forms are to be permitted to express their preferences, for I do not know either answer. If the answer is that certain people are to hold their proxies, then I want to know how those proxy-holders are to be selected: self-appointment does not seem workable to me.

Sixth, and by way of summary of all the foregoing, let me point out that the set of environmental issues under discussion—although they raise very complex technical questions of how to achieve any objective—ultimately raise a normative question: what *ought* we to do? Questions of *ought* are unique to the human mind and world—they are meaningless as applied to a nonhuman situation.

I reject the proposition that we *ought* to respect the "balance of nature" or to "preserve the environment" unless the reason for doing so, express or implied, is the benefit of man.

I reject the idea that there is a "right" or "morally correct" state of nature to which we should return. The word "nature" has no normative connotation. Was it "right" or "wrong" for the earth's crust to heave in contortion and create mountains and seas? Was it "right" for the first amphibian to crawl up out of the primordial ooze? Was it "wrong" for plants to reproduce themselves and alter the

On Pollution
Milton Friedman

In fact, the people responsible for pollution are consumers, not producers. They create, as it were, demand for pollution. People who use electricity are responsible for the smoke that comes out of the stacks of generating plants.

atmospheric composition in favor of oxygen? For animals to alter the atmosphere in favor of carbon dioxide both by breathing oxygen and eating plants? No answers can be given to these questions because they are meaningless questions.

All this may seem obvious to the point of being tedious, but much of the present controversy over environment and pollution rests on tacit normative assumptions about just such nonnormative phenomena: that it is "wrong" to impair penguins with DDT, but not to slaughter cattle for prime rib roasts. That it is wrong to kill stands of sugar pines with industrial fumes, but not to cut sugar pines and build housing for the poor. Every man is entitled to his own preferred definition of Walden Pond, but there is no definition that has any moral superiority over another, except by reference to the selfish needs of the human race.

From the fact that there is no normative definition of the natural state, it follows that there is no normative definition of clean air or pure water—hence no definition of polluted air—or of pollution—except by reference to the needs of man. The "right" composition of the atmosphere is one which has some dust in it and some lead in it and some hydrogen sulfide in it—just those amounts that attend a sensibly organized society thoughtfully and knowledgeably pursuing the greatest possible satisfaction for its human members.

The first and most fundamental step toward solution of our environmental problems is a clear recognition that our objective is not pure air or water but rather some optimal state of pollution. That step immediately suggests the question: How do we define and attain the level of pollution that will yield the maximum possible amount of human satisfaction?

Low levels of pollution contribute to human satisfaction but so do food and shelter and education and music. To attain ever lower levels of pollution, we must pay the cost of having less of these other things. I contrast that view of the cost of pollution control with the more popular statement that pollution control will "cost" very large numbers of dollars. The popular statement is true in some senses, false in others; sorting out the true and false senses is of some importance. The first step in that sorting

process is to achieve a clear understanding of the difference between dollars and resources. Resources are the wealth of our nation; dollars are merely claim checks upon those resources. Resources are of vital importance; dollars are comparatively trivial.

Four categories of resources are sufficient for our purposes: at any given time a nation, or a planet if you prefer, has a stock of labor, of technological skill, of capital goods, and of natural resources (such as mineral deposits, timber, water, land, etc.). These resources can be used in various combinations to yield goods and services of all kinds—in some limited quantity. The quantity will be larger if they are combined efficiently, smaller if combined inefficiently. But in either event the resource stock is limited, the goods and services that they can be made to yield are limited; even the most efficient use of them will yield less than our population, in the aggregate, would like to have.

If one considers building a new dam, it is appropriate to say that it will be costly in the sense that it will require x hours of labor, y tons of steel and concrete, and z amount of capital goods. If these resources are devoted to the dam, then they cannot be used to build hospitals, fishing rigs, schools, or electric can openers. That is the meaningful sense in which the dam is costly.

Quite apart from the very important question of how wisely we can combine our resources to produce goods and services is the very different question of how they get distributed—who gets how many goods? Dollars constitute the claim checks which are distributed among people and which control their share of national output. Dollars are nearly valueless pieces of paper except to the extent that they do represent claim checks to some fraction of the output of goods and services. Viewed as claim checks, all the dollars outstanding during any period of time are worth, in the aggregate, the goods and services that are available to be claimed with them during that period—neither more nor less.

It is far easier to increase the supply of dollars than to increase the production of goods and services—printing dollars is easy. But printing more dollars doesn't help because each dollar then simply becomes a claim to fewer goods, i.e., becomes worth less.

The point is this: many people fall into error upon hearing the statement that the decision to build a dam, or to clean up a river, will cost $X million. It is regrettably easy to say: "It's only money. This is a wealthy country, and we have lots of money." But you cannot build a dam or clean a river with $X million—unless you also have a match, you can't even make a fire. One builds a dam or cleans a river by diverting labor and steel and trucks and factories from making one kind of goods to making another. The cost in dollars is merely a shorthand way of describing the extent of the diversion necessary. If we build a dam for $X million, then we must recognize that we will have $X million less housing and food and medical care and electric can openers as a result.

Similarly, the costs of controlling pollution are best expressed in terms of the other goods we will have to give up to do the job. This is not to say the job should not be done. Badly as we need more housing, more medical care, and more can openers, and more symphony orchestras, we could do with somewhat less of them, in my judgement at least, in exchange for somewhat cleaner air and rivers. But that is the nature of the trade-off, and analysis of the problem is advanced if that unpleasant reality is kept in mind. Once the trade-off relationship is clearly perceived, it is possible to state in a very general way what the optimal level of pollution is. I would state it as follows:

People enjoy watching penguins. They enjoy relatively clean air and smog-free vistas. Their health is improved by relatively clean water and air. Each of these benefits is a type of good or service. As a society we would be well advised to give up one washing machine if the resources that would have gone into that washing machine can yield greater human satisfaction when diverted into pollution control. We should give up one hospital if the resources thereby freed would yield more human satisfaction when devoted to elimination of noise in our cities. And so on, trade-off by trade-off, we should divert our productive capacities from the production of existing goods and services to the production of a cleaner, quieter, more pastoral nation up to—and no further than—the point at which we value more highly the next washing machine or hospital that we would have to do without than we value the next unit of environmental improvement that the diverted resources would create.

Now this proposition seems to me unassailable but so general and abstract as to be unhelpful—at least unadministerable in the form stated. It assumes we can measure in some way the incremental units of human satisfaction yielded by very different types of goods. The proposition must remain a pious abstraction until I can explain how this measurement process can occur. . . . But I insist that the proposition stated describes the result for which we should be striving—and again, that it is always useful to know what your target is even if your weapons are too crude to score a bull's eye.

QUESTIONS

1. Why does Baxter think that there is a choice between people or penguins? Do you agree?

2. What does Baxter mean by "optimal" pollution? What does he say about future generations?

| Norman Bowie | # Morality, Money, and Motor Cars |

Norman Bowie is a professor of management
at the University of Minnesota.

Environmentalists frequently argue that business
has special obligations to protect the environment.
Although I agree with the environmentalists on
this point, I do not agree with them as to where the
obligations lie. Business does not have an obligation
to protect the environment over and above what
is required by law; however, it does have a moral
obligation to avoid intervening in the political arena
in order to defeat or weaken environmental legislation.
In developing this thesis, several points are in order.
First, many businesses have violated important
moral obligations, and the violation has had a severe
negative impact on the environment. For example,
toxic waste haulers have illegally dumped hazardous
material, and the environment has been harmed as a
result. One might argue that those toxic waste haulers
who have illegally dumped have violated a special
obligation to the environment. Isn't it more accurate
to say that these toxic waste haulers have violated
their obligation to obey the law and that in this case
the law that has been broken is one pertaining to the
environment? Businesses have an obligation to obey
the law—environmental laws and all others. Since
there are many well-publicized cases of business
having broken environmental laws, it is easy to think
that business has violated some special obligations
to the environment. In fact, what business has done
is to disobey the law. Environmentalists do not need
a special obligation to the environment to protect the
environment against illegal business activity; they
need only insist that business obey the laws.

Business has broken other obligations beside
the obligation to obey the law and has harmed the
environment as a result. Consider the grounding of the
Exxon oil tanker *Valdez* in Alaska. That grounding
was allegedly caused by the fact that an inadequately
trained crewman was piloting the tanker while the
captain was below deck and had been drinking. What
needs to be determined is whether Exxon's policies
and procedures were sufficiently lax so that it could
be said Exxon was morally at fault. It might be that
Exxon is legally responsible for the accident under
the doctrine of respondent superior, but Exxon is not
thereby morally responsible. Suppose, however, that
Exxon's policies were so lax that the company could
be characterized as morally negligent. In such a
case, the company would violate its moral obligation
to use due care and avoid negligence. Although its
negligence was disastrous to the environment, Exxon
would have violated no special obligation to the
environment. It would have been morally negligent.

A similar analysis could be given to the
environmentalists' charges that Exxon's cleanup
procedures were inadequate. If the charge is true,
either Exxon was morally at fault or not. If the
procedures had not been implemented properly by
Exxon employees, then Exxon is legally culpable,
but not morally culpable. On the other hand, if
Exxon lied to government officials by saying that
its policies were in accord with regulations and/
or were ready for emergencies of this type, then
Exxon violated its moral obligation to tell the truth.
Exxon's immoral conduct would have harmed the
environment, but it violated no special obligation to
the environment. More important, none is needed.
Environmentalists, like government officials,
employees, and stockholders, expect that business
firms and officials have moral obligations to obey
the law, avoid negligent behavior, and tell the truth.
In sum, although many business decisions have
harmed the environment, these decisions violated no

environmental moral obligations. If a corporation is negligent in providing for worker safety, we do not say the corporation violated a special obligation to employees; we say that it violated its obligation to avoid negligent behavior.

The crucial issues concerning business obligations to the environment focus on the excess use of natural resources (the dwindling supply of oil and gas, for instance) and the externalities of production (pollution, for instance). The critics of business want to claim that business has some special obligation to mitigate or solve these problems. I believe this claim is largely mistaken. If business does have a special obligation to help solve the environmental crisis, that obligation results from the special knowledge that business firms have. If they have greater expertise than other constituent groups in society, then it can be argued that, other things being equal, business's responsibilities to mitigate the environmental crisis are somewhat greater. Absent this condition, business's responsibility is no greater than and may be less than that of other social groups. What leads me to think that the critics of business are mistaken? . . .

Consider the harm that results from the production of automobiles. We know statistically that about 50,000 persons per year will die and that nearly 250,000 others will be seriously injured in automobile accidents in the United States alone. Such death and injury, which is harmful, is avoidable. . . . What such arguments point out is that some refinement of the moral minimum standard needs to take place. Take the automobile example. The automobile is itself a good-producing instrument. Because of the advantages of automobiles, society accepts the

possible risks that go in using them. Society also accepts many other types of avoidable harm. We take certain risks—ride in planes, build bridges, and mine coal—to pursue advantageous goals. It seems that the high benefits of some activities justify the resulting harms. As long as the risks are known, it is not wrong that some avoidable harm be permitted so that other social and individual goals can be achieved. . . .

It is a fundamental principle of ethics that "ought" implies "can." That expression means that you can be held morally responsible only for events within your power. In the ought-implies-can principle, the overwhelming majority of highway deaths and injuries is not the responsibility of the automaker. Only those deaths and injuries attributable to unsafe automobile design can be attributed to the automaker. The ought-implies-can principle can also be used to absolve the auto companies of responsibility for death and injury from safety defects that the automakers could not reasonably know existed. The company could not be expected to do anything about them.

Does this mean that a company has an obligation to build a car as safe as it knows how? No. The standards for safety must leave the product's cost within the price range of the consumer ("ought implies can" again). Comments about engineering and equipment capability are obvious enough. But for a business, capability is also a function of profitability. A company that builds a maximally safe car at a cost that puts it at a competitive disadvantage and hence threatens its survival is building a safe car that lies beyond the capability of the company.

Critics of the automobile industry will express horror at these remarks, for by making capability a

Land as a Commodity
Vine Deloria

"Every time we have objected to the use of the land as a commodity, we have been told that progress is necessary to American life. Now the laugh is ours."

function of profitability, society will continue to have avoidable deaths and injuries; however, the situation is not as dire as the critics imagine. Certainly capability should not be sacrificed completely so that profits can be maximized. The decision to build products that are cheaper in cost but are not maximally safe is a social decision that has widespread support. The arguments occur over the line between safety and cost. What we have is a classical trade-off situation. What is desired is some appropriate mix between engineering safety and consumer demand. To say there must be some mix between engineering safety and consumer demand is not to justify all the decisions made by the automobile companies. Ford Motor Company made a morally incorrect choice in placing Pinto gas tanks where it did. Consumers were uninformed, the record of the Pinto in rear-end collisions was worse than that of competitors, and Ford fought government regulations. . . .

As long as business obeys the environmental laws and honors other standard moral obligations, most harm done to the environment by business has been accepted by society. Through their decisions in the marketplace, we can see that most consumers are unwilling to pay extra for products that are more environmentally friendly than less friendly competitive products. Nor is there much evidence that consumers are willing to conserve resources, recycle, or tax themselves for environmental causes.

Consider the following instances reported in the *Wall Street Journal*.[1] The restaurant chain Wendy's tried to replace foam plates and cups with paper, but customers in the test markets balked. Procter and Gamble offered Downy fabric softener in concentrated form that requires less packaging than ready-to-use products; however the concentrate version is less convenient because it has to be mixed with water. Sales have been poor. Procter and Gamble manufactures Vizir and Lenor brands of detergents in concentrate form, which the customer mixes at home in reusable bottles. Europeans will take the trouble; Americans will not. Kodak tried to eliminate its yellow film boxes but met customer resistance. McDonald's has been testing mini-incinerators that convert trash into energy but often meets opposition from community groups that fear the incinerators will pollute the air. A McDonald's spokesperson points out that the emissions are mostly carbon dioxide and water vapor and are "less offensive than a barbecue." Exxon spent approximately $9,200,000 to "save" 230 otters ($40,000 for each otter). Otters in captivity cost $800. Fishermen in Alaska are permitted to shoot otters as pests.[2] Given these facts, doesn't business have every right to assume that public tolerance for environmental damage is quite high . . . .

Recently environmentalists have pointed out the environmental damage caused by the widespread use of disposable diapers. Are Americans ready to give them up and go back to cloth diapers and the diaper pail? Most observers think not . . . . Moreover, if the public wants cloth diapers, business certainly will produce them. If environmentalists want business to produce products that are friendlier to the environment, they must convince Americans to purchase them. Business will respond to the market. It is the consuming public that has the obligation to make the trade-off between cost and environmental integrity.

Data and arguments of the sort described should give environmental critics of business pause. Nonetheless, these critics are not without counter-responses. For example, they might respond that public attitudes are changing. Indeed, they point out, during the Reagan deregulation era, the one area where the public supported government regulations was in the area of environmental law. In addition, *Fortune* predicts environmental integrity as the primary demand of society on business in the 1990s.[3]

More important, they might argue that environmentally friendly products are at a disadvantage in the marketplace because they have public good characteristics. After all, the best situation for the individual is one where most other people use environmentally friendly products but he or she does not, hence reaping the benefit of lower cost and convenience. Since everyone reasons this way, the real demand for environmentally friendly products cannot be registered in the market. Everyone is understating the value of his or her preference for environmentally friendly products. Hence, companies cannot conclude from market behavior that the environmentally unfriendly products are preferred.

Suppose the environmental critics are right that the public goods characteristic of environmentally friendly products creates a market failure. Does that mean the companies are obligated to stop producing these environmentally unfriendly products? I think not. . . . There is a need, and certainly corporations that cause environmental problems are in proximity. However, environmentally clean firms, if there are any, are not in proximity at all, and most business firms are not in proximity with respect to most environmental problems. In other words, the environmental critic must limit his or her argument to the environmental damage a business actually causes. . . . But even narrowing the obligation to damage actually caused will not be sufficient to establish an obligation to pull a product from the market because it damages the environment or even to go beyond what is legally required to protect the environment. Even for damage actually done, both the high cost of protecting the environment and the competitive pressures of business make further action to protect the environment beyond the capability of business. This conclusion would be more serious if business were the last resort, but it is not.

Traditionally it is the function of the government to correct for market failure. If the market cannot register the true desires of consumers, let them register their preferences in the political arena. Even fairly conservative economic thinkers allow government a legitimate role in correcting market failure.

Perhaps the responsibility for energy conservation and pollution control belongs with the government.

Although I think consumers bear a far greater responsibility for preserving and protecting the environment than they have actually exercised, let us assume that the basic responsibility rests with the government. Does that let business off the hook? No. Most of business's unethical conduct regarding the environment occurs in the political arena.

Far too many corporations try to have their cake and eat it too. They argue that it is the job of government to correct for market failure and then use their influence and money to defeat or water down regulations designed to conserve and protect the environment.[4] They argue that consumers should decide how much conservation and protection the environment should have, and then they try to interfere with the exercise of that choice in the political arena. Such behavior is inconsistent and ethically inappropriate. Business has an obligation to avoid intervention in the political process for the purpose of defeating and weakening environmental regulations. Moreover, this is a special obligation to the environment since business does not have a general obligation to avoid pursuing its own parochial interests in the political arena. Business need do nothing wrong when it seeks to influence tariffs, labor policy, or monetary policy. Business does do something wrong when it interferes with the passage of environmental legislation. Why?

To: You
From: The Philosopher
Subject: Who Owns the Earth?

Are we entitled to use the resources available to us? Or are we charging on an account that later generations will have to settle?

"Treat the earth well: it was not given to you by your parents, it was loaned to you by your children. We do not inherit the Earth from our Ancestors, we borrow it from our Children."

Ancient Indian Proverb, source unknown . . . most likely oral tradition handed down over the years.

First, such a noninterventionist policy is dictated by the logic of the business's argument to avoid a special obligation to protect the environment. Put more formally:

1. Business argues that it escapes special obligations to the environment because it is willing to respond to consumer preferences in this matter.
2. Because of externalities and public goods considerations, consumers cannot express their preferences in the market.
3. The only other viable forum for consumers to express their preferences is in the political arena.
4. Business intervention interferes with the expression of these preferences.
5. Since point 4 is inconsistent with point 1, business should not intervene in the political process.

The importance of this obligation in business is even more important when we see that environmental legislation has special disadvantages in the political arena. Public choice reminds us that the primary interest of politicians is being reelected. Government policy will be skewed in favor of policies that provide benefits to an influential minority as long as the greater costs are widely dispersed. Politicians will also favor projects where benefits are immediate and where costs can be postponed to the future. Such strategies increase the likelihood that a politician will be reelected.

What is frightening about the environmental crisis is that both the conservation of scarce resources and pollution abatement require policies that go contrary to a politician's self-interest. The costs of cleaning up the environment are immediate and huge, yet the benefits are relatively long range (many of them exceedingly long range). Moreover, a situation where the benefits are widely dispersed and the costs are large presents a twofold problem. The costs are large enough so that all voters will likely notice them and in certain cases are catastrophic for individuals (e.g., for those who lose their jobs in a plant shutdown).

Given these facts and the political realities they entail, business opposition to environmental legislation makes a very bad situation much worse. Even if consumers could be persuaded to take environmental issues more seriously, the externalities, opportunities to free ride, and public goods characteristics of the environment make it difficult for even enlightened consumers to express their true preference for the environment in the market. The fact that most environmental legislation trades immediate costs for future benefits makes it difficult for politicians concerned about reelection to support it. Hence it is also difficult for enlightened consumers to have their preferences for a better environment honored in the political arena. Since lack of business intervention seems necessary, and might even be sufficient, for adequate environmental legislation, it seems business has an obligation not to intervene. Nonintervention would prevent the harm of not having the true preferences of consumers for a clean environment revealed. Given business's commitment to satisfying preferences, opposition to having these preferences expressed seems inconsistent as well.

The extent of this obligation to avoid intervening in the political process needs considerable discussion by ethicists and other interested parties. Businesspeople will surely object that if they are not permitted to play a role, Congress and state legislators will make decisions that will put them at a severe competitive disadvantage. For example, if the United States develops stricter environmental controls than other countries do, foreign imports will have a competitive advantage over domestic products. Shouldn't business be permitted to point that out? Moreover, any legislation that places costs on one industry rather than another confers advantages on other industries. The cost to the electric utilities from regulations designed to reduce the pollution that causes acid rain will give advantages to natural gas and perhaps even solar energy. Shouldn't the electric utility industry be permitted to point that out?

These questions pose difficult questions, and my answer to them should be considered highly tentative. I believe the answer to the first question is "yes" and the answer to the second is "no." Business does have a right to insist that the regulations apply to all those in the industry. Anything else would seem to violate norms of fairness. Such issues of fairness do not arise in the second case. Since natural gas and solar do not contribute to acid rain and since the costs of acid rain cannot be fully captured in the market, government intervention through regulation is simply correcting a market failure. With respect to acid rain, the electric utilities do have an advantage they do not deserve. Hence they have no right to try to protect it.

Legislative bodies and regulatory agencies need to expand their staffs to include technical experts, economists, and engineers so that the political process can be both neutral and highly informed about environmental matters. To gain the respect of business and the public, its performance needs to improve. Much more needs to be said to make any contention that business ought to stay out of the political debate theoretically and practically possible. Perhaps these suggestions point the way for future discussion.

Ironically business might best improve its situation in the political arena by taking on an additional obligation to the environment. Businesspersons often have more knowledge about environmental harms and the costs of cleaning them up. They may often have special knowledge about how to prevent environmental harm in the first place. Perhaps business has a special duty to educate the public and to promote environmentally responsible behavior.

Business has no reticence about leading consumer preferences in other areas. Advertising is a billion-dollar industry. Rather than blaming consumers for not purchasing environmentally friendly products, perhaps some businesses might make a commitment to capture the environmental niche. I have not seen much imagination on the part of business in this area. Far too many advertisements with an environmental message are reactive and public relations driven. Recall those by oil companies showing fish swimming about the legs of oil rigs. An educational campaign that encourages consumers to make environmentally friendly decisions in the marketplace would limit the necessity for business activity in the political arena. Voluntary behavior that is environmentally friendly is morally preferable to coerced behavior. If business took greater responsibility for educating the public, the government's responsibility would be lessened. An educational campaign aimed at consumers would likely enable many businesses to do good while simultaneously doing very well.

Hence business does have obligations to the environment, although these obligations are not found where the critics of business place them. Business has no special obligation to conserve natural resources or to stop polluting over and above its legal obligations. It does have an obligation to avoid intervening in the political arena to oppose environmental regulations, and it has a positive obligation to educate consumers. The benefits of honoring these obligations should not be underestimated.

NOTES

1. Alicia Swasy, "For Consumers, Ecology Comes Second," *Wall Street Journal*, August 23, 1988, p. B1.

2. Jerry Alder, "Alaska after Exxon," *Newsweek*, September 18, 1989, p. 53.

3. Andrew Kupfer, "Managing Now for the 1990s," *Fortune*, September 26, 1988, pp. 46–47.

4. I owe this point to Gordon Rands, a Ph.D. student in the Carlson School of Management. Indeed the tone of the chapter has shifted considerably as a result of his helpful comments.

QUESTIONS

1. Does business have a special responsibility to protect the environment, according to Bowie? Why or why not? What is his argument?

2. Why might business serve itself well by taking responsibility for the environment?

Peter Singer

The Place of Nonhumans in Environmental Issues

Peter Singer is professor of philosophy at Princeton University. He is America's leading voice on the question of animal rights.

I. HUMANS AND NONHUMANS

When we humans change the environment in which we live, we often harm ourselves. If we discharge cadmium into a bay and eat shellfish from that bay, we become ill and may die. When our industries and automobiles pour noxious fumes into the atmosphere, we find a displeasing smell in the air, the long-term results of which may be every bit as deadly as cadmium poisoning. The harm that humans do the environment, however, does not rebound solely, or even chiefly, on humans. It is nonhumans who bear the most direct burden of human interference with nature.

By "nonhumans" I mean to refer to all living things other than human beings, though for reasons to be given later, it is with nonhuman animals, rather than plants, that I am chiefly concerned. It is also important, in the context of environmental issues, to note that living things may be regarded either collectively or as individuals. In debates about the environment the most important way of regarding living things collectively has been to regard them as species. Thus, when environmentalists worry about the future of the blue whale, they usually are thinking of the blue whale as a species, rather than of individual blue whales. But this is not, of course, the only way in which one can think of blue whales, or other animals, and one of the topics I shall discuss is whether we should be concerned about what we are doing to the environment primarily insofar as it threatens entire species of nonhumans, or primarily insofar as it affects individual nonhuman animals.

The general question, then, is how the effects of our actions on the environment of nonhuman beings should figure in our deliberations about what we ought to do. There is an unlimited variety of contexts in which this issue could arise. To take just one: Suppose that it is considered necessary to build a new power station, and there are two sites, A and B, under consideration. In most respects the sites are equally suitable, but building the power station on site A would be more expensive because the greater depth of shifting soil at that site will require deeper foundations; on the other hand, to build on site B will destroy a favored breeding ground for thousands of wildfowl. Should the presence of the wildfowl enter into the decision as to where to build? And if so, in what manner should it enter, and how heavily should it weigh?

In a case like this the effects of our actions on nonhuman animals could be taken into account in two quite different ways: directly, giving the lives and welfare of nonhuman animals an intrinsic significance which must count in any moral calculation; or indirectly, so that the effects of our actions on nonhumans are morally significant only if they have consequences for humans. . . .

II. SPECIESISM

The view that the effects of our actions on other animals have no direct moral significance is not as

The first five sections of this essay are reprinted from Peter Singer, "Not for Humans Only: The Place of Nonhumans in Environmental Ethics," in K. E. Goodpaster and K. M. Sayre, eds., *Ethics and Problems of the 21st Century* (Notre Dame, Ind.: University of Notre Dame Press, 1979). Reprinted by permission. The final section is reprinted by permission from Peter Singer, "All Animals Are Equal," *Philosophic Exchange*, vol. 1, no. 5 (Summer 1974). Copyright © 1974 the Center for Philosophic Exchange. (Section headings have been added.)

likely to be openly advocated today as it was in the past; yet it is likely to be accepted implicitly and acted upon. When planners perform cost-benefit studies on new projects, the costs and benefits are costs and benefits for human beings only. This does not mean that the impact of [a] power station or highway on wildlife is ignored altogether, but it is included only indirectly. That a new reservoir would drown a valley teeming with wildlife is taken into account only under some such heading as the value of the facilities for recreation that the valley affords. In calculating this value the cost-benefit study will be neutral between forms of recreation like hunting and shooting and those like bird watching and bush walking—in fact hunting and shooting are likely to contribute more to the benefit side of the calculations because larger sums of money are spent on them, and they therefore benefit manufacturers and retailers of firearms as well as the hunters and shooters themselves. The suffering experienced by the animals whose habitat is flooded is not reckoned into the costs of the operation; nor is the recreational value obtained by the hunters and shooters offset by the cost to the animals that their recreation involves.

Despite its venerable origin, the view that the effects of our actions on nonhuman animals have no intrinsic moral significance can be shown to be arbitrary and morally indefensible. If a being suffers, the fact that it is not a member of our own species cannot be a moral reason for failing to take its suffering into account. This becomes obvious if we consider the analogous attempt by white slave-owners to deny consideration to the interests of blacks. These white racists limited their moral concern to their own race, so the suffering of a black did not have the same moral significance as the suffering of a white. We now recognize that in doing so they were making an arbitrary distinction, and that the existence of suffering, rather than the race of the sufferer, is what is really morally significant. The point remains true if "species" is substituted for "race." The logic of racism and the logic of the position we have been discussing, which I have elsewhere referred to as "speciesism," are indistinguishable; and if we reject the former then consistency demands that we reject the latter too.[1]

It should be clearly understood that the rejection of speciesism does not imply that the different species are in fact equal in respect of such characteristics as intelligence, physical strength, ability to communicate, capacity to suffer, ability to damage the environment, or anything else. After all, the moral principle of human equality cannot be taken as implying that all humans are equal in these respects either—if it did, we would have to give up the idea of human equality. That one being is more intelligent than another does not entitle him to enslave, exploit, or disregard the interests of the less intelligent being. The moral basis of equality among humans is not equality in fact, but the principle of equal consideration of interests, and it is this principle that, in consistency, must be extended to any nonhumans who have interests.

III. NONHUMANS HAVE INTERESTS

There may be some doubt about whether any nonhuman beings have interests. This doubt may arise because of uncertainty about what it is to have an interest, or because of uncertainty about the nature of some nonhuman beings. So far as the concept of "interest" is the cause of doubt, I take the view that only a being with subjective experiences, such as the experience of pleasure or the experience of pain, can have interests in the full sense of the term; and that any being with such experiences does have at least one interest, namely, the interest in experiencing pleasure and avoiding pain. Thus consciousness, or the capacity for subjective experience, is both a necessary and a sufficient condition for having an interest. While there may be a loose sense of the term in which we can say that it is in the interests of a tree to be watered, this attenuated sense of the term is not the sense covered by the principle of equal consideration of interests. All we mean when we say that it is in the interests of a tree to be watered is that the tree needs water if it is to continue to live and grow normally; if we regard this as evidence that the tree has interests, we might almost as well say that it is in the interests of a car to be lubricated regularly because the car needs lubrication if it is to run properly. In neither case can we really mean (unless we impute consciousness to trees or cars) that the tree or car has any preference about the matter.

The remaining doubt about whether nonhuman beings have interests is, then, a doubt about whether nonhuman beings have subjective experiences like the experience of pain. I have argued elsewhere that the commonsense view that birds and mammals feel pain is well founded,[2] but more serious doubts arise as we move down the evolutionary scale. Vertebrate animals have nervous systems broadly similar to our own and behave in ways that resemble our own pain behavior when subjected to stimuli that we would find painful; so the inference that vertebrates are capable of feeling pain is a reasonable one, though not as strong as it is if limited to mammals and birds. When we go beyond vertebrates to insects, crustaceans, mollusks and so on, the existence of subjective states becomes more dubious, and with very simple organisms it is difficult to believe that they could be conscious. As for plants, though there have been sensational claims that plants are not only conscious, but even psychic, there is no hard evidence that supports even the more modest claim.[3]

The boundary of beings who may be taken as having interests is therefore not an abrupt boundary, but a broad range in which the assumption that the being has interests shifts from being so strong as to be virtually certain to being so weak as to be highly improbable. The principle of equal consideration of interests must be applied with this in mind, so that where there is a clash between a virtually certain interest and a highly doubtful one, it is the virtually certain interest that ought to prevail.

In this manner our moral concern ought to extend to all beings who have interests. . . .

IV. EQUAL CONSIDERATION OF INTERESTS

Giving equal consideration to the interests of two different beings does not mean treating them alike or holding their lives to be of equal value. We may recognize that the interests of one being are greater than those of another, and equal consideration will then lead us to sacrifice the being with lesser interests, if one or the other must be sacrificed. For instance, if for some reason a choice has to be made between saving the life of a normal human being and that of a dog, we might well decide to save the human because he, with his greater awareness of what is going to happen, will suffer more before he dies; we may also take into account the likelihood that it is the family and friends of the human who will suffer more; and finally, it would be the human who had the greater potential for future happiness. This decision would be in accordance with the principle of equal consideration of interests, for the interests of the dog get the same consideration as those of the human, and the loss to the dog is not discounted because the dog is not a member of our species. The outcome is as it is because the balance of interests favors the human. In a different situation—say, if the human were grossly mentally defective and without family or anyone else who would grieve for it—the balance of interests might favor the nonhuman.[4]

The more positive side of the principle of equal consideration is this: where interests are equal, they must be given equal weight. So where human and nonhuman animals share an interest—as in the case of the interest in avoiding physical pain—we must give as much weight to violations of the interest of the nonhumans as we do to similar violations of the human's interest. This does not mean, of course, that it is as bad to hit a horse with a stick as it is to hit a human being, for the same blow would cause less pain to the animal with the tougher skin. The principle holds between similar amounts of felt pain, and what this is will vary from case to case.

It may be objected that we cannot tell exactly how much pain another animal is suffering, and that therefore the principle is impossible to apply. While I do not deny the difficulty and even, so far as precise measurement is concerned, the impossibility of comparing the subjective experiences of members of different species, I do not think that the problem is different in kind from the problem of comparing the subjective experiences of two members of our own species. Yet this is something we do all the time, for instance when we judge that a wealthy person will suffer less by being taxed at a higher rate than a poor person will gain from the welfare benefits paid for by the tax; or when we decide to take our two children to the beach instead of to a fair, because although the older one would prefer the fair, the younger one has a stronger preference the other way. These comparisons may be very rough, but since there is nothing better, we must use them; it would be irrational to refuse to do so simply because they are rough. More over, rough as they are, there are many situations in which we can be reasonably sure which way the balance of interests lies. While a difference of species may make comparisons rougher still, the basic problem is the same, and the comparisons are still often good enough to use, in the absence of anything more precise. . . .

V. EXAMPLES

We can now draw at least one conclusion as to how the existence of nonhuman living things should enter into our deliberations about actions affecting the environment: Where our actions are likely to make animals suffer, that suffering must count in our deliberations, and it should count equally with a like amount of suffering by human beings, insofar as rough comparisons can be made.

The difficulty of making the required comparison will mean that the application of this conclusion is controversial in many cases, but there will be some situations in which it is clear enough. Take, for instance, the wholesale poisoning of animals that is euphemistically known as "pest control." The authorities who conduct these campaigns give no consideration to the suffering they inflict on the "pests," and invariably use the method of slaughter they believe to be cheapest and most effective. The result is that hundreds of millions of rabbits have died agonizing deaths from the artificially introduced disease, myxomatosis, or from poisons like "ten-eighty"; coyotes and other wild dogs have died painfully from cyanide poisoning; and all manner of wild animals have endured days of thirst, hunger, and fear with a mangled limb caught in a leg-hold trap.[5] Granting, for the sake of argument, the necessity for pest control—though this has rightly been questioned—the fact remains that no serious attempts have been made to introduce alternative means of control and thereby reduce the incalculable amount of suffering caused by present methods. It would not, presumably, be beyond modern science to produce a substance which, when eaten by rabbits or coyotes, produced sterility instead of a drawn-out death. Such methods might be more expensive, but can anyone doubt that if a similar amount of human suffering were at stake, the expense would be borne?

Another clear instance in which the principle of equal consideration of interests would indicate methods different from those presently used is in the timber industry. There are two basic methods of obtaining timber from forests. One is to cut only

The Tame Land
Luther Standing Bear

Only to the white man was nature a "wilderness" and only to him was the land "infested" with "wild" animals and "savage" people. To us it was tame. Earth was bountiful and we were surrounded with the blessings of the Great Mystery.

Luther Standing Bear (1868–1939) from *Land of the Spotted Eagle*, 1933.

selected mature or dead trees, leaving the forest substantially intact. The other, known as clear-cutting, involves chopping down everything that grows in a given area, and then reseeding. Obviously when a large area is clear-cut, wild animals find their whole living area destroyed in a few days, whereas selected felling makes a relatively minor disturbance. But clear-cutting is cheaper, and timber companies therefore use this method and will continue to do so unless forced to do otherwise.[6] . . .

VI. THE MEAT INDUSTRY

For the great majority of human beings, especially in urban, industrialized societies, the most direct form of contact with members of other species is at mealtimes: We eat them. In doing so we treat them purely as means to our ends. We regard their life and well-being as subordinate to our taste for a particular kind of dish. I say "taste" deliberately—this is purely a matter of pleasing our palate. There can be no defenses of eating flesh in terms of satisfying nutritional needs, since it has been established beyond doubt that we could satisfy our need for protein and other essential nutrients far more efficiently with a diet that replaced animal flesh by soy beans, or products derived from soy beans, and other high-protein vegetable products.

It is not merely the act of killing that indicates what we are ready to do to other species in order to gratify our tastes. The suffering we inflict on the animals while they are alive is perhaps an even clearer indication of our speciesism than the fact that we are prepared to kill them.[7] In order to have meat on the table at a price that people can afford, our society tolerates methods of meat production that confine sentient animals in cramped, unsuitable conditions for the entire durations of their lives. Animals are treated like machines that convert fodder into flesh, and any innovation that results in a higher "conversion ratio" is liable to be adopted. As one authority on the subject has said, "cruelty is acknowledged only when profitability ceases."[8] So hens are crowded four or five to a cage with a floor area of twenty inches by eighteen inches, or around the size of a single page of the

New York Times. The cages have wire floors, since this reduces cleaning costs, though wire is unsuitable for the hens' feet; the floors slope, since this makes the eggs roll down for easy collection, although this makes it difficult for the hens to rest comfortably. In these conditions all the birds' natural instincts are thwarted: They cannot stretch their wings fully, walk freely, dust-bathe, scratch the ground, or build a nest. Although they have never known other conditions, observers have noticed that the birds vainly try to perform these actions. Frustrated at their inability to do so, they often develop what farmers call "vices," and peck each other to death. To prevent this, the beaks of young birds are often cut off.

This kind of treatment is not limited to poultry. Pigs are now also being reared in cages inside sheds. These animals are comparable to dogs in intelligence, and need a varied, stimulating environment if they are not to suffer from stress and boredom. Anyone who kept a dog in the way in which pigs are frequently kept would be liable to prosecution, in England at least, but because our interest in exploiting pigs is greater than our interest in exploiting dogs, we object to cruelty to dogs while consuming the produce of cruelty to pigs. Of the other animals, the condition of veal calves is perhaps worst of all, since these animals are so closely confined that they cannot even turn around or get up and lie down freely. In this way they do not develop unpalatable muscle. They are also made anemic and kept short of roughage, to keep their flesh pale, since white veal fetches a higher price; as a result they develop a craving for iron and roughage, and have been observed to gnaw wood off the sides of their stalls, and lick greedily at any rusty hinge that is within reach.

Since, as I have said, none of these practices cater to anything more than our pleasures of taste, our practice of rearing and killing other animals in order to eat them is a clear instance of the sacrifice of the most important interests of other beings in order to satisfy trivial interests of our own. To avoid speciesism we must stop this practice, and each of us has a moral obligation to cease supporting the practice. Our custom is all the support that the meat industry needs. The decision to cease giving it that support may be difficult, but it is no more difficult than it would have been for a white

Southerner to go against the traditions of his society and free his slaves; if we do not change our dietary habits, how can we censure those slaveholders who would not change their own way of living?

NOTES

1. For a fuller statement of this argument, see my *Animal Liberation* (New York: A New York Review Book, 1975), especially Ch. 1.

2. Ibid.

3. See, for instance, the comments by Arthur Galston in *Natural History*, 83, no. 3 (March 1974): 18, on the "evidence" cited in such books as *The Secret Life of Plants*.

4. Singer, *Animal Liberation*, pp. 20–23.

5. See J. Olsen, *Slaughter the Animals, Poison the Earth* (New York: Simon and Schuster, 1971), especially pp. 153–164.

6. See R. and V. Routley, *The Fight for the Forests* (Canberra: Australian National University Press, 1974); for a thoroughly documented indictment of clear-cutting in America, see *Time*, May 17, 1976.

7. Although one might think that killing a being is obviously the ultimate wrong one can do to it, I think that the infliction of suffering is a clearer indication of speciesism because it might be argued that at least part of what is wrong with killing a human is that most humans are conscious of their existence over time, and have desires and purposes that extend into the future—see, for instance, M. Tooley, "Abortion and Infanticide," *Philosophy and Public Affairs*, vol. 2, no. 1 (1972). Of course, if one took this view one would have to hold—as Tooley does—that killing a human infant or mental defective is not in itself wrong, and is less serious than killing certain higher mammals that probably do have a sense of their own existence over time.

8. Ruth Harrison, *Animal Machines* (Stuart, London 1964). This book provides an eye-opening account of intensive farming methods for those unfamiliar with the subject.

QUESTIONS

1. What is the place of nonhumans in environmental issues?

2. Why should we be concerned about "nonhumans"? Isn't our first duty to ourselves?

CASES

CASE 12.1
The Ethics of Dolphin–Human Interaction
Thomas I. White

In tales that reach back to ancient Crete, dolphins are said to be special creatures. We are told that they regularly aid lost ships, save drowning sailors, and form fast friendships with humans. Dolphins were even thought to be gods by some ancient peoples. This fascination with dolphins continues in the present. Even though we no longer consider dolphins to be divine, we have learned that they are surprisingly complex socially, emotionally, and intellectually. Accordingly, we now face a series of questions about the moral justifiability of our behavior toward them.

From Thomas I. White, *Business Ethics: A Philosophical Reader* (New York: Macmillan, 1993). Reprinted with permission.

Research over the last two decades reveals that dolphins are more like humans than was once thought. Dolphins are air-breathing mammals, not fish, and they evidence many of the same higher characteristics as humans. The size and complexity of the dolphin brain compares favorably to that of the human brain. Dolphins can solve difficult, novel problems; they are aware of time; and they can handle abstract and relational concepts. They have a sophisticated level of language comprehension, including the ability to understand syntax, something heretofore thought to be an exclusively human ability. More than one study suggests that dolphins engage in self-reflection. Dolphins appear to experience a range of emotions and to have distinct personalities, and their actions seem to result from deliberation and choice.

At the same time, the fact that dolphins live in the ocean and have an evolutionary history much different from humans leads to important differences between the two species. Dolphins possess a sonar sense that we humans lack, a sense that is superior to anything our technology has been able to devise. They use whistles to communicate with one another at a speed and at frequencies often beyond the ability of human hearing to perceive. Their system of communication may be more nonverbal than ours is, but they live a much more intensely social life than we do.

Both the similarities and the differences between dolphins and humans raise important philosophical questions. For example, we humans have traditionally reserved for ourselves the category of "person," with its special rights and privileges. Yet the advanced characteristics of dolphins suggest that they are probably "nonhuman persons." Does this mean, then, that they have moral standing and "rights"?

The question of whether dolphins have moral standing is an interesting philosophical issue in its own right. The specifics about dolphin/human interaction, however, make it much more than that because it raises the question of the ethical justifiability of our behavior toward the dolphins. Clashes between human and dolphin interests take place daily in the fishing and entertainment industries, and dolphins generally do poorly in the exchange. For example, approximately four hundred dolphins are held in captivity in the United States alone for purposes of research and entertainment at facilities such as Sea World and Marine World. In addition, despite recent progress regarding how tuna is caught in the eastern tropical Pacific, and despite decisions by companies such as Star-Kist to no longer sell tuna caught on dolphins, as many as three hundred dolphins still die each day in the nets of tuna boats. (In the eastern tropical Pacific, dolphins and tuna frequently school together. Tuna boats will often set their nets around a school of dolphin hoping to find tuna beneath them. Dolphins are regularly killed or injured in this process. Approximately 7 million dolphins have died because of this practice.)

The Marine Mammal Protection Act of 1972 allows 20,500 dolphins to die annually from American tuna fishing despite the fact that the original version of the bill aimed to bring the deaths to zero. The law also allows the United States to refuse to import fish from foreign boats causing too many dolphin deaths, and a federal court ordered such an embargo on Mexican tuna in 1990. Mexico objected to the U.S. action and appealed to an international trade body, arguing that the embargo was an unfair trade practice. A panel of the Geneva-based General Agreement on Tariffs and Trade (GATT) sided with Mexico, saying that a GATT member nation has no right to limit trade that harms the environment beyond its borders. For the time being, however, Mexico has agreed to table its case rather than take it to GATT's General Council.

QUESTIONS

1. Do dolphins have rights? If so, which ones? Life? Liberty? Self-determination?

2. How do we evaluate situations in which there is a conflict between human interests and dolphin interests? In trying to resolve such a clash, how do we properly take account of the differences between dolphins and humans and avoid anthropocentrism, that is, irrational prejudice in favor of our own species?

3. Do our need for food and our desire for maximum profit justify the technology we currently employ in tuna fishing? Does human curiosity about dolphins defend keeping them captive for research and education? Does human pleasure at watching dolphins perform (and the ability to make a profit at this) make it ethically justifiable to keep dolphins captive?

CASE 12.2
Made in the U.S.A.—and Dumped
William H. Shaw and Vincent Barry

When it comes to the safety of young children, fire is a parent's nightmare. Just the thought of their young ones trapped in their cribs and beds by a raging nocturnal blaze is enough to make most mothers and fathers take every precaution to ensure their children's safety. Little wonder that when fire-retardant children's pajamas hit the market in the mid-1970s, they proved an overnight success. Within a few short years more than 200 million pairs were sold, and the sales of millions more were all but guaranteed. For their manufacturers, the future could not have been brighter. Then, like a bolt from the blue, came word that the pajamas were killers.

In June 1977, the U.S. Consumer Product Safety Commission (CPSC) banned the sale of these pajamas and ordered the recall of millions of pairs. Reason: The pajamas contained the flame-retardant chemical Tris (2,3-dibromoprophyl), which had been found to cause kidney cancer in children.

Whereas just months earlier the 100 medium-and small-garment manufacturers of the Tris-impregnated pajamas couldn't fill orders fast enough, suddenly they were worrying about how to get rid of the millions of pairs now sitting in warehouses. Because of its toxicity, the sleepwear couldn't even be thrown away, let alone sold. Indeed, the CPSC left no doubt about how the pajamas were to be disposed of—buried or burned or used as industrial wiping cloths. All meant millions of dollars in losses for manufacturers.

The companies affected—mostly small, family-run operations employing fewer than 100 workers—immediately attempted to shift blame to the mills that made the cloth. When that attempt failed, they tried to get the big department stores that sold the pajamas and the chemical companies that produced Tris to share the financial losses. Again, no sale. Finally, in desperation, the companies lobbied in Washington for a bill making the federal government partially responsible for the losses. It was the government, they argued, that originally had required the companies to add Tris to pajamas and then had prohibited their sale. Congress was sympathetic; it passed a bill granting companies relief. But President Carter vetoed it.

While the small firms were waging their political battle in the halls of Congress, ads began appearing in the classified pages of *Women's Wear Daily*. "Tris-Tris-Tris . . . We will buy any fabric containing Tris," read one. Another said, "Tris—we will purchase any large quantities of garments containing Tris." The ads had been placed by exporters, who began buying up the pajamas, usually at 10 to 30 percent of the normal wholesale price. Their intent was clear: to dump the carcinogenic pajamas on overseas markets. ("Dumping" is a term apparently coined by *Mother Jones* magazine to refer to the practice of exporting to overseas countries products that have been banned or declared hazardous in the United States.)

Tris is not the only example of dumping. In 1972, 400 Iraqis died and 5,000 were hospitalized after eating wheat and barley treated with a U.S.-banned organic mercury fungicide. Winstrol, a synthetic male hormone that had been found to stunt the growth of American children, was made available in Brazil as an appetite stimulant for children. Depo-Provera, an injectable contraceptive known to cause malignant tumors in animals, was shipped overseas to seventy countries where it was used in U.S.-sponsored population control programs. And 450,000 baby pacifiers, of the type known to have caused choking deaths, were exported for sale overseas.

Manufacturers that dump products abroad clearly are motivated by profit or at least by the hope of avoiding financial losses resulting from having to withdraw a product from the market. For government

From William H. Shaw and Vincent Barry, *Moral Issues in Business*, 5th ed. (Belmont, CA: Wadsworth, 1996).

and health agencies that cooperate in the exporting of dangerous products, the motives are more complex.

For example, as early as 1971 the dangers of the Dalkon Shield intrauterine device were well documented. Among the adverse reactions were pelvic inflammation, blood poisoning, pregnancies resulting in spontaneous abortions, tubal pregnancies, and uterine perforations. A number of deaths were even attributed to the device. Faced with losing its domestic market, A. H. Robins Co., manufacturer of the Dalkon Shield, worked out a deal with the Office of Population within the U.S. Agency for International Development (AID), whereby AID bought thousands of the devices at a reduced price for use in population-control programs in forty-two countries.

Why do governmental and population-control agencies approve for sale and use overseas birth control devices proved dangerous in the United States? They say their motives are humanitarian. Since the rate of dying in childbirth is high in Third World countries, almost any birth control device is preferable to none. Third World scientists and government officials frequently support this argument. They insist that denying their countries access to the contraceptives of their choice is tantamount to violating their countries' national sovereignty.

Apparently this argument has found a sympathetic ear in Washington, for it turns up in the "notification" system that regulates the export of banned or dangerous products overseas. Based on the principles of national sovereignty, self-determination, and free trade, the notification system requires that foreign governments be notified whenever a product is banned, deregulated, suspended, or canceled by an American regulatory agency. The State Department, which implements the system, has a policy statement on the subject that reads in part: "No country should establish itself as the arbiter of others' health and safety standards. Individual governments are generally in the best position to establish standards of public health and safety."

Critics of the system claim that notifying foreign health officials is virtually useless. For one thing, other governments rarely can establish health standards or even control imports into their countries. Indeed, most of the Third World countries where banned or dangerous products are dumped lack regulatory agencies, adequate testing facilities, and well-staffed customs departments.

Then there's the problem of getting the word out about hazardous products. In theory, when a government agency such as the Environmental Protection Agency or the Food and Drug Administration (FDA) finds a product hazardous, it is supposed to inform the State Department, which is to notify local health officials. But agencies often fail to inform the State Department of the product they have banned or found harmful. And when it is notified, its communiqués typically go no further than the U.S. embassies abroad. One embassy official even told the General Accounting Office that he "did not routinely forward notification of chemicals not registered in the host country because it may adversely affect U.S. exporting." When foreign officials are notified by U.S. embassies, they sometimes find the communiqués vague or ambiguous or too technical to understand.

In an effort to remedy these problems, at the end of his term in office, President Jimmy Carter issued an executive order that (1) improved export notice procedures; (2) called for publishing an annual summary of substances banned or severely restricted for domestic use in the United States; (3) directed the State Department and other federal agencies to participate in the development of international hazards alert systems; and (4) established procedures for placing formal export licensing controls on a limited number of extremely hazardous substances. In one of his first acts as president, however, Ronald Reagan rescinded the order. Later in his administration, the law that formerly prohibited U.S. pharmaceutical companies from exporting drugs that are banned or not registered in this country was weakened to allow the export to twenty-one countries of drugs not yet approved for use in the United States.

But even if communication procedures were improved or the export of dangerous products forbidden, there are ways that companies can circumvent these threats to their profits—for example, by simply changing the name of the product or by exporting the individual ingredients of a product to a plant in a foreign country. Once there, the ingredients can be reassembled and the product dumped. Upjohn, for example, through its Belgian subsidiary, continues to produce Depo-Provera, which the FDA has consistently refused to approve for use in this country. And the prohibition on the export of dangerous drugs is not that hard to sidestep. "Unless the package bursts open on the dock," one drug company executive observes, "you have no chance of being caught."

Unfortunately for us, in the case of pesticides the effects of overseas dumping are now coming home. The Environmental Protection Agency bans from the United States all crop uses of DDT and Dieldrin, which kill fish, cause tumors in animals, and build up in the fatty tissue of humans. It also bans heptachlor, chlordane, leptophos, endrin, and many other pesticides, including 2,4,5-T (which contains the deadly poison dioxin, the active ingredient in Agent Orange, the notorious defoliant used in Vietnam) because they are dangerous to human beings. No law, however, prohibits the sale of DDT and these other U.S.-banned pesticides overseas, where thanks to corporate dumping they are routinely used in agriculture. The FDA now estimates, through spot checks, that 10 percent of our imported food is contaminated with illegal residues of banned pesticides. And the FDA's most commonly used testing procedure does not even check for 70 percent of the pesticides known to cause cancer.

QUESTIONS

1. Do you think dumping involves any moral issues? What are they?

2. Can a moral argument be made in favor of dumping, when doing so does not violate U.S. law? Do any moral considerations support illegal dumping? Speculate on why dumpers dump. Do you think they believe that what they are doing is morally permissible?

CASE 12.3
The Fordasaurus
William H. Shaw and Vincent Barry

Before Ford publicly unveiled the biggest sport-utility vehicle ever, the Sierra Club ran a contest for the best name and marketing slogan for it. Among the entries were "Fordasaurus, powerful enough to pass anything on the highway except a gas station" and "Ford Saddam, the truck that will put America between Iraq and a hard place." But the winner was "Ford Valdez: Have you driven a tanker lately?"

Ford, which decided to name the nine-passenger vehicle the Excursion, was not amused. Sales of sport-utility vehicles (SUVs) exploded in the 1990s, going up nearly sixfold, and the company sees itself as simply responding to consumer demand for ever larger models. Although most SUVs never leave the pavement, their drivers like knowing their vehicles can go anywhere and do anything. They also like their SUVs to be big. The Excursion is now the largest passenger vehicle on the road, putting Ford far ahead of its rivals in the competition to build the biggest and baddest SUV. The Excursion weighs 8,500 pounds, equivalent to two mid-sized sedans or three Honda Civics. It is more than 6 ½ feet wide, nearly 7 feet high, and almost 19 feet long—too big to fit comfortably into some garages or into a single parking space.

Although the Excursion is expensive ($40,000 to $50,000 when loaded with options), it is, like other SUVs, profitable to build. Because Ford based the

William H. Shaw and Vincent Barry, *Moral Issues in Business*, 9th ed. (Belmont, CA: Wadsworth, 2004).

Excursion on the chassis of its Super Duty truck, the company was able to develop the vehicle for a relatively modest investment of about $500 million. With sales of 50,000 to 60,000 per year, Ford earns about $20,000 per vehicle.

Most SUVs are classified as light trucks. Under current rules, they are allowed to emit up to several times more smog-causing gases per mile than automobiles. In 1999, the Clinton administration proposed tighter emissions restrictions on new passenger cars, restrictions that new vehicles in the light-truck category would also have to meet by 2009. However, these rules would not affect the Excursion, which is heavy enough to be classified as a medium-duty truck.

Ford says that the Excursion, with its 44-gallon gas tank, gets 10 to 15 miles per gallon, and that its emission of pollutants is 43 percent below the maximum for its class. By weight, about 85 percent of the vehicle is recyclable, and 20 percent of it comes from recycled metals and plastics. The company thus believes that the Excursion is in keeping with the philosophy of William Clay Ford, Jr. When he became chairman in September 1998, he vowed to make Ford "the world's most environmentally friendly auto maker." He added, however, that "what we do to help the environment must succeed as a business proposition. A zero-emission vehicle that sits unsold on a dealer's lot is not reducing pollution."

The company, however, has failed to win environmentalists to its side. They believe that with the Excursion, the Ford Company is a long way from producing an environmentally friendly product. Daniel Becker of the Sierra Club points out that in the course of an average lifetime of 120,000 miles, each Excursion will emit 130 tons of carbon dioxide, the principal cause of global warming. "It's just bad for the environment any way you look at it," he says.

John DeCicco of the American Council for an Energy-Efficient Economy agrees. He worries further that the Excursion is clearing the way for bigger and bigger vehicles. "This is the antithesis of green leadership."

Stung by criticism of the Excursion, William Clay Ford, Jr., has vowed to make the company a more responsible environmental citizen. Worried that if automobile producers don't clean up their act, they will become as vilified as cigarette companies, in August 2000 Ford promised it would improve the fuel economy of its SUVs by 25 percent over the next five years, smugly inviting other automakers to follow its green leadership. To this GM responded that it was the real green leader and "will still be in five years, or 10 years, or for that matter 20 years. End of story." When they aren't bragging about their greenness, however, both companies continue to lobby Congress to forbid the Department of Transportation from studying fuel economy increases.

Update:

According to media reports, yet to be confirmed by Ford, the company is planning on phasing out the Excursion after 2004.

QUESTIONS

1. Are environmentalists right to be concerned about the environmental impact of SUVs? How do you explain the growing demand for ever larger passenger vehicles?

2. In developing and producing the Excursion, is the Ford Motor Company sacrificing the environment to profits, or is it acting in a socially responsible way by making the Excursion relatively energy efficient for its vehicle class? If you had been on the board of directors, would you have voted for the project? Why/why not? Do Ford's stockholders have a right to insist that it produce the most profitable vehicles it legally can, regardless of their environmental impact?

CASE 12.4
Texaco in the Ecuadorean Amazon
Denis G. Arnold

Ecuador is a small nation on the northwest coast of South America. During its 173-year history, Ecuador has been one of the least politically stable South American nations. In 1830 Ecuador achieved its independence from Spain. Ecuadorean history since that time has been characterized by cycles of republican government and military intervention and rule. The period from 1960 to 1972 was marked by instability and military dominance of political institutions. From 1972 to 1979 Ecuador was governed by military regimes. In 1979 a popularly elected president took office, but the military demanded and was granted important governing powers. The democratic institutional framework of Ecuador remains weak. Decreases in public sector spending, increasing unemployment, and rising inflation have hit the Ecuadorean poor especially hard. World Bank estimates indicate that in 1994 35 percent of the Ecuadorean population lived in poverty, and an additional 17 percent were vulnerable to poverty.

The Ecuadorean Amazon is one of the most biologically diverse forests in the world and is home to an estimated 5 percent of Earth's species. It is home to cicadas, scarlet macaws, squirrel monkeys, freshwater pink dolphins, and thousands of other species. Many of these species have small populations, making them extremely sensitive to disturbance. Indigenous Indian populations have lived in harmony with these species for centuries. They have fished and hunted in and around the rivers and lakes; and they have raised crops of cacao, coffee, fruits, nuts, and tropical woods in *chakras*, models of sustainable agroforestry.

Ten thousand feet beneath the Amazon floor lays one of Ecuador's most important resources: rich deposits of crude oil. Historically, the Ecuadorean government regarded the oil as the best way to keep up with the country's payments on its $12 billion foreign debt obligations. For 20 years American oil companies, lead by Texaco, extracted oil from beneath the Ecuadorean Amazon in partnership with the government of Ecuador. (The United States is the primary importer of Ecuadorean oil.) They constructed 400 drill sites and hundreds of miles of roads and pipelines, including a primary pipeline that extends for 280 miles across the Andes. Large tracts of forest were clear-cut to make way for these facilities. Indian lands, including *chakras*, were taken and bulldozed, often without compensation. In the village of Pacayacu the central square is occupied by a drilling platform.

Officials estimate that the primary pipeline alone has spilled more than 16.8 million gallons of oil into the Amazon over an 18-year period. Spills from secondary pipelines have never been estimated or recorded; however, smaller tertiary pipelines dump 10,000 gallons of petroleum per week into the Amazon, and production pits dump approximately 4.3 million gallons of toxic production wastes and treatment chemicals into the forest's rivers, streams, and groundwater each day. (By comparison, the

This case was prepared by Denis G. Arnold and is based on James Brooke, "New Effort Would Test Possible Coexistence of Oil and Rain Forest," *The New York Times*, February 26, 1991; Dennis M. Hanratty, Ed., *Ecuador: A Country Study*, 3rd ed. (Washington D.C.: Library of Congress, 1991); Anita Isaacs, *Military Rule and Transition in Ecuador, 1972–92* (Pittsburgh: University of Pittsburgh Press, 1993); *Ecuador Poverty Report* (Washington D.C.: The World Bank, 1996); Joe Kane, *Savages* (New York: Vintage Books, 1996); Eyal Press, "Texaco on Trial," *The Nation*, May 31, 1999; and "Texaco and Ecuador," *Texaco: Health, Safety & the Environment*, 27 September 1999, www.texaco.com/she/index.html (16 December, 1999); and *Aguinda v. Texaco, Inc.*, 142 F. Supp. 2d 534 (S.D.N.Y. 2001).

Exxon Valdez spilled 10.8 million gallons of oil into Alaska's Prince William Sound.) Significant portions of these spills have been carried downriver into neighboring Peru.

Critics charge that Texaco ignored prevailing oil industry standards that call for the re-injection of waste deep into the ground. Rivers and lakes were contaminated by oil and petroleum; heavy metals such as arsenic, cadmium, cyanide, lead, and mercury; poisonous industrial solvents; and lethal concentrations of chloride salt, and other highly toxic chemicals. The only treatment these chemicals received occurred when the oil company burned waste pits to reduce petroleum content. Villagers report that the chemicals return as black rain, polluting what little fresh water remains. What is not burned off seeps through the unlined walls of the pits into the groundwater. Cattle are found with their stomachs rotted out, crops are destroyed, animals are gone from the forest, and fish disappear from the lakes and rivers. Health officials and community leaders report adults and children with deformities, skin rashes, abscesses, headaches, dysentery, infections, respiratory ailments, and disproportionately high rates of cancer. In 1972 Texaco signed a contract requiring it to turn over all of its operations to Ecuador's national oil company, Petroecuador, by 1992. Petroecuador inherited antiquated equipment, rusting pipelines, and uncounted toxic waste sites. Independent estimates place the cost of cleaning up the production pits alone at 600 million dollars. From 1995 to 1998 Texaco spent 40 million dollars on cleanup operations in Ecuador. In exchange for these efforts the government of Ecuador relinquished future claims against the company.

Numerous international accords—including the 1972 Stockholm Declaration on the Human Environment signed by over 100 countries, including the United States and Ecuador—identify the right to a clean and healthy environment as a fundamental human right and prohibit both state and private actors from endangering the needs of present and future generations. Ecuadorean and Peruvian plaintiffs, including several indigenous tribes, have filed billion-dollar class-action lawsuits against Texaco in U.S. courts under the Alien Tort Claims Act (ACTA). Enacted in 1789, the law was designed to provide noncitizens access to U.S. courts in cases involving a breach of international law, including accords. Texaco maintains that the case should be tried in Ecuador. However, Ecuador's judicial system does not recognize the concept of a class-action suit and has no history of environmental litigation. Furthermore, Ecuador's judicial system is notoriously corrupt (a poll by George Washington University found that only 16 percent of Ecuadoreans have confidence in their judicial system) and lacks the infrastructure necessary to handle the case (e.g., the city in which the case would be tried lacks a courthouse). Texaco defended its actions by arguing that it is in full compliance with Ecuadorean law and that it had full approval of the Ecuadorean government.

In May 2001 U.S. District Judge Jed Rakoff rejected the applicability of the ACTA and dismissed the case on grounds of forum non conveniens. Judge Rakoff argued that since "no act taken by Texaco in the United States bore materially on the pollution-creating activities," the case should be tried in Ecuador and Peru. In October 2001 Texaco completed a merger with Chevron Corporation. Chevron and Texaco are now known as Chevron Texaco Corporation. In August 2002 the U.S. Court of Appeals for the Second Circuit upheld Judge Rakoff's decision.

QUESTIONS

1. Given the fact that Texaco operated in partnership with the Ecuadorean government, is Texaco's activity in the Amazon morally justifiable? Explain.

2. Does Texaco (now Chevron Texaco) have a moral obligation to provide additional funds and technical expertise to clean up areas of the Amazon it is responsible for polluting? Does it have a moral obligation to provide medical care for the residents of the Amazon region who are suffering from the effects of the pollution? Explain.

CASE 12.5

The Broken "Buy-One, Give-One" Model: 3 Ways To Save Toms Shoes

Cheryl Davenport

Toms has built a popular brand around the buy-one, give-one model. But two critical flaws in that model threaten to undo its social impact and business successes.

Today, April 10, 2012, thousands of people will go barefoot around the world for the second annual "One Day Without Shoes." It's an event organized by Toms Shoes—the company that built a brand around the buy-one, give-one charity model—to raise awareness about the impact a pair of shoes can have on a child's life.

But the day will also shine a light on the Toms model, which is facing two existential flaws that threaten to undo the company's social impact and business success.

The Toms buy-one-give-one model does not actually solve a social problem.

First, the Toms buy-one, give-one model does not actually solve a social problem. Rather, the charitable act of donating a free pair of shoes serves as little more than a short-term fix in a system in need of long-term, multifaceted economic development, health, sanitation, and education solutions.

"What's wrong with giving away shoes?" you might be thinking. "At least they're doing something." The problem, we've learned, is when that "something" can do more harm than good. As *Time* recently noted, an increasing number of foreign aid practitioners and agencies are recognizing that charitable gifts from abroad can distort developing markets and undermine local businesses by creating an entirely unsustainable aid-based economy. By undercutting local prices, Western donations often hurt the farmers, workers, traders, and sellers whose success is critical to lifting entire communities out of poverty. That means every free shoe

donated actually works against the long-term development goals of the communities we are trying to help.

The fact is, Toms isn't designed to build the economies of developing countries. It's designed to make Western consumers feel good. We can see that in the company's origin story, as the Toms website proudly tells it, in which founder Blake Mycoskie saw the problems barefoot children in Argentina faced and decided to start Toms. Mr. Mycoskie didn't ask villagers what they needed most or talk to experts about how to lift villages out of long-term poverty. Instead, he built a company that felt good and that was good enough for him and Toms's nascent consumers.

Toms isn't designed to build the economies of developing countries. It's designed to make Western consumers feel good.

And that brings me to the second flaw. From a business perspective, Toms is at risk. Our research with leading consumer-facing companies has shown that there is a finite and unpredictable market for the feel-good value proposition—consumers are fickle when it comes to committing to brands based on nonfunctional attributes. Toms's core value to its customers is being replicated by an increasing number of companies who can promise the exact same return: feeling good about your purchase. Without a stronger, more differentiated and less replicable product offering, Toms will likely fall out of fashion in the coming years.

And therein lies the real peril. Those "helped" by Toms are, in the long-term, no more able to afford shoes or address the real social, economic, and health issues that they face than they were before. Once their free shoes wear out in a couple years, the children Toms "helped" will be just as susceptible to

From *Fast Company*, December 2012.

the health and economic perils associated with bare feet as they were before.

Toms can do more and do better. In the run-up to "One Day Without Shoes," I challenge the company and its consumers to do three things:

1. *Better understand the problem*: The Toms website points out that those without shoes are at risk of contracting hook worms and suffering from other debilitating injuries and diseases. But a new pair of shoes alone will not eradicate hookworm or protect thousands living in landfills from harm. Toms needs to find out what will. There are surely more cost-effective, enduring solutions that will help those in need not only cover their feet, but also be able to afford shoes and other necessities that improve quality of life in the long term.

2. *Create a solution, not a band-aid*: Toms has donated more than 1 million shoes to date. But to what end? Rather than asking "How many shoes can we give away?" Toms should be trying to figure out "How many lives can we change?" One statistic cited by the company is that there are 30,000 people living in one landfill in the Philippines. For these individuals and families, a free pair of, cloth shoes is nice, but bare feet may be the least of many challenges they face on a day-to-day basis, none of which will be resolved by a pair of Toms. It's the difference between a quick-fix and a cure.

3. *Innovate business models, not marketing campaigns*: The buy-one, give-one model is clever, simple, and consumer-friendly. But the real impact of business often comes behind the scenes and without the sheen of a marketing campaign. Toms should ask: How can we use the whole of our business—including our jobs, our supply chain, our market penetration—to make a difference? I think Oliberté Shoes is really on to something with their approach, in which they manufacture shoes in developing countries and provide an economic boost where it's needed most.

I imagine a Toms that creates jobs and builds economies by sourcing shoes from developing countries, small businesses, and burgeoning entrepreneurs. I imagine a Toms that eradicates hookworms within an entire country by giving not only the gift of shoes, but also the lasting impact of infrastructure and health facilities.

The world doesn't need another advocacy day. We don't need a day without shoes. We need practical, long-term solutions—the kind that only business can engineer. The good people at Toms should keep their shoes on. They'll need them if they're going to find solutions to these intractable problems.

QUESTIONS

1. According to the author, what is wrong with the "buy-one, give-one" model?

2. According to the author, what is a better alternative?

3. Do you agree with the author? Why or why not?

CASE 12.6
Protect Us from Fracking
Morgan Carroll and Rhonda Fields

Colorado's oil and gas resources provoke sharply contrasting feelings. A bonanza for an energy company can be a deep source of worry if you live near a hotbed of drilling and fracking. As companies are encouraged by their return on investment, residents wonder how close to their own home, or to their children's school, the next drilling rig will mar the landscape.

Developers and residents differ sharply on how close is too close. When the state attempted to revise drilling rules in 2008, a lack of consensus forced a delay in setting a new minimum distance between homes and drilling. After four years of inaction, state regulators are taking up the issue again because concerned local governments have moved to issue rules buffering homes from drilling and fracking. The industry no doubt expects a new state-mandated buffer will put the matter to rest.

Unfortunately, the state's proposal is unlikely to reassure nervous homeowners. The state proposal sticks with the status quo: a minimum distance of 350 feet between drilling rigs and homes.

Enshrining the status quo makes no sense. Drilling and fracking are major industrial operations. Chemicals are pumped into the ground; and toxic liquids, laden with heavy metals and cancer-causing compounds, are extracted from deep within the earth. Noxious gases are emitted. Scores of giant trucks move on and off fracking sites. Diesel generators run day and night to power the operations. Conducting industrial activity 350 feet from homes—essentially just down the block and amid parks and schools—threatens health, welfare, and property values.

We need to consider, above all, the health of Colorado residents. Adequate protection for them demands that we adhere to three principles:

- We need to maximize the buffer between industrial sites and homes based on public health

and safety. New technologies enable developers to extract deposits as far as 9000 feet from the drilling site.
- We need to minimize toxic emissions. It makes no sense to allow large quantities of carcinogenic compounds to be released near parks, homes, and schools.
- We need to ensure that affected citizens have a voice in decisions about where to locate and how to manage drilling and fracking. No one who lives near a proposed drilling site should be deprived of a say in its final location.

The state, in fact, acknowledges that potential harms of drilling and fracking extend well beyond the 350-foot limit. The state's proposal recognizes the 1000-foot range as a zone of concern, an area in which companies must work harder to mitigate the impacts of drilling and fracking. We agree. A distance of at least 1000 feet, not 350 feet, is the right starting point.

But we feel that the state must do more to aid and protect citizens within the 1000-foot zone and recognize that many citizens and local governments will want protective measures to stretch further than 1000 feet.

The state should prohibit developers from drilling within this area of concern unless they secure the consent of all affected landowners or work with them to develop a specific local drilling plan.

For proposed drilling sites close to homes, the state should do all it can to bring developers, residents, local government, and other interested parties together to work out solutions that everyone can support. A localized planning process, overseen by the state, stands the best chance of taking into account the range of interests and technical variables that are specific to any given site.

Oil and gas development will be with us for the long haul, but the concerns of Colorado homeowners must not be subordinated to profit over people. As Colorado's population grows and more residents find themselves in the shadow of drilling rigs, it's vital that the state take steps now to create the local planning processes that will reassure communities and not harm our precious quality of life.

QUESTIONS

1. How can legislators establish a safe minimum distance between homes and drilling sites?

2. Should home owners near potential drilling and fracking sites be allowed to decide how close the drilling is to the home? Why?

CHAPTER QUESTIONS

1. What duties do we have to the environment? To future generations? How do we draw the line between our pressing needs and the needs of those who will come after us? What about our needs versus the needs of nonhuman animals? Or should only humans count?

2. Is it hip to be green? Or is it only hip to say you're green while you go on consuming more or less like everyone else? What sacrifices are you willing to make for the environment? And how can we change society's behavior? Who should decide how society ought to behave, vis-à-vis the environment?

13

When the Buck Stops Here

Leadership

Introduction

Imagine that you've finally made it to the top. As CEO, you are now in a position of leadership. Leadership is a funny thing. Some people lead without holding positions of power, and some people hold positions of power but do not really lead. You are probably familiar with the "airport" how-to books on leadership and those numerous biographies and autobiographical books about famous businesspeople. They often tend to make leadership sound easy, a matter of personality or a matter of mastering a few simple techniques. But leadership is about much more than style, expertise, and technique. Leadership is ethically challenging. It requires an enormous amount of self-knowledge and self-control. Power and success can do strange things to people. They can give you a sense of entitlement or make you feel that you no longer have to play by the same rules as others. Many people dream of leading, but the truth is that not everyone is up to the job. No doubt you have noticed how some people, when given authority over others, immediately turn into petty dictators: a teacher's aide when you were in elementary school, one of your playmates who was made captain of your team or leader of your group, a graduate teaching assistant running his or her first class. It is no different in business except that the money tends to be much better. While business leadership brings with it power, money, perks, and prestige, it also brings with it the dangers of overreaching and the burdens of responsibility for the welfare of your company and all its stakeholders. Those who love the perks and ignore or neglect the burdens of caring for the company often fall hard, and the company frequently suffers, sometimes fatally (and too often the abusers float away on "golden parachutes," an enduring blot on the integrity of business and the merits of the market). Attentive leadership is time consuming and stressful. It can take its toll on you and your loved ones. It is not just a chance to enjoy power and its perks.

Corporate leaders do matter. One need only look at business scandals to see how much damage a few executives can do to a company and the people in it. By contrast, a good leader can turn around a failing organization by formulating a compelling vision for the organization. A vision is different from a goal. A company may have the goal of increasing profits by 10 percent in the next year, but the vision is about producing a more environmentally friendly and affordable product, about becoming the powerhouse leader in the industry, about reinventing the way people live or do business or get around town. Behind every vision is some notion of a greater good. It is this moral component that often motivates people in organizations. As a leader, you will not only run a company. You will model the ethical values of the company in your own behavior and demonstrate them in the people with whom you choose to surround yourself. As the leader, you will set the *ethos*, the lifestyle and the customs, as well as the ethics of the company, and set an example for the lives of your employees and perhaps even your customers. It will not be enough for you to be ethical. A corporate leader is responsible for making the company and the people in it flourish and live well. You will have to make sure that everyone who works for you understands the meaning and the moral parameters of their jobs. Managing the moral environment is one of the greatest challenges of leadership in large organizations. While you cannot micromanage or know everything, you have a moral obligation as the leader to have a good sense of what is going on. If the company gets in trouble, you are accountable, even if you did not know about the problem. It is therefore imperative that you keep informed or have a way of sniffing out trouble before it hits the market or the newspapers. We don't mean to take the joy out of your promotion, but people sometimes forget that with power and privilege comes moral responsibility. That is why it is important that you think seriously about the moral challenges of leadership before you get the job that you will probably have worked so hard all those years to get. Until you do actually make it to the top, remember that people at all levels of an organization sometimes exercise leadership, especially when it comes to questions of right and wrong. You will have many years to practice your own leadership and observe firsthand the strengths and weaknesses of how others lead, so practice, watch, and learn.

The first two articles in this chapter are about the relationship between ethics and effectiveness. We all know that good leaders get the job done. Joanne Ciulla argues that we have to ask for more from our leaders—they have to do the right thing, the right way, with the right intentions. Often leaders are ethical in some areas, but not in others. In a different way, Machiavelli was concerned with the same issues, only he is willing to sacrifice the fine points of ethics to get the job done. We then move on to Al Gini's article, which explores the value-laden relationship between leaders and followers. He makes clear the reasons why leadership is always about followership too. Joanne Ciulla's article examines how the virtues and values of a leader influence their organization. She also offers an overview of the role that values play in various theories of leadership. In the article "The Bathsheba Syndrome," the authors use the biblical story about David and Bathsheba to show how success can make leaders less ethical and less effective on the job. The last article on servant leadership offers a moral perspective on leadership that might very well keep leaders from falling prey to the problems that often accompany power and success.

The first two cases in this chapter are about the relationship between leaders and followers. We begin with George Orwell's famous short story about an elephant. For our purposes, the story is about how large, noisy crowds can make leaders do things that they do not want to do. When you read it, think about what personal resources leaders need to have to resist outside pressures to do things that they do not think are right. In the case of Martha Stewart, we see a leader who breaks the law, goes to jail, and manages to regain public support for herself and her business. We then go on to consider the story of Roy Vagelos, the CEO of Merck who decided to produce and give away a drug that cured river blindness. Vagelos' story offers a compelling example of how a CEO can set a moral example that other businesses in his industry begin to copy. Our last case raises a traditional question in business ethics about the drive to succeed. It is about Raj Rajaratnam, a rags-to-riches businessman who built a large and successful hedge fund and got caught doing insider trading. Is he a bad and greedy person, or did he lose sight of what was important in life?

| Joanne B. Ciulla | # What Is Good Leadership? |

The moral triumphs and failures of leaders carry a greater weight and volume than those of nonleaders. In leadership we see morality and immorality magnified, which is why ethics is fundamental to our understanding of leadership. Ethics is about right and wrong and good and evil. It's about what we should do and what we should be like as human beings, members of a group or society, and in the different roles that we play in life. Leadership entails a particular kind of role and moral relationship between people. By understanding the ethics of leadership we gain a better understanding of what constitutes good leadership.

The point of studying leadership is to answer the question, What is good leadership? The point of teaching it is to develop good leaders. The use of the word *good* here has two senses: morally good and technically good (or effective). The problem with this notion of good leadership is that it is sometimes difficult to find both qualities in the same person. Some people are ethical, but not very effective; others are effective, but not very ethical. History only makes things more difficult. Historians don't write about the leader who was ethical but didn't do anything of significance. They rarely write about a general who was a very moral person but never won a battle. Most historians write about leaders who

were winners or who changed history, for better or for worse. While leaders usually bring about change or are successful at doing something, the ethical questions waiting in the wings are: What were the leader's intentions? How did the leader go about bringing change? And was the change itself good? Leadership educators and educators in professional schools face the challenge of seamlessly teaching students to do things right and do the right thing.

OUR FASCINATION WITH PIZZAZZ

Leadership scholars have spilled a lot of ink about the effectiveness of charismatic leaders. But as Rakesh Khurana argues in his book *Searching for a Corporate Savior: The Irrational Quest for Charismatic CEOs*, the mythical belief in the powers of charismatic leaders is overestimated when it comes to their actual effect on corporate performance.[1] Our fascination with charismatic leaders blurs the line between leaders and celebrities. As we have seen in politics, it is almost impossible for a highly competent but dry and boring person to be elected. It's certainly more fun to work with charismatic leaders, and they are more interesting to study,

Joanne B. Ciulla. "What Is Good Leadership?" Center for Public Leadership Working Papers, John F. Kennedy School of Government, Harvard University. Spring, 2004, pp. 116–122. (Author holds copyright.)

but it's not clear that they are always more effective than leaders with less pizzazz.

American writers used to pay more attention to the moral virtues of leaders than to their personality traits. Benjamin Franklin argued that good character was necessary for success. In his autobiography he listed eleven virtues needed for success in business and in life: temperance, silence, order, resolution, sincerity, justice, moderation, cleanliness, tranquility, chastity, and humility.[2] This list does not describe the ideal political candidate or the business leaders who frequently grace the cover of *Fortune* magazine.

In the nineteenth century, William Makepeace Thayer specialized in biographies of business and political leaders. His books focused on how the moral values that leaders formed early in life contributed to their success. Thayer summed up the moral path to success this way: "Man deviseth his own way, but the Lord directeth his steps."[3] Other eighteenth- and nineteenth-century writers preached that strong moral character was the key to leadership and wealth. By the early twentieth century the emphasis on moral character shifted to an emphasis on personality. In Dale Carnegie's 1936 classic *How to Win Friends and Influence People*, personality, not morality, was the key to success in business.[4] Until recently, this was true in the leadership research as well. Scholars were more interested in studying the personality traits of leaders than their ethics.

IT'S GOOD TO BE KING!

When you really think about it, the issue is not that leaders should be held to a *higher* moral standard, but that they should be held to the *same* standards as the rest of us. What we want and hope for are leaders who have a higher rate of success at living up to those standards than the average person. History is littered with leaders who didn't think they were subject to the same rules and standards of honesty, propriety, etc., as the rest of society. Leaders sometimes come to think that they are exceptions to the rules. It's easy to see why, given the perks and privileges that we give to leaders, whether in business,

politics, or government. For example, Tyco's former CEO L. Dennis Kozlowski didn't seem to think that he should have to pay $1 million in New York State taxes on $13 million worth of art that he bought for his Fifth Avenue apartment. He simply arranged to have empty boxes and the invoices for the artwork sent to the Tyco headquarters in Exter, New Hampshire.[5] Commentators have described Kozlowski's behavior in terms of an overblown sense of entitlement or plain and simple greed. But he may have decided that he no longer had to live by the rules.

THE CHALLENGE OF CONSISTENCY

There are some areas, such as moral consistency, where leaders have to be more meticulous than ordinary people—first, because a leader's moral inconsistencies are public and more noticeable than other people's, and second, because a leader's credibility rests on some level of consistency. When leaders' actions do not match their espoused values, they lose the trust they need to be effective with various stakeholders.

Moral consistency is so important to a leader that moral *inconsistency* is the weapon of choice for character assassination. Consider the case of Tim Eyman, leader of the citizen group Permanent Offence. This group has sponsored a number of successful citizen ballot initiatives aimed at holding politicians accountable for how they spent taxpayers' dollars. In February 2002, the *Seattle Post-Intelligencer* revealed that Eyman had paid himself $45,000 of the money raised for one of his ballot initiatives. While this is not illegal, the politicians whom Eyman had often called "corrupt" seized on the issue to damage his credibility and the credibility of the causes that his organization supported. Eyman must have realized how hypocritical he looked because when confronted with the allocations, he denied that he had paid himself the money. He later confessed, saying, "I was in lie mode."[6] We generally think of hypocrites as people who express strong moral values that they do not hold and then act against them. But hypocrites are not always liars. Some really want to live up to the values they talk about, but fail to do so, either intentionally or unintentionally. This may have been Eyman's problem. Sometimes people find it difficult to live up to their own values.

MACHIAVELLIANISM AND ROBINHOODISM

We characterize effective leaders largely in terms of their ability to bring about change, for better or worse. This creates a divide between the ethics of a leader and the ethics of what the leader does. Machiavelli was disgusted by Cesare Borgia the man, but impressed by Borgia as the resolute, ferocious, and cunning prince. Borgia got the job done, but the way he did it was morally repugnant.[7] This is the classic problem of the ends justifying immoral means. Leaders don't have to be evil, greedy, or power hungry to have this moral problem. It even rears its head in charitable organizations. The fact that Robin Hood stole from the rich to give to the poor doesn't get him off the moral hook. Stealing for a good cause looks better than stealing for a bad one, but stealing is still stealing. Robinhoodism is simply Machiavellianism for nonprofits.

There are cases where leaders use appropriate means to serve the needs of some of their constituents effectively, but their beliefs are morally suspect in other areas. Trent Lott's departure as Senate majority leader offers a compelling example of this. Lott was forced to step down from his position because of insensitive racial comments that he made during a speech at the late Senator Strom Thurmond's birthday party. After the incident, some of his African American constituents were interviewed on the news. Several of them said that they would vote for Lott again, regardless of his racist beliefs, because Lott had used his power and influence in Washington to bring jobs and money to the state. In politics, the old saying "He may be a son-of-a-bitch, but he's *our* son of a bitch," captures the trade-off between ethics and effectiveness. In other words, as long as Lott accomplishes the part of the job we're interested in, we don't care about his ethics in other areas. This morally myopic view of a leader explains why people sometimes get the leaders they

deserve when their "son-of-a-bitch" turns out to be a *real* son-of-a-bitch.

THE INTERSECTION OF ETHICS AND EFFECTIVENESS

The distinction between ethics and effectiveness is not always a crisp one. In certain cases being ethical *is* being effective and sometimes being effective *is* being ethical. Sometimes simply being regarded as ethical and trustworthy makes a leader effective, and at other times simply being effective makes a leader ethical. Given the limited power and resources of the secretary-general of the United Nations, it would be very difficult for someone in this position to be effective on the job if he or she did not behave ethically. In some jobs, personal integrity is a leader's sole or primary currency of power and influence. Business leaders have other sources of power that allow them to be effective, but in some situations acting ethically boosts their effectiveness. In the famous Tylenol case, manufacturer Johnson and Johnson actually increased sales of Tylenol by pulling the product off the shelves after some Tylenol had been poisoned. The leaders at Johnson and Johnson were effective at boosting sales of Tylenol *because* of the ethical way that they handled the problem.

In other cases, the sheer competence of a leader has a moral effect. There were many examples of heroism in the aftermath of the terrorist attack on the World Trade Center. The most inspiring and frequently cited were the altruistic acts of rescue workers. Yet consider the case of Alan S. Weil, whose law firm, Sidley, Austin, Brown, & Wood, occupied five floors of the World Trade Center. Immediately after watching the towers fall to the ground and checking to see whether his employees got out safely, Weil got on the phone and within three hours had rented four floors of another building for his employees. By the end of the day he had arranged for an immediate delivery of eight hundred desks and three hundred computers. The next day the firm was open for business with a desk for almost every employee who wanted to work.[8] We don't know whether Mr. Weil's motives were altruistic or avaricious. Mr. Weil may have worked quickly to keep his law firm going because he didn't want to lose a day of billing, but in doing so he also filled the firm's obligations to various stakeholders. We may not like his personal reasons for acting, but in this scenario, the various stakeholders might not care because they benefited.

UNETHICAL OR STUPID?

So what can we say about leaders who do ethical things but for selfish or unethical reasons? In modernity we often separate the inner person from the outer person. John Stuart Mill saw this split between an individual's ethics and the ethics of his or her actions clearly. He said the intentions or reasons for an act tell us something about the morality of the person, but the ends of an act tell us about the morality of the action.[9] This solution doesn't really solve the ethics-and-effectiveness problem. It simply reinforces the split between the personal morality of a leader and what he or she does as a leader. If the various stakeholders knew that Weil had selfish intentions, they would, as Mill said, think less of him but not less of his actions. This is sometimes the case in business. When a business runs a campaign to raise money for the homeless, it may be doing so to sell more of its products or improve its public image. Yet it would be harsh to say that the business shouldn't hold the charity drive and raise needed funds for the homeless. Sometimes it is unethical (and just mean spirited) to demand perfect moral intentions. Nonetheless, personally unethical leaders who do good things for their constituents are still problematic. Even though they might provide for the greatest good, once their unethical intentions are public, people can never really trust them, even if they benefit.

In some situations it is difficult to tell whether leaders are unethical or stupid. They can be incompetent in terms of their knowledge or skill or incompetent in terms of their ability to identify, solve, or prioritize moral problems. There are times when leaders get their facts wrong or think that they are acting ethically when, in fact, they are not. For example, in 2000, President Thabo Mbeki of South Africa issued a statement saying that it was not clear that HIV caused AIDS. He believed the pharmaceutical industry was just trying to scare people so that it could increase its profits.[10] Coming from the leader of a country where about one in five people tests positive for HIV, this was a shocking statement. His stance outraged public health experts and other citizens. Mbeki understood the scientific literature but chose to put political and philosophical reasons ahead of scientific knowledge. (He has since backed away from this position.) When leaders do things like this, we want to know whether they are unethical or misinformed. Mbeki was not misinformed. He knew the AIDS literature but chose to focus on work by researchers who held this minority opinion. His actions appeared unethical, but he may have thought he was taking an ethical stand; however, it was the wrong ethical stand on the wrong ethical issue. His comments demonstrated a misplaced sense of moral priorities. Political concerns about big business and the way the world sees South Africa may have led him to recklessly disregard his more pressing obligations to stop the AIDS epidemic.

In other situations leaders act with moral intentions, but because they are incompetent, the way they solve a problem creates an unethical outcome. For instance, consider the unfortunate case of the Swiss charity Christian Solidarity International. Its goal was to free an estimated 200,000 Dinka children who were enslaved in Sudan. The charity paid between $35 and $75 a head to free the enslaved children. The unintended consequence of their actions was that by creating a market for slavery, they actually encouraged it. The price of slaves and the demand for them went up. Also, some cunning Sudanese found that it paid to pretend that they were slaves; they could make money by being liberated again and again."[11] This deception made it difficult for the charity to distinguish those who really needed help from those who were faking it. Here the charity's intent and the means it used to achieve its goals were not unethical in relation to alleviating suffering in the short run; however, in the long run, the charity inadvertently created more suffering.

BLINDING MORALITY

We want leaders who possess strong moral convictions, but there are times when leaders' moral convictions are too strong and they undercut both their ethics and their effectiveness. Leaders with overzealous moral convictions can be far more dangerous than amoral or immoral leaders. Consider the recent response of the Catholic Church hierarchy to cases of sexual abuse. Many Church leaders still held the medieval view that they could play by different rules than the rest of society, in part because they were the "good guys." The sexual abuse of children is one of the most heinous crimes in our society; however, some church leaders treated it differently because it involved people who "do God's work." Overly moralistic leaders sometimes confuse working for God with being God, usually with disastrous results.

Self-righteousness can also blind leaders to the more mundane things that they need to do in order to be effective. They become so impassioned with the moral rightness of their cause that they forget what they have learned in other areas of life or fail to get the expertise they need to do their job. This is as true today as it was in the past. The story of Magellan, the first navigator to circumvent the globe, is one such case. Magellan led his three ships down the South American coast and on a 12,600-mile journey across the Pacific Ocean. When he arrived in the Philippines, he took up the Spanish cause of spreading Christianity. He began baptizing native leaders and gaining their allegiance to Spain. Magellan's religious fervor became so great that he started to think that he could perform miracles. He then took up the cause of a baptized chief in an unnecessary battle against an unbaptized chief on the island of Mactan. Magellan's seasoned marines would not join him in the battle, so he organized a ragtag group of cooks and other apprentices to fight. The battle was a disaster. Before attacking the island, Magellan failed to get information on the tides. Hence, one of the greatest navigators in the world met his demise waist deep in water, weighed down by heavy armor and unprotected by his ships, which were helplessly anchored outside the reef, too far away to provide him with cover.[12] All this because he thought mundane details and planning were not necessary when you had God on your side.

The story of Magellan shows us how even brilliant leaders can believe so much in the moral rightness

of their goals that they don't listen to others or take mundane precautions to achieve their goals. This case is a dramatic way to think about the mistakes that nonprofit leaders sometimes make, such as having earnest but unqualified volunteers keep the books or assuming that when providing meals for the homeless, it is not necessary to follow standard health procedures in the kitchen. Leaders have a moral obligation to consult with experts, get their facts straight, and take care in planning. This is where ethics and effectiveness converge. The line between being incompetent and unethical is often very thin.

Professional schools are good at teaching students what they know, but they are not as good at teaching them what they don't know. Leadership requires a mixture of confidence and humility. It is about how well leaders understand the limitations of their knowledge and personal perspective. Good leadership calls for people who are confident enough to ask for help, admit they are wrong, and invite debate and discussion. Good leadership also requires humility. Leaders are imperfect human beings who are put in jobs where the moral margin of error is much smaller because the effect of their actions on others is greater. That is why good leaders need knowledge, self-knowledge, ethics, confidence, humility, and a lot of help from people who will tell them the truth.

NOTES

1. Khurana, Rahesh. (2002). *Searching for the Corporate Savior/The Irrational Quest for Charismatic CEOs*. Princeton: Princeton University Press.

2. Franklin, Benjamin (1964). *The Autobiography of Benjamin Franklin*, ed. Leonard W. Larabee, et al. New Haven: Yale University Press.

3. Thayer, quoted in Huber, R. M. (1971). *The American Idea of Success*. New York: McGraw-Hill, p. 53.

4. Carnegie, Dale. (1981). *How to Win Friends and Influence People*. New York: Pocket Books.

5. Maremont, M., & Markon, J. "Ex-Tyco Chief Evaded $1 Million in Taxes on Art, Indictment Says," *Wall Street Journal*, June 5, 2002. Al.

6. "A Watchdog Who Got Watched," *The Economist*, February 9, 2002, p. 29.

7. Prezzolini Giuseppe. (1928). Ralph Roeder (trans.) *Nicolo Machiavelli, the Florentine*. New York: Brentanos.

8. Schwartz, J. "Up from the Ashes, One Firm Rebuilds," *New York Times*, September 16, 2001: Section 3, p. 1.

9. Mill, John Stuart (1987). "What Utilitarianism Is." Alan Ryan (ed.), *Utilitarianism and Other Essays*. New York: Penguin Books, pp. 276–297.

10. Garrett, L. "Added Foe in AIDS War. Skeptics," Newsday, March 29, 2000: News Section, A6.

11. "A Funny Way to End the Slave trade; Slavery in Sudan," *The Economist*, February 9, 2002, p. 42.

12. Manchester, W. (1993). *A World Lit Only by Fire*. Boston: Little, Brown.

QUESTIONS

1. How is ethical leadership related to effective leadership in business?

2. Is it unethical for an incompetent person to hold a leadership position?

3. Is there a preference in business for leaders who are more effective than ethical?

Niccolo Machiavelli

Is It Better to Be Loved than Feared?

Niccolo Machiavelli was the most influential political philosopher of the Italian Renaissance.

And here comes in the question whether it is better to be loved rather than feared, or feared rather than loved. It might perhaps be answered that we should wish to be both; but since love and fear can hardly exist together, if we must choose between them, it is far safer to be feared than loved. For of men it may generally be affirmed that they are thankless, fickle, false, studious to avoid danger, greedy of gain, devoted to you while you are able to confer benefits upon them, and ready, as I said before, while danger is distant, to shed their blood, and sacrifice their property, their lives, and their children for you; but in the hour of need they turn against you. The Prince, therefore, who without otherwise securing himself builds wholly on their professions is undone. For the friendships which we buy with a price, and do not gain by greatness and nobility of character, though they be fairly earned are not made good, but fail us when we have occasion to use them.

Moreover, men are less careful how they offend him who makes himself loved than him who makes himself feared. For love is held by the tie of obligation, which, because men are a sorry breed, is broken on every whisper of private interest; but fear is bound by the apprehension of punishment which never relaxes.

Nevertheless a Prince should inspire fear in such a fashion that if he do not win love he may escape hate. For a man may very well be feared and yet not hated, and this will be the case so long as he does not meddle with the property or with the women of his citizens and subjects. And if constrained to put any to death, he should do so only when there is manifest cause or reasonable justification. But, above all, he must abstain from the property of others. For men will sooner forget the death of their father than the loss of their patrimony. Moreover, pretexts for confiscation are never to seek, and he who has once begun to live by rapine always finds reasons for taking what is not his; whereas reasons for shedding blood are fewer.

But when a Prince is with his army, and has many soldiers under his command, he must needs disregard

Niccolo Machiavelli, *The Prince*, translated by Hill Thompson (The Limited Editions Club, 1954), pp. 123–124 and 127–129.

the reproach of cruelty, for without such a reputation in its Captain, no army can be held together or kept under any kind of control. Among other things remarkable in Hannibal this has been noted, that having a very great army, made up of men of many different nations and brought to fight in a foreign country, no dissension ever arose among the soldiers themselves, nor any mutiny against their leader, either in his good or in his evil fortunes. This we can only ascribe to the transcendent cruelty, which, joined with numberless great qualities, rendered him at once venerable and terrible in the eyes of his soldiers; for without this reputation for cruelty these other virtues would not have produced the like results.

Unreflecting writers, indeed, while they praise his achievements, have condemned the chief cause of them; but that his other merits would not by themselves have been so efficacious we may see from the case of Scipio, one of the greatest Captains, not of his own time only but of all times of which we have record, whose armies rose against him in Spain from no other cause than his too great leniency in allowing them a freedom inconsistent with military strictness. With which weakness Fabius Maximus taxed him in the Senate House, calling him the corrupter of the Roman soldiery. Again, when the Locrians were shamefully outraged by one of his lieutenants, he neither avenged them, nor punished the insolence of his officer, and this from the natural easiness of his disposition. So that it was said in the Senate by one who sought to excuse him, that there were many who knew better how to refrain from doing wrong themselves than how to correct the wrong-doing of others. This temper, however, must in time have marred the name and fame even of Scipio, had he continued in it, and retained his command. But living as he did under the control of the Senate, this hurtful quality was not merely disguised, but came to be regarded as a glory.

Returning to the question of being loved or feared, I sum up by saying, that since his being loved depends upon his subjects, while his being feared depends upon himself, a wise Prince should build on what is his own, and not on what rests with others. Only, as I have said, he must do his utmost to escape hatred.

Be it known, then, that there are two ways of contending, one in accordance with the laws, the other by force; the first of which is proper to men, the second to beasts. But since the first method is often ineffectual, it becomes necessary to resort to the second. A Prince should, therefore, understand how to use well both the man and the beast. And this lesson has been covertly taught by the ancient writers, who relate how Achilles and many others of these old Princes were given over to be brought up and trained by Chiron the Centaur; since the only meaning of their having for instructor one who was half man and half beast is, that it is necessary for a Prince to know how to use both natures, and that the one without the other has no stability.

But since a Prince should know how to use the beast's nature wisely, he ought of beasts to choose both the lion and the fox; for the lion cannot guard himself from the toils, nor the fox from wolves. He must therefore be a fox to discern toils, and a lion to drive off wolves.

To rely wholly on the lion is unwise; and for this reason a prudent Prince neither can nor ought to keep his word when to keep it is hurtful to him and the causes which led him to pledge it are removed. If all men were good, this would not be good advice, but since they are dishonest and do not keep faith with you, you, in return, need not keep faith with them; and no prince was ever at a loss for plausible reasons to cloak a breach of faith. Of this numberless recent instances could be given, and it might be shown how many solemn treaties and engagements have been rendered inoperative and idle through want of faith in Princes, and that he who was best known to play the fox has had the best success. It is necessary, indeed, to put a good colour on this nature, and to be skilful in simulating and dissembling.

But men remain so simple, and governed so absolutely by their present needs, that he who wishes to deceive will never fail in finding willing dupes. One recent example I will not omit. Pope Alexander VI had no care or thought but how to deceive, and always found material to work on. No man ever had a more effective manner of asseverating, or ever made promises with more solemn protestations,

To: You
From: The Philosopher
Subject: "Lao Tzu and *Tao-te-ching*"

Now that you've moved to the corner office, you're going to have to get used to having people dislike you—as a matter of fact, some people will hate you. That's part of the job. People
hate leaders when they behave unethically and sometimes even when they behave ethically.
Leaders have to focus on doing the right thing, not trying to please everyone. That is one
reason why Machiavelli said that it is better to be feared than to be loved, but the ancient
Chinese philosopher Lao Tzu disagreed with him. Lao Tzu believed that leaders should be
loved and that they should respect their followers.

> The best (rulers) are those whose existence is (merely) known by the people.
>   The next best are those who are loved and praised.
>   The next are those who are feared.
>   And the next are those who are despised.
>   It is only when one does not have enough faith in others that others have no faith in him.*

Lao Tzu also realized that when people get power, they act like arrogant jerks. That's why
he thinks that "lovable leaders" are modest. He writes:

> He who stands on tiptoe is not steady.
>   He who strides forward does not go.
>   He who shows himself is not luminous.
>   He who justifies himself is not prominent.
>   He who boasts of himself is not given credit.
>   He who brags does not endure for long.**

*Lao Tzu, "The Lao Tzu (Tao-te-ching)" from Wing-Tist Chan (ed.), *A Source Book in Chinese
Philosophy* (Princeton, N.J.: Princeton University Press, 1963), p. 148.
**Ibid., p. 152.

or observed them less. And yet, because he understood this side of human nature, his frauds always
succeeded.

It is not essential then, that a Prince should have all
the good qualities which I have enumerated above, but
it is most essential that he should seem to have them; I
will even venture to affirm that if he has and invariably
practices them all, they are hurtful, whereas the appearance of having them is useful. Thus, it is well to seem
merciful, faithful, humane, religious, and upright, and
also to be so; but the mind should remain so balanced

that were it needful not to be so, you should be able and
know how to change to the contrary.

QUESTIONS

1. What moral qualities does Machiavelli think a
leader should have?

2. In today's world, is it enough for leaders simply to
appear ethical?

3. In what ways does Machiavelli acknowledge the
importance of ethics in leadership?

Al Gini   # Moral Leadership and Business Ethics

Al Gini is Professor of Business Ethics and Chairman of the Management Department in the Quinlan School of Business at Loyola University Chicago.

LEADERSHIP

Leadership is always about self and others. Like ethics, labor, and business Leadership is a symbiotic, communal relationship. It's about leaders, followers-constituencies, and all stakeholders involved. And, like ethics, labor and business leadership seems to be an intrinsic part of the human experience. Charles DeGaulle once observed that men can no longer survive without direction than they can without eating, drinking, or sleeping. Putting aside the obvious fact that DeGaulle was a proponent of "the great-person theory" of leadership, his point is a basic one. Leadership is a necessary requirement of communal existence. Minimally, it tries to offer perspective, focus, appropriate behavior, guidance, and a plan by which to handle the seemingly random and arbitrary events of life. Depending on the type of leadership/followership involved, it can be achieved by consensus, fiat, or cooperative orchestration. But whatever techniques are employed, leadership is always, at bottom, about stewardship—"a person(s) who manages or directs the affairs of others . . . as the agent or representative of others." To paraphrase the words of St. Augustine, regardless of the outcome, the first and final job of leadership is the attempt to serve the needs and the well-being of the people led.

What is leadership? Although the phenomenon of leadership can and must be distinguishable and definable separately from our understanding of what and who leaders are, I am convinced that leadership can only be known and evaluated in the particular instantiation of a leader doing a job. In other words, even though the terms "leadership" and "leader" are not strictly synonymous, the reality of leadership cannot be separated from the person of the leader and the job of leadership. Given this caveat, and leaning heavily on the research and insights of Joseph C. Rost, we can define leadership as follows: Leadership is a power- and value-laden relationship between leaders and followers/constituents who intend real changes that reflect their mutual purposes and goals. For our purposes, the critical elements of this definition that need to be examined are, in order of importance: followership, values, mutual purposes, and goals.

Followership

As Joseph Rost has pointed out, perhaps the single most important thesis developed in leadership studies in the last twenty years has been the evolution and now almost universal consensus regarding the role of followers in the leadership equation. Pulitzer prize–winning historian Garry Wills argues that we have long had a list of the leader's requisites—determination, focus, a clear goal, a sense of priorities, and so on. But until recently, we overlooked or forgot the first and all-encompassing need. "The leader most needs followers. When those are lacking, the best ideas, the strongest will, the most wonderful smile have no effect." Followers set the terms of acceptance for leadership. Leadership is a "mutually determinative" activity on the part of the leader and the followers. Sometimes it's cooperative, sometimes it's a struggle, and often it's a feud, but it's always collective. Although "the leader is one who mobilizes others toward a goal shared by leaders and followers," leaders are powerless to act without followers. In effect, Wills argues, successful leaders need to understand their followers far more than followers need to understand leaders.

Leadership, like labor and ethics, is always plural; it always occurs in the context of others. E. P. Hollander has argued that even though the leader is the central and often the most vital part of the leadership phenomenon, followers are important and necessary factors in the equation. All leadership is interactive, and all leadership should be collaborative. In fact, except for the negative connotation sometimes associated with the term, perhaps the word "collaborator" is a more precise term than either "follower" or "constituent" to explain the leadership process. But whichever term is used, as James MacGregor Burns wrote, one thing is clear, "leaders and followers are engaged in a common enterprise; they are dependent on each other, their fortunes rise and fall together."

From an ethical perspective, the argument for the stewardship responsibilities of leadership is dependent upon the recognition of the roles and rights of followers. Followership argues against the claim of Louis XIV, "L'état c'est moil" The principle of followership denies the Machiavellian assertions that "politics and ethics don't mix" and that the sole aim of any leader is "the acquisition of personal power." Followership requires that leaders recognize their true role within the commonwealth. The choices and actions of leaders must take into consideration the rights and needs of followers. Leaders are not independent agents simply pursuing personal aggrandizement and career options. Like the "Guardians" of Plato's *Republic,* leaders must see their office as a social responsibility, a trust, a duty, and not as a symbol of their personal identity, prestige, and lofty status. In more contemporary terms, James O'Toole and Lynn Sharp-Paine have separately argued that the central ethical issue in business is the rights of stakeholders and the obligation of business leaders to manage with due consideration for the rights of all stakeholders involved.

In his cult classic *The Fifth Discipline,* management guru Peter Senge has stated that of all the jobs of leadership, being a steward is the most basic. Being a steward means recognizing that the ultimate purpose of one's work is others and not self; that leaders "do what they do" for something larger than themselves; that their "life's work" may be the "ability to lead," but that the final goal of this talent or craft is "other directed." If the real "business of business" is not just to produce a product/service and a profit but to help "produce" people, then the same claim/demand can be made of leadership. Given the reality of the "presence of others," leadership, like ethics, must by definition confront the question, What ought to be done with regard to others?

Values

Ethics is about the assessment and evaluation of values, because all of life is value laden. As Samuel Blumenfeld emphatically pointed out, "You have to be dead to be value-neutral." Values are the ideas and beliefs that influence and direct our choices and actions. Whether they are right or wrong, good or bad, values, both consciously and unconsciously, mobilize and guide how we make decisions and the kinds of decisions we make. Reportedly, Eleanor Roosevelt once said, "If you want to know what people value, check their checkbooks!"

I believe that Tom Peters and Bob Waterman were correct when they asserted, "The real role of leadership is to manage the values of an organization." All leadership is value laden. And all leadership, whether good or bad, is moral leadership at the descriptive if not the normative level. To put it more accurately, all leadership is ideologically driven or motivated by a certain philosophical perspective, which upon analysis and judgment may or may not prove to be morally acceptable in the colloquial sense. All leaders have an agenda, a series of beliefs, proposals, values, ideas, and issues that they wish to "put on the table." In fact, as Burns has suggested, leadership only asserts itself, and followers only become evident, when there is something at stake—ideas to be clarified, issues to be determined, values to be adjudicated. In the words of Eleanor's husband, Franklin D. Roosevelt: "The Presidency is . . . preeminently a place of moral leadership. All our great Presidents were leaders of thought at times when certain historic ideas in the life of the nation had to be clarified."

Although we would prefer to study the moral leadership of Lincoln, Churchill, Gandhi, and Mother Teresa, like it or not, we must also evaluate

Hitler, Stalin, Saddam Hussein, and David Koresh within a moral context.

All ethical judgments are in some sense a values-versus-values or rights-versus-rights confrontation. Unfortunately, the question of what we ought to do in relation to the values and rights of others cannot be reduced to the analogue of a simple litmus test. In fact, I believe that all of ethics is based on what William James called the "will to believe." That is, we choose to believe, despite the ideas, arguments, and reasoning to the contrary, that individuals possess certain basic rights that cannot and should not be willfully disregarded or overridden by others. In "choosing to believe," said James, we establish this belief as a factual baseline of our thought process for all considerations in regard to others. Without this "reasoned choice," says James, the ethical enterprise loses its "vitality" in human interactions.

If ethical behavior intends no harm and respects the rights of all affected, and unethical behavior willfully or negligently tramples on the rights and interests of others, then leaders cannot deny or disregard the rights of others. The leader's worldview cannot be totally solipsistic. The leader's agenda should not be purely self-serving. Leaders should not see followers as potential adversaries to be bested but rather as fellow travelers with similar aspirations and rights to be reckoned with.

Mutual Purposes and Goals

The character, goals, and aspirations of a leader are not developed in a vacuum. Leadership, even in the hands of a strong, confident, charismatic leader remains, at bottom, relational. Leaders, good or bad, great or small, arise out of the needs and opportunities of a specific time and place. Leaders require causes, issues, and—most important—a hungry and willing constituency. Leaders may devise plans, establish an agenda, bring new and often radical ideas to the table, but all of them are a response to the milieu and membership of which they are a part. If leadership is an active and ongoing relationship between leaders and followers, then a central requirement of the leadership process is for leaders to evoke and elicit consensus in their constituencies

and conversely for followers to inform and influence their leaders. This is done through the uses of power and education.

The term "power" comes from the Latin *posse*: to do, to be able, to change, to influence or effect. To have power is to possess the capacity to control or direct change. All forms of leadership must make use of power. The central issue of power in leadership is not Will it be used? but rather Will it be used wisely and well? According to James MacGregor Burns, leadership is not just about directed results; it is also about offering followers a choice among real alternatives. Hence, leadership assumes competition, conflict, and debate, whereas brute power denies it. "Leadership mobilizes," said Burns, "naked power coerces." But power need not be dictatorial or punitive to be effective. Power can also be used in a noncoercive manner to orchestrate, direct, and guide members of an organization in the pursuit of a goal or series of objectives. Leaders must engage followers, not merely direct them. Leaders must serve as models and mentors, not martinets. Or to paraphrase novelist James Baldwin, power without morality is no longer power.

For Peter Senge, teaching is one of the primary jobs of leadership. The "task of leader as teacher" is to empower people with information, offer insights, new knowledge, alternative perspectives on reality. The "leader as teacher" is not just about "teaching" people how "to achieve their vision." Rather, it is about fostering learning, offering choices, and building consensus. Effective leadership recognizes that in order to build and achieve community, followers must become reciprocally coresponsible in the pursuit of a common enterprise. Through their conduct and teaching, leaders must try to make their fellow constituents aware that they are all stakeholders in a conjoint activity that cannot succeed without their involvement and commitment. Successful leadership believes in and communicates some version of the now famous Hewlett Packard motto: "The achievements of an organization are the results of the combined efforts of each individual." In the end, says. Abraham Zaleznik, "leadership is based on a compact that binds those who lead with those who follow into the same moral, intellectual and emotional commitment." However, as both Burns and Rost warn us, the nature of this "compact" is inherently unequal because the influence patterns existing between leaders and followers are not equal. Responsive and responsible leadership requires, as a minimum, that democratic mechanisms be put in place that recognize the right of followers to have adequate knowledge of alternative options, goals, and programs, as well as the capacity to choose among them. "In leadership writ large, mutually agreed upon purposes help people achieve consensus, assume responsibility, work for the common good, and build community."

STRUCTURAL RESTRAINTS

There is, unfortunately, a dark side to the theory of the "witness of others." Howard S. Schwartz, in his radical but underappreciated managerial text *Narcissistic Process and Corporate Decay,* argues that corporations are not bastions of benign, other-directed ethical reasoning; nor can corporations, because of the demands and requirements of business, be models and exemplars of moral behavior. The rule of business, says Schwartz, remains the "law of the jungle," "the survival of the fittest," and the goal of survival engenders a combative "us-against-them mentality" that condones the moral imperative of getting ahead by any means necessary. Schwartz calls this phenomenon "organizational totalitarianism": Organizations and the people who manage them create for themselves a self-contained, self-serving worldview, which rationalizes anything done on their behalf and which does not require justification on any grounds outside of themselves. The psychodynamics of this narcissistic perspective, says Schwartz, impose Draconian requirements on all participants in organizational life: Do your work; achieve organizational goals; obey and exhibit loyalty to your superiors; disregard personal values and beliefs; obey the law when necessary, obfuscate it whenever possible; and deny internal or external discrepant information at odds with the stated organizational worldview. Within such a "totalitarian logic," neither leaders nor followers, rank nor file, operate as independent agents. To "maintain their place,"

to "get ahead," all must conform. The agenda of "organizational totalitarianism" is always the preservation of the status quo. Within such a logic, like begets like, and change is rarely possible. Except for extreme situations in which "systemic ineffectiveness" begins to breed "organization decay," transformation is never an option.

In *Moral Mazes,* Robert Jackall parallels much of Schwartz's analysis of organizational behavior, but from a sociological rather than a psychological perspective. According to critic and commentator Thomas W. Norton, both Jackall and Schwartz seek to understand why and how organizational ethics and behavior are so often reduced to either dumb loyalty or the simple adulation and mimicry of one's superiors. Whereas Schwartz argues that individuals are captives of the impersonal structural logic of "organizational totalitarianism," Jackall contends that "organizational actors become personally loyal to their superiors, always seeking their approval and are committed to them as persons rather than as representatives of the abstractions of organizational authority." But in either case, both authors maintain that organizational operatives are prisoners of the systems they serve.

For Jackall, all American business organizations are examples of "patrimonial bureaucracies" wherein "fealty relations of personal loyalty" are the rule and the glue of organizational life. Jackall argues that all corporations are like fiefdoms of the Middle Ages, wherein the lord of the manor (CEO, president) offers protection, prestige, and status to his vassals (managers) and serfs (workers) in return for homage (commitment) and service (work). In such a system, advancement and promotion are predicated on loyalty, trust, politics, and personality as much as, if not more than, on experience, education, ability, and actual accomplishments. The central concern of the worker/minion is to be known as a "can-do guy," a "team player," being at the right place at the right time and master of all the social rules. That's why in the corporate world, asserts Jackall, 1,000 "attaboys" are wiped away with one "oh, shit!"

Jackall maintains that, as in the model of a feudal system, employees of a corporation are expected to become functionaries of the system and supporters of the status quo. Their loyalty is to the powers that be; their duty is to perpetuate performance and profit; and their values can be none other than those sanctioned by the organization. Jackall contends that the logic of every organization (place of business) and the collective personality of the workplace conspire to override the wants, desires, and aspirations of the individual worker. No matter what a person believes off the job, said Jackall, on the job all of us to a greater or lesser extent are required to suspend, bracket, or only selectively manifest our personal convictions: "What is right in the corporation is not what is right in a man's home or his church. What is right in the corporation is what the guy above you wants from you."

For Jackall the primary imperative of every organization is to succeed. This logic of performance, what he refers to as "institutional logic," leads to the creation of a private moral universe, a moral universe that by definition is totalitarian (self-sustained), solipsistic (self-defined), and narcissistic (self-centered). Within such a milieu, truth is socially defined, and moral behavior is determined solely by organizational needs. The key virtues, for all alike, become the virtues of the organization: goal preoccupation, problem solving, survival/success, and—most important—playing by the house rules. In time, says Jackall, those initiated and invested in the system come to believe that they live in a self-contained world that is above and independent of outside critique and evaluation.

For both Schwartz and Jackall, the logic of organizational life is rigid and unchanging. Corporations perpetuate themselves, both in their strengths and weakness, because corporate cultures clone their own. Even given the scenario of a benign organizational structure that produces positive behavior and beneficial results, the etiology of the problem and the opportunity for abuse that it offers represent the negative possibilities and inherent dangers of the "witness of others" as applied to leadership theory. Within the scope of Schwartz's and Jackall's allied analyses, "normative" moral leadership may not be possible. The model offered is both absolute and inflexible, and only "regular company guys" make

it to the top. The maverick, the radical, and the reformer are not long tolerated. The "institutional logic" of the system does not permit disruption, deviance, or default.

The term "moral leadership" often conjures up images of sternly robed priests, waspishly severe nuns, carelessly bearded philosophers, forbiddingly strict parents, and something ambiguously labeled the "moral majority." These people are seen as confining and dictatorial. They make us do what we should do, not what we want to do. They encourage following the "superego" and not the "id." A moral leader is someone who supposedly tells people the difference between right and wrong from on high. But there is much more to moral leadership than merely telling others what to do.

The vision and values of leadership must have their origins and resolutions in the community of followers, of whom they are a part, and whom they wish to serve. Leaders can drive, lead, orchestrate, and cajole, but they cannot force, dictate, or demand. Leaders can be the catalyst for morally sound behavior, but they are not, by themselves, a sufficient condition. By means of their demeanor and message, leaders must be able to convince, not just tell others, that collaboration serves the conjoint interest and well-being of all involved. Leaders may offer a vision, but followers must buy into it. Leaders may organize a plan, but followers must decide to take it on. Leaders may demonstrate conviction and willpower, but followers, in the new paradigm of leadership, should not allow the leader's will to replace their own.

Joseph C. Rost has argued, both publicly and privately, that the ethical aspects of leadership remain thorny. How, exactly, do leaders and collaborators in an influence relationship make a collective decision about the ethics of a change that they want to implement in an organization or society? Some will say, "option A is ethical," some others will say, "option B is ethical." How are leaders and followers to decide? As I have suggested, ethics is what "ought to be done" as the preferred mode of action in a right-versus-right, values-versus-values confrontation. Ethics is an evaluative enterprise. Judgments must be made in regard to competing points of view. Even in the absence of a belief in the existence of a single universal, absolute set of ethical rules, basic questions can still be asked: How does it affect the self and others? What are the consequences involved? Is it harmful? Is it fair? Is it equitable? Perhaps the best, but by no means most definitive, method suited to the general needs of the ethical enterprise is a modified version of the scientific method: A) *Observation,* the recognition of a problem or conflict; B) *Inquiry,* a critical consideration of facts and issues involved; C) *Hypothesis,* the formulation of a decision or plan of action consistent with the known facts; D) *Experimentation and Evaluation,* the implementation of the decision or plan in order to see if it leads to the resolution of the problem. There are, of course, no perfect answers in ethics or life. The quality of our ethical choices cannot be measured solely in terms of achievements. Ultimately and ethically, intention, commitment, and concerted effort are as important as outcome: What/why did leader/followers try to do? How did they try to do it?

Leadership is hard to define, and moral leadership is even harder. Perhaps, like pornography, we only recognize moral leadership when we see it. The problem is, we so rarely see it. Nevertheless, I am convinced that without the "witness" of moral leadership, standards of ethics in business and organizational life will neither emerge nor be sustained. Leadership, even when defined as a collaborative experience, is still about the influence of individual character and the impact of personal mentoring. Behavior does not always beget like behavior in a one-to-one ratio, but it does establish tone, set the stage, and offer options. Although to achieve ethical behavior, an entire organization, from top to bottom, must make a commitment to it, the model for that commitment has to originate from the top. Labor Secretary Robert Reich recently stated, "The most eloquent moral appeal will be no match for the dispassionate edict of the market." Perhaps the "witness" of moral leadership can prove to be more effective.

QUESTIONS

1. In what ways are the ethics of followers related to the ethics of leaders?

2. Do you think that stewardship is considered an important value for business leaders today?

3. What are some ethical and unethical uses of power and influence in the workplace?

Joanne B. Ciulla | # Why Business Leaders' Values Matter

THE VALUES AND VIRTUES OF BUSINESS LEADERS

Some of our attitudes towards the values of business leaders can be traced to the Protestant work ethic, which included the belief that accumulation of wealth was a sign that one was among God's chosen. One of the Calvinists' favorite Biblical passages was "Seest thou a man diligent in his business? He shall stand before kings" (Proverbs xxii 29). This equation of business success and salvation seemed to stick even in the secular world. In the 18th century. Benjamin Franklin tempered the Protestant work ethic with enlightenment ideals. He believed that business leaders should strive for wealth so that they can use it in a humane way to help society.

Franklin thought good character was necessary for success. In his autobiography he listed eleven virtues needed for success in business and in life temperance, silence, order, resolution, sincerity, justice, moderation, cleanliness, tranquility, chastity, and humility. Virtues tell us what we should be like and what we have to do to be that way. Values are what we believe to be important or morally worthy. We usually assume that values motivate us to act, but this isn't always the case. Some are satisfied to have a value and not act on it. This is not possible with a virtue. A person may value courage, but never do anything brave or heroic. Whereas one cannot possess the virtue of courage unless he or she has done something courageous.

America is somewhat distinct in its history of celebrating the values and character of business leaders. For example, in the 19th century, William Makepeace Thayer specialized in biographies of chief executive officers. His books focused on how the values leaders formed early in life contributed to their success. Thayer summed up the moral path to success this way: "Man deviseth his own way, but the Lord directeth his steps".[1] As the number of business journalists grow in America, some dedicated themselves to lionizing business leaders. The Scottish immigrant Bertie Charles (B.C.) Forbes elevated the moral adulation of business leaders into an enduring art form, imitated by business publications throughout the world. When he started Forbes magazine in 1916. Forbes described it as "a publication that would strive to inject more humanity, more joy, and more satisfaction into business and into life in general".[2] His goal was to convey Franklin's message that work, virtue, and wealth lead to happiness and social benefit.

The 18th and 19th century advocates of the work ethic preached that strong moral character was the key to wealth. By early 20th century the emphasis on moral character shifted to an emphasis on personality. In Dale Carnegie's 1936 classic. *How to Win Friends and Influence People,* psychology, not morality, was the key to success in business. This was true in leadership theory as well, Scholars were more interested in studying the personality traits of leaders than their values. This is in part because through most of the 20th century many prominent leadership scholars were psychologists.

The mythologies of business leaders remain popular, even though many of them are not great philanthropists or particularly morally virtuous or advocates of enlightened self-interest.[3] Today business leaders are more likely to be celebrated in the first person than in the third. Consider, for example, the popularity of autobiographies by Al Dunlap, Donald Trump, and Bill Gates, all of whom enjoy touting their own virtues and values to the public.

Books such as *Business as a Calling,* by Michael Novak, draw the traditional Protestant connection between success in business and God's favor.[4] Novak, who is a Catholic, argues that successful business people are more religious than other professionals. He cites two studies to back up his view. The first looked at church attendance by elites from the news media, business, politics, labor unions, the military, and religion. It found that groups with the highest proportion of weekly church attendance after religious professionals, were the military at 49% and then business at 35%. The second study, a Conference Board survey of senior executives at Fortune 500 companies, reported that 65% of the respondents said they worshipped at churches or synagogues regularly.[5] Novak infers that church going affects business values. However, we need more evidence than church attendance to connect religious values with the values a leader brings to work. After all, for some going to Church is nothing more than *going to Church.*

LEADERSHIP THEORIES AND VALUES

The legacy of the Protestant work ethic and its attitudes toward business present a paradox. Are business leaders successful because of their virtues? or Are they virtuous because they are successful? In the literature of leadership studies both seem to be true, depending on how one defines leadership.

Leadership scholars have spent way too much time worrying about the definition of leadership. Some believe that if they could agree on a common definition of leadership, they would be better able to understand it. Joseph Rost gathered together

221 definitions of leadership. After reviewing all of his definitions, one discovers that the definition problem was not really about definitions *per se*. All 221 definitions say basically the same thing—leadership is about one person getting other people to do something. Where the definitions differ was in how leaders got other followers to act and how leaders came up with the something that was to be done. For example, one definition from the 1920s said. "[Leadership is] the ability to impress the will of the leader on those led and induce obedience, respect, loyalty, and cooperation".[6] Another definition from the 1990s said. "Leadership is an influence relationship between leaders and followers who intend real changes that reflect their mutual purposes".[7] We all can think of leaders who fit both of these descriptions. Some use their power to force people to do what they want, others work with their followers to do what everyone agrees is best for them. The difference between the definitions rests on a normative question: "How should leaders treat followers?"

The scholars who worry about constructing the ultimate definition of leadership are asking the wrong question, but inadvertently trying to answer the right one. The ultimate question about leadership is not "What is the definition of leadership?" The whole point of studying leadership is, "What is good leadership?" The use of word *good* here has two senses, morally good and technically good or effective. If a good leader means *good* in both senses, then the two should form a logical conjunction. In other words, in order for the statement "She is a good leader" to be true, it must be true that she is effective *and* she is ethical.

The question. "What constitutes a good leader?" lies at the heart of many public debates about leadership today. We want our leaders to be good in both ways. Nonetheless we are often more likely to say leaders are good if they are effective, but not moral, than if they are moral, but not effective-Leaders face a paradox. They have to stay in business or get reelected in order to be leaders. If they are not minimally effective at doing these things, their morality as leaders is usually irrelevant, because they are no longer leaders. In leadership, effectiveness sometimes must take priority over ethics. What we hope for are leaders who

know when ethics should and when ethics shouldn't take a back sent to effectiveness. History tends to dismiss as Irrelevant the morally good leaders who are unsuccessful. President Jimmy Carter was a man of great personal integrity, but during his presidency, he was ineffective and generally considered a poor leader. The conflict between ethics and effectiveness and the definition problem are apparent in what I have called, "the Hitler problem"[8] The answer to the question "Was Hitler a good leader?" is yes, if a leader is defined as someone who is effective or gets the job they set out to do done. The answer is no, if the leader gets the job done, but the job itself is immoral, and it is done in an immoral way. In other words leadership is about more than being effective at getting followers to do things. The quality of leadership also depends on the means and the ends of a leader's actions. The same is true for Robin Hood. While in myth some admire him, he still steals from the rich to give to the poor. His purpose is morally worthy, but the way that he does it is not. Most of us would prefer leaders who do the right thing, the right way for the right reasons.

The way that we assess the impact of a leader's values on an organization also depends on one's theory of leadership. Many still carry with them the "Great Man" theory—leaders are born and not made. Personality traits, not values catapult leaders to greatness. This theory has been articulated in different ways. Thomas Carlyle wrote about the trails of heroes such as Napoleon, Niccolo Machiavelli described the strategic cunning of his 'Prince', Frederich Neitszche extolled the will to power of his 'superman'. While the innate qualities of leaders are primary factors in these theories, it is not always clear what makes people want to follow great men.

Charismatic leadership is a close relative to the Great Man Theory, Charismatic leaders have powerful personalities. However the distinguishing feature of charismatic leadership is the emotional relationship that charismatic leaders establish with followers. Charismatic leaders range from a John F. Kennedy, who inspired a generation to try and make the world better, to the cult leader Jim Jones, who lead his followers into suicide. The values of charismatic leaders shape the organization, but in some cases these values do not live on when the charismatic leader is gone.

Other theories of leadership focus on the situation or context of leadership. They emphasize the nature of the task that needs to be done, the external environment, which includes historical, economic and cultural factors, and the characteristics of followers. Lee Iacocca was the right leader for Chrysler when it went bankrupt, but we don't know if he would be the right leader at some other phase of the firm's history. Ross Perot was a good business man, but many doubted his ability to be effective as a political leader. Situational theories don't explicitly say anything about values, but one might surmise that in some situations a person with particularly strong moral values must emerge as a leader. For example, Nelson Mandela and Vaclav Havel seemed to have been the right men at the right time. They both offered the powerful kind of moral leadership required for peaceful revolutions in South Africa and the Czech Republic.

A third group of scholars combine trait theories with situational models and focus on the interaction between leaders and followers. The leader's role is to guide the organization along paths that are rewarding to everyone involved. Here values are sure to play an important role, but again it matters what the values are and what they mean to others in the organization. The Ohio studies and the Michigan studies both measured leadership effectiveness in terms of how leaders treated subordinates and how they got the job done. The Ohio Studies looked at leadership effectiveness in terms of 'consideration' or the degree to which leaders act in friendly and supportive manner, and 'initiating structure' or the way that leaders structure their own role and the role of subordinates in order to obtain group goals.[9] The Michigan Studies measured leaders on the basis of task orientation and relationship orientation.[10] Implicit in these theories and studies is an ethical question. Are leaders more effective when they are kind to people, or are leaders more effective when they use certain techniques for structuring and ordering tasks? Is leadership about moral relationships or techniques?—probably both.[11]

Transforming Leadership and Servant Leadership are normative theories of leadership. Both emphasize the relationship of leaders and followers to each other and the importance values in the process of leadership. James MacGregor Burns' theory of transforming leadership costs on a set of moral assumptions about the relationship between leaders and followers.[12] Burns argues that leaders have to operate at higher need and value levels than those of followers. Charismatic leaders can be transforming leaders, however, unlike many charismatic leaders, the transforming leader engages followers in a dialogue about the tension and conflict within their own value systems. Transforming leaders have very strong values, but they do not force them on others.[13] Ultimately, the transforming leader develops followers so that they can lead themselves.

Burns theory addresses two pressing moral questions. The morality of means (and this also includes the moral use of power) and the morality of ends. Burns' distinction between transforming and transactional leadership, and modal and end-values offers a way to think about the question "What is a good leader?" both in terms of the relationship of leaders to followers and the means and ends of actions. Transactional leadership rests on the values found in the means of an act. These are called modal values which are things like, responsibility, fairness, honesty and promise-keeping, Transactional leadership helps leaders and followers reach their own goals by supplying lower level wants and needs so that they can move up to higher needs. Transforming leadership is concerned with end-values, such as liberty, justice, and equality.

Servant leadership has not gotten as much attention as transformational leadership in the literature, but in recent years interest in it by the business community has grown. Servant leaders lead because they want to serve others. In *Servant Leadership,* Robert K. Greenleaf says people follow servant leaders freely because they trust them. Like the transforming leader, the servant leader also tries to morally elevate followers. Greenleal says servant leadership must pass this test: "Do those served grow as persons? Do they *while being served* become healthier, wiser, freer, more autonomous, more likely themselves to become servants?" He goes on and adds a Rawlsian proviso. *"And,* what is the effect on the least privileged in society?"[14] In both transforming leadership and servant leadership, leaders not only have values, but they help followers develop their own values, which will hopefully overlap or be compatible with those of the organization.

THE PROBLEM ONLY *HAVING* VALUES

Social scientists like to talk about values because they are descriptors. When a poll asks voters if they prefer better schools or lower takes, we assume that if the majority pick better schools, it means most respondents value education. Ask people about their values and they will tell you what they think is important. Different types of moral statements and concepts do different things. For example the statement 'you ought not to kill' prescribes, 'Do not kill' commands, 'Killing is wrong' evaluates, and 'Killing is wrong because I value life' explains, and 'Killing is against my values, which include the value of human life' describes. Values are static concepts. You have to make a lot of assumptions to make a value do something. You have to assume that because people value something they act accordingly, but we know this isn't the case. While values change all the time, having a value does not mean that one has or will do something about it.

Since values themselves do not have agency, the main way that a leader influences the organization is through his or her words and actions. One way to understand a leaders values is through their vision. The CEO who says his or her vision is to double market share by the year 2000 has a goal, not a vision. All businesses want to make profits. Visions must have an implicit or explicit moral component to them.[15] Often the moral component has to do with improving the quality of life, particularly in the case of making a product safer, environmentally friendly, or more affordable to those who need it. A leader's vision should tell us where we want to go, why it's good to go there, and the right way for us to get there.

The only way to understand if a business leader's values have an impact is to look at how his or her values connect with actions. Hypocrisy is the most extreme form of values not meeting up with actions. Hypocrites express strong moral values that they do

not hold and then act against them. For example, a company that advertises its commitment to green products while continuing to sell products that don't meet it's own espoused green standards is hypocritical.[16] What is most odd about some hypocrites is that they are not always complete liars. Some know they should live up to the values they talk about, but simply do not or will not.

Another problem with values and actions is what Frederick B. Bird calls 'moral silence'. Moral silence is the opposite of hypocrisy. Morally silent leaders act and speak as if they do not hold certain moral values. When they actually do. The company president who cuts 1000 jobs from the payroll may publicly state that he cut jobs to fill what he considers his most important obligation to protect shareholder value. When in fact be is guilt ridden because he really believes that his greatest moral obligation is to his employees. Leaders sometimes lack the ability or the moral courage to act on their values. Similarly, there are some who have values, but are either too busy, distracted, or lazy to act on those values. Consider the case of a female corporate executive who has strong convictions about giving women opportunities for career advancement, but does not go out of her way or take advantage of opportunities to ensure that women in her company have these opportunities.

Often leaders don't realize that the values they hold are in practice contradictory or inconsistent. Once a colleague and I conducted an ethics seminar for the presidents of a large conglomerate. The CEO of the corporation was an enthusiastic participant. During the seminar he expressed his feelings about the importance of honesty and integrity in business. However, as the participants discussed our case studies, it became clear that there were a number of situations in which protecting the company's integrity meant losing business or money. The CEO actively agreed with these conclusions. However, the others in the seminar pointed out to him that quarterly sales determined the compensation for each business unit. The CEO set profit targets for each business unit and used a formula to determine compensation. When it came to performance, he valued the numbers more than anything else. What the CEO failed to realize was that he was espousing the value of integrity, but in effect saying that employees would be punished if they did not act with integrity (with bring) *and* punished if they did act with integrity (with reduced compensation). Some thought that if the CEO really valued integrity, he should make some adjustment to the incentive system to take into account business lost for ethical reasons. One brave man wondered out load if the CEO didn't really value profits over integrity.

Often companies write codes of ethics or mission statements but don't to think through what the values in the statement mean in terms of how they manage their businesses. In 1983 the Harvard Business School wrote a glowing case study of how CEO Jim Bere developed the Borg–Warner code of ethics.[17] Borg-Warrier is a conglomerate of automotive. financial services, and security service businesses. Its code began with the statement. "We believe in the dignity of the individual", and "We believe in the commonwealth of Borg Warner and its people". An elegant framed copy of the code was hung offices and factories of Borg–Warner's various businesses. Their ethics code also said, "we must heed the voice of our natural concern for others" and "grant others the same respect, cooperation, and decency we seek for ourselves."[18]

Warner Gear, a division of Borg Warner, manufactured gears for cars and boats. In 1984 it made a text book turn around in labor relations and productivity. After years of losing money and engaging in endless labor disputes, the union and management finally agreed to cooperate. They formed effective quality circles that saved the company millions of dollars in waste and inefficiency. Company profits soared in 1985.[19] However, in July of that year, with no warning to the managers or employees who implemented the turnaround, Borg Warner announced if was shipping part of Warner Gear to Kenfig. Wales to save on labor costs. This meant that the factory would lose 300 jobs. While the business decision may have been warranted, the way that it was implemented did not show decency and respect for those who had worked so hard to make the firm successful. All the energy, good will, and commitment of the employees didn't matter, and neither did the grand values that hung on the wall.

Lastly, there are cases where a business leader acts on values that he has never made any concerted effort to express in words to employees. On 11 December 1995 Malden Mills, a textile factory in Massachusetts, burnt down. The owner, Aaron Feuerstein, immediately decided to give out Christmas bonuses and pay his employees full salaries until the factory was repaired. In the midst of massive corporate downsizings this story of kindness captured the public imagination. Feuerstein was a quiet man running a family business. The business itself was known for treating workers fairly, but Feuerstein had never been one to publicly articulate his own values. Given the publicity of his actions after the fire, he was asked by the press to talk about his values. He then explained that his business values came from his Jewish faith and the teachings of the Talmud. Yet for most employees, *where* he got his values didn't matter as much as *what* he did with them.

The point of these examples is to show that a leaders values do indeed shape the values of the firm when they are paired with policies and actions that breathe life into them. The way in which founders influence the values of the company is by setting out their mission, what they want to do, and how they want to do it. But most importantly, their actions write the story of the organization's values. The story can be a morally good one or an evil one, Either way, the role of leaders who come after the founder is to tell and add to the story of the company and its values. This includes ethical lessons learned from its mistakes as well as its moral triumphs.

Howard Garner believes that great leaders are also great story tellers. He says leadership is a process in the minds of individuals who live in a culture. Some stories tend to become more predominant in this process, such as stories that provide an adequate and timely sense of identity for individuals.[20] The story of the fire at Malden Mills will become part of the company's mythology. It not only conveys a message of moral commitment to employees. but it sets a moral standard for those who will take Feuerstein's place.

Leaders' values matter when they are repeatedly reflected in their actions. However, a leader's values and his or her will to act on them are also shaped by the history and the culture of the organization itself. As I pointed out earlier, we sometimes mythologize business leaders because they are successful or imagine that their lone values are responsible for doing some heroic action. But as we saw earlier, there can be a gap between having values and acting on them. This gap is often narrowed or widened by the values already present in the story of the organization.

QUESTIONS

1. Which of Ben Franklin's virtues would people apply to business leaders today? Which virtues would you add to Franklin's list?

2. What factors make it difficult for business leaders to operationalize their values at work?

3. Do you think that business leaders are successful because of their virtues or are they virtuous because they are successful?

Dean C. Ludwig and
Clinton O. Longenecker

The Bathsheba Syndrome: The Ethical Failure of Successful Leaders

Dean C. Ludwig and Clinton O. Longenecker teach at the University of Toledo.

THE STORY OF DAVID AND BATHSHEBA

Most individuals are at least vaguely familiar with the story of David and Bathsheba, but we would especially like to point out some of the details leading up to David's violation and point out how in many ways the story of David and Bathsheba is paradigmatic for many of the ethical failures of successful leaders which we witness today. How did David, a good, talented, and successful leader, get entangled in this downward spiral of events? The scriptural accounts provide some insight, and offer food for thought for today's leaders.

David loses strategic focus in success. The story of David and Bathsheba begins by noting that David is not where he is supposed to be, doing what he is supposed to be doing. His recent successes in battle have apparently left David complacent—complacent that his overall strategy did not need revision for the time being and complacent that his subordinates were capable of executing the current strategy on their own. Instead of leading his troops into battle as was his role as king, he stayed home, leaving the direction of his troops during critical battles to his right hand man, Joab. David was apparently comfortable that Joab would be able to handle things.

How often today we see executives lead their organizations to the top of the competitive heap, displaying exceptional courage, energy, and leadership, only then to put their organizations on autopilot, kick back, and indulge themselves for all of the

From *Journal of Business Ethics* 12:265–273, 1993. © 1993 Kluwer Academic Publishers. Printed in the Netherlands. References were deleted from the text.

sacrifices they have made along the way. Their set-up for ethical failure begins by not being where they are supposed to be. Not only does this expose the *leader* to potential conflict, but by not being with the troops through a time of crisis and competition, it opens the door to questionable ethical behavior by subordinates.

David's failure of leadership is certainly not that he delegated (though the accounts indicate that it was a king's duty to be with his troops in battle). Rather, David delegated and then ignored what was happening. He did not give supervision to Joab. In addition, David seemed to be delegating not out of a sense of necessity but out of a sense of self-indulgence. That is, David was delegating not because he needed to free time for other duties, but because he wanted more time for leisure (the accounts indicate that David was just rising from bed as evening came). David may have felt he needed or deserved a break after his earlier conquests; it is interesting that he did not feel his troops also needed or deserved to share in this break.

David's success leads to privileged access. As was mentioned, David's leisure allowed him the opportunity, literally, to look around. He was not focused on organizational decision making. Instead, his lack of pre-occupation allowed him to see things he otherwise wouldn't have noticed. Second, his privileged position, high atop the roof of the palace, allowed him to see things that were sheltered to those at lower levels. It would have been clear to someone at a lower level that violation of Bathsheba's privacy was wrong, for they would have somehow had to circumvent the wall that separated her bath from public view. It was easy, however, for David to forget that it was not his right to view this beautiful woman at bath. His privileged vantage point was designed to give him a perspective—a view—that would help him lead his people, not a view that would feed his self-indulgence. By this point, David's lack of involvement in the leadership combined with his privileged position, allowed him to shift his focus to the satisfaction of personal wants.

Many of the scandals we have witnessed in recent years have evolved from privileged access to information, people and objects and from leaders' apparent inability to understand that their privileged position is supposed to give them a perspective from which they can more effectively lead—not from which they can more effectively satisfy personal wants.

David's success leads to control of resources and inflated belief in personal ability to control outcomes. The story of David and Bathsheba unfolds through a degenerate progression of indulgence and cover-up. As the story of David and Bathsheba develops, David sends servants to investigate who this beautiful woman was that he saw from his roof. When he found that she was not only married, but married to one of his officers, he knew it would be a grave offense to take her to his bed. Yet, her husband was off in battle, and the servants, knowing the consequences, could certainly be counted on for silence. David sends for Bathsheba, sleeps with her, and she become pregnant.

In the hopes of covering this violation, David brings Bathsheba's husband in from the battlefield under the false pretense of finding out the state of battle. After months in the field, he hopes Uriah will sleep with his wife, but noble Uriah decides it would be inappropriate while his comrades are still in battle. David then gets Uriah drunk in the hope that he will sleep with his wife, but he doesn't. Finally, David gives Uriah a message to carry back to Joab, the commander of the battle. The message is Uriah's death sentence—it tells Joab to send Uriah to the front of the fiercest battle and then withdraw, leaving Uriah and other innocents to die. After Uriah's death, David sent word to Joab not to let what had just happened seem evil in his sight. Smug in his cover-up, David then took Bathsheba into his house as his wife. It was the prophet Nathan, an outsider to the events, who finally exposed David.

David, in short, chose to do something he knew was clearly wrong in the firm belief that through his personal power and control over resources he could cover up. David's inflated, self-confident belief in his own personal ability to manipulate the outcome of this story is probably representative of the attitude of many of today's professionally trained managers of business. Trained in attitude and technique to "get things done" and "make things happen," today's business school graduates often possess a dangerously inflated self-confidence. Reinforced

	Positive/Benefit	Negative/Disadvantage
Personal Level	**Privileged Access** Position Influence Status Rewards/Perks Recognition Latitude Associations Access	**Inflated Belief in Personal Ability** Emotionally Expansive Unbalanced Personal Life Inflated Ego Isolation Stress Transference Emptiness Fear of Failure
Organizational Level	**Control of Resources** No Direct Supervision Ability to Influence Ability to set Agenda Control Over Decision Making	**Loss of Strategic Focus** Org on Autopilot Delegation without Supervision Strategic Complacency Neglect of Strategy

FIGURE **13-1** Possible outcomes experienced by successful leaders.

by success, given increasing control of resources, and subjected to decreasing levels of supervision, these managers too often stumble as they move into leadership roles.

SUCCESS AS AN ANTECEDENT TO ETHICAL FAILURE

We have outlined four by-products of success—loss of strategic focus, privileged access, control of resources, and inflated belief in ability to manipulate outcomes—and we have looked at the dynamics of these by-products in the life of David. We have noted that privileged access and control of resources are, when kept within reason, positive, justified, strategic perquisites of success. Privileged access is essential for comprehensive strategic vision. Control of resources is necessary for the execution of strategy.

On the other hand, we have suggested that the other two by-products—loss of strategic focus and inflated belief in personal ability to control outcomes—are essentially negative. Further, we suggest (as shown in Figure 13-1) that privileged access and inflated belief in personal ability are primarily

personal issues, while control of resources and loss of strategic focus are primarily organizational issues.

We suggest that several explosive combinations can be found within this matrix. First, when loss of strategic focus is coupled with privileged access, the door is opened for real abuse of some of the personal perquisites associated with success. Position and status are suddenly used to promote non-strategic, non-organizational purposes. An even more explosive combination occurs when control of resources is coupled with an inflated belief in personal ability to manipulate outcomes.

THE DARK SIDE OF SUCCESS

Success is the goal of every leader—both personal success and organizational success. Very often the two are intimately intertwined. Paradoxically, embedded in success may be the very seeds that could lead to the downfall of both the leader and the organization.

On a *personal* level the *benefits* of success to a leader are obvious to even the casual observer. Greater power and influence, increased status, a heightened sense of personal achievement, greater rewards and perks, and more personal latitude on the job are all by-products that come to leaders who can make things happen in their organization. We have summed all of these under the heading "privileged access." When a leader has proven him or herself to the organization, a host of *organizational* benefits tend to accompany this status. Leaders are granted greater control of resources and decision processes; they have increased access to information, people, and things; they are permitted to set their own agendas and have every worker's dream come true—no direct supervision. The combination of personal and organizational benefits that accompany success are indeed the very reasons all of us want to be successful. In a nutshell, success leads to increasing levels of power, influence, rewards, status, and control. None of these should in and of themselves be seen as negative.

Less readily apparent is the personal "dark side" of success—a side that is only recently being addressed by executive psychologists and is still seldom talked about. When leaders climb the organizational ladder and appear to have it all, they are confronted with a host of negatives that affect them on a very personal level. These negatives come in a variety of shapes and forms and affect leaders differently. The negatives of success may not appear to be obvious to most of us, but they nonetheless come with the territory of successful leadership. Collectively, they might be labeled as factors that are associated with an unbalanced personal life and a loss of touch with reality. In this paper we have focused on one of their major manifestations: an inflated sense of personal ability (and sometimes desire) to manipulate outcomes.

Literature on executive psychology describes a variety of negative dynamics associated with success. Successful leaders can often become emotionally expansive, which is to say that their appetite for success, thrills, gratification, and control becomes insatiable. Thus they lose their ability to be satisfied with their current status and they desire more of everything. Secondly, they can experience personal isolation and a lack of intimacy in their lives. Inability to share their problems and long hours away from home can cause leaders to be isolated from their families and friends, losing a valuable source of personal balance. In addition, leaders find themselves without peers at work and can find

making friends at work difficult. Many of these leaders literally lose touch with reality.

Furthermore, the status can bring with it increased stress and, at times, the fear of failure which can cause a leader to experience extreme levels of anxiety. It is one thing to make it to the top, but many leaders are not prepared for what it takes to stay there. At the same time leaders can experience the "emptiness syndrome"—after working hard for years and finally "making it," they take a step back and ask themselves "is this all there is to success?" They have success, but they don't experience it in a meaningful way on a personal level which can cause them to seek other ways to satisfy their needs.

Many times all of this simply adds up to an inflated sense of ego. This egocentricity can cause the leader to become abrasive, close-minded, disrespectful, and prone to extreme displays of negative emotion, all of which are warning signs along the road to megalomania (or the "I am the center of the universe phenomenon").

We are not suggesting that all successful leaders fall prey to these negatives that are frequently associated with success, but rather want to make the case that success can bring with it some very negative emotional baggage. When we couple these negatives that affect leaders on a very personal basis with the organizational benefits of success discussed earlier, they create a rather potent combination for unethical behavior on the part of the successful leader. When we combine extreme organizational autonomy and control with a personal emotional state that is possibly inflated, isolated, or emotionally expansive, it is not hard to see how successful leaders frequently make unethical choices which not only harm them personally but contain the potential to destroy or severely damage the organizations they are responsible for protecting.

In in the case of King David, we see both of these propensities in operation. We see a leader with complete free rein and a man who was apparently more concerned with personal gratification (at this particular moment in time) than with the responsibilities of being an effective leader. David clearly believed in his own ability to cover-up his wrong-doing. And as was addressed at length earlier in this paper, we also saw in David the explosive combination of privileged access combined with a loss of focus. David's inability to handle the by-products of success left him extremely vulnerable to ethical failure.

This ethical failure cost David dearly: the death of the child he bore with Bathsheba; the loss of his commander, Joab, who would later betray him; internal strife and conflict in his household for years to come; the loss of respect in his kingdom that led to future leadership problems; the loss of valuable fighting men and morale among his troops; and extreme personal guilt that he was continually forced to live with. All of these dynamics created even less balance in David's life. David was finally confronted with his ethical failure by the prophet Nathan (who was in this case the equivalent of a modern-day whistle-blower) who led David to realize that his cover-up had been a failure. Even kings who fail to provide ethical leadership are eventually found out.

Whenever a modern leader falls prey to the Bathsheba Syndrome they are knowingly setting themselves and their organizations up for a fall whether they believe it or not. The lessons from David's sad experience are obvious:

1. Leaders are in their positions to focus on doing what is right for their organization's short-term and long-term success. This can't happen if they aren't where they are supposed to be, doing what they are supposed to be doing.
2. There will always be temptations that come in a variety of shapes and forms that will tempt leaders to make decisions they know they shouldn't make. With success will come additional ethical trials.
3. Perpetrating an unethical act is a personal, conscious choice on the part of the leader that frequently places a greater emphasis on personal gratification rather than on the organization's needs.
4. It is difficult if not impossible to partake in unethical behavior without implicating and/or involving others in the organization.
5. Attempts to cover-up unethical practices can have dire organizational consequences including innocent people getting hurt, power being abused, trust being violated, other individuals being corrupted, and the diversion of needed resources.
6. Not getting caught initially can produce self-delusion and increase the likelihood of future unethical behavior.
7. Getting caught can destroy the leader, the organization, innocent people, and everything the leader has spent his/her life working for.

CONCLUSIONS

In closing, some advice to successful leaders is warranted. First, it could happen to you. David was an intelligent, principled individual. So, too, are many of your colleagues that you read about in the paper these days. It is not simply the unprincipled and those under competitive pressure who fall victim to ethical violation. Stand forewarned of David's painful experience and read the papers for constant reminders that the chances of being caught have never been greater. Second, realize that living a balanced life reduces the likelihood of the negatives of success causing you to lose touch with reality. Family, relationships, and interests other than work must all be cultivated for long-term success to be meaningful. Third, understand that your primary function is to provide strategic direction and leadership at all levels. Avoid becoming complacent with strategic direction and current performance. Strategic direction is never "set," no matter how successful. The privilege and status that has been granted to you is designed to enhance your strategic vision. It is not simply reward for a job already accomplished. Likewise, control of organizational resources has been given to you so that you can execute strategy–not to feed personal gratification. Fourth, build an ethical team of managers around you who will inspire you to lead by example and who will challenge or comfort you when you need either. Finally, ethical leadership is simply part of good leadership and requires focus, the appropriate use of resources, trust, effective decision making, and provision of model behavior that is worth following. Once it is lost it is difficult if not impossible to regain.

To: You
From: The Philosopher
Subject: "Plato on Why Ethical People Don't Want to Be Leaders"

I think that you've wanted to move up into this job for a long time, but you've been very careful not to say it out loud. You've probably noticed that people are sometimes uncomfortable with those who seem a little too eager to take on leadership roles. Plato said that we are uneasy with such people because we worry that they are in it for their own interests, not the interests of their constituencies. According to Plato, ethical people have to be compelled to lead. Here is what he says:

> Therefore good people won't be willing to rule for the sake of either money or honor. They don't want to be paid wages openly for ruling and get called hired hands nor take them in secret from their rule and be called thieves. And they won't rule for the sake of honor, because they aren't ambitious honor-lovers. So, if they are willing to rule, some compulsion or punishment must be brought to bear on them—perhaps that's why it is thought shameful to seek to rule before one is compelled to. Now, the greatest punishment, if one isn't willing to rule, is to be ruled by someone worse than one-self. And I think that it's fear of this that makes decent people rule when they do. They approach ruling not as something good or something to be enjoyed, but as something necessary, since it can't be entrusted to anyone better than—or even as good as—themselves. In a city of good men, if it came into being, citizens would fight in order not to rule, just as they do now in order to rule. There it would be quite clear that anyone who is really a true ruler doesn't by nature seek his own advantage, but that of his subjects. And everyone knowing this, would rather be benefited by others than take the trouble to benefit them.

—Plato (*Republic*, 347b3–347e5)

Several observations are also in order for boards of directors and others responsible for overseeing organizational leaders. First, board involvement should include concern for the leader's personal/psychological balance. Support for the leader's psychological well-being can be displayed via forced vacations, outside activities, and periodic visits to counselors and/or psychologists to help the leader keep both feet firmly planted on the ground. Second, boards should erect guard-rails. Detection is the primary factor that deters unethical behavior. Organizations should thus make prudent use of such devices as regularly scheduled audits of critical organizational decision processes and resources. Organizations should also consider the use of ombudsmen for employees who might be willing to uncover unethical acts. Third, boards must clearly establish and implement ethical codes of conduct for organizational leaders and take steps to regularly heighten both the awareness and compliance with such standards. Clearly even successful leaders need both the input, direction, and support of a governing body to be prevented from falling into the dark side of success.

Finally, for those engaged in business ethics training we suggest a broadened understanding of why leaders/managers sometimes abandon their own principles. Do we too quickly focus on the maintenance of ethical behavior in the face of competitive pressure? Should we also discuss the maintenance of ethical behavior in the face of success? Is adherence to principle in either the face of competitive pressure or the wake of success a matter of ethics or of virtue? If success leads to increased levels of power, then we must take steps to deal with the phenomenon that "power corrupts." Researchers and academicians must look for creative ways to prevent this from occurring while not limiting the ability of leaders to lead.

QUESTIONS

1. In the story of David and Bathsheba, where does King David most abuse his power as a leader?

2. In recent business and political scandals, what leaders seem to have fallen prey to the Bathsheba syndrome?

3. What role can spouses, friends, boards, and other stakeholders play in preventing business leaders from falling prey to the Bathsheba syndrome?

Robert Greenleaf

Servant Leadership: A Journey into the Nature of Legitimate Power and Greatness

Robert Greenleaf was a pioneer in leadership studies. He taught and consulted at the Harvard Business School and the Ford Foundation.

Servant and leader—can these two roles be fused in one real person, in all levels of status or calling? If so, can that person live and be productive in the real world of the present? My sense of the present leads me to say yes to both questions. This chapter is an attempt to explain why and to suggest how.

The idea of *The Servant as Leader* came out of reading Hermann Hesse's *Journey to the East*. In this story we see a band of men on a mythical journey, probably also Hesse's own journey. The central figure of the story is Leo who accompanies the party as the *servant* who does their menial chores, but who also sustains them with his spirit and his song. He is a person of extraordinary presence. All goes well until Leo disappears. Then the group falls into disarray and the journey is abandoned. They cannot make it without the servant Leo. The narrator, one of the party, after some years of wandering finds Leo and is taken into the Order that had sponsored the journey. There he discovers that Leo, whom he had known first as *servant*, was in fact the titular head of the Order, its guiding spirit, a great and noble *leader*.

WHO IS THE SERVANT-LEADER?

The servant-leader *is* servant first—as Leo was portrayed. It begins with the natural feeling that one wants to serve, to serve *first*. Then conscious choice brings one to aspire to lead. That person is sharply different from one who is *leader* first, perhaps because of the need to assuage an unusual power drive or to acquire material possessions. For such it will be a later choice to serve—after leadership is established. The leader-first and the servant-first are two extreme types. Between them there are shadings and blends that are part of the infinite variety of human nature.

The difference manifests itself in the care taken by the servant-first to make sure that other people's highest priority needs are being served. The best test,

From Robert Greenleaf, *Servant Leadership: A Journey into the Nature of Legitimate Power and Greatness* (New York: Paulist Press, 1977), pp. 213, 217–19.

and difficult to administer, is: Do those served grow as persons? Do they, *while being served*, become healthier, wiser, freer, more autonomous, more likely themselves to become servants? *and*, what is the effect on the least privileged in society; will they benefit, or, at least, not be further deprived?

As one sets out to serve, how can one know that this will be the result? This is part of the human dilemma; one cannot know for sure. One must, after some study and experience, hypothesize—but leave the hypothesis under a shadow of doubt. Then one acts on the hypothesis and examines the result. One continues to study and learn and periodically one reexamines the hypothesis itself.

Finally, one chooses again. Perhaps one chooses the same hypothesis again and again. But it is always a fresh open choice. And it is always an hypothesis under a shadow of doubt. "Faith is the choice of the nobler hypothesis." Not the *noblest;* one never knows what that is. But the *nobler*, the best one can see when the choice is made. Since the test of results of one's actions is usually long delayed, the faith that sustains the choice of the nobler hypothesis is psychological self-insight. This is the most dependable part of the true servant.

The natural servant, the person who is *servant first*, is more likely to persevere and refine a particular hypothesis on what serves another's highest priority needs than is the person who is *leader first* and who later serves out of promptings of conscience or in conformity with normative expectations.

My hope for the future rests in part on my belief that among the legions of deprived and unsophisticated people are many true servants who will lead, and that most of them can learn to discriminate among those who presume to serve them and identify the true servants whom they will follow.

EVERYTHING BEGINS WITH THE INITIATIVE OF AN INDIVIDUAL

The forces for good and evil in the world are propelled by the thoughts, attitudes, and actions of individual beings. What happens to our values, and therefore to the quality of our civilization in the future, will be shaped by the conceptions of individuals that are born of inspiration. Perhaps only a few will receive this inspiration (insight) and the rest will learn from them. The very essence of leadership, going out ahead to show the way, derives from more than usual openness to inspiration. Why would anybody accept the leadership of another except that the other sees more clearly where it is best to go? Perhaps this is the current problem: too many who presume to lead do not see more clearly and, in defense of their inadequacy, they all the more strongly argue that the "system" must be preserved—a fatal error in this day of candor.

But the leader needs more than inspiration. A leader ventures to say: "I will go; come with me!" A leader initiates, provides the ideas and the structure, and takes the risk of failure along with the chance of success. A leader says: "I will go; follow me!" while knowing that the path is uncertain, even dangerous. One then trusts those who go with one's leadership.

Paul Goodman, speaking through a character in *Making Do*, has said, "If there is no community for you, young man, young man, make it yourself."

WHAT ARE YOU TRYING TO DO?

"What are you trying to do?" is one of the easiest to ask and most difficult to answer of questions.

A mark of leaders, an attribute that puts them in a position to show the way for others, is that they are better than most at pointing the direction. As long as one is leading, one always has a goal. It may be a goal arrived at by group consensus, or the leader, acting on inspiration, may simply have said, "Let's go this way." But the leader always knows what it is and can articulate it for any who are unsure. By clearly stating and restating the goal the leader gives certainty and purpose to others who may have difficulty in achieving it for themselves.

The word *goal* is used here in the special sense of the overarching purpose, the big dream, the visionary concept, the ultimate consummation which one approaches but never really achieves. It is something presently out of reach; it is something to strive for, to move toward, or become. It is so stated that it excites the imagination and challenges people to work for something they do not yet know how to do, something they can be proud of as they move toward it.

Every achievement starts with a goal—but not just any goal and not just anybody stating it. The one who states the goal must elicit trust, especially if it is a high risk or visionary goal, because those who follow are asked to accept the risk along with the leader. Leaders do not elicit trust unless one has confidence in their values and competence (including judgment) and unless they have a sustaining spirit (entheos) that will support the tenacious pursuit of a goal.

Not much happens without a dream. And for something great to happen, there must be a great dream. Behind every great achievement is a dreamer of great dreams. Much more than a dreamer is required to bring it to reality; but the dream must be there first.

QUESTIONS

1. What are the virtues of a servant leader?
2. Are there any problems with the application of this leadership model in business?
3. Why do you think employees would like working for a servant leader?

CASES

CASE 13.1
Shooting an Elephant
George Orwell

In Moulmein, in lower Burma, I was hated by large numbers of people—the only time in my life that I have been important enough for this to happen to me. I was subdivisional police officer of the town, and in an aimless, petty kind of way anti-European feeling was very bitter. No one had the guts to raise a riot, but if a European woman went through the bazaars alone somebody would probably spit betel juice over her dress. As a police officer I was an obvious target and was baited whenever it seemed safe to do so. When a nimble Burman tripped me up on the football field and the referee (another Burman) looked the other way, the crowd yelled with hideous laughter. This happened more than once. In the end the sneering yellow faces of young men that met me everywhere, the insults hooted after me when I was at a safe distance, got badly on my nerves. The young Buddhist priests were the worst of all. There were several thousands of them in the town and none of them seemed to have anything to do except stand on street corners and jeer at Europeans.

All this was perplexing and upsetting. For at that time I had already made up my mind that imperialism was an evil thing and the sooner I chucked up my job and got out of it the better. Theoretically—and secretly, of course—I was all for the Burmese and all against their oppressors, the British. As for the job I was doing, I hated it more bitterly than I can perhaps make clear. In a job like that you see the dirty work of Empire at close quarters. The wretched prisoners huddling in the stinking cages of the lock-ups, the gray, cowed faces of the long-term convicts, the scarred buttocks of the men who had been flogged with bamboos—all these oppressed me with an intolerable sense of guilt. But I could get nothing into perspective. I was young and ill educated and I had had to think out my problems in the utter silence that is imposed on every Englishman in the East. I did not even know that the British Empire is dying, still less did I know that it is a great deal better than the younger empires that are going to supplant it. All I knew was that I was stuck between my hatred of the empire I served and my rage against the evil-spirited little beasts who tried to make my job impossible. With one part of my mind I thought of the British Raj as an unbreakable tyranny, as something clamped down, in *saecula saeculorum*, upon the will of prostrate peoples; with another part I thought that the greatest joy in the world would be to drive a bayonet into a Buddhist priest's guts. Feelings like these are the normal by-products of imperialism; ask any Anglo-Indian official, if you can catch him off duty.

One day something happened which in a round-about way was enlightening. It was a tiny incident in itself, but it gave me a better glimpse than I had had before of the real nature of imperialism—the real motives for which despotic governments act. Early one morning the subinspector at a police station the other end of the town rang me up on the phone and said that an elephant was ravaging the bazaar. Would I please come and do something about it? I did not know what I could do, but I wanted to see what was happening and I got on to a pony and started out. I took my rifle, an old .44 Winchester and much too small to kill an elephant, but I thought the noise might be useful in *terrorem*. Various Burmans stopped me on the way and told me about the elephant's doings. It was not, of course, a wild elephant, but a tame one which had gone "must." It had been chained up, as tame elephants always are when their attack of "must" is due, but on the previous night it had broken its chain and escaped. Its mahout, the only person who could manage it when it was in that state, had set out in pursuit, but had taken the wrong direction and was now twelve hours' journey away, and in the morning the elephant had suddenly reappeared in the town. The Burmese population had no weapons and were quite helpless against it. It had already destroyed somebody's bamboo hut, killed a cow and raided some fruit-stalls and devoured the stock; also it had met the municipal rubbish van and, when the driver jumped out and took to his heels, had turned the van over and inflicted violences upon it.

The Burmese subinspector and some Indian constables were waiting for me in the quarter where the elephant had been seen. It was a very poor quarter, a labyrinth of squalid bamboo huts, thatched with palm-leaf, winding all over a steep hillside. I remember that it was a cloudy, stuffy morning at the beginning of the rains. We began questioning the people as to where the elephant had gone and, as usual, failed to get any definite information. That is invariably the case in the East; a story always sounds clear enough at a distance, but the nearer you get to the scene of events the vaguer it becomes. Some of the people said that the elephant had gone in one direction, some said that he had gone in another, some professed not even to have heard of any elephant. I had almost made up my mind that the whole story was a pack of lies, when we heard yells a little distance away. There was a loud, scandalized cry of "Go away, child! Go away this instant!" and an old woman with a switch in her hand came round the corner of a hut, violently shooing away a crowd of naked children. Some more women followed, clicking their tongues and exclaiming; evidently there was something that the children ought not to have seen. I rounded the hut and saw a man's dead body sprawling in the mud. He was an Indian, a black Dravidian coolie, almost naked, and he could not have been dead many minutes. The people said that the elephant had come suddenly upon him round the corner of the hut, caught him with its trunk, put its foot on his back and ground him into the earth. This was the rainy season and the ground was soft, and his face had scored a trench a foot deep and a couple of yards long. He was lying on his belly with arms crucified and head sharply twisted to one side. His face was coated with mud, the eyes wide open, the teeth bared and grinning with an expression of unendurable agony. (Never tell me, by the way, that the dead look peaceful. Most of the corpses I have seen looked devilish.) The friction of the great beast's foot had stripped the skin from his back as neatly as one skins a rabbit. As soon as I saw the dead man I sent an orderly to a friend's house nearby to borrow an elephant rifle. I had already sent back the pony, not wanting it to go mad with fright and throw me if it smelled the elephant.

The orderly came back in a few minutes with a rifle and five cartridges, and meanwhile some Burmans had arrived and told us that the elephant was in the paddy fields below, only a few hundred yards away. As I started forward practically the whole population of the quarter flocked out of the houses and followed me. They had seen the rifle and were all shouting excitedly that I was going to shoot the elephant. They had not shown much interest in the elephant when he was merely ravaging their homes, but it was different now that he was going to be shot. It was a bit of fun to them, as it would be to an English crowd; besides they wanted the meat. It made me vaguely uneasy. I had no intention of shooting the elephant—I had merely sent for the rifle to defend myself if necessary—and it is always unnerving to have a crowd following you. I marched down the hill, looking and feeling a fool, with the rifle over my shoulder and an ever-growing army of people jostling at my heels. At the bottom, when you got away from the huts, there was a metaled road and beyond that a miry waste of paddy fields a thousand yards across; not yet plowed but soggy from the first rains and dotted with coarse grass. The elephant was standing eight yards from the road, his left side toward us. He took not the slightest notice of the crowd's approach. He was tearing up bunches of grass, beating them against his knees to clean them, and stuffing them into his mouth:

I had halted on the road. As soon as I saw the elephant I knew with perfect certainty that I ought not to shoot him. It is a serious matter to shoot a working elephant—it is comparable to destroying a huge and costly piece of machinery—and obviously one ought not to do it if it can possibly be avoided. And at that distance, peacefully eating, the elephant looked no more dangerous than a cow. I thought then and I think now that his attack of "must" was already passing off; in which case he would merely wander harmlessly about until the mahout came back and caught him. Moreover, I did not in the least want to shoot him. I decided that I would watch him for a little while to make sure that he did hot turn savage again, and then go home.

But at that moment I glanced round at the crowd that had followed me. It was an immense crowd, two thousand at the least and growing every minute. It blocked the road for a long distance on either side. I looked at the sea of yellow faces above the garish clothes—faces all happy and excited over this bit of fun, all certain that the elephant was going to be shot. They were watching me as they would watch a conjurer about to perform a trick. They did not like me, but with the magical rifle in my hands I was momentarily worth watching. And suddenly I realized that I should have to shoot the elephant after all. The people expected it of me and I had got to do it; I could feel their two thousand wills pressing me forward, irresistibly. And it was at this moment, as I stood there with the rifle in my hands, that I first grasped the hollowness, the futility of the white man's dominion in the East. Here was I, the white man with his gun, standing in front of the unarmed native crowd—seemingly the leading actor of the piece; but in reality I was only an absurd puppet pushed to and fro by the will of those yellow faces behind. I perceived in this moment that when the white man turns tyrant it is his own freedom that he destroys. He becomes a sort of hollow, posing dummy, the conventionalized figure of a sahib. For it is the condition of his rule that he shall spend his life in trying to impress the "natives," and so in every crisis he has got to do what the "natives" expect of him. He wears a mask, and his face grows to fit it. I had got to shoot the elephant. I had committed myself to doing it when I sent for the rifle. A sahib has got to act like a sahib; he has got to appear resolute, to know his own mind and do definite things. To come all that way, rifle in hand, with two thousand people marching at my heels, and then to trail feebly away, having done nothing—no, that was impossible. The crowd would laugh at me. And my whole life, every white man's life in the East, was one long struggle not to be laughed at.

But I did not want to shoot the elephant. I watched him beating his bunch of grass against his knees with that preoccupied grandmotherly air that elephants have. It seemed to me that it would be murder to shoot him. At that age I was not squeamish about killing animals, but I had never shot an elephant and never wanted to. (Somehow it always seems worse to kill a *large* animal.) Besides, there was the beast's owner to be considered. Alive, the elephant was worth at least a hundred pounds; dead, he would only be worth the value of his tusks, five pounds, possibly. But I had got to act quickly. I turned to some experienced-looking Burmans who had been there when we arrived, and asked them how the elephant had been behaving. They all said the same thing: he took no notice of you if you left him alone, but he might charge if you went too close to him.

It was perfectly clear to me what I ought to do. I ought to walk up to within, say, twenty-five yards of the elephant and test his behavior. If he charged, I could shoot; if he took no notice of me, it would be safe to leave him until the mahout came back. But also I knew that I was going to do no such thing. I was a poor shot with a rifle and the ground was soft mud into which one would sink at every step. If the elephant charged and I missed him, I should have about as much chance as a toad under a steam-roller. But even then I was not thinking particularly of my own skin, only of the watchful yellow faces behind. For at that moment, with the crowd watching me, I was not afraid in the ordinary sense, as I would have been if I had been alone. A white man mustn't be frightened in front of "natives"; and so, in general, he isn't frightened. The sole thought in my mind was that if anything went wrong those two thousand Burmans would see me pursued, caught, trampled on, and reduced to a grinning corpse like that Indian up the hill. And if that happened it was quite probable that some of them would laugh. That would never do. There was only one alternative. I shoved the cartridges into the magazine and lay down on the road to get a better aim.

The crowd grew very still, and a deep, low, happy sigh, as of people who see the theater curtain go up at last, breathed from innumerable throats. They were going to have their bit of fun after all. The rifle was a beautiful German thing with cross-hair sights. I did not then know that in shooting an elephant one would shoot to cut an imaginary bar running from ear-hole to ear-hole. I ought, therefore, as the elephant was sideways on, to have aimed straight at his ear-hole; actually I aimed several inches in front of this, thinking the brain would be further forward.

When I pulled the trigger I did not hear the bang or feel the kick—one never does when a shot goes home—but I heard the devilish roar of glee that went up from the crowd. In that instant, in too short a time, one would have thought, even for the bullet to get there, a mysterious, terrible change had come over the elephant. He neither stirred nor fell, but every line of his body had altered. He looked suddenly stricken, shrunken, immensely old, as though the frightful impact of the bullet had paralyzed him without knocking him down. At last, after what seemed a long time—it might have been five seconds, I dare say—he sagged flabbily to his knees. His mouth slobbered. An enormous senility seemed to have settled upon him. One could have imagined him thousands of years old. I fired again into the same spot. At the second shot he did not collapse but climbed with desperate slowness to his feet and stood weakly upright, with legs sagging and head drooping. I fired a third time. That was the shot that did it for him. You could see the agony of it jolt his whole body and knock the last remnant of strength from his legs. But in falling he seemed for a moment to rise, for as his hind legs collapsed beneath him he seemed to tower upward like a huge rock toppling, his trunk reaching skyward like a tree. He trumpeted, for the first and only time. And then down he came, his belly toward me, with a crash that seemed to shake the ground even where I lay.

I got up. The Burmans were already racing past me across the mud. It was obvious that the elephant would never rise again, but he was not dead. He was breathing very rhythmically with long rattling gasps, his great mound of a side painfully rising and falling. His mouth was wide open—I could see far down into caverns of pale pink throat. I waited a long time for him to die, but his breathing did not weaken. Finally I fired my two remaining shots into the spot where I thought his heart must be.

The thick blood welled out of him like red velvet, but still he did not die. His body did not even jerk when the shot hit him, the tortured breathing continued without a pause. He was dying, very slowly and in great agony, but in some world remote from me where not even a bullet could damage him further. I felt that I had got to put an end to that dreadful noise. It seemed dreadful to see the great beast lying there, powerless to move and yet powerless to die, and not even to be able to finish him. I sent back for my small rifle and poured shot after shot into his heart and down his throat. They seemed to make no impression. The tortured gasps continued as steadily as the ticking of a clock.

In the end I could not stand it any longer and went away. I heard later that it took him half an hour to die. Burmans were bringing dahs and baskets even before I left, and I was told they had stripped his body almost to the bones by the afternoon.

Afterward, of course, there were endless discussions about the shooting of the elephant. The owner was furious, but he was only an Indian and could do nothing. Besides, legally I had done the right thing, for a mad elephant has to be killed, like a mad dog, if its owner fails to control to it. Among the Europeans opinion was divided. The older men said I was right, the younger men said it was a damn shame to shoot an elephant for killing a coolie, because an elephant was worth more than any damn Coringhee coolie. And afterward I was very glad that the coolie had been killed; it put me legally in the right and it gave me a sufficient pretext for shooting the elephant. I often wondered whether any of the others grasped that I had done it solely to avoid looking a fool.

QUESTIONS

1. Why was the policeman unable to do what he thought was right?

2. Did the policeman fail as a leader?

3. To what extent do followers influence the behavior of business leaders? What makes leaders follow their followers and not act on their own values and preferences?

CASE 13.2

Martha Stewart Focuses on Her Salad

Mary Ann Glynn and Timothy J. Dowd

In 1982, Martha Stewart published what would become the touchstone for her namesake company: her first cookbook, *Entertaining*. It was an immediate bestseller, and it foreshadowed what MSLO pioneered, the "lifestyle category," which not only captured the values and mission she touted but claimed an important source of her charismatic authority:

> With its publication, we began to combine what had been distinct and relatively small media niches—

cooking, gardening, entertaining, crafts, and holidays, into one single new powerhouse category: LIFESTYLE. *We believe that the pursuit of lifestyle leading to a deeper relationship with one's family and home is a serious creative and educational pursuit* [italics added]. We have built our entire business around this principle. (Stewart, 1990, p. 4)

The Wall Street Journal christened Martha Stewart "America's 'Goddess of Graciousness'"

From *Journal of Applied Behavioral Science* 44, No. 1 (March 2008), pp. 71–93. © 2008 NTL Institute.

(Chesnoff, 1985), and soon after, Kmart (which had hired Stewart as a spokesperson) boasted "It will be almost impossible for 76 million households to not be aware of the name Martha Stewart. We'll make her the next Betty Crocker, only she's a real, live person" (Ingrassia, 1987). They succeeded all too well; years later, Stewart reportedly claimed this cultural leadership as hers:

> I'm a brand. . . . My niche (domestic life) is bigger than anyone's. Remember when those shows "Dallas" and "Dynasty" were really popular? People were living vicariously through them. I think my approach is so much more simple and so much nicer a lifestyle. People understand. (Sabulis, 1995, p. E1)

Stewart established her expertise with both her products and her proclamations; Stewart embodied and demonstrated the knowledge and skills that enabled her readers to have an aesthetic, tasteful "lifestyle." Thus, her expert power (French & Raven, 1960) established her cultural authority, but her charisma enabled the identification of her followers. Early on, Stewart, the persona and leader, was connecting to her audience, cultivating referent power (French & Raven, 1960) that later defined her celebrity:

> I gave a lecture to 700 in Fresno on Wednesday. The point is that I made 700 real friends. They all call me Martha and I call them by their first names and we are friends and that's what I want it to be like . . . *like I'm one of them* [italics added]. (Gammon, 1989, p. B1)

In the winter of 1990, Stewart published a trial issue of the magazine that was to become her signature product, *Martha Stewart Living*, under the auspices of Time Warner. Initially, Time was hesitant, doubting the potential success of yet another woman's magazine in an already saturated market. However, the inaugural issue sold out quickly, as did a subsequent issue, far exceeding Time's expectations. Stewart effused about her parent organization in the pages of that first issue:

> In the Time Warner family, I found great support for my ideas. Friends joined me in my new venture, and we set out together to make the magazine you hold in your hands: one filled with inspiration and information. (Stewart, 1990, p. 4)

A decade after publishing the inaugural issue, Stewart reflected on her beginnings in the celebratory 10th anniversary issue:

> I think it was 1987 or 1988, after I had become a moderately well known author, that I decided I would like to do an entire series of books devoted to "beautiful how-to." . . . I submitted the list [of subjects] with brief outlines to my publisher's office. My editor took a while to answer, then replied, sorry: The series was too ambitious; it was a library, not a book project. I felt a bit dejected, to be sure, but being the optimist that I am, I thought about how I could accomplish what I had envisioned, and it occurred to me that what I was really thinking about creating was a magazine. (Stewart, 2001, p. 196)

In 1991, Stewart launched both the magazine and her business. The magazine remains the centerpiece of MSLO; in 2006, it accounted for 54% of the company's total revenue and still retains Stewart's founding passion for "how-to":

> Our flagship magazine, *Martha Stewart Living*, is the foundation of our publishing business . . . *Martha Stewart Living* seeks to offer reference-quality and original "how-to" information from our core content areas for the homemaker and other consumers in an upscale editorial and aesthetic environment. *Martha Stewart Living* has won numerous prestigious awards. (Martha Stewart Living Omnimedia, 2006, p. 14)

Stewart was at the helm of her enterprise from the start. She was recognized early on for her achievements, named to prestigious lists including the "50 Most Powerful Women" (*Fortune*, October 1988) and "America's 25 Most Influential People" (*Time*, June 1996; Church, 2007). In 1997, Stewart purchased the magazine from Time Warner for a reported $75 million. The move propelled her fortunes upward, and the media's coverage of her business (and business savvy) intensified, overshadowing earlier criticisms of her perfectionism and sometimes caustic personality. In 1999, MSLO went public, making Stewart an overnight billionaire (at least on paper). This initiated a positive, upward trajectory for the company as MSLO expanded to television and radio shows, a syndicated newspaper column, an expanded line of books and publications, and a successful Kmart product line. Thus, the MSLO organization succeeded in its change effort to go public. However, the ascendancy was interrupted abruptly and shockingly just a few years later.

On December 27, 2001, Martha Stewart sold her 3,928 shares in the pharmaceutical company, ImClone, on the eve of the critical FDA ruling on its cancer drug, Erbitux. The next day, the FDA announced its rejection of Erbitux, causing ImClone stock to plummet. In less than 6 months, *The New York Times* (Pollack, 2002) and *The Washington Post* (Gillis, 2002) broke stories questioning the circumstances of Stewart's stock sale; public allegations of insider trading surfaced. Martha Stewart, the embodiment of upscale gentility, was facing potentially criminal charges, and this was national news. When Stewart made a regularly scheduled cooking appearance on the CBS *Early Show* a few weeks later (June 25, 2002), she responded to inquiries by saying, "I think this will all be resolved in the very near future and I will be exonerated of any ridiculousness" ("Martha Stewart Focuses on Her Salad," 2002).

Although Stewart's company was never implicated in any of the charges, MSLO stock plunged dramatically. By July 2002, it lost $300 million in market valuation, and her company acknowledged that the founder's legal problems were taking a toll. In September 2002, the U.S. House of Representatives asked the Department of Justice to investigate the possibility of Stewart's insider trading. That same month, MSLO took the extraordinary step of issuing a press release that publicly denied a *New York Times* story that a new CEO search was underway at the firm. Then, 9 months later, on June 4, 2003, Stewart was indicted on charges of obstructing justice and securities fraud related to the sale of ImClone stock but not insider trading. She immediately resigned as chairwoman and CEO of her company but continued on in a newly appointed position: creative director. On June 5, 2003, Stewart took out a $79,000 full-page ad in *USA Today* proclaiming her innocence, titled *An Open Letter From Martha Stewart* and addressed "To My Friends and Loyal Supporters."

After more than a year, the government has decided to bring charges against me for matters that are personal and entirely unrelated to the business of Martha Stewart Living Omnimedia. I want you to know that I am innocent—and that I will fight to clear my name.

I am confident I will be exonerated of these baseless charges, but a trial unfortunately won't take place for months. I want to thank you for your extraordinary support during the past year— I appreciate it more than you will ever know. (Fournier, 2004)

In spite of Stewart's protestations of innocence and attempts to separate her personal life from her company, MSLO stock prices did not recover immediately. MSLO's television and publishing efforts now commanded a smaller audience and fewer advertisers: In the aftermath of the scandal, ad revenue dropped 54% and the magazine lost 22% of its subscribers. For instance, Unilever spent close to $5 million in advertising in 2002 but only $130,000 in 2003 (Crawford, 2004a).

Stewart was convicted of obstruction of justice on March 15, 2004. She authored her final "Letter From Martha" (May 2004) in her magazine. She apologized "for the upset that my personal legal troubles have caused for all of you" (Stewart, 2004a, p. 6) but remained stalwart in her optimism for the future: "This is not an end to anything, but a kind of fresh start, I believe" (Stewart, 2004c, p. 160). Stewart made a point of reaching out to her audience and followers, thanking everyone—"readers, advertisers, business partners, family, friends, staff—for the outpouring of affection and support that you have shown me recently, just as you have consistently done for nearly two years" (Stewart, 2004a, p. 6). And, her audience took note. In the *New Yorker*, Jeffrey Toobin (2004) asked "Why did Martha Stewart lose?" and answered it by referencing the then-current "A Letter From Martha":

In a note to readers in the March, 2004, issue of *Martha Stewart Living*—the issue that was on newsstands when the testimony in her trial began— Stewart described the period leading up to the trial this way: "For the past several months, I have been happily immersed in scores of wonderfully written and beautifully illustrated garden catalogues." The trilling adverbs are a touchstone of Stewart's style. There was defiance in that "happily," too— Stewart's insistence that not even the power of the United States government could prevent her from extracting the soil's bounty.

Stewart communicated with her followers not only through the magazine but through other outlets as well, conducting interviews, appearing on talk shows, and creating her personal Web site: www.marthatalks .com. Her reach seemed to be broad and effective. Media analysts reported that "on the front page, Stewart thanks her audience for its support, mentioning the more than 9 million hits and nearly 50,000 visitors that the site logged in just a few days" (*Martha Talks*, 2003).

On July 16, 2004, she was sentenced to 5 months in a minimum security prison, the least possible sentence (Masters, 2004). She expressed her reactions publicly (to the press) outside the courthouse:

> Today is a shameful day, shameful for me, and for my family and for my beloved company and for all of its employees and partners. What was a small personal matter came, became over the last two years an almost fateful circus event of unprecedented proportions. I have been choked and almost suffocated to death during that time, all the while more concerned about the well-being of others than for myself, more hurt for them and for their losses than my own, more worried for their futures than the future of Martha Stewart the person. More than 200 people have lost their jobs at my company, and as a result of this situation, I want them to know how very very sorry I am for them and their families. I would like to thank everybody who stood by me, who wished me well, waved to me on the streets like these lovely people over here, smiled at me, called me, wrote to me. We received thousands of support letters and more than 170,000 emails to marthatalks.com and I appreciate each and every one of those correspondence. I feel really good about it.
>
> Whatever I have to do in the next few months I hope the months go by quickly, I'm used to all kind of hard work as you know and I'm not afraid, I'm not afraid whatsoever. I'm just very very sorry that it has come to this, that a small personal matter has been able to be blown out of all proportion and with

such venom and such gore, I mean it's just terrible. ("Transcript of Martha Stewart Statement," 2004)

Two months later, on September 15, 2004, Martha Stewart made the surprising announcement that she would serve her sentence as soon as possible because of her "intense desire and need to put this nightmare behind" (Crawford, 2004b). With the announcement, MSLO stock prices spiked 12%, signaling investors' approval. During Stewart's incarceration, she continued to communicate with her followers through her personal Web site, www.marthatalks.com. Her "Thanksgiving" message blended positive and negative feelings about her experience but ended with optimism and strength.

> Dear Friends,
>
> As the Thanksgiving holiday approaches, I want to extend my deepest thanks and appreciation for the steadfast support I continue to receive from so many of you. I am told this web page has logged nearly 8 million hits since I began serving my sentence last month, and that supporters have sent more than 15,000 emails. I have also received thousands of letters. I cherish them all.
>
> While I can't answer each note personally, I want you to know that I am well. As you would expect, the loss of freedom and the lack of privacy are extremely difficult. But I am safe, fit and healthy, and I am pleased to report that, contrary to rumors you might have heard, my daily interactions with the staff and fellow inmates here at Alderson are marked by fair treatment and mutual respect.
>
> In short, I am in good spirits and making the best of this difficult situation. Visits from my friends, family and colleagues—together with your goodwill and best wishes—will get me through this chapter in my life. For this friendship and support, I am very grateful this Thanksgiving. (Stewart, 2004b)

Stewart completed her jail term on March 4, 2005. Upon release, she immediately began working for her company again; MSLO embraced her return, featuring her photo on the next cover of the magazine, announcing "Welcome Back Martha" (April 2005). Although Stewart never wrote another "Letter" or "Remembering" for the magazine, she created a new column, "From My Home to Yours," which she still contributes regularly.

REFERENCES

Chesnoff, R. Z. (1985, March 11). America's "goddess of graciousness." *The Wall Street Journal*. Retrieved January 9, 2008, from Factiva.com database.

Church, D. (2007). *Einstein's business: Engaging soul, imagination and excellence in the workplace.* Retrieved January 9, 2008, from http://www.einsteinsbusiness.com/Contributors.html

Crawford, K. (2004, October 15). Martha: No more money, please! *Fortune*. Retrieved January 9, 2008, from http://money.cnn.com/2004/10/15/news/midcaps/martha openletter/index.htm

Crawford, K. (2004b, September 15). Martha ready to do time. *Fortune*. Retrieved January 9, 2008, from http://money.cnn.com/2004/09/15/news/newsmakers/martha/index.htm

Fournier, S. (2004). *Martha Stewart and the ImClone Scandal* (Tuck School of Business at Dartmouth Teaching Case No. 1-0083). Retrieved January 8, 2008, from http://mba.tuck.dartmouth.edu/pdf/2004-1-0083.pdf

French, J., & Raven, B. (1960). *The bases of social power.* New York: Harper & Row.

Gammon, M. (1989, June 7). Tastefully speaking: Martha Stewart aiming message at Kmart shoppers. *Atlanta Journal and Constitution*, p. B1.

Gillis, J. (2002, June 8). Martha Stewart's call questioned; Star called ImClone chief on day she sold stock.

The Washington Post. Retrieved January 9, 2008, from Factiva.com database.

Ingrassia, P. (1987, October 6). Attention non-Kmart shoppers: A blue-light special just for you. *The Wall Street Journal*. Retrieved January 9, 2008, from Factiva.com database.

Martha talks—In the dog house. (2003). Retrieved January 9, 2008, from http://gerstmanandmeyers com/features_webwatch.asp?ww_id=128

Martha Stewart focuses on her salad. (2002). *The Early Show*. Retrieved January 9, 2008, from http://www.cbsnews.com/stories/2002/06/26/national/main513464.shtml

Martha Stewart Living Omnimedia. (2006). *Annual report*. Retrieved January 9, 2008, from http://thomson mobular.net/thomson/7/2314/2545/

QUESTIONS

1. What common ethical pitfalls of leaders do we see illustrated in the Martha Stewart case?

2. Martha Stewart's business rebounded not long after she got out of jail. What is it about Stewart and her leadership that made the public forgive her crime?

3. Do you think that Martha Stewart deserved to be forgiven by the public? Why or why not?

CASE 13.3

Merck and Roy Vagelos: The Values of Leaders

Joanne B. Ciulla

Prior to becoming CEO, Vagelos was director of Merck Sharp & Dohme's research laboratories.[1] In 1979 a researcher named William Campbell had a hunch that an antiparasite drug he was working on called Ivermectin might work on the parasite that caused river blindness, a disease that threatens the eyesight and lives of 85 million people in 35 developing countries. He asked Vagelos if he could have the resources to pursue his research. Despite the fact that the market for this drug was essentially the poorest people in the world, Vagelos gave Campbell the go ahead. While the decision was Vagelos's, it was also reinforced by Merck's axiom "health precedes wealth."

Campbell's hunch about Ivermectin proved to be right, and he developed a drug called Mectizan, which was approved for use by the government in 1987. By this time Vagelos had become the CEO of Merck. Now that the drug was approved, he sought public underwriting to produce Mectizan. Vagelos hired Henry Kissenger to help open doors for Merck. They approached several sources, including the U.S. Agency for International Development and the World Health Organization, but couldn't raise money for the drug. Merck was left with a drug that was useful only to people who couldn't buy it. Vagelos recalled, "We faced the possibility that we had a miraculous drug that would sit on a shelf."[2] After reviewing the company's options, Vagelos and his directors announced that they would give Mectizan away for free, forever, on October 21, 1987. A decade later, the drug give-away cost Merck over $200 million. By 1996 Mectizan had reached 19 million people. In Nigeria alone it saved 6 million people from blindness.

Few business leaders ever have the opportunity to do what Vagelos did. When asked how he could commit his company to produce a product that cost rather than generated money, he said he had "no choice. My whole life has been dedicated" to helping people, and "this was *it* for me."[3] His values guided his decisions in this case, but so did the values of the founder. George C. Merck, son of the company's American founder, said that from the very beginning, Merck's founders asserted that medicine was for people, not profits. However, he quickly added that they also believed that if medicine is for people, profits will follow.[4]

Like many corporate mission statements, Merck's says its mission "is to provide society with superior products and services." The statement goes on to assert, "We are in the business of preserving and improving human life. . . . All of our actions must be measured by our success at achieving this goal." It concludes that "We expect profits from work that satisfies customer needs and that benefits humanity.[5] Merck's corporate leaders acted on and hence instilled and reinforced these values long before

Vagelos donated Mectizan. After World War II, tuberculosis thrived in Japan: Most Japanese couldn't afford to buy Merck's powerful drug, Streptomycin, to fight it. Merck gave away a large supply of the drug to the Japanese public. The Japanese did not forget. In 1983 the Japanese government allowed Merck to purchase 50.02 percent of Banyu Pharmaceutical. At the time, this was the largest foreign investment in a Japanese company. Merck is currently the largest American pharmaceutical company in Japan. The story makes Merck's mission statement come alive. It is the kind of story that employees learn and internalize when they come to work there.

Vagelos' moral leadership in this case extended beyond his organization into the industry. As Michael Useem pointed out, Merck has become the benchmark by which the moral behavior of other pharmaceutical companies is judged. Sometimes the moral actions of one CEO or company set the bar higher for others. Useem observed that the message hit home at Glaxo. In comparing Glaxo to Merck, a business writer once called Glaxo "a hollow enterprise lacking purpose and lacking soul."[6] Merck's values seemed to inspire Glaxo's new CEO Richard Sykes. In 1993 Glaxo invested in developing a drug to combat a form of tuberculosis that is connected to AIDS and found mostly among the poor. In 1996 Glaxo donated a potent new product for malaria. Similarly, Dupont is now giving away nylon to filter guinea worms out of drinking water in poor countries, and American Cyanamid is donating a larvacide to control them.

A cynic might regard Merck's donation of Streptomycin and Mectizan as nothing more than public relations stunts. But what is most interesting about the actions of Merck's leaders is that while they believed that "by doing good they would do well," at the time that they acted, it was unclear exactly when and how the company would benefit. Neither the Japanese after the war nor the poor people of the world who are threatened by river blindness seemed likely to return the favor in the near future. While this wasn't an altruistic act, it was not a purely self-interested one either. Since it was unclear if, when, and how Merck would benefit, it is reasonable to assume that Merck's leaders and the values upon which they acted were authentic. They intentionally acted on their values. Any future benefits required a leap of faith on their part.

Business leaders' values matter to the organization only if they act on them. In business ethics and in life, we always hope that doing the right thing, while costly and sometimes painful in the short run, will pay off in the long run.

NOTES

1. The information about this case is from Michael Useem, *The Leadership Moment* (New York: Times Business Books, 1998), chap. 1.

2. Ibid., p. 23.

3. Ibid., p. 42.
4. Ibid., p. 29.
5. Ibid., p. 29.
6. Ibid., p. 31.

QUESTIONS

1. What was it about the corporate culture and Vagelos that made it possible for Merck to donate the drug Mectizan?

2. What does this case tell you about the impact of moral leadership inside and outside the organization?

3. Give some examples of cases where the ethical behavior of one company improved the behavior or raised the ethical standards of other companies in the same industry.

CASE 13.4

How Raj Rajaratnam Gave Galleon Group Its "Edge"

Katherine Burton and Saijel Kishan

Katherine Burton and Saijel Kishan write for Bloomberg.Net.

Every weekday at 8:35 a.m., Galleon Group's 70 analysts, portfolio managers, and traders pack into a conference room on the 34th floor of the IBM Building, a gray-green polished granite skyscraper on New York's Madison Avenue. Tardy arrivals are fined $25.

At the head of the table, Chief Executive Officer Raj Rajaratnam fires off questions to the staff of his $3.7 billion hedge-fund firm: Which companies' margins are peaking? What would change your mind about this stock? What's the risk of that company failing to win an expected contract? The 52-year-old billionaire expects his analysts to have an edge: better information than anyone else, say people who have attended the meetings.

U.S. prosecutors allege that Rajaratnam's own edge was illegal. He was arrested on October 16 at his home on Manhattan's Sutton Place, charged with using inside information to trade shares including Google Inc., Polycom Inc., Hilton Hotels Corp., and Advanced Micro Devices Inc., according to complaints. Five other defendants also were arrested in New York and California in a $20 million scheme that prosecutors say is the largest-ever insider trading case involving hedge funds.

"Every trader wants an edge, and there are many gray areas when it comes to aggressive research," said Ron Geffner, a lawyer at New York-based Sadis & Goldberg LLP, whose clients include hedge funds. "But if you trade on material, non-public information that comes from a company insider who is breaching his fiduciary duty, odds are that it is illegal."

From Bloomberg.net, October 9, 2009.

Rajaratnam's net worth of $1.3 billion makes him the 559th richest person in the world, according to *Forbes Magazine*, on par with the likes of hedge-fund manager Julian Robertson and investor Wilbur Ross. Rajaratnam has invested in at least two New York City restaurants, Opia, in midtown Manhattan, according to people who know him, and Rosa Mexicano.

Galleon was among the 10 largest hedge funds in the world in the early years of this decade, and it managed $7 billion at its peak in 2008. It also was one of the three largest technology hedge funds along with Lawrence Bowman's Bowman Technology Fund, which closed in 2001, and Daniel Benton's Andor Capital Management LLC, which shut down last year.

Galleon's $1.2 billion Diversified fund has climbed 21.5 percent a year, on average, since 1992, according to a September marketing document from the firm, compared with 7.6 percent for the Standard & Poor's 500 Index of the largest U.S. companies. The fund has returned 22.3 percent this year, according to an investor letter.

As Rajaratnam's wealth grew, he and his wife, Asha Pabla, who have three children, created a family foundation and have given money to fight AIDS in India. They donated $5 million to help the 2004 tsunami victims in his home country of Sri Lanka, where Rajaratnam was on vacation with his family when the disaster struck.

The foundation donated $400,000 in 2005 to the Tamils Rehabilitation Organization in Cumberland, Maryland, according to tax forms filed by the foundation with the Internal Revenue Service. Two years later, the U.S. Treasury Department froze the assets of the charity, saying it was a front for the Liberation Tigers of Tamil Eelam, or LTTE, which the State Department had designated as a terrorist group 10 years earlier.

"His donation was responsible for rebuilding thousands of homes for Tamils, Sinhalese, and Muslims without discrimination," Dan Gagnier, a spokesman for Galleon, said in an e-mailed statement.

Sri Lanka authorities will review "significant" transactions carried out by Rajaratnam and Channa De Silva, director general of the Securities and Exchange Commission of Sri Lanka, said in an interview today. The agency will "collaborate" with foreign governments in their investigations.

"We don't want a market glazed with investors of this reputation and will make every attempt to keep the Sri Lankan market clean," De Silva said.

Born in Sri Lanka's capital, Colombo, Rajaratnam was educated there at St. Thomas' Preparatory School before leaving for England, where he studied engineering at the University of Sussex. He came to the United States to get his master's of business administration, graduating from the University of Pennsylvania's Wharton School in 1983.

His first job after graduation was at Chase Manhattan Bank, where he was a lending officer in the group that made loans to high-tech companies. In 1985, he joined Needham & Co., a New York-based investment bank that specialized in technology and health-care companies. He started as an analyst covering the electronics industry and rose through the ranks, becoming head of research in 1987, chief operating officer in 1989 and president in 1991. A year later, at 34, Rajaratnam started a fund, Needham Emerging Growth Partners LP, according to Galleon's marketing documents.

Rajaratnam and Needham colleagues Krishen Sud, Gary Rosenbach, and Ari Arjavalingam formed Galleon Group in January 1997. By the end of that year, they were managing $830 million, much of it from technology company executives that Rajaratnam had gotten to know throughout his career, according to *The New Investment Superstars: 13 Great Investors and Their Strategies for Superior Returns,* written by Lois Peltz (John Wiley & Sons, 2001).

As the Internet bubble burst in 2000, the Galleon Diversified Fund climbed 43.7 percent in the three-year period through 2002, while the S&P 500 dropped 37.6 percent.

Galleon's assets jumped to $5 billion by 2001, making it one of the 10 biggest hedge funds in the world. That year Sud, who was co-head of the firm's health-care fund and who had been friends with Rajaratnam since the two were classmates at Wharton two decades before, left to start his own firm, taking six employees with him.

Rajaratnam faces 13 fraud and conspiracy counts, many of which carry 20-year maximum sentences. Under federal sentencing guidelines, he faces 10 years in prison if convicted at trial, Assistant U.S. Attorney Josh Klein said in court on October 16.

Klein asked Eaton to hold Rajaratnam in jail pending his trial. He said the hedge-fund manager had "enormous incentive" to flee to his native Sri Lanka or elsewhere. The prosecutor said there's additional evidence that there may be more charges against Rajaratnam and that the evidence is "overwhelming."

Defense attorney Jim Walden said in court that prosecutors are misconstruing the evidence against Rajaratnam and that the case isn't as strong as prosecutors allege.

Prosecutors say Rajaratnam traded on leaks from insiders at Polycom, Moody's Investors Service Inc., and Market Street Partners. In another alleged scheme, Chiesi got tips from an unidentified person at Akamai Technologies Inc. and from Moffat, according to one of the criminal complaints. These tips generated others, prosecutors said, as Chiesi passed them onto to Rajaratnam, who in turn gave Chiesi inside information.

The government's complaint quotes conversations between Chiesi and Rajaratnam, including a July 24, 2008 discussion that they allegedly had after she spoke to the person at Akamai. That day, Akamai stock had closed at $32.18.

"Akamai," Chiesi told Rajaratnam, according to the complaint. "They're gonna guide down. I just got a call from my guy."

After Chiesi said that the company's comments would bring the stock down to $25 a share, Rajaratnam replied that he would be "radio silent" and asked when Akamai would report, according to the complaint.

QUESTIONS

1. How do you size up the ethics of a man who gives generously to charity but cheats in his business practices? Is Rajaratnam like a Robin Hood? Was Robin Hood, who stole from the rich and give to the poor, ethical?

2. What do you think happens to hard working successful business leaders like Rajaratnam who go from making money through their hard work to insider trading? Do you think that success changed Rajaratnam or was he unethical from the start?

3. Can a business leader aggressively push for an "edge" without pushing employees in to unethical behavior?

CHAPTER QUESTIONS

1. Why is it difficult to be an ethical and effective leader?

2. What ethical challenges are distinctive to people who hold positions of leadership?

3. What can leaders, followers, organizations, and other stakeholders do to improve and/or maintain the ethical behavior of leaders?

14

Who's Minding the Store?

The Ethics of Corporate Governance

Introduction

It is an old question: Who will guard the guardians? In our giant corporations, many of which are larger and more powerful than most state and national governments, who will see to it that they obey the rules and see to the public interest as well as their own profits? The answer is supposed to be corporate directors, whose job it is to ensure that the corporation follows the rules and acts responsibly. But who keeps an eye on the directors? What assures us that they, too, follow the rules and keep a perspective larger than the corporation and its chief executives? It is difficult enough to govern the corporate superstars that many CEOs have become in today's celebrity-driven media. (Even the business pages read like "lives of the rich and famous" these days.) CEOs today enjoy rock star-like celebrity status and salaries that even rock stars cannot reach, and they develop gigantic (if only sometimes justified) egos to match. To complicate matters even more, a good number of CEOs started their companies themselves. They have a privileged attitude toward their creations, which were once private companies, in which they could, in effect, make all of the rules and formulate uncontradicted policies. When they took those companies public, however, a whole new set of rules and responsibilities came to govern how they could operate and how they could spend the money that now came from their investors. Dennis Koslowski, the extravagant CEO of Tyco who threw multimillion-dollar parties and lived in several multimillion-dollar homes and apartments, all on the company tab (and not declared to his stockholders as part of his compensation), is only a particularly egregious example of what is not an uncommon problem. But imagine, if you were one of Tyco's directors, trying to manage Dennis Koslowski. How do you get him to produce results for the company and serve the public when he is, at least in his mind, the monarch, rather than a mere "officer" of the corporation? You remember, too, that he has an important, if not definitive, say in your own compensation for being a board member as well as on whether or not you continue to serve on the board. Now how do you feel about criticizing his behavior or overseeing his decisions? No matter how conscientious you are, if there is no serious insulation between the executives and the board, it is evident that your views are going to be pressured or compromised.

In response to this problem of interlocking executives and board members, some corporate analysts believe that stockholders, stakeholders, and employees (three groups that should be distinguished and might well disagree) ought to have a strong voice in corporate governance. But this has its problems, too. Democracy may be the best kind of government when it comes to running nations, but successful corporations often have to be swift moving and decisive. There is sometimes no time to debate the issues, form a committee, or take a vote. Furthermore, most successful large companies are run by a single authoritative person or perhaps a small group (a CEO, a COO, and a CFO), not a large group of people with many different voices. We want dissent and disagreement in a democracy, but do we want the same in a large corporation? Most executives, needless to say, want unity, "everybody on the same page." The more dissident voices they try to include in decisions, the more difficult that unity is to achieve. They think, how can a hundred or a thousand only somewhat-informed people make a better decision about the direction of a company than a single expert—or a handful of experts—who made that company the success that it is? On the other hand, multiple perspectives often make decisions more rational. From the executive or director's high perch, the view of the company might be impressive, but it is also limited. A worker on the floor or a line manager may see problems much more clearly than any executive could. And in terms of fairness, too, should a person who has $20,000 invested in a company after working for the company for 30 years have no say in the company's future while someone who recently invested $10 million (and so earned a seat on the board) gets to call the shots?

In this chapter we consider these problems of corporate governance, some of the recent spectacular failures of governance, and some proposals for better models of guiding corporations and their leaders. We are particularly concerned with the kinds of pressures that are placed on corporations, their boards and their CEOs, and how those pressures may be counterbalanced by regulations or other forms of systematic corporate control.

Ralph Nader, Mark Green, and Joel Seligman consider the problem of how power should be exerted in corporations, by whom and on what grounds. They suggest criteria for controlling directors and monitoring the responsibility of directors. Irving Shapiro surveys the recent "state of play" of corporate boards. Rebecca Reisner asks if increased corporate governance may reach a point when it drives away the best CEOs. Tom Dunfee offers a detailed analysis of the various approaches to corporate governance and how they relate to our moral thinking. Dunfee makes specific recommendations for changes in corporate governance. Finally, John McCall argues for a strong employee voice in corporate governance.

Ralph Nader, Mark Green, and Joel Seligman

Who Rules the Corporation?

For years Ralph Nader has been one of the most powerful voices in corporate reform. He is also a prominent independent political figure. Mark Green is a leading democratic author and thinker. His most recent work is *The Book on Bush*. Joel Seligman is dean and Ethan A.H. Shepley University Professor at Washington University School of Law.

All modern state corporation statutes describe a common image of corporate governance, an image pyramidal in form. At the base of the pyramid are the shareholders or owners of the corporation. Their ownership gives them the right to elect representatives to direct the corporation and to approve fundamental corporate actions such as mergers or bylaw amendments. The intermediate level is held by the board of directors, who are required by a provision common to nearly every state corporation law "to manage the business and affairs of the corporation." On behalf of the shareholders, the directors are expected to select and dismiss corporate officers; to approve important financial decisions; to distribute profits; and to see that accurate periodic reports are forwarded to the shareholders. Finally, at the apex of the pyramid are the corporate officers. In the eyes of the law, the officers are the employees of the shareholder owners. Their authority is limited to those responsibilities which the directors delegate to them.

In reality, this legal image is virtually a myth. In nearly every large American business corporation, there exists a management autocracy. One man—variously titled the President, or the Chairman of the Board, or the Chief Executive Officer—or a small coterie of men rules the corporation. Far from being chosen by the directors to run the corporation, this chief executive or executive clique chooses the board of directors and, with the acquiescence of the board, controls the corporation.

The common theme of many instances of mismanagement is a failure to restrain the power of these senior executives. A corporate chief executive's decisions to expand, merge, or even violate the law can often be made without accountability to outside scrutiny. There is, for example, the detailed disclosures of the recent bribery cases. Not only do these reports suggest how widespread corporate foreign and domestic criminality has become; they also provide a unique study in the pathology of American corporate management. . . .

The key to management's hegemony is money. Effectively, only incumbent management can nominate directors—because it has a nearly unlimited power to use corporate funds to win board elections while opponents must prepare separate proxies and campaign literature entirely at their own expense. . . .

REVAMPING THE BOARD

The modern corporation is akin to a political state in which all powers are held by a single clique. The senior executives of a large firm are essentially not accountable to any other officials within the firm. These are precisely the circumstances that, in a democratic political state, require a separation of powers into different branches of authority. As James Madison explained in the *Federalist No. 47*:

> The accumulation of all powers, legislative, executive, and judiciary, in the same hands, whether of one, a few or many, and whether hereditary, self-appointed, or elective, may justly be pronounced the very definition of tyranny. Were the federal

constitution, therefore, really chargeable with this accumulation of power, or with a mixture of powers, having a dangerous tendency to such an accumulation, no further arguments would be necessary to inspire a universal reprobation of the system.

A similar concern over the unaccountability of business executives historically led to the elevation of a board of directors to review and check the actions of operating management. As a practical matter, if corporate governance is to be reformed, it must begin by returning the board to this historical role. The board should serve as an internal auditor of the corporations, responsible for constraining executive management from violations of law and breach of trust. Like a rival branch of government, the board's function must be defined as separate from operating management. Rather than pretending directors can "manage" the corporation, the board's role as disciplinarian should be clearly described. Specifically, the board of directors should:

- establish and monitor procedures that assure that operating executives are informed of and obey applicable federal, state, and local laws;
- approve or veto all important executive management business proposals such as corporate by-laws, mergers, or dividend decisions;
- hire and dismiss the chief executive officer and be able to disapprove the hiring and firing of the principal executives of the corporation; and
- report to the public and the shareholders how well the corporation has obeyed the law and protected the shareholders' investment.

It is not enough, however, to specify what the board should do. State corporations statutes have long provided that "the business and affairs of a corporation shall be managed by a board of directors," yet it has been over a century since the boards of the largest corporations have actually performed this role. To reform the corporation, a federal chartering law must also specify the manner in which the board performs its primary duties.

First, to insure that the corporation obeys federal and state laws, the board should designate executives responsible for compliance with these laws and require periodic signed reports describing the effectiveness of compliance procedures. Mechanisms to administer spot checks on compliance with the principal statutes should be created. Similar mechanisms can insure that corporate "whistle blowers" and nonemployee sources may communicate to the board—in private and without fear of retaliation—knowledge of violations of law.

Second, the board should actively review important executive business proposals to determine their full compliance with law, to preclude conflicts of interest, and to assure that executive decisions are rational and informed of all foreseeable risks and costs. But even though the board's responsibility here is limited to approval or veto of executive initiatives, it should proceed in as well-informed a manner as practicable. To demonstrate rational business judgment, the directorate should require management "to prove its case." It should review the studies upon which management relied to make a decision require management to justify its decision in terms of costs or rebutting dissenting views, and, when necessary, request that outside experts provide an independent business analysis.

Only with respect to two types of business decisions should the board exceed this limited review role. The determination of salary, expense, and benefit schedules inherently possesses such obvious conflicts of interest for executives that only the board should make these decisions. And since the relocation of principal manufacturing facilities tends to have a greater effect on local communities than any other type of business decision, the board should require management to prepare a "community impact statement." This public report would be similar to the environmental impact statements presently required by the National Environmental Policy Act. It would require the corporation to state the purpose of a relocation decision; to compare feasible alternative means; to quantify the costs to the local community; and to consider methods to mitigate these costs. Although it would not prevent a corporation from making a profit-maximizing decision, it would require the corporation to minimize the costs of relocation decisions to local communities.

To accomplish this restructuring of the board requires the institutionalization of a new profession:

the full-time "professional" director. Corporate scholars frequently identify William O. Douglas' 1940 proposal for "salaried, professional experts [who] would bring a new responsibility and authority to directorates and a new safety to stockholders" as the origin of the professional director idea. More recently, corporations including Westinghouse and Texas Instruments have established slots on their boards to be filled by full-time directors. Individuals such as Harvard Business School's Myles Mace and former Federal Reserve Board chairman William McChesney Martin consider their own thoroughgoing approach to boardroom responsibilities to be that of a "professional" director.

To succeed, professional directors must put in the substantial time necessary to get the job done. One cannot monitor the performance of Chrysler's or Gulf's management at a once-a-month meeting; those firms' activities are too sweeping and complicated for such ritual oversight. The obvious minimum here is an adequate salary to attract competent persons to work as full-time directors and to maintain the independence of the board from executive management.

The board must also be sufficiently staffed. A few board members alone cannot oversee the activities of thousands of executives. To be able to appraise operating management, the board needs a trim group of attorneys, economists, and labor and consumer advisors who can analyze complex business proposals, investigate complaints, spot-check accountability, and frame pertinent inquiries.

The board also needs timely access to relevant corporate data. To insure this, the board should be empowered to nominate the corporate financial auditor, select the corporation's counsel, compel the forwarding and preservation of corporate records, require all corporate executives or representatives to answer fully all board questions respecting corporate operations, and dismiss any executive or representative who fails to do so.

This proposed redesign for corporate democracy attempts to make executive management accountable to the law and shareholders without diminishing its operating efficiency. Like a judiciary within the corporation, the board has ultimate powers to judge and sanction. Like a legislature, it oversees executive activity. Yet executive management substantially retains its powers to initiate and administer business operations. The chief executive officer retains control over the organization of the executive hierarchy and the allocation of the corporate budget. The directors are given ultimate control over a narrow jurisdiction: Does the corporation obey the law, avoid exploiting consumers or communities, and protect the shareholders' investment? The executive contingent retains general authority for all corporate operations.

No doubt there will be objections that this structure is too expensive or that it will disturb the "harmony" of executive management. But it is unclear that there would be any increased cost in adopting an effective board. The true cost to the corporation could only be determined by comparing the expense of a fully paid and staffed board with the savings resulting from the elimination of conflicts of interest and corporate waste. In addition, if this should result in a slightly increased corporate expense, the appropriateness must be assessed within a broader social context: should federal and state governments or the corporations themselves bear the primary expense of keeping corporations honest? In our view, this cost should be placed on the corporations as far as reasonably possible.

It is true that an effective board will reduce the "harmony" of executive management in the sense that the power of the chief executive or senior executives will be subject to knowledgeable review. But a board which monitors rather than rubber-stamps management is exactly what is necessary to diminish the unfettered authority of the corporate chief executive or ruling clique. The autocratic power these individuals presently possess has proven unacceptably dangerous: it has led to recurring violations of law, conflicts of interest, productive inefficiency, and pervasive harm to consumers, workers, and the community environment. Under normal circumstances there should be a healthy friction between operating executives and the board to assure that the wisest possible use is made of corporate resources. When corporate executives are breaking the law, there should be no "harmony" whatsoever.

ELECTION OF THE BOARD

Restructuring the board is hardly likely to succeed if boards remain as homogeneously white, male, and narrowly oriented as they are today. Dissatisfaction with current selection of directors is so intense that analysts of corporate governance, including Harvard Laws School's Abram Chayes, Yale political scientist Robert Dahl, and University of Southern California Law School Professor Christopher Stone, have each separately urged that the starting point of corporate reform should be to change the way in which the board is elected.

Professor Chayes, echoing John Locke's principle that no authority is legitimate except that granted "the consent of the governed," argues that employees and other groups substantially affected by corporate operations should have a say in its governance:

> Shareholder democracy, so-called, is misconceived because the shareholders are not the governed of the corporations whose consent must be sought.... Their interests are protected if financial information is made available, fraud and overreaching are prevented, and a market is maintained in which their shares may be sold. A priori, there is no reason for them to have any voice, direct or representational, in [corporate decision making]. They are no more affected than nonshareholding neighbors by these decisions....
>
> A more spacious conception of "membership," and one closer to the facts of corporate life, would include all those having a relation of sufficient intimacy with the corporation or subject to its powers in a sufficiently specialized way. Their rightful share in decisions and the exercise of corporate power would be exercised through an institutional arrangement appropriately designed to represent the interests of a constituency of members having a significant common relation to the corporation and its power.

Professor Dahl holds a similar view: "[W]hy should people who own shares be given the privileges of citizenship in the government of the firm when citizenship is denied to other people who also make vital contributions to the firm?" he asks rhetorically. "The people I have in mind are, of course, employees and customers, without whom the firm could not exist, and the general public, without whose support for (or acquiescence in) the myriad protections and services of the state the firm would instantly disappear...." Yet Dahl finds proposals for interest group representation less desirable than those for worker self-management. He also suggests consideration of co-determination statutes such as those enacted by West Germany and ten other European and South American countries under which shareholders and employees separately elect designated portions of the board.

From a different perspective, Professor Stone has recommended that a federal-agency appoint "general public directors" to serve on the boards of all the largest industrial and financial firms. In certain extreme cases such as where a corporation repeatedly violates the law, Stone recommends that the federal courts appoint "special public directors" to prevent further delinquency.

There are substantial problems with each of those proposals. It seems impossible to design a general "interest group" formula which will assure that all affected constituencies of large industrial corporations will be represented and that all constituencies will be given appropriate weight. Even if such a formula could be designed, however, there is the danger that consumer or community or minority or franchisee representatives would become only special pleaders for their constituents and otherwise lack the loyalty or interest to direct generally. This defect has emerged in West Germany under codetermination. Labor representatives apparently are indifferent to most problems of corporate management that do not directly affect labor. They seem as deferential to operating executive management as present American directors are. Alternatively, federally appointed public directors might be frozen out of critical decision-making by a majority of "privately" elected directors, or the appointing agency itself might be biased....

The homogeneity of the board can only be ended by giving to each director, in addition to a general duty to see that the corporation is profitably administered, a separate oversight responsibility, a separate expertise, and a separate constituency so that each important public concern would be guaranteed at least one informed representative on the board. There might be nine corporate directors, each of whom is elected to a board position with one of the following oversight responsibilities:

1. Employee welfare
2. Consumer protection
3. Environmental protection and community relations
4. Shareholder rights
5. Compliance with law
6. Finances
7. Purchasing and marketing
8. Management efficiency
9. Planning and research

By requiring each director to balance responsibility for representing a particular social concern against responsibility for the overall health of the enterprise, the problem of isolated "public" directors would be avoided. No individual director is likely to be "frozen out" of collegial decision-making because all directors would be of the same character. Each director would spend the greater part of his or her time developing expertise in a different area; each director would have a motivation to insist that a different aspect of a business decision be considered. Yet each would simultaneously be responsible for participating in all board decisions, as directors now are. So the specialized area of each director would supplement but not supplant the director's general duties.

To maintain the independence of the board from the operating management it reviews also requires that each federally chartered corporation shall be directed by a purely "outside" board. No executive, attorney, representative, or agent of a corporation should be allowed to serve simultaneously as a director of that same corporation. Directorial and executive loyalty should be furthered by an absolute prohibition of interlocks. No director, executive, general counsel, or company agent should be allowed to serve more than one corporation subject to the Federal Corporate Chartering Act.

Several objections may be raised. First, how can we be sure that completely outside boards will be competent? Corporate campaign rules should be redesigned to emphasize qualifications. This will allow shareholder voters to make rational decisions based on information clearly presented to them. It is also a fair assumption that shareholders, given an actual choice and role in corporate governance, will want to elect the men and women most likely to safeguard their investments.

A second objection is that once all interlocks are proscribed and a full-time outside board required, there will not be enough qualified directors to staff all major firms. This complaint springs from that corporate mentality which, accustomed to 60-year-old white male bankers and businessmen as directors, makes the norm a virtue. In fact, if we loosen the reins on our imagination, America has a large, rich, and diverse pool of possible directorial talent from academics and public administrators and community leaders to corporate and public interest lawyers.

But directors should be limited to four two-year terms so that boards do not become stale. And no director should be allowed to serve on more than one board at any one time. Although simultaneous service on two or three boards might allow key directors to "pollinize" directorates by comparing their different experiences, this would reduce their loyalty to any one board, jeopardize their ability to fully perform their new directorial responsibilities, and undermine the goal of opening up major boardrooms to as varied a new membership as is reasonable.

The shareholder electoral process should be made more democratic as well. Any shareholder or allied shareholder group which owns .1 percent of the common voting stock in the corporation or comprises 100 or more individuals and does not include a present executive of the corporation, nor act for a present executive, may nominate up to three persons to serve as directors. This will exclude executive management from the nomination process. It also increases the likelihood of a diverse board by preventing any one or two sources from proposing all nominees. To prevent frivolous use of the nominating power, this proposal establishes a minimum shareownership condition.

Six weeks prior to the shareholders' meeting to elect directors, each shareholder should receive a ballot and a written statement on which each candidate for the board sets forth his or her qualifications to hold office and purposes for seeking office. All campaign costs would be borne by the corporation. These strict campaign and funding rules will assure that all nominees will have an equal opportunity to be judged by the shareholders. By preventing directorates from being bought, these provisions will require board elections to be conducted solely on the merit of the candidates.

Finally, additional provisions will require cumulative voting and forbid "staggered" board elections. Thus any shareholder faction capable of jointly voting approximately 10 percent of the total number of shares cast may elect a director.

A NEW ROLE FOR SHAREHOLDERS

The difficulty with this proposal is the one that troubled Juvenal two millennia ago: *Quis custodiet ipsos custodes*, or Who shall watch the watchmen? Without a full-time body to discipline the board, it would be so easy for the board of directors and executive management to become friends. Active vigilance could become routinized into an uncritical partnership. The same board theoretically elected to protect shareholder equity and internalize law might instead become management's lobbyist.

Relying on shareholders to discipline directors may strike many as a dubious approach. Historically, the record of shareholder participation in corporate governance has been an abysmal one. The monumental indifference of most shareholders is worse than that of sheep; sheep at least have some sense of what manner of ram they follow. But taken together, the earlier proposals—an outside, full-time board, nominated by rival shareholder groups and voted on by beneficial owners—will increase involvement by shareholders. And cumulative voting insures that an aroused minority of shareholders—even one as small as 9 or 10 percent of all shareholders—shall have the opportunity to elect at least one member of the board....

Shareholders are not the only ones with an incentive to review decisions of corporate management; nor, as Professors Chayes and Dahl argue, are shareholders the only persons who should be accorded corporate voting rights. The increasing use by American corporations of technologies and materials that pose direct and serious threats to the health of communities surrounding their plants requires the creation of a new form of corporate voting right. When a federally chartered corporation engages, for example, in production or distribution of nuclear fuels or the emission of toxic air, water, or solid waste pollutants, citizens whose health is endangered should not be left, at best, with receiving money damages after a time-consuming trial to compensate them for damaged property, impaired health, or even death.

Instead, upon finding of a public health hazard by three members of the board of directors or 3 percent of the shareholders, a corporate referendum should be held in the political jurisdiction affected by the health hazard. The referendum would be drafted by the unit triggering it—either the three board members or a designate of the shareholders. The affected citizens by majority vote will then decide whether the hazardous practice shall be allowed to continue. This form of direct democracy has obvious parallels to the initiative and referendum procedures familiar to many states—except that the election will be paid for by a business corporation and will not necessarily occur at a regular election.

This type of election procedure is necessary to give enduring meaning to the democratic concept of "consent of the governed." To be sure, this proposal goes beyond the traditional assumption that the only affected or relevant constituents of the corporation are the shareholders. But no longer can we accept the Faustian bargain that the continued toleration of corporate destruction of local health and property is the cost to the public of doing business. In an equitable system of governance, the perpetrators should answer to their victims.

QUESTIONS

1. Is corruption at the highest levels of the corporation inevitable? How can it be guarded against?

2. Why do corporations and corporate boards so often encounter ethical dilemmas?

Irving S. Shapiro

Power and Accountability: The Changing Role of the Corporate Board of Directors

Irving S. Shapiro was a prominent attorney.

Are corporations suitably controlled, and to whom or what are they responsible?

One school of opinion holds that corporations cannot be adequately called to account because there are systemic economic and political failings. In this view, nothing short of a major overhaul will serve. What is envisioned, at least by many in this camp, are new kinds of corporate organizations constructed along the lines of democratic political institutions. The guiding ideology would be communitarian, with the needs and rights of the community emphasized in preference to profit-seeking goals now pursued by corporate leaders (presumably with Darwinian abandon, with natural selection weeding out the weak, and with society left to pick up the external costs).

BOARDS CHANGING FOR BETTER

Other critics take a more temperate view. They regard the present system as sound and its methods of governance as morally defensible. They concede, though, that changes are needed to reflect new conditions. Whether the changes are to be brought about by gentle persuasion, or require the use of a two-by-four to get the mule's attention, is part of the debate.

This paper sides with the gradualists. My position, based on a career in industry and personal observation of corporate boards at work, is that significant improvements have been made in recent years in corporate governance, and that more changes are coming in an orderly way; that with these amendments, corporations are accountable and better monitored

than ever before; and that pat formulas or proposals for massive "restructuring" should be suspect. The formula approach often is based on ignorance of what it takes to run a large enterprise, on false premises as to the corporate role in society, or on a philosophy that misreads the American tradition and leaves no room for large enterprises that are both free and efficient.

The draconian proposals would almost certainly yield the worst of all possibilities, a double-negative tradeoff: They would sacrifice the most valuable qualities of the enterprise system to gain the least attractive features of the governmental system. Privately owned enterprises are geared to a primary economic task, that of joining human talents and natural resources in the production and distribution of goods and services. That task is essential, and two centuries of national experience suggest these conclusions: The United States has been uncommonly successful at meeting economic needs through reliance on private initiative; and the competitive marketplace is a better course-correction device than governmental fiat. The enterprise system would have had to have failed miserably before the case could be made for replacing it with governmental dictum.

Why should the public have any interest in the internal affairs of corporations? Who cares who decides? Part of the answer comes from recent news stories noting such special problems as illegal corporate contributions to political campaigns, and tracking the decline and fall of once-stout companies such as Penn Central. Revelations of that kind raise questions about the probity and competence of the people minding the largest stores. There is more to it than this, though. There have always been cases of corporate failures. Small companies have gone under too, at a rate far higher than their larger brethren.

Excerpted from a paper presented in the Fairless Lecture Series, Carnegie-Mellon University, October 24, 1979. Reprinted by permission.

Instances of corruption have occurred in institutions of all sizes, whether they be commercial enterprises or some other kind.

Corporate behavior and performance are points of attention, and the issue attaches to size, precisely because people do not see the large private corporation as entirely private. People care about what goes on in the corporate interior because they see themselves as affected parties whether they work in such companies or not.

There is no great mystery as to the source of this challenge to the private character of governance. Three trends account for it. First is the growth of very large corporations. They have come to employ a large portion of the workforce, and have become key factors in the nation's technology, wealth and security. They have generated admiration for their prowess, but also fear of their imputed power.

The second contributing trend is the decline of owner-management. Over time, corporate shares have been dispersed. The owners have hired managers, entrusted them with the power to make decisions, and drifted away from involvement in corporate affairs except to meet statutory requirements (as, for example, to approve a stock split or elect a slate of directors).

That raises obvious practical questions. If the owners are on the sidelines, what is to stop the managers from remaining in power indefinitely, using an inside position to control the selection of their own bosses, the directors? Who is looking over management's shoulder to monitor performance?

The third element here is the rise in social expectations regarding corporations. It is no longer considered enough for a company to make products and provide commercial services. The larger it is, the more it is expected to assume various obligations that once were met by individuals or communities, or were not met at all.

With public expectations ratcheting upward, corporations are under pressure to behave more like governments and embrace a universe of problems. That would mean, of necessity, that private institutions would focus less on problems of their own choice.

If corporations succumbed to that pressure, and in effect declared the public's work to be their own, the next step would be to turn them into institutions accountable to the public in the same way that units of government are accountable.

But the corporation does not parallel the government. The assets in corporate hands are more limited and the constituents have options. There are levels of appeal. While the only accountability in government lies within government itself—the celebrated system of checks and balances among the executive, legislative, and judicial branches—the corporation is in a different situation: It has external and plural accountability, codified in the law and reinforced by social pressure. It must "answer" in one way or another to all levels of government, to competitors in the marketplace who would be happy to have the chance to increase their own market share, to employees who can strike or quit, and to consumers who can keep their wallets in their pockets. The checks are formidable even if one excludes for purposes of argument the corporation's initial point of accountability, its stockholders (many of whom do in fact vote their shares, and do not just use their feet).

The case for major reforms in corporate governance rests heavily on the argument that past governmental regulation of large enterprises has been impotent or ineffectual. This is an altogether remarkable assertion, given the fact that the nation has come through a period in which large corporations have been subjected to an unprecedented flood of new legislation and rule making. Regulation now reaches into every corporate nook and cranny—including what some people suppose (erroneously) to be the sanctuary of the boardroom.

Market competition, so lightly dismissed by some critics as fiction or artifact, is in fact a vigorous force in the affairs of almost all corporations. Size lends no immunity to its relentless pressures. The claim that the largest corporations somehow have set themselves above the play of market forces or, more likely, make those forces play for themselves, is widely believed. Public opinion surveys show that. What is lacking is any evidence that this is so. Here too, the evidence goes the other way. Objective studies of concentrated industries (the auto industry, for instance) show that corporate size does not mean declining competitiveness, nor does it give assurance that the products will sell.

Everyday experience confirms this. Consider the hard times of the Chrysler Corporation today, the disappearance of many once-large companies from the American scene, and the constant rollover in the membership list of the "100 Largest," a churning process that has been going on for years and shows no signs of abating.

If indeed the two most prominent overseers of corporate behavior, government and competition, have failed to provide appropriate checks and balances, and if that is to be cited as evidence that corporations lack accountability, the burden of proof should rest with those who so state.

The basics apply to Sears Roebuck as much as to Sam's appliance shop. Wherever you buy the new toaster, it should work when it is plugged in. Whoever services the washing machine, the repairman should arrive at the appointed time, with tools and parts.

Special expectations are added for the largest firms, however. One is that they apply their resources to tasks that invite economies of scale, providing goods and services that would not otherwise be available, or that could be delivered by smaller units only at considerable loss of efficiency. Another is that, like the elephant, they watch where they put their feet and not stamp on smaller creatures through clumsiness or otherwise.

A second set of requirements can be added, related not to the markets selected by corporations individually, but to the larger economic tasks that must be accomplished in the name of the national interest and security. In concert with others in society, including big government, big corporations are expected to husband scarce resources and develop new ones, and to foster strong and diverse programs of research and development, to the end that practical technological improvements will emerge and the nation will be competitive in the international setting.

Beyond this there are softer but nonetheless important obligations: To operate with respect for the environment and with careful attention to the health and safety of people, to honor and give room to the personal qualities employees bring to their jobs, including their need to make an identifiable mark and to realize as much of their potential as possible; to lend assistance in filling community needs in which corporations have some stake; and to help offset community problems which in some measure corporations have helped to create.

This is not an impossible job, only a difficult one. Admitting that the assignment probably is not going

---

Advice for Corporate Directors
Immanuel Kant

1. Act only on the maxim [intention] whereby you can at the same time will that it should become a universal law.
2. Act as if the maxim of your action were to become by your will a universal law of nature.
3. Always act so as to treat humanity, whether in yourself or in others, as an end in itself, never merely as a means.
4. Always act as if to bring about, and as a member of, a Kingdom of Ends [that is, an ideal community in which everyone is always moral].

—*Fundamental Principles of the Metaphysics of Morals*

Corporate-Governance Reform

The certification of company accounts by senior executives should be a non-event. After all, financial statements were always supposed to be true and complete, and lying has long been deemed fraudulent. But in the wake of Enron, WorldCom and a slew of other scandals, America no longer trusts its corporate leaders to tell the truth without being warned by the sound of prison doors slamming. Thus, new rules requiring chief executives and chief financial officers to sign off on their accounts have become the stuff of headlines. All the headlines this week concerned August 14th, the SEC's deadline for the bosses of 695 listed American companies with annual revenue of more than $1.2 billion to swear by their financial statements or admit to problems. They are not the only ones under the microscope. Another 250 or so firms (those that do not have a calendar year-end) are expected to vouch for their numbers later in the year. And under America's new Sarbanes-Oxley act, the senior executives of all 14,000 firms listed in the United States, including those based overseas, will have to certify their accounts from August 29th. As people logged on in their thousands to the SEC's website to check which companies had made the cut—and as the treasury secretary, Paul O'Neill, called business honesty "the new patriotism"—it became clear that several firms would unpatriotically miss the deadline. Not surprisingly, the battered energy and telecoms sectors produced the most laggards (including CMS, Dynergy and Qwest). A big trucking group, Consolidated Freightways, also asked for more time. The penalties these companies face are still not clear.

—*The Economist*, Saturday, August 17, 2002.

---

to be carried out perfectly by any organization, the task is unlikely to be done even half well unless some boundary conditions are met. Large corporations cannot fulfill their duties unless they remain both profitable and flexible. They must be able to attract and hold those volunteer owners; which is to say, there must be the promise of present or future gain. Companies must have the wherewithal to reinvest significant amounts to revitalize their own capital plants, year after year in unending fashion. Otherwise, it is inevitable that they will go into decline versus competitors elsewhere, as will the nation.

Flexibility is no less important. The fields of endeavor engaging large business units today are dynamic in nature. Without an in-and-out flow of products and services, without the mobility to adapt to shifts in opportunities and public preferences,

corporations would face the fate of the buggywhip makers.

Profitability and flexibility are easy words to say, but in practice they make for hard decisions. A company that would close a plant with no more than a passing thought for those left unemployed would and should be charged with irresponsibility; but a firm that vowed never to close any of its plants would be equally irresponsible, for it might be consigning itself to a pattern of stagnation that could ultimately cost the jobs of the people in all of its plants.

The central requirement is not that large corporations take the pledge and bind themselves to stated actions covering all circumstances, but that they do a thoughtful and informed job of balancing competing (and ever changing) claims on corporate resources, mediating among the conflicting (also changing) desires of various constituencies, and not giving in to any one-dimensional perspective however sincerely felt. It is this that describes responsible corporate governance....

Once roles are defined, the key to success in running a large corporation is to lay out a suitable division of labor between the board and the management, make that division crystal clear on both sides, and staff the offices with the right people. Perhaps the best way to make that split is to follow the pattern used in the U.S. Constitution, which stipulates the powers of the Federal Government and specifies that everything not covered there is reserved to the states or the people thereof. The board of directors should lay claim to five basic jobs, and leave the rest to the paid managers.

The duties the board should not delegate are these:

1. The determination of the broad policies and the general direction the efforts of the enterprise should take.
2. The establishment of performance standards — ethical as well as commercial—against which the management will be judged, and the communication of these standards to the management in unambiguous terms.
3. The selection of company officers, and attention to the question of succession.
4. The review of top management's performance in following the overall strategy and meeting the board's standards as well as legal requirements.
5. The communication of the organization's goals and standards to those who have a significant stake in its activities (insiders and outsiders both) and of the steps being taken to keep the organization responsive to the needs of those people.

The establishment of corporate strategy and performance standards denotes a philosophy of active stewardship, rather than passive trusteeship. It is the mission of directors to see that corporate resources are put to creative use, and in the bargain subjected to calculated risks rather than simply being tucked into the countinghouse for safekeeping.

That in turn implies certain prerequisites for board members of large corporations which go beyond those required of a school board member, a trustee of a charitable organization, or a director of a small, local business firm. In any such assignments one would look for personal integrity, interest and intelligence, but beyond these there is a dividing line that marks capability and training.

The stakes are likely to be high in the large corporation, and the factors confronting the board and management usually are complex. The elements weighing heavily in decisions are not those with which people become familiar in the ordinary course of day-to-day life, as might be the case with a school board.

Ordinarily the management of a corporation attends to such matters as product introductions, capital expansions, and supply problems. This in no way reduces the need for directors with extensive business background, though. With few exceptions, corporate boards involve themselves in strategic decisions and those involving large capital commitments. Directors thus need at least as much breadth and perspective as the management, if not as much detailed knowledge.

If the directors are to help provide informed and principled oversight of corporate affairs, a good number of them must provide windows to the outside world. That is at least part of the rationale for outside directors, and especially for directors who can bring unique perspective to the group. There is an equally strong case, though, for directors with an intimate knowledge of the company's business, and insiders may be the best qualified to deliver that. What is important is not that a ratio be established, but that the group contain a full range of the competences needed to set courses of action that will largely determine the long-range success of the enterprise.

BOARDS NEED WINDOWS

The directors also have to be able and willing to invest considerable time in their work. In this day and age, with major resources on the line and tens of thousands of employees affected by each large corporation, there should be no seat in the board-room for people willing only to show up once a month to pour holy water over decisions already made. Corporate boards need windows, not window dressing!

There are two other qualities that may be self-evident from what has been said, but are mentioned for emphasis. Directors must be interested in the job and committed to the overall purpose of the organization. However much they may differ on details of accomplishment, they must be willing to work at the task of working with others on the board. They ought to be able to speak freely in a climate that encourages open discussion, but to recognize the difference between attacking an idea and attacking the person who presents it. No less must they see the difference between compromising tactics to reach consensus and compromising principles.

Structures and procedures, which so often are pushed to the fore in discussions of corporate governance, actually belong last. They are not unimportant, but they are subordinate.

Structure follows purpose, or should, and that is a useful principle for testing some of the proposals for future changes in corporate boards. Today, two-thirds to three-quarters of the directors of most large corporations are outsiders, and it is being proposed that this trend be pushed still farther, with the only insider being the chief executive officer, and with a further stipulation that he not be board chairman. This idea has surfaced from Harold Williams, and variations on it have come from other sources.

The idea bumps into immediate difficulties. High-quality candidates for boards are not in large supply as it is. Conflicts of interest would prohibit selection of many individuals close enough to an industry to be familiar with its problems. The disqualification of insiders would reduce the selection pool to a still smaller number, and the net result could well be corporate boards whose members were less competent and effective than those now sitting.

Experience would also suggest that such a board would be the most easily manipulated of all. That should be no trick at all for a skillful CEO, for he would be the only person in the room with a close, personal knowledge of the business.

The objective is unassailable: Corporate boards need directors with independence of judgment; but in today's business world, independence is not enough. In coping with such problems as those confronting the electronics corporations beset by heavy foreign competition, or those encountered by international banks which have loans outstanding in countries with shaky governments, boards made up almost entirely of outsiders would not just have trouble evaluating nuances of the management's performance; they might not even be able to read the radar and tell whether the helmsman was steering straight for the rocks.

If inadequately prepared individuals are placed on corporate boards, no amount of sincerity on their part can offset the shortcoming. It is pure illusion to suppose that complex business issues and organizational problems can be overseen by people with little or no experience in dealing with such problems. However intelligent such people might be, the effect of their governance would be to expose the people most affected by the organization—employees, owners, customers, suppliers—to leadership that would be (using the word precisely) incompetent.

It is sometimes suggested that the members of corporate boards ought to come from the constituencies—an employee-director, a consumer-director, an environmentalist-director, etc. This Noah's Ark proposal, which is probably not to be taken seriously, is an extension of the false parallel between corporations and elected governments. The flaw in the idea is all but self evident: People representing specific interest groups would by definition be committed to the goals of their groups rather than any others; but it is the responsibility of directors (not simply by tradition but as a matter of law as well) to serve the organization as a whole. The two goals are incompatible.

If there were such boards they would move at glacial speed. The internal political maneuvering would be Byzantine, and it is difficult to see how the directors could avoid an obvious challenge of accountability. Stockholder suits would pop up like dandelions in the spring.

One may also question how many people of ability would stand for election under this arrangement. Quotas are an anathema in a free society, and their indulgence here would insult the constituencies themselves—a woman on the board not because she is competent but only because she is female; a black for black's sake; and so on ad nauseam.

A certain amount of constituency pleading is not all bad, as long as it is part of a corporate commitment. There is something to be said for what Harold Williams labels "tension," referring to the divergence in perspective of those concerned primarily with internal matters and those looking more at the broader questions. However, as has been suggested by James Shepley, the president of Time, Inc., "tension" can lead to paralysis, and is likely to do so if boards are packed with groups known to be unsympathetic to the management's problems and business realities.

As Shepley commented, "The chief executive would be out of his mind who would take a risk-laden business proposition to a group of directors who, whatever their other merits, do not really understand the fine points of the business at hand, and whose official purpose is to create 'tension.'"[1]

Students of corporate affairs have an abundance of suggestions for organizing the work of boards, with detailed structures in mind for committees on audit, finance, and other areas; plus prescriptions for membership. The danger here is not that boards will pick the wrong formula—many organization charts could be made to work—but that boards will put too much emphasis on the wrong details.

The idea of utilizing a committee system in which sub-groups have designated duties is far more important than the particulars of their arrangement. When such committees exist, and they are given known and specific oversight duties, it is a signal to the outside world (and to the management) that performance is being monitored in a no-nonsense fashion.

It is this argument that has produced the rule changes covering companies listed on the New York Stock Exchange, calling for audit committees chaired by outside directors, and including no one currently active in management. Most large firms have moved in that direction, and the move makes sense, for an independently minded audit committee is a potent instrument of corporate oversight. Even a rule of that kind, though, has the potential of backfiring.

Suppose some of the directors best qualified to perform the audit function are not outsiders? Are the analytical skills and knowledge of career employees therefore to be bypassed? Are the corporate constituencies well served by such an exclusionary rule, keeping in mind that all directors, insiders or outsiders, are bound by the same legal codes and corporate books are still subject to independent, outside audit? It is scarcely a case of the corporate purse being placed in the hands of the unwatched.

Repeatedly, the question of structure turns on the basics: If corporations have people with competence and commitment on their boards, structure and process fall into line easily; if people with the needed qualities are missing or the performance standards are unclear, corporations are in trouble no matter whose guidebook they follow. Equally, the question drives to alternatives: The present system is surely not perfect, but what is better?

By the analysis presented here the old fundamentals are still sound, no alternative for radical change has been defended with successful argument, and the best course appears to be to stay within the historical and philosophical traditions of American enterprise, working out the remaining problems one by one.

NOTE

1. Shepley, *The CEO Goes to Washington*, Remarks to Fortune Corporation Communications Seminar, March 28, 1979.

QUESTIONS

1. How is the role of the board of directors changing?
2. What is the relationship between power and accountability? Why do they go hand in hand?

Rebecca Reisner | # When Does the CEO Just Quit?

Rebecca Reisner is a freelance journalist who writes primarily on contemporary business.

Tell members of the general public that (1) CEO compensation is likely to decline in the near future; and (2) this drop may compromise the self-esteem and morale of these chief executives, and most would reply (1) it's about time; and (2) who cares?

But for corporate HR officers and boards, it is something to worry about. According to a new study from the Corporate Executive Board (CEB), an organization in Arlington, Virginia, that provides research and support for executives, human resources officers are deeply concerned that the increased scrutiny CEO pay packages will receive—as well as actual cuts in compensation levels—will cause CEOs to become disengaged and even more likely to quit, imperiling the organizations that need their vision and confidence to make them strong despite a weakened economy.

"A lot of leadership teams are thinking about what to do to retain their senior leaders," says Jean Martin, director of the human resources practice at the CEB. The 2009 CEB study, *Executive Compensation*, found that the percentage of senior leaders who demonstrate high levels of discretionary effort (defined as the willingness to go above and beyond normal duties) dropped from 29% in 2006 to 13% for the second half of 2008.

At the same time, the CEB is seeing "100% of organizations visiting whether CEO pay is deserved," a tenuous situation because compensation is more crucial to senior executives' engagement than it is to that of lower-level employees, according to Martin.

Another problem: Many CEOs already have stock options under water.

With many organizations set to reexamining the metrics used to determine CEO compensation, and with the turmoil over executive compensation in general, it's definitely enough to be of concern

to CEOs, says Pearl Meyer, the senior managing director at Steven Hall & Partners, an executive compensation consulting firm based in New York City, who adds that "I don't necessarily think executive pay will decrease significantly."

Ken Blanchard disagrees. "I think it's almost an ethical imperative that CEO compensation come down," says Blanchard, the author of numerous management books, including the classic *The One-Minute Manager.* "In the old days, the rule was CEO compensation was five times that of the lowest-paid employee." Even by the $500,000 minimum TARP standards, the formula isn't relevant today.

Regardless of whether the threat to CEO pay is grounded in reality or overhyped speculation, human resources officers and board members should be on the lookout for CEO disengagement and learn what they can do to remedy it, according to Meyer.

The signs of CEO disengagement are fairly easy to identify, says Neil Jacobs, head of Northeast America for YSC, a global business psychology consulting firm in New York.

WHEN THICK SKIN BECOMES THIN

"Body language tells you what mode your CEO is in," says Jacobs. "Look at posture and whether the CEO sounds defeated in meetings." Indeed, CEOs who seem uncharacteristically scared or oversensitive to criticism may be heading for a disengagement crisis. "People who manage to graduate to CEO level are pretty thick-skinned," says Roy Cohen, a career counselor and executive coach in Manhattan. "They tend to be confident. They believe in themselves and that they deserve to be in the CEO role. If they don't [act that way], there's been a breakdown."

You may notice the CEO seems psychologically disconnected as a team member. When CEOs become disengaged, "the shift of their leadership starts to move to leading more for themselves than for the organization," says Jacobs. "Engaged CEOs will use the word 'we' a lot. They show honesty and responsibility. They'll say, 'I'm the head of this organization, and we're going to get through this.'"

VANISHING ACTS

The next sign of disengagement is a lack of visibility, conspicuous absences especially during times or in places that call for the CEO's attention. "I was working with a client company in Britain, and they thought one division was inviable," Jacobs recalls. "One of the people who was involved in trying to save the division went on an unrelated side trip. That was a very bad sign. The CEO who is committed to bringing an organization through difficult times has a high degree of visibility, being a role model and making sure his or her voice is heard within the organization."

Little signs, too, can mean a lot, according to Jacobs. If the CEO starts taking a bit longer to return phone calls or messages from anyone in the organization or isn't as quick to set up meetings as usual, it could mean he or she is looking around at other employment opportunities.

For those CEOs who prefer to remain in their jobs, however—while at the same time recognizing their own growing disengagement—there is much they can do to reinvigorate their own morale.

"CEOs need to go back to the front lines of their business," says Jacobs, "and see the people who are manufacturing the cars or bottling the fizzy drink at the plant, so they can remember who they're working for and why. That's very powerful."

ACCEPTING BLAME

A commitment to honesty on the part of the CEOs can bring about a morale-raising renewal of the trust between them and employees at all levels of the organization. Blanchard points to the U.S. President's willingness to accept blame as a good example. "Obama has already apologized three time times

to the U.S. people. That's the first time I know of that happening since Kennedy," Blanchard says. "[Likewise], CEOs need to get real with their people."

Another route to reengagement: a better attitude toward feedback. Whether it's a factory worker complaining about poor working conditions or the board president announcing a proposal to reduce the CEO's salary, the CEO should respond by saying, "Tell me more. How might that help?" Blanchard suggests.

Of course, not all chief executives can be counted on to heal themselves. It's the board's job to counsel the CEOs and guide and teach them, particularly when they see leaders exhibiting another dangerous type of disengagement: an unwillingness to take chances in order to stimulate stagnant business.

"CEOs should not be so paralyzed by the pressures society is putting on them today that they don't take risks in their roles as managers," says George Davis, a Boston-based partner of the executive recruiting firm Egon Zehnder International. "Good engaged CEOs and boards know how to gauge the risks and opportunities."

"Boards need to think about how to encourage senior leaders to take well-thought-out risks," says Brian Kropp, senior director for the human resources practice at the CEB. "And they should look at whether CEOs are making the right decisions—not necessarily whether those decisions are getting results [right away]."

In addition to encouraging the CEO to take well-thought-out risks, the board may also want to hire an executive coach. "Coaches can engage CEOs by unlocking their blind spots," says Jacobs.

A MEASURE OF SUCCESS

And one way or another, boards have to let their CEOs know that they don't subscribe to the negative generalizations made about chief execs because of the financial crisis.

"Pitchfork populism has gone too far," says Davis. "The public is painting the CEO population with too broad a brush. A lot of good CEOs are underappreciated."

Even when economic necessity compels the board to reduce some component of compensation—salary, bonus, or stock and stock options—that they award the CEO, the board should know it won't necessarily disengage the CEO if they handle it correctly.

"If you earn $50 million instead of $70 million, does it really make a difference?" says Jacobs. "Does more money mean more, or is it more important that the CEO feel engaged?"

Cohen believes most CEOs want large compensation packages not because they're greedy for more money but because it represents a measure of their success. "If CEOs believe in their own talent, they're less likely to become demoralized and worried about compensation," he says.

Of course, it wouldn't hurt if the general public's image of CEOs could somehow be rehabbed, says

Meyer: "Many people have the wrong image of CEOs, that they're flying in corporate jets and are in the lap of luxury. The reality is these people are in the hot seat, working strenuously to turn their companies around."

QUESTIONS

1. Can corporate governance kill a business by chasing away the best CEOs?

2. Should CEO compensation be governed only by market factors? Why or why not?

3. Do CEOs truly work harder than, say, a single mom who is working two different jobs just to pay her bills?

Thomas W. Dunfee

Corporate Governance in a Market with Morality

Thomas Dunfee was a professor at The Wharton School, and one of the country's most influential business ethicists.

THE ROLE OF THE CORPORATION: DOES IT ENCOMPASS SOCIAL RESPONSIBILITY?

Competing, mutually exclusive visions exist concerning the ultimate purpose and true nature of the corporation. Variously described as communitarian versus contractarian,[1] the Berle v. Dodd debate[2], the shareholder paradox[3] or the separation thesis,[4] these differing visions reflect conflicting political and moral preferences concerning the nature of corporations. Most famously, the debate is reflected in

the sharply contrasting views of Milton Friedman[5] and his many critics.[6] Ultimately, the basis of the disagreement boils down to a pluralistic versus a monotonic view of corporate objectives.[7]

The Monotonist/Pluralist Debate

The monotonic view emphasizes maximization of shareholder wealth. "(S)hareholders claim the corporation's heart. This shareholder-centric focus of corporate law is often referred to as shareholder primacy."[8] The objective reduces to calculations of short-term results for shareholders. Legal mandates must be followed, but most other extra-shareholder considerations are verboten as reflecting inappropriate social or political considerations, violations of innate property rights, or, even worse, as a subterfuge

From "Corporate Governance in a Market with Morality," 62 *Law and Contemporary Problems*, Duke University Law School, 129–158, Summer 1999.

allowing managers to act in furtherance of their own personal interests. Based upon a view of a corporation as a nexus of contracts, this approach eschews public intervention in support of non-shareholder obligations.[9] Working from a foundation of liberty, monotonists assume that non-shareholders with an interest in corporate decisions can either explicitly contract to protect their interests[10] or be treated as having implicitly contracted with shareholders to represent their interests.[11] Milton Friedman is strongly identified with the monotonic position:

> In a free-enterprise, private-property system a corporate executive is an employee of the owners of the business. He has direct responsibility to his employers. That responsibility is to conduct the business in accordance with their desires, which generally will be to make as much money as possible while conforming to the basic rules of the society, both those embodied in law and those embodied in ethical custom.[12]

The pluralistic view, on the other hand, emphasizes broader constituencies or stakeholders (variously, bondholders, suppliers, distributors, creditors, local communities, consumers, users, state and federal governments, special interest groups, etc.) of the corporation[13] and has even been extended by some to a general obligation to act consistently with the general needs of society.[14] This view is supported in two distinct ways. First, the argument is made that management has an ethical obligation to act in furtherance of the interests of stakeholders. Advocates of ethically based fiduciary-like obligations to stakeholders have even gone so far as to ask "what's so special about shareholders?"[15] Second, an instrumental argument is made that firms will be more successful in achieving their primary objective of enhancing shareholder wealth by adequately reflecting stakeholder interests.[16] The pluralistic view is operationalized in the academic management literature under the rubric of corporate social responsiveness. Corporate social responsiveness focuses on the ability and readiness of a corporation to respond to stakeholders.[17] The literature identifies strategies and processes, such as crisis management teams, to be put in place to insure that proper responses occur.

The debate between monotonists and pluralists has run on for decades and while its character and some of the specific issues have changed, it still remains essentially a debate as to the extent to which corporations should be governed to achieve objectives other than shareholder wealth maximization. The debate has been ably and thoroughly described elsewhere[18] and it is not necessary to go into greater detail here. As a starting point, it should be noted that no serious writings advocate the two extreme positions on the monotonic–pluralistic continuum: nothing should ever constrain shareholder wealth maximization—corporations should be managed solely to benefit non-shareholder stakeholders. Rational people do not advocate the position that corporations have an obligation to do *anything* (such as hiring a hit man to murder a key witness against the firm in a major product liability case) that would increase shareholder wealth. Nor do rational people expect that publicly held corporations will be operated in furtherance of social or altruistic objectives with little or no reference to the interests of investors.

Where then on the continuum does the proper position lie? Should managers seek to balance the long-term and short-term welfare of shareholders? Or, toward the oppositive end, should they actively seek to "balance the interests of all the firm's constituencies"[19] in every decision, a position criticized by A. A. Sommer? Part of the reason for the divergence in viewpoints concerning corporate responsibility stems from the wide variety of activities that fall within its purview. Actions implicating the question of for whom the corporation is to be managed include such things as:

- corporate giving, philanthropy
- considering community interests in deciding on plant location or closure
- rejecting premiums offered in hostile takeovers
- making products safer than the law requires
- putting in environmental controls beyond what the law requires

Two cases help to emphasize the types of issues that underlie the monotonist/pluralist debate.

Case 1: Merck and Mectizan[20]

In the late 1970s, Merck scientists discovered that ivermectin, a drug they produced to control parasites in animals, might help millions of people afflicted by onchocerciasis. This disease, known as river blindness, exists primarily in poorer countries in Africa. The disease is transmitted through the bites of black flies whereby larvae entered the victim's body. The larvae produce offspring which cause itching so severe some people have committed suicide and, if the eyes are affected, blindness. Merck incurred great costs in developing the drug; costs that could not be recouped directly from those who had the disease because they were too poor to pay a profit-generating price. Ultimately, Merck spent ten years developing the drug and then decided to give the drug away without charge, and even to financially support the distribution of the drug to remote areas. The drug provides significant benefits and can be taken orally once a year.

Case 2: Shell Oil and the Brent Spar Rig

In 1995, Shell proposed to sink a decommissioned oil rig in the North Sea. They consulted with various stakeholder groups, engaged noted scientists in the process, and obtained approvals from the British government.[21] Greenpeace challenged the proposed deep sea dumping, claiming that Shell's solution of sinking the rig would cause serious harm to the environment. Shell disputed the claim on scientific grounds and argued that sinking was the best available option.[22] Because Shell refused to abandon its plans, Greenpeace surrounded the rig with small boats and even occupied it in 1995.[23] Due to Greenpeace's pressure and consumer boycotts, Shell abandoned its plans and towed the rig to a Norwegian fiord where it remained for close to three years.[24] The reversal of the original plan cost Shell considerable expense.[25] After Shell abandoned its dumping plans, independent scientists investigated and found that Shell had been correct—the environmental impact from sinking the rig would be "minimal."[26] Greenpeace admitted they were wrong on that specific claim.[27]

Both cases involve decisions that may have an impact on shareholder wealth. Merck spent millions developing the drug and then incurred even greater costs by giving it away and helping support the distribution of the drug. Roy Vagelos, the then Chairman, indicated that he spent an enormous amount of time on the project.[28] True, such an action might help Merck in hiring and retaining research scientists, and could help in their relationship with certain physicians, customers and regulators. On the other hand, few customers may even be aware of their action and the precise benefits are hard to measure against the clear expenditures the decision cost. Assuredly, if Merck were to decide to invest half of all its research and development budget in likely unprofitable drugs it would have a serious negative impact on shareholder wealth.

Shell tried to consider the interests of stakeholders in their decision process and incurred costs in so doing. Yet their efforts were for naught because they apparently failed to correctly evaluate the likely public reaction to their decision.[29] The costs Shell incurred in dealing with the project, coupled with the costs of a consumer boycott, etc. probably had a negative effect on shareholder wealth. A more accurate reading of the "moral market" they faced would have benefitted shareholders.

Does Extant Law Resolve the Monotonist/Pluralist Debate?

Assuming that Merck explicitly considered the interests of stakeholders[30] and that Shell's misreading of stakeholder concerns regarding the Brent Spar cost shareholders money, can one say that the management of the two firms acted in violation of their legal obligations?[31] If one interprets the law as requiring a sterile decision-making process, devoid of any consideration of marketplace morality, then perhaps the answer is yes. If, instead, the law is interpreted to mean that managers must have reasonable grounds for assuming that extra-economic considerations may benefit shareholders, then the answer is no. The Merck and Shell cases demonstrate the difficulty in making a definitive assessment of impact on shareholder wealth. It appears likely that Shell's actions hurt shareholders in that there were identifiable costs and no clear-cut benefits. The Merck case is less clear because a reasonable case can be made that, as a result of the enormous favorable publicity Merck received, plus the potential opening of other markets in Africa, Merck reaped a substantial benefit. The question is whether the benefits exceeded the unquestionably significant costs.

Thus, the legal regime is dependent to some extent upon assumptions concerning the likely effect of managerial consideration of stakeholder interests. The shareholder primacy norm, if fully incorporated into the legal regime, would still require that stakeholder interests be considered when doing so has a foreseeable impact upon shareholder wealth. The legal debate concerning the proper interpretation of extant corporate law reflects this empirical uncertainty with the competing advocates working from diametrically different assumptions concerning the likely impact of acting on behalf of stakeholders.[32] It is not surprising that much of the legal debate pertains to issues where the agency problem is greatest, that is where the potential conflict of interest between the shareholder owners and the managers is likely to be at its greatest. Potential conflicts abound in hostile take-overs where managers may lose perks, even their jobs, if ownership changes hands.[33] The monotonists are rightly concerned that where interests dramatically diverge managers may put their own ahead of those of investors. Managers may do this while covering their self-interest with claims that their actions are in furtherance of the public good or are required by business ethics.

The corporation is a legal entity.[34] As such, debates concerning their role and function must of necessity reflect their legal character. Inevitably the legal arguments revolve around two primary questions: (1) how should extant law be interpreted and applied; and (2) what is the optimal legal regime for corporations? Both are reflected in the current controversy concerning the proper role of corporate constituency statutes.[35] First adopted in Pennsylvania in 1983, the majority of states have enacted them.[36] Most provide that managers and directors "may" consider the effects of any action on some broader constituency such as employees, suppliers, customers, communities and so on. The statutes generally do not mandate that stakeholder interests be considered. Instead,

they are merely permissive; management will not be liable for having demonstratively considered such interests.[37] Most of the statutes were adopted in response to the threat of hostile takeovers[38] and were extensively lobbied for by management of potential target firms.[39] This heritage taints their status as legitimizing a broadly pluralistic approach to corporate governance. Significant issues exist as to how the constituency statutes should be properly interpreted and how they can be enforced. So long as they cannot be directly enforced by stakeholder plaintiffs, they will be of limited impact.[40] Interestingly, they have seen surprisingly little use considering the extent to which, at least upon first impression, they appear to change the substantive law in this area.[41]

The fact that the constituency statute regime has had a limited impact does not necessarily lead to the conclusion that the law fully supports the monotonic approach. To the contrary, there is substantial support for the proposition that corporate law allows management to act to further many types of interests other than pure short-term shareholder wealth maximization.[42] The American Law Institute's Principles on Corporate Governance explicitly approves of managerial actions that are "made on the basis of ethical considerations even when doing so would not enhance corporate profit or shareholder gain."[43] The most well-established use of corporate funds that does not improve short-term shareholder wealth—charitable donations—is approved by statute in every state.[44] In general, the business judgment rule gives management broad discretion in what interests they choose to further so long as managers can present a rational basis for the claim that their business judgment is in the best interests of the corporation.[45] In conclusion, the current legal regime does not appear to provide a definitive resolution to the monotonic/pluralist debate. Instead, as is true of so much United States law, its prophylactic nature allows it to evolve in a manner consistent with changing moral and political expectations.

MORALITY IN MARKETS

Surely moral desires[46] influence the preferences of participants in markets. Moral desires pertain to personal beliefs concerning right and wrong behavior and may be contrasted with purely economic desires to obtain desired goods and services at the lowest possible price. Moral desires may encompass refusing to do business with someone deemed to be unfair, boycotting certain firms on the basis of identification of the firm with disfavored policies, and so on. The claim that there is no discernible impact of moral desires on capital and consumer markets is counter intuitive. It seems similarly implausible to claim that moral desires are a dominant force in many markets for goods and services.[47] Instead, the real question is whether there is some discernible impact.[48] Are there, for example, identifiable contexts in which the price and quantity sold of goods and services are influenced by moral desires? It seems quite plausible to claim that some people trade off moral desires against desires for good quality and low price in their own decision making. Across the universe of those acting on the basis of moral desires, some will hold differing moral desires and some marketplace actions based on moral desires will cancel the effect of those acting on the opposite desires.[49]

Moral desires may be an influence in a variety of circumstances. Familiar capital market examples include buying mutual funds that engage in social screening, or screening personal investments. There are people who refuse to own tobacco or gambling stocks in their own portfolios. Some pension funds eschew securities of certain firms, often on the basis of social criteria that presumably reflect the preferences of their beneficiaries.[50] Although the total impact of all forms of screening is hard to measure, Merrill Lynch estimated that the amount invested in socially screened mutual funds increased from $639 billion in 1995 to $1.18 trillion in 1997.[51] Hylton notes a "persistent inability on the part of all participants in the debate to develop a simple, coherent definition of what is meant by socially responsible investing," while noting with some dismay that many funds purporting to engage in the practice have little in common.[52] However, an exogenous definition of what constitutes socially responsible behavior is inconsistent with the idea that, with disclosure, some investors will invest influenced by their own moral desires. Thus, someone might buy a fund that eschews firms that violate the MacBride Principles in Northern Ireland while another investor might be totally indifferent to that issue and buy a screened fund that includes non-Mac-Bride-observing firms in its portfolio but does not include tobacco and gambling stocks.

Similar actions are found in consumer markets. Consumers supported their desires for a clean environment by paying more for pollution-reducing gasoline at a time when they weren't required by law to purchase it.[53] Similarly the sales of Star Kist tuna went up when it raised its prices as a result of switching to suppliers who protected dolphin.[54] Firms such as the Body Shop, Tom's of Maine and Ben & Jerry's develop strategic responses to these desires by engaging in social cause marketing. They work to identify their firms with social causes, such as saving whales, as a means of attracting consumers who share those beliefs. Consumers may choose to do business with them solely on the basis of an assumed alignment of moral preferences. They may even be willing to pay a higher price or accept less desirable goods in order to realize a desire to support a favored cause through their purchasing decisions. The recent growth of these strategies is reflected in $535 million in payments to well-known charities in order for corporations to associate their names with marketing campaigns.[55] Consumers may also participate in boycotts, as has occurred in opposition to Shell's failure to intercede in the execution of Ken Saro Wiwa in Nigeria, Nestles' marketing practices for selling infant formula in developing countries, and Exxon's handling of the Valdez oil spill. Kahneman et al. found that individuals indicate a willingness to incur additional costs, such as paying a higher price or traveling a greater distance, in order to punish a retailer who in their opinion had acted unfairly by trying to take advantage of a condition of scarcity.[56]

Robert Frank found similar effects in labor markets, identifying the existence of a compensating wage premium for less altruistic jobs.[57] Frank gives as examples the large salary gaps between profit and nonprofit jobs, corporate and public interest law, and between expert witnesses for the tobacco companies and those for the public interest groups in opposition.[58]

Thus, the claim that there is morality in markets in the sense that some market participants are influenced by their own moral desires seems easily supportable.[59] For most markets, it may be that price and quality considerations dominate, but for certain submarkets it may be the case that moral desires are dominant. Attitudes about morality may be a major influence in reference to such products and services as furs, certain types of drugs, prostitution, even the scalping of sports and entertainment tickets.

The use of economic analysis to consider various dimensions of human interaction reinforces the claim that there is discernible morality in markets. Gary Becker[60] is a leading practitioner of this relatively new art. He makes use of a very broad analysis of tastes/preferences including such things as personal and social capital pertaining to future consumption,[61] discounting the future,[62] and desires for things such as religiosity or health.[63] In so doing, Becker gives explicit recognition to the fact that individuals may attempt to satisfy what I have described as moral desires in their decisions concerning current consumption. Even some of the assumptions underlying Richard Posner's[64] controversial analysis of human sexuality and sexual practices is consistent with this core idea.

Does Marketplace Morality Support Monotonists or Pluralists?

In answering the ultimate question we must first determine whether marketplace morality supports either the pluralist or monotonic approach to corporate governance.[65] If it does, then the framework of analysis is determined. If the support is for the monotonic position, then the straightforward norm of shareholder primacy is ethically required. If, instead, there is support for a pluralistic position, then more analysis is required to determine which pluralistic vision is supported by marketplace morality. Survey data is limited, although some appears to support the pluralistic position. One massive study of managers posed the Friedman question directly as follows: Which of these opinions do you think most other people in your own country would think better represents the goals of a company, (a) or (b):

(A) The only real goal of a company is making profit.

(B) A company, besides making profit, has a goal of attaining the well-being of various stakeholders, such as employees, customers, etc.[66]

The question was posed to over 15,000 middle managers from twelve different countries. In no country did a majority of managers agree with answer (a). The United States had the highest percentage of agreement with (a), 40%. This is consistent with an earlier survey that found managers at all levels consistently ranked the general public as more important than shareholders.[67]

Statements by United States and global business groups representing senior managers decisively rejecting the Friedman formulation of the monotonic approach are relatively common. For example, the United States Business Roundtable has stated that "Corporations are chartered to serve both their shareholders and society as a whole.... The other stakeholders in the corporation are its employees, customers, suppliers, creditors, the communities where the corporation does business, and society as a whole."[68] The well-known and widely accepted Principles offered by the global Caux Round Table stress stakeholder obligations throughout by emphasizing responsibilities toward customers, employees, suppliers, social/political communities, and even (controversially) competitors.[69] Monotonists might be expected to question whether these statements represent genuine positions of significant business groups and to claim that they are more in the nature of generic public relations. One would expect that the general public would have an even stronger preference against the monotonic positions, preferring instead that corporate managers seek to act consistently with unambiguous popular morality.

Justifications for Respecting Marketplace Morality

Two basic justifications for incorporating the consideration of marketplace morality into corporate governance are offered, one normative and one instrumental.

The first, normative justification, relies upon a hypothetical social contract that requires managers to identify and act consistently with legitimate ethical norms found in the communities in which their firms operate.

Even if marketplace morality supports the monotonic position, the presence of morality within consumer and capital markets still has implications for the committed monotonic manager. If a manager fails to react to conspicuous signs of moral expectations for her firm, she may implement strategies doomed to underperform or even produce losses for the firm. Both outcomes will have a negative impact on shareholder wealth. The experience of Shell with the Brent Spar provides an example where managers may have detracted from shareholder wealth by failing to anticipate the impact of marketplace morality. Shell may have thought that the issue of how to dispose of the rig was merely a technical one. If so, all they had to do was to explain the science of the decision to relevant stakeholders. It turned out to be a very different type of issue. A sufficiently significant portion of the public chose to believe Greenpeace and thereby supported actions which prevented Shell from carrying out its plans. Public support for Greenpeace occured even though Greenpeace was ultimately proven wrong on critical scientific facts. One explanation for this seemingly irrational result pertains to the nature of trust, particularly in reference to decisions affecting the natural environment. As a result of a series of controversial incidents over time involving Shell,[70] coupled with the potential of a conflict of interest on the part of Shell who stood to profit from actions harmful to the environment, many people apparently concluded that Shell was acting in a manner inconsistent with their moral desires.

A similar analysis may be used in reference to the tobacco companies and to Exxon's handling of the Valdez oil spill. The case may be made that the tobacco companies failed to discern changing public attitudes about their product, particularly in regard to rather cavalier industry attitudes about encouraging teenage smoking. RJR's Joe Camel campaign provoked enormous controversy as being obviously targeted toward children. In spite of the protestations of the industry that they had little to do with it, by the mid-1990s young smokers were the only group in the United States among whom smoking was increasing.[71] It may well be that the enormous costs ultimately incurred by the companies as a result of political and legal actions would have been significantly smaller had the companies acted more responsively when it became clear that public sentiment was changing.

The infamous grounding and subsequent oil spill of the Exxon *Valdez* off the shores of Alaska is a well-known corporate disaster. The manner in which Exxon management responded to the spill has been significantly criticized[72] and Exxon was, for awhile, the poster child for how not to manage a crisis. The company allowed unsafe practices, was not prepared to act quickly to deal with a spill of the type and magnitude in Alaska, issued contradictory statements defending their actions, did not send senior leadership to the site immediately afterwards, and was accused of appearing arrogant about their responsibility for the incident.[73] Exxon paid over $3.4 billion in direct charges, was subject to boycotts (some holders cut up their credit cards and returned them to the company), and was ultimately assessed over $5 billion in punitive damages in a law suit in 1994.[74] Again, the failure to respond adequately to the moral desires in the market cost shareholders.

Principles for Respecting Marketplace Morality: Principles for All Managers

The following four guiding principles for managers derive from the normative and instrumental justifications for respecting marketplace morality. They are not based on assumptions concerning the specific nature of marketplace morality. Instead, they are open to whatever output occurs with an expectation that marketplace morality will change over time.

1. There is a presumption that all corporate actions must be undertaken to maximize shareholder wealth.
2. Managers must respond to and anticipate existing and changing marketplace morality relevant to the firm that may have a negative impact on shareholder wealth.
3. The presumption in Principle 1 may be rebutted where clear and convincing evidence exists that marketplace morality relevant to the firm would justify a decision that cannot be shown to directly maximize shareholder wealth.
4. Managers must act consistently with hypernorms (manifest universal norms and principles).

Principle 1. First Duty Is to Maximize Shareholder Wealth

This principle is supported in law, agency principles, property rights, and moral analysis of the corporation.[75] It is the core of the monotonic approach. Yet, the basic obligation to generate profits for shareholders is recognized in most pluralistic approaches. Note that Principle 1 requires shareholder wealth maximization as a first duty, not as the sole duty. Remembering Milton Friedman's qualification— "while conforming to the basic rules of the society, both those embodied in law and those embodied in ethical custom"—even strong monotonists recognize it only as a first duty, albeit a strong and dominating one. The dispute between the monotonists and pluralists concerns the circumstances and extent to which the first duty may be overridden. This agreement is recognized here by creating a rebuttable presumption in favor of shareholder wealth maximization. The next two principles specify the circumstances in which marketplace morality may overcome the presumption. The fourth principle then indicates the limits placed on both marketplace morality and shareholder wealth maximization by manifest universal ethical norms and principles.

Principle 2. Respond to Market Signals Concerning Moral Preferences

The discussion, *supra*, has emphasized how the interaction between marketplace morality and corporate decision-making can have either a beneficial or negative impact on shareholder wealth. To the extent that this is true, the critical issue becomes how to identify marketplace morality with sufficient specificity to enable responsive strategies. The search must begin with an identification of the relevant communities in which marketplace morality will be contained. The key place to look is in markets directly relevant to the firm. These would include, for example, consumer markets targeted by the firm, the labor markets from which the firm hires, and the capital markets tapped by the firm.

The second question is what to look for. Marketplace morality will be reflected in what was described earlier as authentic norms.[76] Authentic norms represent a consensus pertaining to the propriety of particular actions based on aggregate attitudes and behaviors of individuals within a particular community. An example would be the norm held by the television industry and also apparently the public that hard liquor firms should not advertise on television. This norm was observed for many years through the voluntary behavior of the industry. However, as Seagram's actions in breaking with the long-standing norm by advertising on television in 1996 make clear, such norms may be malleable and susceptible to change.

I suggest the following process for identifying important moral norms:

An authentic norm is presumed to exist when supported by the following sources. The more sources that support a particular candidate for an authentic norm, the stronger the presumption in its favor.

An authentic norm may be presumed to exist on the basis of the following:

- Many people in the community believe it exists and are able to express it in words.
- Inclusion in a formal professional code.
- Inclusion in a corporate code.
- Commonly listed in the media as an ethical standard for the relevant community.
- Commonly referred to as an ethical standard by business leaders.
- Identified as a standard in competent opinion surveys.

The presumption in favor of authentic norm status may be overcome on the basis of:

- Evidence of substantial deviance from the putative norm.
- Evidence of an inconsistent or contrary norm in the same community.
- Evidence of coercion relating to the norm within the relevant community.
- Evidence of deception influencing the emergence or evolution of the norm.

The more proxies supporting the existence of an authentic norm, the stronger the contrary evidence required to conclude that the authentic norm is, in fact, ersatz.

The type of evidence required for these judgments will generally be commonly known and readily available. It will not require an elaborate amount of research. The presumption will not result in perfect judgments and there is always some chance of either failing to identify a genuine authentic norm, or in pronouncing ersatz norms to be authentic. On the other hand, we would expect that the prima facie norms recognized on the basis of the presumption will generally hold up if subjected to an ex post test. Nor do such tests have to be complicated, expensive or elaborate. Common techniques such as the use of focus groups chosen as a valid sample of the target community may be used to test the authenticity of putative norms.[77]

One result of this search may be to discover that the various markets relevant to a given firm send conflicting signals regarding moral preferences. It may be the case, for example, that the marketplace morality of the firm's investors are at odds with those found in labor or consumer markets relevant to the firm. Such a conflict may be resolved by evaluating the issue in the context of the morality existing in a broader market that subsumes the competing submarkets. Thus, if the issue is workplace or product safety, the broader political community may have discernable, clear-cut authentic norms which would establish a priority among any competing norms in the submarket. If no resolution is provided by looking to a broader community, then management needs to assess the relative importance of the different markets in the context of the firm's ability to achieve its goals. There shouldn't be a serious problem of incommeasurability in that under Principle 2 the ultimate test is the welfare of shareholders.

It should be stressed that marketplace morality often indicates profit-making opportunities for the firm. Taking steps to align the firm with the moral desires of important consumer or labor market groups may result in enhanced sales or recruiting. Realizing that judgments concerning the profit potential of such opportunities aren't crystal clear, particular leeway should be given to managers who experiment with reaching these special markets.

There may be circumstances in which a decision may initially appear to maximize shareholder wealth, such as Exxon taking a hard defensive position immediately after the *Valdez* incident, or R. J. Reynolds actively seeking new smokers by finding ways to encourage pre-teens to experiment with smoking. But the action, when considered against evidence of marketplace morality, may be foreseen to actually hurt shareholders in the long run. In such circumstances, managers have an obligation to search for evidence of conflicting morality and to bring their actions into conformity with that of dominant authentic norms. Again, here the test is the ultimate welfare of shareholders.

Principle 3. Justifying Actions Failing to Maximize Shareholder Wealth

We turn now to the pluralist arguments that managers have an ethical or social obligation to act to satisfy objectives other than maximizing shareholder wealth. Following the principles presented here helps to resolve many of these issues. Where there is clear-cut evidence of marketplace morality in support of common practices, then they are perfectly permissible[78] even though they cannot be shown to enhance shareholder wealth. A good example is the widespread and long-standing acceptance of corporate philanthropy. Recognized in law, and supported by well-established and recognized custom, philanthropy is unquestionably supported by an authentic norm.[79] In spite of the neoclassical economic claims that "spending money on corporate giving is wrong because it represents a waste of corporate assets,"[80] the practice is clearly justifiable under this analysis. Presumably this conclusion extends even to giving money to charity in times of operating losses. Ben & Jerry's, following the practice of many other firms, gave $255,384 to charity in 1994, a year in which they incurred operating losses.[81]

The case of the pluralistic manager who wishes to act on behalf of stakeholders on the basis of criteria other than that corresponding to clearly evident community morality is more difficult.[82] The business ethics literature suggests various criteria that might be used as a rationale for incorporating the interests of stakeholders into corporate decision-making. The most elaborate among the attempts at justification has been based upon Kantian-derived stakeholder rights, particularly in the work of Evan and Freeman.[83] Donaldson and Preston[84] suggested, but did not detail, a foundation based upon property rights recognizing that stakeholders possess certain rights that may compete or interrelate with those possessed by shareholders. Earlier, Donaldson had used a social contract theory as a means of "either replacing or augmenting the stakeholder model" in his treatment of international business ethics.[85]

Assume then that our pluralistic manager wishes to follow a Kantian analysis and in so doing is acting in a manner inconsistent with the assumed or actual wishes of the shareholders and in a manner inconsistent with clearly evident marketplace morality.[86] Such an approach is directly inconsistent with Principles 2 and 3. A purposeful strategy of acting inconsistently with shareholder wealth maximization and marketplace morality is highly problematic.

On the other hand, marketplace morality may often be permissive rather than mandatory in the sense that the moral desires of people in markets relevant to the firm may support allowing managers to follow their own morality in many circumstances. Donaldson and I[87] refer to this as the domain of "moral free space" in which one makes choices based upon community norms and personal values. This is probably the case for the Merck example given previously. It was certainly neither legally nor morally mandatory that Merck develop and then give away Mectizan. But it was permissible on both counts. There is no evidence to the effect that Merck's actions were inconsistent with the marketplace morality of any of its relevant communities.

Principle 4. Managers Must Act Consistently with Mandatory Hypernorms

There is one circumstance, however, where following marketplace morality and/or the monotonic approach to shareholder wealth maximization is problematic. That is when the action violates what Donaldson and I have characterized as hypernorms.[88] Hypernorms are second-order norms[89] that serve to judge, and if necessary invalidate, local

laws and local morality. Hypernorms "entail principles...fundamental to human existence.... As such, we would expect them to be reflected in a convergence of religious, philosophical, and cultural beliefs...."[90] This is a high standard for a set of universal principles, and presumably the number and scope of such standards would be limited. Consider the example of selling carcinogen-contaminated pajamas in poor countries with insufficient background institutions to control the sale of such products.[91] This strategy for disposing of the product may well increase shareholder wealth, and overseas sales may not violate clearly identifiable marketplace morality in the firm's relevant markets. On the other hand, the product is prohibited for sale in the United States and in Europe and is potentially harmful to the intended users. Taking DeGeorge's first principle—Multinationals should do no intentional direct harm (unless there is a cardinal overriding justification)[92]—as a hypernorm, it becomes the obligation of all organizations to recognize this principle in regard to stakeholders.

Again, Donaldson and I[93] suggest the use of presumptions as a means for identifying relevant hypernorms. We suggest that if:

> two or more of the following types of evidence confirm widespread recognition of an ethical principle, the decision-maker should operate on the basis of a rebuttable presumption that it constitutes a hypernorm. The more types of evidence in support of a hypernorm, the stronger the presumption.
>
> Evidence in support of a principle having hypernorm status:
>
> - Widespread consensus that the principle is universal
> - Component of well-known global industry standards
> - Supported by prominent non-governmental organizations such as the International Labour Organization or Transparency International
> - Supported by regional government organizations such as the European Community, the OECD, or the Organization of American States
> - Consistently referred to as a global ethical standard by international media
> - Known to be consistent with precepts of major religions

- Supported by global business organizations such as the International Chamber of Commerce or the Caux Round Table
- Known to be consistent with precepts of major philosophies generally supported by a relevant international community of professionals, e.g. accountants or environmental engineers
- Known to be consistent with empirical findings concerning universal human values
- Supported by the laws of many different countries

Once having gone through these steps and having identified a presumptive hypernorm, the decision-maker needs to consider whether evidence exists to overcome the presumption. If two or more of the following are found, then the presumption may be rebutted. However, the more types of evidence there are that support the presumption in favor of hypernorm status, the more types of evidence are necessary to override the presumption.

Evidence countering the hypernorm presumption:

- Evidence from the presumptive list to the contrary, e.g., that the putative hypernorm principle does not represent a universal value.
- Evidence from the presumptive list in support of hypernorm status for a mutually exclusive principle.[94]

The marketplace morality approach places a high standard on those managers who wish to use a claim of stakeholder interests or general morality to act in a manner inconsistent with maximization of shareholder wealth. It requires that managers do more than just assert a consistency between their actions and moral obligation.[95] Instead, they should develop justifications in advance and stand ready to defend their stakeholder-based actions with evidence supporting the existence of hypernorms or objective evidence of validating marketplace morality.

THE IMPLICATIONS OF MARKETPLACE MORALITY FOR LAW AND PUBLIC POLICY

A major foundation for a market morality-based analysis is the liberty of individuals to hold moral desires and to seek to implement them in their daily decision making. For some people, implementing their moral desires is the most significant element of their lives. Each person should have a maximal opportunity to act as they prefer in this domain. Individuals acting on the basis of their moral desires may implement them through a wide variety of economic, political, and social channels. They may vote consistently with their desires, lobby legislatures, boycott products, support social issue shareholder resolutions, buy or sell their stock in certain firms, try to persuade friends and strangers to act in a similar way, and so on. Individuals also face many constraints in exercising their moral desires, particularly in the form of restrictive public policy and laws. Because there are many competing moral desires in political and social markets, this is to be expected. Those who find themselves blocked in one channel (e.g., legal interpretations of corporate governance standards, restrictions limiting social issue shareholder resolutions) may turn to other channels (lobbying for legislation, boycotts) as a means of giving effect to their preferences. Among the many channels open to moral desires, the securities markets appear to be among the most open. One may buy and sell securities, at least for oneself, on the basis of whatever criteria one chooses.

As a general matter, supporting disclosure and individual choice in support of a marketplace of ideas is consistent with American traditions and ideals. As Oliver Wendall Holmes, dissenting in *Abrams v. United States*, put it so nicely: "... the ultimate good desired is better reached by free trade in ideas—that the best test of truth is the power of the thought to get itself accepted in the competition of the market and that truth is the only ground upon which their wishes safely can be carried out. That at any rate is the theory of our Constitution."[96] The concept of market morality is also consistent with the concept of reflexive law which seeks to provide access to information and documentation of statements toward supporting decisions by private actors.[97] On the other hand, market morality is not consistent with the idea of legal endorsement of inauthentic norms. For example, it is not clear that the implied contract for job security argued for by O'Conner,[98] which would require directors to act as mediators between stockholders and employees, would meet the test of authentic norms.

The extreme monotonic view, implemented through the business judgment rule, would have the effect of not only denying managers the ability to respond to marketplace morality, but might, in certain circumstances, result in managers violating mandatory hypernorms. Instead, the business judgment rule and other relevant policies should be interpreted consistently with the four guiding principles:

1. There is a presumption that all corporate actions must be undertaken to maximize shareholder wealth.
2. Managers must respond to and anticipate existing and changing marketplace morality relevant to the firm that may have a negative impact on shareholder wealth.
3. The presumption in Principle 1 may be rebutted where clear and convincing evidence exists that marketplace morality relevant to the firm would justify a decision that cannot be shown to directly maximize shareholder wealth.
4. Managers must act consistently with hypernorms (manifest universal norms and principles).

REFERENCES

Abzug, Rikki, and Natalie J. Webb. 1997. "Rational and Extra-Rational Motivations for Corporate Giving: Complementing Economic Theory with Organizational Science." *New York Law School Law Review* 41: 1035.

Becker, Gary S. 1996. *Accounting for Tastes*. Cambridge, MA: Harvard University Press.

Becker, Gary S., and Guity Nashat Becker. 1997. *The Economics of Life*. New York: McGraw-Hill.

Boatright, John R. "What's So Special About Shareholders?" *Business Ethics Quarterly* 4, no. 4 (1994): 393–407.

Bollier, David. 1991. *Merck & Company*. Stanford, CA: The Business Enterprise Trust.

Business Enterprise Trust. 1991. *Merck & Co. (A)–(D)*.

"Caux Round Table Principles for Business." *Caux Round Table Secretariat*, Washington, DC, 1994.

Donaldson, Thomas, and Thomas W. Dunfee. 1999. *Ties That Bind: A Social Contracts Approach to Business Ethics*. Cambridge, MA: Harvard Business School Press.

Donaldson, Thomas. *The Ethics of International Business*. New York: Oxford University Press, 1989.

Donaldson, Thomas, and Thomas W. Dunfee. "Integrative Social Contracts Theory: A Communitarian Conception of Economic Ethics." *Economics and Philosophy* 11, no. 1 (1995): 85–112.

Donaldson, Thomas, and Lee E. Preston. "The Stakeholder Theory for the Corporation: Concepts, Evidence, Implications." *Academy of Management Review* 20, no. 1 (1995): 65–91.

Dunfee, Thomas W. 1998. The marketplace of morality: First steps toward a theory of moral choice. *Business Ethics Quarterly*, 8(1): 127–145.

Epstein, Edwin M. 1987a. "The Corporate Social Policy Process." *California Management Review*, 29(3), 99–114.

Epstein, Edwin M. 1987b. "The Corporate Social Policy Process and the Process of Corporate Governance", *American Business Law Journal*, 25(3): 361–83.

Evan, William M., and R. Edward Freeman. 1988. "A Stakeholder Theory of the Modern Corporation: Kantian Capitalism." In *Ethical Theory and Business* (4th ed.), edited by T. Beauchamp and N. Bowie (pp. 75–93). Englewood Cliffs, NJ: Prentice Hall.

Frank, Robert H. 1996. "Can Socially Responsible Firms Survive in a Competitive Environment?" In David M. Messick and Ann E. Tenbrunsel, *Codes of Conduct: Behavioral Research Into Business Ethics*. New York: Russell Sage Foundation.

Freeman, R. E. "The Politics of Stakeholder Theory: Some Future Directions." *Business Ethics Quarterly* 4, no. 4 (1994): 409–21.

Frederick, William C. 1986. "Toward CSR3: Why Ethical Analysis Is Indispensable and Unavoidable in Corporate Affairs, *California Management Review*, 28(2) 126–41.

Friedman, Milton "The Social Responsibility of Business Is to Increase Its Profits." *New York Times Magazine*, 13 September 1970, pp. 32–33, 122, 124, 126.

Goodpaster, Kenneth E. "Business Ethics and Stakeholder Analysis." *Business Ethics Quarterly* 1, no. 1 (1991): 53–74.

Goodpaster, Kenneth E., Laura L. Nash, and John B. Matthews. 1998. *Policies and Persons: A Casebook in Business Ethics*. New York: McGraw-Hill. (Case "Exxon *Valdez*: Corporate Recklessness on Trial" written by Beth Goodpaster under supervision of Thomas Holloran.)

Hampden-Turner, Charles, & Fons Trompenaars. *The Seven Cultures of Capitalism*. New York: Doubleday, 1993.

Hylton, Maria O'Brien. " 'Socially Responsible' Investing: Doing Good Versus Doing Well in an Inefficient Market". *American University Law Review* 42 (1992): 1.

Kahneman, D., J. L. Knetsch, & R. Thaler "Fairness as a Constraint on Profit Seeking: Entitlements in the Market." *American Economic Review* 76, no. 4 (September 1986): 728–41.

Langbein, John H. 1985. "Social Investing of Pension Funds and University Endowments: Unprincipled, Futile and Illegal." In John H. Langbein et. al., *Disinvestment: Is It Legal? Is It Moral? Is It Productive?*

Maitland, Ian. "The Morality of the Corporation: An Empirical or Normative Disagreement." *Business Ethics Quarterly* 4, no. 4 (1994): 445–58.

Messick, David M. 1996. "Why Ethics Is Not the Only Thing that Matters." *Business Ethics Quarterly* 6(2): 223–26.

Millon, David. 1993. "Communitarians, Contractarians, and the Crisis in Corporate Law", *Washington and Lee Law Review*, 50(4): 1373–93.

Mitchell, Lawrence E. (Ed.) 1995. *Progressive Corporate Law*. Boulder, CO: Westview Press.

O'Connor, Marlene A. 1995. "Promoting Economic Justice in Plant Closings: Exploring the Fiduciary/Contract Law Distinction to Enforce Implicit Employment Agreements." In Lawrence E. Mitchell (Ed.), *Progressive Corporate Law*. Boulder, CO: Westview Press.

Orts, Eric W. 1992. "Beyond Shareholders: Interpreting Corporate Constituency Statutes," *George Washington Law Review* 61(1): 14–135.

Orts, Eric W. 1993. "The Complexity and Legitimacy of Corporate Law," *Washington and Lee Law Review* 50(4): 1565–1623.

Orts, Eric W. 1995. "Reflexive Environmental Law," *Northwestern Law Review* 89(4): 1227–1340.

Posner, Richard A. 1992. *Sex and Reason*. Cambridge: St. Martin's Press.

Schulze, Robert John. 1997. Book Note. "Can This Marriage Be Saved? Reconcilling Progressivism with Profits in Corporate Governance Laws." *Stanford Law Review* 49, 1607.

Sethi, S. Prakash, and Paul Steidlmeier. 1997. *Up Against the Corporate Wall: Cases in Business and Society* (6th ed.). Upper Saddle River, NJ: Prentice-Hall.

Solomon, Lewis D. 1993. "On the Frontier of Capitalism: Implementation of Humanomics by Modern Public Held Corporations: A Critical Assessment." *Washington & Lee Law Review* 50(4): 1625–71.

NOTES

1. David Millon, "Communitarians, Contractarians, and the Crisis in Corporate Law, "*Washington and Lee Law Review* 50 (1993): 1373 [hereinafter Millon, "Crisis"].

2. *See* A. A. Berle, "Corporate Powers as Powers in Trust," *Harvard Law Review* 44 (1931): 1049; E. Merrick Dodd, "For Whom Are Corporate Managers Trustees?," *Harvard Law Review* 45 (1932): 1145; A. A. Berle, "For Whom Corporate Managers Are Trustees: A Note," *Harvard Law Review* 45 (1932): 1365. See also A. A. Sommer, "Whom Should the Corporaton Serve? The Berle-Dodd Debate Revisited". Sixty Years Later." *Delaware Journal of Corporate Law* 16 (1991): 33.

3. *See Business Ethics Journal* 4, No. 4 (1994) and articles therein.

4. R. Edward Freeman, "The Politics of Stakeholder Theory: Some Future Directions," *Business Ethics Quarterly* 4 (1994): 409.

5. *Milton Friedman,* "The Social Responsibility of Business Is to Increase Its Profits," *New York Times Magazine* (September 13, 1970), pp. 32–33, 122, 124, 126.

6. See, generally, Lawrence E. Mitchell (ed.), *Progressive Corporate Law* (1995); Eric W. Orts, "The Complexity and Legitimacy of Corporate Law," *Washington & Lee Law Review* 50 (1993): 1565; Ronald M. Green, "Shareholders as Stakeholders: Changing Metaphors of Corporate Governance," *Washington & Lee Law Review* 50 (1993): 1409; David Millon, "Redefining Corporate Law," *Indiana Law Review* 24 (1991): 223; Lyman Johnson, "The Delaware Judiciary and the Meaning of Corporate Life and Corporate Law," *Texas Law Review* 68 (1990): 865. For a bibliography of communitarian writing, which rejects the idea of shareholder primacy, see Millon, "Crisis," *supra* note 4, pp. 1391–93.

7. Eric W. Orts is a consistent advocate for a pluralistic view arguing that an "…unidimensional economic view of corporate law is an incorrect empirical description" and that "(t)he policies underlying corporate law cannot (and presumably should not) be reduced to a unidimensional value, such as the economic objective of 'maximizing shareholders' wealth'…." Orts, *supra* note 9, at 1587.

8. D. Gordon Smith, "The Shareholder Primacy Norm," *Journal of Corporate Law* 24 (1998): 277 (challenging the relevancy of the putative norm).

9. See generally, Frank H. Easterbrook & Daniel R. Fischel, *The Economic Structure of Corporate Law* (1991); Larry E. Ribstein, "The Mandatory Nature of the ALI Code," *George Washington Law Review* 61

(1993): 984; Stephen M. Bainbridge, "In Defense of the Shareholder Wealth Maximization Norm: A Reply to Green," *Washington & Lee Law Review* 50 (1993): 1423; Michael E. DeBow & Dwight R. Lee, "Shareholders, Nonshareholders and Corporate Law: Communitarianism and Resource Allocation," *Delaware Journal of Corporate Law* 18 (1993): 393.

10. For example, bondholders, distributors and suppliers may easily contract with the firm to protect their own economic interests.

11. Maitland argues that the disagreement between monotonists and pluralists boils down to different empirical assumptions. "Ian Maitland, The Morality of the Corporation: An Empirical or Normative Disagreement," *Business Ethics Quarterly* 4 (1994): 445. Both sides want to recognize the self-determination of stakeholders. Monotonists conclude that stakeholder self-determination is reflected in their explicit or implied contracts with the shareholders; pluralists disagree and argue that public policy must intervene to protect stakeholder self-determination. *Id.*

12. Friedman, *supra* note 8, p. 33.

13. Millon, "Crisis," *supra* note 4, pp. 1378–79;

14. *Id.* at 1379. Interestingly, the same divergence of viewpoints is reflected in the 1994 Company Law in China, which provides a legal framework for the organization and operation of private stock companies. The new law sends mixed messages concerning corporate objectives and governance. Article 102 provides that shareholders "shall be the organ of authority of the company"; while Article 14 provides that "companies must...strengthen the establishment of a socialist spiritual civilization, and accept the supervision of the government and the public." Michael In Nikkel, "Note: Chinese Characteristics in Corporate Clothing: Questions of Fiduciary Duty in China's Company Law," *Minnesota Law Review* 80 (1995): 503, 523.

15. John R. Boatright, "What's So Special About Shareholders?" *Business Ethics Quarterly* 4 (1994): 393.

16. Kenneth E. Goodpaster, "Business Ethics and Stakeholder Analysis," *Business Ethics Quarterly* 1 (1991): 53.

17. *See* Edwin M. Epstein, "The Corporate Social Policy Process," *California Management Review* 29 (1987a): 99; Edwin M. Epstein, "The Corporate Social Policy Process and the Process of Corporate Governance," *American Business Law Journal* 25 (1987b): 361; William C. Frederick, "Toward CSR3: Why Ethical Analysis Is Indispensable and Unavoidable in Corporate Affairs," *California Management Review* 28 (1986): 126.

18. See generally Millon, "Crisis," *supra* note 4; David Millon, "Theories of the Corporation," *Duke Law Journal* (1990): 210; William W. Bratton, "The Nexus of Contracts Corporation: A Critical Appraisal," *Cornell Law Review* 74 (1989): 407; Stephen M. Bainbridge, "Community and Statism: A Conservative Contractarian Critique of Progressive Corporate Law Scholarship" (book review), *Cornell Law Review* 82 (1997): 856.

19. Cindy Schipani & Jim Walsh, "The Modern Firm: Is There Liberty and Justice for All?" *Dividend* (University of Michigan School) (1997): 19, 23 (quoting A. A. Sommer).

20. The following discussion is taken from Business Enterprise Trust, *Case: Merck & Co. (A)–(D)* (1991), which provides an elaborate discussion of the case and the decision process at Merck.

21. *See* Graeme Smith, "Precedent Feared as Shell Saves 34m: Atlantic Grave Approved for Giant Oil Installation," *The Herald* (Glasgow), Feb. 17, 1995, p. 9.

22. "Greenpeace Admits Error Against Shell," *L. A. Times* (September 6, 1995), p. D2.

23. "Shell Oil Platform to Become a Pier," *The Houston Chronicle* (Jan. 30,1998, Business section), p. 1.

24. *Id.*

25. *Id.* In January 1998, after considering many disposal proposals, Shell decided to cut up the rig and make it into a pier in Norway. This plan will cost Shell around $42 million, which is more than twice what it would cost to dump the rig at sea. *Id.*

26. *LA. Times, supra* note 25, at D2.

27. *Idem.*

28. David Bollier, *Merck & Company* 11 (1991).

29. Shell UK director John Wybrew said that even after spending four years making the decision on what to do with the Brent Spar—which was the technically correct decision—the company failed to understand the public's opinion and the international interest the action would attract. Roger Cowe, "Shell Chief Laments PR Failure in Move to Dump Brent Spar," *The Guardian* (London), Sept. 15, 1995, p. 21.

30. The claim may be made that this decision was made solely in reference to shareholder welfare with the firm calculating the likely benefits from reputation with future employees, customers, and regulators. It is not clear that Merck management considered these factors other than in vague terms: e.g., research on ivermectin might lead to other discoveries. The better view appears to be that a primary motive for Merck was to benefit those afflicted with a horrible condition, regardless of whether or not they were able to realize direct profits from the product.

31. "[A] decision that may be rational on purely business grounds is nonetheless subject to invalidation if management candidly admits that its motives were other than profit-based." Kenneth Davis, "Discretion of Corporate Management to Do Good at the Expense of Shareholder Gain: A Survey of, and Commentary on, the US. Corporate Law," *Canada-U.S. Law Journal* 13 (1988): 7, 32. Professor Bainbridge states that corporate law generally holds to the following proposition. Bainbridge, *supra* note 12, p. 1424.

> A business corporation is organized and carried on primarily for the profit of the stockholders. The powers of the directors are to be employed for that end. The discretion of directors is to be exercised in the choice of means to attain that end, and does not extend to a change in the end itself, to the reduction of profits, or to the nondistribution of profits among stockholders in order to devote them to other purposes.... [I]t is not within the lawful powers of a board of directors to shape and conduct the affairs of a corporation for the merely incidental benefit of shareholders and for the primary purpose of benefitting others ....

Dodge v. Ford Motor Co., 170 N.W. 668,684 (Mich. 1919). This statement is consistent with the traditional view that any consideration of non-shareholder interests must be rationally related to improving shareholder welfare. In some situations, the consideration of other interests (in the absence of an applicable other constituency statute) may be strictly forbidden. For example, in *Revlon v. MacAndrews & Forbes Holding, Inc.*, 506 A.2d 173 (Del. 1985) the court stated that it was inappropriate for the Revlon board to justify its actions by stating that it was protecting the corporation's noteholders when the company was clearly up for sale.

32. For example, see the debate between Ronald Green and Stephen Bainbridge. See Green, *supra* note 9; Bainbridge, *supra* note 12. Green argues that strict adherence to the monotonist view can cause (or even require) managers to ignore small risks to stakeholders if acting on those risks would decrease shareholder wealth. Green, *supra* note 9, at 1419–21 (arguing that Union Carbide's managers would have a difficult time justifying expenditures to take extra safety precautions at their plant in Bhopal, India (which suffered an accident causing the deaths of over 2,000 persons), because the risks of an accident were extremely small and the costs to improve the facility would be great). Bainbridge, however, argues that management acting on behalf of stakeholders can

cause many problems, including a conflict of interest problem. Bainbridge, *supra* note 12, p. 1446. Bainbridge also asks the question "How would I feel about living in a world governed by the moral rules implicit in the shareholder wealth maximization norm?" and responds "pretty good." *Id.* "For many years, the basic rule that shareholder interests come first has governed public corporations. That rule has helped produce an economy that is dominated by public corporations, which in turn has produced the highest standard of living of any society in the history of the world." *Id*

In the business ethics literature, Norman Bowie argues that there are "unenlightened" and "enlightened" Friedmanites. While both types agree that a corporation exists to earn a profit within certain bounds, the unenlightened manager exploits nonshareholder stakeholders to increase short-term profits, but fails in the long-run due to lowered productivity and cooperation of those stakeholders. The enlightened Friedmanite manager, however, is concerned with the well-being of all its stakeholders and is able to sustain or improve long-term performance. Norman Bowie, "New Directions in Corporate Social Responsibility," *Business Horizons* 34 (July/August 1991): 56, *reprinted in* Tom Beauchamp & Norman Bowie, *Ethical Theory & Business* (5th ed., 1997), pp. 96–107.

33. It is interesting that there has not been more of a debate concerning corporate philanthropy. When a corporation gives money to a senior manager's alma mater or favorite cultural charity, a conflict of interest exists. The conflict is exacerbated when the gift results in memorializing the manager, as when a university building or an opera lounge is named for the manager even though the funds are provided by the firm.

34. Corporations may also be natural entities, but that "fact" doesn't detract from their being legal entities.

35. See generally Eric W. Orts, "Beyond Shareholders: Interpreting Corporate Constituency Statutes," *George Washington Law Review* 61 (1992): 14 [Hereinafter Orts, "Beyond Shareholders"].

36. For a list of the states with other constituency statutes, see Wai Shun Wilson Leung, "The Inadequacy of Shareholder Primacy: A Proposed Corporate Regime that Recognizes Non-Shareholder Interests," *Columbia Journal of Law and Social Problems* 30 (1997): 587, 613 n.140; 620 n.171.

37. Connecticut is an exception in that it requires consideration of nonshareholder interests. Conn. Gen. Stat. Ann. Section 33–133(e) (West Supp. 1993); Leung, *supra* note 39, p. 619.

38. Orts, "Beyond Shareholders," *supra* note 38, p. 24.

39. Orts notes that certain labor unions also lobbied for constituency statutes which mitigates the common wisdom that they are purely management self-interest statutes. *Id*. pp. 24–25.

40. On the unenforceability of constituency statutes due to a failure to give nonshareholders standing to enforce a claim, see, e.g., Gary von Stange, "Corporate Social Responsibility through Constituency Statutes: Legend or Lie?," *Hofstra Labor Law Journal* 11 (1994): 461, 488; Orts, "Beyond Shareholders," *supra* note 38, at 55; Rima Fawal Hartman, "Situation-Specific Fiduciary Duties for Corporate Directors: Enforceable Obligations or Toothless Ideals," *Washington & Lee Law Review* 50 (1993): 1761, 178–87; Leung, *supra* note 39, pp. 617–18.

41. *See generally* Orts, "Beyond Shareholders," *supra* note 38, pp. 44, 92 (noting that corporate constituency statutes may not really be a change corporate law).

42. As Solomon puts it, "(t)oday in the Anglo-American legal system, corporations have considerable flexibility in undertaking socially responsible activities." Lewis D. Solomon, "On the Frontier of Capitalism: Implementation of Humanomics by Modern Public Held Corporations: A Critical Assessment," *Washington & Lee Law Review* 50 (1993): 1625–26.

43. *Smith, supra note 11, at 290 (quoting the ALI Principles of Corporate Governance).*

44. For a list of the state statutes, see Edward Adams & Karl Knutsen, "A Charitable Corporate Giving Justification for the Socially Responsible Investment of Pension Funds: A Populist Argument for the Public Use of Private Funds," *Iowa Law Review* 80 (1995): 211, 232. For a discussion of the some of the issues raised by corporate philanthropy, see Faith Stevelman Kahn, "Pandora's Box: Managerial Discretion and the Problem of Corporate Philanthropy," *UCLA Law Review* 44 (1997): 579.

45. Kenneth Davis, "Discretion of Corporate Management to Do Good at the Expense of Shareholder Gain: A Survey of, and Commentary on, the U.S. Corporate Law," *Canada–U.S. Law Journal* 13 (1988): 22–23 (stating that the law faces many hurdles in "developing meaningful limits on management's discretion to pass off voluntarism as enlightened long-term profitmaking").

46. Elsewhere I have defined moral desires as pertaining to personal beliefs concerning right and wrong. Thomas W. Dunfee, "The Marketplace of Morality: First Steps Toward a Theory of Moral Choice," *Business Ethics Quarterly* 8 (1998): 127. They "may be based in religious, ethical or sociopolitical convictions. Examples include observance of religious dietary laws or a religious-based refusal to accept any form of medical assistance. (Moral

desires) may reflect a belief that it is wrong to discriminate on the basis of gender or sexual preferences. (They) may be motivated by a hope for salvation, by an interest in leading a virtuous life, or by a more immediate need for approval by peers." *Id*., p. 129.

47. Messick's observation that ethics is not the only thing that matters is unquestionably true. David M. Messick, "Why Ethics Is Not the Only Thing that Matters," *Business Ethics Quarterly* 6 (1996): 223. It is hard to imagine serious advocacy of either extreme position: ethics never matters; only ethics matters.

48. Richard Posner appears willing to recognize the existence of some morality in the market, but refuses to believe that it would ever have much of an impact. "…people seem to behave morally in situations in which the costs of behaving morally are small, but to respond to incentives in situations in which those costs are large." Richard Posner. *The Problems of Jurisprudence* (1990), p. 195.

49. A personal example helps to demonstrate. When the civil rights movement reached West Virginia in the early 1960s, my parents who had patronized a segregated cafeteria in my home town stopped eating there reflecting their support for integration. Parents of a neighbor, who had rarely ever eaten at the cafeteria, starting eating there regularly while the cafeteria was under pressure to integrate. The overall effect of those boycotting, or supporting, all acting on the basis of their moral desires was to decrease the business for the cafeteria. The issue of whether a desire for segregation can be characterized as a "moral desire" is discussed, *infra*, at note 67.

50. If the screening does not accurately reflect the preferences of the beneficiaries, the fund managers may be in breach of their legal duties. See John H. Langbein, "Social Investing of Pension Funds and University Endowments: Unprincipled, Futile and Illegal," in *Disinvestment: Is It Legal? Is It Moral? Is It Productive?* (John H. Langbein et al., eds., 1985). However, critics such as Langbein appear to extend their opposition to the concept of social investing itself. So long as there is full disclosure and the screening is demonstrably consistent with the overall desires of the beneficiaries, it is consistent with the idea of morality in markets, and as will be argued, *infra*, a highly desirable phenomenon.

51. Merrill Lynch, *Priority Client Investor* (January, 1998).

52. Maria O'Brien Hylton, " 'Socially Responsible' Investing: Doing Good Versus Doing Well in an Inefficient Market," *American University Law Review* 42 (1992): 1, 2.

53. Harold H. Kassarjian. "Incorporating Ecology into Marketing Strategy: The Case of Air Pollution," *Journal*

of Marketing 35 (July 1971): 61,65. "Within six weeks after the introduction of the [pollution-reducing] gasoline, more than half of the population had paid an additional 2 to 12 cents per gallon to try the new brand." *Id.*

54. Robert H. Frank, "Can Socially Responsible Firms Survive in a Competitive Environment?" In *Codes of Conduct: Behavioral Research Into Business Ethics*, David M. Messick and Ann E. Tenbrunsel, eds. (1996), p. 95.

55. Fogarty, Thomas A., "Corporations Use Causes for Effect," *USA Today* (Nov. 10, 1997) p. 7B.

56. D. Kahnerman, J. L. Knetsch, & R. Thaler, "Fairness as a Constraint on Profit Seeking: Entitlements in the Market," *American Economic Review* 76 (1986): 728.

57. Frank, *supra* note 63, at 96.

58. Frank also contrasts attitudes toward being a lawyer for the National Rifle Association and being a lawyer for the Sierra Club. Frank, *supra* note 63. This is apparently based on the assumption that most people would prefer to work for the Sierra Club than the NRA. But there may be people whose moral desires favor the right to own and use guns and who, consistent with the approach taken in this article, would be willing to work for the NRA for a lower salary than they would require to work for Handgun Control. Moral desires come in all hues and tones in the overall market, and within the overall market the effect may be to cancel out the impact of particular competing desires. Some "moral" desires in the market such as the example given earlier of a preference for racial segregation may violate universal moral principles, or hypernorms as discussed *infra*. In many instances they will be canceled out by contrary preferences as was the case in the example of civil rights in West Virginia. If they come to dominate and become a community norm, they are nonetheless illegitimate because they violate hypernorms.

59. Note that I am not making the claim that morality itself should be viewed as the output of a market. There are some interesting possibilities, however, in thinking of morality in market terms. There may be certain moral issues, such as the use of severance packages in downsizing, the use of animals in medical research, even abortion, where the input of competing moral desires operates in a manner similar to if not totally congruent with a market. In such a context, one could consider the demand factor to be a demand for resolution of the particular moral conflict. The supply is the competing moral desires as reflected in a variety of capital, consumer, labor and political market contexts. The outcome is the number of abortions, the typical size of severance packages, the number of animals used in research, and so on. These ideas are tentatively explored in Dunfee, *supra* note 55.

60. *See*, Gary S. Becker and Guity Nashat Becker, *The Economics of Life* (1997); Gary S. Becker, *Accounting for Tastes* (1996).

61. Personal capital refers to "relevant past consumption and other personal experiences that affect current and future utilities," while social capital refers to "the influence of past actions by peers and others in an individual's social network." Becker, *supra* note 69, p. 4.

62. *Id.*, pp. 10–12.

63. *Id.*, pp. 5–6.

64. *See* Richard A. Posner, *Sex and Reason* (1992).

65. One could just engage in a political analysis to determine whether the political system has somehow dictated that pluralistic values should be observed. It is well beyond the scope of this article, but there is obviously a question of how effective the political system is in giving effect to the moral desires of any relevant groups of people.

66. Charles Hampden Turner & Fons Trompenaars, *The Seven Cultures of Capitalism* 32 (1993).

67. Barry Posner & Warren Schmidt, "Values and the American Manager," *California Management Review* 26 (1984): 202, 207.

68. Orts, "Beyond Shareholders," *supra note 38*, p. 21.

69. *Caux Round Table Principles for Business* (Caux Round Table Secretariat, Washington, DC, 1994); The Caux Round Table is an organization comprised of very senior executives from Asia, Europe, and the United States. It takes its name from its practice of holding its annual meetings at the Mountain House in Caux, Switzerland.

70. Shell has been involved in many controversial incidents; a few of the major events are listed here. For a discussion on Shell's public relations history, see Andrew Rowell, "Unlovable Shell, the Goddess of Oil, *The Guardian* (London), November 15, 1997, p. 23. After World War II, Shell manufactured pesticides on a site in the Rocky Mountains that the U.S. military had previously used to make nerve gas. In 1960, a game warden notified Shell of harm to local wildlife that was believed to be caused by Shell's activities, but Shell continued operations in the area until 1982. *Id.* In 1988 and 1989, Shell operations caused a discharge of 440,000 gallons of oil into the San Francisco Bay and 150 tons of crude oil into the River Mersey in the United Kingdom. *Id.* Also in the 1980s, Shell refused to go along with a United Nations and OPEC boycott of oil supplies in South Africa. Yvette Cooper & David Orr, "When the People Take on an Oil Giant," *The Independent* (London), Nov. 14, 1995, p. 15. Beginning in the early 1990s, the Ogoni people in Nigeria

demanded that Shell compensate them for damage done to their homeland caused by Shell's operations. Rowell, *supra* this note, p. 23. This situation became a major international event in 1995 (shortly after the Brent Spar incident) when the Nigerian military government executed Ken Saro-Wiwa, an Ogoni leader protesting Shell's activities, and eight others. The eight had been convicted by the Nigerian government for the murder of opposition tribal leaders. The Nigerian action was very controversial and drew worldwide condemnation. Shell failed to intervene or condemn the actions of the Nigerian government, and many alleged that Shell had supported the military regime. Cooper & Orr, *supra* this note, p. 15.

71. S. Prakash Sethi and Paul Steidlmeier, *Up Against the Corporate Wall: Cases in Business and Society* (6th ed., 1997).

72. Beth Goodpaster (under the supervision of Thomas Holloran), "Case: Exxon Valdez: Corporate Recklessness on Trial," in *Policies and Persons: A Casebook in Business Ethics* (Kenneth E. Goodpaster, Laura L. Nash, and John B. Matthews, eds., 1998).

73. *Id.*

74. Keith Schneider, "Exxon Is Ordered to Pay $5 Billion for Alaska Spill," *New York Times*, Sept. 17, 1994, p. 1.

75. See *supra*, Part I.

76. See *supra*, Part III.B.

77. Donaldson and Dunfee, *Ties that Bind, supra* note 79.

78. Unless, of course, they violate manifest universal ethical norms or principles. See the discussion of principle 4, *infra*.

79. See *supra* note 47 and accompanying text.

80. Rikki Abzug, and Natalie J. Webb, "Rational and Extra-Rational Motivations for Corporate Giving: Complementing Economic Theory with Organizational Science," *New York Law School Law Review* 41 (1997): 1035.

81. Robert John Schulze, "Book Note: Can This Marriage Be Saved? Reconciling Progressivism with Profits in Corporate Governance Laws," *Stanford Law Review* 49 (1997): 1607,1612.

82. Goodpaster incorporates a "Nemo Dat Principle" into his discussion of stakeholder synthesis nothing that investors cannot expect managers to act on their behalf in a manner "that would be inconsistent with the reasonable expectations of the community." Kenneth E. Goodpaster, "Business Ethics and Stakeholder Analysis," *Business Ethics Quarterly* 1 (1991): 65.

83. Evan, William M., and R. Edward Freeman, "A Stakeholder Theory of the Modern Corporation: Kantian Capitalism," in *Ethical Theory and Business* (T. Beauchamp & N. Bowie, eds., 4th ed., 1988), pp. 75–93.

84. Donaldson, Thomas, and Lee E. Preston, "The Stakeholder Theory for the Corporation: Concepts, Evidence, Implications," *Academy of Management Review* 20 (1995): 65.

85. Thomas Donaldson, *The Ethics of International Business* (1989), p. 47.

86. Presumably such cases will be rare and Kantial morality will typically be congruent with marketplace morality in relevant communities.

87. Donaldson and Dunfee, *Ties that Bind, supra* note 79; Donaldson and Dunfee, *ISCT, supra* note 79.

88. See *supra*, Part III.B.

89. By second order, we mean higher. Thus first order norms are judged by and are inferior to second order norms.

90. Donaldson and Dunfee, *ISCT, supra* note 79, p. 265.

91. See Richard T. DeGeorge, *Competing with Integrity in International Business* (1993), p. 46.

92. *Id.*

93. Donaldson and Dunfee, *Ties that Bind, supra* note 79.

94. Donaldson and Dunfee, *Ties that Bind, supra* note 79.

95. The emphasis on objective or manifest evidence is responsive to the concerns of critics such as Schulze who worry that the pluralistic proposals are "unworkable because they eliminate much of the guidance for managerial decision making. Under (the pluralistic) reforms, executives would be free to manage corporations based on caprice or bias. Moreover, the proposals leave no objective legal standard by which to judge and evaluate managerial performance." Schulze, *supra* note 96, at 1612.

96. 250 U.S. 616,630 (1920).

97. *See* Eric W. Orts, "Reflexive Environmental Law," *Northwestern Law Review* 89 (1995): 1227; David W. Hess, *Legislating Corporate Social Responsiveness Reflexively Through Social Reports*, paper presented at the Society of Business Ethics annual meeting (August 7–9, 1998). Reflexive laws can be distinguished from "substantive" law on how they, as regulatory schemes, take responsibility for the outcome of social activity. Substantive law essentially mandates a certain outcome, while reflexive law preserves the freedom of regulated parties to reach their own outcomes but establishes procedures that will force those parties to "take account of various externalities." Gunther Teubner, *Substantive and Reflexive Elements in Modern Law*, 17 Law & Soc. Rev. 239 (1983), 255–57. Orts argues for environmental audits as a reflexive law alternative to substantive regulation (e.g., command-control regulation) because they work towards institutionalizing environmental responsibility within corporations. Orts, *supra* this note, p. 1339. Similar to the National Environmental

Policy Act, which requires agencies to prepare environmental impact statements, environmental audits work on the assumption that the process of preparing an audit will promote responsible decision-making. *Id.*, pp. 1272–75. Some of the key components of an environmental audit regulatory scheme are third party verification and public disclosure. *Id.*, p. 1322–24. Similar to securities regulation, these requirements promote more efficient markets by giving the market participants more information. *Id.*, p. 1312.

98. Marlene A. O'Connor, "Promoting Economic Justice in Plant Closings: Exploring the Fiduciary/Contract Law Distinction to Enforce Implicit Employment Agreements," in *Progressive Corporate Law* (Lawrence E.

Mitchell, ed., 1995), p. 235. *See also* Marleen A. O'Connor, "The Human Capital Era: Reconceptualizing Corporate Law to Facilitate Labor-Management Cooperation," *Cornell Law Review* 78 (1993): 899.

QUESTIONS

1. Does Dunfee solve the problem of corporate governance? What is his solution?

2. Explain the differences between monotonic and pluralistic versions of corporate governance. Can they be reconciled?

John J. McCall

Employee Voice in Corporate Governance: A Defense of Strong Participation Rights

John J. McCall is professor of ethics at St. Joseph's University.

INTRODUCTION

"Participative Management." "Employee Involvement." "Flattened Hierarchies." "Employee Voice." As these current buzzwords of management literature indicate, the topic of employee participation decision making has arrived in the U.S. Once a mantra of left-wingers that was inaudible in mainstream discussions of corporate governance, concern with employee participation promises to spread in the current economic and political climate. It is urged by former Clinton administration players (Labor Secretary Robert Reich and chief economist Laura D'Andrae Tyson), promoted as an essential element of the future American workplace by the

blue ribbon "Dunlop Commission on the Future of Labor–Management Relations" and embraced by some labor leaders.

DEFENSES

Employee participation rights can be defended on a number of grounds.

Dignity

First, most approaches to morality that emphasize rights do so because their adherents believe that persons somehow have inherent value and should be treated with dignity. A long tradition explains that inherent value as deriving from the ability to deliberate rationally and choose freely how to live, that is, from autonomy. Traditional hierarchical

From *Business Ethics Quarterly*, Vol. 11(1), pp. 195–213. Reprinted with permission. References were deleted from the text.

patterns of work organization, of course, treat employees as anonymous and replaceable "human resources" that are to be "managed" for the goal of corporate profit. An authentic social commitment to the dignity and autonomy of individuals would challenge that tradition. Since we spend one-third to one-half of our adult lives at work, since our work experience influences the character of even our non-working hours and since work in our culture plays such a dominant role in defining us as individuals and in establishing our social worth, a commitment to dignity and autonomy should urge that workers have some ability to exercise control over their work lives.... That control can only be more than token when it is possessed in amounts equal to that of management.

Fairness

Second, participation rights can be derived from modern Western moral norms that profess a commitment to the *equal* dignity of each person. While no social system could guarantee that all the interests of its members are accommodated, the commitment to equality requires that decisions affecting those interests, and especially decisions affecting important or basic interests, be made fairly. Clearly, many policy decisions made in corporations are capable of great impact on the most basic interests of workers. What more effective guarantee of fairness and accountability could there be than allowing workers to represent their own interests in the decision-making process...? In order for that guarantee to be effective, however, the mechanism of participation must provide real authority. And, since a balanced and fair consideration of all interests is more likely when opposing parties have roughly equal institutional power, employees deserve an amount of authority that enables them to resist policies that unfairly damage their interests. That, of course, means a right to codetermine policy at all levels.

Self-Respect

Third, it is now a psychological commonplace that a person's sense of self-worth is largely conditioned by the institutional relationships she has and by the responses from others she receives in those relationships. Of course, in contemporary America, the development of both the division of labor and hierarchical authority structures leaves little room for most workers to exercise their autonomy or to feel that their opinions are influential. The frequent consequence of such work structures is worker burnout and alienation. Workers dissociate themselves from a major portion of their lives, often with the consequence of a sense of impotence and unimportance. However, these results are less likely when workers are given opportunities for autonomous action and for the exercise of judgment. Since participation in decision making can reaffirm the employees' sense of influence and self worth, there is a presumptive reason for implementing it in the workplace.

It should be noted that this defense of participation rights does not require that those rights be rights to co-determine policy. The concerns expressed by this defense could potentially be satisfied by forms of participation that were merely advisory, if those advisory mechanisms in fact increased employees' subjective sense of influence and self-worth. It is also worth noting, however, that purely advisory mechanisms of participation carry the danger that workers, after an initial decrease in feelings of alienation, might become cynical about the real impact of the participatory structures. Cases of this abound in corporations that implemented quality circles without a strong commitment to altering traditional hierarchical and autocratic structures....

Health

Fourth, if as was just suggested, contemporary work organization is an important cause of alienation, work may provide the stressors that lead to both physical and mental health problems. Some evidence indicates, however, that stress is inversely related to perceived control over one's work environment...Thus, if employees were granted some measure of control over workplace decisions, stress and attendant health difficulties might be reduced. In fact, data exist which show increased levels of work satisfaction when workers believe they are able to influence corporate policies. Additionally, there is evidence that employee voice in the workplace through participatory committees makes more effective regulatory initiatives aimed at health and safety....Since health is a basic interest, there are presumptive reasons for programs, such as employee participation, that might reduce threats to it.

Democracy

Finally, some have argued that only by increasing citizens' sense of power over more local and immediate aspects of their lives will we be able to reverse trends toward voter apathy and disengagement from active participation in the political process, trends that so threaten the vitality of our democracy.... Of course, the workplace is a prime example of the kind of environment where persons can learn lessons either of impotence or efficacy. Hence, participation mechanisms can be instrumental in protecting the health of democratic politics by encouraging people toward greater civic involvement....

PROPERTY RIGHTS OBJECTIONS

...Some objections to strong forms of worker participation arise from efficiency concerns. The most serious objections from a moral perspective, however, derive from property rights claims and it is on those that the remainder of this paper focuses.

The property objection presents a serious obstacle (at least rhetorically) to the acceptance of a manifesto right to strong employee participation. That objection asserts that extending to workers partial control over enterprise decisions is a violation of the corporate owners' property rights. Clearly, if property rights mean anything, they mean that the title holder has more or less exclusive rights to control the use of property. Of course shareholders might allow their agents, management, to introduce participatory schemes if that were a beneficial strategy. That, however, is a far cry from claiming that employees are entitled to participation as a matter of right. Since rights to private property are so central to the ideology of our culture, this objection has a

rhetorical seriousness that threatens to undermine the presumptive grounds for participation.

Some reject this corporate property rights argument on the basis of a fact that...in contemporary corporations, ownership is separated from control. Some might suggest that since owners have already ceded control to management, there is no conflict between shareholders' property rights and an employee share of decision-making control.

...While it is true that contemporary corporate forms separate owners from substantial control of their property, there are still a number of reasons why corporate property rights might be seen as in conflict with strong employee participation rights.

First, even if owners have ceded control, they arguably have done so under the assumption that management will act as their fiduciary and will promote the interests of shareholders alone. Some ongoing debates about corporate control and the agency problems of corporate structures indicate that there is a serious concern that management might not focus sufficiently on shareholder benefit and might instead opportunistically use their powers to promote their own financial gain.... Thus, the mere separation of ownership and control does not necessarily make it any easier to defend mechanisms of participation, especially if those mechanisms might force corporate decisions to give more consideration to the interests of employees.

Second, one could imagine, as the law sometimes seems to, that the property is the corporation's and that management has a quasi-ownership right to control the corporate assets.... Under this interpretation, the right to control decisions is still vested in another constituency whose interests are in potential conflict with the interests of employees. A defense of strong employee participation rights must still, then, confront a property rights objection.

However...private property has traditionally been justified by appeals to autonomy, democracy, fairness and utility. Private possession of property has been defended as providing the greatest incentive for people to work and invest, thus raising the total amount of economic activity and goods produced and, in turn, increasing the aggregate standard of living (utility). It has been described as the only approach that rewards labor properly because it allows one who "mixes his labor with nature" to enjoy the fruits of that labor (fair return). It has been urged as an external check on government abuse that protects democracy by providing a countervailing locus of power. And it has been presented as maintaining autonomy by allowing property owners to have a stable and secure material base that frees them from over-reliance on the largesse of others.

Whatever one thinks of these traditional defenses of private property, the important thing for our purposes is that they reveal property rights to...have the same moral foundations as do the manifesto right of employee participation. As a consequence, it will not be possible for opponents of participation rights to brush them aside by an appeal to owner's rights to control property.

ADJUDICATING THE RIGHTS CONFLICT

What form must such further argument take? When two claimed rights rest on the same moral grounds, a theoretical defense for the priority of one over the other must show that the justifying values are more centrally at stake in the one taking priority....We must ask whether the values promoted by the property rights would be compromised seriously by allowing encroachment in order to sustain another person's competing right claim. Can it be shown that property will take priority over participation rights, that autonomy, fairness and utility are more jeopardized by granting participation rights than by denying them?

Autonomy

Certainly, there seems little threat to owners' autonomy from the marginal decrease in the owners' control over their property that would be required to recognize a workers' right to co-determine corporate policy. For even if workers were given a right to co-determination, owners still would have a large bundle of rights associated with share ownership.

In addition to a significant right to control through voting privileges, and a representation of their interests by management, owners retain the ability to sell their shares. Further, the evidence indicates that a well-designed program of participation does no necessary damage to productivity or profitability. There is increasing empirical and theoretical evidence that employee participation either improves productivity and/or profitability or is at least neutral with regard to those. (See citations in the immediately following paragraph.) And, so, corporate property owners would still have the financial "cushion" of their investment. Since the autonomy promoting aspect of corporate share ownership is the greater economic independence and greater control over life-choices that such ownership provides, employee participation rights seem to pose no substantial threat to owners' autonomy....

Fairness

One could imagine an argument that with strong participation rights workers gain greater guarantees that their interests will be considered fairly, and individual owners retain rights over their corporate assets substantial enough to provide for a fair return on investment. At the very most, owners might suffer some loss of profits returned as dividends if workers were better able to protect their interests (e.g., by gaining more safety equipment). But in assessing the fairness of this, one could argue that workers with co-determination rights assure a fairer distribution of surplus revenue than would be the case under traditional arrangements where management alone determines the distribution.

The typical replies to this suggestion are that investors deserve the return either because they took the risk or because their investment created the enterprise. This, however, ignores the facts that employees face substantial risks at work and are also essential contributors to the enterprise. Neither risk exposure nor contribution, as we will see presently, will provide grounds sufficient for the claim that investors deserve sole rights to control.

Does Governance Need Government?

As the astonishing wave of corporate scandals continues, the public's distaste for corporate misconduct deepens. The CBS poll, for example, shows just 16 percent of the public expressing a "great deal" or "quite a lot" of confidence in big business. This is the lowest level recorded since pollsters began asking this question in 1986.

More amazing still, 67 percent say that most corporate executives are not honest, compared to only 27 percent who say they are. That is not "some"; that is "most," which is quite an indictment. In addition, 79 percent believe questionable accounting practices are widespread, compared to a mere 16 percent who feel these are isolated instances limited to a few companies. Similar questions about CEOs of large companies and investment professionals also show lopsided majorities believing that wrongdoing is widespread, not confined to isolated instances. Finally, more than half (57 percent) endorse the notion that "committing white-collar crimes to make a dishonest profit for themselves and their companies" happens very often in American business, not just occasionally (39 percent) or hardly ever (2 percent).

Related to these feelings, the public is changing its views about the relationship between government and business. In an intriguing result from the Gallup poll, big business is increasingly seen as the biggest threat to the country in the future. Thirty-eight percent now believe this is the case, compared to 47 percent who believe that big government is the biggest threat. This might not seem so bad until one looks at the trend data and realizes this is the highest "threat" reading for big business since pollsters started asking this question way back in 1965; it also is the smallest gap between big business and big government recorded in those thirty-seven years.

Similarly, since 1981 pollsters have been asking whether there is "too much, too little or about the right amount of government regulation of business and industry." In the Gallup poll, 33 percent said "too little," 32 percent said "too much," and 30 percent said the "right amount" That is the highest "too little" reading since the question was first asked.

The CBS poll shows the same feelings about government regulation of business—in fact, in this instance a little stronger. Thirty-seven percent feel the federal government regulates business too little, 30 percent think too much, and 24 percent say the right amount. This is a turnaround from results of the same question in February, which showed 26 percent believing there was too little regulation and 35 percent saying too much.

Feelings are even stronger about federal regulation of businesses' accounting practices. Seventy-one percent believe the federal government should be doing more to regulate these practices, compared to just 7 percent (!) who think it should be doing less and 17 percent who feel it is doing enough.

—CBS Poll of 685 Adults. Released July 11, 2002 (conducted July 8–9, 2002); Gallup Poll of 1,013 Adults for CNN/USA Today. Released July 11, 2002 (conducted July 5–8, 2002); http://www.rcf.org/Opinions/Public_Opinion_Watch/July8–12.html

Clearly, shareholders and employees are both necessary contributors to the enterprise; the absence of either would mean the corporation would cease to exist. Some might suggest, though, that, since they initiated the process that created the organization, shareholders deserve control over the enterprise. For most contemporary corporations, however, stockholders are not temporally prior participants in the organization. I would hazard that most stock now owned was obtained after the firm was actively involved in production. In any case, it is not clear that being temporally first in involvement with the organization would carry sufficient moral weight to justify exclusion of other contributors from a say in the operation of the firm. What seems more relevant is that the contributions of both constituencies are logically necessary for any production to occur.

As for risk, it is often suggested that shareholders, as the residual risk bearers, deserve greater control. Employees, it is claimed, have already been compensated for their risks by the wage they negotiated. This position, however, fails on a number of grounds. Employees face risks to life and health at work. These risks are differentially distributed across and within occupational categories. No evidence suggests, though, that there is a risk premium given to all whose work is more risky, as this position would imply....

Employees also face risks that the firm will lose money and that they will then be out of a job. While shareholders can diversify against such risk by owning a broad portfolio of stock, employees generally cannot have simultaneous careers in multiple corporations.... Hence, there is reason for finding that employees, too, face significant economic risk in choosing to work for a given corporation.

More importantly, it is problematic to claim that employees have been compensated for their risk and efforts by their past wages. This claim ignores the importance of internal labor markets for understanding the economics of employment. Typically, workers, after some job-hopping while young, develop long-term relationships with firms.... As workers stay in a firm's employment for longer periods, they gradually and increasingly make "investments" in the firm. Clearly, workers develop social attachments in their workplaces that are not easily replaced. They acquire firm specific skills that are not easily transferable nor as valuable in the external labor market as they are within the firm. They also typically gain seniority benefits (increased wages, first preference for new positions, greater opportunities for promotion, less exposure to layoffs when there are cyclic downturns in demand) and pension vesting. Given these firm-specific investments, it is not surprising that evidence indicates that the costs of being laid-off rise with the length of a worker's job tenure.... Workers with all these investments are likely to have a difficult time matching their old income and benefits in a new job, especially since new jobs will often begin at the lowest seniority levels.

Recent economic and industrial relations analyses explain the presence of some of these internal job characteristics by pointing out the benefits firms achieve by structuring their internal labor market in these ways.... Many of these practices serve to bond the worker to the firm by making quitting more expensive. Firms thus reduce the possible loss of hiring and training costs when a worker leaves voluntarily. Firms that increase wages or that increase the value of pension benefits over a worker's job tenure also solve problems associated with monitoring a worker's performance. If future earnings are likely to rise, firms create an incentive mechanism that decreases a worker's probability of slacking on the job while simultaneously decreasing the need for constant and costly performance monitoring. Since workers have more to lose if they are fired for insufficient performance, the frequency of monitoring may be reduced. Essentially, firms promise delayed, future compensation as a vehicle for achieving high productivity at reduced management costs. Thus, the longer workers remain with a firm, the more they have invested in their jobs.

These employee investments, however, are subject to predatory and opportunistic abuse by employers. The implicit bargain of higher future wages and/or benefits for current effort and loyalty to the firm is not an enforceable one. For instance, in recent cases, moneys invested in corporate pension funds on the basis of actuarial projections of future earnings of workers (so as to assure that pension benefits were based on wage levels just before retirement) were raided during hostile take-overs because of a technicality in pension law. After the takeover, employees lost substantial value in the expected pension.... Similarly, in plant closings and layoffs, discharged workers are denied the implicitly promised future benefits. If we recognize, as economists and industrial relations specialists increasingly do, that the promise of higher wages and benefits in the future is part of an economic bargain that employers strike for their own benefit, it is very clear that employees have quite a bit at risk in the corporation. It is also clear that past wages and benefits cannot be seen as sufficient compensation for employees' effort and risk. The claim that they are sufficient treats labor markets as ordinary commodity markets. The above characteristics of internal labor markets, however, cannot be explained if the markets are viewed as simple commodity markets.

Thus, it does not seem that the value of fairness, whether it is understood as grounded in contribution or in risk, can provide easy theoretical grounds for a claim that property rights "trump" the manifesto right of employees to co-determination. Rather, it seems that since risk and contribution are shared between owners and employees, then both ought to be able to exercise control over corporate decisions. That, of course, is tantamount to recognition of co-determination rights for employees....

Utility

The outcome of analysis is substantially the same for the two remaining values that underlie both property and participation: utility and democracy. Whether utility is substantially increased by strong participation rights will depend on data about work satisfaction, health and economic results. There is an emerging literature, both theoretical and empirical, which addresses the consequences of employee involvement for efficiency, profitability and productivity. An adequate assessment of that literature is, however, beyond the scope of this paper and will have to wait for another day.

But even without pursuing that full assessment of consequences, one could argue that the marginal change in current understandings of property rights that would be required to recognize participation rights will not significantly change the incentive to produce or, more to the point for this issue, invest. For, investment in U.S. would be attractive because of the stability and productivity of the economy and because of the sheer size of the American market.

Advice to Outside Auditors
Warren Buffett

1. If the auditor were solely responsible for preparation of the company's financial statements, would they have been done differently? If "differently," the auditor should explain both management's argument and his own.
2. If the auditor were an investor, would he have received the information essential to understanding the company's financial performance during the reporting period?
3. Is the company following the same internal audit procedure that the auditor would if he himself were CEO? If not, what are the differences and why?

From *Fortune* magazine, August 22, 1999.

Moreover, as the evidence in sources cited above indicates, participatory mechanisms can contribute to a firm's efficiency. If it would not substantially alter the investment incentive, the traditional utility-based argument for private property would provide no bar to recognizing rights to co-determine corporate policy.

Democracy

Perhaps least clear is the relation between the two claimed rights (property and participation) and the vitality of democracy. The benefits of participatory processes at work for the health of democracy are speculative at best. However the contemporary role of private corporate property in promoting true democracy is also open to question. Some will claim that in a culture with strongly embedded constitutional rights against government, the real threat to democracy is in concentrated ownership of corporate wealth and its ability to influence the outcome of public debate. (Recall that the distribution of wealth is even more skewed than is the distribution of income.) Whatever may be the case for the respective impacts on democracy of participation rights or marginally changed property rights, I doubt that those impacts, given all of the preceding, would be sufficient to tip the scales away from extending a right to participate.

CONCLUSION

The argument of this paper has been that an employee right to co-determine corporate policy has presumptive force. Its force is based on the very same values that have traditionally been used to support a right to private property. While the former right is not currently recognized, the moral commitments of the culture dictate that it ought to be. Such a recognition sets up a potential conflict between participation and property as it is now understood. I have argued that conflict should be resolved by asking which has the greater impact on the underlying values: rejecting the right to co-determination or marginally changing current understandings of corporate property rights. I have also argued both that the marginal change to property rights does least violence to those underlying values and that those who claim that participatory rights are unnecessary for achieving the underlying values are mistaken.

I would preliminarily conclude, then, since the two rights have the same underlying values and since those underlying values have not been shown more crucially at stake in the case of corporate property rights, that we are obliged to extend recognition to the manifesto right of employees to co-determine corporate policy. That would seem the only theoretically legitimate compromise between the competing rights claims.

I offer this conclusion as only preliminary for several reasons. First, as noted above, some of the arguments presented depend on beliefs that strong employee participation will not have seriously harmful economic consequences. There is solid evidence, much of it from the performance of European firms with employee participation, to support that belief. I have not in this limited space, however, done justice to the debates about that evidence. Second, and relatedly, some questions remain about the possibility of transferring labor market institutions from one environment to another. Serious practical questions, then, must be answered before my arguments are more than preliminary.

QUESTIONS

1. Why should employees have a voice in corporate governance? What are the limits of that voice?

2. Explain the "property rights objections" to strong forms of worker participation. Do you agree with them? Why or why not?

CASES

CASE 14.1
Selling Your Sole at Birkenstock
Michael Lewis

One day this spring, two students from the Haas Business School, imbued with the values of public corporate life, traveled to a small private company to explain why it should reconsider its ways. The company was Birkenstock Footprint Sandals, or, as the employees like to call it, Birkenstock USA. Just to say the name, of course, is to hear the sound of granola crunching and the rustle of female underarm hair in the wind. The shoe company of choice for hippies is slightly more complicated than its reputation. It was founded in 1966 by a woman named Margot Fraser to sell orthopedic shoes manufactured by the German shoemaker Birkenstock. In the beginning the only retail outlets that would stock the sandals Fraser imported were health-food stores (then novel), and so the company's first customers had a counter-cultural flavor. The American distributor now sells many different kinds of shoes, including a line for the striving office worker. It has a strain of hippie in it, but other strains too.

At any rate, Birkenstock USA is still a private company, subject to ordinary market forces but immune to pressures from outside investors. When the Haas Business School students went into the company's headquarters in Novato, California, they found something of a mess, at least by public corporate standards. Birkenstock had been doing good works, willy-nilly, for 30 years. It paid employees to volunteer and gave away sacks of cash to worthy causes without telling a soul about it. The company was reluctant to disclose the recipients of its philanthropy; after all, wouldn't it violate the spirit of good works

to publicize them? But the business-school students were able to uncover a few specifics. For instance, they discovered that Birkenstock gave money to the Elizabeth Glaser Pediatric AIDS Foundation. And that, from the investor-driven corporate point of view, was a problem: sick kids are nice and all, but what do they have to do with selling shoes, especially if you don't spend a lot of time explaining to them why they should be grateful to you?

The students recommended that Birkenstock ditch most of their good works and put all of their energy into a single very public act that connected up naturally to footwear. They shrewdly recommended that Birkenstock sponsor walks for causes. The cause did not matter so much as the fact that potential customers would be walking many miles on its behalf, and, somewhere along the line, encounter a giant sign that said BIRKENSTOCK.

The C.E.O. of Birkenstock, Matt Endriss, listened politely to what the business-school students had to say. "I wrestle with the words and phrases they throw around," he said afterward. " 'Formalize' ... 'standardize' ... 'best practices' ... 'bang for your buck.' Those words don't live in this organization on a daily basis. A lot of them are words we try to abolish." He tells me, "There's a lot of discussion inside Birkenstock about 'authenticity.' " While that concept is notoriously hard to define, its opposite is not. It is inauthentic to seem not to care too much about making money in the interest of making even more of it. It is inauthentic to go bragging about corporate goodness, in hopes of selling more shoes. When you are honest only because honesty

From Michael Lewis, "The Irresponsible Investor," Reprinted with permission.

pays, says Birkenstock's C.E.O., you risk forgetting the meaning of honesty. When you are socially responsible only because social responsibility pays, you lose any real sense of what responsibility means.

Put another way: the instinct to give quietly to a pediatric AIDS foundation is second cousin to the instinct not to use slave labor to make your shoes, or not to manipulate your earnings. It is part of a struggle against the market's relentless pressure on the business executive to behave a bit too selfishly—to become one of those corporate villains whom investors can one day profitably sue. "The whole concept of marketing corporate social responsibility seems odd," Endriss says. "Hit folks over the head and tell them how good we are and, in exchange, there's a monetary return for us."

But the matter is clearly not so simple: the people on the receiving end of Birkenstock's social conscience may be grateful, and there's no law to prevent them from telling others what the company has done. Word spreads. And it's possible that the brand Birkenstock is actually strengthened by a less conventionally corporate approach—that is, that the company, in the long run, makes more money by doing its good works on the sly. "People subconsciously think that the company is doing the right thing," Endriss says. "But you ask them, 'Why do you think it's a good company?' And they can't tell you." If it somehow pays for Birkenstock not to publicize its good works—if stealth charity is just a clever strategy for marketing to hippies—then the company is simply strolling down a different path to the biggest pot of gold. But if so, the path is long and poorly marked. "We're not as profitable as we could be," Endriss says, and then goes on to say that if he wanted to maximize the company's earnings he would fire 60 percent of the workers (the ones who build long-term relationships with customers and vendors) and jack up the price of the shoes.

"Maximizing our profits is not our chief goal", Endriss says. "The exchange of goods and services for money—Birkenstock feels it's here for different reasons." Those reasons can be summarized in a sappy sentence: the happiness of employees and customers and a feeling that it is contributing to the general well-being of the world around it. Make money, yes, but don't make a fetish of it. "If the

company were compelled to answer to shareholders," the C.E.O. says, "it would destroy us."

This kind of talk is daft to most investors. Birkenstock USA has existed for nearly 40 years, but it still has only about $120 million in annual sales. It has grown slowly, generating steady but modest profits and exhibiting no great ambition to grow a lot faster. Who'd want to invest in that? To the financial market these guys are a bunch of mediocrities. But that's the idea: when you make a point of behaving extremely well you are unlikely to make as much money as when you don't. A few highly desirable companies (Google?) might be able to dictate morality to investors, but most cannot. The highest moral standards have a price, and most investors do not wish to pay it. But businesspeople who don't have distant, amoral shareholders to answer to are able to pay whatever price they can afford, for the sake of some other goal. And these goals can include behavior so admirable as to make an investor weep.

Three years ago, the founder of Birkenstock, Margot Fraser, by then a septuagenarian, realized that for her company to survive her it would require another owner. She controlled 60 percent of the outstanding shares, and the question was what to do with them. Rather than take them into the public market and find the highest bidder—who would, of course, demand the fastest-rising share price—Fraser decided that she wanted to sell them all to the company's employees in a way that turned just about every employee into an owner. To calculate the price of her shares, the board, aware of the founder's desires, took the current fair-market value, then reduced it as much as they could without making the price so ridiculously low that it could be construed as a gift. But when they presented her with a price for her shares, Fraser's only question was, "Why can't you make it lower?"

QUESTIONS

1. Should you be honest only when honesty pays? How does that risk destroying the meaning of honesty? The culture of honesty?

2. What do you predict for the future of Birkenstock, with the shares in the hands of the employees? Do you think policies will change? How and why?

CASE 14.2
The Good Old Boys at WorldCom
Dennis Moberg and Edward Romar

The year 2002 saw an unprecedented number of corporate scandals: Enron, Tyco, Global Crossing. In many ways, WorldCom is just another case of failed corporate governance, accounting abuses, and outright greed. But none of these other companies had senior executives as colorful and likable as Bernie Ebbers. A Canadian by birth, the six-foot three-inch former basketball coach and Sunday School teacher emerged from the collapse of WorldCom not only broke but with a personal net worth as a negative nine-digit number.[1] No palace in a gated community, no stable of racehorses, or multi-million dollar yacht to show for the telecommunications giant he created. Only debts and red ink—results some consider inevitable given his unflagging enthusiasm and entrepreneurial flair. There is no question that he did some pretty bad stuff, but he really wasn't like the corporate villains of his day: Andy Fastow of Enron, Dennis Koslowski of Tyco, or Gary Winnick of Global Crossing.

Personally, Bernie is a hard guy not to like. In 1998 when Bernie was in the midst of acquiring the telecommunications firm MCI, Reverend Jesse Jackson, speaking at an all-black college near WorldCom's Mississippi headquarters, asked how Ebbers could afford $35 billion for MCI but hadn't donated funds to local black students. Businessman LeRoy Walker, Jr., was in the audience at Jackson's speech, and afterwards set him straight. Ebbers had given over $1 million plus loads of information technology to that black college. "Bernie Ebbers," Walker reportedly told Jackson, "is my mentor."[2] Rev. Jackson was won over, but who wouldn't be by this erstwhile milkman and bar bouncer who serves meals to the homeless at Frank's Famous Biscuits in downtown Jackson, Mississippi, and

wears jeans, cowboy boots, and a funky turquoise watch to work.

It was 1983 in a coffee shop in Hattiesburg, Mississippi that Mr. Ebbers first helped create the business concept that would become WorldCom. "Who could have thought that a small business in itty bitty Mississippi would one day rival AT&T?" asked an editorial in Jackson, Mississippi's *Clarion-Ledger* newspaper.[3] Bernie's fall and the company's was abrupt. In June, 1999, with WorldCom's shares trading at $64, he was a billionaire, and WorldCom was the darling of The New Economy. By early May of 2002, Ebbers resigned his post as CEO, declaring that he was "1,000 percent convinced in my heart that this is a temporary thing."[4] Two months later, in spite of Bernie's unflagging optimism, WorldCom declared itself the largest bankruptcy in American history.

THE GROWTH THROUGH ACQUISITION MERRY-GO-ROUND

From its humble beginnings as an obscure long distance telephone company WorldCom, through the execution of an aggressive acquisition strategy, evolved into the second largest long distance telephone company in the United States and one of the largest companies handling worldwide Internet data traffic. According to the WorldCom website, at its high point the company:

- Provided mission-critical communications services for tens of thousands of businesses around the world

- Carried more international voice traffic than any other company
- Carried a significant amount of the world's Internet traffic
- Owned and operated a global IP (Internet Protocol) backbone that provided connectivity in more than 2,600 cities, and in more than 100 countries
- Owned and operated 75 data centers...on five continents. [Data centers provide hosting and allocation services to businesses for their mission critical business computer applications.]

WorldCom achieved its position as a significant player in the telecommunications industry through the successful completion of 65 acquisitions. Between 1991 and 1997, WorldCom spent almost $60 billion in the acquisition of many of these companies and accumulated $41 billion in debt.[5] Two of these acquisitions were particularly significant. The MFS Communications acquisition enabled WorldCom to obtain UUNet, a major supplier of Internet services to business, and MCI Communications gave WorldCom one of the largest providers of business and consumer telephone service. By 1997, WorldCom's stock had risen from pennies per share to over $60 a share. Through what appeared to be a prescient and successful business strategy at the height of the Internet boom, WorldCom became a darling of Wall Street. In the heady days of the technology bubble Wall Street took notice of WorldCom and its then visionary CEO, Bernie Ebbers. This was a company "on the make," and Wall Street investment banks, analysts and brokers began to discover WorldCom's value and make "strong buy recommendations" to investors. As this process began to unfold, the analysts recommendations, coupled with the continued rise of the stock market, made World Com stock desirable and the market's view of the stock was that it could only go up. As the stock value went up, it was easier for WorldCom to use stock as the vehicle to continue to purchase additional companies. The acquisition of MFS Communications and MCI Communications were, perhaps, the most significant in the long list of WorldCom acquisitions.

With the acquisition of MFS Communications and its UUNet unit, "WorldCom (s)uddenly had an investment story to offer about the value of combining long distance, local service and data communications."[6] In late 1997, British Telecommunications Corporation made a $19 billion bid for MCI. Very quickly, Ebbers made a counter offer of $30 billion in WorldCom stock. In addition, Ebbers agreed to assume $5 billion in MCI debt, making the deal $35 billion or 1.8 times the value of the British Telecom offer. MCI took WorldCom's offer making WorldCom a truly significant global telecommunications company.

All this would be just another story of a successful growth strategy if it wasn't for one significant business reality—mergers and acquisitions, especially large ones, present significant managerial challenges in at least two areas. First, management must deal with the challenge of integrating new and old organizations into a single smooth functioning business. This is a time-consuming process that involves thoughtful planning and a considerable amount of senior managerial attention if the acquisition process is to increase the value of the firm to both shareholders and stakeholders. With 65 acquisitions in six years and several of them large ones, WorldCom management had a great deal on their plate. The second challenge is the requirement to account for the financial aspects of the acquisition. The complete financial integration of the acquired company must be accomplished, including an accounting of asset, debts, good will and a host of other financially important factors. This must be accomplished through the application of generally accepted accounting practices (GAAP).

In July 2002, WorldCom filed for bankruptcy-protection after several disclosures regarding accounting irregularities. Among them was the admission of improperly accounting for operating expenses as capital expenses in violation of generally accepted accounting practices (GAAP). WorldCom has admitted to a $9 billion adjustment for the period from 1999 thorough the first quarter of 2002.

SWEETHEART LOANS TO SENIOR EXECUTIVES

Bernie Ebbers' passion for his corporate creation loaded him up on common stock. Through generous stock options and purchases Ebbers' WorldCom holdings grew and grew, and he typically financed these purchases with his existing holdings as collateral. This was not a problem until the value of WorldCom stock declined, and Bernie faced margin calls (a demand to put up more collateral for outstanding loans) on some of his purchases. At that point he faced a difficult dilemma. Because his personal assets were insufficient to meet the substantial amount required to meet the call, he could either sell some of his common shares to finance the margin calls or request a loan from the company to cover the calls. Yet, when the board learned of his problem, it refused to let him sell his shares on the grounds that it would depress the stock price and signal a lack of confidence about WorldCom's future.

Had he pressed the matter and sold his stock, he would have escaped the bankruptcy financially whole, but Ebbers honestly thought WorldCom would recover. Thus, it was enthusiasm and not greed that trapped Mr. Ebbers. The executives associated with other corporate scandals sold at the top. In fact, other WorldCom executives did much, much better than Ebbers. Bernie borrowed against his stock. That course of action makes sense if you believe the stock will go up, but it's the road to ruin if the stock goes down. Unlike the others, he intended to make himself rich taking the rest of the shareholders with him. In his entire career, Mr. Ebbers sold company shares only half a dozen times. Detractors may find him irascible and arrogant, but defenders describe him as a principled man.

The policy of boards of directors authorizing loans for senior executives raises eyebrows. The sheer magnitude of the loans to Ebbers was breathtaking. The $341 million loan the board granted Mr. Ebbers is the largest amount any publicly traded company has lent to one of its officers in recent memory. Beyond that, some question whether such loans are ethical. "A large loan to a senior executive epitomizes concerns about conflict of interest and breach of fiduciary duty," said former SEC enforcement official Seth Taube. Nevertheless, 27% of major publicly traded companies had loans outstanding for executive officers in 2000 up from 17% in 1998 (most commonly for stock purchase but also home buying and relocation). Moreover, there is the claim that executive loans are commonly sweetheart deals involving interest rates that constitute a poor rate of return on company assets. WorldCom charged Ebbers slightly more than 2% interest, a rate considerably below that available to "average" borrowers and also below the company's marginal rate of return. Considering such factors, one compensation analyst claims that such lending "should not be part of the general pay scheme of perks for executives...I just think it's the wrong thing to do."

WHAT'S A NOD OR WINK AMONG FRIENDS?

In the autumn of 1998, Securities and Exchange Commissioner Arthur Levitt, Jr. uttered the prescient criticism, "Auditors and analysts are participants in a game of nods and winks. It should come as no surprise that it was Arthur Andersen that endorsed many of the accounting irregularities that contributed to WorldCom's demise. Beyond that, however, were a host of incredibly chummy relationships between WorldCom's management and Wall Street analysts.

Since the Glass-Steagall Act was repealed in 1999, financial institutions have been free to offer an almost limitless range of financial services to its commercial and investment clients. Citigroup, the result of the merger of Citibank and Travelers Insurance Company, who owned the investment bank and brokerage firm Salomon Smith Barney, was an early beneficiary of investment deregulation. Citibank regularly dispensed cheap loans and lines of credit as a means of attracting and rewarding corporate clients for highly lucrative work in mergers and acquisitions. Since WorldCom was so active in that mode, their senior managers were the target of a great deal of influence peddling by their banker, Citibank. For example, Travelers Insurance, a Citigroup unit, lent $134 million to a timber company Bernie Ebbers was heavily invested in. Eight months later, WorldCom chose Salomon Smith Barney, Citigroup's brokerage unit, to be the lead underwriter of $5 billion of it's bond issue.

But the entanglements went both ways. Since the loan to Ebbers was collateralized by his equity holdings, Citigroup had reason to prop up WorldCom stock. And no one was better at that than Jack Grubman, Salomon Smith Barney's telecommunication analyst. Grubman first met Bernie Ebbers in the early 1990's when he was heading up the precursor to WorldCom, LDDS Communications. The two hit it off socially, and Grubman started hyping the company. Investors were handsomely rewarded for following Grubman's buy recommendations until stock reached its high, and Grubman rose financially and by reputation. In fact, *Institutional Investing* magazine gave Jack a Number 1 ranking in 1999, and *Business Week* labeled him "one of the most powerful players on Wall Street.

The investor community has always been ambivalent about the relationship between analysts and the companies they analyze. As long as analyst recommendations are correct, close relations have a positive insider quality, but when their recommendations turn south, corruption is suspected. Certainly Grubman did everything he could to tout his personal relationship with Bernie Ebbers. He bragged about attending Bernie's wedding in 1999. He attended board meeting at WorldCom's headquarters. Analysts at competing firms were annoyed with this chumminess. While the other analysts strained to glimpse any tidbit of information from the company's conference call, Grubman would monopolize the conversation with comments about "dinner last night."

It is not known who picked up the tab for such dinners, but Grubman certainly rewarded executives for their close relationship with him. Both Ebbers and WorldCom CFO Scott Sullivan were granted privileged allocations in IPO (Initial Public Offering) auctions. While the Securities and Exchange Commission allows underwriters like Salomon Smith

Barney to distribute its allotment of new securities as it sees fit among its customers, this sort of favoritism has angered many small investors. Banks defend this practice by contending that providing high net worth individuals with favored access to hot IPOs is just good business. Alternatively, they allege that greasing the palms of distinguished investors creates a marketing "buzz" around an IPO, helping deserving small companies trying to go public get the market attention they deserve. For the record, Mr. Ebbers personally made $11 million in trading profits over a four-year period on shares from initial public offerings he received from Salomon Smith Barney. In contrast, Mr. Sullivan lost $13,000 from IPOs, indicating that they were apparently not "sure things."

There is little question but that friendly relations between Grubman and WorldCom helped investors from 1995 to 1999. Many trusted Grubman's insider status and followed his rosy recommendations to financial success. In a 2000 profile in *Business Week*, he seemed to mock the ethical norm against conflict of interest: "what used to be a conflict is now a synergy," he said at the time. "Someone like me ... would have been looked at disdainfully by the buy side 15 years ago. Now they know that I'm in the flow of what's going on." Yet, when the stock started cratering later that year, Grubman's enthusiasm for WorldCom persisted. Indeed, he maintained the highest rating on WorldCom until March 18, 2002 when he finally raised its risk rating. At that time, the stock had fallen almost 90% from its high two years before. Grubman's mea culpa to clients on April 22 read, "In retrospect the depth and length of the decline in enterprise spending has been stronger and more damaging to WorldCom than we even anticipated." An official statement from Salomon Smith Barney two weeks later seemed to contradict the notion that Grubman's analysis was conflicted, "Mr. Grubman was not alone in his enthusiasm for the future prospects of the company. His coverage was based purely on information yielded during his analysis and was not based on personal relationships." Right.

On August 15, 2002, Jack Grubman resigned from Salomon where he had made as much as $20 million per year. His resignation letter read in part, "I understand the disappointment and anger felt by investors as a result of [the company's] collapse, I am nevertheless proud of the work I and the analysts who work with me did." On December 19, 2002, Jack Grubman was fined $15 million and was banned for securities transactions for life by the Securities and Exchange Commission for such conflicts of interest.

The media vilification that accompanies one's fall from power unearthed one interesting detail about Grubman's character—he repeatedly lied about his personal background. A graduate of Boston University, Mr. Grubman claimed a degree from MIT. Moreover, he claimed to have grown up in colorful South Boston, while his roots were actually in Boston's comparatively bland Oxford Circle neighborhood. What makes a person fib about his personal history is an open question. As it turns out, this is probably the least of Jack Grubman's present worries. New York State Controller H. Carl McCall sued Citicorp, Arthur Andersen, Jack Grubman, and others for conflict of interest. According to Mr. McCall, "this is another case of corporate coziness costing investors billions of dollars and raising troubling questions about the integrity of the information investors receive."

NOTES

1. This is only true if he is liable for the loans he was given by WorldCom. If he avoids those somehow, his net worth may be plus $8.4 million according to the *Wall Street Journal* (see S. Pulliam & J. Sandberg [2002]. Worldcom Seeks SEC Accord As Report Claims Wider Fraud [November 5], A-1).

2. Padgett, T., & Baughn, A. J. (2002), The Rise and Fall of Bernie Ebbers. *Time, 159,* (19 May 12]), 56+.

3. Morse, D., & Harris, N. (2002). In Mississippi, Ebbers is a Man to be Proud Of. *Wall Street Journal*, May 2, 2002, B-1.

4. Young, S., & Solomon, D. (2002). WorldCom Backs Chief Executive For $340 Million. *Wall Street Journal* (February 8), B-1.

5. Romero, Simon, & Atlas, Rava D. (2002). WorldCom's Collapse: The Overview. *New York Times*, (July 22), A-1.

6. Eichenwald, Kurt (2002). For WorldCom, Acquisitions Were Behind Its Rise and Fall, *New York Times*, (August 8), A-3.

CASE 14.3

Corporate Governance and Democracy

Robert Reich

What's happened to democracy? GM and Chrysler say they desperately need money to avoid bankruptcy in the next few weeks. Treasury Secretary Hank Paulson now says the Big Three "will get the money as quickly as we can prudently do it."

But didn't Congress just vote down that money?

Don't get me wrong. I'm among those who think there's good reason to give the automakers a $14 billion bridge loan to stave off immediate bankruptcy until they come up with a restructuring plan (although, as I've said before, the plan ought to demand real sacrifices from every stakeholder). But I have to tell you, I'm deeply troubled by the administration's likely decision to give it to them when last week Congress said they can't have it.

Call me old-fashioned, but I believe in the democratic process. Under our Constitution, Congress is in charge of appropriating taxpayer money. If Congress explicitly decides not to appropriate it for a certain purpose, where does the White House get the right to do so anyway by pulling the money out of another bag?

http://robertreich.blogspot.com/2008/12/big-three-and-tarp-what-happened-to.html December 17, 2008

That other bag, by the way—called the Troubled Assets Relief Program, or TARP for short—was enacted to rescue Wall Street, not the automobile industry. Personally, I think there's more reason to rescue big automakers than big Wall Street banks, but what I want isn't the issue. It's what our representatives voted for. When they voted for TARP, at the start of October, they didn't say to the President: Here's a $700 billion slush fund to use as you wish. They said: Here's $700 billion for Wall Street.

If TARP is a slush fund, everything's arbitrary. We're no longer a nation of laws; we're a nation of Treasury and White House officials with hundreds of billions of dollars of taxpayer money to dispense as they see fit. Why rescue autos and not, say, the newspaper industry, which is heading for oblivion? Better yet, why not rescue state and local governments? They're running short about $100 billion this year and as a result are slashing public services, including the nation's schools.

Even as it is, TARP is shrouded in secrecy. The Treasury has burned through $335 billion so far, and no one knows exactly how or by what criteria. Why, for example, did it set tough conditions on AIG while giving Citigroup the sweetest deal imaginable?

The dictionary meaning of a "tarp" is something used to cover things up, which is exactly we've got.

But our system of government depends on sunlight, transparency, and public awareness. It also depends on Congress exercising its constitutional duty to make laws and the President executing them.

An economic crisis is no excuse for turning our backs on democracy.

QUESTIONS

1. Can you explain what TARP is? In a few sentences, to a friend?

2. Can you similarly explain the dangers of TARP?

3. Detail the tensions that exist between CEOs, Boards of Directors, shareholders, and other stakeholders in the corporation. How do you think the power should be divided? How does compensation play into the picture? And how should company performance be evaluated and rewarded, at the various levels? Imagine your own corporation, and try to arrive at a structure that would maximize both performance and ethical behavior.

4. Does corporate governance need greater governmental regulation? Why or why not? Try to give a list of at least ten reasons for your response.

CASE 14.4
Pump It Up
David Seltzer

Henrietta Bluefish has been an investment banker with Tremper and Co. for four years. Since Henrietta had an undergraduate degree in biomechanical engineering and an M.B.A, degree, she was the ideal candidate to assist medal supplies companies going public for the first time. Through her contacts with her father and brother, both medical doctors, she met John Peoples, Chief Executive Officer of Pump It

Up, a manufacturer of infusion pumps. Impressed by Henrietta, Mr. Peoples confided in her that he was looking for an investment banker to take his company public.

Pump It Up eventually chose Tremper as its investment banker, and the company was scheduled to go public on June 13. The initial prospectus, the "red herring," had been released to the public.

Mr. Peoples, the chief financial officer, and the head of research and development for Pump It Up had just completed a series of meetings ("dog and pony shows") in late May with security analysts from the underwriting group.

Pump It Up is a major supplier of infusion pumps to hospitals and outpatient clinics. Its new line of infusion pumps, Vision Pump, can monitor up to 20 pumps via a computer terminal located at a nurses' station. The FDA had approved the clinical trials of Vision Pump 60 days earlier. Vision Pump will eventually replace the company's current line of infusion pumps, and management expects that this product will substantially increase its share of the market.

On the night of June 11, Henrietta attended a dinner party at a friend's house. She overheard a doctor, in the course of a casual conversation, complaining about his stressful life, in particular the past month. Two of his patients died quite unexpectedly in early May and both patients had been hooked up to Pump It Up's Vision Pump system. The hospital's medical staff investigated the cause of death in both cases and concluded "it was possible" that Vision Pump could

have caused the deaths. Of course, the medical staff had notified Pump It Up in mid-May of the findings, and the company had assured the hospital that it would do its own investigation of the matter. Henrietta was surprised that Pump It Up had never mentioned this investigation to her firm or to any of the members of the underwriting group. After some reflection, she realized that, to protect himself, the doctor may have fabricated or distorted the incident.

On the morning of June 12, Henrietta called Pump It Up to confirm the doctor's story. Sure enough, the company said that these incidents had occurred. Pump It Up had investigated the matter and concluded that the doctor had used the pumps incorrectly. No other deaths had occurred, and the FDA had allowed the trials to continue.

QUESTIONS

1. The initial public offering is scheduled for the next day. What should Henrietta do?

2. If Henrietta says nothing, more people die while hooked to the vision pump system. Should she be punished?

CASE 14.5

Fight Corporate Crimes with More than Fines

Lefteris Pitarakis, AP

These days, the pharmaceutical and banking industries seem to be in a contest to see which is better at flouting the law.

Last week, GlaxoSmithKline agreed to pay the government $3 billion for failing to report safety data on its diabetes drug and for marketing its antidepressants for unauthorized uses, including by children.

This comes after similar deals by Pfizer in 2009 ($2.3 billion) and Abbott Laboratories in May ($1.6 billion). Johnson & Johnson is negotiating a

settlement that could cost it as much as $2 billion. And it has been just five years since the maker of OxyContin admitted lying to doctors about the drug's addictive qualities.

Meanwhile, scandals in the finance industry now seem routine. The savings-and-loan debacle of the 1980s forced a $100 billion bailout but was followed by a succession of scams in the investment banking and mutual fund industries. Then came that minor affair known as the global credit crisis, caused by

USA Today, posted July 8, 2012.

banks putting people into inappropriate mortgages and selling the toxic loans to institutional investors as largely risk-free.

Now comes news of a swindle involving the Libor (London interbank offered rate), a key interest benchmark that has a huge impact on mortgages, credit cards, and other borrowing. Executives at an unknown number of the 16 major institutions whose lending practices determine the rate simply lied about what rate they were offered on short-term loans. This caused the Libor to be artificially high or low, so that traders could bet for or against it on derivatives markets.

With a procession of troubling events like these, can there be any doubt that current efforts to police corporate misbehavior are failing? Is there any doubt that only a credible threat of jail time will get executives to insist that the quest for profits is no reason to break the law?

More than 1000 people were convicted of felonies during the savings-and-loan crisis. Tellingly, thrifts have largely avoided the problems encountered by other institutions in recent years.

By contrast, not one high-level executive has been convicted in connection with the credit hustles and packaging of misrepresented mortgages that brought the world economy to its heels in 2008. Since then, a string of scandals has shown how little the financial-services industry has changed. In the Libor scandal, Barlays CEO Bob Diamond and two other executives resigned, all wealthy enough to suffer only embarrassment.

The jury is still out on the drug companies. Most of the behavior being penalized now occurred years ago. But the principle is the same. Intentionally endangering people for profit is a crime.

One thing is certain: Financial penalties aren't the answer. In fact, they could even help legitimize law-breaking. In their 2005 book *Freakonomics*, authors Steven Levitt and Stephen Dubner point to the unintended consequences when a daycare center imposed fines on parents who were late to pickup. Tardiness actually increased as parents saw the modest fines as buying flexibility in their arrival time.

For huge companies, even a 10-figure penalty can be seen as little more than the cost of doing business. Glaxo's $3 billion penalty amounts to about one-third of one year's profits. Penalties for banks have been even more paltry. Federal judge Jed Rakoff rejected a proposed $285 million settlement between Citibank and the government, calling it "neither fair, nor reasonable, nor adequate, nor in the public interest."

Regulation does not appear to be the solution, either. Most rules can be circumvented by, among other things, going overseas. The recent multibillion dollar trading loss at JPMorgan and the much bigger losses incurred by AIG during the credit crisis were engineered out of London.

The way to change criminal behavior is with criminal penalties. In the finance and drug industry scandals, they've been too scarce.

QUESTIONS

1. Should corporations guilty of crimes be fined? Explain your answer.

2. Should the CEOs of a corporation guilty of a crime be tried as a criminal and sent to jail? Explain your answer.

CHAPTER QUESTIONS

1. Explain how corporate governance structure normally works. Identify at least three possible conflicts "corporate governors" make.

2. Is governing a corporation like governing a country? Explain similarities and differences.

15

Is Everything for Sale?

The Future of the Free Market

Introduction

The enthusiasm for market economies may be justified, but should it have it limits? From the outskirts of medieval towns to the center of downtown today, the market has changed from a marginal activity to an essential social enterprise. Local commercial life has given way to global capitalism, and the question is no longer "does this society have a market economy?" but "what kind of a market economy does this society have and how efficient is it?" Commercial life has expanded and infiltrated almost all human activities, so that virtually everything now may be said to have a market value. To take an obvious but awkward example, the value of a human life is now set in dollar terms for the sake of insurance or in lawsuits. (Ford settled Pinto deaths at a rate of $200,000 per person. Malpractice suits sometimes calculate the value of a life in terms of the loss of expected lifetime income.) But "money can't buy happiness," we are told, and "money can't buy love." To be sure, such bits of folk wisdom have their amusing retorts, but we readily recognize what is right about them. Money can't buy everything. Not everything is part of the market. What is most personal about us is not part of the market—and when it becomes part of the market, it is no longer personal. Prostitution is an example. What is wrong is not the sex or even the promiscuity, but the commercialization of something that should not be commercialized. (Thus, "marrying for money" is often subject to the same charge.) When a person "sells out," he or she gives up part of what is most dear and personally precious. We rightly object when commercialization infects religion, and we certainly should object a lot more than we do when it pervades politics.

Is everything for sale? Most of us would surely say no. But what are the limits? Does the market rule everything? Again, most of us would surely say no. But what are the exceptions? This not an all-or-nothing question. After a devastating hurricane in Florida recently, some local merchants jacked up their prices. They were accused of "price-gouging," in other words, taking advantage of the desperate and distorted demands in an emergency situation and ignoring their obligations to the community. No one objected to the merchants charging a "fair" price for such things as bottled water, batteries, and flashlights, covering their costs and giving them a reasonable profit. But taking advantage of situation was another matter, and at some point (a matter of considerable debate), their sense of solidarity with their neighbors should have kicked in. (If only for the sake of future business. No doubt those neighbors will not be good customers after this.) Religion is off-limits, but from the sale of Indulgences that Luther railed against in the sixteenth century to the obscene mix of religion, politics, and commercialism today, the distinction between the spiritual and the commercial has not always been easy to discern.

The readings in this chapter are necessarily abstract in that they consider the nature of economies in general, rather than the particular workings of any one of them. But they raise a central question of special importance in a society that has confidence in the free market to solve all sorts of social problems. We begin, accordingly, with the great philosopher Aristotle writing about a noncapitalist society, ancient Athens. Aristotle expresses considerable doubt about the virtues of what we call "business" and the motivation of those who practice it. We balance this selection with a reading from the "father" of the modern market economy, Adam Smith, who defends the benefits of the free market in his *Wealth of Nations*. We then balance these selections with an excerpt from one of the most famous critics of capitalism, Karl Marx, and the reflections of a contemporary Marxist, Robert Heilbroner, on the "Triumph of Capitalism." Nineteenth-century philosopher-economist John Stuart Mill makes the connection between laissez-faire economics and education. Then we turn to a different conception of the market economy with *Small Is Beautiful* author E. F. Schumacher, who defends what he calls "Buddhist Economics." Nobel prize winner Amartya Sen speaks on the "The Economics of Poverty," and, by way of contrast, economist Thorstein Veblen comments on our status seeking in "Pecuniary Emulation and Conspicuous Consumption," from his *Theory of the Leisure Class*. Daniel Bell discusses "The Cultural Contradictions of Capitalism," and Robert Reich advances his notion of "supercapitalism," the rapidly emerging capitalism of the future, with all of its dangers and responsibilities. Finally, Robert Kuttner discusses the issue that is the title of this chapter: "Is Everything for Sale?"

| Aristotle | # Two Kinds of Commerce |

Aristotle was one of the two greatest Greek philosophers of ancient times and arguably the first economist. But in his *Politics*, his ethics is wholly devoted to an examination of happiness (eudaimonia) and the good life.

Of the art of acquisition then there is one kind which by nature is a part of the management of a household, in so far as the art of household management must either find ready to hand, or itself provide, such things necessary to life, and useful for the community of the family or state, as can be stored. They are the elements of true riches; for the amount of property which is needed for a good life is not unlimited, although Solon in one of his poems says that

No bound to riches has been fixed for man.

Aristotle, *Politics*, trans. W. S. Ross (Oxford University Press, 1916).

But there is a boundary fixed, just as there is in the other arts; for the instruments of any art are never unlimited, either in number or size, and riches may be defined as a number of instruments to be used in a household or in a state.

There is another variety of the art of acquisition which is commonly and rightly called an art of wealth-getting, and has in fact suggested the notion that riches and property have no limit. Being nearly connected with the preceding, it is often identified with it. But though they are not very different, neither are they the same. The kind already described is given by nature, the other is gained by experience and art.

Let us begin our discussion of the question with the following considerations:

Of everything which we possess there are two uses: both belong to the thing as such, but not in the same manner, for one is the proper, and the other the improper or secondary use of it. For example, a shoe is used for wear, and is used for exchange; both are uses of the shoe. He who gives a shoe in exchange for money or food to him who wants one, does indeed use the shoe as a shoe, but this is not its proper or primary purpose, for a shoe is not made to be an object of barter. The same may be said of all possessions, for the art of exchange extends to all of them, and it arises at first from what is natural, from the circumstance that some have too little, others too much. Hence we may infer that retail trade is not a natural part of the art of getting wealth; had it been so, men would have ceased to exchange when they had enough. In the first community, indeed, which is the family, this art is obviously of no use, but it begins to be useful when the society increases. For the members of the family originally had all things in common; later, when the family divided into parts, the parts shared in many things, and different parts in different things, which they had to give in exchange for what they wanted, a kind of barter which is still practised among barbarous nations who exchange with one another the necessaries of life and nothing more; giving and receiving wine, for example, in exchange for corn, and the like. This sort of barter is not part of the wealth-getting art and is not contrary to nature, but is needed for the satisfaction of men's natural wants. The other or more complex form of exchange grew, as might have been inferred, out of the simpler. When the inhabitants of one country became more dependent on those of another, and they imported what they needed, and exported what they had too much of, money necessarily came into use. For the various necessaries of life are not easily carried about, and hence men agreed to employ in their dealings with each other something which was intrinsically useful and easily applicable to the purposes of life, for example, iron, silver, and the like. Of this the value was at first measured simply by size and weight, but in process of time they put a stamp upon it, to save the trouble of weighing and to mark the value.

When the use of coin had once been discovered, out of the barter of necessary articles arose the other art of wealth-getting, namely, retail trade; which was at first probably a simple matter, but became more complicated as soon as men learned by experience whence and by what exchanges the greatest profit might be made. Originating in the use of coin, the art of getting wealth is generally thought to be chiefly concerned with it, and to be the art which produces riches and wealth; having to consider how they may be accumulated. Indeed, riches is assumed by many to be only a quantity of coin, because the arts of getting wealth and retail trade are concerned with coin. Others maintain that coined money is a mere sham, a thing not natural, but conventional only, because, if the users substitute another commodity for it, it is worthless, and because it is not useful as a means to any of the necessities of life, and, indeed, he who is rich in coin may often be in want of necessary food. But how can that be wealth of which a man may have a great abundance and yet perish with hunger, like Midas in the fable, whose insatiable prayer turned everything that was set before him into gold?

Hence men seek after a better notion of riches and of the art of getting wealth than the mere acquisition of coin, and they are right. For natural riches and the natural art of wealth-getting are a different thing; in their true form they are part of the management of a household; whereas retail trade is the art of producing wealth, not in every way, but by exchange. And it is thought to be concerned with coin; for coin is the unit of exchange and the measure or limit of it. And there is no bound to the riches which spring from this art of wealth-getting. As in the art of medicine there is no limit to the pursuit of health, and as in the other arts there is no limit to the pursuit of their several ends, for they aim at accomplishing their ends to the uttermost (but of the means there is a limit, for the end is always the limit), so, too, in this art of wealth-getting there is no limit of the end, which is riches of the spurious kind, and the acquisition of wealth. But the art of wealth-getting which consists in household management, on the other hand, has a limit; the unlimited acquisition of wealth is not its business. And, therefore, in one point of view, all riches must have a limit; nevertheless, as a matter of fact, we find the opposite to be the case; for all getters of wealth increase their hoard of coin without limit. The source of the confusion is the near connexion between the two kinds of wealth-getting; in either, the instrument is the same, although the use is different, and so they pass into one another; for each is a use of the same property, but with a difference: accumulation is the end in the one case, but there is a further end in the other. Hence some persons are led to believe that getting wealth is the object of household management, and the whole idea of their lives is that they ought either to increase their money without limit, or at any rate not to lose it. The origin of this disposition in men is that they are intent upon living only, and not upon living well; and, as their desires are unlimited, they also desire that the means of gratifying them should be without limit. Those who do aim at a good life seek the means of obtaining bodily pleasures; and, since the enjoyment of these appears to depend on property, they are absorbed in getting wealth: and so there arises the second species of wealth-getting. For, as their enjoyment is in excess, they seek an art which produces the excess of enjoyment; and, if they are not able to supply their pleasures by the art of getting wealth, they try other arts, using in turn every faculty in a manner contrary to nature. The quality of courage, for example, is not intended to make wealth, but to inspire confidence; neither is this the aim of the general's or of the physician's art; but the one aims at victory and the other at health. Nevertheless, some men turn every quality or art into a means of getting wealth; this they conceive to be the end, and to the promotion of the end they think all things must contribute.

Thus, then, we have considered the art of wealth-getting which is unnecessary, and why men want it; and also the necessary art of wealth-getting, which we have seen to be different from the other, and to be a natural part of the art of managing a household, concerned with the provision of food, not, however, like the former kind, unlimited, but having a limit.

And we have found the answer to our original question, Whether the art of getting wealth is the business of the manager of a household and of the statesman or not their business?—viz. that wealth is presupposed by them. For as political science does not make men, but takes them from nature and uses them, so too nature provides them with earth or sea or the like as a source of food. At this stage begins the duty of the manager of a household, who has to order the things which nature supplies;—he may be compared to the weaver who has not to make but to use wool, and to know, too, what sort of wool is good and serviceable or bad and unserviceable. Were this otherwise, it would be difficult to see why the art of getting wealth is a part of the management of a household and the art of medicine not; for surely the members of a household must have health just as they must have life or any other necessary. The answer is that as from one point of view the master of the house and the ruler of the state have to consider about health, from another point of view not they but the physician; so in one way the art of household management, in another way the subordinate art, has to consider about wealth. But, strictly speaking, as I have already said, the means of life must be provided beforehand by nature; for the business of nature is to furnish food to that which is born; and the food of the offspring is always what remains over of that from which it is produced. Wherefore the art of getting wealth out of fruits and animals is always natural.

There are two sorts of wealth-getting, as I have said; one is a part of household management, the other is retail trade: the former necessary and honourable, while that which consists in exchange is justly censured; for it is unnatural, and a mode by which men gain from one another. The most hated sort, and with the greatest reason, is usury, which makes a gain out of money itself, and not from the natural object of it. For money was intended to be used in exchange, but not to increase at interest. And this term interest, which means the birth of money from money, is applied to the breeding of money because the offspring resembles the parent. Wherefore of all modes of getting wealth this is the most unnatural.

QUESTIONS

1. What is the difference between the art of wealth getting and retail trade?
2. Is the art of wealth getting the business of the statesman? Why or why not?

Adam Smith | # The Benefits of Capitalism

Adam Smith was the great classical economist who wrote *An Inquiry into the Nature and Causes of the Wealth of Nations* and invoked the tantalizing image of an "invisible hand" that would organize the sum of (more or less) self-interested economic actions into common prosperity.

Everybody must be sensible how much labor is facilitated and abridged by the application of proper machinery. It is unnecessary to give any example. I shall only observe, therefore, that the invention of all those machines by which labor is so much facilitated and abridged seems to have been originally owning to the division of labor. Men are much more likely to discover easier and readier methods of attaining any object when the whole attention of their minds is directed toward that single object than when it is dissipated among a great variety of things. But in consequence of the division of labor, the whole of every man's attention comes naturally to be directed toward some one very simple object. It is naturally to be expected, therefore, that some one or other of those who are employed in each particular branch of labor should soon find out easier and readier methods of performing their own particular work, wherever the nature of it admits of such improvement. A great part of the machines made use of in those manufactures in which labor is most subdivided were originally the inventions of common workmen, who, being each of them employed in some very simple operation, naturally turned their thoughts toward finding out easier and readier methods of performing it. Whoever has been much accustomed to visit such manufactures must frequently have been shown very pretty machines which were the inventions of such workmen in order to facilitate and quicken their own particular part of the work. In the first fire-engines, a boy was constantly employed to open and shut alternately the communication between the boiler and the cylinder, according as the piston either ascended or descended. One of those boys, who loved to play with his companions, observed that, by tying a string from the handle of the valve which opened this communication to another part of the machine, the valve would open and shut without his assistance, and leave him at liberty to divert himself with his play-fellows. One of the greatest improvements that has been made upon this machine, since it was first invented, was in this manner the discovery of a boy who wanted to save his own labor.

All the improvements in machinery, however, have by no means been the inventions of those who had occasion to use the machines. Many improvements have been made by the ingenuity of the makers of the machines, when to make them became the business of a peculiar trade; and some by that of those who are called philosophers or men of speculation, whose

From Adam Smith, *An Inquiry into the Nature and Causes of the Wealth of Nations* (New York: Hafrer, 1948), pp. 6–9.

trade it is not to do anything, but to observe everything; and who, upon that account, are often capable of combining together the powers of the most distant and dissimilar objects. In the progress of society, philosophy or speculation becomes, like every other employment, the principal or sole trade and occupation of a particular class of citizens. Like every other employment too, it is subdivided into a great number of different branches, each of which affords occupation to a peculiar tribe or class of philosophers; and this subdivision of employment in philosophy, as well as in every other business, improves dexterity, and saves time. Each individual becomes more expert in his own peculiar branch, more work is done upon the whole, and the quantity of science is considerably increased by it.

It is the great multiplication of the productions of all the different arts, in consequence of the division of labor, which occasions, in a well-governed society, that universal opulence which extends itself to the lowest ranks of the people. Every workman has a great quantity of his own work to dispose of beyond what he himself has occasion for; and every other workman being exactly in the same situation, he is enabled to exchange a great quantity of his own goods for a great quantity, or, what comes to the same thing, for the price of a great quantity of theirs. He supplies them abundantly with what they have occasion for, and they accommodate him as amply with what he has occasion for, and a general plenty diffuses itself through all the different ranks of the society.

Observe the accommodation of the most common artificer or day laborer in a civilized and thriving country, and you will perceive that the number of people of whose industry a part, though but a small part, has been employed in procuring him this accommodation, exceeds all computation. The woolen coat, for example, which covers the day laborer, as coarse and rough as it may appear, is the produce of the joint labor of a great multitude of workmen. The shepherd, the sorter of the wool, the wool-comber or carder, the dyer, the scribbler, the spinner, the weaver, the fuller, the dresser, with many others, must all join their different arts in order to complete even this homely production.

How many merchants and carriers, besides, must have been employed in transporting the materials from some of those workmen to others who often live in a very distant part of the country! how much commerce and navigation in particular, how many ship-builders, sailors, sail-makers, rope-makers, must have been employed in order to bring together the different drugs made use of by the dyer, which often come from the remotest corners of the world! What a variety of labor too is necessary in order to produce the tools of the meanest of those workmen! To say nothing of such complicated machines as the ship of the sailor, the mill of the fuller, or even the loom of the weaver, let us consider only what a variety of labor is requisite in order to form that very simple machine, the shears with which the shepherd clips the wool. The miner, the builder of the furnace for smelting the ore, the feller of the timber, the burner of the charcoal to be made use of in the smelting-house, the brick-maker, the brick-layer, the workmen who attend the furnace, the mill-wright, the forger, the smith, must all of them join their different arts in order to produce them. Were we to examine, in the same manner, all the different parts of his dress and household furniture, the coarse linen shirt which he wears next his skin, the shoes which cover his feet, the bed which he lies on, and all the different parts which compose it, the kitchen grate at which he prepares his victuals, the coals which he makes use of for that purpose, dug from the bowels of the earth, and brought to him perhaps by a long sea and a long land carriage, all the other utensils of his kitchen, all the furniture of his table, the knives and forks, the earthen or pewter plates upon which he serves up and divides his victuals, the different hands employed in preparing his bread and his beer, the glass window which lets in the heat and the light, and keeps out the wind and the rain, with all the knowledge and art requisite for preparing that beautiful and happy invention, without which these northern parts of the world could scarce have afforded a very comfortable habitation, together with the tools of all the different workmen employed in producing those different conveniencies; if we examine, I say, all these things, and consider what a variety of labor is employed about each of them, we shall be sensible that without the assistance and co-operation of many thousands, the very meanest person in a civilized country could not be provided, even according to what we very falsely imagine the easy and simple manner in which he is commonly accommodated. Compared, indeed, with the more extravagant luxury of the great, his accommodation must no doubt appear extremely simple and easy; and yet it may be true, perhaps, that the accommodation of an European prince does not always so much exceed that of an industrious and frugal peasant, as the accommodation of the latter exceeds that of many an African king, the absolute master of the lives and liberties of ten thousand naked savages.

QUESTIONS

1. How does Smith explain the improvements in machinery? Why does that matter?
2. Why does Smith discuss the "woolen coat" of a workman? Why is he concerned about the complexity and organization of labor?

| Karl Marx | Commodity Fetishism |

Karl Marx was a brilliant but often misused philosopher-economist in the nineteenth century. His great tome was the three-volume *Das Kapital*, published in 1887, which laid out the ground rules for Marxism and then communism in the twentieth century.

The wealth of those societies in which the capitalist mode of production prevails, presents itself as "an immense accumulation of commodities," its unit being a single commodity. Our investigation must therefore begin with the analysis of a commodity.

A commodity is, in the first place, an object outside us, a thing that by its properties satisfies human wants of some sort or another. The nature of such wants, whether, for instance, they spring from the stomach or from fancy, makes no difference. Neither are we here concerned to know how the object satisfies these wants, whether directly as means of subsistence, or indirectly as means of production.

Every useful thing, as iron, paper, &c., may be looked at from the two points of view of quality and quantity. It is an assemblage of many properties, and may therefore be of use in various ways. To discover the various use of things is the work of history. So also is the establishment of socially-recognised standards of measure for the quantities of these useful objects. The diversity of these measures has its origin partly in the diverse nature of the objects to be measured, partly in convention.

The utility of a thing makes it a use-value. But this utility is not a thing of air. Being limited by the physical properties of the commodity, it has no existence apart from that commodity. A commodity, such as iron, corn, or a diamond, is therefore, so far as it is a material thing, a use-value, something useful. This property of a commodity is independent of the amount of labour required to appropriate its useful qualities. When treating of use-value, we always assume to be dealing with definite quantities, such as dozens of watches, yards of linen, or tons of iron. The use-values of commodities furnish the material for a special study, that of the commercial knowledge of commodities. Use-values become a reality only by use or consumption: they also constitute the substance of all wealth, whatever may be the social

From *Capital* Vol. 1: A Critique of Political Economy (1867).

form of that wealth. In the form of society we are about to consider, they are, in addition, the material depositories of exchange value.

Exchange value, at first sight, presents itself as a quantitative relation, as the proportion in which values in use of one sort are exchanged for those of another sort, a relation constantly changing with time and place. Hence exchange value appears to be something accidental and purely relative, and consequently an intrinsic value, *i.e.*, an exchange value that is inseparably connected with inherent in commodities, seems a contradiction in terms. . . .

If . . . we leave out of consideration the use-value of commodities, they have only one common property left, that of being products of labour. But even the product of labour itself has undergone a change in our hands. If we make abstraction from its use value, we make abstraction at the same time from the material elements and shapes that make the product a use-value; we see in it no longer a table, a house, yarn, or any other useful thing. Its existence as a material thing is put out of sight. Neither can it any longer be regarded as the product of the labour of the joiner, the mason, the spinner, or of any other definite kind of productive labour. Along with the useful qualities of the products themselves, we put out of sight both the useful character of the various kinds of labour embodied in them, and the concrete forms of that labour, there is nothing left but what is common to them all; all are reduced to one and the same sort of labour, human labour in the abstract.

Let us now consider the residue of each of these products; it consists of the same unsubstantial reality in each, a mere congelation of homogeneous human labour, of labour-power expended without regard to the mode of its expenditure. All that these things now tell us is, that human labour-power has been expended in their production, that human labor is embodied in them. When looked at as crystals of this social substance, common to them all, they are—Values.

We have seen that when commodities are exchanged, their exchange value manifests itself as something totally independent of their use-value. But if we abstract from their use-value, there remains their Value as defined above. Therefore, the common substance that manifests itself in the exchange value of commodities, whenever they are exchanged, is their value. The progress of our investigation will show that exchange value is the only form in which the value of commodities can manifest itself or be expressed. For the present, however, we have to consider the nature of value independently of this, its form.

A use-value, or useful article, therefore, has value only because human labour in the abstract has been embodied or materialised in it. How, then, is the magnitude of this value to be measured? Plainly, by the quantity of the value-creating substance, the labour, contained in the article. The quantity of labour, however, is measured by its duration, and labour-time in its turn finds its standard in weeks, days, and hours. . . .

We see then that that which determines the magnitude of the value of any article is the amount of labour socially necessary, or the labour-time socially necessary for its production. Each individual commodity, in this connexion, is to be considered as an average sample of its class. Commodities, therefore, in which equal quantities of labour are embodied, or which can be produced in the same time, have the same value. The value of one commodity is to the value of any other, as the labour-time necessary for the production of the one is to that necessary for the production of the other. "As values, all commodities are only definite masses of congealed labour-time."

A commodity appears, at first sight, a very trivial thing, and easily understood. Its analysis shows that it is, in reality, a very queer thing, abounding in metaphysical subtleties and theological niceties. So far as it is a value in use, there is nothing mysterious about it, whether we consider it from the point of view that by its properties it is capable of satisfying human wants, or from the point that those properties are the product of human labour. It is as clear as noon-day, that man, by his industry, changes the forms of the materials furnished by Nature, in such a way as to make them useful to him. The form of wood, for instance, is altered, by making a table out of it. Yet, for all that, the table continues to be that common, everyday thing, wood. But, so soon as it steps forth as a commodity, it is changed into something transcendent. It not only stands with its feet on the ground, but, in relation to all other commodities, it stands on its head, and evolves out of its wooden brain grotesque ideas, far more wonderful than "table-turning" ever was.

The mystical character of commodities does not originate, therefore, in their use-value. Just as little does it proceed from the nature of the determining factors of value. For, in the first place, however varied the useful kinds of labour, or productive activities, may be, it is a physiological fact, that they are functions of the human organism, and that each such function, whatever may be its nature or form, is essentially the expenditure of human brain, nerves, muscles, etc. Secondly, with regard to that which forms the groundwork for the quantitative determination of value, namely, the duration of that expenditure, or the quantity of labour, it is quite clear that there is a palpable difference between its quantity and quality. In all states of society, the labour-time that it costs to produce the means of subsistence must necessarily be an object of interest to mankind, though not of equal interest in different stages of development. And lastly, from the moment that men in any way work for one another, their labour assumes a social form.

Whence, then, arises the enigmatical character of the product of labour, so soon as it assumes the form of commodities? Clearly from this form itself. The equality of all sorts of human labour is expressed objectively by their products all being equally values; the measure of the expenditure of labour-power by the duration of that expenditure, takes the form of the quantity of value of the products of labour; and finally, the mutual relations of the producers, within which the social character of their labour affirms itself, take the form of a social relation between the products.

A commodity is therefore a mysterious thing, simply because in it the social character of men's labour appears to them as an objective character stamped upon the product of that labour; because the relation of the producers to the sum total of their own labour is presented to them as a social relation, existing not between themselves, but between the products of their labour. This is the reason why the products of labour become commodities, social things whose qualities are at the same time perceptible and imperceptible by the senses. In the same way the light from an object is perceived by us not as the subjective excitation of our optic nerve, but as the objective form of something outside the eye itself. But, in the act of seeing, there is at all events, an actual passage of light from one thing to another, from the external object to the eye. There is a physical relation between physical things. But it is different with commodities. There, the existence of the things qua commodities, and the value relation between the products of labour which stamps them as commodities, have absolutely no connexion with their physical properties and with the material relations arising therefrom. There it is a definite social relation between men, that assumes, in their eyes, the fantastic form of a relation between things. In order, therefore, to find an analogy, we must have recourse to the mist-enveloped regions of the religious world. In that world the productions of the human brain appear as independent beings endowed with life, and entering into relation both with one another and the human race. So it is in the world of commodities with the products of men's hands. This I call the Fetishism which attaches itself to the products of labour, so soon as they are produced as commodities, and which is therefore inseparable from the production of commodities.

This Fetishism of commodities has its origin, as the foregoing analysis has already shown, in the peculiar social character of the labour that produces them.

As a general rule, articles of utility become commodities, only because they are products of the labour of private individuals or groups of individuals who carry on their work independently of each other. The sum total of the labour of all these private individuals forms the aggregate labour of society. Since the producers do not come into social contact with each other until they exchange their products, the specific social character of each producer's labour does not show itself except in the act of exchange. In other words, the labour of the individual asserts itself as a part of the labour of society, only by means of the relations which the act of exchange establishes directly between the products, and indirectly, through them, between the producers. To the latter, therefore, the relations connecting the labour of one individual with that of the rest appear, not as direct social relations between individuals at work, but as what they really are, material relations between persons and social relations between things. It is only by being exchanged that the products of labour acquire, as values, one uniform social status, distinct from their varied forms of existence as objects of utility. This division of a product into a useful thing and a value becomes practically important, only when exchange has acquired such an extension that useful articles are produced for the purpose of being exchanged, and their character as values has therefore to be taken into account, beforehand, during production. From this moment the labour of the individual producer acquires socially a two-fold character. On the one hand, it must, as a definite useful kind of labour, satisfy a definite social want, and thus hold its place as part and parcel of the collective labour of all, as a branch of a social division of labour that has sprung up spontaneously. On the other hand, it can satisfy the manifold wants of the individual producer himself, only in so far as the mutual exchangeability of all kinds of useful private labour is an established social fact, and therefore the private useful labour of each producer ranks on an equality with that of all others. The equalisation of the most different kinds of labour can be the result only of an abstraction from their inequalities, or of reducing them to their common denominator, viz., expenditure of human labour power or human labour in the abstract. The two-fold social character of the labour of the individual appears to him, when reflected in his brain, only under those forms which are impressed upon that labour in everyday practice by the exchange of products. In this way, the character that his own labour possesses of being socially useful takes the form of the condition, that the product must be not only useful, but useful for others, and the social character that his particular labour has of being the equal of all other particular kinds of labour, takes the form that all the physically different articles that are the products of labour, have one common quality, viz., that of having value.

QUESTIONS

1. Why do we tend to "fetishize" commodities?
2. What is the distinction Marx draws between "exchange-value" and "use-value"?

Robert Heilbroner

Reflections on the Triumph of Capitalism

Robert Heilbroner taught at the New School for Social Research in New York. He wrote the classic *The Worldly Philosophers* and has written widely on "the future of capitalism."

Less than seventy-five years after it officially began, the contest between capitalism and socialism is over: capitalism has won. The Soviet Union, China, and Eastern Europe have given us the clearest possible proof that capitalism organizes the material affairs of humankind more satisfactorily than socialism: that however inequitably or irresponsibly the marketplace may distribute goods, it does so better than the queues of a planned economy; however mindless the culture of commercialism, it is more attractive than state moralism; and however deceptive the ideology of a business civilization, it is more believable than that of a socialist one...

Yet I doubt whether the historic drama will conclude, like a great morality play, in the unequivocal victory of one side and the ignominious defeat of the other. The economic enemy of capitalism has always been its own self-generated dynamics, not the presence of an alternative economic system. Socialism, in its embodiments in the Soviet Union and, to a lesser degree, China, [was] a military and political competitor but never an economic threat. Thus, despite the rout of centralized planning. . . one would have to be very incautious to assume that capitalism will now find itself rid of its propensity to generate both inflation and recession, cured of its intermittent speculative fevers, or free of threatening international economic problems. Nevertheless, in one very important respect the triumph of capitalism alters the manner in which we must assess its prospects. The old question "Can capitalism work?" to which endless doubting answers have been given by its critics, becomes "Can capitalism work well enough?" which is quite another thing.

. . . Modern-day economists sedulously avoid scenarios of long-term capitalist development—a caution that was not shared by the great economists of the past, virtually all of whom wrote boldly about prospects for the system. What is perhaps more surprising is that, although they disagreed about many things, those economic thinkers were near-unanimous in depicting the prospects as gloomy. Adam Smith, for example, believed that the society of his time, which had not yet been named capitalism, would have a long run but would end up in decline. Marx, of course, expected the demise of the system, but so did John Stuart Mill, whose *Principles of Political Economy* was published in 1848, the year of Marx's *Manifesto*. The most important Victorian economist, Alfred Marshall, warned against socialism and unconsidered changes, but his very Victorianism—he called for "economic chivalry"—makes us squirm a little as we read the exhortative concluding words of his *Principles*. His pupil and protégé, John Maynard Keynes, was of a different mind. Only a "somewhat comprehensive socialization" of investment, he wrote, would rescue the system from intolerable levels of unemployment. Even Joseph Schumpeter, the most conservative (and the least publicly known)

of these magisterial economists, asked in his famous *Capitalism, Socialism and Democracy*, in 1942, "Can capitalism survive?" and answered, "No. I do not think it can.". . .

Keynes. . . based his prognosis not on material limitations of the system but on economic ones— not on the intrinsic lack of any need for a second line from London to York but on the lack of enough purchasing power to buy all the tickets on the first line and thereby establish a possible demand for a second. Quixotically, this lack of purchasing power was itself the result of a failure on the part of business to undertake enough investment projects— railways and others. A pessimistic appraisal of the investment outlook led to insufficient employment on investment projects; and this, in turn, resulted in an insufficiency of the purchasing power needed to make such projects profitable. Given this catch-22, which is one of Keynes's enduring contributions to economic theory, it is not surprising that he looked to the "socialization" of investment as necessary to avoid economic stagnation.

Marx's scenario was not hobbled by a static view of the capacity of the system for inventing new technologies and developing new commodity wants, but it, too, had its catch-22s. These were based on inherent conflicts—contradictions, Marx called them—between the needs of individual enterprises and the working requirements for the system as a whole. One of them was the tendency of capitalism to undercut the buying power of the working class by the continuous introduction of labor-saving machinery, to which business was driven by the pressures of competition. Each enterprise thereby sought to steal a march on its competitors, but instead all enterprises found themselves facing a condition of underconsumption. It is summed up in the perhaps apocryphal story of Henry Ford II walking through a newly automated engine factory with Walter Reuther, the legendary organizing figure of the United Automobile Workers, and asking, "Walter, how are you going to organize these machines?"—to which Reuther is supposed to have answered, "Henry, how are you going to sell them cars?" Another contradiction foreseen by Marx was the erosion of profit rates—not purchasing power—which stemmed from this same substitution of machinery for labor. According to Marx's analysis, labor power was the goose that laid the golden eggs of profits, because employers were able to extract more value from their workers than they paid out as wages. The replacement of living labor by machinery constricted the base from which profit arose, and thus ultimately reduced the rate of return on capital.

. . . The decisive factor in determining the fate of capitalism must be political, not economic. Schumpeter, for example, expected capitalism to disappear, but not because of any strictly economic difficulties. The stumbling block was cultural. "Capitalism," he wrote, "creates a critical frame of mind which, after having destroyed the moral authority of so many other institutions, in the end turns against its own; the bourgeois finds to his amazement that the rationalist attitude does not stop at the credentials of kings and popes but goes on to attack private property and the whole scheme of bourgeois values." Schumpeter anticipated a painless metamorphosis of capitalism into socialism, by which he meant a presumably democratic, planned economy run by the former managers of capitalism. Marx would have scoffed at Schumpeter's low appraisal of capitalism's self-esteem, but he, too, laid its ultimate downfall on the doorstep of political, not economic, events. Capitalism would be progressively weakened by its economic crises, but, in the famous words of *Capital*, the "knell of capitalist private property" would not sound or the "expropriators" be "expropriated" until the working class arose to take things into its own hands.

Schumpeter obviously did not anticipate the present-day resurgence of conservative self-confidence, nor did Marx expect that working-class attitudes and politics would become middle class. Despite their recognition of the importance of mustering and holding the faith of its participants, neither man fully grasped the capacity of the system to do so. This is so, I believe, because neither sufficiently appreciated that capitalism is a social order built upon a deeply embedded and widely believed principle expressed in the actions and beliefs of its most important representatives. From such a viewpoint it is comparable to imperial or aristocratic or Communist regimes, with their universally accepted principle of kingship or aristocracy or socialism, embodied in the personages of monarchs or lords or sacred texts. Capitalism is not normally thought of as possessing such a principle, but its largely uncritical worship of the idea of economic growth is as central to its nature as the similar veneration of the idea of divine kingship or blue blood or doctrinal orthodoxy has been for other regimes. Suggesting that capitalism can be likened to a "regime" rubs our sensibilities the wrong way, but the word is useful in forcing us to consider capitalism as an order of social life, with distinctive hierarchies, imperatives, loyalties, and beliefs. It is this regime-like aspect of capitalism that turns Schumpeter's feared rational skepticism of its privileges into a rationalization of its rights, and makes the working class, far from the opposition that Marx hoped it would become, into stalwart supporters.

QUESTIONS

1. What does Heilbroner mean when he writes that "the decisive factor in determining the fate of capitalism must be political, not economic"? Use examples from his analysis of economic history in your response.

2. Does Heilbroner favor capitalism as an economic system? Is he suspicious of it? Or does he resist such "normative" claims altogether? Why might he adopt a "descriptive" stance toward economic systems?

John Stuart Mill | # Laissez-faire and Education

John Stuart Mill was perhaps the greatest philosopher and political economist in England in the nineteenth century. The following is from his *Principles of Political Economy*.

We have now reached the last part of our undertaking; the discussion, so far as suited to this treatise... of the limits of the province of government: the question, to what objects governmental intervention in the affairs of society may or should extend, over and above those which necessarily appertain to it. No subject has been more keenly contested in the present age: the contest, however, has chiefly taken place round certain select points, with only flying excursions into the rest of the field. Those indeed who have discussed any particular question of government interference, such as state education (spiritual or secular), regulation of hours of labour, a public provision for the poor, &c., have often dealt largely in general arguments, far outstretching the special application made of them, and have shown a sufficiently strong bias either in favour of letting things alone, or in favour of meddling; but have seldom declared, or apparently decided in their own minds, how far they would carry either principle. The supporters of interference have been content with asserting a general right and duty on the part of government to intervene, wherever its intervention would be useful: and when those who have been called the *laisserfaire* school have attempted any definite limitation of the province of government, they have usually restricted it to the protection of person and property against force and fraud; a definition to which neither they nor any one else can deliberately adhere, since it excludes... some of the most indispensable and unanimously recognised of the duties of government. ...

We must set out by distinguishing between two kinds of intervention by the government, which, though they may relate to the same subject, differ widely in their nature and effects, and require, for their justification, motives of a very different degree of urgency. The intervention may extend to controlling the free agency of individuals. Government may interdict all persons from doing certain things; or from doing them without its authorization; or may prescribe to them certain things to be done, or a certain manner of doing things which it is left optional with them to do or to abstain from. This is the *authoritative* interference of government. There is another kind of intervention which is not authoritative: when a government, instead of issuing a command and enforcing it by penalties, adopts the course so seldom resorted to by governments, and of which such important use might be made, that of giving advice, and promulgating information; or when, leaving individuals free to use their own means of pursuing any object of general interest, the government, not meddling with them, but not trusting the object solely to their care, establishes, side by side with their arrangements, an agency of its own for a like purpose. Thus, it is one thing to maintain a Church Establishment, and another to refuse toleration to other religions, or to persons professing no religion. It is one thing to provide schools or colleges, and another to require that no person shall act as an instructor of youth without a government licence. There might be a national bank, or a government manufactory, without any monopoly against private banks and manufactories. There might be a post-office, without penalties against the conveyance of letters by other means. There may be a corps of government engineers for civil purposes, while the profession of a civil engineer is free to be adopted by every one. There may be public hospitals, without any restriction upon private medical or surgical practice.

It is evident, even at first sight, that the authoritative form of government intervention has a much more limited sphere of legitimate action than the

From *Principles of Political Economy*, D. Appleton & Co., 1887.

other. It requires a much stronger necessity to justify it in any case; while there are large departments of human life from which it must be unreservedly and imperiously excluded. Whatever theory we adopt respecting the foundation of the social union, and under whatever political institutions we live, there is a circle around every individual human being, which no government, be it that of one, of a few, or of the many, ought to be permitted to overstep: there is a part of the life of every person who has come to years of discretion, within which the individuality of that person ought to reign uncontrolled either by any other individual or by the public collectively. That there is, or ought to be, some space in human existence thus entrenched around, and sacred from authoritative intrusion, no one who professes the smallest regard to human freedom or dignity will call in question: the point to be determined is, where the limit should be placed; how large a province of human life this reserved territory should include. I apprehend that it ought to include all that part which concerns only the life, whether inward or outward, of the individual, and does not affect the interests of others, or affects them only through the moral influence of example. With respect to the domain of the inward consciousness, the thoughts and feelings, and as much of external conduct as is personal only, involving no consequences, none at least of a painful or injurious kind, to other people; I hold that it is allowable in all, and in the more thoughtful and cultivated often a duty, to assert and promulgate, with all the force they are capable of, their opinion of what is good or bad, admirable or contemptible, but not to compel others to conform to that opinion; whether the force used is that of extra-legal coercion, or exerts itself by means of the law.

———————

Now, the proposition that the consumer is a competent judge of the commodity, can be admitted only with numerous abatements and exceptions. He is generally the best judge (though even this is not true universally) of the material objects produced for his use. These are destined to supply some physical want, or gratify some taste or inclination, respecting which wants or inclinations there is no appeal from the person who feels them; or they are the means and appliances of some occupation, for the use of the persons engaged in it, who may be presumed to be judges of the things required in their own habitual employment. But there are other things, of the worth of which the demand of the market is by no means a test; things of which the utility does not consist in ministering to inclinations, nor in serving the daily uses of life, and the want of which is least felt where the need is greatest. This is peculiarly true of those things which are chiefly useful as tending to raise the character of human beings. The uncultivated cannot be competent judges of cultivation. Those who most need to be made wiser and better, usually desire it least, and if they desired it, would be incapable of finding the way to it by their own lights. It will continually happen, on the voluntary system, that, the end not being desired, the means will not be provided at all, or that, the persons requiring improvement having an imperfect or altogether erroneous conception of what they want, the supply called forth by the demand of the market will be anything but what is really required. Now any well-intentioned and tolerably civilized government may think, without presumption, that it does or ought to possess a degree of cultivation above the average of the community which it rules, and that it should therefore be capable of offering better education and better instruction to the people, than the greater number of them would spontaneously demand. Education, therefore, is one of those things which it is admissible in principle that a government should provide for the people. The case is one to which the reasons of the non-interference principle do not necessarily or universally extend.

With regard to elementary education, the exception to ordinary rules may, I conceive, justifiably be carried still further. There are certain primary elements and means of knowledge, which it is in the highest degree desirable that all human beings born into the community should acquire during childhood. If their parents, or those on whom they depend, have the power of obtaining for them this instruction, and fail to do it, they commit a double breach of duty, towards the children themselves, and towards the members of the community generally, who are all liable to suffer seriously from the consequences of ignorance and want of education in their fellow-citizens. It is therefore an allowable exercise of the powers of government, to impose on parents the legal obligation of giving elementary instruction to children. This, however, cannot fairly be done, without taking measures to insure that such instruction shall be always accessible to them, either gratuitously or at a trifling expense.

It may indeed be objected that the education of children is one of those expenses which parents, even of the labouring class, ought to defray; that it is desirable that they should feel it incumbent on them to provide by their own means for the fulfilment of their duties, and that by giving education at the cost of others, just as much as by giving subsistence, the standard of necessary wages is proportionally lowered, and the springs of exertion and self-restraint in so much relaxed. This argument could, at best, be only valid if the question were that of substituting a public provision for what individuals would otherwise do for themselves; if all parents in the labouring class recognised and practised the duty of giving instruction to their children at their own expense. But inasmuch as parents do not practise this duty, and do not include education among those necessary expenses which their wages must provide for, therefore the general rate of wages is not high enough to bear those expenses, and they must be borne from some other source. And this is not one of the cases in which the tender of help perpetuates the state of things which renders help necessary. Instruction, when it is really such, does not enervate, but strengthens as well as enlarges the active faculties: in whatever manner acquired, its effect on the mind is favourable to the spirit of independence: and when, unless had gratuitously, it would not be had at all, help in this form has the opposite tendency to that which in so many other cases makes it objectionable; it is help towards doing without help.

In England, and most European countries, elementary instruction cannot be paid for, at its full cost, from the common wages of unskilled labour, and would not if it could. The alternative, therefore, is not between government and private speculation, but between a government provision and voluntary charity: between interference by government, and interference by associations of individuals, subscribing their own money for the purpose, like the two great School Societies. It is, of course, not desirable that anything should be done by funds derived from compulsory taxation, which is already sufficiently well done by individual liberality. How far this is the case with school instruction, is, in each particular instance, a question of fact. The education provided in this country on the voluntary principle has of late been so much discussed, that it is needless in this place to criticise it minutely, and I shall merely express my conviction, that even in quantity it is, and is likely to remain, altogether insufficient, while in quality, though with some slight tendency to improvement, it is never good except by some rare accident, and generally so bad as to be little more than nominal. I hold it therefore the duty of the government to supply the defect, by giving pecuniary support to elementary schools, such as to render them accessible to all the children of the poor, either freely, or for a payment too inconsiderable to be sensibly felt.

One thing must be strenuously insisted on; that the government must claim no monopoly for its education, either in the lower or in the higher branches; must exert neither authority nor influence to induce the people to resort to its teachers in preference to others, and must confer no peculiar advantages on those who have been instructed by them. Though the government teachers will probably be superior to the average of private instructors, they will not embody all the knowledge and sagacity to be found in all instructors taken together, and it is desirable to leave open as many roads as possible to the desired end. It is not endurable that a government should, either *de jure* or *de facto*, have a complete control over the education of the people. To possess such a control, and actually exert it, is to be despotic. A government which can mould the opinions and sentiments of the people from their youth upwards, can do with them whatever it pleases. Though a government, therefore, may, and in many cases ought to, establish schools and colleges, it must neither compel nor bribe any person to come to them; nor ought the power of individuals to set up rival establishments, to depend in any degree upon its authorization. It would be justified in requiring from all the people that they shall possess instruction in certain things, but not in prescribing to them how or from whom they shall obtain it.

John Maynard Keynes | # Economic Possibilities for Our Grandchildren (1930)

I

We are suffering just now from a bad attack of economic pessimism. It is common to hear people say that the epoch of enormous economic progress which characterised the nineteenth century is over; that the rapid improvement in the standard of life is now going to slow down–at any rate in Great Britain; that a decline in prosperity is more likely than an improvement in the decade which lies ahead of us.

I believe that this is a wildly mistaken interpretation of what is happening to us. We are suffering, not from the rheumatics of old age, but from the growing-pains of over-rapid changes, from the painfulness of readjustment between one economic period and another. The increase of technical efficiency has been taking place faster than we can deal with the problem of labour absorption; the improvement in the standard of life has been a little too quick; the banking and monetary system of the world has been preventing the rate of interest from falling as fast as equilibrium requires. And even so, the waste and confusion which ensue relate to not more than 7½ per cent of the national income; we are muddling away one and sixpence in the £, and have only 18s. 6d., when we might, if we were more sensible, have £1; yet, nevertheless, the 18s. 6d. mounts up to as much as the £1

would have been five or six years ago. We forget that in 1929 the physical output of the industry of Great Britain was greater than ever before, and that the net surplus of our foreign balance available for new foreign investment, after paying for all our imports, was greater last year than that of any other country, being indeed 50 per cent greater than the corresponding— surplus of the United States. Or again—if it is to be a matter of comparisons—suppose that we were to reduce our wages by a half, repudiate four fifths of the national debt, and hoard our surplus wealth in barren gold instead of lending it at 6 per cent or more, we should resemble the now much-envied France. But would it be an improvement?

The prevailing world depression, the enormous anomaly of unemployment in a world full of wants, the disastrous mistakes we have made, blind us to what is going on under the surface to the true interpretation. of the trend of things. For I predict that both of the two opposed errors of pessimism which now make so much noise in the world will be proved wrong in our own time-the pessimism of the revolutionaries who think that things are so bad that nothing can save us but violent change, and the pessimism of the reactionaries who consider the balance of our economic and social life so precarious that we must risk no experiments.

Scanned from John Maynard Keynes, *Essays in Persuasion*, New York: W. W. Norton & Co., 1963, pp. 358–373.

My purpose in this essay, however, is not to examine the present or the near future, but to disembarrass myself of short views and take wings into the future. What can we reasonably expect the level of our economic life to be a hundred years hence? What are the economic possibilities for our grandchildren?

From the earliest times of which we have record—back, say, to two thousand years before Christ—down to the beginning of the eighteenth century, there was no very great change in the standard of life of the average man living in the civilised centres of the earth. Ups and downs certainly. Visitations of plague, famine, and war. Golden intervals. But no progressive, violent change. Some periods perhaps 50 per cent better than others—at the utmost 100 per cent better—in the four thousand years which ended (say) in A.D. 1700.

This slow rate of progress, or lack of progress, was due to two reasons—to the remarkable absence of important technical improvements and to the failure of capital to accumulate.

The absence of important technical inventions between the prehistoric age and comparatively modern times is truly remarkable. Almost everything which really matters and which the world possessed at the commencement of the modern age was already known to man at the dawn of history. Language, fire, the same domestic animals which we have to-day, wheat, barley, the vine and the olive, the plough, the wheel, the oar, the sail, leather, linen and cloth, bricks and pots, gold and silver, copper, tin, and lead-and iron was added to the list before 1000 B.C.-banking, statecraft, mathematics, astronomy, and religion. There is no record of when we first possessed these things.

At some epoch before the dawn of history—perhaps even in one of the comfortable intervals before the last ice age—there must have been an era of progress and invention comparable to that in which we live to-day. But through the greater part of recorded history there was nothing of the kind.

The modern age opened; I think, with the accumulation of capital which began in the sixteenth century. I believe—for reasons with which I must not encumber the present argument—that this was initially due to the rise of prices, and the profits to which that led, which resulted from the treasure of gold and silver which Spain brought from the New World into the Old. From that time until to-day the power of accumulation by compound interest, which seems to have been sleeping for many generations, was re-born and renewed its strength. And the power of compound interest over two hundred years is such as to stagger the imagination.

Let me give in illustration of this a sum which I have worked out. The value of Great Britain's foreign investments to-day is estimated at about £4,000,000,000. This yields us an income at the rate of about 6½ per cent. Half of this we bring home and enjoy; the other half, namely, 3¼ per cent, we leave to accumulate abroad at compound interest. Something of this sort has now been going on for about 250 years.

For I trace the beginnings of British foreign investment to the treasure which Drake stole from Spain in 1580. In that year he returned to England bringing with him the prodigious spoils of the *Golden Hind*. Queen Elizabeth was a considerable shareholder in the syndicate which had financed the expedition. Out of her share she paid off the whole of England's foreign debt, balanced her Budget, and found herself with about £40,000 in hand. This she invested in the Levant Company—which prospered. Out of the profits of the Levant Company, the East India Company was founded; and the profits of this great enterprise were the foundation of England's subsequent foreign investment. Now it happens that £40,000 accumulating at 3¼ per cent compound interest approximately corresponds to the actual volume of England's foreign investments at various dates, and would actually amount to-day to the total of £4,000,000,000 which I have already quoted as being what our foreign investments now are. Thus, every £1 which Drake brought home in 1580 has now become £100,000. Such is the power of compound interest!

From the sixteenth century, with a cumulative crescendo after the eighteenth, the great age of science and technical inventions began, which since the beginning of the nineteenth century has been in full flood—coal, steam, electricity, petrol, steel, rubber, cotton, the chemical industries, automatic machinery and the methods of mass production, wireless, printing, Newton, Darwin, and Einstein, and thousands of other things and men too famous and familiar to catalogue.

What is the result? In spite of an enormous growth in the population of the world, which it has been necessary to equip with houses and machines, the average standard of life in Europe and the United States has been raised, I think, about fourfold. The growth of capital has been on a scale which is far beyond a hundredfold of what any previous age had known. And from now on we need not expect so great an increase of population.

If capital increases, say, 2 per cent per annum, the capital equipment of the world will have increased by a half in twenty years, and seven and a half times in a hundred years. Think of this in terms of material things—houses, transport, and the like.

At the same time technical improvements in manufacture and transport have been proceeding at a greater rate in the last ten years than ever before in history. In the United States factory output per head was 40 per cent greater in 1925 than in 1919. In Europe we are held back by temporary obstacles, but even so it is safe to say that technical efficiency is increasing by more than 1 per cent per annum compound. There is evidence that the revolutionary technical changes, which have so far chiefly affected industry, may soon be attacking agriculture. We may be on the eve of improvements in the efficiency of food production as great as those which have already taken place in mining, manufacture, and transport. In quite a few years—in our own lifetimes I mean—we may be able to perform all the operations of agriculture, mining, and manufacture with a quarter of the human effort to which we have been accustomed.

For the moment the very rapidity of these changes is hurting us and bringing difficult problems to solve. Those countries are suffering relatively which are not in the vanguard of progress. We are being afflicted with a new disease of which some readers may not yet have heard the name, but of which they will hear a great deal in the years to come—namely, *technological unemployment*. This means unemployment due to our discovery of means of economising the use of labour outrunning the pace at which we can find new uses for labour.

But this is only a temporary phase of maladjustment. All this means in the long run *that mankind is solving its economic problem*. I would predict that the standard of life in progressive countries one hundred years hence will be between four and eight times as high as it is to-day. There would be nothing surprising in this even in the light of our present knowledge. It would not be foolish to contemplate the possibility of afar greater progress still.

II

Let us, for the sake of argument, suppose that a hundred years hence we are all of us, on the average, eight times better off in the economic sense than we are to-day. Assuredly there need be nothing here to surprise us.

Now it is true that the needs of human beings may seem to be insatiable. But they fall into two classes—those needs which are absolute in the sense that we feel them whatever the situation of our fellow human beings may be, and those which are relative in the sense that we feel them only if their satisfaction lifts us above, makes us feel superior to, our fellows. Needs of the second class, those which satisfy the desire for superiority, may indeed be insatiable; for the higher the general level, the higher still are they. But this is not so true of the absolute needs—a point may soon be reached, much sooner perhaps than we are all of us aware of, when these needs are satisfied in the sense that we prefer to devote our further energies to non-economic purposes.

Now for my conclusion, which you will find, I think, to become more and more startling to the imagination the longer you think about it.

I draw the conclusion that, assuming no important wars and no important increase in population, the *economic problem* may be solved, or be at least within sight of solution, within a hundred years. This means that the economic problem is not—if we look into the *future—the permanent problem of the human race*.

Why, you may ask, is this so startling? It is startling because—if, instead of looking into the future, we look into the past—we find that the economic problem, the struggle for subsistence, always has been hitherto the primary, most pressing problem of the human race—not only of the human race, but of the whole of the biological kingdom from the beginnings of life in its most primitive forms.

Thus we have been expressly evolved by nature-with all our impulses and deepest instincts-for the purpose of solving the economic problem. If the economic problem is solved, mankind will be deprived of its traditional purpose.

Will this be a benefit? If one believes at all in the real values of life, the prospect at least opens up the possibility of benefit. Yet I think with dread of the readjustment of the habits and instincts of the ordinary man, bred into him for countless generations, which he may be asked to discard within a few decades.

To use the language of to-day-must we not expect a general "nervous breakdown"? We already have a little experience of what I mean—a nervous breakdown of the sort which is already common enough in England and the United States amongst the wives of the well-to-do classes, unfortunate women, many of them, who have been deprived by their wealth of their traditional tasks and occupations—who cannot find it sufficiently amusing, when deprived of the spur of economic necessity, to cook and clean and mend, yet are quite unable to find anything more amusing.

To those who sweat for their daily bread leisure is a longed—for sweet—until they get it.

There is the traditional epitaph written for herself by the old charwoman:

Don't mourn for me, friends, don't weep for me never, For I'm going to do nothing for ever and ever.

This was her heaven. Like others who look forward to leisure, she conceived how nice it would be to spend her time listening-in-for there was another couplet which occurred in her poem:

With psalms and sweet music the heavens'll be ringing, But I shall have nothing to do with the singing.

Yet it will only be for those who have to do with the singing that life will be tolerable and how few of us can sing!

Thus for the first time since his creation, man will be faced with his real, his permanent problem—how to use his freedom from pressing economic cares, how to occupy the leisure, which science and compound interest will have won for him, to live wisely and agreeably and well.

The strenuous purposeful money-makers may carry all of us along with them into the lap of economic abundance. But it will be those peoples, who can keep alive, and cultivate into a fuller perfection, the art of life itself and do not sell themselves for the means of life, who will be able to enjoy the abundance when it comes.

Yet there is no country and no people, I think, who can look forward to the age of leisure and of abundance without a dread. For we have been trained too long to strive and not to enjoy. It is a fearful problem for the ordinary person, with no special talents, to occupy himself, especially if he no longer has roots in the soil or in custom or in the beloved conventions of a traditional society. To judge from the behaviour and the achievements of the wealthy classes to-day in any quarter of the world, the outlook is very depressing! For these are, so to speak, our advance guard-those who are spying out the promised land for the rest of us and pitching their camp there. For they have most of them failed disastrously, so it seems to me—those who have an independent income but no associations or duties or ties—to solve the problem which has been set them.

I feel sure that with a little more experience we shall use the new-found bounty of nature quite differently from the way in which the rich use it to-day, and will map out for ourselves a plan of life quite otherwise than theirs.

For many ages to come the old Adam will be so strong in us that everybody will need to do some work if he is to be contented. We shall do more things for ourselves than is usual with the rich to-day, only too glad to have small duties and tasks and routines. But beyond this, we shall endeavour to spread the bread thin on the butter-to make what work there is still to be done to be as widely shared as possible. Three-hour shifts or a fifteen-hour week may put off the problem for a great while. For three hours a day is quite enough to satisfy the old Adam in most of us!

There are changes in other spheres too which we must expect to come. When the accumulation of wealth is no longer of high social importance, there will be great changes in the code of morals. We shall be able to rid ourselves of many of the pseudo-moral principles which have hag-ridden us for two hundred years, by which we have exalted some of the most distasteful of human qualities into the position of the highest virtues. We shall be able to afford to dare to assess the money-motive at its true value. The love of money as a possession—as distinguished from the love of money as a means to the enjoyments and realities of life—will be recognised for what it is, a somewhat disgusting morbidity, one of those semicriminal, semi-pathological propensities which one hands over with a shudder to the specialists in mental disease. All kinds of social customs and economic practices, affecting the distribution of wealth and of economic rewards and penalties, which we now maintain at all costs, however distasteful and unjust they may be in themselves, because they are tremendously useful in promoting the accumulation of capital, we shall then be free, at last, to discard.

Of course there will still be many people with intense, unsatisfied purposiveness who will blindly pursue wealth-unless they can find some plausible substitute. But the rest of us will no longer be under any obligation to applaud and encourage them. For we shall inquire more curiously than is safe to-day into the true character of this "purposiveness" with which in varying degrees Nature has endowed almost all of us. For purposiveness means that we are more concerned with the remote future results of our actions than with their own quality or their immediate effects on our own environment. The "purposive" man is always trying to secure a spurious and delusive immortality for his acts by pushing his interest in them forward into time. He does not love his cat, but his cat's kittens; nor, in truth, the kittens, but only the kittens' kittens, and so on forward forever to the end of cat-dom. For him jam is not jam unless it is a case of jam to-morrow and never jam to-day. Thus by pushing his jam always forward into the future, he strives to secure for his act of boiling it an immortality.

Let me remind you of the Professor in *Sylvie and Bruno*:

"Only the tailor, sir, with your little bill," said a meek voce outside the door.

"Ah, well, I can soon settle his business," the Professor said to the children, "if you'll just wait a minute. How much is it, this year, my man?" The tailor had come in while he was speaking.

"Well, it's been a-doubling so many years, you see," the tailor replied, a little grufy, "and I think I'd like the money now. It's two thousand pound, it is!"

"Oh, that's nothing!" the Professor carelessly remarked, feeling in his pocket, as if he always carried at least that amount about with him. "But wouldn't you like to wait just another year and make it four thousand? Just think how rich you'd be! Why, you might be a king, if you liked!"

"I don't know as I'd care about being a king," the man said thoughtfully. "But it dew sound a powerful sight o' money! Well, I think I'll wait."

"Of course you will!" said the Professor. "There's good sense in you, I see. Good-day to you, my man!"

"Will you ever have to pay him that four thousand pounds?" Sylvie asked as the door closed on the departing creditor.

"Never, my child!" the Professor replied emphatically. "He'll go on doubling it till he dies. You see, it's always worth while waiting another year to get twice as much money!"

Perhaps it is not an accident that the race which did most to bring the promise of immortality into the heart and essence of our religions has also done most for the principle of compound interest and particularly loves this most purposive of human institutions.

I see us free, therefore, to return to some of the most sure and certain principles of religion and traditional virtue-that avarice is a vice, that the exaction of usury is a misdemeanour, and the love of money is detestable, that those walk most truly in the paths of virtue and sane wisdom who take least thought for the morrow. We shall once more value ends above means and prefer the good to the useful. We shall honour those who can teach us how to pluck the hour and the day virtuously and well, the delightful people who are capable of taking direct enjoyment in things, the lilies of the field who toil not, neither do they spin.

But beware! The time for all this is not yet. For at least another hundred years we must pretend to ourselves and to every one that fair is foul and foul is fair; for foul is useful and fair is not. Avarice and usury and precaution must be our gods for a little longer still. For only they can lead us out of the tunnel of economic necessity into daylight.

I look forward, therefore, in days not so very remote, to the greatest change which has ever occurred in the material environment of life for human beings in the aggregate. But, of course, it will all happen gradually, not as a catastrophe. Indeed, it has already begun. The course of affairs will simply be that there will be ever larger and larger classes and groups of people from whom problems of economic necessity have been practically removed. The critical difference will be realised when this condition has become so general that the nature of one's duty to one's neighbour is changed. For it will remain reasonable to be economically purposive for others after it has ceased to be reasonable for oneself.

The pace at which we can reach our destination of economic bliss will be governed by four things— our power to control population, our determination to avoid wars and civil dissensions, our willingness to entrust to science the direction of those matters which are properly the concern of science, and the rate of accumulation as fixed by the margin between our production and our consumption; of which the last will easily look after itself, given the first three.

Meanwhile there will be no harm in making mild preparations for our destiny, in encouraging, and experimenting in, the arts of life as well as the activities of purpose.

But, chiefly, do not let us overestimate the importance of the economic problem, or sacrifice to its supposed necessities other matters of greater and more permanent significance. It should be a matter for specialists—like dentistry. If economists could manage to get themselves thought of as humble, competent people, on a level with dentists, that would be splendid!

QUESTIONS

1. Summarize Keynes' Argument.
2. Identify three flaws in his argument, using outside sources (e.g., Google) if necessary.

E. F. Schumacher | # Buddhist Economics

E. F. Schumacher was an iconoclastic economist who wrote the classic, *Small Is Beautiful.*

"Right Livelihood" is one of the requirements of the Buddha's Noble Eightfold Path. It is clear, therefore, that there must be such a thing as Buddhist economics.

Buddhist countries have often stated that they wish to remain faithful to their heritage. So Burma: "The New Burma sees no conflict between religious values and economic progress. Spiritual health and material well-being are not enemies: they are natural allies." Or: "We can blend successfully the religious and spiritual values of our heritage with the benefits of modern technology." Or: "We Burmans have a sacred duty to conform both our dreams and our acts to our faith. This we shall ever do."

All the same, such countries invariably assume that they can model their economic development plans in accordance with modern economics, and they call upon modern economists from so-called advanced countries to advise them, to formulate the policies to be pursued, and to construct the grand design for development, the Five-Year Plan or

---

whatever it may be called. No one seems to think that a Buddhist way of life would call for Buddhist economics, just as the modern materialist way of life has brought forth modern economics.

Economists themselves, like most specialists, normally suffer from a kind of metaphysical blindness, assuming that theirs is a science of absolute and invariable truths, without any presuppositions. Some go as far as to claim that economic laws are as free from "metaphysics" or "values" as the law of gravitation. We need not, however, get involved in arguments of methodology. Instead, let us take some fundamentals and see what they look like when viewed by a modern economist and a Buddhist economist.

There is universal agreement that a fundamental source of wealth is human labour. Now, the modern economist has been brought up to consider "labour" or work as little more than a necessary evil. From the point of view of the employer, it is in any case simply an item of cost, to be reduced to a minimum if it cannot be eliminated altogether, say, by automation. From the point of view of the workman, it is a "disutility"; to work is to make a sacrifice of one's leisure and comfort, and wages are a kind of compensation for the sacrifice. Hence the ideal from the point of view of the employer is to have output without employees, and the ideal from the point of view of the employee is to have income without employment.

The consequences of these attitudes both in theory and in practice are, of course, extremely far-reaching. If the ideal with regard to work is to get rid of it, every method that "reduces the work load" is a good thing. The most potent method, short of automation, is the so-called division of labour and the classical example is the pin factory eulogised in Adam Smith's *Wealth of Nations*. Here it is not a matter of ordinary specialisation, which mankind has practised from time immemorial, but of dividing up every complete process of production into minute parts, so that the final product can be produced at great speed without anyone having had to contribute more than a totally insignificant and, in most cases, unskilled movement of his limbs.

The Buddhist point of view takes the function of work to be at least threefold: to give a man a chance to utilise and develop his faculties; to enable him to overcome his ego-centredness by joining with other people in a common task; and to bring forth the goods and services needed for a becoming existence. Again, the consequences that flow from this view are endless. To organise work in such a manner that it becomes meaningless, boring, stultifying, or nerve-racking for the worker would be little short of criminal; it would indicate a greater concern with goods than with people, an evil lack of compassion, and a soul-destroying degree of attachment to the most primitive side of this worldly existence. Equally, to strive for leisure as an alternative to work would be considered a complete misunderstanding of one of the basic truths of human existence, namely that work and leisure are complementary parts of the same living process and cannot be separated without destroying the joy of work and the bliss of leisure.

From the Buddhist point of view, there are therefore two types of mechanisation which must be clearly distinguished: one that enhances a man's skill and power and one that turns the work of man over to a mechanical slave, leaving man in a position of having to serve the slave. How to tell the one from the other? "The craftsman himself," says Ananda Coomaraswamy, a man equally competent to talk about the modern west as the ancient east, "can always, if allowed to, draw the delicate distinction between the machine and the tool. The carpet loom is a tool, a contrivance for holding warp threads at a stretch for the pile to be woven round them by the craftsmen's fingers; but the power loom is a machine, and its significance as a destroyer of culture lies in the fact that it does the essentially human part of the work." It is clear, therefore, that Buddhist economics must be very different from the economics of modern materialism, since the Buddhist sees the essence of civilisation not in a multiplication of wants but in the purification of human character. Character, at the same time, is formed primarily by a man's work. And work, properly conducted in conditions of human dignity and freedom, blesses those who do it and equally their products. The Indian philosopher and economist J. C. Kumarappa sums the matter up as follows:

> If the nature of the work is properly appreciated and applied, it will stand in the same relation to the higher faculties as food is to the physical body.

It nourishes and enlivens the higher man and urges him to produce the best he is capable of. It directs his free will along the proper course and disciplines the animal in him into progressive channels. It furnishes an excellent background for man to display his scale of values and develop his personality.

If a man has no chance of obtaining work he is in a desperate position, not simply because he lacks an income but because he lacks this nourishing and enlivening factor of disciplined work which nothing can replace. A modern economist may engage in highly sophisticated calculations on whether full employment "pays" or whether it might be more "economic" to run an economy at less than full employment so as to ensure a greater mobility of labour, a better stability of wages, and so forth. His fundamental criterion of success is simply the total quantity of goods produced during a given period of time. "If the marginal urgency of goods is low," says Professor Galbraith in *The Affluent Society*, "then so is the urgency of employing the last man or the last million men in the labour force." And again: "If. . . we can afford some unemployment in the interest of stability—a proposition, incidentally, of impeccably conservative antecedents—then we can afford to give those who are unemployed the goods that enable them to sustain their accustomed standard of living."

From a Buddhist point of view, this is standing the truth on its head by considering goods as more important than people and consumption as more important than creative activity. It means shifting the emphasis from the worker to the product of work, that is, from the human to the subhuman, a surrender to the forces of evil. The very start of Buddhist economic planning would be a planning for full employment, and the primary purpose of this would in fact be employment for everyone who needs an "outside" job: it would not be the maximisation of employment nor the maximisation of production. Women, on the whole, do not need an "outside" job, and the large-scale employment of women in offices or factories would be considered a sign of serious economic failure. In particular, to let mothers of young children work in factories while the children run wild would be as uneconomic in the eyes of a Buddhist economist as the employment of a skilled worker as a soldier in the eyes of a modern economist.

While the materialist is mainly interested in goods, the Buddhist is mainly interested in liberation. But Buddhism is "The Middle Way" and therefore in no way antagonistic to physical well-being. It is not wealth that stands in the way of liberation but the attachment to wealth; not the enjoyment of pleasurable things but the craving for them. The keynote of Buddhist economics, therefore, is simplicity and non-violence. From an economist's point of view, the marvel of the Buddhist way of life is the utter rationality of its pattern—amazingly small means leading to extraordinarily satisfactory results.

For the modern economist this is very difficult to understand. He is used to measuring the "standard of living" by the amount of annual consumption, assuming all the time that a man who consumes more is "better off" than a man who consumes less. A Buddhist economist would consider this approach excessively irrational: since consumption is merely a means to human well-being, the aim should be to obtain the maximum of well-being with the minimum of consumption. Thus, if the purpose of clothing is a certain amount of temperature comfort and an attractive appearance, the task is to attain this purpose with the smallest possible effort, that is, with the smallest annual destruction of cloth and with the help of designs that involve the smallest possible input of toil. The less toil there is, the more time and strength is left for artistic creativity. It would be highly uneconomic, for instance, to go in for complicated tailoring, like the modern west, when a much more beautiful effect can be achieved by the skillful draping of uncut material. It would be the height of folly to make material so that it should wear out quickly and the height of barbarity to make anything ugly, shabby or mean. What has just been said about clothing applies equally to all other human requirements. The ownership and the consumption of goods is a means to an end, and Buddhist economics is the systematic study of how to attain given ends with the minimum means.

Modern economics, on the other hand, considers consumption to be the sole end and purpose of all economic activity, taking the factors of production—land, labour, and capital—as the means. The former, in short, tries to maximise human satisfactions by the optimal pattern of consumption, while the latter tries to maximise consumption by the optimal pattern of productive effort. It is easy to see that the effort needed to sustain a way of life which seeks to attain the optimal pattern of consumption is likely to be much smaller than the effort needed to sustain a drive for maximum consumption. We need not be surprised, therefore, that the pressure and strain of living is very much less in, say, Burma than it is in the United States, in spite of the fact that the amount of labour-saving machinery used in the former country is only a minute fraction of the amount used in the latter.

Simplicity and non-violence are obviously closely related. The optimal pattern of consumption, producing a high degree of human satisfaction by means of a relatively low rate of consumption, allows people to live without great pressure and strain and to fulfill the primary injunction of Buddhist teaching: "Cease to do evil; try to do good." As physical resources are everywhere limited, people satisfying their needs by means of a modest use of resources are obviously less likely to be at each other's throats than people depending upon a high rate of use. Equally, people who live in highly self-sufficient local communities are less likely to get involved in large-scale violence than people whose existence depends on world-wide systems of trade.

From the point of view of Buddhist economics, therefore, production from local resources for local needs is the most rational way of economic life, while dependence on imports from afar and the consequent need to produce for export to unknown and distant peoples is highly uneconomic and justifiable only in exceptional cases and on a small scale. Just as the modern economist would admit that a high rate of consumption of transport services between a man's home and his place of work signifies a misfortune and not a high standard of life, so the Buddhist economist would hold that to satisfy human wants from faraway sources rather than from sources nearby signifies failure rather than success. The former tends to take statistics showing an increase in the number of ton/miles per head of the population carried by a country's transport system as proof of economic progress, while to the latter—the Buddhist economist—the same statistics would indicate a highly undesirable deterioration in the *pattern* of consumption.

Another striking difference between modern economics and Buddhist economics arises over the use of natural resources. Bertrand de Jouvenel, the eminent French political philosopher, has characterised "western man" in words which may be taken as a fair description of the modern economist:

> He tends to count nothing as an expenditure, other than human effort; he does not seem to mind how much mineral matter he wastes and, far worse, how much living matter he destroys. He does not seem to realise at all that human life is a dependent part of an ecosystem of many different forms of life. As the world is ruled from towns where men are cut off from any form of life other than human, the feeling of belonging to an ecosystem is not revived. This results in a harsh and improvident treatment of things upon which we ultimately depend, such as water and trees.

The teaching of the Buddha, on the other hand, enjoins a reverent and non-violent attitude not only to all sentient beings but also, with great emphasis, to trees. Every follower of the Buddha ought to plant a tree every few years and look after it until it is safely established, and the Buddhist economist can demonstrate without difficulty that the universal observation of this rule would result in a high rate of genuine economic development independent of any foreign aid. Much of the economic decay of south-east Asia (as of many other parts of the world) is undoubtedly due to a heedless and shameful neglect of trees.

Modern economics does not distinguish between renewable and non-renewable materials, as its very method is to equalise and quantify everything by means of a money price. Thus, taking various alternative fuels, like coal, oil, wood, or water-power: the only difference between them recognised by modern economics is relative cost per equivalent unit. The cheapest is automatically the one to be preferred, as to do otherwise would be irrational and "uneconomic." From a Buddhist point of view, of course, this will not do; the essential difference between non-renewable fuels like coal and oil on the one hand and renewable fuels like wood and water-power on the other cannot be simply overlooked. Non-renewable goods must be used only if they are indispensable, and then only with the greatest care and the most meticulous concern for conservation. To use them heedlessly or extravagantly is an act of violence, and while complete nonviolence may not be attainable on this earth, there is nonetheless an ineluctable duty on man to aim at the ideal of non-violence in all he does.

Just as a modern European economist would not consider it a great economic achievement if all European art treasures were sold to America at attractive prices, so the Buddhist economist would insist that a population basing its economic life on non-renewable fuels is living parasitically, on capital instead of income. Such a way of life could have no permanence and could therefore be justi-fied only as a purely temporary expedient. As the world's resources of non-renewable fuels—coal, oil, and natural gas—are exceedingly unevenly distributed over the globe and undoubtedly limited in quantity, it is clear that their exploitation at an ever-increasing rate is an act of violence against nature which must almost inevitably lead to vio-lence between men.

This fact alone might give food for thought even to those people in Buddhist countries who care nothing for the religious and spiritual values of their heritage and ardently desire to embrace the materialism of modern economics at the fastest pos-sible speed. Before they dismiss Buddhist econom-ics as nothing better than a nostalgic dream, they might wish to consider whether the path of eco-nomic development outlined by modem economics is likely to lead them to places where they really want to be. Towards the end of his courageous book *The Challenge of Man's Future*, Professor Harrison Brown of the California Institute of Technology gives the following appraisal:

> Thus we see that, just as industrial society is fun-damentally unstable and subject to reversion to agrarian existence, so within it the conditions which offer individual freedom are unstable in their ability to avoid the conditions which impose rigid organisation and totalitarian control. Indeed, when we examine all of the foreseeable difficulties which threaten the survival of industrial civilisation, it is difficult to see how the achievement of stability and the maintenance of individual liberty can be made compatible.

Even if this were dismissed as a long-term view there is the immediate question of whether "mod-ernisation," as currently practised without regard to religious and spiritual values, is actually producing agreeable results. As far as the masses are concerned, the results appear to be disastrous—a collapse of the rural economy, a rising tide of unemployment in town and country, and the growth of a city prole-tariat without nourishment for either body or soul.

It is in the light of both immediate experience and long-term prospects that the study of Buddhist economics could be recommended even to those who believe that economic growth is more impor-tant than any spiritual or religious values. For it is not a question of choosing between "modern growth" and "traditional stagnation." It is a ques-tion of finding the right path of development, the Middle Way between materialist heedlessness and traditionalist immobility, in short, of finding "Right Livelihood."

QUESTIONS

1. What are "Buddhist economics"?
2. For Schumacher and Buddhism, what is the impor-tance of character in ethics?

Amartya Sen | # The Economics of Poverty

Amartya Sen is based at Trinity College Cambridge and won the Nobel Prize for his work on welfare economics and the causes of famine.

PHIL PONCE: Professor, when one thinks of the field in which Nobel winners in economics often work, it's oftentimes something like money, markets, the capital, and yet you seem to be more interested in how events affect people. Why is that?

AMARTYA SEN: Well, economics is a very broad subject, and the money and capital and the operation of the stock market, these are matters of interest to economists, as well as matters of—the way the lives of people go, and I happen to be concerned primarily with the latter and in particular with the down side of the latter, namely the people who seem to have a worse time than others—the poor, the unemployed, the hungry, the starving, and so on. So this has been something I've been concerned with for a long time.

PHIL PONCE: Professor, one of the specific issues that the Nobel citation talks about is your interest in understanding famine, and it says that your best-known work has to do with understanding that famine isn't just caused by a shortage of food but by other things like unemployment, drop in income. Why the specific interest in famine?

AMARTYA SEN: Well, there are many reasons, of course, because famines are unfortunately still a real phenomenon in the world. And lots of people die from it, systematically, in different parts of the world, but in my case the personal interest arose also from the fact that I happened to observe from inside a major famine of the 20th century—the Bengal famine, which occurred in India in 1943—in fact, the last famine that occurred in India, in which close to 3 million people died. And I was a nine-and-a-half-year-old boy at that time. It had very impressionable—certainly very striking memories I have from that period, and the people who starved, they came from a particular group—in this case rural laborers—but that's a characteristic I later found of many famines, indeed, sometimes food supply may fall, sometimes not. Food supply fell in the Irish famine of the 1840's. It did not fall in the Bengal famine of '43, and it was at a peak height in the Bangladesh famine of '74. But a section of the community lose their ability to command food by not having jobs—not having enough wage and then they cannot buy food and that's what happened—not a really large proportion usually— but it can still kill millions of people.

PHIL PONCE: According to a report that I read, you personally, when you were a boy, personally fed people who were starving refugees.

AMARTYASEN: Well, my parents—you know—since we [were] relatively prosperous, still not rich, lower middle class family—still not rich—a lower middle class family—but quite committed on social matters and come from an academic background. My father was a professor; my grandfather was a professor— we were quite involved in that so I was committed to give anyone who asked for food, a tin, a cigarette tin of rice. But since there are many people asking, I was also told that that's what I could give to anyone. I obviously felt very moral in trying to give as much as I could. And it's a very harrowing experience. Obviously, this didn't do anything to solve the famine, but it's a question that got even more strongly engrained in my mind because of the small participation that I happened to do in this context.

PHIL PONCE: Professor, what does winning this prize mean to you personally?

AMARTYASEN: Well, I was particularly pleased that the prize was given with the citation about social— about welfare economics and social choice because

From the *NewsHour with Jim Lehrer* transcript McNeil NewsHour transcript, Oct. 15, 1998. Reprinted with permission.

these are areas in which very interesting, very important work has occurred, and I'm very proud of what others have done and I've learned from them. I think I was led on to that subject by Kenneth Arrow—a great figure in modern economics. And I had very good students and very good colleagues working in this area. So when they mentioned this area, I took that to be a recognition of the importance of that area, and even though I was lucky enough to get the prize, I did think that it was a much wider recognition and in the way it tried to be more appropriate and fair, if the prize was widely shared. But many people have contributed in this area, and this gives me an opportunity to think about them and to the extent to which my own work has been influenced by and dependent on the work that others have done.

PHIL PONCE: Professor, there is this world economic crisis, a lot of turmoil in the markets, and it's adding a lot of new people to poverty, millions of people. How much do economists know? How much can economists explain what is happening now?

AMARTYA SEN: I think economists—if they set their mind to it—can explain a lot. You know, I think it's really a question of concentrating, the questions—the inquiries—appropriately. We know the nature of the success that some of these economies—for example, the East Asian economies, which are in turmoil now, had. We know the basis of their success, which included using the market mechanism efficiently but open-mindedly, non-dogmatically, letting the government do its job in expanding educational base, doing land reform, helping with the health care. It's a partnership of the public and market arrangement. Now they did not work out pretty well. The financial regularities and there were a lot of lacunae and some of the economies there like Indonesia it didn't work out, what would happen if the economy were to go into a slump, namely, how to deal with those who've been thrown out of the system and given to the wolves, and the kind of social safety net that you need didn't exist. There's a lot to learn from the experience of these countries, both positively as to what they have achieved, as well as negatively as to what to avoid. So I think economists—if they analyze these issues—will have various things to offer. And, indeed, there are a lot of economists who are interested in it. And I would not

accept that economists really don't have very much to say on this question.

PHIL PONCE: Professor, do you think people have lost faith in economists because of the current world financial crisis?

AMARTYA SEN: Well, you know, I think the—economics is not a kind of business whereby you could eliminate these problems. You know, it's—odd thing is that earlier on in late 19th century and early 20th century—one of the subjects people studied was business cycle. From time to time you have slump, and at times you have boom. The job of the economist was meant to be to understand why they are caused, rather than to eliminate them. Now I think it would be nice to eliminate them and, indeed, it is possible certainly to reduce them and eliminate it to a great extent. But the fact that sometimes these things would happen does not indicate that these times of economics is worth nothing. What it does indicate is that we have to pay much more attention than often happens to some of these problems, and since I've spent most of my life on the side of economics, I'm very sympathetic to the view that the economy should spend more time in dealing with the predicament of people who are thrown into turmoil when things go wrong, and also the fact that while there are successes of market economies, there are also needs for supplementation in other fields in terms of public intervention, in terms of political participation, and so forth. So it's a question of taking an adequately broad view of economics, along with its neighboring discipline, and it's also a question of paying more attention to those who are most likely to lose when a crisis hits.

PHIL PONCE: Professor Sen, thank you very much. And, again, congratulations.

AMARTYA SEN: Thank you very much.

QUESTIONS

1. Why does poverty exist, according to Sen? How is it encouraged? Can it be defeated? How? Who has a duty to combat it? Why?

2. Why does Sen have a specific interest in famine? What ethical problems does famine pose to us, as (comparatively) wealthy Westerners?

Pecuniary Emulation and Conspicuous Consumption

Thorstein Veblen

Thorstein Veblen published his classic *The Theory of the Leisure Class* in 1899.

Wherever the institution of private property is found, even in a slightly developed form, the economic process bears the character of a struggle between men for the possession of goods. It has been customary in economic theory, and especially among those economists who adhere with least faltering to the body of modernised classical doctrines, to construe this struggle for wealth as being substantially a struggle for subsistence. Such is, no doubt, its character in large part during the earlier and less efficient phases of industry. Such is also its character in all cases where the "niggardliness of nature" is so strict as to afford but a scanty livelihood to the community in return for strenuous and unremitting application to the business of getting the means of subsistence. But in all progressing communities an advance is presently made beyond this early stage of technological development. Industrial efficiency is presently carried to such a pitch as to afford something appreciably more than a bare livelihood to those engaged in the industrial process. It has not been unusual for economic theory to speak of the further struggle for wealth on this new industrial basis as a competition for an increase of the comforts of life—primarily for an increase of the physical comforts which the consumption of goods affords.

The end of acquisition and accumulation is conventionally held to be the consumption of the goods accumulated—whether it is consumption directly by the owner of the goods or by the household attached to him and for this purpose identified with him in theory. This is at least felt to be the economically legitimate end of acquisition, which alone it is incumbent on the theory to take account of. Such consumption may of course be conceived to serve the consumer's physical wants—his physical comfort—or his so-called higher wants—spiritual, aesthetic, intellectual, or what not; the latter class of wants being served indirectly by an expenditure of goods, after the fashion familiar to all economic readers.

But it is only when taken in a sense far removed from its naïve meaning that consumption of goods can be said to afford the incentive from which accumulation invariably proceeds. The motive that lies at the root of ownership is emulation; and the same motive of emulation continues active in the further development of the institution to which it has given rise and in the development of all those features of the social structure which this institution of ownership touches. The possession of wealth confers honour; it is an invidious distinction. Nothing equally cogent can be said for the consumption of goods, nor for any other conceivable incentive to acquisition, and especially not for any incentive to the accumulation of wealth.

It is of course not to be overlooked that in a community where nearly all goods are private property the necessity of earning a livelihood is a powerful and ever-present incentive for the poorer members of the community. The need of subsistence and of an increase of physical comfort may for a time be the dominant motive of acquisition for those classes who are habitually employed at manual labour, whose subsistence is on a precarious footing, who possess little and ordinarily accumulate little; but it will appear in the course of the discussion that even in the case of these impecunious classes the predominance of the motive of physical want is not so decided as has sometimes been assumed. On

From *The Theory of the Leisure Class*, Macmillan, 1899.

the other hand, so far as regards those members and classes of the community who are chiefly concerned in the accumulation of wealth, the incentive of subsistence or of physical comfort never plays a considerable part. Ownership began and grew into a human institution on grounds unrelated to the subsistence minimum. The dominant incentive was from the outset the invidious distinction attaching to wealth, and, save temporarily and by exception, no other motive has usurped the primacy at any later stage of the development.

Property set out with being booty held as trophies of the successful raid. So long as the group had departed but little from the primitive communal organisation, and so long as it still stood in close contact with other hostile groups, the utility of things or persons owned lay chiefly in an invidious comparison between their possessor and the enemy from whom they were taken. The habit of distinguishing between the interests of the individual and those of the group to which he belongs is apparently a later growth. Invidious comparison between the possessor of the honorific booty and his less successful neighbours within the group was no doubt present early as an element of the utility of the things possessed, though this was not at the outset the chief element of their value. The man's prowess was still primarily the group's prowess, and the possessor of the booty felt himself to be primarily the keeper of the honour of his group. This appreciation of exploit from the communal point of view is met with also at later stages of social growth, especially as regards the laurels of war.

But so soon as the custom of individual ownership begins to gain consistency, the point of view taken in making the invidious comparison on which private property rests will begin to change. Indeed, the one change is but the reflex of the other. The initial phase of ownership, the phase of acquisition by naïve seizure and conversion, begins to pass into the subsequent stage of an incipient organisation of industry on the basis of private property (in slaves); the horde develops into a more or less self-sufficing industrial community; possessions then come to be valued not so much as evidence of successful foray, but rather as evidence of the prepotence of the possessor of

these goods over other individuals within the community. The invidious comparison now becomes primarily a comparison of the owner with the other members of the group. Property is still of the nature of trophy, but, with the cultural advance, it becomes more and more a trophy of successes scored in the game of ownership carried on between the members of the group under the quasi-peaceable methods of nomadic life. . . .

. . . With the growth of settled industry, the possession of wealth gains in relative importance and effectiveness as a customary basis of repute and esteem. Not that esteem ceases to be awarded on the basis of other, more direct evidence of prowess; not that successful predatory aggression or warlike exploit ceases to call out the approval and admiration of the crowd, or to stir the envy of the less successful competitors; but the opportunities for gaining distinction by means of this direct manifestation of superior force grow less available both in scope and frequency. . . . It becomes indispensable to accumulate, to acquire property, in order to retain one's good name. When accumulated goods have in this way once become the accepted badge of efficiency, the possession of wealth presently assumes the character of an independent and definitive basis of esteem. The possession of goods, whether acquired aggressively by one's own exertion or passively by transmission through inheritance from others, becomes a conventional basis of reputability. The possession of wealth, which was at the outset valued simply as an evidence of efficiency, becomes, in popular apprehension, itself a meritorious act. Wealth is now itself intrinsically honourable and confers honour on its possessor. By a further refinement, wealth acquired passively by transmission from ancestors or other antecedents presently becomes even more honorific than wealth acquired by the possessor's own effort. . . .

What has just been said must not be taken to mean that there are no other incentives to acquisition and accumulation than this desire to excel in pecuniary standing and so gain the esteem and envy of one's fellow-men. The desire for added comfort and security from want is present as a motive at every stage of the process of accumulation in a modern industrial community; although the standard of sufficiency in these respects is in turn greatly affected by the habit of pecuniary emulation. To a great extent this emulation shapes the methods and selects the objects of expenditure for personal comfort and decent livelihood.

QUESTIONS

1. What is "pecuniary emulation"?
2. Why do you want an SUV? A Rolex? (If you do). What would Veblen say? Is wanting something because everyone else wants one necessarily bad? Why might it be a good thing?

Daniel Bell | # The Cultural Contradictions of Capitalism

Daniel Bell taught for many years at Harvard University and wrote, among many other works, *The Cultural Contradictions of Capitalism*.

The relationship between a civilization's socioeconomic structure and its culture is perhaps the most complicated of all problems for the sociologist. A nineteenth century tradition, one deeply impregnated with Marxist conceptions, held that changes in social structure determined man's imaginative reach. An earlier vision of man—as *homo pictor*, the symbol-producing animal, rather than as *homo faber*, the tool-making animal—saw him as a creature uniquely able to prefigure what he would later "objectify" or construct in reality. It thus ascribed to the realm of culture the initiative for change. Whatever the truth of these older arguments about the past, today culture has clearly become supreme; what is played out in the imagination of the artist foreshadows, however dimly, the social reality of tomorrow.

Culture has become supreme for two complementary reasons. First, culture has become the most dynamic component of our civilization, outreaching the dynamism of technology itself. There is now in art—as there has increasingly been for the past hundred years—a dominant impulse towards the new and the original, a self-conscious search for future forms and sensations, so that *the idea* of change and novelty overshadows the dimensions of actual change. And secondly, there has come about, in the last fifty years or so, a legitimation of this cultural impulse. Society now accepts this role for the imagination, rather than—as in the past—seeing it as establishing a norm and affirming a moral-philosophic tradition against which the new could be measured and (more often than not) censured. Indeed, society has done more than passively accept—it has provided a market which eagerly gobbles up the new, because it believes it to be superior in value to all older forms. Thus, our culture has an unprecedented mission: it is an official, ceaseless searching for a new sensibility.

It is true, of course, that the idea of change dominates the modern economy and modern technology as well. But changes in the economy and technology are constrained by available resources and financial cost. In politics, too, innovation is constrained by existing institutional structures, by the veto power of contending groups, and to some extent by tradition. But the changes in expressive symbols and forms, difficult as it may be for the mass of people to absorb them readily, meet no resistance in the realm of culture itself.

What is singular about this "tradition of the new" (as Harold Rosenberg has called it) is that it allows art to be unfettered, to break down all genres and to explore all modes of experience and sensation. Fantasy today has few costs (is *anything* deemed

From Daniel Bell, *The Cultural Contradictions of Capitalism* (New York: Basic Books, 1976).

bizarre or opprobrious today?) other than the risk of individual madness. And even madness, in the writings of such social theorists as Michel Foucault and R. D. Laing, is now conceived to be a superior form of truth! The new sensibilities, and the new styles of behavior associated with them, are created by small coteries which are devoted to exploring the new; and because the new has value in and of itself, and meets with so little resistance, the new sensibility and its behavior-styles diffuse rapidly, transforming the thinking and actions of larger masses of people.

Bourgeois society, justified and propelled as it had been in its earliest energies by these older ethics, could not easily admit to the change. It promoted a hedonistic way of life furiously—one has only to look at the transformation of advertising in the 1920's—but could not justify it. It lacked a new religion or a value system to replace the old, and the result was a disjunction.

The "new capitalism"—the phrase was used in the 1920's—continued to demand a Protestant Ethic in the area of production—that is, in the realm of work—but to stimulate a demand for pleasure and play in the area of consumption. The disjunction was bound to widen. The spread of urban life, with its variety of distractions and multiple stimuli; the new roles of women, created by the expansion of office jobs and the freer social and sexual contacts; the rise of a national culture through motion pictures and radio—all contributed to a loss of social authority on the part of the older value system.

The Puritan Ethic might be described most simply by the phrase "delayed gratification," and by restraint in gratification. It is, of course, the Malthusian injunction for prudence in a world of scarcity. But the claim of the American economic system was that it had introduced abundance, and the nature of abundance is to encourage prodigality rather than prudence. The "higher standard of living," not work as an end in itself, then becomes the engine of change. The glorification of plenty, rather than the bending to niggardly nature, becomes the justification of the system. But all of this was highly incongruent with the theological

and sociological foundations of nineteenth century Protestantism, which was in turn the foundation of the American value system.

From a *cultural* point of view, the politics of the 1920's to 1960's was a struggle between tradition and modernity. In the 1960's a new cultural style appeared. Call it psychedelic or call it, as its own protagonists have, a "counter-culture." It announced a strident opposition to bourgeois values and to the traditional codes of American life. "The bourgeoisie," we are told, "is obsessed by greed; its sex life is insipid and prudish; its family patterns are debased; its slavish conformities of dress and grooming are degrading; its mercenary routinization of life is intolerable. . . ."[1]

What is quixotic about such pronouncements is the polemical and ideological caricature of a set of codes that had been trampled on long ago—beginning sixty years earlier, with the Young Intellectuals. Yet such a caricature is necessary to make the new counterculture seem more daring and revolutionary than it is. The new sensibility, with its emphasis on psychedelic experience, sexual freedom, apocalyptic moods and the like, thinks of itself as being against "bourgeois" culture. But in truth, bourgeois culture vanished long ago. What the counter-culture embodies is an extension of the tendencies initiated sixty years ago by political liberalism and modernist culture, and represents, in effect, a split in the camp of modernism. For it now seeks to take the preachments of personal freedom, extreme experience ("kicks," and "the high") and sexual experimentation, to a point in *life-style* that the liberal culture—which would approve of such ideas in *art and imagination*—is not prepared to go. Yet liberalism finds itself uneasy to say why. It approves a basic permissiveness, but cannot with any certainty define the bounds. And this is its dilemma. In culture, as well as in politics, liberalism is now up against the wall.

Liberalism also finds itself in disarray in an arena where it had joined in support of capitalism—in the economy. The economic philosophy of American liberalism had been rooted in the idea of growth. One forgets that in the late 1940's and 1950's Walter Reuther,

Leon Keyserling, and other liberals had attacked the steel companies and much of American industry for being unwilling to expand capacity and had urged the government to set target growth figures. Cartelization, monopoly, and the restriction of production had been historic tendencies of capitalism. The Eisenhower administration consciously chose price stability over growth. It was the liberal economists who instilled in the society the policy of the conscious planning of growth through government inducements (e.g., investment credits, which industry, at first, did not want) and government investment. The idea of potential GNP and the concept of "shortfall"—the posting of a mark of what the economy at full utilization of resources could achieve compared to the actual figure—was introduced in the Council of Economic Advisors by the liberals. The idea of growth has become so fully absorbed as an economic ideology that one realizes no longer, as I said, how much of a liberal innovation it was.

The liberal answer to social problems such as poverty was that growth would provide the resources to raise the incomes of the poor. The thesis that growth was necessary to finance public services was the center of John Kenneth Galbraith's book *The Affluent Society*.

And yet, paradoxically, it is the very idea of economic growth that is now coming under attack—and from liberals. Affluence is no longer seen as an answer. Growth is held responsible for the spoliation of the environment, the voracious use of natural resources, the crowding in the recreation areas, the densities in the city, and the like. One finds, startlingly, the idea of zero economic growth—or John Stuart Mill's idea of the "stationary state"—now proposed as a serious goal of government policy. Just as the counter-culture rejects the traditional problem-solving pragmatism of American politics, it now also rejects the newer, liberal policy of economic growth as a positive goal for the society. But without a commitment to economic growth, what is the *raison d'etre* of capitalism?

TWO CRISES

American society faces a number of crises. Some are more manifest—the alienation of the young, the

militancy of the blacks, the crisis of confidence created by the Vietnam War. Some are structural—the creation of a national society, a communal society, and a post-industrial phase—which are reworking the occupational structure and the social arrangements of the society. These are all aspects of a political torment in the social system. Yet these crises, I believe, are manageable (not solvable; what problems are?) if the political leadership is intelligent and determined. The resources are present (or will be, once the Vietnam War is ended) to relieve many of the obvious tensions and to finance the public needs of the society. The great need here is *time*, for the social changes which are required (a decent welfare and income maintenance system for the poor, the reorganization of the universities, the control of the environment) can only be handled within the space of a decade or more. It is the demand for "instant solutions" which, in this respect, is the source of political trouble.

But the deeper and more lasting crisis is the cultural one. Changes in moral temper and culture—the fusion of imagination and life-styles—are not amenable to "social engineering" or political control. They derive from the value and moral traditions of the society, and these cannot be "designed" by precept. The ultimate sources are the religious conceptions which undergird a society; the proximate sources are the "reward systems" and "motivations" (and their legitimacy) which derive from the arena of work (the social structure).

American capitalism, as I have sought to show, has lost its traditional legitimacy which was based on a moral system of reward, rooted in a Protestant sanctification of work. It has substituted in its place a hedonism which promises a material ease and luxury, yet shies away from all the historic implications which a "voluptuary system"—and all its social permissiveness and libertinism—implies.

This is joined to a more pervasive problem derived from the nature of industrial society. The characteristic style of an industrial society is based on the principles of economics and economizing: on efficiency, least cost, maximization, optimization, and functional rationality. Yet it is at this point that it comes into sharpest conflict with the cultural trends of the day, for the culture emphasizes anticognitive and anti-intellectual currents which are rooted in a return to instinctual modes. The one emphasizes functional rationality, technocratic decision-making, and merito-cratic rewards. The other, apocalyptic moods and anti-rational modes of behavior. It is this disjunction which is the historic crisis of Western society. This cultural contradiction, in the long run, is the deepest challenge to the society.

NOTE

1. T. Roszak, *The Making of a Counter-Culture* (Doubleday, 1969), p. 13.

QUESTIONS

1. What are the cultural contradictions of capitalism?
2. How has the "Puritan Ethic" influenced American capitalism and culture?

| Robert B. Reich | # Supercapitalism |

Robert Reich was the nation's 22nd Secretary of Labor and is a professor at the University of California at Berkeley. He blogs at www .robertreich.org and is author of the best-selling eBook, *Beyond Outrage*.

Supercapitalism has triumphed as power has shifted to consumers and investors. They now have more choice than ever before, and can switch ever more easily to better deals. And competition among com-panies to lure and keep them continues to intensify. This means better and cheaper products, and higher returns. Yet as supercapitalism has triumphed, its negative social consequences have also loomed larger. These include widening inequality as most gains from economic growth go to the very top, reduced job secu-rity, instability of or loss of community, environmen-tal degradation, violations of human rights abroad, and a plethora of products and services pandering to our basest desires. These consequences are larger in the United States than in other advanced economies because America has moved deeper into supercapital-ism. Other economies, following closely behind, have begun to experience many of the same things.

Democracy is the appropriate vehicle for respond-ing to such social consequences. That's where citizen values are supposed to be expressed, where choices are supposed to be made between what we want for ourselves as consumers and investors, and what we want to achieve together. But the same competi-tion that has fueled supercapitalism has spilled over into the political process. Large companies have hired platoons of lobbyists, lawyers, experts, and public relations specialists, and devoted more and more money to electoral campaigns. The result has been to drown out voices and values of citizens. As all of this has transpired, the old institutions through which citizen values had been expressed in the Not Quite Golden Age—industry-wide labor unions, local citizen-based groups, "corporate statesmen" responding to all stakeholders, and regulatory agen-cies—have been largely blown away by the gusts of supercapitalism.

Instead of guarding democracy against the disturb-ing side effects of supercapitalism, many reformers have set their sights on changing the behavior of par-ticular companies—extolling them for being socially virtuous or attacking them for being socially irre-sponsible. The result has been some marginal changes in corporate behavior. But the larger consequence has been to divert the public's attention from fixing democracy.

From Robert B. Reich, *Supercapitalism* (New York: Knopf, 2007). Notes have been omitted from the text.

There is no shortage of policy ideas for coping with the social downsides of supercapitalism. You may disagree, but we're not even debating them seriously because public policy has become less and less relevant to politics. New ideas are trotted out for public viewing in every election season but they have little bearing, on what happens after the election is over. Everyday politics within legislatures, committees, and departments and agencies of government has come to be dominated by corporations seeking competitive advantage. Most new legislation and regulation is at the behest of certain companies or segments of industries; most conflicts and compromises are among competing companies or industries. Should some policy be proposed that might impose costs on many companies or industries, they join together to defeat it.

Without a democracy that will implement them, policy ideas about "what should be done" are beside the point. A more fundamental question, therefore, is how to make democracy work better.

There have been calls to publicly finance election campaigns for all major offices, require broad casters who use the public airwaves to contribute free campaign advertising to candidates in a general election, prohibit lobbyists from soliciting and bundling big-check donations from their business clients, ban gifts to lawmakers by corporations or executives, prohibit privately financed junkets for legislators and aides, ban parties staged to "honor" politicians with corporate contributions, prohibit former legislators and public officials from lobbying for at least five years after they leave office, require lobbyists to disclose all lobbying expenditures, and mandate that all expert witnesses in legislative and regulatory hearings disclose financial relationships with economically interested parties. Any such reforms would have to be monitored and enforced by an independent inspector general with power to investigate abuses and impose stiff penalties on violators.

All such steps would be helpful. But the question of how to enact and implement them only leads to a deeper dilemma. Political reforms cannot be achieved as long as public officials and legislators are dependent on the very corporations whose influence is to be limited. The system cannot repair itself from inside. An occasional revelation of outright political bribery causes enough public outrage to elicit solemn pledges by legislators and officials to reform the system. Such promises are forgotten as soon as public outrage fades and memories dim.

In any event, the fundamental problem does not, for the most part, involve blatant bribes and kickbacks. Rather, it is the intrusion of supercapitalism into every facet of democracy—the dominance of corporate lobbyists, lawyers, and public relations professionals over the entire political process; the corporate money that engulfs the system on a day-to-day basis, making it almost impossible for citizen voices to be heard. Not only do campaign contributions have to be severely limited, but also corporate expenditures on lobbying and public relations intended to influence legislative outcomes.

One possible hope for shielding democracy from supercapitalism is the presumed fact that many corporations would rather not pay these escalating costs if they could be certain their competitors would refrain from paying them as well. Firms, therefore, might be amenable to a truce from the political arms race. A few years ago, before the McCain–Feingold Act put a temporary damper on the flow of "soft money" (donations to political parties for "issue advertisements" that often end up as thinly veiled attacks on opponents), several hundred business executives in the Committee for Economic Development—including those from General Motors, Xerox, Merck, and Sara Lee Corporation—endorsed stronger campaign finance reform. The group's president, Charles Kolb, summarized their view: "These people are saying: We're tired of being hit up and shaken down. Politics ought to be about something besides hitting up companies for more and more money." Their collective support helped pass McCain–Feingold.

It may be possible to craft further deals among corporations to limit the flow of money into politics—perhaps barring lobbyists from soliciting and bundling big-check donations from their business clients and banning gifts to lawmakers from corporations or executives. In 2002, BP's CEO, Lord Browne, announced that the firm was voluntarily ending all contributions to political candidates around the world. "We must be particularly careful about the political process," he said, "not because it is unimportant—quite the reverse—but because the legitimacy of that process is crucial both for society and for us as a company working in that society." Yet it will be far harder to gain agreement among large companies to refrain from flooding Washington and other capital cities with lobbyists, lawyers, and public relations specialists. Notably, BP did not terminate its contracts with such professionals.

To be effective, any such truce would have to be enacted into law. A voluntary truce could not gain the support of every large company. The potential benefits of remaining free to craft advantageous political deals would be too great to pass up. That fact alone would doom any such voluntary effort; as long as some large companies continued to pour money into Washington and other capitals, others would feel compelled to do so as well.

But the largest impediment to reform is one brazen fact: Many politicians and lobbyists want to continue to extort money from the private sector. That's how politicians keep their hold on power, and lobbyists keep their hold on money.

Genuine reform will occur only if and when most citizens demand it. In order for that to happen, the public must understand several truths about the present system that are now obscured. The media must understand them as well, and be prepared to convey them when the occasion arises. The half-truths, mythologies, and distortions that now litter the border between the private sector and the public sector make it impossible for the public to keep straight the distinct roles of corporate executives and public officials. Such muddled thinking confounds efforts to prevent supercapitalism from overrunning democracy.

A citizen's guide to supercapitalism would begin by instructing the public to beware of any politician or advocate who blames corporations and corporate executives for the negative social consequences of supercapitalism, whether it be low or declining wages and benefits, job, losses, widening inequality, loss of community, global warming, indecent products, or any other of the commonly voiced complaints. Corporate executives are responsible for obeying the law, and should be held accountable for any illegality. But they cannot and should not be expected to do anything more. Their job is to satisfy their consumers and thereby make money for their investors. If they fail to do this as well if not better than their rivals they will be penalized by consumers and investors who take their money elsewhere.

Corporate executives are not engaged in a diabolical plot. The negative social consequences are the logical consequence of intensifying competition to give consumers and investors better and better deals. Those deals may require moving jobs abroad where they can be done at lower wages, substituting computers and software for people, or resisting unions. Or the deals may come at the expense of small retailers on Main Street who can't sell items at prices nearly as low, or at the expense of entire communities that lose a major employer who has to outsource abroad to remain competitive. The deals may require the talents of celebrity CEOs who are paid like baseball stars. Or they may come at the expense of the earth's atmosphere. Good deals may depend on filling the air with gunk, filling the airwaves with sex and violence, or filling our stomachs with junk food. The deals may involve trampling human rights abroad or putting young children to work in Southeast Asia. As long as the deals are legal, and as long as they satisfy consumers and investors, corporations and their executives will pursue them.

This doesn't make them right, but the only way to make them *wrong*—the only way to stop companies from giving consumers and investors good deals that depend on such moves—is to make them illegal. It is illogical to criticize companies for playing by the current rules of the game; if we want them to play differently, we have to change the rules.

It follows that the public must also beware of any claim by corporate executives that their company is doing something in order to advance the "public good" or to fulfill the firm's "social responsibility."

Companies are not interested in the public good. It is not their responsibility to be good. They may do good things to improve their brand image, so as to increase sales and profits. They will do profitable things that may happen to have socially beneficial side effects. But they will not do good things because they are considered to be good.

Likewise, when corporate executives or their lobbyists and lawyers fight for certain political or judicial outcomes, do not believe a word they, their spokesmen, or their "experts" say about why the outcome they seek is in the public interest. The outcome may indeed be in the public interest, but you cannot take their word for it because they are not motivated to do anything mainly because it is in the public interest. Their only legitimate motive, again, is to satisfy consumers in order to make profits that will satisfy investors. The only reason they have for advocating a particular political or judicial outcome is to advance or protect their competitive position. The sole reason they have for claiming an outcome is in the public's interest is to gain public support for it as a means of increasing their political leverage to achieve it.

I hope I've made it clear that you should also be skeptical of any politician who claims the public can rely on the "voluntary" cooperation of the private sector to achieve some public purpose or goal. Corporations and their executives have no license to use shareholder money to accomplish public purposes. They may "voluntarily" agree to donate money to a worthy cause, or to forbear from polluting the atmosphere, or to bring more jobs to a particular area—but only if the action is profitable, or if in so doing they burnish their public image and thus improve their bottom lines, or to forestall some new law or regulation that might impose a greater burden. But in the latter instances, such "voluntary" good deeds are likely to be limited and temporary, extending only insofar as the conditions that made such "voluntary" action pay off continue. In all such circumstances, you should ask why, if the public goal is so worthy, the politician is not seeking a law requiring the private sector to achieve it.

Similarly, be skeptical of any politician who blames a corporation for doing something that's legal or failing to do something when no law requires that it do so. Find out if the politician is actively supporting legislation to change the rules of the game so that this company and all others must alter their behavior in the prescribed way. If not, you are safe to assume that the politician's words of condemnation are designed to act as a cover for taking no action on the problem.

Be wary, as well, of concerted efforts by advocates and reformers—in the form of public relations campaigns, boycotts, and citizen movements—to force a particular company to be more socially virtuous. Seek to discover the specific goal of any such effort. If you agree with it, ask yourself whether it might be better served by changing laws or regulations that force all companies to alter their behavior in the same way. Sometimes, as we have seen, reformers target specific companies in order to mobilize the public to take political action; sometimes labor organizers target specific companies in order to force them to accept union representation. These may be useful reform strategies. But broad-scale attacks on specific companies to force them to alter their behavior in ways that will cause their prices to increase or their profits to decline should be suspect. Even if socially beneficial, the desired behavior may not seem worth the resulting higher prices or reduced returns. Besides, once the company's prices are raised or returns lowered, other competitors whose behavior has not been altered and whose prices are lower and returns higher may fill the gap, defeating the whole purpose of the effort.

In general, corporate responsibilities to the public are better addressed in the democratic process than inside corporate boardrooms. Reformers should focus on laws or regulations they seek to change, and mobilize the public around changing them. If the campaign against Wal-Mart, for example, is designed to get Wal-Mart to accept unions, that should be made clear. If it is to mobilize the public to accept changes in labor laws that make it easier for low-wage workers to form unions, that goal should be sought directly. The resulting legislative battle would strengthen democracy rather than divert it.

The most effective thing reformers can do is to reduce the effects of corporate money on politics, and enhance the voices of citizens. No other avenue of reform is as important. Corporate executives who sincerely wish to do good can make no better contribution than keeping their company out of politics. If corporate social responsibility has any meaning at all, it is to refrain from corrupting democracy.

A final truth that needs to be emphasized—the most basic of all—is that corporations are not people. They are legal fictions, nothing more than bundles of contractual agreements. Yes, there are "corporate cultures," dominant styles or norms such as characterize any group. But the corporation itself does not exist in corporeal form. This is especially so under supercapitalism, when companies are quickly morphing into global supply chains. Corporations should have no more legal rights to free speech, due process, or political representation in a democracy than do any other pieces of paper on which contracts are written. Legislators or judges who grant corporations such rights are not being intellectually honest, or they are unaware of the effects of supercapitalism. Only *people* should possess such rights.

When companies are invested with anthropomorphic qualities—when they are described in the media or by political leaders as being noble or scurrilous, patriotic or treasonous, law-abiding or criminal, or other qualities that human beings possess—the public is misled into thinking companies resemble people. Even the grammatical convention in America of attaching verbs directly to a company—as in "Microsoft is trying…" or "Wal-Mart wants…"—subtly reinforces the tendency to think about these entities as having independent volition. (The British, with their typical impeccability, use plural verbs to describe corporate conduct, as in "Rolls-Royce are considering. . . .")

The result of this anthropomorphic fallacy is to give companies duties and rights that properly belong to people instead. This blurs the boundary between capitalism and democracy, and leads to a host of bad public policies. Consider, for example, the corporate income tax. The public has the false impression that corporations pay it, and therefore they should be entitled to participate in the democratic process under the old adage "no taxation without representation." But only people pay taxes. In reality, the corporate income tax is paid—indirectly—by the company's

consumers, shareholders, and employees. Studies have attempted to determine exactly how the tax is allocated among these three groups, but the distribution remains unclear. What is clear is that the corporate income tax is inefficient and inequitable.

It's inefficient because interest payments made by corporations on their debt are deductible from their corporate income tax while dividend payments are not. This creates an incentive for companies to overrely on debt financing relative to shareholder equity, and to retain earnings rather than distribute them as dividends. The result, in recent years, has been for many corporations to accumulate large amounts of money that the company then uses to purchase other companies or to buy back its shares of stock. Capital markets would be more efficient if these accumulated profits were redistributed to shareholders as dividends. Decisions by millions of shareholders about how and when to reinvest these funds are likely to be, as a whole, wiser than decisions made by a relatively small number of corporate executives. Abolishing the corporate income tax would thus help capital markets work better.

The corporate income tax is inequitable in that retained earnings representing the portion held by lower-income investors are taxed at a corporate rate that's often higher than the rate they pay on their other income, while earnings representing the holdings of higher-income shareholders are taxed at a corporate rate often lower than they pay on the rest of their income. As we have seen, under supercapitalism, investors have far more power than they did decades ago. Their decisions about where to put their money to maximize their returns are similar to any other decisions they make about how to increase their earnings. Logically, there is no reason why their "corporate" earnings should be taxed differently than their other earnings. Abolishing the corporate income tax and treating all corporate income as the personal income of shareholders would rectify this anomaly.

An idea advanced by Professor Lester Thurow of MIT is to get rid of the corporate income tax and have shareholders pay personal taxes on all income earned by the corporation on their behalf—whether the income is retained by the corporation or is paid out as dividends. This would essentially reveal the corporation to be what it is in fact—a partnership of shareholders. All corporate earnings would be treated as personal income. But shareholders would not feel the pinch. As their "corporate" earnings accumulated throughout the year, the company would withhold taxes owed based on the shareholder's tax bracket—as did the shareholder's employer on his or her salaried earnings. At the end of the year, shareholders would receive from the company the equivalent of a W-2 form telling them how much income should be added to their other sources of income and how much income tax had been withheld. This way, shareholders would automatically pay taxes on "their" corporate earnings at rates appropriate to their own incomes.

This would rectify the two problems. Corporations would have no artificial incentive to retain earnings, and taxes would be lower for low-income shareholders and higher for higher-income shareholders. One important by-product of this reform would be to puncture the widespread but false notion that corporations pay taxes and therefore deserve to be represented in the political process. Again, companies should have no rights or responsibilities in a democracy. Only people should.

A similar confusion and inequity occurs when companies are held criminally liable for the misdeeds of their executives or other employees. Not only does corporate criminal liability reinforce the anthropomorphic fallacy—after all, criminals have rights under most democratic legal systems—but it ends up hurting lots of innocent people.

There is the case of Arthur Andersen, the former accounting firm convicted of obstruction of justice when certain partners destroyed records of the auditing work they did for Enron as the energy giant was imploding, shortly before the SEC began its investigation. When Andersen was convicted in 2002, its clients abandoned the company and hired other accounting firms. Andersen shrank from 28,000 employees to a skeleton crew of 200, who attended to the final details of shutting it down. The vast majority of Andersen employees had nothing to do with Enron but lost their jobs

nonetheless. Some senior partners moved to other accounting or consulting firms. Joseph Berardino, Andersen's CEO at the time, got a lucrative job at a private equity firm. Some other senior partners formed a new accounting firm. But many lower-level employees were hit hard. Three years after the conviction, a large number were still out of work, according to an Andersen associate who ran a Web site for Andersen alumni. In addition, retired partners and employees lost a substantial portion of their retirement benefits. The Supreme Court eventually reversed the conviction, but by then it was too late. The company was gone. One former employee wrote on the Web site, "Does this mean we can bring a class action against the DOJ [Department of Justice] for ruining our lives?"

Companies cannot act with criminal intent because they have no human capacity for intent. Arthur Andersen may have sounded like a person but the accounting firm was a legal fiction. The Supreme Court reversed the decision because the trial judge had failed to instruct the jury it must find proof Andersen knew its actions were wrong. Yet how can any jury, under any circumstances, find that a company "knew" that "its" actions were wrong? A company cannot know right from wrong; a company is incapable of knowing anything. Nor does a company itself take action. Only people know right from wrong, and only people act. That is a basic tenet of democracy.

On the other hand, corporate civil liability—where a company is fined for illegal actions by certain of its executives or employees that profit the firm—is perfectly consistent with the idea of personal responsibility. There is no good reason why shareholders or other employees should reap the gains from illegal acts, even those of which they had no knowledge. But the fine must be proportional to the illegal gain. Punitive damages that go so far beyond the illegal gains as to jeopardize the company's continued existence are more like criminal penalties, and therefore should not be allowed.

Similarly, it makes no sense to criticize or penalize companies headquartered in the United States for sending jobs abroad or parking their profits in other nations. Nor does it make sense for the U.S. government to favor companies headquartered in the United States over companies headquartered elsewhere, on the assumption that American-based companies are somehow more patriotic than companies headquartered abroad. Companies are not patriotic. To believe they should be—even could be, under the logic of supercapitalism—is to further anthropomorphize the corporation, and confuse the set of legal contracts that comprise a company with rights and responsibilities of citizenship that only people can exercise. Under supercapitalism, all global companies, wherever headquartered, are coming to resemble one another because they are competing against one another for global consumers and investors. All are turning into global supply chains—seeking the best deals from all over the world.

Corporate executives who outsource abroad are not treasonous "Benedict Arnolds." They cannot sacrifice good deals for their customers and investors in the belief that their company has a patriotic duty to hire more Americans or otherwise be a good American citizen. If they did so, customers and investors would abandon them in favor of other companies that provided better deals through outsourcing abroad. By 2006, as has been noted, American-based companies accounted for almost half of American imports. The biggest exporter of German-made washing machines was Whirlpool. Whirlpool's American employment has not increased since 1990, while its overseas workforce has tripled. Yet two-thirds of its revenue still comes from American consumers. Even WalMart is becoming a global company, growing faster abroad than in the United States.

For the same reason, it makes little sense to limit certain military contracts to so-called American companies. The ostensible reason for doing so is that American companies will do their research, design engineering, and manufacturing in the United States, and that the nation's security depends on having such crucial activities done within the nation's borders. But in fact, American-based defense contractors increasingly rely on the same worldwide supply chains that other companies do. A significant amount of military software is developed offshore. In 2006, 90 percent of all printed circuit boards were made overseas. If defense contractors had to custom-make everything inside the United States, defense costs would be even more astronomical than they are today.

The logic of limiting certain public responsibilities to American companies is similarly dubious. It fails to distinguish between who owns a company and who actually works for it, and it assumes that the nationality of a global company's executives or other employees alters its performance. In 2006, Congress succumbed to this fallacious logic when it moved to stop Dubai Ports World, owned by the emir of Dubai, from taking over contracts to run six American ports, fearing a security risk. But at the time, about 80 percent of American ports were already run by foreign-based companies, including the six in question. Most of these companies had hired American nationals to undertake day-to-day management of the ports, because they were the most experienced. Dubai Ports World's chief operating officer was an American, as was its former chief executive, as were the American port executives of the British company that was seeking to sell its contracts to Dubai Ports World. In any event, day-to-day operations of the ports would still be done by American longshoremen, clerks, and technicians. And control over port security would remain with the U.S. government, the Coast Guard, Customs, harbor police, and port authorities, who make and enforce the rules.

Subsidizing the research of American-based companies is just as illogical. It does not make America more competitive, because American-based companies are doing their research and development all over the world. Such subsidies merely underwrite research that would have been undertaken here anyway while freeing up more corporate research money to be spent outside the United States. Microsoft recently announced a $1.7 billion investment in India, about half of which will go to its R&D center in Hyderabad, in southern India. In early 2006, IBM announced it was opening a software laboratory in Bangalore, India. Dow Chemical is building a research center in Shanghai that will employ six hundred engineers when completed in 2007, and a large installation in India. In a survey of more than two hundred American and European global corporations conducted by the National Academies, 38 percent planned to shift more of their R&D work to China and India, and to decrease R&D in the United States and Europe.

The goal of government policy should be to make Americans more competitive, not to make American companies more competitive. This is an important distinction that most corporate executives understand. Big companies are global entities; people are not. "For a company, the reality is that we have a lot of options," says William Banholzer, Dow's chief technology officer. "But *my personal worry* is that an innovative science and engineering workforce is vital to the economy. If that slips, it is going to hurt the United States over the long run" (italics added). The federal government should subsidize the basic R&D of any company regardless of its headquarters as long as it does its work in the United States, developing on-the-job skills of American-based engineers and scientists.

It makes no sense to treat companies as "persons" with legal rights to challenge in court duly enacted laws and regulations. That should be left to real citizens. Investors, consumers, or employees already have the right to go to court—as individuals or as members of a class action—to challenge laws and regulations that allegedly impose economic injuries on them. They do not need the corporation to litigate on their behalf. Moreover, because almost all large companies depend on pools of capital derived from investors all over the world, giving companies standing to sue effectively confers on some non-American investors the right to seek to overturn American laws and regulations. Noncitizens should have no right to do so unless the law or regulations breach some international treaty. Otherwise, decisions arrived at democratically can be overturned by people who are not even American citizens.

Yet this is happening all the time when companies are allowed to sue. In January 2005, nine global automakers sued California to block California's new "clean cars" law, which requires cars sold in California to reduce greenhouse gas emissions 30 percent by model year 2016, on grounds that the legislation amounted to an unconstitutional restraint on interstate commerce. A majority of the shareholders of at least seven of these automakers were not American citizens yet the court gave them standing to challenge, and potentially overturn, a law enacted by the citizens of California. This is nonsensical. Real citizenship should be the criterion—and by allowing only people rather than companies to sue, it can be. Any American citizen or group of American citizens claiming they are injured by California's law should be able to challenge it—including, for example, American investors in Toyota, but not including non-American investors in General Motors.

Finally, and most fundamentally, since only people can be citizens, only people should be allowed to participate in democratic decision making. Consumers, investors, executives, and other employees all have a right to advance their interests within a democracy. But as Yale political scientist Charles Lindblom concluded many years ago, neither ethically nor logically do corporations have a legitimate role in the democratic process.

For many years, anti-union lobbyists have pushed what they call "paycheck protection" laws, supposedly designed to protect union members from being forced, through their dues, to support union political activities they oppose. Under such laws—already in effect in several states—no union dues can be spent for any political purpose, including lobbying, unless union members specifically agree. It would seem logical to apply the same principle to protect shareholders from being forced through their investments to support political activities they oppose. "Stockholder protection" would require that shareholders specifically agree to any corporate political activity. If a company dedicates, say, $100,000 to political action in a given year—including lobbying, campaign contributions, and gifts or junkets for elected officials—shareholders who do not wish their money to be used this way would get a special dividend or additional shares representing their pro rata share of that expenditure. Mutual funds and pension plans would have to notify their shareholders of such political activity, and seek their acquiescence. Such political activity would thereby be paid for by shareholders who wished to spend their portion of company profits on it.

Even if it is assumed that political activities of corporations reflect the consumer and investor in us, the citizen in us has nowhere near the same political clout. Another way to redress the imbalance would be to allow taxpayers a tax credit of up to, say, $1,000 a year, which we could send to any organization that used the money to lobby on behalf of our citizen values—groups seeking, for instance, a higher minimum wage, a cleaner environment, or limits on videos and music featuring lurid sex and violence. The group would have to be nonprofit, but the choice of group and goal would be up to each of us. The point would be to give the citizen in us a louder voice in our democracy.

These are illustrations of how we might better ensure that only people have the rights and responsibilities of citizenship. Along with the other measures—abolishing the corporate income tax, ending the practice of prosecuting corporations for criminal conduct, no longer expecting or insisting that companies be patriotic, not granting them standing to challenge duly enacted laws in court— they offer a realistic and logically coherent view of the corporation as a legal fiction, and of people as citizens. I have used the United States as my primary example here, but the same logic would apply in any democracy.

The triumph of supercapitalism has led, indirectly and unwittingly, to the decline of democracy. But that is not inevitable. We can have a vibrant democracy as well as a vibrant capitalism. To accomplish this, the two spheres must be kept distinct. The purpose of capitalism is to get great deals for consumers and investors. The purpose of democracy is to accomplish ends we cannot achieve as individuals. The border between the two is breached when companies *appear* to take on social responsibilities or when they utilize politics to advance or maintain their competitive standing.

We are all consumers and most of us are investors, and in those roles we try to get the best deals we possibly can. That is how we participate in a market economy and enjoy the benefits of supercapitalism. But those private benefits often come with social costs. We are also citizens who have a right and a responsibility to participate in a democracy. We thus have it in our power to reduce those social costs, thereby making the true price of the goods and services we purchase as low as possible. Yet we can accomplish this larger feat only if we take our responsibilities as citizens seriously, and protect our democracy. The first step, which is often the hardest, is to get our thinking straight.

QUESTIONS

1. How can we "get our thinking straight"? Do business ethics classes help?

2. Is Reich pro-capitalism, anti-capitalism, or neither? Explain your position.

3. Imagine a debate between Marx and Reich. Where would they agree?

Thomas Frank

Too Smart to Fail: Notes on an Age of Folly

Thomas Frank is founding editor of *The Baffler*, a columnist for *Harper's Magazine*, and author of *pity the Billionaire*.

The "sound" banker, alas! is not one who sees danger and avoids it, but one who, when he is ruined, is ruined in a conventional and orthodox way along with his fellows so that no one can really blame him.
—John Maynard Keynes

In the twelve hapless years of the present millennium, we have looked on as three great bubbles of consensus vanity have inflated and burst, each with consequences more dire than the last.

First there was the "New Economy," a millennial fever dream predicated on the twin ideas of a people's stock market and an eternal silicon prosperity; it collapsed eventually under the weight of its own fatuousness.

Second was the war in Iraq, an endeavor whose launch depended for its success on the turpitude of virtually every class of elite in Washington, particularly the tough-minded men of the media; an enterprise that destroyed the country it aimed to save and that helped to bankrupt our nation as well.

And then, Wall Street blew up the global economy. Empowered by bank deregulation and regulatory capture, Wall Street enlisted those tough-minded men of the media again to sell the world on the idea that financial innovations were making the global economy more stable by the minute. Central banks puffed an asset bubble like the world had never seen before, even if every journalist worth his byline was obliged to deny its existence until it was too late.

These episodes were costly and even disastrous, and after each one had run its course and duly exploded, I expected some sort of day of reckoning for their promoters. And, indeed, the last two disasters combined to force the Republican Party from its stranglehold on American government—for a time.

But what rankles now is our failure, after each of these disasters, to come to terms with how we were played. Each separate catastrophe should have been followed by a wave of apologies and resignations. Taken together—and given that a good percentage of the pundit corps signed on to two or even three of these idiotic storylines—they mandated mass firings in the newsrooms and op-ed pages of the nation. Quicker than you could say "Ahmed Chalabi, an entire generation of newsroom fools should have lost their jobs.

But that's not what happened. Plenty of journalists have been pushed out of late, but the ones responsible for deluding the public are not among them. Neocon extraordinaire Bill Kristol won a berth at the *New York Times* (before losing it again), Charles Krauthammer is still the thinking conservative's favorite, George Will drones crankily on, Thomas Friedman remains our leading dispenser of nonsense neologisms, and Niall Ferguson wipes his feet on a welcome mat that will never wear out. The day Larry Kudlow apologizes for slagging bubble-doubters as part of a sinister left-wing trick is the day the world will start spinning in reverse. Standard & Poor's first leads the parade of folly (triple-A's for everyone!), then decides to downgrade U.S. government debt, and is taken seriously in both endeavors. And the prospect of Fox News or CNBC apologizing for their role in puffing war bubbles and financial bubbles is no better than a punch line: what they do is the opposite, launching new movements that stamp their crumbled fables "true" by popular demand.

The real mistake was my own. I believed that our public intelligentsia had succumbed to an amazing series of cognitive failures; that time after time they had gotten the facts wrong, ignored the clanging bullshit detector, made the sort of mistakes that would disqualify them from publishing in *The Baffler*, let alone the *Washington Post*.

http://www.huffingtonpost.com/thomas-frank/too-smart-to-fail-.....

What I didn't understand was that these weren't cognitive failures at all; they were moral failures, mistakes that were hard-wired into the belief systems of the organizations and professions and social classes in question. As such they were mistakes that—from the point of view of those organizations or professions or classes—shed no discredit on the individual chowderheads who made them. Holding them accountable was out of the question, and it remains off the table to- day. These people ignored every flashing red signal, refused to listen to the whistleblowers, blew off the obvious screaming indicators that something was going wrong in the boardrooms of the nation, even talked us into an unnecessary war, for chrissake, and the bailout apparatus still stands ready should they mess things up again.

QUESTIONS

1. According to the author, what should have followed millenial fever, the war in Iraq, and the Wall Street collapse? Why?

2. According to the author, what is the flow that precipitated the three events? Where can it be found?

| Robert Kuttner | Everything for Sale |

Robert Kuttner is cofounder and coeditor of *The American Prospect*.

I

The ideal of a free, self-regulating market is newly triumphant. The historical lessons of market excess, from the Gilded Age to the Great Depression, have all but dropped from the collective memory. Government stands impeached and impoverished, along with democratic politics itself. Unfettered markets are deemed both the essence of human liberty, and the most expedient route to prosperity.

In the United States, the alternative to laissez-faire has never been socialism. Rather, the interventionist party, from Hamilton and Lincoln, through the Progressive era, Franklin Roosevelt and Lyndon Johnson, sponsored what came to be known as a "mixed economy." The idea was that market forces could do many things well—but not everything. Government intervened to promote development, to temper the market's distributive extremes, to counteract its unfortunate tendency to boom-and-bust, to remedy its myopic failure to invest too little in public goods, and to invest too much in processes that harmed the human and natural environment.

Since the constitutional founding, however, the libertarian strain in American life has often overwhelmed the impulse toward collective betterment. Today, after two decades of assault by the marketizers, even the normal defenders of the mixed economy are defensive and uncertain. The last two Democratic presidents have been ambivalent advocates for the mixed economy. Mostly, they offered a more temperate call for the reining in of government and the liberation of the entrepreneur. The current vogue for deregulation began under Jimmy Carter. The insistence on budget balance was embraced by Bill Clinton, whose pledge to "reinvent government" soon became a shared commitment merely to reduce government. And much of the economics profession, after an era of embracing the mixed economy, has reverted to a new fundamentalism cherishing the virtues of markets.

America, in short, is in one of its cyclical romances with a utopian view of laissez-faire. Free markets are famous for overshooting. Real-estate bubbles, tulip

From Robert Kuttner, *Everything for Sale: The Virtues and Limits of Markets* (New York: Knopf, 1998).

manias, and stock-market euphorias invariably lead to crowd psychologies and painful mornings-after. The same, evidentially, is true of ideological fashions.

So this is a good moment for a sober sorting out How does the market, whose first principle is one-dollar/one-vote, properly coexist with a political democracy whose basic rule is "one person/one vote"? When does the market run riot? What are the proper boundaries of market principles? What should not be for sale?

II

Even in a capitalist economy, the marketplace is only one of several means by which society makes decisions, determines worth, allocates resources, maintains a social fabric, and conducts human relations. Actual capitalist nations display a wide variation in the blend of market and nonmarket. A basically capitalist system is clearly superior to a command economy. But the nations where markets have the freest rein do not invariably enjoy the most reliable prosperity, let alone the most attractive society.

In this age of the resurgent market, we are promised that technology, ingenuity, and freedom from the dead hand of government will revive economic efficiency and material progress. Yet, despite the triumph of market principles, market society is no Utopia. Compared with the golden era of the postwar boom and the mixed economy, this is a time of broad economic unease. As society becomes more marketized, it is producing stagnation of living standards for most people, and a fraying of the social fabric that society's best-off are all too able to evade. One thing market society does well is to allow its biggest winners to buy their way out of its pathologies.

Even as the market enjoys new prestige, ordinary people are uneasy with many of the results. With greater marketization comes not just opportunity but opportunism; a society that prizes risk also reaps insecurity. Taken to an extreme, markets devalue and diminish extra-market values and norms—on which viable capitalism depends.

The promise of growth has also run into questions of sustainability. Even mainstream economists wonder about the effect on the natural environment if the third world were to enjoy even half the living standards and the claim on natural systems of the United States and Europe. The standard economic calculus does not know how to measure the costs of depletion of natural systems, since these are not accurately captured in current prices. And in market logic, by definition, what is not reflected in the price system does not exist.

All of this should cast serious doubt on the presumption, so fashionable of late, that the natural form of capitalism is laissez-faire. Beyond a certain point, excessive marketization may not be efficient *even for economic life*. . . .

III

The mixed economy of a generation ago was constructed on the ruins of depression and war. It produced a quarter-century of unprecedented growth and prosperity. It allowed a blend of dynamism and stability, of market and political community. When economic growth faltered after 1973, a new, radically classical economics gradually gained influence in the academy and in politics. Resurgent business groups, once cowed by the New Deal-Great Society era, became unabashed crusaders for laissez-faire. The increasing marketization of global commerce undermined the institutional capacity of nation-states to manage a mixed economy, and discredited center-left parties.

The period of "stagflation" discredited economic management and conferred new prestige on laissez-faire. If further confirmation were needed, the erosion and collapse of communism impeached not just state socialism, but European social democracy and American neo-Keynesianism as well. The political counterrevolution that culminated in the 1980 election of Ronald Reagan enjoyed a rendezvous with an intellectual reversion that had been sweeping the economics profession for at least a decade. Each drew strength from the other.

In scholarly economics, theorists such as Milton Friedman, who had been marginal, became central. The concrete study of economic history and economic institutions became archaic. The smartest rising economists used ever more complex mathematics, based on the premise of a "general equilibrium"—a concept that presumed a smoothly self-correcting market and implicitly urged that markets become purer and that more realms of society become markets. Newly self-confident conservative economic theorists colonized other academic disciplines. Market concepts became widespread in law, political science, and economic history. As experts on public policy, these economists became the intellectual champions of privatization, deregulation, and liberation of the global marketplace. It all boiled down to one very simple core precept: market is better.

I begin with the working hypothesis that a capitalist system is a superior form of economic organization, but even in a market economy there are realms of human life where markets are imperfect, inappropriate, or unattainable. Many forms of human motivation cannot be reduced to the market model of man.

There is at the core of the celebration of markets a relentless tautology. If we begin, by assumption, with the premise that nearly everything can be understood as a market and that markets optimize outcomes, then everything else leads back to the same conclusion—marketize! If, in the event, a particular market doesn't optimize, there is only one possible inference: it must be insufficiently marketlike. This epistemological sleight of hand is an astonishing blend that blurs the descriptive with the normative. It is a no-fail system for guaranteeing that theory trumps evidence. Should some human activity not, in fact, behave like an efficient market, it must be the result of some interference that should be removed or a stubborn human refusal to appreciate markets. It cannot possibly be that the theory fails to specify accurately how human behavior works. The thrust of free-market economics for a quarter-century has been a search to narrow the set of special cases where market solutions cannot be found for market failures. Today, the only difference between the utopian version and the mainstream version is degree.

In interpreting political economy, parsimony—Occam's celebrated razor—is the most overrated tool in the scholarly medicine cabinet. The beauty of the market model is its elegant simplicity. A perfect market can be modeled; the analyst can perform neat simulations, using very sophisticated mathematics. But the more complex the departures from a perfect market, the less relevant is the cherished analytic apparatus or the Platonic ideal of a pure market.

Academic champions of the market concede, often with irritation, that real-world institutions are messy; that labor markets are not like product markets, whose merchandise "clears" based on adjustments of price; that actual bundles of capital equipment are "lumpy," and not prone to smooth, frictionless equilibration as in the algebra. But as the economist ventures into the institutional thicket, she strays from the norms of her profession. She had better be tenured first. Thus, in part because of the attractiveness of its own core model, academic economics has lately become a purer version of itself—almost a lobby for the idea that the real economy should strive to emulate the model. The Cambridge economist John Eatwell once remarked, facetiously, "If the world is not like the model, so much the worse for the world."

. . . I am a believer in a balance between market, state, and civil society. I arrive at this belief primarily from a reading of economic and political history, which suggests that pure laissez-faire is socially and even economically unsustainable. Although defenders of a mixed economy often argue their case on equity grounds, there is significant evidence that, quite apart from questions of distributive justice, the very stability of the system requires departures from laissez-faire. My previous books have all treated, in different ways, the intersection of economics, politics, policy, and ideology. They have all dealt with the boundaries between state, market, and society. In these earlier works, I challenged one of the central claims of the marketizers—that equality necessarily comes at the expense of efficiency. I also examined the corrosive influence of international laissez-faire on the project of operating a mixed economy at home. And I explored the practical political difficulty of center-left parties serving their natural constituency in an era of limited budgets and resurgent laissez-faire.

. . . Where, really, do markets perform roughly as advertised? Where is the market model a reasonable approximation of human motivation, and where is it misleading? By what criteria are we to know when the market has overstepped its proper bounds? How do different kinds of markets fail to optimize outcomes? What patterns of failure recur? How are we to know when we are in a realm where markets produce rough efficiency and rough justice, versus one where markets produce avoidable calamities? When is the best response to market failure to contrive procedures or outcomes that are more "marketlike"? When does that approach only make things worse? Where is the proper boundary between market and nonmarket?

In the search for principles on which to reinvent a mixed economy, one must begin by according great respect to the market. For markets do many things very well. . . . It is evident that command economies are not viable; that prices are indeed potent signals of what it costs to produce a good or a service and what consumers will pay; that when prices unreasonably depart from market discipline they yield too many of the wrong goods or too few of the right ones, and insulate producers from the bracing tonic of competition—leading to stagnation. The trouble is that markets do not reliably yield such results; on the contrary, markets sometimes produce perverse outcomes for fairly prolonged periods.

The quest for a viable mixed economy necessarily leads back to government and politics, for the democratic state remains the prime counterweight to the market. Marketization, of late, has swamped the polity. The dynamics are cumulative. Government has less popular legitimacy, and fewer resources with which to treat escalating problems. The less government is able to achieve, the more it seems a bad bargain. American liberals and European social democrats often seem unable to offer more than a milder version of the conservative program—deregulation, privatization, globalization, fiscal discipline, but at a less zealous extreme. Few have been willing to challenge the premise that nearly everything should revert to a market.

To rebuild an alternative philosophy of political economy, one must first shake the hegemony of the laissez-faire market. I hope to accomplish this with evidence, not tautology. The last intellectual refuge of the marketizer is the claim that, even if markets sometimes fail, political interferences are likely only to compound those failures. Here, also, we must get down to cases. Governments seek to override markets for a variety of purposes—to stabilize, to promote growth, to limit detrimental side effects, to temper inequalities, to cultivate civic virtues. But governments also operate in a political crucible, and require political consent and fiscal resources. In the search for strategies to temper and tame the market, we need to seek ones that are within the competence of the state, that restore vitality to the enterprise of politics, and nourish rather than overload civil society.

QUESTIONS

1. What are some reasons we might be uneasy about the socials results of the market?
2. How does Kuttner argue for a balance between market, state, and civil society?

CASES

CASE 15.1
Blood for Sale
William H. Shaw and Vincent Barry

Sol Levin was a successful stockbroker in Tampa, Florida, when he recognized the potentially profitable market for safe and uncontaminated blood and, with some colleagues, founded Plasma International. Not everybody is willing to make money by selling his or her own blood, and in the beginning Plasma International bought blood from people addicted to wine. Although innovative marketing increased Plasma International's sales dramatically, several cases of hepatitis were reported in recipients. The company then began looking for new sources of blood.

Plasma International searched worldwide and with the advice of a qualified team of medical consultants, did extensive testing. Eventually they found that the blood profiles of several rural West African tribes made them ideal prospective donors. After negotiations with the local government, Plasma International signed an agreement with several tribal chieftains to purchase blood.

Business went smoothly and profitably for Plasma International until a Tampa paper charged that Plasma was purchasing blood for as little as fifteen cents a pint and then reselling it to hospitals in the United States and South America for $25 per pint. In one recent disaster, the newspaper alleged, Plasma International had sold 10,000 pints, netting nearly a quarter of a million dollars.

The newspaper story stirred up controversy in Tampa, but the existence of commercialized blood marketing systems in the United States is nothing new. Approximately half the blood and plasma

obtained in the United States is bought and sold like any other commodity. About 40 percent is given to avoid having to pay for blood received or to build up credit so blood will be available without charge if needed. By contrast, the National Health Service in Britain relies entirely on a voluntary system of blood donation. Blood is neither bought nor sold. It is available to anyone who needs it without charge or obligation, and donors gain no preference over nondonors.

In an important study, economist Richard Titmuss showed that the British system works better than the American one in terms of economic efficiency, administrative efficiency, price, and blood quality. The commercialized blood market, Titmuss argued, is wasteful of blood and plagued by shortages. Bureaucratization, paperwork, and administrative overhead result in a cost per unit of blood that is five to fifteen times higher than in Britain. Hemophiliacs, in particular, are disadvantaged by the American system and have enormous bills to pay. In addition, commercial markets are much more likely to distribute contaminated blood.

Titmuss also argued that the existence of a commercialized system discourages voluntary donors. People are less apt to give blood if they know that others are selling it. Philosopher Peter Singer has elaborated on this point:

> If blood is a commodity with a price, to give blood means merely to save someone money. Blood has a cash value of a certain number of dollars, and the importance of the gift will vary with the wealth of

From William H. Shaw and Vincent Barry, *Moral Issues in Business*, 5th ed. (Belmont, CA: Wadsworth, 1996).

the recipient. If blood cannot be bought, however, the gift's value depends upon the need of the recipient. Often, it will be worth life itself. Under these circumstances blood becomes a very special kind of gift, and giving it means providing for strangers, without hope of reward, something they cannot buy and without which they may die. The gift relates strangers in a manner that is not possible when blood is a commodity.

This may sound like a philosopher's abstraction, far removed from the thoughts of ordinary people. On the contrary, it is an idea spontaneously expressed by British donors in response to Titmuss's questionnaire. As one woman, a machine operator, wrote in reply to the question why she first decided to become a blood donor, "You can't get blood from supermarkets and chain stores. People themselves must come forward; sick people can't get out of bed to ask you for a pint to save their life, so I came forward in hopes to help somebody who needs blood."

The implication of this answer, and others like it, is that even if the formal right to give blood can coexist with commercialized blood banks, the respondent's action would have lost much of its significance to her, and the blood would probably not have been given at all. When blood is a commodity, and can be purchased if it is not given, altruism becomes unnecessary, and so loosens the bonds that can otherwise exist between strangers in a community. The existence of a market in blood does not threaten the formal right to give blood, but it does away with the right to give blood which cannot be bought, has no cash value, and must be given freely if it is to be obtained at all. If there is such a right, it is incompatible with the right to sell blood, and we cannot avoid violating one of these rights when we grant the other.

Both Titmuss and Singer believe that the weakening of the spirit of altruism in this sphere has important repercussions. It marks, they think, the increasing commercialization of our lives and makes similar changes in attitude, motive, and relationships more likely in other fields.

QUESTIONS

1. Is Sol Levin running a business "just like any other business," or is his company open to moral criticism? Defend your answer by appeal to moral principle.

2. What are the contrasting ideals of the British and American blood systems? Which system, in your opinion, best promotes human freedom and respect for persons?

3. Examine the pros and cons of commercial transactions in blood from the egoistic, the utilitarian, and the Kantian perspectives.

4. Are Titmuss and Singer right to suggest that the buying and selling of blood reduces altruism? Does knowing that you can sell your blood (and that others are selling theirs) make you less inclined to donate your blood? Do we have a right to give blood that cannot be bought?

5. Many believe that commercialization is increasing in all areas of modern life. If this is so, is it something to be applauded or condemned? Is it wrong to treat certain things—like human organs—as commodities?

6. Did Plasma International strike a fair bargain with the West Africans who supplied their blood to the company? Or is Plasma guilty of exploiting them in some way? Explain your answer.

7. Do you believe that we have a moral duty to donate blood? If so, why and under what circumstances? If not, why not?

CASE 15.2
Cocaine at the Fortune-500 Level
Tom L. Beauchamp, Jeff Greene, and Sasha Lyuste

Roberto, a pure libertarian in moral and political philosophy, is deeply impressed by his reading of Robert Nozick's account of justice. He lives in Los Angeles and teaches philosophy at a local university. Roberto is also a frequent user of cocaine, which he enjoys immensely and provides to friends at parties. Neither he nor any of his close friends is addicted. Over the years Roberto has become tired of teaching philosophy and now has an opportunity, through old friends who live in Peru, to become a middleman in the cocaine business. Although he is disturbed about the effects cocaine has in some persons, he has never witnessed these effects firsthand. He is giving his friends' business offer serious consideration.

Roberto's research has told him the following: Selling cocaine is a $35 billion plus industry. Although he is interested primarily in a Peruvian connection, his research has shown conclusively that the Colombian cartel alone is large enough to place it among the Fortune 500 corporations. Cocaine production in Peru and Bolivia in 1995 represented about 90 percent of the world's cocaine base; the remaining 10 percent was produced in Columbia (*Journal of Inter-American and World Affairs, 1997*). Cocaine is Latin America's second largest export, accounting for 3–4 percent of the GDP of Peru and Bolivia, and up to 8 percent of that of Columbia. The cocaine industry employs close to half a million people in the Andean region alone. Columbian coca cultivation rose 11 percent in 2000.

Former Peruvian President Alan Garcia once described cocaine as Latin America's "only successful multinational." It can be and has been analyzed in traditional business categories, with its own entrepreneurs, chemists, laboratories, employment agencies, small organizations, distribution systems, market giants, growth phases, and so forth. Cocaine's profit margins have narrowed in some markets, while expanding in others. It often seeks new markets in order to expand its product line. For example, in the mid-1980s "crack," a potent form of smoked cocaine, was moved heavily into new markets in Europe. Between the mid-1960s and the late 1990s the demand for cocaine grew dramatically (weathering some up and down markets) because of successful supply and marketing. Middlemen in Miami and Los Angeles were established to increase already abundant profits. Heavy investments were made in airplanes, efficient modes of production, training managers, and regular schedules of distribution. In the late 1980s there was a downturn in cocaine consumption after the deaths of two prominent athletes. In the early 1990s the market recovered slightly before slipping again in the mid-1990s. However, cocaine remains an enormously powerful industry in many countries.

Roberto sees the cocaine industry as not being subject to taxes, tariffs, or government regulations other than those pertaining to its illegality. It is a pure form of the free market in which supply and demand control transactions. This fact about the business appeals to Roberto, as it seems perfectly suited to his libertarian views. He is well aware that there are severe problems of coercion and violence in some parts of the industry, but he is certain that the wealthy clientele whom he would supply in Los Angeles would neither abuse the drug nor redistribute it to others who might be harmed. Roberto is confident that his Peruvian associates are honorable and that he can escape problems of violence, coercion, and abusive marketing. However, he has just read a newspaper story that cocaine-use emergencies—especially those involving cocaine-induced heart attacks—have tripled in the last five years. It is only this fact that has given him pause before deciding to enter the cocaine business. He views these health emergencies

This case was prepared by Tom L. Beauchamp and updated by Jeff Greene and Sasha Lyutse; it relies in part on accounts in *The Wall Street Journal* and *The Economist*.

as unfortunate but not unfair outcomes of the business. Therefore, it is his humanity and not his theory of justice that gives him pause.

QUESTIONS

1. Would a libertarian—such as Roberto—say that the cocaine business is not unfair so long as no coercion is involved and the system is a pure function of supply and demand?

2. Does justice demand that cocaine be outlawed, or is this not a matter of justice at all? Are questions of justice even meaningful when the activity is beyond the boundaries of law?

3. Is the distinction Roberto draws between what is unfortunate and what is unfair relevant to a decision about whether an activity is just?

CASE 15.3
Right to Work
Megan McArdle

Freddie wants me to talk about the human costs of not having the auto bailout. That's easy: they're terrible. Lots of people will lose their jobs. Those that don't will have their expectations for an upper-middle-class life crushed.

Am I glad to see this? No. Am I rooting for the demise of the UAW? No. I don't buy American cars. I don't work for an American car company. I couldn't care less about the UAW.

I do think that the UAW is perhaps the grossest example of something toxic about what a lot of American unions have turned into. I don't care, particularly, whether unions use their power to wrest higher wages and benefits from companies. Even if they kill the company with excessive demands—hell, they're the majority of the workforce, they can destroy their jobs if they want. I feel bad for the non-union workers. But I don't want to, say, legally prevent unions from forming or negotiating. (I don't want to legally encourage it, either. I think the government should be neutral, unless companies use physical force.)

What bothers me is twofold. First, after the unions have put companies into an untenable position, they come to the rest of us looking for a handout to continue the unsustainable levels of pay and benefits. Almost everyone I know makes less than an autoworker, and has a whole lot less job security. Why should they pay autoworkers for the privilege of making cars no one wants?

I also really loathe and despise the way the unions use work rules and featherbedding to make their companies and industries less productive than they otherwise would be. Salary and benefit negotiations seem to me to be neutral; there's a zone of possible agreement, and I don't care if the unions claim all or most of the value in that zone. But the way economic growth happens—the way we become a richer, more productive society—is to produce more stuff with the same amount of people. The union goal is to keep the number of people at least even, and if possible increase it, regardless of the level of production. Hence the fight between the west coast port operators and their unions, who wanted to keep exactly as many jobs loading ships as they'd ever had, even when there were vastly more productive ways to do things. I don't think any thinking liberal should support this.

Nor am I a fan of seniority rules and job protection. Most of us function perfectly well without these,

From *The Atlantic* (November, 2008).

and I don't think that advancement solely by time-in-grade, or protecting everyone who does not actually set the plant on fire from being sacked, is either reasonable or economically desireable. I understand that people want these things, but I would also like to be able to force other people to buy me dinner at will; this does not mean that I should be given that right. I too would enjoy being protected from ever losing my job no matter what, and having all my raises based on my ability to keep my butt in a chair. But I don't think this would be good for my employers, my readers, or, for that matter, me.

But that doesn't mean I don't understand how awful and terrifying it is to have expected a certain life, and have it stolen away from you by a fate you do not very well control. In June 2001 when I graduated from business school, I had a management consulting gig that was scheduled to pay over $100,000 a year and had just moved back to New York. Two months later, two planes crashed into the World Trade Center, killing a number of people I knew and leaving the rest of us traumatized. Four days after that, I was working at the World Trade Center disaster recovery site, trying to come to grips with what had happened. Four months after that, the consulting firm, having pushed back my start date twice, called my associate class and told all of us that our services would not be required.

For the next eighteen months, I struggled to find a job, in the teeth of a recession that kicked MBAs especially hard. It was awful in a way that is difficult to describe to anyone who hasn't been unemployed long term; the thing makes you question everything about your life. I remember going to see the musical *Avenue Q* on a date, and writhing in humiliation, thinking that my date must be identifying me with the aimless failures on stage. I was 29 years old, and living at home. I had money—I always managed to work. But as far as I could tell, I had no future.

When I finally did get a job, with *The Economist*, it paid about a third of what I'd been expecting as a consultant. I had about a thousand dollars in loan payments, and of course I had to live in New York, where my job was. For the first time in my life, I understood what Victorian novelists meant when they described someone as "shabby." Over the years since I'd had a

steady income, my clothes had stretched out of shape, ripped, become stained, gone out of style. I couldn't afford new ones. And I wasn't one of those whizzy heroines who can make over her own clothes. Instead, I frumped around in clothes that never looked quite right, and felt the way my clothes looked.

It took me a long, long time to crawl out of that hole. I'll never make what I expected to make as a consultant. I'll never have the job security that I had learned to expect in the pre-9/11 world. The universe will always seem a potentially malevolent place to me, ready to unleash some unknown disaster at any moment.

I was in a better position than auto workers in many ways; I didn't own a home in a dying area or have children who needed to be educated. I'm not trying to claim that I managed to overcome with hard work and pluck, so why can't they? What to do with a fifty-year-old who pegged his future to a failing industry is a real question.

Nor do I think it's funny to see autoworkers who lived quite a bit better than most of America get their comeuppance. It really doesn't matter what you make; losing everything, most especially your dreams and your sense of security, is one of the worst things that can happen to a person. Laid-off consultants don't starve, of course, but neither will laid-off auto workers. They'll just be forced several rungs down the economic ladder. It will be humiliating, difficult, and it will sour a number of them permanently on life and their country. If I could stop that from happening to people, without making some other aspect of life much worse, I would.

But whatever your feeling about government intervention in the economy, or the correct level of income inequality, I think there's one thing we can all agree on: for the world to get better, things that don't work have to fail. We cannot keep alive every company, every car, and every job that someone once liked, because that way lies stagnation and death. Places where production decisions are made based on how much labor they can consume, rather than how much value they can produce, make everyone in society worse off in the long run.

So while I fully understand the human cost (I think), it has to be borne, for the same reason we couldn't save all the folks who loved their gentle home-weaving traditions, or their jobs making buggy whips. This is, of course, easy to say, when I am not bearing it. But I'm not against helping the auto workers transition to doing something else; I think unemployment assistance is a good idea, and should be extended during this crisis to at least 52 weeks. I would be fine with a job training program, if we could find one that works (so far, government training programs seem to run from useless to actively harmful). I'd be happy to take some of the money we aren't using bailing out auto companies, and offer relocation assistance to people who are trapped in factory towns.

I understand that this is not what the auto workers want; they want their jobs. But while I am happy to help the auto workers, I am not happy to help them manufacture undesireable cars at massive social cost. I too, would have liked to keep my job as a management consultant. But I didn't have a right to have the job I wanted merely because I liked it. And it wouldn't have been good for America if I had.

QUESTIONS

1. Do you agree with McArdle that "for the world to get better, things that don't work have to fail"? If so, when and why does something become "too big to fail"? Should we allow organizations to get so big that they cannot be allowed to fail? But how would we keep them smaller?

2. Imagine yourself suddenly and unexpectedly without a job, through no fault of your own. Would you want help from the government? Same scenario, but now you have a family of four: does your answer change? Same scenario, but now you're a single mom with no savings: same answer? When, why and how should the government step in to help, if ever?

CHAPTER QUESTIONS

1. Should everything be for sale? What should *not* be for sale (are there some things that should *never* be for sale)? How would you distinguish between those things that ought to be subject to market forces and those that should never be subject to the market?

2. Francis Fukuyama argued that history has effectively come to an end because free markets and free societies are the natural goal of humankind. Do you agree? Has Western society discovered (more or less) the ideal economic and political form? Does a free society depend upon free markets? And is capitalism the best—or only—form that free markets can take?

INDEX

ABC Education Program of
    American Industry, 359–61
absolute poverty, 214–15
abusive sales, 150
accountability
    board of directors relating to,
        588–94
    social responsibility relating
        to, 258–59
accounting
    case studies, 177–88
    ethical, 130
    fraud in, 132–40, 177–79
    money managers and, 131–40
    Tapajna on, 140
accusation, 415–16
acquisition of holdings
    in entitlement theory, 203–4,
        208, 210–14
    Locke on, 210–14
Adelphia Communications,
    178–79
adolescents, 108–9
advertising
    ABC Education Program of
        American Industry, 359–61
    at Better Foods Corporation,
        357–58
    brand, image, and, 345–46
    case studies, 354–62
    dependence effect of, 329–36

energy drinks, 362
flattery in, 346–47
Galbraith on, 333n1
for Generation X, 343
Goldman on, 337–41
integrity, persuasion, and,
    347–54
justification of, 337–41
liquor, 361
lying in, 343, 346
marketing, 361
morality relating to, 339–41
promotions, 345
real, 345–46
Savan on, 342–47
as shepherd, 345
sponsored life, 342–43
tips for resisting, 343–47
women, image, and, 358–59
Aesop, 94–95
The Affluent Society (Galbraith),
    334
AFSCME. See American
    Federation of State, County,
    and Municipal Employees
agency argument, 255
agents, 148–50
The Age of Spiritual Machines
    (Kurzweil), 317
aggression, 15. See also bullying
Aldo, Leopold, 501–3

Allegheny Bottling Company, 285
alternative verification, 72–73
American Federation of State,
    County, and Municipal
    Employees (AFSCME),
    229–31
amusement, 105–7
anarchy. See utopia
Andersen, Arthur, 670
    fraud by, 139–40, 177–79
Anderson, Roy R., 373–77
animals. See also nonhumans
    food for, 215
    humans or, 510–14
    meat industry, 525–26
annuities, 181–82
anthropomorphic fallacy, 669
arbitration, 150
Ariely, Dan, 439–41
Aristotle, xxviii
    on commerce, 634–37
    on good life, 89–93
    on happiness, 90–91
    on honesty, 42
    on justice, 190
    on money, 162
    on pleasure, 91–93
    Politics, 634–37
    on self-sufficiency, 91
    on wealth, 90
Arrow, Kenneth J., 269–73

art of doing good, 347–49
art of wealth-getting, 635–37
asbestos, 403–5
Asian fallout, 160–63
aspartame, 400–402
at-risk investors, 144–45
attitudes
    on environmental ethics, 504
    on ethics, 46–47
attraction, in workplace, 35–36
auditors
    advice for, 621
    Buffett on, 621
    ethics for, 181–82
audits
    environmental, 614n97
    social, 281
authentic trust, 70
automobiles. *See* transportation
autonomous responsible beings, 5
autonomy, 618

bad arguments, 331
bad charity, 245–46
balancing competing interests, 151
Bangladesh, 289
bankruptcy, 626–27
banks. *See also specific banks*
    on free markets, 184–86
    management of, 187–88
    "too smart to fail," 674–75
bargaining
    collective, 49–50
    fair conditions of, 147
basic trust, 70
Bathsheba syndrome, 559–65
Baxter, William F.
    on environmental ethics, 510–14
    on pollution, 511, 513–14
Beech-Nut Nutrition
        Corporation, 284–85
behavior, 504
behavioral space, 15
beliefs, 353. *See also* religion
Bell, Daniel, 662–65

Bentham, Jeremy, 299
Berle, Adolf Augustus, 273–75
Berlin, Isaiah, 458
"best person for job," 35, 237
Better Foods Corporation,
        357–58
Bhagwati, Jagdish, 289
Birkenstock, 623–24
birth control, 529
black market, 165
blame acceptance, 596
blinding morality, 543–44
blind loyalty, 431
blind trust, 70
blood, 679–80
bluffing
    Bok on, 49
    Carr on, 48, 50
    collective bargaining and,
        49–50
    consequences of, 48–50
    ethics of, 43–50
    by insurance companies, 45
    laws relating to, 45–46
    lying compared to, 40, 43
    poker analogy, 44–45, 48–49
    pressure for, 44
    trust relating to, 49
board of directors
    accountability relating to,
        588–94
    advice for, 590
    change for, 588–92
    corporate governance relating
        to, 583–94
    duties, 592
    election of, 585–87
    functions of, 583
    homogeneity of, 585–86
    Kant on, 590
    loyalty in, 586
    management of, 584
    objective of, 593
    power relating to, 588–94
    professional directors, 583–84

reform, 583–84
responsibilities of, 583, 586,
        592
    shareholders relating to,
        586–87, 611n31
    staffing, 584, 593–94
    terms, 586
    on wages, 583
boilerplate language, 397–99
Boisjoly, Roger, 418–22
Bok, Sissela
    on bluffing, 49
    on whistleblowing, 412–17,
        423–24
Borg-Werner, 558
boundaryless careers
    contracts in, 22–23
    definition of, 20
    employability and, 20–25
    ethics of, 20–21, 23–24
    fairness in, 21–22
    harm by, 20–21
    risk in, 21–22
Bowie, Norman, 515–20
brands, 345–46
Brewster Bicycle Shop, 399–400
bribers, 474
bribes
    culture relating to, 473
    FCPA on, 475–76
    history on, 472–73
    in international business,
        472–76
    laws on, 474
    Noonan on, 472–76
    politics relating to, 474–75
    religion relating to, 473
British foreign investments, 649
Brukman textile factory, 233–34
bubbles
    derivatives, 164–65
    inflation relating to, 172–73
    mortgage, 173–74
Buchanan, Elizabeth A., 301–5
Buddhist economics, 653–54

on consumption, 655–56
environmental ethics in,
    656–57
on labor, 654–55
materialism in, 654–55
planning in, 655
Buffett, Warren
on auditors, 621
on derivatives, 163–64
bullshit, 60–61
bullying
in cyberspace, 17–18
by destabilization, 15
duration, 16–17
by isolation, 15
overworking, 15
repeated, 16
threat to personal standing, 15
threat to professional status, 15
in workplace, 2, 15–18
Burns, James MacGregor, 556
business. *See also* international
    business
bullshit in, 60–61
in dangerous places, 18–19
in disadvantaged areas,
    238–39
in environmental ethics,
    515–16, 519–20
expenses, 77
fairness in, 189–90
Friedman on, 248
honesty in, 39–42, 58–67
loyalty in, 437–38
philosophy relating to, xxiv
responsibility, 250
secrecy in, 41, 50–53
standard account of, 437–38
trust in, 41, 68–76

Cacique, 123–24
capitalism
benefits of, 637–39
cultural contradictions of,
    662–65

decision-making under, 676
on equal opportunity, 218
growth of, 650
Heilbroner on, 642–44
history of, 218–20
on justice, 217–23
managerial, 264–65
Marx on, 643–44
reflections on, 642–44
Smith on, 93, 218–19, 637–39
stakeholder theory on,
    264–65
supercapitalism, 665–73
von Hayek on, 224
careers
boundaryless, 20–25
planning, 87–88
Carr, Albert, 48, 50
cars. *See* transportation
case studies
accounting, 177–88
advertising, 354–62
corporate governance, 623–32
environmental ethics, 526–37
on ethics, 30–37
on free markets, 679–84
on good life, 115–26
honesty, 77–83
international business, 481–98
on justice, 233–46
leadership, 567–79
liability, 399–409
social responsibility, 280–89
technology, 321–26
whistleblowing, 442–48
causation, 391–96
CEB. *See* Corporate Executive
    Board
Cendant case, 137–38
CEO. *See* Chief Executive
    Officer
Chamberlain, Wilt, 208–9
change
for board of directors,
    588–92

globalization relating to,
    454–55
through leadership, 542
loyalty relating to, 445
character
leadership relating to, 541
purpose, persuasion, and,
    351–52
charismatic leadership, 540–41,
    555–56
charity, 102
bad, 245–46
clothing for, 245–46
debate about, 245–46
social responsibility relating
    to, 286–88
cheating, 439–41. *See also* fraud
Chief Executive Officer (CEO)
blame acceptance, 596
characteristics of, 595–96
corporate governance relating
    to, 595–97
success of, 596–97
visibility of, 596
wages and compensation, 595
child labor, 7
children
adolescents, 108–9
diapers, 517
economics, for grandchildren,
    648–53
elementary education, 646–47
pajamas for, 528–29
safety for, 402–3, 407, 528–29
toys, 407
CID structure. *See* corporate
    internal decision structure
civil rights, 315–16
civil servants, 251
Clean Air Act, 265
"clean cars" law, 672
Clean Water Act, 265
clothing
for charity, 245–46
made in United States, 235

clothing (*continued*)
  pajamas, 528–29
  sweatshops, 235–36
  teamX, 235–36
cocaine, 681–82
coercion, 367–69
coherence, 110–11
collective bargaining, 49–50
Columbia shuttle disaster, 82–83
commerce, 634–37
commitments
  identity-conferring, 112
  persuasion relating to, 350, 353
commoditization, 303
commodity
  analysis of, 640–41
  blood as, 679–80
  fetishism, 639–42
  labor relating to, 641–42
  land as, 516
  Marx on, 639–42
  use-value relating to, 639–40
common-sense
  ethical pluralism, xxix–xxx
  on loyalty, 429–32
communication, 297
communism, 100
community, 435–39
comparable worth
  cost of, 230
  in free markets, 230
  justice relating to, 229–31
compensation. *See* wages
competition
  fairness in, 225
  in free markets, 226–28
  laws of, 100
  von Hayek on, 225
complicity
  on human rights, 466–67
  in Niger Delta, 469–71
complicity theory
  standard theory compared to,
    420–21
  testing, 421–22
  on whistleblowing, 419–22

computer software
  copying, 296–300
  incentives, 295
  intellectual property rights
    and, 293–300, 321
  morality relating to, 294–95
  ownership, 295
concealment, 51. *See also*
    secrecy
concentration camps, 490–91
confidentiality. *See* privacy
conformity, 253
Confucius, 476–81
connections, 468
  guanxi, 480
consent, 367–69
consequentialist arguments,
    295–96
consistency, 541–42
conspicuous consumption,
    660–62
consumer demand, 329–31
consumer lending, 171–72
consumption
  for adolescents, 108
  Buddhist economics on,
    655–56
  conspicuous, 660–62
  leisure and, 104–9
  Veblen on, 344, 660–62
contamination, 456–57
contracts
  boilerplate language, 397–99
  in boundaryless career, 22–23
  employee rights relating to,
    22–23
  express, 148
  forward, 175
  implied, 148
  trustworthiness in, 479–80
control
  corporate, 582–87
  fraud, 185
  individual, 53
  pest, 524
cookie-jar reserves, 135, 137

Cooper, James Fenimore,
    115–16
copying
  computer software, 296–300
  downloading, 291–92
corporate congestion, 270
corporate crimes, 631–32. *See
    also* fraud
Corporate Executive Board
    (CEB), 595
corporate executives, 250–51.
    See also board of directors;
    Chief Executive Officer
corporate finance law, 274
Corporate Fraud Task Force, 149
corporate governance
  board of directors relating to,
    583–94
  case studies, 623–32
  CEO relating to, 595–97
  control and, 582–87
  democracy and, 629–30
  employee rights in, 615–22
  flexibility relating to, 591–92
  government on, 619
  laws on, 599–600
  management, 582
  in marketplace, 597–615
  monotonist and pluralist debate
    on, 597–600, 602, 610n11
  morality in, 597–615
  reform, 591
  at WorldCom, 625–29
corporate internal decision (CID)
    structure
  of Gulf Oil Corporation,
    260–62
  social responsibility relating
    to, 259–62
corporate philanthropy, 611n33
corporate social responsibility
    (CSR), 263–65, 273–76
  agency argument on, 255
  corporate roles relating to,
    597–600
  definition of, 276

morality relating to, 258–63
of NYSEG, 282–83
polestar argument on, 256–57
promissory argument against, 254–55
role argument on, 255–56
stakeholder theory relating to, 265–69, 276–77
corporations. *See also specific corporations*
Berle on, 273–75
board of directors, 583–94
CEOs, 594–97
CID structure of, 259–62
community, loyalty, and, 435–39
control of, 582–87
crisis relating to, 273–75
ethical codes in, 272–73
French on, 258–63
laws of, 264–65
liability for, 72, 670–71
loyalty in, 426, 438–39
management of, 268–69, 277–78, 592
normative core, 268–69
outsourcing, 671–72
prison for, 285–86
privacy for, 588–89
public on, 588–89
regulation of, 271–72, 589
social expectations on, 589–90
stakeholder theory of, 263–69, 275–79
supercapitalism relating to, 666–73
taxes for, 271–72, 669–70
cost
-benefit analysis, 385–86
of comparable worth, 230
liability, 366, 374
of torts, 366
court cases
AFSCME v. Washington State, 229
Greenman v. Yuba Power, 264

Marsh v. Alabama, 265
pay equity lawsuit, 229
Pinto case, 384–90
Ritter v. Narragansett Electric Co., 402–3
Sindell v. Abbott Laboratories, 391
Summers v. Tice, 391–92
from torts, 378–79, 381–93, 399–409
Vincer v. Esther Williams Swimming Pool Co., 403
on Vioxx, 406
Winterbottom v. Wright, 264
Crako Industries, 354–57
credibility, 352
credit, 171–72
crimes, 631–32. *See also* fraud; insider trading
crisis
corporations relating to, 273–75
energy, 258
financial, 170–71, 174–77
liability, 375–76
social responsibility relating to, 273–75
in United States, 664–65
CSR. *See* corporate social responsibility
The Cultural Contradictions of Capitalism (Bell), 662–65
cultural imperialism, 455–56
culture
bribes relating to, 473
capitalism relating to, 662–65
ethical corporate, 462–64
international business relating to, 459–60
internet, 306
trust relating to, 72
cyber attacks, 322
cyberspace, 17–18

Dalai Lama, 320
Dalkon Shield, 529
Daner, Tom, 354–57

danger, workplace, 2
dangerous places, 18–19
data collection, 324
David and Bathsheba story, 559–61
Davis, Michael, 417–22
Death of a Salesman (Miller), 119–20
decision-making
under capitalism, 676
economic, 503–5
ethical, 136
political, 503–5
deforestation, 524–25
de Grazia, Sebastian, 105
Deloitte & Touche, 178–79
democracy
corporate governance and, 629–30
on employee rights, 617
on property rights, 622
supercapitalism on, 673
Democracy and Technology (Sclove), 304–5
dependence effect
of advertising, 329–36
Galbraith on, 329–36
non sequitur of, 333–36
von Hayek on, 334–36
Depression, 173
derivatives
Asian fallout relating to, 160–63
in black market, 165
bubbles, 164–65
Buffett on, 163–64
financial crisis relating to, 174–77
forward contracts, 175
interest-rate swaps, 175
options, 175
Wall Street on, 160
DES. *See* diethylstilbesterol
descriptive feedback, 55
destabilization, 15
Detroit, 375

diapers, 517
diethylstilbesterol (DES), 391
digital divide, 321
dignity, 615–16
disadvantaged areas, 238–39
disclosure, 425
discrimination
    antidiscrimination laws, 26
    in employee selection, 27–28
    facial, 25–29
    of physical appearance, 25–29
disposable diapers, 517
distributive justice, 190–91
    Nozick on, 203, 205–10
    patterning, 206–10
dolphin-human interaction,
    526–27
Donaldson, Thomas
    on ethical corporate culture,
        462–64
    on ethical imperialism,
        459–60
    on international business,
        458–65
    on leadership guidelines,
        464–65
    on values, 461–62
donations. *See* charity
Doumar, Robert G., 285
Dowie, Mark, 384–87
downloading, 291–92
Drabinsky, Garth, 134
drugs
    cocaine, 681–82
    DES, 391
    Mectizan, 599
    Plavix, 408–9
    propranolol, 316
    PureDrug, 484–85
    testing for, 29
    Vioxx, 406
dumping products, 528–30
Duska, Ronald, 423–27
duty, 435–36
dystopian views, 317–18

earned loyalty, 431
Earth's ownership, 518
Echold, J. C., 386–87
economic decision-making,
    503–5
economics
    British foreign investments, 649
    Buddhist, 653–57
    efficiency of, 269–73
    environmental ethics, politics,
        and, 503–10
    global output, 169–70
    for grandchildren, 648–53
    Hollywood-style, 227–28
    of poverty, 658–59
    problem of, 651–53
    social responsibility relating
        to, 269–73
    technology relating to,
        648–49, 650
Ecuador, 532–33
education
    ABC Education Program of
        American Industry, 359–61
    elementary, 646–47
    free markets, *laissez-faire*,
        and, 645–48
    government relating to,
        647–48
    teaching, through leadership,
        550–51
efficiency
    of economics, 269–73
    environmental ethics on,
        505–6
    trust relating to, 69–70
egalitarianism, 217, 220
egocentricity, 562
elections, board, 585–87
elementary education, 646–47
emotional labor, 9–10
emotions
    in trust, 70–71
    in workplace, 8
employability

boundaryless careers and,
    20–25
    right to, 23–24, 682–84
employee rights
    autonomy relating to, 618
    contracts relating to, 22–23
    in corporate governance,
        615–22
    defenses, 615–17
    democracy on, 617
    dignity relating to, 615–16
    fairness relating to, 616,
        618–21
    health relating to, 616–17
    laws on, 264–65
    property rights objections and,
        617–18
    self-respect and, 616
employees
    Enron, investment risk for,
        183–84
    investing by, 183–84, 620–21
    loyalty of, 423–72
    risk for, 183–84, 618, 620
employee selection
    "best person for job," 35, 237
    board of directors staffing,
        584, 593–94
    physical appearance discrimi-
        nation in, 27–28
    restructuring, 27–28
employment. *See* labor; work
end-result principle, 205–6
energy crisis, 258
energy drinks, 362
Enron, 177–78
    employee investment risk and,
        183–84
    fraud, 139–40
    Lay relating to, 442–43
    whistleblowing at, 442–43
enslavement, 198–99
entitlement theory
    acquisition of holdings in,
        203–4, 208, 210–14

Nozick on, 203–5
transfer of holdings, 203–4
environmental audits, 614n97
environmental ethics. *See also* oil
attitudes on, 504
Baxter on, 510–14
behavior relating to, 504
Bowie on, 515–20
in Buddhist economics, 656–57
business in, 515–16, 519–20
case studies, 526–37
deforestation, 524–25
on dumping products, 528–30
Earth's ownership, 518
on efficiency and safety, 505–6
fracking, 536–37
Greenpeace on, 599
humans or animals, 510–14
land ethic, 501–3
liberty relating to, 506–7
of meat industry, 525–26
morality, money, and motor cars, 515–20
nonhumans in, 521–26
on pesticides, 530
politics, economics, and, 503–10
pollution, 511–14
power relating to, 509
Singer on, 521–26
on Texaco, 532–33
Toms shoes relating to, 534–35
values for, 507–8
environmental harm, 517
environmental laws
Clean Air Act, 265
"clean cars" law, 672
Clean Water Act, 265
environmentally friendly goods, 517–18
environmental resources, 513
Epicurus, 97–99

equal information, 153
equality, 53
equal opportunity, 218
equity
capital, 277
private, 167
Ernst & Young, 178
ethical accounting, 130
ethical codes, 272–73
ethical corporate culture, 462–64
ethical decision-making, 136
ethical failure, 275–79
in leadership, 559–65
success relating to, 561
ethical imperialism, 459–60
ethical intuitionism, xxix
ethical obligations
common-sense ethical pluralism on, xxix–xxx
determining, xxv–xxx
Kantian ethics on, xxviii
rights-based ethics on, xvii–xxviii
utilitarianism on, xxv–xxvii
virtue ethics on, xxviii–xxix
ethics
art of doing good, 347–49
attitudes about, 46–47
for auditors, 181–82
of bluffing, 43–50
of boundaryless career, 20–21, 23–24
case studies on, 30–37
finance, 146–52
gone wrong, 275–79
for good life, 85–86
honesty, trust, and, 72–76
information, 297–98, 301–5
insider trading relating to, 156–59
international business, 458–65
in leadership, 542–43
of persuasion, 353–54
philosophy relating to, xxiv

premises of, xxiii
questions for thinking about, xxv
technology and, 290–93, 305–20
Ethics for the New Millennium (Dalai Lama), 320
evaluative feedback, 55
Everything for Sale (Kuttner), 675–78
executive loans, 627
experience, 59
exploitation
justice and, 198–200
labor, 198–200
of need, 198–200
self-enslavement, 198
express contracts, 148
expression
acts of, 12, 13*f*
freedom of, 11–14
laws on, 14
technology relating to, 13
Exxon oil, 515

facial discrimination, 25–29
fair conditions, 147
Fairlie, Henry, 377–81
fairness
in boundaryless career, 21–22
in business, 189–90
in competition, 225
employee rights relating to, 616, 618–21
equal information, 153
of insider trading, 152–54
justice as, 201–2
property rights relating to, 618–21
Fannie Mae, 173–74
fast-food labor
turnover in, 241–42
wages for, 242–43
FCPA. *See* Foreign Corrupt Practices Act

fear
    of leaders, 545–47
    of living, 377–81
Federal Home Loan Mortgage
    Corporation (Freddie Mac),
    173
Federal Housing Administration
    (F.H.A.), 173
feedback
    clarity and accuracy, 57
    descriptive, 55
    effective, 55–57
    forms of, 54
    honesty in, 54–55
    interpretive, 55
    timeliness, 56–57
    tips on providing, 57–58
    types of, 55
    useful content in, 56
F.H.A. *See* Federal Housing
    Administration
fiduciaries
    definition of, 148
    in financial services, 148–50
    insider trading relating to,
        156, 159
finance ethics
    in financial management,
        150–52
    in financial markets, 146–48
    financial services, 148–50
financial contracting, 147–48.
        See also contracts
financial crisis, 170–71
    derivatives relating to, 174–77
financial management
    balancing competing interests,
        151
    defining, 150–51
    finance ethics in, 150–52
    hostile takeovers, 151–52
financial markets
    fair conditions in, 147
    finance ethics in, 146–48
    financial contracting in,
        147–48

justice on, 223–26
    unfair trading in, 146–47
financial services
    defining, 148
    fiduciaries and agents in,
        148–50
    finance ethics in, 148–50
    firms for, 150
    sales in, 150
financial system, 76
fine print, 397–99
firms, 150
flattery, 346–47
flexibility, 591–92
flipping loans, 150
flying business class, 77
followership, 548–49
food
    for animals, 215
    aspartame, 400–402
    Better Foods Corporation,
        357–58
    fast-, 241–43
    hunger, 214–15
Ford
    Pinto case, 384–90
    transportation by, 530–31
foreign assignments, 483–84
Foreign Corrupt Practices Act
    (FCPA), 475–76
forward contracts, 175
Founders, 367–68
Foxconn, 493–96
fracking, 536–37
Frank, Thomas, 674–75
Franklin, Benjamin, 553–54
fraud, 72. *See also* insider
        trading
    in accounting, 132–40,
        177–79
    by Andersen, 139–40, 177–79
    arbitration for, 150
    Cendant case, 137–38
    control, 185
    cookie-jar reserves, 135, 137
    corporate crimes, 631–32

Corporate Fraud Task Force,
    149
    definition of, 147
    Enron, 139–40
    history, 177–79
    ImClone Systems, 178
    incentives, 185
    by Livent and Bankers Trust,
        133–34
    loans relating to, 185–86
    by NMC, 137
    PDAA, 150
    revenue-recognition schemes,
        134–35
    Rite Aid, 177
    scienter, 138
    SEC on, 132, 134, 137–38
    by Tyco International and
        PricewaterhouseCoopers,
        177
    unfair trading, 146–47
Freddie Mac. *See* Federal Home
    Loan Mortgage Corporation
freedom
    enslavement and, 198–99
    of expression, 11–14
    Kant on, 5–6
    Locke on, 198
    of speech, 12–14
    wages for time and, 200
Freeman, Edward R., 263–69
free markets
    banks on, 184–86
    Buddhist economics, 653–57
    case studies on, 679–84
    commerce in, 634–37
    commodity fetishism, 639–42
    comparable worth in, 230
    competition in, 226–28
    economics, for grandchildren,
        648–53
    Everything for Sale, 675–78
    laissez-faire, education, and,
        645–48
    poverty relating to, 658–59
    sales in, 675–78

"too smart to fail," 674–75
winner-take-all-game in,
226–28
French, Peter A., 258–63
Friedman, Milton
on business, 248
on pollution, 512
on shareholder theory, 276
on social responsibility,
248–53, 276
friendship, 111–12

Galbraith, John Kenneth
on advertising, 333n1
The Affluent Society, 334
on consumer demand, 329–31
on dependence effect, 329–36
on public goods and services,
332–33
G. D. Searle & Co., 400–402
Generation X, 343
genetics, nanotechnology, and
robotics (GNR), 318
Germany. *See* Nazi Germany
Ginnie Mae. *See* Government
National Mortgage
Association
Global Compact, 471–72
Global Crossing, 178
global economic output, 169–70
globalization
change relating to, 454–55
contamination from, 456–57
cultural imperialism and,
455–56
homogeneity relating to,
452–53
international business relating
to, 450, 452–57
GNR. *See* genetics, nanotechnology, and robotics
goals
leadership, 550–51, 566–67
persuasion, 352
servant leadership, 566–67
Goldman, Alan, 337–41

good leadership, 540–45, 555
good life
Aristotle on, 89–93
case studies on, 115–26
ethics for, 85–86
greed in, 86, 103–4
happiness in, 124–25
impersonal interests, 113–14
integrity relating to, 110–12
leisure and consumption in,
104–9
planning for, 87–89
Plato on, 86
pleasure relating to, 97–99
wealth relating to, 99–102
workaholism, 85
work and life, 94–97
government
on corporate governance, 619
education relating to, 647–48
financial system relating to,
76
hedge funds relating to, 168
interventions, 645–46
social justice relating to, 222
Government National Mortgage
Association (Ginnie Mae),
173
Grace, W.R., 137
Great Depression, 173
Great Man theory, 555
greed
definition of, 103
in good life, 86, 103–4
happiness relating to, 103–4
Greenhouse, Bunnatine, 446–47
Greenman, William, 369–70
Greenman v. Yuba Power, 264
Greenpeace, 599
guanxi connections, 480
Gulf Oil Corporation, 258
CID structure, 260–62

hackers, 321–22
Halliburton Co., 178, 446–47
happiness

Aristotle on, 90–91
box, 117
in good life, 124–25
greed relating to, 103–4
Russell on, 113–14
harm
by boundaryless careers,
20–21
environmental, 517
from insider trading, 155–56
whistleblowing relating to,
419
head-in-the-sand syndrome,
297
health, 616–17. *See also* drugs
NMC, 137
hedge funds
description of, 166–67
fee structure of, 167–68
government relating to, 168
mythology of, 167
private equity compared to,
167
psychographic portrait of,
167
risk in, 169
Heilbroner, Robert, 642–44
Hesse, Hermann, 565
historical principle, 205–6
history
on bribes, 472–73
of capitalism, 218–20
fraud, 177–79
holdings
acquisition of, 203–4, 208,
210–14
justice relating to, 203–5, 208,
210–14
transfer of, 203–4
holidays, 241
Hollywood-style economics,
227–28
HomeConnection, 322–23
home life
overtime relating to, 237–38
workplace relating to, 34

homogeneity
  of board of directors, 585–86
  globalization relating to,
    452–53
honesty
  Aristotle on, 42
  in business, 39–42, 58–67
  case studies, 77–83
  in Columbia shuttle disaster,
    82–83
  about dangerous places, 19
  ethics, trust, and, 72–76
  about experience, 59
  in feedback, 54–55
  importance of, 40
  Kant on, 42
  material prosperity and, 78
  Mill on, 42
  Nietzsche on, 48
  with others, 58–59
  privacy relating to, 41
  with self, 59
  steps for, 58–59
  testing for, 79–81
  truth, 297
hostile takeovers, 151–52
Huber, Peter
  on liability, 366–71
  on taxes, 366
human exchange, 194–96
humanity, 4–7
humanness, 306–7
human rights
  complicity about, 466–67
  connections relating to, 468
  in international business,
    466–71
  legitimization requirement,
    469
  in Niger Delta, 469–71
  oil relating to, 481–82
  omission requirement, 467–69
  power relating to, 468–69
  speaking out against viola-
    tions, 467–69

voluntariness relating to,
  468
Wettstein on, 466–71
human-robot team
  attempts at, 309–10
  benchmarking, 310–12
  problems with, 307
  specter of, 308–9
  success of, 307–8
humans
  animals or, 510–14
  dolphin interactions with,
    526–27
  interests of, 523–24
  nonhumans and, 521
  robot interaction with,
    305–12
hunger, 214–15
hypernorms, 606–7
hypocrisy, 557

IBM. See International Business
  Machines
idealists, 428–29
identity-conferring commitment,
  112
image
  advertising, women, and,
    358–59
  brand, and, 345–46
ImClone Systems, 178, 179–80
imperialism
  cultural, 455–56
  ethical, 459–60
impersonal interests, 113–14
implied contracts, 148
incentives
  computer software, 295
  fraud, 185
individual control, 53
individual investor, 141–45
individualism, 100
inflation, 172–73
information
  asymmetry, 147

for at-risk investors, 144–45
  commoditization of, 303
  communication relating to,
    297
  equal, 153
  head-in-the-sand syndrome,
    297
  insider trading relating to,
    154–55, 157–58
  profit maximization relating
    to, 270–71
  property rights in, 154–55
  truth relating to, 297
information ethics
  Buchanan on, 301–5
  commoditization, 303
  information inequity, 301–4
  theses for, 297–98
  worldwide, 301–5
information inequity
  internet relating to, 303–4
  overview of, 301–2
initial situation, 201
In Praise of Idleness (Russell),
  106
insider trading
  arguments against, 152–56
  ethics relating to, 156–59
  fairness of, 152–54
  fiduciaries relating to, 156,
    159
  harm from, 155–56
  information relating to,
    154–55, 157–58
  mergers relating to, 179–81
  property rights in information,
    154–55
  SEC on, 180
  theft compared to, 154
instrumental activity, 97
insurance companies
  bluffing by, 45
  twisting by, 150
insurance liability, 374–75
integrity

advertising, persuasion, and, 347–54
coherence and, 110–11
friendship, the Olaf principle, and, 111–12
good life relating to, 110–12
intellectual property rights
    computer software and, 293–300, 321
    consequentialist arguments on, 295–96
    digital divide, 321
    natural rights arguments on, 293–95
interest-group politics, 278
interest-rate swaps, 175
interests
    balancing competing, 151
    of humans, 523–24
    impersonal, 113–14
    of nonhumans, 522–24
international business
    bribes in, 472–76
    case studies, 481–98
    culture relating to, 459–60
    Donaldson on, 458–65
    ethical corporate culture, 462–64
    ethics, 458–65
    FCPA on, 475–76
    foreign assignments, 483–84
    Global Compact on, 471–72
    globalization relating to, 450, 452–57
    guiding principles, 460–61
    human rights in, 466–71
    leadership guidelines, 464–65
    Texaco, in Ecuador, 532–33
    trustworthiness in, 476–81
    values, 461–62
International Business Machines (IBM), 486–87
    background on, 487–88
    in Nazi Germany, 489–92
    punched card system, 488

under Watson, 488–89, 491–92
internet
    culture, 306
    freedom relating to, 325–26
    information inequity relating to, 303–4
interpretive feedback, 55
investing
    British foreign investments, 649
    by employees, 183–84, 620–21
    by Enron's employees, 183–84
    money, 129–30
    restrictions, 142–45
investors
    at-risk, 144–45
    individual, 141–45
isolation, 15

Jackall, Robert, 551–52
Jewish persecution, 486–87, 490–91
job interview, 30–32
job security, 24–25
Johnson, Deborah C., 293–300
Journey to the East (Hesse), 565
Joy, Bill, 316–20
judgement, 478–79
justice
    anarchy, state, and utopia, 203–14
    Aristotle on, 190
    capitalism relating to, 217–23
    case studies on, 233–46
    comparable worth relating to, 229–31
    distributive, 190–91, 203, 205–10
    end-result principle of, 205–6
    entitlement theory, 203–5
    exploitation and, 198–200
    as fairness, 201–2
    on financial market, 223–26
    historical principle of, 205–6
    holdings relating to, 203–5, 208, 210–14

Latin Trade on, 196–97
moral merit relating to, 206–7
Nozick on, 203–14
obligation to assist, 216
Occupy Wall Street on, 221–22
for 1 percent, 221–22, 231–33
Plato on, 190, 192–94
principles of, 201–2, 205–6
retributive, 190–91
social, 217–18, 220, 222–26
A Theory of Justice, 201–2
von Hayek on, 223–26
for wealthy compared to poor, 214–16
in winner-take-all-game, 226–28

Kaczynski, Theodore, 317–18
Kant, Immanuel, xxviii
    on board of directors, 590
    on freedom, 5–6
    on honesty, 42
    on respect, 2, 4–5
    on values, 508
Kantian ethics, xxviii
Kennedy, Donald, 133
Kingdon, B.J., 134
King Midas story, 86
Kluckhorn, C., 306
Kurzweil, Ray, 317
Kuttner, Robert, 675–78

labor. See also work
    Buddhist economics on, 654–55
    child, 7
    commodity relating to, 641–42
    emotional, 9–10
    exploitation, 198–200
    in fast-food, 241–43
    during holidays, 241
    Marx on, 199, 643–44
    monkey, 199–200
    Nike, 243–44

labor (*continued*)
  overtime, 237–38
  physical, 9–10
  Smith on, 638–39
  in sweatshops, 235–36
  theory, 293–94
  turnover, 241–42
  wealth relating to, 654
  women's, 234
  working poor, 240
laissez-faire
  alternatives to, 675–76
  education, free markets, and,
    645–48
land
  as commodity, 516
  ethic, 501–3
language, boilerplate, 397–99
Lao Tzu, 547
Latin America, 196–97
Latin Trade, 196–97
laws. *See also* torts
  antidiscrimination, 26
  bluffing relating to, 45–46
  on bribes, 474
  "clean cars," 672
  of competition, 100
  corporate finance, 274
  on corporate governance,
    599–600
  of corporations, 264–65
  on employee rights, 264–65
  environmental, 265, 672
  on expression, 14
  on leisure, 106
  on liability, 264
  morality for, 607–8
  for paycheck protection,
    672–73
  prison, for corporations,
    285–86
  on trust, 73–74
  on wages, 230
lawyers, 381–83
Lay, Ken, 442–43

leaders
  egocentricity of, 562
  Franklin on, 553–54
  loved or feared, 545–47
  Michigan Studies on, 556
  mythology of, 554
  Plato on, 564
  unethical, 543
  values of, 553–59
  virtues of, 553–54
leadership
  Bathsheba syndrome, 559–65
  Burns on, 556
  case studies, 567–79
  change through, 542
  character relating to, 541
  charismatic, 540–41, 555–56
  consistency in, 541–42
  definitions, 554–55
  Donaldson on, 464–65
  effectiveness of, 542–43
  ethical failure in, 559–65
  ethics in, 542–43
  followership, 548–49
  goals, 550–51, 566–67
  good, 540–45, 555
  guidelines, 464–65
  for international business,
    464–65
  Lao Tzu on, 547
  Machiavellianism, 542
  Machiavelli on, 545–47
  morality in, 541, 544, 548–53
  outcomes, 561*f*
  power in, 550
  purposes, 550–51
  religion relating to, 554
  responsibility of, 539, 549
  Robinhoodism, 542
  Rost on, 548, 552–53
  servant, 556–57, 565–67
  of Stewart, 571–75
  structural restraints, 551–53
  teaching through, 550–51
  Thayer on, 541

theories, 554–57
  transactional, 556
  in United States, 554
  values, 549–50
  visions, 557
legitimization requirement, 469
leisure
  consumption and, 104–9
  definition of, 104–5
  de Grazia on, 105
  laws on, 106
  In Praise of Idleness, 106
  for women, 107
  work, amusement, and, 105–7
leverage, 172
liability
  Anderson on, 373–77
  boilerplate language, 397–99
  case studies, 399–409
  causation and, 391–96
  for corporations, 72, 670–71
  cost, 366, 374
  crisis, 375–76
  in Detroit, 375
  Dowie on, 384–87
  Fairlie on, 377–81
  Huber on, 366–71
  insurance, 374–75
  issues, 373–77
  laws on, 264
  lawyers on, 381–83
  responsibility relating to, 364
  risk calculations, 371–73
  risk intolerance and, 379–81
  solutions, 376
  strict, 369–71
  Thomson on, 391–96
  torts for, 364–69, 378–79,
    381–92
liberty, 506–7
life. *See also* good life
  Aesop on, 94–95
  fear of living, 377–81
  home, 34, 237–38
  play in, 95

sponsored, 342–43
work and, 94–97
liquor advertising, 361
Livent and Bankers Trust, 133–34
loans
    approvals of, 126
    consumer lending, 171–72
    during Depression, 173
    executive, 627
    flipping, 150
    fraud relating to, 185–86
    mortgages, 173–74
location, 238–39
Locke, John
    on acquisition of holding,
        210–14
    on freedom, 198
    on property rights, 291, 293–94
logic, 552
Long-Term Capital Management,
    176–77
Lott, Trent, 542
loved leaders, 545–47
loyalty
    blind, 431
    in board of directors, 586
    in business, 437–38
    change relating to, 445
    common-sense on, 429–32
    concepts of, 428–35
    corporations, community, and,
        435–39
    in corporations, 426, 438–39
    definition of, 436–37
    duty, virtue, and, 435–36
    earned, 431
    employee, 423–72
    idealists on, 428–29
    luxury relating to, 496–98
    minimalists on, 433–34
    to morality relating to, 432–33
    as norm, 432–33
    Randels on, 435–39
    Soles on, 428–35
Lucas Guide (Ronay), 9

luxury, 496–98
lying
    in advertising, 343, 346
    bluffing compared to, 40, 43
    bullshit compared to, 60
    about business expenses, 77
    cheating, 439–41
    failing at, 61–67
    secrecy compared to, 50
    spin compared to, 40

Machiavelli, Niccolo, 545–47
Machiavellianism, 542
machinery, 637–38
The Age of Spiritual
    Machines, 317
Magellan, 544
management
    of banks, 187–88
    of board of directors, 584
    corporate governance, 582
    of corporations, 268–69,
        277–78, 592
    financial, 150–52
    hypernorms relating to, 606–7
    stakeholder theory relating to,
        268–69, 277–78
    of uncertain employment,
        24–25
managerial capitalism, 264–65
marketing, 361. See also
    advertising
marketplace. See also financial
    markets; free markets; secu-
    rities markets
    corporate governance in,
        597–615
    hypernorms relating to, 606–7
    market signals on moral pref-
        erences, 604–5
    morality in, 601–8
    shareholder wealth relating to,
        604, 605–6
market regulation, 74–75
Marsh v. Alabama, 265

Marx, Karl
    on capitalism, 643–44
    on commodity, 639–42
    on labor, 199, 643–44
materialism, 654–55
material prosperity, 78
Mbeki, Thabo, 543
meaningful work, 96–97
meat industry, 525–26
Mectizan, 599
Médecins Sans Frontières
    (MSF), 18
memory, 316
men's earnings, 229–30
mental privacy, 315–16
Merck, 406
    Mectizan and, 599
Merck Sharp & Dohme, 575–77
mergers, 179–81
Meriwether, John, 176
Michigan Studies, 556
Mickey Mouse, 298
Mill, John Stuart
    on honesty, 42
    on laissez-faire and education,
        645–48
Miller, Arthur, 119–20
minimalists, 433–34
mistrust, 75–76
The Modern Corporation
    (Berle), 273–75
molecular electronics, 319
Mondragon Cooperatives,
    280–81
money. See also wealth
    Aristotle on, 162
    credit as, 171–72
    defining, 128–29
    investing, 129–30
    managers, 131–40
    morality, motor cars, and,
        515–20
    Thai baht, 160–62
    trust relating to, 128–29
monkey labor, 199–200

monotonist debate, 597–600, 602, 610n11

moral consistency, 541–42

morality
  advertising relating to, 339–41
  blinding, 543–44
  computer software relating to, 294–95
  in corporate governance, 597–615
  CSR relating to, 258–63
  hypernorms relating to, 606–7
  justifications for respecting, 602–3
  for law and public policy, 607–8
  in leadership, 541, 544, 548–53
  loyalty relating to, 432–33
  in marketplace, 601–8
  market signals on, 604–5
  money, motor cars, and, 515–20
  monotonist debate relating to, 602
  norms, 604–5
  pluralist debate relating to, 602
  principles for respecting, 603–7
  shareholder wealth relating to, 604, 605–6
  trust relating to, 73
  whistleblowing relating to, 415–18

Moral Mazes (Jackall), 551–52

moral merit, 206–7

Morris, William, 96

mortgages, 173–74

motor cars, 515–20. *See also* transportation

MSF. *See* Médecins Sans Frontières

mythology
  of hedge funds, 167
  of leaders, 554

Nader, Ralph, 414

nanotechnology, 318–19

Narcissistic Process and Corporate Decay (Schwartz), 551

National Medical Care (NMC), 137

natural rights arguments, 293–95

Nazi Germany
  concentration camps, 490–91
  first population census, 489–90
  IBM in, 489–92
  Jewish persecution, 486–87, 490–91
  second population census, 490
  Watson in, 491–92

need, 198–200

Nesmith, John, 371–73

New Deal, 173–74, 676

New York State Electric and Gas (NYSEG), 282–83

Niederhoffer, Victor, 161–63

Nietzsche, Friedrich, 48

Niger Delta, 469–71

Nike, 243–44

Nixon Transportation Secretaries, 386

NMC. *See* National Medical Care

nonhumans
  animals, 215, 510–14, 525–26
  dolphin-human interaction, 526–27
  in environmental ethics, 521–26
  humans and, 521
  interests of, 522–24
  meat industry, 525–26
  pest control, 524
  pesticides and, 530
  speciesism, 521–22

non sequitur, dependence effect, 333–36

Noonan, John T., Jr., 472–76

Noonday Demon, 3

normative core, 268–69

norms

hypernorms, 606–7
  loyalty as, 432–33
  morality, 604–5

Nozick, Robert
  on distributive justice, 203, 205–10
  on entitlement theory, 203–5
  on justice, 203–14

NYSEG. *See* New York State Electric and Gas

obligation to assist, 216

Occupy Wall Street, 221–22

oil
  Exxon, 515
  Gulf Oil Corporation, 258, 260–62
  human rights relating to, 481–82
  Shell Oil, 599, 610n29, 613n70
  Texaco, 532–33

Olaf principle, 111–12

Olson, Walter K., 381–83

omission requirement, 467–69

1 percent
  justice for, 221–22, 231–33
  Occupy Wall Street on, 221–22

The Opportunist (Cooper), 115–16

Orwell, George, 567–71

outsourcing, 671–72

overpayment, 77–78

overtime, 237–38

overworking, bullying, 15

ownership. *See also* property rights
  computer software, 295
  of Earth, 518

pajamas, 528–29

Panopticon, 299

Parker, Richard, 273–75

paternalism, 142–43

paycheck protection laws, 672–73

pay equity lawsuit, 229
PDAA. *See* predispute arbitration agreement
pecuniary emulation, 660–62
Pemón, 120–24
Peoplesoft, 178
Peregrine Systems, 178
personal life. *See* home life
personal standing, 15
person's principle, 5–6
persuasion
    advertising, integrity, and, 347–54
    art of doing good and, 347–49
    barriers to, 349
    beliefs relating to, 353
    character, purpose, and, 351–52
    commitments relating to, 350, 353
    credibility relating to, 352
    ethics of, 353–54
    goals, 352
    making pitch, 349–50
    questions for, 352–53
    review of, 349–50
    style, 352–53
pest control, 524
pesticides, 530
philanthropy, 611n33
philosophy. *See also specific philosophers*
    business relating to, xxiv
    ethics relating to, xxiv
    of property rights, 293
    of Smith, Adam, xxiv
physical appearance
    discrimination of, 25–29
    employee selection relating to, 27–28
    employment relating to, 2
    research on, 26–27
physical labor, 9–10
piggyback trading, 148–49
Pinto case

background on, 384–85, 388–89
    cost-benefit analysis in, 385–86
    Echold on, 386–87
    Rashomon effect and, 387–90
    Werhane on, 387–90
Planet Finance, 169–70
planning
    in Buddhist economics, 655
    career, 87–88
    for good life, 87–89
Plasma International, 679–80
Plato
    on danger of bad arguments, 331
    on good life, 86
    on justice, 190, 192–94
    on leaders, 564
    on play, 95
    "Ring of Gyges," 192–94
Plavix, 408–9
play, 95
pleasure
    Aristotle on, 91–93
    Epicurus on, 97–99
    good life relating to, 97–99
pluralist debate, 597–600, 602, 610n11
poker analogy, 44–45, 48–49
polestar argument, 256–57
political decision-making, 503–5
politics
    bribes relating to, 474–75
    environmental ethics, economics, and, 503–10
    interest-group, 278
    supercapitalism relating to, 666–67
Politics (Aristotle), 634–37
pollution
    Baxter on, 511, 513–14
    Friedman on, 512
pornography, 36–37
poverty

absolute, 214–15
    disadvantaged areas, 238–39
    economics of, 658–59
    facts, 214–16
    free market relating to, 658–59
    justice for, 214–16
    race relating to, 241
    TANF, 240
    in United States, 239–41
    wealth compared to, 214–16
    welfare, 240
    women in, 240–41
    working poor, 240
power
    board of directors relating to, 588–94
    environmental ethics relating to, 509
    human rights relating to, 468–69
    in leadership, 550
    secrecy relating to, 52
predispute arbitration agreement (PDAA), 150
PricewaterhouseCoopers, 177
prison
    for corporations, 285–86
    Panopticon, 299
privacy
    for corporations, 588–89
    data collection relating to, 324
    honesty relating to, 41
    mental, 315–16
    secrecy compared to, 51–52
    technology relating to, 292, 324
    in United States, 298
    in workplace, 36–37
private equity, 167
product dumping, 528–30
professional directors, 583–84
professional status threat, 15
profit maximization, 270–71
profit motive, 247–53, 269–71
promissory argument, 254–55
promotions, in advertising, 345

property rights
    acquisition of holding, 203–5,
        208, 210–14
    democracy on, 622
    downloading and, 291–92
    fairness relating to, 618–21
    in information, 154–55
    intellectual, 293–300, 321
    Johnson on, 293–300
    Locke on, 291, 293–94
    objections to, 617–18
    philosophy of, 293
    technology relating to, 291–92
    transfer of holdings, 203–4
    utility relating to, 621–22
propranolol, 316
public, 588–89
    goods and services, 332–33
    policy, 607–8
Public Utility Commission
        (PUC), 447–48
Pulitzer, Joseph, 425
Pump It Up, 630–31
punched card system, 488
punitive damages, 379
PureDrug, 484–85
purpose, 351–52

Qwest, 178

race, 241
Rajaratnam, Raj, 577–79
Randels, George D., 435–39
Rashomon, 387–88
Rashomon effect, 387–90
Rawls, John, 201–2
real ads, 345–46
reform
    board of directors, 583–84
    corporate governance, 591
    supercapitalism, 668–69
regulation
    of corporations, 271–72, 589
    market, 74–75
Reich, Robert B., 665–73
religion

bribes relating to, 473
    leadership relating to, 554
repeated bullying, 16
respect
    for humanity, 4–7
    Kant on, 2, 4–5
    for person's principle, 5–6
    self-, 616
    in workplace, 1–2
responsibility. *See also* corporate
        social responsibility; social
        responsibility
    of board of directors, 583,
        586, 592
    business, 250
    of corporate executives, 250
    of leadership, 539, 549
    liability relating to, 364
    whistleblowing relating to,
        412–17
retributive justice, 190–91
revenue-recognition schemes,
        134–35
rich. *See* wealthy
rights. *See also* human rights;
        property rights
    -based ethics, xvii–xxviii
    civil, 315–16
    to employability, 23–24,
        682–84
    intellectual property, 293–300,
        321
    to work, 682–84
"Ring of Gyges" (Plato), 192–94
risk
    in boundaryless career, 21–22
    calculating, in liability, 371–73
    for employees, 183–84, 618,
        620
    in Enron employee investments,
        183–84
    in hedge funds, 169
    intolerance, 379–81
    levels of, 151
    Nesmith on, 371–73
    in securities markets, 141–42

Rite Aid, 177
*Ritter v. Narragansett Electric
        Co.*, 402–3
Road to Serfdom (von Hayek),
        223–26
Robinhoodism, 542
robots
    advantages of, 312–13
    applications of, 307
    ethics, technology, and,
        305–15
    GNR, 318
    human interaction with, 305–12
    humanness of, 306–7
    human-robot teams, 307–12
    organizational structures, 307
    trust relating to, 308, 310–11
role argument, 255–56
Ronay, Egon, 9
Roosevelt, Franklin, 173, 274
Roosevelt, Theodore, 274
Rost, Joseph, 548, 552–53
Russell, Bertrand
    on happiness, 113–14
    on impersonal interests,
        113–14
    In Praise of Idleness, 106

sadhu, 116–18
safety. *See also* liability
    for children, 402–3, 407,
        528–29
    in dangerous places, 19
    environmental ethics on, 505–6
salary. *See* wages
sales
    abusive, 150
    in financial services, 150
    in free markets, 675–78
Samaritanism, 418–19
Saro-Wiwa, Ken, 469–71
Savan, Leslie, 342–47
Schumacher, E. F., 653–57
Schwartz, Howard S., 551
scienter, 138
Sclove, Richard, 304–5

SEC. *See* Securities and Exchange Commission
secrecy
 in business, 41, 50–53
 concealment and, 51
 conflicts over, 52
 dangers of, 53
 defining, 50–53
 equality relating to, 53
 individual control relating to, 53
 lying compared to, 50
 power relating to, 52
 privacy compared to, 51–52
 Pulitzer on, 425
Securities and Exchange Commission (SEC)
 on fraud, 132, 134, 137–38
 on insider trading, 180
 responsibilities of, 144
securities markets, 141–45
segregation, 230–31
self
 -enslavement, 198
 -examination, 477–78
 honesty with, 59
 -respect, 616
 -sufficiency, 91
 whistleblowing on, 444
Sen, Amartya, 658–59
seniors, 181–82
servant leadership, 556–57
 description of, 565–66
 goals, 566–67
 Hesse on, 565
 virtues of, 565–66
sexual harassment, 37
shareholders
 board of directors relating to, 586–87, 611n31
 morality relating to, 604, 605–6
 role of, 587
 social responsibility relating to, 254–55
 stakeholders and, 275–76
 wealth of, 151, 604, 605–6
shareholder theory, 276

shareholder wealth maximization (SWM), 151, 604, 605–6
Shell Oil, 599, 610n29, 613n70
Shooting an Elephant and Other Essays (Orwell), 567–71
simmering, 19
simple trust, 70
Sindell v. Abbott Laboratories, 391
Singer, Peter, 521–26
sloth, 3
smiling, 8–9
Smith, Adam
 on capitalism, 93, 218–19, 637–39
 on human exchange, 194–96
 on labor, 638–39
 philosophy of, xxiv
 The Theory of Moral Sentiments, 219
 The Wealth of Nations, 218–19
 on wealthy, 219
social audits, 281
social expectations, 589–90
socialism, 643
 von Hayek on, 224
social justice
 definition of, 217, 220
 egalitarianism, 217, 220
 on equal opportunity, 218
 government relating to, 222
 utopia relating to, 222–23
 von Hayek on, 224–26
social responsibility. *See also* corporate social responsibility
 accountability relating to, 258–59
 agency argument against, 255
 Arrow on, 269–73
 for Beech-Nut Nutrition Corporation, 284–85
 case studies, 280–89
 charity relating to, 286–88
 CID structure relating to, 259–62

conformity relating to, 253
crisis relating to, 273–75
difficulty of, 252
economics relating to, 269–73
ethical codes for, 272–73
French on, 258–63
Friedman on, 248–53, 276
Parker on, 273–75
polestar argument against, 256–57
profit motive relating to, 247–53, 269–71
promissory argument against, 254–55
role argument against, 255–56
shareholders relating to, 254–55
stakeholder theory on, 263–69, 275–79
taxes as, 251
types, 258
society
 The Affluent Society, 334
 profit maximization relating to, 270–71
software. *See* computer software
Soles, David E., 428–35
speaking out, 467–69
speciesism, 521–22
speech, 12–14
spin, 40
sponsored life, 342–43
staffing, 584, 593–94
stakeholders, 275–76
stakeholder theory
 on capitalism, 264–65
 concept, 265–66
 on corporate social responsibility, 263–69, 275–79
 CSR relating to, 265–69, 276–77
 description of, 275–76
 equity capital relating to, 277
 by Freeman, 263–69
 interest-group politics relating to, 278

stakeholder theory (*continued*)
  management relating to,
    268–69, 277–78
  in modern corporation,
    266–67
  normative core of, 268–69
  problems with, 277–78
standard theory
  complicity theory compared
    to, 420–21
  on whistleblowing, 418
Stewart, Martha, 179
  leadership of, 571–75
strict liability, 369–71
success
  by-products, 561
  of CEO, 596–97
  dark side of, 561–63
  in David and Bathsheba story,
    560
  ethical failure relating to, 561
  of human-robot team, 307–8
suicides, 493–96
Summers v. Tice, 391–93
supercapitalism
  corporations relating to, 666–73
  on democracy, 673
  politics relating to, 666–67
  reform, 668–69
Supercapitalism (Reich), 665–73
sweatshops, 235–36
SWM. *See* shareholder wealth
    maximization

TANF. *See* Temporary
    Assistance to Needy
    Families
Tapajna, Joe J., 140
taxes
  for corporations, 271–72,
    669–70
  Huber on, 366
  as social responsibility, 251
  as tort, 366–67
teaching, 550–51

Teal, Mike, 354–57
teams, 307–12
teamX, 235–36
technocrats, 184
technology
  *The Age of Spiritual
    Machines*, 317
  case studies, 321–26
  civil rights relating to, 315–16
  cyber attacks, 322
  cyberspace, 17–18
  dangers of, 319–20
  data collection, 324
  Democracy and Technology,
    304–5
  digital divide, 321
  downloading, 291–92
  dystopian views on, 317–18
  economics relating to, 648–49,
    650
  ethics and, 290–93, 305–20
  *Ethics for the New
    Millennium*, 320
  expression relating to, 13
  GNR, 318
  hackers, 321–22
  HomeConnection, 322–23
  information ethics, worldwide,
    301–5
  intellectual property rights
    and computer software,
    293–300, 321
  internet, 303–4, 306, 325–26
  Joy on, 316–20
  molecular electronics, 319
  nanotechnology, 318–19
  privacy relating to, 292, 324
  property rights relating to,
    291–92
  robots, 305–15
Temporary Assistance to Needy
    Families (TANF), 240
termination, 32–33
testing
  complicity theory, 421–22

  for drugs, 29
  for honesty, 79–81
Texaco, 532–33
Thai baht, 160–62
Thayer, William Makepeace, 541
theft, 154
A Theory of Justice (Rawls),
    201–2
The Theory of Moral Sentiments
    (Smith), 218–19
Thompson, Clive, 315–16
Thomson, Judith Jarvis, 391–96
time
  bullying duration, 16–17
  feedback relating to, 56–57
  overtime, 237–38
  wages for freedom and, 200
Toms shoes, 534–35
"too smart to fail," 674–75
torts
  background on, 367–69
  changes to, 376–77
  consent, coercion, and,
    367–69
  cost of, 366
  court cases from, 378–79,
    381–93, 399–409
  Founders of, 367–68
  for liability, 364–69, 378–79,
    381–92
  punitive damages, 379
  taxes as, 366–67
  winning, 391
toys, 407
trading
  insider, 152–59, 179–81
  piggyback, 148–49
  unfair, 146–47
transactional leadership, 556
transcranial magnetic stimula-
    tion, 316
transfer of holdings, 203–4
transportation
  "clean cars" law, 672
  Ford, 384–90, 530–31

morality, money, and motor
cars, 515–20
Nixon Transportation
Secretaries, 386
Pinto case, 384–90
trust
alternative verification and,
72–73
authentic, 70
basic, 70
blind, 70
bluffing relating to, 49
building, 68–71
in business, 41, 68–76
culture relating to, 72
defining, 69, 72–73
efficiency relating to, 69–70
emotions in, 70–71
honesty, ethics, and, 72–76
laws on, 73–74
market regulation relating to,
74–75
mistrust consequences, 75–76
money relating to, 128–29
morality relating to, 73
overselling, 68–69
reduction, 75
robots relating to, 308, 310–11
simple, 70
types, 68, 70
trustworthiness, 69
Confucius on, 476–81
in contracts, 479–80
guanxi relating to, 480
in international business,
476–81
judgement for, 478–79
self-examination for, 477–78
truth, 297. See also honesty
turnover, 241–42
twisting, 150
Tyco International, 177

uncertain employment, 24–25
unethical leaders, 543

unfair trading, 146–47. See also
fraud
unions, 230–31
United States
clothing made in, 235
crisis in, 664–65
leadership in, 554
poverty in, 239–41
privacy in, 298
use-value, 639–40
utilitarianism, xxv–xxvii
utility, 621–22
utopia
anarchy, state, and, 203–14
social justice relating to,
222–23

Vagelos, Roy, 575–77
values
Berlin on, 458
Donaldson on, 461–62
for environmental ethics,
507–8
hypocrisy and, 557
international business,
461–62
in international business
ethics, 458–65
Kant on, 508
of leaders, 553–59
leadership, 549–50
problems with, 557–58
use-, 639–40
virtue compared to, 554
on work, 95–96
Veblen, Thorstein, 344, 660–62
Vietnam, 243–44
Vincer v. Esther Williams
Swimming Pool Co., 403
Vioxx, 406
virtue ethics, xxviii–xxix
virtues
duty, loyalty, and, 435–36
of leaders, 553–54
of servant leadership, 565–66

value compared to, 554
visibility, 596
visions, 557
voluntariness, 468
von Hayek, Friedrich
on capitalism, 224
on competition, 225
on dependence effect,
334–36
on justice, 223–26
on moral merit, 207
Road to Serfdom, 223–26
on socialism, 224
on social justice, 224–26

wages
board of directors on, 583
for CEO, 595
for fast-food labor, 242–43
laws on, 230
men's earnings compared to
women's, 229–30
overpayment, 77–78
paycheck protection, 672–73
for time and freedom, 200
Wall Street
on derivatives, 160
Occupy Wall Street, 221–22
"too smart to fail," 674–75
Wal-Mart, 196–97
Watson, Thomas J.
IBM under, 488–89, 491–92
in Nazi Germany, 491–92
wealth
Aristotle on, 90
art of wealth-getting,
635–37
good life relating to, 99–102
labor relating to, 654
poverty compared to, 214–16
of shareholders, 151, 604,
605–6
surplus, 101–2
The Wealth of Nations (Smith),
218–19

wealthy
    justice for poor compared to,
        214–16
    1 percent, 221–22, 231–33
    Smith on, 219
welfare, 240
Werhane, Patricia, 387–90
Wettstein, Florian, 466–71
whistleblowing
    accusation relating to, 415–16
    Bok on, 412–17, 423–24
    case studies, 442–48
    complicity theory on, 419–22
    Davis on, 417–22
    discussions on, 423
    Duska on, 423–27
    effective, 413
    employee loyalty relating to,
        423–72
    at Enron, 442–43
    harm relating to, 419
    morality relating to, 415–18
    Nader on, 414
    nature of, 412–15
    paradoxes of, 417–22
    at phone company, 447–48
    responsibility relating to,
        412–17
    Samaritanism relating to,
        418–19

    on self, 444
    standard theory on, 418
    Yardley on, 427
Wicker, Tom, 258
winner-take-all-game, 226–28
Winterbottom v. Wright, 264
women
    advertising, image, and,
        358–59
    in Brukman textile factory, 234
    labor, 234
    leisure for, 107
    men's earnings compared to,
        229–30
    in poverty, 240–41
    segregation of, 230–31
    in unions, 230–31
wooing. *See* persuasion
work
    for adolescents, 108–9
    amusement, leisure, and,
        105–7
    as instrumental activity, 97
    job interview, 30–32
    job security, 24–25
    life and, 94–97
    meaningful, 96–97
    Morris on, 96
    physical appearance and
        employment, 2

    right to, 682–84
    termination, 32–33
    uncertain employment, 24–25
    values on, 95–96
workaholism, 85
working poor, 240
workplace
    attraction in, 35–36
    bullying in, 2, 15–18
    danger, 2
    emotions in, 8
    freedom of expression in, 11–14
    home life relating to, 34
    privacy in, 36–37
    respect in, 1–2
    smiling in, 8–9
work-related speech, 12
WorldCom, 179
    bankruptcy, 626–27
    corporate governance at,
        625–29
    executive loans at, 627
    growth, 625–26
worth, comparable, 229–31

Xerox, 178

Yardley, Jim, 427

Zetter, Kim, 439–41